OFFICIAL RECORDS

OF THE

AUSTRALIAN MILITARY CONTINGENTS

TO THE

WAR IN SOUTH AFRICA

COMPILED AND EDITED FOR THE DEPARTMENT OF
DEFENCE BY LIEUT.-COLONEL P. L. MURRAY, R.A.A. (Ret.)

The Naval & Military Press Ltd

Published by
The Naval & Military Press Ltd
Unit 10, Ridgewood Industrial Park,
Uckfield, East Sussex,
TN22 5QE England
Tel: +44 (0) 1825 749494
Fax: +44 (0) 1825 765701
www.naval-military-press.com
www.military-genealogy.com
© The Naval & Military Press Ltd 2007

In reprinting in facsimile from the original, any imperfections are inevitably reproduced and the quality may fall short of modern type and cartographic standards.

Printed and bound by Lightning Source

PREFACE.

THE late Major-General Sir John Hoad, K.C.M.G., had long been desirous that the great mass of statistics accumulated in the Defence Department relative to the Australian Military Contingents should be tabulated and arranged in a comprehensive yet compact and systematic shape. In this manner there would be an official record for preservation in our annals, as a memorial of the period when Australia poured forth her levies to do battle for the Empire—many of her sons doomed never to return, but fated to take their last rest beneath the veldt upon which they had fought. In the absence of such a memorial, it might be that in process of time little would be recalled of the stirring events of 1899-02 except the mere fact that there once was a war in South Africa in which the Colonies took some share.

The General was at length authorized to realize his wish; though he was not permitted to witness the completion thereof. It involved a task of no ordinary magnitude; comprising, as it did, firstly, the evolution of order from chaos; secondly, the partition of the materials; and, thirdly, a judicious selection of that which it was desirable to preserve, coupled with the rejection of matter which was superfluous or cumbersome. In some instances it was found impossible to complete certain minor particulars; lists having been mislaid, and State-District Staff officers not supplying the information.

It must be understood that this volume is not a history of the war. It is a statistical register and reference. The short narratives which accompany the records of Contingents are intended only as sketches or illustrations of each campeign. For certain portions of the outlines of service of some South Australian, Western Australian, and Tasmanian Contingents, the compiler has been indebted to a work entitled *Colonials in South Africa*, by John Stirling, which is based chiefly upon the despatches of the Commander-in-Chief at the seat of war.

Department of Defence,
    Victoria Barracks, Melbourne,
        30th October, 1911.

NEW SOUTH WALES.

NEW SOUTH WALES.

PREFATORY.

IT has not been considered desirable to detail the preliminary training in the case of each Contingent or draft. It may readily be understood, however, that it would have been impossible to clothe, equip, drill, and despatch 6,000 men and horses to the seat of the war, readily and steadily, without perfect system and regularity of method. The first Contingents embarked were in reality drafts from the three New South Wales mounted regiments; the company of infantry was enrolled entirely from selected men of the Militia and Volunteer Battalions. These were, therefore, a superior class of individuals, from whom considerable was to be expected; and there was little trouble in getting them away. "A" Battery R.A.A. was, of course, under strict discipline; and the same may be said of the Army Medical Corps.

But much rougher material had to be dealt with in the Bushmen's and subsequent Contingents; though, of course, they ultimately became leavened with a proportion of men who had been to the war and gained valuable experience. Many of the recruits, however—a large majority in some cases—were mere rough bushmen, countrymen, handicraftsmen, farm labourers, and the like, who had never soldiered before, and had everything to learn in the way of drill and discipline.

Camps of Instruction were established at Randwick and elsewhere; and the men, having been accepted, passed the tests, and enrolled, were put through such a rapid and comprehensive course as should fit them for duty. Horses were selected and purchased as rapidly as possible, consistently with fair accuracy of judgment, and handed over to their riders, who were taught the routine of stable duty. They were issued with uniforms and equipment, and organized into squadrons; squadrons subdivided into troops, and troops into sections of four. The men were exercised in recruit drill, musketry, marching, and squadron work, and the duties of an irregular horseman, both mounted and dismounted. Finally, the battalion was paraded as such; and officers and sergeants tested in their work. Interior economy, as applied to the routine of camp life and the field, and discipline, also formed important subjects of instruction.

Duly qualified officers and staff-sergeants were selected for the training, and a Camp Commandant appointed for each Camp. Selected officers were likewise detailed to make the necessary arrangements for embarkation of men and horses in the transports available in each case; so that when the day arrived, all things being in readiness, there might not be any hitch.

By these means, and a severe course of what might be termed "forcing," the various Contingents were enabled to make quite a creditable appearance when they marched to the quay for embarkation; usually in the presence of thousands of interested and enthusiastic spectators. Great encomium was due to the Head-Quarter Staff, both the A.A.G. and A.Q.M.G. Departments, and to the Pay Department, under Mr. J. B. Laing, upon which an unusually severe strain was placed. Also to the officers and sergeants instructors for the unanimity and energy with which they worked to bring about so desirable a consummation.

No horses were brought back from South Africa; they were handed over to Remount Depôts prior to embarkation of each Contingent for Australia.

In addition to the articles of uniform noted as issued to Contingents, each man was supplied with boots and a full and complete kit, comprising clothing, underwear, necessaries, &c.

THE NEW SOUTH WALES LANCERS.

THE draft of Lancers which from force of circumstances was the first to go to the front from Australia represented the senior cavalry regiment of New South Wales, now the 1st Australian Light Horse (New South Wales Lancers). It was raised in 1883, first as Light Horse, but in 1885, after the return of the Contingent from the Soudan, it was converted into Lancers, as a compliment to the 5th Royal Irish Lancers, which were encamped with the New South Wales Artillery at Handoub. The uniform of that regiment was also adopted with slight variations; but a few years later it was relinquished for the distinctive drab with scarlet plastrons.*

A squadron of 100, under Captain C. Cox, had proceeded to England in 1899, to take part in the annual military tournament at Islington, and for training at Aldershot; the expense of which was defrayed entirely by the regiment. Upon the war breaking out, permission to volunteer was cabled for and acceded to. The detail, with their horses, then proceeded to Cape Town, where they were enthusiastically received, equipped with the service uniform and accoutrements, and despatched to the scene of hostilities.

The subsequent drafts were supplied with horses, but in many instances spare chargers were taken.

Pay.

Rates of pay (as sanctioned by G.O. 107, 21.10.99) "for members of Partially-paid or Volunteer Forces," were as follow:—Buglers and privates, 2s. 3d. per day, with 2s. 3d. deferred pay; corporals, 4s. 9d. and 2s. 3d.; sergeants, 5s. 9d. and 2s. 3d.; company sergeant-majors or colour-sergeants, 6s. 3d. and 2s. 9d.; staff-sergeants, 6s. 6d. and 3s. 6d.; warrant officers, 7s. 6d. and 4s.; lieutenants, 16s. and 3s. deferred pay; captains, 20s. and 3s. 6d.

N.C. officers and men of the Permanent Forces would receive, from date of landing, Imperial rates of pay in addition to existing rates.

"Separation allowance" was also granted to wives and families of N.C.O.'s and soldiers serving in South Africa, at varying rates according to rank. If in occupation of quarters or drawing lodging allowance, the wife received 4d. per diem; for each girl under 16 years 1½d. per diem; each boy under 14 years, 1¼d. per diem. When not in occupation of quarters or receipt of lodging allowance, payment was made at rates varying from warrant officers' wives 2s. 3d. per diem, to privates' wives, 1s. 1d.

Pay was issued by the Imperial Government after the landing of Contingents at Imperial rates. These varied from lieutenant-colonel, 25s. per diem and 4s, field allowance, to subaltern, 15s. and 2s. 6d.; and from 9s., R. sergeant-major. to 5s. privates. Buglers, saddlers, and farriers, 1s. per diem extra.

Establishment.

The following was the establishment authorized for Lancer Contingent, in the first instance:—1 major (temporary), 1 captain, 3 subalterns, 1 Sq. S.M., 1 Sq. Q.M.S., 2 staff-sergeants, 4 sergeants, 2 sergeant-farriers, 2 shoeing smiths, 2 buglers, 8 corporals, 97 privates, including cooks and bâtmen, 1 saddler. Total, 125.

Men volunteering were required to be from 20 to 40 years of age, preferably single, and good shots. Horses brought in had to be for M.I. work, and pass veterinary examination.

---

* The Regiment is allied with "King Edward's Horse;" the King's Oversea Dominions Regiment.

References to Orders.

Formation	G.O., N.S.W.	.. ..	107/99
Pay	,, ,,	.. ..	107/99, 112/99
Conditions of Service	,, ,,	.. ..	107/99
Command	,, ,,	.. ..	113/99
Establishment	,, ,,	.. ..	108/99
Embarkation	,, ,,	.. ..	109/99
Officers	,, ,,	.. ..	110/99

Detachment.

Embarkation	G.O., N.S.W.	.. ..	8/00, 22/00
Personnel	,, ,,	.. ..	22/00
Separation allowance	,, ,,	.. ..	88/00

Clothing, Arms, Etc.

Uniform consisted of brown F.S. jacket and pants, with puttees and hats.

Arms and equipment: M.E. carbines, swords, shoulder bandoliers, waistbelt, and braces.

Fully horsed and provided with saddles.

Also provided with regimental transport.

Units.

The first draft arrived at Cape Town from England on 2nd November, 1899; it consisted of 2 officers and 69 sergeants and rank and file, with their horses. Of these, 2 were killed or died, 2 were transferred to S.A.C., leaving 2 officers and 65 others, who returned.

The second draft left New South Wales on 28th October, 1899; it consisted of 5 officers, 36 others, with 160 horses. Three were killed or died; 1 was transferred, 1 was commissioned in Imperial Army; 4 officers and 32 others returned.

The third draft left New South Wales on 17th January, 1900; it consisted of 17 sergeants and rank and file, with 15 horses; 1 man was killed or died, 16 returned.

The fourth draft departed 16th February, 1900; it comprised 1 officer and 40 others. Total: 8 officers, 162 others, with 246 horses.

The squadron arrived home on 6th December, 1900, and 8th January, 1901.

Record of Service.

The detachment of this regiment undergoing a course of training at Aldershot at the outbreak of the war volunteered for active service in South Africa; the offer being accepted, they embarked on 10th October, 1899, and arrived at Cape Town 2nd November, 1899.

In order to complete and maintain the service establishment of the unit, detachments embarked at Sydney on transport *Kent* on 28th October, arriving at Cape Town 1st December; on transport *Moravian* on 17th January, arriving at Cape Town on 18th February; and on transport *Australian* on 16th February, arriving at Cape Town 19th March, 1900.

The Aldershot detachment after its arrival was attached to General French's command, and was employed on patrol duty in the Colesberg district. On the 6th December, the detachment, under Major Lee, with remounts for the whole squadron, arrived at Naauwpoort, Major Lee assuming the command of the squadron.

Present at capture of Arundel on 8th December, and took part in several minor actions in the vicinity.

A detachment of 28 men, under Lieutenant Osborne, temporarily attached to Lord Methuen's command, took part in the battles of Belmont, Grasspan, Modder River, and Magersfontein, and afterwards rejoined the squadron.

On 2nd January, 1900, a supply train was, by some means started from Rensburg Siding, and ran on a down grade close to the Boer position; the squadron was ordered to recover or burn the trucks. As some of them were derailed, it was found impossible to recover them; they were, consequently, burned under a very heavy fire from the enemy.

On the 16th January a troop of Lancers and Australian Horse, under Lieutenant Dowling of the latter regiment, when returning to camp at Slingersfontein, was surrounded; and after a sharp fight, in which Sergeant-Major Griffin of the Australian Horse was killed, Corporal Kilpatrick of the Lancers mortally wounded, and Lieutenant Dowling and Trooper Roberts severely wounded, the patrol surrendered.

On the 7th February the squadron proceeded to Belmont, and on the 13th were attached to Scots Greys, forming part of the 1st Cavalry Brigade.

Present at the relief of Kimberly on 15th February, action at Dronfield on 16th February, and at the operations which led to the surrender of General Cronje at Paardeburg. Took part in the battle of Poplar Grove on 7th March, and assisted to turn the enemy's left flank.

Present at Dreifontein on 10th, and at the occupation of Bloemfontein on 12th March.

Captain Nicholson, with a detachment of 40 N.C. officers and men from New South Wales, joined on 5th May.

The squadron was now attached to the Inniskillings, under Major Allamby and took part in the advance on Pretoria. Kroonstadt was occupied on 12th May; the Vaal River crossed on 24th May. Took part in heavy fighting at Klip River on 28th May, when Major Lee was complimented by General French on the excellent work of the squadron while with the advance guard.

Took part in operations in the vicinity of Johannesburg, including the severe action at Valkheuvel Poort on 3rd June, when the Australians were again thanked by General French for their gallant conduct.

Present at the release of prisoners at Waterval on the 6th June. On the 9th July reinforced General Hutton at Oliphantsfontein, and was engaged with the enemy on 11th and 12th.

Took part in various engagements in the eastern Transvaal, including LangKloof and Swartz Kop, also in the operations in the Carolina and Barberton districts.

The squadron embarked at Cape Town on transports *Harlech Castle* on 11th November, and *Orient* on 13th December, and arrived in Sydney on 6th December, 1900 and 8th January, 1901, calling at Albany, Adelaide, and Melbourne *en route*.

ACTIONS IN WHICH THE LANCERS TOOK PARK

Belmont	23rd November, 1899
Grasspan	25th November, 1899
Modder River	28th November, 1899
Magersfontein	11th December, 1899
Arundel	13th January, 1900
Reit River	12th February, 1900
Klip Drift	13th February, 1900
Relief of Kimberly	15th February, 1900
Dronfield	16th February, 1900
Paardeburg	18th February, 1900, to 5th March, 1900
Poplar Grove	7th March, 1900
Dreifontein	10th March, 1900
Bloemfontein	12th March, 1900
Brandfort	29th March, 1900
Ventersburg road	10th May, 1900
Vanwyksrust	27th May, 1900
Doornkop	29th May, 1900
Valkheuvel Poort	3rd June, 1900
Diamond Hill	11th and 12th June, 1900
Olifantsfontein	11th and 12th July, 1900
Lang Kloof	26th August, 1900
Swartz Kop	27th August, 1900
Wartburg Hills	12th September, 1900
Barberton	13th September, 1900
Lake Chrissie	16th October, 1900
Mooiplaats	17th October, 1900
Ermelo	18th October, 1900
Reitvley	19th October, 1900
Bethel	20th October, 1900
Rooipoort	22nd October, 1900
Winklehadt	23rd October, 1900
Kaffir Kuil	24th October, 1900
Witkop	25th October, 1900

WAR SERVICES AND HONOURS.

Lee, Major, G. L.—Relief of Kimberley. Operations in Orange Free State, Transvaal, and Cape Colony, February, 1900, to November, 1900. Actions at Colesberg, Paardeburg, Poplar Grove, Driefontein, Zand River, Johannesburg, Pretoria, Diamond Hill, Lang Kloof, and Swartz Kop. Despatches, *London Gazette*, 10th September, 1901. D.S.O. Queen's Medal with six clasps.

Cox, Captain and Hon. Lieutenant-Colonel C. F.—Relief of Kimberley. Operations in Cape Colony, Orange Free State, and Transvaal, January, 1900, to November, 1900. Actions at Colesberg, Paardeburg, Poplar Grove, Driefontein, Karee Siding, Zand River, Johannesburg, Pretoria, Diamond Hill, Lang Kloof, and Swartz Kop. Despatches. *London Gazette*, 17th June, 1901. *London Gazette*, 26th June, 1902. C.B. Queen's Medal with six clasps. King's Medal with two clasps. (Lieut.-Colonel Cox subsequently commanded the 3rd New South Wales Mounted Rifles. Operations in Orange River Colony and Transvaal, 1901–1902.)

Nicholson, Lieutenant and Hon. Captain C. E.—Operations in Orange Free State and Transvaal, February, 1900, to November, 1900. Actions at Zand River, Johannesburg, Pretoria, Diamond Hills, Lang Kloof, and Swartz Kop. Queen's Medal with five clasps.

Allan, Lieutenant G. H.—As above. Queen's Medal with four clasps.

Osborne, 2nd Lieutenant S. F.—Relief of Kimberley. Operations as above, November, 1899, to August, 1900. Actions at Belmont, Modder River, Magersfontein, Paardeburg, Poplar Grove, Dreifontein, Karee Siding, Zand River, Johannesburg, Pretoria, Diamond Hill, Lang Kloof, and Swartz Kop. Queen's Medal with five clasps.

Roberts, 2nd Lieutenant C. W. P.—Relief of Kimberley. Operations as above, February, 1900, to April, 1900. Paardeburg, Poplar Grove, and Dreifontein. Queen's Medal with three clasps. Commission in Imperial Cavalry.

Heron, 2nd Lieutenant R. M.—Relief of Kimberley. Operations as above, February, 1900, to November, 1900. Actions at Paardeburg, Poplar Grove, Dreifontein, Karee Siding, Zand River, Johannesburg, Pretoria, Diamond Hill, Lang Kloof, and Swartz Kop. Queen's Medal with four clasps. (Lieutenant Heron served subsequently with 3rd Mounted Rifles as Captain.)

Melhuish, Vet. Lieutenant F. W.—Relief of Kimberley. Operations as above, February to November, 1900. Actions at Paardeburg, Karee Siding, Zand River, Johannesburg, Pretoria, Diamond Hill, Lang Kloof, and Swartz Kop. (Served subsequently with 2nd Mounted Rifles as Vet.-Captain.) Queen's Medal with five clasps. King's Medal with two clasps.

There were no promotions in South Africa.

EXTRACTS FROM REPORT OF MAJOR G. L. LEE, NEW SOUTH WALES LANCERS.

Monday, 15th January.—About 5.15 p.m. I saw Colonel Porter with Warrant-Officer Duncan and Private Buckholtz, 1st Australian Horse. The latter reported that Lieutenant Dowling's patrol had been surrounded and cut up, and that he was the only one who had escaped. Warrant-Officer Duncan and two others had been detached by Lieutenant Dowling to examine Foster's farm, and so escaped.

The patrol had reconnoitred, according to instructions, and was about returning to camp when Warrant-Officer Duncan with two men was detached to examine Mr. Foster's farm at Kleinfontein. After doing so, he went in search of Lieutenant Dowling's party, failing to find them, he concluded they had returned to camp. At 4.30 p.m. I was informed that a New South Wales Lancer patrol had been cut up.

Upon examination it was found that Sqdn. Sergeant-Major Griffin, 1st Australian Horse, had been killed, and Corporal Kilpatrick, New South Wales Lancers, was found severely wounded through the lungs, and the lower jaw smashed.

Corporal Kilpatrick expired at 11 a.m.

One officer (Lieutenant Dowling) and 13 men are still missing.

Bloemfontein, 4th May, 1900.—Writing a full report is out of the question, as our position has been continually on the front of the Cavalry Brigade (1st), consequently we have not been off "perpetual motion." On arrival here we were on our last legs so far as clothing, *cleanliness*, and horses were concerned.

We have now been re-fitted afresh, and we start off on the second phase, viz., "Bloemfontein to Pretoria." So we now move off again with the 1st Cavalry Brigade, in the best of trim and spirits. The men are all old soldiers now, and will be very useful.

Jordan's Siding, near Kroonstadt, 15th May, 1900.—The night before leaving Springfield camp for marching northwards, Captain Nicholson marched into camp with 37 N.C.O.'s and men (38) of the New South Wales Lancers, and 39 horses. They had been sent on from Cape Town. We will march from here with about 8 officers and 92 N.C.O.'s and men.

I have pleasure in reporting the arrival of four cases of warm clothing, tobacco, chocolate, &c., from Lady Hampden.

Three boxes of tobacco came from Lady Duff; six cases (puddings, pipes, chocolate, &c.), from F. H. Dangar, Esq.

24th May (Queen's Birthday).—We crossed into Transvaal Territory in the afternoon. A few days' rest and we moved off again north-west for a similar move to the north of Pretoria.

We marched through the Megaliesberg range at Crocodile Pont, about 14 miles west of Pretoria. Then, turning to our right, we camped north of Pretoria some 5 or 6 miles.

The following day, 6th June, we went to "Waterval" and released the British prisoners, or rather, the prisoners released themselves by breaking out on the arrival of our advanced scouts. From the 6th June, we have been operating north-west of where we now camp.

Prisoners.—When the prisoners were released, our lot (who were captured on patrol), with the exception of Ford and Whittington who had escaped, were among the released. They all looked thin, and were destitute of clothing. After being released, a Court of Inquiry was held, and found they were free from all blame. It was the 1st Cavalry Brigade that rescued them, and our squadron was in the advance guard.

(It appeared that there were some 3,000 prisoners altogether; and that they hastened to join the British troops. The sight was characterized by Col. Lee as "novel.")

Eureka City, 12 miles from Barberton, 21st September, 1900.—On the 9th July, our Brigade was suddenly ordered south, to the east of the railway line.

After the engagement with Botha, we kept moving eastward on the south side of the Delagoa railway line, thence towards Carolina, where we joined with General Buller. After a few days there, we moved north (leaving General Buller), keeping Belfast on our right. Our arrival at Waterval-Onder station caused the Boers to release the prisoners (except officers) they had at Noitegacht. Returning through Machadodorp, we re-entered Carolina. Just before reaching here, Trooper Avard (New South Wales Lancers) was shot through the kidneys, and died some time afterwards.

Wittekop Farm, 15 miles east of Heidelberg, 25th October, 1900.—We have just reached this place from Barberton. Returning, we stayed a few days at Machadodorp, and then moved off towards this place, viâ Carolina, Ermelo, and Bethel. We were fighting from Carolina, a rear-guard action, right up to here. I had **two** men wounded. The casualties on the march to here are over 100.

Nominal Roll.

No. and Name.	Rank.	Remarks.
Lee, George Leonard	Major Comdg.	
Cox, Charles Fredk.	Captain	*Vide* 3rd N.S.W. M.R.
Nicholson, Charles Edward	Lieutenant	
Allan, George Henry	,,	
Osborne, Septimus Frank	2nd-Lieutenant	
Roberts, Chas. Wm. Fyshe Palmer	,,	Commissioned Imp. Cavalry
Heron, Reginald Manning	,,	*Vide* 3rd N.S.W. M.R.
Melhuish, Frank Whiddon	Lieutenant Vet. Surgeon	*Vide* 2nd N.S.W. M.R.
Fisher, Charles Edward	Warrant Officer	Burmese War, 1885, 1887, 1889. Taken prisoner, rejoined Waterval, 6.6.00.
Read, Henry Thomas	Staff-Sergeant	Zulu War
Winch, William	,,	Boer War, 1881; Bechuanaland, 1884-5
Morris, George Edward	,,	Despatches, *London Gazette*, 27.9.01: D.C.M.
303. Robson, Henry	Squadron Sergt.-Major	
530. Blow, Ernest Alfred	Squadron Q.M.-Sergt.	
304. McDonald, Peter	Sergeant	Prisoner, Slingersfontein; rejoined Waterval, 6.6.00
218. Williams, Charles James	,,	
263. Livingstone, Angus	,,	
69. Houston, Ernest Arthur Edwin	,,	Despatches, *London Gazette*, 27.9.01: D.C.M.
71. Luke, Elias	,,	
237. Gould, George Edward	,,	
477. Dooley, John Sylvester	,,	
489. Moffatt, William	,,	
325. Morrison, Alfred Gordon Lambert	,,	Invalided, Australia, arr. 13.11.00
271. Campbell, John William Wallace	,,	Wounded, Ermelo, 18.10.00
19. Rose, Ernest	Farrier-Sergeant	Invalided, Australia, arr. 17.2.01
755. Kilpatrick, Frederick Isaac	Corporal	Died of wounds, Slingersfontein
609. Fallick, Samuel Reginald	,,	
742. Hopf, Charles	,,	
182. Mullard, William	,,	
67. Harkus, Rowland Edward	,,	Died, enteric fever, Bloemfontein
948. Junor, Chas. Ernest	,,	
961. Conolly, John Bart.	,,	
882. Moon, Wm. John	,,	
624. Woods, Arthur	Lance-Corporal	
415. Ford, John	,,	
213. Barnett, Alick Steel	Trumpet-Corporal	
222. Papworth, William	Trumpeter	Invalided, Australia, arr. 13.9.00
866. Taylor, Albert Vincent	,,	Taken prisoner, Slingersfontein; joined after release at Waterval, 6.6.00
507. Avard, Frederick	Trooper	Died of wounds, Carolina
885. Artlett, Herbert Arthur	,,	
555. Akers, Stanley Ernest	,,	Invalided, Australia, arr. 30.7.00
414. Ambruster, Otto	,,	
946. Alcock, Joseph Nehemiah	,,	
964. Anderson, Henry	,,	Invalided, Australia, arr. 16.11.00
226. Barclay, Robert David	,,	
817. Brady, Wm. Hope	,,	Invalided, Australia, arr. 13.9.00
890. Bell, George	,,	
450. Bresnahan, Patrick	,,	
145. Blencowe, Arthur Wm.	,,	Invalided, Australia, arr. 6.12.00
887. Borman, Alf. Theodore	,,	
629. Brew, Phillip	,,	

Nominal Roll—continued.

No. and Name.	Rank.	Remarks.
749. Byrne, John Joseph	Trooper	
821. Baily, Allan Griffith	,,	
921. Baily, Sydney Nathay	,,	
935. Braid, John	,,	
936. Breckenridge, Thos. Wm.	,,	
940. Beeching, Hy. Cotton	,,	
895. Burgin, Alf. Arthur	,,	
476. Clarke, James	,,	
805. Chilcott, Osborne	,,	
892. Chapman, William	,,	Invalided, Australia, arr. 21.10.00
725. Cummings, George Richmond	,,	Invalided, Australia, arr. 28.5.00
762. Carter, William Beveridge	,,	
757. Cuthbert, Ronald Hopper	,,	
916. Cuthbert, Herbert Hopper	,,	
939. Cavill, Walter William	,,	
951. Clark, Charles Edward A.	,,	
763. Daley, Arthur Denis	,,	Taken prisoner, Slingersfontein; afterwards re-joined, 6.6.00
449. Davey, Walter George	,,	Invalided, Australia, arr. 6.8.00
520. Dickson, Thomas Alexander	,,	
905. Donohoe, Martin Henry	,,	
750. Doudney, Guy	,,	
911. Dare, Alfred Ernest	,,	Invalided, Australia, arr. 6.8.00
860. Elston, William	,,	
878. Elliott, James	,,	
923. Evans, Bertie Frederick	,,	Invalided, Australia, arr. 6.12.00
891. Ellis, Walter Melrose	,,	Died on transport, *Harlech Castle*, 18.11.00
235. Faulkner, Percy	,,	
317. Fenwick, George Thomas	,,	Invalided, Australia, arr. 13.11.00
599. Fetting, Franz Gustav A. L.	,,	Died enteric fever
635. Fitzsimmons, Alfred	,,	
952. Fitzsimons, Joseph Alexander	,,	
800. Fiaschi, Carlo Ferucho	,,	*Vide* 1st A.C.H.
960. Ferris, Cecil Ernest	,,	
897. Ford, John Milvington	,,	Taken prisoner, Slingersfontein and escaped
893. Griffiths, Lewis Henry	,,	Invalided, Australia, arr. 30.7.00
818. Houston, John	,,	
822. Holborow, Daniel Town	,,	
546. Harrison, Bernard Harry	,,	
724. Haken, George	,,	Corporal, invalided, Australia, arr. 19.9.00
68. Hillis, Wm. Henry	,,	
958. Hillis, Geo. Chas.	,,	
898. Hopkinson, Ernest Fairball	,,	Wounded at Brandfort, 29.3.00; invalided, Australia, arr. 16.11.00
899. Hindmarsh, Henry Ernest	,,	
938. Harley, Thomas	,,	
947. Haigh, Chas. Eric	,,	
780. James, Arthur Willis Stanley	,,	Lance-Corporal, invalided, Australia, arr. 17.8.00
579. Johnson, John	,,	
732. Johnson, James	,,	
880. Johnston, Robt. Morrison	,,	
898. Jones, John Charles	,,	
590. Knight, Thos. Satchell	,,	Invalided, Australia, arr. 17.8.00
919. King, Augustus Hadden	,,	Wounded at Ermelo, 18.10.00; invalided, Australia, arr. 17.2.01
896. Lamb, Chas. Valentine	,,	
1000. Lance, Walter Percy	,,	
802. Lee, Ernest	,,	Invalided, Australia, arr. 17.8.00
941. Lumley, John Everett	,,	
244. Morris, Thos. Chas.	,,	
823. Moylan, Bede John	,,	
1001. Middleton, Chas.	,,	
920. Milling, Oliver Louis	,,	**Invalided, Australia, arr. 30.8.00**

Nominal Roll—continued.

No. and Name.	Rank.	Remarks.
623. Milling, Nathaniel	Trooper	
826. Myers, Albert Ed. Croft	,,	
945. Munro, Edgar Charles	,,	
884. McMillan, Allan W. G.	,,	
494. McGill, Michael	,,	
825. McPherson, Jas. Ballintyne	,,	Invalided, Australia, arr. 30.7.00
922. McPherson, Wm. Neil	,,	
283. McPherson, Kenneth Ross	,,	
824. McManus, Arthur	,,	
788. McBaron, Mathew Montgomery	,,	
953. McGee, John	,,	Invalided, Australia, arr. 6.12.00
957. McKinnon, Norman James	,,	
764. McKinnon, Alexander	,,	
761. Peek, John Harold	,,	
781. Palmer, Roger Wingham	,,	
620. Pestell, Thomas	,,	Invalided, Australia, arr. 30.8.00
886. Pettigrew, Andrew Bannantyne	,,	
574. Roberts, John Alexander	,,	Taken prisoner Slingersfontein; joined after release at Waterval, 6.6.00
498. Rankin, James	,,	
877. Ramsay, Gilbert Edward Layton	,,	Invalided, Australia, arr. 13.11.00
889. Robinson, Arthur	,,	
924. Roderick, Joseph	,,	
888. Sandon, Henry	,,	
502. Sproule, John	,,	
210. Stratford, George James	,,	
795. Stewart, Walter	,,	
733. Seccombe, John Frederick	,,	Invalided, Australia, arr. 30.7.00
734. Saville, Alfred Edward	,,	
754. Slattery, Augustus Joseph	,,	
682. Stuart, Frederick William	,,	
294. Stone, George	,,	
606. Skipper, Harry James	,,	
828. Treatt, Eric Burford	,,	Invalided, Australia, arr. 26.1.01
298. Thomas Harley	,,	Invalided, Australia, arr. 16.11.00
299. Thomas George	,,	
815. Turner, William James	,,	
400. Tooze, Thomas Henry	,,	Invalided, Australia, arr. 6.8.00
942. Thompson, William Martin	,,	
949. Tivey, Thomas Edward	,,	Invalided, Australia, arr. 6.12.00
879. Tunks, Leslie Dagworth	,,	
954. Tyler, Charles Henry	,,	Died, enteric fever, Kroonstadt
659. Vernon, Hugh Venables	,,	Invalided, Australia, arr. 4.8.00
591. Wilks, James	,,	Invalided, Australia, arr. 6.8.00
797. Watts, William Wilson	,,	
705. Waddell, Harold Henry	,,	
740. Webster, Charles Edward	,,	Invalided, Australia, arr. 28.5.00
677. Walsh, Edward	,,	Invalided, Australia, arr. 6.8.00
829. Whitney, Ashley	,,	Invalided, Australia, arr. 13.11.00
85. Watts, James William	,,	Invalided, Australia, arr. 17.8.00
790. Warby, Joseph Hillier	,,	
809. Watson, Alfred	,,	
652. Weston, James Albert	,,	
943. White, James	,,	
944. Whitney, William Henry	,,	
950. Wheller Robert John	,,	
962. Whittington, Allan Watson	,,	Invalided, Australia, arr. 17.9.00
963. Withers, Ernest Arthur Frederick	,,	Invalided, Australia, arr. 12.1.01
881. Whittington, George Robert	,,	Taken prisoner, Slingersfontein and escaped; invalided Australia; arrived 30.7.00
894. Wilson, Euston Wardell	,,	

THE ARMY MEDICAL CORPS.

THE New South Wales Army Medical Corps despatched three Contingents to the war (the third being styled "The Imperial Draft"), and the Australian Army Medical Corps sent one. The division was originally organized and established through the exertions of Colonel (afterwards Surgeon-General) W. D. C. Williams. He had succeeded in placing the various units of Mounted Bearer Companies, Bearer Companies, and Field Hospitals, &c., with their Field Medical Equipment, Ambulance and Wag on Transport, in so efficient a condition as regards *personnel*, material, and horses, that upon the initiation of the war no difficulty was experienced in embarking expeditiously, complete and thoroughly-disciplined details. These comprised officers and men who had been carefully instructed in the technique and training of their arm, and who, therefore, required no hurried supplementary curriculum. They were also supplied with all the essential equipment upon a scale of entire comprehensiveness. These were the causes which enabled the Army Medical Corps to present so fine an appearance upon their arrival at the seat of war, and which insured them so cordial a welcome by Imperial officers, who found their collaboration with the Imperial Army Medical Corps invaluable. It was thus also that they acquitted themselves with skill and gallantry that elicited such an unequalled distribution of honours.

REFERENCE TO ORDERS.

First Contingent.

Pay	G.O. (N.S.W.),	107/99; 112/99; 88/00
Formation	,, ,,	107/99
Conditions of Service	,, ,,	107/99
Establishment	,, ,,	108/99
Embarkation	,, ,,	109/99; 123/99
Officers	,, ,,	110/99

Second Contingent.

Establishment	G.O. (N.S.W.),	1/00
Officers	,, ,,	3/00
Distribution of Officers	,, ,,	10/00
Embarkation	,, ,,	8/00

Third Contingent.

Establishment	G.O. (N.S.W.),	27/01

Commonwealth Contingent.

Formation	G.O.,	15/02
Establishment	,,	16/02
Embarkation	,,	25/02

CLOTHING, ETC.

Uniform consisted of brown F.S. jacket and trousers, with puttees and hat.

Arms and Equipment.—Carbines; officers and sergeant-majors with swords and revolvers, and mounted men with revolvers; waistbelt with supporting braces and ammunition pouch. No arms, however, were taken to the front; they were all left at Cape Town. Regimental and Ambulance Transport was provided. For rates of pay *vide* New South Wales Lancers.

C.4720.

ESTABLISHMENT.

The establishment approved for first Contingent was :—Half-bearer Company—1 captain, 1 lieutenant, 1 warrant officer, 1 quartermaster-sergeant, 4 sergeants, 4 corporals, 2 buglers and trumpeters, 1 collar-maker, 1 shoeing and carriage-smith, 38 privates and drivers; total, 54. Field Hospital—50 beds. 2 captains, 1 lieutenant, 1 staff sergeant, 3 sergeants, 4 corporals, 21 privates and drivers; total, 32. For the Half-bearer Company only strong lusty men were accepted, or trained stretcher-bearers.

SUMMARY.

The first Contingent departed on 28th October, 1899. It comprised 6 officers and 80 of other ranks, with 51 horses, 5 ambulance wagons, and 12 carts. Of these, 4 died; 6 officers and 76 others returned.

The second left on 17th January, 1900—Nine officers and 85 of other ranks, with 52 horses, 5 ambulance wagons, and 12 carts—in the *Moravian*; and the mounted bearer unit—Two officers, 23 other ranks, with 33 horses and 6 carts—in the *Southern Cross*. Of these, 2 died; 11 officers and 106 others returned.

The third (Imperial Draft) went on 17th March, 1901, there being 5 officers. 48 other ranks, with 54 horses and 2 ambulance wagons. Three were struck off the strength in South Africa; 5 officers and 45 others returned.

The fourth (Commonwealth) departed on the 11th February, 1902, consisting of 8 officers and 102 other ranks, with 75 horses, 4 ambulance wagons, and 16 carts. One officer and 24 others were struck off in South Africa; 7 officers and 78 others returned.

Totals: 30 officers, 338 other ranks, 265 horses, 16 ambulance wagons, 46 carts (transport wagons).

Note.—Hon. Majors McCormick and Scot-Skirving were included in the second Contingent as Special Service officers.

NURSING SISTERS.

One Lady Superintendent and 13 nurses accompanied the second contingent in the *Moravian*, namely :—

Gould, Ellen Julia	Lady Superintendent
Johnstone, Julia Bligh	Superintendent
Austin, Anne	Sister
Frater, Penelope	,,
Garden, Anna Gardiner	,,
Hoadley, Emily	,,
Lister, Elizabeth Ward	,,
Martin, Marion Philippe	,,
Matchett, Annie L.	,,
Newton, Nancy	,,
Nixon, Elizabeth	,,
Pocock, Mary Annie	,,
Steel, Mabel	,,
Woodward, Theresa E.	,,

Four remained in South Africa; the Lady Superintendent and the others returned. Nursing Sister E. Nixon was awarded the Royal Red Cross; despatches, *London Gazette*, 27.9.01; and Nursing Sister M. A. Pocock mentioned in despatches, *London Gazette*, 29.7.02.

PROMOTIONS.

Name.	Original Appointment.	Subsequent Changes.	Contingents.
Williams, W. D. C.	Colonel	Surgeon-General, P.M.O.	First
Kelly, R. Vandeleur	Major and Brevet Lieut.-Colonel	Lieutenant-Colonel	Second, and Imperial Draft, 13.2.01
Roth, R. E.	Captain	Promoted Major (P.M.O., 2nd M.I. Brigade)	First
Perkins, Alfred Edward	Captain	Promoted Major	First
Green, Terence Alfred	Captain	Promoted Major	First, and Commonwealth Contingent
Newmarch, Bernard James	Lieutenant	Promoted Captain	Second
Martin, Thomas Morgan	Lieutenant	Promoted Captain	First
Samuelson, G. S.	Lieutenant	Promoted Captain	Second
Howse, Neville Reginald	Lieutenant	Promoted Captain and Major	Second, and A.A.M.C.

For promotions of W.O.'s and N.C.O.'s see Nominal Roll.

RECORD OF SERVICE.

First Contingent.

The first Contingent Army Medical Corps for service in South Africa was mobilized commencing 23rd October, 1899, and embarked on s.s. *Kent*, Saturday, 28th October, 1899, leaving Port Jackson at 5 a.m. on Monday, 30th October, 1899, consisting of 6 officers and 85 N.C.O.'s and men, under the command of Colonel W. D. C. Williams, P.M.O. The s.s. *Kent* reached Port Elizabeth on 30th November, 1899, and received orders to proceed to Cape Town, where she arrived 2nd December, 1899. The corps disembarked the same date, and was camped at Green Point, Cape Town. Entrained for Orange River station 20th December, 1899, and arrived 23rd December, 1899. Established Field Hospital, which was opened 24th December, 1899. Detachments of Bearer Company were stationed at Zoutpans Drift and Belmont. Bearer Company at Belmont, under Major Roth, took part in engagement at Sunnyside, 1st January, 1900. Detachment of Bearer Company under Captain Edwards, took part in the relief of Kimberley, 14th February, 1900.

The corps left Orange River station with the advance of Lord Roberts, 17th February, 1900, and took part in the following engagements:—Paardeburg, 27th February, 1900; Poplar Grove, 7th March, 1900; Dreifontein, 10th March, 1900; Arrived at Bloemfontein. Established Artillery Barracks hospital.

The Bearer Company took part in several engagements around Bloemfontein from 24th April, 1900, to 1st May, 1900, viz.:—Leuwfontein, Slingersfontein, and Thaba N'chu. In beginning of May the Bearer Company, first Contingent, was attached to the Field Hospital of second Contingent, and the Field Hospital of first Contingent to Bearer Company of second Contingent by order of Colonel Williams, P.M.O.

The Contingents were engaged in the following actions:—Lindley, Brandfort, Heilbron, Vet River, Zand River, Johannesburg, 28th and 29th June, 1900; Pretoria, 4th June, 1900; Diamond Hill, 11th and 12th June, 1900; Heidelberg, 23rd June, 1900; Retief's Nek, 23rd and 25th July, 1900; Bethlehem and Caledon Valley, capture of Prinsloo, 30th July, 1900; Spitzkop (near Heilbron), **14th August, 1900**; Bothaville, 16th November, 1900; Groot Dam; **Vredefort**; Olifant's Nek; Relief of Elands River; Heckpoort; **Magalies Valley**; **Krugersdorp**.

Second Contingent.

The second Contingent of the New South Wales Army Medical Corps, under the command of Lt.-Colonel R. Vandeleur Kelly, left Sydney in the s.s. *Moravian*, 17th January, 1900; the Bearer section on the same day in the s.s. *Southern Cross*.

The corps disembarked 22nd February, 1900, at East London, and proceeded the same day to Sterkstroom, and on arrival was attached to General Gatacre's column.

The members of the New South Wales Army Nursing Service Reserve were distributed between hospitals at Cape Town, East London, and Sterkstroom.

Part of the second Contingent remained at Sterkstroom in charge of the Stationary Hospital there, while the remainder advanced with the column *viâ* Bethulie Bridge to Bloemfontein, where the Bearer company and Field Hospital were interchanged with those of the first Contingent.

Part of the Contingent returned in the s.s. *Harlech Castle*, embarked at Cape Town 3rd November, 1900, calling *en route* at Albany, Adelaide, Melbourne, and arriving in Sydney 8th December, 1900, in command of Lt.-Colonel Fiaschi.

The main portion of the two Contingents returned in the s.s. *Orient*, embarking at Cape Town 13th December, 1900; and called at Albany and Melbourne, arriving in Sydney 8th January, 1901, under the command of Surgeon-General W. D. C. Williams, C.B. Smaller units returned in the s.s. *Tongariro* and *Wilcannia* respectively.

The Imperial Draft Contingent.

The Imperial Draft Contingent, New South Wales Army Medical Corps, under the command of Lt.-Colonel R. Vandeleur Kelly, left Sydney in the s.s. *Custodian* and *Maplemore* 17th March, 1901, while a few small details went by the s.s. *British Princess, Ranee,* and *Antillian*.

The corps disembarked at Port Elizabeth, and was attached to Colonel Williams' and Colonel Remington's Columns, which operated in the Western and Eastern Transvaal.

The corps returned in the s.s. *Aurania*, and disembarked at Sydney, 3rd June, 1902.

The Australian Army Medical Corps Contingent.

The Australian Commonwealth Army Medical Corps Contingent was composed of units from all the Australian States, under the command of Major T. A. Green (Field Hospital), and Major Howse, V.C. (Bearer Company).

The corps was mobilized in Sydney, and embarked at that place in the s.s. *Manchester Merchant*, 11th February, 1902, sailing the following day. The transport called at Hobart, Adelaide, and Fremantle, and reached Durban 17th March, 1902.

The corps disembarked 19th March, 1902, and proceeded to Newcastle, Natal, by rail. Remained at Newcastle for three weeks, and proceeded thence by rail to Klerksdorp, Western Transvaal, where the Field Hospital unit established a stationary hospital of 100 beds, while the Bearer Company was attached to Thornycroft's Mounted Infantry Column.

The Field Hospital Unit returned by the s.s. *Norfolk*, embarking at Durban, 5th July, 1902, and the Bearer Company embarked at Durban in the s.s. *Drayton Grange*, 8th July, 1902.

WAR SERVICES AND HONOURS OF OFFICERS

First Contingent.

Williams, Surgeon-General, W. D. C., P.M.O., New South Wales Contingent to Soudan, 1885. Special Despatch, *London Gazette*, 5th July, 1886. Medal with clasp; Khedive's star. South African war, 1899 to 1900. Appointed by Lord Roberts on 11th January, 1900, P.M.O., Australian and New Zealand Contingents; and subsequently P.M.O. to Sir Ian Hamilton's Mounted Infantry Division; and later as P.M.O., Sir Archibald Hunter's Field Force. Operations in Orange Free State, Transvaal, Orange River Colony, and Cape Colony. Actions at Johannesburg, Pretoria, Diamond Hill, Bethlehem, Wittebergen, and Wittepoort. Despatches *London Gazette*, 16th April, 1901. C.B. Queen's Medal with five clasps.

Fiaschi, Major T. H. Served with Italian Army in Abyssinian war, 1897–8. South African war. Operations in Orange Free State, and Transvaal, February to November, 1900. Actions at Paardeburg, Poplar Grove, Dreifontein, Houtnek, Vet River, Zand River, Johannesburg, Pretoria, Diamond Hill, and Belfast. Despatches, *London Gazette*, 8th February, 1901, and 16th April, 1901. D.S.O. Queen's Medal with five clasps. Hon. Surgeon to His Excellency the Governor-General. (*C. of A. Gazette*, 8th August, 1902.)

Roth, Major R. E. Operations in Cape Colony, Orange Free State, Transvaal, and Orange River Colony, February, 1900, to November, 1900. Actions at Paardeburg, Poplar Grove, Dreifontein, Karee Siding, Vet River, Zand River, Johannesburg, Pretoria, Diamond Hill, Eland's River, and Bethlehem. Despatches, *London Gazette*, 19th April, 1901. D.S.O. Queen's Medal with six clasps.

Perkins, Major A. E. As above. Despatches, *London Gazette*, 19th April, 1901. D.S.O. Queen's Medal with six clasps.

Green, Major T. A. Operations in Cape Colony, Orange Free State, Transvaal, and Orange River Colony, December, 1899, to May, 1902. Actions at Paardeburg, Vet River, Zand River, Johannesburg, Pretoria, Diamond Hill, and Bethlehem. Despatches, *London Gazette*, 19th April, 1901. D.S.O. Queen's Medal with five clasps.

Martin, Captain T. M. Operations in Orange Free State, Transvaal, and Orange River Colony, February, 1900, to November, 1900. Actions at Paardeburg, Poplar Grove, Dreifontein, Johannesburg, Pretoria, Diamond Hill, Bethlehem, Wittebergen, and Wittepoort. Queen's Medal with six clasps.

Edwards, Captain C. A. Relief of Kimberley. Operations in Orange Free State, and Orange River Colony, February, 1900, to November, 1900. Actions at Paardeburg, Poplar Grove, Dreifontein, Vet River, Zand River, Bethlehem, Wittebergen. Queen's Medal with five clasps. (Captain Edwards went to South Africa with the Infantry, afterwards E squadron, 1st M.R.)

McDonnell, Lieutenant E. P. Relief of Kimberley. Operations in Orange Free State, February to May, 1900. Actions at Paardeburg, Poplar Grove, Dreifontein, Karee Siding, Vet River, Zand River. Queen's Medal with six clasps. (Lieutenant McDonnell accompanied A squadron, 1st M.R., to South Africa.)

Second Contingent.

Kelly, Major and Bt. Lieut.-Colonel, R. V. Operations in Transvaal, and Orange River Colony, May, 1900, to 31st May, 1902. Actions at Johannesburg, Pretoria, Diamond Hill, and Bethlehem. *London Gazette*, 26th June, 1902. C.B. Queen's Medal with five clasps. King's Medal with two clasps.

Eames, Lieut.-Colonel, W. L'E. Operations in Orange Free State and Transvaal, February, 1900, to 27th August, 1900. Actions at Vet River, Zand River, Johannesberg, Pretoria, Diamond Hill, and Belfast. Despatches, *London Gazette*, 27th September, 1901. C.B. Queen's Medal with five clasps.

McCormick, Hon. Major Alex. As before. Despatches, *London Gazette*, 27.9.01. Queen's Medal with four clasps.

Scot-Skirving, Hon. Major Robt. As above. Actions at Vet River and Zand River. Queen's Medal with four clasps.

Marshall, Captain G. A. As above. Queen's Medal with four clasps.

Marshall, Captain J. As above. Actions at Poplar Grove, Dreifontein, Karee Siding, Vet River, Zand River, Johannesburg, Pretoria, Diamond Hill, and Belfast. Queen's Medal with five clasps.

Cortis, Captain W. R. As above. Also actions at Bethlehem and Bothaville. Queen's Medal with five clasps.

Newmarch, Captain B. J. Operations in Orange Free State, Transvaal, and Orange River Colony, February, 1900, to November, 1900. Actions at Vet River, Zand River, Johannesburg, Pretoria, Diamond Hill, Bethlehem, and Bothaville, *London Gazette*, 27th September, 1901. Queen's Medal with four clasps.

Samuelson, Lieut. G. S. Operations in Orange Free State and Transvaal, February, 1900, to May, 1902. Actions at Paardeburg, Poplar Grove, Dreifontein, Karee Siding, Vet River, Zand River, Johannesburg, Pretoria, Diamond Hill. Queen's Medal with five clasps. King's Medal with two clasps.

Dick, Lieut. J. A. Operations in Orange Free State and Transvaal, February, 1900, to November, 1900. Actions as above. *London Gazette*, 27th September, 1901. Queen's Medal with six clasps.

Horsfall, Lieutenant A. H. Operations in Orange Free State, Transvaal, and Orange River Colony, February, 1900, to November, 1900. Actions at Houtnek-Vet River, Zand River, Johannesburg, Pretoria, Diamond Hill, Bethlehem, Wittenbergen. Despatches, *London Gazette*, 27th September, 1901. D.S.O. Queen's Medal with four clasps.

Howse, Lieutenant, N. R. Operations in Transvaal and Orange River Colony, May, 1900, to May, 1902. Actions at Johannesburg, Pretoria, Diamond Hill, Eland's River, Bethlehem, and Wittebergen. *London Gazette*, 4th June, 1900. 𝖁.𝕮. Queen's Medal with six clasps. King's Medal with two clasps. (Lieutenant afterwards Major) Howse went to South Africa with the A.A.M.C. Contingent.)*

Imperial Draft Contingent.

Kelly, Lieut.-Colonel R. V. *Vide* Second Contingent.

Bean, Lieutenant H. K. Operations in Transvaal, 27th April, 1901, to 22nd September, 1901. Queen's Medal with four clasps.

Freyer, Lieutenant J. K. As above. 16th May, 1901, to July, 1901. Queen's Medal with clasps.

Barker, T. H. (Civil Surgeon Hon. Lieutenant). As above. May, 1901, to November, 1901. Queen's Medal with clasps.

Delohery, H. C. M. (Civil Surgeon Hon. Lieutenant). Operations in Transvaal from May, 1901, to May, 1902. Queen's Medal with clasps.

Commonwealth Contingent.

Green, Major T. A. *Vide* First Contingent.

Howse, Major N. R. *Vide* Second Contingent.

Jermyn, Captain F. D. Operations in Cape Colony, Orange River Colony, and Transvaal, 1900 to 1902. Actions at Johannesburg, Pretoria, and Diamond Hill. Queen's Medal with five clasps.

---

* The conduct for which Major Howse was awarded the V.C. is thus officially recorded: "During the action of Vredefort, 24th July, 1900, Captain Howse went out under a heavy crossfire and picked up a wounded man, and carried him to a place of shelter."—*London Gazette*, 4th June, 1901.

Nyulasy, A. J. (C. S., Hon. Captain). Operations in Transvaal, 19th March, 1902, to 31st May, 1902. Queen's Medal with clasps.

Cade, D. D. (C. S., Hon. Captain). As above.

Formby, H. H. (C. S., Hon. Captain). As above.

James, W. A. (C. S., Hon. Captain). As above.

Eberling, Lieut. Quarter-Master Richard. Operations in Cape Colony, Orange River Colony, and Transvaal, 1899 to 1902. Queen's Medal with four clasps.

EXTRACTS FROM REPORTS OF COLONEL W. D. C. WILLIAMS, PRINCIPAL MEDICAL OFFICER, NEW SOUTH WALES ARMY MEDICAL CORPS.

Orange River, 7th January, 1900.—Our first camp at Green Point, about 1½ miles from the wharf, and about 3 miles from town. After duly reporting arrival to C. of S. and Surgeon-General of Army Corps and the G.O.C. of L. of C., I was informed that they had given the A.A.M. Corps the highest post of honour they could, by attaching us to the Field Army under Sir Redvers Buller.

Our inspection was all that could be desired, and Colonel Stevenson, the Inspecting Officer, was profuse in his compliments.

The order to move on to Orange River came just before dark. I had *reveille* sounded at 3.30 a.m. on 21st December, 1899, and at 7.20 a.m. stores were packed and camp cleaned up, and we were at the railway station at five minutes before 8 a.m.—our orders being to entrain at 8 a.m.

On arriving at Orange River about 8 a.m. on the 23rd December, we detrained and moved down to a point 1½ miles from the station, and pitched the Bearer Company camp and Field Hospitals as two distinct units. The Field Hospital was ready to receive patients at 5 p.m. the same day.

They were very short of Field Hospital accommodation, and we had orders to receive all the sick of the Royal Scots Greys, No. 37 R.F.A. Howitzer Battery, Imperial Mounted Infantry, Queensland Mounted Infantry, Remington's Guides, and the sick and wounded coming in by train from the north.

Naturally, we rapidly filled up, and had to extend our accommodation to nearly double our original scale. Major-General Elliott Wood, R.E., is in command here, and has made great demands on our Bearer company. Captains Roth and Martin, with three ambulances, one cart, and stretcher party, left here 14 days ago with a flying column, and did good work at the Sunnyside fight.

Another wagon and party went with the Scots Greys the next day to Douglas. On Friday, the 5th, Captain Perkins and Lieutenant Edwards, with ambulance and cart transport and stretcher party, moved off at 8 p.m. with a flying column of mixed arms under Colonel Alworth, north of Orange River. Captain Green, with two carts for ambulance transport and one transport cart and stretcher party, moved off at 4 a.m. next day, with another column of 700 men under Lieut.-Colonel Davidson, R.H.A., to a point south of Orange River, meeting the northern force by a R.E. pontoon bridge. This leaves only Major Fiaschi and myself to run the Field Hospital, and as we have twelve cases of enteric fever and over twenty cases of dysentry, besides a large number of other cases, including officers, we are busy to a degree.

I have visited, by direction of the Principal Medical Officer, Orange River, the New South Wales Lancers and the New Zealanders at Arundel, and have adjusted one or two items *re* the medical services there.

The Principal Medical Officer next sent me to Belmont, Enslin, and the Modder, to visit Australian troops there.

23rd February, 1900.—I was instructed by the Principal Medical Officer, South Africa, to proceed from Orange River to Cape Town to meet the New South Wales Army Medical Corps units which arrived at Cape Town on the 17th inst. by the transports *Moravian* and *Southern Cross*. I was instructed to distribute them as follows :—

Moravian unit to proceed by sea to East London, and thence to Sterkstroom, and hand over to General Gatacre. This was in accordance with special instructions from Lord Roberts, Commander-in-Chief. As this unit was most urgently needed, the *Moravian* was turned round and left for East London a few hours after its arrival off Cape Town. Lieutenants Samuelson and Dick, New South Wales Army Medical Corps, remained behind and proceeded north for duty with the New South Wales Lancers and No. 1 Field Hospital (New South Wales).

From the composite Half-Bearer Company and Field Hospital units, I was instructed to detail for special temporary duty at the stationary 100-bedded Field Hospital two officers and twelve N.C.O.'s and men.

This was done, with Lieut.-Colonel Kelly in command. Miss Gould (New South Wales), Lady Superintendent Army Nursing Service Reserve, and three nursing sisters (New South Wales) are at this hospital. Miss Gould is in nursing charge of the District (Orange River).

Four (New South Wales) nursing sisters were detailed for duty at the Base Hospital, East London, and six nursing sisters went to the General Hospital, Wynberg.

Bloemfontein, 4th April, 1900.—The Commander-in-Chief paid an official inspection to the hospital we have established here in the Orange Free State Artillery Barracks. A wretchedly dirty and out-of-repair structure, when we took it over; but by heavy fatigue parties and the help of the Royal Engineers, we have made it passable. We run 150 beds. Lord Roberts went round each ward and cheered up the wounded, and at the end of the inspection graciously informed me that he was extremely pleased with all he had seen, and complimented the staff of the hospital on the manner in which they had carried out their difficult work. His Excellency also spoke in high terms of our New South Wales ambulance wagons, and stated he intended to recommend them as a pattern.

Nominal Roll.

No. and Name.	Rank.	Remarks.
FIRST CONTINGENT.		
Williams, William Duncan Campbell	Colonel	Principal Medical Officer, New South Wales Forces. Soudan Contingent, 1885
Fiaschi, Thomas Henry	Major	
Roth, Reuter Emmerich	,,	
Perkins, Alfred Edward	,,	
Green, Terence Albert	Captain	
Martin, Thomas Morgan	,,	
Edwards, Charles Augustus	,,	Infantry, afterwards "E" Squadron, M.R.C.
McDonnell, Edward Patrick	Lieutenant	"A" Squadron, M.R.C.
Mason, Edmund Percy	Warrant-Officer	Soudan, 1885
Bond, John	,, ,,	
Mills, John Hopping	Quarter-Master Sergeant	
5. Eberling, Richard	Sergeant	Staff Sergeant, 24.1.00; invalided, Australia, arr. 15.9.00

Nominal Roll—continued.

No. and Name.	Rank.	Remarks.

First Contingent—continued.

No. and Name.	Rank.	Remarks.
10. Airey, Francis Charles	Sergeant	
11. Dart, George A.	,,	
4. Hadfield, D.	,,	Staff Sergeant
9. Hindmarsh, Alfred J.	,,	
7. Reuder, Thomas N.	,,	
6. Rose, James Dobson	,,	
8. Walpole, William	,,	
12. Rose, George	Lance Sergeant	
13. Davies, William	Trumpeter	
14. Blair, Arthur	Bugler	
18. Colliver, W. C.	Corporal	
17. Connolly, John	,,	
19. Donnellan, John Joseph	,,	
20. Harkness, Thomas	,,	
15. Regden, Henry W.	,,	
16. Schofield, G.	,,	
21. Strong, Lewis	,,	
25. Colbourne, William	Lance Corporal	
24. Cox, Thomas	,,	
27. Green, James	,,	
23. Hannah, John	,,	
22. Maund, James	,,	
28. Poole, William	,,	
26. Ransom, Henry F.	,,	
38. Aitken, Frederick	Private	
44. Blackball, Thomas	,,	
77. Blestowe, William	,,	
79. Chamberlain, Edwin	,,	
70. Collins, William Wallace	,,	
30. Cousens, William M.	,,	
52. Cronin, D. M.	,,	
32. Daggars, Sydney	,,	
66. Dargin, Alfred	,,	
53. Downey, George	,,	
48. Easby, John Henry	,,	
67. Frazer, John	,,	
51. Gill, William	,,	
36. Goodhall, Thomas	,,	
82. Goodsell, Isaac	,,	
69. Gray, Albert J. H.	,,	
85. Harrison, Charles	,,	
29. Harrison, Joseph	,,	
63. Healey, Joseph H.	,,	
80. Henry, John	,,	
57. Hitchens, Ernest	,,	
75. Howarth, John S.	,,	
55. Inman, Arthur	,,	
83. Justin, Alfred J.	,,	
34. Kenny, Frederick	,,	
42. Legge, Henry Percy	,,	Invalided, Australia, arr. 30.8.00
43. Levido, Otto	,,	
59. Lewis, William David	,,	
84. Linfield, Cornelius	,,	
39. Longbottom, Henrick	,,	
54. Louden, James	,,	Invalided, Australia, arr. 17.8.00
33. McKinley, Ernest Albert	,,	

Nominal Roll—*continued*.

No. and Name.	Rank.	Remarks.
First Contingent—*continued.*		
68. McNamara, Ernest Edward	Private	Invalided, Australia, arr. 6.8.00
71. McNaughton, William	Corporal	
46. Maiers, August	Private	
76. Matheson, Angus	,,	
41. Midgley, Arthur	,,	
45. Newton, George Chapman	,,	Invalided, Australia, arr. 28.5.00
49. Norris, Thomas Henry	,,	
60. Oram, John	,,	Died 22.2.00, Orange River Station, from enteric fever
37. Parkhill, Robert	,,	Invalided, Australia, arr. 19.9.00
56. Riglesford, John	,,	
58. Russell, Alexander Wykes	,,	
81. Selmes, George Francis	,,	Despatches, *London Gazette*, 16.4.01 : D.C.M.
61. Shapter, Alfred Ernest	,,	
74. Smith, Thomas	,,	Died, 26.2.00, Orange River Station, from enteric fever
65. Stanton, Oswald Joseph	,,	Invalided, Australia, arr. 6.8.00
47. Stratton, George	,,	
35. Tait, Alfred Stephen	,,	
50. Timmins, Frederick	,,	
62. Townley, Frank	,,	
31. Walker, John Thomas	,,	
64. Walton, Robert Orlando	,,	
72. Warren, Herbert	,,	
78. White, Charles	,,	
40. Widgery, Edward	,,	
73. Willey, George	,,	
Second Contingent.		
Kelly, Robert Vandeleur	Major and Brevet Lieut.-Colonel	
Eames, William L'Estrange	Major	
McCormick, Alexander	Hon. Major	Special service
Scot-Skirving, Robert	,,	Special service
Marshall, George Archibald	Captain	
Marshall, Joseph	,,	
Cortis, William Richard	,,	
Newmarch, Bernard James	,,	
Samuelson, Gerald Septimus	Lieutenant	
Dick, James Adam	,,	
Horsfall, Alfred Herbert	,,	
Howse, Neville Reginald	,,	
322. Howarth, John	Quarter-Master Sergeant	
323. Jones, John	Staff-Sergeant	Invalided, Australia, arr. 21.1.01
321. Pantlin, Frederick W.	,,	
325. Branston, Charles	Sergeant	Invalided, Australia, arr. 21.1.01
324. Burden, Harry W.	,,	Invalided, Australia, arr. 8.2.01
407. Falconer, Robert B.	,,	
330. Hole, Alfred	,,	Acting Sergeant-Major, 2.5.00
326. Loney, Walter H.	,,	Died, 29.7.00, Frankfort, from enteric fever
327. McKewen, Dominick	,,	
328. Salvatori, George	Sergeant	
329. Sullivan, Thomas	,,	

Nominal Roll—continued.

No. and Name.	Rank.	Remarks.
SECOND CONTINGENT—*continued.*		
323. Avon, George	Farrier-Sergeant	
336. Fidden, Charles W.	Lance-Sergeant	Invalided, Australia, arr. 8.2.01
348. Jordan, George	Private	Corporal, 7.4.00; Lance-Sergeant, 1.11.00
346. McEwen, James Fraser	Private	Corporal, 1.11.00
338. Wilson, Alexander	Corporal	Lance-Sergeant, 28.7.00
333. Brears, Norman Frederick	,,	Invalided, Australia, arr. 17.8.00
332. Buttwell, Henry	,,	
340. Carroll, Thomas	,,	Sergeant, 18.5.00; invalided, Australia, arr. 17.5.01
339. Hayward, Henry	,,	Invalided, Australia, arr. 8.2.01
337. Ladd, William	,,	
408. Lyons, George	,,	Lance-Sergeant, 20.3.00; Quartermaster-Sergeant, invalided to England, 3.7.00; Superintending Clerk, S.O., A. and N.Z. Forces, 22.12.00
334. Watts, Ernest	,,	Lance-Sergeant, 1.4.00
335. Wauhope, Hugh	,,	
427. Willis, A.	,,	
428. Berkley, Sidney	Trumpeter	Invalided, Australia, arr. 30.7.00
405. Hardwick, Edward	,,	
404. Masters, Herbert V.	,,	
385. Ayres, Jesse	Lance-Corporal	
331. Clifford, Robert W.	,,	Corporal; Lance-Sergeant, 27.10.00
358. Coulter, Charles W.	,,	Invalided, Australia, arr. 12.2.00
364. Dadd, Herbert	,,	
360. Fishburn, William R.	,,	
399. Murphy, Francis	,,	
424. Priestly, Percy Roland	,,	Invalided, Australia, arr. 30.7.00
396. Reynell, Henry C.	,,	
341. Taylor, James W.	,,	
400. Warden, Charles Robert	,,	
372. Whelan, John	,,	
352. Bennett, Harry	Private	
357. Blanchard, John	,,	
403. Bosler, James Martin	Driver	Invalided, Australia, arr. 28.5.00
409. Bowman, William	Private	Invalided Australia
398. Burne, Lawford W.	,,	
344. Byrne, Stephen M.	,,	Invalided, Australia, arr. 5.1.01
371. Cox, Albert Edward	,,	
375. Cuddy, John	,,	Invalided, Australia, arr. 11.12.00
411. Darby, Frank A.	,,	
410. Davies, Ernest C.	,,	
401. Devery, Nicholas	,,	
347. Duck, Claude F.	,,	
353. Eaves, Frederick Ernest	,,	
363. Edbrook, Henry T.	,,	Invalided, Australia, arr. 30.7.00
343. Edmunds, Alfred	,,	
414. Finley, Francis A.	,,	
413. Flanagan, Cornelius	,,	
342. Franklin, Walter	,,	Invalided, Australia, arr. 30.7.00
412. Franks, Samuel	,,	
392. Freeman, George E.	,,	
383. Gates, James C.	,,	
350. Gavin, Bede	,,	

Nominal Roll—continued.

No. and Name.	Rank.	Remarks.
SECOND CONTINGENT—*continued.*		
368. Golledge, Halford W.	Private	
388. Gordon, Joseph	,,	Invalided, Australia, arr. 8.2.01
85. Harrison, C. E.	,,	Invalided, Australia, arr. 16.11.00
362. Hale, Thomas	,,	
415. Hambly, William H.	,,	
370. Harris, William	,,	Invalided, Australia, arr. 30.7.00
354. Hartnett, James F.	,,	
416. Heath, William	,,	
429. Hill, Ebenezer	,,	Invalided, Australia, arr. 6.8.00
395. Jones, David	,,	
355. Jones, Ernest J.	,,	
417. Kelly, John Joseph	,,	Died, 19.5.00, Bloemfontein, from enteric fever
420. Kelly, Thomas	,,	
419. Learoyd, William E.	,,	Invalided, Australia, arr. 30.8.00
418. Lees, William J.	,,	Invalided, Australia, arr. 30.7.00
376. McAllister, William	,,	
365. McGowan, Allan J.	,,	
356. McDermott, Gabriel	,,	
377. McKeown, Norman R.	,,	
421. McNamara, Dennis	,,	
420. McNeill, Charles	,,	
393. McNiven, Arthur	,,	
374. McPherson, William	,,	Invalided, Australia, arr. 8.2.01
345. Milson, Frederick	,,	
381. Murray, Patrick	,,	
391. Neisk, John	,,	
359. Newell, Sidney	,,	Invalided, Australia, arr. 8.2.01
390. O'Grady, Stephen J.	,,	
423. Pacey, Charles M.	,,	
422. Parrott, John H.	,,	Invalided, Australia, arr. 5.1.01
351. Pawla, Frederick	,,	
387. Pringle, Andrew	,,	
426. Reardon, William T.	,,	
425. Reid, Robert	,,	
349. Seguss, Arthur Richard	,,	
366. Sloan, Robert	,,	
386. Spence, Arthur R.	,,	
361. Spyer, Haden	,,	
380. Stevens, Norman B.	,,	
367. Stewart, John G.	,,	Invalided, Australia, arr. 17.5.01
389. Taylor, James W.	,,	
373. Thornton, Percy	,,	
379. Thornton, Sylvester	,,	
382. Tressider, William P.	,,	
369. Turner, Harold	,,	
378. Vaughan, Horace	,,	
384. Ward, James	,,	
394. Watson, Thomas	,,	
IMPERIAL DRAFT CONTINGENT.		
Kelly, Robert Vandeleur	Lieut.-Colonel	
Bean, Harold Knowles	Lieutenant	
Freyer, John Kennedy	,,	
Barker, Theodore Hugh	Civil Surgeon	
Delohery, Henry Charles M.	,,	
1649. Mills, John Happing	Quarter-Master Sergeant	

Nominal Roll—continued.

No. and Name.	Rank.	Remarks.
IMPERIAL DRAFT CONTINGENT—continued.		
1711. Martin, Edward Terence	Staff-Sergeant	
3015. Poole, William	Sergeant	Staff-Sergeant, 8.4.02
1712. Eadie, James	Corporal	Lance-Sergeant, 31.7.01; Sergeant, 8.4.02
1209. Green, James	,,	Lance-Sergeant, 31.7.01; Sergeant, 18.9.01
1710. Hawkins, Frederick John	Sergeant	Invalided, Australia, arr. 16.9.01
805. Schofield, George	,,	
2992. Warden, Charles Robert	Sergeant - Compounder	
802. Wray, Renfrew Maxwell Frederick	,,	
1713. Mead, Henry Norman Robert	Corporal	Lance-Sergeant, 23.8.01
3106. Easby, John Henry	Lance-Corporal	Corporal, 8.4.02
2002. Smeed, William	Private	Corporal, 18.9.01
2566. Lawrence, Harry	Lance-Corporal	
1067. Powell, Arthur John	,,	
1955. Anderson, Walter Robert	Private	
3077. Avery, George	,,	
3664. Bentley, Tom	,,	
3636. Brown, John Andrew	,,	
1344. Collyer, Albert James	,,	
3443. Cox, Albert Edward	,,	
1210. Cranney, William Henry	,,	
1137. Denecker, William Granville	,,	
1136. Eaves, Frederick Ernest	,,	
801. Ellis, John Aloysius	,,	
2220. Gaston, Percy Mansfield	,,	
1346. Golding, Hollis	,,	
3076. Griffin, Thomas	,,	
2509. Haddow, Edmund	,,	
795. Harper, Arthur	,,	
798. Honnes, William	,,	
999. Jones, David	,,	
1995. Jones, William J.	,,	
1966. Kennedy, Herbert	,,	
316. Louden, James	,,	
1945. McAllister, William	,,	
3385. McCosker, William Bernard	,,	
3277. McGowan, Frederick Ernest	,,	
3383. Miller, Oliver Francis	,,	
2517. Moore, Harry	,,	
3503. Mullins, Arthur	,,	
3688. O'Reilly, Mathew	,,	
796. Perdriau, Ralph Joseph	,,	
1882. Scott, John	,,	
1731. Shapter, Alfred	,,	
1800. Vaughan, Arthur Ernest	,,	
1176. Wilkins, George Thomas	,,	
1068. Wootten, William Frederick	,,	Invalided, Australia, arr. 23.9.01; severely wounded at Machaieve
800. Wormleaton, Thomas Phillip	,,	
COMMONWEALTH CONTINGENT.		
Green, Terence Albert	Major	
Howse, Neville Reginald	,,	
Jermyn, Frederick D.	Captain	
Nyulasy, Arthur John	,,	

Nominal Roll—*continued*.

No. and Name.	Rank.	Remarks.
COMMONWEALTH CONTINGENT—*continued*.		
Cade, David Duncan	Lieutenant	
Formby, Henry H.	,,	
James, William A.	,,	
Eberling, Richard	Warrant-Officer	Lieut.-Quarter Master, 1.4.02
1264. McEwen, James Fraser	Sergeant	Warrant Officer, 1.4.02
1339. Walker, Frederick	Warrant-Officer	
1292. Hadfield, David	Staff-Sergeant	
1296. Donnellan, John Joseph	,,	
1320. Sellwood, William	,,	
1340. Lowry, Robert Alexander	Sergeant	Staff-Sergeant, 1.4.02
1341. Holliday, James Owen	Collarmaker-Sergeant	
1291. Moon, William John	Farrier-Sergeant	
1294. Moore, John Marston	Sergeant-smith	
1272. Atkinson, Lionel Howard	Sergeant	
1293. Carroll, Thomas	,,	
1323. Elphick, Harold Edward	,,	
1277. Hibberd, Claude Wilfred	,,	
1297. Hutchings, Thomas Stawell	Lance-Sergeant	Sergeant, 1.4.02
1298. Jackson, Henry George	Sergeant	
1286. Ransom, Henry Franklin	,,	
1311. Vernon, William Francis John	,,	
1268. White, Charles	,,	
1284. Harrison, Charles John	Corporal	Lance-Sergeant, 1.4.02
1285. Smith, Edward Adolphus	Bugler	
1274. Campbell, George	Corporal	
1261. Cousens, William Mark	,,	
1357. Jeffers, John Patrick	,,	
1299. Kemp, James	,,	
1306. Loughran, Gerald Henry	,,	
1333. Nation, John Boath	,,	
1342. Quinn, John	,,	
1315. Bisset, Ernest George	Lance-Corporal	
1338. Worthington, Andrew Leonard	,,	
1288. Adam, Herbert Laurie	Private	
1354. Adams, Henry	,,	
1325. Angrave, Alfred James	,,	
1349. Armstrong, William Herbert	,,	
1350. Arnsby, Thomas William	,,	
1326. Ayliff, William Lionel	,,	
1273. Atkins, Arthur Edward	,,	
1319. Bade, Alfred	,,	
1307. Bailey, Percy Francis	,,	
1310. Balmer, Frederick William	,,	
1345. Benjamin, Adolph Bertram	,,	
1300. Beulke, Auguste Edward	,,	
1327. Blackwell, Matthew	,,	
1352. Cavanagh, Thomas	,,	
1328. Chamberlayne, Thomas Cecil	,,	
1309. Chandler, Albert	,,	
1316. Chapman, Alick	,,	
1271. Childe, Frederick William	,,	
1358. Cunningham, Alexander Vincent	,,	
1317. Currie, Albert John	,,	
1289. Darragh, Edward James	,,	

Nominal Roll—*continued.*

No. and Name.	Rank.	Remarks.
COMMONWEALTH CONTINGENT—*continued.*		
1329. Davis, William Frank	Private	
1312. Doonan, John	,,	
1348. Dunsmore, William Wallace	,,	
1322. Emmerson, Walter Thomas	,,	
1347. Farrell, William Arthur	,,	
1318. Fulford, Charles Edward	,,	
1275. Gallagher, Charles	,,	
1262. Gammon, Harry	,,	
1343. Hair, Victor Arthur	,,	
1263. Hale, Thomas Arthur	,,	
1313. Hay, Walter Stewart	,,	
1276. Hayes, Henry Albert	,,	
1331. Higgs, Ernest Alexander	,,	
1267. Hollander, Percy Eneyl	,,	
1330. Hollywood, Simon John	,,	
1324. James, Frederick William	,,	
1278. Johnson, Leslie John	,,	
1359. Kempton, Henry Edgar	,,	
1290. McPherson, Cecil	,,	
1362. Matthews, Samuel	,,	
1314. May, Joseph	,,	
1344. Miller, Andrew Reid	,,	
1279. Moore, Hugh	,,	
1283. Morrissey, Albert	,,	
1332. Muir, Thomas Kerr	,,	
1303. Murray, John Wederburn	,,	
1334. Neville, Henry Beauchamp	,,	
1265. Nixon, Clyde William Pemberton	,,	
1280. O'Sullivan, John	,,	
1335. Paynter, Oliver Arthur	,,	
1304. Phillips, Reginald Stuart	,,	
1351. Polson, Alfred Henderson	,,	
1353. Pringle, Alfred	,,	
1361. Reynolds, Sylvanus	,,	
1270. Roberts, Charles Hardwick	,,	
1321. Roughton, William	,,	
1336. Rule, Vivian Roland	,,	
1269. Shrimpton, Jesse	,,	
1301. Smith, Alfred John	,,	
1266. Spackman, James	,,	
1305. Stein, James Laurie	,,	
1355. Stone, William Charles	,,	
1337. Stone, William Ernest	,,	
1302. Suter, Thomas George	,,	
1356. Thorp, Frank Clarence	,,	Promoted Corporal and Lance-Sergeant, 1.4.02
1346. Tunley, Arthur	,,	
1360. Waterman, Frederick Thomas Samuel	,,	
1287. Webb, Claude Charles	,,	
1308. Williams, Thomas	,,	
1282. Withers, George M.	,,	
1281. Woodward, Sydney Edward R.	,,	
1267. Yann, Frederick	,,	

"A" SQUADRON MOUNTED RIFLES.

THIS was originally a draft from the regiment of New South Wales Mounted Rifles, which had been in existence for some years before the war, and served upon the partial-payment system. It still figures in the Army list as the 2nd Australian Light Horse, "New South Wales Mounted Rifles," on the Militia establishment.* The squadron comprised a picked body of especially smart men; good shots and daring riders, excellently mounted; and it did exceptional service during the war.

The establishment authorized in the first instance was as for Lancers, omitting "Major" and substituting 98 privates for 97.

The squadron at first consisted of 4 officers and 100 others, with 104 horses and 3 carts. It was despatched on 3rd November, 1899, and was shortly afterwards followed by a draft of 25 sergeants and rank and file, with 25 horses. One medical officer joined in South Africa, and 6 men were enrolled there. Of these details, 8 were killed or died, 5 were struck off the strength in South Africa, 1 officer was commissioned in the Imperial Army, and 2 men were sent back respectively from Albany and Cape Town; 4 officers and 113 men returned to Australia.

Subsequent to the departure of the squadron, however, a second Contingent had been formed, comprising "B," "C," and "D" Squadrons, "1st Regiment, New South Wales Mounted Rifles," despatched on 17th January, 1900 (*vide* record). The first Contingent, consisting of the squadron now referred to, and a company of Infantry (*vide* record) which left in the same ship, became absorbed as "A" and "E" squadrons respectively of this regiment; the company being mounted at the seat of war.

As already stated, the squadron embarked at Sydney on the transport *Aberdeen*, 3rd November, 1899, arrived at Cape Town on 6th December, and disembarked on the following day. Embarked again at Cape Town on the Transport *Orient*. 13th December, 1900, called at Albany and Melbourne, arrived at Sydney, and disembarked, 8th January, 1901.

REFERENCES TO ORDERS.

Formation ..	.. G.O., N.S.W.,	107/99
Pay and Allowances ..	,, ,,	107/99, 112/99, 88/00
Command ..	.. ,, ,,	116/99
Conditions of Service ..	,, ,,	107/99
Officers ..	.. ,, ,,	110/99
Establishment	.. ,, ,,	108/99
Embarkation	.. ,, ,,	116/99, 123/99, 124/99

CLOTHING, ETC.

Uniform consisted of brown F.S. jackets and pants, with puttees and hats.

Arms and equipment.—M.E. rifles and long bayonet, bandolier and cartridge-belt, with supporting braces.

Fully horsed and provided with saddles.

Regimental transport was also provided.

PROMOTIONS.

The following officers were promoted or appointed in South Africa:—Captain J. M. Antill to Major; Lieutenant A. A. McLean to Captain. Corporal C. A. Lee, Sergeant H. McIntosh, and Q.M.S. J. Newman: each to Lieutenant. For promotions amongst the N.C. officers and men, see Nominal Roll.

---

* Allied with "King Edward's Horse"; the King's Oversea Dominions Regiment.

War Services and Honours.

Antill, Major J. M. (Brevet Lieut.-Colonel). Relief of Kimberley. Operations in Orange Free State, Transvaal, and Orange River Colony, from February to 30th November, 1900. Actions at Paardeburg, Poplar Grove, Dreifontein, Karee Siding, Vet River, Zand River, Johannesburg, Pretoria, Diamond Hill, Eland's River, Venterskroon, and Wittebergen. *London Gazette*, 8th February, and 16th April, 1901. C.B. Queen's Medal with seven clasps. (Major Antill served subsequently with 2nd New South Wales Mounted Rifles in Transvaal and Orange River Colony, April to August, 1901.)

McLean, Capt. A. A. (Hon. Major). Relief of Kimberley. Operations and actions as stated, except Bothaville in place of Venterskroon. (Captain McLean served subsequently in Transvaal and Orange River Colony between April, 1901, and April, 1902.) *London Gazette*, 27th September, 1901. D.S.O. Queen's Medal with seven clasps. King's Medal with two clasps.

Onslow, Lieutenant A. J. M. Relief of Kimberley. Operations in Orange Free State, February to May, 1900. Actions at Paardeburg, Poplar Grove, Dreifontein, Karee Siding, Vet River, and Zand River. Severely wounded at Groot Vlei, 21st May, 1900. Queen's Medal with three clasps.

Tooth, Lieutenant D. K. L. Relief of Kimberley. Operations and actions as for Major Antill, except subsequent service. Wounded at Palmeitfontein, 19th July, 1900. Mentioned in despatches, 28th August, 1900. Queen's Medal with seven clasps. Commissioned in 9th Lancers.

McDonnell, Lieutenant (Surgeon) E. P. See Army Medical Corps.

Principal Operations.

Left De Aar 30th December, 1899, with Colonel Alderson, for Prieska, to cope with a rising of rebels in the district.

3rd January, 1900.—Colonel Alderson returned to De Aar, leaving the New South Wales Mounted Rifles with a small detachment of the Remington Guides to take charge of the township and district (strength 130).

13th January.—Owing to a large force of Boers (estimated 800) attacking, retired towards De Aar; were reinforced by Colonel Alderson, and again advanced on Prieska, and after remaining a short time, marched to Orange River station.

Unit was sent to a farm at Ramah, about 15 miles east of Orange River station, to clear the Boers from the locality, where it remained till 10th February, when it was taken over by Colonel Hannay, and after fighting a severe action near Ramah, as the rear guard to Lord Roberts' column, advanced with the latter through Ram-dam and Jacobsdal to Klip Drift; where, following French's force to the relief of Kimberley, it was engaged with Cronje's army on 16th February.

Was detailed on the following day to follow Cronje, and located his laager at noon at Paardeburg, sustaining some casualties. Paardeburg followed; the commanding officer (Colonel Hannay) being killed.

On the surrender of General Cronje, the New South Wales Mounted Rifles were personally detailed by Lord Roberts to take over his laager and prisoners. It was then attached to Colonel Le Gallais' command, and joined by Colonel Knight, with the 2nd Contingent at Osfontein, 5th March. Took part in the engagements at Abrahams Kraal and Dreifontein and the march to Bloemfontein, which was reached on 14th March.

Marched to the Glen and engaged the enemy on 29th March; remained here until 1st May on outpost duty, and joined General Hutton, being part of the 2nd Corps (Colonel De Lisle). Occupied Brandfort, and present at the engagements at Vet River, and an important reconnaissance of Botha's army at Zand River, followed by a fight at Ventersburg-road on the 10th May. On arrival at

Kroonstadt on the 12th May, were taken from General Hutton and attached to General Ian Hamilton; marching on the 15th May through Lindley and Heilbron to the Vaal River, which was crossed on 25th May.

Engaged with the enemy at Johannesburg on 28th May, and occupied the city next day. Marched on Pretoria, 2nd June, and were the first troops to reach the city on the evening of 4th June, after some few hours opposition.

Marching through Irene, moved on and fought a severe battle at Diamond Hill on 11th and 12th June; casualties heavy, and the regiment specially mentioned in Divisional Orders by General Ian Hamilton. Followed Botha's army to Bronkhurst Spruit, returning to Pretoria 16th June, from thence south to Heidelberg, which was taken on 23rd June; and thence through Villiersdorp, Frankfort, and Reitz to Bethlehem on 9th June. Here De Wet was hiding in the rough country to the south, from whence he broke out on 17th June. Followed him generally north-west, with numerous rear-guard engagements, when he eventually got away to the railway at Roodeval, where he had passed the day previously, burned a train, and moved on to the Vaal.

Sent out by the General Officer Commanding as a contact squadron to recover touch with De Wet, he having been lost by the Cavalry, and located him 20 miles north-east at Vreedefort, where he was surrounded until 5th August, when, having moved north along the Vaal, the whole force of some five divisions chased him to the Megalesberg, through which at Oliphant's Nek he escaped on 15th August.

Moved westward by forced march, and relieved the Bushmen under Colonel Hore at Elands River on 16th August; thence again to Pretoria through Rustenburg on 25th August.

After taking part in sundry small reconnaissances in this district, the regiment was split into two, one part moving along the railway through Middelberg to Machadodorp, and the remainder south, where it took part in the severe fight at Rustenburg Drift, the regiment capturing a Krupp from De Wet (sent to New South Wales by the Commander-in-Chief); and to Bothaville, where there was a severe fight on 6th November. A large number of Boers were killed and taken prisoners; all their waggons, three Krupps, one 15-pounder, one 12-pounder, a Pom-pom and a Maxim were captured. Reached Kroonstadt on 17th November, joined by the remainder of the Contingent which had come from Machadodorp; entrained to Cape Town, and embarked for Sydney 13th December, Lord Milner and several Generals coming to the transport (*Orient*) to say good-bye. Reached Sydney and disbanded 8th January, 1901. The Contingent lost no horses on their voyage to South Africa. No men were taken prisoners during the campaign. Its strength was 130. Its honours were:—One C.B.; one D.S.O.; three D.C.M.'s.

CORPS ORDER BY COLONEL H. B. DE LISLE (2ND MOUNTED INFANTRY.)

109. Elands River Station, 13th June, 1900.

General Hamilton Commanding the Force has desired the Commandant to express to all ranks of the 2nd Corps and the Pom-Pom Section "A" his congratulations on their achievement on the evening of the 12th instant at Diamond Hill, of which he has made a special report to the Field Marshal Commander-in-Chief. In publishing this, the Commandant wishes to express his high appreciation of the way Captain Antill and the New South Wales Mounted Rifles advanced to take the hill yesterday, and the gallant way the regiment pushed forward beyond the crest under a murderous fire. He deeply regrets the casualties and especially the death of Lieutenant Drage, when bravely leading his men.

By order,

R. FANSHAW, Captain,

S.O. De Lisle's Corps.

COPY OF LETTER FROM GENERAL RIDLEY, COMMANDING 2ND BRIGADE, MOUNTED INFANTRY.

My dear Antill,

I cannot let you leave the country without telling how much I have appreciated the services of yourself and your men. Their gallantry, endurance, and cheeriness under very great stress have been beyond praise, and their skilful handling was admirable. Please remember me to all officers. I shall be glad to assist any of them, as far as I can, especially in any way to further any ideas they may have of making a career in this country.

Yours very sincerely,
C. RIDLEY, Brigadier-General,
2nd Brigade Mounted Infantry.

COPY OF LETTER FROM GENERAL ALDERSON, COMMANDING MOUNTED INFANTRY.

Major J. M. Antill, New South Wales Mounted Infantry, has been under my command on several occasions during the past year, and I have been much impressed with the way in which he has handled and managed his men. I consider that his Contingent has been more under control and in hand than any of the Colonial troops I have seen.

Major Antill is a dashing and capable leader in action, and remarkably cool under fire. I have personally seen him carry out some difficult and dangerous tasks with great success. I am extremely sorry Major Antill and the 1st Contingent New South Wales Mounted Rifles are now leaving my command, and I am very glad to have been able to bring his services especially to the notice of the Field Marshal Commander-in-Chief.

E. A. S. ALDERSON, Brigadier-General,
Commanding Mounted Infantry Brigade.

Pretoria, 16/11/1900.

The majority of the Contingent earned the following clasps :—(1) Relief of Kimberley, (2) Paardeburg, (3) Dreifontein, (4) Johannesburg, (5) Diamond Hill, (6) Wittebergen.

EXTRACTS FROM DIARY OF CAPTAIN J. M. ANTILL, NEW SOUTH WALES MOUNTED RIFLES.

Honwater, 16/1/1900.—My last letter advised departure from De Aar through to Prieska on 30th ult. The column consisted of 80 mounted rifles, one company mounted infantry, one troop Remington's Guides, and two Maxim guns. The march (135 to 140 miles) was done in three days. The water is scarce in this district, necessitating fixed stages. Arrived within 15 miles of Prieska on the Orange River on the evening of the 3rd, finishing our march by 4 a.m. next day. Colonel Alderson in command, directed me to at once occupy the southern bank—the northern being in possession of the rebels—and to attack immediately they made their appearance, which was expected to be at sunrise (5 a.m.) At daylight some twenty of them showed and after a smart fire for some 20 minutes, in which five of them were wounded, they decamped, over the mountainous country towards Grigua-town. I crossed over on foot, and pursued them on foot, with a troop for some distance, but could not get near them. Returning to the huts occupied by them, secured a quantity of arms, ammunition, saddlery, &c., and found a Kaffir of their party badly wounded. Started to-day to make "dampers" from wheat; bread unprocurable.

Omdraau Vlei, 22/1/1900.—Prieska having been attacked by rebels on the 13th, I retired to this place (about 40 miles south), and here I await reinforcements which arrive to-morrow from De Aar. Our relief consists of a battery R.A., one squadron of Imperial Light Horse, two companies infantry, and two companies mounted infantry. I was, fortunately, able to effect retirement without loss of life or mishap; but only evacuated Prieska 1½ hours before it was occupied by the Boers in large numbers. I also got my prisoners away to De Aar, as well as 1,000 sheep. The horses we took were much needed. The men are in splendid health, two only being exempt from work. I am very pleased to state the discipline is all that can be desired, and our commanding officer has expressed his (Colonel Alderson's) very great satisfaction with the work done by our squadron. The duties are arduous for so small a unit, there being 20 miles of front to watch. This means only about two nights a week in "bed." There are also three roads diverging from here to patrol. I greatly miss veterinary assistance, as the country teems with horse sickness.

Zand River, 8/5/1900.—During an engagement yesterday, in which I was in command of the advanced guard, on coming in contact with the enemy numbering 8,000 Boers, the following were wounded :—Sergt.-Major McAlister, Corporal Osborne, Privates Tonkin, Mitchell, and McMillan. These casualties occurred at Zand River at railway crossing. The reconnaissance was for the purpose of gaining information of the enemy, and to prevent, if possible, his destroying the bridges and culverts on the railway line. General Hutton expressed himself as pleased with the manner in which the work was carried out by the New South Wales Mounted Rifles. The men of my unit (all ranks) have done most excellent work, and have earned commendation from the various officers under whom they have worked.

12/6/1900. We are now attached to Colonel Hannay's brigade, *en route* to Modder River. There has been continuous marching and fighting since I last wrote. Our squadrons have acted as advance guards right through and have taken part in almost every action, and have been conspicuously steady under fire.

Nominal Roll.

No. and Name.	Rank.	Remarks.
Antill, John Macquarie	Captain	
McLean, Archibald Alexander	Lieutenant	
Onslow, Arthur John Macarthur	,,	Wounded near Heilbron, 21.5.01 Invalided, Australia, arr 30.8.00
Tooth, Douglas Keith Lucas	,,	Wounded, Palmeitfontein, 19.7.00
Holman, Richard Charles	Sergt.-Major (W.O.)	Despatches, *London Gazette*, 27.9.01 : D.C.M.
Wasson, John	Staff-Sergeant	Despatches, *London Gazette*, 27.9.01 ; 29.7.02: D.C.M.
2. McAllister, Adam	Coy. Sergt.-Major	Wounded, Zand River, 7.5.00. Invalided, Australia, arr. 15.9.00
3. Newman, Joseph	Coy. Q.M.-Sergt.	*Vide* "Promotions"
5. Barham, William Henry	Sergeant	
21. McIntosh, Harold	,,	*Vide* "Promotions"
81. Hawkey, John Martin	Farrier-Sergeant	
6. Seagar, Charles William	,,	
84. Wardrobe, John	Corporal	Q.M.-Sergeant
82. Bateup, Amos Albert	,,	Invalided, Australia, 3.7.00
11. Weekes, Sydney	,,	
9. Apps, James	,,	
83. Osborne, Edmund	,,	Wounded, Zand River, 7.5.00. Invalided, Australia, arr. 13.9.00
10. Allen, Alfred Edward Elkington	,,	Wounded, Spyfontein, 6.4.00 ; died, Pretoria, 18.10.00
80. Gilfillan, John Robert	,,	Sergeant. Invalided, England, 31.7.00
12. Owens, Frank Patrick	,,	Wounded, Paardeburg, 19.2.00. Invalided, Australia, arr. 28.5.00

Nominal Roll—continued.

No. and Name.	Rank.	Remarks.
37. Daly, Verdi Robert	Bugler	Died, Bloemfontein, 11.6.00
14. Mills, Charles George	,,	Invalided, Australia, 26.6.00
106. Arnold, Reginald Thomas	Private	Discharged, Cape Town, 30.11.00
15. Abrahams, William John	,,	Killed, Abraham's Kraal, 10.3.00
85. Axam, Francis William	,,	
69. Ball, Samuel	,,	Wounded, Klip Kraal, 17.2.00; invalided, England, and returned to South Africa, August, 1900
70. Ball, Thomas	,,	Invalided, Australia, 14.7.00
16. Battye, Reg. Rich.	,,	Lance-Corporal; invalided, Australia; returned 17.8.00
17. Bender, William	,,	Killed, Palmersfontein, 19.7.00
18. Bennett, Arthur Thomas	,,	Invalided, Australia, 3.11.00
19. Bird, Thos. George	,,	
86. Blackwood, Jas.	,,	
87. Bollard, Albert John	,,	
78. Bode, Arthur	,,	Invalided, Australia, 3.11.00
20. Bond, Wm.	,,	Wounded, Paardeburg, 22.2.00. Invalided, Australia, arr. 30.7.00
21. Bull, Ed. Counde	,,	
88. Burke, Michael Joseph	,,	Invalided, Australia, 12.7.00
89. Butler, Arthur Albert	,,	
23. Chesher, Geo.	,,	Wounded, Paardeburg, 19.2.00. Invalided, Australia, arr. 30.8.00
90. Cleary, Ed. Thos.	,,	Lance-Corporal; invalided, Australia, 13.8.00
91. Clifford, George	,,	
25. Cox, Austin Clarendon	,,	Invalided, Australia, 23.10.00
77. Corbett, Herbert	,,	Invalided, Australia, 2.6.00
24. Cripps, Wm. Sydney	,,	
26. Darken, Chas. John	,,	Invalided, Australia, 3.11.00
27. Dawson, Walter Henry	,,	Invalided, Australia, 12.7.00
28. Drummond, Dugald	,,	Despatches, *London Gazette*, 27.9.01: D.C.M.
102. Field, John	,,	Invalided, Australia, 3.7.00
29. Flint, Clive	,,	Wounded, Klip Drift, 16.2.00; died Wynberg, 24.6.00
30. Garlick, Hubert	Shoeing-smith	
31. Gosper, Charles	Private	Invalided, Australia, 5.5.00
32. Hackett, Ernest Jas.	,,	
33. Hawes, Edwin George	,,	
43. Hopkins, Jas.	,,	
103. Hughes, John	,,	Invalided, Australia, 17.8.00
34. James, Arthur Herbert	,,	
36. Kelly, John	,,	Died, Bloemfontein, 20.4.00
35. Kirkland, Wilfred John	,,	
37. Lee, Charles Arthur	,,	Corporal. *Vide* "Promotions."
38. Leet, Gifford Caleb	,,	
39. Lindsay, Edward James	,,	Invalided, Australia, 13.8.00
104. Lloyd, William George	,,	Invalided, Australia, 3.11.00
45. Maples, Joseph Henry	,,	Invalided, England, 31.7.00:
74. Maxted, George	,,	
92. Maxwell, John	,,	Promoted Corporal and Sergeant
44. McAllister, David	,,	Returned to Australia, 3.11.00
41. McDonald, John	,,	
40. McDonald, Alexander	,,	Returned to Australia, 3.11.00
42. McGregor, Norman	,,	Promoted Corporal and Sergeant
43. McGregor, Peter	,,	Invalided, Australia, 3.7.00
46. Millar, Charles Robert	,,	
47. Miller, Christian	,,	
93. Moore, Patrick Thomas	,,	Returned to Australia, 3.11.00
50. Mullampy, James	,,	
49. Moss, Michael George	,,	

Nominal Roll—continued.

No. and Name.	Rank.	Remarks.
51. Murray, George	Private	Wounded, Diamond Hill, 12.6.00
52. Nicholson, Tom Renton	,,	
94. Nethery, Robert John	,,	Promoted Corporal and Sergeant
101. Pearce, Wellington Henry	,,	Invalided, Australia, 3.7.00
76. Pitt, Walter Frank	,,	Invalided, England, 19.7.00
53. Potts, Pembroke	,,	Invalided, Australia, 5.5.00
54. Quinn, William Cuff	,,	Invalided, Australia, arr. 20.11.00
48. Reeves, Alfred John	,,	
95. Reilly, Phillip John	,,	Died, Bloemfontein, 30.4.00
79. Savage, Wilfred	,,	Invalided, England, 31.7.00
96. Sharpe, Henry	,,	Invalided, Australia, 5.5.00
97. Sharpe, Robert	,,	
58. Smith, Albert Edward	,,	Died, Bloemfontein, 30.5.00
60. Smith, Rex	,,	Promoted Corporal
98. Spearing, Benjamin Charles	,,	Invalided, Australia, 2.6.00
75. Stewart, Graham	,,	Invalided, Australia, 3.7.00
61. Suttor, Harold Bruce	,,	Invalided, Australia, 12.7.00
56. Swan, James Henry	,,	Invalided, England, 21.10.00
57. Swan, Richard	,,	
62. Symonds, Michael James	,,	Invalided, Australia, 5.5.00
63. Trevitt, George Spurway	,,	Invalided, Australia, 3.7.00
99. Tweedy, William George	,,	Wounded, Klip Kraal, 17.2.00; and again at Thaba N'chu, 30.4.00; Invalided, Australia, arr. 6.8.00
72. Waite, George	,,	
64. Walker, John	,,	
65. Waterson, Lous Charles	,,	Invalided, Australia, 23.10.00
71. Wearne, Albert Ernest	,,	Promoted Corporal and Sergeant; invalided, Australia, 17.8.00
66. West, Leslie		
67. Wilson, Richard Stephen	,,	
458. Wilson, John	,,	
100. Wintle, William Edward	,,	
68. Young, Horace	,,	Invalided, Australia, 3.11.00
DRAFT.		
104. Webster, James	Coy. Q.M.-Sergt.	
107. Agland, Herbert	Private	
116. Alexander, George Edward	,,	Invalided, Australia, 2.6.00
108. Byrne, Patrick James	,,	Attached Royal Engineers, 18.6.00
117. Bull, Walter	,,	Invalided, Australia, 2.8.00
113. Cameron, Hugh James	,,	
122. Gates, Henry George	,,	Returned to Australia, 15.11.00
123. Healey, Michael Henry	,,	Invalided, Australia, 2.6.00
115. Jenkins, Herbert William	,,	
126. Kelaher, Charles Richard	,,	
119. Maxwell, Alfred	,,	Wounded, Thaba N'chu, 30.4.00; invalided, England, 27.11.00
114. Marks, Charles	,,	
124. McAlpine, Alexander	,,	
105. McLeod, William	,,	Invalided, Australia, 3.11.00
125. Perritt, James	,,	Invalided, Australia, 14.7.00
127. Rafter, Frederick William	,,	Invalided, Australia, 14.7.00
128. Ransley, Edwin Horace	,,	Died, Sterkstroom, 27.4.00
129. Robinson, Samuel Geekie	,,	
130. Ross, James	,,	
109. Steel, Watson Augustus	,,	
110. Staines, Robert William	,,	
121. Windeyer, Edward	,,	
111. Zalinski, Ernest	,,	Invalided, Australia, 3.7.00
100. Hayes, Frederick St. Ledger	,,	Invalided, Australia, 3.11.00
128. Mason, George	,,	Invalided, Australia, 23.10.00

NEW SOUTH WALES INFANTRY (SUBSEQUENTLY "E" SQUADRON 1st NEW SOUTH WALES MOUNTED RIFLES).

THIS was the only Infantry Contingent despatched from New South Wales; and it was subsequently mounted in South Africa, and became "E" Squadron of the 1st New South Wales Mounted Rifles. It was recruited from 1st, 2nd, 3rd, and 4th regiments of New South Wales partially-paid infantry, the Scottish, Australian, and St. George's (English) Rifles, the National Guard (these four being Volunteer regiments), besides three men from the Field Artillery as transport drivers.

The recruits were carefully selected, not only on account of physique, but in regard to good character; and no man was enrolled who had not during the previous year classified in the musketry course, as either a marksman or a first-class shot, and been efficient. They were further required to be between 20 and 40 years of age, preferably single, height 5 feet 7 inches and upwards, chest 35 inches and upwards.

The company was embarked in the transport *Aberdeen*, leaving on 3rd November, 1899; and having on board also the squadron of Mounted Rifles that was destined to be "A" Squadron of the 1st Regiment. It comprised 5 officers, and 121 sergeants and rank and file; with 1 machine-gun, 1 horse, and 1 cart. Of these 11 were killed or died, 2 were struck off the strength in South Africa; 5 officers and 108 others returned to Australia.

REFERENCES TO ORDERS.

Formation	.. ..	G.O.'s (N.S.W.)	107/99, 112/99
Pay and allowances	..	,, ,,	107/99, 88/00
Conditions of service	..	,, ,,	107/99, 108/99
Officers	.. ..	,, ,,	110/99
Embarkation	..	,, ,,	116/99

CLOTHING, ETC.

Clothing consisted of brown F.S. jacket and trousers, with puttees and hat.
Arms and equipment.—M.L.E. rifles and sword bayonets.
Infantry valise equipment, together with specially made entrenching tools carried in a frog secured to waistbelt. Regimental transport was provided.

ESTABLISHMENT.

The establishment authorized was—1 captain, 3 subalterns, 1 colour-sergeant, 4 sergeants, 6 corporals, 2 buglers, and 108 privates; total, 125.

RECORD OF SERVICE.

The corps left Sydney by steamship *Aberdeen*, 3rd November, 1899, and called at Melbourne on 5th; left again on 8th. Arrived Port Elizabeth, 3rd December at 10 p.m., left at 8.30 a.m. on 4th, and arrived at Cape Town, 7 a.m., 6th December. Disembarked on 7th December, at 5 a.m.

On the 9th December the Company joined "The Australian Regiment" at Belmont, and served with it until April, when the battalion was broken up. For an account of the excellent service done, *vide* "First Victorian Contingent" under "Australian Regiment."

The company was engaged on outpost duty at Enslin on the line of communications to Kimberley, from 10th December, 1899, to 30th January, 1900.

On 1st February it was converted into Mounted Rifles at Naauwpoort; Indian cavalry remounts being supplied. No difficulty was experienced, as, with the exception of about six, every man was a good rider. On 3rd February the corps was inspected by General J. D. P. French, and put to work as mounted troops next day.

The corps, under the command of Captain J. G. Legge, accompanied General Clements' column from Arundel *viâ* Colesberg to Norval's Pont, Orange River, thence through the south-western portion of the Orange Free State to Bloemfontein.

At Bloemfontein the corps, under the command of Captain W. Holmes, joined General Ian Hamilton's column as portion of De Lisle's (II. M.I.) corps, and proceeded thence to Pretoria, Diamond Hill, &c.

On 13th June, 1900, Captain F. A. Dove assumed command, *vice* Holmes (wounded and invalided). The corps returned to Pretoria and took part in the campaign against De Wet and De La Rey, under Generals Hunter, Broadwood, Lord Kitchener, and Clements respectively, operating in the Transvaal and northern part of Orange River Colony.

Returned to Kroonstadt, thence by rail to Cape Town; embarked December, 1900, on board s.s. *Orient ;* called at Melbourne on 6th January, 1901, and arrived at Sydney on 8th January, 1901.

Detailed list of engagements attached hereto.

The casualties were as follows:—

Killed in action	5
Died of wounds	2
Wounded	14
Died of enteric	4
Total	25

PRINCIPAL ENGAGEMENTS IN WHICH CORPS TOOK PART.

With Major-General Clements' Column :

Relief of Colesberg, 3rd February to 7th March, 1900. Actions at Slingersfontein, 10th February, 1900 ; The Kloof (Cole's Cop), 11th February ; Mader's Aarm, 11th February ; Vaal Kop, 12th February ; Rensburg, 14th February ; Frundel, 15th February ; Plewman's Farm, 17th February ; Kuilfontein, 17th February ; Woolvefontein, 20th February ; Norval's Pont, 7th March.

Advance on Bloemfontein, 15th March to 4th April, 1900. Capture of the following towns in the Orange Free State :—Phillipolis, 21st March ; Jagersfontein, 27th March ; Fauresmith, 27th March ; Koffyfontein, 28th March ; Petrusburg, 2nd April.

With General Ian Hamilton's Column, Bloemfontein to Diamond Hill, 22nd April to 12th June.—Action at Boesman's Kop, 23rd April ; Watervaal Drift, 24th April ; Waterworks, 25th April ; Israel's Poort, 25th April. Battle of Houtnek (Thaba 'Nchu), 30th April and 1st May. Action at Kaffir's Kraal, Roodepoort, 4th May. Capture of Winburg, 5th May. Battle of Zand River, 10th May. Capture of Ventersburg, 11th May. Advanced Guard action, Lindley, 20th May. Rearguard action, Rhenoster River, 21st May. Klipriversburg, Battle of Doornkop, 29th May. Johannesburg, 31st May. Capture of Pretoria, 4th June. Battle of Diamond Hill, 11th and 12th June.

Campaign against De Wet. Capture of Heidelberg.

June.—Capture of Villiersdorp, Frankfort, Reitz, and Bethlehem.

July.—Actions around Bethlehem. Actions at Palmietfontein, Vredefort, ainje, Lindeque Drift.

August.—Relief of Elands River Post. March to Pretoria, *viâ* Rustenburg.

September.—To Machadodorp. Operations against De La Rey in the Magaliesberg. Several actions and skirmishes with General Clements' column. Return to Pretoria.

September.—With De Lisle's force. Operations against De Wet in northern Orange River Colony. Skirmishes about Heilbron and (October) Vredefort.

Two days' fight at Witkoppies and Reitzburg. Capture of Potchefstroom.

27th October.—Successful fight with De Wet at Rensburg Drift. Capture of Krupp gun and wagons.

November.—Action at Bothaville. Capture of seven guns.

SERVICES AND HONOURS.

Legge, Captain J. G. (promoted major and afterwards Lieut.-Colonel).—Operations in Cape Colony, Orange Free State, and Transvaal, December, 1899, to November, 1900. Actions at Colesberg. Advance on Kimberley. Actions at Johannesburg, Pretoria, Diamond Hill, Elands River, Venterskroon, Bethlehem, Wittebergen, and Bothaville. Subsequently Intelligence Officer to Col. De Lisle's column, 1901-2. Queen's Medal with four clasps. King's Medal with two clasps.

Holmes, W., Lieutenant (promoted captain).—Operations in Cape Colony, Orange Free State, and Transvaal, 1899 to November, 1900. Actions at Colesberg. Advance on Kimberley, Houtnek, Vet River, Zand River, Johannesburg, Pretoria, and Diamond Hill, at which latter wounded 12th June, 1900. Despatches, *London Gazette*, 16th April, 1901. D.S.O. Queen's Medal with four clasps.

Dove, Lieutenant F. A.—Operations as above. Wounded at Mader's Farm, 26th February, 1900. Despatches, *London Gazette*, 16th April, 1901. D.S.O. Queen's Medal with five clasps. (Lieutenant Dove was promoted captain and served subsequently as adjutant 3rd Battalion A.C.H., and S.O. to Australian Brigade, Newcastle, Natal.)

Logan, Lieutenant M. W.—Operations in Cape Colony and Orange Free State, December, 1899 to May, 1900. Actions at Colesberg. Advance on Kimberley. Actions at Vet River and Zand River. Queen's Medal with two clasps.

Edwards, Lieutenant (A.M.C.) E. A.—*Vide* A.M.C.

EXTRACTS FROM REPORT OF CAPTAIN J. G. LEGGE.

February, 1900.—On 20th February we went out with a force to repel an attack upon our right rear. One division, under Lieutenant Dove, was escort to some of the guns, where, unfortunately, Private Atchison was killed by a shell, together with his horse; Private Southey was also wounded.

With the other three divisions, reinforced by the Victorian Mounted Rifles, we were sent to occupy some kopjes in front. After crossing with two divisions under fire, and taking two ridges, we received an order to retire, which it appears was never meant for us. The men retired under a very heavy fire and kept their heads well. Finding the order was never intended for us, we again went across, and by evening drove the Boers along 5 miles of ridges. We were assisted greatly by a cross-fire from our artillery.

At dusk we were, with 55 rifles and 20 in reserve, opposed to 200 Boers in a farm and on the opposite ridge. The rest of our men were holding the other part of the ridge already taken. Here we came to a stop, and had a furious rifle duel, which the Boers finished up by firing shrapnel from an invisible gun at about 1,000 yards. They also used explosive bullets. We had good cover, however, and had no other loss. The whole of the company fought well under a heavy fire, and it is really wonderful how we escaped without loss.

As my orders were to secure all the positions I took, I had to move from one point to another, and entrusted the firing line to Lieutenant Holmes, who acted with great dash and coolness. At night we received orders to return to the guns and went back to camp with them. The Boers retired from the vicinity during the night. Major Enthoven, R.A., was kind enough to send over a message saying " We could not have done better."

After a reinforcement of guns on the 22nd February, our force advanced west, and another force from the camp attacked the Boers on the south, and gave them a heavy shell fire. Lieutenant Dove did an excellent piece of scouting on the right with his division, and drove off the Boer patrols, thus rendering the advance of the guns possible.

About 3 p.m. the Boers retired in great haste, making north, and we returned to camp at night.

The last fortnight has been extremely trying on both men and horses, through broken rest, irregular and deficient food and water. The latter is not due to the A.S.C., but to the rapid moves we have to make as mounted men.

EXTRACTS FROM REPORT OF CAPTAIN W. HOLMES.

28th April.—In camp, Israel's Poort. Detailed Lieutenant Dove and 25 men to scout in the vicinity of Thaba Mountain and Houtnek. Lieutenant Dove was instructed to locate the position of the Boer laager. In this duty he was eminently successful, and received the commendation of General Ian Hamilton and Colonel De Lisle. As a result of this reconnaissance, the battle of Houtnek was fought two days later.

30th April.—Marched at daylight, and came into collision with the enemy, who were strongly posted at Thaba Mountain and Houtnek. Lieutenant Dove and 25 men were detached from my command for scouting work ; with the remainder I was ordered to occupy an advanced kopje, which proved to be an important strategical point. Remained in possession all day under very heavy fire (shrapnel and rifle) from front and right flank. At night retired to a farm house. No casualties.

Re-occupied the position of the previous day before dawn. Remained there under an exceedingly heavy fire until about noon, when I was ordered to withdraw as best I could, as the Infantry was advancing to attack. As the best means of leaving the position, I determined to retire at the gallop by groups of four, widely extended, to another hill about ¾-mile in rear. In this retirement Private F. V. Smith was killed and Privates Lewis, Tweedie, and Maxwell, wounded, and two horses killed.

Nominal Roll.

No. and Name.	Rank.	Remarks.
Legge, James Gordon	Captain Comdg.	
Holmes, William	Lieutenant	Wounded, Diamond Hill, 12.6.00. Invalided, Australia, arr. 17.8.00
Dove, Frederick Allan	Lieutenant	Wounded, Mader's Farm, 26.2.00
Logan, Marcus William	,,	Invalided, England, 25.10.00
1. Liggins, Frederick Pontifex	Sergt.-Major	Severely wounded, Diamond Hill, 12.6.00. Commander-in-Chief Despatches, 19.4.01. Invalided Australia, arr. 13.9.00
2. Mowbray, Harry Haire	Sergeant	Severely injured, Johannesburg, 31.5.00. Invalided, Australia, arr. 8.1.01
3. Allen, Ralph Rowland	,,	Quartermaster - Sergeant. Invalided, Australia, arr. 6.8.00
7. Edney, John Robertson	,,	
9. Coles, James Howe	,,	Invalided, Australia, arr. 6.8.00
12. Grace, Harry George	,,	Invalided, Australia, arr. 17.8.00

Nominal Roll—*continued*.

No. and Name.	Rank.	Remarks.
124. Palazzi, Silvio Alfred	Saddler-Sergeant	
97. Reid, Henry Laurie	Farrier-Sergeant	
4. Chant, William	Corporal	Wounded, Ventersberg, 10.5..00. Invalided Australia, arr. 8.1.01
5. Macdonald, William Thomas	Corporal	
8. Martin, Sydney Edgar	,,	Invalided, Australia, arr. 8.10.11
10. Stinson, William Joseph	,,	Wounded near Bethlehem, 13.7.00.
28. Buckleton, Sidney Douglas	,,	Invalided, Australia arr. 17.2.01
6. Wallace, Arthur David	Lance-Corporal	
92. Prior, William Parker	,,	
96. Robison, Alexander Stuart	,,	
74. McCann, Sidney Henry	,,	
105. Strettles, Stephen	,,	
67. Lusher, Augustus Thomas William	Bugler	
75. McNair, Arthur Victor	,,	
13. Annison, William Thomas	Private	Invalided, Australia, ret. 15.9.00
14. Angell, William Arthur	,,	Invalided, Australia, ret. 13.11.00
15. Appleby, Thomas Samuel	,,	
16. Andrews, Alexander	,,	
17. Atchison, Samuel Charles	,,	Killed in action, Woolvefontein, 20.2.00
125. Baxter, Robert Moore	,,	
19. Bowling, George Walter	,,	
22. Bowman, Henry Thomas	,,	
24. Bowditch, Walter Edward	,,	Invalided, Australia, arr. 21.10.00
25. Boulton, George James	,,	Wounded, Mader's Farm, 26.2.00. Invalided, Australia, arr. 15.12.00
18. Brack, Frederick Charles	,,	
26. Brady, Charles Joseph	,,	Invalided, Australia, arr. 17.2.01
20. Bradstock, Sydney Edgar George	,,	Invalided, Australia, arr. 30.8.00
21. Bradstock, Herbert Henry	,,	
23. Braun, Benjamin Henry	,,	
128. Bright, George Claude	,,	Invalided, Australia, arr. 30.7.00
27. Budd, Henry Martin	,,	Died, enteric fever, February, 1900
35. Cameron, Archibald Lochiel	,,	Died, enteric fever, February, 1900
29. Carpenter, George Edward	,,	Invalided, Australia, arr. 17.8.00
36. Clarke, Joseph David	,,	Invalided, Australia, arr. 15.12.00
32. Corns, Alexander	,,	
31. Coupe, James William Ralph	,,	
33. Coxhead, Albert David	,,	
34. Coyle, Edward	,,	Invalided, Australia, arr. 30.7.00
30. Creech, Albert	,,	Invalided, Australia, arr. 6.8.00
37. Davis, Vincent	,,	
39. Dawes, John	,,	Invalided, Australia, arr. 30.7.00
38. Dawson, Francis Scholefield	,,	
130. Devine, William John	,,	
41. Edgar, Bertram Kinmond	,,	
127. Foster, Michael Joseph	,,	Invalided, Australia, arr. 6.8.00
46. Fowler, Cyril	,,	Died of wounds, Colesberg, 28.2.00
45. Fraser, Donald	,,	Died of enteric fever, June, 1900
44. Fraser, John Clarence	,,	
129. Fraser, John Edward	,,	Invalided, Australia, arr. 17.8.00
43. Fraser, William	,,	
49. Gates, Arthur Thomas	,,	
52. Gilbert, William	,,	
51. Goodsall, Sidney Henry	,,	
48. Glanville, Harold Thomas	,,	

Nominal Roll—*continued.*

No. and Name.	Rank.	Remarks.
47. Grey, George Reginald	Private	
50. Grimmond, John Daniel Revel	,,	
55. Hall, Richard	,,	
60. Halley, Belton Andrew	,,	Killed, Elands Kop, 1.10.00
54. Hardie, Alexander Forrester	,,	Invalided, Australia, arr. 26.1.01
59. Hebblewhite, Duncan Edward	,,	Invalided, Australia, arr. 30.7.00
57. Hickey, John Francis	,,	Invalided, Australia, arr. 19.8.00
56. Hill, Leslie Charles	,,	Died, enteric fever
121. Hines, Ellis Elijah	,,	
53. Hoffman, Edward Martin	,,	
58. Howard, James Joseph	,,	Invalided, Australia, arr. 6.12.00
62. Jones, Arthur Francis	,,	
122. Jones, Charles William	,,	
64. Joyce, Charles Stanley	,,	
65. Key, Money Dyason	,,	
66. Key, Sidney Harrison	,,	
68. Lee, Frederick Henry	,,	
69. Low, Walter	,,	
126. Maher, John Edward	,,	Invalided, Australia, arr. 13.9.00
73. Mascord, Ernest Edwin	,,	
71. May, Edward Francis	,,	
76. McCredie, Henry Dixon	,,	Severely injured near Colesberg, 28.2.00. Invalided, Australia, arr. 30.7.00
78. Macdonald, William Chisholm	,,	Severely wounded, Rhenoster River, 21.5.00. Invalided, Australia, arr. 13.9.00
83. McLennan, Simon	,,	Died of wounds, Colesberg, 3.3.00
81. Millington, John Robert	,,	
85. Moore, Wallace Melbourne	,,	
80. Morris, Percy Herbert	,,	
84. Morris, Thomas Loyd	,,	
72. Mowbray, Benjamin	,,	Invalided, Australia, ret. 13.9.00
70. Murphy, William Henry	,,	
79. Murray, Alfred John	,,	
87. Nash, William Henry	,,	
89. Osborn, Edgar	,,	Wounded near Bethlehem, 13.7.00
88. Owens, Ernest Alfred	,,	Invalided, Australia, arr. 8.1.01
90. Palazzi, Joseph	,,	Killed, Palmietfontein, 19.7.00
94. Paul, Harold	,,	
93. Pearce, William Henry	,,	
95. Poole, George William	,,	Invalided, Australia, arr. 15.12.00
91. Potter, Harry	,,	Invalided, Australia, arr. 30.8.00
102. Rex, Alfred George	,,	
98. Richardson, John	,,	
100. Robson, Stewart	,,	
101. Russell, Harold Hector	,,	Invalided, Australia, arr. 15.1.01
99. Russell, John Thomas	,,	Invalided, Australia, arr. 13.9.00
108. Saxelby, Sidney Henry	,,	
104. Scanlan, James	,,	
109. Shaddock, Arthur John	,,	Invalided, Australia, ret. 13.9.00
107. Sharpe, Alfred	,,	Wounded, near Commando Nek, August, 1900
106. Smith, Frederick Victor	,,	Killed, Houtnek, 1.5.00
103. Southey, Clifford Melville	,,	Slightly wounded, Woolvefontein, 20.2.00
110. Spilsbury, George Henry	,,	Invalided, Australia, arr. 15.12.00
111. Storey, John Alexander	,,	
11. Taylor, Prince Richard	,,	

Nominal Roll—*continued.*

No. and Name.	Rank.	Remarks.
114. Taylor, William St. John	Private	Invalided, Australia, arr. 6.8.00
112. Thomas, Edward Davies	,,	
119. Wells, Stephen Leslie	,,	
117. Whiley, Alfred Henry	,,	
120. Wickerson, Phillip Henry	,,	Invalided, Australia, arr. 4.3.01
118. Williams, Thomas Joseph	,,	Wounded, Ventersberg, 10.5.00
116. Willis, David	,,	Killed, Elands Kop, 1.10.00
115. Woods, Patrick John	,,	

THE FIRST AUSTRALIAN HORSE.*

THE "First Australian Horse" should not be confounded with the "Australian Commonwealth Horse," which consisted of service battalions of Mounted Rifles, raised after the establishment of the Commonwealth, and despatched successively to the seat of war; the squadrons being from the different States. The First Australian Horse was Bush Cavalry upon the Volunteer system originally; but subsequently converted to the partial-payment class; and raised in 1895, chiefly by the exertions of Colonel J. H. K. Mackay, their first commanding officer, for service in the remote country districts of New South Wales. The movement became very popular; and several excellent squadrons were enrolled, of a superior class of men, who were admirably mounted. They wore a distinctive and somewhat remarkable uniform of dark green with black embroidery, of the hussar pattern; with handsome belts and accoutrements, including sabretaches. For irregular cavalry they attained a high standard of proficiency; and when the war broke out they were not behind their comrades of the other arms in seeking service, or obtaining honour.

The First Australian Horse despatched two Contingents; the first of which departed on the 14th November, 1899, taking their own horses with them. It consisted of 2 officers and 32 sergeants and rank and file, with 36 horses. Of these, 1 died, 1 officer and 2 others returned to Australia, 28 were transferred to the second Contingent, and 1 officer and 1 trooper were commissioned in the Imperial Army.

The second Contingent or service squadron left on the 17th January, 1900. It comprised 5 officers and 102 others, with 28 that joined subsequently from the first Contingent, and 112 horses. One man joined in Western Australia and one in South Africa. Of these, 2 officers and 8 others were killed or died; 1 officer and 121 others returned to Australia; 1 officer and 1 other quitted the corps in South Africa; and 1 officer and 2 others were commissioned in the Imperial Army. The squadron arrived in Sydney on 2nd May, 1901.

REFERENCES TO ORDERS.

Formation	..	G.O. (N.S.W.) 107/99
Pay	..	,, ,, 107/99, 112/99
Embarkation	..	,, ,, 123/99, 124/99
Officers	..	Govt. Gazette 45 of 17.1.00

Detachment.

Formation	..	G.O. (N.S.W.) 144/99
Conditions of enrolment	..	,, ,, 144/99
Establishment	..	,, ,, 1/00
Embarkation	..	,, ,, 8/00
Separation allowance	..	,, ,, 88/00

For the detachment the conditions were :—Men to be good shots and proficient swordsmen, of superior physique, not under 5 ft. 6 in. or 34 in. chest; good riders and bushmen, accustomed to find their way about in strange country. Horses to be up to 16 or 17 stone, and fit to carry that weight day after day.

---

* Allied with "The King's Colonials" Yeomanry.

CLOTHING, ETC.

Uniform consisted of brown F.S. jacket and pants, with puttees and hat. *Vide* clothing issued to 1st M.R., page 57.

Arms and equipment :—M.E. carbines, swords, cartridge-belts with supporting braces. Fully horsed and provided with saddles.

Also provided with Regimental transport.

PROMOTIONS, ETC.

Lieutenant J. F. M. Wilkinson promoted Captain 1st January, 1901.
Lieutenant W. V. Dowling promoted Captain 1st January, 1901.
Lieutenant K. K. Mackellar was Commissioned in 6th D.G.
Lieutenant J. B. N. Osborne was Commissioned in 16th Lancers 6th March, 1900.
Sergeant G. A. Thomas was Commissioned in Imperial Service.
Corporal J. H. M. Abbott was Commissioned in Imperial Service.
Trooper H. J. Kirkpatrick was Commissioned in Imperial Service.
For Promotions of N.C.O.'s and men *vide* Nominal Roll.

WAR SERVICES AND HONOURS.

Thompson, Captain R. R.—Operations in Orange Free State and Transvaal, February to November, 1900. Actions at Poplar Grove, Dreifontein, Karee Siding, and Belfast. Queen's Medal with four clasps.

Wilkinson, Captain J. F. M.—Operations in Orange Free State and Transvaal, February to November, 1900. Actions at Poplar Grove, Dreifontein, Karee Siding, and Belfast. Queen's Medal with four clasps.

Dowling, Captain W. V.—Relief of Kimberley. Operations in Orange Free State and Transvaal, January, 1900 to November, 1900. Actions at Reit River Klip Drift, Paardeberg, Poplar Grove, Dreifontein, Karee Siding, and Belfast Dangerously wounded at Slingersfontein. Queen's Medal with five clasps.

Osborne, 2nd Lieutenant J. B. N.—Operations as above. Queen's Medal with five clasps.

Vaughan, 2nd Lieutenant P. W.—Operations as above. Queen's Medal with five clasps.

Mackellar, Lieutenant K. K. was killed at Deedepoort, 11th July, 1900; and *Ebsworth*, 2nd Lieutenant A., at Bronkhurst Spruit, 24th July, 1900.

Howse, Lieutenant H. R., A.M.C., accompanied the service squadron in the *Surrey* and served with it subsequently; also with second and Commonwealth Contingents, Army Medical Corps (*vide* Army Medical Corps' record).

Bowker, Lieutenant (Veterinary) H., proceeded to Cape Town in medical charge of horses (*Surrey*); returned next steamer.

RECORD OF SERVICE.

The first Contingent of this regiment, comprising 2 officers and 32 non-commissioned officers and men, with Lieutenant Willoughby Dowling in command, left Newcastle, New South Wales, in s.s. *Langton Grange* on 14th November, and arrived at Cape Town on 13th December, 1899.

On arrival they were attached to the Royal Scots Greys serving in General French's cavalry division. Present at battle of Slingersfontein on 16th January, in which they were sharply handled; Lieutenant Dowling being severely wounded and captured, Sergeant-Major Griffin killed, and Corporal Kirkpatrick severely wounded, afterwards dying of his wounds. Sergeant-Major Griffin was the first Australian soldier who fell in the war. Present at various actions in Cape Colony during February.

Early in March the Service Squadron, which recently arrived from Australia, joined.

The Service Squadron, 1st Australian Horse, embarked at Sydney, on transport *Surrey*, on 17th January, and arrived at Cape Town on 23rd February, 1900.

Ordered to Modder River, arriving there on 3rd March; proceeded to Ossfontein and joined the Royal Scots Greys on 6th. Took part in the battle of Poplar Grove on the 7th March. Present at Dreifontein, 10th March, and occupation of Bloemfontein, 13th March. Formed portion of escort to Thaba 'Nchu under Major Allanby, Inniskilling Dragoons.

Present at Karee Siding, 29th March, under very heavy fire for some time. Present at Sannas Post and at affair at Evans' Farm.

Joined advance to Pretoria, 6th May. Took part in battle of Zand River, 10th May, when the squadron formed part of an attacking force ordered to take some kopjes which were found to be so strongly occupied that the attacking force, after suffering heavy loss, was compelled to retire. In this affair Lieutenant Wilkinson and two men were taken prisoners and two men were killed. Present at capture of Kroonstadt, 12th May. Continued with advance to Pretoria, taking part in various actions *en route*. Present at the surrender of Pretoria, 5th June; release of prisoners at Waterval on 6th; and battle of Diamond Hill on the 7th.

Lieutenant Wilkinson assumed command on 2nd July. On 8th, the squadron moved to Crocodile River and took part in a smart engagement at Zilicats Nek on the 11th inst.; also in affair at Kameel Drift on 16th., and various minor affairs during the remainder of this month.

On 10th August, Lieutenant Vaughan was ordered into hospital at Pretoria, Lieutenant Wilkinson being the only officer left with the squadron.

Present at battle of Belfast on 27th; the splendid scouting of the Australian Horse enabling General French to turn the Boer right flank, and compel them to retire.

The squadron was engaged almost daily during the month of September, including the occupation of Barberton. Took part in operations round Ermelo and Bethel, where some heavy fighting took place; in fact, the squadron was engaged almost every day during October.

Returned to Pretoria for a much needed rest on 29th October, and remained until 12th December, on which date it was ordered to Machadodorp, joining some Queenslanders and South Australians, and employed patrolling railway line. Ordered to Belfast on 10th February, where remounts were obtained; and, on 14th, took part in sharp action near Belfast, the Australian Horse being complimented by General Kitchener on their gallant conduct.

On 25th February the squadron entrained at Middelberg for Pretoria, *en route* for Australia, and on 31st March embarked on s.s. *Tongariro* at Cape Town, and arrived at Sydney on 2nd May, 1901.

ENGAGEMENTS.

First Contingent.

13th January, 1900	Arundel and Colesberg Districts.
12th February, 1900	Reit River.
13th ,, ,,	Klip Drift, Modder River.
15th ,, ,,	Relief of Kimberley.
16th ,, ,,	Dornfield.
18th ,, ,,	Paardeberg.

Both Contingents.

8th March, 1900	Poplar Grove.
10th ,, ,,	Abraham's Krall and Dreifontein.
13th ,, ,,	Surrender of Bloemfontein.
29th ,, ,,	The Glen or Brandfort.
31st ,, ,,	Koorn Spruit or Sannas Post.
10th May, 1900	Zand River (Ventersburg-road).
12th ,, ,,	Kroonstadt.
26th ,, ,,	Hartebeestfontein.
27th ,, ,,	Hartebeestfontein.
28th ,, ,,	Oliphant's Nek.
30th ,, ,,	Doornkop.
2nd June, 1900	Johannesburg.
3rd ,, ,,	Fall of Pretoria.
6th ,, ,,	Waterval—Release of prisoners.
11th ,, ,,	Diamond Hill.
11th July, 1900	Zilicat's or Nitrel's Nek.
16th ,, ,,	Kameel Drift.
20th ,, ,,	Olifantsfontein.
23rd ,, ,,	Olifant's River.
24th ,, ,,	Kromdraai.
27th ,, ,,	Near Middleberg.
31st ,, ,,	Wonderfontein.
24th August, 1900	Geluk's Farm, near Belfast.
25th ,, ,,	Geluk's Farm, near Belfast.
26th ,, ,,	Geluk's Farm, near Belfast.
27th. ,, ,,	Belfast.
29th ,, ,,	Helvetia.
31st ,, ,,	Waterval-Onder.
4th September, 1900	Bonnefoot.
5th ,, ,,	Carolina.

EXTRACTS FROM REPORT OF CAPTAIN R. R. THOMPSON.

At 2 a.m. on 8th March, the squadron marched with the 1st Brigade of the Cavalry Division and took part in the engagement at Poplar Grove. The first shot was fired by our artillery at 5.20 a.m., the Boers replying with shell and rifle fire.

In the afternoon Trooper Palmer was shot in the head (our first casualty).

This trooper behaved very pluckily when wounded; he bandaged his own head and rejoined the ranks, until compelled to retire through loss of blood. He has since been in hospital, and is now invalided to England.

No further casualties occurred amongst the men, but several horses were lost through exhaustion during the rapid advance.

The advance was continued next day; the squadron being detailed to furnish scouts, and when extended, covered in front and flanks about 5 miles of country.

10th March.—Battle of Dreifontein.—The squadron moved off with the Royal Scots Greys at daybreak, and occupied two kopjes in succession and used volley-firing at long ranges, which had the effect of stopping the independent firing and causing the Boers to open fire with artillery. In advancing across some open country, mounted, some Vickers-Maxim shells (pom-poms) dropped between the 2nd and 3rd troops. One horse was killed, and Trooper Owen Taylor wounded in the shoulder. Trooper Parry, whose horse was killed, had his leg broken.

This was a general engagement; 380 casualties—about 200 killed.

On Wednesday, 14th March, I heard certain British prisoners were in Bloemfontein Free State Hospital, and visited it in the hope of finding some of the Australian Horse prisoners who had been captured at Rensburg. I found Lieutenant W. V. Dowling, who had been seriously wounded, now fairly convalescent. He had lost the sight of one eye, his right thumb, and had been wounded in the thigh, but was otherwise in good health. Although he desired to continue serving throughout the campaign, the Medical Board decided that he should return to Australia.

The camp remained at "The Willows" until the 18th, when the brigade moved 4 miles further west to "Wessels Farm"; still without tents.

Nominal Roll.

No. and Name.	Rank.	Remarks.
Thompson, Robert Roland	Captain (Comdg.)	
Mackellar, Keith Kinnaird	Lieutenant	Killed, Deedeport, 11.7.00
Wilkinson, John Frederick Moore	,,	
Dowling, Willoughby Vincent	,,	Dangerously wounded, Slingersfontein
Osborne, James Bunbury Nott	,,	
Ebsworth, Alfred	2nd Lieutenant	Killed, Bronkhurst Spruit, 24.7.00
Vaughan, Percy William	,,	
Duncan, George Charles	Regimental Sergt.-Major	
Dowson, Lancelot Arthur	Regimental Q.M.S.	Invalided, Australia, arr. 6.8.00
367. Griffen, George Allman	Troop Sergt.-Major	Killed, Slingersfontein, 16.1.00
Arnold, Herbert	Squad. Sergt.-Major	
245. Barnes, Sydney Charles	Sergeant	Promoted S. Sergt.-Major, 17.2.00
582. Hargrave, Charles	,,	Promoted Sq. Q.M.S., 6.2.00
38. Doyle, Herbert Frederick	,,	Invalided, Australia, arr. 21.10.00
393. Vaughan, David Douglas	,,	
1055. Thomas, Gilbert Arding	,,	*Vide* "Promotions"
1056. Sayer, Francis Arthur	,,	
1057. Williams, Alfred	Transport-Sergt.	
224. Hanson, George	Farrier-Sergeant	
1107. Gray, William	,,	
323. Wilson, Rufus Roland	Corporal	
137. Mills, Herbert Alfred	,,	Promoted Sergeant, 17.2.00. Invalided, Australia, arr. 17.8.00
275. O'Brien, Harold	,,	Sergeant, 23.4.00; Sq. Q.M.S., 14.12.00
968. Peard, William Ernest	,,	Invalided, Australia, arr. 6.8.00
623. Juleff, James Michael	,,	Promoted Sergeant, 1.12.01
1058. Woods, Harris Dunmore Lang	,,	Promoted Sergeant, 6.2.00. Invalided, Australia, arr. 13.4.01

Nominal Roll—continued.

No. and Name.	Rank.	Remarks.
1059. Pulsford, Hubert Stanley	Corporal	Sergeant; Invalided, Australia, arr. 21.10.00
1060. Ferguson, Alexander Robert Leslie	,,	Invalided, Australia, arr. 16.11.00
504. Strike, Sydney John	Lance-Corporal	Promoted Corporal, 17.2.00
737. Firman, George James	,,	Corporal, 17.2.02; invalided, Australia, arr. 15.9.00
1061. Booth, David Henry Trayer	Corpl.-Trumpeter	Invalided, Australia, arr. 13.11.00
17. Dobson, Ernest Aubrey	Trumpeter	
893. Gilchrist, Charles Anthony	,,	
1062. Hezlett, John Henry	Shoeing-smith	
916. Armstrong, Alfred William	,,	Invalided, Australia, arr. 17.8.00
892. Ford, Michael John	,,	Wounded, Colesberg District. Invalided, Australia, arr. 17.8.00
931. Thrift, Arthur Edward	Saddler	
5. Barnes, Thomas W.	Trooper	Invalided, Australia, arr. 30.7.00
641. Boreland, William	,,	Invalided, Australia, arr. 9.12.00
748. Bossley, Charles Clifton	,,	
208. Bucholtz, James	,,	
1062. Abbott, John Henry Macartney	,,	Corporal. Vide "Promotions." Invalided, Australia, arr. 21.10.00
1063. Alick, John	,,	
1064. Andrew, John Alexander Stewart	,,	Died, Cape Town, 5.3.00
947. Appleby, John Henry	,,	
984. Ball, Wallace Dalton	,,	Invalided, Australia, arr. 17.8.00
1065. Bashford, Frederick Frank	,,	
1066. Bell, Walter Montgomery (or Henry)	,,	Invalided, Australia, arr. 19.11.00
845. Bishop, Alexander	,,	
1067. Bisley, Leslie Stuart	,,	
157. Black, William Henderson	,,	
747. Bonner, John	,,	Killed, Glen Siding, 28.3.00
912. Bonner, William Thomas	,,	
1068. Brosi, Henry Joseph	,,	
1108. Brown, Peter	,,	
990. Bridges, Herbert Throsby	,,	
1069. Cameron, Donald	,,	
1070. Cameron, William	,,	Promoted L. Corpl.; Corpl. 1.12.00
956. Cox, Reginald Belmore	,,	Died, Adelaide, 24.1.00
1070. Cooper, William Valentine	,,	
994. Crowley, James	,,	
391. Cummins, Michael Joseph	,,	Died, Bloemfontein, 27.6.00
996. Cumming, Duncan	,,	Lance-Corporal. Invalided, Australia, arr. 30.8.00
1071. Currie, William Joseph	,,	Wounded, Kroonstad
1072. D'Arcey, Arthur Ernest	,,	Invalided, Australia, arr. 15.9.00
1073. Dolman, Frederick William	,,	
974. Dunn, Samuel John	,,	Invalided, Australia, arr. 30.8.00
812. Eames, William	,,	Invalided, Australia, arr. 17.8.00
999. Ellis, William John	,,	Invalided, Australia, arr. 6.8.00
301. Fogarty, Thomas	,,	Corporal. Invalided, Australia, arr. 17.8.00
431. Fuller, Samuel Charles	,,	
181. Grenenger, Wengel	,,	Died, Bloemfontein, 13.3.00
1007. Gilchrist, Horace William	,,	Invalided, Australia, arr. 13.11.00
1074. Gowland, Richard Henry	,,	Invalided, Australia, arr. 17.8.00
1075. Granville, Cecil Horace	,,	
334. Haydon, John William	,,	
585. Hill, Alexander	,,	Promoted Lance-Corpl., 17.2.00. Invalided, Australia, arr. 6.8.00
1009. Hall, Ebenezer	,,	Invalided, Australia, arr. 8.1.01
1011. Harnett, Harold Laurence	,,	
1013. Hartney, James Patrick	,,	
689. Harmer, John Alfred	,,	

Nominal Roll—*continued*.

No. and Name.	Rank.	Remarks.
1012. Harris, Geoffrey Hamlyn	Trooper	
1076. Hockley, Charles Edward	,,	
1077. Hopkins, Reginald Arthur	,,	
1015. Huxley, Arthur Ernest	,,	Invalided, Australia, arr. 16.11.00
1109. Heaney, Alexander	,,	
1078. James, Walter Joseph	,,	Died, Bloemfontein, 4.5.00
81. Jones, James Allen	,,	Wounded, Colesberg District. Invalided, Australia, arr. 28.5.00
1079. Kirkpatrick, Hedley John	,,	*Vide* "Promotions." Invalided, Australia, arr. 28.4.01
1017. Langsford, William Henry	,,	Invalided, Australia, arr. 30.8.00
191. Louis, Joseph	,,	
965. Legge, Walter Givenap	,,	Promoted L.-Corpl.; Corporal, 23.4.00
376. Luff, William	,,	Invalided, Australia, arr. 30.7.00
680. Lynn, Richard John	,,	
454. Martin, Herbert R.	,,	Severely wounded, Glen Siding. Invalided, Australia, arr. 6.8.00
894. Masters, Curtis	,,	Invalided, Australia, arr. 16.11.00
1080. Malartic, Armand Claude	,,	
1026. Marshall, James Bernard	,,	
1081. Mecham, John Walter	,,	Wounded at Zand River. Invalided, Australia, arr. 13.9.00
1027. Mecham, Maunsel Richard	,,	Wounded at Zand River. Invalided, Australia, arr. 17.8.00
1082. Meehan, William Patrick	,,	Died, Adelaide, 24.1.00
883. Mettam, Albert Abraham	,,	
1083. Moody, Edgar Lionel	,,	
902. Macdonald, Richard	,,	Invalided, Australia, arr. 22.3.01
1084. McJannett, William Vincent	,,	
1085. McMinn, David	,,	Invalided, Australia, arr. 6.8.00
686. Minch, Thomas John	,,	
1025. McWilliams, Crawford	,,	
1109. Maher, James Peter	,,	
538. North, George Campbell	,,	Wounded near Johannesburg
804. Overend, Thomas Edward	,,	
1086. Palmer, Lawrence Alfred	,,	Severely wounded, Poplar Grove. Invalided, Australia, arr. 24.11.00
901. Parry, Sidney Carew McDonald	,,	Wounded near Johannesburg. Invalided, Australia, arr. 28.5.00
1087. Peard, Richard Hawke	,,	
1088. Prior, Ernest Arthur	,,	
837. Pole, Robert Chaffey	,,	
891. Priddle, Norman	,,	Promoted L.-Corporal, 17.2.00
809. Resch, Richard N. J.	,,	Invalided, Australia, arr. 30.7.00
1089. Renehan, William	,,	
1954. Roe, Richard James	,,	
1090. See, Harry David	,,	
1097. Seiffert, Louis	,,	
518. Smith, Charles Frederick	,,	
1092. Spittle, Samuel	,,	
961. Spring, David Hugh	,,	Invalided, Australia, arr. 30.7.00
1094. Stackpoole, Guilford William Jack	,,	Promoted Corporal, 6.2.00; Sergeant, 1.4.01
1095. Stafford, Samuel Thomas	,,	
1108. Stewart, John	,,	
1039. Sweetland, Benjamin David	,,	Invalided, Australia, arr. 13.9.00
1096. Taylor, Frederick John	,,	
811. Taylor, Owen Albert	,,	Wounded, Dreifontein, 10.3.00
1097. Thacker, William Herbert	,,	

Nominal Roll—*continued.*

No. and Name.	Rank.	Remarks.
775. Thomas, Edward	Trooper	
1098. Ussher, Neville James	,,	
1044. Walker, Thomas	,,	
1099. Wells, John	,,	
1100. Wessell, Theodore Vehlmes	,,	Severely wounded, Glen Siding. L.-Corporal. Invalided, Australia, arr. 12.11.00
1101. Williamson, Percy Gordon	,,	Invalided, Australia, arr. 17.8.00
1102. Wilson, Robert Frank	,,	Died, Bloemfontein, 16.5.00
1103. Windsor, Frederick Harold	,,	
1049. Windsor, Eli Alexander	,,	Invalided, Australia, arr. 30.7.00
1104. Winter, Joseph James	,,	
1106. Yarrington, Selwyn Herbert	,,	Invalided, Australia, arr. 13.9.00

"A" BATTERY, ROYAL AUSTRALIAN ARTILLERY.

THIS unit was formed entirely of officers and men belonging to the Royal Australian Artillery, New South Wales; the officers and men of the Field Battery already in existence being taken as the nucleus, and the strength made up from the Garrison companies.

In point of *personnel* it was, probably, in point of discipline it was certainly, the most highly classed detail that left Australia for the war. The Royal Australian Artillery, New South Wales, under their "Naval and Military Forces Act of 1871" were subject to the Imperial Army Act and Regulations, and to the King's (then the Queen's) Regulations for the Army; therefore the code under which they were trained was a complete replica of that of the Royal Artillery. Thus the men were embarked under a perfect system of organization.

The battery was equipped with six 15-pr. B.L. guns, with their wagons, &c., and supplied in all respects as a complete unit of its arm. It was the only Australian Field Battery sent to the front.

REFERENCE TO ORDERS.

Inspection of battery	G.O., N.S.W.,	144/99
Pay and allowances	,, ,,	88/00
Embarkation	,, ,,	146/99
Personnel	,, ,,	149/99

CLOTHING.

This consisted of the brown F.S. uniform, cord pants and puttees, with helmets.

ESTABLISHMENT.

The following was the establishment approved :—One commanding officer; 4 subalterns (1 acting-captain); 1 battery sergeant-major; 1 battery Q.M.-sergeant; 6 sergeants; 1 farrier-sergeant; 4 shoeing-smiths; 2 collar-makers; 2 wheelers; 2 trumpeters; 6 corporals; 6 bombardiers; 76 gunners; 63 drivers. Total Field Battery, 175.

The actual captain of the battery was Captain H. Dangar, who was at the time of departure in South Africa as a Special Service officer. It was expected that he would join the battery there, which he did.

Pay and separation allowance were at the usual rates.

EMBARKATION AND RETURN.

The battery embarked at Sydney on the 30th December, 1899, in the transport *Warrigal*, comprising 7 officers (including Captain G. A. Marshall, A.M.C., and Rev. E. C. Beck, C.E. chaplain, with relative rank of major), and 170 non-commissioned officers, artificers, and rank and file, with 148 horses, 6 guns, 6 wagons, 11 carts. Arrived at Cape Town 5th February, 1900. Two of the men died in South Africa.

Captain Dangar joined at Cape Town on 6th February, and remained with the battery for some months.

On the 15th March, 1901, Lieutenant R. G. King, with a draft of 43 sergeants and rank and file, and 19 horses, left Sydney and proceeded to South Africa, where he joined the battery, and was posted for duty with the section under Captain Antill, serving with Colonel Williams' column in Transvaal.

The battery having completed about 18 months' arduous service, was ordered home, and the various sections (which had been detached for special duty in different parts of the country), having re-united, the embarkation took place on the transport *Harlech Castle* on 12th August, 1901, arriving at Sydney on 15th September; having called at Albany, Adelaide, and Melbourne on the passage.

SERVICE.

"A" Battery, soon after its arrival in South Africa, joined General Settle's column, which was then engaged in clearing the districts of Prieska, Kenhardt, and Goodania, in north-western Cape Colony.

In December, 1900, the left section joined Colonel Crabbe's column, then operating on the Orange River, and remained with him until March, 1901, taking part in the chase after De Wet in the Hopetoun district. Was instrumental in capturing De Wet's guns north of Pompean Pan in February. Also attached to Colonel Grenfell's column in Graff Reinet district, operating against Commandants Malan and Kritzinger.

The battery was subsequently employed in the Transvaal with Colonel Williams' and Colonel Remington's columns, and took part in the operations against the commandoes then in the field.

It was unfortunate that the battery, from beginning to end, was split up, and hardly served at all as a complete unit. Colonel Smith observes in his diary, 25th October, 1900 :—"My battery now has its right section at Vryburg, its left at Prieska, and the centre here (Upington), thus covering a front of 360 miles." The sections, however, individually did especially good service.

SERVICES OF OFFICERS.*

Antill, Lieutenant (afterwards captain and major) E. A.—Operations in Cape Colony, Orange River Colony, and Transvaal between February, 1900, and July, 1901. Queen's Medal with three clasps.

Taylor, Lieutenant H. J. C.—As above. (Lieutenant Taylor was subsequently captain and adjutant to 1st Australian Commonwealth Horse in 1902.) Queen's Medal with three clasps. King's Medal with two clasps.

Christian, Lieutenant S. E.—As above.—Despatches, *London Gazette*, July, 1901. Queen's Medal with four clasps.

Sweetland, Lieutenant H. St. J.—As above. Queen's Medal with four clasps.

King, Lieutenant R. G.—Operations in Transvaal and Orange River Colony from 15th May, 1901, to August, 1901. Queen's Medal with four clasps.

Beck, Rev. E. C.—For this chaplain's services *vide* Colonel Smith's diary attached. Queen's Medal with clasps.

Marshall, Captain G. A. (Army Medical Corps).—Operations in Transvaal and Orange River Colony. Queen's Medal with four clasps. *Vide* Army Medical Corps.

PROMOTIONS.

Lieutenant E. A. Antill was promoted captain, and subsequently major (local rank) from 20th June, 1901.

For promotions of sergeants and rank and file see nominal roll of battery.

---

* Col. S. C. U. Smith, R.F.A.'s services are referred to in the extracts from his **Report**, next page.

EXTRACTS FROM REPORT OF COLONEL S. C. SMITH, ROYAL FIELD ARTILLERY.

7th April, 1900.—Arrived near Draghoender about 6 p.m., in a heavy downpour of rain ; 2 inches in three-quarters of an hour.

31st March, 1900.—Camped awaiting supplies. A small column with one section Royal Australian Artillery, under Lieutenant Sweetland, proceeds to Upington. We are all put on half rations.

1st April, 1900.—A small party with two guns, under Lieutenant Christian, start for Kenhardt.

2nd April, 1900.—General Settle left for Upington, and left me in command here at Draghoender. I am guarding a swinging bridge, which is the only means of crossing the Orange River anywhere for miles, and is known as Coejas Pont. Received a report that the Boers, who are very active north of the river, proposed to cut the wire of the bridge. Sent out a troop of yeomanry to reinforce 40 men of Orpheus' Horse, holding the position.

3rd April, 1900.—Our patrol on the other side of the river had a brush with the enemy—no casualties.

12th May, 1900.—I am still at this station (Draghoender) as military commandant. We are not to shift at present as we are forming a supply depôt for future use. We are confronted by about 400 Boers just across the river, who are anxious to destroy the flying bridge here, so as to check our advance. They attacked us on the 13th of last month. We had two killed and one wounded (none of the Royal Australian Artillery) ; their loss being twelve killed and others wounded.

Owing to the ground on this side of the river being flat, I have made my defences on the other side, as it is hilly. With 120 men and one gun, I can keep the Boers at bay unless they can procure guns, which so far they have failed to do, although they have been trying to get them. Their numbers have been increasing, and we have been expecting further attacks daily.

A patrol was attacked on the 28th April, when we lost six horses. We have about 40 miles of river to guard and patrol.

An apprehended attack on Upington caused General Settle to order the two guns I had at Kenhardt to proceed to Upington, so that now four guns are there under Lieutenants Christian and Sweetland. I have despatched Captain Dangar to take command.

The Royal Australian Artillery lost their first man here on the 1st inst., Gunner W. Edwards, a garrison gunner, a good fellow ; he was kicked by a horse and died of tetanus. He is buried here in our small graveyard, and we are erecting a wooden cross. He behaved throughout with great pluck.

10th July, 1900.—On the 2nd July the two guns stationed here (Draghoender) were ordered to De Aar. This leaves me here " gunless." I have applied to be relieved of my command here, so as to rejoin my four guns at Upington, but up to date have received no reply.

13th August, 1900.—I heard of Lieutenant Antill's safe arrival at De Aar with his section, and the fact that they had been ordered to Petrusville near the Free State border.

20th July, 1900.—Major Mynors arrived, and I handed over my command to him. Lieutenant Taylor, Rev. E. Beck (chaplain), and Head-quarters' Staff preceeded by march route to Upington, where we arrived on the 23rd. Upington is 240 miles from Orange River station—the nearest point of railway. I found the officers and men of the battery all well.

4th August, 1900.—Received orders to proceed with a patrol of 50 men of the Border Scouts, Orpheus' Light Horse, and Imperial Yeomanry, down the Orange River towards German territory.

I was away 8 days and patrolled the country 90 miles west. I marched every morning at 6.45, and made 9 or 10 miles before breakfast, then 14 miles between that and lunch, and 6 or 7 miles in the afternoon. We averaged just over 5 miles per hour. I have just heard from Lieutenant Antill that his section have been ordered back to De Aar.

The officers are worse off for clothes than the men, and wander about in a sort of collection of patches.

25th October, 1900.—Captain (Dr.) Marshall rejoined head-quarters of the battery here (Upington) from Draghoender on 4th October. The need of his medical services being required there till relieved.

Lieutenant Christian, with his section, marched from Kenhardt yesterday for Prieska, there to be stationed.

My battery has now its right section at Vryburg, its left at Prieska, and the centre here, thus covering a front of 360 miles.

The men of the battery continue to keep their health well, and have throughout their stay in this country in this respect shown a marked difference to other troops. Lieutenant Antill reports from Vryburg all well.

21st November, 1900.—On this day the Rev. E. C. Beck, who has been with the battery throughout its service in South Africa, left to return to Sydney. His loss was much felt by the battery and by the inhabitants of Upington. By his kindliness and forethought, by his interest in and assiduous attendance on the sick in the hospitals, he had endeared himself to all ranks, both military and civil. Although it was his misfortune, in common with many of us, to see no fighting, his services were invaluable, particularly to the wounded after the battle of Keis, and also to the many sick, and not a few dying, at Draghoender; and throughout his duties were carried out conscientiously, quietly, and unostentatiously.

On this day also, I subsequently heard that Lieutenant Antill with the right section were engaged in action at Vryburg. With much assistance from these guns, the garrison were enabled to beat off a party of looting Boers, and to recover a quantity of stock. They were in action twice on this day. They have been frequently utilized as mounted infantry, and acted as such on patrol.

10th November, 1900.—Lieutenant Christian with his two guns at Prieska was ordered to Colesberg, but on arrival at De Aar, were sent on to Petrusville.

A wire to-day (21st November) states that a laager of 250 Boers are in the drifts close to Petrusville, where Lieutenant Christian arrived yesterday.

13th November, 1900.—Lieutenant Sweetland with his two guns marched for Prieska.

I left for Prieska to-day (14th November) to take over command of the district.

17th November, 1900.—Arrived in Prieska, which is at present garrisoned by three companies, 3rd Welsh, one squadron Nesbitt's Horse, a few Border Scouts, and Cape Police.

19th November, 1900.—Lieutenant Sweetland, with the centre section Royal Australian Artillery, marched into Prieska, having marched 130 miles over very bad roads, in 6 days, bringing all his horses in fit—a capital performance, especially compared with our outward journey, through horse sickness.

4th December, 1900.—I received report from Lieutenant Christian that his section had been twice in action on the drifts near Petrusville, and had no casualties (24th November). **29th November, 1900.**—Report from Vryburg states the right section Royal Australian Artillery had sent one gun, under Lieutenant Antill, as part of escort to a convoy to Schweizer-Rencke. On its way back, the convoy was attacked by a superior force of Boers, during which I regret to have to report Gunner B. Gowing of the battery was dangerously wounded and died shortly after. The gun did capital work.

A native runner was sent 16 miles into Vryburg for reinforcements, and the other gun, with some of the Australian Bushmen, proceeded to the scene of action, when the Boers retired.

No. 2 gun on this occasion fired 190 rounds, the engagement lasting from 7 a.m. till 7 p.m. Two battery horses were wounded and had to be destroyed.

Gunner B. Gowing is a great loss to the battery; he was a good shoeing-smith, a good and cheery soldier, and his death is much deplored by his officers and comrades.

4th December, 1900.—Heavy rain fell to-day, $1\frac{3}{4}$ inches. Our Christmas beer *en route* to here (Prieska) was intercepted by the Boers, and a convoy of much needed clothes was also " commandeered " by them.

25th December, 1900 (Christmas Day).—Still no reported advance of the Boers. Men had a capital Christmas dinner, with plum pudding and beer.

5th February, 1901.—In my last I was not in a position to say what was happening in the two outlying sections of the battery. It appears the right section, under Lieutenant Antill, went off with a column to Kuruman. On the 2nd January the Boers had surrounded the town. They arrived and relieved the town without opposition. On their way back they were attacked, and drove the Boers off without any Royal Australian Artillery casualties. They are now back to Vryburg, which was attacked on the 2nd of this month; the Boers being again easily repulsed.

Lieutenant Christian and his two guns from Petrusville joined Colonel Crabbe's column operating between Orange River and De Aar, to oppose any further incursions of the Boers.

The battery is doing very well indeed, and the men's behaviour is exceptionally good compared with other troops with which they are quartered, and I have every reason to be proud of them.

Lieutenant Sweetland's men fired the Royal salute here on the accession of King Edward the Seventh.

We have been improving our defences, which is work that interests the men and at which the Royal Australian Artillery are *facile princeps*.

Nominal Roll.

No. and Name.	Rank.	Remarks.
Smith, Sydenham Campbell Urquhart	Colonel	Major R.F.A.
Antill, Edward Augustus	Lieut. (Acting Captain)	
Taylor, Herbert James Cox	Lieutenant	
Christian, Sydney Ernest	,,	
Sweetland, Henry St. John	,,	
King, Robert Guy Cyril	,,	
Marshall, George	Captain (A.M.C.)	
Beck, Revd. Ernest C.	Hon. Major	Chaplain
304. Coleman, William	Batty. Sgt.-Major	N.S.W. Battery to Soudan, 1885
1200. Rauchle, George	Batty. Q.M.-Sergt.	N.S.W. Battery to Soudan, 1885
1295. Buffery, William	Wheeler-Sergeant	South Africa, 1879
2605. Ross, Matthew	Farrier-Sergeant	South Africa, 1879
2351. Jansen, Thomas	Collarmaker-Sergeant	
814. Kennedy, John Dunne	Sergeant	N.S.W. Battery to Soudan, 1885; invalided, Australia, 13.12.00
2226. Lawrie, Robert	,,	
1426. Colbourne, Robert	,,	
1662. Holland, Thomas	,,	N.S.W. Battery to Soudan, 1885
2300. Bridge, John	,,	
2211. Shankland, Robert	Corporal	Sergeant, 30.12.99
2336. Abbott, John	,,	Sergeant, 13.12.00
2533. McLeod, John	,,	Invalided, Australia, arr. 16.9.01
2523. Higgins, Richard	,,	Invalided, Australia
2466. Porteus, Arthur	,,	Returned to Australia, 24.1.01
2535. Black, Colin	,,	
2667. Hicks, George	Bombardier	Corporal, 13.12.00.; invalided, Australia, arr. 11.6.01
2485. Gleeson, John	,,	Corporal, 30.12.99.; invalided, Australia, arr. 30.8.00
2493. Leape, George Sebastian	Acting Bombr.	
2665. Cowburn, Chas.	,,	Bombardier; and Corporal, 13.12.00
2496. McElwee, Ed. Spencer	,,	Corporal, 30.3.01.; invalided, Australia, arr. 6.7.01
2691. McLean, David	,,	
2809. Fairlamb, Frank	,,	Bombardier; and Corporal, 5.6.01
2836. Colless, Frederick Jocelyn	,,	
2037. Farrell, Wm.	Trumpeter	
2908. Gillard, Leonard Percival		
1134. Abdy, Charles John	Gunner	
2799. Aplin, Chas.	,,	Invalided, Australia, arr. 6.7.01
2819. Anderson, Chas.	Driver	Invalided, Australia, arr. 23.9.01
2871. Abel, John McNabb	,,	
2916. Arthur, Charles Amery	,,	Invalided, Australia, 23.10.00
2483. Bailey, Harry William	Gunner	
2646. Brown, William John	,,	
2513. Bennett, Charles Alfred	,,	Invalided, Australia, 3.5.00
2297. Bastin, Henry John	Driver	
2495. Butt, George James	,,	
2655. Brook, Henry Gilbert	,,	Acting Bombardier; and Bombardier, 22.5.01
2656. Barrett, Arthur Sydney	,,	
2841. Brownfield, Douglas	,,	
2893. Burrows, John Edward	,,	
2901. Breen, Neil William	,,	
2922. Brain, Arthur Albert	,,	
2933. Bradley, George	,,	
2958. Burkett, Cyril Theodore	,,	
2945. Bultitude, William James	,,	

Nominal Roll—*continued*.

No. and Name.	Rank.	Remarks.
2974. Behan, Maurice James	Driver	
1296. Brush, Wm.	Gunner	Invalided, Australia, arr. 2.11.01
2668. Clare, William Ernest	,,	
2747. Campbell, George	,,	
2751. Clarke, Patrick James	,,	Invalided, Australia, 13.12.00
2833. Carradus, Charles	,,	
2834. Cotter, Edward	,,	
2895. Connell, John	Driver	
2878. Cederberg, Charles	,,	
2975. Coggins, William	,,	
2976. Colter, John	,,	
2650. Dark, Edward	Gunner	
2713. DeClouet, James	,,	Bombardier. Invalided, Australia, arr. 2.8.01
2459. Donaldson, Arch. Henry	Driver	
2716. Dunn, Reginald	Gunner	
2708. Edwards, Walter	,,	Died, Draghoender, 1.5.00
1090. Forrest, George	,,	N.S.W. Battery to Soudan, 1885
2313. Flower, Percy Charles	Driver	
2855. Fisher, Frederick	Gunner	
2260. Gilshannon, Cornelius	,,	
2610. Gowing, Bernard	,,	Killed in action, 29.11.00
1716. Gazzard, Ambrose	Driver	
2798. Gillard, Thomas Michael	,,	
2854. Gallagher, Charles	,,	
2883. Gardiner, Clifford Stephen	,,	
2937. Gill, Edward	,,	
2977. Gurd, Harry James	,,	
2978. Gilmore, William J.	,,	
2689. Hamilton, William	Gunner	
2240. Holmes, James	,,	
2581. Hickey, Walter	,,	
2589. Hadfield, William Frank	,,	
2740. Hodson, William	,,	
2774. Hill, Arthur Chilton	,,	
2583. Hibberd, Claude	,,	Bombardier, 5.6.01
2906. Howarth, Horace Maitland	,,	
2952. Howe, Patrick John	,,	Invalided, Australia, 3.7.00
2647. Hinds, Alfred	,,	
2826. Hart, John	,,	Invalided, Australia, 2.8.00
2832. Hughes, George Russell	,,	
2884. Hatter, Albert Thomas	,,	Invalided, Australia, arr. 16.9.01
2885. Hughes, Thomas Russell	,,	
2892. Hogan, Owen Eugene Joseph	,,	
2904. Henebury, Wm. James	,,	
2969. Hanney, James	,,	
2649. Hinds, Joseph	,,	Invalided, Australia, arr. 2.8.01
2857. Ives, Alexander Robert	,,	
2914. Jones, Walter Thomas	,,	Invalided, Australia, arr. 18.5.01
2971. Jones, Septimus	Driver	
2442. Kelly, Michael	Gunner	
2864. King, Arthur Luxmore	,,	Invalided, Australia, arr. 16.9.01
2600. Kennelly, James Daniel	,,	
2548. Knight, Wm.	,,	Bombardier, 13.12.00
2746. Leonard, Herbert Henry	,,	Invalided, Australia, 13.8.00
2072. La Touche, Gerald George	,,	
2815. Lawrence, Alfred Henry	,,	
2882. Lynch, Philip James	,,	
2894. Loveday, Laurence	,,	
2927. Locke, Ernest Escott	Driver	Invalided, Australia, 23.10.00
2298. Lang, Wm. Chas.	,,	
2598. McCormack, Wm. Henry	Gunner	Bombardier, 30.3.01. Invalided, Australia, arr. 23.9.01
2874. McDonnell, Martin	,,	

Nominal Roll—continued.

No. and Name.	Rank.	Remarks.
2930. Murray, Claude	Gunner	
2687. McCarthy, Wm.	,,	
2606. Mullen, John	,,	
2435. McGrath, James John	,,	Bombardier, 23.1.00. Invalided, Australia, arr. 16.9.01
2759. McFarlane, Patrick		
2382. Murray, Cameron	,,	
2903. Milwood, George Edward	Driver	Invalided, Australia, 28.12.00
2900. Morris, Arthur Thomas	Gunner	
2898. McWilliams, Fred. Arthur	,,	
2800. Mohr, Philip Charles		Invalided, Australia, arr. 2.8.01
2972. McLean, James	Driver	
2552. Murray, Ernest Edward		Invalided, Australia, 13.12.00
2844. O'Toole, Walter	Gunner	
2949. O'Brien, Wilfred		
2859. Pheeney, David	,,	
2915. Perrin, Augustus	,,	Invalided, Australia, arr. 2.8.01
2860. Pugh, Ernest	,,	
2973. Parker, Herbert	Driver	
2534. Quinn, James	,,	Invalided, Australia, arr. 11.6.01
2530. Reilly, Patrick	Gunner	Invalided, Australia, arr. 5.3.01
2673. Ralphs, Samuel	,,	
2567. Ryan, John	,,	
2599. Ridge, Leo	,,	Invalided, Australia
2727. Ringwood, William Travers	,,	
2872. Rice, Percy	Driver	Invalided, Australia, arr. 18.5.01
2910. Rossi, Thomas	,,	Invalided, Australia, 13.12.00
2666. Robertson, Donald	,,	
2014. Ridgway, Fred. William	,,	
2642. Steward, Edward	Gunner	
2616. Simon, William	,,	
2614. Seymour, George	,,	
2332. Skuse, Richard Daniel	,,	
2766. Smyth, Henry Edward	,,	
2410. Smith, Saml...	,,	Invalided, Australia, arr. 22.3.01
675. Sykes, Geo.	,,	
2189. Stewart, John Neil	,,	
2791. Sare, Wm.	Driver	
2601. Skalla, John Peter Paul	Gunner	Invalided, Australia, 13.12.00
2721. Sheedy, Michael James	,,	
2853. Sturrock, And.	,,	
2871. Seward, Samuel Geo.	Driver	
2928. Stopp, Geo. Wm.		Invalided, Australia, 23.10.00
2153. Seage, Jas.	,,	Invalided, Australia, arr. 15.7.01
2965. Selmes, Jeremiah Chas.	,,	
2865. Townsend, Arthur Ashton	Gunner	
2213. Tristram, Thomas Chas.	,,	
2754. Turner, Jas.	,,	
2775. Thornton, Algernon	,,	
2966. Trevenar, Jas. Walter	Driver	Invalided, England, 25.7.00
2202. Valentine, John	Gunner	
2086. Vincent, Wm. Chas.	Driver	Invalided, Australia, arr. 15.7.01
2862. Warner, Walter	Gunner	
1569. Wakerley, John	,,	
2551. Wilson, Chas. Richard	,,	Acting-Bombardier. Invalided, Australia, 23.10.00
2888. White, John	,,	
2603. White, Alfred Richard	,,	
1613. Willis, Wm.	,,	
2863. White, Joseph		
2932. Walsh, Joseph Grafton	Driver	
2941. Woodward, Colin Campbell	,,	

Nominal Roll—*continued*.

No. and Name.	Rank.	Remarks.
2979. Wiseman, Wm.	Driver	Invalided, Australia, 16.11.00
2310. Whitbread, Arthur	,,	
116. Whitton, John	,,	
2967. Watson, William Harry	,,	
2968. Wheeler, James	,,	Invalided, Australia, 13.8.00

DRAFT FOR "A" BATTERY.

B.A.A. No.	Rank.	Name.	Coy.	Remarks.
	Lieutenant	King, R. G.	2	In charge of Draft
2429	Sergeant	Kelaher, C.	1	
2401	Corporal	Batten, W. J.	2	
2728	Acting Bombardier	Hewitt, I.	3	
2699	,,	Sercombe, H.	1	
2683	,,	McKenzie, J. T.	2	Died
2846	,,	Randall, E.	3	
2897	,,	McLaurin, H.	1	
2981	,,	Connochie, W.	1	
3016	,,	Kavanagh, B.	"A" Bty.	
3000	,,	Callan, T. H.	,,	
3053	,,	Bourke, W. T.	,,	
3043	Gunner	Allen, G. A.	3	
2929	,,	Hessian, E.	1	
3067	,,	Horne, H. J.	2	
3139	,,	Howarth, H.	3	
3026	,,	Kremer, C.	2	
2732	,,	Leonard, J.	2	
3100	,,	McCauley, A. H.	3	
3069	,,	McMaugh, A.	2	
3124	,,	Macdonnell, C. P.	3	Servant to Lieut. King
2935	,,	Robinson, T. R.	2	
3123	,,	Vlaeminck, H.	2	
3034	,,	Walsh, L. C.	3	
3078	,,	Weaver, T.	2	Invalided, Australia, arr. 23.9.01
3120	,,	Younger, T.	2	
3136	,,	Younger, E.	3	
3111	Driver	Anderson, A. J.	"A" Bty.	
3046	,,	Bush, S. P.	,,	
3128	,,	Coulcher, E. H.	,,	
3143	,,	Cooke, F.	,,	
3155	,,	Ellis, E. C. B.	,,	Invalided, Australia, arr. 23.9.01
3022	,,	Easterbrook, W. H.	,,	
3047	,,	Gunning, W. J.	,,	
3141	,,	Hickey, J.	,,	
3021	,,	Lane, H.	,,	
3013	,,	Moran, C.	,,	
3008	,,	Mackay, J. H.	,,	
3138	,,	Mulhearn, J. M.	,,	
3146	,,	Rice, W.	,,	
3017	,,	Stephenson, R. J.	,,	
3020	,,	Sharpe, P.	,,	
3031	,,	Verdon, F. J.	,,	
3045	,,	Watkins, G. A.	,,	
3030	,,	Wonson, A. H.	,,	
3005	,,	Withers, E. A.	,,	
3182	,,	Johnston, J.	,,	

FIRST NEW SOUTH WALES MOUNTED RIFLES.

THIS was the first Contingent despatched from New South Wales which did not consist entirely of drafts from local regiments or of men recruited from different local infantry regiments. One squadron from the Mounted Rifle Regiment had already been sent, together with a company of infantry which was mounted in South Africa. It was now resolved that three squadrons of Mounted Rifles should be raised; to be " B," " C," and " D " squadrons of the 1st Regiment, and that the squadron and company at the seat of war should be " A " and " E " squadrons respectively. Men who were good shots and good riders were required, and preference was given to those serving, or who had served, in the local forces, provided they fulfilled the necessary qualifications. Reservists and men of civilian rifle clubs were also eligible on the same terms.

The establishment authorized was:—Staff: 1 major, 1 adjutant and quartermaster, 3 sergeants, 2 drivers, 3 batmen; total, 10, with 11 horses. Details of a company (or squadron): 1 captain, 4 subalterns, 1 colour-sergeant, 4 sergeants, 1 farrier-sergeant, 4 shoeing-smiths, 2 buglers, 6 corporals, 92 privates (including batmen), 5 drivers; total, 120, with 130 horses. Dismounted: 1 saddler, 5 batmen riding spare horses), 2 cooks, 2 wagon-men; total, 10.

REFERENCE TO ORDERS.

Formation	G.O., N.S.W., 141/99
Pay and allowances	,, ,, 6/00, 88/00
Establishment	,, ,, 1/00, 2/00
Clothing, &c.	,, ,, 142/99; 146/99
Officers	,, ,, 4/00; G. Gazette, 45, 17th January, 1900
Ammunition	,, ,, 3/00
Outfit for officers	,, ,, 4/00
Embarkation	,, ,, 8/00
Veterinary-surgeon	,, ,, 9/00

CLOTHING, ETC.

Articles of uniform supplied as authorized by G.O. 146 (27th December, 1899) were as follows:—Two F.S. jackets, khaki tweed, without facings; 2 pairs Bedford cord pants; 1 large F.S. hat; 1 F.S. cap; 2 pairs puttees; 2 pairs Cossack boots; 1 great coat.

Arms and equipment.—M.L.E. rifles and sword-bayonet, cartridge-belt with supporting-braces. Fully horsed and provided with saddles. Regimental transport was also provided. Officers were granted £25 towards outfit.

EMBARKATION AND RETURN.

The three squadrons of the regiment, under the command of Lieut.-Colonel Knight, embarked at Sydney on the transport *Southern Cross* on the 17th January, 1900, and arrived at Cape Town on 17th February, disembarking on the 19th. It comprised 20 officers, 385 sergeants and rank and file, with 404 horses and 17 carts. Of these, 3 officers and 20 others were killed or died, 3 officers and 4 others were transferred to 2nd and 3rd Mounted Rifles, 2 officers and 21 others were struck off the strength in South Africa, 1 officer and 4 others were commissioned in the Imperial Army; 11 officers and 336 others returned to Australia.

As thus reduced, the regiment again embarked at Cape Town on 30th March, 1901, and arrived at Sydney on 29th April, disembarking on the 1st May. The only port of call was Fremantle.

Promotions, Etc.

Name.	Original Appointment.	Subsequent Changes.	Contingents.
Lenehan, Robert William	Captain	Promoted Major	Bushveldt Carbineers
Bennett, Alfred Joshua ..	Captain	Promoted Major	Transferred to 3rd M.R.
Anderson, Charles Godfrey	Lieutenant	Promoted Captain	
Lee, Charles Arthur ..	Lieutenant	Previously served as Corporal in "A" Squadron	Subsequently with 2nd Mounted Rifles as Captain
McGlinn, John Patrick ..	Lieutenant	Promoted Captain	
Watson, William Walker Russell	Lieutenant	Promoted Captain	
Lydiard, Charles Geo. Sydney	Lieutenant	.. .. ..	Subsequently with 2nd M.R. as Captain
Kelly, Robt. H. Vandeleur	Lieutenant	.. .. ..	Commissioned in R.F.A.
Learmonth, F. L. ..	Corporal	Promoted Lieutenant	
Stirton, P. E. ..	Private	Promoted Lieutenant	
Antill, S. R. ..	Sergeant	Promoted Lieutenant	Subsequently as Captain with 1st A.C.H.

Troopers and N.C.O.'s who received Commissions in Imperial and Irregular Corps.

In Imperial Army:—Troopers W. S. Rich, J. E. F. D'Apice, C. T. Woods, Lance-Corporal J. B. Mitchell.

In 2nd and 3rd New South Wales Mounted Rifles:—Sergeants J. B. Bent and C. L. Braun, Q.M.-Sergeant D. J. Stewart, Lance-Corporal Cuthbert Fetherstonhaugh.

In Bushveldt Carbineers:—Sergeant J. H. V. Edwards, Q.M.-Sergeant H. S. Mortimer, Farrier-Sergeant Handcock.

Commands to which Attached.

Le Gallais' Brigade, Lord Roberts' main column, Modder River to Bloemfontein—4th to 14th March, 1900. Le Gallais' Brigade, General Tucker's force—advanced post near Brandfort. With General Hutton's force, 1st to 13th May, 1900, Bloemfontein to Kroonstadt—general advance to Pretoria. With De Lisle's Column, Ridley's Brigade, General Ian Hamilton's Force, Kroonstadt to Pretoria, in general advance.

Remainder of period of service, viz., to March, 1901, with De Lisle's column.

Principal Operations in which Engaged.

Poplar Grove	7th March, 1900.
Dreifontein	10th March, 1900.
Bloemfontein	14th March, 1900.
Karee Siding	29th March, 1900.
Thaba 'Nchu	April, 1900 (detachment only).
Brandfort	3rd May, 1900.
Vet River	5th May, 1900.
Zand River	10th May, 1900.
Kroonstad	12th May, 1900.
Lindley	20th May, 1900.
Near Johannesburg	29th May, 1900.

Principal Operations in which Engaged—*continued*.

Pretoria	4th June, 1900.
Diamond Hill	11th and 12th June, 1900.
Heidelberg	23rd June, 1900.
Wittebergen	July, 1900.
Palmietfontein	19th July, 1900.
Vredefort	24th July, 1900.
Venterskroom	7th August, 1900.
Alexanderfontein	14th August, 1900
Boschfontein	10th September, 1900.
Schoeman's Drift	7th October, 1900.
Rensburg Drift	27th October, 1900 (captured Boer Krupp gun).
Bothaville	5th and 6th November, 1900.
Honwater (C.C.)	26th December, 1900.
Machadodorp	October and November, 1900.

Operations in Orange River Colony between 30th November, 1900, and 19th December, 1900. Operations in Cape Colony between 20th December, 1900, and 30th March, 1901.

WAR SERVICES AND HONOURS.

Knight, Lieut.-Colonel G. C.—Operations in Orange Free State, Transvaal, Orange River Colony, and Cape Colony, February, 1900, to March, 1901. Actions—at Poplar Grove, Dreifontein, Karee Siding, Vet River, Zand River, Johannesburg, Elands River, Venterskroom, Wittebergen, and Bothaville. Wounded at Honwater, 26th December, 1900. Despatches, *London Gazette*, 19th April, 1901. Queen's Medal with six clasps.

McGlinn, Captain (Adjutant) J. P.—Operations as above. Actions at Poplar Grove, Dreifontein, Karee Siding, Vet River, Zand River, Johannesburg, Pretoria, Diamond Hill, and Wittebergen. Queen's Medal with six clasps.

Cortis, Captain (A.M.C.) W. R.—*Vide* Army Medical Corps.

Gribben, Captain (Vet.) A. P.—Operations in Orange Free State and Orange River Colony, February to December, 1900. Actions at Poplar Grove, Dreifontein, and Karee Siding. Accidentally injured at Rensburg Drift, 26th October, 1900. Queen's Medal with three clasps.

Fagan, Rev. P. (R.C. chaplain).—Operations as above. Actions as stated. Queen's Medal with six clasps.

Lenehan, Captain R. W.—Operations and actions as above. Queen's Medal with six clasps.

Hilliard, Captain M. A.—Operations in Orange River Colony and Transvaal, February, 1900, to June, 1900. Actions at Poplar Grove, Dreifontein, Karee Siding, Vet River, Zand River, Johannesburg, Pretoria, and Diamond Hill. Accidentally injured at Heidelberg, 27th June, 1900. Despatches, *London Gazette*, 18th April, 1901. D.S.O. Queen's Medal with four clasps.

Anderson, Captain C. G.—Operations and actions as first stated. Queen's Medal with four clasps.

Bennett, Captain A. J.—Soudan Contingent, 1885. **Medal and clasp. Khedive's Star.** Operations in Orange Free State, Transvaal, Orange River Colony, and Cape Colony, February, 1900, to March, 1901. Actions at Poplar Grove, Dreifontein, Karee Siding, and Bothaville. Severely wounded at Dreifontein, 10th March, 1900. Despatches, *London Gazette*, 19th April, 1901, and 29th July, 1902. D.S.O. Queen's Medal with three clasps. King's Medal with two clasps. (Captain Bennett was promoted to major, and subsequently joined 3rd Mounted Rifles.)

Watson, Captain W. W. R.—Operations and actions as first stated. S.O. De Lisle's 2nd Imperial Mounted Infantry Corps (South Africa), 14th August, 1900, to 31st March, 1901. Despatches, *London Gazette*, 18th April, 1901. Queen's Medal with six clasps.

Lydiard, Lieutenant C. G. S.—Operations and actions as first stated. Despatches, *London Gazette*, 25th April, 1901, and 29th July, 1902. Queen's Medal with seven clasps. (Subsequently joined 2nd Mounted Rifles.)

Basche, Lieutenant C. O.—Operations in Orange Free State, February to April, 1900. Actions at Poplar Grove and Dreifontein. Died of enteric fever at Bloemfontein, 16th April, 1900.

Kelly, Lieutenant R. H. V.—Operations and actions as above. Queen's Medal with six clasps. Obtained commission in Royal Field Artillery.

Lee, Lieutenant C. A.—Operations as above. Actions at Poplar Grove, Dreifontein and Karee Siding. Queen's Medal with four clasps. (Subsequently joined 2nd Mounted Rifles.)

Learmouth, Lieutenant F. L.—Operations as above. Actions at Poplar Grove, Dreifontein, Karee Siding, Vet River, Zand River, Johannesburg, Pretoria, Diamond Hill, and Bothaville. Despatches, *London Gazette*, 25th April, 1901. D.S.O. Queen's Medal with four clasps.

Stirton, Lieutenant P. E.—Operations and actions as above. Queen's Medal with four clasps.

Harriott, Lieutenant W. R.—Operations in Orange River Colony and Transvaal, February, 1900, to June, 1900. Actions at Poplar Grove, Vet River, Zand River, Johannesburg, Pretoria, and Diamond Hill. Died of wounds, Diamond Hill, 13th June, 1900.

Newman, Lieutenant W. A.—Operations and actions as stated. Queen's Medal with five clasps.

Garvan, Lieutenant Jas. C.—Operations and actions generally as stated. Queen's Medal with four clasps.

Antill, Lieutenant S. R. — Operations and actions as stated. Despatches, *London Gazette*, 19th April, 1901. Queen's Medal with four clasps. (Subsequently joined Australian Commonwealth Horse.)

Legge, Lieutenant G. H.—Operations and actions as stated. Queen's Medal with four clasps.

Holborow, Lieutenant G. A. H.—Operations in Orange Free State, February to March, 1900, including action at Klip Drift. Wounded near Klip Drift, 6th March, 1900. Queen's Medal with two clasps.

Drage, Lieutenant P. W. C.—Operations in Orange Free State and Transvaal, February to June, 1900. Actions at Poplar Grove, Dreifontein, Karee Siding, Vet River, Zand River, Johannesburg, Pretoria, and Diamond Hill. Killed at Diamond Hill, 12th June, 1900.

Legge, Captain (now Lieut.-Colonel) J. G., was adjutant from April, 1900, to November, 1900. For war services, *vide* Infantry Contingent (" E " Squadron).

Extracts from Diary of Lieut.-Colonel G. C. Knight.

12th June, 1900 (second day, Diamond Hill).—Regiment engaged in a hot position all day; incessant artillery and rifle fire. Towards evening an order was given for the regiment to take a kopje. The men, led by their officers, advanced steadily in the face of a most severe fire. The kopje was taken, but at a heavy cost to the regiment, as Lieutenants Drage and Harriott were killed, and Captain Holmes, Sergeant-Major Liggins, Lance-Corporal Bowler, Privates A. Cameron, D. G. Campbell, and G. Murray, were wounded. Captain Cortis (Australian Medical Corps), under heavy fire, did splendid work in attending to the wounded.

Camped for the night near the scene of the day's engagement.

13th June, 1900.—Corps pushed on to Shietport. Two companies of 6th (Imperial) Mounted Infantry and " C " Squadron (Captain Hilliard) met with heavy rifle and shell fire, but our " pom-pom " effectively replied. Buried Lieutenant Drage in a garden at Rhenosterfontein Farm. Regiment returned to Elands River station and camped.

14th June, 1900.—Camped at Elands River station. News of Lieutenant Harriott's death received this morning. General Ridley reviewed the corps and complimented all hands on work done. The Gordon Highlanders and 6th (Imperial) Mounted Infantry cheered the New South Wales men for the gallantry displayed by them at Diamond Hill on the 12th inst.

27th June, 1900.—Lieutenant Newman, in charge of a small reconnoitering party, left camp at 4 a.m. in the direction of Heidelberg. Finding entrance to town clear the party entered, and amidst much enthusiasm hoisted the British flag. A number of Boers handed in their arms to Lieutenant Newman. The main body of troops entered Heidelberg before noon.

19th July, 1900.—Marched at daylight. Regiment acting as right flank guard to General Broadwood's force. On finding Boers in front, the regiment pushed on, and was directed to clear the right of the advance. This they did, and in the advance on the enemy's position Private Palazzi was shot through the heart. A small party of " B " Squadron lost touch owing to ground formation, and getting temporarily blocked by a wire fence found themselves exposed to a strong fire at short range. Private Biddle was killed and Sergeant Nicholson severely wounded. After this, " A " Squadron was sent, under orders from the commanding officer (Colonel De Lisle), to my left front, when they became so hotly engaged that for a time it was doubtful whether we would not lose heavily, but by the timely arrival of reinforcements, the enemy retired. Private Bennett, " A " squadron, was killed, and Lieutenant Tooth wounded.

20th July, 1900.—Bodies of Privates Bennett, Biddle, and Palazzi buried this morning; graves marked with crosses. Burial services read by Father Patrick.

23rd July, 1900.—Regiment marched at noon and camped for the night within 8 miles of Vredefort. On outpost all night; bitterly cold.

Nominal Roll.

No. and Name.	Rank.	Remarks.

REGIMENTAL STAFF.

No. and Name.	Rank.	Remarks.
Knight, Guy Cunninghame	Lieut.-Colonel	
McGlinn, John Patrick	Captain (Adjutant)	
Gribben, Andrew Pitt	Captain (Vet. Surgeon)	
Cortis, William Richard	Captain (A.M.C.)	
Fagan, Patrick	Captain (Chaplain)	
524. Lacey, Henry Noel	Regtl. Q.M.-Sergt.	
534. Sullivan, Edward John	Transport Sergeant	N.S.W. Contingent to Soudan, 1885; died, Kroonstadt, 26.5.00

"B" SQUADRON.

No. and Name.	Rank.	Remarks.
Lenehan, Robert Wm.	Captain	
Lydiard, Chas. Geo. Sydney	Lieutenant	
Basche, Carl Oswald	,,	Died, Bloemfontein, 16.4.00
Kelly, Robt. H. Vandeleur	,,	Vide "Promotions"
Lee, Chas. Arthur	,,	
Learmonth, Frederick L.	,,	Vide "Promotions"
Stirton, Percy Edward	,,	Vide "Promotions"
520. Abel, Martin	Private	Invalided, Australia, arr. 6.8.00
531. Andrews, George Thos.	,,	
447. Ashton, Ernest E. Allen	,,	
126. Asquith, Walter	,,	
360. Apps, Wm. John Robt.	Sergeant	
308. Avern, Henry Charles	Corporal	
425. Antill, Arthur Johnston	,,	
258. Andrews, Wm. Henry	Private	
303. Binns, Christopher S.	Bugler	
285. Bates, Alfred	Private	
193. Buckley, Ernest James	Farrier-Sergeant	
511. Bassiere, Louis Phillip	Private	
231. Biddle, John Wright	,,	Killed in action, Palmietfontein, 19.7.00
344. Bentley, Clarence W. G.	,,	Invalided, Australia, arr. 17.2.01
467. Barber, Charles Hulme	,,	Invalided, Australia, arr. 17.8.00
519. Bathurst, Seymour	,,	Invalided, Australia, arr. 30.7.00
218. Broadhurst, Hill Roland	,,	
346. Button, Walter Jas.	,,	
129. Brown, Charles	,,	Invalided, Australia, arr. 9.12.00
361. Bird, Sydney	,,	
461. Coulson, Walter Arnold	,,	Invalided, Australia, arr. 9.12.00
343. Cripps, John Clinch	,,	
351. Cripps, Charles G.	,,	Died, Bloemfontein, 5.5.00
223. Carver, William	Q.M.-Sergeant	
236. Cunningham, W. J.	Private	Invalided, Australia, arr. 30.7.00
487. Callaghan, Clendon C.	,,	
205. Cradick, Albert E.	,,	
244. Carter, John Hugh	,,	
165. Campbell, William	Corporal	
220. Constantine, Alexander	Private	Invalided, Australia, arr. 13.9.00

Nominal Roll—continued.

No. and Name.	Rank.	Remarks.
"B" SQUADRON—continued.		
342. Curby, Ernest Joseph	Private	
366. Coucom, Arthur	Corporal	
261. Clements, Percy Gregory	Private	
207. Cleary, Thomas James	,,	Invalided, Australia, arr. 30.7.00
235. Cavanagh, Walter	,,	
298. Cardell, James	,,	
477. Conybeare, Edwin Jas.	,,	Died, Bloemfontein, 16.6.00
532. Coombes, Charles Jos.	,,	
307. Donovan, Thos. Wm.	Sergeant	Invalided, Australia, arr. 27.4.01
521. Degner, Cumming A. A. B.	Private	Invalided, Australia, arr. 6.12.00
195. Dockrell, Wm. Maynard	Sergeant	Invalided, Australia, arr. 21.10.00
179. Duprez, Arthur Offord	Private	Invalided, Australia, arr. 30.8.00
317. English, Patk. Joseph	Corporal	Despatches, *London Gazette*, 25.5.01. Invalided, Australia, arr. 30.8.00
206. Edwards, James H. V.	Sergeant	Vide " Promotions "
180. Eager, John Francis	Private	Invalided, Australia, arr. 30.8.00
530. Fanton, James	,,	Died at Glen, near Bloemfontein, 15.4.00
375. Fraser, Archibald	,,	
516. Flynn, John Joseph	,,	Invalided, Australia, arr. 6.8.00
490. Finch, William Henry	Farrier-Sergeant	
312. Fox, Kirk Stanley	Private	
216. Gilshanen, Patrick J.	,,	
315. Godsell, David	,,	
237. Graham, John Joseph	,,	
131. Glanham, Thomas D. Y.	,,	N.S.W. Contingent to Soudan, 1885
132. Glover, William H.	,,	
238. Greenow, Alfred E. R.	,,	Invalided, Australia, arr. 16.11.00
304. Hamilton, Joseph Alex.	Bugler	
352. Holm, Louis Harry	Private	
134. Hunt, Herbert	,,	
321. Henery, William Downer	,,	
319. Hays, Francis Reginald	,,	
286. Hanson, Henry Syvert	,,	
378. Hanson, Charles Bent	,,	
156. Henry, John William	,,	Invalided, Australia, arr. 30.8.00
224. Halliwell, Robert	,,	Invalided, Australia, arr. 30.8.00
135. Howell, Athol Norman	,,	
322. Hughes, Thomas	,,	
504. Hardwell, Samuel Moss	Farrier	Sergeant-Farrier. Invalided, Australia, arr. 30.8.00
246. Holland, Edward P.	Private	Invalided, Australia, arr. 30.8.00
555. Harrison, Saml. Ernest	,,	
247. Jones, Henry Harold	,,	
326. James, Edward	,,	Invalided, Australia, arr. 9.12.00
507. Kendall, Joseph	Sergeant-Major	Invalided, Australia, arr. 26.1.01
470. Kiddle, Barnett	Private	
327. Kennedy, Fredk. Adolphus	,,	
430. Kite, George Harold	,,	Died, Bloemfontein, 24.5.00
431. Kite, Charles Norman	,,	Invalided, Australia, arr. 30.7.00
523. Lynch, David William	,,	Invalided, Australia, arr. 15.9.00
183. Lye, George Albert	,,	Invalided, Australia, arr. 6.12.00
139. Lindon, Francis Sydney	,,	
290. Lynch, Richard Thos.	,,	
381. Lenehan, Alfred Henry	,,	
283. Larman, Herbert	,,	Invalided, Australia, arr. 21.10.00

Nominal Roll—*continued.*

No. and Name.	Rank.	Remarks.
"B" SQUADRON—*continued.*		
333. McSweeney, Joseph	Corporal	Invalided, Australia, arr. 6.12.00
140. Munro, Robt. Thomas	,,	Invalided, Australia, arr. 30.7.00
275. Martin, Wm. Henry	Private	Invalided, Australia, arr. 17.8.00
270. Mitchell, John Basil	Lance-Corporal	*Vide* "Promotions"
313. Metcalfe, Henry J. T.	Private	
335. Mackay, Andrew Hector	,,	Invalided, Australia, arr. 30.7.00
142. McClelland, Ernest Edwd.	,,	Invalided, Australia, arr. 6.8.00
276. McGill, Richd. Webb	,,	Accidentally killed, Cape Town, 11.3.01
510. McGrath, Henry James	,,	Invalided, Australia, arr. 6.8.00
272. McFerran, A. B.	,,	
338. Morrow, Thos. Hamilton	,,	
209. McLean, John Hector	,,	
161. Mooney, Wm. Henry	,,	
508. Nicholson, John	Sergeant	
339. Neilsen, Robert	Private	
174. O'Brien, Wm. Smith	,,	
440. Oakes, Walter Edward	,,	
144. Parkes, Sydney Ernest	Sergeant	
239. Podmore, Henry Benyon	Corporal	
241. Pickleson, William	Private	Invalided, Australia, arr. 6.8.00
350. Pope, Walter Wm. Edwin	,,	Invalided, Australia, arr. 15.9.00
213. Paul, George	,,	Invalided, Australia, arr. 13.9.00
175. Pateman, Charles Irving	,,	
552. Peek, Arthur Richd.	,,	
202. Ross, Thomas Wm.	,,	Invalided, Australia, arr. 15.9.00
289. Rogerson, William Jno.	,,	
400. Rolleston, George	,,	
279. Sheffield, John Arthur	,,	
146. Spring, Reginald	,,	
396. Sandon, Robert Alfred	,,	Invalided, Australia, arr. 17.8.00
399. Simpson, George A. D.	,,	
397. Sinclair, Frank L.	,,	
229. Tepper, Harold Lewis	,,	
515. Tarlington, John	,,	Invalided, Australia, arr. 13.9.00
455. Thompson, Norman E.	,,	Died, Kroonstadt, 4.12.00
505. Watson, Thomas H.	Sergt.-Major	
187. Ward, Walter	Private	
408. Wilson, John	,,	Invalided, Australia, arr. 30.8.00
456. Ward, Edward George	,,	Invalided, Australia, arr. 30.8.00
409. Williams, Austin	,,	
518. White, James Ginger	,,	
186. Whinfield, Frederick Wm.	,,	Died, Bloemfontein, 25.4.00
347. Wheeler, Albert Simmends	,,	Invalided to England, 11.8.00
411. Yeo, William George	Lance-Corporal	Invalided, Australia, arr. 16.11.00
481. Young, John William	Private	
"C" SQUADRON.		
Hilliard, Maurice Alfred	Captain	Invalided, Australia, arr. 17.8.00
Anderson, Charles Godfrey	,,	
Harriott, William Rupert	Lieutenant	Died of wounds, Diamond Hill, 13.6.00

Nominal Roll—continued.

No. and Name.	Rank.	Remarks.
"C" SQUADRON—continued.		
Newman, William A.	Lieutenant	
Garvan, James C.	,,	Invalided, Australia, arr. 11.10.00
Antill, Stanley Ross	,,	*Vide* " Promotions "
468. Alley, George Fraser	Private	
453. Anderson, George	Corporal	N.S.W. Contingent to Soudan, 1885. Invalided, Australia, arr. 21.10.00
354. Anderson, George Wm.	Private	
349. Allwood, Fredk. Thos.	,,	
359. Attwood, Francis	,,	Invalided, Australia, arr. 30.8.00
358. Argaet, Charles W.	,,	
432. Barnes, Walter	,,	
442. Beatty, Henry Jno.	,,	
454. Beck, William	,,	Invalided, Australia, arr. 17.8.00
118. Bellamy, Thomas C.	,,	Invalided, Australia, arr. 18.5.01
364. Bennetts, James	Shoeing-smith	
497. Benson, Harold Edgar	Private	
365. Bent, James B. L.	Sergeant	*Vide* " Promotions "
219. Blackman, Wm. Harold	Private	
362. Bratten, Thomas H.	,,	Invalided, Australia, arr. 13.9.00
153. Braun, Charles L.	Sergeant	*Vide* " Promotions "
525. Browe, William Jno.	Private	Invalided, Australia, arr. 17.8.00
292. Burns, Edward	,,	
233. Burns, James	,,	
296. Callagher, Joseph H.	,,	
426. Cameron, Allan	,,	
262. Campbell, Dalgety G.	,,	Invalided, Australia, arr. 30.8.00
297. Campbell, Robert B.	,,	Died, Cape Town, 14.3.00
294. Christison, John H.	,,	
232. Carr, Henry Stedman	,,	Invalided, Australia, arr. 13.9.00
243. Crisp, Henry Garlick	,,	Invalided, Australia, arr. 15.12.00
166. Crapp, Wm. Alfred	,,	Invalided, Australia, arr. 30.7.00
368. Collins, Mark Fredk.	Lance-Corporal	
222. Dale, Henry John	Private	
249. Dale, William	,,	
475. Divall, William	,,	
300. Dowse, Arthur T.	,,	
103. Du Frayer, Alfred Henry	,,	Invalided, Australia, arr. 17.9.00
479. Evans, Sydney L.	,,	
167. Ferrie, Albert E.	,,	
353. Ferris, Hugo Chas. Jno.	,,	
478. Fetherstonhaugh, Cuthbert	Lance-Corporal	*Vide* " Promotions "
374. Fisher, William J. W.	Private	
197. Fleming, George Henry	Corporal	
528. Fogg, Rudolph W.	Private	Invalided, Australia, arr. 12.11.00
101. Freeman, Samuel Fredk.	Corporal	
106. Freeman, George R.	Private	Invalided, Australia, arr. 22.12.00
208. Fuller, George G.	,,	Invalided, Australia, arr. 28.5.11
376. Fulton, Thomas A.	,,	Died of wounds, Kroonstadt, 23.11.00
168. Gaites, Henry George	,,	
314. Gilmour, Ernest	,,	
316. Gray, John Wm.	,,	
489. Gribben, Henry St. J.	Farrier-Sergeant	
154. Gribble, Joseph Wm.	Private	**Invalided, Australia, arr. 22.3.01**
155. Gribble, William	Lance-Corporal	**Invalided, Australia, arr. 17.8.00**

Nominal Roll—*continued.*

No. and Name.	Rank.	Remarks.
"C" SQUADRON—*continued.*		
488. Handcock, Peter Joseph	Shoeing-smith	Farrier-Sergeant. *Vide* "Promotions"
265. Hart, Alexander J.	Private	Invalided, Australia, arr. 15.9.00
499. Hart, William John	,,	Invalided, Australia, arr. 21.10.00
320. Hayward, Lessian F.	,,	Despatches, *London Gazette*, 19.4.01: D.C.M.
323. Hazel, William	,,	Invalided, Australia, arr. 30.7.00
157. Hughes, Charles Alfred	,,	
182. Jeffrey, Edmund	,,	
325. Jones, Collin	,,	
330. Keay, Wm. Jas. Fraser	Corporal	
355. Kelly, John Ross	Private	
445. Kelman, John Percival	,,	
444. Kessell, John Rattray	,,	Corporal and Sergeant. Invalided, Australia, arr. 5.3.01
805. Kimbell, William Martin	Bugler	Invalided, Australia, arr. 22.3.01
112. King, Joseph Robert	Private	
158. Kortlang, Arthur Henry	,,	Invalided, Australia, arr. 11.12.00
328. Kremer, Edward Victor	,,	Invalided, Australia, arr. 5.1.01
159. Lees, Thomas James	Lance-Corporal	Invalided, Australia, arr. 30.7.00
268. Legge, Franklin H.	Corporal	Died, Bloemfontein, 20.5.00
251. Legh, William M.	Private	
463. Lennon, Robert Hugh	,,	Invalided, Australia, arr. 17.8.00
267. Lennon, Thomas B.	,,	Died, Bloemfontein, 30.4.00
160. Linn, Joseph Chas.	,,	Invalided, Australia, arr. 13.9.00
274. McAlpine, Alexander	Shoeing-smith	
211. Macarthur, Ebbie J.	Private	
433. McLean, Fredk. Stephen	Sergeant	Invalided, Australia, arr. 30.7.00
210. McCracken, John	Private	Despatches, *London Gazette*, 19.4.01
254. Macdonald, Allan M.	,,	
527. Moore, David Thomas	,,	Invalided, Australia, arr. 6.12.00
340. Neild, William James	,,	Despatches, *London Gazette*, 19.4.01
491. Noakes, David Peter	Shoeing-smith	
173. Norris, Charles Tucker	Corporal	
306. Nugent, George	Bugler	
464. Ogle, Ernest Chalmer	Private	Died, Bloemfontein, 16.5.00
163. Parkinson, James	Corporal	Invalided, Australia, arr. 30.8.00
145. Plasto, Augustine Dennis	Private	
449. Palmer, Rupert T. S.	,,	
386. Parrott, Arthur Kercy	,,	
225. Phillips, Allan L.	,,	
240. Picot, Arthur Henry	,,	
242. Plowman, Sinclair	,,	Invalided, Australia, arr. 30.7.00
277. Porter, Fredk. Stanley	,,	Invalided, Australia, arr. 6.12.00
419. Porter, Lionel B. O.	,,	Invalided, Australia, arr. 17.8.00
383. Power, Patrick	,,	
401. Reid, Thomas Jas.	,,	
392. Rich, William Suttor	,,	*Vide* "Promotions"
226. Robertson, David	,,	N.S.W. Contingent to Soudan, 1885
391. Ross, William H.	,,	
123. Rudd, Francis Wm. P.	,,	Despatches, *London Gazette*, 19.4.01: D.C.M.
228. Sewell, Francis	,,	Invalided, Australia, arr. 16.11.00
148. Smith, Arthur E.	,,	
443. Smith, Sydney J.	,,	

Nominal Roll—*continued*.

No. and Name.	Rank.	Remarks.
"C" SQUADRON—*continued*.		
498. Spooner, Chas. Greenwood	Private	Invalided, Australia, arr. 6.12.00
394. St. Clair, Charles A.	,,	
393. Steel, James Alex.	,,	Invalided, Australia, arr. 6.8.00
395. Stewart, David John	Q.M.-Sergeant	*Vide* "Promotions"
214. Swanston, John P.	Private	Invalided, Australia, arr. 12.8.00
398. Symons, Henry	,,	Invalided, Australia, arr. 30.8.00
410. Taylor, Wm. Graham	,,	Died of wounds, Koetzee's Drift, 30.6.00
485. Treatt, Graham V. O.	,,	
434. Tyrrell, Joseph V.	Sergeant	
553. Tullidge, Herbert L.	Shoeing-smith	
452. Vacchini, Caleb F.	Sergeant	
407. Walker, George	Private	
405. Wallace, William	Lance-Sergeant	
509. White, Thomas W.	Sergeant-Major	
151. Woods, Cecil Talbot	Private	*Vide* "Promotions"
466. Whitehead, Henry Carr	,,	
472. Wilson, John James	,,	Invalided, Australia, arr. 13.9.00
512. Wilson, James L.	,,	
457. Wolpert, Emanuel	,,	Invalided, Australia, arr. 13.9.00
473. Wright, David Stanley	,,	
284. Yates, Victor	,,	
373. D'Apice, John E. F.	,,	*Vide* "Promotions"
"D" SQUADRON.		
Bennett, Alfred Joshua	Captain	N.S.W. Contingent to Soudan, 1885
Watson, Wm. Walker Russell	,,	
Legge, George Herbert	Lieutenant	
Holborrow, Grantley A. H.	,,	
Drage, Percy Wm. Chanter	,,	Bechuanaland Expedition, 1884-5; killed in action at Diamond Hill, 12.6.00
506. Fraser, Robert Donald	Sergeant-Major	
526. Lindsell, Frederick Wm.	Sergeant	
170. Humphries, Fredk. James	,,	
177. Smiley, Alexander	,,	Died of wounds, Dreifontein, Kroonstad, 17.11.00
203. Spalding, Warner Edward	,,	Commissioned in S.A. Field Force
421. Mortimer, Hugh Stanley	Q.M.-Sergeant	*Vide* Promotions
264. Gribben, Sydney Alexander	Farrier-Sergeant	
199. King, Frederick	Lance-Sergeant	
428. Bowler, Ernest A. H.	,,	
379. Helsham, Somerville	Corporal	Invalided, Australia, arr. 9.12.00
147. Smillie, James	,,	Sergeant. Invalided, Australia, arr. 16.11.00
185. Smith, Edward Selwyn	,,	
459. Taplin, Thomas Kells	Sergeant	
437. Bates, James	Corporal	N.S.W. Contingent to Soudan, 1885
137. Johnson, Charles	Sergeant	
278. Reynolds, Mark H.	Lance-Corporal	
184. Roberts, Ralph Ernest	,,	
476. Taylor, Charles F.	,,	
480. Cotter, Sydney T.	Bugler	Invalided, Australia, arr. 17.8.00
299. Melville, William A.	,,	Invalided, Australia, arr. 17.9.00
332. Mason, George	Saddler	Invalided, Australia, arr. 6.8.00
496. Smith, Charles Roy	,,	

Nominal Roll—*continued.*

No. and Name.	Rank.	Remarks.
"D" SQUADRON—*continued.*		
492. Hatton, George J.	Shoeing-smith	Invalided, Australia, arr. 30.7.00
136. Ireland, Wm. Edward	,,	
336. Murphy, John James	,,	
483. Webster, Joseph	,,	
451. Abbott, Archibald	Private	
257. Appleyard, Richard	,,	
191. Baker, Herbert O.	,,	Invalided, Australia, arr. 17.8.00
128. Baldwin, Thos. Wm.	,,	Invalided, Australia, arr. 6.8.00
469. Bartlett, James	,,	Invalided, Australia, arr. 30.7.00
192. Best, Fredk. Wm.	,,	Invalided, Australia, arr. 30.8.00
190. Bowden, Thomas Leslie	,,	Invalided, Australia, arr. 30.7.00
291. Brien, Robert	,,	
551. Brewer, Charles Art.	,,	Invalided, Australia, arr. 16.11.00
448. Buchanan, Frank W.	,,	
363. Burmeister, August H.	,,	Invalided, Australia, arr. 15.9.00
260. Cameron, Patrick Ewen	,,	Invalided, Australia, arr. 6.12.00
295. Christie, James	Acting Sergeant	
370. Clark, Frank	Private	
194. Cook, Silas	,,	Invalided, Australia, arr. 6.3.01
372. Dalley, James R.	,,	
245. Davidson, Walter T.	,,	Invalided, Australia, arr. 28.5.01
221. Dennison, Thomas E.	,,	Invalided, Australia, arr. 16.11.00
309. Doherty, Patrick J.	,,	Invalided, Australia, arr. 5.3.01
310. Douglas, Roland A.	,,	
371. Drum, Patrick I.	,,	Missing, Kareefontein, 23.4.00
513. Duffy, Edwin H.	,,	
302. Duffy, Oliver A.	,,	Invalided, Australia, arr. 9.12.00
215. Dwan, James	,,	
196. Ellis, Geo. Arthur	,,	Invalided, Australia, arr. 17.8.00
438. Ezzy, Leslie	,,	Invalided, Australia, arr. 15.7.01
263. Finch, Walter Henry	,,	
377. Foulstone, John Wm. Ed.	,,	
311. Freeman, William	,,	Died, Bloemfontein, 29.6.00
287. Fry, Robert A.	,,	
369. Cranfield, William I.	,,	
495. Gaggin, Harry L. M.	,,	Invalided, Australia, arr. 6.12.00
169. Gates, Thomas	,,	N.S.W. Contingent to Soudan, 1885
471. Galloway, Guy Spencer F.	,,	
133. Gannon, John	,,	
181. Grace, Reginald	,,	Invalided, Australia, arr. 13.9.00
486. Greame, Cecil Richd.	,,	Invalided, Australia, arr. 6.12.00
198. Gunning, Thomas	,,	N.S.W. Contingent to Soudan, 1885. Invalided, Australia, arr. 6.12.00
357. Henshaw, Henry	,,	Invalided, Australia, arr. 17.8.00
529. Hopkinson, Leslie R. A.	,,	Invalided, Australia, arr. 17.8.00
266. Hodges, Alfred John	,,	Invalided, Australia, arr. 30.7.00
171. Ireland, Arthur C.	,,	Invalided, Australia, arr. 15.9.00
517. Irvine, Gerald	,,	
324. Jamieson, Fredk. Wm.	,,	
248. Johnston, Reginald	,,	Invalided, Australia, arr. 6.12.00
422. Johnston, Thomas	,,	
356. Jones, John	,,	Invalided, Australia, arr. 21.10.00
329. Key, Charles	,,	Invalided, Australia, arr. 21.10.00
138. Lake, Arthur R.	,,	
514. Lake, Percy Wm.	,,	
250. Larkin, John Joseph	,,	

Nominal Roll—continued.

"D" Squadron—continued.

No. and Name.	Rank.	Remarks.
474. Leggett, William E.	Private	Invalided, Australia, arr. 15.9.00
172. Lewis, Henry Jones	,,	
334. Matthews, Frank Reg.	,,	
269. Maund, Lewis Earl	,,	
253. Maxwell, William M.	,,	
271. Mills, Edward Jas.	,,	
255. Mitchell, Allan B.	,,	
141. Mitchell, Charles H.	,,	N.S.W. Contingent to Soudan, 1885. Invalided, Australia, arr. 24.11.00
435. Mulhearn, Wm. Joseph	,,	
429. Maccabe, Joseph	,,	
436. Macgregor, James H.	,,	
462. McJannett, John Blumer	,,	Invalided, Australia, arr. 30.8.00
337. McKellor, Peter Fraser	,,	
200. McMillan, Alexander W.	,,	
503. McMillan, John Maher	,,	Invalided, Australia, arr. 13.9.00
331. McPhee, Aubrey	,,	
143. McRae, James	,,	
441. Nixon, Horace P.	,,	Invalided, Australia, arr. 17.8.00
460. Oldfield, Henry Joseph	,,	
259. O'Neill, Charles T.	,,	
201. Osborne, Alexander H.	,,	
384. Phillips, Edward	,,	Invalided, Australia, arr. 22.3.01
418. Pickering, Alfred	,,	Invalided, Australia, arr. 6.12.00
380. Rawe, George	,,	Died, Bloemfontein, 10.5.00
494. Reynolds, John Robert	,,	
500. Richardson, Wm. Henry	,,	Invalided, Australia, arr. 17.8.00
390. Rigg, Malcolm	,,	Invalided, Australia, arr. 30.8.00
176. Roberts, Caleb James	,,	Invalided, Australia, arr. 17.9.00
465. Robertson, Thomas C.	,,	Killed in action, Rhenoster Kop, 21.11.00
417. Sharp, Albert Jas.	,,	
446. Silk, Edward Volney	,,	
439. Small, Robert	,,	
280. Smith, Albert Geo.	,,	
149. Stanton, Ernest Walter	,,	
150. Thorndike, John	,,	Corporal. Invalided, Australia, arr. 28.5.11
178. Thoroughgood, Henry	,,	
186. Thompson, Wm. Athol	,,	Invalided, Australia, arr. 30.8.00
403. Tidy, Richard Henry	,,	Invalided, Australia, arr. 17.8.00
281. Tonkin, Charles John	,,	Invalided, Australia, arr. 15.9.00
402. Tonkin, Francis H.	,,	Invalided, Australia, arr. 6.8.00
404. Trim, Dominic Joseph	,,	Invalided, Australia, arr. 6.8.00
484. Wallace, John Casse	,,	
188. Wells, George Taylor	,,	Invalided, Australia, arr. 28.5.01
282. Warburton, Charles Henry	,,	
533. Watts, Hubert	,,	Invalided, Australia, arr. 30.8.00
427. Weatherly, Frederick	,,	
412. Weiss, Alfred Osmond	,,	
414. Williams, Phillip	,,	
415. Wilshire, Norman	,,	Invalided, Australia, arr. 13.9.00
204. Wirth, Daniel	,,	
502. Young, James A.	,,	
230. Young, Wm. Frederick	,,	Invalided, Australia, arr. 17.8.00 and died at Sydney, 4.10.00

NEW SOUTH WALES CITIZENS' BUSHMEN.

THE New South Wales Contingent of Citizens' Bushmen was raised in the first instance by public subscription; whence the name. The object was to enrol a regiment of countrymen acquainted with the vicissitudes of bush life; good shots, good riders, and of sound physique—such a class of men, in fact, as would be fitted to cope with the enemy, according to the methods of the latter. Preference, therefore, was given to men who had previously served in South Africa, and those having experience of country work in Australia, management of horses, and bush travelling.

The following establishment was approved:—One lieutenant-colonel, 1 major, 1 adjutant, 1 quartermaster, 1 veterinary officer, 1 regimental sergeant-major, 1 quartermaster-sergeant, 1 transport-sergeant, 1 orderly-room sergeant, 1 orderly-room clerk, 2 drivers, 6 batmen, 1 cook, 1 wagonman; total regimental staff, 5 officers, 15 N.C.O.'s and men, with 14 riding and 4 draught horses. For each squadron:— One captain, 2 lieutenants, two 2nd lieutenants, 1 squadron sergeant-major, 1 squadron quartermaster-sergeant, 6 sergeants, 1 sergeant-farrier, 2 shoeing smiths, 2 trumpeters, 6 corporals, 87 privates, 4 drivers, 5 batmen, 2 cooks, 1 saddler, 2 wagonmen; total, 5 officers, 120 N.C.O.'s and men, with 117 riding and 8 draught horses, besides 4 pack and 9 spare. Four squadrons; grand total, 25 officers, 495 others; 482 riding horses, 36 draught, 16 pack, 36 spare.

Pay was issued at cavalry rates up to disembarkation and afterwards from 25s., with 4s. to commanding officers, to 15s. and 2s. 6d. subalterns; and from 9s. to sergeant-majors to 5s. to privates; buglers, saddlers, and farriers, 1s. per diem extra. Colonial allowance to all officers, 3s. per diem; on A.S. Corps duty, 5s. per diem additional. "Separation allowance" was also paid to wives and families of soldiers at the front. *Vide* also p. 85.

The Contingent left Sydney on the 28th February, 1900, at a strength of 30 officers and 495 of other ranks, with 570 horses and 10 carts. Of these, 1 officer and 29 others died or were killed, 6 officers and 8 others were transferred, 3 officers and 49 others were struck off the strength in South Africa, 1 officer and 1 other were commissioned in the Imperial army; 23 officers and 404 others returned to Sydney. The 4 officers additional in the total accounted for were appointed in South Africa.

REFERENCE TO ORDERS.

Establishment	.. ..	G.O. (N.S.W.), 21/00
Accounts ..	.. .. ..	,, ,, 6/00
Inspection ..	.. .. ..	,, ,, 28/00
Command ..	.. .. ..	,, ,, 28/00
Embarkation	.. .. ..	,, ,, 29/00
Separation allowance	.. ..	,, ,, 88/00
Staff officer	.. .. ..	,, ,, 5/00
Officers	..	*Gov. Gazette*, N.S.W., 139, 15th February, 1900, and 173, of 23rd February, 1900

CLOTHING, ETC.

Clothing consisted of F.S. jacket and pants, with leggings and helmet. *Vide* p. 57.

Arms and equipment:—M.L.E. rifles and sword bayonet, bandolier, and waistbelt. Fully horsed and supplied with saddlery.

Regimental transport was provided.

OUTLINE OF SERVICES.

The Citizens' Bushmen embarked at Sydney on transports *Atlantian* and *Maplemore*, on 28th February, 1900; arrived at Cape Town 2nd April, and proceeded to Biera, where they disembarked on 12th April, and proceeded, *viâ* Marandellas, to Bulawayo.

Staff and "A" squadron served under General Plumer at relief of Mafeking. Served in General Plumer's Brigade, in General Baden-Powell's column, at the relief of Rustenburg. After a smart engagement, occupied the town 7th July, 1900.

"B," "C," and "D" squadrons, under Lt.-Colonel Airey, D.S.O., took part in a severe engagement at Koster's River on 22nd July, in attempting to relieve the Eland's River garrison.

"A" squadron, assisted by about 50 men of other details, defended Eland's River post against De la Rey with 1,000 men and guns for 13 days, refusing to surrender on any terms. They were eventually relieved by Lord Kitchener's force on 15th August, and Lord Methuen's column arrived from the north, 18th August, 1900.

GENERAL ORDERS.

By Major-General R. S. S. Baden-Powell, Commanding Frontier Force.

Rustenburg, Monday, 9th July, 1900.

The General Officer Commanding desires to thank Colonel Airey on the prompt and efficient measures taken by him to maintain Her Majesty's supremacy in Rustenburg, at a critical time, and the Australian Squadrons, C.B.C., for the dash and gallantry with which they made the affair a brilliant success.

By order,

A. J. GODLEY, Lt.-Colonel,
A.A.G. Frontier Force.

The Citizen's Bushmen embarked at Cape Town on their return to Australia, 9th May, 1901, and disembarked at Sydney, 11th June. They called at Fremantle, Adelaide, and Melbourne *en route*.

PROMOTIONS, ETC.

Name.	Original Appointment.	Subsequent Changes.	Contingents.
Thomas, James Francis	Captain	Promoted major	
Baker, Arthur Brander	,,	,, ,,	
Ryrie, Stanley Stewart	Lieutenant	Promoted captain	
Eckford, Arthur Grant	,,	Promoted captain and major	
Mullins, Thomas Lane	,,	Promoted captain	Subsequently with 1st Battalion Australian Commonwealth Horse
Westgarth, John Ellesmere	,,	Imperial commission, Royal Field Artillery	
Cape, Charles Scarvell	,,	Promoted captain	
Lynch, Thomas Joseph	2nd Lieutenant	,, ,,	
Airey, H. G	Sergeant	Promoted lieutenant	
Hallett, J. W.	Regtl. Sergeant-Major	,, ,,	
Ryrie, O. B.	Sq. Sergeant-Major	,, ,,	
Broinowski, F. J.	Sq. Quartermaster Sergeant	,, ,,	
Fitzharding, A. F.	Corporal	Received Imperial commission	
C. Cornwall	Lieut.	Transferred to S.A. Constabulary, 6.11.00	
H. B. Christie	Lieut.	Transferred to S.A. Constabulary, 3.11.00	

For promotions of N.C. Officers and Troopers, see Nominal Roll.

War Services and Honours.

Airey, Lieut.-Colonel H. P.—With Field Battery, New South Wales Artillery, to Soudan, 1885. Medal and clasp, and Khedive's Star. Burmah, 1886. Dangerously wounded. D.S.O. Medal and clasp. Relief of Mafeking. Operations in Rhodesia and Transvaal, April, 1900, to November, 1900. Despatches, *London Gazette*, 19th April, 1901. C.M.G. Queen's Medal with four clasps.

Dangar, Major H. P.—Relief of Mafeking. Operations in Rhodesia, April, 1900, to June, 1900. Invalided, 1st July, 1900. Queen's Medal with two clasps.

Thomas, Major J. F.—Relief of Mafeking. Operations as stated, and from April, 1900, to 31st May, 1901. Actions at Rhenoster Kop and Eland's River. Queen's Medal with four clasps.

Machattie, Captain T. A.—Relief of Mafeking. Operations as stated. Wounded at Rustenberg, 7th July, 1900. Queen's Medal with four clasps.

Robertson, Captain C. W.—Relief of Mafeking. Operations in Rhodesia and Transvaal, April, 1900, to June, 1900. Killed, 22nd July, 1900.

Ryrie, Captain-Adjutant S. S.—Relief of Mafeking. Operations in Rhodesia-Transvaal, and Cape Colony, April, 1900, to March, 1901. Queen's Medal with five clasps.

Baker, Captain A. B.—Relief of Mafeking. Operations in Rhodesia and Transvaal. *London Gazette*, 19th April, 1901. D.S.O. Queen's Medal with four clasps.

Eckford, Captain A. G.—Relief of Mafeking. Operations as stated in Rhodesia and Transvaal, and from 30th November, 1900, to 31st May, 1901. Queen's Medal with four clasps.

Fraser, Captain C. S.—Relief of Mafeking. Operations as stated in Rhodesia and Transvaal, and from November, 1900, to May, 1901. Queen's Medal with four clasps.

Cape, Captain C. S.—Relief of Mafeking. Operations as stated. Despatches, *London Gazette*, 19th April, 1901. D.S.O. Queen's Medal with four clasps.

Mullins, Lieutenant T. L.—Relief of Mafeking. Operations as stated, including action at Rhenoster Kop. (Lieutenant Mullins was promoted Captain and served subsequently with the 1st Australian Commonwealth Horse.) Queen's Medal with five clasps.

Cope, Lieutenant D. W.—Contingent to Soudan, 1885. Medal and clasp, Khedive's Star. Relief of Mafeking. Operations as stated, including action at Eland's River. Queen's Medal with four clasps. (Invalided, 27th September, 1900.)

Battye, Lieutenant A. E. M.—Relief of Mafeking. Operations as stated. Queen's Medal with four clasps. (Invalided, 10th October, 1900.)

Allen, Lieutenant W. B.—Relief of Mafeking. Operations as stated, and between 30th November, 1900, and 31st May, 1901. Queen's Medal with four clasps. (Invalided, 14th November, 1900.)

Gell, Lieutenant S. L.—Relief of Mafeking. Operations as above. Queen's Medal with four clasps.

Cornwall, Lieutenant C.—Relief of Mafeking. Operations as stated. Queen's Medal with four clasps.

Pockley, Lieutenant H. R.—Relief of Mafeking. Operations as stated, and between 30th November, 1900, and 31st May, 1901. Queen's Medal with four clasps.

Christie, Lieutenant H. B.—Relief of Mafeking. Operations as stated. Despatches, *London Gazette*, 19th April, 1901. D.S.O. Queen's Medal with four clasps.

Hutton, Lieutenant A. W.—Relief of Mafeking. Operations as stated, and between 30th November, 1900, and 31st May, 1901. Queen's Medal with four clasps.

Moore, Lieutenant T. M.—Relief of Mafeking. Operations as above. Despatches, *London Gazette*, 19th April, 1901. D.S.O. Queen's Medal with four clasps.

Zouch, Lieutenant R. E.—Relief of Mafeking. Operations as above, including actions at Rhenoster Kop and Eland's River. Despatches, *London Gazette*, 14.4.01. Queen's Medal with five clasps.

Westgarth, Lieutenant J. E.—Relief of Mafeking. Operations in Rhodesia and Transvaal, April and May, 1900. Queen's Medal with two clasps. (Transferred to Royal Field Artillery, 8th May, 1900.)

Lynch, Captain T. J.—With Field Battery, New South Wales Artillery, to Soudan, 1885. Medal with clasp. Khedive's Star. Relief of Mafeking. Operations as stated, including action at Eland's River, and operations in Transvaal between 30th November, 1900, and 31st May, 1901. Queen's Medal with five clasps.

Airey, Lieutenant H. G. F.—Relief of Mafeking. Operations as above. Queen's Medal with four clasps.

Hallett, Lieutenant J. W.—With Field Battery, New South Wales Artillery, to Soudan, 1885. Medal with clasp. Khedive's Star. Relief of Mafeking. Operations as above, including action at Rhenoster Kop. Queen's Medal with five clasps.

Ryrie, Lieutenant O. B.—Relief of Mafeking. Operations as stated. Queen's Medal with four clasps.

Broinowski, Lieutenant F. J.—Relief of Mafeking. Operations as stated, including action at Eland's River. Queen's Medal with four clasps.

Rouse, Lieutenant T. H. R.—With Field Battery, New South Wales Artillery, to Soudan, 1885. Medal and clasp. Khedive's Star. Relief of Mafeking. Operations as stated. Queen's Medal with four clasps.

Meredith, Lieutenant J. B. (A.M.C.)—Relief of Mafeking. Operations as stated. Queen's Medal with four clasps.

Cherry, Vet.-Lieutenant C. C.—Relief of Mafeking. Operations as stated. Queen's Medal with four clasps.

Boardman, Rev. J., *Timoney*, Rev. F., *Auld*, Rev. J. H., and *Green*, Rev. J. (chaplains ranking as captains), were present at the relief of Mafeking and operations as stated (Rev. J. Green present at Eland's River), and including Transvaal, 30th November, 1900, to 31st May, 1901. Queen's Medal with four clasps.

EXTRACTS FROM REPORT OF MAJOR W. HOWARD TUNBRIDGE, OFFICER COMMANDING 2ND REGIMENT RHODESIAN FIELD FORCE.

The Eland's River camp was attacked by Commandant De la Rey on 4th August, at daybreak.

The garrison consisted of 105 of the 1st Regiment Rhodesian Field Force (New South Wales), 145 of the 2nd Regiment, Rhodesian Field Force (141 Queenslanders, 2 Tasmanians, and 2 Rifle Brigade), 51 of the 3rd Regiment, Rhodesian Field Force (42 Victorians, 9 West Australians), and 201 Rhodesian and other South African volunteers, with two Canadians and 1 Army Service Corps man attached. One 7-lb. screw gun, 1 ·303 Maxim, and 1 ·45 Maxim. The attacking force consisted, as far as we could learn, of from 2,000 to 3,000 men, with 5 guns, 3 pom-poms, and 1 Maxim. As the camp was only a rest camp, and an attack in force had not been anticipated, the defences were not at all complete, consisting only of a series of half-moon loose stone walls on two sides of the main camp, and on a kopje held by Captain Butters and 80 men. As soon, however, as the sun had set, and shelling had ceased, the men not required for picket and watering guard were at once got to work throwing up earth on the outside of the walls, and trenching on the inside. Stores were also used to protect the back of the trenches, banked with earth on the reverse side, as, the camp being very small, a large proportion of the wounds were from the reverse fire.

The hospital was inside the camp, and was composed of the three ambulances of my regiment, covered by buck sheets, and on the first day of attack was only protected by a double row of biscuit boxes, about 5 feet high. This was raised afterwards and strengthened by another row of boxes and earth banked to the top on the outside.

The horses, oxen, and mules, being on an exposed slope, suffered very heavily, over 1,500 being killed altogether; but it was impossible to protect them.

A picket from Captain Butters' post first discovered the enemy, and opened rifle fire, which was immediately responded to by shell fire, which was kept up the whole day until dark.

The enemy shelled us daily until the 9th August, on which date only a few shells fell.

Over 1,700 shells were counted the first day, and about 480 the second day; but after that the firing gradually slackened until the afternoon of the 9th, when it ceased altogether.

Besides the shell fire, which was from all sides, rifle fire commenced on the morning of the 4th, and was kept up all day and night for eleven days, at distances varying from 300 to nearly 3,000 yards; the riflemen being in every case well protected by natural cover and seldom showing themselves.

The enemy brought up their guns to within 2,100 yards on the 5th, but were compelled to retire by our volleys, and finally took up a position out of range of rifle fire.

The gun we had was only an old 7-pounder muzzle-loading screw gun, mounted on a 9-pounder gun carriage, and we only had 100 rounds in all.

The gun was constantly getting jammed, and I had to take it to pieces four times, and finally filed the gas-checks on the shells, which had become burred up. The cartridges were black powder. The ·303 Maxim also continually jammed with the ammunition served to them. Captain Hockings informed me of this, and asked if I would allow our ammunition to be used, which I did; the elevation had to be increased about 200 yards, and after this the gun worked excellently.

The ·45 Maxim with Captain Butters also jammed once or twice, but was got to work well afterwards; this also had black powder.

On the 8th, Commandant De la Rey summoned Colonel Hore to surrender, officers to be allowed their arms and to be permitted to march the men to the nearest British post. This was refused.

The siege was raised on the evening of the 14th. Lord Kitchener's advance guard was seen approaching about sundown on the 15th, and he marched into camp on the 16th. Lord Methuen arrived from Magato Pass on the 18th, and the garrison returned to Mafeking with him next day.

I am sorry to have to report a rather heavy casualty list of New South Wales men under my command—4 killed and 6 wounded.

The casualties were very heavy on the first day; nearly all being from fragments of shells, and were very bad wounds.

Surgeon-Captain Duka and his staff—one of them, Trooper W. Hunt of your Colony—were untiring in their work, which was all done under shell fire. Captain Duka did splendid work the whole time, and had his hands very full.

Nominal Roll.

No. and Name.	Rank.	Remarks.
REGIMENTAL STAFF.		
Airey, Henry Parke	Lieut.-Colonel Commanding	Royal Australian Artillery
Dangar, Henry Phelps	Major, 2nd in command	Invalided to England, 1.7.00
Ryrie, Stanley Stewart	Lieutenant and Adjutant	Royal Australian Artillery
Rouse, Thomas Henry	Lieutenant and Quartermaster	,, ,,
Meredith, John Baldwin	Lieutenant A.M.C.	Invalided to Australia, 26.10.00
Cherry, Chas. Cummins	Veterinary Lieut.	
Boardman, John	Chaplain (C.E.)	
Timoney, Francis	Chaplain (R.C.)	
Green, James	Chaplain (Wesleyan)	
Auld, John Hay Goodlet	Chaplain (Presbyterian)	
Hallett, James William	Regtl. Sergeant-Major (W.O.)	Vide "Promotions"
532. Coleman, Thomas Fulton	Regtl. Quartermaster-Sergeant	
315. Sherrifs, Charles Macken	Orderly Sergeant	Invalided, Australia, 13.12.00
140. Wentworth, Buckwell Lionel	Transport Sergt.	Invalided, Australia, 30.3.01
529. Grahame, Edward Phillip	Orderly-room clerk	Lance-Sergeant, 7.6.00
527. Brennan, Joseph John	Trooper	Lance-Corporal, Invalided, Australia, arr. 11.6.01
528. Gardner, Charles Andrew	,,	
479. George, Richard	,,	
498. Ellis, John	,,	
33. White, Robert	,,	
429. Ryan, Thomas	,,	
399. Cooper, Granville Thomas	,,	Killed, 14.10.00
473. Nicholson, John	,,	
510. Haybittle, Percy Arnold	,,	
540. Huddart, W. H.	,,	Invalided, Australia, 20.2.01
539. Cantwell, Reginald	,,	
545. Copeland, Reginald Heber	,,	
532. Christianson, James Oca	,,	
"A" SQUADRON.		
Thomas, James Francis	Captain	
Cope, William	Lieutenant	Invalided, Australia, 27.9.00
Allen, William Bell	,,	Invalided, Australia, 14.11.00
Zouch, Richard Essington	2nd Lieutenant	
Cornwall, Charles	,,	Vide "Promotions"
508. Mitchell, James	Sqn. Sergeant-Major	Killed, Eland's River, 17.8.00
458. Broinowski, Felix James	Sqn. Quartermaster Sergeant	Vide "Promotions"
122. Burrow, John Cuthbert	Sergeant	
132. Wheeler, George Henry	,,	Sergeant-Major, Transferred South African Constabulary, 8.10.00. Invalided, Australia, arr. 22.3.01
106. Raymond, Erskine North	,,	Invalided, Australia, 24.1.01
15. Weir, Frank V.	,,	Sqn. Quartermaster-Sergeant, 13.8.00; C. in C's. despatches, 8.5.01; invalided, England, 7.3.01

C.4720.   F

Nominal Roll—continued.

"A" SQUADRON—continued.

No. and Name.	Rank.	Remarks.
14. Druitt, Charles Hafed Conrad	Sergeant	Invalided, Australia, 30.3.01
40. Sproat, John Barber	,,	
55. White, John	Farrier-Sergeant	Invalided to England
67. McGuinness, George Reginald	Corporal	Sergeant, 1.3.01; killed near Vet River, 15.3.01
115. Buckleton, Fitzroy Augustus	,,	Invalided, Australia, 24.1.01
16. Kelman, William Nivison	,,	
99. Morrow, Edwin James	,,	Sergeant, 16.3.01
77. Macarthur, Lionel George	,,	Sergeant, 8.10.01
97. Keene, Thomas Evans	,,	Sqn. Quartermaster-Sergeant, 1.8.00
130. McCullough, Harold Edwin	Lance-Corporal	Corporal, 13.1.01
11. Pounceby, Alfred	,,	Invalided, Australia, 13.12.00
129. Reynolds, James	,,	Corporal, 19.8.00
32. Bohlsen, Henry	,,	Invalided, Australia, arr. 11.12.00
39. Gibb, Thomas Reuben Hamilton	,,	Corporal, 1.8.00; joined Johannesberg Railway Service, 4.2.01
22. Mankey, William Henry	Trumpeter	
21. Peek, Rupert de Lacey	,,	Invalided, Australia, 13.12.00
71. Anderson, Edward Christopher	Trooper	
83. Ansling, Charles	,,	Invalided, Australia, 24.1.01
61. Aitcheson, John Carlton	,,	Killed, 20.2.01
502. Allen, Alexander William	,,	Transferred to Q. Infantry Brigade, 30.4.00
2. Brigden, Edward Ernest	,,	
107. Burke, Patrick	,,	Invalided, Australia, arr. 18.5.01
38. Burrow, Richard William Peard	,,	
108. Buchanan, Angus McLeod	,,	
120. Bunton, William Wallace	,,	Invalided, Australia, arr. 11.6.01
81. Borlase, Thomas	,,	Despatches, *London Gazette*, 26.6.01: D.C.M. Invalided, Australia, arr. 18.5.01
41. Brunning, John Theodore	,,	
451. Brown, A. H.	,,	Invalided, Australia, 28.12.00
13. Barnes, Joseph William	,,	
12. Barnes, Claude	,,	
73. Clarke, James Edmund	,,	
86. Cummings, William Joseph	,,	
91. Corbett, William Edmund	,,	
109. Cusack, Joseph Michael	,,	
42. Charles, George	,,	Invalided, Australia, arr. 18.5.01
52. Campbell, Beresford Frederick	,,	Invalided, Australia, 28.12.00
105. Campbell, Ernest	,,	
522. Dodd, Walter Charles	,,	Invalided, Australia, 1.2.01
181. Duffy, Edward Michael	,,	
34. Duff, James Daniel	,,	Killed, Eland's River, 17.8.00
30. Davidson, Frank Lomas	,,	Invalided, Australia, 3.11.00
49. Douglas, Allen	,,	
112. Dowe, Hedley Vicars	,,	
85. Davenport, Robert George	,,	Promoted Sergeant for gallantry in action, 12.1.01; despatches, *London Gazette*, 26.6.01: D.C.M.
45. Dickinson, Philip	,,	
4. Elly, George William	,,	
89. Eastcott, John Edward Henry	,,	
535. Fimister, Herbert James	,,	
26. Frater, Fergus Stewart	,,	
53. Fowler, Patrick John	,,	

Nominal Roll—*continued.*

No. and Name.	Rank.	Remarks.
"A" SQUADRON—*continued.*		
36. Farnell, Arthur Hilton	Trooper	
82. Fraser, Donald	,,	Killed, 26.2.01
127. Gibson, George Henry Flood	,,	Killed, Ottoshoop, 16.8.00
84. Gulson, Kelvedon	,,	
201. Grey, Arthur Percy Briton	,,	Died at Pretoria, 9.11.00
48. Holm, Herman	,,	
64. Hewitt, John William	,,	Invalided, Australia, 13.12.00
31. Hodge, Robert	,,	Invalided, Australia, 13.12.00
96. Hunt, William Francis	,,	Corporal, 16.3.00; Sergeant; despatches, *London Gazette*, 26.6.01. D.C.M.
9. Hurtz, Charles Joseph	,,	Invalided, Australia, 18.9.00
10. Illife, Tom	,,	
178. Lawer, Samuel James	,,	
68. Logan, James Miles	,,	Died, Pretoria, 13.1.01
72. Lees, David	,,	Corporal, 19.8.00. Invalided, Australia, arr. 18.5.01
8. Macdonald, Allan	,,	
60. McGrath, William	,,	Invalided, Australia, arr. 18.5.01
76. McPhee, Claude Malcolm	,,	
87. Mills, Ernest Noel	,,	
78. Murray, Adam	,,	Corporal, 16.3.01
110. Murray, Frederick John	,,	Invalided, Australia, 24.1.01
66. Mayne, Alfred	,,	Invalided, Australia, arr. 13.4.01
29. Marks, Frederic William	,,	Discharged, Cape Town, 1.4.00
118. Middleton, Osman Frederick Hume	,,	Lance-Corporal, Invalided, Australia, 6.2.01
98. Mansergh, Charles James	,,	Invalided, Australia, 16.11.00
88. McLean, William Paul	,,	
1. Mackenzie, Donald	,,	Invalided, Australia, arr. 18.5.01
25. Neville, Arthur Thomas	,,	Invalided, Australia, 27.9.00
56. Nicholls, John	,,	
259. Nolan, Albert Edward	,,	
137. O'Malley, William	,,	Invalided, Australia, 30.3.01
104. Meehan, Daniel Peter	,,	Died, Pretoria, 18.1.01
100. Onus, Albert Edward	,,	
116. O'Connell, John	,,	
37. Ormsby, Lewis Gore	,,	Invalided, Australia, 1.2.01
69. Perrin, Patrick	,,	
90. Plonges, Henry	,,	Invalided, Australia, 13.12.00
240. Putney, Henry George	,,	Invalided, Australia, 30.3.01
74. Prussing, Alfred	,,	
63. Robb, Walter	,,	
543. Rawlings, George	,,	Invalided, Australia, arr. 13.9.00
50. Rosen, Leslie William	,,	
47. Rankin, Neil	,,	
126. Ralston, George Henry	,,	Invalided, Australia, 30.3.01
3. Stanton, Frederick William	,,	Invalided, Australia, 24.1.01
51. Struck, James Thomas	,,	
103. Smith, Michael	,,	
121. Shannon, Richard	,,	
95. Sloey, C. P. S.	,,	Invalided, Australia, 13.12.00
43. Smith, Edwin	,,	
44. Sutton, Thomas	,,	
101. Shannon, William	,,	
65. Shepherd, George	,,	Invalided, Australia, 13.12.00
94. Salisbury, Ernest	,,	Invalided, Australia, 1.2.01
79. Stoppelbein, John Archibald	,,	

Nominal Roll—*continued*.

No. and Name.	Rank.	Remarks.
"A" SQUADRON—*continued*.		
28. Thomas, Ernest	Trooper	
125. Thompson, Andrew	,,	
54. Taylor, Sydney James	,,	
92. Tarvis, James	,,	
117. Turner, George Tindall	,,	Transferred, Rhodesian Artillery, 1.5.00. Invalided, Australia, arr. 15.7.01
521. Verdon, Patrick	,,	Died, Pretoria, 17.1.01
7. Wherratt, Alfred Charles	,,	
27. Wilson, Harry Zouch	,,	
62. Winnette, Charles	,,	Invalided, Australia, 16.11.00
75. Walker, James Edwin	,,	Killed, Eland's River, 17.8.00
503. Woods, Thomas Edward	,,	
57. Williams, George	,,	
"B" SQUADRON.		
Robertson, Claude William	Captain (R.M.L.1)	Killed, Koster's River, 22.7.00
Eckford, Arthur Grant	Lieutenant	
Fraser, Charles Stuart	,,	Invalided, England, 7.2.01
Lynch, Thomas Joseph	,,	Invalided, Australia, 25.10.00; returned; invalided, Australia, arr. 23.9.01
Gell, Sherbrooke Leigh	,,	
133. Mason, Archibald	Sqdn. Sergeant-Major	Invalided, Australia, 16.11.00
235. Shayler, John Leonard	Sqn. Quartermaster Sergeant	Regimental Quartermaster-Sergeant, 13.7.00
236. Bennett, Joseph	Sergeant	
220. Kerr, William Joseph	,,	
197. Nicholson, Sidney Thomas	,,	
189. Payne, John Henry	,,	
148. Foster, Ernest G.	,,	S. Sergeant-Major, 19.10.00
233. Huon, Walter	,,	
445. Towner, Benjamin	Farrier-Sergeant	Transferred, Rhodesian Artillery, 1.5.00
174. De Loré, James Reuben	Corporal	Invalided, Australia, 3.11.00
442. Downing, Frederick	,,	Invalided, Australia, 1.2.01
194. De Mestre, Hurtle E.	,,	Sergeant, 26.3.01
195. Murray, Walter	,,	Killed, Rustenberg, 7.7.00
152. Spier, Walter Laishley	,,	Died, Cape Town, 23.1.01
135. Ryrie, Wallace	,,	Sergeant, 22.6.01
237. Parkes, Adam	Lance-Corporal	Corporal, 30.7.00
196. Reece, Ernest William	,,	
193. Gordon, Thomas Spencer	,,	
198. Davis, Herbert	,,	
150. Nance, Frank P.	,,	
18. Threlfall, Robert	Trumpeter	Invalided, Australia, 3.11.00
17. McKoy, Alfred Herbert	,,	
155. Aitcheson, George William	Trooper	
203. Ayre, William Myles	,,	Died, Pretoria, 16.11.00
134. Alphen, Henry Arthur	,,	
167. Anderson, Vernon George	,,	
456. Bryant, Alfred John	,,	
136. Burr, Jack Andrew	,,	
204. Broad, Ernest	,,	
153. Bingham, Ernest	,,	
525. Benson, Alfred Ernest Arthur	,,	Discharged, 4.2.01
179. Baldwin, Walter Hearns	,,	
214. Booth, William Joseph	,,	

Nominal Roll—*continued.*

No. and Name.	Rank.	Remarks.
"B" SQUADRON—*continued.*		
212. Bodkin, James Edward	Trooper	
454. Bentley, Joseph	,,	Invalided, Australia, 24.1.01
536. Buchback, Henry	Saddler	Invalided, Australia, 23.8.00
176. Cauvin, Charles	Trooper	Invalided, Australia, arr. 18.5.01
230. Chandler, Albert Henry	,,	Invalided, Australia, 1.10.00
163. Cobby, George Arthur	,,	
206. Cordwell, Joseph Charles	,,	
229. Corderoy, Percy William	,,	
183. Charlton, John	,,	
227. Cartwright, Charles Lewis	,,	
443. Collins, Patrick	,,	Invalided, Australia, 1.10.00
516. Campbell, Norman	,,	Invalided, England, 2.10.00
139. Dennis, Leslie Thomas Anderson	,,	
186. Dunn, James Joseph	,,	Invalided, Australia, 13.12.00
173. Duval, Ferdinand Francis	,,	Invalided, Australia, 14.9.00
177. Duval, Francis William	,,	
447. Dwyer, Edmund	,,	
448. Duncan, George Frederick	,,	
145. Duff, Edward John	,,	
70. Eastaughffe, Albert John	,,	Invalided, Australia, arr. 6.8.00
515. Eyre, Leslie George	,,	Invalided, Australia, 2.8.00
142. Evans, Sidney Charles	,,	
215. Edwards, Thomas	,,	Invalided, Australia, arr. 11.6.01
234. Emery, Louis	,,	
185. Ellis, John	,,	
494. Fitzpatrick, John Joseph	,,	
526. Fryer, Alexander Urquhart	,,	
495. Gourley, Arthur Charles Gordon	,,	
160. Glissan, William Henry	,,	
462. Hughes, William Martin	,,	
219. Houchen, Arthur	,,	
209. Holmes, William Edward	,,	
157. Hudson, Harry Alfred	,,	Corporal, 23.10.00
231. Hoy, Laurence	,,	Invalided, Australia, 24.1.01
261. Hunt, Charles Eastaway	,,	Invalided, Australia, 15.9.00
224. Howard, Leslie	,,	
211. Home, Walter Davidson	,,	Invalided, Australia, 24.1.01
507. Jeffrey, William Knibb	,,	Invalided, Australia, 13.12.00
464. Jackson, J.	,,	Invalided, Australia, 23.8.00
463. Jones, Walter	,,	Died, Pretoria, 22.4.01
175. King, William Joseph	,,	
158. Leathart, William	,,	
147. Layburn, John	,,	
182. Levett, Robert	,,	
180. Low, Gavin	,,	
437. Lamb, James	,,	Corporal, 20.6.00 ; died, Pretoria, 16.11.00
386. Manus, George	,,	
216. Manning, James	,,	
154. Marshall, Lewis Perryman	,,	Invalided, Australia, 13.12.00
166. Milligan, John Eyers	,,	
222. Mottashaw, John	,,	Invalided, Australia, arr. 11.6.01
207. Manser, Charles John	,,	
549. Maitland, James Simpson	,,	
143. Matthews, Ernest	,,	
164. McRae, Lachlan	,,	
217. Mackinnon, Roderick	,,	
170. McColl, Archibald	,,	

Nominal Roll—*continued*.

No. and Name.	Rank.	Remarks.
"B" Squadron—*continued*.		
191. McMillan, Robert	Trooper	
202. McPhail, Thomas	,,	Invalided, Australia, 16.11.00
228. McIntyre, Duncan Kennedy	,,	
188. McKinnon, Frederick William	,,	Invalided, Australia, arr. 11.6.01
190. Macdonald, William Wallace	,,	Invalided, Australia, 30.3.01
444. McWilliams, Thomas Morris	,,	
151. Newell, Vincent	,,	Corporal; and Sergeant, 26.6.01; invalided, Australia, 13.12.01
213. Neich, Arthur Joseph	,,	Invalided, Australia, arr. 11.6.01
113. Pateman, Wilfred Stuart	,,	Invalided, Australia, 13.12.00
199. Quinlan, William	,,	Invalided, Australia, 13.12.00
168. Rowland, William Frederick	,,	
141. Rolley, George	,,	
210. Rudder, Wilfred Valentine	,,	
205. Rudder, Archie	,,	
149. Russell, Joseph	,,	Killed, Rustenberg, 7.7.00
200. Sloane, Benjamin	,,	Invalided, Australia, 13.12.00
144. Stewart, Peter	,,	Invalided, Australia, 3.11.00
169. Smith, James	,,	Invalided, Australia, 30.3.01
165. Sheppard, Henry	,,	Invalided, Australia, 1.2.01
482. Smallhorn, Ernest Robert	,,	
208. Tyrell, Frederick William	,,	
238. Trotman, William Timbrel	,,	Invalided, Australia, 30.3.01
159. Tough, William Alfred	,,	
232. Treatt, Harold Rome	,,	
221. Von Hammer, Frederick	,,	
156. Waddell, Herbert William	,,	Killed, Pienaar's River, 22.9.00
138. Watson, Oswald Victor	,,	Invalided, Australia, 16.11.00
162. Wyse, Frederick Hutchinson	,,	
223. Woodley, George Edward Mitchell	,,	Invalided, Australia, 13.12.00
517. Walker, Richard Thomas	,,	
484. Walsh, William Matthew	,,	Invalided, Australia, 3.11.00
"C" Squadron.		
Machattie, Thos. Alfred	Captain	Invalided, Australia, 5.10.00
Battye, Arthur E. Montague	Lieutenant	Invalided, Australia, 10.10.00
Mullins, Thomas Lane	,,	
Pockley, Henry Richardson	2nd Lieutenant	
Christie, Henry Bertram	,,	Transferred to South African Constabulary, 3.10.00
314. Ryrie, Oswald Bruce	Sqn. Sergeant-Major	*Vide* "Promotions"
275. Walton, John Nathaniel	Sqn. Quartermaster-Sergeant	Died, Ironmine Hill, 22.5.00
339. Mullampy, John Ernest	Sergeant	Invalided, Australia, 5.10.00
441. Holmes, Richard John	,,	Sqn. Quartermaster-Sergeant, 22.5.00
239. Geary, Godfrey George	,,	Sqn. Sergeant-Major, 22.6.00
321. Seale, Harold	,,	Invalided, Australia, 1.2.01
256. Weston, Clive Condor	,,	
341. Curr, Hubert	,,	
450. Stewart Frederick William	Farrier-Sergeant	
336. Egan, Arthur Peter	Corporal	Invalided, Australia, 1.2.01
276. Waters, Horace C. Philip	,,	Sergeant, 22.6.01
319. Cadden, Reginald Naylor	,,	Sergeant, 22.6.01
290. McKinnon, George Robert	,,	Invalided, Australia, 24.1.01
279. Fitzhardinge, Arthur Frederick	,,	*Vide* "Promotions"
323. Cobcroft, Percy Henry	,,	
280. Cortis, Percival Fyam	Lance-Corporal	Discharged, 14.3.01

Nominal Roll—*continued.*

No. and Name.	Rank.	Remarks.
"C" Squadron—*continued.*		
324 Aitken, James	Lance Corporal	
322. May, Mavon John	,,	Invalided, Australia, 13.12.00
249. Legh, Gilbert	,,	Invalided, England, 14.11.00
333. Chesher, Edward Brown	,,	Killed, Kaneel Poort, 2.9.00
23. Preston, George William	Trumpeter	Invalided, England, 22.12.00
19. Brown, Arthur Thornton	,,	
309. Ahern, Eugene	Trooper	Invalided, Australia, 30.3.01
171. Alston, Alexander Kenneth	,,	Invalided, Australia, 13.12.00
244. Burne, Henry Francis..	,,	Corporal, 14.9.00
271. Blanche, Matthew	,,	Invalided, Australia, 3.11.00
269. Biddlecombe, Charles ..	,,	Invalided, Australia, arr. 18.5.01
293. Bewers, Thomas	,,	
342. Battye, Arthur Frederick	,,	Invalided to Australia, 26.10.00
453. Bailey, George	,,	
351. Bentley, F. W.	,,	Invalided, Australia, 15.10.00
258. Carpenter, George	,,	
297. Cox, William Richard	,,	Invalided, Australia, 13.12.00
312. Cottrell, Charles	,,	
320. Cameron, Robert	,,	Killed, Koster's River, 22.7.00
285. Druitt, Thomas Henry Cyril	,,	Invalided, Australia, arr. 22.11.00
288. Druitt, Frederick Clement	,,	Invalided to Australia, 26.10.00
294. Darling, Thomas	,,	
287. Drinkwater, Harold	,,	Died, 1.2.01
311. Emery, Arthur	,,	
504. Fox, John Smith	,,	Invalided, Australia, arr. 11.6.01
274. Forbes, Christopher Owen	,,	
277. Fortescue, Arthur Henry	,,	
325. Finnigan, James	,,	
328. Ferguson, Leslie	,,	
329. Foster, Charles Frederick	,,	
449. Fackender, Alfred Herbert	,,	Invalided, Australia, 13.12.00
243. Guy, Paul James	,,	
461. Graham, William Johnstone	,,	
246. Gillies, Neil Patrick	,,	
283. Gregory, William James	,,	
300. Glennon, John Andrew	,,	
335. Godfrey, James	,,	Invalided, Australia, 30.3.01
496. Grubel, Albert	,,	
497. Hudson, Herbert	,,	
296. Holden, Frank Herbert	,,	Invalided, Australia, 23.12.00
439. Hayes, Arthur Ernest	,,	
434. Hickey, Edwin Patrick	,,	
464. Jackson, James William	,,	Transferred to Rhodesian Artillery, 1.5.00
289. Kelleher, Charles Edward	,,	Invalided, Australia, 30.3.01
466. Kennedy, Thomas	,,	
465. King, Horatio	,,	Corporal, 21.10.00
192. King, Frank	,,	Invalided, Australia, arr. 18.5.01
310. Lawes, Charles	,,	
308. Lyall, Albert..	,,	Invalided, Australia, 13.12.00
313. Lord, John Norton	,,	Invalided, Australia, 22.12.00
304. Luckie, Samuel	,,	
330. Lovatt, Joseph	,,	Invalided, Australia, 13.12.00
254. Matthews, J.	,,	
264. Macdonald, Harry Stewart	,,	
270. McDougall, John	,,	
278. McPherson, William Antill	,,	
281. Maguire, Duncan	,,	Invalided, Australia, 3.11.00

Nominal Roll—continued.

No. and Name.	Rank.	Remarks.
"C" Squadron—continued.		
471. McGrath, John William	Trooper	Invalided, Australia, 23.10.00
470. Mason, Charles	,,	Invalided, Australia, 1.2.01
291. Muir, William Miller	,,	
301. Meares, William Scott	,,	Invalided, Australia, 20.2.01
302. Monk, Charles Frederick Holes	,,	
331. Maling, William Alfred	,,	
332. Morris, Richard James	,,	Invalided, Australia, 30.3.01
309. Middleton, Archibald James	,,	
259. Nolan, Albert Edward	,,	Invalided, Australia, 1.2.01
337. O'Connell, William Joseph	,,	
474. O'Brien, Michael	,,	Invalided, Australia, 13.12.00
477. Payne, Joseph Henry	,,	Invalided, Australia, 30.3.01
475. Payne, George	,,	Invalided, Australia, arr. 18.5.01
273. Porter, Joseph Arthur	,,	Invalided, Australia, arr. 30.8.00
298. Pound, William James	,,	
299. Pound, Edwin	,,	
305. Parr, William Andrew	,,	Invalided, Australia, 13.12.00
489. Quine, John Henry	,,	
251. Quick, Albert Edward	,,	
374. Ross, G.	Corporal	Invalided, Australia, arr. 26.1.01
306. Reid, Henry Roderick	Trooper	
313. Ratten, Aubrey George	,,	
260. Ryan, Patrick Albert	,,	
480. Thorpe, William Edward John	,,	
338. Robertson, John Campbell	,,	Invalided, Australia, 13.12.00
340. Robertson, Edward	,,	
247. Sergeant, Thomas Wilson	,,	
250. Stibbards, Fred	,,	
252. Sadler, John Frederick	,,	Invalided, Australia, arr. 18.5.01
254. Sweeney, Edward	,,	
262. Stevens, Henry George	,,	
266. Storey, Mark Faucett	,,	
268. Smith, Edward Alexander	,,	
272. Spraggs, Richard William	,,	Corporal, 26.9.00
295. Sutherland, George	,,	
307. Staunton, Oscar Patrick	,,	
282. Thompson, Henry	,,	
286. Tindale, Albert Owen	,,	Invalided, Australia, 28.12.00
267. Treweek, James	,,	
334. Toohey, Frank	,,	Died, Ottoshoop, 26.10.00
248. Watson, William James	,,	Invalided, Australia, 26.10.00
253. Witts, Frederick Theodore	,,	
255. Wise, William Albert	,,	
263. Willmott, John Andrew	,,	
485. Walther, Thomas Henry	,,	Invalided, Australia, 3.11.00
327. Waddell, John	,,	Despatches, *London Gazette*, 4.9.01; killed, Eland's River, 17.8.00
284. Young, Robert	,,	
488. Zaccheus, Gustavus Henry	,,	Invalided, Australia, arr. 17.8.00
518. Woods, Theodore Alfred	,,	
"D" Squadron.		
Baker, Arthur Brander	Captain	
Westgarth, John Ellesmere	Lieutenant (R.A.A.)	Transferred, Royal Field Artillery, 1.5.00
Cape, Charles Scarvall	,,	
Moore, Thomas Mitchell	2nd Lieutenant	
Hutton, Arthur William	,,	

Nominal Roll—continued.

No. and Name.	Rank.	Remarks.
"D" SQUADRON—continued.		
530. Pearce, Henry	Sqn. Sergeant-Major	
506. McMillan, Murdoch Evans	Sqn. Quartermaster-Sergeant	
379. Airey, Henry George	Sergeant	Vide "Promotions"
114. Hurley, Thomas	,,	
397. Barrett, Dennis Joseph	,,	Died, 16.2.01
344. Davidson, George William	,,	Died, Mafeking, 7.3.01
458. Cox, Frederick William Sloper	,,	
46. Myers, Walter	,,	Died, Umtali, Mashonaland, 24.4.00
446. Grace, Martin Joseph	Farrier-Sergeant	
387. Bell, Albert John	Corporal	Invalided, Australia, 30.3.01
440. Johns, Digby Noy	,,	
430. Capell, Harry	,,	
419. Osborne, Duncan Campbell	,,	
433. Atkinson, William	,,	
424. Lloyd, Charles Richard Campbell	,,	
404. Heath, Samuel	Lance-Corporal	
413. Mair, Alexander William	,,	
380. Mair, Henry James Drepas	,,	
353. Burns, John	,,	
414. Andrews, Charles	,,	
422. Scott, John	,,	Invalided, Australia, arr. 11.6.01
20. Taylor, Sidney John	Trumpeter	Invalided, Australia, 30.3.01
24. Mason, Albert Edward	,,	
377. Ayshford, Ewart Aaron	Trooper	Invalided, Australia, arr. 11.6.01
391. Allison, Thomas	,,	Corporal, 30.7.00
59. Barnes, George John	,,	
352. Bullock, Frederick G.	,,	
362. Billsborough, Ralph Seymour Arthur	,,	Invalided, Australia, arr. 30.7.00
372. Blackman, Harold	,,	
376. Baker, William	,,	Invalided, Australia, arr. 30.7.00
394. Boyd, Robert Patrick Quin	,,	
396. Brett, John Theodore	,,	Invalided, Australia, arr. 11.6.01
420. Burke, William	,,	
431. Butler, Charles	,,	Invalided, Australia, 13.11.00
457. Beaumont, Albert	,,	Invalided, Australia, 23.12.00
455. Black, Robert	,,	Invalided, Australia, 2.8.00
5. Baker, Herbert James	,,	
410. Cox, George Frederick	,,	
346. Collins, James Joseph	,,	
347. Clements, Ernest	,,	Invalided, Australia, arr. 18.5.01
546. Charlton, John Leydon	,,	
403. Chown, George Henry	,,	Invalided, Australia, 15.10.00
411. Carey, John Patrick	,,	
417. Cummins, Philip Penrose	,,	
418. Cummins, Edward Augustus	,,	
459. Chanter, John Courtney	,,	
548. Corkhill, Joseph D.	,,	
423. Darcey, Robert Joseph	,,	
533. Davis, Harry H.	,,	Invalided, Australia, arr. 2.8.01
345. Duffy, Victor Herman Herbert	,,	
415. Duckett, Arthur	,,	
407. Eggleton, Roland John	,,	Invalided, Australia, 30.3.01
401. Freer, Robert	,,	
509. Fogarty, William James	,,	
364. Galwey, Frank	,,	
427. Gunter, Thomas Neville	,,	

Nominal Roll—*continued*.

No. and Name.	Rank.	Remarks.
"D" Squadron—*continued*.		
460. Gunning, Thomas Francis	Trooper	
358. Hardy, Thomas	,,	
723. Hassell, J. P.	,,	Invalided, Australia, arr. 6.12.00
367. Hall, Joseph	,,	
373. Howarth, Ernest	,,	
385. Holt, Hugh Morton	,,	
416. Hocking, James Richard	,,	Invalided Australia, arr. 5.3.01
490. Hampson, Wright	,,	Invalided, Australia, 16.11.00
523. Horseman, William Profit	,,	
524. Harrison, John Charles	,,	
416. Hocking, J. R.	,,	Invalided, Australia, 6.2.01
355. Ingrey, Arthur	,,	
366. Jackson, Frederick Joseph	,,	Invalided, Australia, 1.2.01
383. Jensen, Francis Ernest	,,	
421. James, Reginald Venables	,,	
514. Jones, Henry	,,	
389. Klein, Godfrey	,,	
467. Kirby, John	,,	
395. Long, Walter	,,	
349. Lidster, Edward A.	,,	
436. Libbesson, Gustave	,,	Invalided, Australia, 15.10.00
406. Middlemus, Thomas Patrick	,,	
356. Monk, Herbert Charles	,,	
370. Martin, Sydney Alfred	,,	
348. McSpadden, Frederick	,,	
425. McGowan, Alfred James	,,	
361. McLeod, Alexander	,,	
541. Macfarlane, James	,,	
428. Macdonald, John	,,	
292. Miller, A. H.	,,	Invalided, Australia, 13.11.00
472. Mooney, Archibald Patrick	,,	Invalided, Australia, 30.3.01
469. Mannser, Francis Richard Homer	,,	
547. Morrison, Henry Sproule	,,	
468. McCusker, William Francis	,,	Invalided, Australia, 13.12.00
438. Mackenzie, Donald	,,	
405. Nicholson, Angus	,,	Invalided Australia, arr. 11.6.01
501. Nicholls, Frederick Vincent	,,	Invalided, Australia, 6.2.01
512. Piddington, George Busby	,,	
476. Perrott, Harold Athelston	,,	Invalided, Australia, 23.12.00
398. Quigly, Benjamin Joseph	,,	Died, Lichtenberg, 20.12.00
131. Quinlivan, John	,,	
369. Rhall, Sydney Francis	,,	
365. Ritchie, Charles	,,	
384. Rowley, Samuel	,,	
408. Russell, Frederick Charles	,,	
409. Rush, James	,,	
478. Ryan, Joseph	,,	
491. Reid, George Thomas	,,	
1041. Reid, S. S.	,,	Invalided Australia, arr. 26.1.01
359. Sinclair, Duncan	,,	Corporal, 30.7.00
360. Smith, Reginald Montagu	,,	
363. Stokes, Charles Lawrence	,,	Invalided, Australia, 30.3.01
371. Spring, Arthur Francis	,,	
513. Sproule, Andrew	,,	
381. Stevenson, Charles	,,	
393. Stevenson, Robert Edward	,,	
382. Street, John Rendell	,,	Invalided, Australia, 6.2.01
426. Stanley, Richard	,,	

Nominal Roll—*continued*.

No. and Name.	Rank.	Remarks.
"D" SQUADRON—*continued*.		
483. Sutherland, William John	Trooper	Corporal. Invalided, Australia, 16.11.00
520. Smith, Ignatius Loyala	,,	
400. Thomson, Bertie John	,,	
481. Thomson, William John	,,	
432. Taylor, Joseph	,,	Sergeant, 12.6.00
519. Thomas, William Charles Frederick	,,	
374. Vigors, Richard Stanley	,,	
368. Watt, William	,,	
375. Wilson, Robert	,,	
388. Wilkinson, James	,,	
412. Walker, James	,,	
354. Watson, Vivian	,,	Invalided, Australia, 1.2.01
357. Wootten, Thomas Edward	,,	Invalided, Australia, 30.3.01
379. Waters, John	,,	
242. Weaver, Fredk. Egerton Pigon	,,	

IMPERIAL BUSHMEN.

THE New South Wales Imperial Bushmen was one of the regiments raised in response to an invitation from the British Government, which (the second phase of the war having commenced) now asked the Colonies for hardy bushmen—men who could ride, shoot, and find their way about—in order to fight the Boers with their own weapons.

Volunteers were tested and subsequently enrolled in Cootamundra, Gundagai, Wagga, Young, Hay, Cooma, Moree, Cobar, Tenterfield, and Bourke.

Pay.

Pay was issued by the New South Wales Government at Imperial Cavalry rates until landed in South Africa. These ranged from 23s. per diem with 4s. field allowance in camp to lieut.-colonel, to 9s. 10d. and 2s. 6d. to 2nd lieutenant; and from 6s. 4d. per diem to regimental sergeant-major, with 1s. field allowance, to 2s. 3d. to buglers and privates. After disembarkation, pay was as follows:—Brigadier-general, 50s. and 12s. per diem; commandant, 25s. and 4s.; major, 23s. and 4s.; captain, 21s. and 3s.; adjutant and quartermaster, the same; subalterns, 15s. and 2s. 6d.; medical officers, 20s. and 3s.; veterinary officers, 20s. and 3s. Colonial allowance for all officers, 3s. per diem. Officers employed in Army Service Corps duties, 5s. per diem, additional. Regimental sergeant-major, 9s. per diem; quartermaster-sergeant, 8s. 6d.; company sergeant-major, 8s.; other sergeants, 7s.; corporals, 6s.; privates, 5s.; buglers, saddlers, and farriers, 1s. per diem extra.

"Separation allowance" was also granted to wives and families of soldiers serving in South Africa, from 2s. 3d. to warrant-officers' wives to 1s. 1d. those of privates; and 2d. per diem each child, or 4d. per diem to wife, with 1½d. each child, if in quarters or drawing lodging allowance.

Establishment.

The following establishment was approved:—Regimental Staff—One lieut.-colonel, 1 major, 1 adjutant, 1 quartermaster, 1 medical officer, 1 veterinary officer, 1 sergeant-major (W.O.), 1 quartermaster sergeant, 2 clerks, 2 medical orderlies, 12 batmen; total, 24, with 15 riding horses and 7 spare; total, 22.

Detail of a company or squadron:—One major or captain, 4 subalterns, 1 colour-sergeant, 1 farrier-sergeant, 5 sergeants, 3 shoeing smiths, 1 saddler, 2 buglers, 6 corporals, 97 privates (including 5 drivers, 5 batmen, 2 cooks, 2 wagon men); total, 121, with 112 riding horses, 4 pack-horses, 4 spare horses; total, 120.

Total of staff and 6 companies:—36 officers, 714 N.C.O.'s and men; total, 750, with 687 riding horses, 24 pack horses, 31 spare horses; total, 742. To this was added as an estimate, 66 mules, to be provided by the Imperial authorities in South Africa.

Reference to Orders.

Enrolment	G.O. (N.S.W.), 37/00
Pay and allowances	,, ,, 43/00; 88/00
Establishment	,, ,, 52/00
Nominal roll	,, ,, 57/00
Embarkation	,, ,, 57/00
Officers	*Gov. Gazette* (N.S.W.) 342, 12th April, 1900

Clothing, Etc.

Uniform consisted of F.S. jacket, pants, puttees, and hat. Arms were supplied in South Africa. Cartridge belts with supporting-braces issued in Sydney. Fully horsed and supplied with saddlery. Regimental transport was provided.

Departure and Return.

The regiment embarked at Sydney on transport *Armenian*, on 23rd April, 1900, comprising 40 officers, 722 sergeants and rank and file, with 800 horses and 6 carts. Of these, 1 officer, 20 others were killed or died, 1 was transferred to South African constabulary, 9 officers and 95 others were struck off in South Africa, 1 was commissioned in Imperial Army; 30 officers and 605 others returned to Australia by transport *Orient*, embarking at East London 23rd June, and arriving in Sydney 17th July, 1901, having called at Albany and Melbourne.

Prior to his departure from Cape Town, Colonel Mackay was entertained by the Mayor at a banquet, where there was a large and representative gathering. The Mayor, in proposing the toast of his guest, referred to the valuable services rendered by the Contingent.

Service.

The New South Wales Imperial Bushmen served with—(*a*) 2nd Brigade Rhodesian Field Force, under Lieut.-General Sir F. Carrington, K.C.B., K.C.M.G., from 22nd June, 1900, to 31st August, 1900; (*b*) Lord Methuen's No. 2 Column, under Major-General C. W. Douglas, from 7th September, 1900, to 25th December, 1900; (*c*) Mounted Brigade, under Colonel R. G. Kekowich, from 25th December, 1900, to 12th January, 1901; (*d*) Mounted Brigade, under Major-General J. M. Babington, from 12th January, 1901, to 29th May, 1901.

It was brigaded with 4th and 5th Contingents, New Zealand; 2nd Imperial Light Horse; 2nd Mounted Infantry; and two squadrons 14th Hussars. Brigade was commanded by Lieut.-Colonel R. Grey, C.M.G., from 17th July, 1900, to 6th May, 1901; and by Colonel W. B. Hickie from 7th to 29th May, 1901.

"D" Squadron served as personal bodyguard to Lieut.-General Lord Methuen, K.C.V.O., C.B., C.M.G., from 17th September, 1900, to 31st May, 1901.

The following were the principal operations in which this Contingent was engaged:—Relief of garrison, Eland's River, 5th August, 1900; Marico River, 6th August, 1900; occupation of Ottoshoop, 14th August, 1900; Buffel's Hoek, 18th and 19th August, 1900; Jacobsdal, 22nd August, 1900; Malmani, 27th August, 1900; Wonderfontein, 10th and 11th September, 1900; Manana and Lewerpan, at which place one 15-pr. and one pom-pom were captured from the enemy, 12th September, 1900; re-occupation of Lichtenberg, 28th September, 1900; Oliphant's Nek, 5th October, 1900; Magatas Pass, 10th October, 1900; Riekertodam, 16th October, 1900; Lead Mines, 24th October, 1900; Kaffir Kraal, 1st November, 1900; Klerksdorp (re-occupation of), 16th November, 1900; Wittepoort and Bulkop, 26th and 27th December, 1900; Syferfontein, 5th January, 1901; occupation of Ventersdorp, 10th January, 1901; Klip Drift, 17th January, 1901; Valkfontein, 26th January, 1901; Magalisburg Valley, where one 9-pr. and one pom-pom were captured from enemy, 3rd March, 1901; relief of Lichtenberg, 7th March, 1901; Hartebeestfontein, 20th, 21st, 22nd March, 1901; Veldfontein, where the whole of De la Rey's convoy was captured, including 9 guns and 142 prisoners, 24th March, 1901; Wittepoort, two 15-prs. being captured from the enemy, 14th April, 1901; Hartebeestfontein, 18th April, 1901; Geduld (one 9-pr. Krupp captured), 3rd May, 1901; Palmietfontein, 8th April, 1901; here Kemp and Smutts' convoy was captured.

Promotions, Etc.

Captain and Adjutant H. Le Mesurier to Major, 11th April, 1900; Lieut.-Colonel, 12th November, 1900.

Captain G. De L. Ryrie to Major, 10th November, 1900.

Captain W. E. O'Brien to Major, 12th November, 1900.

Lieutenant H. Caines to Captain, 11th September, 1900.

Lieutenant J. E. Oxley to Captain, 11th September, 1900.

Lieutenant (A.M.C.) G. L. L. Lawson to Captain, 11th April, 1900.

2nd Lieutenant V. W. Ryrie to 1st Lieutenant, 11th September, 1900.

2nd Lieutenant A. C. Michell, Acting Adjutant, 29th March, 1901, to 8th April, 1901.

2nd Lieutenant C. M. Macpherson, Acting Adjutant, 9th April, 1901, to 7th June, 1901.

Warrant-Officer W. Butler, Lieutenant and Adjutant, 11th May, 1900; Captain, 24th September, 1900.

345. Sergeant A. C. M. Gould to 2nd Lieutenant, 1st June, 1900.

547. Squadron Sergeant-Major T. Hungerford, 2nd Lieutenant, 13th September, 1900.

1339. Sergeant A. C. Thompson to 2nd Lieutenant, 24th March, 1901. For distinguished gallantry in the field. A.O., 25th April, 1901.

R.Q.M.Sergeant G. H. Helbert, Lieutenant Quartermaster, 26th August, 1900; Captain, South African Constabulary, 1st January, 1901.

1406. Transport Sergeant W. Foley, Lieutenant Quartermaster, 1st January, 1901.

For promotions of N.C.O.'s and troopers, see nominal roll.

War Services and Honours of Officers.

Regimental Staff.

Mackay, Colonel Hon. J. A. K.—Operations in Rhodesia, 17th to 21st May; 1900. Transvaal, July to November, 1900, including action at Eland's River, Orange River Colony, and Cape Colony, November, 1900, to June, 1901. Staff Officer Oversea Colonials, Cape Town, November, 1900, to July, 1901. Despatches *London Gazette*, 19th April, 1901. C.B. Queen's Medal with four clasps.

Le Mesurier, Lieut.-Colonel H. (originally Adjutant).—Operations Rhodesia, Transvaal, Orange River Colony, and Cape Colony, May, 1900, to June, 1901. Commanded Regiment from 12th November, 1900, to — July, 1901. Queen's Medal with four clasps.

Butler, Captain Adjutant W.—Operations as above. Despatches, *London Gazette*, 19th April, 1901. D.S.O. Queen's Medal with four clasps.

Miller, Major David (acting Paymaster).—Operations as above. Staff Officer Oversea Colonials, Cape Town, July to October, 1901. Queen's Medal with four clasps.

Holmes, Captain Quartermaster, Arthur.—As above. Queen's Medal with four clasps.

Greig, Lieutenant F. E. (Transport Officer).—As above. Queen's Medal with four clasps.

Lawson, Lieutenant (A.M.C.) G. L. L.—As above. Queen's Medal with five clasps.

Kane, Lieutenant (A.M.C.) F. W.—As above. Queen's Medal with four clasps.

Barbeta, Lieutenant (Veterinary) Estevan.—As above. Queen's Medal with four clasps. (Vet. Lieut. Barbeta served subsequently with 1st A.C.H.)

Reynolds, J. A. (Chaplain, Anglican).—As above. Queen's Medal with four clasps.

Caine, Clement (Chaplain, R.C.)—As above. Queen's Medal with four clasps.

"A" Company.

Ryrie, Captain G. De L.—Operations in Rhodesia, Transvaal Cape Colony, and Orange River Colony, May, 1900, to June, 1901. Wounded at Wonderfontein, 11th September, 1900. Queen's Medal with four clasps.

Mackenzie, Lieutenant K. D.—Operations as above. Queen's Medal with four clasps.

Doyle, Lieutenant R. D.—Operations as above. Despatches, *London Gazette*, 19th April, 1901. (Lieutenant Doyle served subsequently in 1902. Despatches, *London Gazette*, 29th July, 1902.) Queen's Medal with four clasps. King's Medal with two clasps. D.S.O.

Ryrie, 2nd Lieutenant V. W.—Operations as above. Queen's Medal with four clasps.

Robinson, 2nd Lieutenant H. F.—Operations as above. Queen's Medal with four clasps.

"B" Company.

O'Brien, Captain W. E.—Operations as above. Despatches, *London Gazette*, 24th March 1901. Queen's Medal with four clasps. D.S.O.

Caines, Lieutenant Herbert.—Operations as above. Queen's Medal with four clasps.

Irving, Lieutenant G. R.—Operations as above. Queen's Medal with four clasps.

Gibson, 2nd Lieutenant C. H.—Operations as above. Queen's Medal with four clasps.

Rainey, 2nd Lieutenant A. P.—Operations as above. Queen's Medal with four clasps.

"C" Company.

Wray, Captain K. M.—Operations as above. Despatches. *London Gazette*, 27th September, 1901. D.S.O. Queen's Medal with five clasps.

Muhs, Lieutenant A. C.—Operations as above. Queen's Medal with five clasps.

Rudken, Lieutenant C. M. C.—Operations as above. Queen's Medal with four clasps.

White, 2nd Lieutenant R. J. L.—Killed in action, Manana, 12th September, 1900.

Michell, 2nd Lieutenant H. C.—Operations as above. Queen's Medal with four clasps.

"D" Company.

Waldron, Captain T. W. K.—Operations as above. Queen's Medal with four clasps.

Oxley, Lieutenant J. E.—Operations as above. Queen's Medal with four clasps.

Cosgrove, Lieutenant A. R.—Operations as above. Queen's Medal with four clasps.

King, 2nd Lieutenant A. E. G.—Operations as above. Queen's Medal with four clasps.

Wentworth, 2nd Lieutenant F.—Operations as above. Queen's Medal with four clasps.

"E" Company.

Browne, H. H.—Operations as above. Despatches, *London Gazette*, 27th September, 1901. (Captain Browne served subsequently as Major in 3rd Imperial Bushmen.) Queen's Medal with four clasps. King's Medal with two clasps. D.S.O.

Miller, Lieutenant D. F.—Operations as above. Queen's Medal with four clasps.

Thomas, Lieutenant E. H.—Operations as above. Despatches, *London Gazette*, 29th July, 1902. Queen's Medal with four clasps.

Maclean, 2nd Lieutenant A. L.—Operations as above. Queen's Medal with four clasps.

Macpherson, 2nd Lieutenant C. M.—Operations as above. Queen's Medal with four clasps.

"F" Company.

Soane, Captain E. W. R.—Operations as above. Slightly wounded Ottoshoop, 29th August, 1900, and at Maganspan, 4th April, 1901. *London Gazette*, 29th July, 1901. (Captain Soane served subsequently in 5th Australian Commonwealth Horse.) Queen's Medal with four clasps. King's Medal with two clasps.

Mylne, Lieutenant G. E.—Operations as above. Queen's Medal with four clasps.

Hanley, Lieutenant C.—Operations as above. Queen's Medal with four clasps.

Mackenzie, 2nd Lieutenant S. L.—Operations as above. Queen's Medal with four clasps.

Learmouth, 2nd Lieutenant M. C. L.—Operations as above. Queen's Medal with four clasps.

EXTRACT FROM REPORT OF MAJOR D. MILLER.

Ottoshoop, 4th September, 1900.—Since my last report we have been continually engaged in sniping, skirmishes, or heavier engagements daily, and are now awaiting orders for another advance.

General Carrington and staff left us, and are now at Buluwayo, organizing a force there to repel a threatened Boer invasion of Rhodesia.

Lord Errol, in command of our first brigade, has assumed command of our division, which is under the orders of Lord Methuen, who marched through here (Ottoshoop) a few days ago with his force, which had been on march since early in May.

The horses have suffered terribly up to now; we have lost nearly 200; some of our very best amongst them.

Leeupan, 20th September, 1900.—We are now in Lord Methuen's division, General Douglas' column, operating in the north-west corner of the Transvaal in the Marico and Lichtenburg districts. We marched out of Ottoshoop in the direction of Lichtenburg on the 9th inst., since when we have had five encounters with the Boers, who bolted each time.

The immediate results of the fights consist of 50 prisoners, 40 wagons with spans complete, a number of cattle and sheep, besides rifles, ammunition, &c.

On our side we lost Lieutenant White, killed in action, also two troopers; and one officer, Captain Ryrie, with several troopers, were wounded.

Lord Methuen joined us on Tuesday, but marched out the same day, taking 200 of our regiment to act as scouts for his column.

On Wednesday he had a fight, in which he captured 27 prisoners, 28 wagons, 1 15-pr. which the British lost some time ago at Colenso, 1 Maxim, 20,000 rounds of ammunition, sundry rifles, 3,000 sheep, and 500 oxen.

He then continued to march south to relieve some 300 troops who are held up by 2,600 Boers.

We are now camped about 35 miles south-west of Lichtenburg.

Cape Town, 6th November, 1900.—Colonel Mackay returned on the 23rd September from Lord Methuen's command. The General was delighted with the work done by the "Bushmen," and retained "D" Squadron for his personal bodyguard.

27th September.—Moved out at 4 a.m., marched until noon, covered 12 miles; occupied Reitkuil. The result of the day's work was—9 prisoners, 95 oxen, 1 wagon, some rifles and ammunition. At 5 p.m. the Boers attacked our outposts. Mounted troops turned out and engaged the enemy, volley-firing at long ranges. Pom-poms were brought into action, also our 15-prs. with shrapnel. The enemy, as usual, dispersed.

29th September.—Convoy moved out at 2.30 a.m. and marched 15 miles to Dinkfontein. Commandant Lemner attacked Lord Methuen's force, which is marching parallel to ours; several casualties. These Boers have now adopted precisely similar formations, columns of troops, &c., to ours, the result being most confusing. They are also dressed in khaki.

30th September.—Moved out at 2.30 a.m. Arrived at Rietpan at 10 a.m., 14 miles; found Lord Methuen's column here.

12th October.—Moved off at 2 a.m., trekked 10 miles, and surprised the residents at Waterval. Captured 9 prisoners, 500 oxen, 300 sheep, several trek wagons, 1 ammunition wagon, also large quantities of mealies, hay, &c.

17th October.—Moved out at 3.15 a.m.; arrived at Dammenburg at 8.30 a.m. (10 miles), again overtaking Lord Methuen's column. The Boer gun shelled Lord Methuen's camp, with serious results.

18th October.—Moved off at 3 a.m.; arrived at Zeerust at noon.

19th October.—Moved out at 3.30 a.m.; halted at noon.

20th October.—Moved out at 4 a.m. General Douglas engaged the enemy at daybreak. Lord Methuen assisted.

Arrived at Mafeking at 3 p.m., 21st inst.

Nominal Roll.

No. and Name.	Rank.	Remarks.
REGIMENTAL STAFF.		
Mackay, James Alexander Kenneth	Colonel (O.C.)	
Miller, David	Major (Acting Paymaster)	
Le Mesurier, Haviland	Captain (Adjutant)	Royal Aust. Artillery
Holmes, Arthur	Captain (Quartermaster)	
Greig, Francis Ernest	Lieutenant (Transport Officer)	
Lawson, George Langrigg Leathes	Lieutenant (A.M.C.)	
Kane, Francis William	,, ,,	Invalided Australia, arr. 21.10.00
Barbeta, Estevan	Lieutenant (Veterinary)	

C.4720.   G

Nominal Roll—continued.

No. and Name.	Rank.	Remarks.
REGIMENTAL STAFF—continued.		
Reynolds, Joseph Auburn	Hon. Captain (Chaplain, Anglican)	
Caine, Clement	Hon. Captain (Chaplain, Roman Catholic)	Invalided, Australia, arr. 8.1.01
Butler, Walter	Regtl. Sergeant-Major	Vide "Promotions"
1395. Helbert, Geoffrey Helbert	Quartermaster-Sergeant	Vide "Promotions"
1401. Foley, William	Transport Sergeant	Vide "Promotions"
1400. Anderson, Laurence Martin	Sergeant Bugler	
1389. Sharpe, Edward McManus	Staff-Sergeant (O.R.C.)	
426. Ward, Stanley Cullen	Sergeant (O.R.C.)	
1399. Neild, James..	Sergeant Cook	
"A" COMPANY.		
Ryrie, Granville De Laure	Captain	Slightly wounded, Wonderfontein 11.9.00. Invalided, Australia arr. 15.7.01
Mackenzie, Keith Douglas	Lieutenant	
Doyle, Richard Dines	,,	
Ryrie, Vincent Wallace	2nd Lieutenant	
Robinson, Harry Fletcher	..	Invalided, Australia, arr. 8.2.01
1347. Duke, Charles Edward	Coy. Sergeant-Major	Reg. Sergeant-Major, 22.6.01
3. Ashworth, Albert Henry	Coy. Quartermaster-Sergeant	
136. Fletcher, Laidley Shepherd	Sergeant	Staff Sergeant-Major, 22.6.01
240. King, Herbert	,,	
44. Godson, William James	,,	
11. Blackwell, George Robert	,,	
140. Guy, Thomas Lloyd	,,	
15. Cortese, Frank	,,	
220. Dalton, William	Lance-Sergeant	Severely wounded, Eland's River, 5.8.00
417. McKeon, George Henry	,,	
114. Annetts, Thomas	Corporal	
388. Lee, Albert Edward	,,	
269. Payne, Robert	,,	
113. Milner, Joseph Thomas	,,	
284. Curry, Thomas Shafton	,,	Lance-Sergeant, 1.1.01
681. Cambridge, William Henry	,,	
71. Mansfield, Horatio Stanley S.	Lance-Corporal	
85. Ransley, Thomas Walter	,,	
62. Lloyd, Norman Montgomery	,,	
43. Gardiner, Frederick James	,,	Corporal; Lance-Sergeant, 2.10.00
64. McKenny, William John	,,	
84. Rostron, Alexander	,,	
55. Holmes, Aubrey Harenutt	,,	
425. Horsley, Charles Joseph	,,	
2. Aitken, Robert	Private	
333. Anderton, David James	,,	
1405. Andrews, Frank	,,	Killed in action, Ottoshoop, 27.8.00

Nominal Roll—*continued*.

No. and Name.	Rank.	Remarks.
"A" COMPANY—*continued.*		
288. Alcock, Edwin Lawrence	Private	Sqn. Quartermaster-Sergeant, 1.1.01
10. Beatty, James	,,	
9. Briley, John	,,	
14. Boland, George	,,	
119. Brown, Henry	,,	
202. Beacham, William	,,	
355. Bosanquet, Lancelot George Vivian	,,	
409. Begg, George Alfred	,,	
418. Bradley, Charles	,,	
294. Burcher, Harvey Stephen	,,	
1360. Clancy, William James	,,	
17. Capp, Alfred	,,	
22. Cronk, William	,,	
23. Cox, George Henry Frederick	,,	Invalided, Australia, arr. 11.12.00
124. Cripps, Alfred Ernest	,,	
335. Cox, William James	,,	
26. Derrill, David	,,	Severely wounded, Kaffir's Kraal, 1.4.00. Invalided, Australia, arr. 5.3.01
28. Doran, Walter	,,	
29. Dalrymple, Martin	,,	
31. Davison, Henry	,,	Sergeant, 3.10.00; Reg. Chemist
1413. De Boos, Henry	,,	Invalided, Australia, arr. 11.10.00
131. Doney, Eustace Octavius Herbert	,,	Dangerously wounded, Ottoshoop, 23.8.00. Lance-Corporal. Specially mentioned for gallantry in B.O. by Lieutenant-Colonel Grey, 30.8.00
93. Dumont, Leslie Eugene	,,	
1409. Earl, William	,,	
35. Elletson, Robert	,,	
36. Edmunds, Frederick John	,,	Slightly wounded, Wonderfontein, 11.9.00
420. Eisenmanger, Charles Henry	,,	Lance-Corporal, 9.2.01
38. Fletcher, George	,,	
40. Filby, Thomas	,,	Invalided, Australia, arr. 11.6.01
137. Forrester, David	,,	
1411. Fuller, William	,,	Lance-Corporal, 9.2.01
1358. Fotheringhame, James	,,	
139. Graham, Alfred Adolphus	,,	
714. Gillies, Wallace Thomas	Shoeing-smith	Farrier-Sergeant, 4.3.01
140. Gilman, Hugh Rusden	Private	
363. Gunter, John Cornelius	,,	
144. Goodfellow, Sydney	,,	
47. Hockings, John Abraham	,,	
49. Hudson, Albert	,,	
50. Hazlewood, William Sydney	,,	Lance-Corporal, 13.1.01. Invalided, Australia, arr. 15.7.01
53. Hardy, Henry Cullum	,,	Died, Cape Town, 8.9.00
233. Hooworth, Claude Henry	,,	Invalided, Australia, arr. 11.10.00
234. Henson, William	,,	
148. Horner, William	,,	
1247. Hodges, Henry	,,	
56. Jones, Benjamin	,,	
257. Jennings, James William	,,	Lance-Corporal, 10.10.00. **Invalided, Australia, arr. 11.6.01**

Nominal Roll—*continued.*

No. and Name.	Rank.	Remarks.
"A" Company—*continued.*		
1408. Kelly, Michael Joseph	Private	
238. King, Frederick William	,,	
156. Kennedy, Donald Cameron	,,	
63. Leacock, James Freeland	,,	
1441. Lindsay, Colin Hunter	,,	
159. Logan, John Stuart	,,	
160. Luckie, Frederick William	,,	
66. Mather, Sydney	,,	
67. McGuire, Frederick	,,	
73. Mortimer, Edmund	,,	Invalided, Australia, arr. 19.9.00
75. Montgomery, George Arthur	,,	Died of wounds, Zeerust, 27.10.00
72. Murray, John Rowan	,,	Killed in action, Kaffir's Kraal, 1.11.00
258. Morgan, Alfred	,,	
263. Mickelson, Francis	,,	
1361. Mathews, William	,,	
168. McCarthy, Frederick John	,,	
170. McColgan, James	,,	
249. McCrea, Thomas James	,,	
1406. McKenna, John Alexander	,,	
61. McKenzie, Hugh Bailey	,,	
471. McCarthy, Alfred Stephen	,,	
589. O'Brien, William	,,	
1412. Peters, Ernest Francis James	,,	
78. Pringle, Huntley George	,,	Lance-Sergeant, 2.2.01; Staff-Clerk
303. Puxty, Alfred	,,	Specially mentioned for gallantry in B.O. by Lieutenant-Colonel Grey, 30.8.00
421. Paine, George	,,	Lance-Corporal, 10.10.00
423. Palmer, James Robert	,,	
1436. Powell, Alexander Allman	,,	Invalided, Australia, arr. 5.3.01
88. Riddell, William	,,	
940. Rawcliffe, James	,,	
95. Seaborn, George Hugh Merbyn	,,	Invalided, Australia, arr. 26.1.01
1435. Saunders, Ernest Valdreut	,,	
184. Sturgess, Frederick William	,,	
309. Stewart, Malcolm	,,	
276. Scard, Benjamin	,,	Invalided, Australia, arr. 5.3.01
275. Sargent, Thomas	,,	
453. Stables, Jonathan	,,	
99. Taylor, John	,,	
279. Tuft, Francis John	,,	
103. Witt, Edward	,,	
107. Wainwright, John Henry	,,	
108. Wallace, Alexander Campbell	,,	
190. Williams, Albert Henry Oscar	,,	
191. Woods, George James	,,	
327. Wilshire, Brisbane Challis	,,	
422. Ward, Alfred Edmund Thomas	,,	
1318. Watt, Joseph	,,	
112. Webb, George Frederick	,,	
1362. Williams, Edward	,,	
1438. Whiddon, Eustace	,,	
1410. Williams, Edward Samuel	,,	

Nominal Roll—*continued.*

No. and Name.	Rank.	Remarks.
"B" COMPANY.		
O'Brien, William Edward	Captain	
Caines, Herbert	Lieutenant	
Irving, George Richard	,,	Invalided, Australia, arr. 15.7.01
Gibson, Clarence Hyne	2nd Lieutenant	
Rainey, Arthur Pigon	,,	
1348. Murphy, Charles Thomas	Coy. Sergeant-Major	Reg. Quartermaster-Sergeant 1.1.01. Despatches, *London Gazette*, 29.7.01
16. Campbell, Irvine Flemming	Coy. Quartermaster-Sergeant	Invalided, Australia, arr. 22.3.01
494. Beckhaus, Frederick	Sergeant	Invalided, Australia, arr. 12.8.01
429. Moyes, Alexander Henry	,,	
428. Blackett, Robert George	,,	
440. Kelly, Robert	,,	
470. Hyndman, James Archibald	,,	Died, Enkeldoorn, R., 3.7.00
1404. Wall, John Felix	,,	
106. Wallace, Arthur Selwyn	Lance-Sergeant	Severely wounded, Reit Kuil, 28.9.00
241. King, Thomas	,,	
117. Best, Henry Alfred	Corporal	Lance-Sergeant, 2.10.01
430. Treloar, William Symons	,,	
135. Davie, Robert George	,,	Sergeant. Invalided, Australia, arr. 2.8.01
134. Dolman, Herbert Henry	,,	Sqn. Sergeant-Major, 22.6.01
1344. Norris, Samuel Edward	,,	
450. Hutchinson, Robert George Edgworth	,,	Sergeant, 4.8.00; O.R.C.
456. Morgan, John Stanton	,,	
602. Rathven, Edward Southwell Gowrie	Lance-Corporal	
457. Travers, Augustus Loftus	,,	
452. Fubbs, Samuel George	,,	
123. Challis, George	,,	Died, Johannesburg, 9.2.01
161. Leishman, Robert	,,	
441. Priestley, Charles Turton	,,	
175. Quintal, Fletcher Evelyn	,,	Lance-Sergeant, 1.12.00; slightly wounded, Buffel's Hoek, 18.8.00. C. in C.'s despatches, 8.10.01
478. Ashwin, George James	Private	
432. Atkins, Daniel	,,	
1392. Ball, Herbert Mugliston	,,	Severely wounded, **Reit Kuil**, 28.9.00
6. Benns, George	,,	
345. Bridge, Benjamin William	,,	
809. Brunsden, Thomas Henry	,,	
122. Bowden, William Campbell	,,	
489. Bolger, Robert Charles	,,	
447. Boyd, Michael John	,,	Invalided, Australia, arr. 22.3.01
469. Brown, William Stewart	,,	
485. Burke, Thomas Augustine	,,	
1337. Bode, Theodore Charles	,,	Severely wounded, Buffel's **Hoek**, 18.8.00
128. Carter, George James	,,	
116. Conolly, Thomas James	,,	
513. Campling, Albert Edward	,,	Invalided, Australia, **arr. 22.3.01**
410. Campbell, James William	,,	
1439. Cochrane, Lachlan	,,	
1065. Comben, Henry	,,	

Nominal Roll—*continued.*

No. and Name.	Rank.	Remarks.
"B" COMPANY—*continued.*		
511. Connorton, John Riddle	Private	
81. Cressy, Thomas Wentworth	,,	Died, Klerksdorp, 22.5.01
525. Dixie, Richard Thomas	,,	
218. De Smet, Charles Emanuel	,,	
437. Denny, Henry	,,	
521. Dunn, Joseph Windsor	,,	
1395. Dunnett, Francis Ernest	,,	
295. Elliott, William Walter	,,	Shoeing-smith, 1.6.00
1393. Fortescue, Francis Arthur	,,	Sergeant; Squ. Sergeant-Major, 1.1.01
853. Fitzpatrick, Percy	,,	
436. Garland, George	,,	
543. Gibson, Frederick	,,	
1402. Gibson, John Cooper	,,	
544. Greenway, Thomas Clarence	,,	
316. Goldring, Henry	,,	
448. Gammidge, Thomas Alexander	,,	
438. Gillespie, Alfred Stawell	,,	
459. Godden, William E.	,,	
431. Glenn, Alfred John	,,	Invalided, Australia, arr. 11.12.00
1415. Green, Alfred	,,	
48. Hillbrick, Walter Herbert	,,	
800. Hart, Charles Edward	,,	
262. Hasson, Thomas	,,	
329. Jamieson, Thomas	,,	Shoeing-smith, 18.10.00
442. Jensen, Australian Peter	,,	
1440. Legge, Charles Ernest	,,	Invalided, Australia, arr. 2.8.01
245. Lowing, Bertie	,,	
1346. Larkin, Henry Vincent	,,	Lance-Corporal, 2.2.01. Invalided, Australia, arr. 11.6.01
164. McMahon, William Francis	,,	
317. Meaney, Joseph Patrick	,,	
458. Mohr, Frederick William	,,	
443. Mohr, Christopher Bernard	,,	Invalided, Australia, arr. 11.6.01
431. McElroy, John	,,	
464. Murphy, Charles Peter	,,	
575. Munn, William F.	,,	Invalided, Australia, arr. 18.5.01
576. Moore, John	,,	
580. Mould, Albert Edward	,,	
413. Murphy, William	,,	Invalided, Australia, arr. 12.8.01
126. Nelson, Thomas Absolom	,,	Invalided, Australia, arr. 12.11.00
456. Nolan, Thomas Joseph	,,	
588. Newell, Edward Cecil	,,	
813. Nelmes, Archibald Granville	,,	
451. Ogden, Hubert George	,,	
463. Owens, Leslie	,,	
468. Oswald, Ernest D.	,,	Invalided, Australia, arr. 11.6.01
590. Owen, James Benjamin	,,	
272. Perry, Edward John	,,	
593. Pollock, Robert	,,	
462. Ryan, John	,,	
86. Roberts, Francis	,,	
179. Rushton, Thomas	,,	
374. Ross, George	,,	
446. Robinson, Walter Edward	,,	
82. Ryan, Patrick Joseph Stanislaus	,,	
605. Ratcliffe, Alfred Henry	,,	
606. Richardson, William James Reid	,,	

Nominal Roll—continued.

No. and Name.	Rank.	Remarks.
"B" COMPANY—continued.		
1041. Read, Samuel Stevenson	Private	
96. Smith, Arthur Herbert	,,	
183. Sullivan, John	,,	
439. Sale, Edward Frederick	,,	
444. Selby, Harold Isaac	,,	C. in C.'s despatches, 8.5.01
454. Sheedy, Michael	,,	
460. Souter, Thomas	,,	
466. Schussler, John Peter	,,	
1407. Smith, Edward	,,	
618. Stacey, Albert Edward	,,	Invalided, Australia, arr. 6.12.00
1359. Stapleton, Edwin	,,	
1414. Sullivan, Patrick James	,,	
780. Taylor, Herbert Wallace	Shoeing-smith	Farrier-Sergeant, 1.1.01
638. Usher, Daniel	Private	
195. Wright, William	,,	
449. Watt, Peter	,,	
648. Wilson, Henry	,,	Slightly wounded, Buffel's Hoek, 4.6.00
1394. Winters, Henry Charles	,,	
419. Yates, John Percival	,,	
287. Young, Rupert	,,	
"C" COMPANY.		
Wray, Kenneth Mackenzie	Captain	
Muhs, Albert Christian	Lieutenant	Invalided, Australia, arr. 15.7.01
Rudkin, Charles Mark Clement	,,	
White, Robert James Little	2nd Lieutenant	Killed in action, Manana, 12.9.00
Michell, Henry Carhayes	,,	
1349. Clark, Walter	Coy. Sergeant-Major	
151. Kelly, George Edward Ecclestack	Sergeant	
65. Macdonald, Hugh	,,	
255. Main, Boyan Thomas S.	,,	
91. Simes, Charles Nelson	,,	
18. Clarke, Frederick Henry	Corporal	
182. Starling, William Henry	,,	Slightly wounded, Klerksdorp, 16.11.00
231. Herfort, Gustavus Adolphus	,,	Sqn. Sergeant-Major, 22.6.01
97. Scott, Edwin Irvine Charles	,,	
223. Fleetwood, John	,,	
246. Lowing, Walter Harold	,,	
312. Warner, John Frederick	,,	
796. Anderson, Alfred	Private	
204. Buffett, David	,,	Invalided, Australia, arr. 5.3.01
147. Bradford, Sidney Edward	,,	
334. Bourke, Desmond Gerald	,,	
491. Bellamy, Arthur Joseph	,,	
490. Bellamy, Oswald	,,	
493. Barnes, John Alexander	,,	
501. Barber, Alexander Herbert	,,	
1366. Baker, William Salisbury	,,	
1422. Bondsfield, Henry Richard	,,	Lance-Corporal, 1.4.01. Invalided, Australia, arr. 15.7.01
25. Connors, Francis	,,	
127. Clark, Alexander	,,	
213. Curtis, William Ernest	,,	
214. Crittenden, Edward	,,	

Nominal Roll—continued.

No. and Name.	Rank.	Remarks.
"C" COMPANY—continued.		
216. Curtis, Arthur John	Private	Invalided, Australia, arr. 6.7.01
289. Caunt, Walter John	,,	
54. Cairnes, John	,,	Severely wounded, Kaffir's Kraal, 24.10.00. Invalided, Australia, arrived 22.3.01
358. Clyde, Frederick	,,	
397. Cameron, Frederick Edward	,,	
1365. Carey, James Joseph	,,	Slightly wounded, Jameson's Store, 9.9.00
512. Cook, William Frederick	,,	
514. Chadwick, John Colin	,,	
87. Cameron, Donald Wilson	,,	
27. Dunn, William Joseph	,,	
1421. Duffy, Michael Bernard	,,	
132. Darnley, Edward	,,	Slightly wounded, Jameson's Store, 9.9.00
336. Daggar, Edward	,,	Died of wounds, Ventersdorp, 11.1.01
347. Drummond, Donald	,,	
520. Dugan, James	,,	
33. Epple, Andrew William	,,	
310. Evans, Ralph	,,	
360. Elliott, Curtis Dyce	,,	
1416. Elliott, Rowland	,,	
361. Edmunds, George	,,	
433. Eather, Robert	,,	
39. Forster, Francis Joseph	,,	
328. Foulkes, Ernest	,,	
154. Ferguson, Leonard Tordiffe	,,	Slightly wounded, Eland's River, 6.8.00
1363. Fox, Alexander Henry	,,	Sergeant. Invalided, Australia, arr. 11.12.00
226. Gray, Frederick Charles	,,	Invalided, Australia, arr. 6.12.00
296. Gunston, George Washington	,,	Invalided, Australia, arr. 18.5.01
545. Guthrie, John William	,,	
546. Green, James William	,,	
1021. Giddins, Robert Samuel	,,	Shoeing-smith, 18.10.00
46. Healey, Sidney	,,	
298. Henwood, Arthur	,,	
473. Handcock, Hugh Hunter	,,	Killed in action, Reneke, 29.11.00
556. Hynes, Peter	,,	Lance-Corporal, 1.1.00
559. Hill, Archibald Usher	,,	Sqn. Quartermaster-Sergeant, 22.6.01
935. Holland, Simon	,,	
1434. Holmes, Robert Arthur	,,	
157. James, Henry David	,,	
299. Jennings, Horace Hocking	,,	
153. Kerr, Charles	,,	
239. King, Alexander	,,	Died of wounds, Manana, 12.9.00
804. King, Samuel	,,	
367. Logan, John	,,	
382. Lawrence, Edwin James	,,	Invalided, Australia, arr. 11.10.00
802. Luther, Edward	,,	Lance-Sergeant, 2.10.10; slightly wounded, Buffel's Hoek, 18.8.00
805. Lyford, George	,,	
369. Matthews, William James	,,	
74. Meaker, George	,,	Invalided, Australia, arr. 15.7.01
250. Moore, George William	,,	

Nominal Roll—continued.

No. and Name.	Rank.	Remarks.
"C" COMPANY—continued.		
251. McMillan, William Edward	Private	
254. Moy, Patrick Joseph	,,	Lance-Sergeant, 2.5.01. C. in C.'s despatches, 8.5.01. D.C.M.
260. McClymont, George	,,	Corporal, 24.3.01. C. in C.'s despatches, 8.5.01
261. Miggins, James	,,	
129. Mortimer, David Francis	,,	
400. McCarthy, William	,,	
435. Moore, Frank Ernest	,,	Shoeing-smith, 18.10.00
811. McGrath, Thomas	,,	
812. Norman, James	,,	Lance-Corporal, 3.9.00
1419. Nicholls, John Lane	,,	
1418. Nicholls, Francis Edward	,,	
371. O'Connor, Thomas	,,	
80. Prendergast, Henry Patrick	,,	
270. Phillipson, John	,,	
801. Powell, Edward Charles	,,	
83. Robertson, James Robert	,,	
177. Rhoderick, Edward	,,	Lance-Corporal, 10.10.00. Invalided, Australia, arr. 15.7.01
339. Rose, Hamilton Francis	,,	
372. Rawlings, James	,,	
1420. Richardson, Walter Claude Charles	,,	
90. Stevens, Alfred George Vivian	,,	
186. Sayers, John	,,	
109. Smyth, Peter	,,	
278. Seton, Hubert Canston	,,	
401. Skehan, John Cornelius	,,	Corporal. Invalided, Australia, arr. 11.12.00
406. Skehan, Park George	,,	Invalided, Australia, arr. 18.5.01
420. Smith, William Alexander	,,	
629. Smith, Alexander	,,	Severely wounded, Reneke, 29.11.00
630. Smith, George Franklin	,,	
1364. Simpson, Edward	,,	
1417. Tudor, William Hunter	,,	
343. Usher, Robert	,,	
110. Watts, Leslie Llewellyn	,,	Invalided, Australia, arr. 22.3.01
282. Wilmot, Alfred Rosewell John	,,	Corporal-Trumpeter. Invalided, Australia, arr. 21.1.01
285. Whinfield, Felix Edgar	,,	Invalided, Australia, arr. 22.3.01
286. Watt, Hubert Martel	,,	
375. Warbrick, Arthur	,,	
383. Warwick, Lewis Alfred	,,	Invalided, Australia, arr. 26.1.01
404. Ward, R. A.	,,	
807. Watson, Walter	,,	
353. Young, Robert	,,	
"D" COMPANY.		
Waldron, Thos. Walter King	Captain	Invalided, Australia, arr. 8.1.01
Oxley, John Evelyn	Lieutenant	
Cosgrove, Arthur Raymond	,,	Invalided, Australia, arr. 15.7.01
King, Allan Essington Gidley	2nd Lieutenant	Dangerously wounded, Buffel's Hoek, 4.6.01. Invalided, Australia, arr. 23.9.01
Wentworth, Fitzwilliam	,,	
1292. Cooke, Charles	Cov. Sergeant-Major	

Nominal Roll—*continued.*

No. and Name.	Rank.	Remarks.
"D" Company—*continued.*		
1343. Sheriff, George Towry	Sergeant	
1028. Russell, Christopher Stuart	Lance-Sergeant	
37. Fields, John Thomas	,,	
158. Lassetter, William Arthur	,,	Killed in action, Buffel's Hoek, 23.10.00
320. Willis, Patrick Peter	Corporal	
934. Marshall, Robert Paton	,,	
710. Gibbs, Frederick Meade	Lance-Corporal	
947. Murphy, Patrick Richard	,,	
281. Vivers, Robert	,,	Invalided, Australia, arr. 15.7.01
984. Williams, Jonathan	,,	
1005. Sullivan, William John	,,	
583. McFarland, George	,,	
874. McNamara, Michael Joseph	,,	
1160. Tutty, Robert	,,	
480. Abbott, Albert Barker	Private	Severely wounded, Cyferfontein, 16.2.01
660. Alexander, William Grant	,,	
332. Anderson, Alexander Thorburn	,,	
115. Anglim, Edward	,,	
381. Armstrong, Sidney George	,,	
5. Ash, Wallace Wood	,,	
427. Baker, Frank	,,	Invalided, Australia, arr. 11.10.00
672. Bell, Robert	,,	
936. Bell, Arthur David	,,	
499. Black, David	,,	Died, Mafeking, 12.9.00
986. Bliss, Ernest	,,	
1260. Bornholt, Nicholas	,,	
8. Bowman, George Sydney	,,	
205. Buffett, John Edward	,,	
142. Butler, Arthur Vernon	,,	Slightly wounded, Leerust, 13.5.00
509. Carroll, Michael	,,	Invalided, Australia, arr. 21.10.00
504. Cayford, Ross	,,	
510. Colenutt, George Pulham	,,	
893. Cook, Frederick	,,	
997. Cooper, William Thomas Meroyhung	,,	Invalided, Australia, arr. 17.2.01
1371. Cooper, William Arthur	,,	
19. Cureton, Harold	,,	Severely wounded, Buffel's Hoek, 4.6.01
976. Clark, John Matthew	,,	
892. Clarke, John	,,	
519. Dewson, Thomas William	,,	
217. Dransfield, Andrew	,,	
529. Dunsmore, William	,,	
695. Daly, John Joseph	,,	
120. Davis, William George	,,	
337. Dowse, Ernest William	,,	
944. Elliott, John Robins	,,	Shoeing-smith, 1.4.01
1246. Emery, James Thomas	,,	
702. Edwards, Arthur Robert	,,	Invalided, Australia, arr. 26.1.01
949. Egan, Arthur	,,	
867. Fawcett, Thomas Liddle	,,	
926. French, Matthew	,,	
1437. Fuller, Frederick Waldron	,,	
145. Gordon, Charles Thomas	,,	
715. Greggery, Robert	,,	
51. Hemmie, Reginald	,,	

Nominal Roll—*continued.*

No. and Name.	Rank.	Remarks.
"D" COMPANY—*continued.*		
1085. Hoffman, John Thomas	Private	
921. Holland, William	,,	Invalided, Australia, arr. 17.2.01
1007. Hill, Frederick Dorset	,,	
392. Hadfield, Edward Albert	,,	
366. Huckstepp, George Edwin	,,	
146. Harris, William Edward	,,	
360. Hopkins, Harold	,,	
52. Helmkamp, Frederick Henry	,,	
121. Humphreys, Thomas Francis	,,	
229. Huthwaite, Allan Stokham	,,	
914. Iverach, Peter Donald	,,	Invalided, Australia, arr. 26.1.01
57. Jay, Charles Alfred	,,	
731. Jenner, William Thomas	,,	
163. Jackson, Harry Vernon	,,	
738. Kelton, Harry McLean	,,	
993. Kinred, Hubert Cowley	,,	
814. Laing, John	,,	
916. Lanes, Albert Victor	,,	
978. Leonard, David Blake	,,	
1017. Lambert, Frank Herbert	,,	
1370. Lipscombe, Stanley	,,	
569. Marchant, George	,,	Invalided, Australia, arr. 21.10.00
167. Murdoch, William Henderson	,,	
578. McCarthy, John Hamilton	,,	Provost Sergeant, 24.10.00
69. McGrane, John Arthur	,,	
579. McCann, Reuben	,,	
166. McCormack, James	,,	
415. Macdonald, John	,,	
747. Milgate, James	,,	
259. Morris, Arthur	,,	
752. Mitchell, Thomas Moore	,,	
68. Mitchell, Thomas Dewar	,,	
939. Morris, Edward James	,,	Died, Klerksdorp, 29.11.00
942. Moclair, John	,,	
252. Munro, James	,,	Invalided, Australia, arr. 15.7.01
882. Naughton, Bernard John	,,	
173. O'Brien, William	,,	
822. O'Malley, Charles	,,	
1372. Robinson, James	,,	Invalided, Australia, arr. 11.6.01
1074. Ritchie, George	,,	
957. Ryan, Thomas William	,,	
1388. Roy, Benjamin	,,	
185. Sturgiss, George Herbert	,,	
180. Simpkins, Charles	,,	
623. Single, Arthur Percy Creswell	,,	
834. Squire, Herbert Charles	,,	Slightly wounded, Vaalkop, 17.10.00
966. Smith, Samuel Joseph	,,	
1023. Seccombe, Edgar Gerald	,,	Invalided, Australia, arr. 21.10.00
1043. Schramm, Thomas	,,	
94. Shepherd, Norman Hugh	,,	
274. Smallwood, William John	,,	
806. Stanton, John James	,,	
1044. Seymour, John	,,	
898. Sullivan, John Timothy	,,	
279. Stephens, Arthur	,,	
1369. Taylor, David Henry	,,	
100. Thomson, Thomas Mackenzie	,,	
783. Tierney, Michael	,,	

Nominal Roll—continued.

No. and Name.	Rank.	Remarks.
"D" COMPANY—continued.		
1387. Walls, Hugh Benedict	Private	Corporal; and Sergeant. C. in C.'s despatches, 1.6.02
102. Ward, Francis Hiller	,,	
101. Whitaker, Barrington	,,	
788. West, Thomas	,,	Severely wounded, Reit Kuil, 28.9.00. Invalided, Australia, arr. 22.3.01
962. Wotherspoon, Ernest	,,	Invalided, Australia, arr. 16.11.00
1008. Woods, George Edward	,,	
1019. Wilson, George Hay	,,	
1029. Williams, Frederick Blackham	,,	
196. Ward, Horton	,,	
"E" COMPANY.		
Browne, Henry Hamilton	Captain	Wounded, Kaffir's Kraal, 24.10.00
Miller, David Frederick	Lieutenant	Severely wounded, Wittepoort, 26.12.00
Thomas Edward Haslan	,,	
Maclean, Allan Lloyd	2nd Lieutenant	
Macpherson, Clarence Montrose	,,	
1053. Messenger, Reginald William James	Coy. Sergeant-Major	Warrant Officer and R. Sergeant-Major, 11.5.00; Brig. Sergeant-Major, 22.6.01; slightly wounded, Malmani, 27.8.00
645. Whinfield, John Richard Seymour	Coy. Quartermaster-Sergeant	Transport Sergeant, 1.1.01
507. Christie, Tilden	Sergeant	Sqn. Sergeant-Major, 11.5.00
547. Hungerford, Thomas	,,	Sqn. Sergeant-Major, 1.9.00; mentioned in B.O. for gallantry by Lieut.-Col. Grey, 30.8.00 *Vide* "Promotions"
883. Tebbutt, Henry Leslie	,,	Slightly wounded, Kaffir's Kraal, 24.10.00
1340. Wearne, William Stewart	,,	
837. Thomas, Herbert William	Corporal	
486. Bennett, Henry Augustus	,,	Killed in action, Reickersdam, 16.10.00
795. Lanes, Arthur Frederick	,,	
745. Matheson, Frank	,,	Sergeant, 5.9.00
689. Dowler, Anstall Charles	,,	
678. Crawford, George Robert	,,	Invalided, Australia, arr. 4.3.01
653. Adams, William John	Private	
474. Adrian, Robert Edward	,,	Sergeant, 1.1.01
75. Aggett, Joseph	,,	
77. Andrews, Frederick Lorimer	,,	
55. Argyle, Harry	,,	Slightly wounded, Roodeval, 15.10.00
656. Arnold, James	,,	
479. Ashwin, William	,,	
1378. Bartlett, Thomas Smith	,,	
483. Baldwin, John Henry	,,	
484. Bargh, John Munro	,,	
667. Barton, Harold Hindmarsh	,,	
663. Benson, John	,,	
492. Board, Osbert William Francis	,,	
664. Blunden, Harry Herbert	,,	
502. Bohle, Bernard Fitzwilliam	,,	
855. Bridges, William Throsby	,,	

Nominal Roll—*continued*.

No. and Name.	Rank.	Remarks.
"E" COMPANY—*continued*.		
1379. Brooks, Harold Herbert	Private	
165. Campbell, Oliver James	,,	Sergeant. Invalided, Australia, arr. 18.5.01
674. Carroll, Phillip Joseph	,,	
679. Chapman, William	,,	
505. Coffill, Harold James	,,	
92. Conlon, John	,,	
516. Coulter, Edward Albert	,,	
527. Dhu, Roderick	,,	
690. Diamond, Thomas William	,,	
532. Eggleton, John Robert	,,	
534. Elliott, George Alexander	,,	
1376. Fenton, Edward	,,	
1705. Fewkes, William Newton	,,	Corporal, 24.3.01 ; C. in C.'s despatches, 8.5.01 ; distinguished conduct in the field
709. Foster, William Macquarie	,,	
706. Freitas, Francis	,,	
1377. Glazier, James John	,,	Shoeing-smith, 1.12.00
539. Gall, Frank Joseph	,,	Lance-Sergeant, 20.5.01
537. Giddins, Robert Samuel	,,	Shoeing-smith, 18.10.00 ; slightly wounded at Klip Drift, 13.11.00. Invalided, Australia, arr. 15.7.01
542. Grimshaw, John	,,	Invalided, Australia, arr. 6.12.00
1066. Gutterson, George	,,	
555. Hamilton, William Henry	,,	Invalided, Australia, arr. 22.3.01
720. Harden, Alan Scott	,,	Sergeant, 1.10.00. C. in C.'s despatches, 1.6.02
723. Hassett, James Patrick	,,	
845. Huggins, Thomas Alfred	,,	Lance-Sergeant, 8.11.00
76. Hull, Ernest	,,	
561. Jessup, Arthur William	,,	Corporal. Invalided, Australia, arr. 15.7.01
1355. Jobson, Alfred Henry	,,	
496. Jones, Emil Henry	,,	
248. Johnson, Sydney Arthur	,,	
562. Kirkwood, James Hunter	,,	
564. Leatherday, William John	,,	
917. Leeke, James Edward	,,	
568. Lewis, Thomas	,,	
918. Lindsay, Arthur	,,	
746. Manson, John Alexander	,,	
818. Martin, Cecil Charles	,,	
582. McKinlay, Edward	,,	Lance-Sergeant, 1.12.00
572. Moore, Caleb Thomas	,,	
1374. Moran, Arthur	,,	
1104. Moreton, Thomas John	,,	
1354. Munson, Thomas Arthur	,,	
881. Nelmes, William Henry	,,	
587. New, George	,,	
1344. Newport, George Charles	,,	
758. O'Grady, Patrick	,,	Died of wounds, Ottoshoop, 29.9.00
757. Osborn, Leonard	,,	Invalided, Australia, arr. 16.9.01
592. Parish, Leslie Robert	,,	
403. Partridge, William Benjamin Henry	,,	
764. Perry, Wilfred Henry	,,	

Nominal Roll—*continued*.

No. and Name.	Rank.	Remarks.
"E" COMPANY—*continued*.		
598. Pestell, Richard	Private	Slightly wounded, Reitfontein, 5.1.01
841. Pierce, Stanley Hope	,,	
594. Piesley, Hercules John	,,	
1286. Poole, Frederick Plunkett	,,	
1348. Pringle, Thomas Alexander	,,	Invalided, Australia, arr. 15.7.01
1373. Rhodenback, Henry	,,	Corporal, 24.3.01; C. in C.'s despatches, 8.5.01
601. Renehan, Michael Joseph	,,	
331. Roberts, Clarence Victor	,,	
765. Roberts, Ward Francis Egbert	,,	Lance-Corporal, 1.12.00
977. Robinson, Hercules Elliott	,,	
305. Rolfe, Sydney Samuel	,,	Shoeing-smith, 1.6.00
178. Ryan, Edward	,,	
1375. Squire, Osborn Abram	,,	
625. Shalvey, Andrew	,,	
621. Schaeche, Alfred William	,,	
848. Sidney, John William	,,	Lance-Corporal, 1.11.00
771. Slade, James	,,	
770. Small, David George	,,	
612. Smith, Pierce Eaglesfield	,,	
1127. Smith, William	,,	
622. Stiles, Arthur Tarlton	,,	Lance-Corporal, 1.12.00
1251. Stewart, John	,,	Invalided, Australia, arr. 18.5.01
1434. Stewart, Edward Henry	,,	
831. Stubbs, William James	,,	Lance-Corporal, 5.9.00
611. Sutton, Joseph Henry	,,	
849. Targett, Harold Scott	,,	Invalided, Australia, arr. 18.5.01
838. Thompson, Frederick Louis	,,	Shoeing-smith, 1.4.01
1339. Thompson, Albert Charles	,,	Sergeant, 1.4.00; *vide* "Promotions"
631. Trim, William Patrick	,,	
637. Todd, Cecil Harry	,,	
782. Tasker, David Henry	,,	
810. Trulock, George Marshal	,,	
786. Ward, Peter George	,,	
650. Webber, William James	,,	
118. Wills, John	,,	
889. Wilson, Ira	,,	
104. Wynn, Walter Watkin	,,	Slightly wounded, Reit Kuil, 28.9.00
850. Younger, William Broughton	,,	Severely wounded, Wittepoort, 26.12.00 Invalided, Australia, arr. 18.5.01
"F" COMPANY.		
Soane, Ernest William Reading	Captain	Slightly wounded, Ottoshoop, 29.8.00; and Maganspan, 4.4.01 Invalided, Australia, arr. 15.7.01
Mylne, Graham Ernest	Lieutenant	
Hanley, Charles	,,	
Mackenzie, Stuart Leopold	2nd Lieutenant	
Learmouth, Maxwell C. L.	,,	Invalided to England
Robinson, George Mansfield	Coy. Sergeant-Major	
798. Dixon, James	Coy. Quartermaster-Sergeant	

Nominal Roll—*continued*.

No. and Name.	Rank.	Remarks.
"F" COMPANY—*continued*.		
1178. Body, Elice Arthur	Sergeant	
1134. Wilson, Thomas	,,	
1341. Macgregor, Neil Archibald	,,	
1123. Paul, George	,,	
387. Gjedsted, Charles	,,	
267. O'Shea, William Andrew	,,	
1144. Walker, James David	Lance-Sergeant	Invalided, Australia, arr. 30.8.00
603. Ruthven, Charles Kenneth Gowrie	,,	
1210. Bice, Luke	Corporal	Lance-Sergeant, 1.7.00
176. Rayment, Robert	,,	
1319. Shields, William John	,,	
1212. Ranclaud, Ernest Boscawen	Lance-Corporal	
1345. Gould, Albert Clarence Montrose	,,	Sergeant, 1.4.00; *vide* "Promotions"
125. Coggins, Henry Clark	,,	Sergeant, 23.7.00
1126. Rose, Frank	,,	Slightly wounded, Wonderfontein, 11.9.00
1225. Aberline, Alexander McFarlane	Private	Died of wounds, Lichtenburg, 4.10.00
900. Babington, James Henry	,,	
1080. Ball, George Austin	,,	
1162. Beit, Walter Scott	,,	Invalided, Australia, arr. 5.3.01
946. Byrne, Frederick Beaumont	,,	
1050. Butler, William	,,	
1227. Brown, James Edward	,,	
1233. Brooks, Frederick William	,,	
1232. Baxter, Albert	,,	
1236. Butler, James	,,	
1300. Byrne, Matthew	,,	
1163. Ball, Lucius Edward	,,	Severely wounded, Reit Kuil 28.9.00
1135. Brown, William Andrew	,,	
1261. Creswick, Charles Francis	,,	
1237. Collins, James	,,	
1258. Cain, Alexander	,,	
1301. Colless, Horace Arthur	,,	
1321. Cody, William Roger	,,	Severely wounded, Cyferkeil, 3.5.01
1102. Cain, Michael Joseph	,,	
1103. Clifton, John James	,,	
20. Cox, Frederick	,,	
105. Carney, George	,,	
1305. Dopson, Joseph John	,,	
1302. Dodd, Henry George	,,	
1357. Deane, Albert Joseph	,,	
1385. Ezzy, Albert	,,	Slightly wounded, Reit Kuli, 28.9.00
1192. Fahey, James Joseph	,,	Died of wounds, Lichtenberg 2.10.00
1216. Ford, Arthur Samuel	,,	
1194. Fahey, Joseph	,,	
868. Forsyth, Sydney Joseph	,,	Lance-Corporal, 1.1.01
39. Farrell, Walter	,,	
1297. Fisher, James	,,	Shoeing-smith, 24.7.00
1381. Fyfe, William Germain	,,	Sergeant, 25.4.01; distinguished conduct in field. C. in C.'s, despatches, 8.5.01
1230. Goldby, Henry	,,	

Nominal Roll—continued.

No. and Name.	Rank.	Remarks.
"F" COMPANY—continued.		
1264. Garvie, John	Private	Invalided, Australia, arr. 21.1.01
45. Giles, Charles	,,	
930. Haynes, Edward Charles	,,	Severely wounded, Reit Kuil, 28.9.00. Invalided, Australia, arr. 22.3.01
992. Harding, Charles Robert	,,	
994. Hoad, William Thomas	,,	
1432. Holmes, Iredell Decourt	,,	
1138. Humphries, William Frederick	,,	
1242. Hickey, Henry	,,	Invalided, Australia, arr. 18.5.01
1279. Hogan, John	,,	Invalided, Australia, arr. 15.7.01
1280. Havers, William	,,	
1311. Horne, John William	,,	Invalided, Australia, arr. 17.2.01
1314. Jeffreys, Arthur Lionel	,,	Lance-Sergeant, 2.2.01
1078. Johnson, Albert John	,,	Slightly wounded, Jameson's Store, 9.9.00
149. Jones, Sydney Edward	,,	
980. Kelly, Patrick Richard	,,	
1235. Kilgour, Robert William	,,	Severely wounded, Ottoshoop, 19.8.00. Invalided, Australia, arr. 11.12.00
1053. King, Walter Stephen	,,	
150. Kelk, William Brooks	,,	Lance-Sergeant, 25.8.00
1101. Littlewood, George	,,	
1396. Lord, Austin Southwell	,,	
1354. Lovie, Alfred Edward	,,	
943. Murray, Denis Joseph	,,	Died, Krugersdorp, 10.1.01
1190. Morgan, Llewellyn	,,	Died of wounds, Klerksdorp, 30.12.00
1214. Morris, James William	,,	
1316. Malone, Andrew	,,	Lance-Corporal, 22.4.01
391. Medcalf, James	,,	
1299. Mullins, John	,,	
1356. Milwain, George Finlay	,,	
1380. Moore, Thomas Sydney	,,	
1248. Macdougall, Ormond Butler	,,	
1353. McNamara, William	,,	
1383. Mackellar, Andrew Ross	,,	Died of wounds, Lichtenberg, 29.9.00
1254. Norton, Edward	,,	
1308. Neal, Gordon Hubert	,,	
884. Newlands, Robert George	,,	Sergeant, 25.4.01; distinguished conduct in field. C. in C.'s despatches, 8.5.01
1197. Price, Ernest Richard	,,	Invalided, Australia, arr. 15.7.01
1430. Pynsent, Alfred Thomas	,,	
988. Ruddle, Harry	,,	Corporal. C. in C.'s despatches, 8.7.01
1018. Roots, Walter Arthur	,,	
1141. Ryan, James	,,	
1294. Richardson, Charles Frederick	,,	Shoeing-smith, 1.6.00; severely wounded, Reit Kuil, 28.9.00
1317. Ross, William Patterson	,,	
1181. Ryrie, Cecil James	,,	
42. Robron, Matthew William	,,	
1382. Rudder, Lindsay Ernest	,,	
1047. Shelley, Walter Mansfield	,,	
1057. Scott, Thomas	,,	

Nominal Roll—*continued*.

No. and Name.	Rank.	Remarks.
"F" COMPANY—*continued*		
1058. Spence, William	Private	
1059. Shepherd, David	,,	Invalided, Australia, arr. 18.5.01
1142. Sweeney, Michael	,,	
1143. Smith, William	,,	
1244. Scott, Thomas John	,,	Invalided, Australia, arr. 6.12.00
1075. Shelley, Hector Harold	,,	Lance-Corporal. Invalided, Australia, arr. 11.6.01
373. Sands, James	,,	Lance-Corporal, 22.4.01
1394. Smith, Sydney	,,	
1403. Toes, Alfred Howard	,,	Severely wounded, Jameson's Store, 9.9.00. Invalided, Australia, arr. 15.7.01
885. Trainor, Henry George	,,	Severely wounded, Hartebeestfontein, 18.2.00. Invalided, Australia, arr. 11.6.01
416. Thick, James	,,	
1433. Tyler, George William	,,	
789. White, John Tremaine	,,	
1296. Watson, Henry	,,	
1384. Westbury, George Robert	,,	
1226. Watson, Thomas Gammol	,,	Severely wounded, Ottoshoop, 19.8.00
1307. White, George	,,	
1182. Wallace, Albert Norman	,,	

SECOND NEW SOUTH WALES MOUNTED RIFLES.

THIS regiment was established at Sydney upon pretty much the same lines as the 1st Mounted Rifles; except that, as no service squadrons were away, the whole corps was embodied in New South Wales.

Preference was given to trained men who were good shots and good riders, subject to tests as ordered. The age limit was 20 to 40 years; standard height, 5 feet 6 inches and upwards; minimum chest measurement, 34 inches. Applicants were also required to be single men and to pass a military medical examination. Rates of pay as for Citizen's Bushmen.

Establishment authorized :—1 lieut.-colonel, 1 major, 1 adjutant, 1 quartermaster, 1 transport officer, 1 veterinary officer, 1 sergeant-major (warrant-officer), 1 quartermaster-sergeant, 2 clerks, 2 medical orderlies, 12 batmen. Machine gun section :—2 officers, 2 sergeants, 2 corporals, 12 gunners, 12 drivers, 4 batmen; total, 8 officers, 1 warrant-officer, 49 N.C.O.'s and men; total 58, with 34 horses.

Five squadrons. Each—1 major or captain, 4 subalterns, 1 S. sergeant-major, 1 farrier-sergeant, 5 sergeants, 3 shoeing smiths, 1 saddler, 2 buglers, 6 corporals, 106 troopers (including 5 drivers, 5 batmen, 2 cooks, 2 wagon-men). Total of a squadron, 5 officers, 125 sergeants and rank and file, with 125 horses. Total of the regiment, 33 officers, 1 warrant-officer, 674 N.C.O.'s and men (708), with 659 horses.

REFERENCE TO ORDERS.

Formation	G.O. (N.S.W.), 4/01
Pay and allowances	,, ,, 4/01, 31, 34/01
Officers	,, ,, 18/01
Change of camp	,, ,, 22/01
Outfit allowance	,, ,, 23/01
Seconded	,, ,, 29/01
Establishment	,, ,, 34/01
Embarkation	,, ,, 37/01, 43/01
Officers	Govt. Gazette, 185, 2nd March, 1901

CLOTHING.

Uniform consisted of F.S. jacket, pants, puttees, and hat. Equipped partially with saddles.

DEPARTURE AND RETURN.

The regiment left Sydney on 15th March, 1901. It consisted of 33 officers and 673 of other ranks, with 700 horses, and disembarked at Port Elizabeth, 17th April. Of these, 2 officers and 23 others were killed or died, 3 officers and 10 others were struck off the strength in South Africa, 28 officers and 640 others returned to Australia. Embarked at Cape Town on 4th May, 1902; called at Albany on 21st May, Melbourne, 29th May, and disembarked at Sydney, 4th June.

A draft for the regiment was despatched on 21st March, 1901, of 9 officers and 281 others, with 320 horses; 7 were killed or died; 2 officers, 27 others were struck off in South Africa, and 7 officers and 207 others returned.

LIST OF OFFICERS promoted from other Contingents and attached to 2nd Mounted Rifles, supernumerary to establishment:—

Rank and Name.		Corps in which previously served.	Date of Promotion.	Remarks.
Major	Eckford, C. G.	New South Wales Bushmen	8th May, 1901	Staff employ
,,	Browne, H. H.	New South Wales Imperial Bushmen	9th May, 1901	Transferred to 3rd New South Wales Bushmen
Captain	Gell, S. L.	New South Wales Bushmen	8th May, 1901	Staff employ
,,	Johns, D. N.	New South Wales Bushmen	,, ,,	Recruiting staff
Lieutenant	de Mestre, H.	New South Wales Bushmen	,, ,,	
,,	Cox, F. W. S.	,, ,,	,, ,,	
,,	Robinson, G. M.	New South Wales Imperial Bushmen	22nd June, 1901	
,,	Stevens, A. G. V	,, ,,	,, ,,	
,,	Gjedstead, C. E.	,, ,,	,, ,,	
,,	McDonald, H.	,, ,,	,, ,,	
,,	Coggins, H. C.	,, ,,	,, ,,	
,,	McFarlane, G.	,, ,,	,, ,,	
,,	Moyes, A. H.	,, ,,	,, ,,	
,,	Adrian, R. E.	,, ,,	,, ,,	
,,	Wearne, W. S.	,, ,,	,, ,,	
,,	Simes, C. N.	,, ,,	,, ,,	
Lt. and Qr.-M.	Nield, J.	,, ,,	,, ,,	

OPERATIONS.

The 2nd New South Wales Mounted Rifles were engaged in operations against Generals De La Rey, Kemp, Potgeitiers, and Vermaas:—

(a) Served in the Western Transvaal, under the command of Major-General Fetherstonhaugh, from 23rd April to the 1st October, the principal operations being the capture of Potgeitiers' convoy on the Vaal, 24th May, 1901; capture by the regiment of General De La Rey's convoy of 106 waggons, a large quantity of cattle, ammunition, &c.

(b) Served in the Eastern Transvaal, under Major-General Fetherstonhaugh; engaged in many night marches, resulting in over 1,000 prisoners being captured.

The regiment served under Colonel E. T. C. Williams, of the "Buffs," throughout, with the exception of six weeks, when the column was commanded by Lieut.-Colonel Lassetter.

Special Remarks.

Her Most Gracious Majesty Queen Alexandra was pleased to award pipes to the following warrant-officers, non-commissioned officers, and men for gallantry and distinguished conduct in the field :—

No.	Rank and Name.	Particulars.
3683	R.S.M. Wasson, J.	For gallant conduct and conspicuous bravery at various times
1620	S.S.M. Digby, A. E.	
678	,, Sutherland, W. J.	
3680	,, Webster, J.	For general, good, and consistent work
208	,, White, A. W.	
3571	,, Wintle, W. E.	
876	Sergeant Corlette, E. A. C.	
75	,, Hill, T. J.	Distinguished behaviour Boshman's Hoek, 13th December, 1901, and The Magaliesberg, 5th September, 1901
214	,, Love, E. P.	General good work, especially at Beestelaagte, 19th August, 1901
1668	,, Smith, R.	Distinguished behaviour at all times, especially 24th May, 30th May, 19th July, 27th October, 10th December, 1901
724	,, Taylor, T. G.	General good work
249	Corporal Edwards, R.	Gallant conduct at Korranafontein, 10th May, 1901, and Tweedrai, 10th December, 1901
2369	,, Stewart, C. G.	Good work at Beesulaagte, 19th August, 1901
874	L.-Cpl. McRae, F.	Good behaviour in bringing in cattle under difficult circumstances, 4th December, 1901
1086	,, Smith, R.	For good scouting and conspicuous gallantry, 24th May, 19th August, 30th June, 27th October, 1901, and 20th February, 1902
862	Private Brown, A. E.	For good behaviour generally under fire
222	,, Davis, A.	Gallantry at Korranafontein, 10th May, 1901, in bringing in wounded officer out of action under heavy fire
644	,, Snowdon, W. S.	Gallantry at Korranafontein, 10th May, 1901, in connexion with wounded comrade
584	,, Swadling, D. W.	Good work at Rhenoster Spruit, 21st August, 1901

List of N.C.O.'s and men selected by the Commander-in-Chief to attend the coronation of His Most Gracious Majesty King Edward VII. :—Sergeant Corlette, Corporals McSpeddan and Pasco, Privates Hutchings and Farrell.

Extracts from Column Orders, issued 17th April, 1902, at Standerton.

The command of this, a purely Australian Column, has been a great pleasure to the officer commanding, and he desires to thank every one for their cordial support and unfailing loyalty at all times.

During the year the Column has been in existence it has travelled upwards of 4,000 miles in every part of the Transvaal, doing much fighting and hard work, all of which has been most cheerfully carried out. One specially noteworthy feature is that, though constantly engaged with the enemy, only 18 men have been taken prisoners, and of them the larger number were taken on the first fight at Korranafontein and through no fault of the men. This record, which it is impossible to beat, speaks volumes for the spirit and soldierly qualities of the Australian soldier. No column has made more night marches; and one march, made on the night of 11th March, 1902, from Brugspruit, over the difficult Wilge River to Doornek (230), a distance of 45 miles, which, with the return journey, makes a distance of

75 miles, is worthy of mention.   Finally, to Lieut.-Colonel Lassetter, Commanding 2nd New South Wales Mounted Rifles, and to Major Lydiard, 2nd Mounted Rifles, the officer commanding Column desires to express his grateful thanks.

One hundred and forty-one officers, N.C.O.'s, and men, never missed a trek during the regiment's service in the field.

Officers Mentioned in "Despatches" with "Honours" Awarded.

No.	Rank and Name.	Honour.
..	Lt.-Col. Lassetter, H. B.	Companion of the Order of the Bath (*London Gazette*, 31st October, 1902)
..	Major Lydiard, C. G. S.	Despatches, *London Gazette*, 25th April, 1902, and 29th July, 1902
..	Captain Holman, R. C.	Companion of the Distinguished Service Order (*London Gazette*, 31st October, 1902)

Promotions.

Captain A. A. McLean to be Major, 15th October, 1901.
Captain C. G. Lydiard to Major, 20th June, 1901.
Lieutenant H. McIntosh to Captain, 4th May, 1901.
Lieutenant R. C. Holman to Captain, 19th May, 1901.
For promotions of N.C.O.'s, see nominal roll.

War Services and Honours.

Lassetter, Lieut.-Colonel H. B.—Soudan Expedition, 1884–1885. Nile medal with clasp. Khedive's Star. Operations in Transvaal and Orange River Colony, April, 1901, to April, 1902. Despatches *London Gazette*, 29th July, 1902, 31st October, 1902. C.B. Queen's Medal with five clasps.

Antill, Major J. M.—*Vide* " A " Squadron Mounted Rifles.
McLean, Major A. A.—*Vide* " A " Squadron Mounted Rifles.
Lydiard, Major C. G. S.
Jenkins, Captain R. L.
McIntosh, Captain Harold
Holman, Captain-Adjutant R. C., D.S.O.
Griffiths, Lieutenant O. R.
Tedder, Lieutenant Jas. G.
Murray, Lieutenant P. L.
Airey, Lieutenant C. F.
Lyons, Lieut. Quartermaster M.
Molloy, Lieutenant Laurence, T. O.
Coyle, Lieutenant J. E. F.
Edie, Lieutenant J. G.
McColl, Lieutenant J. P.
Kater, Lieutenant E. D.
Lassetter, Lieutenant F. O.
Griffiths, Lieutenant C. T.

Operations as stated, April, 1901, to April, 1902. Major Antill served to July, 1901 ; Major McLean to June, 1901 ; Lieutenant Airey to December, 1901 ; Lieutenant Lyons was stationed at the base, Klerksdorp, to August, 1901, he was then transferred to Staff duty (" Oversea Colonials ") at Cape Town. The officers received Queen's Medal (and nearly all) with five clasps.

Melhuish, Veterinary-Captain.—*Vide* New South Wales Lancers.

The names of officers are omitted from this list who, though originally posted to this regiment, were subsequently posted to other regiments in South Africa.

Second Regiment New South Wales Mounted Rifles.
Nominal Roll.

No. and Name.	Rank.	Remarks.
Lassetter, Harry Beauchamp	Lieut.-Colonel	Nile Expedition, 1884–1885
Antill, John Macquarie	Major	
Carington, Rupert	,,	
McLean, Arch. Alexander	Captain	Wounded, 10.5.01
Newman, Joseph	,,	
Lydiard, Chas. George Sydney	,,	
Jenkins, Richard Lewis	,,	
Lee, Charles Arthur	,,	
Holman, Richard Charles	Lieutenant	Bechuanaland Expedition, 1884–1885
McIntosh, Harold	,,	
Griffiths, Owen Rhys	,,	
Forster, George Brooke	,,	Killed, 10.12.01
Tedder, James George	,,	
Murray, Pembroke Lathrop	,,	
Campbell, Dalgetty Gordon	,,	
Middleton, Cecil Ernest	,,	
Airey, Charles Francis	,,	Wounded, 10.12.01
Wearne, Albert Ernest	,,	
Atkinson, Stephen Herbert	,,	
Battye, Reginald Richard	,,	
Stewart, David John	,,	
Lyons, Miles	2nd Lieutenant	Egyptian Campaign
Molloy, Laurence	,,	
Mills, Charles George	,,	
Coyle, James Edward	,,	
Edie, James Gibson	,,	
McColl, John Patrick	,,	Bechuanaland Expedition, 1884–1885
Suttor, Harold Bruce	,,	
Kater, Edward Darvall	,,	
Lamb, Edward Allister	,,	Killed, 10.5.01
Bremner, Horace Malcolm	,,	
Lassetter, Fredk. Oswald	,,	
Griffiths, Cyril Tracey	,,	
Melhuish, Frank	Veterinary - Captain	
Nield, James Henry	Lieutenant and Quartermaster	

N.C.O.'s and Men.

No. and Name.	Rank.	Remarks.
1406. Abbott, George Henry	Trooper	
547. Aburrow, Francis William	,,	
1093. Adams, Charles Francis	,,	
884. Adams, Sydney Robert	,,	
121. Adamson, George Herriott	,,	
653. Ahrens, Sydney	,,	Died, 19.11.01
1563. Alldridge, Ernest	,,	
1348. Alting, Joseph	Corporal	
808. Anderson, Alic	Sergeant	Sqn. Quartermaster-Sergeant, 1.11.01
489. Anderson, Arthur	Trooper	
474. Anderson, John Leslie	,,	
162. Anderson, William	,,	
362. Anderson, William James	,,	

Nominal Roll—*continued.*

No. and Name.	Rank.	Remarks.
N.C.O.'s AND MEN—*continued.*		
74. Andrus, Percival Edward	Trooper	
1189. Appleby, Percy William	,,	
1023. Appleby, Thomas	,,	
85. Archibald, Wilton Carlisle	,,	
671. Arkenstall, Joseph Henry	,,	
774. Armstrong, Percy	,,	
161. Armstrong, William	,,	
1510. Arthur, Clifton Sherman	,,	Corporal, 13.12.01; sergeant, 1.5.02
106. Ashford, Thomas	,,	
22. Attwood, Francis	,,	
436. Baghurst, William James	Corporal	Lance-Sergeant, 15.5.01
478. Bailes, Cooper	Trooper	
215. Baker, Frank Cargill	,,	Invalided, Australia, arr. 2.8.01
772. Baker, Robert	Sergeant	
3475. Balchin, John	Trooper	
970. Balmer, Archibald	Sergeant	
163. Bannon, John	Trooper	
2706. Barker, Benjamin Allen	,,	
494. Barker, Thomas Percy	,,	Killed, 10.5.01
143. Barlow, Ernest Edwin	,,	
643. Barnby, Sydney Norfolk	,,	
895. Barnes, Sydney Charles	,,	Lance-Corporal, 3.3.01
1304. Barnes, William Arthur	,,	Corporal, 19.5.01
1123. Barnett, William	,,	
990. Bartlett, James Walker	,,	
164. Baskerville, Fredk. William	,,	
1307. Bastick, Michael	,,	Died, 5.12.01
727. Bathie, Albert	,,	
1490. Bathie, Charles George	,,	
250. Bathie, Frederick James	Corporal	Sergeant, 19.5.01
2795. Bayliss, Phillip James	Trooper	Wounded, 28.7.01
971. Beadman, Thomas	,,	
972. Beadman, William	,,	
1033. Bell, Walter Hugh	,,	
715. Bellwood, Harry Mason	,,	
906. Bentley, Frank David	,,	
614. Berrie, Thomas Alexander	Sergeant	
706. Beston, Percy	Trooper	
166. Beswick, John Franklin	Corporal	
588. Bevill, Robert Royston	Trooper	
3507. Bickle, Ernest	,,	
353. Biddle, Thomas John	,,	
165. Biggs, George Henry	,,	Corporal, 1.5.02
167. Blade, Frank Sydney	,,	Corporal, 1.5.02
103. Blair, Richard John	,,	
273. Blanchard, Chas. Edward	,,	
955. Bloomfield, Charles John	,,	
824. Blunden, James Edward	,,	
1342. Bond, Charles Joseph	,,	
1166. Boon, Herbert Edward	,,	
1301. Boon, Walter George	,,	
337. Boss, George	,,	
843. Bourne, Henry Ottaman	Corporal	
3676. Bowden, James Henry	Trooper	
589. Bowron, Frederick James	,,	
1048. Boyd, Frederick	,,	
1260. Bornholt, N.	,,	Invalided, Australia, arr. 2.8.01

Nominal Roll—*continued.*

No. and Name.	Rank.	Remarks.

N.C.O.'s AND MEN—*continued.*

No. and Name.	Rank.	Remarks.
381. Boyd, Malcolm	Trooper	
1449. Bracey, Stanley Paget	,,	
854. Bradsheet, Theodore	,,	
1541. Brady, James	,,	
583. Braithwaite, Daniel	,,	
1619. Bridges, Wm. Frederick	,,	
534. Briggs, Vivian Radford	,,	
1418. Brown, Arthur	,,	Died, 2.12.01
862. Brown, Arthur Ernest	,,	
1467. Brown, Fredk. Edwin	,,	
1385. Brown, James Edward	,,	
1277. Brown, John	,,	
915. Brown, Sydney Ernest	,,	
349. Browne, Percy A. de Courcey	,,	
348. Browne, William de Courcey	,,	
743. Brownlee, Frederick	,,	
1308. Bryant, William	,,	Wounded, 28.7.01
651. Buckley, William	,,	
2930. Burcher, Richmond	,,	Corporal, 1.5.02
24. Burrows, George Francis	Sergeant	
104. Bursill, Douglas Victor	Trooper	
927. Bussell, Harold	,,	
3480. Butcher, Fred	,,	
1070. Butcher, Frederick William	,,	
810. Butcher, Rowland Phillip	,,	
1103. Butler, Reuben Joseph	,,	
1123. Barnett, William	,,	
532. Cameron, Charles	,,	
1764. Cameron, Hugh James	Sergeant	
301. Canning, William Joseph	Trooper	
449. Carey, Samuel John	,,	
2539. Carey, William Thomas	,,	
1019. Carlile, Robert Sherman	,,	
603. Carmichael, John Henry	,,	
1398. Carmody, John	,,	
1491. Chandler, Albert Henry	,,	
901. Chandler, Charles	,,	Corporal, 19.5.01
649. Chapman, Oscar Fredk.	,,	
1006. Charet, Alfred George	,,	
760. Charles, William	,,	
446. Charlton, James Robert	Corporal	Sergeant, 19.5.01
272. Church, Charles John	Trooper	
908. Clancy, William Edward	,,	Died, 15.5.01
1051. Clark, James Joseph	,,	
152. Clark, Lancelot Walter	,,	
72. Clark, Noel Lester Sayers	,,	
3672. Clayton, Thomas Hutton	Regtl. Sergeant-Major	
510. Clements, John	Trooper	
509. Clibborn, George Holmes	Corporal	
628. Clissold, Chas. Stuart	Trooper	
97. Coady, William	,,	
3517. Coates, Fredk. William	,,	Invalided, Australia, arr. 12.8.01
1487. Cockran, Ben	,,	Corporal, 1.5.02
2880. Cocks, Charles	,,	
946. Collins, Edward Thomas	,,	Invalided, Australia, arr. 16.9.01
594. Commens, John Henry	,,	Corporal, 1.5.02

Nominal Roll—*continued.*

No. and Name.	Rank.	Remarks.
N.C.O.'s AND MEN—*continued.*		
1473. Conley, Augustus Charles	Trooper	
882. Conlon, Thomas Edward	,,	
579. Conn, John Alfred	,,	
475. Constable, Sydney Oswald	,,	
217. Cook, Alfred Hercules	Corporal	Sergeant, 19.5.01
1081. Cook, Jacob	Trooper	
659. Cook, William Albert	,,	
238. Cook, William Wilson	,,	
961. Cooke, Ira	,,	
504. Cooke, Percy James	,,	
696. Cooke, Samuel Charles	,,	
893. Cooper, Leonard	,,	
168. Coppock, Herbert Fitzroy	,,	
978. Corbett, Frank James	,,	
820. Corbett, John Joseph	,,	
876. Corlette, Edwin Arthur	Corporal	Sergeant, 11.4.01
998. Costley, John Thomas	Trooper	
1034. Cotter, Bertie	,,	
638. Cotterill, Phillip Graham	,,	Sergeant, 7.2.02
1106. Courtney, George	,,	
1549. Cousley, John Woods	,,	
1760. Coyle, George Francis	,,	Died, 25.9.01
417. Creagh, Arthur Gething	,,	
664. Crichton, David Ross	,,	Died, 2.2.02
564. Crick, Thomas Farley	,,	Corporal, 19.5.01
1555. Cripps, William Sydney	Sergeant	Sqn. Quartermaster - Sergeant, 17.4.01
1565. Crowell, John	Farrier-Sergeant	Farrier-Major, 24.6.01
718. Crewys, George Walter	Trooper	
1299. Cummings, Edwin Joseph	,,	
496. Curnow, Wm. Henry	,,	
169. Curr, Arthur	Corporal	
71. Daly, John Charles	Trooper	
596. Dalziel, Alex. Andrew	,,	
344. Dart, Richard	Corporal	
1323. Davidson, Thomas Keith	Trooper	
222. Davies, Arthur James	,,	
831. Davis, George David	,,	
975. Dawson, Arthur	,,	Corporal, 1.5.02
73. Day, Edward Waldron	,,	
296. Denman, Wm. Rowan	,,	
1644. Dennis, John	,,	
1325. Dicks, George Llewellyn	,,	
1620. Digby, Arthur Edward	Sqn. Sergeant-Major	Commander-in-Chief's despatches, 8.4.02
1178. Druitt, Robert Mayo	Trooper	Invalided, Australia, arr. 16.9.01
711. Duncan, Jas. Francis	,,	
55. Dunstan, Richard Edward	,,	Invalided, Australia, arr. 12.8.01
809. Eade, Henry	,,	
1335. Eades, Michael	,,	Farrier-Sergeant, 16.4.01
135. Eadie, Charles	,,	Wounded, 10.5.01
535. Eather, James	,,	
1169. Edmonds, Michael	,,	
3478. Edwards, John Gunn	,,	
249. Edwards, Richard Edward	,,	Corporal, 1.5.02; wounded, 10.12.01
949. **Edwell, Horace**	Lance-Corporal	

Nominal Roll—*continued.*

No. and Name.	Rank.	Remarks.

N.C.O.'s AND MEN—*continued.*

No. and Name.	Rank.	Remarks.
2699. Egan, Norman William	Trooper	
880. Egan, Thomas Kennedy	,,	
308. Elvin, Thomas Henry	,,	Invalided, Australia, arr. 16.9.01
1001. Elwell, Paul Leonard	,,	Wounded, 7.9.01
703. Erratt, Cyril Poulton	,,	Corporal, 1.5.02
1280. Esler, Alexander	,,	
170. Ezzy, Fredk. James	,,	
10. Ellis, James Mathew	,,	
645. Farrell, Edward	,,	
3499. Farrell, Martin	,,	Died, 13.6.01
929. Farrell, Thomas Mathew	,,	
710. Farry, Gregory	Lance-Corporal	
171. Faulkner, Wm. Edward	Trooper	
356. Fennessey, Jno. Edmund	,,	
109. Fenton, Lindsay Charles	,,	
666. Ferguson, Henry Donald	,,	
268. Ferguson, Max Beresford	,,	
490. Ferrier, John Meredith	Lance-Corporal	
172. Finlayson, George James	Sergeant	Sqn. Quartermaster-Sergeant, 17.4.01
1593. Fisk, Walter	Corporal	
469. Fitzell, Sydney	Trooper	
3512. Fitzgerald, Edward	,,	
2743. Fletcher, Henry Leonard	,,	
124. Flynn, John Sidney	,,	
897. Foran, Robert	,,	Died 5.10.01
324. Ford, Arthur Thomas	,,	
451. Ford, John	,,	
60. Ford, John Bernard	Sergeant	
921. Foreman, John Francis	Trooper	Died, 5.4.01
1104. Foster, William	,,	
821. Fox, Ernest Devenish	,,	
1182. Fray, George	,,	
834. Freer, Roland St. Lawrence	,,	
890. Friend, Alexander Joseph	,,	
497. Fry, George Lovelock	,,	
445. Gaddee, Arthur Alfred	,,	
92. Galloway, John Elder	,,	
325. Galloway, William	,,	
229. Gardner, James	Lance-Corporal	
129. Gardner, Hunley George	Trooper	
900. Garrood, John Charles	Sergeant	
823. Gavin, Lewis Norman	Trooper	
269. Geake, Ernest George	,,	
350. Gee, Arthur	,,	
437. George, Malcolm	Corporal	Sergeant, 1.5.02
3501. George, Samuel John	Trooper	
1138. Gibb, Henry James	Sergeant	
271. Gibson, James	Trooper	
36. Gilchrist, Jno. Hay Goodlet	Corporal	
466. Glanville, Harry	Trooper	
1145. Glenfield, Walter Herbert	Corporal	Sergeant, 15.5.01
704. Gooch, Fredk. James	Trooper	
502. Goodwin, Arthur Cuthbert	,,	
447. Gordon, George	,,	
2933. Gordon, Meldrum Guy	,,	
174. Gorey, William	,,	Sergeant, 18.1.02

Nominal Roll—continued.

No. and Name.	Rank.	Remarks.
N.C.O.'s AND MEN—continued.		
725. Goss, Albert Edward	Trooper	
386. Gould, James Edward	,,	
175. Gracie, Thomas	,,	
918. Grant, Frank	,,	
51. Grant, Henry Alfred	,,	
1357. Grant, Percival Lindfell	,,	
909. Gray, Herbert Edward	,,	
95. Green, Charles Lewis	,,	
396. Green, Ernest William	,,	Wounded, 10.5.01; died, 11.5.01
2584. Green, Henry	,,	
700. Green, Thomas Wilkinson	,,	
2583. Green, Alfred William	,,	
537. Greentree, Alfred Harold	,,	
465. Greenwood, Nimrod	,,	
2374. Greenwood, Robert William	,,	
2233. Grieve, John Anslem	,,	
606. Griffin, Richard James	,,	
945. Griffiths, Henry James	,,	
6. Griffiths, Lewis Henry	Lance-Corporal	Corporal, 28.9.01; sergeant, 1.5.02
45. Griffiths, Robert	Trooper	
66. Grundie, Charles	,,	
1353. Grundie, John	Lance-Corporal	Corporal, 1.8.01
648. Gubbins, William	Trooper	
674. Guerin, John Aloysius	,,	
173. Griffen, Ernest	,,	
2553. Hagarty, Denis	,,	
591. Halsted, Arthur Stan...	Lance-Corporal	Corporal, 1.5.02
1459. Halsted, Francis Gilbert	Trooper	
869. Hamilton, James Richard	Corporal	Sergeant, 19.5.01
540. Hamilton, William John	Trooper	Farrier-Sergeant, 20.1.02
197. Harbord, Alfred King	Sergeant	
397. Harding, Henry	Trooper	
2435. Harding, William John	,,	
176. Hardy, Alfred	,,	
412. Harker, Walter	,,	Killed, 10.5.01
1100. Harris, William	,,	
82. Harrison, John	,,	
1551. Hart, John	,,	
956. Hart, Percy Shadrock	,,	
566. Hartley, William John	,,	
148. Hawkshaw, Wm. Theodore	,,	
3487. Hay, James Thomas	,,	Died, 12.10.01
491. Hayden, Thomas Joseph	Corporal	
689. Hayes, Caleb Donald	Lance-Corporal	
155. Hayes, Francis Henry	Trooper	
608. Hedrick, David Brydon	Corporal	
607. Hession, Thomas Frank	Farrier-Sergeant	
2852. Hickey, Michael James	Trooper	
225. Hill, Compton Thomas	,,	
321. Hill, James Henry	,,	
75. Hill, Thomas John	Sergeant	
139. Hilzinger, Clarence	Trooper	
44. Hine, Gilbert Edward	,,	
333. Hobson, George Louis	,,	Corporal, 1.5.02; wounded, 10.5.01. Despatches, *London Gazette*, 31.10.02. D.C.M.
405. Hogan, Arthur	,,	
248. Hollingsworth, George	,,	
986. Holm, Peter Thomas	,,	

Nominal Roll—continued.

N.C.O.'s AND MEN—continued.

No. and Name.	Rank.	Remarks.
2454. Hughes, G.	Trooper	Invalided, Australia, arr. 2.8.01
2995. Holmes, Hugh Urish	,,	
480. Hood, John Ulrick	,,	Corporal, 19.5.02
960. Hopkins, Ben. Clarence	,,	
7. Hopkinson, Leslie Reginald	,,	
399. Howard, Henry Cecil	,,	
452. Howes, John Harper	,,	
127. Hoye, Wm. Cunningham	,,	
742. Hoyle, George Edward	Lance-Corporal	Corporal, 7.4.01 ; Sergeant, 1.5.02
662. Hubbard, Alfred Montrose	Trooper	Corporal, 7.4.02
567. Huer, Edward	,,	
767. Hume, James Edward	,,	
230. Hunt, Arthur	,,	
281. Hunt, Richard Henry	,,	
3485. Hutchings, Edward Thomas	,,	
521. Hutchinson, Wm. Edward	,,	
3. Hutchinson, Evelyn Granville	,,	
4. Hughes, Thomas Arthur	,,	
1249. Ings, James	,,	
851. Irwin, Patrick Thomas	,,	
3483. Jackson, Thomas Alexander	,,	
959. Jacobson, Ernest Hilton	,,	
104. James, Fredk. William	,,	
556. James, Gilbert	,,	
598. James, Samuel	,,	
555. James, William John	,,	
434. Jeffery, Henry Ernest	,,	
2860. Jessop, Joseph	,,	
467. Johnson, Gerald	Corporal	
468. Johnson, George	Trooper	Died, 21.5.01
673. Johnson, George Thomas	,,	
917. Johnston, Cyril Gainer	Corporal	Sergeant, 28.11.01
649. Johnston, Frank Hall	Trooper	
783. Johnston, George Augustus		
2781. Jones, Alfred Herbert	Sergeant	S. Quartermaster-Sergeant, 1.5.02
766. Jones, George Alfred	Trooper	
629. Jones, Joseph Patrick	,,	
178. Kaye, William Henry	,,	
2408. Keelty, Thomas Francis	,,	
1002. Kelly, Thomas Henry	,,	
581. Kennedy, John Michael	,,	
730. Kenny, John Patrick	,,	
841. Kenny, Francis Charles	,,	Invalided, Australia, arr. 16.9.01
1229. Kensell, William	,,	
650. Kerr, James Somerville	,,	
663. King, William Henry	,,	
2568. Kirby, Jeremiah	,,	
857. Kofoed, George T.	,,	
849. Kohler, Walter Henry	,,	Died, 12.12.01
832. Lake, Percy Frederick	,,	
2359. Lamb, James John	,,	
966. Lawler, Charles Fredk.	,,	
503. Lawton, John	,,	Lance-Corporal, 13.9.01
1095. Leahey, Patrick Joseph	,,	
585. Leer, Charles Edward	Sergeant	
2794. Leigh, Henry Stracey	Trooper	
1075. Leonard, John Joseph	Lance-Corporal	Corporal, 1.8.01 ; Sergeant, 13.12.01

Nominal Roll—*continued*.

No. and Name.	Rank.	Remarks.
N.C.O.'s AND MEN—*continued*.		
1022. Leonard, Thomas Patrick	Trooper	
587. Lidster, Thomas Alfred	,,	
387. Lightbody, Albert	Corporal	
459. Lister, Albert Langford	Trooper	
119. Little, Frank Henry	,,	
623. Locke, Herbert Jabez	,,	Wounded, 10.5.01
675. Lofts, Alfred	,,	
214. Love, Eden Percy	Lance-Corporal	Corporal, 15.5.01; Sergeant, 19.5.01
1476. Low, Thomas	Farrier-Sergeant	
3606. Lucey, Walter James	Trooper	
842. Lynch, John William	,,	
179. Lynch, Richard	,,	
226. McAlpine, Frank	,,	
825. McAuliffe, Henry James	,,	
199. McCann, Robert James	,,	
514. McCarthy, Patrick Joseph	,,	
2515. McClure, James Howe	,,	
150. McCoy, William James	,,	
261. McCristol, Timothy William	,,	
1080. Macdonald, Alex. Joseph	,,	
1157. Macdonald, David	,,	
492. Macdonald, Denis	Corporal	Lance-Sergeant, 1.6.01
1607. McGowan, Meal	Trooper	Corporal, 11.4.01
948. McGrath, John	,,	
240. McIllveen, James	,,	
398. McKay, Albert	,,	
455. McKay, Thomas	,,	Killed, 10.5.01
539. McKee, Trevor Allan	,,	
345. McKellar, Duncan	,,	
613. Mackenzie, John	,,	
425. McKinley, Alfred John	,,	
3476. McLeod, William Donald	,,	
1643. McNamara, Patrick	,,	
874. McRae, Finlay	,,	Corporal, 1.5.02
1331. McShane, Francis Andrew	,,	
390. McSpeddan, Archibald	,,	Corporal, 12.12.01
722. Macauley, Arthur	,,	
218. Macdonald, John	,,	
34. McIntosh, Lindsay	Lance-Corporal	Corporal, 24.5.01; Sergeant, 1.5.02
67. Macken, William Thomas	Trooper	
2436. Macpherson, John	Lance-Corporal	
938. Maddison, John Ernest	,,	Corporal, 19.5.01
758. Mainstone, C. Beresford	Trooper	
3675. Mallard, John	,,	
495. Mallyon, John Brunker	,,	
87. Mann, Benjamin F.	,,	
833. Mansfield, Fredk. Holmes	,,	Corporal, 19.5.01; Sergeant, 20.3.02
160. Marcroft, Wm. Lindley	,,	
548. Marlin, Robert George	,,	
443. Mansfield, Joseph	,,	
2354. Marshall, Edward	,,	
837. Marshall, George Lowes	,,	
1168. Marshall, William Henry	,,	
635. Mason, Thomas	,,	
18. Masters, Samuel Curtis	Lance-Corporal	Corporal, 3.10.01
2016. Macmahon, T. J.	Trooper	**Invalided, Australia, arr. 2.8.01**

Nominal Roll—*continued.*

No. and Name.	Rank.	Remarks.

N.C.O.'S AND MEN—*continued.*

No. and Name.	Rank.	Remarks.
1027. Masters, Wm. Alfred	Trooper	
375. Matterson, Stephen Henry	Corporal	Sergeant, 13.12.01
695. Matthews, Lionel	Trooper	Invalided, Australia, arr. 12.8.01
826. Maxwell, Thos. Reynold	,,	
933. Mayo, Leslie Howard	,,	
1812. Mayo, Sydney Selwyn	,,	Died, 11.3.02
1333. Meldrum, John Albert	,,	
212. Miles, Robert Hardham	,,	
846. Miller, Harry Frank	,,	
739. Miller, Henry Hensen	Lance-Corporal	Corporal, 18.1.02
654. Miller, James Saul	,,	Corporal, 20.8.01; Sergeant, 1.5.02
682. Miller, Robert Atcheson	Trooper	
570. Miller, Thomas Croker	Corporal	
339. Milne, Thomas Gibb	Trooper	
31. Mills, George Frederick	,,	
47. Mills, Richard	,,	
182. Mitchell, William Joseph	,,	
181. Mizzi, Charles	,,	
96. Molineaux, Bolton William	,,	
91. Monro, Robert Thomas	Sergeant	Sqn. Sergeant-Major, 1.5.02
78. Montgomery, John	Trooper	Wounded, 7.9.01
180. Moore, George Henry	,,	
402. Moore, James Alix	,,	
476. Morris, Fergus Richard	,,	
81. Morris, Henry	,,	
384. Mortimer, Geo. Frederick	,,	
391. Mortimer, Harold Michael	,,	
630. Mortimer, Harry	,,	
253. Moulds, Edgar John	,,	Invalided, Australia, arr. 16.9.01
3508. Muggwan, Patrick	,,	
2869. Mulampy, Thomas Francis	,,	Invalided, Australia, arr. 12.8.01
1734. Mulampy, James Paul	Farrier-Sergeant	
1233. Mulampy, Wm. Reynold	Trooper	
86. Mundey, Bernard	Lance-Corporal	
597. Murphy, George William	Trooper	
112. Murphy, Ernest Albert	,,	
2836. Murphy, Thomas	,,	
3108. Murray, James Bernard	,,	
698. Myler, Harold Hilton	,,	
5. McPherson, James	,,	
3567. May, Harry	,,	
1616. Napier, James Henry	,,	
263. Newell, Frank	,,	
158. Newman, Charles John	,,	
968. Nix, Thomas	,,	
881. Nixon, John	,,	
907. Northover, Charles Henry	,,	Wounded, 27.10.01
2612. O'Brien, Albert	,,	
981. O'Keefe, John Joseph	,,	
438. Olsen, George Daniel	,,	
1648. O'Niell, Henry Michael	,,	
1008. O'Rourke, Francis	,,	
994. Orr, David	,,	Corporal, 1.5.02
327. Orvad, John Peter	,,	
839. Osborn, William	Lance-Corporal	Corporal, 20.3.02
3491. Oswald, Norman	Trooper	
720. O'Sullivan, Denis	Lance-Corporal	

Nominal Roll—continued.

No. and Name.	Rank.	Remarks.
N.C.O.'S AND MEN—continued.		
183. Owen, James	Trooper	
687. Owers, James Henry	,,	
1035. Pascoe, Hilton Harcourt	,,	
811. Payne, Henry William	,,	
717. Pegg, Edward	,,	
1053. Perritt, James	,,	
844. Philbrook, John	,,	
586. Phillips, Arthur George	,,	
731. Phillips, Percy Walter	,,	
573. Phipps, George Edward	,,	
154. Pidgeon, Percival Jos.	,,	
314. Piper, Harry Aubrey	,,	
740. Platt, Adam	Lance-Corporal	
461. Playford, William George	Trooper	
370. Porter, John Archd.	,,	Invalided, Australia, arr. 23.9.01
371. Porter, Leslie Myles	,,	Invalided, Australia, arr. 16.9.01
636. Porter, Samuel James	,,	
1031. Powell, Benjamin Lloyd	,,	
2564. Powell, Mervyn Lealand	,,	
2985. Power, Henry	,,	
2950. Price, Edward	,,	
924. Price, Henry Richard	,,	
996. Price, Norman	,,	
670. Primrose, Carlton	,,	
786. Prior, Fredk. John	,,	
3290. Pritchard, James	,,	
26. Pritchard, Lewis George	,,	Corporal, 15.11.01
184. Pritchard, Walter Henry	,,	Bechuanaland Expedition, 1884–1885
1121. Pullen, James	,,	
201. Quinlan, Patrick Francis	,,	
1124. Radburn, Archd. Peter	Lance-Corporal	
3479. Randell, George Washington	Trooper	
593. Ransom, George Herbert	,,	
755. Reardon, Eugene John	,,	Wounded, 5.12.01
1062. Reed, Henry	,,	
616. Reid, Arthur Alexander	,,	
439. Reid, Joseph	,,	
860. Reid, Thomas	,,	
752. Rice, George	,,	
1518. Richardson, James	,,	Died, 22.3.02
969. Riley, George Joseph	,,	
499. Ritchie, Andrew David	,,	
751. Roberts, John	,,	
444. Robinson, Edward	,,	Invalided, Australia, arr. 2.8.01
3509. Robinson, John	,,	
3152. Robinson, Reynold S.	,,	
780. Rosen, Eric Canute	,,	
827. Ross, Henry	,,	
373. Rouse, Harry Lionel	,,	
622. Rowe, John	,,	Died, 20.5.01
943. Rowley, George William	,,	Corporal, 1.5.02
641. Ruthven, John	,,	
507. Ryan, Charles George	,,	
925. Ryan, John	Corporal	Sergeant, 19.5.01
1. Ridley, James	Trooper	
8. Ramsay, Frederick	,,	

Nominal Roll—continued.

No. and Name.	Rank.	Remarks.

N.C.O.'s AND MEN—continued.

No. and Name.	Rank.	Remarks.
1386. Sandstrom, Svenadvin..	Trooper	
852. Saunders, Robert John	,,	
3521. Scanlan, Boyd	Sergeant	S. Sergeant-Major, 1.12.01; Reg. Quartermaster-Sergeant, 1.4.02
1313. Schmich, William	Lance-Corporal	Corporal, 11.4.01
639. Scholes, Mark	Trooper	Corporal, 7.2.02
259. Scott, Roland	,,	
470. Scott, William	Lance-Corporal	
686. Scott, William Bruce	Trooper	
20. Seguss, Arthur Richard	Sqn. Sergeant-Major	
2806. Seaward, William	Trooper	
574. Seymour, Frank	,,	Wounded, 10.5.01
153. Sharkey, John Alexander	,,	
1206. Shea, Thomas	,,	
1349. Sheehan, Cornelius	,,	
919. Sheens, Peter	,,	
647. Shoobert, Frederick	,,	
3066. Silcock, John	,,	
563. Simpson, Claude Francis	,,	
747. Simpson, James Victor	,,	
1076. Simpson, William Ross	Lance-Corporal	Corporal 1.5.02
792. Sinclair, Robert	Trooper	
930. Sisley, Albert William	Farrier-Sergeant	Died, 20.1.02
460. Skipper, Alfred John	Trooper	
560. Sloane, Bernard	,,	
420. Smart, William George	,,	Wounded, 11.1.02
911. Smee, Ernest	,,	
697. Smith, Alfred Robert	,,	
500. Smith, Alfred	,,	
1109. Smith, Carl Wm.	,,	
1589. Smith, Carlton	,,	
203. Smith, George Alexander	,,	
32. Smith, Harry	,,	
2430. Smith, Henry	,,	
479. Smith, James	,,	
186. Smith, John Henry	Lance-Corporal	Corporal, 1.5.02
1668. Smith, Rex	Sergeant	
1086. Smith, Robert	Trooper	
699. Smith, Thomas	,,	
1038. Smith, Victor H.	,,	
609. Smith, Walter Charles	,,	
694. Snelgrove, David	,,	
644. Snowdon, Walter	,,	
850. Solomon, Judah Moss	,,	
488. Solomon, Sydney	,,	
920. Sommerville, Jno. Samuel	,,	
954. Sparks, Edward	,,	
1650. Speer, Arthur James	,,	
655. Spencer, Arthur George	,,	
1016. Spiers, Harry	,,	Died, 20.2.02
376. Spinks, William John	,,	
2945. Sprich, Paul	,,	
721. Stanton, Claude	,,	
572. Stanton, Herbert Robert	,,	
962. Stark, William Wilson	,,	
224. Starkey, Joseph Samuel	,,	

Nominal Roll—*continued.*

No. and Name.	Rank.	Remarks.
N.C.O.'s AND MEN—*continued.*		
764. Starr, Joseph Eliz	Trooper	
898. Steele, George Harry Edward	,,	
185. Steele, John Frost	Sergeant	
735. Stevens, Arthur Archd.	,,	Sqn. Quartermaster - Sergeant, 1.5.02
221. Stevenson, Walter Ormond	,,	Sqn. Quartermaster - Sergeant, 17.4.01
2369. Stewart, Charles Grant	Trooper	Corporal, 24.2.02
1117. Stewart, Donald	,,	
541. Stewart, James Arthur	,,	
202. Stuart, Charles Cameron	,,	
657. Suppel, James Joseph	,,	
678. Sutherland, Wm. John	,,	
584. Swadling, Danl. William	,,	
626. Swainson, John William	,,	Corporal, 22.6.01
2508. Swords, William Edward	,,	Wounded, 2.2.01
2. Symons, Henry	Lance-Corporal	Corporal, 13.12.01
724. Taylor, Thomas George	Sergeant	
845. Terone, Chris. John	Trooper	
1999. Thomas, Richard O.	,,	
2332. Thompson, Arthur B.	,,	
865. Thompson, Alfred	,,	
187. Thompson, Herbert Edward	,,	
873. Thompson, Wm. Michael	,,	Lance-Corporal, 8.4.01
705. Thompson, Wellyn	,,	
2368. Toll, John Joseph	,,	
206. Tonkin, James Samuel	Sergeant	
677. Tonkin, Septimus	Trooper	
204. Totten, Edward	,,	Lance-Corporal, 3.6.01
716. Tourle, Edgar	,,	Invalided, Australia, arr. 16.9.01
205. Towle, John Herbert	,,	
188. Trescott, William	,,	
646. Tresillian, John	,,	
2464. Triggs, James Ernest	,,	Invalided, Australia, arr. 23.9.01
1015. Turner, Harry Wingate	,,	
2887. Tutill, Robert John	,,	
3552. Thomas, Evan	,,	
822. Veiscery, Otto Alfred	Sergeant	
982. Verrinder, Wm. Henry	Trooper	Invalided, Australia, arr. 2.8.01
902. Vickery, George Henry	,,	
519. Vidler, Cecil Byron	,,	
498. Vine, John Daniel	,,	
190. Walker, George	Corporal	
189. Walker, Hamilton	Lance-Corporal	Corporal, 15.5.01; Sergeant, 1.5.02
193. Wallace, Alexander	,,	Corporal, 19.5.01; Sergeant, 13.12.01
1013. Walsh, Harold	Trooper	Died, 7.11.01
995. Ward, Wm. Barrington	,,	
815. Wardell, Basil	,,	
3683. Wasson, John	Regl. Sergeant-Major	Despatches, *London Gazette*, 27.9.01. D.C.M.
2955. Watriama, William Jacob	Trooper	
84. Watson, Fredk. Bowen	,,	
440. Watson, Oswald Victor	Corporal	Sergeant, 16.3.01
1771. Watt, Herbert Crook	Trooper	
806. Watt, Sydney George	,,	
652. Watt, William Redfern	,,	
640. Webber, Harry	,,	Invalided, Australia, arr. 16.9.01

C.4720.   I

Nominal Roll—continued.

No. and Name.	Rank.	Remarks.
N.C.O.'s AND MEN—continued.		
40. Webster, Edward Charles	Trooper	Wounded, 10.5.01
3680. Webster, James	Sqn. Sergeant-Major	Acting Reg. Sergeant-Major, left wing, 4.5.01
3327. Weekes, Sydney	Sergeant	Sqn. Quartermaster-Sergeant, 17.4.01
257. Weeks, Richard	Trooper	Lance-Corporal, 1.2.02; killed, 31.3.02
624. Weidemier, Alfred	,,	
98. Weir, James	,,	
886. Wells, George Reuben	,,	
191. West, Harrie..	,,	
757. Westoby, John Ellison	,,	
456. Weston, Lintorn Brook	Sergeant	Sqn. Quartermaster-Sergeant, 1.5.02
515. Whelan, James Joseph	Trooper	
2397. Whelan, Stephen Francis	,,	
1237. Whinfield, Charles Albert	,,	
642. Whitaker, Thomas Wm.	,,	Corporal, 1.5.02
208. White, Arthur William	Sqn. Sergeant-Major	
389. White, Bert ..	Corporal	Sergeant, 5.12.01
262. White, Peter Francis ..	Trooper	
557. Whitford, Wm. Ernest	,,	
42. Whitney, Victor Harry	,,	
192. Whitty, Percival C. ..	,,	
1147. Wicking, Cornelius B.	,,	
1515. Wilding, Frank Sydney	,,	
768. Wilkins, Herbert Granville	Corporal	Sergeant, 1.5.02
637. Williams, Alfred	Trooper	
1026. Williams, Ernest John	,,	
709. Williams, Harold	,,	
550. Williams, George Vincent	,,	
554. Williams, Isaac	,,	
3488. Williams, John	,,	Corporal, 1.5.02
521A. Williams, Leslie James	,,	
707. Williams, Patrick	,,	
471. Wilmette, Franklin	Lance-Corporal	Corporal, 19.3.01
688. Wilson, Andrew	Trooper	
3673. Wilson, Joseph Walter	Regl. Quartermaster-Sergeant	Afghan War, 1879; Bechuanaland, 1884–1885
633. Wilson, William Coombes	Trooper	
518. Wintle, Alfred	Sergeant	Sqn. Sergeant-Major, 4.11.01
592. Wiseman, Herbert George	Trooper	
450. Witt, Morris	Lance-Corporal	Corporal, 14.1.02; Sergeant, 1.5.02
762. Wolstenholme, Chas. M.	Trooper	
658. Wonson, William Edward	,,	
1306. Woods, James Joseph..	,,	
1010. Wright, Arthur John ..	,,	
414. Wright, Hugh	,,	Corporal, 1.5.02
756. Wright, Percival Ernest	,,	
894. Wright, Wilfred John	,,	
559. Wrightson, Walter C.	,,	
558. Wrightson, Wm. Robert	Corporal	
400. Wynne, Edwin Charles	Trooper	
448. Wythes, Vivian George	,,	
888. Young, Arthur	,,	Farrier-Sergeant, 14.12.01
952. Young, Roy Gordon ..	,,	

THIRD NEW SOUTH WALES MOUNTED RIFLES.

THIS Regiment was raised upon the same lines as its predecessors, preference being given to trained men who were good shots and good riders; age, 20 to 40 years; height, 5 feet 6 inches and upwards; minimum chest measurement, 34 inches. Applicants were required to be single men and to pass a military medical examination. Establishment and rates of pay as for 2nd Mounted Rifles.

REFERENCE TO ORDERS.

Formation	G.O. (N.S.W.), 4/01
Pay, &c.	,, ,, 4/01, 31/01, 34/01
Officers	,, ,, 18/01, 27/01
Outfit allowance	,, ,, 23/01
Seconded	,, ,, 29/01
Establishment	,, ,, 34/01
Embarkation	,, ,, 37/01, 43/01
Officers	Govt. Gazette, New South Wales, 219, 12th March, 1901

CLOTHING, ETC.

Uniform consisted of F.S. jacket, pants, puttees, and hat. Equipped with saddles (portion only).

DEPARTURE AND RETURN.

"B" and "D" squadrons of this regiment embarked at Sydney on the transport *Maplemore* on the 15th March, and arrived at Port Elizabeth on 12th April, 1901, with 8 officers and 251 others.

"A," "C," and "E" squadrons, with Regimental Staff, embarked on transport *British Princess* on 21st March, and arrived at Durban on 17th April, 1901, with 17 officers and 401 other ranks.

Machine-gun section embarked on transport *Ranee* on 21st March, and arrived at Durban on 23rd April, 1901. Strength, 2 officers, 34 others.

Drafts embarked on transport *Antillian* on 5th April, and arrived at Durban on 12th May, 1901—10 officers, 294 others. Total strength of regiment, 37 officers, 980 of other ranks, besides supernumeraries with 1,000 horses.

One officer, 36 Sergeants and rank and file were killed or died; and 6 officers, 46 others were struck off in South Africa.

The regiment embarked at Cape Town for Australia on 4th May, and arrived at Sydney on 3rd June, 1902, calling at Albany, Adelaide, and Melbourne *en route*.

LIST OF OFFICERS promoted from other Contingents attached as Supernumeraries to Third Mounted Rifles.

Rank and Name.		Corps in which previously served.	Date of Promotion.	Remarks.
Major	Bennett, A. J.	1st New South Wales Mounted Rifles	30th March, 1901	
Captain	Mackenzie, S. L.	New South Wales Imperial Bushmen	22nd June, 1901	
,,	Hungerford, T.	,, ,,	,, ,,	
,,	Miller, D. F.	,, ,,	,, ,,	Died, Harrismith, 29th March, 1902
,,	Greig, F. E.	,, ,,	,, ,,	Staff
,,	Gibson, C. H.	,, ,,	,, ,,	
Lieutenant	Bent, J. B. L.	1st New South Wales Mounted Rifles	30th March, 1901	
,,	Braun, C. L.	,, ,,	,, ,,	
,,	Lyons, G.	Oversea Staff	1st April, 1901	Attached to A.S.C.
,,	Foster, E. G.	New South Wales Citizen Bushmen	8th May, 1901	
,,	Waters, H.	,, ,,	,, ,,	
,,	Cadden, R.	,, ,,	,, ,,	
,,	Grahame, E. P.	,, ,,	,, ,,	

Service.

This regiment was attached to Colonel Remington's column from 2nd May, 1901, to 28th April, 1902.

The regiment took part in operations in the Eastern Transvaal and Eastern Orange River Colony in 1901-2. It also took part in several drives in the early part of 1902; the principal one, the Harrismith drive, resulting in the capture of 251 prisoners, 26,000 head of cattle, and 2,000 horses.

A Machine-gun section was attached to it, *vide* Nominal Roll.

Promotion of Officers.

Major C. F. Cox to Lieutenant-Colonel, 29th June, 1901.
Captain H. P. R. Copeland to Major, 13th December, 1901.
Lieutenant H. Peek to Captain, 28th February, 1901.
Lieutenant R. Scobie, to Captain, 18th June, 1901.
Lieutenant P. Macdonald to Captain, 28th February, 1901.
Lieutenant T. R. Richards to Captain, 18th June, 1901.
Sergeant O. A. Taylor to Lieutenant, 28th February, 1901.
Sergeant-Major G. Lyons to Lieutenant, 1st April, 1901.
Sergeant W. A. Brees to Lieutenant, 5th October, 1901.
Sergeant A. G. Gordon to Lieutenant, 11th June, 1901.
Sergeant Barnett to Lieutenant, 1st October, 1901.
Sergeant E. F. Hopkinson to 2nd Lieutenant, 28th February, 1901.

(For promotions of non-commissioned officers and troopers, *vide* Nominal Roll.)

Mentioned in Despatches and Honours Awarded.

Cox, Lieut.-Colonel C. F.—Despatches, *London Gazette*, 17th June, 1902. C.B. *London Gazette*, 26th June, 1902.

Bennett, Major A. J.—Despatches, *London Gazette*, 29th July, 1902. D.S.O.

Macdonald, Captain P.—Despatches, *London Gazette*, 29th July, 1902. *London Gazette*, 29th October, 1902.

Heron, Captain R. M.—Despatches, *London Gazette*, 29th July, 1902.

For honours awarded to W.O. and N.C.O.'s, *vide* Nominal Roll.

War Services of Officers.

Cox, Lieut.-Colonel C. F.—*Vide* New South Wales Lancers.

The officers had nearly all seen service with previous Contingents, for which *vide* those Contingents. The service reckoned with this regiment was from 2nd May, 1901, to 28th April, 1902. Operations in Eastern Transvaal and Eastern Orange River Colony.

Officers who had not served previously obtained the Q.M. with clasps.

Nominal Roll.

No. and Name.	Rank.	Remarks.
REGIMENTAL STAFF.		
Cox, Charles Frederick	Major	
Copeland, Henry Paul Ramsay	Captain, Adjutant	*Vide* SPECIAL SERVICE OFFICERS
Symonds, Stanley Leplastrier	Lieutenant (Vet.)	
Robson, Henry	Lieutenant	
Allen, Ralph Rowland	2nd Lieutenant	
3671. McColl, John Thomas	Regtl. Sergeant-Major Warrant Officer	Despatches, *London Gazette*, 29.7.02
3674. Bruggy, Stephen	Regtl. Quartermaster-Sergeant	
3259. Brady, Phillip Patrick	Orderly-room Clerk	
3589. Crow, John	Corporal	Sergeant, 15.5.01
3716. Williams, Henry	Quartermaster-Sergeant	Died, Standerton, 8.5.01
3341. Butwell, Henry James Francis	Sergeant	
2127. Clarke, John James	Trooper	
2870. Chadwick, David Oliver	,,	Corporal, 5.5.01
941. Fitzgerald, Michael	,,	
1784. Hayes, Percy Thomas	,,	
338. Heymoure, Sydney Charles	,,	
2302. Holt, Donald Lea	,,	
2730. Kennedy, William	,,	
128. Lyons, William James	,,	Sergeant, 23.5.01
1542. McGrath, James	,,	
3113. Schofield, Edwin	,,	Armourer-Sergeant 18.6.01
2012. Yard, Edward Sidney	,,	
"A" SQUADRON.		
Peek, John Harold	Lieutenant	
Stuart, Frederick William	,,	
Pearce, Norman Matthew	,,	
2005. Watt, Edward Chorley	Sqn. Sergeant-Major	
2210. Heery, Thomas Joseph	Quartermaster-Sergeant	Sqn. Sergeant-Major, 7.1.02
1954. Burgis, Thomas Persehouse	Sergeant	
2106. Hamilton, Francis Benjamin	,,	
1875. Lockett, George Hugh	,,	
3094. Taylor, Owen Albert	,,	*Vide* Promotions
3381. Neenan, John Francis Patrick	Farrier-Sergeant	
2019. Dent, Charles Edwin	Corporal	Sergeant, 15.3.02
1981. Johnson, Alfred William	,,	Sqn. Quartermaster-Sergeant, 18.6.01
2014. Dransfield, Edgar Septimus	,,	
2016. McMahon, Thomas Joseph	,,	
1923. Clancy, William	,,	
782. Hodges, Herbert Ernest	,,	Sergeant, 11.12.01
2066. Mason, Daniel James	,,	Sergeant, 7.1.02
1906. Meecham, Herbert Joseph	,,	
1938. Donn, Joseph	Shoeing-smith	
1969. Dean, Patrick Silvester	,,	
1630. McMahon, Terance Charles	,,	Farrier-Sergeant, 18.6.01
1947. Lee, Sydney	Trumpeter	
1886. Matthews, Percy Clarke	,,	
1936. Apthorpe, Aubrey Vincent	Trooper	Died, 31.1.02
1937. **Angove**, William Paul	,,	

Nominal Roll—*continued.*

No. and Name.	Rank.	Remarks.
"A" SQUADRON—*continued.*		
2070. Adams, John Francis Henry	Trooper	
1926. Andrews, Arthur Edgar	,,	
3486. Boyd, Edgar Reginald	,,	
1877. Broderick, John Francis	,,	
1838. Byers, Samuel	,,	
1909. Barsley, Robert Edward	,,	Corporal, 4.8.01; Sergeant, 7.4.02
1919. Browne, George Charles	,,	
1922. Baxter, Samuel Lyson	,,	
848. Butler, Allan	,,	
1962. Banks, William	,,	
1940. Bates, Frederick Charles	,,	
2060. Batson, James Valentine	,,	
2086. Bayliss, Harry Monsell	,,	Died, 3.3.02
422. Beatty, H. J.	,,	Sergeant, 6.5.01; Sqn. Quartermaster-Sergeant, 21.11.01
3474. Boreland, Archibald	,,	
3472. Boreland, John King	,,	
3528. Brown, John	,,	
2009. Bosler, John Martin	,,	
1430. Cronin, George Martin	,,	
2121. Coleman, Robert Parmenas	,,	
2091. Crago, Alexander Henry	,,	
2101. Carbine, Sydney Edward	,,	
2018. Carroll, William John	,,	
791. Clark, Ernest	,,	
1972. Christiansen, David	,,	
2017. Donehue, Edward Douglas	,,	
2006. Dwyer, Edward	,,	
1729. Downes, James Sterling	,,	
916. Duke, Sidney William	,,	
1976. Davidson, Douglas Gordon	,,	
2104. Dennis, Walter	,,	
1944. Easey, Fred	,,	
3466. Faulkner, Wellington Thomas	,,	
1821. Farrar, Wilfred	,,	
2339. Farren, Thomas	,,	
1957. Frazer, Walter George	,,	
1859. Flynn, Lancelot	,,	
2074. Grant, William Francis	,,	
1963. Grant, Duncan	,,	
2093. Gleeson, James	,,	
1874. Gibb, Adam Murray	,,	
1927. Hall, David	,,	
2123. Hayes, James Henry	,,	
2079. Hughes, John James	,,	
785. Haines, Edward	,,	
817. Heine, Claude Frederick Henry Russel	,,	
1974. Hodgson, Harold Hepworth	,,	
2088. Hockings, Albert Charles	,,	
965. Hird, Thomas	,,	
2015. Holmes, Hector	,,	
1908. Hayman, William Boyne	,,	
157. Hodgson, Charles Christopher	,,	
1980. Jolliffe, Frederick	,,	
1894. Jones, John Jonathan	,,	
1990. Kirby, George Amos	,,	
2081. Keys, Herbert Alonzo	,,	

Nominal Roll—*continued.*

No. and Name.	Rank.	Remarks.
"A" Squadron—*continued.*		
1832. Lane, Henry Joseph	Trooper	
2094. Locke, Charles Lionel	,,	
1933. Linden, John	,,	
1903. Lennon, James	,,	Corporal, 7.1.02
1823. McKenzie, Joseph	,,	
1924. McPherson, Neil	,,	
2128. McCook, John George	,,	
1959. McClymont, Donald Norman	,,	Corporal, 11.12.01
1907. McBride, Hugh	,,	
1420. McAlpine, George Rodney	,,	Corporal, 15.3.02
1994. McCrossin, John Alexander	,,	
1998. Morris, Major	,,	
1942. Mason, Robert	,,	
1633. Macdonald, Alexander John	,,	
3397. O'Niell, William	,,	
2110. Noakes, William Arthur	,,	
2089. Nelson, William Wallace	,,	
2120. Ogilvie, Charles	,,	
2118. Ogilvie, William Ernest	,,	
1991. Penny, William Henry	,,	
2004. Pallier, Joseph	,,	
879. Pallier, William	,,	
2188. Page, Frank	,,	
2090. Richards, Robert Harris	,,	
2080. Richards, Alfred	,,	Killed, 7.2.02
2139. Reynolds, James	,,	
903. Rogers, Thomas Bray	,,	
926. Ryan, Henry Patrick	,,	
1472. Russell, Frederick Winter	,,	Died, 12.10.01
2339. Scott, Sidney	,,	
1941. Smith, James	,,	
2009. Smythe, David George	,,	
2072. Strickland, Joseph	,,	
775. Stitt, Samuel George	,,	
1998. Simeon, Frederick Taylor	,,	
988. Townsend, Thomas Edward	,,	
1987. Trafford, Robert	,,	
2013. Turner, Frederick Thomas	,,	
3451. Turner, William	,,	
3465. Tarlington, Herbert	,,	
2008. Williamson, John	,,	
2067. Willmette, Fulton Barvelle Hooper	,,	
2068. White, Edward Charles	,,	
2092. Wilson, Robert Percy	,,	
2124. Williams, William	,,	
107. Williams, Alexander Joseph	,,	
868. Wright, Gilbert	,,	
1925. Wood, Thomas Henry	,,	
2011. Wood, William	,,	Died, 26.11.01
2145. Weston, Norman	,,	
"B" Squadron.		
Burnage, Granville John	Major	Invalided to Australia
Scobie, Robert	Lieutenant	
Moffitt, William	2nd Lieutenant	
Bullock, Charles Cyrus	,,	

Nominal Roll—*continued.*

No. and Name.	Rank.	Remarks.
"B" SQUADRON—*continued.*		
1455. Black, William Henderson	Sqn. Sergeant-Major	
1045. Berry, William Ronald Stuart	Quartermaster-Sergeant	
2134. Gordon, Alec. Gilligar	Sergeant	*Vide* Promotions
1789. Taylor, Albert Bentley	,,	
991. Scott, Arthur	,,	Sqn. Quartermaster-Sergeant, 21.12.01
2130. Miller, John William	,,	
2199. Edge, Percy	Corporal	Sergeant, 4.3.02
101. Nossiter, Robert Anthony	,,	
816. Smith, David Owen Leslie	,,	
1239. Stevens, Edwin Marcus	,,	
2058. Smith, Cecil Selwyn	,,	Sergeant, 12.11.01; died, 27.7.02
1750. Zalinski, Ernest	,,	Sergeant, 18.6.01
1370. Greer, Hubert	,,	
1141. Armstrong, William Alec	Trooper	
1375. Armstrong, Frederick	,,	
1340. Armstrong, John Frederick	,,	
1537. Allingham, Alfred John	,,	Died, 28.5.01
1410. Amy, Alexander	,,	
1471. Appleby, Ernest Albert	,,	
1102. Browne, Robert James	,,	
1059. Butcher, Albert Henry	Shoeing-smith	
1462. Barlow, John	Trooper	
2132. Besnard, Jack	Sergeant	Sqn. Sergeant-Major, 24.1.02
2137. Berriman, John Arthur	Trooper	
2135. Berriman, William Thomas	,,	Died, 7.3.02
2180. Brennan, John Thomas	,,	
2173. Boyd, George	,,	
1802. Brophy, Arthur Matthew	,,	
1918. Brown, Henry Austin	,,	
2349. Bradley, Francis	,,	
1440. Clark, Alfred	,,	
1208. Cheetham, John George	,,	Invalided, Australia, arr. 16.9.01
2160. Cowham, Joseph Ashton	,,	
2190. Casey, John Herbert	,,	
2172. Carpenter, Stanley Leslie	,,	
1090. Douglass, James Edward	,,	
1857. Doull, Lewis	,,	
2078. Duffy, Joseph	,,	
2175. Dowdell, William Joseph	,,	Lance-Corporal, 7.4.01
2102. Eurell, Patrick	,,	
1101. Fraser, Alexander	,,	
2149. Farrell, Patrick	,,	
913. Geering, George	,,	
947. Grinstead, Frederick Albert	,,	
1030. Guthrie, Robert	,,	
1867. Gilbert, William Henry	,,	
2147. Graham, George Ethelbert	,,	
1036. Horton, Sydney James	,,	
931. Hehir, John	,,	
1891. House, Herbert	Corporal	Sergeant, 4.5.02
1895. Howard, Edgar Vincent	Trooper	
2133. Hill, William	,,	
1743. Harper, Frederick	,,	
2119. Isbister, Robert Crighton	,,	
1020. Jennings, Charles Edward	,,	

Nominal Roll—*continued.*

No. and Name.	Rank.	Remarks.
"B" SQUADRON—*continued.*		
2103. Joyce, Reginald Milton	Trooper	
2502. Johnson, Alfred	,,	
2201. Kingsmill, Stanley Horace	,,	
2138. Kerton, George Findon	,,	
2183. Kinsela, William Joseph	,,	
2254. Kidson, William Giles	,,	
2557. Kenna, Edgar Aloysius	,,	
1025. Lucas, John	,,	Corporal, 7.4.02
1869. Lucey, Joseph Alphonsus	,,	
2169. Lewis, William Herbert	,,	
1899. Ley, Wallace George	,,	
1005. Mason, Ernest	Bugler	
1825. McWilliam, Thomas	Trooper	
1860. Mead, Herbert Ernest	,,	
836. McDermott, Leslie William Hugh	,,	
1865. Medaris, James	,,	
1914. Martin, Charles Gilbert	,,	
2142. McHugh, William	,,	
2165. Moore, Frederick George	,,	Corporal, 18.6.01
2136. McArthur, George Kirby	,,	
2000. McIntyre, Charles William	,,	
1917. Nixon, Percy	,,	
2167. Norton, James	,,	
1843. Neale, Thomas William	,,	
944. O'Neil, Martin	Shoeing-smith	
2063. O'Keefe, John Ernest	Trooper	Missing, 22.9.01
1798. Parkinson, Thomas	,,	
1781. Powell, Thomas Hilton	,,	Died, 7.12.01
1887. Pugh, Walter Charles	Bugler	
1893. Porter, Arthur James	Trooper	
2087. Pedrotta, Hugh	,,	
2198. Pretty, Edgar Gerald	,,	
2194. Phillips, Peter	,,	
3433. Rolleston, Samuel	,,	
1099. Roy, Robert James	,,	
1890. Royal, Thomas	,,	
940. Rock, Michael	,,	
2415. Robinson, John	,,	
1757. Sterritt, Albert George	,,	
1810. Sutherland, Donald	Farrier-Sergeant	
1822. Smith, Matthew	Trooper	
1751. Stannard, Frank Alfred	,,	
1684. Sandy, Hastings	,,	
1826. Seard, Jasper James	,,	
1896. Simpson, Edgar Whetter	,,	
2166. Sales, Frank Francis	,,	
984. Thompson, Harry Miller	,,	
987. Taylor, Ernest Alexander	Shoeing-smith	
912. Taylor, Leslie	Trooper	
1094. Tubberty, James Peter	,,	Corporal, 4.5.02
3387. Turvey, Robert	,,	
1836. Twiss, James	,,	
2085. Toovey, John	,,	
1827. Uren, James	,,	
1892. Urquhart, Frederick Ernest	,,	
108. Waine, Arthur Henry Charles	,,	
1804. Walker, Edward William	,,	
1745. Walton, William	Saddler	

Nominal Roll—*continued.*

No. and Name.	Rank.	Remarks.
"B" Squadron—*continued.*		
1718. Walsh, Thomas	Trooper	
1792. Wallace, William Richard	,,	
1904. White, Frederick	,,	
1900. Wilkes, Harold John	,,	
1920. Wallace, John	,,	
2107. Watson, William	,,	
2109. Westling, Charles	,,	
2164. Walton, Richard	,,	
2140. Whitehead, Roland George	,,	
2777. Whitton, Robert	,,	
2178. Wallace, Charles John	,,	
3421. Wyburn, Ernest	,,	
1142. Yarrow, Stanley Australia	,,	
"C" Squadron.		
Chapman, Alfred Ernest	Captain	
Thompson, John Alfred Malbon Windeyer	Lieutenant	
Treatt, Graham Voller Dalhousie	,,	Died, 14.5.01
Meecham, Maunsel Richard	,,	
2203. Black, John	Sergeant-Major	
1164. Adrien, John James	Quartermaster-Sergeant	
1286. Hopkinson, Ernest Fairhall	Farrier-Sergeant	*Vide* Promotions
1177. Rice, Joseph	Sergeant	
1358. Hodson, John George	,,	
369. Cranfield, T.	Sergeant	Sqn. Sergeant-Major, 13.9.01
1041. Crawford, James	,,	
1120. Brodie, Alexander Neil	,,	
1347. Ryan, James Alfred	Corporal	
1445. Coulter, Arthur Ernest Cody	,,	Sergeant, 18.6.01
1063. Grimson, Charles	,,	
1061. Meeham, Reginald Pentland	,,	Sergeant, 11.12.01
305. Sharp, Henry	,,	Sergeant, 13.10.01
1190. Nathan, Vernour Vigne	,,	Lance-Sergeant, 4.8.01
1132. Lupton, George Darlow	Lance-Corporal	
1217. George, Sydney	,,	Corporal, 7.2.02
728. Huggins, Edgar Idem	Shoeing-smith	
928. Forrester, Landen Edgar	,,	
1501. Doyle, Andrew Edwin	,,	
1421. Daley, Joseph	Saddler	Died, 5.2.02
2399. Moore, Frederick John	Bugler	
1910. Worthington, Sydney Herbert	,,	
1592. Angel, Henry George William	Trooper	
1606. Allen, Francis Frederick	,,	
1279. Byrne, Frank Patrick	,,	
1155. Berry, Samuel Magor	,,	
1083. Brooks, Thomas Henry	,,	
1114. Butler, James Richard	,,	
1046. Boot, William Alfred Sydney	,,	
1134. Benham, George	,,	
1144. Bing, William Edward	,,	
1219. Byron, Robert Walter Herbert	,,	
1236. Beckhouse, Hume Phillip	,,	
1150. Black, Henry Alexander	,,	
2098. Braggs, Joseph Orton	,,	
2099. Braggs, Phillip	,,	

Nominal Roll—continued.

No. and Name.	Rank.	Remarks.
"C" SQUADRON—continued.		
2979. Burrows, George Walter	Trooper	
1131. Coveney, Norbert Francis	,,	
1248. Collins, Edward Thomas	,,	
1153. Carter, Arthur G. P.	,,	
1520. Coates, George Donald	Lance-Corporal	Corporal, 29.12.01; Farrier-Sergeant, 9.1.02
1456. Cullen, Fred	Trooper	
1425. Chapman, Alfred	,,	
1230. Cox, Carl Mackenzie	,,	
1066. Daley, Roland Earl	,,	
1498. Duckering, Bertie	,,	
1284. Doak, William	,,	
1938. Donn, Edwin	,,	
49. Dickson, George Jennings	Corporal	Farrier-Sergeant, 13.4.01; died 9.1.02
1359. Davis, Charles Austin	Trooper	
1461. Dwyer, Stanley Arthur	,,	
1140. Eagle, Alfred	,,	
1535. Elliott, Arthur	,,	
1077. Fuller, Charles John	,,	
1505. Ford, Leslie	,,	
1322. Fletcher, John	,,	
1232. Goode, Norman William	,,	
1198. Gilligan, Ambrose Gregory	,,	
1292. Gimbert, Alfred	,,	
1373. Godber, Arthur Davis	,,	
1289. Gallegos, Albert	,,	
1412. Gafney, Edward	,,	
52. Gosper, Charles John	,,	Drowned, 26.11.01
1111. Huggins, Aubrey William	,,	
1497. Harris, William John	,,	
1242. Howard, Alan Aubrey	,,	
1126. Huff, John Edward	,,	
1367. Hamilton, David Alexander	,,	
1417. Hodge, Philip	,,	
1534. Hands, Alfred	,,	
1451. Heuchman, Godfrey Davanant	,,	Corporal, 14.2.02
1044. Innes, James	,,	
2153. Jones, Herbert Ernest	,,	
1392. Jones, Harry	,,	
1252. Jacobs, James Henry	,,	Died, 16.8.01
1234. Jackson, William Charles	,,	Died, 4.2.02
1329. Johnston, William Joseph	,,	
1087. Kerwin, John	,,	
1499. King, William	,,	
1496. King, John Thomas	,,	
1407. Kelly, Henry	,,	
1159. Mullaly, Thomas	,,	
1160. McNamara, Bernard Francis	,,	
1688. Maher, James Peter	,,	
1354. McInnes, Charles Hugh	,,	
1341. Murray, Hugh Miller	,,	
1146. Mullarkey, Michael	,,	
1285. Morris, Joseph Brabazon Cavendish	,,	
1439. McKenzie, Samuel Francis	,,	
1401. Meyers, Frederick	,,	
1092. Monish, William	,,	

Nominal Roll—continued.

No. and Name.	Rank.	Remarks.
"C" Squadron—continued.		
1652. Montgomery, Harry	Trooper	
302. Muston, John	,,	
1149. Neville, James	,,	
1127. Nolan, Patrick	,,	
2213. Nicholson, Walter Herbert	,,	
1091. O'Donnell, Michael Thomas	,,	
1384. O'Brien, William	,,	
1230. Oborn, Harry	,,	
2061. Olive, Albert Richard	,,	
1364. Patton, Arthur Charles	,,	
1118. Pounceby, Thomas	,,	
1254. Patterson, Richard	,,	
2182. Patison, Douglas Fawcett	,,	
1161. Rodgers, Nichol H.	,,	
1039. Ray, Walter Thomas	,,	
1084. Ray, Herbert George	,,	
2227. Ray, Daniel	,,	
1297. Ryan, Walter John	,,	Corporal, 8.4.02
3699. Shannon, Ernest Herbert	Corporal	Sergeant, 4.5.02
1113. Strickland, Norman Hylton	Trooper	
1128. Sams, Edwin	,,	Died, 1.2.02
1073. Short, Thomas	,,	
1148. Stevens, Bertram Alfred	,,	
1312. Skinner, Samuel William	,,	
1326. Stead, Alfred Mansfield	,,	
1897. Stanton, Major	,,	
2177. Smith, Pierce Seall	,,	
2191. Sheens, Henry	,,	Corporal, 11.12.01
1011. Taylor, Frank Harold	,,	
406. Taplin, George Richard	,,	
1336. Tubnor, Arthur Leopold	,,	
2239. Thomson, Daniel Watson	,,	
1500. Woollett, William Henry	,,	
1403. Welsh, Thomas	,,	
2141. Williams, Joseph Robert	,,	
1776. Williams, Joseph	,,	
2005. Watt, E. C.	,,	Corporal, 5.6.01
1400. Young, John	,,	
"D" Squadron.		
Heron, Reginald Manning	Captain	
Macdonald, Peter	Lieutenant	
Stewart, John	,,	
Doudney, Guy L. H.	,,	
3651. Moore, James William	Sqn. Sergeant-Major	
1328. Gordon, Robert Charles	Quartermaster-Sergeant	
729. Chapman, William	Sergeant	Sqn. Sergeant-Major, 18.6.01
264. Smith, Sydney James	,,	Died, 12.10.01
1452. Walsh, John Edmund	,,	
3186. Kelaher, Charles Richard	Corporal	Sergeant, 7.12.01
484. Lees, Thomas James	,,	
1256. Isaacs, Edward Rogers	,,	
1475. Richardson, James Fraser	,,	
1458. Reardon, John James	,,	Sergeant, 15.10.01

Nominal Roll—*continued.*

No. and Name.	Rank.	Remarks.
"D" Squadron—*continued.*		
1246. McClurg, Thomas William Wallace	Corporal	Sergeant, 5.6.01
1253. Gribble, Benjamin Martin	Lance-Corporal	Corporal, 27.8.01
1460. McShane, William	,,	Corporal, 19.12.01
1261. Alexander, William John	Trooper	
1790. Alley, Reginald Ralph	,,	
1753. Atkinson, Walter John	,,	
1744. Billot, John Ernest Edward	Farrier-Sergeant	Farrier Quartermaster-Sergeant 18.6.01
932. Bennett, Thomas	Trooper	
2214. Bell, George	,,	
2126. Benton, Charles	,,	
1224. Cain, William	,,	Corporal, 13.11.01
1196. Clark, John	Shoeing-smith	
1258. Cufley, Alfred Edward	Trooper	Corporal, 14.1.02
1218. Coady, James Cornelius	,,	
1235. Cameron, Peter	,,	
2152. Cook, Douglass	,,	
2822. Carmichael, David Joseph	Bugler	
2606. Clarke, Edwin James	Trooper	
2607. Clarke, William Francis	,,	
2266. Cooper, William Lockwood	,,	
2250. Dobbie, Edward Ernest	,,	
2357. Donnelly, James Thomas	,,	
1244. Fox, Thomas Patrick	,,	
685. Fulton, Joseph	,,	
1946. Fitzhenry, Patrick Michael	,,	
2069. Foulkes, Horace Saker	,,	
1197. Gregory, Percy Hobart	,,	
1391. Gander, George	,,	Died, 19.3.02
1570. Gallagher, John William	,,	
1231. Griffin, Patrick	,,	
2257. Gilliard, Henry James	,,	
2367. Garven, John Hill	,,	
3464. Gosper, Frederick William	,,	
1228. Hayes, Norman Richard	,,	
1379. Hodgson, Samuel George	,,	
1226. Hiscock, Edward	,,	
1486. Hornby, Richard Johnson	,,	
1415. Holswick, Cyril James	,,	
2274. Higgins, Frederick Harold	,,	
2111. Harper, Charles Ernest	,,	
2402. Hines, Herbert Edward	,,	
2297. Hammond, Alexander Henry	Shoeing-smith	
17. Hart, William John	Trooper	
1320. Hiscock, John	,,	
1018. Illsley, James William	,,	
1508. Jeffrey, William John	,,	Corporal, 16.5.01
1463. Jones, Albert Henry	,,	
2218. Jones, Edwin Walter	,,	
2208. Kelly, Joseph Augustine	,,	
1307. Lane, Henry Herbert	,,	
1270. Lefoe, Joseph Edward	,,	Died, 6.6.01
1193. Larden, Albert Victor	,,	
1402. Lyon, Alfred Rudolph	,,	
1324. Long, Walter	,,	
1511. Lovett, Herbert P.	,,	
1437. Luscombe, John	,,	

Nominal Roll—*continued.*

No. and Name.	Rank.	Remarks.
"D" Squadron—*continued.*		
2259. Leeks, Bazel	Trooper	
2376. Logan, Ernest Charles	,,	
1560. Mitchell, Stanley Oswald	,,	
1540. Mobberly, George Edward Cyril	,,	
1360. McCann, John	,,	
1677. Murtagh, Alexander Patrick	,,	Invalided, Australia, arr. 2.8.01
1564. Mallon, Alexander	,,	
1509. Murphy, Oliver Charles	,,	
1442. Murphy, Hubert	,,	
1424. McGrath, John	,,	
1485. Mason, Thomas	,,	
1318. McLaughlin, John	,,	
1278. Matthews, William John	,,	
1180. Maunsell, George	,,	
2182. McMahon, Mortimer Patrick	,,	
2234. Morris, Thomas	,,	
1556. Parr, Samuel Herbert	,,	
1298. Prussian, George Henry	,,	Corporal, 17.10.01
2236. Penny, Charles Maxian	,,	
2205. Perrin, Benjamin George	,,	
2401. Plucknett, Edgar Ewart	,,	Corporal, 13.10.01
2385. Plummer, Frederick Charles	,,	
1381. Read, Thomas Rolls	,,	Corporal, 17.12.01
1339. Rolfe, Anthony	,,	
1454. Roach, James Samuel	,,	
1523. Rollason, William	,,	
1305. Reid, James	,,	
2240. Ruane, Valentine	,,	
2253. Rogers, Oliver John	,,	
2241. Rush, Charles Orr	,,	
1383. Smith, Matthew George	Saddler	
1519. Stuart, Charles Gordon Grant	Trooper	
1521. Sullings, Leonard Oinan	,,	
1465. Starr, William	Farrier	Farrier-Sergeant, 15.6.01
1516. Seymour, George Robert	Trooper	
1614. Stewart, Ewen Gore	,,	
1533. Stubbings, William James	,,	
2273. Simpson, George Achison	,,	
1399. Smith, William Samuel	,,	
3218. Smith, Lennox Walter Macquarie	Sergeant	Sqn. Sergeant-Major, 4.5.02
2400. Sims, Douglas	Trooper	
2328. Shearston, Albert Edward	,,	
1262. Smith, James	,,	
1222. Thompson, George	,,	
1240. Wilson, Sidney	,,	
1295. Walsh, Arthur Patrick	,,	
1272. West, Charles Henry	,,	
1187. Wilson, John	,,	
1223. Wells, Thomas	,,	
1571. Whitbread, Joseph William	Shoeing-smith	
1314. Wilson, Charles	Trooper	Died of wounds, 8.9.01
1484. Waters, Joseph	,,	
1408. Wall, George Henry	,,	
1755. Ward, Bert Thomas	,,	
2252. Williams, Walter Henry Burns	,,	
3393. Wickham, James	,,	
3388. Wells, Edward	,,	
1186. Young, Ernest	,,	
2209. Young, James	,,	

Nominal Roll—*continued.*

No. and Name.	Rank.	Remarks.
" E " SQUADRON.		
Stokes, Stanley Frederick	Captain	
Palmer, Roger Wingham	Lieutenant	
Drummond, Dugald	2nd Lieutenant	
Price, David C. W. Howell	,,	
Thomas, Henry	,,	
2276. Norman, George William	Sqn. Sergeant-Major	
1738. Staunton, John Baston	Quartermaster-Sergeant	
1645. Barnes, Alfred Henry	Sergeant	
1624. Nowland, Archibald Frederick	,,	
1586. McNabb, Edward James	,,	Sqn. Sergeant-Major, 27.8.01
1558. Sturgeon, Thomas	,,	Died, 7.1.02
2708. Brees, William Angelo	Sergeant-Trumpeter	*Vide* Promotions
595. Nixon, Horace P. C.	Corporal	
1358. Hodson, J. G.	,,	Lance-Sergeant, 4.8.01
1638. Wilson, Edgar A.	,,	Sergeant, 5.3.02
1566. Thomas, Arthur Samuel	,,	
1631. Ellwood, Thomas Frederick	,,	
1413. Johnson, Eugene Vigil	Lance-Corporal	Corporal, 4.5.02
1676. Kimmorley, Alfred Ernest	Corporal	Sergeant, 4.5.02
1590. Brims, John Augustus	Lance-Corporal	
1557. Gallagher, John Edward	,,	
3696. McPherson, Kenneth Ross	Sergeant-Farrier	
1625. Garretty, Charles Arthur	Shoeing-smith	
2325. Clifford, Charles	,,	
1512. Arneil, Thomas John	Trooper	
1528. Alexander, William	,,	
1603. Ashton, James Richard	,,	
1700. Allison, Charles Walter	,,	
1353. Bewley, Isaac	,,	Died, 1.2.02
1429. Brodie, John Alexander	,,	
1687. Bentley, Charles Arthur	,,	
1575. Brooker, Samuel George	,,	
1663. Budd, Alfred Joshua	,,	
1681. Bremner, Kenneth	,,	
1446. Ballinger, Frederick	,,	
1685. Britton, Charles	,,	Corporal, 24.1.02
1824. Braddock, John	,,	
2291. Boulais, Joseph Pierce	,,	
2475. Best, John	,,	
2316. Clements, Henry Edward	,,	
2222. Clarke, William	,,	
2280. Clout, Samuel	,,	
1666. Cameron, Norman Victor	,,	Died, 19.2.02
1716. Capper, William Thomas	,,	
1834. Cameron, Thomas John	,,	
1594. Caddow, Ernest Arthur	,,	
1581. Claffey, Michael Farrell	,,	
1702. Campbell, Andrew McKenzie	,,	Died, 21.5.01
1698. Carey, Frank	,,	
1642. Culshaw, Richard Mathew	,,	
1703. Cumming, Ralph	,,	Died, 6.5.02
3460. Cains, S.	,,	
1513. Donnolly, Albert Aloysius	,,	
1507. Dwight, Joseph	,,	
1735. Dowling, Edward Thomas	,,	

Nominal Roll—*continued.*

No. and Name.	Rank.	Remarks.
"E" SQUADRON—*continued.*		
1741. Doak, James	Trooper	
1818. Dransfield, Reginald Gustavus	,,	
1808. Donovan, Edward	,,	
2321. Dunn, John James	,,	
1754. Evans, John Frederick	,,	
1628. Ellwood, John Edmond	,,	
1708. Edgar, Joseph Henry	,,	
1600. Farr, Herbert Alfred	,,	
1690. Francis, George Cuthbert	,,	
1682. Flannery, James	,,	
1730. Foley, William	,,	
1608. Fowler, James George	,,	
1731. Griffiths, William	,,	
1514. Green, Henry Burnet	,,	
1531. Gibson, Thomas Henry	,,	
1629. Graham, William Abell	,,	Saddler-Sergeant, 18.6.0
1695. George, Reginald St. John	,,	
2504. Gormley, Alfred Patrick	,,	
1767. Hoffman, Albert Everard	,,	
1840. Hawes, William Robert	,,	
1723. Hutchinson, John	,,	
1574. Hayes, Michael	,,	
1699. Harris, Charles William	,,	
1691. Hughes, Hugh Llewellyn	,,	Lance-Corporal, 30.6.01, Corporal, 24.1.02
2283. Hall, William John	,,	
2324. Hurley, Martin	,,	
2510. Hill, Christopher	,,	
2505. Hill, William Henry	,,	
2454. Hughes, George Hugh	,,	
1831. Jarman, Thompson	,,	
1525. Jones, William	,,	
2278. Jones, Gustavus Travers	,,	
2262. Jones, John	,,	
1794. Kain, George Charles	,,	
1727. Knobel, Jacob	,,	
1579. Kelly, James	,,	Corporal, 29.5.02
1634. Kilpatrick, James Alexander	,,	
1276. Keady, Patrick John	,,	
1431. Lynch, Archibald	,,	
1758. Lane, Henry Walter	,,	
1787. Lett, Septimus George	,,	
1595. Lenon, Herbert William	,,	
1626. Loader, Arthur Charles	,,	
2982. Lawler, E. A.	,,	
1814. Mulholland, C. H. S.	,,	
1752. McKee, W.	,,	
1807. McLean, D. J. F.	,,	
1773. McGirr, M.	,,	
1778. Macdonald, D.	,,	
1553. Morrison, R. J.	,,	
1543. Millar, J.	,,	
1538. Mundy, T. C.	,,	
1696. Macgregor, H. H.	,,	
1704. McIntyre, J.	,,	
3244. McIntyre, R. D.	,,	
2217. McKeown, J.	,,	

Nominal Roll—*continued.*

No. and Name.	Rank.	Remarks.

"E" SQUADRON—*continued.*

No. and Name.	Rank.	Remarks.
1602. Montgomerie, William	Trooper	Died, 30.5.02
2587. Maxwell, William Morley	Corporal	Sergeant, 5.5.01 Despatches, *London Gazette*, 29.7.02. D.C.M.
2588. Mitchell, George Absalom	Trooper	
1661. Neill, Ernest Edwin	,,	
2264. Norwood, William John	,,	
1583. Pleydell, Herbert Leslie	,,	
1714. Parkinson, Frederick William	,,	
2322. Richardson, George Henry Archibald	,,	
1597. Ryan, John Henry	,,	
1529. Reid, Duncan Robert	,,	
569. Sutton, James Duncan	Corporal	Sergeant, 5.5.01 Invalided, Australia, arr. 23.9.01
1707. Sherringham, Joseph George	Trooper	
1683. Smith, George William	,,	
1662. Spedding, Richard	,,	
1705. Stevenson, Thomas	,,	
2231. Stoneham, Samuel John	,,	
1582. Turner, Henry Ernest	,,	
2277. Thompson, James William	,,	
1706. Thompson, Arthur	,,	
1371. Treweek, Stacy Beauchamp	,,	
1544. Williamson, Percival Claude	,,	
1527. Wilson, Charles Brinsley	,,	

DRAFTS.

No. and Name.	Rank.	Remarks.
Bennett, Alfred Joshua	Major	From 1st N.S.W. Mounted Rifles
Simmons, Turton English	Lieutenant	
Hindmarsh, Henry Ernest	,,	
Richards, Thomas Robert	,,	
Greenwell, George Malcolm	2nd Lieutenant	
Dart, George Anderson	,,	
Shaw, Lindsay John	,,	
Holland, Frederick Henry	,,	
Brooke, Herbert Edward	,,	
Binstead, John William	,,	
2676. Anker, Alexander	Trooper	
2823. Arkinstall, Ernest	,,	
2813. Antill, Elwyn D.	Sergeant	
2948. Anderson, Charles Alexander	Trooper	
2954. Anderson, John Edward	,,	
3020. Amor, Edgar Walter	Lance-Corporal	Corporal, 4.5.02
3007. Allingham, John Worthington	Trooper	
3140. Atherton, Alfred Joseph	Farrier	Farrier-Sergeant, 18.6.01
3174. Anderson, John	Trooper	
3317. Armfield, George Henry	,,	
3682. Amos, Douglas James	,,	
3718. Anderson, Walter Charles	,,	
3647. Alfreds, Walter	,,	
2672. Broomham, William George	,,	
2658. Bell, Wentworth L.	,,	
2681. Bonham, William James	,,	
3360. Bowen, James	,,	
3010. Banan, Richard	,,	Corporal, 13.11.01
3345. Billin, Joseph	,,	
3367. Bush, Edgar William	,,	
3046. Brodie, William Walter	,,	

C.4720.

Nominal Roll—*continued*.

No. and Name.	Rank.	Remarks.
DRAFTS—continued.		
3293. Baker, Arthur	Lance-Corporal	Corporal, 13.11.01
3083. Booth, William	Trooper	
3143. Boyd, John	,,	
3144. Buckley, Albert	Sergeant	Sqn. Sergeant-Major, 4.5.02
3065. Beel, Jacob	Trooper	
3213. Bamford, Charles	,,	
3429. Byrne, Bernard	,,	
3060. Boyd, Robert	,,	
2754. Banks, Charles Henry	Corporal	
2747. Budgen, Charles Mathews	Trooper	
2359. Brackenrigg, Trevelyn Lyons	,,	
2909. Bailey, Edward	,,	
2913. Browning, Edgar	Corporal	Sergeant, 4.5.02
3270. Bayliss, George Walter	Trooper	
3278. Boardman, William John	,,	
3307. Burt, Samuel	,,	
3577. Brown, Albert Jordan	,,	
3605. Bowerning, John Ernest Pushman	,,	
3720. Birchall, Kingsley Charles	,,	
3550. Brien, Frank Albert	,,	
345. Clare, William Everard	Sergeant	
2997. Crouch, Joseph Blackstone	Trooper	
3009. Cameron, Charles	,,	
3008. Clancy, Michael Vincent Bond	,,	
3134. Coady, John	,,	
3115. Collins, William Henry	,,	
3150. Cleary, George Valentine	,,	
3073. Cardwell, Walter Francis	,,	
3034. Clancy, John Patrick	,,	
2746. Chambers, James Richard	,,	
2799. Cranney, Augustine Joseph	,,	
2810. Conlon, Sidney	,,	
2824. Clements, James Lionel	,,	
2843. Carter, Frank Anderson	,,	
2923. Cone, Charles William	,,	
2865. Clarke, James Stephens	,,	
2939. Cates, William Henry Bright	,,	
3281. Clark, Frederick Henry	,,	Corporal, 19.12.01
3276. Caban, James Valentine	,,	
2554. Clayton, Charles Clifford	,,	
2740. Carroll, George	,,	
2720. Cameron, Richard	,,	
3581. Corbett, Joseph	,,	
3620. Carew, William	,,	
3687. Claffey, James	,,	
3690. Crane, Henry Ernest	,,	
3704. Capner, Ernest Edgar	,,	
2918. Davis, Thomas Charles	,,	
2793. Davis, George Frederick	Lance-Corporal	
2818. Duggan, Edward	Trooper	
2758. Dein, Walter Henry	,,	
2815. Davis, Thomas Theodore	,,	
2871. Dando, James Hayes	,,	
3265. Dryburgh, Robert Samuel	,,	
3399. Downs, Matthew	,,	
3003. Davis, Robert Edward	,,	
3346. Doherty, Patrick Joseph	,,	

Nominal Roll—continued.

No. and Name.	Rank.	Remarks.

DRAFTS—continued.

No. and Name.	Rank.	Remarks.
3350. Dhu, James	Trooper	
3413. Dix, Arthur Edward	,,	Corporal, 18.6.01
3706. Dobson, Sydney	,,	
3700. Davies, Arthur Irwin	,,	
3243. Elliott, James	,,	Corporal, 14.2.02
3524. Edwards, Arthur Robert	,,	Corporal. Invalided, Australia, arr. 16.9.01
2744. Elliott, Leslie Herbert Daniel	,,	
2770. Ellis, William Charles	,,	
3332. Elliott, Edwin Robert	,,	
3272. Everett, John William	,,	
2974. Francis, Edward Frederick	,,	
3062. Fuller, William Walter	,,	
3359. Fryer, Edwin Henry	,,	
3185. Fitton, William James	Bugler	
3276. Field, George	Trooper	
3541. Goode, William Norman	,,	
3698. Goodsell, David	,,	
2589. Gordon, Wilfred	Lance-Corporal	
3389. Grumbleton, William Charles	Trooper	
3398. Gamble, George Henry	,,	
3403. Gibbons, John	,,	
3335. Goold, Charles	,,	
3342. Glen, Herbert Anthony	,,	
3366. Graham, Ross	,,	
2845. Garrard, Richard Milton	,,	
3228. Gray, James Mackey	Corporal	Sqn. Quartermaster-Sergeant, 9.12.01; died, 28.1.02
3266. Green, George Henry	Trooper	
2862. Griffith, Albert Edward Murhall	,,	
3719. Gardner, Norman Leslie	,,	
2567. Hulks, William Robert	,,	
3405. Hughes, George	,,	
3015. Hudson, John	,,	
3001. Hartwell, Percy	,,	
3081. Hargreaves, William John	,,	
3039. Halliday, William	,,	
3104. Hamilton, Joseph	,,	
2797. Hill, Alexander James	,,	
2938. Hansby, William	,,	
2924. Humphries, Walter Vincent Victor	,,	
3303. Heydon, George Thomas	,,	
3308. Horsley, Ernest Francis	Lance-Corporal	
2157. Hall, Ellis	Trooper	
3639. Hobson, Frank Foley	Bugler	
3593. Hart, Ernest Watkins	Sergeant-Major	
2774. Jones, Henry	Trooper	
2763. Jones, Hugh Trevor	Corporal	Died, 19.12.01
2892. Jones, Alfred Richard	Trooper	
2893. Jones, Arthur	,,	
3299. Joyce, Albert John	,,	
3298. Johnson, William Reuben	,,	
3400. Jackson, Thomas	,,	
3119. Jones, Robert	,,	
3118. Johnson, David Charles	Corporal	Sergeant, 24.1.02
3091. Johnston, Christopher Robert	Trooper	
3334. Jones, Edward	,,	

K 2

Nominal Roll—continued.

No. and Name.	Rank.	Remarks.
Drafts—continued.		
3162. Kuchler, William	Lance-Corporal	
3061. Knight, Harry	Trooper	
3125. Kelly, William	,,	
3114. Keady, Michael	,,	
2895. Kemp, Hugh William	,,	
2765. Kerr, Arthur Andrew	,,	
2857. Knight, Charles Goswell	,,	
2884. King, Thomas	,,	Corporal, 29.1.02
3274. Kay, Serle Francis	,,	
3318. Kennedy, Roger	,,	
3273. Knight, Alfred Thomas	,,	
2511. Langrish, William John	,,	
1390. Le Seur, Leslie Joseph	,,	
3426. Low, Charles	,,	
3126. Lewis, John William Nelson	,,	
3019. Lloyd, Charles James	,,	
3717. Lewis, Albert Ernest	,,	
3055. Lesslie, Thomas Arthur	,,	
2971. Littley, Henry James	,,	
3068. Lloyd, Herbert Brisbane	,,	
3411. Lithgo, Charles Edward	,,	
2782. Lane, James Augustus	,,	
2838. Laiken, Charles	,,	
3652. McCauley, Norman	,,	Died, 27.12.01
3710. McLachlan, William Henry	,,	
2524. Moore, Charles Herbert	,,	
2671. McGowan, James	,,	
3188. Mould, William George	,,	
784. Moore, William Archibald	Corporal	
2702. McClelland, William	,,	
2817. McPhee, Hector	Trooper	
3422. Morton, James Reginald	,,	
435. Mulhean, W. J.	Sergeant	Squ. Sergeant-Major, 4.5.02
3005. McDiarmid, Donald Angus	Trooper	
3056. McAllister, Thomas Romanus Patricia	,,	
3054. Muntz, Albert Henry	,,	
1766. McMahon, John	,,	
3070. Mason, Walter	,,	Missing, 22.9.01
3096. Mackenzie, John Thomas Evendon	,,	
3037. McIntyre, Alexander Donald	,,	
2686. McDonnell, George Alfred	,,	
3035. Mackenzie, Archie	,,	
3373. McDermid, William Duncan	,,	
2756. Martin, Thomas Henry Alexander	,,	
2776. Mackenzie, Hugh Fraser	,,	
2775. Manusa, Alfred Aristides	Lance-Corporal	Corporal, 24.1.01
3722. Musgrave, Thomas Thomson	,,	
2804. Marshall, James Gregory	Trooper	
2759. McLachlan, Bertie	,,	
2888. McIvor, Bernard Francis	,,	
2875. McClung, Norman Hunt	,,	
2942. Meredith, Thomas Frederick	,,	
2936. McMahon, Thomas James	,,	
3292. McFarlane, Stephen	,,	Corporal, 23.11.01
3282. McAlier, Frank	,,	

Nominal Roll—*continued.*

No. and Name.	Rank.	Remarks.
DRAFTS—*continued.*		
3315. Matthews, James P.	Corporal	
3200. May, David	Trooper	
3597. McCormack, Michael	,,	
2690. Nicholson, William	Sergeant	Sqn. Sergeant-Major, 21.11.01
3117. Nichols, Frederick George	Corporal	
3057. Nash, James	Trooper	Corporal, 13.11.01
3988. Nash, William Henry	,,	
3030. Nichols, Edward Joseph	,,	
3124. Neilan, John	,,	
3240. Neary, John Francis	,,	Died, 3.2.02
3560. Norris, Arthur George	,,	
2640. Owens, John	,,	Lance-Corporal, 12.11.01
3102. O'Brien, Michael	,,	
3024. Oborn, Benjamin Henry	,,	
3354. Owen, Lewis	,,	
3631. Parker, Hilton Thomas	,,	
2731. Parrish, Lewis Cornelius	,,	
2856. Paine, Alfred	Corporal	Sergeant, 23.11.01
2917. Pollock, Walter	Trooper	
2903. Powers, Nicholas	,,	
2940. Peck, William Edward	,,	
2983. Probert, Albert Henry	Sergeant	Sqn. Quartermaster-Sergeant, 18.6.01
2949. Page, William	Trooper	
3132. Porter, John	,,	Corporal, 4.12.01
3128. Porter, Edward	,,	
3340. Piggott, William Henry	,,	
2745. Pateman, Stephen Thomas	,,	
3211. Pederson, Anthony	,,	
2981. Quetcher, Phillip Alexander	,,	
3669. Rowland, William Henry	,,	
2632. Ryan, Lawrence	,,	
2701. Robbins, George	,,	
3522. Richards, Robert	,,	Died, 19.2.02
3022. Rasmussen, Joseph	,,	
3362. Robinson, Harry	,,	
3288. Rolfe, Joseph	,,	
2967. Rankin, William Edward	Lance-Corporal	
3325. Ridgway, John	Trooper	
3313. Sheffield, William Arthur	,,	
2617. Seymour, William Christopher	,,	
2629. Smith, William James	,,	
2576. Stevens, Raymond Douglas	,,	
2796. Stafford, Herbert Edwin	,,	
2581. Smith, Donald Sidney	Farrier	Farrier-Sergeant, 14.2.02
2786. Smith, Alfred Edgar	Trooper	
2894. Smith, George William	,,	
3279. Strauss, Albert Edward	,,	
2882. Simpson, William	,,	
2868. Shearman, Cecil Woodford	,,	
2891. Smith, William Oscar	,,	
2958. Stynes, Clement Joseph	,,	
2919. Stewart, Hugh Hill	Corporal	
3311. Stevenson, Harry John	Trooper	
3314. Stevenson, Joseph	,,	
3302. Stacey, Archibald Sidney	,,	
3264. Seach, William	,,	

Nominal Roll—continued.

No. and Name.	Rank.	Remarks.

DRAFTS—continued.

No. and Name.	Rank.	Remarks.
3027. Spurway, Robert William	Corporal	Sergeant, 13.9.01
2989. Smith, William Frank	Trooper	Corporal, 13.11.01
537. Stapleton, John Patrick	,,	Lance-Corporal, 13.11.01
3063. Shepherd, William Henry	Sergeant	Sqn. Sergeant-Major, 4.5.02
3086. Summerfield, Ernest Alfred	Trooper	
3017. Swan, Charles James	,,	
3031. Simmons, John Thomas	Corporal	Sergeant, 13.11.02
3064. Savage, Albert Alexander	Trooper	
2998. Stratton, William Henry	,,	
3138. Sedgwick, William Mervyn	Lance-Corporal	Corporal, 13.9.01
2625. Toogood, George Charles	Corporal	
2711. Tipper, Thomas James	,,	
2718. Trollope, Harry Reginald	Trooper	
3601. Townsend, Arthur	,,	
2771. Tindall, Clarence Edward	,,	
2766. Turner, Charles Thomas Elisha	,,	Died, 21.3.02
2931. Tenison, George	Sergeant	Sqn. Sergeant-Major, 3.4.01
3275. Tuddenham, Herbert Lionel	Trooper	
3052. Teague, Linden	,,	
3103. Trinder, Albert Ernest	,,	
3079. Thomas, William Edward	Lance-Corporal	
3349. Tiers, Bernard	Trooper	
3285. Thomson, Arthur Clarence	,,	
3286. Underwood, Septimus Richard	,,	
2649. Williams, James Bennett	,,	
3544. Webb, Arthur Ernest	,,	
3582. Whitford, James Henry	,,	
3344. Wheeler, James	,,	
2755. Walker, William	,,	
2816. Westwood, Frank	,,	
2834. Weston, William Charles	,,	
2916. Williams, Albert	,,	
2872. Wells, Edward Henry	,,	
3347. Westwood, Benjamin	,,	
2911. Woodhill, Herbert Stanley	,,	
3296. Whitty, Upton	,,	
3109. Walker, John William	,,	
2987. Walkling, Charles John	,,	
2878. Woodward, Fred Hewlett	,,	
2975. Williams, Edward	,,	
3078. Wickham, John William	,,	
3067. Whye, Alfred	,,	
3041. Whyn, James John	,,	
3130. Wetherall, Harry	,,	
3051. Wetherall, William Thomas	,,	
3153. Wells, George Taylor	Sergeant	
2427. Wonson, Albert Monday	Farrier-Sergeant	

MACHINE GUN SECTION.

No. and Name.	Rank.	Remarks.
Schwabe, James Harry	Lieutenant	
Hill, Norton Gordon	,,	
2381. Taylor, Murray Joseph	Sergeant	
3469. Clark, George Henry James	,,	Sqn. Sergeant-Major, 4.5.02
2460. Hopkinson, Victor Burchall	Corporal	Sergeant, 18.6.01
2362. Arnold, Herman Augustus	,,	

Nominal Roll—*continued.*

No. and Name.	Rank.	Remarks.
MACHINE GUN SECTION—*continued.*		
3526. Easterbrook, William Herbert	Lance-Corporal	Corporal, 10.9.01
2748. Strachan, William	,,	
2446. Lawrence, Charles William	,,	Corporal, 18.6.01
2448. Rosten, Charles	,,	
2520. Blake, Sydney Frederick Joseph	Gunner	Lance-Corporal, 4.4.02
2470. Booker, Charles Edward	,,	
2474. Bratt, William	,,	
2475. Best, John	,,	
2441. Browne, Henry Frederick	,,	
2438. Chisholm, Thomas John	Driver	
2437. Chisholm, Alexander John Henry	,,	Died, 15.9.01
2432. Clutton, William Frederick	,,	
2444. Cox, James	Gunner	
1573. Deane, Morgan Robert Fitzmaurice	Driver	
2541. Fitzgerald, Martin Henry	,,	
2479. Gallagher, John	Gunner	
2469. Glover, William Ralph	,,	Invalided, Australia, arr. 23.9.01
2411. Hattersley, Arthur Edward	,,	
2519. Heapy, Frederick James	Bugler	
2454. Hughes, George Hugh	Driver	
2449. Jaggers, George	,,	
2486. Kebblewhite, Daniel	,,	
2378. Pederson, John James	,,	
2439. Philp, Ernest Alfred	,,	
891. Pitt, Oswald Saunders	Gunner	Died, 18.12.01
2023. Sharpe, Paul	,,	
2452. Westbury, William	,,	
1658. Williams, John Heitman	,,	
2457. Wilson, Alfred Ernest	Driver	
2468. Wyer, James	,,	

THIRD NEW SOUTH WALES IMPERIAL BUSHMEN.
Record of Regiment.

THE Third New South Wales Imperial Bushmen was a regiment formed at Klerksdorp, Transvaal, on 4th May, 1901, from drafts consisting of 230 officers, N.C.O.'s and men intended for the New South Wales Imperial Bushmen and the Citizens' Bushmen; but owing to these two regiments being under orders for home, the men were formed into a separate regiment under the command of Major Hon. Rupert Carington.

This regiment was attached to Lieut.-Colonel E. C. Williams D.S.O's. Column, and took part in all the engagements of that Column (with the exception of Karanafontein), and during the year marched over 4,000 miles.

During the months of May, June, July, August, September, and part of October, they operated in the Western Transvaal, where numerous captures of prisoners, wagons, and stock were made. On 24th October, the Column left Klerksdorp and went to Eastern Transvaal, where they took part in General Bruce Hamilton's operations, resulting in heavy loss to the enemy.

In January, 1902, another squadron was formed from Australians, recruited in Cape Town, and in February another was formed, bringing the strength of the regiment up to over 500 men.

On 4th May, 1902, some of the time-expired men of the regiment proceeded home in the transport *Ansonia*; but many of the men and nearly all the officers volunteered for further service.

A draft of 200 Riverina bushmen, raised by Mr. J. S. Horsfall, of Widgewa, New South Wales, and the volunteers for further service, joined the regiment at Klerksdorp, Transvaal, and were attached to Colonel Williams' Column, who again was operating in the Western Transvaal, and served until peace was declared in June, 1902.

The regiment sailed from Durban, Natal, under the command of Lieut.-Colonel Hon. Rupert Carington, in the transport *Drayton Grange*, 12th July, for Sydney, calling *en route* at Albany and Melbourne, and arriving 11th August.

Promotions of Officers.

Rank and Name.		To what Rank Promoted.	Date.	Remarks.
Major	Carington, The Hon. Rupert, D.S.O.	Lieut.-Colonel	15th May, 1902	
,,	Browne, H. H.	Major	Transferred from 2nd Mounted Rifles	
Lieutenant	Mylne, C. E.	Captain	22nd June, 1901	From N.S.W. Imperial Bushmen
,,	Thompson, A. C.	,,	,, ,,	,, ,,
,,	Doyle, R. D.	,,	,, ,,	,, ,,
,,	Caines, H.	,,	,, ,,	,, ,,
Sq. S.M.	Clarke, W.	Lieutenant	,, ,,	,, ,,
,,	Fortescue, F. A.	,,	,, ,,	,, ,,
Sq. Q.M.S.	Dixon, J.	,,	,, ,,	,, ,,
,,	Dransfield, A.	,,	,, ,,	,, ,,
Sergeant	McGregor, N. A.	,,	,, ,,	,, ,,
,,	Thomas, H. W.	,,	,, ,,	,, ,,
,,	Kelly, G. E. E.	,,	,, ,,	,, ,,
,,	O'Shea, W. A.	,,	,, ,,	,, ,,
,,	Newlands, R. G.	,,	,, ,,	,, ,,
,,	Russell, C. S.	,,	,, ,,	,, ,,
,,	Hyndman, J. A	,,	,, ,,	,, ,,

Promotions of Officers—*continued*.

Rank and Name.		To what Rank Promoted.	Date.	Remarks.
Sergeant	Sheppard, H. H.	Lieutenant	22nd June, 1901	From N.S.W. Imperial Bushmen
,,	Ranclaud, E. B.	,,	,, ,,	
R.S.M.	Scott, E. J. C.	,,	4th November, 1901	
,,	Porter, J. W.	,,	5th May, 1902	
Sq. S.M.	Moy, P. J.	,,	,, ,,	
Sq. Q.M.S.	Finlayson, —	,,	,, ,,	From 2nd Mounted Rifles
Sq. S.M.	Wintle, —	,,	,, ,,	,, ,,
,,	Taylor, T. G.	,,	,, ,,	,, ,,
Sergeant	Smith, R.	,,	,, ,,	,, ,,
R.Q.M.S.	Ritchie, A. M.	Lieutenant and Qtr.-Master	,, ,,	

For promotions of N.C.O.'s and men *vide* Nominal Roll.

SERVICES.

24th May, 1901.—After a running fight of 12 miles at Koldersdrai, and a skirmish, captured 30 waggons, 19 prisoners, 600 cattle, and 1,000 sheep; 2 Boers killed.

20th August, 1901.—Near Wolmanstadt, after a 50-miles night march, ending with a skirmish, captured 100 waggons, with stock; many Boers wounded and taken, and several killed.

23rd September, 1901.—Broke up Boer meeting between De la Rey and Kemp at Doornkop.

25th September, 1901.—Pursued up the Toilani Valley, after a skirmish at the head of the pass. Boer ambulances were allowed to take their wounded, and were full. Pursued the enemy until night.

27th October, 1901.—Engaged Muller's commando at the head of Kaultsfont Nek, and took 64 prisoners.

20th February, 1902.—Attacked Trichart's commando, and took 164 prisoners.

The regiment was present at General Bruce Hamilton's operations from Ermelo in January and February, and also took part in the "drives" subsequently, until mobilization at Standerton in April, 1902. It was in a "drive" under Lieut.-General Sir Ian Hamilton from Klerksdorp in May, 1902. Only three men of the regiment were taken prisoners during the twelve months it was in the field.

EXTRACT FROM FORCE ORDERS, KLERKSDORP, 4TH JUNE, 1902, PARA. 2.

The following telegram from Sir Ian Hamilton is published for information :—

"I am ordered to revert to my post as Chief of Staff, Head-Quarters, and must, therefore, bid you and your gallant troops farewell. Convey to them my very good wishes, and congratulate them from me in having played so distinguished a part in the closing scenes of the South African War, whereby I am convinced you have contributed in a very special degree to the termination of hostilities."

EXTRACT FROM FORCE ORDERS, KLERKSDORP, 16TH JUNE, 1902, PARA. 3.

The officer commanding Column wishes to express his regret at the departure of the 3rd New South Wales Imperial Bushmen, who have been under his command for over a year in the field, during which time they have gained an excellent reputation for the good work they have done, and well maintained the credit of Australian soldiers. He wishes all ranks a safe voyage and good luck.

Letter from Major-General R. S. Fetherstonhaugh.

To Colonel Carington, officers and men of the 3rd Imperial Bushmen.

Now that you are on your way home I wish to thank you for your good and gallant services in the Western and Eastern Transvaal, especially for your gallant conduct in the Tellawa Valley, and also for the capture of the Middelberg commando on the Bothasberg in the Eastern Transvaal.

I have written to General Hutton, commanding troops in Australia, and sent him a diary of the combats and skirmishes in which you took part, and I have told him that your conduct was most gallant, and that no night or day march was too long for you.

I hope that your friends and relations in New South Wales will hear of your distinguished services, and that you will live many years to wear the medal that you have so well earned. I shall always look back to the time I served with the 3rd Imperial Bushmen with the greatest pride, and I wish you a good voyage and a happy and prosperous future.

R. S. FETHERSTONHAUGH,
Major-General.

War Services of Officers.

Carington, Lieut.-Colonel Hon. R.—Served in Grenadier Guards; was acting-adjutant with the 1st battalion 24th regiment in the Zulu war, 1879, and afterwards with Mounted Infantry in Colonel Baker Russell's Column. Medal with clasp. Operations in Cape Colony, Orange River Colony, and Transvaal, May, 1901, to May, 1902. Despatches, *London Gazette*, 29th July, 1902. D.S.O. *London Gazette*, 31st October, 1902. Queen's Medal with five clasps. C.V.O.

Brown, Major H. Hamilton.—*Vide* Imperial Bushmen.

Most of the officers served previously either with Imperial Bushmen, Citizen's Bushmen, 1st or 2nd Mounted Rifles, or other Contingents, for which *vide* those Contingents. The service now reckoned was, generally, as stated.

Most of the N.C.O.'s and men had also served with previous details,

Mentioned in Despatches and Honours Awarded.

Carington, Major the Hon. Rupert.—Mentioned in despatches, *London Gazette*, 29th July, 1902. Companion Distinguished Service Order. *London Gazette*, 31st October, 1902. Commander Royal Victorian Order.

Middleton, Captain C. E.—Mentioned in despatches, *London Gazette*, 29th July, 1902.

Dixon, Lieutenant J.—Mentioned in despatches, *London Gazette*, 29th July, 1902.

Fortescue, Lieutenant F. A.—Mentioned in despatches, *London Gazette*, 29th July, 1902.

The following officers were mentioned by the Commander-in-Chief, **Lord Kitchener** :—

    Major H. Hamilton Brown, D.S.O.

    Lieutenant **F. A. Fortescue.**

Officers who had not had previous service received the Q.M. with clasps.

Nominal Roll.

No. and Name.	Rank.	Remarks.
Carington, The Hon. Rupert (D.S.O.),	Lieut.-Colonel	*Vide* War Service.
Hamilton-Browne, Henry (D.S.O.)	Major	
Mylne, Graham Ernest	Captain	From Imperial Bushmen
Lee, Charles Albert	,,	From 1st and 2nd Mounted Rifles
Thompson, Albert Charles	,,	From Imperial Bushmen
Middleton, Cecil Ernest Albert	,,	From 1st and 2nd Mounted Rifles
Newman, Joseph	,,	From 1st and 2nd Mounted Rifles
Johns, Digby Noy	,,	From Citizens' Bushmen
Cairnes, Herbert	,,	From Imperial Bushmen
Doyle, Richard Dines	,,	From Imperial Bushmen
Foreman, Henry Clifton	Chaplain	
Southey, Clifford Melville	Lieutenant	From 1st Mounted Rifles
Breckenridge, Thomas William	,,	From New South Wales Lancers
Wearne, Albert Ernest	,,	From 1st and 2nd Mounted Rifles
Battye, Reginald Richard	,,	From 1st and 2nd Mounted Rifles
Carter, William B.	,,	From New South Wales Lancers
D'Arcey, Arthur Ernest	,,	From 1st Australian Horse
Bowden, Thomas Leslie	,,	From 1st N.S.W. Mounted Rifles
Cameron, Donald	,,	From 1st Australian Horse
Blossey, Francis Victor	,,	
Buchanan, Donald	,,	
Cox, Carl Mackenzie	,,	From Citizens' Bushmen
de Mestre, Hurtle	,,	From Citizens' Bushmen
Clarke, Walter	,,	From Imperial Bushmen
Robinson, George Masfield	,,	From Imperial Bushmen
Dixon, James	,,	Adjutant, from Imperial Bushmen
Mills, Charles George	,,	From 1st and 2nd Mounted Rifles
Dransfield, Andrew	,,	From Imperial Bushmen
Fortescue, Francis Arthur	,,	From Imperial Bushmen
McGregor, Neild Archibald	,,	From Imperial Bushmen
Hyndman, James Archibald	,,	From Imperial Bushmen
Thomas Herbert	,,	From Imperial Bushmen
Wearne, William Stewart	,,	From Imperial Bushmen
Kelly, George Edward Eccleston	,,	From Imperial Bushmen
O'Shea, William Andrew	,,	From Imperial Bushmen
Newlands, Robert George	,,	From Imperial Bushmen
Russell, Christopher Stuart	,,	From Imperial Bushmen
Sheppard, Norman Hugh	,,	From Imperial Bushmen
Coggins, Harry Clark	,,	From Imperial Bushmen
Macdonald, Hugh	,,	From Imperial Bushmen
MacFarland, George	,,	From Imperial Bushmen
Gjedsted, Charles	,,	From Imperial Bushmen
Suttor, Harold Bruce	,,	From 1st and 2nd Mounted Rifles
Scott, Edward J. C.	,,	From Imperial Bushmen
Taylor, John Sinclair	,,	
Evans, Tyrell George	,,	From Victorian Mounted Rifles
Wintle, William Edward	,,	From 1st and 2nd Mounted Rifles
Taylor, Thomas George	,,	From Imperial Light Horse, and 2nd Mounted Rifles
Ranclaud, Ernest Boscawen	,,	From Imperial Bushmen
Smith, Rex	,,	From 1st and 2nd Mounted Rifles
Finlayson, George James	,,	From 2nd Mounted Rifles
Ritchie, Andrew McLean	,,	Quartermaster
Porter, James William	Reg. Sergeant-Major	Despatches. *London Gazette*, 29.7.02 D.C.M. *Vide* "Promotions"
Kelk, William Brookes (W.O.)	,,	From Sqn. Sergeant-Major, 5.5.02
3208. Ahern, Hugh Jordan	Shoeing-smith	
5001. Anderson, Aleck Tonkin	Sqn. Sergeant-Major	

Nominal Roll—continued.

No. and Name.	Rank.	Remarks.
103. Annison, Christopher Isaac	Sergeant	Sqn. Sergeant-Major, 6.7.02
3. Ashworth, Henry	,,	
2527. Allingham, George Robert	Corporal	Invalided, Australia, 2.11.01
5. Adams, George Oxley	Trooper	
105. Allen, Thomas	,,	
178. Allen, James Edward	,,	
104. Alsopp, Thomas Ernest	,,	
102. Angel, Arthur Edward	,,	
216. Armstrong, William Alexander	,,	
215. Algie, Ernest	,,	
217. Anderson, William James	,,	
2682. Ackland, James	,,	
3645. Adams, Ernest Joseph	,,	
3647. Alfreds, Walter	,,	Invalided, Australia, 21.9.01
3214. Alderton, John	,,	Invalided, Australia, 13.10.01
2569. Arndell, Douglas James	,,	Killed in action, Naauwpoort, 10.10.01
2394. Armstrong, Thomas William	,,	
3160. Ashwin, Arthur Edward	,,	
3262. Avery, Michael Albert	,,	
4001. Aines, Charles	,,	
2632. Ackerman, Lawrence	,,	
2117. Armstrong, Frederick	,,	
2234. Apps, William	,,	
2631. Adrian, Laurence J.	,,	
2634. Anderson, John Leslie	,,	
2084. Archer, George	,,	
3063. Andrews, Arthur	,,	
1093. Adams, Frederic Charles	,,	
1261. Alexander, William John	,,	
180. Bartley, Mic. Squire	Shoeing-smith	
1183. Butler, Reuben Joseph	,,	
2076. Burcher, Henry Stephen	Sqn. Quartermaster-Sergeant	
6001. Beatty, Henry John	,,	
664. Blunden, Henry	Sergeant	W.O. Sup. Clerk, Staff, 1.11.01
3206. Bollard, Arthur Benjamin	Corporal	Lance-Sergeant, 1.9.01; invalided, Australia, 14.1.02
5008. Balmer, Archibald	,,	
946. Byrne, Frederick Beaumont	,,	
2611. Blunt, Richard Henry Thomas	Sergeant	Saddler-Sergeant, 24.5.02
3206. Bord, Albert	Corporal	Lance-Sergeant, 1.9.01
4. Brown, George	,,	
158. Baldwin, James Henry	,,	Sergeant, 6.8.02
181. Bennett, John	,,	
9. Button, Horace Dacre	Lance-Corporal	Corporal, 6.8.02
3125. Barnett, George	,,	
900. Barnett, William	Trumpeter	
44. Burton, Hubert James	Trooper	
106. Bloxham, George Arthur	,,	
11. Bell, James William	,,	
161. Barnes, Henry	,,	
112. Bain, John	,,	
118. Barrass, William Alfred	,,	
179. Birkin, William	,,	
111. Bower, James	,,	
162. Brackenrigg, George Royden	,,	
157. Brading, John	,,	
2075. Banks, A. E.	,,	
2652. Britain, P. W.	,,	

Nominal Roll—*continued.*

No. and Name.	Rank.	Remarks.
326. Barnes, William Arthur	Trooper	
218. Bell, Francis Charles	,,	
36. Burton, A.	,,	
220. Barnett, George B.	,,	
3635. Bartlett, George	Corporal	
2640. Bulmer, Charles	Trooper	
276. Basterfield, George	,,	
277. Basterfield, William	,,	
278. Buhler, Norman	,,	
2643. Bremner, John Alexander	,,	
2641. Brandon, George	,,	
2271. Baird, John	,,	
2649. Blakeney, Edward John	,,	
2642. Bowers, James	,,	
2630. Barnes, Thomas	,,	
2637. Brown, Frederick Arthur	,,	
288. Bracey, Stanley Paget	,,	
319. Beaumont, James	,,	
5114. Ball, Thomas Alfred	,,	
2635. Blencowe, Arthur William	,,	
5115. Baskerville, Frederick William	,,	
326. Barnes, William	,,	
2728. Brown, Alfred George	,,	
2081. Brown, Horatio	,,	
3010. Ball, George Alfred	,,	
1619. Bridges, William Frederick	,,	
2700. Black, Edward John	,,	
2600. Barnes, William John	,,	
2619. Bellamy, John Leo	,,	Died of wounds, 9.9.01
3419. Berriman, Herbert	,,	
2560. Bennett, Arthur Jules	,,	
3666. Black, Hector Norman	,,	Died of enteric, Pretoria, 12.2.02
3239. Biggs, Arthur John Thomas	,,	
3075. Blackman, Alfred Valentine	,,	
2701. Barrett, Thomas William	,,	
3601. Boyd, Frederic Joseph	,,	
2389. Boles, George Livingstone	,,	
2694. Bouchier, Patrick James	,,	
3204. Box, Joseph Stanley	,,	
2428. Broughton, George	,,	
2675. Boyd, Edward	,,	
3566. Brown, James	,,	
1304. Barnes, William Arthur	,,	
3456. Braddon, John	,,	
3250. Brown, John	,,	
3224. Brown, Frederic Charles	,,	
3550. Brien, Frank Albert	,,	Invalided, Australia 14.1.02
3644. Brodie, Victor Algin	,,	Lance-Corporal, 10.4.02
3542. Bridges, William	,,	
3641. Bresnahan, Edward Patrick	,,	
2412. Bruce, John Albert	,,	Invalided, Australia, 14.1.02
2644. Black, George	,,	
2599. Burns, George Herbert	,,	Died of enteric, 22.7.01
2645. Burrows, William	,,	
2739. Burns, Robert James	,,	
2563. Burns, John	,,	
3258. Bourke, Stewart	,,	
23. Braun, Benjamin Henry	,,	
20. Bord, William	,,	
4002. Bosworth, George	Shoeing-smith	

Nominal Roll—continued.

No. and Name.	Rank.	Remarks.
1120. Bailey, William	Trooper	
226. Blake, David John	,,	
2269. Bethune, Arthur	Corporal	
2280. Blake, John	Trooper	
2283. Barron, William	,,	
2286. Booth, Alfred Edward	,,	
3224. Brown, Frederick	,,	
67. Bowden, William Campbell	,,	
318. Clibborn, George Holmes	Corporal	O.R. Sergeant, 24.5.02
1. Cobden, John	Shoeing-smith	
549. Carter, William Henry	Sqn. Sergeant-Major	
2606. Carter, Samuel Henry	,,	
76. Chenery, Albert	Sqn. Quartermas-Sergeant	
137. Campbell, Arthur Leslie	Corporal	R. Quartermaster-Sergeant, 10.7.02
18. Clarke, George	Sergeant	
39. Cooper, James	,,	
2208. Coulls, Arthur Frederick	Trooper	Sergeant, 10.1.02
2607. Cairnes, Charles Beresford	,,	Sergeant, 16.4.02
294. Cummings, Edwin Joseph	Sergeant	
281. Cue, Henry	Farrier-Sergeant	
120. Clarke, John Wishart	Lance-Sergeant	
207. Chandler, Albert Henry	,,	
107. Craft, John Ebenezer	Corporal	
2522. Clutton, Walter Henry	,,	Invalided, Australia, 4.11.01
2681. Connors, Stephen Henry	,,	Sergeant, 16.4.02
110. Crockett, Edward	,,	
1237. Collins, John	,,	
68. Clyde, Fred	,,	Lance-Sergeant, 6.8.02
291. Capell, Claude Charles	Lance-Corporal	
10. Carter, George	Trooper	
2. Clyde, James	,,	
33. Cross, Sydney James	,,	
86. Carter, Henry	,,	
87. Campbell, Charles Ernest	,,	
6. Curtain, John James	,,	Corporal, 6.8.02
119. Cartis, Charles	,,	
187. Carey, James Joseph	,,	
160. Cartwright, Michael Augustine	,,	
146. Church, Edward Charles	,,	
15. Clarke, Charles Leo	,,	
196. Collins, Henry James	,,	
221. Cockroft, Arthur William	,,	
2654. Cullen, Francis	,,	
322. Cullen, George Henry	,,	
2098. Clive, George Arthur	,,	
301. Collings, Morton	,,	
207. Conway, James	,,	
2222. Caldwell, William	,,	
1718. Cruwys, George Walter	,,	
1010. Cox, Robert	,,	
2660. Cole, Henry M. V.	,,	
223. Coupland, John Robert	,,	
224. Copeland, Edward	,,	
226. Coady, William	,,	
665. Cox, George Henry F.	,,	
2225. Coppock, Herbert Fitzroy	,,	
268. Cullinan, James	,,	

Nominal Roll—*continued*.

No. and Name.	Rank.	Remarks.
261. Colley, Henry	Trooper	
2658. Campbell, James B.	,,	
2669. Cochrane, James	,,	
2667. Crawford, Thomas	,,	
2656. Crawford, John	,,	
1022. Costigan, Michael W.	,,	
878. Crayshaw, William	,,	
2666. Cakebread, Thomas	,,	
3545. Campbell, Patrick Frederick	,,	
3632. Campbell, Charles Ernest	,,	Invalided, Australia, 7.2.02
3247. Campbell, Henry Albert	,,	
3714. Cantwell, Michael James Joseph	,,	
2659. Camper, William Valentine	,,	
105. Carney, George	,,	
2609. Carter, Henry	,,	Invalided, Australia, 9.11.01
3234. Cavanough, William	,,	
3563. Christie, John	,,	
3558. Clarke, William Robert	,,	
2590. Cliff, Albert	,,	Invalided, Australia, 12.10.01
3245. Cliff, George	,,	Invalided, Australia, 6.2.02
2232. Clifford, James	,,	Invalided, Australia, 14.11.01
3200. Clough, John William	,,	Died of enteric, Ventersdorp, 17.10.01
2598. Connelly, Joseph	,,	
2655. Cusker, Alfred	,,	
3599. Connell, Henry	,,	
2662. Crawford, Charles	,,	Died of enteric, Middelberg, 18.3.02
3248. Cook, Mountford	,,	
2494. Cooper, Oswald Hunter	,,	
2333. Collins, James William	,,	
2329. Cross, George	,,	
3161. Cross, William Edward	,,	
2592. Cross, George Albert	,,	Invalided, Australia, 24.2.02
2523. Crossland, Wright	,,	
2521. Crummy, Arthur Albert	,,	
2525. Cunningham, Alexander	,,	
509. Carroll, Michael	,,	
1926. Catt, Alfred John	,,	
516. Coulter, Edward Albert	,,	
4005. Cook, George Paul	,,	
28. Collins, Charles	,,	
4004. Cross, Henry S.	,,	
4003. Clarke, James R.	,,	
2306. Craig, Albert	,,	
2309. Claye, Charles	,,	
2671. Crockett, Lawrence	,,	
2670. Cockbill, William Ernest	,,	
297. Chalmers, Charles William	,,	
2535. Dowsett, Frederick Ernest	O.R. Sergeant	
193. Duffy, Victor Sherman	Sqn. Sergeant-Major	
115. Donahoe, Herbert Bede	Corporal	
296. Denman, William Rowan	,,	
117. Dartwell, George Orion	,,	
7. Dunstan, Bert	Trooper	
3002. Daley, Herbert	,,	
99. Donald, James	,,	
2074. Davis, Percy	,,	
123. Davis, David Ellis	,,	

Nominal Roll—continued.

No. and Name.	Rank.	Remarks.
124. Dutton, Edwin James	Trooper	
228. Donovan, James	,,	
229. Dalton, Charles Sydney	,,	
230. Davis, Henry Cradoc	,,	
2667. Daley, Charles	,,	
2678. Dreux, David	,,	
2676. Douglas, John Charles	,,	
2672. Dobson, Leslie	,,	
290. Driscoll, William	,,	
3112. Dunn, Arthur	,,	
9776. Dugan, Edward	,,	
116. Davis, George	,,	
3197. Deane, Albert George	,,	
3711. Downes, James Stirling	,,	Died of enteric, Pretoria, 27.12.01
2709. Doy, James	,,	
3167. Done, Percival Frederick	,,	
2409. Dovey, Thomas Freman	,,	Invalided, Australia, 21.11.01
2405. Donaldson, Leslie Sinclair	,,	Invalided, Australia, 11.12.01
2366. Donkin, Ernest Francis	,,	Lance-Corporal, 16.4.02
3625. Dunning, Walter Reuben	,,	Invalided, Australia, 11.12.01
3684. Dunrich, Ellis	,,	
2594. Dunn, Thomas Henry	,,	Invalided, Australia, 14.11.01
2623. Durbridge, John	,,	
4006. Dubbe, James	,,	
1106. Duncan, James Francis	,,	
9776. Deegan, Henry James	,,	
4007. Dodds, James S.	,,	
4049. Davidson, Charles	,,	
2314. Davidson, Edward	,,	
2331. Dale, Frank	,,	
2679. Darke, Edward	,,	
3463. Delaney, James	,,	
5116. Duncan, James Francis	,,	
2562. Evans, George Fitzroy	Shoeing-smith	
479. Evans, James	Sqn. Quartermaster-Sergeant	
8. Emery, James Thomas	Sergeant	
1210. Elliott, Jobe Robin	Farrier-Sergeant	
5118. Essler, Alexander	Saddler-Sergeant	
121. Edmunds, Thomas	Trooper	
122. Espie, Beecher	,,	
231. Eather, James	,,	
5117. Eade, Henry Hazell	,,	
3468. Eastcott, Henry Ernest	,,	Invalided, Australia, 9.9.01
3568. Ebery, William James	,,	
3598. Edwards, Garrett John	,,	
2573. Egan, Samuel Robert	,,	
556. Edwards, Arthur	,,	Invalided, Australia, 7.11.01
306. Edwards, Louis Ernest	,,	
125. Evans, Edgar	,,	
2633. Furber, Frederick William	,,	Sergeant, 4.5.01
1212. Fisher, James	Farrier Sergeant	
234. Fitzell, Sydney Martin	Saddler-Sergeant	
2693. Fenton, James Thomas	Trooper	Corporal, 6.12.01
2392. Felts, David	Corporal	Sergeant, 18.2.02 Despatches, London Gazette, 20.7.02
108. Fitzgerald, Andrew	,,	
209. Ferrier, John Meredith	,,	
13. Findlay, James George	Trooper	
12. Friend, James Jacob	,,	
176. Fenn, Enoch Elijah	,,	

Nominal Roll—*continued.*

No. and Name.	Rank.	Remarks.
798. Fitzhardinge, William	Trooper	
190. Fleming, John	,,	
128. Friend, William	,,	
2685. Finn, William	,,	
232. Farrant, Thomas Montague	,,	
2680. Farrant, William	,,	
233. Fisk, Walter	,,	
2684. Freebairn, Richard	,,	
18. Fitzgerald, Alfred	,,	
38. Fletcher, George	,,	
5127. Fletcher, Henry Leonard	,,	
3341. Freyburg, Oscar	,,	
298. Freyburg, Paul Milton	,,	
296. Finn, William	,,	
5119. Ford, John	,,	
2083. Foggan, Charles	,,	
3610. Farrell, John	,,	
2727. Fallon, Richard	,,	
3665. Fitzgerald, Harry	,,	
3530. Fitzpatrick, Michael	Lance-Corporal	Corporal, 10.4.02
3709. Fitz, John Henry	Trooper	
2495. Flack, Frederick	,,	Sqn. Quartermaster-Sergeant, 24.3.02
2633. Foley, Patrick	,,	
3141. Frazer, Harold Campbell	,,	Invalided, Australia, 11.12.01
494. Fitzpatrick, James	,,	
4008. Fitzgerald, William	,,	
3454. Glover, Philip John	Sergeant	
1934. Graham, John Joseph	,,	
5005. Gibb, Henry James	,,	
229. Gardiner, James	Corporal	
127. Galvin, Alfred George	Lance-Corporal	
2697. Gandy, William	Trooper	
313. Gibson, William	,,	
2704. Goss, Arthur	,,	
308. Grassham, James	,,	
18. Grundy, Sydney	,,	
303. Gregory, Charles	,,	
17. Green, James	,,	
293. Guy, Roland	,,	
88. Goodman, Albert	,,	Lance-Corporal, 6.8.02
2547. Garforth, Leonard	,,	
14. Gardiner, Robert	,,	
2701. Goodrich, Henry	,,	
130. Gibbs, Henry Edmond	,,	
2705. Gray, Henry	,,	
147. Gittoes, Ernest Claude	,,	
2088. Gilham, Thomas	,,	
171. Graham, Arthur James	,,	
199. Grimshaw, John William	,,	
2687. Gilchrist, Robert Arthur	,,	
235. Gilchrist, Robert John	,,	
236. Glennon, John Francis	,,	
237. Grier, Charles	,,	
238. Gillanders, George	,,	
2702. Green, William	,,	
3452. Gartlan, John	,,	
3231. Garling, George Frederick	,,	
3229. German, John Phillip	,,	
3230. German, Harold Arthur	,,	

C.4720.   L

154

Nominal Roll—continued.

No. and Name.	Rank.	Remarks.
2664. Gilligan, Alfred Charles	Trooper	
2674. Glennie, Herbert Frederick	,,	
2696. Griffiths, Arthur	,,	
3541. Goode, William Norman	,,	Invalided, Australia, 8.3.02
3713. Groom, Alick Everett	,,	
3207. Grant, John	,,	
2352. Gray, Edward	,,	
4010. Gray, Henry	,,	
2706. Gladding, John	,,	
4011. Gay, Edward	,,	Died of enteric, Ermelo, 26.1.02
2335. Griffiths, George	,,	
2339. Griffiths, Percival O.	,,	
2341. Gardiner, Henry Walter	,,	
4016. Hackett, Alfred John	Corporal	
2281. Humphries, Thomas Joseph	Sergeant	
317. Hales, Matthew D.	,,	Reg. Quartermaster-Sergeant, 24.5.02
3578. Hoskin, Alfred	Shoeing-smith	
3241. Hearne, Patrick	,,	
2207. Harbourne, Robert	,,	
2663. Heffernan, George Jonas	Sqn. Sergeant-Major	Invalided, Australia, 14.1.02
3220. Hardy, John	Sergeant	Sqn. Sergeant-Major, 6.2.02. Despatches, *London Gazette*, 29.7.02
2330. Henderson, Lachlan MacAlister	,,	
2345. Hicks, Thomas John	,,	
3220. Harvey, John	,,	
2714. Henry, James McTiernay	,,	
201. Hill, Thomas John	,,	
229. Huthwaite, Allen Stephen	,,	
1247. Hodges, Harry	Saddler-Sergeant	
110. Healey, Florence Alfred	Lance-Sergeant	
3681. Hobson, John Charles	Corporal	Sergeant, 1.12.01; invalided, Australia, 24.2.02
3455. Hogan, Edward John	,,	
114. Harris, William John	,,	
2710. Hill, Robert	,,	
4000. Hartill, William	,,	
5110. Hood, John Ulrich	,,	
2434. Hamilton, James Henry	Trooper	Lance-Corporal, 1.9.01
298. Henwood, Alfred	Corporal	
2740. Hall, Percival	,,	
208. Horner, Horace Russell	,,	
23. Hudson, Percy Horatio	Trooper	
20. Hodge, Edward		
16. Hansell, Joseph	,,	
19. Hindle, Herbert	,,	
21. Harvey, John	,,	
71. Holland, Frank	,,	
78. Horgan, Joseph John	,,	
239. Horton, Charles	,,	
2711. Holford, Frederick	,,	
210. Higham, Joseph Matthew	,,	
240. Horning, Frederick	,,	
241. Hewitt, Frank Rupert	,,	
307. Hill, James Henry	,,	
2707. Hogan, George A.	,,	
2708. Hogan, George M.	,,	
242. Hislop, James Scott Hunter	,,	
243. Huxtable, William James	,,	
2716. Hyland, James	,,	

Nominal Roll—*continued*.

No. and Name.	Rank.	Remarks.
231. Hoy, L.	Trooper	
2729. Harrington, Thomas	,,	
2733. Howard, Arthur	,,	
2730. Hill, Arthur	,,	
22. Hanna, William David	,,	
131. Halloran, Rowland	,,	
135. Harris, James	,,	
115. Hicks, George	,,	
129. Hilton, Albert	,,	
2718. Harrison, William	,,	
134. Hill, Edwin Henry	,,	
133. Hoye, William John	,,	
126. Hudson, Henry	,,	
2731. Holmes, Charles Henry	,,	
2812. Hepner, William	,,	
3689. Harpur, Charles William	,,	
3450. Hadfield, Henry Foster	,,	
3159. Hamilton, William	,,	
2577. Hamilton, George F. C.	,,	
3021. Harrison, William Paul	,,	
3471. Heathwood, Samuel John	,,	
3688. Henderson, William	,,	
3462. Hibberd, Joseph	,,	Lance-Corporal, 16.4.02
2445. Hurst, Arthur Percival	,,	
3708. Hobson, Mark	,,	
2163. Hogan, Edward	,,	
3444. Huxley, Albert	,,	Wounded and invalided, Australia, 21.11.01
2614. Harris, Alfred	,,	
4013. Hayes, James	,,	
800. Hart, Charles Ernest	,,	
4014. Healey, William	,,	
4015. Harris, Sydney	,,	
4017. Henson, Charles	,,	
4019. Hicks, Thomas John	,,	
2347. Hobson, Charles William	,,	
2735. Hawley, Charles	,,	
2351. Hood, Arthur	,,	
3740. Hall, William	,,	Lance-Corporal, 26.5.02
2631. Hutchinson, George	,,	
2395. Halliday, George	,,	
2367. Howlett, James Henry	,,	
2390. Harley, Thomas	,,	
2371. Hawksby, James Edward	,,	
2388. Henderson, William	,,	
2378. Howe, Henry	,,	
2788. Hooper, Charles William	,,	
4012. Hughes, Phillip	,,	
304. Hove, William John	,,	
292. Holswick, Cyril	,,	
2086. Hokin, Walter Edward	,,	
2082. Hughes, Richard Joseph	,,	
3009. Holland, George	,,	
79. Holt, Thomas William	Corporal	Lance-Sergeant, 6.8.02
3022. Irwin, Oram	Trooper	
5120. Irvine, Patrick Thomas	,,	
691. Inch, Richard Jeffrey	,,	Drowned at sea, 13.6.02
6000. Johnson, Alfred William	Sqn. Quartermaster Sergeant	
137. Johnson, Charles B.	Sergeant	
596. Jones, Emil Henry	Corporal	Sergeant, 10.1.02; wounded

L 2

Nominal Roll—*continued*.

No. and Name.	Rank.	Remarks.
89. Jacka, Frank	Saddler-Sergeant	
2413. Jones, Stanley Albert	Corporal	
325. Jones, Charles	,,	
2422. Jones, Frederick George	Lance-Corporal	Corporal, 16.4.02
75. Jennings, John George	Trooper	
3024. Joyce, James	,,	
3023. Jones, Frank	,,	
3025. Jones, William	,,	
36. Johns, David	,,	
25. Josephs, Alfred	,,	
195. Jones, James Ambrose	,,	
138. Jack, David	,,	
132. Jenkins, David	,,	
163. Jolley, Edward James	,,	
99. Jude, James	,,	
300. Jones, Ernest	,,	
2089. Jordan, John	,,	
2090. Johnston, Hubert	,,	
2093. Jacobson, Victor	,,	
2624. Jarvis, Samuel	,,	
1363. Jardine, William Englis	,,	
3203. Jackson, Frederick	,,	
3656. Jones, Edward John	,,	
2423. Jones, Thomas Edmund Norris	,,	
2393. Jones, Henry Arthur	,,	
2424. Jones, Thomas Richard	,,	
3232. Jones, Harold John	,,	Invalided, Australia, 7.2.02
2507. Johnston, Phillip	,,	
2578. Jordan, Arthur Archibald	,,	Invalided, Australia, 4.3.02
4020. Johnston, Robert James	,,	Invalided, Australia, 4.3.02
442. Jensen, Australian Peter	,,	
842. Jansen, William James	,,	
2406. Johnston, Robert Arthur	,,	
2410. Jardine, Richard	,,	
3069. Josephson, Edward A.	,,	
2612. Knight, George Frederick	,,	Farrier-Sergeant, 26.5.02
294. Kessell, William Henry	Lance-Corporal	
214. Knight, Edward	Trumpeter	
306. Kimbel, William	,,	
27. Kennewell, Frederick	Trooper	
34. Kelly, Michael O'Connor	,,	
182. Koenig, Wilhelm Frederick	,,	
3070. Kelly, Thomas Henry	,,	
244. Kohler, William	,,	
3189. King, Alfred Leslie	,,	
2342. Kaysley, Henry John	,,	Invalided, Australia, 11.12.01
2653. Kennedy, Patrick	,,	
2346. Kelly, William Patrick	,,	Died of enteric, Zeerust, 24.7.01
2370. Kerr, Thomas	,,	
3436. Kimpton, Reuben	,,	Died of enteric, Pretoria, 28.12.01
2435. Kerr, James	,,	
3070. Kelly, John	,,	
3009. King, William Henry	,,	
26. Logan, James	Shoeing-smith	
184. Lampe, Albert	,,	
183. Lampe, Charles	,,	
212. Lindsay, John	,,	
275. Leonard, William	,,	
28. Lindsay, Colin Hunter	Sergeant	
5006. Lees, Thomas	,,	
2618. Leitch, Samuel R.	Trooper	Lance-Sergeant, 26.5.02

Nominal Roll—*continued.*

No. and Name.	Rank.	Remarks.
139. Latham, Alfred Joseph	Lance-Corporal	
3072. Lake, James S.	Trooper	Corporal, 26.5.02
30. Lindner, Alfred	,,	Lance-Corporal, 6.8.02; died of pneumonia, Albany, 9.9.02
29. Lindner, Walter	,,	
40. Leslie, Sylvester Francis	,,	
1212. Little, James L.	,,	
140. Lawson, George	,,	
136. Lewitz, Frank Ernest	,,	
3071. Lambert, Charles B.	,,	
246. Lowery, Daniel Alexander	,,	
247. Lurman, Henry Arthur	,,	
3076. Lightbody, Thomas	,,	
3094. Lyall, James	,,	
4023. Lee, William	,,	
285. Lloyd, Richard	,,	
3006. Laffan, Thomas	,,	
2078. Lilford, Alfred	,,	
2079. Lilford, George	,,	
3095. Lee, James	,,	
3538. Lane, Richard Clifton	,,	
1933. Lindon, Jack Cuthbert	,,	
3172. Lord, Frank	,,	
2621. Lynam, Edmund Yates	,,	
3540. Lyons, John Llewellyn	,,	
4021. Libby, Alfred	,,	
4022. Lipman, James William	,,	
3071. Lambert, Charles	,,	
2407. Luther, Martin	,,	
2420. Langford, Arthur	,,	
2425. Lawrence, Charles	,,	
3073. Lawler, Patrick	,,	
3074. Laseron, Martin	,,	
5002. Maddison, John Ernest	Sergeant	
200. Maguire, George	Trooper	
319. Munro, James	Pay Sergeant	
74. Mackay, Andrew Hector	Sqn. Sergeant-Major	
2116. Macdonald, James	Sqn. Quartermaster-Sergeant	
2630. Morton, George	Sergeant	
2610. Morrison, Henry James	Trooper	Sergeant, 10.1.02
5003. Maxwell, William Marley	Sergeant	
5009. Mansfield, Frederick Holmes	,,	
2628. Morrison, James	,,	
80. Mackay, Eric Reay	Lance-Sergeant	Sergeant, 6.8.02
204. Masters, Samuel Curtis	,,	
3096. Mathieson, James M.	,,	
2377. Mawhinney, Hugh Arthur	Corporal	Sergeant, 16.4.02
2467. Morris, Fergus Richard	,,	
2285. Mitchell, Henry	Lance-Corporal	Invalided, Australia, 14.1.02
2095. Mackie, William	,,	
3155. Moran, Christopher	Shoeing-smith	Invalided, Australia, 11.12.01
2599. Mitchell, Arthur Walter	,,	
1734. Mullampy, James	,,	
2340. Mulvihill, Thomas Patrick	Trooper	
35. Meaney, John Joseph	,,	
90. Miller, James	,,	
96. Miller, John	,,	
32. Matthews, Charles	,,	

Nominal Roll—*continued*.

No, and Name.	Rank.	Remarks.
Moy, Patrick Joseph	Sqn. Sergeant Major	Wounded. Despatches, *London Gazette*, 29.7.02. *Vide* "Promotions"
83. Miller, Joseph John	Trooper	
197. Maguire, Hugh Peter	,,	
185. Malcolm, Hamilton	,,	
3253. Milligan, Thomas Martin	,,	
145. Minty, George James	,,	
249. Mews, Frank	,,	
250. Murphy, Michael	,,	
2855. Munroe, James	,,	
3142. Mulligan, William	,,	
3099. Murphy, Arthur S.	,,	
3143. Miller, Charles	,,	
3144. Morgan, Richard	,,	
3165. Morrison, Arthur	,,	
3164. May, Tasker	,,	
2620. Maim, James	,,	
3100. Michie, David	,,	
3162. Murray, James	,,	
295. Murphy, James Joseph	,,	
248. Meyrick, Leonard John	,,	
251. Murray, David	,,	
2474. Marr, Edward	,,	
6002. Maher, James Peter	,,	
2097. Maloney, James	,,	
3000. Miles, Charles	,,	
3661. Marshall, Joseph Amos	,,	Invalided, Australia, 11.12.01
3382. Maberley, Charles	,,	Invalided, Australia, 13.10.01
2334. Martin, David Alexander	,,	Invalided, Australia, 6.2.02
2605. Matthews, Alexander	,,	Invalided, Australia, 8.11.01
3198. Meredith, Rex	,,	
3712. Mitchell, Robert Bruce	,,	Invalided, Australia, 21.11.01
3223. Moss, Aubrey	,,	
2616. Macintosh, Andrew William	,,	Invalided, Australia, 4.3.02
3176. Morrison, Frederick	,,	
3495. Murnane, Augustus Wenceslaus	,,	
2734. Murphy, Dennis	,,	
2419. Muirfield, William	,,	
4024. Milligan, Arthur	,,	
4025. Magee, John	,,	
536. Menser, Louis	,,	
4026. Mitchell, George	,,	
4027. Miller, Edward	,,	
3096. Mathieson, John	,,	
4028. Manning, George	,,	
3097. Martin, Thomas	,,	
4029. Morrison, Richard	,,	Invalided, Australia, 8.3.02
4030. Morton, David Alexander	,,	
4031. Minton, William	,,	
4032. Melby, Matthew	,,	
2467. Morris, Thomas	,,	
2472. Miller, Edward	,,	
3158. Mason, James	,,	
3156. Murphy, Charles	,,	
3157. Mitten, John Henry	,,	
2080. Matthews, William	Sergeant	
3573. Mackay, Walter Arthur	Trooper	
2615. McArthur, Henry	,,	Sqn.Quartermaster-Sergeant, 10.1.02
3600. McCulloch, Peter	Corporal	Sergeant, 1.12.01
174. McMahon, George	Sergeant	
2268. McIntyre, Frederick	,,	

Nominal Roll—*continued*.

No. and Name.	Rank.	Remarks.
2629. McGregor, F. A. R. C.	Sergeant	
2613. McDougall, Archibald	Trooper	Sergeant, 10.1.02
440. McWilliams, Thomas Morris	Sergeant	
62. McKell, Hamilton Kerr	Corporal	
142. McNevin, Thomas Butler	,,	
253. McAlpine, William	,,	
811. McGrath, Thomas	,,	
3249. McNamara, Patrick John	Lance-Corporal	Killed in action, Holfontein, 26.6.01
2386. McClelland, Ernest Edward	Trooper	Lance-Corporal, 1.9.02
5112. McAllister, Thomas Romanus Patricia	Shoeing-smith	
2087. McNamara, Patrick	,,	
31. Macdonald, James	Trooper	
151. Macfarlane, William	,,	Died of pneumonia, Melbourne, 28.8.02
143. Macintosh, William James	,,	
144. McLean, James Arthur	,,	
166. McLennon, Arthur	,,	
141. McNicholl, Thomas	,,	
341. McCarthy, Allen	,,	
3168. McLean, Richard	,,	
3166. Macintyre, John	Trooper	
279. Macfarlane, John	,,	
352. McCarthy, Alfred	,,	
3008. Mackenzie, Robert	,,	
3652. McAuley, Norman	,,	
2270. Macarthur, John James	,,	Invalided, Australia, 13.2.02
2418. Macdonald, Bartholomew	,,	
3573. McKay, Walter Arthur	,,	
2471. McGee, Joseph Patrick	,,	
3710. McLachlan, William Henry	,,	Invalided, Australia, 7.1.02
3233. McLean, Robert	,,	
3537. McNab, Joseph Alexander	Lance-Corporal	Corporal, 10.4.02
3649. McNamara, Thomas Walter	Trooper	
331. McPhee, Arthur	,,	
2446. McIntyre, Alexander Donald	,,	
3169. McLister, Hugh	,,	
3170. McKerr, William	,,	Killed in action, Wittbank, 31.3.02
1607. McGowan, Neal	,,	
390. McSpedden, Archibald	Corporal	
76. Nolan, Edward	Sergeant	
85. Norman, James	Trooper	
39. Newton, John Edward	Corporal	
81. Nolan, Sydney Herbert	Trooper	
82. Neve, William Patrick	,,	
37. Nicholls, John	,,	
175. Norman, Lionel Dewhurst	,,	
3098. Newland, William	,,	Died of enteric, Zeerust, 10.7.01
2712. Newton, George Henry	,,	Invalided, Australia, 7.2.02
2305. Neill, William Arthur	,,	
3572. Nicholls, Edward Alfred	,,	Lance-Corporal, 10.4.02
3536. Nott, James Joshua	,,	Lance-Corporal, 10.4.02
2657. Nolan, Edward Joseph	Trooper	
881. Nelmes, William Henry	Farrier-Sergeant	
2485. Newman, Reginald Thomas	Trooper	
2608. O'Reilly, Matthew	,,	
3595. O'Connor, James	,,	
213. O'Hey, John Henry	Shoeing-smith	
109. Owens, Arthur	Sergeant	

Nominal Roll—*continued*.

No. and Name.	Rank.	Remarks.
36. Osborne, Charles	Trooper	
194. O'Brien, William	,,	
38. O'Brien, William	,,	
177. Olsen, George William	,,	
173. O'Neill, Frederick	,,	
3175. Owens, Arthur William James	,,	
5121. Owers, James Henry	,,	
1681. Oldham, John	,,	
2234. Oldham, Charles	,,	Killed in action, Tweefontein, 13.12.01
305. O'Dwyer, James	,,	
2537. O'Loughlin, Charles	,,	Died at Standerton, 4.4.02
3174. Osborne, Patrick	,,	
3093. O'Shea, Thomas Pierce	,,	
3171. Olsen, Alfred	,,	
88. Owens, Charles	,,	
325. Pringle, Huntley Gordon	Sergeant	Sqn. Quartermaster-Sergeant, 21.3.02; invalided, Australia, 14.1.02
4030. Pringle, R.	Trooper	
3481. Porter, Joseph Arthur	Sergeant	
78. Pringle, Thomas	,,	
321. Pritchard, Louis George	,,	
202. Phillips, Thomas William	,,	
272. Perry, Edward John	Corporal	
156. Parkinson, William Frederick	Lance-Corporal	
3202. Pether, William Henry	,,	
1833. Pryor, John Hubert	Trumpeter	
50. Poppleton, John	Trooper	
41. Payne, John Edward	,,	
42. Powell, Frederick James	,,	
44. Parnaby, Thomas William	,,	
153. Palmer, William Thomas	,,	
145. Pearson, William Clarence	,,	
155. Perry, Alfred Samuel	,,	
149. Pringle, Alexander Frazer	,,	
167. Power, Claude Ashley	,,	
254. Phillips, Thomas William	,,	
255. Post, Alfred Joseph	,,	
256. Prestwich, Frederick William	,,	
3470. Purdie, Donald	,,	
3209. Parsons, Samuel	,,	
280. Pulman, Thomas Henry	,,	
3205. Peterson, James	,,	
2717. Perry, Edward	,,	
289. Platt, Adam	,,	
257. Pryor, Lawrence	,,	
5000. Perrin, Patrick	,,	
3631. Parker, Hilton Thomas	,,	
186. Price, George Henry	,,	
2703. Painter, William Henry	,,	
3219. Padman, Horace Lelliott	,,	
3679. Pearson, Herbert William	,,	Invalided, Australia
2716. Perry, Lawrence	,,	
3226. Perkins, Francis Sydney	,,	Died of enteric, Ermelo, 28.1.01
3210. Provost, Charles James	,,	Invalided, Australia, 11.12.01
4033. Pilliner, Alfred	,,	
1035. Pascoe, Hilton Harcourt	,,	
2626. Paul, A. W.	,,	Corporal, 26.5.02
258. Quine, Frederick	,,	
259. Quine, Samuel	,,	

Nominal Roll—continued.

No. and Name.	Rank.	Remarks.
3553. Quick, David	Trooper	
5496. Ryan, George Edward	Sergeant	Sqn. Sergeant-Major, 24.5.02
2636. Roche, Thomas	Trooper	
3489. Rennell, John Martin	Lance-Corporal	Sergeant, 10.4.02
3677. Ryrie, Wallace	Sergeant	
188. Rhodenback, Harry	,,	
158. Riley, James St. C.	,,	
2625. Ryan, John Alexander	Trooper	Sergeant, 26.5.02
606. Richardson, William James Reid	Sergeant	
3641. Rennie, William Thompson	Corporal	Farrier-Sergeant, 24.5.02; invalided, Australia, 7.2.02
2279. Russell, Alexander Nicholas	Sergeant	
944. Roots, William Arthur	,,	
97. Reid, Henry Laurie	,,	
73. Reid, Albert Henry	,,	
2624. Reid, Frederick William	Trooper	Corporal, 24.5.02
3261. Ryder, Thomas	Corporal	
85. Ransley, Thomas William	Lance-Corporal	
47. Rennie, Richard	Trooper	
43. Ryan, Edward	,,	
49. Ross, Hugh Benjamin	,,	
84. Rowland, Joseph	,,	
33. Rawlings, Harold John	,,	
53. Rohrick, Bernard	,,	Lance-Corporal, 6.8.02
46. Ryan, Thomas	,,	
54. Regan, Michael	,,	
48. Reid, David	,,	
198. Roach, William Henry	,,	
159. Ryan, Henry	,,	
260. Reid, Ernest	,,	
3211. Rees, Arthur	,,	
1229. Ronald, Henry	,,	
299. Regan, John Bede	,,	
3007. Reid, Alexander	,,	
2099. Robinson, William Ralph	,,	
3519. Reid, James	,,	
3547. Reynolds, Hubert	,,	Lance-Corporal, 10.4.02
2308. Reid, George Frederick	,,	Invalided, Australia, 7.2.02
2473. Riley, Andrew William	,,	Invalided, Australia, 7.2.02
3669. Rowland, William Henry	,,	
2811. Robertson, Thomas	,,	
2370. Roberts, John	,,	
2350. Rush, Phillip Charles	,,	
3199. Ryan, Phillip	,,	
1317. Ross, Henry	,,	
4035. Russell, James Henry	,,	Accidentally killed, Vlaaklaagte, 26.3.02
2526. Reid, Henry David	Corporal	
2495. Ryder, Charles	Trooper	
2508. Robinson, Sydney	,,	
2528. Robey, Cecil	,,	
3212. Rankin, Neil	,,	
323. Sargent, Thomas	Farrier-Major	
2619. Sullivan, Thomas	Shoeing-smith	
3445. Sullivan, Eric Mackay	Sqn. Sergeant-Major	
439. Sale, Frederick	Sqn. Quartermaster-Sergeant	
72. Smale, Basil Lionel	Sergeant	
101. Stevens, Charles Henry	,,	

Nominal Roll—continued.

No. and Name.	Rank.	Remarks.
1044. Seymour, James	Sergeant	Killed in action, Lieuwfontein 28.7.01
107. Strettles, Stephen	,,	
5004. Spurway, Robert William	,,	
1086. Smith, Robert	,,	
206. Smith, John Henry	Lance-Sergeant	
433. Sellars, James	,,	
2627. Sheedy, Edward John	Trooper	Lance-Sergeant, 26.5.02
77. Solomon, Solomon	Corporal	
3201. Shelley, Cecil Harcourt	,,	
2426. Savage, John O'Brien		Sergeant, 16.4.02
789. Smith, William	Trooper	Corporal, 22.6.01; died of enteric, Middelberg, 11.12.01
2617. Souter, James R.	,,	Corporal, 26.5.02
3227. Sinclair, James	,,	Corporal, 26.5.02. Imperial service in Egypt **V.C.**
3240. Sandeman, Thomas George	,,	Corporal, 26.5.02
5122. Stewart, Donald	Corporal	
1386. Sandstrom, Ewen Addoin	,,	
584. Swadling, Daniel William	,,	
94. Shannon, William	Lance-Corporal	Corporal, 6.8.02
2221. Sexton, George	Trooper	Lance-Corporal, 26.5.02
2387. Steele, George	Lance-Corporal	Corporal, 16.4.02
205. Stockley, William S.	,,	
5111. Sedgewick, William Mervyn	,,	
58. Stokes, Samuel Pitt	Trooper	
52. Simpson, Archibald	,,	
97. Sinclair, Hector	,,	
56. Shelley, Daniel	,,	
95. Shannon, Richard	,,	
57. Shannon, Robert	,,	
55. Sheppard, William	,,	
51. Smith, George Sylvester	,,	
113. Shaw, Charles James	,,	Died at Newcastle, 17.7.02
169. Sheppard, Charles	,,	
152. Sheppard, Walter Leslie	,,	
172. Swansborough, Thomas Edward	,,	
262. Soden, Richard	,,	
261. Smith, Robert	,,	
3216. Sheen, Charles	,,	
211. Sheppard, Alfred George	,,	
263. Saunders, William	,,	
264. Sanders, George	,,	
265. Spencer, Bernard H. A.	,,	
266. Sparsholt, Henry William	,,	
267. Silcock, John	,,	
329. Shaw, Oswald Robert	,,	
3244. Snoxhill, William	,,	
3225. Skerry, Charles	,,	
3237. Smith, Walter Charles	,,	
3218. Sparkes, William	,,	
3228. Stapleton, Percival	,,	
3231. Stewart, Donald	,,	
3235. Symmonds, Henry James	,,	
310. Summons, Edward	,,	
256. Stephenson, Robert John	,,	
2092. Smith, Robert	,,	
2097. Sheridan, Samuel Alexander Patrick	,,	
2789. Scott, William Frederick	,,	

Nominal Roll—*continued*.

No. and Name.	Rank.	Remarks.
2622. Scully, Daniel	Trooper	Invalided, Australia, 7.1.02
3238. Seabrook, John Henry	,,	
3163. Sheehan, Thomas	,,	Invalided, Australia 9.7.01
3215. Shield, Joseph	,,	
2582. Shirley, Robert Henry	,,	Invalided, Australia, 6.2.02
2496. Simons, Edward	,,	
2465. Simpson, Louis Vivian	,,	
3539. Smith, Albert Edward	,,	
3655. Smith, William	,,	Invalided, Australia, 13.10.01
2732. Smith, Richard William	,,	
3154. Smith, Abraham Gordon	,,	Lance-Corporal, 16.4.02
3194. Smith, Alfred George	,,	
3386. Smith, Sydney Fletcher	,,	Invalided, Australia 11.12.01
3222. Smyth, Alfred	,,	
3561. Stibberd, Henry Norman	,,	
2484. Stack, Frederick Henry	,,	
3510. Summerfield, Edward	,,	
3686. St. George, Arthur	,,	Invalided, Australia, 11.12.01
2673. St. George, Frederick	,,	
4036. Spooner, John	,,	
4453. Stevens, Arthur J.	,,	Died of enteric, Johannesburg, 13.6.02
434. Stirling, James	,,	
3217. Smith, James	,,	
3242. Stevens, James Frederick S.	,,	
2561. Smith, Thomas F.	,,	
2571. Scott, William	,,	Died of enteric, Standerton, 3.3.02
2574. Shorter, Septimus Arthur	,,	
3243. Stimpson, George	,,	
3614. Stuart, William	Lance-Corporal	Corporal, 10.4.02
920. Somerville, John Samuel	Trooper	
4039. Tanner, Harrie	Saddler	Saddler-Sergeant, 1.12.01
3616. Tame, Henry	Sqn. Quartermaster-Sergeant	Died of enteric, Middelberg, 23.3.02
3618. Tame, Albert Edward	Farrier-Sergeant	
2650. Taylor, George	Corporal	Died of enteric, Middelberg, 29.11.01
268. Tonkin, James Samuel	,,	
5123. Towle, Edgar Austin	,,	
325. Tepper, Hubert Alfred	,,	
323. Taylor, Charles Henry	Lance-Corporal	
3640. Thomas, Edward J. C.	Trumpeter	
60. Tooth, Frank William	Trooper	
59. Tuscilian, Frederick Robertson	,,	Lance-Corporal, 6.8.02
168. Talbot, John Joseph	,,	
100. Topprell, Duncan John	,,	
150. Topprell, William McPherson	,,	
3490. Tew, Edward	,,	
3246. Tollis, Frank	,,	
3255. Tuvey, James	,,	
3257. Taylor, Arthur James	,,	
2277. Thompson, James William	,,	
3692. Tame, Herbert Bernden	Farrier-Sergeant	Died of enteric, Standerton, 7.2.02
3111. Thomas, George	Trooper	
2084. Taylor, William	,,	
2085. Thompson, David	,,	
3617. Tame, Walter	,,	Died of enteric, Standerton, 20.10.01
2647. Taylor, Charles	,,	
2648. Taylor, Edward	,,	

Nominal Roll—continued.

No. and Name.	Rank.	Remarks.
2360. Taylor, William	Trooper	Invalided, Australia, 11.12.01
2638. Thornley, Robert Hubert	,,	
2692. Thurlow, Charles	,,	Invalided, Australia, 19.7.01
2338. Thackery, Herbert	,,	
3678. Thompson, Joseph	,,	
3643. Turner, James	,,	
4037. Taylor, Sydney H.	,,	
4038. Towler, James	,,	
309. Timewell, William	,,	
4049. Trigwell, Henry J.	,,	
3068. Turner, Alfred	,,	
4009. Travis, William	,,	
2580. Thomas, Henry James	,,	
2583. Turner, Albert	,,	
2591. Turnbull, John	,,	
3251. Tully, William P. J.	,,	
3252. Tendt, Henry	,,	
457. Travers, Alfred L.	,,	
3256. Thompson, George	,,	
64. Underwood, John	,,	
309. Uril, Alfred Ernest	,,	
5124. Underwood, Septimus Richard	,,	
2593. Uhr, George Arthur	,,	
65. Vernon, Frederick Henry	,,	
3263. Vesper, Joseph	,,	
3502. Vince, Richard Henry	,,	
203. Varney, Sydney George	Farrier-Sergeant	
63. Westhorpe, Frederick Henry	Shoeing-smith	
5002. Weeks, Sidney	Sqn. Quartermaster-Sergeant	
77. Wilson, Norman	Sergeant	
3260. Watt, Robert Graham	,,	Transport-Sergeant
164. Wright, Edward	,,	
191. Watt, Joseph	Farrier-Sergeant	Farrier-Major, 11.7.02
3520. Webb, Aleck	Lance-Sergeant	
93. Wilson, Edwin Thomas	,,	Sergeant, 6.8.02
272. Wilmette, Franklyn Henry Eardley	Corporal	
274. White, Edward Henry	,,	
5125. Wallace, Alexander	,,	
62. Watson, Alfred James	Lance-Corporal	Corporal, 6.8.02
2466. Walsh, Christopher	,,	Invalided, Australia, 8.11.01
3383. Ward, Bernard Thomas	,,	
270. Wren, Frank W. W.	,,	
327. Wiltshire, Bernard	,,	
273. Wolstenholme, Charles Matthew	,,	
3507. Worthington, Allen Valentine	Trumpeter	
3196. Walker, Brighton St. Kilda	Trooper	
2536. Walker, John	,,	
3569. Walsh, Arthur Winifred	,,	
3254. Wall, John Thomas	,,	
2633. Watson, Algernon Bemerton	,,	
3236. Wasson, Johnston	,,	Invalided, Australia, 7.2.02
3619. Williams, Robert	,,	
3518. Williamson, Leslie Cecil	,,	
3515. Wilmott, Frederick Horace	,,	
3579. Wilson, David	,,	
3663. Wood, Randolph Colin	,,	
3383. Ward, Benjamin Thomas	,,	
4041. Whiskin, David Charles	,,	

Nominal Roll—*continued*.

No. and Name.	Rank.	Remarks.
4042. Wallace, Thomas	,,	
4043. Walter, Henry Charles	,,	
4044. Wallace, Edward	,,	
4045. Watson, Frederick Robert	,,	
4046. Williams, Peter	,,	
4047. Ward, James	,,	
4048. Webber, Victor P.	,,	
2596. Wiseman, Henry	,,	
2595. Williams, James	,,	
3601. Woods, Edward	,,	
3387. Wyatt, David J. A.	,,	
3446. Webb, William Robert	,,	
3543. Williams, John	,,	Invalided, Australia, 7.3.01
3447. Williams, John Richard	,,	
66. Walsh, James	,,	
61. Watson, William John	,,	
71. Webb, Michael	,,	
69. West, Thomas	,,	
24. Wheeler, John	,,	
98. Williamson, James	,,	
92. Wilson, Ernest James	,,	
322. Winters, Frederick M.	,,	
154. Waller, George Henry	,,	
148. Welsh, William Henry	,,	
137. Wharton, James Joseph	,,	
189. Wilson, George Theophilus Warby	,,	
172. Wilson, David Patrick	,,	
192. Wilson, James Wentworth Gordon	,,	
165. Woodhouse, Robert Benjamin	,,	
164. Wright, Edward	,,	
269. Wright, John	,,	
3385. White, Lawrence D.	,,	
271. Williams, Arthur	,,	
3384. Whitford, Edward B.	,,	
324. Weston, William Chester	,,	
3448. Warne, James	,,	
3449. Wilkinson, Edward	,,	
3437. Wilkie, William S.	,,	
3420. Winger, James	,,	
3451. Woods, Arthur	,,	
315. Wells, John Arthur Ernest	,,	
5126. Watt, William Redfern	,,	
3446. Webb, William	,,	
3609. Wheeler, Robert John	,,	
4040. Wonters, John	,,	
2268. Williams, F.	Corporal	Sergeant, 16.4.02
3580. Young, Edward Stuart	Trooper	

FIRST BATTALION AUSTRALIAN COMMONWEALTH HORSE.

AFTER the Commonwealth had been established and the Australian Defences handed over to the Federal Government, it was decided to send further Contingents of Mounted Rifles to the war; and that battalions of a representative character should be formed, with squadrons from the different States. Then the first of these was made up of three units from New South Wales, one from Queensland, and one from Tasmania.

The establishment of each unit authorized was 121 of all ranks. Pay at cavalry rates for all ranks, viz., basis of 1s. 2d. for privates till date of embarkation, and from date of embarkation 5s. per diem for privates; other ranks at the rate allowed to Imperial (Australian) Contingents. Officers were granted an allowance of £30 to provide uniform, equipment, and saddlery. *Vide* also 2nd A.C.H., Victoria.

The men selected were required to be good shots and good horsemen; men of previous service having preference, if medically fit. Only single men were taken, and unmarried officers had preference, other conditions being equal.

The system of selection and purchase of horses was left to State Commandants, as with previous Contingents. Officers were allowed two horses; and 10 per cent. spare horses were to be sent with each unit.

The battalions were in the first instance known as "——— Battalion Commonwealth Contingent," but this was altered to "Australian Commonwealth Horse."

Details of Establishment.

Staff:—1 lieut.-colonel, 1 major, 1 adjutant, 1 quartermaster, 1 medical officer, 1 veterinary officer, 1 regimental sergeant-major, 1 regimental quartermaster-sergeant, 1 orderly room sergeant.

Each company (or squadron):—1 major or captain, 4 subalterns, 1 company sergeant-major, 1 company quartermaster-sergeant, 1 farrier-sergeant, 4 sergeants, 3 shoeing-smiths, 1 saddler, 2 buglers, 6 corporals (including paid lance-sergeants) at the rate of two per battalion), 97 privates, including 4 paid lance-corporals.

Reference to Orders.

Formation	G.O., 1/02
Establishment	,, 1 and 2/02
Pay and allowances	,, 1, 3, and 4/02
Conditions of service	,, 1/02
Allotment of pay	,, 1 and 10/02
Clothing	,, 1 and 2/02
Equipment officers	,, 4/02
Officers	,, 10/02
Paymaster	,, 24/02
Nomenclature	D.O., 239 of 22nd April, 1902
Personnel (N.S.W. units)	G.O., 39/02
Adjutant	,, 34/02
Embarkation	,, 31 and 32/02

Clothing Etc.

Uniform consisted of F.S. jacket, pants, puttees, and hats. Equipped with M.L.E. rifles, bayonets, bandoliers, and saddlery, and fully horsed.

Departure and Return.

The 1st Australian Commonwealth Horse (New South Wales units) embarked at Sydney on the transport *Custodian* on 18th February, 1902, and disembarked at Durban on 19th March, 1902. It comprised 21 officers and 354 of other ranks, with 372 horses. Of these, 4 died, and 20 were struck off in South Africa. Twenty-one officers and 330 others returned by transport *Drayton Grange*—which left Durban on 11th July, and arrived at Sydney on 11th August, 1902, having called at Albany and Melbourne on the way.

Operations.

This battalion proceeded on 19th March, 1902, by train from Durban to Newcastle, and thence to Klerksdorp on 10th April, arriving at the latter place on the 13th. Joined Column under the command of Colonel De Lisle, which formed part of Thornycroft's brigade.

This Column was inspected by Lord Kitchener on 22nd April, who expressed himself as pleased with the appearance of men and horses.

The Column was employed clearing the district north of Klerksdorp, and took part in a drive which commenced on 7th May, moving westward to the Kimberley-Mafeking railway blockhouse line. In this, 251 prisoners, including General De la Rey's brother, were captured, also 300 horses, 144 rifles and bandoliers, 6,000 rounds ammunition, and a large quantity of stock.

Colonel De Lisle, who was leaving for England, handed over his command to Colonel Williams. The Column then returned to Klerksdorp, reaching that place on the 21st May, where the regiment remained until the declaration of peace, when they were ordered to Elandsfontein to prepare for return to Australia.

The regiment proceeded by rail to Newcastle on 29th June, and to Durban on 9th July, for embarkation.

Promotions.

Major J. H. Lee to Lieut.-Colonel, 5th June, 1902.
(For promotions of N.C.O.'s and men, *vide* nominal roll.)

War Service.

The service which officers were entitled to reckon was:—Operations in Western Transvaal and British Bechuanaland, April to May, 1902. Queen's Medal with three clasps was awarded in most cases to officers who had not served before, but many of them had done so.

The majority of the N.C.O.'s and men had also served in previous details.

Nominal Roll.

No. and Name.	Rank.	Remarks.
Regimental Staff.		
Lyster, James Sanderson	Lieut.-Colonel	Military Staff
Lee, John Henry Alexander	Major	Royal Australian Engineers
Taylor, Herbert James Cox	Captain and Adjutant	From " A " Battery, Royal Australian Artillery
Grace, Harry George	Lieutenant and Quartermaster	Served 1st Mounted Rifles
Gillies, J.	Captain (A.M.C.)	
Barbeta, E.	Veterinary Officer	Served N.S.W. Imperial Bushmen
Oakes, Rev. Spencer	Chaplain C. of E. (Captain)	

Nominal Roll—*continued*.

No. and Name.	Rank.	Remarks.
REGIMENTAL STAFF—*continued*.		
Green, Rev. James	Chaplain Wesleyan (Captain)	
117. Edney, John R.	Reg. Sergeant-Major	
177. Foley, William	Reg. Quartermaster-Sergeant	
350. Boam, Harry N.	Orderly-Room Sergeant	
"A" SQUADRON.		
Zouch, Richard Essington	Captain	Citizens' Bushmen Contingent
Bowden, Thomas Leslie	Lieutenant	1st Mounted Rifles and 3rd Imperial Bushmen
Curr, Hubert	,,	Citizens' Bushmen Contingent
Roberts, Ward Francis Egbert	,,	Imperial Bushmen
Harris, Geoffrey Hamlyn Saviscount	,,	1st Australian Horse
44. Brittsworth, Charles M.	Sqn. Sergeant-Major	
297. Ward, Frank H.	Sqn. Quartermaster-Sergeant	
230. Duffy, Edward H.	Sergeant	
19. McConnell, James	,,	
158. Tipper, Edwin J.	,,	
6. Dwyer, Edward	Farrier-Sergeant	
14. Hamilton, Joseph G.	Lance-Sergeant	
27. Symonds, Michael J. P.	,,	
29. Sutton, Joseph H.	Corporal	Sergeant, 7.7.02
24. Rose, Frank	,,	Sergeant, 6.6.02
12. Hulbert, James H.	,,	
45. Fenton, Edward	,,	
109. Feehily, Roger B.	,,	
47. Gall, Frank J.	,,	Sergeant, 7.7.02
1. Bartlett, James	Lance-Corporal	
2. Bowling, George W.	,,	
59. Bohlson, Harry A.	,,	Corporal, 6.6.02
46. Dalton, William	,,	Corporal, 7.7.02
8. Glasscock, Edward S.	Bugler	
73. Baker, Thomas	Saddler	
68. McMillan, William T.	Shoeing-smith	Farrier-Sergeant, 7.7.02
384. Sayers, G. E.	,,	
85. Moore, William T.	,,	
13. Ayshford, Edward A.	Trooper	
57. Almond, Peter	,,	
112. Atkins, Archibald C.	,,	
3. Baker, Arthur	,,	
4. Coban, Thomas	,,	
43. Charleton, Albert G.	,,	
100. Champion, George H.	,,	
107. Charles, Robert	,,	
120. Cahill, Timothy P.	,,	
5. Dawson, Walter H.	,,	
74. Dumont, Norman A.	,,	
76. Davidson, Archibald	,,	
103. Dwyer, John R. J.	,,	
110. Donaldson, J.	,,	
7. Elley, George	,,	
40. Evans, Walter E.	,,	

Nominal Roll—*continued.*

"A" SQUADRON—*continued.*

No. and Name.	Rank.	Remarks.
89. Ford, Arthur	Trooper	
91. Feeney, J. P.	,,	
93. Fleetwood, John	,,	
104. Franklin, Alfred	,,	
105. Fardell, Thomas E.	,,	
113. Foat, Frederick J.	,,	
9. Gunter, Thomas N.	,,	
41. Gildea, Montague S.	,,	
50. Green, John	,,	
67. Gall, Cecil G.	,,	
77. Grove, Frederick W.	,,	
92. Gunn, Richard	,,	
99. Glasson, William	,,	
11. Healey, S.	,,	Lance-Corporal, 7.7.02
60. Heron, Eden H.	,,	
83. Holm, Lewis H.	,,	
116. Holland, William H.	,,	
15. Johnson, R. Morrison	,,	Lance-Corporal, 15.4.02
64. Jackson, John S.	,,	
96. Jackson, John H.	,,	
97. Kay, Henry	,,	
17. Luxton, Robert J.	,,	
39. Linfoot, George B.	,,	
385. Leacock, James Freeland	,,	Lance-Corporal, 1.4.02
49. Lamb, Malcolm J.	,,	
78. Long, Hugh	,,	
101. Love, Edwin	,,	Lance-Corporal, 6.6.02
18. Mayne, Alfred	,,	Lance-Corporal, 6.6.02
20. Morris, Thomas L.	,,	
21. Mitchell, Arthur	,,	
119. Mealing, George	,,	
53. Millwood, George	,,	
69. Morris, Arthur T.	,,	
72. Morgan, Frank G.	,,	
82. Murray, Arthur J.	,,	
94. Maguire, Duncan	,,	
125. McAndrew, Alexander	,,	
106. Mealing, H.	,,	
114. McCarthy, William	,,	
102. Neal, James E.	,,	
52. O'Brien, Albert	,,	
51. Osborne, Arthur E.	,,	
95. O'Malley, Walter B.	,,	
283. O'Malley, William	,,	
23. Paul, G.	,,	
34. Poole, Frederick	,,	Lance-Corporal, 7.7.02
26. Richardson, John	,,	
25. Robertson, James R.	,,	
38. Read, Arthur L.	,,	
48. Ross, Charles	,,	
63. Randell, William F. W.	,,	
88. Robinson, James W.	,,	
108. Rosewell, Thomas	,,	
28. Spencer, Sydney	,,	
56. Shirley, Andrew	,,	Lance-Corporal, 6.6.02
30. Shepherd, George	,,	
37. Stopp, George W.	,,	
61. Sutherland, Hector J.	,,	Lance-Corporal, 7.7.02

Nominal Roll—*continued.*

No. and Name.	Rank.	Remarks.
"A" Squadron—*continued.*		
75. Smith, John	Trooper	
80. Slater, Arthur	,,	
98. Smith, Thomas	,,	
111. Sheehan, Alphonso N.	,,	
31. Thomas, Wm. C. F.	,,	
86. Troy, Patrick W.	,,	
87. Tamsett, Edgar	,,	
81. Vallins, George	,,	Lance-Corporal, 7.7.02
33. Watt, Thomas R.	,,	
42. Watson, Charles W.	,,	Lance-Corporal, 7.7.02
62. Woods, William	,,	
65. Whalley, Thomas	,,	
66. Wheeler, Robert J.	,,	
79. Wall, John W.	,,	
84. Watkins, William J.	,,	
71. Williams, William J.	,,	
90. Wilson, John G.	,,	
35. Yates, Percival J.	,,	
"B" Squadron.		
Forrest, Arthur E.	Captain	B.M.S.
Mullins, Thomas Lane	Lieutenant	Citizens' Bushmen
Norris, Charles Tucker	,,	1st N.S.W. Mounted Rifles
Weir, Frank Valentine	,,	Citizens' Bushmen
Johnson, Sedbar Bradshaw	,,	
143. Mansfield, Horatio	Coy. Sergeant-Major	
218. Bowler, Adolphus	Coy. Quartermaster-Sergeant	
147. Curry, Thomas	Sergeant	
169. Lorenzo, Frank	,,	
150. McAlpine, Archibald	,,	
137. Tullidge, Herbert	,,	
144. Meaney, Joseph	Farrier-Sergeant	
148. Braddock, Alfred E.	Corporal	
135. Leape, George S.	,,	Acting Sergeant, 8.7.02
139. Payne, George	,,	
186. Sare, William	,,	Sergeant, 5.7.02
184. Sheedy, Martin	,,	
233. Staunton, Oscar	,,	Sergeant, 5.7.02
178. Brown, Albert H.	Lance-Corporal	
189. Frost, Sydney	,,	Corporal, 5.7.02
172. Glenn, Alfred	,,	Corporal, 5.7.02
245. Saunders, Matthews	,,	
193. Brears, George	Bugler	
191. Evans, Howard	Saddler	
138. Alexander William	Shoeing-smith	
235. Grey, George (*alias* Cousens)	,,	Farrier-Sergeant
183. Abel, Garnet	Trooper	
239. Akhurst, Mathew	,,	
168. Allason, Sidney	,,	
225. Amor, Archie	,,	
162. Ausling, Frederick	,,	
171. Barsley, Henry W.	,,	
199. Barnard, David L.	,,	Lance-Corporal, 23.3.02
248. Barrett, Jabez	,,	
251. Barber, Bert	,,	
391. Behan, Maurice J.	,,	

Nominal Roll—*continued.*

No. and Name.	Rank.	Remarks.
"B" SQUADRON—*continued.*		
209. Blackman, George	Trooper	
213. Bolton, Harry	,,	
217. Boswell, Ernest E.	,,	
149. Biddlecombe, Charles	,,	
208. Brown, William	,,	
206. Brown, Robert T.	,,	Lance-Corporal, 5.7.02
210. Callan, Thomas H.	,,	
185. Coulcher, Ernest H.	,,	Lance-Corporal, 8.7.02
247. Collins, Daniel	,,	Lance-Corporal, 8.7.02
222. Croome, William	,,	
241. Croucher, Arthur C.	,,	
261. Donaldson, Archibald	,,	
151. Evans, Sidney	,,	
118. Fisk, Edward	,,	
234. Geer, William	,,	
263. Glessner, Ernest	,,	
190. Haybittle, Percy	,,	
224. Hadden, John E.	,,	
227. Hackett, Samuel	,,	
246. Handy, Frederick	,,	
164. Hagney, Frank	,,	
170. Humphreys, John E.	,,	
252. Hickson, T.	,,	
221. Hill, Charles	,,	
228. Hornby, Charles	,,	
256. Jackson, John C.	,,	
264. Johnston, Percy H.	,,	
197. Kremer, Cecil	,,	
392. Kay, Searle F.	,,	
136. Leeke, James	,,	
394. Lynch, Patrick M.	,,	
156. Malone, James	,,	
141. McCarthy, William	,,	
146. McJannett, William V.	,,	
255. Mackay, George S.	,,	Died, Newcastle, 15.5.02
192. Mitchell, Leonard	,,	
238. McAllum, William	,,	Lance-Corporal, 8.7.02
240. McAlister, Narcissi	,,	
226. Murphy, Lionel	,,	
242. Mulhall, Joseph	,,	
159. Porteous, James	,,	
262. Phinn, William	,,	
236. Porter, John	,,	
243. Powell, George	,,	
220. Reynolds, Ernest	,,	
121. McDonald, George	,,	
166. Moate, George H.	,,	
160. Norris, Alfred	,,	
188. Noakes, Robert R.	,,	
173. O'Brien, Edward	,,	Died at sea, 10.3.02
216. Paul, Henry H.	,,	
165. Philpott, Frederick	,,	
262. Phinn, William	,,	
167. Robins, Aubrey D.	,,	
187. Robinson, Robinson Wm.	,,	
249. Rowley, Walter C.	,,	
253. Ryan, William	,,	
231. Rushworth, Henry	,,	

Nominal Roll—*continued*.

No. and Name.	Rank.	Remarks.
"B" SQUADRON—*continued*.		
223. Sayers, John	Trooper	
201. See, Henry D.	,,	
214. Sherritt, Charles	,,	
250. Sheehan, James	,,	
202. Smith, Arthur	,,	
140. Stanton, John	,,	
123. Slack, Thomas G.	,,	
174. Stewart, John	,,	
145. Stoppelbein, John	,,	
219. Strang, Alexander	,,	
161. Tooth, Stewart A.	,,	
200. Ward, Horton	,,	Lance-Corporal, 5.7.02
122. Williams, John	,,	Lance-Corporal, 5.7.02
204. Ward, Martin	,,	
229. Watson, Walter	,,	
154. White, James	,,	
195. White, Joseph	,,	
180. Wilson, Joseph	,,	
232. Williams, R. H.	,,	
215. Wise, Arthur	,,	
393. Watkins, James	,,	
237. Wickerson, Phillip	,,	Died, Elandsfontein, 12.6.02
260. Whitbread, Arthur J.	,,	
244. Witton, Alfred	,,	
155. Wilson, William	,,	
182. Wilson, Herbert	,,	
181. Woodgate, Edward	,,	
205. Wood, Thomas	,,	
"C" SQUADRON.		
Antill, Stanley Ross	Captain	1st Mounted Rifles
Fiaschi, Carlo Ferruccio	Lieutenant	Lancer Contingent
Holmes, Richard John	,,	
O'Brien, Harold	,,	
Apps, James	,,	
54. Hopkins, James William	Coy. Sergeant-Major	
281. Miller, Christian	Coy. Quartermaster-Sergeant	
311. Hetherington, Christopher	Sergeant	
134. McMahon, William	,,	
290. Taplin, Thomas Kells	,,	Died Elandsfontein, 12.7.02
293. Weston, James Albert	,,	
196. Maund, James Hamilton	,,	
198. White, John	Farrier-Sergeant	
325. Abel, John McNab	Corporal	
310. Annison, William Thomas	,,	Sergeant, 5.7.02
313. Bridge, Benjamin William	,,	
327. Loveday, Lawrence Arthur	,,	
344. Mitchell, Thomas Dewar	,,	
286. Parry, Sydney	,,	
322. Harper, Herbert Edward	Lance-Corporal	Corporal, 27.6.02
287. Shepherd, Albert Ezekiel	,,	Corporal, 18.5.02
355. Stafford, Samuel Thomas	,,	
365. Woods, Frederick Talbot	,,	
163. Dansey, Colin R.	Saddler	
321. Davis, Percy	Shoeing-smith	
379. Meeve, Joseph Angus	,,	

Nominal Roll—*continued.*

No. and Name.	Rank.	Remarks.
"C" SQUADRON—*continued.*		
254. Smith, James F.	Bugler	
324. Grey, Lairman Ashby	,,	Lance-Corporal, 7.7.02
294. Goodfellow, Sydney	,,	
356. Alick, John	Trooper	
267. Anderton, David James	,,	
268. Annetts, Thomas	,,	
386. Beatty, Alexander	,,	
375. Beatty, James	,,	
394. Lynch, P. M.	,,	
340. Brown, Harry William	,,	
367. Byrne, Patrick James	,,	
334. Carsons, Frank	,,	
347. Campbell, Jack Leslie	,,	
270. Comben, Henry	,,	
377. Crowley, George A.	,,	
318. Clark, Charles	,,	
258. Campbell, James	,,	
296. Cross, James Robert	,,	
343. Currie, William Joseph	,,	
374. Cunningham, Thomas G.	,,	
317. Dawes, Sydney	,,	
298. Denmead, Percy Loftus	,,	
315. Dopson, John Joseph	,,	
370. Eagar, Frank Wm. Austin	,,	Lance-Corporal. 5.7.02
361. Fineran, Charles	,,	
271. Freer, Robert	,,	
380. Fogarty, George	,,	
302. Giles, Alfred Percy	,,	
331. Gillen, Alfred Henry	,,	
389. Galway, Edward K.	,,	
295. Glanham, Thomas D.	,,	Lance-Corporal, 2.4.02
272. Haley, Arthur	,,	
332. Harris, William David	,,	
333. Harris, Arnold Joseph	,,	
346. Hart, William John	,,	
358. Hart, Thomas Francis	,,	
381. Hart, Herbert William	,,	
364. Hamilton, William	,,	Lance-Corporal, 27.6.02
273. Hopkins, Edward	,,	
304. Hodges, Frederick	,,	
339. Hoey, Reuben Levy	,,	
382. Johnstone, L. R.	,,	
378. Johnson, John	,,	
274. Kennedy, Thomas	,,	Lance-Corporal, 2.4.02 ; Corporal, 18.5.02
265. Kohn, Charles Henry	,,	
338. Knight, Walter Osmond	,,	
349. Knowler, Thomas Watson	,,	
337. Lachmund, Charles Albert	,,	
387. Laycock, John E.	,,	
345. Laycock, Maurice Connell	,,	
275. Leaman, Edward Charles	,,	
351. Lewis, George	,,	
276. Littlewood, George Edward	,,	
257. Long, William F.	,,	
383. Lynch, P. J.	,,	
279. Mason, George	,,	
277. Matheson, Angus	,,	

Nominal Roll—*continued.*

No. and Name.	Rank.	Remarks.
"C" SQUADRON—*continued.*		
278. Mascord, Ernest Edward	Trooper	
312. Maston, Henry	,,	
335. Mangan, Francis Joseph	,,	
314. McKenzie, Donald	,,	
354. McKinnon, William John	,,	
299. McPhee, Hugh Duncan	,,	Lance-Corporal, 18.5.02
300. McLean, Neal	,,	
357. McLean, John	,,	
396. Meagher, Harold	,,	
280. Mooney, Archie Patrick	,,	
282. Newport, George Charles	,,	Lance-Corporal, 2.4.02
363. Newland, Bernard James	,,	
320. Osborn, Hugh Leslie	,,	
285. Payne, John Henry	,,	
366. Page, Frank	,,	
336. Pickett, William Rowland	,,	
309. Ralphs, Samuel	,,	
348. Rae, Garner G. W.	,,	
305. Reimar, Edward	,,	
323. Ridge, William	,,	
266. Raphael, Ralph	,,	
326. Rice, Percy	,,	
288. Skehan, Patrick	,,	
308. Skelly, Clements Joseph	,,	
126. Shepherd, Henry Ernest	,,	
303. Stokes, William Hugh	,,	
362. Stokes, John	,,	
373. Stokes, Arthur	,,	
328. Sutherland, John Thomas	,,	
368. Taylor, George Henry	,,	
352. Tovey, James John	,,	
353. Tanko, William	,,	
390. Woodham, Harry	,,	
359. Trulock, George Marshall	,,	
329. Upton, James Thomas	,,	
360. Wallace, James	,,	
291. Williams, Austin	,,	
372. Williams, Amos Edward	,,	
388. Wells, Matthew G.	,,	
319. Wiseman, Edward Francis	,,	
259. Walters, Walter	,,	
292. Whitton, John	,,	
341. Woods, Victor Henry	,,	
371. Woods, Henry Robert	,,	
124. Williamson, Farquhar G.	,,	

COMMONWEALTH ARMY MEDICAL CORPS.
Nominal Roll—New South Wales Details.

No. and Name.	Rank.	Remarks.
Green, Terence Albert	Major	
Howse, Neville Reginald	,,	
Eberling, Richard	Warrant-Officer	Lieut., Quartermaster, 1.4.02
1292. Hadfield, David	Staff Sergeant	
1295. Donnellan, John Joseph	,,	
1291. Moon, Wm. John	Farrier-Sergeant	
1294. Moore, John Marston	Sergeant-Smith	
1264. McEwan, James Fraser	Sergeant	
1272. Atkinson, Lionel Howard	,,	
1293. Carroll, Thomas	,,	
1277. Hibberd, Claude Wilfred	,,	
1286. Ransom, Henry Franklin	,,	
1268. White, Charles	,,	
1285. Smith, Edward Adolphus	Bugler	
1274. Campbell, George	Corporal	
1261. Cousens, Wm. Mark	,,	
1284. Harrison, Charles John	,,	Lance-Sergeant, 1.4.02
1288. Adams, Henry	Private	
1273. Atkins, Arthur Edward	,,	
1271. Childe, Frederick Wm.	,,	
1289. Darragh, Edward James	,,	
1275. Gallagher, Charles	,,	
1262. Gammon, Harry	,,	
1263. Hale, Thomas Arthur	,,	
1276. Hayes, Henry Albert	,,	
1267. Hollander, Percy Evelyn	,,	
1278. Johnson, Leslie John	,,	
1290. Macpherson, Cecil	Bugler	
1279. Moore, Hugh	Private	
1283. Morrissey, Albert	,,	
1280. O'Sullivan, John	,,	
1351. Polson, Alfred Henderson	,,	
1270. Robarts, Charles Hardwick	,,	
1269. Shrimpton, Jesse	,,	
1266. Spackman, James	,,	
1287. Webb, Claude Charles	,,	
1282. Withers, George M.	,,	
1281. Woodward, Sydney Edward R.	,,	

Vide Army Medical Corps, Fourth Contingent, p. 16, 25.

THIRD BATTALION AUSTRALIAN COMMONWEALTH HORSE.

THIS was formed upon the same basis as the first, viz., three units from New South Wales, one from Queensland, and one from Tasmania.

Establishment, rates of pay, &c., were as for the other regiment.

Applicants to enrol were required to be able to ride and shoot and to pass military medical examination. Only single men were accepted; the period of service being one year, or the duration of the war. Applicants for commissions were required to state age, physique, previous military service (especially in South Africa), occupation, if accustomed to country life and travelling in the bush, whether any knowledge of map reading, and general experience of country life in Australia.

REFERENCE TO ORDERS.

Formation	G.O. 27/02
Pay and allowances	„ 3, 4 and 14/02 ——
Allotment of pay	„ 10/02
Equipment	„ 4/02
Accounts	„ 10/02
Enrolment, conditions of	„ 14/02
Establishment	„ 1/02, and 2/02
Embarkation	D.O. 111, of 26th March, 1902
Nomenclature	„ 239, of 22nd April, 1902

CLOTHING, ETC.

Uniform consisted of F.S. jacket, pants, puttees, and hat. Equipped with rifles, bayonets, bandoliers, saddlery, and fully horsed.

SUMMARY.

The staff and head-quarter companies left Sydney on 2nd April, 1902, comprising 19 officers and 352 non-commissioned officers and rank and file, with 372 horses. Six died, 4 officers and 62 others were struck off in South Africa, 15 officers, 284 others returned to New South Wales, arriving on 11th August, 1902.

SERVICE.

The New South Wales division of the 3rd Battalion, Australian Commonwealth Horse, embarked at Sydney on transport *Manhattan* on 1st April, and arrived at Durban on 30th April, 1902.

At Durban it entrained a few days afterwards for Newcastle, where it proceeded into camp at Kitchener's Kop, in the vicinity of that town, awaiting orders to proceed to the Transvaal. Here the Queensland and Tasmanian squadrons joined. *Vide* those Contingents.

Upon peace being concluded, the battalion returned to Durban on 11th July, and embarked on transport *Drayton Grange* on the following day. Called at Albany and Melbourne *en route*, and arrived at Sydney on 11th August.

As in previous Contingents, most of the officers, N.C.O.'s, and men had served before. Those who had not were awarded Queen's Medal, with one clasp.

Nominal Roll.

No. and Name.	Rank.	Remarks.
STAFF.		
Wallace, Robert	Lieut.-Colonel	Royal Australian Artillery
Clark, Walter J.	Major	,, ,,
Murray, Pembroke Lathrop	Major and Paymaster	Royal Australian Artillery. South Africa, 1901
Dove, Frederick Allen	Captain and Adjutant	New South Wales Mounted Rifle Contingent
Wynne, George	Captain and Quartermaster	China, 1900
Fullerton, A. Y.	Captain and Medical Officer	
Leitch, J. B.	Captain and Veterinary Officer	Victorian Imperial Bushmen
SQUADRON OFFICERS.		
Nicholson, Sydney Howard	Captain	Citizens' Bushmen Contingent
Shadler, Reinhold	,,	
Creer, Reginald Charles	,,	China, 1900
Cross, Edwin Herbert	Lieutenant	Imperial Light Horse
Millard, Godfrey William	,,	
Macarthur, Lionel George	,,	Citizens' Bushmen Contingent
McMillan, Murdock Evan	,,	
Connolly, John Bartholomew	,,	New South Wales Lancer Contingent
Gilchrist, Horace William	,,	1st Australian Horse Contingent
Doudney, R. V.	,,	
Cory, George Charles	,,	
Forsythe, William Alfred	,,	
Rankin, James	,,	New South Wales Lancer Contingent
Morgan, John Stanton	,,	Imperial Bushmen
Woods, Harris B.	,,	Brabant's Horse
N.C.O.'S AND MEN.		
1427. Martin, William H.	Coy. Sergeant-Major	
1416. McRae, James	,,	
1813. Black, John	,,	Regimental Sergeant-Major
1418. Ryan, James	Coy. Quartermaster-Sergeant	Died, 6.9.02, after return to New South Wales
1587. Mair, Henry J.	,,	
1743. Clark, Charles E.	,,	
1474. Dalziel, Joseph George	Sergeant	
1486. McDonald, Henry S.	,,	
1411. West, Thomas	,,	
1498. Whitney, W. H.	,,	
1552. Antwis, William E. L.	,,	
1642. Humphreys, Thomas J.	,,	
1603. Rostron, Alexander	,,	
1732. Burke, Michael J.	,,	
1754. Stubbs, William J.	,,	
1729. Whereat, A. C.	,,	
1741. Wilson, Thomas	,,	
1406. Gillies, Wallaa T.	Farrier-Sergeant	
1812. Connors, Francis	,,	
1573. Hanson, George	,,	

Nominal Roll—*continued.*

No. and Name.	Rank.	Remarks.

N.C.O's AND MEN—*continued.*

No. and Name.	Rank.	Remarks.
1483. Ward, George	Lance-Sergeant	
1572. Trafford Alfred B.	,,	R. Pay-Sergeant
1441. Blackwell, R. T.	Corporal	
1408. Eggleton, John Robert	,,	
1502. Rouse, Morris H.	,,	
1412. Russell, Harold	,,	
1424. Reynolds, James	,,	
1414. Whiddon, Eustace	,,	Sergeant
1634. Knight, James H.	,,	
1589. Lamb, James	,,	
1646. Mann, Arthur C.	,,	
1566. Smith, Edward	,,	
1609. Smith, Arthur	,,	
1746. Huckstopp, George E.	,,	
1711. Layburn, John	,,	
1751. Logan, Edward D.	,,	
1733. Robinson, William O.	,,	
1757. Tebbutt, Herbert S.	,,	
1740. Wilson, Charles F.	,,	
1451. Hardwick, Edward H.	Bugler-Corporal	
1420. Everett, Frederick A.	Lance-Corporal	
1449. McDougall, A. W.	,,	
1667. Robertson, H.	,,	Corporal
1623. Gilham, Edward	,,	
1551. Hogg, Charles H.	,,	Corporal
1592. Medcalf, William C.	,,	
1639. Worthington, Sydney H.	,,	Corporal
1779. Curtis, Percy H. M.	,,	Corporal
1799. Jones, George	,,	
1798. Morris, Frank A.	,,	Corporal
1766. Shead, George H.	,,	Corporal
1447. Milwain, George	Bugler	
1664. Tideswell, Phillip	,,	
1665. Waugh, Leslie	,,	
1808. Collins, Norman L.	,,	
1807. Julius, Harry George	,,	
1459. Aldridge, Robert B.	Saddler	
1804. Moran, Martin	Farrier	
1805. Smith, Dan O.	,,	
1478. Thompson, Archibald	,,	
1568. Gutterson, Stephen J.	,,	
1613. Hoy, William	,,	
1768. Harland, Thomas	,,	Died at sea, —.7.02
1806. Henry, Richard	,,	
1803. O'Keefe, Timothy	,,	
1473. Sulter, David B.	,,	
1467. Atkins Arthur	Trooper	
1470. Andrews, William	,,	
1484. Allen, George	,,	
1708. Arnold, Harold A.	,,	
1710. Alderson, Seymour	,,	
1434. Barker, Charles	,,	
1443. Brown, Samuel	,,	
1445. Brook, William E.	,,	
1468. Briggs, Joseph B.	,,	
1485. Brown, Alick	,,	
1562. Bell, John Thomas	,,	
1605. Bibbey, John	,,	

Nominal Roll—continued.

No. and Name.	Rank.	Remarks.
\multicolumn{3}{c}{N.C.O.'s AND MEN—continued.}		
1617. Bradley, Clifford	Trooper	
1628. Beyer, Peter A.	,,	
1640. Brown, Norman	,,	
1827. Bell, W. J.	Farrier	Farrier-Sergeant
1641. Biddle, James T.	Trooper	
1673. Barber, Norman E.	,,	
1742. Brattan, Thomas H.	,,	
1745. Bonsfield, Henry R.	,,	
1756. Beehag, Sam. C.	,,	
1777. Black, William J.	,,	
1683. Bowker, J. C.	,,	
1818. Boyd, John	,,	
1822. Bignell, Frank G.	,,	
1436. Castray, James	,,	
1452. Coady, Richard	,,	
1469. Crispe, Edmond H.	,,	
1479. Crozier, M. B.	,,	
1495. Colless, George	,,	
1527. Chisholm, A. F.	,,	Corporal
1834. Cronin, T.	,,	
1524. Campbell, D.	,,	
1677. Cockroft, Alfred	,,	
1679. Cross, T. H.	,,	
1423. Curtin, William McCarthy	,,	
1659. Carroll, Henry I.	,,	
1662. Combes, Charles J.	,,	
1666. Cliff, James	,,	
1720. Corbett, William E.	,,	
1723. Chambers, Arthur	,,	
1721. Connell, Daniel	,,	
1727. Chambers, William	,,	
1728. Corby, Leslie M.	,,	
1748. Cavanagh, Daniel	,,	
1772. Cook, Francis F.	,,	
1775. Campbell, Horace G. C.	,,	
1678. Cardwell, Walter	,,	
1785. Carpenter, Alfred S.	,,	
1800. Cowx, John F.	,,	
1810. Corderoy, Sydney C.	,,	
1407. Dean, George	,,	
1500. Dyer, W. A.	,,	
1569. Denshire, Rupert C.	,,	
1663. Douglas, Robert	,,	
1704. Drury, A. E.	,,	
1680. Docherty, Andrew	,,	
1784. Dawson, William I.	,,	
1795. De Smet, Charles E.	,,	
1820. Devane, John B.	,,	
1505. Eather, James	,,	
1674. Evans, Ralph	,,	
1633. Evans, Harry	,,	
1688. Ellis, J.	,,	
1462. Fraser, Benjamin D.	,,	
1491. Foreman, Thomas	,,	
1492. Furber, John B.	,,	
1594. Findlay, Alexander	,,	
1624. Frawley, Daniel	,,	
1638. Fitzpatrick, Fredk. F.	,,	

Nominal Roll—*continued.*

No. and Name.	Rank.	Remarks.
N.C.O.'s AND MEN—*continued.*		
1653. Francis, William C.	Trooper	
1816. Finch, D. D.	,,	
1761. Freeman, George G.	,,	
1405. Gunn, Arthur	,,	
1453. Girdler, William H.	,,	
1463. Gaudin, August	,,	
1471. Gardiner, John S.	,,	
1499. Gannoni, Frederick	,,	
1596. Glasgow, Alexander J.	,,	
1630. Gribble, Arthur A.	,,	
1712. Gourlay, David B.	,,	
1817. Garvay, William J.	,,	
1684. Gilbert, W. H.	,,	
1437. Hickie, Arthur J.	,,	
1454. Harman, Robert	,,	
1489. Hanna, John A.	,,	
1497. Hurn, Richard	,,	
1501. Herberton, Harry T.	,,	
1556. Hay, W.	,,	
1584. Hail, Joseph	,,	
1599. Hay, George H.	,,	Corporal
1611. Hogan, John	,,	
1622. Hindmarsh, John A.	,,	
1631. Hampson, Harry W.	,,	
1715. Hunter, Sam F. H.	,,	
1724. Hart, Herbert	,,	
1735. Hibberd, David	,,	
1738. Hardie, Edward	,,	
1790. Handley, Herbert	,,	
1801. Hillis, George C.	,,	
1819. Hemme, Reginald	,,	
1824. Howard, Alfred E.	,,	
1829. Healey, Joseph	,,	Quartermaster-Sergeant
1404. Isherwood, Robert	,,	
1433. Jeffreys, Charles H.	,,	
1435. Jack, James H.	,,	
1466. Jacobs, Frank	,,	
1647. Joiner, Daniel A.	,,	
1650. Jacobs, Edward J.	,,	
1654. Johnson, Luke	,,	
1759. Jones, Edmond O.	,,	
1671. Jones, Charles	,,	Corporal
1660. Johnston, Stanley G.	,,	
1670. Johnston, A. G.	,,	
1830. Jones, Robert	,,	
1425. Knudson, G. J. H. G.	,,	
1595. Kelly, William M.	,,	
1563. King, Edward R.	,,	
1581. Kuhne, Charles W.	,,	
1523. Kennedy, Thomas	,,	Corporal
1809. Kenny, Francis T.	,,	
1448. Lemon, Thomas S. H.	,,	
1444. Laws, Charles	,,	
1455. Lagerlow, H. W.	,,	
1477. Lee, Thomas T.	,,	
1519. Leigh, J. T.	,,	
1528. Leathart, William	,,	
1627. Laughton, Herbert S.	,,	

Nominal Roll—*continued.*

No. and Name.	Rank.	Remarks.
N.C.O.'s AND MEN—*continued.*		
1570. Lewis, W. C.	Trooper	
1576. Lucas, William	,,	
1583. Leonard, Walter	,,	
1656. Lee, Thomas C.	,,	
1625. Logan, David James	,,	
1529. Locke, H. E.	,,	Died, 24.6.02
1737. Lea, Archibald	,,	
1739. Lynch, George	,,	
1780. Lea, Robert	,,	
1802. Lees, Beale	,,	
1421. Moon, William	,,	
1426. Marshall, John H.	,,	
1456. Miller, Montague C.	,,	Lance-Corporal
1458. Mason, John E.	,,	
1461. Marsh, Thomas G.	,,	
1510. Merriman, Frederick	,,	
1513. Manson, John A.	,,	Lance-Corporal
1417. McGrath, Henry	,,	
1431. McKee, William F.	,,	
1480. McKenzie, M. C.	,,	
1561. Mooney, Thomas T.	,,	
1586. Mair, Allan H.	,,	
1643. Mather, James	,,	
1672. Morris, Frank	,,	Lance-Corporal
1550. McDuff, Victor J.	,,	
1635. McDougall, F.	,,	
1705. Molloy, Frank A.	,,	
1716. Mace, George	,,	
1717. Martin, Arthur H.	,,	
1750. Manning, William E.	,,	
1753. Mychael, T. E.	,,	
1776. Malcolm, Albert	,,	
1831. Mansergh, Charles	,,	
1832. Morrow, E.	,,	
1718. McEvoy, Edward	,,	
1752. McLean, A. K.	,,	Corporal
1758. McDonald, Albert J.	,,	
1778. McKay, Charles	,,	
1676. Miller, O. T. B.	,,	
1685. McComb, David	,,	
1490. Neil, William	,,	
1669. Norton, Charles	,,	Remained in hospital, Sydney
1598. Naughton, Charles E.	,,	
1821. Newham, Wm. H.	,,	
1707. Nolan, Daniel	,,	
1165. Organ, James	,,	
1713. Onus, John G.	,,	
1755. Osborne, Thomas	,,	
1792. O'Donnell, Eugene	,,	
1481. Powe, Waverley G.	,,	
1482. Parkes, W. E.	,,	
1508. Perry, George	,,	
1511. Pooley, Sydney	,,	
1526. Potter, Henry	,,	
1553. Percy, Thomas	,,	
1560. Pye, William John	,,	
1618. Pease, Albert W.	,,	
1637. Parsons, William Frederick	,,	

Nominal Roll—*continued.*

No. and Name.	Rank.	Remarks.
N.C.O.'s AND MEN—*continued.*		
1655. Peno, Henry	Trooper	
1657. Phillips, Albert	,,	
1661. Preston, George	,,	
1730. Parkhill, Robert	,,	
1760. Powell, William G. A.	,,	
1781. Pritzler, William J.	,,	
1794. Putney, Henry G.	,,	
1619. Quinn, Patrick J.	,,	
1709. Quinn, Michael Joseph	,,	
1774. Quinn, Charles O.	,,	
1507. Riddle, William C.	,,	
1488. Rose, Ernest	,,	
1682. Ross, Edwin A.	,,	
1557. Roberts, Thomas	,,	
1558. Reynolds, Claude O.	,,	
1590. Reed, Murray M.	,,	
1686. Roberts, F. G.	,,	
1687. Reynolds, F. M.	,,	
1736. Roe, Edm. A.	,,	
1749. Reid, Archibald H.	,,	
1796. Rosewell, James T.	,,	
1825. Reynolds, William	,,	
1465. Smedley, William	,,	Corporal
1460. Saunders, Charles	,,	
1402. Smith, Samuel	,,	
1413. Sherwood, Fredk. R.	,,	
1432. Stanton, Harold M.	,,	
1439. Smith, D'Arcy	,,	Died at sea, –.7.02
1442. Smith, Harry P.	,,	
1457. Sullivan, Fred. W.	,,	
1476. St. George, Robert E.	,,	
1487. Smith, Fredk W.	,,	
1494. Storey, Sam	,,	
1530. Simpson, O., J.	,,	
1565. Sheedy, Michael	,,	Corporal
1575. Smith Henry J.	,,	
1580. Sneddon, Richard	,,	
1597. Shaw, Frederick	,,	
1600. Stockall, Leo J.	Saddler	
1601. Shaw, Henry	Trooper	
1620. Schroeder, Alfred C.	,,	
1621. Sullivan, Edward J. N.	,,	
1652. Seaton, George H.	,,	
1681. Skillen, F.	,,	
1675. Stubbs, Ephraim C.	,,	
1706. Sweep, Bernard	,,	
1762. Slade, Albert J.	,,	
1764. Spring, William E.	,,	
1773. Swan, William P.	,,	
1786. Savory, Frederick	,,	
1823. Schade, Christian	,,	
1814. Sutton, J. D.	,,	Promoted Sergeant-Major, O.R.C.; died, 3.2.03, after return to New South Wales
1496. Smith, Thomas W.	,,	
1503. Spence, Mervyn	,,	
1509. Sherringham, H. R.	,,	Died, 12.8.02
1521. Scott, Robert F.	,,	

Nominal Roll—*continued*.

No. and Name.	Rank.	Remarks.
N.C.O's AND MEN—*continued*.		
1593. Toms, John G.	Trooper	
1604. Tattersall, Joseph J.	,,	
1607. Thomson, D. A.	,,	Corporal
1428. Talbot, Hugh	,,	
1747. Tarrant, Edwin W.	,,	
1771. Twist, Henry E.	,,	
1787. Turner, John	,,	Corporal
1833. Toovey, John	,,	
1719. Upton, W. G.		
1578. Vale, Percy M.	,,	
1701. Vercoe, John A.	,,	
1450. Walters, Thomas E.	,,	
1506. Woods, James W.	,,	
1520. Williams, F. J.	,,	
1518. White, George	,,	
1555. Weston, Joe H.	,,	
1571. Wyborn, Edward	,,	
1574. Wilson, Herbert F.	,,	
1577. Williamson, Arthur	,,	
1606. Williams, George G.	,,	
1608. Wyld, Herbert T.	,,	
1610. Wells, John	,,	
1626. Walcott, Frank E.	,,	
1629. Walker, Ninian	,,	
1648. Wolstenholme, William F.	,,	
1649. Wright, George	,,	
1722. Woof, William	,,	
1734. Ward, John J.	,,	
1765. Ward, James B.	,,	
1767. Walsh, M. E.	,,	
1788. Williams, Frederick M.	,,	
1789. Winch, John A.	,,	
1797. Webb, William T.	,,	
1504. Young, James	,,	

FIFTH BATTALION AUSTRALIAN COMMONWEALTH HORSE.

THIS consisted of four squadrons, with the following establishment:—Staff— 1 lieut-colonel, 1 major, 1 adjutant, 1 quartermaster, 1 medical officer, 1 veterinary officer, 1 regimental sergeant-major, 1 quartermaster-sergeant, 1 O.R. sergeant; total, 6 officers, 1 warrant-officer, 2 sergeants, with 9 horses. Squadron of 4 troops— 1 major or captain, 4 subalterns, 1 squadron sergeant-major, 1 squadron quartermaster-sergeant, 4 sergeants, 1 sergeant-farrier, 3 shoeing-smiths, 1 saddler, 2 trumpeters, 6 corporals, 97 privates; total, one squadron, 5 officers, 6 sergeants, 5 artificers, 2 trumpeters, 103 rank and file—in all, 121, with an equal number of horses. Total of battalion of 4 squadrons, 26 officers, 1 warrant-officer, 26 sergeants, 20 artificers, 8 trumpeters, 412 rank and file; in all, 493, with 493 horses.

ORGANIZATION.

It was resolved no longer to create composite battalions representing different States, but to raise the whole corps in New South Wales on a territorial basis, in order to associate defined districts, and the military units existing in those districts, with each battalion, squadron, and troop. By such means it was considered the battalion would consist of officers and men who represented the State. Each squadron would represent a distinct district, and the troops in that district; and each troop would further represent a particular corps or military unit in a defined locality. Officers and men would thus bring with them to the squadrons and troops so formed (representative of defined districts and the troops belonging to such districts), all the cohesion, comradeship, and local association which are such valuable elements in promoting the highest standard of discipline in the field, and gallantry before the enemy.

Enrolment, therefore, was carried out under the General Officer Commanding Commonwealth Forces, New South Wales, by the commissioned officers of regiments and squadrons of the districts and localities selected to furnish a quota of men; and, as soon as appointed, the officers commanding battalion, squadrons, and troops assisted. Preference in selecting men was given (1) to those then serving in existing military units in each of the districts named; (2) to those who had served in South Africa; (3) to civilians possessing the most valuable military qualities. Enrolling officers were required to ascertain that the applicant fulfilled the required conditions, and that he was a suitable representative of the district troops; upon which he was furnished with a certificate and directed to present himself at the place of concentration of the squadron upon a given date. Candidates were then medically examined, tested in horsemanship and rifle practice; and finally, if passed, enrolled and attested.

Upon this principle "A" Squadron represented New South Wales Lancers and troops in localities covered by this regiment; "B" Squadron—New South Wales Mounted Rifles and troops in such localities; "C" Squadron—Australian Horse and troops in localities covered by half this regiment; "D" Squadron—Australian Horse and troops in localities covered by half this regiment.

The four "troops" into which each squadron was divided were thus recruited:—

"*A*" *Squadron* (*Lancers*)—1st troop—Sydney squadron, enrolled at Sydney; 2nd troop—Camden-Berry squadron, enrolled at Berry; 3rd troop—Maitland, Singleton, and Newcastle squadron, enrolled at Newcastle; 4th troop—Parramatta, Richmond, and Windsor squadron, enrolled at Parramatta.

"*B*" *Squadron* (*Mounted Rifles*)—1st troop—Tenterfield, Inverell, Lismore, and Casino squadron, enrolled at Tenterfield; 2nd troop—Bathurst-Molong squadron and Forbes half-squadron, enrolled at Bathurst; 3rd troop—Picton-Camden squadron, enrolled at Camden; 4th troop—Bega and Canterbury half-squadrons, enrolled at Canterbury.

"*C*" *Squadron* (*Australian Horse*)—1st troop—Armidale, Glen-Innes squadron, enrolled at Armidale; 2nd troop—Tamworth-Gunnedah squadron, enrolled at Tamworth; 3rd troop—Scone, Belltrees, and Muswellbrook squadron, enrolled at Scone; 4th troop—Mudgee, Lue, and Rylstone squadron, enrolled at Mudgee.

"*D*" *Squadron* (*Australian Horse*)—1st troop—Goulburn squadron, enrolled at Goulburn; 2nd troop—Braidwood-Araluen squadron, enrolled at Araluen; 3rd troop—Bungendore and Michelago squadron, enrolled at Bungendore; 4th troop—Gundagai, Cootamundra, and Murrumburrah squadron, enrolled at Murrummurrah.

QUALIFICATIONS AND PAY.

Qualifications were :—Height, not less than 5 feet 3 inches ; chest measurement, not less than 34 inches ; age, not under 20 ; to pass medical examination ; ride and shoot well ; single men only, except in case of senior N.C.O.'s of exceptional merit, who, if enlisted, were warned that their widows and children had claims on Patriotic Fund only, and not on Imperial funds, for pensions.

Pay and field allowances as for former Contingents.

Preference for horses was given to those bought by men who enrolled. Qualification : standard 15 to 15.3 ; age, 5 to 12 years.

REFERENCE TO ORDERS.

Pay and allowances ..	.. D.O. 159, of 9th April, 1902
Formation ..	,, ,, ,, ,,
Equipment	,, ,, ,, ,,
Enrolment ..	,, ,, ,, ,,
Establishment	,, ,, ,, ,,
Clothing and equipment	,, ,, ,, ,,
Embarkation	,, ,, ,, ,,

CLOTHING, ETC.

Uniform consisted of brown F.S. jacket and pants, puttees, and hat. Equipped with bandoliers, and saddlery, and fully horsed.

SERVICE.

The battalion embarked on transport *Columbian* at Sydney, on 22nd May, 1902, and disembarked on 18th June, at Durban. It comprised 22 officers, 465 other ranks, with 490 horses ; 91 were struck off in South Africa, and 22 officers, 374 others, returned.

This splendid battalion had no chance of displaying its capabilities, the war having ended before its arrival. During its short stay in South Africa, half the battalion was stationed at Newcastle, Natal, and the other half at Durban, and subsequently at Gillett's, Natal.

The battalion again embarked at Durban on the transport *Manchester Merchant* on 1st July, and disembarked at Sydney on 1st August, 1902, having called at Albany, Adelaide, Melbourne, and Hobart *en route*.

NOMINAL ROLL.

No. and Name.	Rank.	Remarks.
BATTALION STAFF.		
Onslow, James William Macarthur	Lieut.-Colonel	Served as S.S. Officer
O'Brien, William Edward	Major	With Imperial Bushmen
Soane, Ernest William Reading	Captain and Adjutant	,, ,, ,,
Crane, Frederick William Charlesworth	Captain and Quartermaster	
Bell, George Lawaluk	Lieutenant Medical Officer	
Murphy, Charles Thomas	Regt. Sergeant-Major	
Young, Edward	Regt. Quartermaster Sergeant	
McGrath, James John	Staff-Sergeant O.R.C.	
"A" SQUADRON.		
Blow, Ernest Alfred	Captain	
Filney, Leslie Edward	Lieutenant	
Gould, George Edward	,,	
Innes, Percival Selwyn Long	,,	
28. McCormac, William Henry	Squadron Sergeant-Major	
45. Appleyard, Richard	Sergeant	
10. Crisp, Herbert Edward	,,	
15. Duffy, Edwin Herbert	,,	
93. Vandenbergh, William	,,	
60. Whinfield, Felix Edgar	,,	
61. Avon, George	Farrier Sergeant	
6. Baker, Frank Cargill	Corporal	
83. Brownlee, Thomas James	,,	
16. Dunstan, Richard Edwin	,,	
30. Nicholson, Alexander Douglas	,,	
56. Smith, David Owen Leslie	,,	
58. Vivers, Robert	,,	
32. Quinn, Terence	Paid Lance-Corporal	
43. Alderson, Frank Barry Strauss	Lance-Corporal (unpaid)	
118. Hardy, Victor John	Trumpeter	
50. Jobson, Alfred Henry	,,	
49. Henderson, George	Farrier	
86. Lofts, Alfred	,,	
55. Sinclair, Frank Leighton	,,	
57. Sinclair, Samuel	,,	
4. Akers, Stanley	Trooper	
44. Allman, Daniel John	,,	
62. Appleby, Thomas Samuel	,,	
5. Armstrong, Robert Montgomery	,,	
100. Ashley, William Patrick	,,	
46. Auliff, Herbert	,,	
90. Blundell, George Manning	,,	
117. Bossley, Sydney Burdekin	,,	
7. Bowen, Henry William	,,	
113. Brodie, William Richard	,,	
8. Burston, John Stewart	,,	
89. Byrne, George	,,	

Nominal Roll—*continued.*

No. and Name.	Rank.	Remarks.
"A" SQUADRON—*continued.*		
112. Browne, Charles Simon	Trooper	
94. Brown, George Alfred	,,	
63. Carne, Thomas Broughton	,,	
65. Clarke, Joseph James	,,	
66. Cook, Joseph William	,,	
64. Cogan, John Livingstone	,,	
95. Carrick, James	,,	
99. Craig, Charles Wm. Leslie	,,	
9. Challen, Frederic	,,	
121. Chatfield, Leslie	,,	
11. Day, Arthur Thomas	,,	
67. Douglas, Oliver George	,,	
14. Duffy, Oliver Andrew	,,	
47. Davis, John Walter	,,	
48. Deal, John William	,,	
12. Dodds, Herbert Sydney	,,	
124. Dare, Arthur Edwin	,,	
68. Davies, David Morgan	,,	
13. Drayton, Walter Roland	,,	
123. Deane, Albert Joseph	,,	
69. Eather, Harry	,,	
17. Ezzy, Frederick James	,,	
70. Farlow, Joseph James	,,	
101. Forsyth, Walter	,,	
19. Gibson, Harold	,,	
18. Greentree, Harry Arthur	,,	
120. Garvan, William	,,	
105. Howell, Edgar Robert	,,	
20. Hibbert, Daniel Richard	,,	
97. Hadlow, Stephen	,,	
116. Hatton, William	,,	
22. King, Robert Edwin	,,	
119. Kirkland, Reginald Charles	,,	
21. Kelly, Michael Joseph	,,	
51. Lowe, Arthur Melbourne	,,	
73. Lacey, John Henry	,,	
24. Lethbridge, Fredk. Augustus	,,	
72. Lackey, Albert Mathew	,,	
23. Lambke, Peter John	,,	
74. Mallett, Raymond Robert	,,	
53. Munro, George	,,	
106. Mackel, Joseph Francis	,,	
122. McCann, Robert James	,,	
25. Markham, Charles	,,	
52. Mills, Robert James	,,	
27. McKenzie, Alexander	,,	
77. McPherson, John Wilks	,,	
91. McNamara, Thomas	,,	
76. Martin, Albert Ernest	,,	
26. Martin, William George	,,	
102. Murphy, John James	,,	
114. McPhee, Charles Malcolm	,,	
29. Missingham, John	,,	
75. Missingham, Robert	,,	
54. Nimmett, Robert	,,	
78. Norton, Charles	,,	
31. O'Brien, William Stephen	,,	
108. Osmond, Thomas	Saddler	

Nominal Roll—*continued*.

No. and Name.	Rank.	Remarks.

"A" Squadron—*continued*.

No. and Name.	Rank.	Remarks.
103. Parker, Edwin	Trooper	
33. Reeves, Albert	,,	
98. Roberts, Frederick	,,	
109. Roberts, Leslie	,,	
34. Robinson, Edwin	,,	
79. Ryan, William Augustus	,,	
37. Somer, Phillip James	,,	
87. Somerville, Robert Walter Brewer	,,	
92. Smithson, Harold Aubrey	,,	
111. Scott, Percy	,,	
36. Smith, Ernest Edward	,,	
35. Sly, William Henry	,,	
38. Thoroughgood, Henry	,,	
107. Turner, Alfred	,,	
80. Tait, Sydney James	,,	
39. Vanderbergh, Charles William	,,	
59. Voller, Algie	,,	
82. Webber, Henry	,,	
41. Walton, Robert Orlando	,,	
81. Wells, Daniel	,,	
84. White, Francis William	,,	
110. Woollard, Arthur	,,	
42. Woodworth, William George	,,	
40. Wareham, Harry Dunlop	,,	

"B" Squadron.

No. and Name.	Rank.	Remarks.
Everett, William Frank	Captain	
Bathgate, John Douglas	Lieutenant	
Bossley, Frederick Vincent	,,	Contingent, S.A.
Neild, William James	,,	1st N.S.W. Mounted Rifles
129. Atkinson, William	Sqn. Sergeant-Major	,, ,,
107. Alexander, George Edward	Sqn. Quartermaster-General	
137. Fraser, Samuel	Sergeant	
157. Fryer, Alexander	,,	
165. Stewart, Graham	,,	
144. Shearman, Charles Woodford	,,	
135. Finch, William Henry	Farrier-Sergeant	
139. Lynch, Robert Thomas	Lance-Sergeant	
226. Attrill, Charles Henry	Corporal	
228. Bolger, Robert Charles	,,	
133. Davey, George Allan	,,	
138. Gillfillan, John Robert	,,	
166. Shields, William John	,,	
130. Beacham, William Edley	Lance-Corporal	
170. Bennett, Henry Stephen	,,	
212. Kennedy, George Alexander	,,	
193. See, Garnet Edward	,,	
236. Wall, John Felix	,,	
244. Bode, Charles Theodore	Trumpeter	
159. Hughes, Victor Russell	,,	
154. Darcy, Robert Joseph	Saddler	
180. Ingrey, Arthur	,,	
142. McNamara, William	,,	

Nominal Roll—*continued.*

No. and Name.	Rank.	Remarks.
"B" Squadron—*continued.*		
179. Hamilton, Benjamin	Shoeing-smith	
225. Ross, William	,,	
235. Schafer, Thomas Abraham	,,	
146. Armstrong, William James	Trooper	
145. Armstrong, Wilson	,,	
167. Armstrong, George Waddell	,,	
206. Burge, Arthur Macaffie	,,	
169. Bentley, Thomas	,,	
199. Bush, Edgar William	,,	
147. Bartley, Herbert Wilford	,,	
168. Burgess, Theodore Fredk.	,,	
151. Clarke, Robert Henry	,,	
149. Clark, Charles Henry	,,	
150. Crisp, Henry	,,	
132. Collins, James Joseph	,,	
148. Cortis, William Henry	,,	
153. Cahill, William	,,	
171. Clemson, Ernest	,,	
229. Crouch, Henry Wolsey	,,	
200. Clarke, Lancelot Walter	,,	
152. Casey, Edwin	,,	
208. Childs, Julian	,,	
131. Coates, Leslie Herbert	,,	
210. Davies, John Edward	,,	
174. Donn, Francis	,,	
201. Davies, John Northam	,,	
134. Dennis, Leslie Thomas A.	,,	
209. Davis, Edwin	,,	
156. Diamond, William	,,	
175. Eisenmanger, Charles	,,	
230. Edwards, Henry William	,,	
176. Fraser, Henry Campbell	,,	
136. Forrester, David	,,	
238. Fogarty, Thomas Joseph	,,	
211. Fraser, Innis	,,	
239. Gaskell, Ivor Augustus	,,	
249. Griffin, Walter T.	,,	
248. Goldfinch, Philip Henry Macarthur	,,	
202. Gilbert, William John	,,	
246. Gribble, James	,,	
178. Hughes, Roland	,,	
222. Hobbs, Edwin	,,	
177. Hardy, Henry George L. R.	,,	
240. Hurley, Norman Sydney	,,	
158. Hill, Arthur	,,	
223. Hopkins, Edward John	,,	
221. Hobden, Arthur Albert	,,	
231. Hayden, Percival	,,	
224. Johnston, Charles	,,	
160. Judge, Frederick William	,,	
181. James, Arthur	,,	
213. Kelly, James	,,	
215. Leis, George	,,	
182. Luther, Bertie Murray	,,	
214. Lyons, Joseph	,,	
161. Legge, Charles Ernest	,,	
216. Lacey, Albert	,,	

Nominal Roll—*continued.*

No. and Name.	Rank.	Remarks.
"B" SQUADRON—*continued.*		
163. Marsden, Frederick Wm.	Trooper	
203. Mawkes, George	,,	
242. McDonald, Donald	,,	
217. Merchant, Francis	,,	
184. Maunsell, William Stewart	,,	
188. Medcalf, Edward Ernest	,,	
141. McGrath, John William	,,	
140. McAnnalty, Paul Albert	,,	
186. McLeod, William	,,	
232. McKenzie, Robert Henry	,,	
187. Mestre, John C. Prosper de	,,	
185. Morrice, Osborn	,,	
243. Murray, Ernest	,,	
162. McDonald, William	,,	
183. McDonald, John	,,	
143. Morgan, Robert Thomas	,,	
189. Nicholson, Duncan	,,	
190. Ordoyne, George Edward	,,	
191. Parkinson, Edward	,,	
164. Parnell, Lawrence	,,	
233. Quigley, Charles	,,	
218. Ryan, James Albert	,,	
204. Rouse, Henry Lionel	,,	
234. Rixon, Percy	,,	
195. Stidolph, Washington	,,	
219. Smith, Henry Samuel	,,	
194. Starling, Bob	,,	
192. Samuels, Robert Osenel	,,	
205. Smith, James	,,	
196. Smith, Amos Anthony	,,	
220. Wolstenholme, Arthur A. E.	,,	
245. Wynne, William Joseph	,,	
198. Williams, John	,,	
237. Wall, Edward Patrick	,,	
241. Webb, Francis	,,	
197. Williams, William Charles	,,	
"C" SQUADRON.		
Ryrie, V. W.	Captain	Imperial Bushmen
King, A. E. G.	Lieutenant	,,
Geary, G. G.	,,	Citizens' Bushmen
Ryder, A. O.	,,	
256. Deane, Harry	Sqn. Sergeant-Major	Kitchener's Scouts
273. Simpson, Frederick Fowler	Sqn. Quartermaster-Sergeant	
301. Bossley, Charles Clifton	Sergeant	
325. Cusack, Joseph Michael	,,	
361. Harkness, Thomas	,,	
359. Ryrie, Harold S.	,,	
338. Berwick, William Henry	Farrier-Sergeant	
326. Campbell, James	,,	
253. Allwood, Frederick Theodore	Corporal	
303. Brown, Wm. Chas. Agnew	,,	
312. Jones, Benjamin	,,	
263. Jamieson, William Jan	,,	
296. Price, Richard Ernest	,,	

Nominal Roll—*continued.*

No. and Name.	Rank.	Remarks.
"C" SQUADRON—*continued.*		
271. Ridge, Merwyn Claude	Corporal	
302. Aurisch, Bernard Frank	Lance-Corporal	
288. Jackson, Herbert Joseph	,,	
362. Hawes, Theophilus Octavius	Trumpeter	
330. Prott, Leonard Clyde	,,	
350. Osmond, Albert	Saddler	
277. Bowman, Thomas	Farrier	
304. Clarke, Ernest Martin	,,	
349. Newman, Thomas	,,	
254. Alcorn, Raymond Leslie	Trooper	
275. Alcorn, Charles Albert	,,	
352. Armstrong, Alf. William	,,	
335. Armstrong, Joseph John	,,	
276. Ambler, Herbert William	,,	
336. Beer, Walter George	,,	
337. Bower, Walter	,,	
255. Bullen, Charles	,,	
280. Bracken, James Edward	,,	
357. Bowman, George Sydney	,,	
279. Brodie, Reginald Wm. Finch	,,	
339. Blake, William	,,	
281. Brassell, Thomas Joseph	,,	
278. Beckton, Clarence Edw.	,,	
341. Cameron, Duncan Alexander	,,	
340. Coughlin, Henry Edward	,,	
284. Chisholm, Henry Alexander	,,	
283. Connaughton, Thomas Joseph	,,	
305. Curran, J. F.	,,	
282. Clay, William Henry	,,	
363. Chalmers, Arthur	,,	
342. Dwyer, William	,,	
358. Doran, Walter	,,	
306. Douglas, Francis	,,	
286. Davis, Edward James	,,	
285. Davis, Mathew	,,	
343. Dwyer, Victor Robert	,,	
366. Demery, John	,,	
327. Davis, Richard	,,	
328. Farrell, Stanislaus Joseph	,,	
368. Foran, George	,,	
307. Foench, James Hooper	,,	
308. French, Oswald Ernest	,,	
331. Fitzgerald, Patrick	,,	
258. Gimbert, William Ephraim	,,	
285. Grinsell, Albert	,,	
259. Gurd, Robert	,,	
260. Gurran, Henry	,,	
257. Gillan, George Francis	,,	
311. Harrison, John Emanuel	,,	
262. Heagney, Richard	,,	
261. Hughes, Percy Ince	,,	
309. Harrison, Walter	,,	
310. Harrison, Ernest Thomas	,,	
367. Hocking, J. A.	,,	
364. Hindmarsh, George	,,	
344. Johnstone, Norman	,,	
353. James, William John	,,	
313. Kennedy, John	,,	

Nominal Roll—continued.

No. and Name.	Rank.	Remarks.
"C" Squadron—continued.		
345. Keegan, Henry	Trooper	
289. Kerr, Sydney	,,	
314. Kerr, Clarence Paget	,,	
264. Lewis, Hyman	,,	
265. Lonsdale, William Thomas	,,	
315. Leonard, Henry Herbert	,,	
346. Larpent, Arthur John	,,	
269. McHugh, James	,,	
348. McKenzie, Arthur	,,	
266. Morson, Henry	,,	
317. Murray, Henry Joseph	,,	
316. Murtagh, Alexander Patk.	,,	
291. McMillan, Robert Baker	,,	
292. McFerran, Arthur Blair	,,	
290. McGovern, Walter Reginald	,,	
268. McKenzie, John Norman	,,	
329. McNeill, Robert	,,	
267. McLean, Hector Ronald	,,	
347. Molloy, Henry	,,	
354. Morrison, Wilfred	,,	
293. North, Archibald H. Fleming	,,	
270. Oldfield, Sydney Livingstone	,,	
318. O'Connell, John	,,	
294. Parry, Henry John	,,	
297. Partridge, Wm. Benjamin Henry	,,	
332. Pipe, Herbert Alfred	,,	
295. Phelan, Patrick	,,	
324. Percival, Frederick John	,,	
319. Robertson, Donald	,,	
360. Ryan, Thomas	,,	
351. Robins, Alfred Charles	,,	
298. See, Frederick	,,	
320. Sewell, Thomas	,,	
321. Snell, Oliver Edward	,,	
274. Sweeney, Edward	,,	
322. Stewart, Thomas	,,	
274. Slapp, Henry Frederick	,,	
299. Stilwell, John	,,	
323. Taylor, William	,,	
365. Taylor, Wesley Joseph	,,	
333. Threlfall, Robert	,,	
334. Ussher, John Lachlan	,,	
356. Westaway, George	,,	
355. Williams, James	,,	
300. Worrad, William Henry	,,	
"D" Squadron.		
Ryrie, Oswald Bruce	Captain	Imperial Bushmen
Dickson, B. B.	Lieutenant	
Martin, W. P.	,,	
Ussher, Neville James	2nd Lieutenant	1st Australian Horse Contingent
431. Hunt, E. W.	Sqn. Sergeant-Major	
486. Monkley, Percy Hamilton	Sqn. Quartermaster-Sergeant	
382. Hill, Alexander	Sergeant	

Nominal Roll—*continued*.

"D" SQUADRON—*continued*.

No. and Name.	Rank.	Remarks.
383. King, Samuel	Sergeant	
400. Macansh, Duncan	,,	
443. Smith, C. W.	,,	
391. Williams, Jonathan	,,	
378. Barker, A. H.	Corporal	
380. Chalker, William Edward	,,	
399. Lyttleton, W.	,,	
387. Overend, Thomas Edward	,,	
477. Thompson, J. B.	,,	
413. Gandy, Noah	Trumpeter	
485. Gray, Arthur Horace Leslie	,,	
428. Foy, Charles	Farrier	
396. Gutterson, George William Bertie	,,	
442. Rogan, James	,,	
388. Renehan, Michael Joseph	,,	
417. Abbey, Wilfred	Trooper	
445. Ayre, Thomas Bell	,,	
416. Aikin, William Andrew	,,	
447. Barrett, W.	,,	
446. Boxall, F.	,,	
405. Beckhouse, Jacob	,,	
419. Beckhouse, James	,,	
407. Brooker, F.	,,	
406. Beatty, William	,,	
377. Bridges, Herbert	,,	
418. Bungate, Robert Hamilton	,,	
420. Barrington, Donald Henry	,,	
408. Bennett, Ernest Alexander	,,	
422. Collins, T. J.	,,	
487. Crittle, J.	,,	
410. Craig, Robert Henry	,,	
379. Crawford, Reginald Calder	,,	
394. Clayton, Walter	,,	
411. Coles, William	,,	
409. Creswick, F. W.	,,	
393. Cassey, Michael	,,	
381. Chalker, John Henry	,,	
392. Chalker, William Arthur	,,	
423. Case, T. E. W.	,,	
448. Charlesworth, Arthur Joseph	,,	
450. Dennett, John	,,	
424. Daft, Edward	,,	
395. Dunn, James	,,	
412. Dixon, William	,,	
426. Dunlop, Robert	,,	
425. Dunlop, Charles	,,	
452. Finch, H. W.	,,	
427. Fenn, William Thomas	,,	
415. Gordon, Hugh	,,	
414. Goodman, A. J.	,,	
397. Guy, William Henry	,,	
429. Grenenger, Leslie Augustus	,,	
496. Hart, J. W.	,,	
430. Hourn, N. F.	,,	
488. Hill, A. W.	,,	
398. Haydon, James	,,	
433. Jobson, Frank	,,	
453. Jones, Lance	,,	

Nominal Roll—continued.

No. and Name.	Rank.	Remarks.
"D" SQUADRON—continued.		
434. Jeffs, George	Trooper	
432. Johnston, T. A.	,,	
454. Kreamer, A. E.	,,	
435. Keane, Patrick John	,,	
436. Large, R. A.	,,	
456. Lynch, J. W.	,,	
384. Lynn, Richard John	,,	
456. Ledger, Alfred	,,	
494. McGowan, A. J.	,,	
438. Matthews, William Charles	,,	
440. McAllister, Patrick Edward	,,	
458. Moore, Joseph Charles	,,	
489. Maher, Michael	,,	
437. Mallard, Edward	,,	
385. McMahon, Thomas James	,,	
461. McGuire, Thomas Bernard	,,	
495. Murphy, Daniel	,,	
462. Myers, Kenrick William	,,	
441. McLean, W. J.	,,	
460. McDonnell, William Paul	,,	
439. McGrath, Robert	,,	
491. Murphy, Henry	,,	
490. Murphy, William	,,	
463. Nash, Albert	,,	
386. Neich, Arthur Joseph	,,	
464. Payton, E.	,,	
492. Powell, F.	,,	
465. Pope, John	,,	
466. Quinn, Henry	,,	
471. Ryan, James Daniel	,,	
389. Robson, Matthew William Chas.	,,	
468. Riley, William James	,,	
467. Renehan, James Patrick	,,	
469. Renehan, Martin	,,	
470. Reid, Robert David	,,	
472. Simons, W.	,,	
475. Stewart, John James	,,	
401. Sparks, M.	,,	
498. Sullivan, John	,,	
455. Siebert, George Augustus	,,	
474. Sheehan, Arthur Edward	,,	
473. Shennech, Thomas	,,	
402. Tyrrell, Leo. John	,,	
390. Verrender, William Henry	,,	
444. Webb, W.	,,	
404. Williams, F.	,,	
403. Walker, Thomas	,,	
497. Wynne, Clifford E. C.	,,	
482. Webber, Edward Henry	,,	
480. Walters, Robert Frederick	,,	
478. West, Arthur	,,	
479. White, Alfred	,,	
483. White, Edward	,,	
481. Ware, Michael John Joseph	,,	
484. Younie, Hugh	,,	
499. Rush, James	,,	

SPECIAL SERVICE OFFICERS.

A CERTAIN number of officers were sent to the war, with the sanction of the Imperial War Office, not detailed to Contingents, but independently, for the purpose of employment at the theatre of operations, as authorized by the Commander-in-Chief. Thus, either in staff employ or attached to Columns in the field they would gain valuable experience in the many changes and chances which occur during active service. They would also be afforded opportunity to observe and sustain the vicissitudes and privations of warfare, and to note the value of initiative, and capability to act promptly upon any available resources in each and every emergency.

It should be noted that four of the officers whose record is included in the subjoined series, did not originally proceed to South Africa as Special Service officers, but were, nevertheless, employed as such, and could not, therefore, properly be omitted. These were:—

Onslow, Lieut.-Colonel.—Went to South Africa at his own expense, and was attached to Field Force as Special Service officer.

Rose, Rev. H. J.—Went as chaplain with Second Contingent, Australian Horse; and was attached to South African Field Force.

Morris, Major.—Was in charge of troops on *Antillian*, and was employed at the base.

Niesigh, Captain.—Went with draft of "Spare" details, and was employed with staff, Oversea Colonials.

Nine N.C.O.'s and men went as officers' servants.

Bayly, Major (afterwards Lieut.-Colonel) M. W.—Proceeded to South Africa 3rd November, 1899, by the transport *Aberdeen*. He saw service in various capacities, and was taken prisoner. Subjoined is his own account of his experience:—

"Cape Town, 23rd August, 1900.—I have been with Lord Methuen's force attached to his staff, and then to Lord Chesham with the 1st Imperial Yeomanry Brigade of the same division. Briefly, events were as follows:—Actions, Swartz Kopjesfontein, Spitzkop, about April (the dates were in my diary which I had to destroy when captured); then Ville Bois Mareuil; then marched to Hoopstad, Bothaville (south bank of Vaal River), to Kroonstad, where we arrived on the 28th May. This was the longest march without coming in contact with the Boers during the campaign—250 miles. We had a convoy of six miles of waggons, and lost 3,000 oxen *en route*. I was temporarily attached to the A.S.C., and learned a good deal *re* transport. Thence on to Lindley, where we were too late to relieve the 13th Yeomanry, but defeated De Wet and recaptured Lindley. From there we marched to Colville and on to Heilbron, arriving on the 7th June. Thence along the main line (where we fought C. De Wet at Kopjesfontein) and Rhenoster, but again too late to rescue the Sherwood Foresters. Marched on to Kroonstad and back in a hurry to help Colonel Spence at Kopjesfontein, and chased De Wet, who still had 800 Sherwood Foresters in tow. Thence to Eland's Laagte, where De Wet got away on the 19th June. Ordered to Kroonstad once more, and here I was captured *en route* while foraging for cattle, &c. My mate's horse was shot and I couldn't get him away, hence capture. The Boers took us to Rietz and Bethlehem where we met Steyn; re-arrested by Theron and taken to the mountains during the fight at Bethlehem, before the British got in. We were then permitted by Steyn to try and get back to Bethlehem, which we eventually succeeded in doing. We were heartily glad to be once more with 'our own.' General Hunter was very kind to us. Meanwhile the 1st Division trekked to the Vaal, and I returned to Cape Town."

Grieve, Lieutenant G. J.—Embarked at Sydney on transport *Kent* on 28th October; arrived at Cape Town, 1st December, 1899. Attached to Royal Highlanders (Black Watch). Killed at Paardeberg Drift, 18th February, 1900.

Extracts from Report of Lieutenant G. J. Grieve.

Modder River, 1st January, 1900.—On arrival at Cape Town on the 6th December last, I was detailed by the Chief Staff Officer, line of communications, as railway staff officer, Cape Town.

As I felt that this position would not enable me to see active service, I interviewed the Chief Staff Officer, who informed me that I must remain in the position referred to for the time being.

On the 13th I heard of the losses sustained at Magersfontein; I immediately called on the Chief Staff Officer who, after a large amount of hesitation, gave me orders to leave at once and report to the Officer Commanding Highland Brigade here. I left at an hour's notice, and on arrival was appointed to the command of "T" Company, 2nd Black Watch.

Since my arrival I have been constantly employed on outpost duty and working parties, owing to the shortness of officers (only eight) four of whom are under six months' service) in the battalion; I am on outpost every second day.

The great loss sustained by the battalion has seriously affected its *morale*, and I think it will be left here (Modder River) when an advance takes place. In that case I intend to apply to join another battalion of the brigade or get appointed to the staff of Brigadier-General Macdonald, to whom I am known.

The position of the enemy is very strong. I have been twice on escort to the guns with my company on reconnaissance, and have been within 2,000 yards of their trenches, which are in tiers with good head cover. Shelling on both sides goes on daily, but their shells are very defective, while our 4·7 naval guns always silence their guns. I have been under fire on four occasions, but only of a very trivial nature.

General Order (New South Wales) 146, 19th October, 1900.

The General Officer Commanding has much pleasure in making known through General Order the following opinions expressed by the immediate Commanding Officers of the late Lieutenant Grieve, and which have only recently been received:—

From Major-General H. A. Macdonald, C.B., D.S.O., Commanding Highland Brigade.

"You should all be proud of Lieutenant Grieve. He was ever foremost in his desire to show that those from Australia would not be behind in the attack; and thus he was always ahead gallantly leading his men to victory, men who deplore his loss and who knew his skill as a leader. The officers and men of the famous battalion to which he was attached—a battalion whose record is second to none—mourn for him as for one of themselves, and in the history of the Royal Highlanders, the name of Lieutenant Grieve will find honorable mention and abiding record, an honour to his people and to his country."

From Lieut.-Colonel A. M. Carthew-Yorstoun, Commanding 2nd "The Black Watch."

Bethlehem, 9th August, 1900.

To the Brigade Major, Highland Brigade.

Sir,—I have the honour to submit the following report concerning late Lieutenant Grieve of the New South Wales Forces, as it might be of use or give pleasure to his relatives :—

"Lieutenant Grieve was attached to the battalion under my command in January, 1900. He was a most useful officer, full of resource and energy. He knew his work thoroughly, and was in command of a company for some time. He was present at the action at Koodesburg, as well as at Paardeberg, and on each occasion distinguished himself by untiring energy and zeal. His loss was much regretted by this battalion, with whom he was most popular, on account of his genial temperament, as well as his sterling qualifications as an officer and a soldier. He had much influence with the men, in whose welfare he took great interest.

I have the honour to be, &c.,

A. M. CARTHEW-YORSTOUN, Lieut.-Colonel,
Commanding 2nd 'The Black Watch.'"

Bridges, Major (now Brigadier-General) W. T.—Embarked at Sydney on transport *Aberdeen*, 3rd November, arrived at Cape Town, 6th December, 1899.

Attached to R.A. Cavalry division while in South Africa. Brigadier-General Bridges was present at the operations in Cape Colony, south of Orange River, 1899–1900, including action at Colesberg. He was also with the army at the relief of Kimberley. Present at operations in Orange Free State, February to May, 1900, including Paardeberg, Poplar Grove, Driefontein, and Karee Siding. Being taken with enteric fever was sent to hospital in Bloemfontein, and upon becoming convalescent, was invalided to England, from whence he returned to Sydney, *via* Cape Town, arriving 21st September, 1900. Queen's Medal with three clasps.

Extract from Major W. T. Bridges' Report.

Bloemspruit, near Bloemfontein, Orange Free State, 20th March, 1900.—I left Orange River and proceeded to Modder River Station on 5th February. At this place I saw the siege guns in action against the trenches of Magersfontein. It was the custom to fire a few rounds at sunrise and sunset. The guns (5" B.L.) were laid by means of General G. A. French's telescopic sights, *i.e.*, a telescope was attached to a bar fixed to the fore and hind sights. The arrangement I was told acted satisfactorily, though it was only roughly made on the spot.

The cavalry division was re-organized at Modder as follows :—

1st Brigade (Colonel Pater in command).—Carbineers, Scot's Greys, Inniskillings, New South Wales Lancers; R.H.A., T, Q, and U; Lieut.-Colonel Rochford.

2nd Brigade (Colonel Broadwood).—Household Cavalry; 12th Lancers; R.H.A., G and P (P battery joined at Ram Dam) ; Major Barmatyne-Allison.

3rd Brigade (Colonel Gordon).—9th and 16th Lancers, Mounted Infantry, Colonel Hannay's Brigade; R.H.A., O and R Batteries, Lieut.-Colonel Eustace.

Colonel Davidson, R.H.A., on whose staff I am, was appointed C.R.A. on General French's staff. The division marched from Modder at 3 a.m. on 11th February, and reached Ram Dam about 10 a.m.

On 12th, moved at 1.45 a.m., and the first Boer gun opened at 6.30 a.m. The Reit River, between Waterval Drift and De Kiel's farm, was reached about 10 a.m., and after a slight resistance the Drift was secured.

The division moved off next day at 10 a.m., and secured the passage of the Modder about 5 p.m. Halted at Modder during the 14th.

It was decided here not to have a C.R.A. for the division, and Colonel Davidson took command of the 2nd Brigade division; consequently, I have since remained with the 2nd Cavalry brigade.

On 15th February we moved off at 10.15, and came into action about twenty minutes later. Obtained first sight of Kimberley at 2.45 p.m., and bivouacked some 7 miles south of it about sunset. Here it was understood we were to remain a few days to refit and rest the horses, many of whom had died, *e.g.*, G battery lost 12 on 13th, and 1st Brigade Division 39 horses on the same day. My second charger was stolen at De Kiel's farm, and the other, which I brought from Australia, had to be shot at Kimberley. However, at 2.30 a.m. on 17th, orders were suddenly received to march at 3 a.m. The brigade started at 3.30 a.m.; watered at a dam, such horses as would drink the water, at 8.30 a.m., and reached Rannefontein at 11.45 a.m. Here we saw Cronje's force and laager which had got away from the infantry, and which we engaged at 12.5 p.m. and forced to halt. The guns remained unlimbered until 10 a.m., 18th, when the horses were watered for the second time since leaving Kimberly.

I entered the laager of Paardeberg on the afternoon of 27th, the day of Cronje's surrender. Considering the bombardment it had been exposed to, the material damage was very slight. The effect of lyddite seemed to be *nil*. None of the damage I saw was of any extent, *e.g.*, one lyddite shell fell within 12 inches of the back of a wheel, and did no damage beyond bending slightly the front of the fork. Several Boer prisoners I spoke to told me that they did not mind lyddite shells in the open as the usual resultant effect was small upon material. I heard General Albrecht was knocked down by a lyddite shell that burst close to them, but suffered no injury from it.

From the time we left Kimberley until getting here, both men and horses have been on half, quarter, and, sometimes, three-quarter rations; the horses generally getting 8 lbs. of oats per diem. It is generally estimated that we have lost at least 50 per cent. of the horses we started with.

The Cavalry division left Osfontein on 7th March and marched to Salderpoort, a few miles east of Poplar Grove on Modder River, making a turning movement which enabled the infantry to enter the trenches of the "Seven Kopjes" without having to fire a shot. The 2nd brigade were in action off and on from 6 a.m. to 2.30 p.m.

The 1st brigade marched to Abram's Kraal on 9th March; the 2nd brigade to Driefontein on 10th; and the 3rd brigade to Petersburg. About half of the casualties in the Cavalry Division on the 10th, occurred in the 2nd brigade.

On the 12th, orders arrived at 2.30 a.m. for the 2nd brigade, which was bivouacked at Blanbosch Pan, to march at 5 a.m. This day was one of the hardest marches we have had. There were no halts practically until we got to Venter's

Vallie at 12.45 a.m., where the water so dirty the horses would not drink. **We moved** again at 2.30, and bivouacked at 8.30 p.m., the horses being 13½ hours in the collar. I have no doubt that our loss in horses would have been much less and our pace more rapid had regular halts been made, and when we reached good grazing the horses allowed to graze for 15 minutes.

On 13th inst. we reached Bloemfontein and bivouacked at this farm, where we understand we are likely to remain until the batteries get remounts, and stores are brought up.

Nearly all the ammunition and supply waggons have been left behind on the veldt, batteries having in many cases only three ammunition waggons with them, and most guns are drawn by eight horses. The buck waggons have been more efficient than ammunition and supply. The delay at Koodesrand, after the surrender of Cronje at Paardeburg, was due to the shortness of supplies. The deficiency of supplies is due chiefly to the fact that after we seized Klip Drift on the Modder River, Cronje decided to evacuate Magersfontein, and thereupon the army had to march east instead of west.

Shortly after Lord Kitchener's arrival regimental transport was abolished.

Dangar, Captain (now Lieut.-Colonel) H. W., R.A.A.—Embarked at Sydney on transport *Aberdeen*, 3rd November; arrived at Cape Town, 6th December, 1899. Attached to Headquarters R.H.A. Was present at operations in Cape Colony, south of Orange River, 1899–1900, including actions at Colesberg, 5th to 9th January. On 6th February joined A Battery Royal Australian Artillery (which see). Embarked at Cape Town on transport *Sophocles*, 16th November; arrived Sydney, 8th December, 1900. Queen's Medal with two clasps.

Lamb, Captain C. W., R.A.A.—Embarked at Sydney on transport *Warrigal*, 30th December, 1899; arrived at Cape Town, 5th February, 1900. Temporarily employed on Embarkation staff at Cape Town, 8th February. On 19th February appointed staff officer and Provost Marshal at Orange River station and surrounding district. 21st May, appointed district commissioner Fauresmith and Philippolis districts, Orange River Colony. Mentioned in despatches by General Pretyman. Military Governor, Orange River Colony. Staff officer to Colonel King-Hall in operations 3rd to 18th October; defence of Fauresmith and Jagersfontein, relief of Philippolis, and operations in vicinity, action at Blaauwheuvel 28th October, 1900. Embarked at Cape Town on transport *Orient*, 13th December, 1900; arrived at Sydney, 9th January, 1901. Queen's Medal with two clasps.

Jenkins, Captain R. L. H. B., R.A.A.—Embarked at Sydney on transport *Moravian*, 17th January; arrived Cape Town, 17th February, 1900. On 27th February was ordered to Orange River Colony. Took charge of a machine-gun section of Royal Garrison Artillery at Fort Munster. Commanded a detachment of Royal Garrison Artillery with two 9-pr. guns at Zuit Pan drift. Admitted to hospital suffering from dysentery, 20th March; returned to duty on 12th April, and took command of mounted infantry details at Fort Munster. On 19th May was appointed staff-officer and Provost Marshal. Returned to Australia, invalided, 17th August, 1900. Captain Jenkins subsequently commanded machine-gun section in 2nd Mounted Rifles (New South Wales Regiment), which see. Queen's Medal with three clasps. King's Medal with two clasps.

Brace, Lieutenant C. F.—Embarked at Sydney on transport *Moravian*, **17th** January; arrived at Cape Town, 16th February, 1900. Attached to **23rd Company**

Royal Artillery at Cape Town. On 6th March joined pom-pom depôt at Stellenbosch as staff officer to Colonel Crampton, Royal Artillery. On 17th June received command of "V" section pom-poms, and proceeded to Johannesburg. On 8th July was placed in command of an armoured train operating between Pretoria and Kroonstad. In October was sent to reinforce Spring's, and assumed command of garrison. On 10th January, 1901, returned to Pretoria for duty, and was invalided to England on 8th July of same year. In February, 1902, took charge of shipment of horses from Fiume, Hungary, for Durban; went from thence to Pretoria, and joined remount department. Embarked at Cape Town on s.s. *Damascus*, 23rd August; arrived Sydney, 16th September, 1902. Queen's Medal with three clasps. King's Medal with two clasps.

Rose, Rev. J. H. (Chaplain).—Embarked at Sydney on transport *Moravian* on 17th January; arrived Cape Town, 17th February, 1900. Appointed chaplain Orange River hospital. Chaplain to Sir C. Warren's column, Griqualand West, and British Bechuanaland. Divisional chaplain to General French. Chaplain to s.s. *Yorkshire*. Embarked at Cape Town for England, 14th November, arrived 10th December, 1900. Returned to Sydney, March, 1901. Queen's Medal with clasps.

Parrott, Lieut.-Colonel T. S.—Embarked at Sydney on transport *Moravian* on 17th January; arrived Cape Town, 18th February, 1900. Attached to Royal Engineers and employed on engineering works in Orange River Colony. Formed Australian Pioneers (Flying Sappers) in May, 1900, at Bloemfontein. Embarked at Cape Town on transport *Orient* on 13th December, and arrived at Sydney on 9th January, 1901. Queen's Medal with two clasps. (Lieut.-Colonel Parrott had served on the staff of the New South Wales Contingent to Suakin, 1885, and received medal with clasp and Khedive's star.)

Murray, Major (now Lieut.-Colonel) J. H. P.—Embarked at Sydney on transport *Moravian*, 17th January; arrived at Cape Town, 17th February, 1900. Appointed to command Tasmanian details. Appointed Commandant Rustfontein Camp at Bloemfontein. Provost Marshal, 2nd corps, 1st Mounted Infantry Brigade. Provost Marshal, 2nd Mounted Infantry Brigade. Operations in Cape Colony and Orange River Colony, February to May, 1900. Operations in the Transvaal, May and June, 1900, including actions near Johannesburg, Pretoria, and Diamond Hill, 11th and 12th June. Orange River Colony, July to August, 1900, including actions at Bethlehem and Witteberg. Operations west of Pretoria, including action at Venterskroon. Embarked at Cape Town for England, 17th October, 1900, and returned to Sydney by R.M.S. *Oroya*, 19th January, 1901. Queen's Medal, with four clasps.

Kyngdon, Captain (now Lieut.-Colonel) L. H., R.A.A.—Embarked at Sydney on transport *Moravian*, 17th January, arrived at Cape Town, 17th February, 1900. Attached to Royal Artillery, Cape Town. Employed as railway staff officer, Bethulie Bridge; station staff officer, Bethulie Bridge; station staff officer, Norval's Pont. Graded as staff captain, *vide London Gazette*, 10th July, 1900. Embarked at Cape Town on s.s. *Sophocles*, 16th November, and arrived at Sydney 10th December, 1900. Queen's Medal with two clasps. (Captain Kyngdon had served as a subaltern with the New South Wales Battalion of Infantry in the Soudan, 1885, and received medal with clasp and Khedive's star.)

Luscombe, Captain (now Major) A. P., R.A.A.—Embarked at Sydney on transport *Moravian*, 17th January; arrived Cape Town, 17th February, 1900. Appointed staff officer to the Base Commandant, Cape Town, 1st March. Attached to Army

Transport and appointed officer commanding 33rd Company, Army Service Corps, 16th March. Graded D.A.A.G., from same date. In command of Divisional Transport, advance to Bethlehem, Orange River Colony, under Lieut.-General Hunter, June, 1900. Actions at Ratif's Nek, Stabaat's Nek, Vet River, Zand River, Spitzkop, Bultfontein, Winburg, and Lindley. With General Bruce Hamilton, operations between Lindley, Reitz, Heilbron, Wolverhoek, and Vaal River. Mentioned in despatches by General Sir H. Macdonald, General Sir A. Hunter, and Colonel Barter, K.O.Y.L.I., generally for transport work. Captain Luscombe received much commendation in regard to a large convoy of about 300 waggons of which he was placed in command at Heilbron on 1st July, with Major-General Hector Macdonald's brigade. On the way to Frankfort there was a good deal of sniping. At Frankfort he was placed in charge of another convoy of 140 waggons, with which he proceeded to Winberg, arriving on 21st.; but they encountered the enemy under De Wet on 16th, and a fight ensued, during which the convoy was shelled a good deal. Colonel Baxter, who commanded the escort, sent a special report of the manner in which Captain Luscombe got the convoy along under great difficulties to General Hunter. He embarked at Cape Town on transport *Orient*, 13th December, 1900, and arrived at Sydney, 9th January, 1901. Queen's Medal with three clasps.

Copeland, Captain (now Major) H. P. R.—Embarked at Sydney on transport *Moravian*, 17th January; arrived Cape Town, 17th February, 1900. Appointed divisional officer, Royal Engineers, Cape Town. Proceeded to East London, 22nd March, and from there to Bethulie, Orange River Colony, as staff officer to Cape Royal Engineers (Gatacre's division). Proceeded to Bloemfontein in May, and assisted Colonel Parrot, New South Wales Engineers, to form Australian Pioneers (Flying Sappers), attached to General Hutton's column. Left Bloemfontein 24th May, in the march to Pretoria. Actions at Brandfontein and Vet River. Proceeded to Kimberley as staff officer, Royal Engineers, from Orange River to Mafeking. Embarked at Cape Town, 25th October, on s.s. *Australian*, and arrived at Sydney, 17th November, 1900. Major Copeland served subsequently as adjutant to 3rd New South Wales Mounted Rifles (q.v.) Queen's Medal with three clasps. King's Medal with two clasps.

Pearce, Captain (now Major) R. St. J.—Embarked at Sydney on transport *Moravian*, 17th January; arrived at Cape Town, 17th February, 1900. Attached to Royal Horse Artillery, 1st Cavalry Brigade, to 30th April. Present at all engagements to occupation of Bloemfontein. Joined Field Artillery, 11th Division, May, 1900, attached to 83rd Field Battery; afterwards transferred to 84th Field Battery, and remained with it to 10th August. Appointed Intelligence Officer to Military Governor, Orange River Colony, and acted as Chief Intelligence Officer, Orange River Colony. Graded as D.A.A.G. Actions at Driefontein, Vet River, Zand River, Johannesburg, Pretoria, and Diamond Hill. Embarked at Cape Town on s.s. *Sophocles* on 16th November, and arrived at Sydney 10th December, 1900. Returned to South Africa by s.s. *Orient*, leaving Sydney 23rd July, 1901, and arriving at Cape Town, 16th August. Employed as railway staff officer, Naauwpoort. Embarked at Cape Town on transport *Manchester Merchant*, 7th January, and arrived at Sydney, 31st January, 1902. Queen's Medal with six clasps.

Owen, Major (now Lieut.-Colonel) P. T.—Embarked at Sydney on transport *Australasian*, 20th February; arrived at Cape Town, 19th March, 1900. Employed as staff officer to Major General Hutton, commanding 20th Brigade, until 31st

March. Staff officer, Kimberley, 1st April to 4th May. Invalided to England, 19th May. Returned to Sydney, 16th September, 1900. Queen's Medal with clasp.

Savage, Major (afterwards Lieut.-Colonel) A. H. P.—Embarked at Sydney on transport *Maplemore*, 28th February; arrived at Beira, 11th April, 1900. Appointed Camp Commandant, Marendellas. Took charge of convoy to Bulawayo. Attached to New Zealand 15-pr. battery at Ottoshoop, under Lord Methuen, in August, and took part in operations in Western Transvaal in August, September, and October, 1900. Embarked at Cape Town in s.s. *Sophocles*, 14th November; arrived at Sydney, 11th December, 1900. Queen's Medal with two clasps.

Dibbs, Captain T. B.—Embarked at Sydney on transport *Atlantian* on 28th February, 1900; arrived Cape Town, 31st March. Ordered thence to Beira, arriving at that place on 11th April. Employed as ordnance officer at Umtali, and in charge of depôt at Bulawayo. Was also employed as transport officer and supply officer to 1st Brigade, Australian Bushmen. Commanded General Paget's dismounted details. Employed as galloper on brigade staff. Embarked at Cape Town on transport *Orient*, 13th December; arrived at Sydney, 9th January, 1901. Queen's Medal with four clasps.

Conroy, Captain J. M.—Embarked at Sydney on transport *Atlantian*, 28th February; arrived at Cape Town, 31st March, 1900. Ordered to Beira, and arrived at that place, 11th April, 1900. Employed on engineering work at Marendellas, Bulawayo, and Mafeking. Afterwards employed in similar capacity with Lord Methuen's column. Embarked at Cape Town on s.s. *Nineveh*, 24th January; arrived Sydney, 17th February, 1901. Queen's Medal with four clasps.

Onslow, Lieut.-Colonel J. W. M.—Embarked at Sydney on s.s. *Salamis*, 7th March; arrived at Cape Town, 11th April, 1900. He proceeded to South Africa at his own expense. Employed on staff of 7th Division to June 30th. Afterwards served as aide-de-camp to Major-General Hutton until date of departure from South Africa. Embarked at Cape Town for England, 10th October, on s.s. *Norman*, arriving on 30th November, 1900. Returned to Sydney by s.s. *Australia*, 21st March, 1901. Operations in Orange Free State and Transvaal, including actions at Vet River, Zand River, Johannesburg, Pretoria, and Belfast. Despatches *London Gazette*. He subsequently commanded 5th Commonwealth Horse (q.v.). Queen's Medal with four clasps. (Lieut.-Colonel Onslow also served with the Chitral Relief Force, 29th March to 15th July, 1895, including the storming of Malakand Pass, and the action at Khar. Medal with clasp.)

Niesigh, Captain J. W.—Embarked at Sydney on transport *Antillian*, 5th April; arrived at Cape Town, 14th May, 1901. Employed as assistant staff officer, Oversea Colonials, Cape Town and East London; afterwards commanding Oversea Colonial Details at the base. Invalided to Australia, December, 1901. Queen's Medal with clasp.

Morris, Captain (afterwards Major) A. G. H., R.A.A.—Embarked at Sydney on transport *Antillian*, 5th April, arrived Cape Town, 14th May, 1901. Appointed commandant depôt, Royal Artillery, Cape Town, 24th June, 1901, to 11th July, 1902. Officer commanding troops, The Castle, Cape Town, 24th June, 1901, to 11th July, 1902. Armament officer, Table Bay Defences, 5th October, 1901, to 11th July, 1902. Adjutant Royal Artillery, Cape Colony District, 1st March, 1901, to 31st May, 1902. Acting Commandant Royal Artillery, Cape Colony District, 2nd May, 1902, to 29th May, 1902. Appointed a member of Permanent Military Court, Cape Town, on declaration of martial law. Embarked at Cape Town on s.s. *Salamis*, 11th July; arrived Sydney, 5th August, 1902. Queen's Medal with three clasps.

PENSIONS AWARDED BY THE NEW SOUTH WALES GOVERNMENT.

No.	Rank.	Name.	Regiment.	Remarks.
171	Corporal	Alston, A. K.	Citizens Bushmen	Ceased 31.5.07
	Captain	Anderson, C. G.	1st Mounted Rifles	to 31.1.04
358	Private	Argent, C. W.	,, ,,	31.10.04
		Basche, Mrs. E. J. (wife Lt. C. Basche)	,, ,,	—.4.05
115	Corporal	Buckleton, F. A.	Citizens Bushmen	to 30.4.08
107	Trooper	Burke, P.	,, ,,	to 31.1.04
361	Private	Bird, S.	1st Mounted Rifles	to date
231	,,	Biddle, Mrs. M. A. (widow of J. W. Biddle)	,, ,,	to 31.5.08
387	Corporal	Bell, A. J.	Citizens Bushmen	to 31.12.05
641	Trooper	Boreland, W.	1st Australian Horse	to 12.1.04
455	,,	Black, R. P.	Citizens Bushmen	to date
984	,,	Ball, W. D.	1st Australian Horse	to 12.1.04
218	Private	Broadhurst-Hill, R.	1st Mounted Rifles	to 16.9.04
353	Trooper	Burns, J.	Citizens Bushmen	to 12.1.04
409	Private	Bowman, W.	Army Medical Corps	to 31.1.04
956	,,	Conybeare, Miss M., (daughter late E. Conybeare)	1st Mounted Rifles	to date
298	..	Cordell, J.	1st Mounted Rifles	to 30.6.05
516	Trooper	Campbell, N.	Citizens Bushmen	to 31.3.06
347	,,	Clements, E.	,, ,,	to 9.1.03
86	..	Cummings, M. (widow of late W. J. Cummings)	,, ,,	to date
		Drage, Mrs. M. B. (widow of late Lt. Drage)	1st Mounted Rifles	to date
521	Private	Degner, C.	,, ,,	to 31.12.06
310	,,	Douglas, R. A.	,, ,,	to date
515	Trooper	Eyre, L. G.	Citizens Bushmen	to dath
		Grieve, Mrs. J. A., (widow of late Lieutenant G. J. Grieve)	Special Service Officer	to date
127	Trooper	Gibson, Miss M. (daughter of late G. H. F. Gibson)	Citizens Bushmen	to date
2485	Corporal	Gleeson, J.	"A" Battery, R.A.A.	to 17.2.08*
29	Private	Harrison, Mrs. S. J. (widow of J. Harrison)	Army Medical Corps	to date
555	,,	Harrison, S. E.	1st Mounted Rifles	to 30.9.05
462	Lance-Corporal	Hughes, W. M.	Citizens Bushmen	to date
2864	Gunner	King, A. L.	"A" Battery, R.A.A.	to 20.2.03*
3	Staff Sergeant	Jones, J.	Army Medical Corps	to date
461	Trooper	Jackson, J. W.	Citizens Bushmen	to 31.12.04
19	..	Jones, J. A.	1st Australian Horse	to 3.6.03
2415	Gunner	Lindsell, F. C.	"A" Battery, R.A.A.	to date
1	Warrant Officer	Liggins, F. P.	1st Mounted Rifles	to 31.1.04
470	Private	Mason, Mrs. M., widow of late C. Mason)	Citizens Bushmen	to date
508	Sergt.-Major	Mitchell, Mrs. E. E. (widow of Mitchell, J.)	,, ,,	to date
119	Private	Maxwell, A.	1st Mounted Rifles	to 18.6.02
1083	Trooper	Moody, Mrs. E. A. (widow of late E. Moody)	1st Australian Horse	to 28.10.03 then to Mrs. Moody
276	,,	McGill, Mrs. J. (widow of R. W. McGill)	1st Mounted Rifles	to date
333	Corporal	McSweeney, J.	,, ,,	to 9.7.07*

* Signifies that the person mentioned is deceased.

Pensions awarded by the New South Wales Government—*continued*.

No.	Rank.	Name.	Regiment.	Remarks.
503	Private	McMillan, J. M.	1st Mounted Rifles	to 31.8.04
290	Corporal	McKinnon, G. R.	Citizens Bushmen	to 26.12.10
65	Private	Oram, Mrs. E. E. (widow of J. J. Oram)	Army Medical Corps	to date
12	Corporal	Owens, F. P.	1st Mounted Rifles	to 28.2.03
2949	Gunner	O'Brien, W. J.	"A" Battery, R.A.A.	to date
405	Trooper	Nicholson, A.	Citizens Bushmen	to date
501	,,	Nicholls, F. V.	,, ,,	to 31.1.05
1086	,,	Palmer, A.	1st Australian Horse	to date
552	Private	Peek, A. R.	1st Mounted Rifles	to date
2534	Gunner	Quin, J.	"A" Battery, R.A.A.	to 31.1.08
826	Trooper	Ralston, G. H.	Citizens Bushmen	to date
		Robertson, Mrs. E. H. (widow of late Capt. Robertson)	,, ,,	to date
534	W.O.	Sullivan, Mrs. A. M. (widow of Sullivan, E. J.)	1st Mounted Rifles	to date
489	Trooper	Thorpe, Mrs. S. A. (widow of W. Thorpe)	Citizens Bushmen	to 30.6.02
2086	Gunner	Vincent, W. C.	"A" Battery, R.A.A.	to date
275	S.Q.M.S.	Walton, Mrs. L. (widow of J. M. Walton)	Citizens Bushmen	to date
484	Trooper	Walsh, W. M.	,, ,,	to 31.5.08
485	Private	Walther, T. H.	,, ,,	to 31.5.08

NOTE.—This List is exclusive of members of South African Irregulars that were assisted by the New South Wales Government, or Imperial and Commonwealth Contingents raised in New South Wales.

List of Officers and Others of New South Wales Contingents who were Killed or Died on Service during the South African War.

New South Wales Lancers.

Corporal F. I. Kilpatrick
,, R. E. Harkus
Private F. Avard
,, W. M. Ellis
,, F. G. A. L. Fetting
,, C. H. Tyler
,, L. D. Tunks

Army Medical Corps Contingent.

Private I. Goodsell
,, J. A. Harrison
,, J. Oram
,, T. Smith
Sergeant W. H. Loney
Private J. J. Kelly

"A" Squadron Mounted Rifles.

Bugler V. R. Daly
Private W. J. Abrahams
,, W. Bender
,, W. J. Kirkland
,, P. J. Reilly
,, A. E. Smith
,, E. H. Ransley
Corpl. A. E. E. Al'en
Private C. Flint
,, A. T. Bennett

Special Service Officer.

Lieut. G. J. Grieve

New South Wales Infantry.

Private S. C. Atchison
,, H. M. Budd
,, A. L. Cameron
,, D. Fraser
,, J. C. Fraser
,, B. A. Halley
,, L. C. Hill
,, S. McLennan
,, J. Palazzi
,, F. V. Smith
,, D. Willis

1st Australian Horse.

Lieut. K. K. Mackellar
2nd Lieut. A. Ebsworth
Ser.-Major G. A. Griffen
Private J. A. S. Andrew
,, J. Bonner
,, R. B. Cox
,, M. J. Cummins
,, H. W. Gilchrist
,, W. J. James
,, M. P. Meehan
,, R. F. Wilson

"A" Battery, Royal Australian Artillery.

Gunner W. Edwards
,, B. Gowing
Actg. Bomb. J. T. McKenzie

1st New South Wales Mounted Rifles.

Sergeant E. J. Sullivan
Lieut. C. O. Basche
Private J. W. Biddle
,, C. G. Cripps
,, E. J. Conybeare
,, J. Fanton
,, G. H. Kite
,, R. W. McGill
,, N. E. Thompson
,, F. W. Whinfield
Lieut. W. R. Harriott
Private R. B. Campbell
,, T. A. Fulton
Corporal F. H. Legge
Private T. B. Lennon
,, E. O. Ogle
,, W. G. Taylor
Lieut. P. W. C. Drage
Sergeant A. Smiley
Private W. Freeman
,, G. Rawe
,, T. C. Robertson
,, W. F. Young
,, J. Drum
,, H. L. N. Gaggin

List of Officers and Others of New South Wales Contingents, &c.—*continued.*

New South Wales Citizens Bushmen.

Private	G. T. Cooper
S. S. Major	J. Mitchell
Corporal	G. R. McGuiness
Private	J. C. Aitcheson
,,	J. D. Duff
,,	D. Fraser
,,	G. H. F. Gibson
,,	A. P. B. Grey
,,	J. M. Logan
,,	D. P. Meehan
,,	P. Verdon
,,	J. E. Walker
Captain	C. W. Robertson
Sergt.	W. Murray
Corpl.	W. L. Spier
Private	W. M. Ayre
,,	D. Jones
,,	J. Lamb
,,	J. Russell
,,	H. W. Waddell
S.Q.M.S.	J. N. Walton
Corporal	E. B. Chesher
Private	R. Cameron
,,	H. Drinkwater
,,	F. Toohey
,,	J. Waddell
Sergeant	D. J. Barrett
,,	G. W. Davidson
,,	W. Myers
Private	B. J. Quigley
,,	W. J. Cummings
,,	J. Finnegan
,,	G. Manns
,,	C. Mason
L.-Corpl.	N. C. Dodd

Imperial Bushmen.

Private	F. Andrews
,,	H. C. Hardy
,,	G. A. Montgomery
,,	J. R. Murray
Sergeant	J. A. Hyndman
L.-Corpl.	G. Challis
Private	T. W. Cressy
2nd Lieut.	R. J. L. White
Private	E. Daggar
,,	H. H. Handcock
,,	A. King

Imperial Bushmen—continued.

Sergeant	W. A. Lassetter
Private	D. Black
,,	E. J. Morris
Corporal	H. A. Bennett
Private	A. Aberline
,,	J. J. Fahey
,,	D. J. Murray
,,	L. Morgan
,,	A. R. Mackellar
,,	P. O'Grady
Sergeant	F. J. Gardiner
Private	J. Hogan
,,	S. Lipscombe
Sergeant	R. Kelly

2nd New South Wales Mounted Rifles.

Lieut.	G. B. Forster
2nd Lieut.	E. A. Lamb
Private	S. Ahrens
,,	T. P. Barker
,,	M. Bastick
,,	A. Brown
,,	W. E. Clancy
,,	G. F. Coyle
,,	D. R. Crichton
,,	M. Farrell
,,	R. Foran
,,	J. F. Foreman
,,	E. W. Green
,,	W. Harker
,,	J. T. Hay
,,	G. Johnson
,,	W. H. Kohler
,,	T. Mackay
,,	S. S. Mayo
,,	J. Richardson
,,	J. Rowe
F.-Sergt.	A. W. Sisley
Private	H. Spiers
,,	H. Walsh
,,	R. Weeks

3rd New South Wales Mounted Rifles.

Captain	D. F. Miller
Q.M. Sergt.	H. Williams
Private	A. V. Apthorpe

List of Officers and Others of New South Wales Contingents, &c.—*continued*.

3rd New South Wales Mounted Rifles—continued.

Private	H. M. Bayliss
,,	A. Richards
,,	F. W. Russell
,,	W. Wood
Corporal	C. S. Smith
Private	A. J. Allingham
,,	W. T. Berriman
,,	T. H. Powell
Lieutenant	G. V. D. Treatt
Saddler	J. Daley
Farr.-Sergt.	G. J. Dickson
Private	C. J. Gosper
,,	J. H. Jacobs
,,	W. C. Jackson
,,	R. Sams
Sergeant	S. J. Smith
Private	G. Gander
,,	J. E. Lefoe
,,	C. Wilson
Sergeant	T. Sturgeon
Private	I. Bewley
,,	N. V. Cameron
,,	A. M. Campbell
,,	R. Cumming
,,	H. W. Lenon
,,	R. J. Morrison
,,	W. Montgomerie
Q.M.-Sergt.	J. M. Gray
Corporal	H. T. Jones
Private	N. McCauley
,,	J. F. Neary
,,	R. Richards
,,	C. T. E. Turner
Driver	A. J. Chisholm
Gunner	O. S. Pitt
Private	A. Eagle
,,	W. Mason
,,	J. F. O'Keefe
,,	J. H. Starr
L.-Corpl.	W. Strachan

3rd Imperial Bushmen.

Private	D. J. Arndell
,,	J. L. Bellamy
,,	H. N. Black
,,	G. H. Burns
,,	J. W. Clough

3rd Imperial Bushmen—continued.

Private	G. Crawford
,,	J. S. Downs
,,	E. Gay
,,	R. J. Inch
,,	W. P. Kelly
,,	R. Kimpton
,,	A. Lindner
L.-Corpl.	P. J. McNamara
Private	W. Macfarlane
,,	W. McKenn
,,	W. Newland
,,	C. Oldham
,,	C. O'Loughlin
,,	F. S. Perkins
,,	J. H. Russell
,,	J. Seymour
,,	W. Smith
,,	C. J. Shaw
,,	A. J. Stevens
,,	W. Scott
Q.M.S.	H. Tame
Corpl.	G. Taylor
F.-Sergt.	H. B. Tame
Private	W. Tame

1st Battalion Australian Commonwealth Horse.

Private	W. Wickerson
Sergeant	T. K. Taplin
Private	G. S. Mackay
,,	E. O'Brien
,,	W. Croom
,,	J. Green
,,	A. McAndrew

3rd Battalion Australian Commonwealth Horse.

Private	H. R. Sherringham
,,	H. E. Locke
,,	D'A. Smith
Farrier	T. Harland
Q.M.S.	J. S. Ryan
Sergt.-Major	J. D. Sutton

5th Australian Commonwealth Horse.

Nil.

NEW SOUTH WALES.

No. 1.

SUMMARY OF ALL MILITARY CONTINGENTS SENT FROM NEW SOUTH WALES TO SOUTH AFRICA.

Transports, &c.

Name of Transport.	Date of embarkation.	Date of disembarkation.	Officers.	N.C. Officers and men.	Total.	Horses.	Carts and Waggons.	Guns.
s.s. *Nineveh*	1899. 9 Oct.	1899. 2 Nov.	2	69	71	..	..	..
s.s. *Kent*	28 ,,	1 Dec.	11	119	130	180	22	..
s.s. *Aberdeen*	3 Nov.	7 ,,	11	193	204	49	8	1
s.s. *Langton Grange*	14 ,,	13 ,,	4	57	61	117	1	..
s.s. *Warrigal*	30 Dec.	1900. 5 Feb.	9	170	179	141	17	6
s.s. *Southern Cross*	1900. 17 Jan.	17 Feb.	20	433	453	475	17	..
s.s. *Moravian*	17 ,,	18 ,,	18	120	138	81	17	..
s.s. *Surrey*	17 ,,	23 ,,	8	103	111	117	5	..
s.s. *Australasian*	16 Feb.	19 Mar.	2	41	43	45	1	..
s.s. *Maplemore*	28 ,,	4 Apr.	10	172	182	211	6	..
s.s. *Atlantian*	28 ,,	2 ,,	23	327	350	396	11	..
s.s. *Armenian*	23 Apr.	17 May	40	722	762	748	32	..
s.s. *Custodian*	1901. 15 Mar.	1901. 13 Apr.	25	496	521	518	..	..
s.s. *Maplemore*	15 ,,	12 ,,	22	488	510	481	2	..
s.s. *British Princess*	21 ,,	17 ,,	18	397	415	408	..	..
s.s. *Ranee*	21 ,,	23 ,,	13	234	247	234	..	..
s.s. *Antillian*	5 Apr.	12 May	12	367	379	356	..	..
s.s. *Manchester Merchant*	1902. 11 Feb.	1902. 17 Mar.	8	97	105	70	4	..
s.s. *Custodian*	18 Feb.	17 ,,	20	355	375	375	..	..
s.s. *Manhattan*	1 Apr.	2 May	25	569	594	385	..	..
s.s. *Menelaus*	10 May	11 June	3	25	28	147	..	..
s.s. *Columbian*	22 ,,	19 ,,	23	446	469	343	..	..
Total	..	..	327	6,000	6,327	5,877	143	7

NEW SOUTH WALES.

No. 2.

SUMMARY OF ALL MILITARY CONTINGENTS SENT FROM NEW SOUTH WALES TO SOUTH AFRICA.

Classification.

Classification.	Officers.	N.C. Officers and men.	Total.	Horses.
Lancers	7	158	165	190
Australian Horse	7	132	139	152
Mounted Rifles	59	1,450	1,509	1,477
Mounted Infantry	16	383	399	413
Bushmen	142	3,090	3,232	3,116
Artillery	6	214	220	160
Infantry	4	121	125	9
Army Medical Corps and Medical Officers	37	340	377	275
Nurses (Women)	2	12	14	..
Chaplains	16	2	18	1
Special Service	17	9	26	14
Veterinary Department	11	4	15	2
Spare—				
Draft	1	85	86	..
Unallotted	2	..	2	68
Total	327	6,000	6,327	5,877

VICTORIA.

VICTORIA.

PREFATORY.

ON the 28th September, 1899, and following days, a Conference of Military Commandants was held at Victoria Barracks, Melbourne. This had been convened at the invitation of the Government of Victoria for the purpose of submitting a scheme for the consideration of the various Governments, by which, should they decide to do so, a United Australian Military Contingent could be organized for service in South Africa in the event of a war with the Boers.

President:
Major-General Sir Charles Holled Smith, K.C.M.G., Commandant, Victoria.

Members:
Major-General G. A. French, C.M.G., Commandant, New South Wales.
Major-General Hunter, Commandant, Queensland.
Colonel G. H. Chippindall, Commandant, Western Australia.
Colonel W. V. Legge, Commandant, Tasmania.
Colonel J. Stuart, Commandant, South Australia.

Secretary:
Colonel J. C. Hoad, A.A.G., Victoria.

It was decided (*inter alia*) that in the opinion of the Conference the necessary Acts should be passed without delay by each of the several Colonies to enable their respective Military Contingents to act, either as a combined force or otherwise, for service outside Australia.

Further, that pay should be recommended on the following scale :—Gunners and privates, 4s. 6d. per diem; acting bombardiers, 5s.; bombardiers, 6s. 6d.; corporals, 7s.; sergeants, 8s.; coy. sergeant-majors, 9s.; staff sergeants, 10s.; warrant officers, 11s. 6d.

And that a force of about 2,000 of all ranks should be sent, divided as follows :—New South Wales 745, viz.—Horse Artillery 120, Cavalry and Mounted Rifles 300, Infantry 265, Department Corps and Engineers 60. Queensland—Mounted Rifles and Machine Gun Section, 275. South Australia 140, namely—Mounted Rifles 60, Infantry 80. Tasmania—Infantry 160. Western Australia—Infantry, 160. Victoria, 543; thus disposed—Mounted Rifles 198, Infantry 345. General Staff, 30, to be made up amongst the Colonies.

No result followed, however, other than that when the war broke out, an Australian Regiment was formed (for details of which see 1st Victorian Contingent). This was an administrative, not a consolidated battalion.

Victoria passed the following enabling Acts :—63 Vict. No. 1619 (Victorian Military Contingent Act), enabling forces to be raised under Defences and Discipline Acts, and to come under Imperial Army Act of '81, when serving with Her Majesty's regular troops. £30,000 was appropriated for this purpose. 63 Vict. No. 1627 appropriated £35,000 for the purposes of a second Contingent; 63 Vict. No. 1655 appropriated £30,000 for a third Contingent; 64 Vict. No. 1698 appropriated £45,000 for further Contingents. 63 Vict. No. 1640 authorized contributions by Municipal Councils, banks, and other bodies towards military Contingents, or any members thereof, or their relatives, or in aid of the Patriotic Fund.

CAMP OF INSTRUCTION.

The Camp of Instruction where the various Contingents were stationed, under Colonel Otter and other selected and experienced officers and staff-sergeants, prior to being despatched to the theatre of war, was at Langwarrin. There the men, after having been tested and enrolled, were drilled, trained, organized, disciplined, clothed, equipped, and supplied with horses. When the celerity with which the battalions were raised and sent away is considered, it may readily be judged that more than ordinarily strenuous exertions must have been made by all concerned, including the Commissary and Veterinary Departments and the embarkation officers, whose duty it was to see that all was in readiness on board the transports.

Not a great deal of instruction was required for the earlier Contingents, because the officers and men were mostly drawn from the local regiments; but in the case of the Bushmen's and successive battalions, usually several weeks became necessary to make something like soldiers of these very raw levies before they could be embarked for the front.

No horses were brought back from South Africa. Contingents handed them over into Remount depôts prior to embarkation for Australia.

FIRST VICTORIAN CONTINGENT.

G.O. 77 of 28th October, 1899—" Colonel Hoad, Assistant Adjutant-General, proceeds on 30th instant by train to Adelaide to join s.s. *Medic en route* to South Africa, for duty there."

The following troops embarked on the s.s. *Medic* at Melbourne on the 28th October, 1899 :—

Victoria.—

 Special Service Officer, Colonel J. C. Hoad, A.A.G. Victorian Forces ; and 2 horses.
 Transport Officer, Commander W. J. Colquhoun, V.N.
 One Company Mounted Rifles—125 officers, N.C. officers, and men ; 156 horses.
 Commanding Officer, Captain D. McLeish.
 One Company Infantry—125 officers, N.C. officers, and men ; 9 horses.
 Commanding Officer, Major G. A. Eddy.

Tasmania.—

 One Company Infantry—80 officers, N.C. officers, and men ; 4 horses.
 Commanding Officer, Captain C. St. C. Cameron.

South Australia.—

 Embarked at Adelaide on 2nd November, 1899. One Company Infantry—127 officers, N.C. officers, and men ; 3 horses and 9 mules.
 Commanding Officer, Captain F. H. Howland.

Western Australia.—

 Embarked at Albany on 7th November, 1899. One Company Infantry—130 officers, N.C. officers, and men ; 17 horses.
 Commanding Officer, Captain H. G. Moor, R.A.

Total—588 officers, N.C. officers, and men ; 189 horses, and 9 mules.

Arrived at Cape Town on 26th November, 1899.

Lines of Communication Orders, dated 28th November, 1899 :—

 " (9) The undermentioned details having arrived per s.s. *Medic* and disembarked at Cape Town on 25th November, 1899, are taken on the strength of the Command accordingly :—Tasmanian Infantry, Western Australian Infantry, South Australian Infantry, Victorian Mounted Rifles, Victorian Infantry."

Colonel Hoad, and the Commanding Officers of the Contingents were invited by Sir Alfred Milner to dine at Government House, on the evening of arrival at Cape Town.

FIRST AUSTRALIAN REGIMENT.

South African Campaign, October, 1899, to April, 1900.

THE "Australian Regiment" was formed at Cape Town on the 26th November, 1899. by the amalgamation of the companies sent to South Africa from the Australian Colonies, as follows:—1 Company of Mounted Rifles, Victoria; 1 Company of Infantry, Victoria; 1 Company of Infantry, South Australia; 1 Company of Infantry, Western Australia; 1 Company of Infantry, Tasmania.

Commanding Officer—Colonel J. C. Hoad, Victoria.

Second in Command—Major G. A. Eddy, Victoria.

Captains—C. St. C. Cameron, Tasmania (promoted major, 17th December, 1899); H. G. Moor, Western Australia (promoted major, 14th October, 1899); G. R. Lascelles, A.D.C., South Australia, "Royal Fusiliers" (adjutant); D. McLeish, Victoria (promoted major, 29th March, 1900); F. H. Howland, South Australia; R. W. Salmon, Victoria.

Lieutenants—T. McInerney, Victoria; J. H. Stapleton, South Australia; F. N. Blair, South Australia; Wallace Brown, Tasmania; H. W. Pendlebury, Victoria (acting quartermaster); G. F. Thorn, Victoria; A. J. N. Tremearne, Victoria; F. B. Heritage, Tasmania; J. W. Powell, South Australia; F. M. Parker, Western Australia; S. T. Staughton, Victoria; G. G. F. Chomley, Victoria; J. C. Roberts, Victoria; H. F. Darling, Western Australia; J. Campbell, Western Australia; G. E. Reid, Tasmania.

Medical Officers—Major G. F. McWilliams, Western Australia; Captain J. T. Toll, South Australia; Captain W. F. Hopkins, Victoria.

Veterinary Officer—Captain E. A. Kendall, Victoria.

Attached for duty—Commander Colquhoun, V.N., Victoria.

Regimental Sergeant-Major—A. W. Johnston, South Australia.

Regimental Quartermaster-Sergeant—J. Paul, Victoria.

The following officers subsequently joined the Regiment:—(9.12.99) New South Wales—Captain J. G. Legge, Lieutenants W. Holmes, F. A. Dove, and M. W. Logan; Captain Sellheim (Queensland), was attached to the Regiment for duty from 17.12.99 to 31.1.00; Captain J. H. Bruche (Victoria), 1.1.00 (appointed quartermaster); Major C. D. W. Rankin (Queensland), 2.3.00. Strength of the regiment, 716, and 3 maxim guns.

This was the first occasion on which a regiment was formed for active service of troops representative of the various Colonies of Australia.

27th to 30th November, 1899.—The Regiment was stationed at Maitland Camp, Cape Town, re-equipping, &c.

28th November.—Sir Alfred Milner inspected the Regiment at Maitland, and the officers were presented to him. He said—"Colonel Hoad—I am delighted to see the Australians here. They are a fine lot of men, and look very fit indeed. The horses are in excellent condition, and I am surprised that you only lost one on so long a sea journey. I shall cable to the Government of the several Colonies represented, the pleasure I feel seeing you here in camp to-day."

29th November.—Major-Generals Brabazon and Babington visited the camp.

1st December.—The Regiment entrained at Cape Town, under orders to proceed to De Aar, to join the Kimberley Relief Force. 3rd.—Arrived at De Aar, and ordered on, without detraining, to Orange River, where the Regiment arrived the same day and detrained. Major-General Wauchope, C.B., C.M.G., in command of the troops at Orange River. 6th.—Four Rimington Guides, under Corporal Clements, were attached to the Regiment. Corporal Clements was awarded the V.C. during the campaign. 7th.—Marched to Witteputs, starting at 5 a.m. Ordered to start at midnight for Belmont.

8th.—Arrived at Belmont at daylight. The march to Witteputs was most trying; the distance was only 11 miles, but it was very hot. The distance to Belmont was 10 miles. It rained heavily during the night, and we had to take all our transport with us. The transport consisted of—13 buck wagons, 4 Scotch carts, 4 small arm ammunition carts, 11 water carts, 1 spring cart, 190 mules, and 9 horses. The following message was received from the Commanding Officer at Orange River:—" 8.12.99 O.C. Australians, Belmont—I am pleased to hear you have surmounted difficulties of night march and heavy rain, and will be glad to receive short account of your experiences.—O.C. Troops, Orange River."

9th.—The strength of the Regiment was increased by the arrival of a company of infantry from New South Wales, under the command of Captain Legge. 10th.— Marched to Enslin, accompanied by two guns Royal Horse Artillery. Camp formed under command of Colonel Hoad.

16th.—The 1st Battalion Gordon Highlanders joined at Enslin camp from the Modder River; also two guns field artillery, section of field engineers, and a detachment of Rimington's Guides.

23rd.—The following message was received by Colonel Hoad from Cape Town :— "18th December, 12.20 a.m.—It is officially announced that Field Marshal Lord Roberts has been appointed to supreme command of the British Army in South Africa, and that General Lord Kitchener will act as Chief of his Staff. It is assumed that Sir Redvers Buller will continue to hold the Chief Command of the Forces operating in Natal."

25th.—The following telegram was received from Her Majesty the Queen :— " I wish you and all my brave soldiers a happy Christmas. God protect and bless you all.—Victoria R.I."

27th.—The following telegram was received from the Lord Mayor of London :— " Kindly convey troops hearty Christmas greeting from citizens of London. Admiration and sympathy with their struggles."

1st January, 1900.—Captain J. H. Bruche (Victoria), joined Regiment; appointed quartermaster *vice* Captain Pendlebury. Fifty Mounted Rifles, with Captain McLeish in command, reconnoitred towards Douglas, and got touch of a Boer laager. The " Queen's chocolate " distributed.

6th.—The following cable message was received from Melbourne :—" Victoria sends New Year's greetings, and God speed to Colonel Hoad and his brave soldiers now fighting for the Empire." 8th.—Major-General Babington visited Enslin Camp. 9th.—The mounted company took part in a reconnaissance into the Orange Free State, under Major-General Babington. The following extract from a memo. sent to Colonel Hoad by Major-General Babington was inserted in Regimental Orders :—" I would like to tell you how pleased I was with the men of the Victorian Mounted Rifles that were out with me. I hope you will convey this to their immediate Commanding Officer and men, and I wish you were all up at Modder River."

Colonel Hoad, accompanied by Captain McLeish, visited General Lord Methuen at Modder River, having in contemplation the conversion of the whole Regiment into mounted infantry.

17th.—12th Lancers, under the command of Lieutenant-Colonel Lord Airlie, joined at Enslin. The troops then under Colonel Hoad's command were :—12th Lancers, four field guns, the Australian Regiment, 1st Battalion Gordon Highlanders, detachment of Royal Engineers, detachment of Rimington Guides.

21st.—First casualty of Australian Regiment occurred, Private P. Falls being wounded while on patrol duty. 29th.—Orders were received to proceed to Naauwpoort to take over horses to mount the Regiment. 30th.—The Regiment marched to Belmont. 31st.—Entrained at Belmont for Naauwpoort. 1st February.—

Arrived at Naauwpoort. The regiment was inspected by Major-General Kelly-Kenny, who said :—" Colonel Hoad, I am delighted to have seen those Australians and to notice the excellent physique of the men and the fit condition in which you have brought them to this station. I congratulate you on having such a command, and I would impress on you all the importance of the duties you are called upon to discharge here. There are large quantities of stores at this station, and it is one of strategic value. It is your duty to help in guarding it just now, but very soon you will be sent where you will get plenty of work of the kind which I know you want."

The Regiment took over the first detail of 260 horses and 260 men were equipped and mounted.

2nd.—182 officers and men (mounted), under Colonel Hoad, proceeded by rail to Rensburg. 3rd.—The portion of Regiment at Rensburg was inspected by General French at daylight, and a further draft of 150 men (mounted) arrived at Rensburg, under Major Eddy. General French left Rensburg, and the Australian Regiment formed part of the force, under the command of Major-General Clements, D.S.O.

4th.—Captain McLeish's company ordered to Maeder's Farm on outpost duty. Remainder of regiment from Naauwpoort arrived at Rensburg (not yet horsed), as the horses could not be got through from Cape Town. 5th.—The New South Wales, Victorian and South Australian companies were ordered to Maeder's Farm; the Western Australian company to Slingersfontein; and 40 of the Tasmanian company to Jasfontein. Skirmishing with enemy was general all round on the outpost line. Wounded—Private J. M. Cunningham, Western Australia.

6th.—A further draft of 256 remounts received, and the Regiment was now fully horsed. A company of 50 mounted men was detailed for special duty with Major-General Clements. 9th.—A detachment, under Captain Salmon, sent to Jasfontein to support the Tasmanian company. Heavy engagement. The Western Australians at Slingersfontein also were hotly engaged. Casualties :—Killed—Western Australia—Privates Conway, T. Gilham, and T. Button (originally reported as missing). Wounded—Western Australia—Sergeant Hensman, promoted lieutenant (subsequently died in hospital), Sergeant Unkles, Privates L. France, J. Bird, J. Ansell, and G. Gifford. Mr. Lambie, war correspondent of the *Age*, who was attached to the regiment, was killed at Jasfontein. Major W. T. Reay, the war correspondent of the *Herald*, rendered valuable assistance during the engagement at Jasfontein. He was awarded the South African war medal. Mr. A. G. Hales, war correspondent, was taken prisoner by the Boers.

Order issued by Major-General Clements, D.S.O. :—" Operations at Slingersfontein, 9th February, 1900. The General Officer Commanding wishes to place on record his high appreciation of the courage and determination shown by a party of 20 men of the Western Australians, under Captain Moor, in the above operations. By their determined stand against 300 or 400 men they entirely frustrated the enemy's attempt to turn the flank of the position."

The position defended by the Western Australians was named " West Australia Hill."

10th.—The Victorian Company was heavily engaged at Bastard's Nek. Killed—Sergeant Grant and Private Wilson, Victoria. Wounded and taken prisoners—Privates Suttie (subsequently died in Boer hospital), Burrows, and Gifford.

12th.—Very heavy engagement at Pink Hill. Casualties :—Killed—Major Eddy, Victoria; Lieutenant Powell, South Australia; Corporal Ross, Privates Williams and T. Stock, Victoria. Mortally wounded—Lieutenant Roberts (died following day). Wounded and taken prisoners—Captain McInerney, Lieutenant Tremearne. Severely wounded—Privates S. W. Edwards and H. J. Colley.

Wounded—Privates Inglis, Lawdorn, Maxwell, Byers, Elms, Wallace, Bush, Meagher, Hamilton, Michel, Hagan, Peters, Gamble, Williamson, McCance, Stanford, Roberts, and Corporal McCauley. Taken prisoner—Lance-Corporal Mawley.

13th.—Lieutenant Tremearne released by Boers and handed over to Captain Hopkins (Victoria), medical officer.

14th.—General Clements' column (including Australian Regiment) retired to Arundel; the Advance Guard being formed of the New South Wales and Tasmanian companies; Right Flank Guard, Victorian company; Left Flank Guard Western Australian company; and Rear Guard, South Australian company. Boers attacked Arundel position, but were repulsed.

The following order was issued by General Clements:—" Operations, 9th to 14th February, 1900. The General Officer Commanding wishes to place on record his appreciation of the spirit and determination of the troops in the operations of the 9th to the 14th instant. The powers and endurance of the troops were fully taxed, and they well sustained the strain. The resistance which the Worcester Regiment offered to a large number of the attacking force at Slingersfontein was highly creditable, as was that offered by the Wiltshire Regiment at Hobkirk's Farm. The assistance rendered to their dismounted comrades of the Wiltshire Regiment by the Victorian Rifles is deserving of the highest praise. The General Officer Commanding wishes his thanks conveyed to all ranks of the forces."

19th and 20th.—Lord Kitchener, Chief of Staff, visited camp of Australian Regiment at Arundel, and desired that the officers be introduced to him. He referred specially to the good work done by the Regiment in the Colesberg district.

20th.—Boers attacked Arundel camp; fighting lasted all day. Enemy's attempt to invest Arundel camp defeated. Casualties:—Killed—Private S. C. Atchison, New South Wales. Slightly wounded—Private Southey.

21st.—Desultory fighting during whole day. Killed—Private W. C. Smith, South Australia.

22nd and 23rd.—The Boer positions around Arundel were shelled and attacked. 24th.—Captain Cameron (Tasmania) was wounded and captured by the enemy while on reconnaissance duty. One hundred and forty-eight additional remounts were received by Regiment to supply losses at Rensburg, &c.

26th.—The Boers commenced retirement from the neighbourhood of Arundel. New South Wales company engaged while on reconnaissance. Casualties:—Slightly wounded—Lieutenant Dove. Wounded and taken prisoners—Privates F. McLennan and D. Fraser (subsequently died of wounds at Colesberg). Taken prisoners—Private Brack (wounded), Corporal J. E. Fraser, Private Goodsall.

27th.—Boers complete retirement from Arundel. 28th.—Major-General Clements' column, keeping touch with Boers, again advanced to Rensburg and occupied old positions, also pushed on advanced troops (including Australian Regiment) to Colesberg Junction.

4th March.—Victorian companies and Western Australian company reconnoitred towards Norval's Pont. Engaged with Boer detachment. Casualties:—Wounded—Private A. H. Baker, Western Australia. 5th.—The column advanced to Achtertang. 7th.—Advance party reached Norval's Pont. 8th.—Advance of column continued to Van Zyl's Siding. 12th.—News received that Sergeant Hensman had succumbed to his wounds at the military hospital, Maitland. 14th.—A Colt gun attached to the Regiment. 15th to 27th.—Regiment crossed the river into Orange Free State, with Major-General Clements' column. Communication opened up with Lord Roberts at Bloemfontein. Captain R. Salmon (Victoria) died of fever at Naauwpoort. Advance continued to Donkerspoort. Column arrived at Longkop. Column marched through Philippolis. The Regiment marched with the column through Fauresmith, and a detachment of the Regiment, under Colonel

Hoad, detached to Jagersfontein. Captain W. F. Hopkins, Medical Staff (Victoria), died of fever at Naauwpoort. 29th to 31st.—Column left Fauresmith and marched to Riet River. March continued to Beisjesbult (Bettyput). March continued to Boschkop (near Petrusburg). 1st to 3rd April—March continued to Briekop. Advance to Bloemfontein continued (by night march on 2nd), and on following day (4th) the regiment, with General Clements' column, arrived at Bloemfontein.

6th.—Major-General Hutton inspected the regiment and said:—" Colonel Hoad, Officers, Non-commissioned Officers, and Men of the Australian Regiment, I wish to explain to you the circumstances which have led up to an alteration now to be made in the constitution of the various Contingents from the Australian Colonies. As you are no doubt aware the Australian Regiment was formed in the first instance with a view of simplifying the administrative work of the units from Australia. This object, I may tell you, has been fully achieved, and the organization has been a complete success. I may further express to you my high appreciation, not only of the administrative work, but of that done in the field by the Regiment since its formation. That work redounds to the credit of Colonel Hoad and of every officer and man in the Regiment. As later Contingents have arrived, it has been thought desirable that in future troops from individual Colonies should, as far as possible, work together. The advantages of this arrangement are, no doubt, obvious. While small units engaged in a large campaign like this are unquestionably doing good work—most admirable work—they can scarcely, while acting separately, make their work sufficiently pronounced and distinctive of the several Colonies they come from. By becoming units in a larger sense they may be able to play a much more important part in operations in the field.

" I am sure that every officer and man present desires to add to the honour of the Colony from which he comes. The formation of a Colonial Division, comprising, as it will do, two brigades of about 6,000 men each, should materially assist you in accomplishing that object.

" I am very pleased indeed to renew my acquaintanceship with my old friend, Colonel Hoad, and also with Australian troops generally. Some of your faces are well known to me, and recall pleasant recollections of the time I spent in Australia. I feel sure that the disposition of troops from the several Colonies which has been decided upon will considerably increase your volume of usefulness.

" I have appointed Colonel Hoad my A.A.G., and he will represent me here in camp."

6th.—Colonel Hoad, in bidding good-bye to the Regiment, said:—" Officers and men of the Australian Regiment, as this is the last parade on which you appear as a regiment, I desire to express to you my appreciation of the loyal support and assistance I have received from you during the period of my command. The work done by the Regiment speaks for itself. I may tell you that General Clements yesterday informed me that he was going to report to Lord Roberts on the admirable character of that work performed by you in the field. The organization of this regiment at Enslin on a new basis as a mounted infantry corps, needless to say, involved a great deal of work. I desire to express my personal indebtedness to Captain Lascelles who, as you know, wrought like a Trojan as our adjutant, at a period when there was very much to do. In saying good-bye to you as a regiment, I am pleased to know I am not to be disassociated from you, and can only express the hope that every officer and man may be able to look back to the time we have spent together, and think of me not so much as a commanding officer, but as a friend and comrade, as one who has slept beside him on the South African veldt. I may tell you that the alteration now to be made, and which the General has described to you, is one about which I was consulted, and in which I have at every stage most heartily concurred, and I feel that it will be a great advantage to the troops from Australia. I wish you all good-bye and good luck, and I pray that if God wills you may all be spared to return to your wives, families, and dear ones in Australia."

8th.—The Australian Regiment with several other corps, was absorbed in the 1st Mounted Infantry Brigade, formed under the command of Major-General Hutton, C.B., A.D.C.

The regiment served under the following General Officers:—Lieutenant-General Sir F. W. E. F. Forestier-Walker, G.C.M.G., K.C.B.; Major-General A. G. Wauchope, C.B., C.M.G.; Major-General Elliott Wood, R.E., K.C.B.; Lieutenant-General P. S. Lord Methuen, K.C.B., K.C.V.O., C.M.G.; Lieutenant-General T. Kelly-Kenny, C.B., *p.s.c.*; Lieutenant-General Sir J. D. P. French, K.C.B., K.C.M.G.; Major-General R. A. P. Clements, D.S.O., A.D.C., and formed part of the Kimberley Relief Force, under Lord Methuen, K.C.B., K.C.V.O., C.M.G.

Operations in Cape Colony, south of Orange River, including actions round Colesberg, operations in the Orange Free State, and the advance to Bloemfontein.

Extract from Lines of Communication Orders, dated 1st August, 1900 (Cape Town):—

"*Command*—
> Colonel J. C. Hoad, Australian Regiment, commanded the Australian Regiment from 27th November, 1899, to 7th April, 1900, inclusive. C.R., No. A3265–107A."

CASUALTY LIST.

Killed in Action.

State.	No.	Rank.	Name.	Place.	Date.
Tasmania	30	Private	Button, A.	Jasfontein	9.2.00
,,	50	,,	Gilham, A.	,,	,,
Western Australia	96	,,	Conway, M.	Slingersfontein	,,
Victoria	2	Sergeant	Grant, N.	Rensburg	10.2.00
,,	74	Private	Willson, A. H.	,,	,,
,,	..	Major	Eddy, G. A.	,,	12.2.00
,,	4	Corporal	Ross, A.	,,	,,
,,	55	Private	Williams, C. E.	,,	,,
,,	89	,,	Stock, T.	,,	,,
New South Wales	17	,,	Atchison, S. C.	Woolvefontein	20.2.00
South Australia	118	,,	Smith, W. F.	Arundel	21.2.00
,,	..	Lieutenant	Powell, J. W.	Rensburg	12.2.00

Died of Wounds.

State.	No.	Rank.	Name.	Wounded.		Died.	
				Place.	Date.	Place.	Date.
Victoria	88	Private	*Suttie, F.	Bastard's Nek	10.2.00	Boer Hospital, Rensburg	12.2.00
,,	..	Lieutenant	Roberts, J. C.	Rensburg	12.2.00	Rensburg	13.2.00
New South Wales	45	Private	†Fraser, D.	Arundel	26.2.00	Colesberg	28.2.00
,,	83	,,	†McLennan, S.	,,	,,	,,	3.3.00
Western Australia	..	Lieutenant	Hensman, G. G. W.	Jasfontein	9.2.00	Cape Town	7.3.00

* Taken prisoner by enemy.
† Taken prisoner by enemy; re-captured at Colesberg.

Casualty List—continued.
Other Deaths.

State.	No.	Rank.	Name.	Cause.	Place.	Date.
Western Australia	18	Corporal	Bishop, G. N.	Sunstroke	De Aar	16.2.00
New South Wales	27	Private	Budd, H. M.	Enteric fever	..	—.2.00
,,	35	,,	Cameron, A. L.	,,	..	—.2.00
Victoria	43	,,	Coulson, A. E.	,,	De Aar	26.2.00
,,	..	Captain	Salmon, R. W.	,,	Naauwpoort	16.3.00
,,	..	,,	Hopkins, W. F. (Medical Staff)	,,	,,	27.3.00

Wounded in Action.

State.	No.	Rank.	Name.	Place.	Date
Western Australia	74	Private	Cunningham, J. M.	Slingersfontein	5.2.00
,,	112	Sergeant	Unkles, S. J.	,,	9.2.00
,,	51	Private	France, L.	,,	,,
,,	104	,,	Bird, J.	,,	,,
,,	97	,,	Ansell, J.	,,	,,
Tasmania	15	,,	Peers, V. S.	,,	,,
Victoria	33	,,	*Burrows, W. J.	Rensburg	10.2.00
,,	70	,,	*Gifford, A. E.	,,	,,
,,	..	Captain	*McInerney, T. N.	,,	12.2.00
,,	..	Lieutenant	†Tremearne, A. J. N.	,,	,,
,,	98	Sergeant	*Byers, R. J.	,,	,,
,,	57	Corporal	McCauley, D. H.	,,	,,
,,	37	Private	Michel, F.	,,	,,
,,	35	,,	Gamble, W.	,,	,,
,,	43	,,	Hagon, M. W.	,,	,,
,,	51	,,	Elmes, J. T.	,,	,,
,,	49	,,	Inglis, L. M.	,,	,,
,,	56	,,	Wallace, F. W.	,,	,,
,,	61	,,	Williamson, W. G.	,,	,,
,,	64	,,	Lawdorn, A.	,,	,,
,,	78	,,	*McCance, J.	,,	,,
,,	80	,,	Meagher, F. M.	,,	,,
,,	85	,,	Maxwell, T. J.	,,	,,
,,	87	,,	*Standford, W.	,,	,,
,,	90	,,	Bush, H.	,,	,,
,,	97	,,	Colley, H. J.	,,	,,
,,	100	,,	*Roberts, R.	,,	,,
,,	108	,,	Falla, P.	Rooipan	22.1.00
,,	112	,,	Edwards, S. W.	Rensburg	12.2.00
,,	114	,,	*Hamilton, S. G.	,,	,,
,,	117	,,	Peters, E.	,,	,,
Tasmania	..	Captain	Cameron, C. St. C.	Kulfontein	24.2.00
New South Wales	..	Lieutenant	Dove, F. A.	Maeder's Farm	26.2.00
,,	18	Private	Brack, F. C.	,,	,,
,,	103	,,	Southey, C. M.	Rensburg	12.2.00
Western Australia	65	,,	Baker, A. H.	Slingersfontein	4.3.00

* Taken prisoner by enemy; released at Pretoria.
† Taken prisoner by enemy; released following day.

Other Casualties.

State.	No.	Rank.	Name.	Casualty.	Place.	Date.
Tasmania	54	Lance-Corporal	Hynes, C. W.	Taken prisoners by enemy	Jasfontein	9.2.00
,,	9	Private	Swan, M. H.			
,,	53	,,	Hutton, J.			
,,	58	,,	Brothers, C.			
Western Australia	101	Lance-Corporal	Gifford, G.	Injured through fall from horse	Slingersfontein	,,
Victoria	69	,,	Mawley, E.	Taken prisoner by enemy	Rensburg	12.2.00
New South Wales	129	Corporal	Fraser, J. E.	,, ,, ,,	Arundel	26.2.00
,,	51	Private	Goodsall, S. H.	,, ,, ,,	,,	,,
,,	76	,,	McCredie, H. D.	Severe injury in action	Near Colesberg	28.2.00

Summary of Casualties.

Killed in action—Officers, 2; other ranks, 10. Died of wounds—Officers, 2; other ranks, 3. Other deaths—Officers, 2; other ranks, 4. Total deaths—Officers, 6; others, 17. Wounded in action—Officers, 4; others, 32. Other casualties—Officers, nil; others, 9. Total—Officers, 4; others, 41.

The following officers, non-commissioned officers and men, who belonged to the "1st Australian Regiment" from November, 1899, to April, 1900, were subsequently "Mentioned in Despatches" and awarded "Honours":—

MENTIONED IN DESPATCHES.

Colonel J. C. Hoad, Major G. A. Eddy, Captains G. R. Lascelles, C. St. C. Cameron, D. McLeish, W. Holmes, F. A. Dove, S. T. Staughton, J. H. Stapleton, and F. M. W. Parker, Lieutenant H. F. Darling, Sergeant-Majors J. P. Liggins, P. M. Edwards, and J. Costello, Sergeant J. Barry, Lance-Corporal J. Burley, Privates R. Corkill, J. H. Cooke, R. G. Gardiner, F. Starkey, H. Force, and F. C. Cornish.

HONOURS.

C.M.G. and A.D.C. to the Governor-General.—Colonel J. C. Hoad (since Major-General and K.C.M.G.). *C.B., and A.D.C. to the Governor-General.*—Captain (now Lieutenant-Colonel) C. St. C. Cameron; C.M.G., Captain (now Colonel) D. McLeish. D.S.O., and Extra A.D.C. to the General Officer Commanding.—Captain S. T. Staughton. *D.S.O.*—Lieutenants (now Lieutenant-Colonel) W. Holmes, (now Major) F. M. W. Parker, (now Major) F. A. Dove, (now Captain) J. H. Stapleton, and (now Captain) H. F. Darling. *Brevet Rank.*—Captain C. St. C. Cameron, C.B., A.D.C., to the Governor-General to Brevet Lieutenant-Colonel; Captain D. McLeish, C.M.G., to Brevet Lieutenant-Colonel; Lieutenant W. Holmes, D.S.O., to Brevet Lieutenant-Colonel; Lieutenant F. M. W. Parker, D.S.O., to Brever-Major; Captain J. G. Legge, to Brevet-Major; Captain J. Campbell, to Brevet-Major.

D.C.M.—Sergeant-Majors J. Costello and P. M. Edwards, Sergeant J. Barry, Lance-Corporal J. Burley, Privates R. Corkill, H. Force, J. G. Cooke, R. G. Gardiner, and F. Starkey.

FIRST VICTORIAN CONTINGENT—*continued*.

AFTER the Australian Regiment had been broken up, the 1st Victorians were placed under Colonel Price, who had the 2nd Victorians, and they formed part of the 4th Mounted Infantry Corps, under Colonel Henry (*vide* 2nd Contingent). They took part in all the operations with the main line of advance from Bloemfontein to Komati Poort, being present at Brandfort, Klip River, Zand River, Johannesberg, Pretoria, Diamond Hill, Belfast, and many other fights. During the fighting east of Karee on 1st May, several men whose horses had been killed were carried out by their comrades. Colonel Price and Captain Staughton each carried one out of fire during the retirement.

On 5th November, the Contingent embarked at Cape Town in the *Harlech Castle*, and arrived at Melbourne on 4th December, having called at Albany and Adelaide *en route*.

SUPPLEMENTARY LIST OF DEATHS.

54. Corporal King, O.D.	Killed in action at Edenvale, 16.7.00.
94. Private Barbour, R.	Died of enteric at Bloemfontein, 6.5.00.
65. Private Atkinson, M. W.	Died of enteric at Smithfield, 27.6.00.
94. Farrier Rose, T. J.	Died of enteric at Pretoria, 29.6.00.
26. Private Jones, A.	Died of inflammation of intestines at Kroonstadt, 24.10.00.
86. Private Ross, D.	Died of bronchitis at Hamilton, Victoria, 16.11.00.

SUPPLEMENTARY LIST OF CASUALTIES.

27. Private Anderson, J. W.	Severely wounded at Johannesburg, 30.5.00.
114. Private Gazzard, S. E.	Severley wounded at Brandfort, 6.5.00.
1. Rgt. Serg.-Major Healy, J. W.	Taken prisoner, 6.5.00; re-captured on occupation of Pretoria.
7. Corpl. Henessy, H. S.	Wounded, 3.5.00.
112. Private Kilbeg, J.	Arm broken, 4.5.00.
72. Private Kingston, G.	Taken prisoner, 29.5.00; recaptured at Pretoria, 6.6.00.
10. Private Lindsay, R. T.	Accidentally shot in leg at Houdenbeck, 28.4.00.
44. Private Lyle, R. G.	Severely wounded during siege of Philippolis.
42. Saddler-Sergt. Morton, J. H.	Slightly wounded at Kroonstadt, 11.5.00.
50. Q.-M. Sergt. Pearce, W. J.	Slightly wounded, 4.5.00.
81. Private Rogers, J.	Missing at Thaba N'Chu, 8.9.00.
15. Private Seymour, W.	Missing at Thaba N'Chu, 8.9.00.

PROMOTIONS, ETC.

Captain D. McLeish, C.M.G.	Promoted Major, 29.3.00.
Lieutenant T. M. McInerney	Promoted Captain, 8.11.99; provisionally appointed Chief Magistrate, at Pretoria, 11.6.00; promoted Major, 10.2.01.
,, H. W. Pendlebury	Promoted Captain, 1.1.00.
,, A. J. N. Tremearne	Struck off strength of Contingent on joining Ashanti Field Force.

Promotions, &c.—*continued.*

Lt. and Adjt. R. W. Salmon	Promoted Captain, 8.1.00, *deceased.*
Lieutenant G. F. Thorn	Promoted Captain, 9.3.00.
,, G. G. F. Chomley	Captain, 5th Contingent.
,, S. T. Staughton, D.S.O.	Promoted Captain, 22.6.00.
Sergeant E. E. Righetti	Lieutenant, 27.8.00; Captain, 5th Contingent.
Lance-Corpl. E. C. Tatchell	2nd Lieutenant, 29.3.00; Captain, 5th Contingent.
Private N. Smith	2nd Lieutenant, 29.3.00; Lieutenant, 5th Contingent.
Sergeant A. P. Ahern	2nd Lieutenant, 29.3.00.
,, A. Sindel	Lieutenant, 1st Scottish Horse, 28.4.01.

NOMINAL ROLL.

First Victorian Mounted Infantry Company.

No. and Name.	Rank.	Remarks.
McLeish, Duncan	Captain	
Salmon, Robert Westrup	Lieutenant and Adjutant	
Thorn, George Francis	Lieutenant	Invalided, Australia, arr. 26.8.00
Chomley, George Griffith Floyd	,,	
Staughton, Samuel Thomas	,,	
Roberts, James Clarke	,,	
Kendall, Ernest Arthur	Veterinary-Captain	

N.C.O.'s AND MEN.

1. Healy, John Walton	a/Coy. Sergeant-Major	Reg. Sergeant-Major, 8.4.00
4. Patterson, Charles	Sergeant	
3. Wallace, Peter J. C.	,,	Coy. Sergeant-Major, 14.4.00
5. Geary, Edward	,,	
2. Grant, Neil	,,	
52. Hennessy, Victor J.	Corporal	Sergeant, 11.2.00
6. Linsley, Thomas	,,	
48. Malcolm, John A.	,,	
71. Connor, John Wright	,,	
79. McAlpine, Robert Stephen	,,	Invalided, Australia, arr. 21.11.00
8. Daniel, Giles Francis	,,	Reduced, Private, C.M., 19.11.00
9. Satchwell, Albert Edwin	Saddler-Sergeant	Invalided, Australia, arr. 29.7.00
42. Morton, John H.	Saddler	Lance-Corporal, 1.5.00; Saddler-Sergeant, 10.6.00
93. Punshon, Richard James	Farrier-Sergeant	
101. Buchanan, William Thomas	Farrier	
94. Rose, Thomas Joel	,,	
11. Thomas, Edgar E.	Bugler	Lance-Corporal
10. Pleasents, Ormond William	,,	
37. Michel, Frederick	Private	Invalided, Australia, arr. 29.7.00
38. Squires, David	,,	Lance-Corporal, 1.3.00
39. Lyle, David	,,	
40. Prowse, Stephen Robert	,,	Lance-Corporal, 14.11.99; Sergeant, 1.5.00
41. Payne, Victor Harold	,,	
43. Coulson, Arthur Edward	,,	
44. Lyle, Robert G.	,,	

Nominal Roll—*continued*.
First Victorian Mounted Infantry Company—continued.

No. and Name.	Rank.	Remarks.
N.C.O.'s AND MEN—*continued*.		
45. Vallance, Packington J.	Private	Invalided, Australia, arr. 17.11.00
46. Ferris, Frederick A.	,,	
47. Towt, John Ford	,,	Invalided, Australia, arr. 24.5.00
49. Inglis, Lindsay Morrow	,,	Invalided, Australia, arr. 24.5.00. Awarded pension
50. Pearce, William John	,,	Quartermaster-Sergeant, 1.12.99
51. Elms, John Turner	,,	Lance-Corporal, 1.5.00
12. Bidstrup, Charles N.	,,	Lance-Corporal, 14.11.99; Corporal, 1.5.00; Sergeant, 22.7.00
13. Fletcher, John	,,	
14. Vearing, James	,,	
15. Seymour, William	,,	Invalided, Australia, arr. 5.1.01. Awarded pension
16. Miller, Charles	,,	
17. Newby, Thomas R.	,,	Invalided, Australia, arr. 29.7.00
18. Campbell, Archibald	,,	
63. Griggs, James	,,	
64. Lawdorn, Alphonsus	,,	Invalided, Australia, arr. 24.5.00; Awarded pension
65. Atkinson, Marmaduke W.	,,	
66. McLean, Norman	,,	
67. Kirwin, Henry May	,,	Lance-Corporal, 1.10.00
68. Bell, George John	,,	Corporal, 1.5.00; sergeant, 1.9.00
69. Mawley, Edward	,,	Lance-Corporal, 14.11.99
70. Gifford, Alfred Ernest	,,	
72. Kingston, George	,,	
73. Brain, Charles H.	,,	
74. Willson, Albert Herbert	,,	
53. Killeen, Christopher	,,	
54. McFarlane, John Duncan	,,	
7. Henessy, Henry Stephen	,,	Lance-Corporal, 1.3.00; Corporal, Invalided, Australia, arr. 10.7.00. Awarded pension
55. Williams, Charles E.	,,	
56. Wallace, Frederick William	,,	Invalided, Australia, arr. 24.5.00. Awarded pension
57. McCauley, Denis Henry	,,	Corporal, 1.2.00. Invalided, Australia, arr. 12.2.00. Awarded pension
58. Ve'all, George Fairfax	,,	Invalided, Australia, arr. 2.8.00
75. Breen, John	,,	
76. Welch, John McPherson	,,	Invalided, Australia, 29.7.00 arr.
77. Pattison, Henry	,,	
78. Brooks, John	,,	
22. Robinson, Stuart	,,	Lance-Corporal, 1.5.00; Corporal, 1.10.00
23. Crothers, Gavin W.	,,	
24. Hessian, Thomas	,,	
25. Wilson, Henry R.	,,	
26. Jones, Arthur	,,	
27. Burnie, Reginald M.	,,	
28. McDonald, Alexander Norman	,,	
80. Meagher, Francis Michael	,,	Invalided, Australia, arr. 29.7.00. Awarded pension (temporary)
81. Rogers, James	,,	
82. Brand, Horatio George	,,	
83. Righetti, Edward Edmund	,,	Lance-Corporal, 14.11.99; Corporal, 11.2.00; Sergeant, 1.5.00, *Vide* "Promotions."

Nominal Roll—*continued.*
First Victorian Mounted Infantry Company—continued.

No. and Name.	Rank.	Remarks.
N.C.O.'s and Men—continued.		
84. Stock, Duncan	Private	Lance-Corporal, 8.9.00; Corporal 1.10.00
85. Maxwell, Thomas James	,,	Invalided, Australia, arr. 9.8.00. Awarded pension
86. Ross, Donald	,,	Invalided, Australia, 9.8.00 arr.
87. Stanford, William	,,	
88. Suttie, Frank	,,	
89. Stock, Thomas	,,	
90. Bush, Henry	,,	Invalided, Australia, arr. 24.5.00. Discharged to pension (temporary)
59. McLay, Henry Devine	,,	
62. Kortum, Herbert James	,,	
60. Butcher, Albert John	,,	
36. Williamson, George Sutherland	,,	
61. Williamson, William George	,,	
35. Gamble, William	,,	Invalided, Australia, arr. 24.5.00. Awarded pension (temporary)
33. Burrows, William John	,,	Invalided, Australia, arr. 6.9.00. Awarded pension
34. Slatter, Alfred Henry	,,	
19. Ebling, Gustave	,,	
20. Kemmis, Walter	,,	Invalided, Australia, arr. 24.5.00
118. Ditchburn, Ernest N. V.	,,	Invalided, Australia, arr. 29.7.00
115. Robey, Cecil Vincent T.	,,	Invalided, Australia, arr. 9.8.00
21. Hicks, William	,,	Invalided, Australia, arr. 29.7.00
114. Gazzard, Stanley Edwin	,,	Invalided, Australia, arr. 12.9.00
104. Ross, Malcolm	,,	Lance-Corporal, 14.11.99. Invalided, Australia, arr. 9.8.00.
109. Kashow, Daniel A.	,,	
108. Falla, Peter	,,	Discharged from Netley, medically unfit, 7.5.01. Awarded pension
112. Edwards, Samuel William	,,	Invalided, Australia, arr. 24.5.00. Awarded pension (temporary)
100. Anderson, Charles A. W.	,,	Invalided, Australia, arr. 25.9.00
99. Dobson, Ernest Street	,,	
101. Fisher, Albert	,,	
29. Tackaberry, William Thomas	,,	Invalided, Australia, arr. 29.7.00
32. Keeble, John Walter	,,	
30. Streitberg, Charles Gosclar	,,	Invalided, Australia, arr. 29.7.00
102. Bolding, John	,,	
103. Nadenbousch, John	,,	
91. Hornsby, Arthur Gilbert	,,	Invalided, Australia, arr. 17.11.00
107. Hull, William E.	,,	
111. Earnshaw, Claude Tasman	,,	
92. McGrowther, Robert	,,	
98. Dobson, John	,,	Lance-Corporal, 1.10.00
106. Stayner, George Alexander	,,	
95. Holmes, Thomas Harold	,,	
96. Cook, Henry E.	,,	
97. Colley, Henry James	,,	Invalided, Australia, arr. 24.5.00. Awarded pension
31. Shearn, James	,,	Lance-Corporal, 8.9.00
105. Robinson, Alfred J.	,,	
116. Lethlean, William	,,	
117. Winsor, Charles	,,	
113. Dickson, Charles	,,	

NOMINAL ROLL.
First Victorian Infantry Company.

No. and Name.	Rank.	Remarks.
Eddy, George Albert	Major	
Hopkins, William Fleming	Captain (Medical Staff)	
McInerney, Timothy Marcus	Lieutenant	
Pendlebury, Henry William	,,	
Tremearne, Arthur John Newman	,,	Invalided to England, 1.6.00

N.C.O.'s AND MEN.

No. and Name.	Rank.	Remarks.
1. Coffey, Ernest Norman	Coy. Sergeant-Major	Reg. Sergeant-Major, 1.5.00. Invalided, Australia, 6.9.00 Awarded pension
2. Paul, John Keating	Coy. Quartermaster Sergeant	Reg. Quartermaster-Sergeant, 27.11.99
3. Walker, William Samuel	Sergeant	Coy. Quartermaster - Sergeant, 1.2.00
32. Buzzini, Angelo Francis	,,	
62. Everall, William John	,,	Saddler-Sergeant, 1.2.00; Private C.M., 10.6.00
92. Miller, William John	,,	Farrier-Sergeant, 1.2.00
33. Lynch, Charles Daniel	Corporal	Sergeant, 1.2.00
63. Archer, Charles Benjamin	,,	Invalided, Australia, arr. 2.8.00
64. Curnow, John Treloar	,,	Sergeant, 1.2.00
4. Ross, Alexander	,,	
93. Keck, Alfred Harry	,,	Sergeant, 1.2.00
65. Bottle, Albert John	Bugler	
34. Brenchley, William Jesse Henry	,,	
98. Byers, Robert James	Private	
70. Boyes, Reginald Cummins	,,	
31. Sindel, Alfred	,,	Lance-Corporal, 1.2.00; Provost Corporal, 1.5.00; Provost Sergeant, 1.6.00. Vide "Promotions."
54. King, Oscar David	,,	Lance-Corporal, –.11.99; Corporal, 1.2.00
26. Young, William Murray	,,	Lance-Corporal, –.11.99; Corporal, 1.2.00
12. Hendrie, Andrew	,,	
30. Hull, Frank	,,	Invalided, Australia, arr. 29.7.00
5. Cambridge, Owen	,,	
11. Mahy, Charles Harold	,,	
9. Capper, Charles Edward	,,	
15. Jennings, John Thomas	,,	
16. Macartney, Robert Augustine	,,	
68. Robin, Robert	,,	
20. Tomlinson, William Edward Holliday	,,	Lance-Corporal, 1.2.00
19. Ziesche, Lawrence	,,	
22. Quick, Malcolm Henry	,,	
23. Lambert, Vincent Robert	,,	
24. Pike, William George	,,	
27. Anderson, James William	,,	Invalided, Australia, arr. 16.1.01. Discharged to pension
25. Eyres, Thomas	,,	
91. Fraher, Philip	,,	
6. Gibbons, Alfred Sidney	,,	
8. Jenkinson, Thomas Walker	,,	Invalided, Australia, arr. 2.8.00
7. Sanders, Ernest William	,,	
21. Meadows, John	,,	

Nominal Roll—*continued.*
First Victorian Infantry Company—continued.

No. and Name.	Rank.	Remarks.
N.C.O.'s AND MEN—*continued.*		
18. Whitwam, Thomas Walker	Private	
14. Robertson, Albert Arthur	,,	
17. Milne, Albert William	,,	
29. Somerville, Edward George	,,	
28. Smith, Norman	,,	*Vide* "Promotions"
69. Hughes, James Lawrence	,,	
10. Lindsay, Richard Thomas	,,	
13. Chiron, Eugene	,,	Invalided, Australia, arr. 29.7.00
37. Tracey, Charles Joseph	,,	
41. Pettit, Alfred	,,	
35. Blunden, Thomas	,,	
36. Foster, John	,,	
38. Ryan, John Philip	,,	
39. De Kuyper, Albert Henry	,,	Invalided, Australia, arr. 29.7.00
56. McCracken, Ralph	,,	
58. Newham, Collingwood	,,	Invalided, Australia, arr. 5.1.01
51. Mackenzie, Herbert Archibald	,,	
46. Hunter, Robert	,,	
55. Roach, Charles Frederick	,,	
47. Murray, John	,,	
50. Gray, William Henry	,,	
59. Jennings, Thomas Edwin	,,	
44. Mason, Thomas	,,	
42. Wright, George Mountford	,,	
43. Hagon, Harry William	,,	
49. Brownrigg, John	,,	
67. Cooke, Herbert James	,,	
60. Browning, Herbert Samuel	,,	Invalided, Australia, arr. 6.12.00
90. Will, William Thomas	,,	
52. Smith, Edward Alfred	,,	
57. Plumridge, Charles Albert	,,	
61. Hart, Frederick Charles	,,	
53. Matson, Thomas	,,	
45. Hatchard, Ernest A.	,,	
40. Watson, Arthur H.	,,	Invalided, Australia, arr. 6.9.00
48. Kirby, Walter	,,	
66. Wright, Alfred William	,,	
83. James, William Henry	,,	
85. Lawn, James Edward	,,	
84. Coulter, Graham	,,	
86. Ross, John	,,	
80. Brough, William Thomas	,,	
88. Thomas, Gwillim Treharne	,,	
82. Starkey, Arthur Eli	,,	
81. Hockey, Edward	,,	
87. McMillan, William George	,,	
75. Dyer, Henry	,,	
78. McCance, John	,,	Invalided, Australia, arr. 6.9.00. Awarded pension (temporary)
71. Duggan, James	,,	
72. Sampson, Francis Horatio	,,	Corporal, 26.8.00
74. Webber, Albert	,,	
77. Topham, Charles Robert	,,	Invalided, Australia, arr. 2.8.00
89. McMinn, Robert	,,	
76. Jackson, Jesse Jabe	,,	
73. McMinn, Robert	,,	**Invalided, Australia, arr. 17.10.00**

Nominal Roll—*continued.*
First Victorian Infantry Company—continued.

No. and Name.	Rank.	Remarks.
N.C.O.'s AND MEN—continued.		
79. Hughes, Arthur Walker Joseph	Private	Lance-Corporal, –.11.99; Private, 18.6.00
96. Shearer, Hugh	,,	
97. Walton, Jackson Stanley	,,	
94. Barbour, Robert	,,	
95. Friswell, Harry Hain	,,	
104. Ordish, Harold	,,	Lance-Corporal, –.11.99; Lance-Sergeant, 1.2.00; Acting C.S.M., 1.5.00
113. Tyers, Egbert William	,,	Invalided, Australia, arr. 26.8.00
105. Rule, James Henry	,,	
103. Kerans, Henry	,,	Corporal, 1.11.99; Sergeant
112. Kilbeg, James	,,	
101. Collins, Leonard Thomas	,,	
99. Wilks, William Allan	,,	
102. McDonald, Donald	,,	
114. Hamilton, Samuel George	,,	
111. Waites, Frederick	,,	
115. Schaeche, Oscar	,,	
100. Roberts, Richard	,,	
107. Tatchell, Edward Charles	,,	Lance-Corporal, 1.2.00, *vide* "Promotions"
116. Jewell, Edwin C.	,,	Invalided, Australia, arr. 26.8.00. Awarded pension
108. McGhie, James A.	,,	Invalided, Australia, arr. 10.7.00
110. Henshaw, William J.	,,	Invalided, Australia, arr. 24.5.00
109. Rochester, Charles Henry	,,	
117. Peters, Ezich	,,	Invalided, Australia, arr. 24.5.00. Awarded pension
118. Gardiner, Richard Joseph	,,	Lance-Corporal, –.11.99; Private, 12.10.00
119. Crawford, Frederick	,,	
116. Lucas, Gordon	,,	
120. Ahern, Albert P.	,,	Lance-Corporal, –.11.99; Sergeant, 1.12.99, *vide* "Promotions." Invalided, — Australia; and awarded pension

Note.—This company was converted into Mounted Infantry at Naauwpoort on 1st February, 1900.

(For nominal rolls of New South Wales, South Australia, Western Australia, and Tasmanian Companies, see under those States).

THE SECOND (MOUNTED RIFLES) CONTINGENT.

EXCEPT that no infantry was raised, the second Contingent was formed upon much the same principles as the first. Under G.O. 94 (Vic.) '99, the Commanding Officer Mounted Rifles was directed to submit a return of officers, N.C.O.'s, and men of his corps who volunteered for active service. They were required to be good shots, and medically fit. Applications were also received from officers, N.C.O.'s, and men of the Militia and Volunteer Forces, to be considered in the event of an insufficient number of Mounted Rifles being available to complete a Contingent of 250. Such candidates to be riflemen, hardy riders, medically fit, and preferably unmarried. In addition to men from the Mounted Rifles, a considerable proportion were thus enrolled from the Rangers (an infantry regiment of similar organization), Militia, and Volunteer regiments, and a few from the Royal Australian Artillery.

The Mounted Rifle Regiment was raised in 1885 by Colonel T. Price, who now obtained the command of the Contingent.

CLOTHING, ETC.

The men were issued with khaki tweed uniform, comprising F.S. jackets, cord pants, puttees, F.S. hat, F.S. cap, and greatcoat; besides boots and a complete kit of clothing, underclothing, necessaries, &c.

Fully horsed and supplied with bandoliers and saddlery, rifles, and bayonets.

ESTABLISHMENT.

The following establishment was approved :—1 commanding officer, 2 captains, 8 subalterns, 1 adjutant, 1 medical officer, 1 veterinary officer, 2 coy. sergeant-majors, 2 quartermaster-sergeants, 8 sergeants, 12 corporals, 2 saddler-sergeants, 2 saddlers, 2 farrier-sergeants, 4 shoeing-smiths, 4 buglers, 200 privates, 12 drivers. Total—14 officers, 12 sergeants, 10 artificers, 4 buglers, 224 rank and file. In all, 264, with 305 horses (28 officers' horses, 238 other ranks, 24 spare, and 15 transport and pack).

RATES OF PAY.

Pay to all ranks was approved as under :—Privates, 4s. 6d. per diem; corporals, 7s.; sergeants, 8s.; company sergeant-majors, 9s.; staff sergeants, 10s.; warrant officers, 11s. 6d.; lieutenants, 16s. and 3s. field allowance; captains, 20s. and 3s. 6d.; majors, 25s. and 4s. 6d.; adjutants, 5s. per day in addition to pay of their ranks. These rates, it was stated, were to be considered as in full; and any payments made by the Imperial Government would be deducted therefrom. Members of medical or veterinary staff to be paid according to relative rank. Portion of pay might be drawn by authorized persons in Victoria; and one month's pay, in advance, could be drawn by any member of Contingent desiring to do so.

DEPARTURE AND RETURN.

The 2nd Victorian Mounted Rifles left on the 13th January, 1900, comprising 15 officers, 250 of other ranks, with 305 horses, and 6 wagons. Of these, 1 officer and 9 others were killed or died; 2 officers and 4 others were transferred; 2 officers and 13 others were struck off the strength in South Africa; 1 officer was commissioned in the Imperial Army; 10 officers and 223 others returned to Australia.

Promotions, Etc.

Lieutenant T. H. Sergeant, promoted Captain, 8th January, 1900.
Lieutenant M. T. Kirby, promoted Captain, 23rd October, 1900.
Lieutenant E. S. Norton, promoted Captain, 23rd October, 1900.
Lieutenant T. F. Umphelby, promoted Captain, 22nd June, 1900; Major, 23rd October, 1900.
R.Q.M. Sergt. J. R. Mathews, lieutenant, 27.3.01; Australian Base Details, 16th September, 1901.
Sergt.-Major H. Macdonald became Lieutenant in 4th A.C.H.
Corporal G. H. Hood, 2nd lieutenant, 29th March, 1900.
Sergeant J. H. Brabazon, 2nd lieutenant, 29th March, 1901.
Corporal M. Wood, 2nd lieutenant, 29th March, 1901.
Lieutenant E. O. Anderson was commissioned in Royal Field Artillery.
Private A. Kelly was commissioned in Scottish Horse.
For promotions of N.C.O.'s and men, *vide* nominal roll.

Service.

The Second Contingent embarked in the *Euryalus* on the 13th January, 1900, and arrived at Cape Town on 5th February. There the ship was inspected by Lord Roberts, who expressed himself in complimentary terms. Only three horses had been lost on the passage. On the 7th, the troops proceeded to Maitland Camp, and on the 10th, entrained and arrived at Naauwpoort on the morning of the 14th. The Tasmanian Contingent, under Captain Cameron came in that evening. Colonel Price was placed in command of what was known as the "Hanover Road Field Force," consisting in the first instance of about 80 Prince Albert's Guards, 60 Tasmanians, 230 Victorians, and one battalion of 8 companies of the Lancashire Militia; they were without artillery. They were constantly in touch with the enemy and patrolling work was very heavy. On the 21st, Colonel Price broke two of his ribs by falling down a donga in the dark, but he still continued at his duty. On the 24th, it was determined to shell Kuilfontein Kopje, which was very strongly held; it being the key to the position of the advance upon Colesberg. Colonel Page Henderson, 6th Inniskilling Dragoons, commanded the left attack, Colonel Price the centre, and General Clements, under whose direction the whole operations were conducted, the right. Lord Kitchener was present to watch the proceedings. Colonel Price's command was reinforced by one battery of artillery, and about 150 Eastern Province Horse; but he gave Colonel Page Henderson two companies—Victorians and Tasmanians. This column met with very heavy fighting, and 1 officer, West Riding Mounted Infantry, was killed, and Captain (now Major) Cameron wounded and taken prisoner; 15 rank and file of the West Riding were reported killed; 20 wounded. The shelling comemnced about 6.30 a.m., and was sustained by 24 field guns, 2 howitzers, and 1 5" R.M.L. It was carried on until about 5.30 p.m., but no impression was made on the enemy; though (as was afterwards ascertained) they suffered severely. They remained on the hill until dusk, when they began to draw away in small parties, making towards Colesberg.

On the 26th, the Hanover Road Field Force again moved on Kuilfontein, and occupied it without opposition. On the 28th, they participated in the relief of Colesberg. On the 14th March, the passage of the Orange River was carried out; the pontoon bridge being 260 yards long, upon which the whole army crossed into Orange Free State. On the 17th, news was obtained of the death of Captain Salmon, of enteric, at Naauwpoort. Colonel Price received orders to march on Bloemfontein *viâ* Philippolis and Fauresmith, with the Head-Quarters Flying

Column, which consisted of the Victorians (2nd contingent), Grahamstown and E.P. Horse, and one battery artillery; in all, about 1,000. This command was broken up on the 20th, and the Contingent then joined the main column at Donkerspoort and formed part of the advanced guard. On the 23rd, Philippolis was occupied, on the 26th, Wittevreden; and on the 27th, Fauresmith.

On 4th April, General Clements' column reached Tempe, outside Bloemfontein, where it was broken up; and the whole of the Mounted Infantry, both Imperial and Colonial, was placed under the command of Colonel Price, and marched into Bloemfontein, where there was a re-organization. The Victorians, South Australians, Tasmanians, and 4th Mounted Infantry Corps, were formed into the 4th Mounted Infantry Corps, under the command of Colonel Henry, 5th Fusiliers. The Australian Regiment was severed, and the troops of all the Colonies formed into their own Colonial regiments. The Victorians were placed under their own commanding officer, the Tasmanians under Major Cameron (who had been released), and the South Australians under Major Reade. These remained at Bloemfontein refitting and rehorsing, until the 20th. Enteric now began to develop itself, and amongst the victims was Lieutenant Bree, who died on the 26th.

On the 21st, the 4th Mounted Infantry marched on the glen to the north of Bloemfontein, this being the first step in the great main advance of Lord Roberts. On the 22nd, the Victorians relieved Kitchener's Horse at Houdenbeck, about 6 miles from Karee Kloof, where the remainder of the corps had gone, and had to hold the extreme left of the line of outposts; the Boers occupying the Modderspruit, along the front of the Victorian position. The work was very heavy and involved constant skirmishing with the enemy. On the 29th, the Contingent joined Colonel Henry at Karee Kloof, where these experiences were continued.

On the 30th, the Victorians were attacked by a force of about 1,500 Boers, and retired about $2\frac{1}{2}$ miles, under shell, pom pom, and rifle fire. Lieutenant Lilley was dangerously wounded, Private Coughlan's leg broken, and Reg. S. M. Healy was captured. Many men went back under pom pom fire, and carried out those whose horses had been killed.

There was fighting all the way to Mooifontein, where they bivouacked on the ground, 4th May. On the 5th, there was the action at Vet River, in which the Victorians participated; being on the right. From this on, until the 10th, they were with the advance, and no resistance of any moment was offered. The weather was extremely cold by night and hot by day. Twice the troops were without any rations, and so knocked up by work and starvation that they had to be halted at Lewkville for a day. At the Zand River, Virginia Siding, the Boers were driven in after contesting the whole way, and the Victorians advanced and made good their lodgment in a deep donga, under very heavy fire. From the 12th to the 21st, they remained outside Kroonstadt, which had surrendered. On the 22nd, the advance on the Vaal River was continued, and though the enemy were frequently seen, there was no engagement until Vereeniging was arrived at, where the troops were opposed by the Irish Brigade, who made good their retreat, blowing up the bridge over the river after they had crossed it. On the 27th, the Vaal was crossed.

On the 29th, the Victorians were engaged at the Black Reef Mine, Witwatersrand, where they were met with a heavy rifle fire; and subsequently shell fire when endeavouring to turn the enemy's flank; nevertheless, they accomplished the movement. During the day a company was detached, under Lieutenant Kirby to assist a mixed party of Lumsden's Horse and Imperial Mounted Infantry, who, were hard-pressed at the railway station, close to Germiston Junction. Lieutenant Kirby pushed in, and, after a fairly sharp struggle, captured several engines, a considerable amount of rolling stock, and an ambulance train that was going out. For this he received the D.S.O. About this time no less than 79 Victorian horses succumbed to the privations and severity of the weather.

In June, they moved to a bivouac near Orange Grove, north of Johannesburg. On the 4th, they were heavily engaged at the 6-Mile Spruit, and advanced, fighting all the way, to the outskirts of Pretoria, which were reached on the following day, and the Victorians, owing to the formation of the march, were the first to enter. They remained there until the 7th (Pretoria having surrendered), when they were marched into Perraarspoort, where they remained until 22nd July, doing very severe patrol and picket duty. On the 23rd, they commenced the march to Middelburg, halting at Brugspruit and Howard's Colliery from 27th to 4th August. From Middelburg they went to Doornkop, which they held from 7th to 17th August. On the 24th, Bester's Farm was reached, and on the 25th, the enemy was again come into contact with, and a brilliant reconnaisance was made under Captains Staughton and Umphelby. There was fighting all the way to Waterval Onder, which was arrived at on the 30th, the enemy holding the hill across the ravine of Eland's River.

On 6th September, the 4th Mounted Infantry were ordered back to Machadodorp and on the 7th were engaged with the enemy, when severe fighting took place On the 14th, the force arrived at Kapsche Hoop, after advancing over most difficult country and being constantly intercepted by the enemy. On the 16th, the march to Komati Poort was commenced; and on the 18th, the enemy was encountered near Avoca, taking away a convoy. On the 20th, a halt was made to recuperate the horses, which were suffering greatly from fatigue and want of forage. On the 24th, arrived at Komati Poort, the horses being barely able to stagger in, and the heat excessive. A camp was selected close to the junction of the Crocodile and Komati Rivers. The whole of the Portuguese frontier was marked with flags, and Portuguese soldiers were seen patrolling in every direction. On the 28th, the whole of the troops in camp were reviewed in honour of the birthdays of the King and Queen of Portugal; the Portuguese Commandant attended by a strong escort riding over from his territory to attend. A great quantity of ammunition, which had been left by the Boers on the right bank of Komati River, near Rosario Garcia (the Portuguese having prevented them from taking it any further), was blown up by the British.

On 3rd October, the Victorians entrained for Pretoria, and at Machadodorp handed over all the horses to General French. On the 7th, arrived at Pretoria, remaining there until the 23rd, when the bulk of the Victorians were permitted to return to Australia, under Colonel Price.

The journey to Cape Town was uneventful, except that on the 26th, the line between Edenburg and Norval's Pont was blown up. The Boers held the hill at this place, and evidently intended to wreck the train. They were driven off by the Victorians; the line was repaired, and the farm house which had sheltered the enemy burnt.

Arrived at Cape Town on the 29th, and on the 5th November embarked in the *Harlech Castle*, which reached Melbourne on 4th December. Disbandment followed.

War Services of Officers.

Price, Colonel T.—Operations in Cape Colony, Orange Free State, and Transvaal, between February, 1900, and September, 1900, including actions at Colesberg, Karee Siding (horse wounded), Vet River, Zand River, Johannesberg, Pretoria, Diamond Hill, and Belfast. Despatches, *London Gazette*, 16th April, 1901. C.B. Queen's Medal with five clasps.

Jenkins, Captain D. H.—Operations in Cape Colony and Orange River Colony. Queen's Medal with two clasps.

Sergeant, Captain T. H.—Operations as above. Actions at Houtnek, Vet River, Zand River, Johannesburg, Pretoria, Diamond Hill, and Belfast. Queen's Medal with five clasps.

Kirby, Captain M. T.—Operations and actions as above. Despatches, *London Gazette*, 16th April, 1901. D.S.O. Queen's Medal with six clasps.

Norton, Captain E. S.—Operations and actions as above. Queen's Medal with clasps.

Umphelby, Major T. F.—Operations and actions as above. Queen's Medal and King's Medal with clasps. Served subsequently with 5th Contingent.

Bruce, Lieutenant G. O.—Operations and actions as above. Queen's Medal with four clasps.

Holdsworth, Lieutenant A. A.—Operations and actions as above. Queen's Medal with six clasps. (Lieutenant Holdsworth was attached to A.S.C. for twelve months.)

Bree, Lieutenant R. S. R. S.—Operations and actions in Cape Colony and Orange River Colony. Died of enteric, 26th May, 1900.

Umphelby, Lieutenant T. A.—Operations as above. Actions at Houtnek, Vet River, Zand River, and Johannesburg. (Lieutenant Umphelby saw subsequent service with 5th Contingent.) Queen's Medal with four clasps. King's Medal with two clasps.

Lilley, Lieutenant and Adjutant J. L.—Operations and actions in Cape Colony and Orange River Colony. Dangerously wounded at Houtnek, and taken prisoner, 4th May, 1900. Re-captured at Brandfort, 7th May, 1900. Despatches, *London Gazette*, 16th April, 1901. D.S.O. Queen's Medal with two clasps.

Honman, Major A. (Medical Staff).—Operations and actions as above. Queen's Medal with clasps.

Rudduck, Veterinary-Captain H. S.—Operations and actions as above. Queen's Medal with clasps.

Wray, Rev. F. W.—Operations and actions as above. Queen's Medal with five clasps.

Mathews, Lieutenant J. R.—Operations and actions as above. Queen's Medal with clasps.

Hood, Lieutenant G. H.—Operations and actions as above. Queen's Medal with clasps.

Brabazon, Lieutenant J. H.—Operations and actions as above. (Lieutenant Brabazon saw subsequent service with 5th Contingent.) Queen's Medal with six clasps. King's Medal with two clasps.

Wood, Lieutenant M.—Operations and actions as above. Queen's Medal with clasps.

Nominal Roll.

No. and Name.	Rank.	Remarks.
Price, Thomas	Colonel	
Jenkins, Donald Halley	Captain	
Sergeant, Theophilus Hengist	Lieutenant	
Umphelby, Thomas Frederick	,,	
Bruce, George Owen	,,	Invalided to England, 19.7.00
Holdsworth, Albert Armytage	,,	Invalided, Australia, 30.9.01
Kirby, Mark Thomas	,,	
Anderson, Edgar Oswald	,,	
Umphelby, Thomas Austin	,,	Invalided, Australia, arr. 13.8.00
Norton, Edward Stuart	,,	
Bree, Reginald Stephen Robert Stapylton	,,	Died of enteric at Bloemfontein, 26.5.00
Lilley, James Lindsay	Lieutenant and Adjutant	Awarded pension (temporary)
Honman, Andrew	Major (Medical Staff)	Invalided, Australia, arr. 17.11.00
Wray, Rev. Frederick William	Chaplain	
Rudduck, Harold Sugden	Veterinary-Captain	

N.C.O.'s AND MEN.

No. and Name.	Rank.	Remarks.
370. Macdonald, Hugh	Coy. Sergeant-Major	
127. Jeffery, John	,,	Reverted to Sergeant, 8.2.00
266. Fawns, James Robertson	Quartermaster-Sergeant	Coy. Sergeant-Major, 8.2.00
371. Mathews, John Robert	,,	Reg. Quartermaster-Sergeant, 8.4.00, vide " Promotions " and " War Services "
294. Masters, Charles John	Sergeant	Invalided, Australia, arr. 17.10.00
139. Baldry, Robert John	,,	
243. Murray, Daniel	,,	Coy. Sergeant-Major, 20.12.00
237. Challenger, William Samuel	,,	Reduced Corporal by C.M., 31.8.00
187. Cahill, Thomas Stewart	,,	Quartermaster-Sergeant, 23.10.00
340. Watts, Arthur John	,,	
214. Hiscock, Henry James	,,	Reduced Private, by resignation, 20.2.00. Died of enteric at Bloemfontein, 19.5.00
344. Warden, Andrew Duncan	,,	
132. Miller, William Grant	Corporal	Sergeant, 25.2.00. Invalided, Australia, arr. 26.8.00. Awarded pension
305. Francis, George William	,,	Sergeant, 1.9.00. Killed in action Eland's Drift, 3.12.00
349. Wilson, Andrew	,,	Saddler-Sergeant, 20.12.00
240. Dowd, Albert Henry	,,	Invalided, Australia, arr. 24.5.00
324. Whelan, Urban	,,	Taken prisoner, Dinaarspoort, Lockhart, 7.7.00; released, 2.9.00; returned Victoria, 1.3.01
138. Mountjoy, Ernest Lindsay	,,	Sergeant, 4.12.00
234. Sutherland, Alexander Robert	,,	Sergeant, 16.11.00
338. Sutherland, Charles Hector	,,	Sergeant, 20.3.01
292. Carr, William Maitland	,,	Invalided, Australia, arr. 24.5.00. Awarded pension
328. Fawcett, John Lowe	,,	Reduced Private, C.M., 5.9.00
364. McGowan, John	,,	Died of enteric at Rustenburg, 1.12.00
326. Fox, James Peter	,,	

Nominal Roll—*continued*.

No. and Name.	Rank.	Remarks.
N.C.O.'s AND MEN—*continued*.		
154. Allinson, John Thomas	Saddler-Sergeant	
356. Everall, Albert	,,	Reduced Private, C.M., 10.6.00
157. McLachlan, Hugh Alexander	,,	Invalided, Australia, arr. 17.10.00
362. Tate, William Henry	,,	Lance-Corporal, 26.4.00. Invalided, Australia, arr. 29.7.00
269. Woodbridge, John James	Farrier-Sergeant	
258. Smith, William Henry	,,	Invalided, Australia, arr. 9.8.00
361. Mason, Denman Etherley	Shoeing-Smith	
182. Carey, Patrick Joseph	,,	
203. Hortle, Frank William	Bugler	Taken prisoner, 3.5.00; recaptured at Pretoria
264. Akins, Donald Gordon	,,	Reported missing, 3.5.00; rejoined 16.5.00
267. Oakley, David	,,	Corporal-Bugler, 19.3.01
210. Bell, Henry Henderson	,,	Sergeant, 25.8.00. Commander-in-Chief's Despatches, 2.4.01
126. Wallace, Douglas Edwin	Private	Despatches, *London Gazette*, 7.5.01
128. Booth, Frederick Harper	,,	
129. Kelly, Alured	,,	*Vide* "Promotions"
130. Lear, Guy Wishart	,,	Invalided, Australia, arr. 29.7.00
131. Dalgarno, Frederick Joseph	,,	Invalided, Australia, arr. 29.7.00
133. Oliver, David	,,	
134. Browning, Frederick Sydney	,,	
135. Banks, William James	,,	
136. Selman, Sydney	,,	Lance-Corporal, 10.4.00; Corporal, 8.9.00
137. Hutton, Walter John	,,	Invalided, Australia, arr. 17.11.00
140. Caton, Alexander John King	,,	Lance Corporal, 2.4.00; Corporal 8.4.00; Lance-Sergeant, 1.10.00
141. Prowse, William Henry	,,	Lance-Corporal, 8.9.00
142. Woods, Thomas Brassey	,,	Invalided, Australia, 6.9.00
143. Ogilvy, Arthur James	,,	
144. Duff, Charles De Vertus	,,	Slightly wounded, Bethseda, 10.8.01
145. Davies, John Hugh, jun.	,,	
146. Jeffreys, Richard Broughton	,,	
147. Ferguson, Kenneth	,,	
148. Baker, George Tarrant	,,	
149. Tait, Ralph	,,	Invalided, Australia, arr. 4.8.00
150. Turnley, Harold Eric	,,	
151. Lockwood, James Benjamin Edward	,,	Slightly wounded, Belfast, 26.8.00
152. Sandilands, John Graham	,,	
153. Martyn, Frederick	,,	
155. Johnstone, Robert	,,	
156. Peters, Robert Brookes	,,	
158. Hall, Thomas Patrick Joseph	,,	Lance-Corporal, 20.2.01
159. Gooch, Hampton Alexander	,,	Invalided, Australia, arr. 29.7.00
160. Macdonald, George Langlands	,,	Lance-Corporal, 8.6.00
161. Greenwood, Albert	,,	Lance-Corporal, 10.4.00; Corporal 8.9.00. Slightly wounded, Elandsfontein, 29.5.00
162. Taylor, Thomas Charles	,,	
163. Howard, Albert Edward	,,	
164. Wilson, Edgar George	,,	Lance-Corporal, 8.9.00; Corporal, 4.12.00
165. Lancaster, Arthur Ernest	,,	
166. McPherson, Alexander	,,	Invalided, Australia, arr. 17.10.00

Nominal Roll—continued.

No. and Name.	Rank.	Remarks.
N.C.O.'s AND MEN—continued.		
167. Macleod, Charles William Campbell	Private	Invalided, Australia, 6.9.00
168. Bell, William Robert	,,	
169. Hasthorpe, John Jesse	,,	
170. Lawdorn, Conrad	,,	
171. Fechner, Gustavus Henry	,,	
172. Fechner, John William	,,	
173. Bayley, Henry	,,	Attached to Pioneer Corps, 21.4.00
174. Lydiard, George Evelyn	,,	Lance-Corporal, 10.4.00
175. Kitson, John Sidney	,,	
176. Pinder, Peter	,,	
177. Rennie, Charles Edward	,,	
178. Mallett, Thomas Gardiner	,,	
179. Morley, Alexander	,,	Lance-Corporal, 10.4.00. Invalided, Australia, arr. 29.7.00
180. Clements, Charles Edward	,,	
181. Crosbie, Matthew Robert	,,	Invalided, Australia, arr. 24.5.00
183. Brooks, William Henry	,,	
184. Yorston, Kenneth	,,	
185. Knott, George Henry	,,	Invalided, Australia, arr. 12.9.00. Awarded Pension. Died, 1.5.02
186. Wakley, Victor Oak	,,	Died of enteric at Kroonstadt, 21.5.00
188. Buckingham, Alfred George Kernan	,,	
189. Welch, Thomas McKenzie	,,	Invalided, Australia, arr. 6.9.00
190. Bethune, Leo William	,,	Invalided, Australia, 29.7.00
191. Tubb, Frank Reid	,,	
192. Hennebery, Thomas James	,,	
193. Grant, James Highmore	,,	
194. Campbell, John Norman	,,	Invalided, Australia, arr. 6.12.00
195. Crothers, Richard	,,	Invalided, Australia, arr. 5.6.01
196. Dallimore, Peter James	,,	Sergeant, 25.8.00. Despatches, *London Gazette*, 16.4.01
197. Clark, Walter Ernest	,,	Killed in action, at Pienaarspoort, 7.7.00
198. Jewell, Thomas	,,	
199. Campbell, Archibald Lachlan	,,	
200. Coustley, Robert	,,	Invalided, Australia, arr. 29.7.00. Awarded, pension (temporary)
201. Thomas, Robert	,,	Invalided, Australia, arr. 9.8.00
202. Meagher, Daniel	,,	
204. Bourke, Abedi Michael	Lance-Corporal	Despatches, *London Gazette*, 7.5.01
205. Elmore, Ernest Theophilus	Private	Wounded near Pretoria, 6.6.00
206. Sealey, Herbert Albert	,,	Died of enteric at Bloemfontein, 30.4.00
207. Coustley, Frederick	,,	
208. Morrison, William Alexander	,,	Invalided, Australia, arr. 29.7.00
209. Dobson, David	,,	Lance-Corporal, 8.9.00
211. Meharry, William	,,	Invalided, Australia, arr. 29.7.00
212. Aicken, Thomas Edwin	,,	
213. Penno, William Henry (jun.)	,,	
215. Williamson, Hubert James	,,	Invalided, Australia, arr. 29.7.00
216. Dennis, George	,,	
217. Towt, Charles	,,	
218. Reardon, Thomas	,,	
219. **Robertson**, Robert Henry	,,	Invalided, Australia, arr. 2.8.00

Nominal Roll—*continued.*

No. and Name.	Rank.	Remarks.
N.C.O.'s AND MEN—*continued.*		
220. Cullen, George James	Private	Lance-Corporal, 10.4.00. Died of typhoid at Pretoria, 3.9.00
221. Henderson, William John	,,	
222. Redfern, Joseph Thomas	,,	
223. Payne, Edwin Ernest Horace	,,	Attached to Pioneer Corps, 21.4.00
226. Dureau, Francis Edward	,,	Taken prisoner, Dinaarspoort, Lockhart, 7.7.00; released, 2.9.00
228. Fahle, Conrad	,,	
231. Boys, Frederick Arthur	,,	Taken prisoner, 29.5.00; recaptured at Pretoria, 6.6.00
232. Dawson, Robert Foster	,,	
235. Ryan, Edwin Christie	,,	
236. Brooks, Henry	,,	Invalided, Australia, arr. 31.7.00
238. Bowman, George Alfred	,,	
242. Baird, William	,,	Invalided, Australia, arr. 10.9.00
244. Taylor, George May	,,	Lance - Corporal, 2.4.00. Invalided, Australia, 26.8.00
245. Johnson, Albert Alfred Goodsman	,,	
246. Sheppard, William George	,,	
247. Corlett, Cæsar Stephen	,,	Lance-Corporal, 10.4.00; Corporal 3.12.00
248. Treacy, Thomas Paul	,,	
249. Warne, Joseph John	,,	
250. McKenzie, William	,,	
251. Strahan, Simon William	,,	
252. Wilkinson, George	,,	
253. Roberts, James Eckersley	,,	Lance-Corporal, 10.4.00. Invalided, Australia, arr. 17.10.00
254. Goodwin, John Ephriam	,,	Invalided, Australia, arr. 6.9.00
255. Moyle, Edwin	,,	Invalided, Australia, arr. 17.11.00
256. Wood, John Frederick	,,	Invalided, Australia, arr. 9.8.00
257. Gardiner, Edgar Robert Watson	,,	Invalided, Australia, arr. 29.7.00
259. Young, George James	,,	
260. McNulty, J.	,,	Lance-Corporal, 19.2.00; reduced Private, 3.4.00. Attached to Pioneer Corps, 20.4.00
261. Wells, David Reid	,,	Invalided, Australia, arr. 31.7.00
262. Davies, John Hugh	,,	
263. Bristow, George Edwin	,,	Died of enteric at Brandfort, 10.5.00
265. White, David	,,	Corporal, 20.3.01
270. Cotter, Hurtle Plummer	,,	Invalided, Australia, arr. 9.8.00
271. Walker, Percy	,,	Invalided, Australia, arr. 9.8.00
272. Smart, Henry James	,,	Died of enteric at Kroonstadt, 3.6.00
273. Battye, Arthur James	,,	
274. Harper, Sedgewick Percy	,,	
275. Waterson, Ernest Edward	,,	
276. Brown, Walter James	,,	
277. Ramsay, Finlay George	,,	Taken prisoner, Dinaarspoort, 7.7.00; released, 2.9.00; discharged, South Africa, 8.2.01
278. Wood, Matthew	,,	Corporal, *vide* " Promotions " and " War Services "
279. Ross, William Thomas	,,	
280. Summer, James Ziba	,,	
281. Tonkin, Arthur William	,,	

Nominal Roll—*continued*.

No. and Name.	Rank.	Remarks.
N.C.O.'s AND MEN—*continued*.		
282. Wilson, James Edward	Private	Slightly wounded, Modderfontein, 24.1.00. Invalided, arr. 5.6.01
283. Ferguson, Samuel	,,	
284. Coughlan, Arthur William	,,	Leg broken through fall from horse; taken prisoner, 4.5.00; recaptured at Pretoria. Invalided, Australia, arr. 6.9.00
285. Higgins, Leslie Lyndhurst	,,	Invalided to Australia, arr. 6.9.00
286. Stroud, Thomas	,,	Invalided to Australia, arr. 17.11.00
287. Tweedie, James	,,	Corporal, 20.3.01
288. Neaves, Andrew Campbell	,,	Lance-Corporal, 20.3.01
289. Turpie, John Henry	,,	Lance-Corporal, 20.3.01
290. Beecher, James Alexander	,,	Invalided, Australia, arr. 6.9.00
291. Smyth, Francis Sydney	,,	
293. Brabazon, Joseph Henry	,,	Lance-Corporal, 10.4.00; Sergeant, 3.12.00. *Vide* "Promotions" and "War Services"
295. Lethlean, Elisha Alexander	,,	
296. Pummeroy, Robert	,,	Lance-Corporal (cook), 3.4.00; reduced private, 8.6.00 (cook)
297. O'Mullane, William Norman Percy	,,	
298. Carey, David John	,,	
299. Mackin, Terence	,,	
300. Treloar, Charles	,,	
301. Broadfoot, John	,,	
302. Philpot, William Thomas	,,	
303. Barr, William Francis	,,	
304. Nankivell, John Thomas	,,	
306. Rogers, Llewellyn Edward	,,	
307. Weir, William Hamilton	,,	Invalided, Australia, arr. 5.6.01
308. Beck, Edward Hue	,,	
309. Cochrane, William James	,,	Lance-Corporal, 10.4.00; Corporal, 16.11.00
310. Davis, George	,,	Invalided, Australia, arr. 29.7.00
311. Cox, Albert Henry	,,	
312. Loder, Joseph	,,	
313. Duff, John	,,	Invalided, Australia, arr. 8.11.00
314. Cook, Ernest Robert	,,	
315. Firth, John	,,	
316. Bradford, David James	,,	Taken prisoner at Dinaarspoort, 7.7.00; released, 2.9.00
317. Wilson, Henry Alexander	,,	Mentioned in Despatches, *London Gazette*, 20.8.01, and promoted Corporal by Commander-in-Chief
318. Mitchell, Henry Richard Perris	,,	
319. Earnshaw, Edwin Walter	,,	Accidentally shot in foot, Merrifontel, 9.5.00. Invalided, Australia, arr. 26.8.00
320. Rough, William George	,,	
321. Murray, Augustus Richard	,,	
322. Williamson, Charles	,,	Invalided, Australia, arr. 9.8.00
323. Quirk, Joseph Edward	,,	
325. Watt, Alfred	,,	Lance-Corporal, 10.4.00
327. Norwebb, Hubert Scott	,,	Invalided, Australia, arr. 9.8.00
329. Kent, John Charles	,,	

Nominal Roll—*continued*.

No. and Name.	Rank.	Remarks.
N.C.O.'s and Men—continued.		
330. Sommerville, Miller Robert	Private	Invalided, Australia, arr. 29.7.00
332. Burn, Frederick George	,,	
333. Crouch, John	,,	Lance-Corporal, 10.4.00; reduced Private, 14.8.00. Invalided, Australia, arr. 8.11.01
334. Young, Alfred Ernest	,,	
335. Redwood, Hugh Richard	,,	
336. Bruhn, Charles	,,	
337. Pettit, George	,,	Invalided, Australia, arr. 9.8.00
339. Shaw, Michael Charles Alfred	,,	Attached to Pioneer Corps, 1.4.00
341. Greening, Richard Joseph	,,	Invalided, Australia, arr. 29.7.00
342. Carter, Herbert	,,	Attached to Pioneer Corps, 21.4.00
343. Monsborough, Alexander Edward	,,	Lance-Corporal, 10.4.00
345. Kerans, Edwin	,,	
346. Barnes, John Christopher	,,	
347. Daff, William Frank	,,	Taken prisoner, 29.5.00; recaptured at Pretoria, 6.6.00
348. Sheehan, Daniel	,,	
350. Pettman, Frederick	,,	
351. Osgood, Harry Albert	,,	Corporal, 10.2.00. Invalided, Australia, arr. 9.8.00
352. Hillman, Alfred Ernest	,,	
353. Murcutt, Joseph	,,	
354. Dalton, William James	,,	
355. Cock, William Arnold	,,	
357. Carter, Charles Reginald	,,	
358. Lawrie, John Robert	,,	Corporal, 6.9.00
359. Rolfe, Charles Dudley	,,	
360. Grant, Ebenezer	,,	
363. Westcott, Frederick Tom	,,	
367. Hood, George Hamilton	,,	Corporal, 25.2.00. *Vide* "Promotions" and "War Services"
368. Lacey, Joseph Charles	,,	Lance-Corporal, 3.6.00; reduced Private, 14.8.00; Lance-Corporal, 3.12.00
369. Fuller, Charles Herbert	,,	
372. Wilkins, George Wade	,,	Awarded pension
373. Fogarty, James	,,	
374. Roberts, William John	,,	
375. Rigg, William George Webster	,,	Invalided, Australia, arr. 29.7.00
224. Dennis, George	Driver	
225. Gilbert, George Augustus	,,	Lance-Corporal, 10.4.00; Corporal, 20.12.00
227. Foot, Walter Edward	,,	
229. Hamilton, Henry	,,	
230. Stocks, William Kent	,,	
233. Tredrea, Henry	,,	Lance-Corporal, 10.4.00; reduced Private, 26.4.00; Lance-Corporal, 8.6.00 (cook); Saddler-Sergeant, 22.10.00
239. Treyvaud, Albert John	,,	
241. Mulcahy, Arthur Henry	,,	Lance-Corporal, 20.3.01
268. Hennett, Albert Henry Joseph	,,	Farrier-Corporal, 20.3.01
331. Tweedle, Arthur James	,,	Invalided, Australia, arr. 29.7.00
365. Daniel Edwin Stuart	,,	
366. Deegan, Leslie	,,	Lance-Corporal, 19.2.00; Corporal, 23.10.00

THE THIRD (BUSHMEN'S) CONTINGENT.

LIKE the "Citizen's Bushmen's" Contingent in New South Wales, this corps was largely subscribed for by the public. It was resolved that, in lieu of drawing the men exclusively from the local forces, a class of Australian yeomen and bushmen should be obtained; hardy riders, straight shots, accustomed to find their way about in difficult country, and likely to make an expert figure in the vicissitudes of such a campaign as was being conducted. There was an enormous number of candidates for enlistment. Those selected were, practically, untrained in military matters; no less than 230 being farmers, or connected with that industry. They were selected by a committee, and passed a strict test in riding and shooting; as also, of course, medical examination.

General Order 6 (Victoria), 1900, directed Commanding Officers of Militia and Volunteer Corps to submit names of officers under their command who volunteered for service with the Bushmen's Corps, and were recommended. Applicants were required to be skilled bushmen, good riders, medically fit, and, preferably, unmarried.

Rates of pay were as in previous Contingents.

The eminent surgeon, Sir Thomas Fitzgerald, accompanied the Contingent to South Africa, as an indulgence passenger, for the purpose of visiting the hospitals there.

CAMERON'S SCOUTS.

This was a party of 24 men raised by Mr. John McLeod Cameron for special service, and for whom he obtained horses, except when they provided themselves with mounts. They were attached to the Contingent, and similarly armed and equipped.

ESTABLISHMENT.

The following establishment was authorized:—Two captains, 8 lieutenants, 1 adjutant, 1 medical officer, 1 veterinary officer, 1 chaplain, 2 company sergeant-majors, 2 company quartermaster-sergeants, 8 sergeants, 12 corporals, 2 saddler-sergeants, 2 saddlers, 2 farrier-sergeants, 4 shoeing-smiths, 4 buglers, 195 privates, 4 drivers; total, 14 officers, 12 sergeants, 10 artificers, 4 buglers, 211 rank and file; in all, 251. Horses—26 officers', 233 N.C.O.'s and men's, 24 spare. Four wagons, with 8 horses and 2 spare, 31 pack horses; total, 41.

Cameron's Scouts.—One lieutenant, 1 sergeant, 2 corporals, 21 privates; total, 25, with 33 horses.

Grand total—15 officers, 13 sergeants, 10 artificers, 4 buglers, 234 rank and file; in all, 276, with 357 horses. In addition, 2 horses were taken for Mr. Staughton, and 1 for Mr. Hood, bringing the total to 360.

CLOTHING, ETC.

Uniform consisted of khaki "Garibaldi" jacket, and pants, with leggings, F.S. hat, and F.S. cap. Provided with boots and greatcoats.

Arms and equipment.—M.L.E. magazine rifles, and sword bayonet (provided in South Africa), bandolier and waistbelt. They were fully horsed, but, in many instances, the men brought their own horses; in some cases, more than one per man.

Supplied with saddlery, and regimental transport. Each man also received a full kit, comprising underclothing, necessaries, &c.

This was the only Contingent to wear "Garibaldies"—a jacket with a fold or pleat over a waistband, falling somewhat after the fashion of a shirt. It was considered an appropriate costume for bushmen, and rather suggested the uniform worn by Victorian Volunteers in the early sixties.

Nursing Sisters.

The following nursing sisters proceeded to South Africa with this Contingent, for service under the Imperial Government, in terms of the cablegram from the High Commissioner of the Cape, dated 3rd February, 1900 :—

Rawson, Marianne (in charge).
Tiddy, Diana.
Smith, Ethel Mary Bernhard.
Langlands, Eleanor Augusta Victoria.
Smith, Dorothy F.
Hines, Frances Emma.
Anderson, Julia B.
Walter, Ellen.
Thomson, Annie Eliza Helen.
Ivey, Isabel.

These ladies were all single. They did excellent work in the hospitals, developing the best qualities of professional nurses. Sister Hines died in South Africa. Sister Rawson was awarded the Royal Red Cross. Sister Ivey was mentioned in Commander-in-Chief's despatches, 26th June, 1902. In both cases, despatches, *London Gazette*, 29th July, 1902.

Departure and Return.

The Contingent left on 10th March, 1900, comprising 15 officers, 261 other ranks, with 357 horses and 4 wagons Seventeen were killed or died; 5 officers were transferred; 3 officers, 12 others were struck off the strength in South Africa; 1 officer, 1 other commissioned in the Imperial Army; 9 officers, 228 others returned.

Promotions, Etc.

Dobbin, Captain W. W.—Promoted Major while serving with the Rhodesian Field Force, 18th May, 1900.

McKnight, Captain-Adjutant W.—Promoted Major, 5th Contingent in South Africa.

Hill, Lieutenant C.—Promoted Captain, 1st May, 1900.

Trew, Lieutenant H. F.—Promoted Captain, 5th Contingent, in South Africa. Services placed at disposal of Inspector-General, South African Constabulary, 11th July, 1901.

Carstairs, Lieutenant H. G.—Promoted Captain, 5th Contingent, in South Africa.

Holdsworth, Lieutenant J. H. B.—Promoted Captain, 5th Contingent, South Africa.

Cameron, Lieut. J. McL.—Promoted Captain while serving with Rhodesian Field Force, 22nd June, 1900; Major in Cape Colony Colonial Force.

McCulloch, 2nd Lieutenant W.—Commissioned Royal Irish Rifles, 29th August, 1900.

Fletcher, Veterinary-Lieutenant S.—Transferred to South Australian Imperial Bushmen.

De Haviland, Sergeant T. L.—Lieutenant, 20th May, 1900; Adjutant, 13th December, 1900; Captain, 5th Contingent, in South Africa; services placed at disposal of Inspector-General, South African Constabulary, 11th July, 1901.

Howe, Sergeant R. W.—Promoted Lieutenant, 13th July, 1900; Captain in Rhodesian Field Force, 8th May, 1901.

Chrisp, Corporal H. McD.—Promoted Lieutenant, in 5th Contingent, in South Africa, 8th May, 1901.

Horne, Sergeant H. R.—Promoted Lieutenant, 19th June, 1900.

Sherlock, R.Q.M.-Sergeant H. H.—Quartermaster and Hon. Lieutenant, 25th October, 1900.

Gayer, Private A. V.—Commissioned Derbyshire Regiment; struck off Contingent, 30th September, 1901.

For promotions of N.C.O.'s and men, *vide* nominal roll.

Vide note to " Promotions," 4th Contingent.

SERVICE.

The Contingent left Melbourne on 10th March, 1900, in the transport *Euryalus*, and touched at Cape Town, from whence they preceeded to Beira, arriving on 3rd April, and disembarked. From Beira their route lay to Marandellas, in Rhodesia, where all the Colonial Bushmen were formed into regiments known as the Rhodesian Field Force; the Victorians and West Australians forming the 3rd, under Major Vialls. Except Cameron's Scouts, which remained at Marandellas, they marched by squadrons through Rhodesia to Buluwayo; and from there to Mafeking, where they were again mobilized, equipped, and moved out in regiments, under General Baden-Powell, their destination being Rustenburg.

In that district on 22nd July, the Victorians, under Captain Hill, and other Contingents, encountered the enemy at Koster River, and lost 7 men killed, and many wounded. In Rustenburg district also, a party of Victorians, under Captain Ham, with Bushmen from New South Wales and Queensland, were attacked and besieged by General De la Rey at Eland's River; the siege lasting thirteen days, and the casualty list being heavy. After enduring great hardships, and losing all their horses by the fire of the enemy, the garrison was relieved by Lord Kitchener on 17th August (*vide* 3rd Queensland Mounted Infantry).

Here the Contingent was divided, and those with Captain Ham were attached to Lord Methuen's Force until they reached Mafeking, to which place from Eland's River they marched on foot, no horses being available. The other portion of the Victorian Contingent, under Major Vialls, moved from Rustenburg to Pretoria and thence to Warmbad and Nylstroom; which, under General Baden-Powell, was captured, and then retired to Pienaars River. The party under Captain Ham, after being partially equipped at Mafeking, left that place at the end of August, and travelled south through Kimberley to De Aar, and from there to Naauwpoort, Bloemfontein, and Pretoria, where after a few days' rest they moved north and, rejoined the Regiment at Pienaars River. From here the Regiment operated through the north-western portion of the Transvaal, and south as far as Rustenburg; and from there back once more to Pretoria. Several engagements took place in these operations, and what with killed, wounded, and sick men, the column, under General Plumer, who was now in command, was sadly weakened. At Pretoria the column was strengthened by the New Zealanders, portion of the 4th Queenslanders, and some South Australians, and General Paget with two companies of Munster Fusiliers (as infantry); also two batteries of Royal Artillery, pom pom battery, and several maxims. Operations were undertaken this time in an easterly direction from Pretoria. Several engagements at Silbrants' Kraal, Wagon Drift, and other places, culminated in the action at Rhenoster Kop on the 29th November, where the enemy, under Viljoen and Botha, made a firm stand. All the force was engaged from 4 o'clock in the morning until 7 in the evening, and the fighting line extended for a distance of four miles, and all of it under a hot fire. At times the attack was pushed to within 600 yards of the Boer position, but it was impossible to dislodge them from the naturally strong position which they held, and the darkness of evening ended the battle. The Victorians, under the command of Captain Ham, were towards the left flank, and the New Zealanders were on the right. The casualty list was a heavy one, but, compared with the Bushmen, the Victorians may be considered lucky.

From Rhenoster Kop the column moved north and west, and gave the commandoes under Viljoen and Botha a routing on several occasions, and once more camped at Pienaars River, north of Pretoria. From here they started to clear up the north-western portion of the Transvaal, moving by forced marches to Rustenburg, Commando Nek, Hekpoort, and Nooitgedacht, arriving at the latter place soon after De lâ Rey and Beyers had attacked General Clements and the Northumberland Fusiliers. Several smart engagements took place along the Magliesberg and Witwatersrand Ranges, and continued south to Krugersdorp and east to the outskirts of Pretoria, where the Bushmen again camped for four days. From here they were ordered to Balmoral, east of Pretoria, and towards Middelburg. The Bushmen were ordered to De Aar to check De Wet and other Boer generals from invading Cape Colony. It was a big move from Middelburg to De Aar, but the Bushmen did it; and in the swift and oppressive march that General Plumer made after De Wet, when other columns were tired out or withdrawn, the 3rd Regiment were with him to the last, and lost heavily in their attacks on the enemy. The Victorians had the majority of the wounded, including Lieutenant Gartside; only 60 men answered the roll call when orders came for the 3rd Regiment to be withdrawn. These men had been on short rations: six biscuits for six days being their share, and 18 lbs. of oats for the horses. A few days recruiting in Bloemfontein, Weinberg, and Brandfort, and orders came to move once more to Pretoria, and from there to Pienaars River, where forces were once more concentrated with the object of attacking the enemy at Warmbad, Nylstrom, and Pietersburg. These places were captured one after the other after considerable resistance, and General Plumer's Bushmen had the honour of capturing the last Boer capital.

CAMERON'S SCOUTS.

These proceeded from Marandellas to Buluwayo and were appointed bodyguard to Sir Frederick Carrington; Sergeant R. W. Howe was promoted to Lieutenant. They entrained from Buluwayo to Mafeking, where the main body of the Rhodesian Field Force was mobilized, and marched from there to Ottoshoop and Zeerust, where there was a reconnaissance in force of 2,000 men. These marched to Marico River, thence to Brakfontein, near Eland's River, where an engagement lasting eight hours took place against a commando of De la Rey. A rearguard action was fought back to Marico River, and two days after the order was given to return to Zeerust. A rearguard action was fought for three or four miles along the road to Zeerust. From thence they proceeded to Ottoshoop; and after remaining there two days, advanced again on Zeerust. After proceeding about four miles a commando, under General Lemmer, opened fire on them, and held them in check for about six hours. They remained on the firing line all night; and, on advancing in the morning, found that the Boers had retired, leaving several dead upon the field. The Scouts returned to Ottoshoop next day, remaining there nearly two weeks, during which time there were several small sniping engagements, in which a few officers and men were killed.

General Carrington was then ordered to return to Rhodesia, and the Cameron Scouts were practically disbanded. Their leader, however, saw that all who desired to return to Victoria were sent back. Both he and Lieutenant Howe remained (*vide* War services).

RETURN OF CONTINGENT.

The Victorian Bushmen embarked at Cape Town on transport *Morayshire*, on 9th May, 1901, and arrived at Melbourne on 6th June, having called at Albany and Adelaide *en route*. Captain Ham returned in charge. Disbanded shortly after return.

WAR SERVICES AND HONOURS.

Dobbin, Captain W. W.—Specially employed shortly after his arrival in South Africa. Operations in Rhodesia, Transvaal, and Orange River Colony. Temporarily attached to Remount Depot. He served throughout the war in various capacities. Queen's Medal with four clasps. King's Medal with two clasps.

Ham, Captain D. J.—Operations in Rhodesia, Transvaal, Orange River Colony, and Cape Colony. Queen's Medal with four clasps.

McKnight, Captain W.—Operations as above. Captain McKnight served subsequently as Major in 5th Contingent. Queen's Medal with five clasps.

Hill, Captain C.—Operations in Rhodesia, Transvaal, and Orange River Colony. Queen's Medal with four clasps.

Trew, Lieutenant H. F.—Operations as above, and in Natal. Slightly wounded at Wolve Kuil. Lieutenant Trew was posted as Captain to 5th Contingent, and served throughout the war. Queen's Medal with four clasps. King's Medal with two clasps.

Gartside, Lieutenant R.—Operations in Rhodesia and Transvaal. Severely wounded at Wolve Kuil. Queen's Medal with three clasps.

Moore, Lieutenant G. A.—Operations as above. Queen's Medal with clasps.

Strong, Lieutenant W. J. W.—Operations in Rhodesia, Transvaal, Orange River Colony, and Cape Colony. Queen's Medal with four clasps.

Carstairs, Lieutenant H. G.—Operations in Rhodesia, Transvaal, and Orange River Colony. He served as Captain in 5th Contingent. Queen's Medal with three clasps. King's Medal with two clasps.

Holdsworth, Lieutenant J. H. B.—Operations as stated. He was posted as Captain in 5th Contingent. Queen's Medal with three clasps. King's Medal with two clasps.

Cameron, Lieutenant J. McL.—Operations as stated. Joined Cape Colonial Forces. Became Commandant of Aberdeen and Carnarvon, with rank of Major. Served until termination of war. Queen's Medal with four clasps. King's Medal with two clasps.

Griffith, Captain J. de B. (Medical Staff).—Operations in Rhodesia and Transvaal. Queen's Medal with four clasps.

Fletcher, Vet.-Lieutenant S.—Operations as stated. Queen's Medal with clasps.

MacBain, Rev. S.—Operations in Rhodesia and Transvaal. Queen's Medal, with two clasps.

De Haviland, Lieutenant T. L.—Operations in Rhodesia, Transvaal, Orange River Colony, and Cape Colony. Served as Captain in 5th Contingent. Attached to staff of Inspector-General of South African Constabulary, 11th July, 1901. Queen's Medal with four clasps. King's Medal with two clasps.

Howe, Captain R. W.—Operations as stated. Attached to Imperial Regiment, and acted as Scouting Officer, under Generals Dixon and Reeves, until termination of war. Queen's Medal with four clasps. King's Medal with two clasps.

Horne, Lieutenant H. R.—Operations as stated. Dangerously wounded at Tuli, 21st October, 1900. Returned to Victoria, 28th December, 1900. Returned to South Africa. Severely wounded at Aliwal North, 25th March, 1901. Invalided to Australia. Arrived, 9th May, 1901. Queen's Medal with four clasps.

Sherlock, Lieutenant H. H.—Operations as stated. Queen's Medal with clasps.

Nominal Roll.

No. and Name.	Rank.	Remarks.
Dobbin, William Wood	Captain	
Ham, David John	,,	
McKnight, William	Captain and Adjutant	
Hill, Charles	Lieutenant	
Trew, Henry Freame	,,	Slightly wounded at Wolve Kuil, 14.2.01
Gartside, Robert	,,	Severely wounded at Wolve Kuil, 14.2.01. Invalided, Australia, arr. 9.5.01. Awarded gratuity
Moore, George Alfred	,,	Invalided, Australia, arr. 2.5.01
Strong, William John Whitley	,,	
Carstairs, Harold Grafton	,,	
Holdsworth, John Henry Beard	,,	
McCulloch, William	2nd Lieutenant	
Griffith, James de Burgh	Captain (Medical Staff)	
Fletcher, Stanley	Veterinary-Lieutenant	
MacBain, the Rev. Smith	Chaplain	

N.C.O.'s AND MEN.

No. and Name.	Rank.	Remarks.
376. De Baugh, Ernest Charles Hill	Private	Invalided to England; returned Victoria, 31.7.01. Awarded gratuity
378. Goddard, William Walter	,,	
379. Fisher, William Newton	,,	Severely wounded at Hout Kraal, 15.2.01. Invalided, Australia, arr. 30.7.01. Awarded pension
380. Bellmer, George	,,	
381. Butler, Lilford Thomas	,,	Slightly wounded at Koster River, 21.7.00. Invalided, Australia, arr. 4.12.00
382. Fenton, Charles Henry	,,	
383. Brooker, Sydney Benjamin	,,	Slightly wounded at Koster River, 21.7.00. Invalided, Australia, arr. 17.11.00
384. Brent, Herbert	Sergeant	Killed in railway accident at Mandigras, 14.5.00
385. Davis, Thomas Cecil	Sergeant-Saddler	Severely wounded at Wolve Kuil, 14.2.01. Invalided, Australia arr. 2.5.01
386. Garing, David	Private	
387. Gordon, Francis Christopher	,,	Hon. Corporal, 13.5.01
388. Burt, Thomas	,,	
389. Chambers, Henry McKean	,,	
390. Graham, David Burgoyne	,,	
391. Cuttriss, Alfred Percival	,,	
392. Byrne, Charles D'Arcy	,,	
393. Geary, Ambrose	,,	
394. Bartlett, William Henry	,,	
395. Goodman, Herbert John	Sergeant	Killed in action at Koster River, 22.7.00
396. Fortune, John Francis	Private	Invalided, Australia, arr. 2.5.01
397. Sadler, Lewis Arthur	,,	
398. Speers, Charles Walter	Driver	Lance-Corporal, 21.5.00; Farrier-Sergeant, 31.3.01; Hon. Farrier-Sergeant-major, 3.5.01
399. Inwood, James	Private	

Nominal Roll—*continued*.

No. and Name.	Rank.	Remarks.
N.C.O.'s AND MEN—*continued*.		
401. Clinnick, Richard James	Private	
402. Lewis, William Henry	Driver	Severely wounded at Pietersburg, 9.4.01. Awarded pension.
403. Fyfe, James	Private	
404. Pruden, David Hamitlon	Sergeant	Killed in action at Koster River 22.7.00
405. Raggatt, Thomas Henry	Shoeing-Smith	Died of enteric at Pretoria, 3.1.01
406. Sutherland, John	Private	
407. Orchard, Alfred	,,	
408. Perry, Percy	,,	
409. Bottle, Edward John	,,	
410. McPherson, Frank	,,	
411. Roberts, Matthew Henry	,,	
412. Kelly, William Irvine	,,	Invalided, Australia, arr. 4.12.00,
413. McFarlane, James Robert	,,	
414. De Haviland, Thomas Lyttleton	Sergeant	*Vide* "Promotions" and "War Services"
415. Shannon, Thomas	Private	
416. Mailer, James Melrose	,,	Invalided, Australia, arr. 9.5.01
417. Smith, William Raymond	,,	
418. Oliver, Samuel Joseph	,,	Killed in action at Koster River, 22.7.00
419. Nicholson, George	,,	
420. Howard, Richard James	,,	
421. Reaper, Charles	,,	
422. McCausland, Ancrum	,,	Invalided, Australia, arr. 9.5.01
424. McMurtrie, David	,,	Lance-Corporal, 22.7.00; Hon. Corporal, 13.5.01
425. Sutherland, Benjamin	,,	
427. Finlayson, William Randolph	,,	
428. Jones, Arthur	,,	
429. Morphett, David James	,,	
430. Cooper, Charles Herbert	,,	Hon. Lance-Corporal, 13.5.01
431. Kennedy, John	,,	Slightly wounded at Koster River, 21.7.00. Invalided, Australia, arr. 8.11.00. Awarded pension
432. McClure, James	Lance-Corporal	Died of wounds at Rustenburg Hospital, 26.7.00
433. Gardiner, John Fraser	Private	Invalided, Australia, arr. 2.5.01
434. Jones, John Joseph	,,	Corporal, 21.5.00; Lance-Sergeant, 19.11.00; Sergeant, 14.12.00; Acting C.S.M., 14.12.00
435. Best, Henry (jun.)	Sergeant	
437. Ross, Andrew	Corporal	Sergeant, 22.7.00. Slightly wounded at Rust de Winter, 2.9.00; severely wounded at Wolve Kuil, 14.2.01
438. Hartley, Hugh Francis James	Private	
439. Towers, Ernest Alfred Thomas	,,	Sergeant, 18.1.01
440. McCartney, John Irwin	,,	Died of wounds at Rustenburg Hospital, 31.7.00
441. Morris, Frederick	,,	
442. Lloyd, John	,,	
443. Loutit, George Henry	,,	
444. Hamilton, William Hugh	,,	
445. Sharry, Michael Thomas	Farrier	Invalided, Australia, arr. 2.5.01
446. Blanchard, Charles	Private	
447. McDonald, Archibald	,,	
449. McCallum, John Campbell	,,	
450. Knox, Edwin	,,	Drowned at Wanderboom 26.2.01

Nominal Roll—*continued*.

No. and Name.	Rank.	Remarks.
N.C.O.'S AND MEN—*continued*.		
451. Meldrum, Frederic James	Private	
452. Davey, J. M.	,,	
453. Lloyd, Thomas	,,	Slightly wounded at Rust de Winter, 2.9.00. Invalided, Australia, arr. 1.3.01. Awarded pension
454. Davies, Arnold Mercer	,,	
455. Anderson, William Woods	,,	Slightly wounded at Koster River, 21.7.00
457. Dobson, Charles Hill	,,	
458. Johnston, Sidney John	,,	Invalided, Australia, arr. 2.5.01
460. Johnson, William	Shoeing-Smith	Hon. Farrier-Corporal, 13.5.00
461. Knox, Frederick	Private	Invalided, Australia, arr. 12.9.00
462. James, Francis	,,	Hon. Lance-Corporal, 13.5.01
463. Millar, Albert James Robert	Corporal	Invalided, Australia, arr. 2.5.01
464. Moffatt, George	Private	Invalided, Australia, arr. 2.5.01
465. Balfour-Ogilvy, Walter Mansel	Coy. Sergeant-Major	
466. Donleavey, James	Private	Lance-Corporal, 16.6.00; Corporal, 22.7.00; Hon. Sergeant, 13.5.01
467. Johnston, Arthur Charles	,,	
468. Clarke, William Ewart Gladstone	,,	
469. McNamara, William	Corporal	Sergeant, 22.7.00; invalided, Australia, arr. 6.12.00
470. Meyer, James Edward	Private	
471. Miles, Percival Benjamin	,,	
472. McInnes, John	,,	Lance-Corporal, 22.7.00; Hon. Corporal, 13.5.01
473. Bates, Frederick Michael	,,	Invalided, Australia, arr. 1.3.01
474. Harris, Wright	,,	
476. Harris, William	,,	Severely wounded at Koster River, 21.7.00. Invalided, Australia, arr. 8.11.00. Awarded pension
477. Blezard, Ivie	,,	Severely wounded near Fauresmith, 4.3.01. Invalided, Australia, arr. 8.7.01. Awarded pension
478. Gibson, Richard	Saddler	Invalided, Australia, arr. 3.3.01. Awarded gratuity
479. Glynn, Thomas	Private	
481. Smith, Stephen	,,	
482. Holman, Thomas Henry	,,	
483. Furniss, Thomas Henry	,,	Lance-Corporal, 31.7.00
484. Rudd, William	,,	Invalided, Australia, arr. 23.3.01
485. Hillier, Joseph Frederick	,,	Severely wounded, Marico River, 22.8.00; reported dangerously ill at Kimberley, 14.9.00. Awarded pension
486. Gillespie, William Thomas	,,	Invalided, Australia, arr. 2.5.01
487. Carlile, Frank	,,	Invalided, Australia, arr. 1.3.01
488. Walford, Henry Oliver	,,	Died of wounds at Koster River, 23.7.00
489. Casement, William Wilson	Sergeant	
490. Bell, Alexander Duncan	Bugler	Hon. Bugler-Sergeant, 10.5.01; reduced Private, 12.4.00; Trumpeter, 19.6.00
491. Christie, James William	Private	Died of enteric at Rustenburg, 7.12.00

Nominal Roll—continued.

No. and Name.	Rank.	Remarks.
N.C.O.'s AND MEN—continued.		
492. Gillett, William John	Private	
494. Merritt, Walter	,,	
495. Greenaway, Arthur James	,,	
496. Allison, Ernest Charles	,,	Lance-Corporal, 20.5.00; Corporal, 5.8.00; Hon. Sergeant, 10.5.01
497. James, Albert Henry	Corporal	Hon. Sergeant, 10.5.01
498. Chadwick, George Alfred	Private	Quartermaster-Sergeant, 19.6.00.
499. McKenzie, John Hugh Robert	,,	Invalided, Australia, arr. 8.11.00. Awarded pension
500. Bastian, William Henry	,,	Slightly wounded at Koster River, 22.7.00
501. McPherson, William	,,	
502. Millar, Leslie John	,,	
503. Brand, William Henry	,,	Invalided, Australia, arr. 6.12.00
505. Cochran, Frank Eardley	,,	Invalided, Australia, arr. 2.5.01
506. Johnstone, Andrew	,,	
507. Jarrett, Norman Gerald	,,	
508. Wilson, Gervase Mason	,,	
509. Mackenzie, Archibald	,,	Killed in action at Rhenoster Kop, 29.11.00
510. Carroll, Thomas	,,	Invalided, Australia, arr. 8.11.00
511. Gayer, Aubrey Vivian	,,	Vide "Promotions"
512. Hiscock, Percy Herbert	,,	
513. Mackenzie, Robert Sime	,,	
514. Murphy, Francis	,,	Invalided, Australia, arr. 9.5.01
515. Martin, Henry	,,	Invalided, Australia, arr. 7.10.00
516. Kidgell, James Ernest	,,	Joined Army Service Corps, 30.11.00
517. Hazel, Henry	,,	Slightly wounded at Rust de Winter, 2.9.00. Invalided, Australia, arr. 5.1.01
518. Goullet, Arthur Thomas	,,	
519. Cain, Frank Helps	,,	Lance-Corporal, 20.5.00
520. Bailey, Frank Andrew Lewis	Corporal	
521. Beard, Walter Frederick	Private	
522. James, Frederick John Edward	Sergeant	Invalided, Australia, arr. 5.6.01. Awarded gratuity
523. Mitchell, William	Private	
524. McPherson, Duncan	,,	
525. Hay, David James	,,	
526. Lang, Benjamin Peter	,,	
527. Tracey, Cornelius	Corporal	Sergeant, 19.5.00
528. Honan, Edward	Private	
529. Christensen, Duncan Neil	,,	Lance-Corporal, 13.5.01
530. Hughes, John James	,,	
531. Thomson, Thomas Edward	,,	Hon. Lance-Corporal, 3.5.01
534. Jesse, Edward Charles	Corporal	Reduced Private, 19.4.00. Hon. Corporal, 10.5.01. **Missing at Eland's River**, 2.9.00; released, 11.10.00
535. Bolding, George William	Private	Died of enteric at Pretoria, 24.10.00
536. Bird, Frank John	,,	Severely wounded at Eland's River, 4.8.00; right leg amputated. Awarded pension
537. Brown, Harry Alexander	,,	

Nominal Roll—continued.

No. and Name.	Rank.	Remarks.
N.C.O.'s AND MEN—continued.		
538. Cane, Elfeck Arthur	Private	Slightly wounded at Ottoshoop, 22.8.00. Invalided, Australia, arr. 2.5.01
539. Robertson, George Victor	,,	Hon. Lance-Corporal, 13.5.01
540. Peters, John James William Errol	,,	Lance-Corporal. Severely wounded at Koster River, 22.7.00. Awarded pension
542. Dale, Frank	,,	
543. James, Holman	Coy. Sergeant-Major	
544. Ryan, Louis	Private	
545. Morris, Henry Robert	,,	
546. Harris, Shelley	,,	
547. O'Loghlen, Bryan	,,	
548. Baird, John Nicol	Shoeing-Smith	
549. Ebbs, John	Private	Lance-Corporal
550. Dyamond, George Benjamin	,,	Lance-Corporal, 1.5.00; Corporal, 7.1.01
551. Wellan, Richard	,,	Transferred, Marandellas Artillery, 21.5.00. Invalided, Australia, arr. 3.3.01
552. Gardiner, Thomas	,,	
553. Bake, Harman Collingwood	,,	Hon. Corporal, 13.5.01
554. Boulton, William John	,,	Invalided, Australia, arr. 9.5.01
555. Mackin, Arthur Alban	,,	
556. Beecher, Henry Ward	Shoeing-Smith	Invalided, Australia, arr. 9.5.01
557. Beecher, George Andrew	Private	
558. Blandford, Charles Walter	,,	
559. Milne, George Henry	,,	
560. Delany, Thomas Stephen	,,	
561. Haycroft, Harry	,,	Trumpeter, 12.4.00. Missing at Koster River, 22.7.00; released at Nooitgedacht, 5.9.00
562. Grant, Worthey Bailey	,,	Invalided, Australia, arr. 23.3.01
564. Henty, James Reginald	Corporal	Sqn. Quartermaster-Sergeant, 15.6.00. Invalided, Australia, arr. 9.5.01
565. Hunt, Percy Clark	Sergeant	Transferred to Marandellas Artillery. Returned, Victoria, 5.6.01
566. Roberts, Thomas Frederick	Private	
567. Fryer, George Edward	,,	Hon. Lance.-Corporal, 13.5.01
568. Morey, James Matthew	,,	Lance-Corporal, 20.5.00; Hon. Sergeant, 13.5.01
569. D'Alton, Charles Wylde	,,	
570. Sherlock, Harold Herbert	Corporal	Quartermaster-Sergeant, 21.5.00; Reg. Quartermaster-Sergeant, 19.6.00. Vide "Promotions" and "War Services"
571. Moyle, John Joseph	Private	
572. Chester, Henry	,,	Invalided, Australia, arr. 1.3.01
573. Morey, Alfred Charles	Driver	
574. Murphy, Peter William	Private	
575. Jameson, Patrick Graham	Driver	Invalided, Australia, arr. 1.3.01. Awarded pension (temporary)
576. Douglas, Arthur Henry	Private	Hon. Lance-Corporal, 13.5.01. Slightly wounded at Eland's River, 2.9.00
577. Gullan, James Stirling	,,	Lance-Corporal, 5.8.00; Reg. Quartermaster-Sergt., 25.10.00

Nominal Roll—continued.

No. and Name.	Rank.	Remarks.
N.C.O.s AND MEN—*continued.*		
578. Williamson, Walter	Private	Lance-Corporal, 21.5.00; Corporal, 23.7.00; Hon. Sergeant, 10.5.01
579. Thompson, Henry Joseph	,,	
580. Turner, Charles Wentworth	,,	
581. Ronald, Hugh Jomes	,,	
582. Powell, Frederick John	,,	Invalided, Australia, arr. 2.5.01
583. Norton, Charles William	Corporal	Died of wounds at Eland's River, 4.8.00
584. Swan, John Campbell Duncan McPherson	Private	Died of malarial fever, at Umtali, 28.5.00
585. Grace, Thomas Deloris	,,	Taken prisoner at Buffalo Hoek, 2.8.00; released by enemy, 30.8.00
586. McEldrew, George	,,	Missing at Eland's River, 2.9.00; released, 11.10.00
588. Carolan, Charles	Sergeant-Saddler	
589. Williams, George Wheadon	Private	
590. Seymour, Edwin Sutherland	,,	
591. Siddle, John	,,	Hon. Corporal, 10.5.01. Missing at Eland's River, 2.9.00; released, 11.10.00; severely wounded, Wolve Kuil, 14.2.01
593. Hammond, Stanley Forrest	,,	
594. Newton, John Thomas	,,	
595. McManus, Patrick William	,,	
596. Shanks, George James	,,	Hon. Corporal, 10.5.01
597. Tinker, Alfred John	Saddler	Lance-Corporal, 19.5.00; Corporal, 23.12.00; Hon. Sergeant, 10.5.01
598. Leach, Frederick Roger	Private	
599. Dennis, Stanley Fred Jenner	,,	
600. Heywood, Frederick	,,	
601. Ridley, Charles	,,	
602. Wilson, James	,,	
603. Stevens, Charles Henry	,,	Lance-Corporal, 25.10.00. Missing at Eland's River, 2.9.00; released, 11.10.00. Severely wounded at Wolve Kuil, 14.2.01
604. Williams, William Ernest	,,	Invalided, Australia, arr. 5.1.01
605. Courtier, Sydney Ernest	Corporal	Sergeant, 21.6.00
606. Thorpe, Frederick Beal	Private	Died of dysentery at Pretoria, 13.1.01
608. Thomson, Walker Henderson	,,	Corporal, 21.5.00; Lance-Sergeant, 21.10.00; Sergeant, 8.1.01
609. Lee, Leonard Jonathan	,,	Taken prisoner at Buffalo Hoek, 2.8.00; reported released, 22.10.00
610. Richards, Jabez	,,	
611. McCurdy, Samuel John	,,	Severely wounded at Rhenoster Kop, 29.11.00. Invalided, Australia, arr. 1.3.01. Awarded pension
612. Holmes, Robert James Carter	,,	
613. Wainwright, Alfred Sydney	,,	Corporal, 20.5.00; Hon. Sergeant, 13.5.01
614. LePatourel, Arthur McGregor	,,	

Nominal Roll—continued.

No. and Name.	Rank.	Remarks.

N.C.O.'s AND MEN—continued.

No. and Name.	Rank.	Remarks.
615. O'Toole, William Edmund	Private	
616. Petty, William	,,	Died of enteric at Pretoria, 27.12.00
617. Palmer, Richard	,,	
618. Thompson, William Samuel	,,	
619. Thorburn, George Farquharson	,,	Quartermaster-Sergeant, 14.12.00
620. Gilbert, Samuel (jun.)	,,	Lance-Corporal, 10.5.01
621. McSwain, Roderick	,,	Transferred South African constabulary; struck off Contingent, 30.9.01
622. Thompson, James	,,	
623. Baillot, Charles Henry	,,	Invalided, Australia, arr. 2.5.01
624. Green, John	Corporal	Sergeant, 21.6.00
625. Essex, William Henry	Private	Corporal (acting Quartermaster-Sergeant), 16.4.00; Quartermaster-Sergeant, 16.4.01
626. Kennedy, Napier	Coy. Quartermaster-Sergeant	Reg. Sergeant-Major, 19.6.00
627. Beattie, James Patrick	,,	
628. Ockenden, Palmer	Farrier-Sergeant	Invalided, Australia, arr. 1.3.01
629. Williamson, Jas. Wm. Nicholas	,,	Died of dysentery at Pretoria, 27.12.00
630. Ward, Jas. Adelbert	Lance-Corporal	Sergeant-Trumpeter, 19.6.00. Invalided, Australia, arr. 9.5.01
631. Dwyer, Andrew Jas.	Bugler	
632. Esdale, Wm.	,,	Transferred to Marandellas Artillery, 21.5.00; ret. Victoria, 5.6.01

CAMERON'S SCOUTS.

No. and Name.	Rank.	Remarks.
Cameron, John McLeod	Lieutenant	
701. Shaw, Arthur James	Corporal	Quartermaster-Sergeant, 26.10.00
702. Negri, Joseph Francis	Private	Invalided, Australia, arr. 3.3.01
703. Calder, Roy Hacking	,,	
704. MacMillan, Alexander Campbell	,,	
705. Chrisp, Hugh Macdonald	Corporal	Vide "Promotions"
706. McCausland, John Coleridge	Private	Quartermaster-Sergeant,
707. Edgar, William Rae	,,	Invalided, Australia, arr. 5.1.01
708. Finlay, John Gordon	,,	
709. Campbell, John Alexander	,,	
710. Canty, David Michael	,,	Sergeant
711. Dolan, Henry	,,	
712. Yuille, Stephen	,,	
713. Griffiths, Harry David	,,	
714. Still, James Oliver Alexander	,,	
715. Graham, Henry	,,	Invalided, Australia, arr. 3.3.01
716. Howe, Roderick William	Sergeant	Vide "Promotions" and "War Services"
717. Macleod, John Davison	Private	
718. Horne, Herbert Roger	Sergeant	Vide "Promotions" and "War Services"
719. Valantine, Alexander	Private	
720. Sharkey, Robert	,,	Sergeant
721. Phillips, Louis Eleazer	,,	
722. Nicholls, Athelstone	,,	
723. Cameron, Ewen	,,	
724. Clarke, Horatio St. John	,,	

THE FOURTH (IMPERIAL) CONTINGENT.

AT the request of the Imperial Government, which desired that a corps of seasoned bushmen, bold riders, and sharpshooters, should be enrolled, capable of successfully contending with a guerilla enemy, this Contingent was raised. The officers and men were to serve directly under the Imperial Government and be subject entirely to it. The period of service was limited to twelve months or the duration of the war.

General Order 16 (Victoria), 1900, notified that applications would be received from officers of the Forces and those who had previous military service as officers, for appointment to this Contingent. Candidates were required to be capable horsemen, and to have had a certain amount of bush experience.

CLOTHING, ETC.

Uniform consisted of khaki cloth F.S. jacket, pants, puttees, hat, F.S. cap. Greatcoats and boots were also issued ; and a full kit (underclothing and necessaries). *Vide* Appendix II., p. 578.

Rifles and bayonets were supplied in South Africa. Cartridge belts, with supporting braces, issued in Victoria. Fully horsed and supplied with saddlery.

Regimental transport was provided.

PAY.

Pay was issued at Imperial rates. This, in the first instance, prior to service outside the borders of Cape Colony and Natal, varied from £1 1s. 6d. per diem, lieutenant-colonel, to 1s. 2d. private.

The rates of pay when serving in South Africa outside such borders were as follow :—Brigadier-General, £2 10s. per diem, with 12s. field allowance ; commandant, £1 5s. and 4s ; major, £1 3s. and 4s. ; captain, adjutant, quartermaster, each £1 1s. and 3s. ; subaltern, 15s. and 2s. 6d. ; medical officer, veterinary officer, each £1 and 3s. Colonial allowance for all officers, 3s. per diem ; officers employed on Army Service Corps, 5s. per diem additional.

Warrant and N.C.O.'s and men.—Regimental sergeant-major, 9s. per diem ; quartermaster-sergeant, 8s. 6d. ; company sergeant-major, 8s. ; other sergeants, 7s. ; corporals, 6s. ; privates, 5s. ; buglers, saddlers, and farriers, 1s. per diem extra.

N.C.O.'s and men were entitled to a gratuity of £5 if discharged medically unfit, or on account of services being no longer required in connexion with the war, or on termination of engagement. In case of death when serving, the gratuity to be credited to the estate. This gratuity to be in addition to the gratuity (if any) at the end of the war. (A.O., July, 1900.)

ESTABLISHMENT.

The establishment authorized was as follows, being five companies of Mounted Rifles, with staff for one battalion of four companies :—

Regimental staff.—1 lieutenant-colonel, 1 major, 1 adjutant, 1 quartermaster, 1 medical officer, 1 veterinary officer, 1 regimental-sergeant major, 1 regimental quartermaster-sergeant, 2 orderly-room clerks, 2 medical orderlies, 12 batmen ; total, 24, with 18 horses and 1 wagon.

Details of a company.—1 captain, 4 lieutenants, 1 colour-sergeant, 1 farrier-sergeant, 5 sergeants, 3 shoeing-smiths, 1 saddler, 6 corporals, 2 buglers, 97 privates ; total, 121, with 126 riding horses, 15 pack horses, and 2 wagons

Total of five companies.—25 officers, 30 staff-sergeants and sergeants, 25 artificers, 10 buglers, 515 rank and file; in all, 605, with 630 riding, 75 pack horses, 10 wagons. To these were added 50 spare riding horses, 5 pack horses.

Grand total, with staff.—31 officers, 34 staff-sergeants and sergeants, 25 artificers, 10 buglers, 529 rank and file; in all, 629, of all ranks, with 778 horses and 11 wagons.

Departure and Return.

The Contingent left on 1st May, 1900, consisting of 31 officers (and 2 supernumeraries), 598 other ranks, with 778 horses and 11 wagons. One officer, 22 others were killed or died; 14 officers, 9 others were transferred; 4 officers, 25 others were struck off in South Africa; 1 officer, 1 other were commissioned in the Imperial Army; 17 officers, 504 other ranks returned to Australia.

Promotions, Etc.

Clarke, Major L. F.—Promoted Lieutenant-Colonel, 22nd June, 1901.

O'Farrell, Capt.-Adjutant M.—Promoted Major in 5th Contingent in South Africa.

Tivey, Captain E.—Promoted Major in 5th Contingent in South Africa.

Downes, Captain H. M.—Promoted Major in 5th Contingent in South Africa.

Chalmers, Captain H. B.—Promoted Major in 5th Contingent in South Africa; appointed President of Military Compensation Board, Pretoria.

Purcell, Lieutenant F. G.—Promoted Captain; and Major in 5th Contingent in South Africa.

Code, Lieutenant F. G.—Promoted Captain in 5th Contingent in South Africa.

Coltman, Lieutenant C. S.—Promoted Captain, 5th Contingent, in South Africa.

Whidborne, Lieutenant H. E.—Promoted Captain in 5th Contingent in South Africa.

Mason, Lieutenant C. J. C.—Promoted Captain in 5th Contingent in South Africa; appointed A.D.C. to Lieut.-General Lord Methuen.

Moseley, Lieutenant F. W.—Promoted Captain in 5th Contingent in South Africa.

Pounds, Lieutenant H. H.—Promoted Captain in 5th Contingent in South Africa.

Ffrench, Lieutenant E. A. W.—Commissioned in Royal Artillery.

Parkin, Lieutenant T.—Promoted Captain in 5th Contingent in South Africa.

Cleveland, Lieutenant L. A.—Promoted Captain, 5th Contingent in South Africa.

Appleby, Sergeant-Major H. O.—Promoted Lieutenant, 5th Contingent.

King, Private A. T.—Appointed 2nd Lieutenant, Royal Artillery, 21st November, 1900.

Wanliss, Private E.—Promoted Lieutenant, 20th August, 1900.

D'Arcy, Private C. B.—Promoted Lieutenant, 25th July, 1900; posted to 5th Contingent in South Africa.

Mason, Private J. W.—Promoted Lieutenant, 1st August, 1900; promoted Captain in 5th Contingent in South Africa.

Duncan, Sergeant R. L.—Promoted Lieutenant, 5th Contingent, in South Africa.

Esler, Sergeant H. J.—Promoted Lieutenant, 5th Contingent, in South Africa.

Gregg, Sergeant A. N.—Promoted Lieutenant, 5th Contingent, in South Africa.

McFarlane, Sergeant J.—Promoted Lieutenant, 5th Contingent, in South Africa.

McIntyre, Sergeant H.—Promoted Lieutenant, 5th Contingent, in South Africa.

McKaige, Sergeant E. J.—Promoted Lieutenant, 5th Contingent, in South Africa.
Watts, Sergeant-Major B.—Promoted Lieutenant, 5th Contingent, in South Africa.
Borwick, Private W. H.—Promoted Lieutenant, 15th February, 1901.
Heywood, Private P. G.—Promoted Lieutenant.
Kelly, Private J. P.—Promoted Lientenant.
O'Brien, Private J.—Promoted Lieutenant, 23rd May, 1901.

For promotions of N.C.O.'s and men, *vide* nominal roll.

Note.—It is to be observed that many of the officers specified as having been posted or promoted to the 5th Contingent never actually joined it. They were, apparently, appointed pursuant to the following South African Army Order:—

"Army Headquarters, South Africa,
Pretoria, 10th April, 1901.

The following is approved as regards all officers, N.C.O.'s and men of oversea corps, who desire to continue to serve in South Africa on the departure of their Contingents:—

(1) All corporals and privates to be promoted to the rank of sergeant if recommended by their commanding officer.
(2) All sergeants to be promoted to lieutenants, if recommended by their commanding officer.
(3) All officers to be given a step in rank if recommended by their commanding officer.
(4) Pay for all ranks to be on the scale of South African Mounted Irregular Forces.
(5) Officers, N.C.O.'s and men will be posted to the new Contingents from their respective Colonies, as far as possible.
(6) They will be borne in excess of establishment until absorbed.

Approved,

KITCHENER, General.

(Compare with nominal roll, 5th Contingent.)

SERVICE.

This Contingent left on 1st May, 1900, by the transport *Victorian*, and arrived on the 23rd at Beira; disembarked, entrained to Umtali, and marched to Marandellas, reaching there on 11th July.

"A" and "B" squadrons, under Lieutenant-Colonel Kelly, were sent to Buluwayo, and thence by rail to Mafeking. They were then despatched to Ottoshoop, and formed part of Brigadier-General Lord Erroll's Brigade, under Lieutenant-General Sir Frederick Carrington.

The three remaining squadrons, "C," "D," and "E," under Major Clarke, remained in Rhodesia at Marandellas, Fort Charter, Fort Victoria, Tuli, and Buluwayo; being engaged on the lines of communication until the end of the year, when they were ordered to Cape Colony.

During the months of August and September, 1900, the Transvaal detachment assisted in clearing the enemy out of Ottoshoop; also in combined operations at Zeerust and Jacobsdal; defended convoy at Lowe's Farm, and assisted to capture a large convoy at Malopo Oog. In October a great quantity of supplies was taken, and the enemy driven from a strong position. From 24th October the detachment formed part of the 2nd Mounted Brigade of the 1st Division, under Lieutenant-General Lord Methuen.

On 9th November, surprised a laager at Wonderfontein, and after a lively skirmish, seized their wagons and took a number of prisoners. On 10th, at Manana, captured a pom pom and assisted to secure a large quantity of stock. During the remainder of the month at Lichtenberg, Ottoshoof, Leeuwfontein, Jacobsdal, and Zeerust, engaged in various operations.

During December, besides minor operations, assisted in repulsing an attack upon a convoy, and surprised and captured a laager—portion of De la Rey's.

On 7th January, 1901, relieved garrison at Schwezer Reneke, after some opposition, and captured a large convoy at Uitral's Kop. In February, the progress of the column was impeded by the enemy several times, with losses on both sides, especially at Doornbult. On the 11th and 12th, the Victorians occupied the town of Wolmaranstad, after some resistance, making many prisoners, and capturing arms, ammunition, and supplies. At Harteb, on the 18th, the enemy opened the attack at 7.30 a.m.. The Victorians advanced on the left flank, and the enemy kept up a continuous fire until 1.30 p.m., when they were driven from their positions—losses very heavy on both sides. A huge convoy was brought safely into Klerksdorp, comprising upwards of 16,000 sheep, 6,000 cattle, besides horses, donkeys, wagons, &c.

There were continuous operations until 6th March, when the town of Wolmaranstad was again occupied. During the remainder of the month, and in April, the enemy was constantly engaged, the garrison at Hoopstad was released, and various operations ensued in Orange River Colony. On the 23rd, at Warrenton, ordered to join the other portion of the regiment in Cape Colony.

In October, 1900, " C " squadron left Buluwayo and marched to Tuli, arriving on the 18th. It was in garrison until 23rd November, when they marched to Pont Drift, arriving on 25th; garrisoned it, and patrolled the country until 12th December, when ordered to return to Buluwayo.

In Cape Colony.

" C," " D," and " E " squadrons, under Major Clarke, were engaged at Matjesfontein, collecting stock, removing undesirables, etc., until early in February, when they entrained for De Aar, being attached to Colonel Hon. A. H. Henniker's column.

On 11th February, 40 men of " C " squadron, under Captain Tivey, made a forced march of 40 miles to Philipstown, and surprised the enemy, who numbered upwards of 300, occupying the adjacent kopjes, and who were driven back and kept in check until reinforcements arrived, when they retired. (*Vide* extract from Column Order, 14th February.) Captain Tivey subsequently received the D.S.O.

Engaged following up De Wet, and on the 23rd came in contact with the enemy at Read's Drift, Orange River, where one 15-pr. B.L. gun and one pom pom fell into the hands of the Victorians; three troopers (Sheehan, Green, and O'Brien) being promoted for their share in this. The pursuit was still maintained; the Victorians marching 380 miles in 15 days, and being very highly complimented by Colonel Plumer.

On 1st March, at the junction of Orange and Sea Cow Rivers, Captain Dallimore and a party of 16 men surprised and captured a party of 33 armed Boers, and 54 horses. During the month the Victorians were operating in Colesberg district, in the vicinity of Fort Brown, and thence to Schoombes, and were in constant touch with the enemy. On the 30th, Sergeant Sandford, Lance-Corporal Ledgerwood, and Trooper Browning rescued, under fire, a comrade whose horse had been lost. Sergeant Sandford received D.C.M.; the others mentioned in despatches.

During the months of April and May, from Zurberg to Somerset East District pursued the enemy all the time, kept in touch with them, and prevented them from joining forces or doing much damage to towns or farms. On 12th May, a party of 40 encountered a large number of the enemy near Doornbosch, and after a sharp engagement drove them back. From the 28th May to June 22nd, engaged in Queenstown, Tonkastad, and Dordrecht District.

EXTRACTS FROM ORDERS.

Column Order by Lieut.-Colonel Hon. A. Henniker, C.B., Coldstream Guards.

Philipstown, 14th February, 1901.

The officer commanding Column has great pleasure in expressing his appreciation of the excellent work carried out by squadron Victorian Imperial Regiment under command of Captain Tivey, on 12th inst. Captain Tivey, by his well-timed advance and skilful handling of his small force, prevented a greatly superior number of the enemy from occupying a position which forms the key to Philipstown, and forced them to evacuate the town with loss. The way in which the whole operation was executed speaks well for the good training and discipline of the Victorian Imperial Regiment."

Extract from Divisional Order, 16th April, 1901, by Lieut.-General Lord Methuen on the occasion of the departure of the detachment from his column.

"The Lieut.-General cannot allow the occasion to pass without expressing to his mounted forces his heartfelt gratitude for the splendid service they have performed for their country. Their courage has been undeniable, and there has been an entire absence of any discontent; the hardships of a campaign, during which the division has trekked over 2,900 miles, having been cheerfully faced."

Extract from Brigade Order, 18th April, 1901, by Brigadier-General Lord Erroll.

"Brigadier-General the Earl of Erroll, regrets that the time has come when he must say good-bye to the mounted troops. He wishes to take this opportunity of thanking all ranks for the cheerful manner in which they have carried out his orders during the time they have been under his command; and to express his admiration of the way they have behaved on all occasions, both in the camp and in the field."

Extract from Column Order, 25th April, 1901, by Lieut.-Colonel Hon. A. Henniker C.B.

"Colonel Henniker cannot permit the Victorian Imperial Regiment to leave his command without expressing to them his thanks for the way in which they encountered and overcome all difficulties during the time they have been with the Column and for their gallant conduct on all occasions. The Contingent has made a name for itself which will be second to none among the many fine bodies of men who have given their services to His Majesty from Australia."

Telegram from Lord Kitchener, Commander-in-Chief, 20th April, 1901.

"Before the *Orient* sails, please express to the Victorian Imperial Regiment my best thanks for their services to the Empire whilst in South Africa. I lose them with the greatest regret, and shall always remember with gratitude the good work they have done in this arduous campaign. Please say good-bye to all ranks for me, and wish them good luck."

On 22nd June, the regiment embarked at East London on the *Orient* transport and arrived at Melbourne on 12th July, having called at Albany on the way. They were forthwith paid off.

War Services and Honours.

Kelly, Lieut.-Colonel N. W.—Operations at Rhodesia, Transvaal, and Cape Colony, 1900–01. Wounded at Hartebeestfontein, 16th February, 1901. Despatches, *London Gazette*, 16th April, 1901, and 7th May, 1901. C.B. Queen's Medal with four clasps.

Clarke, Major L. F.—Operations in Rhodesia, Transvaal, and Cape Colony Commanded North-western Districts. Administrator, No. 13 area, Cape Colony Commanded Contingent, 23rd February, 1901, to 23rd June, 1901. Despatches, *London Gazette*, 23rd April, 1901, and 9th July, 1901. D.S.O. Promoted Lieut.-Colonel, and served until the end of the war. Queen's Medal with four clasps. King's Medal with two clasps.

O'Farrell, Captain-Adjutant M.—Operations in Rhodesia, Transvaal, and Cape Colony. Staff-Officer North-western District, and No. 13 Area, Cape Colony. Served until the end of the war. Despatches, *London Gazette*, 29th July, 1902. D.S.O. Queen's Medal with five clasps. King's Medal with two clasps.

Alfred, Captain-Quartermaster W.—Operations in Rhodesia, Orange River Colony, and Transvaal. Queen's Medal with three clasps.

Sturdee, Captain A. H. (Medical Staff)—Operations as stated. Despatches, *London Gazette*, 9th July, 1901. Served until the end of the war. Queen's Medal with three clasps. King's Medal with two clasps.

Leitch, Veterinary-Lieutenant J. B.—Operations as stated, and in Cape Colony. Served subsequently as Veterinary-Captain with 3rd Australian Commonwealth Horse. Queen's Medal with four clasps. King's Medal with two clasps.

Lang, Lieutenant P. H. (Medical Staff)—Operations in Rhodesia, Transvaal, and Orange River Colony. Queen's Medal with three clasps.

Sherlock, Veterinary-Lieutenant S.—*Vide* 5th Contingent.

Tivey, Captain E.—Operations in Rhodesia, Transvaal, Orange River Colony, and Cape Colony. Despatches, *London Gazette* (supplement), 22nd March, 1901. *London Gazette*, 7th May, 1901. D.S.O. Queen's Medal with six clasps.

Dallimore, Captain J.—Operations as stated. Despatches, *London Gazette*, 7th May, 1901. D.S.O. Queen's Medal with three clasps.

Downes, Captain H. M.—Operations as stated. Served until the end of the war. Queen's Medal with four clasps. King's Medal with two clasps.

Wollaston, Captain H. N. S.—Operations as stated. Queen's Medal with four clasps.

Chalmers, Captain H. B.—Operations as stated. Queen's Medal with clasps.

Purcell, Captain F. G.—Operations as stated. Served until end of war. Queen's Medal with four clasps. King's Medal with two clasps.

Mann, Lieutenant F. W.—Operations in Rhodesia and Transvaal. Wounded at Hartebeestfontein. Queen's Medal with three clasps.

Code, Lieutenant F. G.—Operations in Rhodesia, Transvaal, Orange River Colony, and Cape Colony. Slightly wounded at Philipstown. Served until end of war. Queen's Medal with four clasps. King's Medal with two clasps.

Macdonald, Lieutenant A. C.—Operations as stated. Queen's Medal with six clasps.

Gilpin, Lieutenant T. J.—Operations in Rhodesia, Transvaal, and Cape Colony. Queen's Medal with two clasps.

Ulbrich, Lieutenant F. W.—Operations in Rhodesia and Transvaal. Employed in remount depot. Queen's Medal with two clasps.

Gilpin, Lieutenant A. G.—Operations in Rhodesia and Transvaal. Killed in action at Ottoshoop, 20th August, 1900.

Coltman, Lieutenant C. S.—Operations in Rhodesia, Transvaal, Orange River Colony, and Cape Colony. Served with 5th Contingent. Queen's Medal with four clasps. King's Medal with two clasps.

Boyd, Lieutenant C. J. K.—Operations as stated. Queen's Medal with three clasps.

Whidborne, Lieutenant H. E.—Operations as stated. Station Commandant Aberdeen and Steynsberg. Served until end of war. Queen's Medal with four clasps. King's Medal with two clasps.

Nicholl, Lieutenant J. A.—Operations as stated. Queen's Medal with clasps.

Mason, Lieutenant C. J. C.—Operations as stated. Slightly wounded at Philipstown. Queen's Medal with clasps.

Hutchings, Lieutenant F. H.—Operations as stated. Queen's Medal with clasps.

Moseley, Lieutenant F. W.—Operations as stated. Served with 5th Contingent. Queen's Medal with four clasps. King's Medal with two clasps.

Pounds, Lieutenant H. H.—As above.

Ffrench, Lieutenant E. A. W.—Operations in Rhodesia and Transvaal. Commissioned in Royal Artillery.

Parkin, Lieutenant T.—Operations in Rhodesia and Transvaal. Wounded at Hartebeestfontein. Queen's Medal with two clasps.

Embling, Lieutenant H. A. A.—Operations in Rhodesia, Transvaal, Orange River Colony, and Cape Colony. Queen's Medal with four clasps.

Cleveland, Lieutenant L. A.—As above.

Chomley, Lieutenant W. B.—Operations as above. Served until end of war Queen's Medal with four clasps. King's Medal with two clasps.

Mason, Lieutenant J. W.—As above.

Heywood, Lieutenant P. G.—Operations as stated. Queen's Medal with clasps.

D'Arcy, Lieutenant C. B.—Operations as stated. Invalided to Victoria; arrived 3rd March, 1901. Reported fit. Returned to South Africa, 4th April, 1901, and rejoined. Queen's Medal with clasps.

Wanliss, Lieutenant E.—Operations as stated. Queen's Medal with four clasps.

Borwick, Lieutenant W. H.—Operations as stated. Severely wounded near Hoopstad, 30th March, 1901. Queen's Medal with four clasps.

Kelly, Lieutenant J. P.—Operations as stated. Queen's Medal with clasps.

O'Brien, Lieutenant J.—Operations as stated. Queen's Medal with clasps.

Nominal Roll.

No. and Name.	Rank.	Remarks.
Battalion Staff.		
Kelly, Nicholas Wm.	Lieut.-Colonel	Wounded at Hartebeestfontein, 16.2.01
Clarke, Lancelot Fox	Major	
O'Farrell, Michael	Captain and Adjutant	
Alfred, Wm.	Captain and Quartermaster	
Sturdee, Alfd. Hobart	Captain (Medical Staff)	
Leitch, John Black	Veterinary-Lieutenant	
Lang, P. H.	Lieutenant (Medical Staff)	
Sherlock, Samuel	Veterinary-Lieutenant	
Company Officers.		
Tivey, Edwin	Captain	Granted passage to England, and struck off strength on arrival
Dallimore, Joseph	,,	
Downes, Herbert Major	,,	
Wollaston, Herbert Newton Spencer	,,	Granted passage to England; struck off on arrival
Chalmers, Hy. Black (jun.)	,,	
Purcell, Fredk. George	Lieutenant	
Mann, Fredk. Wollaston	,,	Wounded at Hartebeestfontein, 16.2.01
Code, Fredk. George	,,	Slightly wounded at Philipstown, 13.2.01
Macdonald, Alexr. Campbell	,,	
Gilpin, Thos. John	,,	Granted passage to England, and struck off on arrival
Ulbrich, Fredk. Wm.	,,	
Gilpin, Alex. Geo.	,,	Killed in action at Ottoshoop, 20.8.00
Coltman, Chas. Stanley	,,	
Boyd, Chas. Jas. Kingsley	,,	
Whidborne, Hy. Elderton	,,	
Nicholl, Jas. Alexr.	,,	
Mason, Chas. Joseph Conway	,,	Slight scalp wound at Philipstown, 13.2.01
Hutchings, Fredk. Hawthorn	,,	Granted passage to England, and struck off on arrival
Moseley, Francis Wm.	,,	
Pounds, Herbert Healy	,,	
Ffrench, Evelyn Alexr. Wilson	,,	*Vide* " Promotions "
Parkin, Thos.	,,	Wounded at Hartebeestfontein, 16.2.01. Granted passage to England, and struck off strength on arrival
Embling, Herbert Arthur Austin	,,	
Cleveland, Lancelot Arthur	,,	
Chomley, Wm. Burgh	,,	Granted passage to England; struck off on arrival

Nominal Roll—continued.

No. and Name.	Rank.	Remarks.
N.C.O.'s AND MEN.		
1. Howat, Chas. Thos.	Private	Invalided, Australia, arr. 7.10.00
2. Frazer Samuel	Corporal	Sergeant. Invalided, Australia, arr. 2.5.01. Pension
3. Midgley, Percival Edwin	,,	Sergeant
4. Smartt, Alexr. Wm.	,,	
5. Esler, Hugh Jas.	Sergeant	Vide "Promotions"
6. Blair, Hy. Chas.	Corporal	Sergeant
7. Wall, Wm. Saml.	,,	Sergeant
8. Neyland, John Wm.	,,	
9. Walkden, Percy Babbington	Sergeant	
10. Sweeney, Edwd. Chas.	Private	Shoeing-Smith
11. Whiting, Albt. Clarence	,,	Lance-Corporal
12. Kivlighon, Thos.	,,	Corporal
13. Rowan, Wm.	,,	Lance-Corporal
14. Tennant, Percy Ponsonby	,,	Corporal. Discharged in South Africa
15. Parker, Richd. Wilson	,,	Corporal
16. Lee, Herbert Frank	,,	Corporal
17. Middleditch, Geo.	,,	Corporal
18. Neville, Henry Percy	,,	Corporal
19. Wemyss, Benjn.	Bugler	
20. Rhodes, Harold	,,	Granted passage to England, and discharged on arrival there, 9.8.01
21. Quinn, Robt.	Private	Returned, Victoria, 18.1.01; reported fit, returned South Africa and rejoined, 15.2.01
22. Allsop, John	,,	
23. Burley, Thos.	,,	Invalided, Australia, arr. 9.5.01
24. Barry, Herbert	,,	
25. Alder, Francis Robt.	Corporal	Sergeant
26. Edwards, Edward Emml.	Private	
27. O'Brien, Jas.	,,	Vide "Promotions" and "War Services"
28. McPherson, Alfd. Wm. Glenelg	,,	Corporal
29. Madden, Wilfred	,,	Lance-Corporal. Granted passage to England, and discharged on arrival, 9.8.01
30. Burns, Robt.	,,	Lance-Corporal
31. Bloxham, Andw.	,,	
32. Cameron, John Alexr.	,,	Farrier-Sergeant
33. Finlayson, Thos. Wm.	Corporal	Sergeant
34. O'Brien, Percy	,,	Sergeant; promoted Corporal from Farrier by Commander-in-Chief for bravery, Orange River, 23.2.01. Despatches, London Gazette, 7.5.01
35. Scott, Geo. Robt.	Private	
36. Thompson, Peter Wm.	,,	
37. Baird, Matthew	,,	
38. St. John, Eugene Bolingbroke	,,	Died of malarial fever at Buluwayo, 1.1.01
39. Baird, George	,,	
40. Richards, Wm. Chas.	Corporal	
41. Sedunary, Edward	,,	Invalided, Australia, arr. 6.12.00. Reported fit; returned, 23.1.01, and rejoined

Nominal Roll—*continued.*

No. and Name.	Rank.	Remarks.
N.C.O.'s AND MEN—*continued.*		
42. McNamara, John Francis	Private	
43. Vogel, Thos.	,,	
44. Appleby, Thos.	Bugler	
45. Adams, Wm. John	Corporal	Sergeant-Major
46. Johnstone, Arthur Leslie	Corporal	Quartermaster-Sergeant; D.C.M. for gallantry at Waterkloop, 12.5.01. Despatches, *London Gazette*, 20.8.01
47. Cooke, Joseph Henry	Private	Lance-Corporal
48. Ellis, Thos.	,,	
49. Smith, Robert Golding	,,	Invalided, Australia, arr. 2.5.01
50. D'Arcy, Chas. Bingham	,,	*Vide* "Promotions" and "War Services"
51. Bannister, Thos.	,,	
52. Creelman, Wm. John	,,	Lance-Corporal. Died of enteric at Erkeldroon, 17.9.00
53. Dalton, Sydney Atkins	,,	Farrier-Sergeant
54. Mallett, Robt. Alfd.	,,	Lance-Corporal
55. Connell, Patk.	,,	
56. Collins, Wm. Hy.	,,	Severely wounded at Quaggashoek, 12.5.01
57. Long, Alfd. Wm.	Corporal	Sergeant
58. Evans, Alfred	Private	
59. Peveril, Geo. Wm.	,,	
60. Felstead, Frank Best	,,	
61. Crosthwaite, Robt. Jarratt	,,	Corporal
62. McIntosh, Jonathan	,,	
63. Dwyer, Thos.	,,	Invalided, Australia, arr. 7.10.00; reported fit; returned to South Africa, and rejoined, 23.1.01
64. Button, Cecil Harncis	,,	
65. Dinneen, Danl. Joseph	,,	Corporal. Invalided, Australia, arr. 9.5.01
66. Durbridge, Alfred Peter	,,	
67. Cantwell, Timothy John	,,	
68. McKinnon, Chas.	,,	Died in Melbourne Hospital, 18.7.01
69. Sandford, David	Corporal	Sergeant. D.C.M. for gallantry at Zuurberg Mounts, 30.3.01. Despatches, *London Gazette*, 20.8.01
70. Gessner, Richd. Ernest	Private	
71. Lyons, John	,,	
72. Caple, Wm. Hy.	,,	Discharged in South Africa, 22.7.01
73. Smyth, Richd. Joseph	,,	
74. Smith, Wm. Rennie	Farrier	Discharged in South Africa, 22.6.01
75. Howard, Wm.	Private	Corporal. Invalided, Australia arr. 3.3.01
76. Green, Jas.	,,	Corporal by Commander-in-Chief, for bravery, Orange River, when two guns were captured from De Wet, 23.2.01. Despatches *London Gazette*, 7.5.01
77. Kollosche, Fredk. Paul	,,	
78. Stone, Ernest Wm.	,,	Invalided, Australia, arr. 7.10.00. Reported fit; returned to South Africa, and rejoined, 23.1.01
79. Trippitt, Arthur	,,	
80. McKinnon, Geo. W.	,,	Wounded in Cape Colony, 23.3.01

Nominal Roll—*continued*.

No. and Name.	Rank.	Remarks.

N.C.O.'s AND MEN—*continued*.

No. and Name.	Rank.	Remarks.
81. Jenkins, Saml. Sampson Joseph..	Corporal	Sergeant, 18.10.01
82. O'Brien, James	Private	
83. O'Brien, Edwd. Howard	,,	
84. Garlick, David Lord	,,	
85. Ward, Jas. Ernest	,,	Returned, Victoria, 5.1.01; reported fit; returned South Africa, 4.4.01, and rejoined
86. Wilton, Geo. Ramsdale	Corporal	Sergeant, 30.4.01
87. Hurst, John Stephen	,,	Sergeant. Killed in action at Zuulfontein, 27.4.01
88. Bishop, Wm. Robt.	Private	
89. Elligate, Edwd. Patk.	,,	
90. Cameron, John	,,	
91. Post, Peter Jas.	,,	
92. O'Reilly, John	,,	Lance-Corporal
93. Small, Duncan Wm.	,,	Lance-Corporal. Invalided, Australia, and died of enteric at Mortlake, Victoria, 2.2.01
94. O'Reilly, Laurence Joseph	,,	Slightly wounded at Elandsputtie, 12.11.00
95. White, Arthur Alfd.	,,	
96. Stone, Ernt. Joseph	,,	
97. Gorman, Geo. Hy.	,,	
98. Ryan, Michl. Francis	Corporal	Sergeant
99. Watts, Bertram	Sergeant	Reg. Sergeant-Major. *Vide* "Promotions"
100. Marshall, Laurence Geo.	Private	
101. Irvine, Wm.	Corporal	Sergeant. Slightly wounded at Philipstown, 13.2.01
102. Jenner, Thos.	Private	
103. Haigh, Wm.	,,	
104. Love, Herbert	Corporal	Sergeant
105. Thomas, William	Private	
106. Spooner, Wm.	Corporal	Sergeant
107. Morrison, Chas. John	Private	Granted passage to England, and discharged on arrival, 9.8.01
108. Borwick, Wm. Heron	,,	*Vide* "Promotions" and "War Services"
109. Weidemann, Geo. Nicholas Gustav Vasa	,,	Lance-Corporal
110. Wells, Geo. Murray	,,	
111. Wells, Thos. Hy.	,,	
112. Rankin, Wm.	,,	
113. Riley, Wm. Hy.	,,	
114. Sloan, Hamilton Hughes	,,	
115. Hall, John	,,	
116. Ferguson, Saml. Cornelius	,,	Corporal
117. Dwyer, Thos.	,,	
118. Casey, Jas. Desmond	,,	
119. Fagan, Wm.	,,	
120. Bailey, Andrew	,,	
121. Elliott, Harold Edwd.	,,	Corporal. Awarded D.C.M. for gallantry on Sea Cow River, 1.3.01. *London Gazette*, 7.5.01
122. Bawden, Edwin Chas. Matthew..	Farrier	Died in Melbourne Hospital, 7.8.01
123. Barton, Fredk. St. John	Private	Lance-Corporal
124. Costin, Richard	,,	Lance-Corporal
125. Simsen, Chas.	,,	

Nominal Roll—*continued.*

No. and Name.	Rank.	Remarks.
N.C.O.'s AND MEN—*continued.*		
126. Bloxsome, Chas. Enos	Private	
127. Bradford, Robt. Edwd.	,,	
128. Finlayson, John McKay	Corporal	Quartermaster-Sergeant
129. Arnott, Wm. Hy.	Private	Corporal
130. Glennon, Edwd. John	Sergeant	Reg. Quartermaster-Sergeant
131. Byron, Wm. Archer	Private	
132. Beattie, Francis Patk.	,,	Lance-Corporal
133. Hollington, Francis Geo.	,,	Granted passage to England and discharged there, 9.8.01
134. Lindsay, Wm.	,,	
135. Goebel, Chas. John	,,	Lance-Corporal. Killed in action at Zuilfontein, 27.4.01
136. Gregg, Angus Nicholson	Lance-Corporal	Sergeant by Commander-in-Chief, for rescuing a comrade under fire, 7.3.01. Despatches, *London Gazette*, 9.7.01. *Vide* " Promotions "
137. O'Neill, Louis	Private	
138. Wakeman, Hy.	,,	
139. Cox, Spencer Drummond	,,	Corporal
140. Rhodes, Chas. Jas.	Corporal	Sergeant
141. Mesley, George	,,	
142. Rawson, Percy	Bugler	
143. Willis, Wm. Organ	Private	Invalided, Australia, arr. 8.11.00; reported fit; returned and rejoined, 23.1.01
144. Williams, Thos. Fredk.	,,	Corporal
145. Walker, John Robert Milne	,,	Lance-Corporal
146. Sinclair, Percy Edwd. Turton	,,	
147. Henderson, Lestue Jas.	Bugler	
148. Weibye, Lewis Sumner	Private	
149. Weibye, Thos. Wm.	,,	Lance-Corporal
150. Tulloch, Gerald Geo.	,,	Granted passage to England, and discharged there, 9.8.01
151. Trotman, Leslie Joseph	,,	
152. Seymour, Percy Callan	,,	Corporal. Died at enteric of Graaff Reinet, 20.5.01
153. Langslow, Richd. Chas.	,,	
154. Savage, Hy. Geo.	Sergeant	Sergeant-Major
155. Kelly, Geo. Arthur	Private	Corporal
156. O'Keefe, John	,,	
157. Watson, Anthony Edwin	,,	
158. Willing, Justin Wm.	,,	Lance-Corporal. Mentioned in Despatches for gallantry at Middle Water, 22.4.01, *London Gazette*, 9.7.01
159. Stening, Wm. Walter Jewell	,,	
160. Nelson, Edgar John	Sergeant	Sergeant-Major. Invalided, Australia, arr. 3.3.01; reported fit; returned, and rejoined, 4.4.01
161. Dawe, Spencer Augustus	Private	Returned to Victoria, 5.1.01; reported fit; returned to South Africa, 4.4.01, and rejoined
162. Wyatt, Geo. Hadfield	,,	
163. Tennant, Arthur Jas.	,,	
164. Richardson, Geo. Edwd.	,,	Invalided, Australia, arr. 12.7.01. **Pension**
165. Tope, John	,,	

Nominal Roll—*continued*.

No. and Name.	Rank.	Remarks.
N.C.O.'s AND MEN—*continued.*		
166. Martin, John	Corporal	Sergeant
167. Gardner, Wm. John	Private	
168. Gore, Robert	,,	
169. Scott, John Thos.	,,	
170. Castle, Thos. Jas.	,,	
171. Thomas, Vernon Albert Edwd.	,,	Discharged in South Africa, 10.5.01
172. Bushby, Benjamin	,,	Invalided, Australia, arr. 1.3.01; returned to South Africa, and rejoined
173. Paul, Andrew Cameron	,,	
174. Thomas, John Bevan	,,	
175. Loveridge, Andrew H.	,,	Invalided, Australia, arr. 9.5.01
176. Robins, Mortimer Harold	,,	
177. Tebbs, Geo.	,,	Invalided, Australia, arr. 7.10.00
178. Duncan, Robt. Lewis	Corporal	Sergeant. *Vide* "Promotions." Despatches, 6.3.01
179. Smale, Walter	Private	Dangerously wounded. Hartebeestfontein, 16.2.01. Invalided, Australia, arr. 31.7.01. Pension
180. Lee, John	,,	
181. Windsor, Edwd. Jas.	,,	
182. Ousley, Wm.	,,	Corporal
183. Rogers, Frank	,,	
184. Brown, James	,,	Corporal
185. Ferries, Duncan	,,	
186. Cockroft, Alfred	,,	Slightly wounded at Hartebeestfontein, 16.2.01
187. McKee, Saml. Bates	,,	Lance-Corporal
188. Harvey, Herbert Wm.	,,	Reported dangerously ill at Jarkastad, 14.6.01
189. Caldin, Thomas	,,	Invalided, Australia, arr. 23.3.01
190. Barlow, Bertram Fredk.	,,	
191. Sandford, John Windridge	,,	Reported dangerously wounded. Paarde Kraal, 15.5.01
192. Cooke, Clement Herbert Kernot	,,	
193. Jenkins, Walter Herbert	,,	
194. Anderson, Bright Oliver	,,	Lance-Corporal
195. Johnson, Wm.	Corporal	Quartermaster-Sergeant
196. Hill, Alexr. Wm.	Private	Corporal
197. Waugh, Ralph Wilson	Corporal	Sergeant
198. Campbell, Clive Ogilvy	Private	Invalided, Australia, arr. 23.3.01
199. South, Alfred	,,	
200. Thomas, Wm.	,,	
201. Horsley, Sydney	,,	
202. Whelan, Arthur Jas.	,,	
203. Rush, Arthur Dudley	,,	Corporal. Invalided, Australia, arr. 7.10.00
204. Smith, Jas. Anderson	,,	Lance-Corporal. Died of enteric fever at Mafeking, 11.1.01
205. Kavanagh, Thos. John	,,	Lance-Corporal
206. Egan, William Thos.	,,	Invalided, Australia, arr. 6.12.00
207. Nicholson, Ernest Chas.	,,	
208. McColley, Alexr.	,,	
209. Clarke, Thos. Mathew	,,	Invalided, Australia, arr. 8.11.00
210. Healy, Patrick	,,	
211. Warman, Ronald Wm.	,,	
212. Gorman, Thos.	,,	

Nominal Roll—*continued*.

No. and Name.	Rank.	Remarks.
N.C.O.'s and Men—continued.		
213. Williams, Arthur Geo.	Private	Invalided, Australia, arr. 8.11.00; reported fit; returned, and rejoined, 23.1.01
214. O'Rourke, Patk. Michael	,,	Invalided, Australia, arr. 7.10.00; reported fit; returned, South Africa, and rejoined, 23.1.01
215. Scouller, Edwin Hy.	Sergeant	Coy. Sergeant-Major. Invalided, Australia, arr. 2.5.01
216. Pendlebury, Chas. Thos.	Private	
217. Sleddon, John Exley Crowther	,,	
218. Walton, Chas. Stewart	,,	Granted passage to England, and discharged there, 9.8.01
219. Collie, John	,,	
220. McCaughey, Edward	,,	
221. Wallace, Alexander Henderson	,,	
222. MacDonald, Ronald	,,	Corporal
223. Walker, Alexr.	Corporal	Sergeant. Mentioned in Despatches for gallantry at Wolmaranstad, 6.3.01, *London Gazette*, 9.7.01
224. McCormack, James	Private	Invalided, Australia, arr. 3.3.01
225. Molloy, Edwd. Patk.	,,	
226. McIntyre, Alexr.	,,	
227. Clay, Jas. Alexr.	,,	Corporal, for bravery at Sea Cow River, 1.3.01, by Commander-in-Chief. *London Gazette*, 7.5.01. Dangerous injury at Wagon Hill, 29.4.01
228. Guest, Edwin	,,	
229. Skoglund, Gustav Vasa	,,	
230. Mohan, Thos. Peter	Corporal	Sergeant. Died of pneumonia at Jarkasdat, 16.6.01
231. Rule, Donald Allen	,,	Farrier-Sergeant
232. Mulavin, Charles	Private	
233. Hampton, George	,,	
234. Lang, Thos. Geo.	,,	Corporal
235. Threlfall, James	Corporal	Quartermaster-Sergeant
236. King, Alexr. Trevelyn	Private	*Vide* " Promotions "
237. Edwards, Hy. John	,,	
238. Brymer, Thos. Reid	,,	
239. Gordon, Hy.	Corporal	Sergeant
240. Hammond, Wm. Gladstone	Private	
241. McKaige, Edwd. Jas.	Corporal	Sergeant. *Vide* " Promotions "
242. Toy, Ralph Stephens	,,	Reported dangerously ill at Kimberley, 16.2.01; invalided, Australia, arr. 2.5.01
243. Williams, Geo. Stanley	,,	
244. Naylor, Fredk. Hy.	,,	Lance-Corporal, Invalided, Australia, arr. 7.10.00; reported fit; returned, and rejoined, 23.1.01
245. Turrell, Edgar	,,	
246. Reid, Wm. Arnold Vivian	,,	
247. Trevethick, Edwd.	,,	Lance-Corporal
248. Latham, John	,,	
249. Ball, James	,,	Lance-Corporal
250. Thorpe, Cecil Jas.	,,	Invalided, Australia, arr. 3.3.01
251. Coyne, Alfred	Sergeant	Sergeant-Major

Nominal Roll—*continued.*

No. and Name.	Rank.	Remarks.
N.C.O.'s AND MEN—*continued.*		
252. Rickard, Geo. Wm.	Private	Severely wounded at Wonderfontein, 9.11.00; invalided, Australia, arr. 12.7.01
253. Yates, Thomas	,,	Died in Melbourne Hospital, 16.7.01
254. McIntyre, Hector	Corporal	Sergeant. *Vide* "Promotions"
255. Dalton, Cecil	Private	
256. Mahoney, Arthur	,,	
257. Sheehan, Wm. Thos.	,,	Corporal, by Commander-in-Chief, for bravery, Orange River, 23.2.01. Despatches, *London Gazette*, 7.5.01
258. Rafferty, Peter	,,	Invalided, Australia, arr. 1.3.01
259. McFarlane, John	Corporal	Sergeant. *Vide* "Promotions"
260. Sones, John Lindsay	Private	
261. McCulloch, John Wm.	,,	Corporal. Slightly wounded at Doornbult, 9.2.01
262. Jacobs, John	,,	
263. Phillips, Arthur Jas.	,,	Discharged in South Africa, 22.6.01
264. Hollingsworth, Wm. Edwd.	,,	
265. Ousley, Wm. John	,,	
266. Powell, James	Corporal	Sergeant. Granted passage to England, and discharged on arrival, 10.8.01
267. Roscoe, Alfred	Private	Lance-Corporal
268. Holloway, Reginald James	,,	Dangerously wounded at Wolverhinten, 14.2.01. Invalided, Australia, arr. 5.6.01
269. Powell, Jas. Llewellyn	Corporal	Sergeant. Died of enteric at Graaff Reinet, 13.6.01
270. Webster, Alexr.	Farrier	Invalided, Australia, arr. 2.5.01
271. Woodland, Sydney	Corporal	Sergeant
272. Sharp, Thomas	Private	
273. Jones, David Henry	,,	Slightly wounded at Wolverhinton, 14.2.01
274. Lumsden, Adam Murray	,,	Lance-Corporal
275. Paul, Hy.	Corporal	Sqn. Sergeant-Major
276. McClelland, Jas.	,,	
277. McRae, Roderick	Lance-Corporal	Corporal, for bravery at Sea Cow River, 1.3.01, by Commander-in-Chief. Despatches, *London Gazette*, 7.5.01
278. Kerr, John	Private	Lance-Corporal
279. Candy, Arthur Jas.	,,	
280. Holland, Jas. Edwd.	,,	Corporal
281. Wynes, David Alma	,,	
282. Pooley, Oscar Vincent	,,	Corporal
283. Lysaght, Hy. Geo. Wm.	,,	Invalided, Australia, arr. 3.3.01
284. Rockliff, Ernest	,,	
285. Holmes, Gordon Du Be Dat	,,	
286. Sheridan, Thos. Herbert	,,	Lance-Corporal
287. Showers, Alfd. Jas.	,,	
288. Reid, Donald Chas. Leonard	,,	Lance-Corporal
289. Yelland, Wm. Gleadow	Bugler	
290. Sutherland, Robt.	Private	Lance-Corporal. Invalided, Australia, arr. 3.3.01; returned, and rejoined, 4.4.01; discharged in South Africa, 22.5.01

Nominal Roll—*continued.*

No. and Name.	Rank.	Remarks.
N.C.O.'s AND MEN—*continued.*		
291. Hooper, John	Private	Lance-Corporal. Invalided, Australia, arr. 23.3.01
292. Buckland, Philip Percival	,,	Invalided, Australia, arr. 3.3.01
293. Hawker, Mark	,,	Farrier-Sergeant
294. Walsh, Chas...	,,	
295. Hewitt, Hector Norman Simson	Corporal	Sergeant, by Commander-in-Chief, for distinguished gallantry, at Waterkloof, 12.5.01. Despatches, *London Gazette*, 20.9.01
296. Ford, Herbert Geo. Jas.	Private	
297. Rogerson, Arthur	,,	
298. Jones, John	,,	
299. Harvey, Thos.	,,	
300. Fisher, Edward	Corporal	Sergeant
301. Moore, Chas.	Private	Died of wounds at Quaggashoek, 12.5.01
302. Woolcott, Wm. York	,,	
303. Capp, Frederick	,,	
304. Rodgers, Robert	,,	
305. Pritchard, Geo.	,,	Returned, Victoria, 5.1.01; reported fit; returned to South Africa, and rejoined, 4.4.01
306. Dennis, Chas. Stanley	,,	
307. Woods, Jas. McKenzie	,,	
308. Harrison, Thos.	,,	
309. Rudd, Rupert	,,	Corporal. Returned, Victoria, 18.1.01; reported fit; returned, 4.4.01, and rejoined
310. Horsburgh, Ernest	,,	Dangerously wounded near Warrenton, 18.4.01
311. Young, Gilbert Benjn.	,,	Severely wounded at Philipstown, 13.2.01
312. Nicholls, Regind. Walter	,,	Corporal
313. Heywood, Percy Geo.	,,	*Vide* "Promotions" and "War Services"
314. Wilson, Thos. Wm.	,,	Lance-Corporal
315. Bennett, John Isaac	,,	Farrier-Major
316. Campbell, Norman	,,	Lance-Corporal
317. Tyson, Alfred	,,	
318. Press, Alfred Howard	Corporal	Sergeant
319. Candy, Chas. Hy.	Private	Lance-Corporal
320. Rankin, John Robt.	Corporal	Sergeant
321. Symonds, Llewellyn Claude	,,	Sergeant
322. Unsworth, Thos.	,,	Quartermaster-Sergeant
323. Geddes, James	Private	Lance-Corporal
324. Appleby, Herbert Oliver	Sergeant	Sergeant-Major. *Vide* "Promotions"
325. Ayre, James	Private	
326. Gange, Geo. Mitchell (jun.)	,,	
327. Wanliss, Ewen	,,	*Vide* "Promotions" and "War Services"
328. Poulter, Francis Herbert	,,	
329. Fry, Frank	,,	Invalided, Australia, arr. 7.10.00
330. Elder, Jas. Hugh Clifford	,,	
331. Green, Geo. Joseph	Sergeant	Sergeant-Major
332. Burke, Edmund Peter	Private	
333. Anderson, Andrew Percival	,,	Lance-Corporal
334. Neilson, Alexander	,,	

Nominal Roll—*continued*.

No. and Name.	Rank.	Remarks.
N.C.O.'S AND MEN—*continued*.		
335. Walker, Hy. Andw.	Private	Invalided, Australia, arr. 2.5.01
336. Pattinson, Arthur Thos. Abraham	,,	
337. Lehmann, Orla Gustav	,,	Granted passage to England, and discharged on arrival
338. Jones, George	,,	Farrier-Sergeant
339. Burgoyne, James John	,,	
340. Lancashire, Leslie Francis	,,	
341. Burke, Joseph Bernard	,,	Severely wounded at Bavian's Drift, 7.5.01
342. Edwards, Edward	,,	
343. Woodman, Andw. Thos.	,,	Killed in action at Ottoshoop, 20.8.00
344. Geary, Edmund	,,	Discharged in South Africa, 2.8.01
345. Oliver, Jas. Hy.	,,	
346. Davey, Thos. Mathew	,,	
347. Neal, Chas. Fredk.	,,	
248. Abrahamson, Soren Martin	,,	
349. Germaine, Thos. Hyland	Sergeant	Sergeant-Major
350. Ede, Hy.	Private	Corporal
351. Young, Arthur Charlton	,,	
352. Halliday, Robt.	,,	
353. Perry, Jacob	,,	Corporal
354. Davis, Arthur Hy.	,,	
355. Rich, Edmund Press	,,	Returned, Victoria, 5.1.01; returned South Africa, and rejoined, 15.2.01; granted passage to England, discharged there
356. Bradstreet, Joseph	,,	Lance-Corporal
357. Young, Jas. Wm. Coffey	,,	
358. Potter, Wm. Lockyer	,,	
359. Watson, Chas. Geo. Arthur	Bugler	
360. Cullen, James	Private	Corporal
361. Newton, Herbert Geo.	,,	
362. Thomson, Cornelius	,,	
363. Bird, John Hy. Maldon	Bugler	
364. Wilmot, Geoffrey Edwin Winchester	Private	
365. Thorpe, Arthur Hy.	Corporal	Sergeant
366. Burkitt, John	Private	Lance-Corporal
367. Foster, Thos. Barham	,,	Died of enteric at Umtali, 22.8.00
368. Fuller, David	,,	Lance-Corporal
369. Ffrench, Robert	,,	Lance-Corporal
370. Aeschlimann, Louis Chas.	,,	Lance-Corporal
371. Good, Jas. McMillan	,,	
372. Whitaker, Ernest Wm.	,,	
373. Cameron, Alexr.	,,	
374. McDonald, Findlay Norman	,,	
375. Pitches, Jas. Wm.	,,	
376. Millar, Geo. Leighton	,,	Invalided, Australia, arr. 5.6.01
377. Wilson, Jas. Joseph	,,	
378. Row, Hy. Thos.	,,	Invalided, Australia, arr. 1.3.01
379. Drane, John Robt.	,,	
380. Hayes, John Thos.	,,	Returned to Victoria, 5.1.01; reported fit; returned to South Africa, and rejoined, 4.4.01
381. Jonson, Jephthah	,,	Killed in action at Hartebeestfontein, 18.2.01
382. Thorpe, Arthur Hale	,,	Lance-Corporal

Nominal Roll—*continued.*

No. and Name.	Rank.	Remarks.
N.C.O.'s AND MEN—continued.		
383. Drane, George	Private	Lance-Corporal
384. Bruce, Hugh Andrew	,,	
385. Kivlighon, John	,,	Reported dangerously ill at Jarkastad, 13.6.01
386. Gooding, Frank	,,	
387. Spencer, Thomas	,,	
388. Davis, Hy. Ernest	,,	
389. King, Thos. Hy.	,,	Corporal
390. Searle, Chas. John	,,	Discharged in South Africa, 5.8.02
391. Bolton, Edwy	,,	
392. Williamson, William	,,	
393. Jude, James	,,	
394. Darcy, John	,,	Corporal
395. Langley, Jas. Circuit	,,	
396. Ford, Cyrus Fredk.	,,	
397. Baldwin, Thomas	,,	
398. Nolan, Michael	,,	Severely wounded near Mafeking, 9.4.00
399. Southern, Chas. Wm. Hy.	,,	
400. Halse, Edward Geo.	,,	
401. Wilson, Hy. Alfred	,,	
402. Crighton, John Wyllie	,,	Died of enteric at Mafeking, 18.9.00
403. Russell, James Paul	Corporal	Sergeant. Discharged in South Africa, 27.8.01
404. Hassett, John Joseph	,,	Sergeant
405. Bodey, Walter	Private	
406. Claridge, Jas. Edwd.	,,	
407. Fidge, Albert Edwd.	,,	
408. Currey, John Phillip	,,	
409. Field, Matthew Jas.	,,	Lance-Corporal
410. Bodey, Mathew Geo.	,,	
411. Lancaster, Aubrey John	,,	Wounded at Hartebeestfontein, 16.2.01
412. Field, Hy. Francis	,,	
413. Burgess, Wm. Servant	,,	Lance-Corporal
414. Sims, Edwd. John	,,	
415. Smith, Robt. Jas. Holderness	Bugler	
416. McDonald, Jas. Stephen	Private	
417. Ryan, James Cue	,,	
418. Kiley, John	,,	Died of pneumonia at Marandellas, 13.10.00
419. McRae, Christopher Albert	,,	
420. Williams, Wilfred Wall	,,	
421. Tauer, Edwd. Thos.	,,	
422. Morton, Wm. John	,,	
423. Greenwood, Ernest	,,	
424. Francis, Wm. Collier	,,	Corporal
425. Davis, Alfd. Alexr.	,,	
426. Campbell, Archd.	,,	
427. Collister, David Geo.	,,	Returned to Victoria, 5.1.01; reported fit; returned to South Africa, 15.2.01, and rejoined
428. Berry, George	,,	
429. Enright, Michael	,,	Invalided, to Australia, arr. 5.6.01
430. Butler, John Jeremiah	,,	Mentioned in Despatches, for gallantry at Wolmaranstad, 6.3.01, *London Gazette,* 9.7.01

Nominal Roll—*continued.*

No. and Name.	Rank.	Remarks.
N.C.O.'s AND MEN—*continued.*		
431. Browning, Reuben Frank	Private	Mentioned in Despatches, for gallantry at Zuurberg Mounts, 30.3.01, *London Gazette*, 9.7.01
432. Pearson, Chas.	Bugler	Sergeant-Trumpeter
433. Allen, Thomas William	Private	
434. Murphy, Denis	Corporal	Lance-Sergeant
435. Smith, Geo. Barnett	Private	
436. Hodden, Oliver Foster	,,	Corporal
437. Westerguard, Francis Chas.	,,	
438. Hadden, Arthur Graham	,,	Lance-Corporal
439. McGrath, Thos. Walter	,,	Corporal
440. Riley, William	,,	
441. Crowder, William John	,,	
442. Kinley, Robt. Creteny	,,	
443. Tweedie, John Anderson	,,	Severely wounded at Ottoshoop, near Mafeking, 4.9.00
444. Killeen, Peter Augustus	,,	Discharged in South Africa
445. Mays, Wm. David	,,	Lance-Corporal. Died of enteric fever at Mafeking, 11.1.01
446. Quiney, Joseph Howell	Corporal	Sergeant
447. Watts, Horace	Private	
448. Johnson, Alfd. Herbert	,,	
449. Dunlop, Matthew	,,	Returned to Victoria, 18.1.01; reported fit; returned to South Africa, and rejoined, 4.4.01
450. Killeen, Maurice Gerald	,,	Discharged in South Africa
451. Caughey, Francis John	,,	
452. Chapman, Chas. Ernest	,,	Discharged in South Africa, 2.8.01
453. Young, Walter Ivan	,,	Corporal
454. Collins, Francis Wm. Packenham	,,	
455. Bruce, Geo. Richmond	,,	Lance-Corporal
456. Buckham, Jas. Robt.	,,	
457. Sullivan, Alfred	,,	
458. Bruce, Geo. Alexr.	,,	Corporal
459. Fitzpatrick, John	,,	Invalided, Australia, arr. 3.3.01
460. Clark, James	,,	
461. Noonan, Edwd. Joseph	,,	
462. Cameron, John	,,	
463. Burrows, Albert	,,	
464. Ford, Thos. Hy.	,,	
465. Ireland, Frank	,,	Corporal
466. Poppleton, John Henry	,,	
467. Watkins, Frederick	,,	Corporal
468. Clinton, Robert	,,	Lance-Corporal
469. Pearson, Joseph Kirkby	,,	Slightly wounded at Wolverhinton, 14.2.01; invalided, Australia, arr. 5.6.01
470. Pacholli, John Dennis	,,	Invalided, Australia, arr. 7.10.00; reported fit; returned to South Africa, and rejoined, 23.1.01
471. Shinnick, Peter Edwd.	,,	
472. Odgers, Wm. Hy. (jun.)	,,	
473. O'Reilly, James	,,	
474. Neville, George Albert	,,	Invalided, Australia, arr. 26.8.00;
475. Hierons, Charles	,,	Corporal. Invalided, Australia, arr. 3.1.02. Pension
476. Skinner, Edmund Robt.	,,	Invalided, Australia, arr. 5.6.01
477. Clark, James	Corporal	Sergeant

Nominal Roll—continued.

No. and Name.	Rank.	Remarks.
N.C.O.'s AND MEN—continued.		
478. Norton, Reginald Percy	Private	
479. Boyd, William	,,	Invalided, Australia, arr. 7.10.00
480. Fenton, Hy. Clarke	,,	
481. Black, Ernest Edwd.	,,	
482. Sharpe, Edwd. John	,,	
483. Drummond, Robt. Reid	,,	
484. Wall, Jas. Joseph	,,	
485. McKay, Samuel	Sergeant	Sqn. Sergeant-Major
486. Mason, John Willmore	Private	*Vide* " Promotions " and " War Services "
487. Kelly, Joseph Peter	,,	*Vide* " Promotions " and " War Services "
488. Slatter, Chas. Silverwood	,,	
489. Somer, Philip Jas.	,,	
490. Robertson, Edwd. Bruce	,,	
491. Smith, Frankland	,,	
492. Ellis, James	Corporal	Quartermaster-Sergeant
493. Duncan, Jas. Thos.	Private	Lance-Corporal. Mentioned in Despatches for gallantry at Wolmaranstad, 6.3.01, *London Gazette*, 9.7.01
494. Telford, Chas. Alexr.	,,	
495. Hicks, John Alexr.	,,	
496. Runnalls, John Trewin	,,	
497. Shepherdson, Wm. Fredk.	,,	Invalided, Australia, arr. 7.10.00 ; reported fit ; returned South Africa, and rejoined, 23.1.01
498. Jeffery, Geo. Edminstone	,,	Lance-Corporal
499. Taylor, Robt. Wm.	,,	
500. Smith, Thos. Ignatius	,,	
501. Angus, Geo. Whitfield	,,	
502. Stephenson, Rowland Joseph	,,	Invalided, Australia, arr. 9.5.01
503. Jefferyes, John	,,	Invalided, Australia, arr. 12.7.01. Pension
504. Beggs, Angus	,,	
505. Fowler, Theodore Percival	,,	
506. Watkins, John	,,	
507. Park, Andrew	,,	
508. Michael, Alexr. Thos.	,,	
509. Wingate, Robert John	,,	
510. Lindsay, Frank	,,	
511. McPherson, John	,,	
512. Herschell, John Wren	Bugler	Invalided, Australia, arr. 5.6.01
513. McLennan, Duncan Jas.	,,	Lance-Corporal. Invalided, Australia, arr. 24.8.01
514. Lugg, Jas. Saml.	,,	
515. Dineen, Cornelius Patk.	Farrier	Discharged in South Africa, 22.6.01
516. Ryan, John	Private	Invalided, Australia, arr. 17.10.00 ; reported fit ; returned, and rejoined, 23.1.01
517. O'Shea, Arthur Patk.	,,	
518. Morris, Thomas	,,	Lance-Corporal
519. Vernon, Fredk. Geo.	,,	
520. Valentine, Jas. Robt.	,,	
521. Fitzgibbon, Henry	,,	Invalided, Australia, arr. 3.3.01
522. Lowe, Rupert	,,	Lance-Corporal
523. Lyons, Thomas	,,	Invalided, Australia, arr. 1.3.01
524. Midgley, Chas. Victor	,,	Invalided, Australia, arr. 2.5.01

Nominal Roll—*continued.*

No. and Name.	Rank.	Remarks.
N.C.O.'s and Men—continued.		
525. McKenzie, Henry Jas.	Private	
526. Farrell, Alexander	,,	Invalided, Australia, arr. 12.7.01 Pension
527. Pike, Charles Wm.	,,	Corporal, by Commander-in-Chief, for bravery. Despatches, *London Gazette*, 15.11.01. Sergeant
528. Bloomfield, Jas. Patk.	,,	Wounded near Philipstown, 15.2.01
529. Jamieson, Jas. Young..	,,	Mentioned in Despatches, for gallantry at Wolmaranstad, 6.3.01, *London Gazette*, 9.7.01
530. Stanley, Ernest	,,	Discharged to pension at Shorncliffe, 16.5.01
531. Mulcahy, Joseph Ignatius	,,	Corporal
532. Ledgerwood, Ernest	,,	Lance-Corporal. Mentioned in Despatches for gallantry at Zuurberg Mounts, 30.3.01, *London Gazette*, 9.7.01
533. Hoare, John Richard	,,	Lance-Corporal
534. Kemmis, Fredk. Jas.	,,	Corporal
535. Bell, John	,,	
536. Riseborough, Jas. Archd.	,,	Invalided Australia, arr. 17.10.00 reported fit; returned South Africa, 23.1.01, and rejoined
537. Guyther, Geo. Francis Arthur Wm.	,,	
538. Brennan, James	,,	
539. Morton, William	,,	Corporal
540. Milne, Robert	,,	
541. Gardner, Robt. Thos.	,,	
542. Bartlett, Robt. Jas.	,,	
543. Olle, Chas. Advent	,,	Lance-Corporal
544. Christie, William	,,	Discharged in South Africa, 10.5.01
545. Munro, Claude Bland	,,	
546. Axford, Thomas	,,	Lance-Corporal
547. Coleman, Daniel	,,	
548. Bonner, John	,,	
549. Wallace, Andw. Henderson	,,	
550. Schaeche, David	,,	
551. Howe, Wm. Hy.	,,	
552. Gordon, Adolphus	,,	
553. Cutton, Peter Chas.	,,	
554. Richards, Chas.	Bugler	Lance-Corporal. Severely wounded near Warrenton, 18.4.01
555. Vaughan, Charles	Corporal	Sergeant. Killed in action at Hartebeestfontein, 18.2.01
556. Sands, Fredk. Owen	Private	
557. Farrer, Jas. Farish	,,	
558. Ward, Christopher Norman	,,	Lance-Corporal. Wounded at Hartebeestfontein, 16.2.01
559. Gillanders, Alexr. John	,,	Invalided, Australia, arr. 7.10.00; reported fit; returned to South Africa, and rejoined, 23.1.01
560. Hesketh, John Smith	,,	Killed in action at Hartebeestfontein, 18.2.01
561. **Kelly**, Mark John	,,	

Nominal Roll—*continued.*

No. and Name.	Rank.	Remarks.
N.C.O.'s AND MEN—*continued.*		
562. Paterson, Andrew	Private	
563. Walker, Wm. Francis	,,	
564. McSweeney, John Joseph	,,	Farrier-Sergeant. Invalided, Australia, arr. 8.11.00; reported fit; returned and rejoined, 23.1.01
565. Gardiner, Robert	,,	
566. Winchester, Charles	,,	
567. Moloney, Danl. Jas.	,,	Lance-Corproal
568. O'Shea, Walter	,,	Wounded at Hartebeestfontein, 16.2.01
569. Beauvais, Francis Joseph	Corporal	Sergeant
570. Craig, David	Private	
571. Gomalle, Richd.	,,	
572. Evans, Tyrrell George	Corporal	Lance-Sergeant. Invalided, Australia, arr. 23.3.01
573. Evans, Wm. Turrell	,,	Corporal
574. Poole, William Thos.	,,	
575. Whidburn, Jas. Marchant	,,	
576. Lennox, John	,,	Lance-Corporal. Invalided, Australia, arr. 17.10.00; reported fit; returned to South Africa, and rejoined, 15.2.01
577. McGurgan, James	,,	
578. Thomson, Christopher	Corporal	Sergeant
579. Tidyman, William	Private	Corporal
580. Eddy, Edwin Thos.	,,	
581. Crisfield, Henry	,,	
582. Donaldson, Mark Edwd.	,,	Returned to Victoria, 17.1.01; reported fit; returned to South Africa, and rejoined, 4.4.01
583. Hayes, Wm. Joseph	,,	
584. Irvine, Fredk. Wm.	,,	
585. Jordan, James	,,	
586. Hyland, Louis	,,	Corporal, for bravery at Waterkloof, by Commander-in-Chief, 12.5.01. Slightly wounded. Despatches, *London Gazette*, 20.8.01
587. Newman, Frederick	Corporal	Sergeant. Discharged to pension at Shorncliffe, 10.5.01
588. Muntz, John Nelson	,,	Sergeant
589. Harding, Geo. Aaron	Private	
590. Morrison, James Chas.	,,	Corporal
591. Miller, Andrew	,,	
592. Ryan, John Laurence	,,	Drowned at Warrenton, 26.3.01
593. Barton, Henry George	Corporal	Sergeant. Slightly wounded at H'lobane, 27.8.01
594. Quinlan, Patk. John	,,	
595. Burgess, Wm. Joseph	,,	Lance-Corporal
596. Mackenzie, Andw. Symington	Farrier	Mentioned in Despatches for gallantry at Wolmaranstad, 6.3.01, *London Gazette*, 9.7.01
597. Carter, Fredk. Howard	Private	Corporal
598. Friend, Joseph	Corporal	Lance-Sergeant

THE FIFTH (MOUNTED RIFLES) CONTINGENT.

ENROLLED in February, 1901, and consisted of eight companies of Mounted Rifles, enlisted under the following conditions:—(1) Engagement to be for twelve months, or the duration of the war; (2) preference to be given to those who had returned from active service in South Africa; (3) single men to be preferred; (4) pay to be at the rate of 5s. per diem from date of joining the Camp of Instruction at Langwarrin. No man over 12 stone in weight was eligible, and candidates to pass riding, shooting, and physical tests. Members of the Victorian Military Forces who fulfilled all conditions were accorded preference over civilians.

For rates of pay *vide* 4th Contingent.

CLOTHING, ETC.

Uniform consisted of khaki cloth F.S. jacket, pants, puttees, hat, F.S. cap. Greatcoats and boots were also provided. L.M. rifles and bayonets issued at Cape Town. Cartridge belts were issued in Victoria. Fully horsed and provided with saddlery.

Regimental transport was also provided.

Each man received a full kit, comprising clothing, boots, underclothing, necessaries, &c.

ESTABLISHMENT.

This was as follows:—Staff—Commanding officer, 1; adjutant, 1; quartermaster, 1; medical officers, 2; veterinary officers, 2; reg. sergeant-major (W.O.), 1; reg. quartermaster-sergeant, 1; orderly-room sergeant, 1; with 15 horses.

Detail of a company.—Captain, 1; lieutenants, 4; company sergeant-major, 1; company quartermaster-sergeant, 1; sergeant-farrier, 1; sergeant-saddler, 1; sergeants, 5; corporals, 6; shoeing-smiths, 3; saddlers, 3; bugler, 1; privates, 99. Total, 126, with 131 horses.

Total of eight companies.—40 officers, 56 staff sergeants and sergeants; 64 artificers; 8 buglers; 840 rank and file. Total—1,008, with 1,048 horses.

Add staff as stated:—Grand total—46 officers, 1 warrant officer, 58 staff-sergeants and sergeants, 64 artificers, 8 buglers, 840 rank and file; in all, 1,017, with 1,099 horses.

This return is exclusive of the Commanding Officer who was, in the first instance, detailed to take the troops to the Cape only.

DETAILS OF DEPARTURE AND RETURN.

The Contingent departed on 15th February, 1901, consisting of 46 officers, 971 other ranks, with 1,099 horses. Six officers, 48 other ranks were killed or died; 14 officers, 69 others were struck off in South Africa; 60 officers, 854 others returned to Australia.

PROMOTIONS, ETC.

Captain C. Hutton, promoted Major, 27th March, 1902.
Lieutenant C. A. P. Gardiner, promoted Captain, 12th March, 1901.
Lieutenant T. S. L. O'Reilly, promoted Captain, *vide* "Service."
Lieutenant G. J. H. Clements, promoted Captain.
Lieutenant H. Henwood, promoted Captain.
Lieutenant G. J. Bell, promoted Captain, *vide* "Service."
Lieutenant J. H. Patterson (M.S.), promoted Captain, *vide* "Service."
Sergeant H. H. Bell, promoted Lieutenant, 19th February, 1902.
Sergeant W. J. Cochrane, promoted Lieutenant, 19th February, 1902.
See also "Promotions," 3rd and 4th Contingents.
For promotions of N.C.O.'s and men, see nominal roll.

Service.

This large Contingent required three transports to convey it to the war, namely, the *Orient*, the *Argus*, and the *City of Lincoln*, leaving 15th February, 1901. The bulk of the Regiment went in the former ship, the horses and a horse-deck guard of about 100 in the two latter. They also went different routes on arriving at Cape Town; for the horses (one shipment having rested at Maitland Camp) were sent along the coast to Durban, and there landed and entrained for Pretoria; whilst the men finally disembarked at Port Elizabeth and entrained there, proceeding through Cape Colony and Orange River Colony to Pretoria, where the Regiment was mobilized between 24th March and 4th April, 1901.

On the 10th, they went to Middelburg, East Transvaal, to join General Beatson's column, and started on the first trek, moving north from the Delagoa Bay line on the 13th. Between that date and 23rd, they were constantly in touch with the enemy, and captured a convoy of 21 wagons, 16 prisoners, at Leeuwfontein. The horses were greatly knocked up and many died from wounds received in action. Four companies returned to Middelburg for remounts, the other four remaining with the column.

On the 7th May, in action at Rhenoster Kop, Captain Kelly was mortally wounded, Lieutenant Johnston killed, and one N.C.O. and two men dangerously wounded. Lieutenant and Adjutant Patterson and Sergeant Carlisle were recommended in Army Orders for bravery.

On the 11th, the Regiment was divided into two wings; the right, "A," "B," "C," "D" squadrons, under Major Umphelby; the left, "E," "F," "G," "H" under Major McKnight. They were united at Bronkhurst Spruit; and the total results of the trek were—6 Boers killed, 124 prisoners, 17 surrenders, 163 rifles, 31,450 rounds small arm ammunition, 212 wagons, 58 Cape carts, 100 horses, 65 mules and donkeys, 2,460 cattle, 5,600 sheep, 800 trek oxen, 4,700 bags mealies, &c.—all the work of the Fifth. This return is presented as an example of what was usually accomplished in these treks.

On the 18th, the Regiment received 780 remounts, and Colonel Otter went ino hospital. He was subsequently invalided to Australia; but Lord Kitchener cabled to the Governor of Victoria that this officer had done excellent work whilst in charge of the Contingent. Major Umphelby took over the command.

Between the 18th May and 10th June, there were constant engagements at Rhenoster Kop, Klippan, Kornfontein, and Drivelfontein, where Lieutenant Murphy was killed (29th May), besides one N.C.O. and two men. Major Daly, West Yorks, and Major Fraser, Bengal Lancers, took command of right and left wings.

The left wing moved out from Vandyke's Drift; and, on the 12th, encamped at Wilmansrust, where the camp was rushed by the Boers at 8 p.m., and the wing suffered severely; 1 officer (Lieutenant Palmer, M.S.), 18 N.C.O.'s and men were killed; 5 officers, 36 N.C.O.'s and men wounded. The Boer casualties were stated to be 11 killed and 14 wounded. On the 15th, at Nooitgedacht, the enemy again on all sides attacked the Column on the march, but were beaten off.

On the 18th, joined the Column under Sir Bindon Blood, including General Babington's, General W. Kitchener's, and Colonel Campbell's Columns at Kranspoort. The Regiment united again at Middelburg on 2nd July, and Major Umphelby went into hospital. From then until 9th August, constant trekking, and frequent encounters with the enemy. Sergeant-Major Keeble was recommended for bravery.

On 10th August, left General Beatson's command at Bronkhurst Spruit, and trekked to Wittebank; entrained to Newcastle, Natal, to assist in operations against General L. Botha. Joined Colonel Pulteney's Column, and made Newcastle their base depot,

On the 21st, Major Daly was badly wounded in an advance-guard action at Kambuladraai. The enemy were driven out of their position, and papers and Boer flag captured. Captain Hutton, commanding right wing, moved to Vryheid, and thence towards Zululand. The regiment was heavily engaged at H'lobane, where Lieutenant Coulter was killed (27th); and at Reit Vlei they camped at Good Hoek, L. Botha's farm, which was blown up. There were constant operations until 6th September, when moved into Zululand at N'gutu; Major Vallentin taking command of the right wing. From thence to Dundee; entrained for Volkrust, and trekked to Wakkerstroom; and thence across the Drakensberg to Utrecht in heavy rain, taking three days. From Utrecht to Cattle Drift, Column was without blankets for six days, and on half rations; heavy rain most of the time.

On 25th, moved off with several Columns (General Clements in command) to De Jager's Drift; marched through N'gutu, Nondweni, Vryheid, Grootvlei, arriving at Utrecht on 14th October. On 16th October, in action at Luchiel's Nek, and on the 17th heavy fighting, holding Loch's Kraal. The united Columns captured 200 prisoners and 8,000 head of cattle in the Pongola Bosch. On 22nd, marched through Limeberg over Intombi River in action. On very short rations. On the 26th, reconnaissance: Commandant Potgeiter captured. On the 28th, night march; several farms rushed; 16 Boers captured, and many horses, saddles, and rifles.

On 3rd November, night march to Matjes Kop, and several farms rushed. Lieutenant Chrisp and two men killed, four wounded. 14th November, arrived at Vryheid; and on the 23rd, Lieutenant Maygar was recommended for the Victoria Cross (which he afterwards received), for bringing Saddler Short out of action. On 25th, at Donkerhook, joined General Plumer. On 6th December, running fight of night march with big commando under Generals L. and C. Botha. From that date to 22nd December, constant operations. Captain Chomley was recommended for bravery in bringing Corporal Cummins out of action. Returned to Rotterdam, which had been previously occupied on the 19th. On 26th, Captain Hutton took over command of the right wing from Major Vallentin, who was appointed to command Colonel Sir John Jarvis's column.

Major Daly took command of the right wing on 1st January. Night march and another commando chased. Moved from Balmoral on three days' reconnaissance, and encountered Chris. Botha and Opperman at Onverwacht; fighting all day. Advance guard (Queenslanders and Hants Mounted Infantry) suffered severely. The Fifth took up advance of flank guards. The Boers endeavoured to rush the pom pom, but were repulsed. They suffered severely, Opperman being among the killed. The Victorians were complimented by General Plumer for their share in the day's work.

Arrived at Wakkerstroom on the 8th, where the Column rested until the 22nd owing to the loss of horses. Then night march through Grootfontein, and on the 24th, night march to Johnston Hoek. Engaged all day, and in conjunction with blockhouses, killed 3 and captured 55 Boers. Between that date and 8th February, when Lieutenant Patterson (Med. Staff) was promoted to Captain, night marches and running fights; and same to 12th, when night march to Elandsberg, and slight fighting. Three days' reconnaisance followed.

On the 18th, Lieutenant McFarlane and party captured 12 Boers and 40 horses. On 19th, Lieutenants O'Reilly and Bell promoted to Captains. Sergeants Cochrane and Bell promoted to commissions. On 24th, night march to Wilhelm Hendricks; on 25th, moved across Matusa; on 28th, night march; and following day engaged in running fight. 2nd March, moved towards Standerton; night march at 5.30

p.m., and held Roberts' Drift, "C" and "D" companies engaged. On the 8th, trekked to Standerton, where the Column broke up. Captain Hutton took command of the Regiment. He was promoted to Major on 27th March.

On 11th March the Fifth arrived at Cape Town.

Telegram from General Lord Kitchener, Commander-in-Chief, to General Settle, Cape Town.

" Please convey to Australians my warm appreciation of their gallant and arduous service in this country. In the name of the army in South Africa, I wish them good luck and God speed.

To officer commanding 5th Victorian Mounted Rifles."

On 27th March, two Companies embarked in the *St. Andrew* for Melbourne, and arrived on 25th April. The remainder on the following day embarked in the *Montrose* for Durban, there transhipped into the *Custodian*, and arrived at Melbourne on 26th April, 1902, shortly after which the Contingent was disbanded.

Note.—The following is the official report of the deed for which Lieutenant Maygar received the Victoria Cross:—" At Geelhoutboom, 23rd November, 1901, Lieutenant Maygar galloped out and ordered the men of a detached post, which was being outflanked, to retire. The horse of one of them being shot under him, when the enemy was within 200 yards, Lieutenant Maygar dismounted and lifted him upon his own horse, which bolted into boggy ground, causing both of them to dismount. On extricating the horse, and finding that it could not carry both Lieutenant Maygar again put the man on its back, and told him to gallop for cover at once; he himself proceeding on foot. All this took place under a very heavy fire."—*London Gazette*, 11th February, 1902.

WAR SERVICES AND HONOURS.

Otter, Colonel A. E.—Commanded the Regiment until 18th May, 1901. Was present during operations in N.E. Transvaal. Queen's Medal with three clasps

McKnight, Major W.—Operations in N.E. Transvaal. *Vide* 3rd Contingent.

Umphelby, Major T. F.—Operations in N.E. Transvaal. *Vide* 2nd Contingent.

Hutton, Major C.—Operations in Transvaal, Orange River Colony, and Cape Colony, 1901–1902. Queen's Medal with four clasps.

Meadows, Captain A. J. H.—As above.

Kelly, Captain J.—Operations in N.E. Transvaal. Mortally wounded in action at Rhenoster Kop, 7th May, 1901; died two days afterwards.

Chomley, Captain G. G. F.—Served previously in the 1st Victorian Contingent (*vide* that Contingent). Operations in Transvaal, Orange River Colony, and Cape Colony, 1901–1902. Despatches, *London Gazette*, 29th July, 1902. Queen's Medal with six clasps. King's Medal with two clasps.

Tatchell, Captain E. C.—Served previously in 1st Victorian Contingent (*vide* that contingent). Operations and medals as above. Served subsequently in 6th Australian Commonwealth Horse.

Righetti, Captain E. E.—Served previously in 1st Victorian Contingent (which see). Operations in Transvaal. Severely wounded at Wilmansrust. Queen's Medal with six clasps. Subsequent service in 6th Australian Commonwealth Horse.

Gardiner, Captain C. A. P.—Operations in Transvaal, 1901. Queen's Medal with one clasp.

Bell, Captain G. J.—Served previously in 1st Victorian Contingent (which see). Operations in Transvaal, Orange River Colony, and Cape Colony. Severely wounded at Bakkop, 4th January, 1902. Despatches, *London Gazette*, 29th July, 1902. D.S.O. Queen's Medal with six clasps. King's Medal with two clasps.

Carstairs, Captain H. G.—Operations as stated. *Vide* 3rd Contingent.

De Haviland, Captain T. L.—Operations in N.E. Transvaal. *Vide* 3rd Contingent.

Coltman, Captain C. S.—Operations in Transvaal, Orange River Colony, and Cape Colony. *Vide* 4th Contingent.

Moseley, Captain F. W.—Operations as stated. *Vide* 4th Contingent.

Clements, Captain G. J. H.—Operations as stated. Queen's Medal with four clasps.

O'Reilly, Captain T. S. L.—Operations and medal as above. Slightly wounded at Poulteney's Column, 5th March, 1902. Despatches, *London Gazette*, 29th July, 1902.

Henwood, Captain H.—Operations and medal as stated. Slightly wounded at Wilmansrust.

Robertson, Lieutenant S. A.—Operations as stated. Queen's Medal with three clasps.

Redford, Lieutenant P. W.—Operations as stated. Queen's Medal with four clasps.

Smith, Lieutenant N.—Served previously in 1st Victorian Contingent (which see). Operations as stated. Queen's Medal with six clasps. King's Medal with two clasps.

Farlow, Lieutenant F. C. E.—Operations in Transvaal and Orange River Colony. Attached to Army Service Corps. Queen's Medal with three clasps.

Walton, Lieutenant E. R. N.—Served in the Afghan war, 1879. Medal with clasps. Operations in Transvaal and Orange River Colony. Queen's Medal with two clasps.

Coulter, Lieutenant S. R.—Operations in Transvaal. Killed in action H'lobane, near Vryheid, 27th August, 1901.

Chrisp, Lieutenant J. G.—Operations in Transvaal. Killed in action at Vryheid, 27th August, 1901.

Wedd, Lieutenant W. S.—Operations as stated. Severely wounded near Klippan, 25th May, 1901. Queen's Medal with clasps.

Maygar, Lieutenant L. C.—Operations in Transvaal, Orange River Colony. and Cape Colony. *Vide* "Summary of Service" *ante.* Despatches, *London Gazette*, 29th July, 1902. V.C. Queen's Medal with four clasps.

Johnston, Lieutenant A. G.—Operations in Transvaal. Killed in action at Rhenoster Kop, 7th May, 1901.

Power, Lieutenant T. H.—Operations in Transvaal, Orange River Colony, and Cape Colony. Queen's Medal with three clasps.

Garland, Lieutenant R. R.—Operations and medal as stated.

Henessy, Lieutenant V. J. P.—Served previously with 1st Contingent (which see). Operations and medals as stated. Promoted in 6th Australian Commonwealth Horse.

Dallimore, Lieutenant P. J.—Served previously with 2nd Contingent (which see). Severely wounded at Wilmansrust, 12th June, 1901. Operations and medals as stated.

Sergeant, Lieutenant J. E.—Operations as stated. Queen's Medal with clasps.

Stebbins, Lieutenant J. F.—Operations and medal as stated. Served subsequently in 6th Australian Commonwealth Horse.

Clark, Lieutenant W. F.—Operations in Transvaal. Queen's Medal with one clasp.

Gubbins, Lieutenant S.—Operations in Transvaal, Orange River Colony, and Cape Colony. Queen's Medal with clasps.

Brace, Lieutenant E.—Operations as stated. Severely wounded at Wilmansrust, 12th June, 1901. Queen's Medal with three clasps. (Lieutenant Brace served subsequently in Zulu rebellion, 1906. Medal and clasp).

Stock, Lieutenant D.—Served previously in 1st Contingent (which see). Operations and medal as stated.

Selman, Lieutenant S.—Served previously in 1st Contingent. Operations in Transvaal. Wounded, 16th June, 1901, and again 20th August, 1901. Queen's Medal with clasps.

Burnie, Lieutenant R. M.—Served previously in 1st Contingent. Operations in Transvaal, Orange River Colony, and Cape Colony. Medals as stated.

Ebeling, Lieutenant G.—Served previously with 1st Contingent. Operations and medals as stated.

O'Loghlen, Lieutenant B.—Served previously with 3rd Contingent (which see). Operations as stated. Queen's Medal with clasps.

Grover, Lieutenant H. C.—Operations in Transvaal and Orange River Colony. Queen's Medal with two clasps.

Murphy, Lieutenant A. E.—Operations in Transvaal. Killed in action at Drivelfontein, 29th May, 1901.

Rowan, Lieutenant A. P.—Operations in Transvaal, Orange River Colony, and Cape Colony. Queen's Medal with three clasps.

Beatty, Lieutenant K. J.—Operations and medal as stated.

Osborne, Lieutenant H. H.—Operations and medal as stated.

Kessell, Lieutenant H.—Operations as stated. Despatches, *London Gazette*, 29th July, 1902. Queen's Medal with four clasps. Subsequent service in 6th Australian Commonwealth Horse.

Cochrane, W. J., *Bell*, H. H. (Lieutenants)—(*Vide* "Summary of Service.") Served previously with 2nd Contingent. Queen's Medal with five clasps. King's Medal with two clasps. Lieutenant Cochrane served subsequently with 6th Australian Commonwealth Horse. Lieutenant Bell reported commissioned in Scottish Horse.

Brabazon, Lieutenant J. H.—Served previously with 2nd Contingent. Operations as stated. Wounded at Wilmansrust, 12th June, 1901. Queen's Medal with six clasps. King's Medal with two clasps. Promoted for service with 6th Australian Commonwealth Horse.

Appleby, H. O., *Duncan*, R. L., *Esler*, H. J. (Lieutenants).—Served also with 4th Contingent (which see), and obtained both Queen's Medal and King's Medal with clasps.

Gregg, Lieutenant A. N.—Also served previously with 4th Contingent. Despatches, *London Gazette*, 9th July, 1901. Queen's Medal with six clasps. King's Medal with two clasps. Served subsequently in 6th Australian Commonwealth Horse.

Umphelby, Lieutenant T. A.—*Vide* 2nd Contingent.

MacFarlane, J., *McIntyre*, H., *McKaige*, E. J., and *Watts*, B. (Lieutenants).— Served previously with 4th Contingent. The former obtained Queen's Medal the three latter both Queen's Medal and King's Medal with clasps.

Anderson, Lieutenant and Adjutant H. A.—Operations in Transvaal, Orange River Colony, and Cape Colony. Despatches, *London Gazette*, 29th July, 1902. Queen's Medal with clasps.

Akins, Lieut.-Quartermaster C. H.—Operations as stated. Queen's Medal with clasps.

Patterson, Captain (M.S.) J. H.—Operations as stated. Despatches, *London Gazette*, 29th July, 1902. Queen's Medal with four clasps.

Palmer, Lieutenant (M.S.) H. A.—Operations in Transvaal. Killed in action at Wilmansrust, 12th June, 1901.

Strong, Veterinary-Lieutenant C. D.—Operations in Transvaal and Orange River Colony. Queen's Medal with two clasps.

Sherlock, Veterinary-Captain S.—Operations in Transvaal, Orange River Colony, and Cape Colony. Slightly wounded at Wilmansrust, 12th June, 1901. Despatches, *London Gazette*, 20th August, 1901. Served previously with 4th Contingent. Queen's Medal with four clasps. King's Medal with two clasps.

Kendall, Veterinary-Captain E. A., and *McDonnell*, Chaplain Rev. G. N.—Were attached for the voyage out only.

Nominal Roll.

No. and Name.	Rank.	Remarks.
Otter, Alfred Emanuel	Colonel	Returned to Victoria, 5.8.01 (invalided)
Meadows, Abraham James Howlin	Captain	
Kelly, John	,,	Killed in action at Rhenoster Kop, 7.5.01
Hutton, Charles	,,	
Chomley, George Griffith Ffloyd	,,	
Tatchell, Edward Charles	,,	
Righetti, Edmond Edward	,,	Severely wounded at Wilmansrust, 12.6.01; invalided Australia; arr. 3.11.01
Clements, George Justin Hill	Lieutenant	
O'Reilly, Thomas Stephen Leo	,,	Slightly wounded at Pulteney's Column, 5.3.02
Henwood, Harold	,,	Wounded at Wilmansrust, 12.6.01
Robertson, Septimus Archdale	,,	
Redford, Percy William	,,	
Smith, Norman	,,	
Farlow, Frederick Charles Edward	,,	
Walton, Edward Reginald Norcliffe	,,	Invalided, Australia, arr. 3.11.01
Coulter, Sydney Richard	,,	Killed in action at H'lobane, near Vryheid, 27.8.01
Chrisp, John George	,,	Killed in action at Vryheid, 5.11.01
Wedd, Walter Stockbridge	,,	Severely wounded near Klippan, 25.5.01
Maygar, Leslie Cecil	,,	
Gardiner, Charles Alfred Percy	,,	
Johnston, Alfred Gresham	,,	Killed in action at Rhenoster Kop, 7.5.01
Power, Thomas Henry	,,	Adjutant of wing
Garland, Richard Reginald	,,	

Nominal Roll—*continued*.

No. and Name.	Rank.	Remarks.
Hennessy, Victor Jerome Patrick	Lieutenant	Wounded at Groot Oliphant's River (accident), 12.7.01
Bell, George John	,,	Severely wounded at Bakkop, 4.1.02
Dallimore, Peter James	,,	Severely wounded at Wilmansrust, 12.6.01
Sergeant, John E.	,,	
Stebbins, James Frederick	,,	
Clark, William Forbes	,,	Invalided, Australia, arr. 7.12.01
Gubbins, Stamer	,,	
Brace, Edgar	,,	Severely wounded at Wilmansrust, 12.6.01
Stock, Duncan	,,	
Selman, Sydney	,,	Slightly wounded, 16.6.01 ; severely wounded at Travanspoort, 20.8.01 ; invalided, Australia, arr. 3.11.01
Burnie, Reginald Mortimer	,,	
Ebeling, Gus.	,,	
O'Loghlen, Bryan	,,	
Grover, Henry Chaplyn	,,	
Murphy, Arthur Edward	,,	Killed in action at Drivelfontein, 29.5.01
Rowan, Andrew Percival	,,	
Beatty, Kenneth James	,,	Wounded at Leeuwfontein, 19.4.01
Osborne, Henry Houston		
Anderson, Herbert Alfred	Lieut.-Adjutant	
Akins, Charles Henry	Lieut. Quartermaster	
Patterson, James Harold	Lieutenant (M.S.)	
Palmer, Herbert Appleton	,,	Killed in action at Wilmansrust, 12.6.01
Sherlock, Samuel	Vet.-Captain	
Strong, Charles Denniston	Vet.-Lieutenant	Slightly wounded at Wilmansrust, 12.6.01

The following officers from 2nd, 3rd, and 4th Contingents (which see), were posted to 5th Contingent in South Africa, and served with it approximately as stated :—

Major	W. McKnight		From about	March to June, 1901
,,	T. F. Umphelby		,, ,,	March to 18th June, 1901
Captain	H. G. Carstairs		,, ,,	22.3.01 to 5.5.02
,,	T. L. De Haviland		,, ,,	22.3.01 to 30.4.01
,,	C. S. Coltman		,, ,,	22.6.01 to 27.3.02
,,	F. W. Moseley		,, ,,	22.6.01 to 6.5.02
Lieut.	J. H. Brabazon		,, ,,	20.3.01 to 6.5.02
,,	H. O. Appleby		,, ,,	22.6.01 to 6.5.02
,,	A. N. Gregg		,, ,,	22.6.01 to 5.5.02
* ,,	H. Kessell		,, ,,	22.6.01 to 6.5.02
,,	T. A. Umphelby		,, ,,	22.6.01 to 6.5.02
,,	R. L. Duncan			
,,	H. J. Esler			
,,	J. MacFarlane		,, ,,	22.6.01 to 27.3.02
,,	H. McIntyre			
,,	E. J. McKaige			
,,	B. A. G. Watts		,, ,,	22.6.01 to 6.5.02

* Lieutenant Kessell had no previous war service.

C. 4720. T

Nominal Roll—continued.

No. and Name.	Rank.	Remarks.
N.C.O.'s AND MEN.		
725. Kroschel, Charles Frederick William	Sergeant	
726. Cleland, Henry Charles	Corporal	Sergeant
727. McCorkell, John	Private	Died of enteric at Wakkerstroom, 21.1.02
728. Collins, Walter John	,,	
729. O'Donnell, Charles Edward Somerset	Corporal	Invalided, Australia, arr. 25.3.02
730. Whyte, James	Private	
731. Cleland, George Francis Hudson	,,	
732. Clugston, John Andrew Ross	Corporal	Quartermaster-Sergeant
733. Nuttall, Mark Cyril	Private	Lance-Corporal
734. Blackwood, William Biddulph	Sergeant	
735. Watson, Harold Edgar	Bugler	
736. Hockley, Walter Norman	Sergeant	
737. Burman, Alfred Edward	,,	Invalided, Australia, arr. 3.1.02
738. Burman, William	Private	
739. Sheehan, Harry	Corporal	
740. Short, Arthur James	Saddler	
741. McGee, Ernest	Sergeant	
742. Macarthur, Archibald	Private	Dangerously ill at Wakkerstroom, 12.2.02, and 17.2.02
743. Carter, William Henry	Lance-Corporal	Slightly wounded at Wagon Drift, 19.4.01
744. Laurie, John Cameron	Private	
745. Vogel, Ernest	,,	
746. Cooper, Charles Oscar	Corporal	
747. Wheeler, David Jesse	Private	
748. Patrick, William	,,	
749. Purchase, Albert Hazelwood	Lance-Corporal	
750. Cleeland, Arthur Herbert McCarthy	Private	
751. Patterson, Ernest Edward	,,	
752. Goodwill, Charles Henry	,,	
753. Kissane, Charles	Corporal	Invalided, Australia, arr. 29.1.02
754. Lanyon, Raymond Rivers	Private	
755. Doodt, Ernest Anthony	Saddler	
756. Lovelace, Alfred John	Private	
757. Wight, Phillip Francis	,,	Lance-Corporal
758. Smart, Arthur	,,	Corporal
759. Heron, John	,,	
760. Thorpe, Stanley James	,,	
761. Prosser, Charles Robert	Farrier-Sergeant	
762. McMillan, Joseph Rea	Private	
763. Hawkins, John	,,	Invalided, Australia, arr. 29.1.02
764. McDonald, William Nicol	,,	
765. Johnson, James Newling	,,	
766. Shanks, Thomas	,,	
767. Tennick, William Matthew	,,	
768. Needham, John Valentine	,,	
769. Hornby, Francis James	,,	
770. Bull, Percy Thurlow	Sergeant	
771. McLellan, Ernest George	Private	Lance-Corporal
772. Esmore, Bertie	,,	
773. Dillon, Harry James	,,	Severely wounded at Wilmansrust, 12.6.01; also at Schimmelhoek, 4.1.02
774. Allan, Frederick Humphrey	,,	

Nominal Roll—*continued.*

No. and Name.	Rank.	Remarks.
N.C.O.'s AND MEN—*continued.*		
775. Clark, George Edward	Private	
776. Dyke, Samuel	,,	Lance-Corporal
777. Higgins, Leslie Lyndhurst	,,	Invalided, Australia, arr. 3.01.01
778. Bell, Harry Henderson	Corporal	Sergeant. *Vide* "Promotions" and "War Services"
779. Buckley, Patrick Craig	Private	
780. Craig, Andrew Frederick	,,	
781. Barry, Edgar Charles	,,	Severely wounded at H'loblane, near Vryheid, 27.8.01
782. Seymour, Charles Tudor	,,	Invalided, Australia, arr. 29.1.02
783. Boxall, Henry John	,,	Reported missing, and afterwards reported dead by Court of Inquiry, 17.4.01
784. Boake, Alfred Hogarth	Sergeant	Coy. Sergeant-Major. Severely wounded at Wilmansrust, 12.6.01
785. Reisenaner, Edward Alexander	Private	Killed in railway accident near Cape Town, 11.3.01
786. Manning, George	,,	
787. Wilson, John Henry	,,	
788. McKimmie, Walter	,,	Invalided, Australia, 29.1.02
789. Sherar, C.	Corporal	
790. Woodbridge, Arthur	Private	
791. Trippet, Charles Samuel	,,	
792. Massie, William	,,	
793. Roach, Charles Herbert	,,	
794. Shearer, Alfred George	,,	
795. Dow, Frederick George	,,	Killed in action at Schueveberg Hoek, 23.8.01
796. Osborne, Terence Joseph	,,	
797. Haywood, Edwin	Corporal	Quartermaster-Sergeant
798. Parker, John	Private	Invalided, Australia, arr. 11.12.01
799. Jeffery, Albert	Coy. Sergeant-Major	Slightly wounded at Wilmansrust, 12.6.01
800. Hoffmann, Frederick Victor	Private	
801. Kennedy, Cecil Taylor	Sergeant	
802. Speers, Isaac	Private	
803. Farmer, Fred William	,,	
804. Borcham, Alfred William	,,	
805. McCoy, William John	,,	Silghtly wounded at Leeuwin Kop, 17.4.01; invalided, Australia, arr. 12.9.01
806. Patterson, James Benjamin	,,	
807. Gregory, Henry Ernest	,,	
808. Jack, Thomas William	,,	
809. Cardwell, Charles Henry	,,	Slightly wounded near Middelburg, 8.7.01
810. Kerr, William Henry	,,	
811. Hodgson, Henry William	,,	
812. Parsons, Wesley	,,	
813. Pentland, William Christie	Lance-Corporal	Corporal
814. Male, William Alex.	Private	
815. Ruddle, Arthur Exley	,,	Corporal
816. Black, Sidney Rupert	,,	
817. Lumley, Arthur Charles	Coy. Quartermaster-Sergeant	
818. Smith, William Edward	Private	
819. Collins, Frank William	,,	

Nominal Roll—*continued.*

No. and Name.	Rank.	Remarks.
N.C.O.'s AND MEN—*continued.*		
820. Olsen, William	Private	
821. Mangan, James Patrick	,,	
822. Rankin, Robert	,,	Lance-Corporal
823. Ireland, John	,,	
824. Maynard, John	,,	Corporal
825. McGregor, Alex.	,,	
826. Edwards, Robert	,,	
827. Salmon, John Henry William	Coy. Quartermaster-Sergeant	Battalion Quartermaster-Sergeant
828. Goodsir, William Alexander	Private	
829. Richards, Joseph	,,	
830. Ennis, David Francis	,,	
831. Colles, Clive Dana	,,	
832. Sullivan, George Daniel	,,	
833. Temple, William Francis	,,	
834. McKay, Charles	,,	
835. Kiddle, Harold Leigh	Sergeant	
836. Taylor, Frederick Norman	Private	
837. Stainborough, Ernest William	,,	
838. Day, William Gregory	,,	Corporal
839. Banbrook, Alfred	Corporal	Invalided, Australia, arr. 7.2.02
840. Thomas, Charles Hugh	Private	
841. Robinson, Arthur Leslie	Sergeant and Orderly Room Clerk	Reg. Quartermaster-Sergeant
842. Meagher, William Patrick	Private	Dangerously ill at Charlestown, 7.2.02, and 23.2.02
843. Evans, Graham Berry	,,	
844. Taylor, George May	Corporal	
845. Cass, Walter Edmund	,,	Sergeant
846. Strong, Wm. Henry	Sergeant	
847. Haddock, Joseph	Private	
848. Cavanagh, George	,,	Dangerously ill at Charlestown, 23.2.02
849. Judd, Walter Wm. Mitchell	Corporal	Sergeant
850. Moore, George Wright	Private	
851. Ethell, Edmund	,,	Corporal
852. Sullivan, William N.	Coy. Quartermaster-Sergeant	
853. Gallagher, James Farrell	Private	
854. Hammond, Maxwell Charles Lefebre	Corporal	Severely wounded at Rhenoster Kop, 7.5.01; invalided, Australia, arr. 3.11.01
855. Healy, William James	Private	Died of enteric at Pretoria, 2.8.01
856. Ridd, Charles William	,,	Lance-Corporal
857. Bowman, Walton	,,	
858. McKay, William Henry	,,	Invalided, Australia, arr. 3.1.02
859. Crean, Francis	,,	
860. Monk, Arthur James	,,	
861. Arkle, William	,,	
862. Young, Edward	,,	
863. Fay, John	,,	
864. Lockhart, Cecil	,,	
865. Biram, Ben. Entwistle	,,	
866. Howell, Edgar Earnest	,,	Lance-Corporal
867. McCracken, Ralph	Sergeant	
868. Dwyer, Philip	Private	
869. Winter, Albert	,,	

Nominal Roll—*continued.*

No. and Name.	Rank.	Remarks.
N.C.O.'S AND MEN—*continued.*		
8870. Orgill, Ernest Alfred	Private	
71. Bailey, William Henry	,,	Dangerously ill at Standerton, 10.3.02
872. McLachlan, Hector	,,	
873. McKay, David Wm.	,,	
874. Maguire, Edward James	,,	Lance-Corporal
875. Steele, Henry Darragh	,,	
876. Thomas, Robert	,,	
877. Keys, Frederick	,,	
878. Paterson, Albert	,,	
879. Turner, Frederick John	,,	Invalided, Australia, arr. 25.2.02
880. Gordon, George Grosvenor	Corporal	Sergeant
881. Stewart, James	Private	Corporal
882. Mackay, Norman	,,	Corporal. Seriously wounded, 28.6.01, at Bethel
883. Mackay, John	,,	
884. Bennett, George Albert	,,	
885. Fullarton, George Watson	Coy. Sergeant-Major	
886. Birmingham, Francis John	Bugler	
887. McGrath, Patrick Daniel	Private	Dangerously ill at Charlestown, 7.2.02
888. Young, Arthur Edward	,,	Lance-Corporal
889. Dear, John Thomas	Corporal	Sergeant
890. McPhee, Angus	,,	Sergeant
891. O'Shea, Thomas Martin	,,	
892. Thorne, William Henry	Private	Lance-Corporal
893. McCann, John Bernard	,,	Died of enteric at Pretoria, 19.6.01
894. Pontin, Albert	Coy. Quartermaster-Sergeant	Regimental Sergeant-Major
895. O'Dea, Thomas Michael	Corporal	Quartermaster-Sergeant
896. Harrison, Thomas Jas. Irwin	Farrier	Farrier-Sergeant
897. Gonsalves, Alfred James	Private	
898. Matthews, Albert Edwin	,,	
899. Moran, John Thomas	Corporal	Sergeant. Reported dangerously ill at Wakkerstroom, 19.1.02, 25.1.02, and 4.2.02
900. Hutchinson, Henry Hall	Lance-Corporal	Corporal. Severely wounded, 28.6.01, at Bethel. Despatches, *London Gazette,* 29.7.02
901. Tivendale, Robert Anglin	Private	Corporal
902. Glass, David	,,	
903. Burley, Albert Edward	,,	Lance-Corporal. Reported missing near Kaferstadt; reported dead by Court of Inquiry, 2.12.02
904. Williamson, David	,,	
905. Dalgarno, Frederick Joseph	,,	Corporal
906. Dalgarno, John Stockton	,,	
907. Cunningham, Robert	Lance-Corporal	Invalided, Australia, arr. 3.1.02
908. Eden, William Valentine	Private	Dangerously ill at Charlestown, 2.2.02; also on 9.2.02, and 23.2.02
909. Streitberg, Charles	Sergeant	Coy. Sergeant-Major
910. Keeble, John Walter	,,	Coy. Sergeant-Major. Despatches, *London Gazette,* 29.7.02. D.C.M.
911. Fletcher, Gordon Mackie	Lance-Corporal	
912. Paulett, Alfred Edward	Private	

Nominal Roll—continued.

No. and Name.	Rank.	Remarks.
\	N.C.O.'s AND MEN—continued.	
913. Greenaway, Frederick	Private	
914. Corteen, Thomas James	,,	Slightly wounded at Klippan, 25.5.01
915. Parsell, Alexander James	,,	
916. Wilson, John	,,	
917. Blyth, Robert	Corporal	
918. Towt, William Finlay	Private	Slightly wounded near Klippan, 25.5.01; dangerously ill at Charlestown, 14.4.02
919. Davis, George	Corporal	Sergeant
920. Topham, Charles Robert	Private	
921. Cameron, Donald	,,	
922. Bugg, William James	,,	
923. Archer, Thomas	,,	
924. Clancy, Peter John	,,	
925. Wellington, Arthur	,,	Invalided, Australia, arr. 29.1.02
926. Wilckens, Valentine Randolph	Lance-Corporal	Corporal
927. Osgood, Harry A.	Coy. Sergeant-Major	Bat. Sergeant-Major
928. Beecher, James Alexander	Sergeant	
929. Pettit, George	Private	
930. Kidson, Frank	,,	
931. McCutchan, William	,,	Lance-Corporal
932. Godfrey, Rowland Tapley	,,	Resigned, 19.1.01
933. Beecher, William Walter	,,	
934. Cummins, Edward Francis	Lance-Corporal	Corporal
935. Homel, Frederick Charles	Private	
936. McDonald, Michael Terence	Sergeant	Died of debility at Pretoria, 10.4.01
937. Bent, James Ernest	,,	
938. Weeding, Herbert	Private	Invalided, Australia, arr. 29.1.02
939. Bird, Claude Manston L.	Sergeant	Dangerously ill at Charlestown, 11.3.02
940. Cox, Harold	Corporal	Quartermaster-Sergt. Invalided to England, 13.1.02
941. Walker, James Rowan	Private	Corporal
942. Adams, Edward Ernest	,,	
943. Muir, William	Saddler	Saddler-Sergeant
944. Whelan, John	Private	Died of wounds at Grootvlei, 16.12.01
945. Kerr, Albert George	,,	Invalided, Australia, arr. 12.9.01. Awarded pension
946. Davies, Peter	,,	Invalided, Australia, arr. 11.12.01
947. Kennedy, Thomas Henry	,,	
948. Lowther, Louis Anthony John	,,	
949. Lee, John	,,	
950. Jarrett, Cyrill Charmers	,,	
951. Warren, Thomas Gordon	,,	
952. Costello, John	,,	Died of wounds at Middelburg, 5.7.01
953. Clarke, Alexander	,,	
954. Kennedy, James Robert	,,	
955. Hamilton, John Melrose	,,	Reported dangerously ill at Kozi River, 28.9.01.
956. Grinham, Roy McNeill	,,	Wounded, Klipplaat, 7.6.01. Invalided, Australia, arr. 3.10.01
957. Carr, James Patrick	Corporal	Coy. Quartermaster-Sergeant

Nominal Roll—*continued.*

No. and Name.	Rank.	Remarks.
N.C.O.'s AND MEN—*continued.*		
958. Knights, William James	Sergeant	C. Sergeant-Major
959. Mullen, Leslie Miltiades	Private	
960. Smith, Guy Haddon	,,	
961. Mullen, George Percy	,,	
962. Smith, William Sydney	,,	Reported dangerously ill at Mosi River, 28.9.01
963. Sievers, Richard Lewis	,,	
964. Blair, William John	,,	
965. Emmett, Robert John	,,	Invalided, Australia, arr. 30.7.01
966. Watson, Thomas William	,,	Reported dangerously ill at Wakkerstroom, 25.1.02, 4.2.02 and 17.2.02
967. Dearden, Thomas	Saddler	
968. Harrison, Albert	Corporal	
969. Hickey, John	Private	
970. Mullen, Clarence Alka	,,	
971. Stein, David John	Sergeant	
972. McRae, Godfrey Francis	Private	
973. Martin, John Frederick	Shoeing-Smith	
974. Houghton, Albert	,,	Killed in action at Utrecht, 16.10.01
975. Grassham, Frederick	Private	Corporal
976. McMicking, Gilbert James	,,	
977. Purdue, Harold Egbert	Corporal	
978. Purdue, Horace Josiah	Private	
979. Reckenberg, William Augustus	,,	
980. Crocker, Albert Hugh	,,	Slightly wounded near Balmoral, 10.8.01. Invalided, Australia, arr. 29.1.02
981. Crowl, George	,,	
982. Muir, Ronald Thomas	,,	
983. Glowski, Henry	,,	
984. Drysdale, John James	,,	Corporal
985. Phillips, Fennel	,,	
986. Lewis, Albert Francis	,,	
987. Purdey, William	,,	
988. Glinn, Carlyon	,,	Died of enteric at Charlestown, 14.2.02
989. Smith, Theo.	,,	
990. Judd, Thomas	,,	
991. McPhee, Angus	,,	
992. Hulme, Herbert James	,,	
993. Thurgood, Alfred George	,,	Corporal
994. Bell, Richard Chambers	,,	
995. Campbell, Ormond Leslie	,,	
996. Hawkes, Robert	,,	
997. O'Brien, Michael	,,	
998. Davies, John	,,	
999. Gibson, Thomas Edward	,,	
1000. Phillips, Francis Percy	,,	
1001. Newton, John	,,	
1002. Biggins, Ernest	,,	
1003. Kennedy, Thomas	,,	
1004. Kerwin, Thomas Edward	,,	
1005. Chisholm, Arthur Augustine	,,	
1006. Reid, Frederick George	,,	
1007. Collins, James	,,	Killed in action at Wilmansrust, 12.6.01
1008. Fry, Percy	,,	Corporal

Nominal Roll—*continued*.

No. and Name.	Rank.	Remarks.
N.C.O.'s AND MEN—*continued.*		
1009. O'Loughlan, James William	Private	
1010. Lord, James Roderick	,,	
1011. Clarke, James	,,	Severely wounded at Vryheid, 5.11.01
1012. Shirley, William Samuel	,,	
1013. Coustley, Robert	,,	
1014. Miller, Samuel	Shoeing-Smith	
1015. Samers, William Robert	Private	Corporal
1016. Head, Kerwin	,,	
1017. Newell, Frederic Lord	Lance-Corporal	Corporal
1018. Callender, Herbert Victor	Private	
1019. Powis, Harry	,,	
1020. Crane, Ernest	Shoeing-Smith	
1021. Tickell, Windsor Herbert	Bugler	
1022. Lewis, John	Private	
1023. Martin, Cecil Leslie	,,	
1024. McKeown, Ernest Edward	,,	
1025. Sarkies, Andrew	Reg. Quartermaster-Sergeant	
1026. Sweeny, John	Private	Invalided, Australia, arr. 27.2.02
1027. de Valle, Harold	,,	
1028. Cottrell, Thomas	,,	
1029. Campbell, Donald	Sergeant	Invalided, Australia, arr. 29.1.02
1030. Swain, Edward	Private	
1031. Steele, James	,,	
1032. Daff, John Fawcett	,,	Lance-Corporal. Severely wounded near Wakkerstroom, 21.12.01
1033. Dare, Samuel Carlisle	,,	
1034. Davidson, Albert Benjamin	,,	Died of enteric at Charlestown, 15.2.02
1035. Dare, James Nankiville	,,	Severely wounded at Schimmelhoek, 4.2.02
1036. McGrath, Albert James	,,	
1037. Wilson, James Leslie	,,	
1038. Jenkinson, Thomas Walter	,,	Slightly wounded at Grootvlei, 16.12.01
1039. Halsall, Frank	,,	
1040. Supple, John	,,	Dangerously wounded at Schueveberg Hoek, 23.8.01; wounded at Howick, 24.11.01; dangerously ill at Howick, 30.11.01
1041. Leekamp, Frederick Herbert	,,	
1042. Thomson, James Peter	,,	
1043. Forrester, Robert	,,	
1044. Puzey, William Joseph	Coy. Quartermaster-Sergeant	Battalion Quartermaster-Sergeant
1045. Mills, John Matthew	Private	
1046. Wyndham, Arthur	,,	
1047. McLennan, Donald	Farrier-Sergeant	
1048. Mawley, Edward	Sergeant	
1049. Campbell, Garnet	Private	
1050. McIntosh, John Daniel	,,	
1051. McIntosh, John Thomas	,,	
1052. Bryant, Harry Cornelius	Farrier-Sergeant	
1053. Cook, Charles William	Private	
1054. Wilson, William	,,	
1055. Simcox, Henry Charles	,,	
1056. Payne, William John	,,	

Nominal Roll—*continued*.

No. and Name.	Rank.	Remarks.
N.C.O.'s AND MEN—*continued.*		
1057. McNabb, Alexander Stuart	Private	Lance-Corporal
1058. Weidner, William John	,,	
1059. Borland, Louis Boyd	,,	
1060. Nicolson, Donald	,,	
1061. Davey, Leslie	,,	Lance-Corporal. Invalided, Australia, arr. 29.1.02
1062. Linacre, James Abrahams	,,	Invalided, Australia, arr. 29.1.02
1063. Hodges, Frederick Charles	,,	
1064. Bolton, George	,,	
1065. Tighe, Thomas Terence	,,	
1066. McAlpine, George	,,	
1067. Mitchell, James Bevan	,,	
1068. Slater, Joseph	Corporal	Sergeant
1069. Symmonds, John	Coy. Quartermaster-Sergeant	
1070. Scriven, Henry John Fenton	Private	
1071. Wallace, William	,,	
1072. Wooster, Henry Victor	,,	
1073. Osborne, Richard	,,	
1074. Serjeant, William Thompson	Shoeing-Smith	
1075. Deacon, Charles	Saddler	
1076. Ross, William	Private	
1077. Muller, Otto Emil	Corporal	Sergeant
1078. Waite, William Albert	Coy. Sergeant-Major	Slightly wounded at Nooitgedacht, 15.6.01
1079. King, George Albert	Private	
1080. Phelan, Michael	,,	
1081. King, Percy Robert Henry Grierson	,,	
	Farrier-Sergeant	
1082. Weir, John Lewis	Private	
1083. Fitzpatrick, Samuel	,,	
1084. Brooks, Henry Ralph	,,	Lance-Corporal
1085. Chambers, Michael James	,,	Lance-Corporal
1086. Lowe, Arthur Albert	,,	Lance-Corporal
1087. Giles, Arthur Horace	,,	
1088. Jefferys, Owen James	,,	
1089. McNally, John	,,	Accidentally killed at Naauwpoort, 2.1.02
1090. Canty, Alexander	,,	
1091. Williamson, Thomas Peter	,,	Lance-Corporal
1092. Maher, John	,,	
1093. Matthews, Louis Henry	,,	
1094. Berry, Archie James	Coy. Quartermaster-Sergeant	
1095. Topham, Richard	Private	Killed in action at Wilmansrust, 12.6.01
1096. Carlisle, Robert	Sergeant	Slightly wounded at Kaalhoek, 23.11.01. Mentioned in Despatches
1097. Rutledge, John Horace Douglas	Corporal	Invalided, Australia, arr. 19.9.01; Awarded pension
1098. Davies, Charles	Private	
1099. McLean, Alexander	,,	
1100. Kimpton, Harold Stanley	,,	
1101. Lawrence, John James	,,	Killed in action at Schueveberg Hoek, 23.8.01
1102. Dudley, William	,,	
1103. Dudley, Edward James	,,	

Nominal Roll—*continued.*

No. and Name.	Rank.	Remarks.
N.C.O.'s AND MEN—*continued.*		
1104. Barr, John	Private	
1105. Cook, William Henry	,,	
1106. Noble, Richard William	,,	
1107. Smith, Shorland H.	,,	
1108. Smith, Ernest	,,	Invalided, Australia, arr. 29.1.02
1109. Clingin, James Archibald	,,	
1110. Gambold, George Thomas	Corporal	Sergeant
1111. Smith, Horace Fellowes	Private	
1112. Ross, David Bain	,,	
1113. Thompson, James Barrett	,,	
1114. Gilbert, Edmund Burke	,,	
1115. Ramsay, Samuel William	Coy. Quartermaster-Sergeant	
1116. Payne, Walter Ernest	Private	
1117. Brace, James	,,	
1118. Steele, Thomas Alexander	,,	Invalided, Australia, arr. 9.5.01
1119. Maine, Henry	,,	
1120. Browning, Herbert Samuel	,,	
1121. Goodwin, John E.	Corporal	Lance-Sergeant
1122. Ross, Malcolm	Sergeant	
1123. Roberts, Richard	,,	Slightly wounded at Leeuwin Kop, 16.4.01
1124. McNeill, James	Private	
1125. Baker, Arthur Herbert	Sergeant	Invalided, Australia, arr. 7.2.02
1126. Williamson, Charles	Private	Lance-Corporal
1127. Lear, Guy Wishart	,,	
1128. Wilson, Edward	Bugler	
1129. McCormack, Henry Charles	Private	
1130. Watt, Alfred	Sergeant	Coy. Sergeant-Major. Despatches *London Gazette,* 29.7.02
1131. Carter, Alfred Percy	Private	
1132. Shields, Thomas Lackey Cunningham	,,	Lance-Corporal
1133. Neyland, Nevin	,,	
1134. Ross, John	,,	
1135. Roney, George	,,	
1136. Quinn, William Joseph	Saddler	Saddler-Sergeant
1137. McLean, George	Private	
1138. Clinton, George	,,	
1139. Everall, William John	Saddler	Saddler-Sergeant. Wounded at Wagon Drift, 19.4.01; reported suffering from gunshot wound at Pretoria, 15.6.01; invalided, Australia, arr. 3.1.02
1140. Shields, John	Private	
1141. Wood, William Alfred	,,	
1142. Steele, James	,,	
1143. Prentice, William	,,	Invalided, Australia, arr. 29.1.02
1144. Newton, Samuel	,,	
1145. Harkness, Walter	Lance-Corporal	Pay Sergeant
1146. Bowman, George Alfred	Private	
1147. Thomas, Gwillim Trehara	Sergeant	
1148. Jones, Richard	Shoeing-Smith	Slightly wounded at Blood River, 16.4.01
1149. Harte, Edward	Private	Corporal
1150. Wright, Arthur Ernest	,,	
1151. Strachan, Charles	,,	

Nominal Roll—*continued.*

No. and Name.	Rank.	Remarks.
N.C.O.'s AND MEN—*continued.*		
1152. Freeman, George	Private	Reported dangerously ill at Charlestown, 6.12.01, also 21.12.01, 28.12.01, and at Pietermaritzburg, 23.2.02 and 9.3.02. Returned to Victoria, 31.5.02
1153. Bishop, Edward John	Farrier	Farrier-Corporal
1154. Kelly, James	Private	Lance-Corporal. Severely wounded at Rhenoster Kop, 7.5.01
1155. Brunet, Herbert Foster	,,	Severely wounded at Schueveberg Hoek, 23.8.01
1156. Campbell, Addison John	,,	
1157. Bunny, Gavin	Farrier	
1158. Bird, Frank	Private	
1159. Morgan, Walter	,,	Lance-Corporal
1160. Handlen, William	,,	Reported dangerously ill, 4.6.01
1161. West, Thomas Robertson	Coy. Sergeant-Major	
1162. Clarke, Arthur	Private	
1163. Dow, George	,,	
1164. Coughlan, Arthur William	Sergeant	
1165. Rawlins, William Henry	Private	
1166. Simpson, George Edward	,,	
1167. Seaborn, William James	Farrier-Sergeant	
1168. Cunnington, William Sheeton	Private	
1169. Edington, William James	,,	
1170. Ashton, Edward Johnson	Farrier	
1171. Chamings, William	Private	
1172. Dartnall, William	,,	
1173. Smith, Robert Boyle	,,	
1174. Grayton, Henry Havelock	,,	
1175. Cock, William Henry	,,	
1176. Collins, John	,,	
1177. Moore, Henry	,,	
1178. Lawton, Walter Jack	,,	
1179. Kemp, William Matthew	,,	Invalided, Australia, arr. 13.12.01.
1180. Bates, Anthony	,,	
1181. James, William Walter	,,	Died of pneumonia at sea, s.s. *Nineveh*, 6.12.01
1182. Yager, Harry	,,	
1183. Kelland, Robert	,,	
1184. Campbell, William	Saddler	Saddler-Sergeant
1185. Espie, Daniel	Private	
1186. Connal, William Graham	,,	
1187. Cuthbert, James	,,	
1188. Ferguson, Kenneth	Corporal	Sergeant
1189. Beamish, William John	Private	
1190. Martyn, Fred.	,,	Lance-Corporal
1191. McFee, Fred Aspinall	,,	
1192. Thomas, Walter Edward	,,	
1193. Conquest, James	,,	
1194. Lyon, Arthur Ernest	,,	
1195. Harris, Herbert	,,	
1196. Bambrook, George	,,	
1197. Rose, Harry Morgan	,,	Accidentally severely wounded at Biviaan's Poort, 21.8.00. Invalided, Australia, arr. 11.12.01
1198. Ford, Henry Edward	,,	

Nominal Roll—continued.

No. and Name.	Rank.	Remarks.

N.C.O.'S AND MEN—continued.

No. and Name.	Rank.	Remarks.
1199. Moran, Edward Dalton	Private	Dangerously ill at Charlestown, 9.2.02
1200. Littlejohn, Arthur James	,,	Severely wounded at Rhenoster Kop, 7.5.01
1201. Fletcher, Charles Edward	,,	
1202. Bryant, Walter	,,	Invalided, Australia, arr. 3.10.01
1203. Grant, Alfred	,,	
1204. Ruddle, Frank Ernest	,,	Corporal. Slightly wounded near Middelburg, 8.7.01
1205. Brace, Reginald Filson	Saddler	Saddler-Sergeant
1206. Cox, John William	Private	Lance-Corporal
1207. O'Brien, Timothy	,,	
1208. Graham, Peter	,,	Lance-Corporal
1209. Mahoney, James Francis	,,	
1210. Mackenzie, Wm.	,,	Lance-Corporal
1211. Sherar, E. C.	,,	Lance-Corporal
1212. Hillard, George Thomas	,,	
1213. Parrott, Henry	,,	Invalided, Australia, arr. 11.12.01
1214. Bruce, Henry Homeward	,,	
1215. Evans, R. M.	,,	
1216. Pearse, Leslie Osbourne	,,	Reported dangerously ill at Vryheid, 15.11.01. Invalided, Australia, arr. 25.3.02
1217. Bryant, Robert George	,,	
1218. Craig, Cowan James	,,	Lance-Corporal
1219. Willan, Digby Hoskins	,,	
1220. Hewitt, John	,,	
1221. Vercoe, John Edward	,,	Slightly wounded at Brouktrolal Spruit, 1.8.01. Invalided, Australia, arr. 3.1.02
1222. Willett, Percy	,,	Dangerously wounded at Brouktrolal Spruit, 1.8.01
1223. Datson, George	,,	Corporal
1224. Kickie, Henry John	,,	
1225. Phillips, Arnold	,,	
1226. Hobson, Richard Francis	,,	
1227. MacDonald, Laurence William	,,	Lance-Corporal
1228. Ross, Thomas Scott	,,	Died of enteric at Wakkerstroom, 4.3.02
1229. Smith, Frederick James	,,	
1230. Hockley, Bertram	,,	Invalided, Australia, arr. 29.1.01
1231. Passmore, William Forest	,,	
1232. Rafferty, Matthew	,,	
1233. Anthony, Henry Thomas	,,	
1234. Chambers, Samuel	,,	Lance-Corporal
1235. Hesketh, Henry Richmond	Sergeant	Coy. Sergeant-Major
1236. Simons, Felix Leonard	Private	
1237. Birch, James	,,	Slightly wounded at Brereton, 28.11.01. Despatches, *London Gazette*, 29.7.02
1238. Reeve, John Coas	,,	Slightly wounded at Wilmansrust, 12.6.01
1239. Reynolds, Stanley Moore	,,	
1240. Hicks, Sydney James	Corporal	Invalided, Australia, arr. 12.9.01
1241. Croy, Joseph Gipson	Private	Invalided, Australia, arr. 3.1.02
1242. Holt, Thomas	,,	Lance-Corporal
1243. Newham, Henry S.	,,	Lance-Corporal
1244. Stevenson, Edward Henry	,,	Invalided, Australia, arr. 29.1.02

Nominal Roll—continued.

No. and Name.	Rank.	Remarks.

N.C.O.'s AND MEN—continued.

No. and Name.	Rank.	Remarks.
1245. O'Farrell, John	Private	
1246. Steege, Allan	,,	
1247. Hayes, William George	,,	Slightly wounded at Wilmansrust, 12.6.01
1248. Paulin, Norman	,,	
1249. Maher, William	,,	
1250. Thistleton, James	,,	
1251. Barton, William James	Shoeing-Smith	
1252. Hodges, Charles Albert	Private	
1253. Gaynor, John	,,	
1254. Davis, Mark	,,	Wounded at Zwartfontein, 1.8.01
1255. Outhwaite, Joseph	Sergeant	
1256. Stanley, William Charles	Private	
1257. Smith, Thomas Cadzow	,,	
1258. Steele, George	,,	Lance-Corporal
1259. Jones, James Wm. Beever	Shoeing-Smith	
1260. Holliday, Albert Ernest	Private	
1261. Spowart, Albert Edward	,,	Shoeing-Smith. Died of enteric at Charlestown. 15.2.02
1262. Culliton, Fred. Samuel	Sergeant	Slightly wounded at Wilmansrust, 12.6.01
1263. Pitt, Thomas	Private	Corporal
1264. Turner, Horace Bulwer	,,	Invalided, Australia, arr. 3.10.01
1265. Bauld, James Patrick	,,	Invalided, Australia, arr. 12.9.01
1266. Peters, John Julius	,,	
1267. Murray, Charles	,,	
1268. Cochran, Frederick John	Saddler	
1269. Tweedle, Frederick	Private	Invalided, Australia, arr. 29.1.02
1270. Bridgeland, Frederick C. Lionel	,,	
1271. Quinton, Alfred George	,,	
1272. Richards, Arthur	,,	
1273. Collins, Willie Arthur	,,	Invalided, Australia, arr. 30.7.01
1274. Attfield, Charles	,,	Invalided, Australia, arr. 3.11.01
1275. Hedley, John	,,	Reported dangerously ill at Charlestown, 28.12.01, 4.1.02, 19.1.02, and 4.2.02
1276. Watson, A. E.	,,	Corporal
1277. May, Edward Sherwood	Corporal	O.R. Sergeant
1278. Anderson, David	Farrier-Sergeant	
1279. Alexander, Ernest Plunkett	Private	
1280. Alexander, Frank Plunkett	,,	
1281. Gavagan, Charles John	Bugler	Invalided, Australia, arr. 3.10.01
1282. Carolin, John Paul	,,	
1283. Whitford, Thomas E.	,,	
1284. Cahir, Thomas Francis	Private	
1285. Noble, John	,,	
1286. Christie, Henry	,,	
1287. Pike, Edward	,,	
1288. Brailsford, Henry	,,	
1289. Murray, Alfred	,,	Accidentally severely wounded at Vryheid, 9.10.01. Invalided, Australia, arr. 25.3.02
1290. Browne, William	,,	
1291. Gooney, Thomas	,,	
1292. Mahoney, Thomas Henry	Shoeing-Smith	Killed in action at Wilmansrust, 12.6.01
1293. Bowen, William	Private	

Nominal Roll—*continued.*

No. and Name.	Rank.	Remarks.

N.C.O.'s AND MEN—*continued.*

No. and Name.	Rank.	Remarks.
1294. Carnegie, William Brown	Private	Dangerously ill at Wakkerstroom, 23.2.02
1295. Gibbs, William Albion	Corporal	
1296. Wood, Thomas James	Private	Corporal
1297. Martinson, Willie	Sergeant	Slightly wounded at Wilmansrust, 12.6.01
1298. Biggs, Algernon Burnett	Corporal	
1299. Sampson, Percy Fred.	Private	Reported dangerously ill, 9.11.01
1300. Herbert, Henry	,,	Invalided, Australia, arr. 9.10.01. Awarded pension
1301. Edwards, Frederick William	,,	
1302. Waldie, William Fenton	,,	
1303. Purves, Robert	,,	
1304. McPherson, Ronald V.	Corporal	Pay-Sergeant
1305. Christensen, Valdemar Witt	,,	
1306. Stirling, James Johnson	Private	
1307. Stratton, George William	,,	Killed in action at Wilmansrust, 12.6.01
1308. Sharpe, Charles Henry	,,	Severely wounded at Middle Kraal, 29.5.01
1309. Wilson, Thomas	,,	Slightly wounded at Wilmansrust, 12.6.01
1310. Hall, Sidney	Corporal	
1311. Donald, James Wilson	Private	Invalided, Australia, arr. 29.1.02
1312. McDonald, Donald	,,	
1313. Mackenzie, Robert Arch.	Sergeant	
1314. Ellsworth, George	Bugler	
1315. Moore, James Webber	Corporal	Sergeant
1316. Jones, David Elliot	Private	
1317. Cowan, John	,,	Severely wounded at Wilmansrust, 12.6.01
1318. Brearley, Frederick	,,	
1319. Troyel, John William	,,	
1320. McNamara, Albert Edward	,,	
1321. Joughin, Frederick Daniel	,,	
1322. Ross, William	,,	Corporal
1323. Wyatt, Albert Wm. Joseph	,,	Lance-Corporal
1324. Bolwell, Percy Herbert Alfred	,,	
1325. Weir, John Charles	Saddler	
1326. Rickards, John Henry	Private	
1327. Melican, David	,,	
1328. Gauld, Thomas	,,	Reported dangerously ill at Standerton, 22.3.02
1329. Barnett, Edwin Allan	,,	
1330. Combe, Ernest	,,	
1331. Swan, John	,,	
1332. Lynch, Thomas Francis	,,	
1333. Tackaberry, William Thomas	Sergeant	Coy. Sergeant-Major
1334. Krodstedt, Verne	Private	
1335. Parry, Herbert Henry	,,	
1336. Lucas, Gordon	Lance-Corporal	Corporal
1337. Pearsall, William Joseph	Private	Invalided, Australia, arr. 11.12.01
1338. Tilley, Frederick Gladman	,,	
1339. Crowle, George	,,	Invalided, Australia, arr. 11.12.01
1340. Warren, Alfred George	,,	Lance-Corporal. Accidentally injured kneecap at Utrecht, 15.8.01. Invalided, Australia, arr. 11.12.01

Nominal Roll—*continued*.

No. and Name.	Rank.	Remarks.
N.C.O.'s AND MEN—*continued*.		
1341. Johnson, Harry	Private	
1342. Ingram, Andrew	,,	
1343. Walker, Edward Gordon	,,	
1344. Robertson, Robert Patrick Norton	Corporal	Killed in action at Middle Kraal, 29.5.01
1345. Jarvie, Peter James	Private	
1346. Larpent, Lionel Herbert	,,	
1347. Hopkins, Albert	,,	
1348. Crosby, William Fowler	,,	Lance-Corporal
1349. Stead, Frederick William	,,	
1350. Cullen, Thos.	,,	
1351. Miller, William	Corporal	Sergeant. Severely wounded at Middle Kraal, 29.5.01
1352. Clareborough, Walter Charles Alfred	Private	
1353. Lowenthal, Mark	,,	
1354. Mays, Harry Victor	,,	
1355. Anderson, Herbert	,,	
1356. Rankin, George	,,	
1357. Fisher, Harold Arthur	,,	Accident to collar-bone, Amersfort, 12.12.01
1358. Lamb, Henry Spencer	,,	Killed in action at Wagoner's Drift, 30.4.01
1359. Barnard, Stanley John	,,	Killed in action at Wilmansrust, 12.6.01
1360. Hennelly, Peter Francis	,,	
1361. Graham, George	,,	
1362. Brown, Henry	,,	
1363. Robinson, Edgar Edward	,,	
1364. Pfeffer, Joseph V.	,,	
1365. Heath, Arthur	,,	
1366. Harrison, Henry	,,	Corporal. Killed in action at Wilmansrust, 12.6.01
1367. Pope, Louis	,,	
1368. Gourlay, Albert Wm.	,,	
1369. Chalmers, Claude	,,	Corporal
1370. Rice, Edward Henry David	,,	
1371. Barber, George Thomas	,,	Lance-Corporal
1372. Bunney, Charles	,,	
1373. Grady, William Keir	Corporal	Saddler-Sergeant
1374. Filcar, Arthur	Saddler	Saddler-Sergeant
1375. Weir, William Rich.	Corporal	Sergeant
1376. Leffler, Frank	Private	Invalided to England, 13.1.02
1377. Hardie, James Frew	,,	
1378. Logan, James Robert	Sergeant	
1379. Fleming, Laurence	Private	
1380. Hendy, Herbert Henry	,,	Killed in action at Wilmansrust, 12.6.01
1381. Salmon, Charles Thomas	,,	Slightly wounded at Wilmansrust, 12.6.01
1382. Moorehouse, Frederick Thomas	,,	
1383. Luckwall, Otto J.	,,	
1384. Scott, Robert Wm.	,,	
1385. Kilbeg, James	Sergeant	Despatches, *London Gazette*, 29.7.02
1386. Townsend, George	Private	
1387. Linden, Charles	Saddler	
1388. Atkinson, Horace Garrett	Private	

Nominal Roll—continued.

No. and Name.	Rank.	Remarks.
	N.C.O.'s AND MEN—continued.	
1389. Herry, Leopold Francis	Private	
1390. Love, Alex. Henry	,,	Slightly wounded at Vryheid, 5.11.01
1391. Freeman, Arnold W.	,,	
1392. Esler, Samuel	,,	Lance-Corporal
1393. Warner, Angus Atty	,,	Invalided, Australia, arr. 26.2.02
1394. Byford, Thomas Frank	,,	
1395. Dennis, Hubert James	,,	
1396. Stanborough, Alfred Henry	,,	Chest accident at Latking's Shoe, 1.10.01
1397. Miles, Thomas William	,,	
1398. Smith, Robert Sydney	,,	
1399. Lamb, Alexander Joseph	,,	
1400. Carey, William	,,	
1401. Simmons, Albert	,,	
1402. Hewett, John T.	,,	
1403. Ellis, L.	,,	Dangerously wounded at H'lobane, 27.8.01 ; reported dangerously ill. 13.10.01. Invalided, Australia, arr. 29.1 02
1404. Newlands, Henry	Corporal	Killed in action at Wilmansrust, 12.6..01
1405. Molyneux, Frederick Harold	Private	
1406. Forbes, Duncan William	,,	
1407. Gill, John James	,,	
1408. Spurr, William Henry	,,	Corporal. Invalided, Australia, arr. 29.1.02
1409. Sherar, James Henry	,,	
1410. McDonnell, John Thomas	Farrier-Sergeant	Invalided, Australia, arr. 29.1.02
1411. Shaw, Fred	Corporal	Sergeant
1412. Strike, Ernest James	Private	Invalided Australia, arr. 30.7.01
1413. Redston, Charles Richard Henry	,,	
1414. Revell, George	Saddler	
1415. Miller, Herbert	Private	
1416. Norwood, Francis Elton	,,	
1417. Murray, James	,,	Invalided, Australia, arr. 11.12.01
1418. Chivers, Alex. Forbes	,,	
1419. Sadler, James Robert	Shoeing-Smith	
1420. O'Keefe, James William	Private	
1421. Reddan, David William	,,	
1422. Whittaker, Albert Walter	,,	Lance-Corporal
1423. Gilbert, Thomas Nicklas	,,	Lance-Corporal
1424. Marshall, Albert Henry	Saddler	Invalided, Australia, arr. 29.1.02
1425. Brunsdon, William Thomas	Private	
1426. Bradley, Charles	,,	
1227. Pagden, William Gering	,,	Slightly wounded at Wilmansrust, 12.6.01. Awarded pension
1428. Crocker, Joseph Ernest	,,	Wounded at Balmoral, 10.8.01
1429. McDonald, John George	,,	
1430. Goudie, Laurence James Watt	,,	Killed in action at Wilmansrust, 12.6.01
1431. Dare, Douglas Henry	Corporal	Sergeant
1432. Born, Percy Harold	Private	
1433. Mackley, William	,,	
1434. Kuhle, Gus	,,	
1435. Duffell, Sidney	,,	
1436. Barnett, Alfred Ernest	,,	Invalided, Australia, 25.3.02 arr.

Nominal Roll—*continued.*

No. and Name.	Rank.	Remarks.
N.C.O.'s AND MEN—*continued.*		
1437. Bechaz, John	Private	Slightly wounded at Wilmansrust 12.6.01
1438. Blandford, Ernest Henry	,,	Killed in action at Wilmansrust, 12.6.01
1439. Hardie, Malcolm Kenneth	,,	
1440. Jones, William Sydney	,,	Corporal
1441. Young, Thomas Joseph	,,	
1442. Alexander, Albert Reddon	,,	
1443. McKenzie, Francis Gurley	,,	
1444. Finn, Bertram S.	,,	Lance-Corporal
1445. Manallack, William	,,	Invalided, Australia, arr. 3.1.02
1446. Hadley, Harry	,,	Corporal. Died of enteric at Wakkerstroom, 10.2.02
1447. Blannin, Arthur Lyndhurst	Corporal	Sergeant
1448. Goodall, John	Private	
1449. Saunders, Charles Alex.	,,	
1450. Cavanagh, John Patrick	,,	
1451. Anderson, William	,,	
1452. Ferguson, Hare	,,	
1453. Duncan, William Gordon	Private	
1454. Rice, Alfred John	,,	
1455. Hewins, Herbert Vincent	,,	Killed in action at Middle Kraal, 29.5.01
1456. Foley, William Laurence	,,	Dangerously ill at Charlestown, 7.2.02. Returned to Victoria, 25.4.02
1457. Simpson, Arthur Henry	,,	Lance-Corporal
1458. Morrison, Thomas	,,	
1459. Aitken, Walter Hugh	,,	
1460. Pollock, Samuel	,,	Corporal. Slightly wounded at Wilmansrust, 12.6.01
1461. McNeill, Colin	,,	
1462. Anderson, David	,,	Severely wounded at Wilmansrust, 12.6.01
1463. Barkell, Henry L.	,,	
1464. Dennehy, John	,,	
1465. Sheehan, Patrick	,,	
1466. Lindan, Charles Alex.	,,	
1467. Charlton, John	,,	Died of enteric at Pretoria, 16.8.01
1468. Evans, David	,,	Lance-Corproal
1469. Tootell, William Ernest	,,	Lance-Corporal. Invalided, Australia, arr. 29.1.02
1470. Guy, Arthur	,,	Reported missing between Belfontein and Rotterdam, 13.2.02; afterwards rejoined
1471. Thomson, Albert Wm.	Corporal	Lance-Sergeant. Slightly wounded at Wilmansrust, 12.6.01
1472. Bain, Walter Albert	Private	Slightly wounded at Wilmansrust, 12.6.01
1473. Phillips, Richard	Shoeing-Smith	
1474. Honeybone, Frederick George	Sergeant	
1475. White, James Edwin	Private	Killed in action at Middle Kraal, 29.5.01
1476. Kemp, Francis Hubert	,,	Wounded at Klippan, 31.5.01
1477. Gay, Richard Horace	,,	Wounded at Klippan, 31.5.01. Invalided, Australia, arr. 3.10.01
1478. Noye, Martin Herbert	Corporal	Sergeant

C.4720.   U

Nominal Roll—*continued*.

No. and Name.	Rank.	Remarks.

N.C.O.'s AND MEN—*continued*.

No. and Name.	Rank.	Remarks.
1479. Sheppard, George Herbert	Corporal	Farrier-Sergeant
1480. Marshall, Wm. John	Private	Slightly wounded at Wilmansrust, 12.6.01
1481. Rowe, Ernest James	,,	Killed in action at Wilmansrust, 12.6.01
1482. O'Donoghue, John	,,	
1483. Bulluss, Walter Herbert	,,	
1484. Olsen, Francis Errick	,,	
1485. Houlihan, John Francis	Farrier-Sergeant	Killed in action at Wilmansrust, 12.6.01
1486. Potter, Charles	Private	
1487. Rayner, Herbert William Leslie	Corporal	Sergeant
1488. Mitchell, Benjamin Francis	Private	Lance-Corporal. Dangerously wounded at Wilmansrust, 12.6.01
1489. Soultry, William	,,	Died of enteric at Charlestown, 11.1.02
1490. Bartlett, Frederick William	,,	
1491. Birch, Ormond Winstanley	Sergeant	
1492. Hellens, Richard	Private	Invalided, Australia, arr. 30.7.01
1493. Hellens, Alexander	,,	
1494. Bott, John William	,,	
1495. Thorne, Charles Edward	,,	
1496. Bloom, William	,,	
1497. Lamard, Ernest George	,,	
1498. Stainsby, Leslie Robert	,,	Lance-Corporal
1499. Murray, Cecil Bertie	Saddler	Invalided, Australia, arr. 29.1.02
1500. Hutchison, Oswald Nelson	Private	
1501. Smith, Charles Francis	,,	Slightly wounded at Wilmansrust, 12.6.01; leg since amputated
1502. Riley, Marshall	,,	
1503. Riley, William Charles	,,	
1504. Duggan, John	,,	Accident to foot, Vryheid, 7.11.01
1505. Nugent, John Joseph	,,	Invalided, Australia, arr. 29.1.02
1506. Spears, William Henry	,,	
1507. Pedler, William Gage	Saddler	Invalided, Australia, arr. 6.1.02
1508. Taylor, Andrew	,,	
1509. Barbor, Richard Dawson	,,	Invalided, Australia, arr. 12.7.01,
1510. Carey, James	,,	Dangerously ill at Charlestown, 30.1.0.1
1511. Chapman, John	Sergeant	Invalided, Australia, arr. 29.3.02 Awarded pension
1512. Gardner, William	Private	Invalided, Australia, arr. 3.10.01
1513. Chrimes, Henry	,,	
1514. Drysdale, Robert Alexander	,,	
1515. Keen, William	,,	
1516. Craven, William Henry	,,	Lance-Corporal
1517. Hogan, James Samuel	,,	
1518. Dwyer, Ernest Patrick	,,	
1519. McClaren, Robinson Abram	Farrier	
1520. Wilcock, Thomas	Private	
1521. Melans, Bernard	,,	
1522. Nolan, William	,,	
1523. Carroll, James William	Corporal	Sergeant
1524. Shaw, John	Private	
1525. Bud, Frederick James	,,	
1526. Trigger, Francis Henry	,,	

Nominal Roll—*continued*.

No. and Name.	Rank.	Remarks.

N.C.O.'s AND MEN—*continued*.

No. and Name.	Rank.	Remarks.
1527. Scott, Walter Frost	Private	
1528. Hughes, Michael	,,	
1529. Messeroy, Ralph Norman	,,	
1530. Newman, Abel Ernest	,,	
1531. Down, George	,,	
1532. Blyth, John	,,	
1533. Mills, Arthur Lewis	,,	Dangerously ill at Wakkerstroom, 23.2.02
1534. Southern, Arthur	,,	
1535. Willett, Stephen	,,	
1536. Simpson, Henry	Farrier	
1537. Handley, William Thomas	Private	Corporal
1538. Spence, George Watson	,,	
1539. Pleydell, Stephen Richardson	Shoeing-Smith	
1540. Lightfoot, Thomas Austin	,,	
1541. Fyans, Harold Richard Napier	,,	
1542. Purse, Hugh Landler	,,	Corporal
1543. Bunting, George E. Ernest	,,	
1544. Ramsay, Samuel John	,,	Corporal
1545. Good, Herbert	,,	
1546. McMahon, William Joseph	,,	
1547. McLean, Archibald Hardy	,,	
1548. Conway, John	,,	
1549. Walton, Joseph	,,	
1550. Smith, William Alexander	,,	Killed in action at Wilmansrust, 12.6.01
1551. Hutton, William Liddordale	Corporal	Sergeant
1552. Dargie, Percy	Private	
1553. McCallum, Thomas	,,	Severely wounded at Vryheid, 5.11.01; reported dangerously ill there, 7.11.01. Invalided, Australia, arr. 29.11.02
1554. Stafford, Ernest	,,	
1555. Abbott, Herbert James	Saddler	
1556. Moule, Gordon Osborne	Private	
1557. Macdonald, William Hector	,,	Reported dangerously ill at Charlestown, 4.1.02; also at Newcastle, 11.1.02
1558. Lewis, Henry James	,,	
1559. Bourke, Frank	,,	
1560. Bond, Louis	,,	Killed in action at Wilmansrust, 12.6.01
1561. Bond, William Henry	,,	Invalided, Australia, arr. 29.1.02
1562. McBride, George	,,	
1563. Flannery, Michael Vincent	,,	
1564. Preston, Richard	,,	
1565. Cullen, William	,,	
1566. Schoman, Herman	,,	
1567. Herbert, William Barker	Coy. Sergeant-Major	Reported dangerously ill at Middelburg, 2.7.01
1568. Hall, Frank Leslie	Private	Corporal
1569. Burrows, Thomas Ross	Corporal	
1570. Harrison, Robert Glenn	Private	Killed in action at Vryheid, 5.11.01
1571. Ritchards, John Vernon	,,	
1572. Grimes, William	,,	**Slightly wounded at Wilmansrust, 12.6.01**

Nominal Roll—continued.

No. and Name.	Rank.	Remarks.

N.C.O.'s AND MEN—continued.

No. and Name.	Rank.	Remarks.
1573. Grimes, Herbert	Private	Severely wounded at Wilmansrust, 12.6.01; reported dangerously ill at Middelburg, 19.6.01. Returned to Victoria, 26.11.01
1574. Jencke, Ernest Otto	,,	Slightly wounded as above
1575. Allan, Percy James	,,	
1576. Caughey, F. H.	,,	Killed in action at Vryheid, 5.11.01
1577. Hardiman, Timothy Patrick	,,	
1578. Wallace, Charles William	Farrier	Farrier-Sergeant. Wounded at H'lobane, 27.8.01
1579. Clarke, David Joseph	Private	Corporal
1580. Corrigan, Robert William	,,	Slightly wounded at Wilmansrust, 12.6.01
1581. Corrigan, John	,,	
1582. Valpied, E. A.	,,	Died of enteric at Pretoria, 18.8.01
1583. Fitzgibbon, Maurice Dawson	,,	
1584. De Tracy, George Samuel	Corporal	
1585. Samuels, Otto Felix	Private	Invalided, Australia, arr. 6.1.02
1586. Newell, Albert Henry	Sergeant	Coy. Sergeant-Major
1587. Carey, Andrew	Private	
1588. George, Thomas Moore	,,	Dangerously wounded at Wilmansrust, 12.6.01. Invalided, Australia, arr. 3.10.01
1589. McKerlie, James	,,	
1590. Watson, Robert Alfred	,,	Died of enteric at Middelburg, 6.12.01 (previously wounded at Wilmansrust)
1591. Duell, David	,,	Dangerously ill at Utrecht, 22.10.01 (fractured leg)
1592. Spark, Austin Jeremiah	,,	
1593. Smart, Nathaniel Augustus	,,	
1594. Dent, Robert	Corporal	Sergeant. Slightly wounded at Vryheid, 5.11.01
1595. Timewell, George Thomas	Private	
1596. Chambers, Francis Joseph	,,	
1597. Rogers, George Morton	,,	Lance-Corporal
1598. Thompson, Robert	,,	
1599. Dawson, Frederick	,,	Lance-Corporal
1600. Murphy, William David	,,	
1601. Wilson, Charles	,,	Dangerously wounded at Wilmansrust, 12.6.01. Invalided, Australia, arr. 3.1.02
1602. Thornton, Rupert Melbourne	,,	Killed in action at Wilmansrust, 12.6.01
1603. Fischer, Henry M. Matheison	,,	
1604. Chandler, Percival Samuel	,,	Invalided, Australia, arr. 25.3.02
1605. McPherson, Archibald Robert	,,	Slightly wounded at Wilmansrust, 12.6.01
1606. Weiss, Llewellyn	,,	Corporal
1607. White, Albert Thomas	,,	Slightly wounded at Wilmansrust, 12.6.01
1608. Driver, James Henry	,,	Invalided, Australia, arr. 13.12.01
1609. Sprigg, James	,,	Lance-Corporal. Slightly wounded at Wilmansrust, 12.6.01
1610. Mack, Archibald Edward	,,	Died of wounds at Wilmansrust, 12.6.01
1611. Edge, John William Davis	,,	Lance-Corporal

Nominal Roll—*continued.*

No. and Name.	Rank.	Remarks.
N.C.O.'s and Men—continued.		
1612. Kemmis, William Albert	Private	
1613. Dodson, Frank	,,	
1614. Games, Robert Somerton	,,	
1615. Matheson, John Cameron	,,	Severely wounded at Travanspoort, 20.8.01. Invalided, Australia, arr. 7.12.01
1616. Baxter, Ernest George Nelson	,,	
1617. Slater, Walter	,,	
1618. Amor, Albert George	,,	
1619. Sheppard, J. J.	,,	
1620. Sloper, Seymour	Saddler	
1621. Stark, Atholstan	Private	Invalided, Australia, arr. 29.1.02
1622. Hassett, John	,,	Slightly wounded at Wilmansrust, 12.6.01
1623. Nunan, Matthew	,,	
1624. Biscaya, John	Farrier	Farrier-Sergeant
1625. McNamara, Joseph	Saddler	Slightly wounded at Wilmansrust,, 12.6.01. Invalided, Australia, arr. 3.11.01
1626. Murray, George William	,,	Saddler-Sergeant
1627. Bandewig, Michael Joseph Jacob	,,	
1628. Reddoch, Robert Boyle	Private	Severely wounded at Wilmansrust, 12.6.01. Invalided, Australia, arr. 3.11.01
1629. Ross, Arthur William	Corporal	
1630. Ashley, Aubrey Frederick	Private	Slightly wounded at Wilmansrust, 12.6.01. Awarded pension
1631. Fanning, John	,,	Dangerously wounded at Wilmansrust, 12.6.01. Awarded pension
1362. Engelke, Henry	,,	
1633. Gray, Matthew	Corporal	Sergeant. Invalided, Australia, arr. 30.7.01
1634. Rankin, James	Shoeing-Smith	Died from wounds at Wakkerstroom, 28.11.01
1635. Duncan, George	Private	
1636. Miles, James	,,	
1637. Foster, Ernest Alfred	,,	
1638. Johnson, Farmer	,,	
1639. Jones, Hedley	Corporal	Sergeant
1640. Goodwin, George Craig	Corporal	
1641. Bregenza, Ernest Raymond	Private	
1642. Curnow, John Treloar	Sergeant	
1643. Crapper, Charles	Private	
1644. Dow, Robert Alexander	,,	Fractured arm accidentally, Grootfontein, 25.1.02
1645. Nuttall, Isaac	,,	
1646. Munro, Alexander	,,	
1647. Noonan, John James	,,	
1648. Johnson, David Allan	,,	Invalided, Australia, arr. 29.1.02
1649. Johnson, Edmund Sheldrick	,,	Corporal. Slightly wounded, H'lobane, 27.3.01
1650. Reetman, Ernest	Shoeing-Smith	
1651. Thomas, James Faulkner	Saddler	Saddler-Sergeant
1652. Walsh, Joseph	Private	
1653. Newton, Alfred John	,,	Severely wounded at Wilmansrust, 12.6.01

Nominal Roll—*continued*.

No. and Name.	Rank.	Remarks.
N.C.O.'s AND MEN—*continued*.		
1654. Tomkins, Henry Holton	Saddler	
1655. Jolliffe, Albert Ernest	,,	
1656. Wilson, Arthur Reginald	Private	
1657. Hickey, Timothy	,,	
1658. Robertson, Ernest	,,	
1659. Brownhill, Joseph Henry	,,	
1660. Giles, Nathaniel Oliver	,,	Slightly wounded at Wilmansrust, 12.6.01 ; also accidentally dangerously wounded at Nguter 2.10.01. Invalided Australia, arr. 29.1.02
1661. Naylor, Richard Rooke	,,	Lance-Corporal
1662. Newham, William Herbert	,,	
1663. Wilson, Peter	,,	Invalided, Australia, arr. 30.7.01
1664. Hinton, William John	,,	
1665. Wright, John Christopher	Saddler	Saddler-Sergeant
1666. Thompson, Daniel	,,	
1667. McCaskill, H.	,,	
1668. Kirby, James J.	,,	Saddler-Sergeant
1669. Timbury, Cyril Douglas	Private	
1670. Carr, Arthur	,,	
1671. Jenkins, Fred	,,	Dangerously ill at Charlestown, 23.2.02, and 9.3.02
1672. Baillie, James	,,	
1673. Dibbs, Thomas	,,	
1674. Healey, Edward	,,	
1675. Cockran, Arthur	,,	Invalided, Australia, arr. 11.12.01
1676. Anderson, James Percy	,,	
1677. Coward, William	,,	
1678. Leith, Robert William	,,	
1679. Lynch, Michael James	,,	
1680. Croy, William Davis	,,	Reported dangerously ill at Middelburg, 6.5.01
1681. Manuell, James	,,	
1682. Godby, John Heitland	Corporal	Coy. Quartermaster-Sergeant
1683. Miller, Albert	Private	
1684. Cook, Harold Victor	Saddler	Severely wounded at Scheuveberg Hoek, 23.8.01. Invalided, Australia, arr. 29.1.02. Awarded pension
1685. Jewell, George	,,	Slightly wounded at Wilmansrust, 12.6.01
1686. Cattanach, Harry	Private	Corporal
1687. McClymont, John Joseph	,,	
1688. Smith, John Hartley	,,	
1689. Briggs, William George	,,	
1690. Capper, Frederick Hanison	Saddler	Dangerously ill at Charlestown, 9.12.01
1691. Button, George Rowland	Private	Lance-Corporal Killed in action at Wilmansrust, 12.6.01
1692. Gallagher, James	,,	Invalided, Australia, arr. 29.1.02
1693. Cross, Frederick William Burney	,,	
1694. Stewart, Charles John	,,	Invalided, Australia, arr. 29.1.02
1695. Turner, Richard Marsden	,,	Lance-Corporal. Reported dangerously ill at Charlestown, 12.1.02

Nominal Roll—*continued*.

No. and Name.	Rank.	Remarks.
N.C.O.'s AND MEN—continued.		
*38. Sanders, J.	Private	
151. Trotman, L. J.	,,	
197. Waugh, R. W.	Sergeant	
391. Doulton, E.	Private	
480. Fenton, H. L.	Corporal	
593. Barton, H.	Sergeant	Slightly wounded at H'lobane, 27.8.01
785. Carey, P. T.	,,	
791. M'Phee, A.	Private	
844. Bennett, G. A.	Lance-Corporal	
1143. Mackley, W.	Private	
1696. Jordon, D.	,,	
1697. White, D. C.	Sergeant	Wounded at Wilmansrust, 12.6.01.
1700. Buckingham, A. G. K.	,,	Killed in action at Rhenoster Kop, 23.7.01
1844. Ramsay, S.	Private	
1876. Wallacan, C. N.	,,	Slightly wounded at H'lobane, 27.8.01 ; severe accident, Grootvlei, 16.12.01

* Numbers from this were enlisted in South Africa. In this respect, however, the returns are incomplete.

RECRUITS FOR SCOTTISH HORSE.

IN addition to the Contingents, authority was given for enrolment of 250 men for the Marquis of Tullibardine's Scottish Horse, in South Africa.

These men were selected by the acting Assistant Adjutant-General, Victoria, and handed over to Lieut.-Colonel Creagh, who acted for the Marquis of Tullibardine.

A large portion of those chosen were men who had passed all tests for the 5th Victorian Contingent, but who were thrown out in the ballot.

This Contingent proceeded to South Africa in the *Orient* as indulgence passengers, 15th February, 1901. They were noted by the Officer Commanding troops as amongst the very best on board. On arrival they were all accepted for the 2nd Battalion, and they gave a good account of themselves during their service. Many of them were in the heroic defence of the guns at Brakenlaagte, 30th October, 1901, of which Lord Tullibardine in his despatch, wrote :—" The next fight was a big one at Brakenlaagte, where Colonel Benson and Major Murray were both killed. The men did magnificently, trying to save the guns ; only 96 were engaged at this point, and they stuck it out until only 6 were left unhit. Their casualties were—5 officers, 28 men killed ; 4 officers, 36 men wounded ; total, 73 out of 96—all the officers being hit. I don't think I ever heard of better or more determined fighting. Although we lost the guns, the camp was saved by the delay, and the men really did cover themselves with glory." The officers killed were—Major F. D. Murray, Captains M. W. H. Lindsay, A. Inglis, Lieutenants C. Woodman, J. B. Kelly. Wounded—Captain A. C. Murray, Lieutenants W. Campbell, T. Finis, A. C. Wardrop. Captain Murray, though wounded, was the on'y senior officer available to take temporary charge of the residue of the party. He was subsequently elected to proceed to England in charge of the detail of Scottish Horse to attend the coronation of King Edward VII.

SPECIAL SERVICE OFFICERS.

FOR description of this species of service, *vide* New South Wales, under that heading, p. 195.

Major-General (then Colonel) Sir John Hoad, K.C.M.G.
Vide 1st Victorian Contingent.

Lieut.-Colonel C. E. Umphelby.

Lieut.-Colonel Umphelby, Royal Australian Artillery, proceeded to South Africa by the transport *Aberdeen*, on 8th November, 1899, and arrived at Cape Town early in December. He was, in the first instance, employed as Press Censor at the base; a post for which his acquirements as a linguist especially fitted him. It was his desire, however, to go to the front, with a view of gaining experience with field artillery on active service. He therefore applied to be so employed, and was appointed Staff Officer to Colonel Barker, who commanded the howitzer battery at Modder River.

Shortly after Lord Roberts' advance from the west through the Free State, Colonel Barker obtained the command of the 76th, 81st, and 82nd Batteries, Royal Field Artillery; and on the 28th February, Colonel Umphelby started from the Modder River to join him at the camp about 5 miles from Paardeburg. The army moved from thence on 9th March. The division in which Umphelby served was under General Kelly-Kenny; and, during the earlier part of Roberts' advance was the southern force. As such it fought at Osfontein on the day of the advance. The Boers fell back and were followed about 5 miles further by the troops, which halted at Driefontein, 36 miles west of Bloemfontein. At daylight on the following morning, 10th March, Kelly-Kenny's division, becoming the centre one, advanced against the Boer position, a long low ridge running across the front, which they occupied in force. The guns of Barker's brigade came into action at about 3,000 yards. After fighting obstinately all day, the Boers retired little by little; and the guns, as they followed, gradually reduced the range to about 2,000 yards. About 5.30 p.m., and near sunset, the artillery dashed forward again, and came under a smart rifle fire at a range of less than 1,000 yards, it having been supposed, apparently, that the enemy had fallen back further than they actually did. The Boers were posted on a ridge commanding the hollow within which the guns re-opened; and they commenced a brisk fusillade, raining bullets upon the batteries.

Colonel Umphelby had been employed all day on staff duty, carrying orders and helping to direct the movements of the three batteries. He was now seated upon an ant-hill, examining the enemy's position through his glasses, and having his horses' reins slung over his left arm. In this position he was struck by one of the last shots fired; the bullet passing through his body diagonally from the right front to the left side in rear, and perforating the liver.

First aid was administered, and he was taken to the field hospital, about 1½ miles away. He lingered during the subsequent day; but, owing to the removal of the field hospital, it became necessary to convey him on a wagon to a farm house, where quarters had been found for him, about ¾ mile distant. He arrived in a very exhausted condition; and though he received some medical attendance, he died about 1.30 a.m. on the following morning.

Major (now Lieut.-Colonel) G. J. Johnston.

Major Johnston proceeded to South Africa on the 8th November, 1899, by the transport *Aberdeen*, in company with the late Lieutenant-Colonel Umphelby, Major Bruche, and the New South Wales "A" Squadron Mounted Rifles. On arrival at Cape Town he was engaged for a few days as a Railway Staff Officer, and then attached to 62nd Battery Royal Field Artillery, and joined them at Modder River. He did regimental duty with this battery as a section commander, and was with them on many reconnaissances, several side expeditions, and the great trek, during which several engagements were fought, including Klip Drift, Paardeburg, Osfontein, and many others, before reaching Bloemfontein.

He proceeded with the 62nd battery to Karee; and, after that engagement, was left in Bloemfontein with a section without horses. After getting remounts, he rejoined the battery, and then received a telegram from Colonel (afterwards Major-General) Hoad, inviting him to accept the command of an Australian squadron. Major Johnston met Colonel Hoad in Bloemfontein; but finding that his (Major Johnston's) services were not necessary with the Australians, he rejoined the Royal Field Artillery, and was attached to a howitzer brigade. He took part in several expeditions round about Bloemfontein, and did duty with the Corps Artillery until he was sent into hospital and invalided. He was granted three months' leave of absence, placed in charge of about 150 invalided Australians and New Zealanders, and proceeded with them to Hobart, by the s.s. *Karamea*. There he left them and returned to Melbourne, viâ Launceston, arriving on the 29th July, 1900.

He was afterwards promoted Lieut.-Colonel and appointed to the command of the 4th Australian Commonwealth Horse (which see). Queen's Medal with three clasps.

Captain (now Major) J. H. Bruche.

Left Melbourne per s.s. *Aberdeen* on 8th November, 1899; landed at Cape Town 6th December. Attached to 3rd Battalion Grenadier Guards at Modder River from 8th December, 1899, to 10th January, 1900.

Attached to "The Australian Regiment" from 11th January to 6th April, acting as Quartermaster. Attached to Victorian Mounted Rifles, 7th April. Adjutant Victorian Mounted Rifles, 1st May to 12th December, 1900. Returned to Australia by s.s. *Harlech Castle*, leaving Cape Town in October, 1900, arriving at Melbourne 4th December, 1900.

Present at operations in Cape Colony, advance on Kimberley, action at Magersfontein. Orange River Colony, including actions at Houtnek, Vet River, and Zand River. Transvaal, including actions at Johannesberg, Pretoria, Diamond Hill, and Belfast. Transvaal, 12th March, to 31st May, 1902.

Major Bruche commanded "A" Squadron in 2nd Battalion Australian Commonwealth Horse. *Vide* that Contingent. Appointed to command Thornycroft's depot at Klerksdorp, 1st April to 28th May. Returned to Australia with 2nd Battalion Australian Commonwealth Horse in s.s. *Norfolk*, leaving Durban 8th July, arriving Melbourne, 2nd August, 1902.

Queen's Medal with six clasps.

Major A. J. Christie.

Lieutenant A. J. Christie proceeded to South Africa with the 2nd Contingent, on 13th January, 1900, by the transport *Euryalus*, which arrived at Cape Town on 5th February. Attached for special service to the Army Service Corps. Was present at operations in Cape Colony, Orange Free State, and Transvaal. Actions at Paardeburg (severely wounded), Jacobsdal, Poplar Grove, Driefontein, and Karee Siding. Commanded "P" Transport Company in operations in East Transvaal, Orange River Colony, and Cape Colony, from March, 1901, to May, 1902. Slightly wounded at Spreeuwfontein and Kamiesberg. Promoted captain, 9th March, 1901. Despatches, *London Gazette*, 29th July, 1902. Queen's Medal with five clasps. King's Medal with two clasps

THE SECOND BATTALION AUSTRALIAN COMMONWEALTH HORSE.—VICTORIAN UNITS.

THIS Battalion was raised after Federation, to represent Australian troops, upon the same principles as the first battalion. It consisted of three Victorian units (or companies), one from South Australia, and one (half-company) from Western Australia, together with the battalion staff.

Preference was given to men who had had experience in the war, but candidates were also eligible who were acquainted with country life in Australia, also the management of horses, and were good shots. As a matter of fact, almost the whole of the staff, the company officers, and the N.C.O.'s and men had served in previous Contingents. Some had belonged to South African regiments. Married men were not selected except for N.C.O.'s of exceptional merit.

CLOTHING, ETC.

Uniform consisted of F.S. jacket, pants, puttees, F.S. hat, F.S. cap, greatcoat, together with boots and a full kit of underclothing, necessaries, &c.

Equipped with rifles and bayonets, and bandolier belts; fully horsed and provided with saddlery. *Vide* Appendix II.

Regimental transport was also provided.

PAY.

Up to date of embarkation, this was at Imperial cavalry rates. After embarkation as follows:—

Colonel or lieut.-colonel, £1 5s. per diem, with 4s. field allowance; major, £1 3s., and 4s.; captain, £1 1s., and 3s.; lieutenant, 15s., and 2s. 6d.; adjutant, as for captain or lieutenant, according to rank; quartermaster, as for captain; paymaster, if captain, same; medical officer, £1, and 3s.; veterinary officer, £1, and 3s.; chaplain, £1 1s., and 3s.; regimental sergeant-major, 9s.; quartermaster-sergeant, 8s. 6d.; farrier-sergeant, 8s. 6d.; farrier staff-sergeant, 8s. 6d.; company sergeant-major, 8s; company quartermaster-sergeant, 8s; sergeants, 7s.; corporals (if paid lance-sergeants), 6s. 6d.; corporals and paid lance-corporals, 6s.; buglers, 6s.; privates, 5s. N.C. officers not above the rank of sergeant, acting as farrier-sergeant, or farrier staff-sergeant, and privates, acting as buglers, saddlers, or shoeing-smiths, 1s. per diem extra.

Officers were allowed £30 to provide equipment, &c.

ESTABLISHMENT.

Detail of a company:—1 major or captain, 4 lieutenants, 1 company sergeant-major, 1 company quartermaster-sergeant, 1 farrier-sergeant, 4 sergeants, 3 shoeing-smiths, 1 saddler, 2 buglers, 6 corporals, 97 privates; total, 5 officers, 6 staff-sergeants and sergeants, 5 artificers, 2 buglers, 103 rank and file; total, 121, with the like number of horses.

Add battalion staff—5 officers, 3 staff-sergeants, with 8 horses. Total of staff and three companies—20 officers, 21 staff-sergeants and sergeants, 15 artificers, 6 buglers, 309 rank and file; in all, 371, with 401 horses, including 30 spare.

A chaplain accompanied the battalion.

DEPARTURE AND RETURN.

The staff and Victorian units left 12th Feburary, 1902, comprising—21 officers, 351 others, with 401 horses. One died, 2 officers, 77 others were struck off in South Africa; 19 officers, 273 others returned.

SERVICE.

The staff and three Victorian companies embarked on 12th February, 1902, on the transport *St. Andrew*, and arrived at Durban on 10th March. On the following day they entrained for Newcastle, arriving on the 13th; and on the 18th they were joined by the South Australian and Western Australian units, "D" and "E." On the 22nd, the battalion was inspected by General Lyttelton, General Officer Commanding, Natal; and General Burn-Murdoch, Officer Commanding Newcastle sub-district, visited the camp and inspected the horses. On the 6th April, the battalion started for Klerksdorp, and arrived on the 10th. There they were brigaded under Lieut.-Colonel De Lisle, who commanded portion of Colonel Thorneycroft's force. The 1st Battalion Australian Commonwealth Horse also was under Colonel De Lisle, his brigade being styled "De Lisle's Australian Brigade," altered afterwards to "De Lisle's Column," as Thorneycroft's Mounted Infantry, and two guns R.F.A. and a pom-pom were added. Colonel Thorneycroft had likewise the New Zealand Brigade with which were the New South Wales Bushmen, and Hasler's Scouts, a South African corps.

On the 22nd, Lord Kitchener inspected the battalion and expressed his satisfaction. The whole of the troops were under General Sir Ian Hamilton. On the 23rd April, a general move took place. The trek passed through Paardeplatts, Hartebeestfontein, Palmfontein, and Boschepoort.

On 7th May, a "drive" was commenced, starting from Noitverwacht, to the Hartz River. The 2nd Commonwealth Horse occupied about 1½ miles of the driving line, distributed thus:—"C" squadron, under Captain Kirby, on the right, Captain De Passey's "D" squadron and one pom-pom in the centre; "A" squadron; under Lieutenant Day, in rear of centre in reserve; Captain Pendlebury's "B" squadron on the left. When the line halted for the night, the various portions camped where they halted; squadron wagons and watercarts being sent to them from regimental transport.

The advance was through Joubert's Rust (8th) and Rapoli, Boesman's Pan (9th), and Bodenstein, Wonderfontein, and Kaal Platts (10th), on which date the line taken up was on the border of British Bechuanaland and the Transvaal.

Considerable numbers of Boers were seen in front of the driving line; but no fighting took place. On the night of the 10th, they made a determined attempt to break through, but without success. On the 11th, Bazendekout's commando announced their surrender by a flag of truce; and Captain Roberts, Adjutant of the 2nd, was sent to bring them in. There were 191 prisoners, and over 200 horses. Shortly afterwards 52 others surrendered to Captain Kirby.

The drive terminated about 3 p.m. on the 11th, arriving at the railway line Kimberley to Mafeking, Vryburg being near the centre of the line. After examining the ground thoroughly, the battalion rejoined the main body, encamped at Leeuwspruit, about 4 miles from Devondale Siding.

On the 12th, Colonel De Lisle said farewell, as he was going to England on sick leave; and Lieutenant-Colonel Williams took over the brigade. The general result of operations, as officially announced, was:—Killed, 1; prisoners, 326; mules, 95; donkeys, 20; wagons, 175; Cape carts, 61; sheep, 300; small arm ammunition, 6,340 rounds; oxen, 106. Amongst the prisoners was Jan De La Rey, brother of the general. Lord Kitchener telegraphed to General Hamilton: "Capital result. Tell troops I highly appreciate their exertions and consider result very satisfactory." This, it was explained, was to be considered a high compliment, as the G.O. Commanding-in-Chief was not in the habit of bestowing indiscriminate praise,

The Contingent returned to Klerksdorp, arriving on 21st May, and remained there after peace was concluded, until 20th June, when they marched to Elandsfontein, arriving on 25th. There the horses, equipment, saddlery, rifles, &c., and all transport were handed over. On 29th, entrained for Newcastle, arriving next day.

On 5th July, entrained for Durban, and on the 6th, the battalion embarked on the transport *Norfolk*. Left on the 8th; arrived at Albany on the 25th, Adelaide on the 30th, and Melbourne on 2nd August. Paid off and discharged the same day.

WAR SERVICES.

For war services of officers, *vide* 1st, 2nd, 3rd, 4th, and 5th Contingents, also under "Remarks" column of nominal roll. Lieutenant Day served previously in Brabant's Horse (South African corps), Lieutenant Lockett in 2nd Western Australian contingent, Lieutenant Holmes in South African Light Horse, and Captain-Adjutant Roberts in 4th South Australian Contingent. The three officers who had not served before were awarded Queen's Medal with two clasps.

Nominal Roll.

No. and Name.	Rank.	Remarks.
BATTALION STAFF.		
McLeish, Duncan, C.M.G.	Lieut.-Colonel	Commanded 1st Victorian Mounted Infantry (1st Victorian Contingent)
Tivey, Edwin, D.S.O.	Major (2nd in command)	Served in 4th Victorian Contingent
Barnard, James Fox	Lieut. (Medical Staff)	
Roberts, Ernest Alfred	Lieutenant and Adjutant	Promoted Captain, 26.1.02. Previously 4th South Australian Contingent
Loel, Bertram Benjamin	Veterinary-Lieutenant	
McInerney, Rev. John, S.J.	Chaplain	
751. Richardson, James	Regimental Sergt. Major	
592. Kidgell, James Ernest	Regtl. Quartermaster-Sergeant	
406. Seymour, Edwin Sutherland	Staff - Sergeant, O.R. Clerk	
COMPANY OFFICERS.		
Bruche, Julius Henry	Captain	Previously Special Service Officer
Pendlebury, Henry William	,,	Served in 1st Victorian Contingent
Kirby, Mark Thomas	,,	Served in 2nd Victorian Contingent
Day, Albert Thomas	Lieutenant	Served in 1st Brabant's Horse
Garland, Richard Reginald	,,	Served in 5th Victorian Contingent
Bell, Harry Henderson	,,	Served in 2nd and 5th Victorian Contingents, also 2nd Scottish Horse
Lockett, Harry	,,	Served in 2nd Western Australian Contingent and 2nd Scottish Horse
Germaine, Thomas Hyland	,,	Served in 4th Victorian Contingent

Nominal Roll—continued.

No. and Name.	Rank.	Remarks.
COMPANY OFFICERS—continued.		
Holmes, Francis Joseph	Lieutenant	Served in South African Light Horse
Cahill, Thomas Stewart	,,	Served in 2nd Victorian Contingent
Press, Alfred Howard	,,	Served in 4th Victorian Contingent
Sandford, David	,,	Served in 4th Victorian Contingent
Bidstrup, Charles Neils	,,	Served in 1st Victorian Contingent
Powell, James	,,	Served in 4th Victorian Contingent
Thomson, Walter Henderson	,,	Served in 3rd Victorian Contingent
N.C.O.'s AND MEN.		
401. Shaw, Harold	Private	
402. Tweedie, James	Corporal	
403. Tweedie, John Anderson	Private	
404. Speers, Charles Wm.	Sergeant	
405. Smyth, Francis Sydney	Private	
407. Selby, Percy	,,	
408. Robinson, William Joseph	,,	
409. Rouse, Charles Wm.	,,	
410. Heron, George	,,	
411. McCoy, William John	,,	
412. McPherson, William	Lance-Corporal	
413. Merchant, William	Private	
414. Miles, Percival Benjamin	Saddler	
415. Lee, Maurice	Private	
416. Cook, William James	,,	
417. Hilbrick, Walter Herbert	,,	
418. Hooley, Albert	,,	
419. Cantwell, Timothy John	,,	
420. Giles, Frederick John	,,	
421. Briggs, Charles	,,	
422. Ford, Herbert	,,	
423. Fitzpatrick, Edward	,,	
424. Dalton, Robert James	,,	
425. Ditchburn, Ernest Norman Vere	,,	
426. Daley, Daniel Henry	,,	
427. Chiron, Victor	,,	
428. Corlett, Cæsar Stephen	Lance-Corporal	
429. Baldwin, Thomas	Private	
430. Bradford, David James	Saddler	
431. Bellmer, George	Private	
432. Buchanan, Angus McLeod	,,	
433. Blair, Henry	,,	
434. King, Walter Litchfield	,,	
435. Treadrea, Henry	,,	
436. Pattinson, David Simpson	,,	
437. Walker, Alexander	Sergeant	
438. Madden, Thomas George	Private	
439. McCallum, John Campbell	,,	
440. Tomlinson, William	,,	
441. Stacey, Alfred John	Sergeant	
442. Byron, William Archer	Private	
443. Strahan, Simon William	,,	
444. Rogers, Llewellyn Edward	,,	
445. Loder, Joseph	,,	
446. Rofe, Albert Frederick	,,	

Nominal Roll—*continued.*

No. and Name.	Rank.	Remarks.
N.C.O.'s AND MEN—*continued.*		
447. Irvine, Gilbert Arthur	Private	
448. Quirk, John Michael	,,	
449. Herbert, Henry	,,	
450. Harris, Thomas William	,,	Died at South Melbourne, 15.10.02
451. Hawker, Mark	Farrier-Sergeant	
452. Geddes, Thomas	Private	
453. Fitzpatrick, John	,,	
454. Fox, James Peter	Corporal	
455. Fishlock, John	Private	
456. Carey David John	Farrier-Sergeant	
457. Asker, William	Private	
458. Anderson, Andrew Frederick	,,	
459. Baird, William	,,	
460. Cooke, Herbert James	Lance-Corporal	
461. Cochran, Frank Eardley	Private	
462. Browne, Walter James	,,	
463. Perry, Jacob	Coy. Quartermaster-Sergeant	
464. Steele, Thomas Alexander	Private	
465. Sanson, Albert Henry	,,	
466. Mulcahy, Joseph Ignatius	Corporal	
467. Webb, William Henry	Private	
468. Lamb, Frederick Thomas	,,	
469. Weibye, Thomas William	Corporal	
470. Fairlie, Archibald Douglas	Shoeing-Smith	
471. Woodland, Sydney	Coy. Quartermaster-Sergeant	
472. Williams, Francis James	Private	
473. Rees, Charles	,,	
474. Rogers, Frank	,,	
475. Jenner, Thomas	Corporal	
476. South, Alfred	Private	
477. Smith, Thomas Ignatius	Lance-Corporal	
478. Gardiner, Arthur Joseph	Private	
479. Clarke, Reginald Valentine	Bugler	
480. Adams, Phipps Alexander	Private	
481. Wallis, William Henry	,,	
482. Murphy, Herbert Richard	,,	
483. Anderson, David	,,	
484. Parrott, Stanley Hamilton	Lance-Corporal	
485. Hughes, James Lawrence	Private	
486. Bertrand, Louis Henry	,,	
487. Skirving, Charles Reginald	Corporal	
488. Barker, Edward	Private	
489. Tubb, Frank Reid	Corporal	
490. Dureau, Francis Edward	Sergeant	
491. Carnie, Robert	Private	
492. Carsons, Samuel Henry	,,	
493. Jefferyes, John	Bugler	
494. Allsopp, John	Lance-Corporal	
495. Love, Herbert	Coy. Quartermaster-Sergeant	
496. Ryan, James Joseph	Private	
497. Thomas, Arthur Edward	,,	
498. Scott, Geo. Robert	,,	
499. Lee, Hugh	,,	
500. Morrell, Wm. Ernest	,,	
501. Sussex, Joshua David	,,	

Nominal Roll—continued.

No. and Name.	Rank.	Remarks.
N.C.O.'s AND MEN—continued.		
502. Boyes, Reginald Cummins	Coy. Sergeant Major	
503. Stock, Alexander	Private	
504. Pearson, Joseph Kirkby	,,	
505. Feckner, Gustavus Henry	,,	
506. Rudd, William	,,	
507. Spooner, William	Coy. Sergeant Major	
508. Pilkington, James	Private	
509. Sheehan, William Thomas	Corporal	
510. Capp, Frederick	Private	
511. Condy, George	,,	
512. Meagher, Daniel	,,	
513. Ede, Harry	Sergeant	
514. Harley, Charles George	Private	
515. Brooks, John	Corporal	
516. Coustley, Frederick	Private	
517. Dixon, Ambrose	,,	
518. Quirk, Joseph Edward	,,	
519. McDonald, Alexander	,,	
520. Mathews, Frank Reginald	,,	
521. Griggs, James Wallace	,,	
522. Williamson, William	,,	
523. Williamson, George Sutherland	,,	
524. Waterston, John Walker	,,	
525. Ryan, Edwin Christie	Sergeant	
526. Summer, James Ziba	Private	
527. Uchtman, Frederick	,,	
528. Toy, Ralph Stephen	,,	
529. Tidyman, William	Sergeant	
530. Savage, Henry George	Coy. Sergeant-Major	
531. Pinder, Peter	Private	
532. Mallett, Thomas Gardiner	,,	
533. Quiney, Joseph Howells	Sergeant	
534. McCance, John	Private	
535. Curtiss, William	,,	
536. Quinn, Robert	,,	
537. O'Toole, William Edmond	,,	
538. Heywood, Frederick	,,	
539. Butt, Thomas Charles	,,	
540. Valpied, Henry John	,,	
541. McAlpin, Robert Stephen	Corporal	Lance-Sergeant
542. McClelland, James	Shoeing-Smith	
543. Munro, Claude Bland	Private	
544. Lurman, Ernest Gustive John	,,	
545. Moon, William James	,,	
546. Milne, Frederick Thomas	,,	
547. Jordan, Robert	,,	
548. Herschell, John William	Bugler	
549. Hammond, Charles Stewart	Private	
550. Bailey, George	,,	
551. Pedder, Robert James	,,	
552. Ellis, Frank Mortimer	,,	
553. Bowler, William Arthur	,,	
554. De Wardt, Thomas Ewen	,,	
555. Davies, John Hugh	,,	
556. Dalton, William James	,,	

Nominal Roll—*continued.*

No. and Name.	Rank.	Remarks.

N.C.O.'s AND MEN—*continued.*

No. and Name.	Rank.	Remarks.
557. Deegan, Leslie	Sergeant	
558. Crawford, Frederick	Private	
559. Bonnett, William	,,	
560. Bannister, Thomas	,,	
561. Howard, George	,,	
562. Absalom, Edward	,,	
563. Geddes, James	,,	
564. McLay, Henry Devine	Lance-Corporal	
565. Ve'All, George Fairfax	Sergeant	
566. Butcher, Albert John	Private	
567. Lyons, John	,,	
568. Paul, Andrew Cameron	,,	
569. Miller, Herman	,,	
570. Somerville, Samuel	,,	
571. Wright, George Mountford	,,	
572. Calk, George Edwin	,,	
573. Valpied, James Arthur	,,	
574. Dennis, George Edward	Shoeing-Smith	
575. Bourke, Abed Michael	Corporal	
576. Kelly, William Irvine	Private	
577. Martin, Henry	,,	
578. Cooper, Edward Garden	,,	
579. Moore, Arthur Thomas	,,	
580. Heaney, James	,,	
581. Hyland, Louis	Corporal	
582. Hughes, Arthur Walter Joseph	,,	
583. Poor, Robert Henry	Private	
584. Crooke, William	,,	
585. Gayer, Oswald Ventry	,,	
586. Sabelberg, Joseph Francis	,,	
587. Ryan, Michael Francis	Sergeant	
588. McDonald, Angus	Private	
589. Bell, William	,,	
590. Callaway, Edward Arthur	,,	
591. Jordan, John	Corporal	
593. Cochran, John	Private	
594. Cook, Charles Frederick Mills	,,	
595. Ryan, James Cue	,,	
596. Christensen, Charles	,,	
597. Sands, Frederick Owen	,,	
598. McGinty, Alfred James	,,	
599. Elligate, Edward Patrick	,,	
600. Harper, Sedgwick Percy	,,	
601. Grant, F. R.	,,	
602. Swayn, Robert	,,	
603. Carter, Herbert	,,	
604. Poulter, Francis Herbert	,,	
605. Beggs, Angus	,,	
606. Conway, James	,,	
607. Trapp, Henry	,,	
608. Roberts, William Aitkin	,,	
609. Mitchelmore, William Alfred	,,	
610. Gray, William Henry	,,	
611. McPherson, Duncan	Lance-Corporal	
612. Scott, Alfred	Private	
613. Burkitt, Harold Mortimer	,,	
614. Russell, William Benjamin	,,	

C. 4720.

Nominal Roll—*continued.*

No. and Name.	Rank.	Remarks.
N.C.O.'s AND MEN—*continued.*		
615. Stronge, St. Clair	Private	
616. Taylor, John Edwin	,,	
617. Tinker, Alfred John	Sergeant	
618. Slattery, James Joseph	Private	
619. Mahoney, Arthur	,,	
620. Woolcott, Arthur Francis	,,	
621. McGrouther, Robert	Lance-Corporal	
622. Campbell, Archibald Lachlan	Private	
623. Porter, Albert Thomas	,,	
624. Conway, Francis Bernhardt	,,	
625. Runnalls, John Trewin	,,	Promoted Lance-Corporal
626. Routley, Charles Thomas	,,	
627. Were, Eric Laurenny	,,	
628. Shaw, Archibald Samuel	,,	
629. Ralph, Roy Moore	,,	
630. Watts, James Joseph	,,	
631. Anderson, Clifford Harry	Lance-Corporal	
632. Hamilton, John Henry	,,	
633. Potton, Walter John	Private	
634. Turnley, Harold Eric	,,	
635. Jeffreys, Richard Broughton	,,	
636. Morrison, Henry Sproule	,,	
637. O'Linn, John Thomas Joseph	Shoeing-Smith	
638. Hanks, Samuel	Private	
639. Baptie, James	,,	
640. Clark, John	,,	
641. Bruce, George Richmond	Corporal	
642. Duff, James Robert	Private	
643. Palmer, George Robert	,,	Promoted Lance-Corporal
644. Trew, William Merriman	,,	
645. Chalmers, James McCracken	,,	
646. Cameron, John	,,	
647. Hayes, Harry James	,,	
648. Hayes, Edward Geo.	,,	
649. McIntyre, Thomas John	,,	
650. Newson, Arthur Ernest	,,	
651. Brain, George	,,	
652. Wishart, Joseph	,,	
653. Dobson, Frank Leslie	,,	
654. Grigg, Arthur Ernest	,,	
655. Scott, Thos.	,,	
656. Swan, William	,,	
657. Sweeting, George	,,	
658. Brooks, Charles	,,	
659. O'Brien, Henry	,,	
660. Albon, Jesse Frederick	,,	
661. Vanlawick, James	,,	
662. O'Donnell, Hugh Alexander	,,	Promoted Lance-Corporal
663. Shreeve, James William	,,	
664. Smart, Benjamin	,,	
665. Groves, David	,,	
666. Trevan, Carew	,,	
667. Freeme, William	,,	
668. Toogood, Thomas	Shoeing-Smith	
669. Smith, Joseph Andrew	Private	
670. McRae, Edward	,,	
671. O'Brien, John James	,,	

Nominal Roll—*continued*.

No. and Name.	Rank.	Remarks.

N.C.O.'S AND MEN—*continued*.

No. and Name.	Rank.
672. Thomson, Percy William	,,
673. Kerr, Samuel Teale	,,
674. Cooper, Reginald John	,,
675. Baptie, Thomas Richard	,,
676. Baptie, Charles Henry	,,
677. Thomas, William	,,
678. Gray, James Gordon	Bugler
679. Butler, Percy Vivian	Private
680. Trevascus, William Charles	,,
681. Fitzpatrick, Mathew George	,,
682. Spencer, Thomas	Farrier-Sergeant
683. Wilson, William Henry	Private
684. Skillecorn, George	,,
685. Pitt, Thomas	Corporal
686. Wright, Alfred William	Private
687. Cooke, Harry Ernest	,,
688. Fryer, George Edward	,,
689. Trickey, Frederick Victor	Bugler
690. Rose, Harry Morgan	Private
691. Spencer, J. S.	Shoeing-Smith
692. Ievers, Herbert Francis Kearney	Private
693. Arnold, John	,,
694. Newton, John Thomas	,,
695. Beyer, Harry Peter	,,
696. Bollen, Alfred John	,,
697. McLean, Norman	,,
698. Eunson, Donald Wallace	,,
699. Wheeler, Louis James	,,
700. Tompsitt, Sydney	,,
701. Oliver, Charles Henry	,,
702. Travers, Keith	,,
703. Herald, William Theodore	,,
704. Smith, George Barnet	,,
705. Norman, William Oscar	,,
706. Sutcliffe, Charles	,,
707. Anderson, Leslie	,,
708. Robertson, Robert	,,
709. Breen, John	,,
710. Kelly, John	,,
711. Turner, Robert	,,
712. Gardner, William	,,
713. Gordon, Adolphus	,,
714. Hortle, Frank	Bugler
715. Hazel, Henry	Private
716. Wells, Thomas Henry	,,
717. Parker, Charles	,,
718. Ferguson, John	Saddler
719. Lovelace, Alfred John	Private
720. Powell, William	,,
721. McDonald, Hugh	,,
722. Miller, Robert	,,
723. Weire, Augustus William	,,
724. Sides, Ferdinand James	,,
725. Johnstone, Alexander	,,
726. Payne, Reuben	,,
727. Gardiner, John Fraser	,,
728. Bloomfield, Walter John James	,,

Nominal Roll—*continued.*

No. and Name.	Rank.	Remarks.
N.C.O.'s AND MEN—*continued.*		
729. Olholm, Neil	Private	
730. White, Thomas	,,	
731. Emmett, William George	,,	
732. Smith, William Ambrose	,,	
733. Burrows, Albert	,,	
734. Pearce, Frederick James	,,	
735. Drew, Michael	,,	
736. Skene, Thomas	,,	
737. Moore, Francis Richard	,,	
738. Hayes, Matthew	,,	
739. McKee, Daniel Thomas	,,	
740. Sutherland, George	,,	
741. Moore, William	,,	
742. Goodwin, George Craig	Lance-Corporal	
743. Mason, Joseph Ernest	Private	
744. Farrant, Arthur	,,	
745. Cleverley, Robert Duncan	,,	
746. Coe, Ferdinand John	,,	
747. Woods, Samuel Mullen	Shoeing-Smith	
748. Haydon, William Henry	,,	
749. Seymour, James Dudly	Private	
750. Hoad, Aubrey Geo. Denniston	,,	

COMMONWEALTH ARMY MEDICAL CORPS—VICTORIAN DETAILS.

THESE comprised the Victorian portion of the Australian Commonwealth Army Medical Corps. For organization, pay, equipment, service, &c., *vide* Army Medical Corps, New South Wales, in which also a complete roll of this Contingent will be found. The Victorian section included 3 officers, 1 staff-sergeant, 2 sergeants, and 25 rank and file.

Nominal Roll.

No. and Name.	Rank.	Remarks.
Cade, David Duncan	Lieutenant	Hon. Captain
Formby, Henry H.	,,	,, ,,
James, William A.	,,	,, ,,
1320. Sellwood, William	Staff-Sergeant	
1398. Jackson, Henry George	Sergeant	
1311. Vernon, Wm. Francis John	,,	
1297. Hutchings, Thomas Stawell	Corporal	Lance-Sergeant; Sergeant, 1.4.02
1299. Kemp, James	,,	
1306. Langhran, Gerald Henry	,,	
1300. Beulke, Auguste Edward	Private	
1301. Smith, Alfred John	,,	
1302. Suter, Thomas George	,,	
1303. Murray, John Waderburn	,,	
1304. Phillips, Reginald Stewart	,,	
1305. Stein, James Laurie	,,	
1307. Bailey, Percy Francis	,,	
1309. Chandler, Albert	,,	
1310. Balmer, Frederick William	,,	
1312. Doonan, John	,,	
1313. Hay, Walter Stewart	,,	
1314. May, Joseph	,,	
1315. Bisset, Ernest George	,,	Lance-Corporal
1316. Chapman, Alick	,,	
1317. Currie, Albert John	,,	
1318. Fulford, Charles Edward	,,	
1319. Bade, Alfred	,,	
1321. Roughton, William	,,	
1322. Emmerson, Walter Thomas	,,	
1355. Stone, William Charles	,,	
1356. Thorpe, Frank Clarence	,,	
1265. Nixon, Clyde William Pemberton	,,	

THE FOURTH BATTALION AUSTRALIAN COMMONWEALTH HORSE—VICTORIAN UNITS.

A BATTALION organized upon the same system as the Second, except that its establishment consisted of two companies from Victoria, one from South Australia, and one from Western Australia.

For details of pay, establishment, and clothing, *vide* 2nd Battalion. The battalion staff, prior to embarkation, also comprised a lieutenant-quartermaster (Western Australian officer), making six officers in all, plus a chaplain. In the other battalion the quartermaster had come with the Western Australian unit.

DEPARTURE AND RETURN.

The battalion staff and Victorian units embarked on 26th March, 1902, comprising 17 officers, 235 others, with 276 horses. One died; 2 officers, 30 others were struck off in South Africa; 15 officers, 204 others returned.

SERVICE.

The battalion staff and Victorian units left in the transport *Templemore*, on 26th March, 1902. On 2nd April, arrived at Adelaide, and received the South Australian squadron; proceeded to Fremantle, and there, on 7th, half the West Australian squadron was embarked; the remainder to follow in the transport *Englishman*.

Arrived at Durban on 22nd April, and disembarked on the following morning. Encamped at the Show Grounds until 24th; then entrained for Newcastle, Natal, and arrived on 26th, and encamped at Kitchener's Kop on the veldt, about 3 miles from the town. On 27th, the battalion was inspected by General Burn-Murdoch, Commandant. On 10th May, paraded at 2 a.m., and proceeded by order to Wool's bridge, Buffalo River, where some Boer delegates were to cross on their way to Vereeniging, the scene of the peace confederation.

On 13th, started to march for Volksrust, Transvaal, thence to entrain for Elandsfontein, which was arrived at on the 16th; and there the battalion remained until 24th June, during which time it was engaged in refitting, sending sick horses to sick horse farms, and obtaining remounts. On 28th May, General Oliphant inspected the battalion, and spoke in complimentary terms of the drill, and the cleanliness of the horse lines. On 1st June, news was received of the peace proclamation: subsequently officially confirmed, with a notification that every N.C.O. and man was to receive 1s. 6d. worth of stores, free, from the Field Force canteens—a concession to the troops which is said to have cost £20,000. On 7th June, a squadron, under Captain Collins, proceeded to Pretoria to take part in the service which was held next day to celebrate the cessation of hostilities. The Commanding Officer, the Second in Command, the Adjutant, and Captains Thorn and Macdonald also attended.

On 23rd, all horses were handed in to the remount depot. On 24th, the battalion entrained for Newcastle, arriving on 25th, and encamping on their former ground. Here the Australian troops were mobilizing previous to their return. On 28th, three officers and about 250 N.C.O.'s and men of the battalion entrained for Durban, there to embark on the *Manchester Merchant*; these were followed on 2nd July by ten officers, to join the *Britannic*. The remainder were ordered to embark in the *Norfolk* on 7th; but this transport being unable to accommodate all, Colonel Johnston and Lieutenant Robertson, with the balance, took passage by the *Drayton Grange*, which arrived at Port Melbourne on 7th August.

WAR SERVICES.

Many of the officers (as also N.C.O.'s and men) had seen previous service: *vide* nominal roll, also under various Contingents. Those who had not, received the Queen's Medal with two clasps.

Nominal Roll.

No. and Name.	Rank.	Remarks.
BATTALION STAFF.		
Johnston, George Jamieson	Lieut.-Colonel	Previously Special Service Officer
Patterson, William George	Major (2nd in command)	
Mailer, William	Captain and Adjutant	
Houston, John James	Lieutenant and Quartermaster	Served in 4th Western Australian Mounted Infantry Contingent
Stacpoole, Adam Richard	Captain (Medical Staff)	
Jones, David Thomas	Veterinary-Lieutenant	
Milne, Rev. Frank	Chaplain	
2240. Southby, Henry	Reg. Sergeant-Major	
2310. Jarrett, Norman Gerald	Reg. Quartermaster-Sergeant	
2245. Peters, Robert Brooks	Staff Sergeant, O.R. Clerk	
COMPANY OFFICERS.		
Macdonald, Alexander Campbell	Captain	Previously 4th Victorian Contingent
Thorn, George Francis	,,	Previously 1st Victorian Contingent
Rodd, Francis Charles	Lieutenant	
Robertson, William St. Leonard	,,	
Bailey, Harry Stephen	,,	
Clarke, Cyril Wilberforce St. John	,,	
Healy, John Walton	,,	Previously 1st Victorian Contingent
Macdonald, Hugh	,,	Previously 2nd Victorian Contingent
Pearce, John William	,,	Previously 1st Victorian Contingent
Fawns, James Robertson	,,	Previously 2nd Victorian Contingent
N.C.O.'S. AND MEN.		
2201. Hibberd, William Frederick	Private	
2202. Burgess, William Joseph	Sergeant	
2203. Cantlon, Peter Charles	Corporal	
2204. Donaldson, Mark Edward	Private	
2205. Douglas, George Henry Allen	,,	
2206. Dennis, Stanley Fred Jenner	Coy. Quartermaster-Sergeant	
2207. Donnan, James	Private	
2208. Davies, William	Corporal	
2209. Ellis, James	Coy. Quartermaster-Sergeant	
2210. Calcutt, Robert Knaggs	Private	
2211. Gilbert, George Augustus	Corporal	
2212. Stephenson, Rowland Joseph	Private	
2213. Sharman, Ernest Arthur	,,	
2214. Ferguson, Augustus Theodore	,,	
2215. Jeffery, George Edminston	Sergeant	
2216. Massie, William	Private	

Nominal Roll—*continued.*

No. and Name.	Rank.	Remarks.
N.C.O.'s AND MEN—*continued.*		
2217. Kerr, Albert George	Private	
2218. McKeone, Daniel	,,	
2219. Hall, Albert	,,	
2220. Wilkins, Harrie	,,	
2221. Newland, William	,,	
2222. Pittard, Edward William	,,	
2223. Parsons, Wesley	,,	
2224. Harris, George	,,	
2225. Post, Peter James	Corporal	
2226. Robins, Albert Christopher	Private	
2227. Stevenson, George Ingram	,,	
2228. St. John, William	Corporal	
2229. Sutherland, James	Private	
2230. Taylor, Thomas Charles	,,	
2231. Walker, Charles Frederick	Corporal	
2232. Fitzgibbon, Henry	Private	
2233. Collister, David George	,,	
2234. Butler, Charles Henry Felix	Corporal	
2235. Collins, William	Private	
2236. Cleeves, Geo. Lewis	,,	
2237. Duncan, Robert George	,,	
2238. Morrison, Duncan	,,	
2239. McKenzie, William	,,	
2241. Smith, William Henry	Farrier-Sergeant	
2242. McNulty, James	Sergeant	
2243. Daniel, Edwin Stewart	Private	
2244. Geary, Ambrose	,,	
2246. Robertson, Edward Bruce	,,	
2247. Robertson, Robert Henry	,,	
2248. Harris, Wright	,,	
2249. Midgley, Percival Edwin	Coy. Sergeant-Major	
2250. Wallace, John	Private	Deserted at Albany *en route* to South Africa
2251. Negri, Joseph Francis	,,	
2252. Sleddon, John Exley Crouther	Lance-Corporal	
2253. Campbell, Norman	Sergeant	
2254. Armstrong, James Ernest Lorraine	Private	
2255. Aitken, Magnus Miller	,,	
2256. Anderson, Percival Wm. Henry	,,	
2257. Bennet, Henry George	,,	
2258. Broderick, Frank	,,	
2259. Butler, Vivian George	,,	
2260. Bullock, James	,,	
2261. Baragwanath, Guy	,,	
2262. Bourke, Michael	Corporal	
2263. Brady, Charles	Private	
2264. Belcher, Edward Norman	,,	
2265. Brumley, Victor	,,	
2266. Butler, Archie	Sergeant	
2267. Beer, Walter	Saddler	
2268. Bandy, William Thos.	Private	
2269. Brown, Alexander	,,	
2270. Butler, Herbert Augustus Kingsbury	,,	
2271. Cope, Arthur James Poole	,,	
2272. Cassidy, John Patrick	,,	

Nominal Roll—*continued.*

No. and Name.	Rank.	Remarks.
N.C.O.'s AND MEN—*continued.*		
2273. Clinton, John	Private	
2274. Cattanach, Alfred James	,,	
2275. Campbell, James William	Lance-Corporal	
2276. Clarke, Ernest Hislop	Private	
2277. Cameron, William Kennedy	,,	
2278. Cameron, Ewen Anthony	Corporal	
2279. Charleson, Archibald	Private	
2280. Creber, Frederick	,,	
2281. Carson, Walter Eastwood	,,	
2282. Chudleigh, Henry Clement	,,	
2283. Davern, Arthur	,,	
2284. Davies, Isaac	,,	
2285. Davey, George Francis	,,	
2286. Degner, Francis Carl August	,,	
2287. Daldy, Jas. Thos.	,,	
2288. Davidson, Christopher	,,	
2289. Dixon, Charles Harold	,,	
2290. Dare, Miles	Sergeant	
2291. Hearnden, Edward	Private	
2292. Dodd, Joseph Allen	Corporal	
2293. Enright, Edward Patrick	Private	
2294. Fowler, Walter Rufus	,,	
2295. Foy, Charles James	,,	
2296. Fletcher, James	,,	
2297. Flynn, Christopher	Lance-Corporal	
2298. Fawcett, Thomas	Bugler	
2299. Glass, John	Private	
2300. Gadd, Sampson Burton	,,	
2301. Graham, Percival Thomas	,,	
2302. Gordon, John George Gay	Shoeing-Smith	
2303. Grant, John Christopher	Private	
2304. Hunt, Henry	,,	
2305. Hodgins, George Ernest	Shoeing-Smith	
2306. Hill, William Henry	Private	
2307. Gordon, Huntly Campbell	Lance-Corporal	
2308. Herschell, George Alexander	Bugler	
2309. Harvey, Thomas James	Private	
2311. Hehir, Timothy Edward	,,	
2312. Hurle, Thomas	,,	
2313. Hennebery, John	,,	
2314. Hazlett, George Connolly	,,	
2315. McLeod, Norman	,,	
2316. Hoad, Fred J. S.	,,	
2317. Hughes, George Henry	,,	
2318. Hussey, Herbert Alfred	Shoeing-Smith	
2319. Jones, William John	Private	
2320. Jillett, Tasman	,,	
2321. Jeffreys, Dodsworth	,,	
2322. Jones, George Joseph	,,	
2323. Jeffreys, Frederick Guin	,,	Died of pyæmia at Pine Town Bridge, 1.5.02
2324. Keating, Samuel Francis	,,	
2325. Kilgour, William	,,	
2326. Keys, Percival William	,,	
2327. Keys, David	,,	
2328. King, John Liddington	,,	
2329. Leith, John	,,	
2330. Lindsay, Joseph Herbert	,,	

Nominal Roll—continued.

No. and Name.	Rank.	Remarks.

N.C.O.'s AND MEN—continued.

No. and Name.	Rank.
2331. Littlejohn, Wm. Alfred	Private
2332. Lowes, John Geo.	,,
2333. Leeke, James	,,
2334. Marshall, William Francis	Lance-Corporal
2335. Mills, Robert	Private
2336. Morris, Henry	,,
2337. Middleton, James Andrew	,,
2338. Millar, Lionel	,,
2339. Murrie, Alexander James	Shoeing-Smith
2340. Marsden, Frederick Chas.	Private
2341. Miller, George Graylin	,,
2342. Molloy, David	,,
2343. Murphy, James	,,
2344. Morrison, James	,,
2345. McLean, Leslie Gordon	,,
2346. McMillan, Ernest Schultz	,,
2347. McDonald, John Phillip	,,
2348. McLean, Neil Allen Thomas	,,
2349. Macdonald, Robert Bruce	Lance-Corporal
2350. McPherson, Albert Henry	Private
2351. McAleer, James	Sergeant
2352. McFarlane, Herbert	Private
2353. Nickols, Robert Francis	,,
2354. Newland, James Ernest	,,
2355. O'Connor, Arthur Edward	,,
2356. Old, Ernest	,,
2357. Ohloff, Paul	,,
2358. Prime, Charles Edward	,,
2359. Poore, Henry Ernest	,,
2360. Penny, Lytton Wm.	,,
2361. Piera, Charles Joseph	Corporal
2362. Richardson, Bernard	Private
2363. Ross, Robert Cuthbertson	,,
2364. Rede, Paston Hubert	,,
2365. Richardson, William John	,,
2366. Roberts, Frederick John	,,
2367. Riley, Robert	,,
2368. Ross, George	,,
2369. Roberts, Henry	,,
2370. Richards, Thomas Arthur	,,
2371. Regan, Christopher	Farrier-Sergeant
2372. Swan, Archibald Robert Campbell	Private
2373. Shannon, James	,,
2374. Stephens, Frank	,,
2375. Sharman, Henry James	,,
2376. Sheldon, George Frederick Rainsford	,,
2377. Savige, Garfield Ralph	,,
2378. Sharwood, Sydney Macalister	Corporal
2379. Schonell, Joyce Henry	Private
2380. Sheldrake, Charles	,,
2381. Staff, Herbert Nicol	,,
2382. Soar, Robert	,,
2383. Thomas, William John	,,
2384. Thomson, George	,,
2385. Slattery, Patrick John	,,
2386. Tegart, Charles Edward	,,
2387. Towt, Arthur Edward	,,

Nominal Roll—*continued.*

No. and Name.	Rank.	Remarks.
N.C.O.'s AND MEN—*continued.*		
2388. Turner, William	Bugler	
2389. Vickery, Ernest Henry	Shoeing-Smith	
2390. Withers, Robert	Private	
2391. Williams, Thomas	,,	
2392. Wilson, Robert Muscott	,,	
2393. Watson, Reginald Moses	,,	
2394. Weiland, Ernest	,,	
2395. Willcockson, Frederick Ernest	,,	
2396. Saunders, Edward	,,	
2397. Westwood, Robert	Shoeing-Smith	
2398. Wittingslow, William Joseph	Private	
2399. Welsford, Thomas Arthur	,,	
2400. Whiting, James Frederick	,,	
2401. Withers, James	,,	
2402. White, Alexander Henry	Sergeant	
2403. Wills, Herbert Sydney Norman	Private	
2404. Wilson, James Evan	,,	
2405. Wilson, Percy	,,	
2406. Wells, George Clement	,,	
2407. Young, Francis	Coy. Sergeant Major	
2408. Mulavin, Charles	Private	
2409. McIntosh, Jonathan	,,	
2410. Sanders, Ernest William	,,	
2411. Brand, William Henry	,,	
2412. Brown, George	,,	
2413. Vincent, Leslie Moore	,,	
2414. Vincent, Rubin Jacob	,,	
2415. Mulavin, Frank	,,	
2416. Eadie, William Aitken	Lance-Corporal	
2417. Williams, Wilfred Wall	Saddler	
2418. Coleman, William	Bugler	
2419. Henderson, William	Private	
2420. McLaren, William James	,,	
2421. Trezise, Martin Edwards	,,	
2422. Mills, James Robt.	,,	
2423. Amott, Henry Albert	,,	
2424. Abberton, James Ignatius	Lance-Corporal	
2425. Elliott, Walter	Private	
2426. Meatchem Thomas Henry	,,	
2427. Wilton, Frederick George	,,	
2428. Jones, Henry	,,	
2429. Mumford, James Hugh	,,	
2430. Harrison, John	,,	
2431. Crowe, William Albert	,,	
2432. Ryan, James	,,	
2433. Moir, Albert Edwin	,,	
2434. Kronk, Edward George	,,	
2435. Flegg, Albert	,,	

THE SIXTH BATTALION AUSTRALIAN COMMONWEALTH HORSE.

WAS authorized upon the same system as the Fifth (see under New South Wales); the formation of composite battalions, each representing three States, having been altered to a territorial basis. Thus each battalion, or part of a battalion, represented a State; each squadron a distinct district, and the troops in that district; and each troop (or section of a squadron) a particular corps, or military unit in a defined locality.

Establishment (four squadrons), rates of pay, clothing and equipment, as for 4th Australian Commonwealth Horse. The companies were now officially styled "squadrons," divisions became "troops," and groups "sections." (General Order 60 of 1902.) This was judicious; for previously both expressions had been used indiscriminately.

ORGANIZATION.

The organization was as follows:—" A " Squadron.—1st Troop : " A " Company Victorian Mounted Rifles and Melbourne Military District (32 men and horses). 2nd Troop: Same (27 men and horses). 3rd Troop : " C " Company Victorian Mounted Rifles, " H " Company Rangers, and Military District, Warragul (29 men and horses). 4th Troop : " C " Company Victorian Mounted Rifles, " I " Company Rangers, and Military District, Sale (28 men and horses). Horses were supplied.

" B " Squadron.—1st Troop : " J " Company Victorian Mounted Rifles and Military District, Wangaratta (32 men and horses). 2nd Troop : " E " Company Victorian Mounted Rifles, and Military District, Euroa (27 men and horses). 3rd Troop : " F " Company Victorian Mounted Rifles and Military District, Yea (29 men and horses). 4th Troop : " B " Company Victorian Mounted Rifles, and Military District, Murchison (28 men and horses).

" C " Squadron.—1st Troop : " I " Company Victorian Mounted Rifles, 5th Battalion Infantry Brigade, " E " Company Rangers, and Military District, Bendigo (32 men and horses). 2nd Troop : " I " Company Victorian Mounted Rifles, " K " Company Rangers, and Military District, Kerang (27 men and horses). 3rd Troop : " K " Company Victorian Mounted Rifles, 3rd Battalion Infantry Brigade, and Military District, Ballarat (29 men and horses). 4th Troop : " K " Company Victorian Mounted Rifles, 4th Battalion Infantry Brigade, " B " Company Rangers, and Military District, Maryborough (28 men and horses).

" D " Squadron.—1st Troop : " G " Company Victorian Mounted Rifles, Detachments Western Artillery, and Military District, Warrnambool (32 men and horses). 2nd Troop : " G " Company Victorian Mounted Rifles, and Military District, Colac (27 men and horses). 3rd Troop : " H " Company Victorian Mounted Rifles, and Military District, Hamilton (29 men and horses). 4th Troop : " A," " C," and " D " Company Rangers, and Military District, Stawell (28 men and horses).

Ten per cent. extra were provisionally enrolled to allow for rejections.

Many of those who joined had served in previous Contingents and in local South African regiments.

DEPARTURE AND RETURN.

The Contingent left on 19th May, 1902, comprising 22 officers, 467 of other ranks, with 489 horses. Four commissions were left vacant for officers to be appointed in South Africa. Of those who went, 2 died, 66 were struck off in Natal; 22 officers, 399 others returned.

SERVICE.

The battalion embarked on 19th May on the transport *Manchester Merchant*; a detachment, consisting of Lieutenant Kessell, 47 N.C.O.'s and men, and 123 horses, having previously departed on the 16th by the freight ship *Menelaus*.

Arrived at Durban on 13th June, and landed on the following day, proceeding at once to Newcastle, Natal, at which town they arrived on the 18th. Orders were almost immediately received for return to Australia, owing to the termination of the war. The horses were handed over, and the following three weeks were spent preparing for the return journey. On 9th July, entrained for Durban, and re-embarked there on the following day in the transport *Drayton Grange*, which left on the following day. Major F. J. Hayter and 11 lieutenants had departed on 5th July by H.M.T. *Britannic*.

Arrived at Melbourne on 7th August, and disembarked the same day. Disbanded on the 8th.

NOMINAL ROLL.

No. and Name.	Rank.	Remarks.
BATTALION STAFF.		
Irving, G. G. H.	Lieut.-Colonel	
Hayter, F. J.	Major	
Strong, W. J. W.	Captain and Adjutant	Previous service in 3rd Victorian Contingent
Shields, D. A.	Medical Officer (Captain)	
Coghill, A. J.	Quartermaster Lieutenant	
Wilson, A. C.	Veterinary - Lieutenant	
250. Ordish, H.	Regtl. Sergeant-Major	
242. Puzey, W. J.	Regtl. Quartermaster-Sergeant	
43. Paul, H.	Staff Sergeant, O.R. Clerk	
"A" SQUADRON.		
Brabazon, J. F.	Captain	Served with 2nd and 5th Contingents
No. 1 TROOP (MELBOURNE).		
Stebbins, J. F.	Lieutenant	5th Victorian Contingent
N.C.O.'s and Men.		
33. Walkden, P. B.	Sqn. Sergeant-Major	
58. Burman, A. E.	Quartermaster-Sergeant	
56. Clinton, R.	Sergeant	
41. Lindsay, F.	Sergeant-Farrier	
201. Tait, R.	Saddler	
17. Collett, E. E.	Trumpeter	
36. Dickson, C.	Lance-Sergeant	
7. Robertson, D. G.	Corporal	
8. Rust, S.	Private	
2. Robinson, G.	,,	

Nominal Roll—*continued.*

No. and Name.	Rank.	Remarks.

"A" Squadron—No. 1 Troop (Melbourne)—*continued.*

N.C.O.'s and Men—continued.

3. O'Sullivan, J. J.	Private	
4. Stowe, A. R.	,,	
5. Younge, G. J.	,,	
9. Harris, E. C.	,,	
12. Kennedy, J. V.	,,	
13. Howard, T.	,,	
14. Booth, D.	,,	
15. Burman, W. J.	,,	
16. Crawley, E. H.	,,	
18. Dubois, A. J.	,,	
19. Traill, J.	,,	
21. Raper, P. C.	,,	
22. Palmer, B. B.	,,	
25. Morton, R.	,,	
26. Gatliff, H. E.	,,	
29. Hogg, W. C.	,,	
30. Weir, C. W.	,,	
31. Wilson, S. C.	,,	
32. Wood, T. R.	,,	
117. Chapman, F. J.	,,	
118. Tobin, M.	,,	
37. Hanlon, R. A.	,,	

No. 2 Troop (Melbourne).

Power, J. E.	Lieutenant	

N.C.O.'s and Men.

53. Barr, A.	Sergeant	
69. Murie, D.	Shoeing-smith	
11. Dennis, F.	Corporal	
49. Roche, F. J. G.	Lance-Corporal	
38. Flannery, M. V.	Private	
39. Neilson, A.	,,	
40. Jordan, J.	,,	
42. Robertson, A. A.	,,	
44. Hawdon, T.	,,	
45. Gardiner, T.	,,	
46. Rigg, W. G.	,,	
47. Evans, G. B.	,,	
48. Croy, J. G.	,,	
51. Treacy, T. P.	,,	
52. Fawcett, J. L.	,,	
54. Coleman, D.	,,	
55. Lindsay, W. M.	Lance-Corporal	
57. Hede, J.	Private	
119. Azzopardi, G.	,,	
60. Colley, H. J.	,,	
61. Riley, W.	,,	
62. Mitchell, J.	,,	
63. Robinson, G. W.	,,	
64. Whelan, A. J.	,,	
65. Meagher, J. T.	,,	
66. Kennedy, A.	,,	
67. Betts, G.	,,	

Nominal Roll—continued.

No. and Name.	Rank.	Remarks.

"A" SQUADRON—continued.

No. 3 TROOP (WARRAGUL).
N.C.O.'s and Men.

No. and Name.	Rank.	Remarks.
87. Burton, H. J.	Sergeant	
104. Austin, A.	Shoeing-Smith	
20. Jenkins, D.	Trumpeter	
27. Larkins, F. D.	Corporal	
88. Charles, R. H.	Lance-Corporal	
68. Elliott, G. W.	Private	
70. Houlahan, J. J.	,,	
71. Mitchell, H.	,,	
72. Bickford, A.	,,	
73. Jordan, T.	,,	
74. Jordan, E. F.	,,	
75. Ward, R. H.	,,	
76. Pavitt, J. W.	,,	
77. Andrews, A.	,,	
78. Farrant, F. E.	,,	
79. Rees, G.	,,	
80. Hasthorp, R.	,,	
81. Lewis, T. F.	,,	
82. Fechner, C. A.	,,	
83. Adkins, S.	,,	
84. Stone, C.	,,	
85. Pedersen, C. S.	,,	
86. Monger, E. T.	,,	
89. Burgoyne, J. J.	,,	
95. Burgoyne, W. F.	,,	
90. Carrigg, F.	,,	
91. Fitzpatrick, S.	,,	
92. Edwards, E.	,,	
484. Anderson, D. S.	,,	
489. McNaughton, H. J.	,,	

No. 4 TROOP (SALE).

Name	Rank	Remarks
Rowan, A. H.	Lieutenant	

N.C.O.'s and Men.

No. and Name.	Rank.	Remarks.
34. Sandford, J. W.	Sergeant	
137. Dudley, S. W.	Shoeing-Smith	Died of pneumonia, Melbourne Hospital, 11.8.02
28. Jolley, F. R.	Corporal	
35. O'Brien, E. H.	,,	
102. Buchanan, N.	Lance-Corporal	
93. Ryan, W. E.	Private	
94. Fidler, W. H.	,,	
96. Johnson, M.	,,	
98. Ray, S.	,,	
99. Lett, R. W.	,,	
100. Peterson, H. F.	,,	
101. Archibald, J. R. H.	,,	
103. Manning, J. L.	,,	
105. Archibald, A. T. J.	,,	
106. Scott, T. J.	,,	
107. McGregor, R.	,,	Died at sea, returning, 4.8.02

Nominal Roll—continued.

No. and Name.	Rank.	Remarks.

"A" Squadron—No. 4 Troop (Sale)—continued.

N.C.O.'s and Men—continued.

108. Winnett, W. H.	Private	
109. Lewis, J.	,,	
110. Ralston, M.	,,	
111. Galbally, W.	,,	
112. Bennett, W.	,,	
113. Hill, G. F.	,,	
114. Blackshaw, J. F.	,,	
116. McColl, J. B. S.	,,	
115. May, R. W.	,,	
485. Forsythe, G.	,,	
491. Filbey, W.	,,	
490. Cheeseman, A. W.	,,	

"B" Squadron.

Hennessy, V. J. P.	Captain	Previously 5th Victorian Cont.

No. 1 Troop (Wangaratta).

Cochrane, W. J.	Lieutenant	5th Victorian Contingent.

N.C.O.'s and Men.

189. Rogers, H. A.	Sergeant-Major	
243. Sullivan, W. N.	Quartermaster-Sergeant	
126. Sharry, M.	Sergeant	
204. Richards, P.	Sergeant-Farrier	
160. Willis, G. A.	Saddler	
241. Chandler, E. R.	Bugler	
127. Vincent, A.	Corporal	
129. Dare, S. H.	Private	
156. Webster, W. C.	,,	
131. Meadway, C. B.	,,	
132. Collins, W.	,,	
133. Hannam, H. G.	,,	
134. Archbold, J. T.	,,	
135. Keat, W.	,,	
136. Woolley, H.	,,	
138. Anderson, R. F.	,,	
139. Keane, G.	,,	
140. Howard, L. H.	,,	
141. Condron, R.	,,	
142. Richards, G.	,,	
143. Bell, B. E.	,,	
144. Canny, D. E.	,,	
237. Cummins, J. M.	,,	
146. Ashley, W. J. C.	,,	
147. Morrell, H. C.	,,	
148. Gilbert, A. N.	Lance-Corporal	
149. Ashley, E. A.	Private	
150. Wadeson, S.	,,	
151. Cunningham, W.	,,	
152. Burns, W.	,,	
153. Chester, H. J.	,,	

Nominal Roll—*continued.*

No. and Name.	Rank.	Remarks.

"B" SQUADRON—*continued.*

No. 2 Troop (Euroa).

Beattie, J. P.	Lieutenant	

N.C.O.'s and Men.

173. Goode, E. A.	Sergeant	
162. Drury, C. W.	Corporal	
175. Benson, A.	Lance-Corporal	
130. Clark, G.	Shoeing-Smith	
157. Rogash, F. J.	Private	
159. Dick, F. A. J.	,,	
161. McNay, S. T.	,,	
163. Anker, J.	,,	
164. Morley, J.	,,	
165. Ditchfield, T.	,,	
166. Martin, E. W.	,,	
167. Hartshorn, J. W.	,,	
168. Smith, J. J.	,,	
169. Cramer, C.	,,	
170. Sargeant, W.	,,	
171. Webb, G. H.	,,	
172. Roe, H. E.	,,	
174. Lowden, A.	,,	
176. Fossey, A.	,,	
177. Gordon, P. J.	,,	
178. Savage, A. R.	,,	
239. Campbell, M. A.	,,	
234. Morley, E. J.	,,	
235. Little, A.	,,	
158. Graham, P.	,,	
230. Blaney, W. J.	,,	
145. Terry, W. F.	,,	

No. 3 Troop (Yea).

191. Snodgrass, A. A. H.	Sergeant	
194. Hardy, N. J.	Corporal	
128. Sloan, H. H.	,,	
240. Watson, W.	Bugler	
180. Burns, P. J.	Private	
181. Davis, S. H.	,,	
182. Sheppard, W. J.	,,	
183. Norman, M. P.	,,	
184. Brooks, T. J.	,,	
185. McKay, W.	,,	
186. Reardon, D.	,,	
187. Callaghan, J.	,,	
190. Clark, W.	,,	
192. O'Connor, J. J.	,,	
193. Reardon, D.	,,	
195. Fenton, T.	,,	
196. Johnston, W.	,,	
197. McCaskell, J. A.	,,	
198. Smith, J. R.	,,	
199. O'Connor, D.	,,	
223. Brasher, H.	,,	

Nominal Roll—*continued*.

No. and Name.	Rank.	Remarks.
"B" SQUADRON—No. 3 TROOP (YEA)—*continued*.		
N.C.O.'s and Men—*continued*.		
224. Pocknee, R.	Private	
225. Walker, D. H.	,,	
227. Kelly, F. M.	,,	
188. McKinnon, J.	Lance-Corporal	
179. Morton, C. J.	Private	
228. Byrne, A.	,,	
155. Murphy, P. J.	Shoeing-Smith	
No. 4 TROOP (MURCHISON).		
Bell, W. R.	Lieutenant	
N.C.O.'s and Men.		
231. Ferrie, A. E.	Sergeant	
200. Mackenzie, W. A.	Corporal	
470. Sproule, J. E.	,,	
219. McBean, P.	Lance-Corporal	
216. Pavey, S.	Shoeing-Smith	
202. Ross, D. J.	Private	
203. Currey, J. P.	,,	
205. Stocks, W.	,,	
206. Taylor, J. H.	,,	
207. Fosternelli, P. J.	,,	
208. Armstrong, C. E.	,,	
209. Conway, W. A.	,,	
210. Bliss, F.	,,	
211. Driver, A.	,,	
212. Downie, F. W.	,,	
213. March, R.	,,	
214. Shadforth, W.	,,	
215. Morrison, W. D.	,,	
217. Frater, W. T.	,,	
218. Hamilton, C.	,,	
226. Russell, H.	,,	
229. Casey, T.	,,	
232. McKerlie, J.	,,	
233. Mason, E. E.	,,	
220. Calman, C.	,,	
238. Gormley, W. J.	,,	
236. Broad, A.	,,	
244. Evans, R. J.	,,	
"C" SQUADRON.		
Tatchell, E. C.	Captain	Previously 1st and 5th Vic. Conts.
No. 1 TROOP (BENDIGO).		
Gregg, A. N.	Lieutenant	4th and 5th Vic. Conts.
N.C.O.'s and Men.		
24. Ryan, T. J.	Sergeant-Major	
251. Earnshaw, E. W.	Quartermaster-Sergeant	
256. Davis, G. W.	Sergeant	
253. McGregor, W.	Corporal	
281. Stanley, A.	,,	
275. Anderson, A. G.	Lance-Corporal	

Nominal Roll—*continued*.

No. and Name.	Rank.	Remarks.

"C" SQUADRON—No. 1 TROOP (BENDIGO)—*continued*.

N.C.O.'s and Men—*continued*.

252. Trewick, R.		Private
254. Hensen, F. C.		,,
255. Toner, J.		,,
257. Kidney, T.		,,
258. McDowell, F.		,,
259. Waugh, L.		Shoeing-Smith
261. Drysdale, D. H.		Private
262. Brown, J. H.		,,
264. McKenzie, W.		,,
265. Mitchell, W. T.		,,
266. Thornley, P. H.		Trumpeter
267. Boyd, J. L.		Private
268. Tulloch, A. F.		,,
269. Howell, G. W.		,,
270. Jones, G.		,,
271. Flannagan, W. J.		,,
272. Eeles, A.		,,
274. Peters, E. C.		Saddler
273. Dwyer, E. J.		Private
276. Jeal, J.		,,
277. Thompson, H. J.		,,
278. Binnie, A. T.		,,
279. O'Brien, L. K.		,,
280. Reid, T. C.		,,
282. Williams, E. B.		,,

No. 2 TROOP (KERANG).

Mountjoy, E. L.		Lieutenant

N.C.O.'s and Men.

304. McIvor, J. K.		Sergeant
285. Slatter, A. H.		Lance-Sergeant
308. Butler, E. C.		Lance-Corporal
287. Belsar, R. H.		Private
286. Henry, H.		,,
288. Moser, E.		,,
289. Rohan, J.		,,
290. Copeland, A.		,,
291. Lucas, H.		,,
292. Reaper, W.		,,
293. Heil, A.		,,
294. Kirk, M. D.		,,
295. Ritcher, F.		,,
296. Hare, G.		,,
297. Muir, J.		,,
298. Grimley, G. F.		,,
299. Blake, R.		,,
300. Ralph, H.		,,
301. Stevens, R. F.		,,
302. Morgan, J. E.		,,
303. Scow, L. H.		,,
305. Ryan, J. T.		,,
306. Brook, J. H.		,,

Nominal Roll—*continued.*

No. and Name.	Rank.	Remarks.
"C" SQUADRON"—No. 2 TROOP (KERANG)—*continued.*		
N.C.O.'s and Men—*continued.*		
307. Jenner, T. G.	Private	
309. Roe, W.	,,	
310. Routley, J. J.	,,	
311. McGrath, W.	,,	
368. Byrne, Charles D'Arcy	,,	
No. 3 TROOP (BALLARAT).		
Henty, J. R.	Lieutenant	
N.C.O.'s and Men.		
313. Hocking, E.	Sergeant	
329. Strike, E. J.	Farrier-Sergeant	
335. Hilcke, J.	Corporal	
341. Geddes, J. A.	Lance-Corporal	
314. Velten, A. J.	Private	
315. Jones, C. E.	,,	
316. Magor, W. J.	,,	
317. Gordon, A. V.	,,	
318. Tainsh, J.	,,	
319. Penhallurick, E. W.	,,	
320. Donaldson, C.	,,	
321. Dermoody, J.	,,	
322. McGregor, J.	,,	Promoted Corporal, 9.5.02
323. Dorizzi, P. F.	,,	
324. Eltringham, W.	,,	
325. Flood, J.	,,	
326. Arch, W. J.	,,	
327. Reynolds, W. J.	,,	
328. Johnson, F. G.	,,	
330. McDonald, T. C.	,,	
331. Allen, W. E.	,,	
332. Starkey, J. P.	,,	
334. Carnell, S. J.	,,	
336. Sneddon, W.	,,	
337. Diamond, C. H.	,,	
338. Glover, J.	,,	
339. McGill, A. J.	,,	
340. Smith, H. J.	,,	
97. Gabbitt, E. P.	Trumpeter	
No. 4 TROOP (MARYBOROUGH).		
345. Peacock, A. T.	Sergeant	
347. Gillanders, A. J.	Corporal	
355. Johnson, P. R.	,,	
361. Woolley, H. T.	Lance-Corporal	
343. Pitts, A. T.	Private	
344. House, T. E.	,,	
346. Cook, C.	,,	
348. Giles, F. W.	,,	
349. Murphy, J. A.	,,	
350. Williams, R. J.	,,	
351. Emmett, J. H.	,,	

Nominal Roll—*continued*.

No. and Name.	Rank.	Remarks.

"C" SQUADRON—No. 4 TROOP (MARYBOROUGH)—*continued*.

N.C.O.'s and Men—*continued*.

352. Renkin, A. W.	Private	
353. Mathews, H.	,,	
354. Wightwick, A. N.	,,	
356. Marcos, R.	,,	
357. Eagle, A. E.	,,	
358. Rose, J. A.	,,	
359. Cousens, B. E.	,,	
360. Cock, G. F.	,,	
362. Mason, R. A.	,,	
363. Kemm, J.	,,	
364. Ayars, W. J.	,,	
365. Canning, J. R.	,,	
366. Hammer, W. J.	,,	
283. Bennett, J. A.	,,	
284. Wemyss, J. M.	,,	
312. Dunstan, T. E.	,,	
342. Game, W.	,,	
367. Price, F. D.	,,	

"D" SQUADRON.

Righetti, E. E.	Captain	1st and 5th Vict. Contingents.

No. 1 TROOP (WARRNAMBOOL).

Kessell, H.	Lieutenant	5th Vict. Contingent.

N.C.O.'s and Men.

23. Bawden, R.	Sergeant-Major	
416. O'Connor, F. G.	Sqn. Quartermaster-Sergeant	
6. Bush, H.	Sergeant	
50. White, J. E.	Sergeant-Farrier	
514. Thomson, F. M.	Saddler	
391. Wainwright, H. J.	Bugler	
487. Tulley, H. E.	Corporal	
379. Bull, E. A. O. E.	Private	
380. Clingan, E.	,,	
381. Harris, W. H.	,,	
382. Fabian, W. A.	,,	
383. Swan, D. E.	,,	
384. Bartlett, J.	,,	
385. Rutter, G.	,,	
386. Fleming, D.	,,	
387. Burleigh, W.	,,	
388. Milne, P. A.	Lance-Corporal	
389. Evans, J.	Private	
390. Brown, F. E. A.	,,	
392. Stanley, G. T. S.	,,	
393. Williams, G. K.	,,	
395. Marfell, H. G.	,,	
396. Mansell, G. H.	,,	
397. Nettleton, J. F.	,,	
398. Jenkins, R. D.	,,	
399. Brown, J.	,,	
400. Bourke, J.	,,	

Nominal Roll—continued.

No. and Name.	Rank.	Remarks.

"D" Squadron—No. 1 Troop (Warrnambool)—continued.

N.C.O.'s and Men—continued.

401. Wallace, D. A.	,,	
402. Wallace, J. H.	,,	
403. Oakley, L. C.	,,	
404. Howe, W. H.	,,	
405. Blake, J.	,,	

No. 2 Troop (Colac).

Dobson, D.	Lieutenant	

N.C.O.'s and Men.

376. Rankin, C.	Sergeant	
333. Hunt, E. A.	Shoeing-Smith	
417. O'Donnell, M. J.	Corporal	
406. Collins, E.	Private	
408. Kemp, E. A.	,,	
409. Riordan, G. F.	,,	
410. Williams, W.	,,	
411. Swan, E.	,,	
412. Michel, L.	,,	
413. Strong, G.	,,	
414. Kett, V.	,,	
415. Pennefather, K.	,,	
418. Jones, R. P.	,,	
420. Harper, S.	,,	
421. King, T.	,,	
422. Williamson, F.	,,	
423. Michel, A. N.	,,	
424. Ritchie, F.	,,	
425. Gillett, T. J.	,,	
426. Keates, T. J.	,,	
486. Harricks, —.	,,	
429. Rose, G.	,,	
430. McKinley, W.	,,	
431. Morgan, H.	,,	
432. Morris, F.	,,	
433. Jones, J.	,,	
434. Yates, C.	,,	
488. Gray, H.	,,	

No. 3 Troop (Hamilton.)

Rogers, J.	Lieutenant	

N.C.O.'s and Men.

407. Schultze, C. W.	Sergeant	
263. Ellis, A. E.	Shoeing-Smith	
437. Donelan, R.	Corporal	
435. Garton, G.	,,	
1. Brenchley, H. T.	Bugler	
394. Rankin, T.	Private	

Nominal Roll—*continued*.

No. and Name.	Rank.	Remarks.

"D" SQUADRON—NO. 3 TROOP (HAMILTON)—*continued*.

N.C.O.'s and Men—*continued*.

No. and Name.	Rank.
436. Stanford, W.	Private
438. Watson, J. L.	,,
439. Arnott, J.	,,
440. Allan, W.	,,
441. Pennefather, V.	,,
442. Tilley, M. J.	,,
443. Haylock, C. E.	,,
444. O'Brien, J.	,,
445. Chapple, C.	,,
446. McLean, D.	,,
447. Pollard, C.	,,
448. Pirie, A.	,,
449. Redfern, W.	,,
450. Wash, C,	,,
451. Tilley, P. H.	,,
452. Stagoll, W.	,,
453. Gordon. E.	,,
454. Dunbar, H.	,,
455. Peskett, A.	,,
456. Victor, W. J.	Lance-Corporal
457. Drummond, —.	Private
459. McLeod, N.	,,

NO. 4 TROOP (STAWELL).

No. and Name.	Rank.
377. Axford, T. A.	Lance-Sergeant
460. Meagher, J.	Shoeing-Smith
419. Hevey, S. A.	Corporal
427. Johnson, G. S.	,,
458. McAdam, E.	Private
461. McGregor, D.	,,
462. Tucker, A.	,,
463. Darling, G.	,,
10. Maxwell, T.	,,
464. Williamson, V.	,,
465. Edwards, C. H.	,,
466. Williams, V. P.	,,
467. Battye, A. J.	,,
468. Noonan, E. J.	,,
469. Cooper, F. P.	,,
471. Coutts, A.	,,
472. Mills, W. R.	,,
473. Gange, W. H.	,,
474. Abbott, W.	,,
475. Richards, A.	,,
476. McMurtrie, T. J.	,,
477. Smith, W. J.	,,
478. Gray, R.	,,
479. Green, H. A.	,,
480. Green, W. H.	,,
481. Lester, M.	,,
482. Allan, V.	,,
483. Sloan, G.	,,

List of Officers and Others of Victorian Contingents who were Killed or Died.

Regimental Number, Rank, and Name.	Regimental Number, Rank, and Name.

First Victorian Contingent.

*Lieut-Colonel Umphelby, C. E.
Major Eddy, G. A.
Captain Salmon, R. W.
   „   Hopkins, W. F. (Med. Staff)
Lieutenant Roberts, J. C
2. Sergeant Grant, N.
4. Corporal Ross, A.
74. Private Wilson, A. H.
88.   „   Suttie F.
89.   „   Stock, T.
55.   „   Williams, C. E.
54. Corporal King, O.D.
43. Private Coulson, A. E.
94.   „   Barbour, R.
65.   „   Atkinson, M. W.
94. Farrier Rose, T. J.
26. Private Jones, A.
86.   „   Ross, D.

Second Victorian Contingent.

Lieutenant Bree, R. S., R. S.
197. Private Clarke, W. E.
206.   „   Sealey, H. A.
263.   „   Bristowe, G. E.
214. Sergeant Hiscock, H. J.
186. Private Wakly, V. O.
272.   „   Smart, H. J.
220.   „   Cullen, G. J.
364. Corporal McGowan, J.
305. Sergeant Francis, G. W.

Third (Bushmen's) Contingent.

384. Sergeant Brent, H.
395.   „   Goodman, H. J.
404.   „   Pruden, D. H.
418. Private Oliver, S. J.
488.   „   Walford, H. O.
432. Lance-Corporal McClure, J.
440. Private McCartney, J. I.
583. Corporal Norton, C. W.
584. Private Swan, J. C. D. McP.
535.   „   Bolding, G. W.
509.   „   Mackenzie, A.
491.   „   Christie, J. W.
629. Farrier-Sergt. Williamson, J. W. N.
616. Private Petty, W.
405. Shoeing-Smith Raggatt, T. H.
606. Private Thorpe, F. B.
450.   „   Knox, E.

Fourth (Imperial) Contingent.

Lieutenant Gilpin, A. G.
343. Private Woodman, A. T.
367.   „   Foster, T. B.
52.   „   Creelman, W. J.
402.   „   Crighton, J. W.

Fourth (Imperial) Contingent—continued.

418. Private Kiley, J.
38.   „   St. John, E. B.
445. Lance-Corporal Mays, W. D.
204. Lance-Corporal Smith, J. A.
93. Lance-Corporal Small, D. W.
555. Sergeant Vaughan, C.
560. Private Hesketh, J. S.
381.   „   Jonson, J.
592.   „   Ryan, J. L
87. Sergeant Hurst, J. S.
135. Lance-Corporal Goebel, C. J.
301. Private Moore, C.
269. Sergeant Powell, J. L.
230.   „   Mohan, T. P.
152. Corporal Seymour, P. C.
253. Private Yates, T.
68.   „   McKinnon, C.
122. Farrier Bawden, E. C. M.

Fifth (Mounted Rifle) Contingent.

785. Private Riesenaner, E. A.
936. Sergeant McDonald, M. T.
Lieutenant Johnston, A. G.
Captain Kelly, J.
1358. Private Lamb, H. S.
Lieutenant Murphy, A. E.
1344. Corporal Robertson, R. P. N.
1455. Private Hewins, H. V.
1475.   „   White, J. E.
Lieutenant Palmer, H. A.
1307. Private Stratton, G. W.
1292. Shoeing-Smith Mahoney, T. H.
1438. Private Blandford, E. H.
1404. Corporal Newlands, H.
1602. Private Thorton, R. M.
1485. Farrier-Sergeant Houlihan, J. F.
1691. Lance-Corporal Button, G. R.
1560. Private Bond, L.
1359.   „   Barnard, S. J.
1430.   „   Goudie, L. J. W.
1481.   „   Rowe, E. J.
1380.   „   Hendy, H. H.
1366. Corporal Harrison, H.
1550. Private Smith, W. A.
1095.   „   Topham, R.
1007.   „   Collins, J.
1610.   „   Mack, A. E.
893.   „   McCann, J. B.
783.   „   Boxall, H. J.
952.   „   Costello, J.
1700. Sergeant Buckingham, A. G. K.
855. Private Healy, W. J.
1582.   „   Valpeid, E. A.
1467.   „   Charlton, J.
1101.   „   Lawrence, J. J.
795.   „   Dow, F. G.
Lieutenant Coulter, S. R.

*Special Service Officer.

List of Officers and Others of Victorian Contingents who were Killed or Died—continued.

Regimental Number, Rank, and Name.	Regimental Number, Rank, and Name.
Fifth (Mounted Rifle) Contingent—contd.	
974. Shoeing-Smith Houghton, A.	*2nd Battalion Australian Commonwealth Horse.*
Lieutenant Chrisp, J. G.	
1570. Private Harrison, R. G.	450. Private T. W. Harris
1576. ,, Caughey, F. H.	
1634. Shoeing-Smith Rankin, J.	
1590. Private Watson, R. A.	*4th Battalion Australian Commonwealth Horse.*
1181. ,, James, W. W.	
944. ,, Whelan, J.	
1089. ,, McNally, J.	2323. Private F. G. Jeffreys
1489. ,, Soultry, W.	
1446. Corporal Hadley, H.	
727. Private McCorkell, J.	
1261. Shoeing-Smith Spowart, A. E.	*6th Battalion Australian Commonwealth Horse.*
1034. Private Davidson, A. B.	
903. Lance-Corporal Burley, A. E.	
1228. Private Ross, T. S.	107. Private R. McGregor
988. ,, Glinn, C.	137. Shoeing-Smith S. W. Dudley

SUMMARY OF CONTINGENTS DESPATCHED.*

Transport.	Date.	Contingent.	Officers.	Others.	Horses.	Wagons.
Medic	28th Oct., 1899	First	12	240	168	6
Euryalus	13th Jan., 1900	Second	15	250	305	6
,,	10th Mar., 1900	Bushmen	15	261	357	4
Victorian	1st May, 1900	Imperial	33	598	778	11
Orient, Argus, City of Lincoln	15th Feb., 1901	Fifth (M.R.)	46	971	1,099	..
St. Andrew	12th Feb., 1902	2nd Batt. A.C.H.	20	351	401	..
Manchester Merchant	,, ,,	A.C.A.M.C.	3	28	..	..
Templemore	26th Mar., 1902	4th Batt. A.C.H.	16	235	276	..
Manchester Merchant and Menelaus	19th May, 1902	6th Batt. A.C.H.	22	467	489	..
		Special Service Officers	5	..	..	..
		Batt. Staff A.C.H.	4	..	..	..
		Total	191	3,401	3,873	27

* This is exclusive of 250 recruits for Scottish Horse. *vide* p. 304.

DISPOSITION.*

	Officers.	Other Ranks.
Died or were killed	13	113
Transferred	21	13
Discharged in South Africa, or embarked for England and struck off in South Africa	28	305
Commissioned in Imperial Army	3	2
Returned to Australia	205	2,923
Total	270	3,356

* These figures are in some respects approximate only; it having been found impossible to obtain exact statements, owing to promotions to commissions, attachments, enlistments, and discharges in South Africa, of which no adequate returns have been made.

SOUTH AUSTRALIA.

SOUTH AUSTRALIA.

PREFATORY.

LIKE the Contingents despatched from other territories those sent to the war by South Australia may be divided into three classes: namely, the early ones, paid by local Government or by private subscription; the Imperial Bushmen, subsidised by the Imperial War Office; and the Commonwealth Contingents, raised after Federation, but also under British pay. The earlier companies were drawn from citizens and members of territorial forces, but (except in New South Wales), none of them were composed of drafts from such troops. In all cases, volunteers were desired, and preference was given to men with military service; but no whole units proceeded to the front. Afterwards, bushmen were enrolled; men accustomed to the exigencies of rough life in the backwoods, daring riders, expert shots, experienced in finding their way in tangled country, and hardened against privations. Then, as time went on, and the war still proceeded, the ranks of the Contingents became leavened with men who had already heard the click-clack of the Mauser, and the snarl of the pom-pom; and officers and others presented themselves who had tried conclusions with the Boers and were desirous to do so again. Finally, the Commonwealth Horse. These were, in the first instance, constituted of squadrons from separate States united in battalions, and afterwards of battalions enrolled upon a territorial basis, as already set forth. Only the first and second battalions, of eight that proceeded, were in time to join in the operations.

South Australia embarked six Contingents for the front, and contributed her quota to the Australian Commonwealth Horse. The pay of the First and Second Contingents was debited to the revenue of South Australia. The Third Contingent (Bushmen's) was entirely equipped and partly paid from private contributions. The pay of the Fourth, Fifth, and Sixth Contingents (other than paid by the Imperial Government in South Africa) was refunded to South Australia by the Imperial Government. It ranged from 25s. and 4s. field allowance per diem to major in command, to 5s. per diem to trooper.

The officers and members of all the six Contingents were also paid war gratuities as under, by South Australia; the amount being afterwards refunded by the Imperial Government.

SPECIAL WAR GRATUITY FOR SERVICES IN SOUTH AFRICA.

		£ s. d.	£ s. d.
Colonel and graded as A.A.G., 40 shares at		5 0 0	200 0 0
Colonel	32 ,,	,,	160 0 0
Major	16 ,,	,,	80 0 0
Captain	12 ,,	,,	60 0 0
Lieutenant	7½ ,,	,,	37 10 0
Quartermaster	2½ ,,	,,	12 10 0
Sergeant-Major	2½ ,,	,,	12 10 0
Sergeant	2 ,,	,,	10 0 0
Corporal	1½ ,,	,,	7 10 0
Lance-Corporal	1¼ ,,	,,	6 5 0
Trooper	1 ,,	,,	5 0 0

Additional to all Colonial officers serving in South Africa at £100 per annum paid by the Imperial Government.

Plain clothing allowance to all men in Imperial contingents, 25s. each.

DAILY RATES OF PAY AND ALLOWANCES CONTRIBUTED BY THE SOUTH AUSTRALIAN GOVERNMENT TO THE FIRST AND SECOND CONTINGENTS SENT TO THE SOUTH AFRICAN WAR:—

	First Contingent			Second Contingent	
	In South Australia and on Voyages to and from South Africa.	In South Africa.*		In South Australia and on Voyages to and from South Africa.	In South Africa.*
		Foot.	Mounted.		Pay.
	s. d.	s. d.	s. d.	s. d.	s. d.
Major	25 0	..	..	25 0	11 5
Captain	20 0	8 5	7 0 and 10 0	†20 0	7 0
Lieutenant	16 0	9 6	8 4 and 7 0	‡16 0	8 4
Sergeant-Major	9 0	6 0	4 8	9 0	4 8
Sergeant	8 0	5 8	5 4	8 0	5 4
Corporal	7 0	5 0	5 4	7 0	5 0
Lance-Corporal	5 0	3 9	3 10	5 0	3 10
Corporal-Bugler	7 0	5 4	5 8	..	..
Trooper	..	..	..	5 0	3 10
Private	5 0	3 10	4 0	..	..
Quartermaster-Sergeant	9 0	5 4	5 8	9 0	5 8
Farrier-Sergeant	8 0	5 4	5 2	8 0	5 2
Trumpeter	..	..	..	5 0	3 10
Shoeing-Smith	..	..	..	5 0	3 10
Lance Corporal-Bugler	5 0	3 9	..	..	..
Sergeant-Bugler	8 0	6 6	..	..	..
Saddler-Sergeant	8 0	5 4	..	..	..
Corporal-Farrier	7 0	5 4	..	..	..
Sergeant-Major and Warrant-Officer	..	..	..	11 6	5 4
Surgeon-Lieutenant	..	..	..	16 0	16 0
Surgeon-Captain	..	..	..	20 0	..
Farrier-Major	..	..	..	..	5 0

* Balance of pay was paid by the Imperial Government.
† And 3s. 6d. per diem Field Allowance to date of leaving South Australia.
‡ And 3s.   „   „   „   „   „   „

THIRD SOUTH AFRICAN CONTINGENT.—SOUTH AUSTRALIAN BUSHMEN'S CORPS.

DAILY RATES OF PAY.

Captain—Imperial, 13s.; Colonial, 10s. 6d.; total, £1 3s. 6d. Lieutenant, Lieutenant-Surgeon, and Lieutenant Veterinary-Surgeon—Imperial, 7s. 8d.; Colonial, 11s. 4d.; total, 19s. Sergeant-Major and Quartermaster-Sergeant—Imperial, 4s.; Colonial, 5s.; total, 9s. Sergeant—Imperial, 2s. 8d.; Colonial, 5s. 4d.; total, 8s. Corporal—Imperial, 2s.; Colonial, 5s.; total, 7s. Trooper—Imperial, 1s. 2d.; Colonial, 3s. 4d.; total, 4s. 6d.

The pay issued by the Imperial Government to the Imperial Contingents has already been quoted in the New South Wales and Victorian Contingents.

Uniform consisted of brown F.S. jacket, cord pants, puttees, F.S. hat and cap. Great coats and boots were also supplied, together with a full kit of working clothes, under garments, and necessaries. Rifles, bayonets, and bandolier-belts were issued. Fully horsed and supplied with saddlery; and (the early Contingents) regimental transport.

The training camp for the Contingents was at the old Exhibition Grounds, Adelaide.

FIRST (MOUNTED RIFLES) CONTINGENT.

ENROLLED, in the first instance, as a company of infantry; but mounted in South Africa. Preference was given to men who were or had been serving in the local or other military forces. They were also required to be good shots, and to pass a medical examination as regards physical fitness.

Establishment.—1 captain, 3 subalterns, 1 medical officer, 1 colour-sergeant, 7 sergeants, 7 corporals, 6 lance-corporals, 1 bugler, 99 privates; total, 5 officers, 121 of other ranks. Captain G. R. Lascelles, Royal Fusiliers, accompanied the Contingent for special service, and acted as adjutant of the combined battalion.

For pay, uniform, etc., *vide* p. 342.

PROMOTIONS.

Captain F. H. Howland, to be Major, 5th September, 1900.
Lieutenant J. H. Stapleton, to be Captain, 5th September, 1900.
Lieutenant F. M. Blair, recommended and approved for Captain, 10th December, 1900.
Sergeant A. W. Johnstone, to be Lieutenant, 21st March, 1900.
Corporals G. E. H. Noblett, W. C. N. Waite, and Trooper J. H. Shearer, were promoted Lieutenants in Fifth and Sixth Contingents.
Sergeant F. Laycock, promoted Lieutenant, 8th Australian Commonwealth Horse.

For promotions of N.C.O.'s and men, *vide* nominal roll.

SERVICE.

The company embarked at Port Adelaide on the transport *Medic*, 2nd November, 1899, and disembarked at Cape Town on 25th November. They were encamped at Maitland until 1st December, on which day they entrained and proceeded to De Aar; from there marched to Belmont, where the Contingent formed part of the Australian Regiment under Colonel J. C. Hoad; *vide* 1st Victorian Contingent. On 10th December, marched to Enslin, under orders from Lieutenant-General Lord Methuen, to relieve the Gordon Highlanders. At Enslin the Regiment was held in reserve for Magersfontein, but was not required.

Returned to Naauwpoort about the end of January; then went to Rensburg, and from there to Maeder's Farm, where they were supplied with horses, and converted into Mounted Infantry. In the fighting which took place at Hopkirk's Farm (when the Boers with a very strong force attacked the whole of Clements' extended line), Lieutenant J. W. Powell was killed. Owing to the superior strength of the Boers, the force to which the regiment was attached had to fall back on Rensburg, and, eventually, to Arundel, where some casualties were sustained. From there the Contingent was sent to join the Berkshire Regiment, under Major M'Cracken. On the retirement of the Boers, the Column, under General Clements, advanced to Norval's Pont, where the Contingent crossed the Orange River and took part in the march to Bloemfontein, under Major Dauncey of the Inniskillings. At Bloemfontein the First and Second Contingents formed the South Australian Mounted Rifles.

In the retirement on Arundel, which commenced at midnight, 13th–14th February, 1900, the South Australians formed the rear-guard; a position of honour and responsibility, as General Clements' men had been without rest or sleep for nearly 48 hours. Notwithstanding these great exertions, Captain Lascelles, Royal Fusiliers, who was acting as adjutant, on arriving in the neighbourhood of Arundel, went back with a mixed body of volunteers, mostly South Australians to endeavour to bring in or assist some infantry who had been left behind. On the 20th, the Boers again attacked Clements, but were driven back. During the next eight days there was constant fighting, in which the Contingent took their share. In the advance from Arundel on the 28th, they again formed the rear-guard. When General Clements was preparing to cross the Orange River (8th March), the South Australians were sent forward to the front at Norval's Pont, where they were in contact with the enemy until the 15th, when the force crossed. During the march through the Orange State, the squadron was on the right of the Column.

For further particulars of service, *vide* Second Contingent.

The Contingent embarked at Cape Town on 3rd November, 1900, in the transport *Harlech Castle*, and disembarked at Adelaide on 30th November. Granted a bonus of 30 days' pay by the South Australian Government. Disbanded, 30th November, 1900.

Captain Humphris and 25 men of the Second Contingent, having urgent private business, returned to Australia with the First Contingent.

WAR SERVICES AND HONOURS.

Howland, Major F. H.—Operations in Cape Colony, Transvaal, and Orange River Colony, between December, 1899, and October, 1900. Actions at Colesberg, Johannesburg, Pretoria, Diamond Hill, and Belfast. Queen's Medal with five clasps.

Stapleton, Captain J. H.—Operations as stated. Actions at Diamond Hill and Belfast. Despatches, *London Gazette*, 16th April, 1901. D.S.O. Queen's Medal with four clasps.

Blair, Lieutenant F. M.—Operations and actions as stated first above. Queen's Medal with five clasps.

Powell, Lieutenant J. W.—Operations in Cape Colony. Killed in action 9th February, 1900.

Toll, Captain (Medical Staff) J. T.—Operations as stated. Died at sea on s.s. *Australasia*, 20th June, 1900, when returning to Australia, invalided.

Johnstone, Lieutenant A. W. Operations as stated. Queen's Medal with three clasps.

Nominal Roll.

No. and Name.	Rank.	Remarks.
OFFICERS.		
Howland, Frederick Henry	Captain	In command
Lascelles, G. R.	Captain (Royal Fusiliers)	Adjutant
Toll, J. T.	Captain (Medical Staff)	Died at sea on s.s. *Australasia*, when returning invalided
Stapleton, John Henry	Lieutenant	
Blair, Francis Malcolm	,,	
Powell, J. W.	,,	Killed at Rensburg, 9.2.00
N.C.O.'s AND MEN.		
1 Kubale, J. C.	Colour-Sergeant	Slightly wounded at Wanderlover 7.9.00
119. Johnstone, A. W.	Sergeant	*Vide* "Promotions"
3. Watson, A. W.	,,	
4. Laycock, F.	,,	*Vide* "Promotions"
6. Schwan, W.	,,	
7. Thomas, W.	,,	Quartermaster-Sergeant. Invalided, to Australia, arrived 10.8.00
2. Doherty, H. P.	,,	
68. Hanley, T.	,,	
5. Heinjus, J. H.	Corporal	Died of enteric at Naauwpoort, 26.4.00
10. Klaffer, T. J.	,,	Died at Wynberg, 12.10.00
9. McGillvray, James	,,	Sergeant
86. McIntosh, N. A.	,,	
14. Noblett, G. E. H.	,,	*Vide* "**Promotions**"

Nominal Roll—continued.

No. and Name.	Rank.	Remarks.
N.C.O.'s AND MEN—continued.		
11. Waite, W. C. N.	Corporal	Vide "Promotions"
8. Wilson, F. M. E. O.	,,	Invalided to Australia, arr. 10.8.00
78. Barron, R. T.	Lance-Corporal	
13. Cooper, A. W. R.	,,	
73. Muir, F.	,,	
12. Oldham, D. C.	,,	
70. Rispin, A. C.	,,	
16. Walter, J. C.	,,	
15. Glieman, T. W.	Corporal-Bugler	Sergeant
18. Aiston, G.	Private	
66. Angrove, A.	,,	
77. Aldersey, W. E.	,,	Invalided to Australia, arr. 19.11.00
29. Alexander, J. J.	,,	
81. Butefisch, W.	,,	
32. Beecken, A. N.	,,	
47. Brown, J. R.	,,	
93. Burton, T. P.	,,	Invalided to Australia, arr. 11.6.00
48. Bennett, J.	,,	
59. Bradshaw, C. H.	,,	
64. Bristow, E.	,,	
88. Bates, A. S.	,,	
112. Bothe, A.	,,	Invalided to Australia, arr. 11.6.00
84. Brisbane, A.	,,	
17. Cornish, F. C.	,,	
21. Carson, A. E.	,,	Lance-Corporal
43. Collins, F. W.	,,	Invalided to Australia, arr. 11.6.00
100. Cameron, A. D. K.	,,	Invalided to Australia, arr. 10.8.00
19. Duncan, E. T.	,,	Invalided to Australia, arr. 19.11.00
92. Davis, G. C.	,,	
35. Dawson, T.	,,	
87. Dew, M. J.	,,	
103. Earle, J.	,,	
98. Eversley, H. E.	,,	
101. Ewens, A. E.	,,	
80. Edge, A.	,,	
115. Forbes, J.	,,	Missing; date not recorded
26. Foreman, W. J.	,,	
89. Gilbert, L.	,,	
31. Hanson, E. H.	,,	
37. Hood, T.	,,	
53. Holland, T.	,,	
60. Hay, J. G.	,,	Corporal
61. Hill, R.	,,	Invalided to Australia, arr. 19.11.00
105. Hare, J. L.	,,	
49. Holland, W.	,,	
33. Hawke, H. E.	,,	
25. Howe, S.	,,	Invalided to Australia, arr. 10.8.00
44. Jenkinson, T. R.	,,	
71. Jones, S. R.	,,	
116. Justice, W.	,,	
24. Kelly, W. J.	,,	
34. Keith, C. J.	,,	
91. Kilsby, A. J.	,,	
75. Leane, F. T.		
106. Larson, J. B. T.	,,	Invalided to Australia, arr. 10.8.00
20. Malone, M.	,,	
22. McBeth, J. C. J.	,,	

C.4720.

Nominal Roll—*continued.*

No. and Name.	Rank.	Remarks.
N.C.O.'s AND MEN—*continued.*		
113. Murch, A. E.	Private	Missing; date not recorded
42. Merrotsy, G. L.	,,	
50. Macdonald, R.	,,	
55. Marshall, T.	,,	Slightly wounded at Wanderlover, 7.9.00. Invalided to Australia; arr. 28.2.01
58. McGarish, A.	,,	
94. Macarthur, D.	,,	Invalided to Australia, arr. 10.8.00
102. Malone, R. A.	,,	Invalided to Australia, arr. 19.11.00
107. Moloney, C.	,,	
108. McLeod, D.	,,	
104. Mackenzie, W. H.	,,	Invalided to Australia, arr. 17.12.00
45. Mason, C. F.	,,	
109. Morphett, H. L. A.	,,	
110. Mander, J. G.	,,	Invalided to Australia, arr. 10.8.00
27. Maley, J.	,,	,, ,, ,,
96. Matthews, F. G.	,,	Died of fever, Deelfontein, 7.4.00
41. Nelson, O.	,,	
97. Naughton, T. A.	,,	
56. Nixon, A. R.	,,	Invalided to Australia arr. 11.6.00
74. Noblett, J. E.	,,	Lance-Corporal
54. Owen, R. W.	,,	Invalided to Australia, arr. 17.12.00
28. Paltridge, G. R.	,,	
30. Provis, F. H.	,,	Taken prisoner by the enemy. Invalided to Australia, arr. 23.7.01
76. Pinstney, S. C.	,,	
65. Pope, J.	,,	Missing; date not recorded
120. Parsons, J. W.	,,	Invalided to Australia, arr. 11.6.00
121. Petrie, J. E.	,,	
79. Raymond, L. S.	,,	
23. Rust, W.	,,	Lance-Corporal
38. Reid, J.	,,	
52. Ruddock, J. W.	,,	
39. Suffolk, W. C.	,,	
40. Stephens, T. H.	,,	
63. Simpson, A.	,,	
36. Swanson, J. H.	,,	
51. Short, R.	,,	
46. Smith, G.	,,	Invalided to Australia, arr. 10.8.00
82. Shearer, J. H.	,,	*Vide* " Promotions "
95. Stacey, N. A. J.	,,	
114. Scott, A. E.	,,	Lance-Corporal
118. Smith, W. E.	,,	Killed in action, 18.2.00
62. Schmidt, S. J.	,,	
57. Taverner, J. G.	,,	
69. Thompson, D.	,,	
83. Toole, J.	,,	Invalided to Australia, arr. 19.11.00
67. Ware, W. T.	,,	
72. Warnes, E. C.	,,	Invalided to Australia, arr. 10.8.00
85. Whitehead, W.	,,	
90. Wauchope, F. H.	,,	
111. Whitley, F.	,,	
117. Walters, W.	,,	
99. Wilkie, W. H.	,,	Invalided to Australia, arr. 10.8.00

SECOND (MOUNTED RIFLES) CONTINGENT.

THIS consisted of a squadron enrolled and organized upon the same principles (so far as they were applicable to mounted men) as that which had preceded it to the war, and which it joined in South Africa, as stated, under the head of "Service."

Establishment.—1 captain, 4 subalterns, 1 medical officer, 2 warrant-officers, 1 quartermaster-sergeant, 6 sergeants, 2 farrier-sergeants, 6 corporals, 4 lance-corporals, 3 shoeing-smiths, 1 saddler, 2 trumpeters, 85 troopers. Total, 6 officers, 112 of other ranks. One subaltern was attached, and one veterinary-lieutenant was appointed for the passage. A machine gun, and also wagons were taken.

For pay, uniform, etc., *vide* p. 342.

DEPARTURE AND RETURN.

The Contingent left on 26th January, 1900, comprising 7 officers, 112 others, with 120 horses. Died or were killed, 4. Two (warrant-officers) were promoted to commissions; 4 others obtained commissions in the Imperial Service; 1 in South African Light Horse; 7 were granted commissions for service with the 5th and 6th Contingents; 1 officer, 25 others, returned to Australia with 1st Contingent. Number struck off in South Africa not known.

PROMOTIONS, ETC.

Captain C. J. Reade, to Major, 7th June, 1900.
Lieutenant J. F. Humphris, to Captain, 1st July, 1900.
Lieutenant F. D. Jermyn (Medical Staff), to Captain, 3rd April, 1900.
Lieutenant F. M. Rowell, to Captain (for further service), 31st March, 1901.
Lieutenant G. J. R. Walter, to Captain (for further service), 31st March, 1901.
Warrant-Officer W. J. Press, to Lieutenant, 15th May, 1900.
Warrant-Officer W. De Passey, to Lieutenant, 13th March, 1901.
Troopers James Way, Leonard W. Gordon, W. H. Gosse, and F. G. Sanders, obtained commissions in the Imperial Army.
Corporal F. F. Solly-Flood, to be Lieutenant, South African Light Horse.
Quartermaster-Sergeant H. E. Francis, Sergeant E. J. F. Langley, Corporal D. W. Brock, Troopers H. A. Tolmer, S. Blue, J. D. Tolmer, and R. A. Hamilton, were promoted to commissions for service with 5th and 6th South Australian Contingents.
Sergeant H. L. S. B. Ogilvy, was promoted Lieutenant, 2nd Australian Commonwealth Horse. (S.A. unit.)
Corporal W. G. R. P. Nordman, was promoted Lieutenant, 8th Australian Commonwealth Horse.
Lance-Corporal R. C. H. Walker, was promoted Lieutenant, 8th Australian Commonwealth Horse.
For promotions of N.C.O.'s and men, *vide* nominal roll.

SERVICE.

The squadron left Adelaide on the transport *Surrey* on 26th January, 1900, and disembarked at Cape Town, 25th February. Encamped at Maitland, and entrained for De Aar on 2nd March; arrived on the 6th. Three hours later, marched to Britstown to join Column under Colonel Adye. Marched to and assisted in the relief of Prieska; the Column being under Colonel Adye, Colonel Mahon in charge of the mounted troops, and Lord Kitchener accompanying. Returned to De Aar and entrained for Norval's Pont. Marched to Bloemfontein, under Major Euthoven of "J" Battery, Royal Horse Artillery. Acted under orders from General Gatacre, and General Pole-Carew.

On arrival at Bloemfontein, the squadron united with the First Contingent to form the South Australian Mounted Rifles, and were ordered to join the Fourth Corps of First Mounted Infantry Brigade, under the command of Major-General E. T. H. Hutton. Colonel J. M. Gordon was appointed Deputy Adjutant-General to the Brigade, which numbered 6,215 officers and men.

The First Mounted Infantry Brigade (Hutton's) was formed of eight Mounted Infantry Corps; the Fourth Corps, under Colonel St. G. C. Henry, included the Victorian Mounted Rifles, South Australian Mounted Rifles, Tasmanian Mounted Infantry, and 500 Imperial Mounted Infantry, "J" Battery Royal Horse Artillery, and two pom-poms. Took part in the Karee-Brandfort fight, under General Tucker. Trooper Campbell was shot through the lungs, but recovered, and Trooper Provis (First Contingent) was taken prisoner. Marched to Johannesburg as advanced guard to XI. Division, under Lieutenant-General Pole-Carew, with whom were Lord Roberts and staff. Participated in the taking of Johannesburg, and were first into the fort; also in the taking of Pretoria, and the battle of Diamond Hill, under Lieutenant-General Pole-Carew.

The South Australians camped at Donker Hoek and Rhenoster Fontein, 13th June, to 28th July. Marched through Bronkhurst Spruit to Middelburg. Took their share in the engagement at Belfast, in which Generals Buller, French, Pole-Carew, Hamilton, and Stevenson were concerned. Marched through Helvetia, Machadodorp, Nooitgedacht, Kapsche Hoop, Barberton, and Hectorspruit to Komati Poort, at which place took part in a review in honour of the King of Portugal's birthday. Returned by train to Pretoria, 9th October, and encamped at Sunnyside.

Part of the Second Contingent, as already stated (*vide* First Contingent), left for Australia with the First Contingent on 3rd November. The remainder were attached to Mounted Infantry Brigade, under Brigadier-General E. A. Alderson, and returned for further service in east and north-east Transvaal until March, 1901.

The squadron embarked at Cape Town in the transport *Tongariro*, which steamed for Australia on 29th March. Landed in Sydney on 1st May; proceeded overland to Melbourne, and took part in the Commonwealth celebrations, reaching Adelaide, 12th May.

The Contingent was granted a bonus of 30 days' pay by the South Australian Government. Disbanded on 15th May, 1901.

War Services and Honours.

Reade, Major C. J.—Operations in Cape Colony, Orange River Colony, and Transvaal, between March, 1900, and March, 1901, including actions at Vet River, Zand River, Johannesburg, Pretoria, Diamond Hill, and Belfast. Despatches, *London Gazette*, 16th April, 1901. C.B. Queen's Medal with six clasps.

Humphris, Captain J. F.—Operations as stated. Actions at Johannesburg, Pretoria, Diamond Hill, and Belfast. Despatches, *London Gazette*, 16th April, 1901. D.S.O. Queen's Medal with five clasps.

Lynch, Lieutenant G. H.—Operations and actions as stated. Queen's Medal with clasps.

Rowell, Lieutenant F. M.—Operations as stated. Actions as Johannesburg, Pretoria, Diamond Hill, and Belfast. Lieutenant Rowell was promoted Captain after departure of the Contingent, and served until the end of the war. King's Medal with two clasps. Queen's Medal with five clasps.

Walter, Lieutenant G. J. R.—Operations and actions as stated, including Colesberg. Served until end of war. King's Medal with two clasps. Queen's Medal with five clasps.

Allan, Lieutenant W.—Operations and actions as stated. Queen's Medal with clasps.

Lieutenants W. J. Press and W. De Passey participated in operations and actions generally, and obtained the Queen's Medal, with clasps. Lieutenant De Passey had served in the Zulu campaign, 1879. Medal with clasp. He commanded the South Australian Squadron 2nd Australian Commonwealth Horse. Operations in Transvaal from 12th March, 1902, to 31st May, 1902. Seven clasps.

Jermyn, Captain (A.M.C.) F. D.—*Vide* Army Medical Corps (New South Wales) Commonwealth Contingent.

Nominal Roll.

No. and Name.	Rank.	Remarks.
OFFICERS.		
Reade, Charles James	Captain	Commanding
Humphris, Joseph Francis	Lieutenant	
Lynch, George Herbert	,,	
Rowell, Frank Milton	,,	
Walter, George Joseph Ristall	,,	
Allan, W.	,,	Attached
Jermyn, Frederick David	Lieutenant (Medical Staff)	
Bickford, William John	Veterinary-Lieutenant	For voyage only (*vide* 4th Imperial Bushmen)
W.O.'s, N.C.O.'s AND MEN.		
1. De Passey, William	Regimental-Sergeant-Major	*Vide* " Promotions "
112. Press, William Joseph	Sergeant-Major	,, ,,
110. Francis, Henry Ernest	Quartermaster-Sergeant	,, ,,
24. Langley, Edgar John Flynn	Sergeant	,, ,,
48. Dochrell, John	,,	Quartermaster-Sergeant
52. Read, James	,,	Sergeant-Major
87. Knapman, Leonard	,,	Despatches, *London Gazette*, 14.4.01. D.C.M.
41. Fay, Francis Xavier	,,	
65. Allan, Thomas Howard	,,	
26. Goodall, George Henry	Farrier-Sergeant	Farrier Quartermaster-Sergeant
107. Carter, Thomas James	,,	
29. Brock, Denzil William	Corporal	*Vide* " Promotions "
23. Butler, Charles Philip	,,	
83. Grosser, Chas. Alex. Constantine	,,	Sergeant
19. Solly-Flood, Frederick Frere	,,	*Vide* " Promotions "
Napier, Archibald George	,,	
22. White, Robert	,,	Invalided to Australia, arr. 10.8.00
16. Coffey, Maurice James	Lance-Corporal	Corporal
60. Castine, Claude Clement	,,	Sergeant
37. Morrant, Henry Horland	,,	
62. Rowell, Thomas Hubert	,,	
98. Burford, George	Shoeing-Smith	
10. Skinner, Thomas Nixon	,,	
11. Richardson, Thomas Walker	,,	
94. Marshall, Edward Sherman	Trumpeter	Died of fever, Pretoria, 17.6.01
17. Wright, Allen O'Halloran	,,	
86. Aldridge, George Richard	Trooper	Lance-Corporal
33. Barnett, Samuel	,,	Invalided to Australia, arr. 17.12.00

Nominal Roll—*continued*.

No. and Name.	Rank.	Remarks.
N.C.O.'s AND MEN—*continued*.		
75. Bostock, Robert Vernon	Trooper	Sergeant
76. Brown, Herbert Woolmer	,,	Despatches, *London Gazette*, 16.4.01. D.C.M.
91. Blue, Sinclair	,,	*Vide* "Promotions"
97. Bail, Henry	,,	Lance-Corporal
103. Bateson, Frederick Westbrook	,,	
34. Bartlett, Francis	,,	Died of fever, Pretoria, 26.12.00
Belt, Francis Walter	,,	
85. Campbell, John Angus	,,	
93. Campbell, Donald Angus	,,	Invalided to Australia, arr. 10.8.00
69. Carter, William Daniel	,,	
50. Clarke, James Gregory	,,	
30. Corpe, Hugh Robertson	,,	
14. Cook, William Arthur	,,	
108. Coon, John A.	,,	Lance-Corporal
9. Croucher, Joseph Erskine	,,	Severely wounded near Pretoria, 4.6.01
2. Cuttle, William George	,,	
61. Davies, Albert Chas. William	,,	
101. Dayman, Arthur Shorer	,,	
58. Douglas, James	,,	
18. Evans, Edward James	,,	
84. Ferbrache, Charles	,,	
51. Fetch, Hubert Harry	,,	Corporal. Despatches, *London Gazette*, 16.4.01
77. Florence, James	,,	
109. Goode, Stanley Livingstone	Lance-Corporal	Corporal
82. Gordon, Leonard William	Trooper	*Vide* "Promotions"
104. Gosse, William Hay	,,	,, ,,
6. Halliday, William Arthur	,,	Invalided to Australia, arr. 10.8.00
68. Hamilton, Reginald Alexander	,,	*Vide* "Promotions"
88. Hancock, Edmund Joseph	,,	
39. Hillman, Alfred Stanley	,,	
5. Hardy, George Lawrence	,,	Died of enteric at Bloemfontein, 4.6.00
Hawker, Henry Colley	,,	
38. Henderson, Leo Morphett	,,	
27. Horne, William Bannister	,,	
7. Huskisson, Arthur Frederick	,,	
66. Jenner, Edward	,,	
95. Jones, Philip	,,	Corporal
81. Lee, Arthur John	,,	Invalided to Australia, arr. 10.8.00
47. Loller, James Leslie	,,	
78. Lowe, Percy Thomas	,,	Invalided to Australia, arr. 10.8.00
43. Lynskey, Michael Frank	,,	
4. Macauley, Anlay Babington	,,	
13. Marsden, Thomas Bradshaw	,,	Died of pneumonia at Britstown, 5.4.00
149. Makin, Frank Humphrey	,,	Corporal
111. Malcolm, Wilfred Walter	,,	
35. Millar, James Hay	,,	
Moore, Albert Walter	,,	
74. Morrow, John Henry	,,	
28. Mounsey, John	,,	Invalided to Australia, arr. 27.10.00
64. Morton, Daniel	,,	
99. McInerney, William	,,	Corporal
46. Newbold, Hartlet Herman	Shoeing-Smith	Corporal

Nominal Roll—*continued.*

No. and Name.	Rank.	Remarks.
N.C.O.'s and Men—*continued.*		
59. Newland, Victor Mara	Trooper	Despatches *London Gazette*, 16.4.01. D.C.M.
40. Nober, William Sterling	,,	
36. Nordmann, Wilfred G. R. P.	,,	Corporal, *vide* " Promotions "
8. Nunneley, Wilfred Alexander	,,	Invalided to Australia, arr. 12.4.01
49. Nuttall, Ramsay	,,	Invalided to Australia, arr. 28.2.01
45. Ogilvy, Harry Lort S. B.	,,	Sergeant. Despatches, *London Gazette*, 16.4.01. D.C.M. *Vide* " Promotions "
72. Pether, William Henry	,,	Invalided to Australia, arr. 28.2.01
105. Pettitt, Percival Arthur Chas.	,,	
32. Pflaum, Frederick Conrad	,,	Invalided to Australia, arr. 19.11.00
56. Rankine, Peter Bruce	,,	
31. Reidy, James	,,	Sergeant
25. Robson, Horace Daniel	,,	
3. Sanders, Frank Gordon	,,	*Vide* " Promotions "
70. Shepherd, John	Saddler	Corporal
53. Simper, Hector	Trooper	
106. Sobels, Oscar Carl	,,	
102. Stock, Alfred Douglas	,,	
100. Stoyel, William Gilbert	,,	
96. Tavernor, George	,,	
79. Taylor, Alfred	,,	
44. Tolmer, Herbert Alexander	,,	*Vide* " Promotions " Invalided to Australia; arr. 17.12.00
54. Tolmer, James Douglas	,,	*Vide* " Promotions "
21. Toseland, William James	,,	
71. Ward, William Henry	,,	
57. Way, James	,,	*Vide* " Promotions "
67. Wauchope, Leslie Alexander	,,	
90. Walker, Reginald C. Henderson	,,	Lance-Corporal. *Vide* " Promotions "
92. Webb, Edward Dugald	,,	
89. Webb, Robert Dutton	,,	
Williams, Frank	,,	Invalided to Australia, arr. 28.2.01
12. Wood, Richard Edward	,,	
63. Wormleighton, Frederick	,,	

THIRD BUSHMEN'S CONTINGENT.

LIKE similar Corps elsewhere, the cost of this Contingent was defrayed by subscriptions from the citizens; a Committee being formed for administrative purposes, but the enrolment and organization being carried on by the military authorities. Men were required to be good riders and expert shots, and to be familiar with the ordinary conditions of bush life.

Establishment.—1 captain, 3 subalterns, 1 medical officer, 1 veterinary officer, 1 sergeant-major, 1 quartermaster-sergeant, 4 sergeants, 1 farrier-sergeant, 8 corporals, 6 lance-corporals, 1 corporal trumpeter, 1 corporal cook, 1 saddler, 69 privates. Total, 6 officers, 93 of other ranks.

For pay, uniform, &c., *vide* p. 342.

Departure and Return.

The Contingent left 27th February, 1900, comprising—6 officers and 93 other ranks, with 100 horses. Five died or were killed; 1 N.C.O. was promoted to a commission. Number struck off in South Africa not known.

Promotions.

Lieutenant A. E. Collins, to Captain, 16th October, 1900.
Sergeant-Major J. I. Dempsey, to Lieutenant, 16th October, 1900.
For promotions of N.C.O.'s and men, *vide* nominal roll.

Service.

The Bushmen's Contingent embarked in the transport *Maplemore*, which steamed from Port Adelaide on 27th February, 1900, and called at Fremantle to pick up the Western Australian Bushmen. Disembarked at Beira, 1st April. This squadron participated in operations in Western Transvaal from June, 1900, to April, 1901, under Lord Methuen, "No. 1" Division. If formed part of General Carrington's force, which crossed Rhodesia and entered the Transvaal from about Mafeking.

Between 4th July and 9th August, the squadron was patrolling the Marico and working towards Eland's River district. On the 9th, they retired to Mafeking with General Carrington. On the 13th, they were in a skirmish, and next day in a fight at Buffel's Hoek. On the 15th, the squadron was made part of a composite regiment of Bushmen with "D" Squadron New South Wales 1st Mounted Rifles, Captain Polson's squadron 5th New Zealanders, and the 3rd Tasmanians. For a long time the Regiment did excellent work in the Western Transvaal, as part of Lord Methuen's division. At Buffel's Hoek there was fighting, and they sustained casualties. For the second time they were in action at Ottoshoop on 12th September, when Captain S. G. Hubbe was killed; and there were other losses.

At Lichtenberg on the 26th, there were again casualties. Lieutenant Collins, who had been wounded near Ottoshoop on 6th August, but had recovered and rejoined, took command with the rank of captain. Throughout the latter part of 1900, and the first quarter of 1901, the composite regiment was in many engagements, chiefly in the Western Transvaal, and also north of the Orange River Colony; and losses were frequent, the enemy being alert and ably led. At Uitralskop, 3rd February, the squadron lost one man; and Lieutenant Dempsey and others were wounded. At a very severely contested action near Rietfontein, 16th February, Captain Collins was wounded for the second time; besides one other man.

Lord Methuen, in a letter to the Secretary of the Bushmen's Committee, South Australia, written after the departure of the Contingent, expressed praise for the "splendid work performed by the squadron," their cheerfulness in hardship, and their discipline. "I cannot conceive any body of men of whom a commander has greater reason to be proud," he wrote.

The squadron embarked at Cape Town on the transport *Morayshire*, 29th April, 1901, and arrived at Adelaide about 25th June.

War Services and Honours.

Hubbe, Captain S. G.—Operations in Western Transvaal between June and 12th September, 1900. Despatches, *London Gazette*, 16th April, 1901. Killed in action at Ottoshoop, 12th September, 1900.

Collins, Captain A. E.—Operations in Transvaal, Orange River Colony, and Rhodesia. Twice wounded. Despatches, *London Gazette*, 16th April, 1901. D.S.O. Queen's Medal with six clasps. He subsequently commanded "C" squadron, 4th Australian Commonwealth Horse.

Ives, Lieutenant C. M.—Operations in Cape Colony, Orange River Colony, Transvaal, and Rhodesia. Despatches, *London Gazette*, 16th April, 1901. D.S.O. Queen's Medal with five clasps.

Arnot, Lieutenant W. O.—Operations as stated. Queen's Medal with clasps.

Dempsey, Lieutenant J. I.—Operations as stated. Wounded at Uitralskop. Despatches, *London Gazette*, 16th April, 1901. Queen's Medal with five clasps.

Douglas, Lieutenant (Medical Staff) F. J.—Operations as stated. Queen's Medal with five clasps.

Burns, Veterinary Lieutenant J. L.—Operations in Cape Colony. Queen's Medal with one clasp.

Nominal Roll.

No. and Name.	Rank.	Remarks.
Officers.		
Hubbe, Samuel Grau	Captain Commanding	Killed at Ottoshoop, 12.9.00.
Collins, Angus Edward	Lieutenant	Wounded near Ottoshoop, 6.8.00; slightly wounded near Rietfontein, 16.2.01
Ives, Charles Marsh	,,	
Arnot, Walter Oliphant	,,	
Douglas, Francis John	Lieutenant (Medical Staff)	
Burns, Jerome Lawrence	Veterinary Lieutenant	
N.C.O.'s and Men.		
26. Dempsey, J. I.	S. Sergeant-Major	*Vide* "Promotions." Wounded at Uitralskop, 3.2.01. Invalided to Australia, arr. 23.7.01
85. Blackmore, G. E.	Quartermaster-Sergeant	
2. Kerr, J. M.	Sergeant	Sergeant-Major, 16.10.00
77. Mair, G. H. M.	,,	
3. Rundle, J.	,,	Despatches *London Gazette*, 29.7.02. Invalided to Australia, arr. 31.5.01
94. Kent, T. D.	,,	
32. Westley, J. A.	Farrier-Sergeant	Invalided to Australia, arr. **23.7.01**
56. Beck, J. R.	Corporal	Wounded at Uitralskop, **3.2.01.** Invalided to Australia, **arr.** 23.7.01
15. Clark, J. J.	,,	
84. Mitchell, P.	,,	

Nominal Roll—*continued.*

No. and Name.	Rank.	Remarks.
N.C.O.'s AND MEN—*continued.*		
34. Currie, C. W. B.	Corporal	Despatches, *London Gazette*, 16.4.01. Killed at Uitralskop, 3.2.01
27. Anthes, J. J.	,,	
21. Attiwell, E. H.	,,	Slightly wounded, Ottoshoop, 12.9.00
91. Rickaby, T. N.	,,	Slightly wounded near Kaffirs Kraal, 29.10.00
69. Ive, H. P.	,,	Sergeant, 16.10.00. Despatches, *London Gazette*, 16.4.01
44. Formby, H. J.	Lance-Corporal	Corporal, —.10.00. Despatches, *London Gazette*, 16.4.01
40. Fenwick, W. E.	,,	Corporal, 10.0.00. Despatches, *London Gazette*, 16.4.01. Invalided to Australia, arr. 30.5.01
4. Wickens, E. A.	,,	Taken prisoner, 18.8.00
19. Stanners, G. E.	,,	
88. McLachlan, J. F.	,,	
53. Lyons, T. P.	,,	
33. Gay, H.	Corporal Trumpeter	Sergeant-Trumpeter, —.6.00
31. Gilbert, W. J.	Corporal-Cook	
28. Anderson, W. F.	Trooper	
71. Batten, A. C.	Saddler	
29. Barnes, J. L.	Trooper	
51. Brown, F.	,,	
30. Cabot, A.	,,	
67. Churches, A. E.	,,	Slightly wounded at Ottoshoop, 12.9.00
72. Coutts, A. F.	,,	
59. Cradock, W.	,,	
8. Donnelly, J.	,,	
37. Dunkley, G. H.	,,	
38. Denman, E.	,,	
35. Denman, H. R.	,,	
39. Elliot, J. W.	,,	
25. Emmerton, W. H.	,,	
10. Ewens, C. E.	,,	
42. Forbes, G. S.	,,	Invalided to Australia, arr. 28.2.01
43. Fortherby, J.	,,	
41. Ford, J.	,,	Severely wounded at Uitralskop, 2.3.01. Invalided to Australia, arr. 23.7.01
45. Flynn, T. W.	,,	
16. Gaylard, J. H.	,,	
58. Gooley, J. B.	,,	Invalided to Australia, arr. 31.5.01
14. Hayward, H.	,,	Slightly wounded near Mafeking, 13.8.00. Invalided to Australia, arr. 28.2.01
11. Hayward, R.	,,	
60. Horne, R. J.	,,	
73. Holland, A.	,,	Dangerously ill, pneumonia, **near** Ottoshoop, 6.8.00. **Invalided** to Australia, arr. 28.2.01
55. Hunter, T. F.	,,	
22. Hoban, M. P.	,,	
70. Hodge, E. P.	,,	Invalided to Australia, arr. 12.4.01
47. Harrington, H. J.	,,	

Nominal Roll—*continued*.

No. and Name.	Rank.	Remarks.
N.C.O.'S AND MEN—*continued*.		
24. Higgins, J.	Trooper	
23. Japper, J.	,,	
48. Johnstone, W. G.	,,	Severely wounded near Wonderfontein, 9.11.00. Invalided to Australia, arr. 28.5.01
49. Keitel, C.	,,	Invalided to Australia, arr. 23.7.01
64. Laughton, J. E.	,,	
68. Lowe, F. G. H.	,,	
62. Litchfield, W. M.	,,	
80. Lovelock, C. S. A.	,,	Severely wounded at Uitralskop, 2.3.01. Invalided to Australia, arr. 23.7.01
50. Leonard, A.	,,	
82. Mann, P. A.	,,	
83. Martin, H.	,,	
89. Maccabe, J.	,,	
65. Millman, C. F.	,,	Killed at Kaffirs Kraal, 31.10.00
86. Mullins, J. B.	,,	
7. Mullins, J. E.	,,	
81. Matthews, A.	,,	
52. Matthews, C.	,,	Invalided to Australia, arr. 28.2.01
61. Mercer, C. J. B.	,,	Sergeant. Died of enteric at Kroonstadt, 21.12.01
87. Munro, A.	,,	
Morphett, C. E.	,,	
12. Nickels, A. G.	,,	
13. Nickels, H. H.	,,	Invalided to Australia arr. 28.2.01
90. Page, H. J.	,,	Orderlyroom-Sergeant, —.10.00
92. Ridley, W. E.	,,	
93. Rowell, C. F.	,,	
18. Rutherford, D. D.	,,	Severely wounded at Uitralskop, 2.3.01
5. Skene, T.	,,	Taken prisoner, 18.8.00
74. Searle, W. W.	,,	
20. Sullivan, T.	,,	
57. Simmons, E. F.	,,	
16. Spendor, E. C.	,,	Taken prisoner, 18.8.00
9. Swan, S. P. W.	,,	Invalided to Australia, arr. 31.5.01
95. Sloan, J. D.	,,	Injured by fall from horse; died of injuries, Cape Town, 1.1.01
66. Staples, A.	,,	
98. Treloar, C. R.	,,	
77. Turner, J. W.	,,	
96. Thomas, M. E.	,,	
99. Usher, T.	,,	
6. Valpien. J. A.	,,	
19. Virgo, J. H.	,,	
100. Ward, R. R.	,,	Invalided to Australia, arr. 31.5.01

FOURTH (IMPERIAL BUSHMEN) CONTINGENT.

FOR pay, equipment, organization, conditions of enrolment, etc., *vide* Imperial Bushmen, New South Wales or Victoria; also p. 341. This was the first South Australian Contingent receiving entire Imperial pay. It consisted of two squadrons, "A" and "B," under a lieutenant-colonel, with a major second in command, who likewise acted as adjutant. There were also a medical officer and a veterinary officer on battalion staff. The establishment comprised—2 captains, 6 lieutenants, 2 sergeant-majors, 2 quartermaster-sergeants, 13 sergeants, 1 sergeant-farrier, 13 corporals, 12 lance-corporals, 1 sergeant-cook, 1 sergeant-trumpeter, 7 trumpeters, 1 corporal-farrier, 6 farriers, 2 saddlers, and 161 privates. Total, 12 officers, 222 of other ranks.

DEPARTURE AND RETURN.

The Contingent left on 1st May, 1900, comprising—12 officers, 222 others, with 240 horses. Thirteen died or were killed; 5 N.C.O.'s were promoted to commissions, 1 N.C.O. obtained a commission in the Imperial service; 2 officers struck off in South Africa. Number of other ranks not known.

PROMOTIONS, ETC.

Captain H. L. D. Wilson, to Major, 10th January, 1901.
Lieutenant F. W. Hurcombe, to Captain, 20th February, 1901.
Sergeant H. J. Russell, to Lieutenant, 20th February, 1901; Captain, 22nd April, 1901.
Sergeant-Major H. L. Keckwick, to Lieutenant, 20th February, 1901.
Lance-Corporal F. O. Thorne, to Lieutenant, 20th February, 1901.
Sergeant H. A. Reid, to Lieutenant, 4th March, 1901.
Sergeant G. E. Catchlove, to Lieutenant, 25th May, 1901.
Quartermaster-Sergeant G. Lewis, commissioned in the West Riding Regiment (Duke of Wellington's Own), 4th January, 1901.
Quartermaster-Sergeant F. C. Sickmann was appointed a Lieutenant in 2nd Australian Commonwealth Horse.
Lance-Corporal J. H. Downer became a Lieutenant in 4th Australian Commonwealth Horse.
Trooper G. De Reyher became a Lieutenant in 4th Australian Commonwealth Horse.
Sergeant W. F. Spencer was appointed Lieutenant in 8th Australian Commonwealth Horse.
Lance-Corporal B. T. Ward was similarly appointed.
For promotions of N.C.O.'s and men, *vide* nominal roll.

SERVICE.

The Fourth Imperial Bushmen left Port Adelaide in the transport *Manhattan* on 1st May, 1900. Called at Fremantle to embark the Fourth Western Australians: Beira, Durban, and disembarked at Port Elizabeth on 19th June. Lieutenant-Colonel Rowell was placed in command of an Australian regiment comprising some 400 Bushmen; there being the two squadrons of South Australians, one Western Australian, and one Tasmanian. For some account of the excellent service rendered, *vide* Fourth Western Australian and Third Tasmanian Contingents.

Bethlehem was taken on 7th July, when 300 Bushmen, mostly South and Western Australians, joined in the attack. When De Wet broke through the cordon on 16th, the Contingent took part in his pursuit to the Reitzburg hills. At Palmietfontein on 19th, there was an engagement; and on the 24th, at Stinkhoutboom, where the South Australians sustained losses. The Contingent followed De Wet to the Transvaal. In November, they joined General Plumer. In February, 1901, they sustained several casualties in Cape Colony, during the pursuit of De Wet; and in March, April, and May, they distinguished themselves in operations between Pretoria and Pietersberg. When General Plumer, after the occupation of the latter town, was moving southwards, Captain F. W. Hurcombe was commended for his successful leading. During May, the Contingent suffered casualties on various occasions in the Eastern Transvaal.

The service may thus be summarized:—June, 1900—Formed escort to convoy from Kroonstadt to Lindley. Attached to General Paget in operations against De Wet from Lindley to Bethlehem; and took part in the capture of the latter town. July and August—Attached to General Broadwood, in pursuit of De Wet, from Bethlehem through Oliphant's Nek and the Magaliesberg Range. Took part in the relief of Eland's River garrison. 29th November—Engagement at Rhenoster Kop; attached to General Plumer, and participated in General French's operations in the Eastern Transvaal. February and March, 1901—Operations in pursuit of De Wet in Cape Colony and Orange River Colony. April, May, and June—With General Plumer to Pietersburg; in operations in Northern Transvaal, and from thence to Bethel, Standerton, and Piet Retief.

The Contingent embarked on 5th July, 1901, at East London, in the transport *Britannic*, and arrived at Adelaide, 27th July. Disbanded shortly afterwards.

WAR SERVICES AND HONOURS.

Rowell, Lieut.-Colonel J.—Operations in Cape Colony, Transvaal, and Orange River Colony, between July, 1900, and July, 1901, including action at Wittebergen. Despatches, *London Gazette*, 16th April, 1901. C.B. Queen's Medal with four clasps. Aide-de-Camp to the Governor-General.

Hawker, Major J. C.—Operations and action as stated. Queen's Medal with four clasps.

Wilson, Major H. L. D.—Operations and action as stated. Despatches, *London Gazette*, 16th April, 1901. Queen's Medal with four clasps. Remained for further service with 5th and 6th Imperial Bushmen.

Norton, Captain A. E. M.—Operations in Cape Colony and Orange River Colony, and action as stated. Despatches, *London Gazette*, 10th September, 1901. D.S.O. Queen's Medal with two clasps.

Hurcombe, Captain F. W.—Operations in Transvaal and Orange River Colony, including Wittebergen. Subsequently promoted Major (served with 5th and 6th Imperial Bushmen). Queen's Medal with three clasps. King's Medal with two clasps.

Cook, Lieutenant A. E.—Operations and actions as first stated. Queen's Medal with four clasps. Became Captain in 8th Australian Commonwealth Horse.

Leane, Lieutenant E. T.—Operations in Transvaal and Orange River Colony, including Wittebergen. Despatches, *London Gazette*, 10th September, 1901. Queen's Medal with three clasps.

Ferguson, Lieutenant R. H.—Operations in Orange River Colony and Transvaal, and action as stated. Queen's Medal with three clasps.

Roberts, Lieutenant E. A.—Operations and action as first stated. Queen's Medal with four clasps.

White, Lieutenant S. A.—Operations in Transvaal and **Orange River Colony**. Staff Officer to Commandant of an Area, 1901-2. Queen's Medal with **three** clasps. King's Medal with two clasps.

Dunn, Captain (Medical Staff) S. S., and *Bickford*, Veterinary-Lieutenant W. J.—Operations as stated. Queen's Medal with clasps.

Russell, Captain H. J., *Keckwick*, Lieutenant H. L., and *Thorne*, Lieutenant F. O.—Operations and action as stated. Queen's Medal with four clasps.

Reid, Lieutenant H. A.—Operations and action as stated. Despatches, *London Gazette*, 16th April, 1901. D.S.O. Queen's Medal with three clasps. He subsequently became Captain and Adjutant, 8th Australian Commonwealth Horse.

Catchlove, Lieutenant G. E.—Operations in Transvaal and Orange River Colony, and Wittebergen. Queen's Medal with four clasps (*vide* also nominal roll, Corporal Catchlove.)

Nominal Roll.

No. and Name.	Rank.	Remarks.
OFFICERS.		
Rowell, James	Lieut.-Colonel	
Hawker, James Clarence	Major-Adjutant	Permanent Artillery. Invalided to Australia, arr. 28.2.01
Wilson, Howard Locke Dexter	Captain	
Norton, A. Edward Marston	,,	
Dunn, Spencer Smithson	Captain (Medical Staff)	
Hurcombe, Frederick William	Lieutenant	
Cook, Alfred Edward	,,	Invalided to Australia, arr. 28.2.01
Leane, Edwin Thomas	,,	
Ferguson, Ross Hayter	,,	Invalided to Australia, arr. 31.5.01
Roberts, Ernest Alfred	,,	
White, Samuel Albert	,,	
Bickford, W. J.	Veterinary-Lieutenant	
N.C.O.'S AND MEN.		
1. Baker, Charles Frederick	Sergeant-Major	
124. Mitchell, Thomas John Henwood	,,	Invalided to Australia, arr. 28.2.01
6. Varley, George Albert	Quartermaster-Sergeant	
117. Siekmann, Francis Charles	,,	Invalided to Australia, arr. 12.4.01. *Vide* " Promotions "
120. Coulter, Frederick	Sergeant	
118. Carruthers, Charles George	,,	
5. Bridgeman, Jno. Samuel	,,	
131. Harrington, Howard Jos.	,,	
2. Keckwick, Hubert Lydiard	,,	Sergeant-Major, 1.11.00. *Vide* " Promotions "
121. Harrington, Edgar Randolph	,,	
11. Lewis, Gilbert	,,	Quartermaster-Sergeant, 1.11.00. *Vide* " Promotions "
77. Maccabe, Chas. Edward	,,	Killed in action, Reitfontein, 29.11.00
122. Owen, Samuel Hugh	,,	
152. Ogilvy, Graham Balfour	,,	
8. Reid, Herbert Ambrose	,,	*Vide* " Promotions "
134. Spencer, Wm. Frederick	,,	Wounded at Grasfontein, 13.2.01. Despatches, *London Gazette*, 10.9.01. D.C.M. *Vide* " Promotions "
3. **Wilson, Almeric Fitzroy**	,,	

Nominal Roll—continued.

No. and Name.	Rank.	Remarks.
N.C.O.'s AND MEN—continued.		
4. Phillifant, Benjamin Charles	Sergeant-Farrier	
15. Wilkin, Fred. Barrett	Corporal	
135. Tratham, Henry Harold	,,	Sergeant. Invalided to Australia, arr. 31.5.01
21. Russell, Herbert James	,,	Sergeant, 1.11.00. *Vide* "Promotions"
79. O'Halloran, Nicholas Bayley	,,	
12. Hey, Tom Henry	,,	Sergeant, 1.11.00
14. Jones, Jno. Thomas	,,	
130. Jones, David George	,,	
132. McLeod, Fred. John	,,	
13. Cox, Robert Christopher	,,	
10. Denholm, Alexr. Charles	,,	Invalided to Australia, arr. 17.12.00
133. Allnutt, George Stephen	,,	Despatches, *London Gazette*, 10.9.01. D.C.M. Invalided to Australia, arr. 28.2.01
89. Bosworth, Jno. Henry Ward	,,	Invalided to Australia, arr. 17.12.01
128. Catchlove, George Edwin	,,	Sergeant, 1.11.00. *Vide* "Promotions." Slightly wounded at Stinkhontboom, 24.7.00, again at Vredefort, 18.8.00. Despatches, *London Gazette*, 10.9.01
19. Alexander, Philip	Lance-Corporal	Invalided to Australia, arr. 23.7.01
16. Downer, Jno. Henry	,,	*Vide* "Promotions"
136. Farley, Frederick Hammond	,,	Corporal, 1.11.00
138. Holthouse, Fred. Reginald	,,	Corporal, 1.11.00
139. Knowles, Jno. Frederick	,,	
22. Love, Richard Thomas	,,	
23. Mutch, Thomas Henry	,,	
18. Nicholls, Charles Alfred	,,	
140. Read, Wm. Bowman	,,	Enteric at Bloemfontein, 27.4.01
17. Sandell, Neil	,,	
137. Sandison, Henry George	,,	
20. Wilson, Clarence	,,	
119. Miller, William	Sergeant-Cook	Invalided to Australia, arr. 31.5.01
24. Harris, Ernest James	Sergeant-Trumpeter	
87. Weman, David Henry	Trumpeter	
125. White, Horatio	,,	
82. Stoneham, R. A. A.	,,	Invalided to Australia, arr. 12.4.01
25. Gent, Percy Athelstone	,,	
72. Jergens, John	,,	
198. Errington, Jas. John	,,	Invalided to Australia, arr. 17.12.00
126. Davis, Cornelius George	,,	Died of fever, Pretoria, 4.1.01
129. Simper, Sydney James	Corporal-Farrier	
191. Wynne, Michael	Shoeing-Smith	
187. Schramm, Thomas Horan	,,	Invalided to Australia, arr. 28.2.01
209. Lewis, George Wilson	,,	Corporal-Farrier. Invalided to Australia, arr. 17.12.00
44. Muir, James Percival	,,	Invalided to Australia, arr. 17.12.00
37. Hanchant, Alfred Walter Thomas	,,	
33. Fooks, William	,,	
115. Wadsham, Jno. Henry	Saddler	
178. Mitchell, Edmund Henry	,,	**Killed at Welverdiend, 4.9.00**

Nominal Roll—*continued.*

No. and Name.	Rank.	Remarks.
N.C.O.'s AND MEN—*continued.*		
194. Albon, William Robert	Trooper	
168. Allen, Fred. William	,,	Invalided to Australia, arr. 28.2.01
167. Atkinson, Alfred	,,	
59. Atkinson, Chas. Harvey	,,	
58. Allen, Walter Henry	,,	
57. Alfred, Jno. Westley	,,	
26. Adams, Wm. James	,,	
88. Batten, Jno. Lawrence	,,	
61. Brackinreg, Walter Colin	,,	Invalided to Australia, arr. 28.2.01
60. Becker, Herbert Lionel	,,	Invalided to Australia, arr. 17.12.00
27. Bolt, Allen Christopher	,,	
171. Bolitho, Wilfred	,,	
170. Bleechmore, Edgar James	,,	
147. Burton, Fred. Charles	,,	
141. Bunn, Richard William	,,	
196. Clark, Kenneth	,,	Invalided to Australia, arr. 12.4.01
195. Comley, Joseph	,,	
181. Champion, Harry	,,	Lance-Corporal, 30.8.00
172. Croft, William Henry	,,	
158. Cullen, William	,,	
90. Cornwall, Robert Jno.	,,	
29. Cowan, Wm. Jas. Trafford	,,	
28. Cowan, Fred Hamilton	,,	Invalided to Asutralia, arr. 28.2.01
7. Cowan, Jno. George	,,	
93. Donaghy, Vincent Gerald Jos.	,,	
90. Dunn, Lionel William	,,	Invalided to Australia, arr. 17.12.00
31. Dickson, George Isaac	,,	Invalided to Australia, arr. 12.4.01
30. Davis, Edgar Chas. Patterson	,,	Invalided to Australia, arr. 28.2.01
62. De Reyher, Gordon	,,	*Vide* " Promotions "
197. Dolley, Charles John	,,	
193. Dwyer, Daniel Jos.	,,	
144. Doody, Patrick	,,	
143. Daffey, Michael Thomas	,,	Invalided to Australia, arr. 28.2.01
142. Dale, Henry Stewart	,,	Invalided to Australia, arr. 17.12.00
63. Ewens, Clifford Woolley	,,	
174. Edwards, Thomas	,,	Invalided to Australia, arr. 31.1.02
95. Ford, Archibald Harris	,,	
32. Foale, Stanley Archy	,,	
200. Freebairn, William Lewis	,,	
199. Fisher, David Roaden	,,	
64. Follett, Walter Herbert	,,	
98. Goodes, Herbert Ernest	,,	Killed in action at Bethel, 23.5.01
97. Glennie, Charles John	,,	Invalided to Australia, arr. 17.12.00
67. Gray, William Henry	,,	
65. Giles, Henry Arthur	,,	
35. Gully, Harold Percy	,,	
34. Guerin, Michael Martin	,,	
145. Gardiner, Robert Cornelius	,,	Despatches, *London Gazette,* 10.9.01. Invalided to Australia, arr. 28.2.01
73. Hanley, William Henry	,,	
68. Henzenroeder, Edmund Gerald	,,	Invalided to Australia, arr. 12.4.01
66. Horner, Charles Forbes	,,	Died of fever, Hebron, 24.12.00
36. Hendrie, James Herbert	,,	

Nominal Roll—continued.

No. and Name.	Rank.	Remarks.
N.C.O.'S AND MEN—continued.		
24. Harris, Ernest James	Trooper	
203. Haydon, Edward	,,	
202. Herriman, Wm. James	,,	Invalided to Australia, arr. 28.2.01
201. Hawksby, Jackson Ebenezer	,,	Invalided to Australia, arr. 28.2.01
175. Hecht, Henry Frederick	,,	
169. Hastie, Percy Ronald Stuart	,,	Invalided to Australia, 31.5.01 arr.
146. Hall, Howard Frank	,,	Lance-Corporal. Severely wounded at Bethlehem, 25.7.00. Invalided to Australia, arr. 31.5.01
73. Jones, Edward Wilcox	,,	
71. Johnston, Archibald Wm.	,,	
70. Johnston, Charles Bert	,,	Invalided to Australia, arr. 23.7.01
39. Johnston, Frederick James	,,	
38. Jewell, Joseph	,,	
176. James, John George	,,	
130. Johns, David George	,,	
74. Landsdale, Sydney	,,	Severely wounded at Bethel, 23.5.01; died next day
205. Lewis, George Wilson	,,	
204. Lemon, James Richard	,,	
103. Macfarlane, Percy Muir	,,	
102. McBeth, Alexdr. Francis	,,	
101. Mitchell, George John	,,	
99. McCall, James	,,	Invalided to Australia
78. Moulden, Albert	,,	
218. McBean, John Alexr.	,,	
76. Mathews, Charles Angus	,,	
75. Meny, Arnold Barnard	,,	
52. Manning, Wm. Joseph	,,	
43. Mackareth, Frederick J.	,,	Invalided to Australia, arr. 17.12.00
42. Macdougal, Ewen	,,	
41. Murray, Enos	,,	
40. Marchant, Tom Octavius	,,	
216. Marshall, Herbert Spencer	,,	Invalided to Australia, arr. 28.2.01
207. Menzel, Otto R.	,,	Invalided to Australia, arr. 31.5.01
206. Maxwell, John Strachan	,,	Invalided to Australia, arr. 28.2.01
179. Moore, John Hartly	,,	Killed at Palmietfontein, 12.7.00
177. Modra, Rudolph Fredk. Martin	,,	
150. Muir, Thomas Ker	,,	Invalided to Australia, arr. 28.2.01
149. Magor, Ernest Howard	,,	Invalided to Australia, arr. 12.4.01
148. Mayfield, Stanley Howard	,,	Despatches, *London Gazette*, 10.9.01. Invalided to Australia, arr. 12.4.01
106. Newman, Archibald John	,,	
47. Norman, Frederick	,,	
46. Noblett, Geo. Edwin	,,	
208. Nicholas, Alexander Wm.	,,	Killed at Stinkhontboom, 24.7.00
151. Nation, Wylie	,,	
107. Ogilvie, Wm. Henry	,,	
123. Prosser, Henry Clifton	,,	Sergeant. Severely wounded at Palmietfontein, 19.7.00. Invalided to Australia, arr. 23.7.01
80. Prosser, Herbert Edgar	,,	Died from injuries near Durban, 12.6.00
48. Page, Albert Stephen	,,	Killed in action, Rietfontein, 29.11.00

Nominal Roll—*continued.*

No. and Name.	Rank.	Remarks.
N.C.O.'s AND MEN—*continued.*		
211. Plunkett, Wm. Gladstone	Trooper	Invalided to Australia, arr. 31.5.01
210. Potter, Harry	,,	
209. Palmer, Harold Prelin	,,	
180. Packard, Charles Harrison	,,	Invalided to Australia, arr. 28.2.01
157. Palmer, Albert Thomas	,,	Died of enteric, Pretoria, 10.3.01
156. Plate, Frederick Wm.	,,	
155. Painter, Wm. Arundel	,,	
154. Payne, John Rudolph Stuart	,,	Invalided to Australia, arr. 12.4.01
153. Pearce, Walter Henry	,,	
81. Richardson, Frank Sinclair	,,	
49. Redman, Charles	,,	Invalided to Australia, arr. 23.7.01
45. Roy, Robert Thompson	,,	Invalided to Australia, arr. 17.12.00
212. Reid, Francis Wm.	,,	
160. Richardson, John Percival	,,	Severely wounded at Bethlehem, 3.7.00
159. Rowe, David	,,	
17. Sondell, Neil	,,	
9. Smith, Walter	,,	
111. Stone, Wm. Ernest	,,	
110. Smythe, James Herbert	,,	
109. Smith, George Quorn	,,	
94. Smart, James Henry	,,	
91. Scott, Walter Hamilton	,,	
185. Sayers, Wm. Samuel	,,	Slightly wounded at Palmietfontien, 12.7.00
50. Skinner, John Arthur	,,	
51. Smith, Rupert Sydney	,,	
215. Swinden, Edwin Glenelg	,,	
214. Short, Augustus Egerton	,,	
213. Stott, Thomas	,,	Despatches, *London Gazette*, 10.9.01. Invalided to Australia, arr. 17.12.00
185. Smythe, David Hugh C.	,,	Invalided to Australia, arr. 31.5.01
184. Sabine, Charles Glen	,,	
183. Scott, Thomas Stephen	,,	
182. Stone, James Cornelius	,,	Invalided to Australia, arr 17.12.00
162. Schimdt, Henry Giles	,,	
161. Sandford, John Edgar Fk.	,,	
127. Siebert, Francis Joseph	,,	
113. Trevenen, Frank Bert	,,	
108. Trower, William	,,	Invalided to Australia, arr. 31.5.01
105. Thomas, Harry	,,	
104. Thorne, Frederick Otto	,,	Lance-Corporal. *Vide* "Promotions." Slightly wounded at Stinkhontboom, 24.7.00. Despatches, *London Gazette*, 10.9.01. D.C.M.
84. Thompson, Andrew Jamieson	,,	
83. Thyer, Frank	,,	
217. Tollmer, Horace Foster	,,	
189. Tyrrell, Charles Frank	,,	
188. Taits, Arthur Randolph S.	,,	Wounded at Stinkhontboom. 24.7.00
163. Tothill, Fredk. Joseph	,,	Killed, 25.7.00
164. Thompson, Wm. Henry	,,	
112. Van Damme, Thomas Edwin	,,	

Nominal Roll—*continued.*

No. and Name.	Rank.	Remarks.
N.C.O.'S AND MEN—*continued.*		
53. Wilcox, Thomas James	Trooper	
54. Walsh, Patrick	,,	
55. Wickens, Eugene Wilson	,,	
56. Wallace, Arthur Knight	,,	Invalided to Australia, arr. 23.7.01
85. Walsh, Michael John	,,	Invalided to Australia, arr. 12.4.01
86. Wilson, Percy Nagor Graham	,,	Hospital, Cape Town, 7.4.01
96. Wickens, Geo. Wm.	,,	Invalided to Australia, arr. 28.2.01
100. Wright, Sydney Murray	,,	Invalided to Australia, arr. 17.12.00
114. Wilkens, Thomas Walter	,,	Invalided to Australia, arr. 31.5.01
116. Ward, Barnard Torrens	,,	Lance.Corporal, 30.8.00. *Vide* "Promotions."
193. Walter, Wm. Henry Leslie	,,	Severely wounded at Bethlehem, 3.7.00
192. Wagstaffe, John Gifford	,,	Severely wounded at Bethlehem, 3.7.00. Invalided to Australia, arr. 28.2.01
190. Woodward, Hubert Mowbray	,,	
165. Wyman, Alfred Albert	,,	
166. Woodham, Hugh Prior	,,	Invalided to Australia, and died on s.s. *Britannic* at Albany, of measles and bronchitis, 28.2.01

FIFTH AND SIXTH (IMPERIAL) CONTINGENTS.

ALTHOUGH these Contingents were separately enrolled and despatched, yet they amalgamated into one battalion in South Africa, so that the latter was more in the nature of a fully-officered draft for the former than a separate corps. The Fifth was established under authorization from the South Australian Government, published in General Order No. 2, 1901, 10th January, 1901; and a Military Board was appointed to select members of the Contingent. A local Military Board was also appointed to assist in the preliminary selection of men living in the Mount Gambier, Naracoorte, and Millicent Districts. Selection was regulated by the following conditions :—(1) All returned soldiers of good character, and passing medical examination were accepted; (2) members of local forces fulfilling all conditions had preference over civilians; (3) all things being equal, single men preferred to married men; (4) men over 12 stone in weight not accepted, except to complete the number; (5) men between 18 and 27 years of age preferred, all else being equal; (6) after selection, men to be medically examined and tested in horsemanship and rifle shooting. A Board was appointed to purchase horses. A local solicitor proffered his services for making, gratuitously, the Wills of men joining; and arrangements were effected accordingly.

The Sixth Contingent was raised under similar conditions (General Order No. 4, 1901). Both Contingents contained a proportion of officers and others that had already served in the war.

For pay, &c., *vide* p. 341.

ESTABLISHMENTS.

The Fifth consisted of two and a half squadrons, "C," "D" and "E," and was officered as follows :—2 captains, 1 lieutenant-adjutant, 1 lieutenant-quartermaster, 15 lieutenants, 1 medical officer, 1 veterinary officer—the two latter appointed for the voyage only. Other ranks—1 regimental sergeant-major, 2 squadron sergeant-majors, 2 quartermaster-sergeants, 1 farrier-sergeant, 21 sergeants, 21 corporals, 20 lance-corporals, and 227 others; total, 19 officers, 295 other ranks.

The Sixth comprised "F" squadron, containing—1 captain, 6 lieutenants, 1 lieutenant transit-officer, 1 medical officer (voyage only), 1 veterinary-lieutenant, 1 sergeant-major, 1 quartermaster-sergeant, 5 sergeants, 6 corporals, 5 lance-corporals, 1 saddler, and 107 others; total, 9 officers, 126 others.

Additional men were enrolled in South Africa.

DEPARTURE AND RETURN.

The Fifth Contingent left on 9th February, 1901, comprising—21 officers, 295 other ranks, with 320 horses. One officer, 20 others died or were killed. Number struck off in South Africa not known.

The Sixth left on 6th April, 1901, at a strength of 10 officers, 126 others, with 146 horses. Six died, or were killed. Number struck off not known. Twenty-one N.C.O.'s and men of the two Contingents were left in hospital in South Africa. The balance of both Contingents returned to Australia.

PROMOTIONS, ETC.

Fifth Contingent.

Lieutenant J. R. B. O'Sullivan, to Captain.

Sixth Contingent.

Lieutenant S. C. Macfarlane, to Captain.

For promotions of N.C.O.'s and men, *vide* **nominal roll.**

SERVICE.

The Fifth Contingent embarked at Port Adelaide in the transport *Ormazan*, on 9th February, 1901, called at Albany and Cape Town, and disembarked at Port Elizabeth on 23rd March. They proceeded to the Kroonstadt district, where they joined Colonel De Lisle's Column. The Sixth Contingent left Port Adelaide on the transport *Warrigal*, on 6th April, 1901, and disembarked at Durban on 25th April. They proceeded at once to join the Fifth, which in the meantime had already trekked 291 miles. They were formed into one regiment under Major Shea, Indian Staff Corps, with Majors Wilson and Hurcombe, formerly Fourth Contingent. The regiment came under Lieut.-Colonel R. Fanshawe's command, and was in General E. Locke Elliott's division. From May, 1901, to May, 1902, Colonel De Lisle's Column did outstanding work in the north-eastern corner of the Orange River Colony.

On 25th May, Captain Hipwell died of enteric, and Lieutenant O'Sullivan was promoted in his place.

On 6th June, 1901, a composite force of 100 mounted infantry, and the same number of South Australians, made an early morning march and captured the whole of De Wet's convoy with six months' supplies. For four hours 160 men held out against the notable Boer leader and between 300 and 400 burghers, who attempted to re-capture it; eight men being killed and six wounded. The Boers lost heavily; 15 dead and a number of wounded being picked up.

From the Harrismith district, trekked to Klerksdorp, and from thence to Bloemfontein. An attack was made upon General Smut's laager at Grootvallier. Lord Kitchener, in his despatch of the 8th August, stated that—" Broadwood on the 29th July, made a night march on Bothaville, which resulted in his driving a number of Boers into the arms of Colonel De Lisle's South Australians, who captured 18 prisoners and 12 wagons. Major Shea, with 200 South Australians, made a gallant attack on Smut's commando at Grootvallier Farm, near the Vet River. Wire fencing, unseen in the darkness, prevented complete success of the plans, and enabled the Boers to escape, despite the fact that the South Australians pressed forward on foot, with fixed bayonets. Five Boers were left dead and 11 captured, including Field-Cornet Wolmarans, of Potchefstroom. By the 6th and 7th, Colonel De Lisle had accounted for 40 prisoners, 147 stand of arms, 600 horses, and 2,000 cattle." Three separate convoys were captured. Colonel De Lisle on 2nd August, congratulated the regiment on the successful night enterprises, and said that "the very dashing night attack at Grootvallier was worthy of the best traditions of Australian troops in the war."

After leaving Bloemfontein in August, trekked along the Basuto border, taking a number of prisoners, in addition to capturing the convoy of the Ficksburg commando. For the next two months they scoured the south-eastern portion of the Orange River Colony, then went north, where fighting and night marches were experienced. Then proceeded to Standerton, and from thence sent to relieve the late Colonel Benson's force after the Brakenlaagte disaster. The South Australians were the first to get to that place, after riding 75 miles in 22 hours.

In October, Captain Cornish was invalided to Australia, and Lieutenant Macfarlane promoted to succeed him.

The blockhouses were completed by February, and the Columns, abandoning the former system of operating individually, adopted the plan of moving together and driving the enemy on the railway or blockhouses. This involved hardships and trying work, long marches, and the digging of entrenchments along the front. The duties of keeping watch on the always alert enemy became so arduous that even the officers were ordered by the General to take their turns on sentry. In the first drive 405 Boers were captured; and, in the second, which Lord Kitchener himself directed, no less than 1,100 of the enemy were accounted for, including General Jan Meyer and Jacobus De Wet's son. The next drive was from Harrismith to Wolvehoek, but owing to the inefficiency of the blockhouses the Boers crossed the line in two places and escaped.

On 18th March, at Kroonstadt, orders were received to mobilize for home. The men had not been three consecutive days in one place. In conjunction, the two Contingents trekked 3,825 miles. The men caught, and broke in for themselves, 867 veldt ponies; in addition, they received 630 remounts, so that it was a rarity for a man to be dismounted longer than a day or two.

The Contingents embarked at Cape Town on 27th March, 1902, in the transport *Montrose*, and proceeded to Durban, where they transferred to the transport *Manchester Merchant*. Left Durban on 5th April, called at Albany, and disembarked at Port Adelaide on 27th April. Subsequently disbanded.

WAR SERVICES AND HONOURS.
Fifth Contingent.

Hipwell, Captain M. G. P.—Operations in Cape Colony. Died of enteric at Kroonstadt, 25th May, 1901.

Watt, Captain J. A.—Operations in Cape Colony and Orange River Colony between April, 1901, and March, 1902. Despatches, *London Gazette*, 15th November, 1901. D.S.O. Queen's Medal with four clasps.

O'Sullivan, Captain J. R. B.—Operations as stated. Queen's Medal with four clasps.

Richman, Lieutenant-Adjutant E.—Operations as stated. Queen's Medal with three clasps.

Gleeman, Lieutenant-Quartermaster T. W.—Previous service with First Contingent. Operations as stated Queen's Medal with five clasps. King's Medal with two clasps.

Langley, Lieutenant E. J. F.—Previous service with Second Contingent. Operations as stated. Despatches, *London Gazette*, 2nd July, 1901. D.S.O. Queen's Medal with five clasps. King's Medal with two clasps. He served subsequently as Captain in 8th Australian Commonwealth Horse.

Carter, Lieutenant A. C., and *Priestly*, Lieutenant P. H.—Operations as stated. Queen's Medal with four clasps.

Shearer, Lieutenant J. H.—Previous service with First Contingent. Operations as stated. Despatches, *London Gazette*, 29th July, 1902. Queen's Medal with five clasps. King's Medal with two clasps.

Miell, Lieutenant A.—Operations in Transvaal and Orange River Colony Queen's Medal with four clasps.

Ferguson, Lieutenant C. C.—Operations in Transvaal, Cape Colony, and Orange River Colony. Queen's Medal with five clasps.

Edmunds, Lieutenant W. H., and *Fotheringham*, Lieutenant R. S.—Operations in Cape Colony and Orange River Colony. Queen's Medal with four clasps.

Muir, Lieutenant F. B.—Previous service with First Contingent. Operations as stated. Despatches, *London Gazette*, 29th July, 1902. Queen's Medal with five clasps. King's Medal with two clasps.

Cudmore, Lieutenant R. H.—Operations as stated. Queen's Medal with four clasps.

Tolmer, Lieutenant H. A.—Previous service with Second Contingent. Operations as stated. Queen's Medal with five clasps. King's Medal with two clasps.

Ayliffe, Lieutenant G. G.—Operations in Cape Colony. Queen's Medal with two clasps.

Brock, Lieutenant D. W.—Previous service with Second Contingent. Operations in Cape Colony and Orange River Colony. Queen's Medal with three clasps. King's Medal with two clasps.

Campbell, Lieutenant N.—Operations in Transvaal and Orange River Colony. Queen's Medal with four clasps.

Smith, Captain (Medical Staff) W. R.—Principal Medical Officer, Plague Administration, Cape Town. Queen's Medal with two clasps.

Desmond, Lieutenant (Veterinary) J.—War Service. Queen's Medal with one clasp.

Sixth Contingent.

Cornish, Captain A. F.—Operations in Transvaal and Orange River Colony. Queen's Medal with three clasps.

Macfarlane, Captain S. C.—Operations as stated. Despatches, *London Gazette*, 29th July, 1902. Queen's Medal with four clasps.

Bagot, Lieutenant C. G. S.—Operations as stated. Queen's Medal with clasps.

Waite, Lieutenant W. C. N.—Previous service with Third Contingent. Operations as stated. Despatches, *London Gazette*, 29th July, 1902. Queen's Medal with five clasps. King's Medal with two clasps.

Nunneley, Lieutenant W. A.—Previous service with Second Contingent. Operations as stated. Queen's Medal with five clasps. King's Medal with two clasps.

Harvey, Lieutenant A. K. Le R.—Operations as stated. Queen's Medal with four clasps.

Blue, Lieutenant S.—Previous service with Second Contingent. Operations as stated. Queen's Medal with four clasps. King's Medal with two clasps.

Cossins, Lieutenant G. H.—Operations as stated. Severely wounded, 6th June, 1901. Queen's Medal with four clasps.

Stirling, Lieutenant (Veterinary) N. W.—Operations as stated. Queen's Medal with four clasps.

Nominal Roll—Fifth Contingent.

No. and Name.	Rank.	Remarks.
OFFICERS.		
Hipwell, Malcolm George Patrick	Captain	Commanded "C" squadron. Died of enteric, Kroonstadt 25.5.01
Watt, John Alexander	"	Commanded "D" squadron
Richman, Edward	Lieut.-Adjutant	
Gleeman, Thomas W.	Lieut.-Quartermaster	Previous service, 1st Contingent
O'Sullivan, Julian Roger Bede	Lieutenant	
Langley, Edgar John Flynn	"	Previous service, 2nd Contingent
Carter, Alleyne Charles	"	
Priestly, Philip Henry	"	
Shearer, John H.	"	Previous service, 1st Contingent
Miell, Albert	"	
Ferguson, Charles C.	"	
Edmunds, William H.	"	
Fotheringham, Roy S.	"	
Muir, Frank B.	"	Previous service, **1st Contingent**
Cudmore, Roland Herbert	"	Commanded " **E** " **half-squadron**

Nominal Roll—*continued.*

No. and Name.	Rank.	Remarks.
OFFICERS—*continued.*		
Tolmer, Herbert Alexander	Lieutenant	Previous service, 2nd Contingent. Invalided to Australia, arr. 13.12.01
Ayliffe, Gerald Gleeson	,,	Invalided to Australia, arr. 23.7.01
Brock, Denzil William	,,	Previous service, 2nd Contingent
Campbell, Neil	,,	
Smith, William Ramsay	Captain (Medical Staff)	For voyage only
Desmond, John	Veterinary-Lieutenant	For voyage only
N.C.O.'s AND MEN.		
419. McGillivray, James	Reg. Sergeant-Major	Killed, Vankollensfontein, 21.7.01.
244. Ryan, William John	Sergeant-Major	
464. Walter, John Charles	,,	
414. Congreve, Alfred George	Quartermaster-Sergeant	
281. Schumann, Otto Frederick	,,	Killed at Venterspruit, 6.5.01
273. Leane, Frederick Thomas	Sergeant-Major	
278. Goodall, Edwin Ray	Farrier-Sergeant	
220. Edge, Arthur	Sergeant	
258. Rust, William	,,	Died; date not recorded
386. Hammond, Henry	,,	
411. Lee, Arthur John	,,	
249. Simpson, Freebairn Liddon	,,	
410. Dawson, Thomas	,,	
295. Fitzgerald, John Christopher	,,	Quartermaster-Sergeant
320. Ferry, Roland Jaspar	,,	Regimental Sergeant-Major
308. Ownsworth, William Henry	,,	
428. Ewens, Arthur Edwin	,,	Squadron Sergeant-Major
240. Naughton, Thomas Augustine	,,	Quartermaster-Sergeant
489. Leech, Frederick William	,,	
429. Tollner, Charles Gustave	,,	
358. Hamilton, James	,,	Drowned at Kroonstadt, 3.4.01
460. Gréwar, Leonard Dangar	,,	Sqn. Sergeant-Major. Despatches, *London Gazette*, 2.7.01
453. Luckett, George Ernest	,,	
457. Harrington, Albert Bernard	,,	
452. Evans, Edward James	,,	
450. White, Robert	,,	
228. Hood, Thomas	,,	
221. Bartlett, Ebenezer Culliford	Corporal	
222. Malcolm, Cecil Bertram	,,	Lance-Sergeant
413. Noblett, William Chamney	,,	
246. Bergin, Edward Joseph	,,	
250. Bristowe, Alfred Charles	,,	Quartermaster-Sergeant
245. Slattery, J. William	,,	Trumpeter
406. Egan, Cornelius Joseph	,,	Cook
380. Wilke, Walwin Harold	,,	
379. Brisbane, Alexander	,,	Sergeant
415. Ruddock, John Wilfred	,,	Sergeant
277. McNamee, Wm. John Bern	,,	Sergeant
276. Collins, John James	,,	
309. Horne, Wilfred Bannister	,,	Sergeant
310. Inglis, Elliott Maxwell	,,	
344. Mackenzie, Kenneth	,,	Sergeant

Nominal Roll—*continued.*

No. and Name.	Rank.	Remarks.
N.C.O.'s AND MEN—*continued.*		
333. Semple, George	Corporal	
359. Heaslip, Sydney	,,	
454. Kilsby, Albert John	,,	Sergeant
440. Hodgson, Frank Vincent D.	,,	
451. Cruickshank, Percival	,,	Sergeant
458. Milne, Leslie Hugh	,,	
224. Sommerville, Malcolm	Lance-Corporal	Corporal
223. Bell, William Sanders	,,	Corporal
267. Frost, George	,,	Invalided to Australia, arr. 28.8.01
259. Murphy, Robert	,,	
381. Hannam, William Charles	,,	Lance-Sergeant
387. Pizey, Edward John	,,	
412. Rybeig, John Philip	,,	
229. Hill, James	,,	
279. White, Frederick Sylvester	,,	Corporal. Died; date not recorded
301. De Laine, Horace Chas. Caspar	,,	
294. Suffolk, William Charles	,,	Sergeant
311. Noblett, Charles Herbert	,,	Corporal
313. Boucaut, Leonard Harris	,,	Corporal
434. Arnott, Archibald Sandy	,,	
480. Campbell, Donald John	,,	
376. Gardner, Walter	,,	Corporal
456. Taylor, Francis Augustine	,,	
455. Boucaut, Max Arthur	,,	
459. Bayly, Alfred Lanzel	,,	
512. Hamp, Richard Frank	,,	Killed at Rietz, 6.6.01
500. Heaney, Roderick Henry	Trumpeter	
505. Jeanes, Hurtle Sylvester	,,	
225. Alexander, Alexander	Trooper	Invalided to Australia, arr. 11.2.02
513. Aird, William Alexander	,,	
227. Berg, William Christian	,,	
230. Bayley, Harold Sydney	,,	
417. Boon, Albert	,,	
418. Boscence, Arthur Henry	,,	
498. Bowen, Percy Bernard G.	,,	
425. Butler, Arthur Wm. Thomas	,,	
488. Baird, John Marshall	,,	Invalided to Australia, arr. 28.8.01
316. Birchmore, Wm. John	,,	
323. Brown, Joseph	,,	Lance-Corporal. Slightly wounded at Kaffirstad, 22.10.01
351. Benson, Alexander	,,	
348. Berry, John	,,	Lance - Corporal. Despatches, *London Gazette*, 29.7.02. D.C.M.
335. Barnes, Edward James	,,	
338. Barnes, Horace Newton	,,	Slightly wounded, 5.12.01
433. Beale, Walker Osmond	,,	
369. Burgess, Stanley Stephen	,,	
373. Baker, Richard Ernest	,,	Dangerously ill with fever, Harrismith, 21.7.01. Invalided to Australia, arr. 13.12.01
363. Brinkman, Ernest Albert	,,	
444. Bean, James	,,	
461. Bradbury, Chas. Lewis W. B.	,,	
518. Brown, Frank	,,	Lance-Corporal
519. Becker, Ernest Alexander	,,	Corporal
226. Coulls, Joseph Charles	,,	
231. Cook, Ronald McNeil	,,	

Nominal Roll—*continued*.

No. and Name.	Rank.	Remarks.
N.C.O.'s AND MEN—*continued.*		
233. Cameron, John	Trooper	
234. Champness, Leslie	,,	
476. Coffey, Sylvester Plunkett	,,	
256. Collins, Charles	,,	
497. Crawford, Samuel Cecil	,,	
407. Conrad, Herbert Selman	,,	
302. Clarke, William George	,,	
300. Clarke, Henry Charles	,,	
318. Chapman, Leslie John	,,	
319. Curgenven, William Edgar	,,	
327. Cleveland, Albert Bruce	,,	Invalided to Australia, arr. 31.1.02
355. Clark, Albert Henry	,,	
346. Cochrane, Bertram H.	,,	Died of dysentery at Cape Town, 27.1.02
352. Casseltine, Frederick	,,	
337. Clayton, Ernest	,,	
336. Cattermole, Thos. Joseph	,,	Invalided to Australia, arr. 28.8.01
363. Chisholm, Alexander Garn	,,	
370. Cantwell, Robert Michael	,,	
372. Cunninghame, James	,,	
377. Clark, Alfred	,,	
374. Cook, Henry George	,,	
467. Crawford, James	,,	
445. Copley, Frank Wallace	,,	
509. Clines, James	,,	
232. Dunn, Chas. Henry Wm.	,,	
235. Davis, Jacob John	,,	
237. Drury, Frederick Walter	,,	
241. Donovan, John	,,	
420. De Longville, Charles	,,	Invalided to Australia, arr. 31.1.02
282. Dowsett, William Herbert	,,	
329. Dunn, Frederick Charles	,,	
305. Deers, Louis	,,	Lance-Corporal
343. Davey, William Henry	Shoeing-Smith	
364. Du Bois, Eugene Rupert	Trooper	Sergeant
371. Davis, Archibald Hiram	,,	
367. Dugan, Thomas James	,,	
378. Dowler, George	,,	
438. Donovan, Frederick James	,,	
269. Erroch, Charles	,,	
253. Easther, Ronald Edward	,,	
298. Errington, Philip	,,	
287. Eyre, Ernest James Stratford	,,	
349. Edwards, Frederick Herbert	,,	
347. Edmunds, Robert Hugh	,,	
368. Ellis, Joseph Albert	,,	
365. Errington, Arthur William	,,	
437. Everett, Charles Manuel	,,	
506. Evans, Archie Albert	,,	
255. Fleetwood, Charles Rufus	,,	Invalided to Australia, arr. 5.11.01
264. Flatman, John Henry	,,	
499. Fuller, Sydney Walter	,,	
478. Foster, Harry Isaac	,,	Invalided to Australia, arr. 28.8.01
462. Frankel, George William	,,	
254. Goode, Samuel J. Mortimer	,,	
257. Goode, James William	,,	
422. Gower, Frederick Davidson	,,	
482. Gillis, Heaton George	,,	

Nominal Roll—continued.

No. and Name.	Rank.	Remarks.
N.C.O.'s AND MEN—continued.		
289. Gluyas, John Edgar	Trooper	Died of enteric at Kroonstadt, 25.1.02
280. Guymer, James	,,	
317. Gribble, John Curthen	,,	
339. Gough, William George	,,	
485. Goode, Charles Henry	,,	Lance-Corporal
490. Giles, Edgar Malcolm	,,	Lance-Corporal
491. Gibb, David Haxton	,,	Killed at Rietz, 6.6.01
511. Gooch, Walter Malcolm Craig	,,	
332. Greenfield, Henry Richard	,,	
517. Granleese, John Thomas	,,	
342. Humbey, Herbert James	,,	Invalided to Australia, arr. 7.1.02
238. Henry, Ernest Alfred	,,	
239. Harris, Percy Godfrey	,,	
251. Hawke, Hedley Charles	,,	
261. Hutchison, Luke	,,	
479. Haines, Albert James	,,	
280. Hannaford, John James	,,	
324. Hinze, Sydney William	,,	
357. Haywood, Jack	,,	
431. Hirth, Fred. William	,,	Died of enteric at Kroonstadt, 27.2.02
465. Hill, William George	,,	
442. Hannaford, Frank Elliot	,,	
508. Hosking, Herbert Ralph	,,	
448. Halden, Alexander	,,	
470. Harry, William James	,,	
487. Howie, James Edgar	,,	
248. Horsfall, Nathaniel	,,	Slightly wounded at Lindley, 24.1.01; killed at Standerton, 9.6.01
492. Ireland, Eric William	,,	
242. Jennings, David Absolom	,,	
439. Jones, Charles Frederick	,,	
514. Jessop, Harold Newton	,,	
243. Kelly, William A. McCleand	,,	
430. Kavanagh, Peter John	,,	Invalided to Australia, arr. 12.4.01
469. Kollosche, Matthew	,,	
504. Klopper, William	,,	
495. Kermode, Thomas	,,	Corporal. Despatches, *London Gazette*, 15.11.01. D.C.M.
240. Lintern, William Albert	,,	Invalided to Australia, arr. 26.3.02
260. Lowe, William Charles	,,	Slightly wounded at Liebenbegsvlei, 10.12.01
314. Lewis, John Bavard	,,	
299. Lee, Arthur Murray	,,	Invalided to Australia, arr. 31.1.02
366. Lush, George Amos	,,	
449. Litchfield, Burnel Murray	,,	Lance-Corporal
486. Lovell, George	,,	
252. Messenger, Alfred James	,,	
262. Mase, Samuel Archibald	,,	
391. Moulden, Frederick	,,	
392. Maley, Alfred Charles	,,	
385. Matthews, Jack McGregor	,,	
270. Maley, John	,,	
481. McFayden, Allen	,,	
384. McCawley, Christopher	,,	

Nominal Roll—continued.

No. and Name.	Rank.	Remarks.

N.C.O.'s AND MEN—continued.

No. and Name.	Rank.	Remarks.
271. Matters, Leonard Warburton	Trooper	
272. McNally, George Sylvester	,,	
293. Muecke, Emile Hugo Franz	,,	
304. Malone, Richard Alexander	,,	
288. Matthews, Albert	,,	
306. McKenna, James	,,	
312. Muloney, Thomas	,,	
321. McLean, Walter Hugh	,,	
326. Maloney, William James	,,	
375. May, Bruce Harold	,,	Killed; date not recorded
466. Munt, Frederick Wm. Dixon	,,	Severely wounded near Reitz, 6.6.01
463. McInerney, William Joseph	,,	
443. McPhee, Edward Duncan	,,	Invalided to Australia, arr. 31.1.02
247. Nash, John Drummond	,,	
266. Nation, Henry Albert	,,	
295. Nation, Percy Eastwood	,,	
356. Nicholls, Albert Samuel	,,	Invalided to Australia, arr. 2.11.01
423. O'Halloran, Edward Clanfurgal	,,	
390. O'Shea, James Thomas	,,	
361. O'Connor, Arthur Lewis	,,	Lance-Corporal
290. Ozanne, George William	,,	
447. O'Brien, William John	,,	
473. Ogilvie, Ralph Joseph	,,	
502. Palmer, Percy George Caspar	,,	
263. Pickering, John Basil	,,	Lance-Corporal
268. Pleader, Edward Andrew	,,	
395. Parmitter, Arthur Philip	,,	
389. Patterson, John Alexander	,,	
396. Pryor, Alfred	,,	Slightly wounded at Lindley, 24.1.01
397. Pope, William Ernest	,,	
394. Peake, George Alfred	,,	
330. Pryor, Thomas	,,	Invalided to Australia, arr. 23.7.01
331. Pearce, Frederick Gibbs	,,	
354. Phelps, Edgar	,,	
334. Petrie, Albert Benjamin	,,	
446. Parsons, Edwin George	,,	
516. Patten, Arthur John	,,	
484. Peake, Albert Henry Prince	,,	
501. Reid, James Lawrence	,,	
503. Richards, Edgar	,,	
403. Rehn, Henry	,,	
405. Richards, William James	,,	
408. Russell, William	,,	
399. Richardson, Walter Rupert	,,	
404. Richardson, George Henry	,,	
297. Reynolds, Sydney	,,	
292. Ranford, Joseph Marmion	,,	Slightly wounded at Lindley 24.1.01
291. Rogers, John	,,	
307. Randall, John	,,	
435. Ruwoldt, John Chas. Henry	,,	Lance-Corporal
471. Rankine, Henry Gimmel	,,	
483. Rickaby, Ralph	,,	
493. Richter, Peter George	,,	
515. Richter, Charles Ernest	,,	

Nominal Roll—*continued.*

No. and Name.	Rank.	Remarks.

N.C.O.'s AND MEN—*continued.*

No. and Name.	Rank.	Remarks.
409. Searles, Richard Tusson	Trooper	
400. Simmonds, Ralph	,,	Died of enteric at Springford
401. Stanton, Frederick Theodore	,,	Severely wounded near Honing Spruit, 11.4.01
383. Skinner, George Henry	,,	
427. Smith, Donald Henry	,,	
283. Stuckey, David	,,	
432. Sampson, Frederick	,,	
315. Sparshott, George Vick	,,	
322. Souter, Harry	,,	
328. Searle, Alfred Wallace	,,	Invalided to Australia, arr. 2.11.01
507. Slattery, Michael	,,	
441. Smith, Edwin John	,,	
475. Shakes, Alfred	,,	
494. Shepherd, Clarence	,,	Slightly wounded near Reitz, 6.6.01
284. Tucker, Bethold August A.	,,	
496. Toole, James Patrick	,,	
426. Thompson, George	,,	
382. Turner, Alex. John Stanley	,,	
303. Thomas, Arnold Joseph	,,	
341. Taverner, George Alfred	,,	Invalided to Australia, arr. 5.11.01
350. Taverner, William Charles	,,	
398. Uhlson, Frederick Laurence	,,	
402. Vickery, Albert Arthur	,,	Died; date not recorded
510. Vile, Henry Worthy	,,	
236. Whittle, Clemen Cyril George	,,	Died of enteric, Truter's Drift, 10.8.01
416. Winfield, Ernest Alfred	,,	Invalided to Australia, arr. 5.11.01
265. Weinerlein, Ernest Henry Leonard	,,	
421. Wellington, Albert Gibon	,,	
477. Wellington, Clement Wellesley	,,	
388. Wood, Arthur Montgomery	,,	
424. Wilson, Peter Henry	,,	Invalided to Australia, arr. 8.1.02
296. Walters, Walter	,,	
286. Whitfield, Alexander	,,	Lance-Corporal
353. Woodforde, John Roy	,,	
345. Webster, Albert Charles	,,	Invalided to Australia, arr. 31.1.02
360. Waller, James Patrick	,,	Invalided to Australia, arr. 2.11.01
468. Wilson, Frederick Clarke	,,	
472. Wilson, George Richard	,,	
474. White, William Henry	,,	
302. Carter, W. George	,,	Lance-Corporal
520. McGuire, C. H.	,,	Severely wounded near Reitz, 6.6.01
61. Mercer, C. J. B.	Sergeant	Died; date not recorded
647. Barron, R. T.	Lance-Corporal	Killed at Standerton, 9.6.01
586. Bennier, A. J.	Trooper	Died of wounds received in action 27.5.01
598. Croft, F. G.	,,	Killed in action at Standerton, 9.6.01
599. Main, H. G.	,,	Killed at Standerton, 9.6.01
268. Steader, E. A.	,,	
521. Skinner, L. V.	,,	

Nominal Roll—Sixth Contingent.

No. and Name.	Rank.	Remarks.
OFFICERS.		
Cornish, Augustus Frederick	Captain	Invalided to Australia arr., 27.11.01
Bagot, Christopher George Seymour	Lieutenant	
Waite, William Charles Nightingale	,,	Previous service, 1st Contingent
Nunneley, Wilfred Alexander	,,	Previous service, 2nd Contingent
Macfarlane, Sydney Colin	,,	
Harvey, Arthur Kenneth Le Rei	,,	
Blue, Sinclair	,,	Previous service, 2nd Contingent
Cossins, George Herbert	,,	Transport Officer. Severely wounded at Rietz, 6.6.01
Stirling, Norman William	Veterinary-Lieutenant	
Rogers, R. S.	Civ. Surgeon	For voyage only
N.C.O.'s AND MEN.		
661. Cocker, Edward John	Sergeant-Major	
617. Glover, Alfred James	Sergeant	Quartermaster-Sergeant. Invalided, to Australia, arr. 28.8.01
522. Murrie, Peter	,,	Died of fever at Standerton, 9.6.01
541. Partington, Albert	,,	
629. Ridings, Reginald	,,	
615. Swanson, James Hamilton	,,	
569. Smith, Harold Tobias	,,	Severely wounded at Rietz, 6.6.01
627. Williams, Edwin	Corporal	Invalided to Australia, arr. 7.1.02
621. Millar, James Alexander	,,	Sergeant
572. Merry, Morton Peto	,,	Sergeant
612. Cockburn, Walter	,,	Lance-Sergeant
638. Angrave, Andrew	,,	
648. Wells, Percy M.	,,	Severely wounded at Rietz, 6.6.01 Invalided to Australia, arr. 5.11.01
540. Boyton, Frederick Ernest	Lance-Corporal	
579. Jackman, Sydney	,,	Sergeant
602. King, Lewis Augustine	,,	Sergeant
619. Stephens, Thomas Henry	,,	Lance-Corporal. Forearm fractured, 13.7.01. Invalided to Australia, arr. 7.1.02
583. Wauchope, Leslie Alexander	,,	
534. McNamara, John Lewis	Saddler	Corporal-Saddler
523. Hannam, Horace Henry	Trumpeter	
614. Alexander, John James	Trooper	Corporal
558. Angel, Henry Atcham	,,	
637. Brewer, Ernest Hammond	,,	
603. Brandt, Phillis	,,	Corporal. Despatches, *London Gazette,* 29.7.02
620. Beare, Harold Egbert	,,	Died; date not recorded
586. Bennear, Alfred James	,,	
531. Black, Ernest Grant	,,	Invalided to Australia, arr. 7.1.02
574. Bray, Harry	,,	
647. Barron, Robert Thomas	,,	Lance-Corporal
636. Clues, Herbert Reuben	,,	
598. Croft, Frederick George	,,	
591. Collins, Frederick Albert	,,	Lance-Corporal. Invalided to Australia, arr. 8.1.02
565. Cullen, Wesley John	,,	

Nominal Roll—*continued*.

No. and Name.	Rank.	Remarks.
N.C.O.'s AND MEN—*continued*.		
592. Carter, Joel Brien	Trooper	
576. Donnell, Henry	,,	
555. Evans, Frederick William	,,	Invalided to Australia, arr. 31.5.01
557. Ewens, William Reynolds	,,	Killed at Standerton, 9.6.01
568. Foale, Percy	,,	
581. Forgan, Robert Hugh	,,	
589. Fryar, Walter Ernest	,,	
597. Freer, Augustine George	,,	Invalided to Australia, arr. 31.5.01
601. Fuller, Albert Ernest	,,	
605. Fawk, George Richard	,,	
561. Faulkner, Edwin Benjamin	,,	
543. Frost, Ernest Walter	,,	
539. Fletcher, George Bailey	,,	Lance-Sergeant
536. Grant, George Porter	,,	
538. Goldsmith, Douglas Eard	,,	
552. Glenn, George	,,	Severely wounded at Rietz, 6.6.01
588. Guerin, Thomas Lawrence	,,	Lance-Corporal
590. Gooch, Hugh Lowden	,,	Sergeant
596. Gulley, Richard	,,	Corporal. Despatches, *London Gazette*, 29.7.02
624. Growden, Hamley Maynard	,,	
564. Hunt, Sydney	,,	
628. Hancock, Harold	,,	
625. Harder, Franciscus John	,,	
623. Heffernan, Robertson	,,	
575. Halls, Sappho	,,	Lance-Corporal
573. Henderson, Ernest John	,,	Invalided to Australia, arr. 27.11.01
554. Hemming, Thomas George	,,	Lance-Sergeant
542. Hehir, Dennis	,,	
618. Ingerson, Sydney	,,	
545. Ingleton, James	,,	
582. Jones, Howard Thomas	,,	
548. Joseph, Francis William	,,	
532. Jordan, Harry Eustace	,,	
533. Leamey, David Alexander	,,	Lance-Corporal
556. Lomas, William Ernest	,,	
525. Lock, Frank Harry	,,	
526. Latimer, Robert Turner	,,	
634. Morton, Charles	,,	
626. Marshall, William Percy	,,	
610. Maloney, John Joseph	,,	
608. Medlen, Arthur Edward	,,	Corporal
609. Macdougall, Angus	,,	Quartermaster-Sergeant
599. Main, Harry George	,,	
585. Martin, Harold Bernard	,,	
584. Mundy, Charles Ebenezer	,,	
580. Myatt, John Charles	,,	
571. Mattfield, Edward William C. T.	,,	
549. Mansfield, Waldemar Otto C.	,,	Invalided to Australia, arr. 31.5.01
535. Marshall, Albert Edward Charles	,,	Killed at Standerton, 9.6.01
551. Noblett, George Newman	,,	
550. Nicholls, Henry	,,	Slightly wounded at Spitzkop
578. Nelson, Oscar	,,	Invalided to Australia, arr. 5.11.01
528. O'Brien, Peter James	,,	
639. Oliphant, Frank Arnold	,,	
527. Owen, Thomas	,,	
593. Pamienter, John Snow	,,	

Nominal Roll—continued.

No. and Name.	Rank.	Remarks.
N.C.O.'s AND MEN—continued.		
524. Pretty, Samuel Hainsworth	Trooper	
577. Reece, George Wm. Melrose	,,	
559. Rowe, Thomas Matthew	,,	
529. Rankine, Arthur Gamell	,,	
635. Randle, James Kinnear	,,	
633. Reid, Henry D'Arcy	,,	
613. Simpson, Alexander	,,	
587. Spreech, Percival Alfred	,,	
562. Shepherd, Stanley	,,	
546. Teate, William David	,,	Died; date not recorded
547. Taylor, Arthur Gerald	,,	
537. Tucker, Walter George Ewen	,,	
530. Thompson, Harry	,,	
563. Thomas, Percival Armstrong	,,	
606. Tucker, James Hannam	,,	
622. Thomas, William Joseph	,,	
631. Williams, Arthur Thomas	,,	Severely wounded at Brakenlaagte, 30.10.01. Invalided to Australia, arr. 31.1.02
630. Webber, Andrew James	,,	Invalided to Australia, arr. 5.1.02
616. Wigley, John	,,	
607. Williamson, Charles	,,	
604. Walker, John	,,	
595. Wilson, Alfred Hedley	,,	
594. Warnes, Ernest Edwin	,,	Quartermaster-Sergeant
570. Webster, Arthur Edward	,,	
567. Walter, Nathaniel	,,	
566. Warmington, Kenneth Allen	,,	
560. Wilkie, Charles Gilbert	,,	
553. Walter, Charles Richard Douglas	,,	Killed at Standerton, 9.6.01
600. Wadge, Albert George	,,	Lance-Corporal
544. Sobels, Richard Julius	,,	Severely wounded at Lindley, 24.1.02
640. Summers, John Chestnut	,,	
644. Sangster, Cecil Ingham	,,	
641. McDonald, Herbert Ernest	,,	
642. McDonald, Lewis Beaton	,,	
643. Perry, Alfred James	,,	Invalided to Australia, arr. 27.11.01
645. Thorpe, Joseph Prentice	,,	Invalided to Australia, arr. 31.1.02
646. Whittington, James Campbell N.	,,	Invalided to Australia, arr. 5.1.02
274. Phillips, J. W.	,,	Fractured collarbone, 4.7.01
316. Birchmore, W. J.	,,	Invalided to Australia, arr. 23.6.02

SPECIAL SERVICE OFFICERS.

GORDON, Colonel (now Brigadier-General) J. M.—This officer proceeded to South Africa with the Second Contingent by the transport *Surrey*, and arrived at Cape Town on 25th February, 1900. He was appointed Staff Officer for Oversea Colonials. He served as Deputy Adjutant-General to the First Mounted Infantry Brigade, commanded by Major-General E. T. H. Hutton, which numbered 6,215 officers and men. He also commanded a Column 1,200 strong (composed of mounted men who belonged to the First and Second Mounted Infantry Brigades of General Ian Hamilton's Division), from Bloemfontein to Kroonstadt; and he accompanied General Hutton in the march from Kroonstadt to Pretoria, and afterwards from Pretoria to Belfast. Operations in Cape Colony. Operations in Orange Free State, including action at Karee Siding. Operations in the Transvaal, including action near Johannesburg. Despatches, *London Gazette*, 16th April, 1901. C.B. Queen's Medal with four clasps.

Edwards, Major Vernon Harridge.—Proceeded to South Africa with the Fifth Contingent, which arrived at Port Elizabeth on 23rd March, 1901. He was present at operations in Cape Colony, and Orange River Colony, and was ultimately invalided to Australia, arriving at Adelaide on 5th August, 1901. Queen's Medal with three clasps.

Scriven, Major Walter, V.D.—Embarked in the transport *Ormazan* on 9th February, 1901, with the Fifth Imperial Bushmen, having charge of the Contingent until its arrival in South Africa. It was his desire to obtain an appointment in the artillery, if possible, that being the branch of the service to which he belonged. The Contingent proceeded to Kroonstadt, Orange Free State. As, however, there was no special work for an officer of his rank with the artillery, he remained with the Fifth for a considerable time, operating all over Orange Free State, under the command of Colonel De Lisle. He then returned to Kroonstadt, and was officer commanding Colonel De Lisle's details for some time, after which he returned to Australia. Queen's Medal with three clasps.

AUSTRALIAN ARMY MEDICAL CORPS CONTINGENT.

SOUTH AUSTRALIAN DETAILS.

COMPRISED 1 officer, 1 sergeant, 1 corporal, 1 bugler, and 14 privates. For organization, equipment, pay, service, etc., *vide* Army Medical Corps, New South Wales, page 13, *et seq.*

Nominal Roll.

No. and Name.	Rank.	Remarks.
Jermyn, Frederick D.	Captain	
1323. Elphick, Harold Edward	Sergeant	
1333. Nation, John Boath	Corporal	
1285. Smith, Edward Adolphus	Bugler	
1324. James, Frederick William	Private	
1325. Angrave, Alfred James	,,	
1326. Ayliffe, William Lionel	,,	
1327. Blackwell, Matthew	,,	
1328. Chamberlayne, Thomas Cecil	,,	
1329. Davis, William Frank M.	,,	
1330. Hollywood, Simon John	,,	
1331. Higgs, Ernest Alexander	,,	
1332. Muir, Thomas Kerr	,,	
1334. Neville, Henry Beauchamp	,,	
1335. Paynter, Oliver Arthur	,,	
1336. Rule, Vivian Roland	,,	
1337. Stone, William Ernest	,,	
1338. Worthington, Andrew Leonard	,,	Lance-Corporal

In this connexion it may be mentioned that Nursing Sisters M. S. Bidmead, Glenie, and N. S. Harris, proceeded from Adelaide to South Africa at an early stage of the war. Sister Bidmead obtained the Royal Red Cross (Despatches, *London Gazette*, 10th September, 1901). Sisters Bidmead and Glenie were presented with Devoted Service Crosses at the Review on Coronation Day, 26th June, 1902. Sister Harris returned by the transport *Tongariro* from Cape Town, leaving on 31st March, 1901. No further records of S. A. Nursing Sisters could be obtained,

SECOND BATTALION AUSTRALIAN COMMONWEALTH HORSE.
SOUTH AUSTRALIAN UNIT.

"D" SQUADRON was authorized on 6th January, 1902, and formed in Adelaide. For pay, equipment, establishment, organization, etc., *vide* 2nd Battalion, Australian Commonwealth Horse, Victoria. By notification in the public press, returned South African soldiers, single, and of good character, were invited to join. All the officers, and many of the sergeants and rank and file had served in previous Contingents, or in local South African corps. One officer was promoted from the ranks, *vide* nominal roll; as also for promotions of N.C.O.'s and men. There were no casualties.

SERVICE.

The squadron left Port Adelaide on 20th February, 1902, by the transport *Manchester Merchant*, comprising—5 officers and 116 other ranks, with 121 horses. Disembarked at Durban on 14th March, and proceeded by rail to Newcastle. Took part in operations round Newcastle and Botha's Post until 8th April; then marched to Volksrust, and entrained to Klerksdorp. Participated in operations from Klerksdorp to Devondale Siding as part of De Lisle's Australian Brigade (which was portion of Lieutenant-General Sir Ian Hamilton's Mobile Force), in the last great drive of the war. Marched back to Klerksdorp, and were included with the 2nd Battalion in the complimentary General Order issued by the Commander-in-Chief, and also in the Orders by General Ian Hamilton, and Brigadier-General Thornycroft. Marched to Elandsfontein and handed over horses, saddlery, &c.; entrained to Newcastle, and thence to Durban. Embarked in the transport *Norfolk*, 5th July; called at Albany, and disembarked at Largs Bay, South Australia, 31st July. Disbanded, 14th August, 1902.

WAR SERVICES AND HONOURS.

See First, Second, and Fourth Contingents for previous service of officers. That with the squadron was as already detailed. An additional clasp for the medal was granted, for "South Africa, 1902."

Nominal Roll.

No. and Name.	Rank.	Remarks.
OFFICERS.		
De Passey, William	Captain	Previous service, 2nd Contingent
Thorne, Frederick Otto	Lieutenant	Previous service, 4th Contingent
Siekmann, Francis Charles	,,	Previous service, 4th Contingent
Ogilvy, Harry Lort Spencer Balfour	,,	Previous service, 2nd Contingent
Johnson, Charles Frederick Maison	,,	Previous service, 1st Contingent
N.C.O.'S AND MEN.		
1058. Read, James	Sergeant-Major	
1012. Dockrell, John	Quartermaster-Sergeant	
966. Gay, Howard	Sergeant	
1019. Hey, Thomas Henry	,,	
1034. Wickens, Eugene Albert	,,	
1020. Love, Richard Thomas	,,	

Nominal Roll—continued.

No. and Name.	Rank.	Remarks.
N.C.O.'s AND MEN—continued.		
986. Wickens, George William	Farrier-Sergeant	
960. Cabot, Alfred	Shoeing-Smith	
1006. Castles, Joseph	,,	
983. Strother, Arthur John	,,	
1050. Higgs, Horace	Bugler	
1066. Heaney, Roderick Henry	,,	
971. Luxmoore, Edgar Alexander	Corporal	
967. Gooley, John Byrne	,,	Promoted Sergeant
1021. Lovely, Lewis Howard	,,	Promoted Lieutenant, 4th Battalion Australian Commonwealth Horse
976. McBean, John Alexander	,,	
965. Foreman, Walter John	Lance-Corporal	Promoted Corporal
984. Stanmers, George Edward	,,	
1015. House, Robert James	,,	
954. Ayliffe, Sydney Hamilton	,,	
1023. Caire, Martin James	Saddler	
970. Atkinson, Clement	Private	
991. Adams, Bertrand	,,	
951. Adams, William James	,,	
953. Adams, Clarence Matthew	,,	
955. Ayliffe, James Burton	,,	
994. Barnes, Edward George	,,	
1001. Bath, William Murray	,,	
959. Bolitho, Wilfred	,,	
990. Bell, Francis	,,	
1002. Barry, Laurence Du Bois	,,	
1035. Brown, John Riddle	,,	
956. Bateson, Frederick Westbroke	,,	
957. Barnes, John Leo	,,	
995. Butcher, Osmund	,,	
1036. Bennett, Walter James	,,	
1064. Barrett, Albert Alfred	,,	
958. Bowden, John Herbert	,,	
1038. Cooper, Percival Daniel Squibb	,,	
1003. Cole, Arthur Edward	,,	
1039. Clarke, Albert Ernest	,,	
961. Cradock, William	,,	
1004. Clark, Peter	,,	
1005. Catchlove, George James Leyland	,,	Promoted Transport-Sergeant
1007. Clarke, George Francis	,,	
1008. Cox, Albert Edward	,,	
1009. Cobby, George Arthur	,,	
1010. Clark, Kenneth	,,	
962. Croucher, John Erskine	,,	
1040. Carter, William Daniel	,,	
963. Cornish, Francis Clement	,,	
1042. Dodd, Fleming William	,,	
1011. Dolley, Charles John	,,	Promoted Mess-Sergeant
1043. Derrick, Robert Francis	,,	
1044. Elliott, Ronald	,,	
1045. Ellison, William Erskine	,,	
1013. Freer, Austin George	,,	
964. Florence, James	,,	
993. Flannigan, James	,,	
968. Holland, William Henry	,,	
969. Holland, Thomas Everard	,,	
1046. Hunter, Albert John	,,	

Nominal Roll—*continued.*

No. and Name.	Rank.	Remarks.

N.C.O.'s AND MEN—*continued.*

No. and Name.	Rank.	Remarks.
1014. Harris, John Arthur	Private	
1062. Hisgrove, Frederick James	,,	
1016. Harrison, James Francis	,,	
1017. Holland, Albert	,,	
1018. Henderson, Ernest John	,,	
1047. Hamilton, Stanley	,,	
1048. Harris, Frederick George	,,	
1049. Heading, Charles Shaw	,,	
987. James, Bennett	,,	
1051. Jones, Edward Whitlock Hesketh	,,	
1052. Jones, Edgar	,,	
1053. Knopka, John Andrew	,,	
1041. Kruger, Will Heinrich	,,	
1054. Killicoat, John Cave	,,	
972. Loller, Harold Stanley	,,	
973. Loller, James Leslie	,,	
952. Laugenberg, Albert Frederick James	,,	
979. Menzell, Otto Anton	,,	
992. Main, George	,,	
1055. Moore, Thomas Richard	,,	
980. Manning, William Joseph	,,	
974. Mann, Peter Augustine	,,	
975. McLean, Walter Hugh	,,	
1024. Macdonald, Robert	,,	
1025. Manning, Horold Aldersey	,,	
1026. McNicol, Donald Lorne	,,	
1027. Marsson, Harry Horace	,,	
997. Mogg, Sidney	,,	
977. Macfarlane, Herbert Samuel	,,	
1056. McDermott, Charles Ernest	,,	
978. Macfarlane, Herbert	,,	
1063. Moran, Michael Patrick	,,	
1030. Morant, Arthur Franklin	,,	
1065. Nash, Allan Moyles	,,	
981. O'Dea, William	,,	
1022. Ogilvy, Inglebram Balfour	,,	
1037. Olorenshaw, Francis Joseph	,,	
989. Paddick, Bernard Henry	,,	
1028. Packard, Charles Harrison	,,	
1057. Peckham, Charles	,,	
1029. Reid, James	,,	
982. Ragless, Benjamin Brookman	,,	
1031. Searle, William Woodland	,,	
1032. Sandford, John Edward Frank	,,	
1059. Summers, Frederick Charles	,,	
996. Siviour, Richard	,,	
1033. Solly-Flood, Frederick Fiere	,,	
1000. Thomas, Henry Carlin	,,	
998. Whitehorn, Stanley	,,	
985. Weman, David Henry	,,	
999. Wickens, Thomas Hall	,,	
1060. Worrall, Ernest	,,	
988. Wundenberg, Frederick	,,	
1061. Webling, Norrie	,,	

FOURTH BATTALION AUSTRALIAN COMMONWEALTH HORSE.
SOUTH AUSTRALIAN UNIT.

"C" SQUADRON of this Battalion was raised under circumstances which did not differ in any essential from those under which that preceding it was enrolled. Authority was received on 23rd January, 1902; and men were selected, medically examined, tested, and finally accepted in the usual manner. The strength was —4 officers, 116 others, with 121 horses.

The Contingent left Port Adelaide on 1st April, 1902, in the transport *Templemore*, which carried the Victorian units and staff, and part of the Western Australian unit. Landed at Durban, 21st April, and encamped there for two days; then entrained for Newcastle, and encamped at Kitchener's Kop, with the 3rd Battalion. Subsequently trekked, *viâ* Laing's Nek and Majuba, to Volksrust. Entrained from there (Charleston) to Elandsfontein, and encamped there until ordered to return to Australia, after having returned horses into Remount Camp. There was but one casualty (*vide* Nominal Roll); and not any promotions.

Embarked at Durban on 7th July, in the transport *Norfolk*. Lieutenant Watson and portion of the Contingent arrived in South Australia on 24th July, *viâ* Albany; Captain Collins, D.S.O., with remainder, arrived *viâ* Albany, 31st July. Disbanded, 15th August.

Nominal Roll.

No. and Name.	Rank.	Remarks.
OFFICERS.		
Collins, Angus Edward	Captain	Previous service with 3rd Contingent
Watson, William Wauchope	Lieutenant	
Downer, John Henry	,,	Previous service with 4th Contingent
De Reyher, Gordon	,,	,, ,, ,, ,,
N.C.O.'s AND MEN.		
2750. Kerr, John McRae	Sergeant-Major	
2734. Donnelly, Joseph	Quartermaster-Sergeant	
2682. Hawke, Horace Ernest	Sergeant	
2751. Marchant, Tom Octavius	,,	
2719. Peakle, Frank Arthur		
2740. Pillifant, Benjamin Charles	Farrier-Sergeant	
2726. Wright, William	Shoeing-Smith	
2729. Williams, Thomas George	,,	
2704. Ploeuges, Henry	,,	
2739. Plunkett, William Civiall	,,	
2718. Trathan, Gilbert William	Saddler	
2732. Willcocks, Thomas James	Corporal	
2705. Powell, Frederick Christopher	,,	
2653. Bates, Arthur Samuel	,,	
2759. Sayer, William Samuel		
2678. Griffin, Francis Thomas	Lance-Corporal	
2735. McGavisk, Andrew Boys	,,	
2745. Stone, Frederick Stuckey	,,	
2728. Whitehead, William	,,	
2662. Cole, Herbert George Mitchell	Bugler	
2717. Scales, Henry Thomas	,,	
2710. Seymour, Charles Randolph	Orderly-Clerk	

Nominal Roll—*continued.*

No. and Name.	Rank.	Remarks.
N.C.O.'s AND MEN—*continued.*		
2650. Adams, James Lacy Lawson	Private	
2692. Angell, Charles William	,,	
2651. Andrews, David	,,	
2652. Agnew, Joseph	,,	
2654. Brymer, Thomas Reid	,,	
2655. Baird, Harold Robert	,,	
2656. Bidjood, Arthur Edward Frank	,,	
2657. Bryant, John Charles	,,	
2658. Barber, William Samuel	,,	Killed; date not recorded
2659. Birrell, Frederick	,,	
2724. Bennett, Claude Ernest	,,	
2660. Colbey, Reginald	,,	
2663. Callaghan, William John	,,	
2664. Chatfield, Alfred Charles	,,	
2665. Currie, Charles	,,	
2666. Chick, Philip Bertram	,,	
2667. Creber, John Roberts	,,	
2668. Cornish, George Campbell	,,	
2661. Cahill, Martin	,,	
2687. Cox, Robert Emanuel	,,	
2669. Dayman, Frederick Hastelow	,,	
2747. Davy, Oliver Leopold	,,	
2670. Drayton, Arthur Job	,,	
2672. Donovan, Michael	,,	
2673. Dunstall, Charles Guy	,,	
2761. Eckersley, Percy Cyril Wheaton	,,	
2752. Fowler, Fred	,,	
2674. Flett, William Peter	,,	
2765. Furze, William Lewarn, jun.	,,	
2748. Gordon, William John	,,	
2675. Galloway, Garvoc Bouchier	,,	
2676. Gill, Edward Charles	,,	
2677. Gilbert George Allen	,,	
2679. Gordon, William Matthew Alexder	,,	
2680. Goldner, Charles Frederick Francis	,,	
2681. Goodhart, Albert Thomas Nelson	,,	
2758. Hood, George	,,	
2683. Hay, William Loutit	,,	
2749. Hood, Samuel	,,	
2671. Hine, Charles Henry	,,	
2684. Jones, Samuel Hedley	,,	
2685. Jarrad, Edward	,,	
2686. Jury, William John	,,	
2688. Kell, Lewis Smith	,,	
2689. King, Alexander	,,	
2690. Ludlow, Thomas Herbert	,,	
2691. Lehsew, William Henry	,,	
2756. Lawrie, Allen Austin	,,	
2764. Lennon, James Michael	,,	
2693. McLeod, Roderick James	,,	
2694. Munn, Philip	,,	
2755. Mohr, Samuel	,,	
2695. Mutrie, Hugh, jun.	,,	
2696. Mutrie, James	,,	
2697. Mackenzie, Kenneth	,,	
2698. Mitchell, William	,,	

Nominal Roll—*continued.*

No. and Name.	Rank.	Remarks.
N.C.O.'s AND MEN—*continued.*		
2699. May, Herbert Harris	Private	
2700. Mara, Alfred Joseph	,,	
2701. McNeil, Alexander Peter	,,	
2702. McLaren, Robert	,,	
2733. McInerney, William	,,	
2737. McAloney, James	,,	
2736. Macfarlane, Horace Edward	,,	
2746. Moyle, Sidney	,,	
2703. Osborne, Henry	,,	
2738. O'Connell, John Lawrence	,,	
2753. Phelan, William George	,,	
2706. Pettitt, Randolph George	,,	
2741. Plunkett, William Gladstone	,,	
2708. Pierson, John Edward	,,	
2762. Pierson, James Benjamin	,,	
2763. Pengilly, Henry Albert Ernest Raymond	,,	
2707. Prior, Thomas	,,	
2709. Richardson, Kenneth Cornelius	,,	
2742. Ryan, Ernest	,,	
2711. Sinclair, Neal	,,	
2714. Stevens, James Francis	,,	
2712. Shanahan, Joseph	,,	
2713. Sinclair, Ronald Lincoln Clement	,,	
2715. Silley, Alfred Thomas	,,	
2716. Spicer, Frederick Wallace	,,	
2744. Shegog, George	,,	
2757. Sawyers, Charles Edward Sylvester	,,	
2720. Trower, William	,,	
2721. Taylor, Edgar George	,,	
2722. Todd, Robert Stanley	,,	
2723. Thompson, Henry	,,	
2760. Thomas, Malcolm Edward	,,	
2743. Vivian, Edgar Vyvyan	,,	
2725. Virgo, George William	,,	
2754. White, Arthur	,,	
2727. Warren, Percy	,,	
2730. Wilson, Samuel	,,	
2731. White, Ambrose John Alphonsus	,,	

EIGHTH BATTALION AUSTRALIAN COMMONWEALTH HORSE.

THIS Contingent comprised the Battalion Staff and "A" and "B" Squadrons; "C" and "D" being Tasmanian and Western Australian respectively. It was raised, like the 5th, 6th, and 7th, upon a territorial basis, for which and other particulars of organization, &c., *vide* page 184. Preference in selecting men, qualification, age, term of engagement, conditions, pay, horse selection, &c., as for other battalions, which see.

Regimental staff consisted of 1 lieut.-colonel, 1 major, second-in-command, 1 adjutant, 1 quartermaster, 1 medical officer, 1 veterinary officer, 1 regimental sergeant-major, 1 regimental quartermaster-sergeant, 1 orderly-room sergeant (staff sergeant). One paymaster was appointed for two Battalions. Each Squadron included 1 captain, 4 subalterns, 1 sergeant-major, 1 quartermaster-sergeant, 4 sergeants, 1 sergeant-farrier, 6 corporals, 1 saddler, 3 shoeing-smiths, 2 trumpeters, 97 troopers; in all, 5 officers, 116 others. One Squadron was divided into four troops, each under the immediate command of a subaltern officer, and comprising about 29 N.C.O.'s and men. Most of the officers and many of the men had served in previous Contingents or South African corps. The appointment of one subaltern in each Squadron was left vacant.

The four troops of "A" Squadron were raised in Adelaide, and the country within a radius of 80 miles; "B" Squadron as follows—1st troop in the south-eastern district (headquarters, Mount Gambier, comprising Naracoorte, Penola, Millicent, and surrounding country); 2nd troop in the central north-eastern district (headquarters, The Burra, comprising Petersburg, Broken Hill, and the country between); 3rd troop in the Peninsula district (headquarters, Wallaroo, comprising Moonta, Kadina, Bute, and surrounding country); 4th troop in the northern district (headquarters, Port Pirie, comprising Jamestown, Gladstone, Port Germien, Spalding, Laura, and surrounding country).

SERVICE.

Like the three previous Battalions, this one was not destined to see anything of the war. The Contingent, comprising 13 officers, 232 others, with 250 horses, left Port Adelaide by the transport *St. Andrew* on the 26th May, 1902, taking also the Tasmanian and Western Australian Squadrons, and arrived at Durban on 19th June. The left wing proceeded to Newcastle, under Major Osborne; the right wing remained at Durban. The Battalion (less those struck off in South Africa) embarked at Durban on 1st July, in the transport *Manchester Merchant*, and arrived in South Australia, *viâ* Albany, on 24th. South Australian Squadrons were disbanded on 9th August, 1902.

Nominal Roll.

No. and Name.	Rank.	Remarks.
	BATTALION STAFF.	
Le Mesurier, Haviland	Lieut.-Colonel Commanding	Royal Australian Artillery. Previous service with New South Wales Imperial Bushmen
Osborne, Fredk. William	Major, 2nd in Command	Royal Australian Artillery

Nominal Roll—continued.

No. and Name.	Rank.	Remarks.

Battalion Staff—continued.

No. and Name.	Rank.	Remarks.
Reid (D.S.O.), Herbert Ambrose	Captain and Adjutant	Previous service with 4th Contingent
Jones, Philip Wm.	Captain - Quartermaster	
Healey, Walter James	Lieutenant (Army Medical Corps)	
Goucher, Thomas	Sergeant-Major	Warrant Officer
Glen, Alexander H.	Quartermaster-Sergeant	
Harrington, Maurice Lionel	Orderly-room-Sergeant	

"A" Squadron.

No. and Name.	Rank.	Remarks.
Cook, Alfred Edward	Captain	Previous service with 4th Contingent

1st Troop (Adelaide, &c.)

No. and Name.	Rank.	Remarks.
Spencer, William Fredk.	Lieutenant	Previous service with 4th Contingent
78. Blanc, Victor	Sergeant-Major	
77. Muirhead, Francis Alexander	Quartermaster-Sergeant	
14. Cleland, William Lander	Sergeant	
99. Smith, Walter	Sergeant-Farrier	
86. Quinn, William Henry	Saddler	
12. Casey, Daniel	Trumpeter	
37. Harrington, Sydney William	Corporal	
117. Henry, Ernest Alfred	,,	
5. Bryant, Paul Hugget	Private	
11. Cragen, Geo. Garnet	,,	
22. Cockrum, William George Hiles	,,	
28. Fewings, Ernest John	,,	
35. Harrison, Henry	,,	
41. Hall, Charles Arthur	,,	
49. Jackson, George Victor	,,	
58. Lawson, Hurtle Vivian	,,	
66. Marchant, Malcolm John	,,	
70. Moore, Tom Oliver	,,	
71. Martin, Harold James	,,	
60. McBride, Norman Harrold	,,	
67. Macdonald, Richard Augustin	,,	
87. Round, Henry Brinley	,,	
90. Robinson, Ben Foxhall	,,	
92. Smallacombe, Henry	,,	
93. Scragg, Arthur	,,	
98. Stafford, Howard	,,	
100. Tilley, Tom	,,	
103. Thomas, Albert William	,,	
106. Thomas, George Campbell	,,	
15. Cock, Albert William	,,	

Nominal Roll—continued.

No. and Name.	Rank.	Remarks.
"A" Squadron—continued.		
2nd Troop (Adelaide, &c.)		
Laycock, Frank	Lieutenant	Previous service with 1st Contingent
30. Farley, Frederick Hammond	Sergeant	
25. Evans, Walter Clement	Corporal	
54. Le Lievre, Horatio Charles	Private	
8. Bailey, Charles Albert	,,	
10. Barrow, John Vivian	,,	
16. Colbey, Percy	,,	
20. Casey, Jeremiah Joseph	,,	
18. Colgan, James	,,	
36. Harris, Charles James	,,	
40. Hill, Harry	,,	
43. Heffernan, Charles Ernest	,,	
53. Krogdale, Michael Christian	,,	
56. Leitchfield, William Lyle	,,	
69. McAloney, Alexander	,,	
80. Norman, John Edward Rudolph	,,	
79. Noble, Fredk. John	,,	
75. Norman, Herbert	,,	
27. Rivett, Hurtle John	,,	
94. Symonds, Walter	,,	
104. Tomkins, Edward John	,,	
105. Tacuber, Herbert	,,	Died of enteric at Durban; date not recorded
108. Tuit, Harry James	,,	
115. Wilson, Arthur John	,,	
38. McBean, William Peter	,,	
111. Wheatland, William	,,	
31. O'Dea, Robert	,,	
4. Brown, Herbert Lewin	Shoeing-Smith	
3rd Troop (Adelaide, &c.)		
Walker, Reginald Charles Henderson	Lieutenant	Previous service with 2nd Contingent
110. Wilson, Peter Henry	Sergeant	
42. Hunt, Henry Vincent	Shoeing-Smith	
23. Jones, George Phillip	Trumpeter	
13. Coleman, William John	Corporal	
63. Merrotsy, George Lawrence	Private	
3. Baker, Frederick Allen	,,	
7. Bowie, Archibald Duncan	,,	
9. Buchanan, Alfred Henry	,,	
17. Coley, George	,,	
21. Carman, Alfred Ernest	,,	
24. Daulby, Hurtle Herbert	,,	
29. Fisher, John James	,,	
83. Fenwick, William Edward	,,	
32. Gilbert, Robert	,,	
54. Gunderson, Henry	,,	
39. Hazzalin, John Edward	,,	
44. Haseldine, Oliver	,,	
47. Jackson, Richard Bestall	,,	
51. Knox, Anthony	,,	
52. Kaiser, William Martin	,,	
57. Lock, Clarence Osborne	,,	
68. Manson, William James	,,	

Nominal Roll—continued.

No. and Name.	Rank.	Remarks.
"A" Squadron—*continued.*		
3rd Troop (Adelaide, &c.)—continued.		
72. Marshall, Joseph Thomas	Private	
74. Macdougall, Duncan Henry	,,	
91. Rehn, Charles	,,	
231. Spencer, Frank Athol	,,	
102. Thorpe, Joseph Prentice	,,	
109. Webbling, Darcy	,,	
4th Troop (Adelaide, &c.)		
59. Lyall, Harold Arthur	Sergeant	
65. Mueller, Herbert Walderman	Shoeing-Smith	
62. Mitchell, Geo. John	Corporal	
101. Whitfield, Alexander	,,	
73. McNamara, Andrew Patrick	Private	
113. Winfield, Ernest Alfred	,,	
1. Aish, Frederick Geo.	,,	
2. Brooker, William	,,	
19. Coulter, Elliott Herbert	,,	
33. Greenwood, John	,,	
82. Haydon, Edward Thomas	,,	
48. Jarmyn, Robert Henry	,,	
50. Klaus, William	,,	
55. Lamshed, Harold	,,	
61. Miller, William Charles	,,	
76. Markham, William Thomas	,,	
81. Oatway, Alfred	,,	
84. Philps, Richard Jeffrey	,,	
85. Pointon, Alexander	,,	
88. Rollbush, Albert Frederick	,,	
89. Robinson, William	,,	
95. Scott, Fred	,,	
96. Sounders, Albert James	,,	
97. Spillane, John	,,	Died at sea; date not recorded
112. Webber, Harry	,,	
114. Williams, Edgar William	,,	
6. Birch, William	,,	
45. Hart, Percy Alfred	,,	
"B" Squadron.		
Langley, Edgar John Flynn	Captain	Previous service with 2nd and 5th Contingents
1st Troop (Mount Gambier).		
Reid, Lister Livingston	Lieutenant	Previous service with 4th Western Australian Contingent
177. McLean, David	Sergeant-Major	
134. Newman, Marcus Richard	Quartermaster-Sergeant	
191. McLachlan, James Francis	Sergeant	
137. Clifford, Henry	Sergeant-Farrier	
118. Bawden, Ernest	Corporal	
227. Warren, Edwin Wyatt	Saddler	
152. Blair, Henry Dougald	Trumpeter	
169. King, George	Private	
119. Anderson, Alexander	,,	
131. Barber, Alfred Douglas	,,	
130. Burton, Jack Field	,,	
127. Blagg, Charles Henry	,,	

Nominal Roll—*continued.*

No. and Name.	Rank.	Remarks.
"B" Squadron—*continued.*		
1st Troop (Mount Gambier)—*continued.*		
126. Brammer, William Frederic	Private	
230. Cavell, Frank	,,	
138. Carter, William Thomas	,,	
141. Daniels, David Owen	,,	
146. Farmer, Alfred James	,,	
153. Grant, Samuel	,,	
167. Kidman, Sidney Munn	,,	
168. Kennedy, Colin Duncan	,,	
170. Lyons, Thomas William	,,	
174. Leitch, Robert	,,	
192. Millhouse, John Scott	,,	
190. Macfarlane, Roderick Andrew	,,	
199. O'Neill, John Francis	,,	
202. Pickett, John Allen	,,	
207. Rackham, Frederick Richard	,,	
144. Summers, John Chestnute	,,	
216. Smith, Walter John	,,	
220. Taylor, Edward Alfred	,,	
225. Wyatt, Charles William	,,	
228. Williams, Arthur Thomas	,,	
2nd Troop (The Burra, &c.)		
Ward, Bernard Torrens	Lieutenant	Previous service with 4th Contingent
176. Lyons, Thomas Patrick	Sergeant	
129. Bates, Robert	Corporal	
128. Bell, George Herbert	Shoeing-Smith	
148. Gray, James	Private	
135. Casey, Edward Joseph	,,	
142. Dalrymple, William Herbert Elphinstone	,,	
150. Gorman, John	,,	
149. Giles, William	,,	
151. Gillespie, Wilfred Neil	,,	
159. Harrold, Albert Edwin	,,	
160. Hales, Thos. Hillary	,,	
187. Maloney, Lawrence	,,	
188. Masters, Joseph Henry	,,	
189. Mitchell, Francis Henry	,,	
195. Neilson, Carl	,,	
197. O'Grady, John	,,	
198. Oke, William Henry	,,	
206. Ramage, Archibald	,,	
213. Scott, Robert Oliver	,,	
214. Smith, James Alexander	,,	
215. Starr, Benjamin	,,	
222. Wehrman, Charles Gustave	,,	
224. Weatherill, William Arthur	,,	
219. Thomas, William Joseph	,,	
203. Rowett, Thomas Charles	,,	
186. Mannix, James	,,	
145. Footer, William Thomas	,,	
3rd Troop (Wallaroo, &c.)		
136. Coe, Robert Henry	Sergeant	
165. James, Richard Alfred	Corporal	
173. Lander, Arthur Hamilton	Shoeing-Smith	
201. Pearce, Clement Andrew	Trumpeter	

Nominal Roll—continued.

No. and Name.	Rank.	Remarks.
"B" SQUADRON—continued.		
3rd Troop (Wallaroo, &c.)—continued.		
204. Rubenicht, Joseph William	Private	
125. Brennan, Mortimer Bert	,,	
124. Badock, Alick James	,,	
123. Bos, Jacob Henry	,,	
122. Brock, John	,,	
133. Chandler, Joseph William	,,	
157. Heard, John James	,,	
158. Hornhardt, Fredk.	,,	
163. Jocelyn, Arthur S.	,,	
164. James, James	,,	
166. Knevitt, William Joseph	,,	
172. Lines, John Thomas	,,	
185. Madigan, Andrew Francis	,,	
182. Morton, Howard Francis	,,	
183. Montgomery, Albert John	,,	
184. McAveney, John	,,	
194. Nairn, James William	,,	
200. Phelan, Thomas Pickworth	,,	
205. Rose, Richard John	,,	
210. Sims, Daniel	,,	
211. Slattery, James William	,,	
218. Tucker, William James	,,	
226. Winterfield, Walter	,,	
116. Watts, Richard George	,,	
221. Walker, John Elliott	,,	
4th Troop (Port Pirie, &c.)		
Nordman, Wilfred Gottlick Roland Patrick	Lieutenant	Previous service with 2nd Contingent
120. Bleechmore, Edgar James	Sergeant	
154. Healey, William John	Corporal	
193. Moroney, Edmund	Shoeing-Smith	
181. Hudd, Edmund William	,,	
64. Adams, John Hemsworth	Private	
26. Beauchamp, Frederic Arthur	,,	
121. Brownley, William Alexander	,,	Died at sea; date not recorded
132. Collison, John Cleeve	,,	
139. Cottrell, Vincent	,,	
140. Dearlove, Ernest	,,	
212. Fowler, Thomas	,,	
143. Ferguson, Thomas	,,	
147. Gainer, Robert George	,,	
155. Hussey, Charles Edward	,,	
156. Hagel, William Charles	,,	
46. Hetley, Ernest	,,	
161. Joyce, James Joseph	,,	
162. Johnston, Walter	,,	
171. Litster, David	,,	
175. Lyons, James Clifford	,,	
179. Murray, Wallace Bruce	,,	
180. Martin, George	,,	
178. Macdonald, Allan	,,	
196. O'Brien, John	,,	
208. Shannon, Peter	,,	
209. Skinner, Alfred	,,	
223. Wilson, Andrew Arthur	,,	
229. Zschorn, Gustave	,,	

LIST OF OFFICERS AND OTHERS OF SOUTH AUSTRALIAN CONTINGENTS WHO DIED OR WERE KILLED.

1st Contingent.

	Captain	Toll, J. T.
	Lieut.	Powell, J. W.
5.	Corporal	Heinjus, J. H.
10.	,,	Klaffer, T. J.
118.	Trooper	Smith, W. E.
96.	,,	Matthews, F. G.

2nd Contingent.

94.	Trumpeter	Marshall, E. S.
13.	Trooper	Marsden, T. B.
5.	,,	Hardy, G. L.
34.	,,	Bartlett, F.

3rd Contingent.

	Captain	Hubbe, S. G.
34.	Corporal	Currie, C. W. B.
65.	Trooper	Millman, C. F.
95.	,,	Sloan, J. D.
61.	Sergeant	Mercer, C. J. B.

4th Contingent.

77.	Sergeant	Maccabe, C. E.
178.	Saddler	Mitchell, E. H. E.
126.	Trumpeter	Davis, C. G.
80.	Trooper	Prosser, H. E.
179.	,,	Moore, J. H.
208.	,,	Nicholas, A. W.
48.	,,	Page, A. S.
66.	,,	Horner, C. F.
157.	,,	Palmer, A. T.
98.	,,	Goodes, H. E.
166.	,,	Woodham, H. P.
163.	,,	Tothill, F. J.
74.	,,	Landsdale, S.

5th Contingent.

	Captain	Hipwell, M. G. P.
419.	R.S.M.	McGillivray, J.
281.	Q.M.S.	Schumann, O. F.
358.	Sergeant	Hamilton, J.
258.	,,	Rust, W.
61.	,,	Mercer, C. J. B.
279.	Corporal	White, F. S.
512.	Lance-Cpl.	Hamp, R. F.
647.	,,	Barron, R. T.
586.	Trooper	Bennier, A. J.
491.	,,	Gibb, D. H.
598.	,,	Croft, F. G.
599.	,,	Main, H. G.
236.	,,	Whittle, C. C. G.
375.	,,	May, B. H.
248.	,,	Horsfall, N.
285.	,,	Gluyas, J. E.
346.	,,	Cochrane, B. H.
431.	,,	Hirth, F. W.
402.	,,	Vickery, A. A.
400.	,,	Simmonds, R.

6th Contingent.

522.	Sergeant	Murrie, P.
553.	Trooper	Walter, C. R. D.
557.	,,	Ewens, W. R.
535.	,,	Marshall, A. E. C.
546.	,,	Teate, W. D.
620.	,,	Beare, H. E.

4th Battalion, A.C.H.

2658.	Trooper	Barber, W. S.

8th Battalion, A.C.H.

97.	Trooper	Spillane, J.
121.	,,	Brownley, W. A.
105.	,,	Tacuber, H.

Summary of Contingents Despatched.

Transport.	Date.	Contingent.	Officers.	Others.	Horses.	Wagons, &c.
Medic	2 Nov., 1899	1st Mounted Rifle Contingent	5	121	*12	
Surrey	26 Jan., 1900	2nd Mounted Rifle Contingent	7	112	120	
Maplemore	27 Feb., 1900	3rd Bushmen	6	93	100	
Manhattan	1 May, 1900	4th Imperial Bushmen	12	222	240	
Ormazan	9 Feb., 1901	5th Imperial Bushmen	21	295	320	No returns.
Warrigal	6 Apr., 1901	6th Imperial Bushmen	9	126	146	
Manchester Merchant	11 Feb., 1902	Army Medical Corps..	1	17	..	
,, ,,	20 Feb., 1902	2nd Australian Commonwealth Horse	5	116	121	
Templemore	1 Apr., 1902	4th Australian Commonwealth Horse	4	116	121	
St. Andrew	26 May, 1902	8th Australian Commonwealth Horse	13	232	250	
	Staff	Australian Commonwealth Horse	1	..	..	
	Total	..	84	1,450	1,430	

* Three horses, nine mules.

Even approximate returns of the ultimate disposition of these troops could not be made out owing to there not being any lists of officers and others struck off in South Africa. Casualties and changes will be found under each Contingent.

WESTERN AUSTRALIA.

WESTERN AUSTRALIA.

PREFATORY.

WESTERN Australia despatched six Contingents to the war, besides her quota of the Commonwealth Contingents. The first three, consisting of one Company each, were paid by the Colonial Government; the remainder by the Imperial; and horses and saddlery were provided, as well as (in the earlier Contingents) regimental transport. The 4th Contingent consisted of one Company; the 5th and 6th, of two Companies each; and the two latter Contingents amalgamated in South Africa. One half-Company ("E") was contributed to 2nd Battalion, Australian Commonwealth Horse; one Company ("D") to 4th Battalion, Australian Commonwealth Horse; and one Squadron ("D") to 8th Battalion, Australian Commonwealth Horse.

The Camp for preliminary training and organization was at Karrakatta.

The first Contingent served with General Clements' Column near Colesberg and Orange Free State. With Major-General Hutton's Column on advance from Bloemfontein to occupation of Pretoria. With Colonel De Lisle's Column from capture of Pretoria to departure from South Africa, 13th December, 1900. Claimed as per medal roll for Johannesburg, Diamond Hill, Wittebergen, and Cape Colony.

The second Contingent was with General Pole-Carew's Column from advance from Bloemfontein to engagement at Belfast. With Colonel De Lisle's Column afterwards until departure. Claimed medal roll for Johannesburg, Diamond Hill, Cape Colony, Orange Free State, and Belfast.

The third Contingent did duty with General Carrington's Column through Rhodesia, until after relief of Eland's River; subsequently with Lord Methuen's Column, and afterwards with General Plumer. Claimed medal roll, Cape Colony, Orange Free State, Transvaal, and Rhodesia.

The fourth Contingent served with General Clements' Column, including Wittebergen and Bethlehem. Medal roll for Wittebergen, Cape Colony, and Transvaal.

The fifth Contingent was with General W. Kitchener's Column in Eastern Transvaal; Natal, and Orange Free State; with Colonel Campbell's and Colonel Wing's Columns in Eastern Transvaal. Medal roll for Transvaal.

The sixth Contingent served with General W. Kitchener's Column in Eastern Transvaal, Natal, and Orange Free State; with Colonel Campbell's, Colonel Benson's, and Colonel Wing's Columns in Eastern Transvaal. Medal roll for Transvaal.

The half unit in 2nd Battalion, Australian Commonwealth Horse, participated in the great "drive," terminating at the railway line near Vryburg, which practically brought the war to a conclusion.

FIRST (MOUNTED INFANTRY) CONTINGENT.

IN the Western Australian *Government Gazette* of 13th October, 1899, appeared a notification that His Excellency the Governor in Council had been pleased to sanction the formation of a Company of Infantry, with an establishment of 1 captain, 3 lieutenants, and 125 other ranks, for service with Her Majesty's Imperial Forces in South Africa. The period of engagement to be for one year, but this was subsequently extended (Western Australian *Government Gazette*, 19th October, 1900). Men between the ages of 20 and 30 were qualified for enlistment. There was a Machine Gun Section.

PAY.

For officers, upon the same scale as in other States; for warrant officers, N.C.O.'s, and men, as follows:—Company sergeant-major, 9s. per diem; sergeants 8s.; corporals, 7s.; paid lance-corporals, 5s.; privates and buglers, 4s. 6d.; 2s. 6d. per diem to be retained as deferred pay and handed over on completion of engagement, but forfeited in case of desertion or dismissal for misconduct, and for every day on which actual pay was forfeited.

It was stipulated also that pay and allowances were to be considered as in full; and that any payments made by the Imperial Government to members of the Contingent for service in South Africa, would be deducted therefrom.

CLOTHING AND EQUIPMENT.

Uniform consisted of khaki drill jacket (2), drill trousers (3), F.S. hat, and forage-cap (glengarry). Greatcoat, ankle-boots, and blue guernsey were also provided, together with the following kit:—1 tin blacking, 1 pair braces, 1 set brushes, 1 button-holder, comb, knife, fork, and spoon, holdall, clasp-knife and lanyard, canvas kit-bag, razor and case, 3 flannel shirts, 3 pairs woollen socks, 1 piece soap, sponge, 2 towels.

Arms and equipment.—M.L.E. rifle and bayonet, infantry valise equipment and entrenching tools.

Regimental transport was provided.

DEPARTURE AND RETURN.

The Contingent went away on 7th November, 1899, consisting of 5 officers, 125 others, with 17 horses, 2 maxim guns, 1 spring-cart, and 2 wagons. Two officers, 4 others, died or were killed; 4 were struck off in South Africa; 5 officers, 115 others, returned to Australia. Two promotions from ranks.

PROMOTIONS, ETC.

Captain H. G. Moor, promoted Major, 14th October, 1899.
Lieutenant F. M. W. Parker, promoted Captain, 1st January, 1901.
Lieutenant H. F. Darling, promoted Captain, 5th Contingent, 11th December, 1900.
Lieutenant J. Campbell, Captain, 11th December, 1900; to 6th Contingent, 8th March, 1901.
Major G. F. McWilliams (Medical Staff), promoted Lieut.-Colonel, 12th December, 1900.
Sergeant A. J. B. Brown, promoted Lieutenant, 22nd April, 1900. Captain, 5th Contingent, 25th June, 1901.
Sergeant G. G. W. Hensman, Lieutenant, 1st January, 1900.
Lance-Corporal A. E. Maley, became Lieutenant (6th Contingent), 8th March, 1901.

Lance-Corporal J. F. Messer, Lieutenant, 5th Contingent, 11th December, 1900.
Private N. Sherard, commissioned Lieutenant, 5th Contingent, 11th December, 1900.
Private F. W. Bell, commissioned Lieutenant, 6th Contingent, 8th March, 1901.
Private G. A. Moris, commissioned Lieutenant, 6th Contingent, 21st August 1901.
For promotions of N.C.O.'s and men, *vide* nominal roll.

SERVICE.

The Contingent left Albany on the 7th November, 1899, in the transport *Medic*, together with Victorian, South Australian, and Tasmanian units, and arrived at Cape Town on 27th November. These companies were there formed into "The Australian Regiment," and were joined subsequently by a Company from New South Wales. On 1st December, the Regiment entrained for De Aar to join the Kimberley Relief Force; and were employed on the lines of communication between De Aar and Modder River. On 1st February, 1900, the Western Australian Company was converted into Mounted Infantry at Naauwpoort, as were also the others.

For details of service between November, 1899, and April, 1900, when the Regiment was broken up, *vide* 1st Victorian Contingent, under "Australian Regiment." Reference may be directed to General Order, 10th February, 1900, quoted therein. with regard to the gallant defence of a kopje at Slingersfontein (afterwards known as "West Australia Hill") by Captain Moor, with Lieutenants Darling and Hensman, 2 sergeants, and 23 rank and file, against 300 or 400 of the enemy. Mention should be made of Private Krygger's gallantry. After Lieutenant Hensman had fallen mortally wounded, this soldier, under very heavy fire, endeavoured to build a sangar or wall round his officer, as a screen.

Subsequently the 1st Western Australians participated in operations in the Transvaal, Orange Free State, and Cape Colony, including actions at Johannesburg, Pretoria, Diamond Hill, Wittebergen, Vet River, Zand River, Waterval Onder, and Colesberg, and many skirmishes. They were with General Clements' Column (as part of the Australian Regiment); with Major-General Hutton's Column on advance from Bloemfontein to occupation of Pretoria; and with Colonel De Lisle's Column, from capture of Pretoria to departure from South Africa.

"At Diamond Hill, 12th June, 1900, the New South Wales Mounted Rifles were ordered to support the 6th Mounted Infantry battalion, and the 1st Western Australian Mounted Infantry were held in reserve. About 2 p.m. the advance began, under cover of the pom-pom fire, which was directed on the Boer gun. As soon as De Lisle saw that the battalion had gained a footing on the hill, he brought the pom-poms under shelter of the wall of Rhenosterfontein Farm, at a range of 1,400 yards, and let go the New South Wales Mounted Rifles. Leaving their horses under cover of the dead ground, the Australians came on to the attack in column of troops, the men being opened out at intervals of 30 yards, with 50 yards distance between troops. Extended in this way, the 350 men of the corps created the appearance of a much larger force, and as they swarmed over the crest of the hill with fixed bayonets, the Boers, without waiting for the attack, retired to a second position, some 1,200 yards away. Darkness was just closing over Diamond Hill when the Boers beyond opened a furious fusilade all down the line; the 2nd Coldstream Guards responded with equal energy. The sound as of a *feu de joie* was heard over the whole field. But this was the end; for the English had captured the key of the Boer position."—*Times* **History of the War.**

On the 27th June, a post on the railway near Roodeval station was attacked, but the enemy were repulsed by a detachment of the Shropshire Light Infantry with the 1st Western Australian Mounted Infantry, with the aid of a 15-pr. gun on an armoured train.

Ridley's Mounted Infantry Brigade, including the 1st Western Australians, formed part of the force which Sir Archibald Hunter led into the north-east Orange River Colony, with a view of surrounding, if possible, the enemy under De Wet, and Prinsloo, in the Wittebergen, or Brandwater Basin, as the district was more generally called. On the night of the 15th July, De Wet, with about 1,600 men and some guns, escaped from Slabbert's Nek. General Broadwood, with the 2nd Cavalry Brigade and Ridley's Mounted Infantry, were sent in pursuit. The Boers succeeded in cutting the railway line. On 22nd July, General Knox, at Kroonstad, wired to the General in Command, Central Transvaal, the following from General Broadwood, sent by despatch-rider to Honingspruit, and telegraphed from there to Lord Kitchener :—" Have followed commando since 16th July. Had sharp fight at Palmietfontein on 19th July ; prevented from pursuing by darkness. Eight dead Boers found. Our casualties—Killed, Major Moor, Western Australian Mounted Infantry, and four men ; wounded—Lieutenant Stanley, 10th Hussars, Lieutenant Tooth, Australian Contingent, and fourteen men." Major Moor's death was a heavy loss to the 1st Western Australians. His fine leadership had brought his corps into great prominence, considering their small number. There were, besides him, one killed, six wounded.

In the fighting at Stinkhontboom, 24th July, there were several casualties. At the relief of Colonel Hore at Eland's River, 16th August, the first troops to ride in and receive the thanks of the garrison were De Lisle's Western Australians, here scouting in front of Lord Kitchener's force, which comprised six regiments of regular cavalry. De Lisle's corps reached Pretoria on 28th August, and were thereafter employed in the Central Transvaal. At Waterval Onder, 3rd September, Lieutenant Darling and four men were wounded. On the 15th October, the 1st Western Australians were inspected by Lord Roberts in Pretoria, and were complimented on their work.

On 13th December, 1900, the Contingent left Cape Town in the transport *Orient*, and arrived at Albany on the 29th. Disbanded on 29th March, 1901.

War Services and Honours.

Moor, Major H. G. (Captain, Royal Artillery).—Served in Rhodesian Campaign, 1897. Medal. Operations and actions in Transvaal and Orange Free State. Killed in action, 19th July, 1900.

Parker, Captain F. M. W.—Operations in Transvaal, Orange Free State and Cape Colony, between December, 1899, and December, 1900. Actions at Johannesburg, Pretoria, Diamond Hill, Vet River, Zand River, and Colesberg. Despatches, *London Gazette*, 19th April, 1901. D.S.O. Queen's Medal with four clasps.

Darling, Lieutenant H. F.—Operations and actions as stated, and in Natal. Slightly wounded, 3rd September, 1900. Subsequently promoted Captain and appointed to the command of the 5th Contingent, 11th December, 1900. Operations in Eastern Transvaal, including actions at Belfast and Rhenoster Kop. Despatches, *London Gazette*, 16th April, 1901, and 29th July, 1902. D.S.O. Queen's Medal with four clasps.

Campbell, Lieutenant J.—Operations and actions as stated. Commanded Maxim Gun Section. Promoted Captain, and appointed to command of 6th Contingent, 8th March, 1901. Operations in Eastern Transvaal. Mentioned in Commander-in-Chief's despatches, 8th July, 1901. Queen's Medal with four clasps.

Hensman, Lieutenant G. G. W. (Sergeant, 1st November, 1899; Lieutenant, 1st January, 1900).—Operations and actions as stated. Specially mentioned in Commanding Officer's despatches, 25th February, 1900. Died at Rondebosch, 12th March, 1900, of wounds received at Slingersfontein, 9th February, 1900.

Brown, Lieutenant A. J. B. (Lance-Corporal, 1st November, 1899; Corporal, 15th February, 1900; Sergeant, 17th March, 1900; Lieutenant, 22nd April, 1900).—Operations and actions as stated. Subsequently appointed to 5th Western Australian Mounted Infantry. Adjutant, 5th and 6th Western Australian Mounted Infantry, and promoted Captain. Operations in Eastern Transvaal. Despatches, *London Gazette*, 8th July, 1901, and 31st September, 1902. D.S.O. Queen's Medal with four clasps.

McWilliams, Lieut.-Colonel G. F. (Medical Staff).—Operations and actions as stated. Queen's Medal with clasps.

Nominal Roll.

No. and Name.	Rank.	Remarks.
Moor, Hatherly George	Major (Captain R A.)	Killed in action at Palmietfontein, 19.7.00
Parker, Francis Maitland W.	Lieutenant	
Darling, Herbert Frederick	,,	Slightly wounded at Waterval Onder, 3.9.00
Campbell, John	,,	
Hensman, Geoffrey Gordon William	,,	From Sergeant, 1.1.00. Died of wounds (Slingersfontein, 9.2.00) at Cape Town, 12.3.00
Brown, Arthur J. Bessel	,,	From Sergeant, 22.4.00
McWilliams, George Frederick	Major (Medical Staff)	
Fraser, John Arthur	Sergeant-Major (Warrant Officer)	Specially mentioned by C.O. in despatches, 24.1.00; 25.2.00, and 24.6.00

N.C.O.'s AND MEN.

No. and Name.	Rank.	Remarks.
41. Edwards, Percy M.	Coy. Sergeant-Major	Despatches, *London Gazette*, 27.9.01 D.C.M.
38. Lessey, Barton Scobell	Sergeant	Dangerously wounded at Palmietfontein, 19.7.00. Specially mentioned by C.O. in despatches, 7.6.00, 25.2.01; invalided to Australia; and awarded pension
112. Unkles, Samuel John	,,	
75. Barry, John	,,	Despatches, *London Gazette*, 27.9.01. D.C.M.
118. Copeland, Thomas	,,	
56. Vernon, John George Warren	Corporal	Sergeant, 25.10.00
119. McWhirter, Samuel George	,,	
60. Tratham, John Edwin	Lance-Corporal	Specially mentioned by C.O. in despatches, 25.2.00; Corporal, 17.3.00; captured at Vaal River, 29.5.00; recaptured at Pretoria, 7.6.00
80. Hamilton, Thomas	,,	Broken ankle through horse being shot at Wagenfontein, 20.8.00; Corporal, 25.10.00. **Invalided** to Australia, and awarded pension

Nominal Roll—*continued*.

No. and Name.	Rank.	Remarks.
N.C.O.'s AND MEN—*continued.*		
124. Sherrifs, George H.	Corporal	
88. Callicot, William	,,	Burmese War, 8.7.88. Invalided to Australia, arr. 3.6.00
79. Loane, George	,,	Invalided to Australia, arr. 31.9.00
106. Maley, Albert Edward	Private	Lance-Corporal, 17.3.00. *Vide* "Promotions"
78. Bayley, George Stanley	Lance-Corporal	Specially mentioned by C.O. in despatch, 25.2.00
101. Gifford, Graves	,,	Injured through falling from horse in action, Slingersfontein, 9.2.00; three ribs broken previously at Enslin
90. Mitchell, Charles	,,	
4. Burley, Johnston Edward	Private	Lance-Corporal, 1.1.01. Despatches, *London Gazette*, 27.9.01. D.C.M.
87. Campbell, Edward Robson	,,	Lance-Corporal, 15.2.00
35. Day, Leo	Lance-Corporal	
99. Messer, James Farquharson	Private	Lance-Corporal, 25.10.00. Dangerously wounded at Diamond Hill, 11.6.00. *Vide* "Promotions"
63. Smith, Michael Patrick	Lance-Corporal	
86. White, William Richard	,,	
18. Bishop, George Neville	Corporal	Quartermaster-Sergeant. Died from sunstroke and fever, De Aar, 14.2.00, result of exposure, Slingersfontein, 9.2.00
15. Attwood, Joseph Sidwick	Private	
26. Allingham, John	,,	
49. Austin, Richard	,,	
38. Allen, Phillip	,,	
81. Ashmore, Thomas	,,	Slightly wounded at Palmeitfontein, 19.7.00
97. Ansell, James	,,	Slightly wounded, Slingersfontein, 9.2.00. Invalided to Australia, arr. 24.9.00
3. Baird, Herbert Matthew	,,	
8. Bell, Frederick W.	,,	Dangerously wounded, Palmeitfontein, 19.7.00. *Vide* "Promotions"
24. Body, Charles Sydney	,,	
28. Balding, Frank	,,	
44. Bowden, Albert Charles	,,	
50. Bedwell, Alexander	,,	Captured at Vaal River, 29.5.00; recaptured at Pretoria, 7.6.00
65. Baker, Arthur Herbert	,,	Severely wounded, Achterlang, 4.3.00. Invalided, 30.7.00
66. Brown, Walter	,,	
104. Bird, John	,,	Slightly wounded, Slingersfontein, 9.2.00
110. Birch, Walter Richard	,,	
111. Brown, Frederick Simon Cecil	,,	
2. Cobb, Charles	,,	
5. Clare, Sydney George	,,	Captured at Bethlehem, 9.7.00; released by Commandant Oliver, 12.8.00

Nominal Roll—*continued*.

No. and Name.	Rank.	Remarks.
N.C.O.'s AND MEN—*continued.*		
11. Clarke, George	Private	
16. Cullen, John	,,	
27. Clarke, George Francis	,,	
29. Campbell, Charles F.	,,	Invalided to Australia, arr. 24.9.00
30. Collett, Murray William	,,	Killed in action at Palmeitfontein, 19.7.00
37. Coward, John	,,	
52. Corkill, Robert	,,	Despatches, *London Gazette*, 27.9.01. D.C.M.
68. Cunningham, Edward Joseph	,,	
74. Cunningham, James Michael	,,	Corporal. Severely wounded at Slingersfontein, 7.2.00. Invalided to Australia, arr. 18.6.00; awarded pension
96. Conway, Michael	,,	Corporal. Killed in action at Slingersfontein, 9.2.00
43. Davis, Evan	,,	
54. Dickman, Charles	,,	Slightly wounded at Palmeitfontein, 19.7.00
67. Davies, William	,,	
76. Dunn, Graham	,,	
77. Dunn, John	,,	
115. Douglas, Alexander	,,	
17. Ekert, Harry	,,	
36. Edwards, Frederick Francis	,,	
13. Force, Harold	,,	Dangerously wounded at Waterval Onder, 3.9.00; died of wounds, 14.9.00. Despatches, *London Gazette*, 19.4.01; recommended for D.C.M.
51. France, Levi	,,	Wounded at Slingersfontein, 9.2.00
71. Fosberg, Carl Alfred	,,	
109. Ferguson, Charles	,,	
114. Ferguson, John Maxwell	,,	
58. Gellatly, Arthur Vivian	,,	Slightly wounded at Waterval Onder, 3.9.00
59. Green, Arthur	,,	Captured at Vaal River, 29.5.00; released at Pretoria, 7.6.00. Invalided to Australia, arr. 24.9.00
64. Golden, Thomas Sydney	,,	
91. Groser, Arthur Wentworth	,,	Invalided to England
121. Geale, Alfred	,,	Injured by horse falling on him, —.8.00
6. Hutchinson, Thomas	,,	
23. Hart, Nathaniel	,,	In hospital with fever, Bloemfontein, 9.6.00
19. Jones, George	,,	Invalided to Australia, arr. 31.7.00
84. Jones, Philip John	,,	Invalided to Australia, arr. 31.7.00
93. Johnstone, George	Bugler	
48. Kenny, Stephen	Private	
57. Kay, Martin Bulmer	,,	
61. Kelly, Albert Edwin	,,	Invalided to Australia, arr. 31.7.00
94. Krygger, Alexander	,,	Specially mentioned by C.O. in despatches, 10.2.00 and 17.2.00. Invalided to Australia, arr. **20.8.00**

Nominal Roll—continued.

No. and Name.	Rank.	Remarks.
N.C.O.'s AND MEN—continued.		
105. Kidd, Thomas Arthur	Private	
1. Love, Alexander	,,	Missing. Rejoined
12. Lowe, George	,,	
42. Leigh, Charles	,,	Slightly injured at Tygerfontein, 25.10.00
53. Loughton, Herbert	,,	
7. Mountjoy, Adam	,,	Captured at Vaal River, 29.5.00; recaptured at Pretoria, 7.6.00
22. Marshall, George	,,	Slightly wounded at Palmeitfontein, 19.7.00
25. Morrison, Alexander	,,	
31. Moris, George Augustus	,,	Vide "Promotions"
47. McSwain, Malcolm	,,	
46. Murray, William Alexander	,,	
82. Minchin, Joseph Henry	,,	
83. Millis, William Checkley	,,	
92. McComb, David	,,	Slightly wounded at Waterval Onder, 3.9.00
116. McFarlane, Thomas	,,	Severely wounded at Zand River, 11.5.00. Invalided to Australia, arr. 31.7.00
102. Monger, Lionel	,,	Severely wounded at Waterval Onder, 3.9.00
113. Moore, Godfrey	,,	
107. North, John	,,	Wounded slightly at Erste Fabritan, 4.5.00
32. O'Connell, John	,,	
39. Pye, Robert S.	,,	
122. Paul, George Henry	,,	
9. Robinson, Arthur	,,	
85. Richardson, James	,,	
103. Reynolds, John	,,	
123. Reynolds, Henry Victor	,,	
14. Saunders, David	,,	
34. Spreadbury, Arthur	,,	
40. Scott, Charles	,,	Severely wounded at Vet River, 9.5.00. Invalided to Australia, arr. 31.7.00
62. Sherrard, Norman	,,	Vide "Promotions." Invalided to England, 1.9.00
69. Smith, James Arthur	,,	
70. Shannon, Thomas	,,	
89. Sweeney, Alexander	,,	
108. Shaw, Septimus Lachlan	,,	
117. Shaw, David John	,,	
72. Teare, John Samuel	,,	Slightly wounded at Palmeitfontein, 19.7.00
75. Thompson, Alfred	,,	
120. Trebilcock, Henry	,,	
10. Watson, Thomas Frederick	,,	In hospital, Cape Town, with enteric, 9.6.00
20. Williams, Frederick	,,	
55. Wheeler, George	,,	
95. Wark, Alexander	,,	
98. Wauchope, Robert	,,	
45. Yeo, John Charles	,,	

SECOND (MOUNTED INFANTRY) CONTINGENT.

ON 20th December, 1899, the formation of a second Company of Mounted Infantry for service in the war, was sanctioned by the Western Australian Government. Period of engagement, one year, but subsequently extended (Western Australian *Government Gazette*, 8th March, 1901). Establishment—One captain, 3 subalterns, and 50 other ranks. Clothing, kit, etc., as before, but adapted to mounted men; also rates of pay, except that there was an addition of staff sergeants, 10s. per diem, and warrant officers, 11s. 6d. per diem. It was further notified that pensions to widows of officers and warrant officers, and compassionate allowance to their children, pensions for wounded, etc., would be such as might be considered and allowed by the Imperial Government from Imperial funds; and that officers, warrant officers, N.C.O.'s, and privates had no claim on the Western Australian Government in such respect.

An increase in the establishment to 125 of all ranks was sanctioned on 8th January, 1900. Men between the ages of 20 and 34 were qualified for enlistment.

Departure and Return.

The Company departed on 3rd February, 1900, comprising—6 officers and 97 others, with 125 horses, 1 spring cart, and 1 wagon. Five officers, 21 others, were struck off in South Africa; 5 officers, 72 others, returned to Australia. (Four officers promoted from ranks.)

Promotions, Etc.

Captain H. L. Pilkington to Major, 21st December, 1899; to Lieut.-Colonel, (local in South Africa), 15th August, 1900.

Lieutenant R. T. McMasters, to Captain, 1st March, 1900.

Lieutenant S. Harris, to Captain (local in South Africa), 1st March, 1900.

Lieutenant S. A. Oliver, to Lieutenant, 1st March, 1900; to Captain, 25th February, 1901. Joined South African Constabulary, 12th April, 1901.

Lieutenant L. D. P. Potter, Sergeant, ———; Lieutenant, 1st March, 1900. Joined South African Constabulary.

Sergeant A. H. Barclay, to Lieutenant, 29th May, 1900.

Sergeant J. S. Duffy, to Lieutenant, 25th March, 1901.

Corporal P. C. Collins obtained a Lieutenancy in South African Constabulary, 7th March, 1901.

Corporal J. A. Bullock, promoted Lieutenant, Bush Veldt Carbineers, 7th March, 1901.

Private C. W. Williams, to Lieutenant, 11th December, 1900; served in **5th** Contingent.

Private S. S. Reid, to Lieutenant, 8th March, 1901; served in 6th Contingent.

Quartermaster-Sergeant G. St. G. R. Beresford became Lieutenant, 8th Australian Commonwealth Horse, 5th May, 1902.

Private R. D. W. Esdaile became Lieutenant, 4th Australian Commonwealth **Horse.**

For promotions of N.C.O.'s and men, *vide* nominal roll.

Service.

This Contingent embarked in the transport *Surrey* on 3rd February, 1900, at Fremantle, and arrived at Cape Town on the 24th. They proceeded to the Prieska district in March, and were amongst the troops engaged in dealing with an organized disaffection. The rising having been put down, some of the Western Australian force continued to operate in that district during part of April.

The 2nd Western Australians were with General Pole-Carew's Column from the advance from Bloemfontein to the engagement at Belfast; and with Colonel De Lisle's Column after engagement at Belfast during the remainder of their term. It is rather difficult in some respects to disassociate their service from that of the 1st.

The Company arrived at Bloemfontein in time to take part in the advance to Pretoria in May. At Bloemfontein they were attached to General Pole-Carew's 11th Division, in which they served from 1st May to the end of October, with the exception of a few weeks about the end of June and beginning of July, when they were detached to assist on the lines of communication in the Orange River Colony, The 2nd were in action at Brandfort, 3rd May; Vet River, 4th; Zand River. 9th and 10th; Vaal, 26th; Johannesburg, 28th, 29th, 30th; 6-Mile Spruit, 4th June; Silverton, 8th; Diamond Hill, 11th and 12th June; and Belfast, 27th August.

The Westralians were heavily engaged at Diamond Hill. In his telegram of the 16th June, Lord Roberts said:—"Botha's army has retired, believed to Middelburg. His rearguard was surprised and thoroughly routed by Ian Hamilton's Mounted Infantry, chiefly Western Australians, and the 6th Battalion."

On the 16th July, a party of the 2nd Western Australians at Pienaar's Pont, on the left of General Pole-Carew's position east of Pretoria, successfully repelled a Boer attack.

The 2nd took part, under General Pole-Carew, in the advance from Pretoria to Komati Poort, starting about the 23rd July. They had fighting in the Belfast district on 27th August, and frequently thereafter. In his telegram of 13th September, Lord Roberts remarked that the Western Australian had been scouting in front of Pole-Carew's Division. They were said to have been the first to discover much railway material and other valuable stores near the Poort. They were present at a review on a large scale held there on 28th September. After their stay in that neighbourhood, they were employed about Machadodorp, where they suffered some casualties throughout October.

On the 7th November the Company left Cape Town in the transport *Wooloomooloo*, and arrived, on the 8th December, at Fremantle. Disbanded on 7th March, 1901.

Note:—Although the bulk of the Company left as stated, some remained and were employed in Cape Colony, assisting to drive out the invaders. At Klipplaat, on 5th February, 1901, Lieutenant Oliver had been sent in command of a small force of twelve of the 7th Dragoon Guards, twelve Western Australians, and three Cape Police, to carry despatches from Colonel Haig to another leader. The little party was surprised by several hundred of the enemy. They kept up a steady fire, as occasion served, from 11 a.m. until sundown, but eventually were all overpowered. Four dragoons were killed, and Lieutenant Oliver and several others wounded.

The last of the Contingent appear to have steamed for Australia, under Lieutenant Duffy, on 31st March.

WAR SERVICES AND HONOURS.

Pilkington, Lieut.-Colonel H. L.—Operations in Orange Free State, Transvaal, and Cape Colony, between March and October, 1900, including actions at Vet River, Zand River, Johannesburg, Diamond Hill, and Belfast. Despatches, *London Gazette*, 19th April, 1901. C.B. Queen's Medal with four clasps.

McMasters, Captain R. T.—Operations and actions as stated. Queen's Medal with clasps.

Harris, Captain S.—Operations and actions as stated. Despatches, *London Gazette*, 16th April, 1901. Queen's Medal with clasps.

Inglis, Lieutenant S.—Operations and actions as stated. Queen's Medal with clasps.

De Castilla, Lieutenant J.—Operations and actions as stated. Served until the end of war. Despatches, *London Gazette*, 19th April, 1901. D.S.O. Queen's Medal with five clasps. King's Medal with two clasps.

Oliver, Lieutenant S. A.—Operations and actions as stated. Despatches, *London Gazette*, 19th April, 1901. D.S.O. Queen's Medal with clasps.

Lieutenants L. D. P. *Potter*, A. H. *Barclay*, and J. S. *Duffy*, and Captain J. M. Y. *Stewart* (Medical Staff) served through the various operations and obtained the Queen's Medal with clasps.

Nominal Roll.

No. and Name.	Rank.	Remarks.
Pilkington, H. L.	Major Commanding	
McMasters, Robert Thomas	Lieutenant	
Harris, Samuel	,,	
Inglis, S.	,,	
De Castilla, John	,,	
Oliver, Spencer Alwyne	,,	
Potter, Lewis Dudley Paul	,,	Slightly wounded, Johannesburg, 29.5.00. *Vide* " Promotions "
Barclay, Archibald Henry	,,	*Vide* " Promotions "
Duffy, Jarlath Stephen	,,	*Vide* " Promotions "
Stewart, John Mitchel Young	Captain (M.S.)	
Comrie, Alexander N.	Sergeant-Major (W.O.)	
N.C.O.'s AND MEN.		
27. Draper, Edward Henry	Corporal	Sergeant, 3.3.00 ; Sergeant-Major, 19.12.00. C.-in-C.'s despatches, 2.4.01
46. Beresford, George St. George R.	Lance-Corporal	Quartermaster-Sergeant, 18.12.00. *Vide* " Promotions "
94. Campbell, Henry Alexander	Quartermaster-Sergeant	
93. Bishop, Archibald	Farrier Sergeant-Major	
55. Robertson, James Huntley	Corporal	Sergeant, 3.3.00
6. Clarkson, Henry Wilberforce	Private	Corporal, 3.3.00 ; Sergeant, 15.3.01. Mentioned in C.-in-C.'s despatches, 2.4.01
52. Mills, John Brien	,,	Corporal, 3.3.00 ; sergeant, 30.3.01
74. Brown, Maitland Howard	,,	Corporal, 3.3.00 ; sergeant, 18.7.00
51. Connolly, John Richard Arthur	,,	**Corporal, 3.3.00 ; sergeant, 16.5.00**
31. Northcott, Cecil	,,	**Corporal. 3.3.00**

Nominal Roll—*continued.*

No. and Name.	Rank.	Remarks.
N.C.O.'s AND MEN—*continued.*		
17. O'Mara, John Joseph	Corporal	Wounded at Vet River, 4.5.00
63. Kyle, John Austin Joseph	Lance-Corporal	
95. Abbott, Charles Edgar	,,	
54. Ayre, William Webster	,,	Corporal, 22.3.00
61. Andrews, Edward Rupertsberger	Private	
28. Arthur, George	,,	
14. Barlee, Alan Haynes	,,	
82. Birch, Harold	,,	
79. Bretag, Frederick William	,,	
45. Bunny, Bryce Victor Eric	,,	Lance-Corporal, 22.3.00
57. Bullock, John Aiton	,,	Corporal, 30.3.01. *Vide* "Promotions"
59. Buttermer, Ernest Archdall	,,	Slightly wounded at Waterval Onder, 3.9.00
96. Campbell, John Bruce Stewart	,,	Reported missing at Rhenoster, 28.7.00; rejoined, 9.8.00
83. Chase, Richard Henry	,,	
67. Collins, Percy Carpendale	,,	Lance-Corporal, 22.3.00; Corporal, 6.7.00. *Vide* "Promotions"
48. Cornish, Gordon Anthony Robinson	,,	
84. Cramond, James Dickson	,,	Corporal, 30.3.01
80. Crawford, Angus	,,	
5. Curtis, Richard	,,	
69. Dawson, Eric Blakeney	,,	
8. Doig, Frederick John	,,	Severely wounded at Belfast, 2.8.00
49. Esdaile, Ronald Douglas Walley	,,	*Vide* "Promotions"
40. Farley, Patrick Henry	,,	
24. Firns, Thomas	,,	Slightly wounded at Vet River, 5.5.00
62. Glen, Alexander Henry	,,	
15. Greene, Arthur Henry	,,	Severely wounded at Vet River, 5.5.00. Invalided to Australia, arr. 31.7.00
43. Hardie, James	,,	
21. Harrington, William	,,	Slightly wounded at Belfast, 2.8.00
13. Holles, Arthur	,,	
81. Innes, Olive Selwyn Long	,,	
1. James, Frederick Edward	,,	
25. Jeffers, John Patrick	,,	
60. Jeffers, Edward	,,	
78. Jones, Arthur Belmont	,,	Slightly wounded at Kroomdraai, 2.8.00
56. Kelby, Oliver William	,,	Lance-Corporal, 18.7.00
23. Kennerly, Thomas	,,	
58. Kirkaldy, John	,,	
75. Lockett, Harry	,,	
29. Longman, Edward Robert	,,	Slightly wounded at Kroomdraai, 2.8.00
11. Maley, Henry Kennedy	,,	
34. McCarthy, James Joseph	,,	
77. McFarlane, Sydney Collin	,,	Slightly wounded at Vet River, 5.5.00
2. McKenna, Walter John	,,	

Nominal Roll—*continued*.

No. and Name.	Rank.	Remarks.
N.C.O.'s AND MEN—*continued*.		
65. McLean, Angus Lachlan	Private	Wounded at Val River, 5.5.00. Invalided to Australia, arr. 31.7.00
26. McRobinson, Edward	,,	
20. Messer, Arthur S. B.	,,	
89. Mitchell, Charles Douglas	,,	Lance-Corporal, 30.3.01
90. Moran, William Armstrong	,,	
66. Morrison, James de Burgh	,,	
3. Morrison, Alexander de Burgh	,,	
47. Musgrove, Mandeville	,,	
71. Neville, Frederick Hugh Rother	,,	Invalided to Australia, arr. 21.8.00
76. Nolan, Edward	,,	
72. O'Brien, Edward Dunegh	,,	
44. Palmer, Henry Geoffry	,,	
53. Perkins, Stanley Millbank	,,	Lance-Corporal, 3.3.00
73. Pooley, Reginald William Price	,,	
33. Power, William	,,	Injured through horse accident; Invalided to Australia, arr. Victoria, 10.8.00
41. Reid, Stanley Spencer	,,	*Vide* " Promotions." Reported missing at Rhenoster, 28.7.00. rejoined, 9.8.00
32. Rose, Percy Cooper	,,	
37. Rokby, James Augustus	,,	
7. Ryan, Timothy Joseph	,,	Wounded severely at Pan, 17.8.00
22. Salmon, Algernon	,,	
38. Schroder, Ernest	,,	
50. Skipwith, Edward Renan	,,	
4. Slawson, George	,,	
19. Speers, Alfred Ernest	,,	Severely wounded at Vet River, 5.5.00. Mentioned in C.-in-C.'s despatches, 2.4.01
9. Stewart, Sydney William	,,	
10. Stewart, Duncan John	,,	
70. Strickland, Arthur James	,,	
35. Stubbs, Gerald Salkeld	,,	
97. Thorburn, Ernest Smet	,,	
92. Thurston, John Bates Milne	,,	
87. Uniacke, Gerald L.	,,	
88. Watson, Arthur John	,,	
85. White, Charles	,,	
68. Whiteman, William Leighton	,,	
16. Williams, Claude William	,,	*Vide* " Promotions "
12. Wilson, George Ernest	,,	
91. Withnell, Ernest Willmott	,,	Slightly wounded at Pretoria 5.6.00
18. Woodman, Charles	,,	
64. Zeitsch, Arthur Clarence	,,	Invalided to Australia, arr. 31.7.00

THIRD (BUSHMEN'S) CONTINGENT.

THE Western Australian *Government Gazette*, of 16th February, 1900, contained a General Order to the effect that the Government had sanctioned a further increase in the establishment of the Mounted Infantry Corps by 125 of all ranks. Pay, clothing, equipment, &c., as for previous Contingents.

It was notified that members of the Bushmen's Company who might provide their own horses and saddles, if passed fit for service by the military authorities, would be granted a sum of £15 as compensation, and a refund of any rail freight that might have been paid in bringing such horses to Perth. At the termination of hostilities, if the horses were sold, any excess over £15 obtained by such sale, would be given to the owner.

The same announcement was made in regard to pensions, etc., as previously (*vide* 2nd Contingent).

Each man enlisted was required to be in possession of a certificate from a Committee appointed by the Government as expert judges of the qualifications of an Australian bushman.

DEPARTURE AND RETURN.

The Contingent left on 13th March, 1900, with 7 officers, 109 others, and 127 horses. Four died or were killed ; 6 officers, 13 others, were struck off in South Africa ; 2 officers, 91 others returned to Australia (1 officer promoted from ranks ; 2 men died after return) ; 2 officers appointed to Imperial service.

PROMOTIONS, ETC.

Captain H. G. Vialls, to Major, 13th February, 1900 ; to Lieut.-Colonel (local rank in South Africa).

Lieutenant A. F. Thunder, to Captain, 8th May, 1901 ; posted to 6th Contingent.

Captain (Medical Staff) F. J. Ingoldby, to Major, 12th December, 1900.

Company Sergeant-Major S. J. Chipper, to Lieutenant and Quartermaster, 18th June, 1900.

Private B. H. Andrews became Lieutenant and Quartermaster, 2nd Australian Commonwealth Horse, 11th February, 1902.

Private F. P. Strickland, to Lieutenant, 4th Australian Commonwealth Horse, 27th March, 1902.

Lieutenant R. R. C. Vernon accepted commission in City of London Regiment, 19th May, 1900.

Lieutenant M. R. P. Gledhill was commissioned in Lancashire Fusiliers, 19th May, 1900.

For promotions of N.C.O.'s and men, *vide* nominal roll.

SERVICE.

The 3rd Company of Western Australian Mounted Infantry for the war, left Fremantle on 13th March, 1900, in the transport *Maplemore*, and arrived at Beira on the 18th April. The Contingents which landed at Beira were divided into regiments as follows :—1st Regiment, New South Wales; 2nd Regiment, Victorians and Western Australians ; 3rd Regiment, Queenslanders. But the Victorian and Western Australian Regiment was more generally designated the " 3rd Bushmen." The different corps were very much mixed up before they had gone far into the Transvaal.

The 3rd Western Australians formed part of the force of Bushmen which, under General Carrington, crossed Rhodesia and entered the Transvaal from Mafeking. They served in the first instance with General Carrington's Column through Rhodesia, until after the relief of Eland's River; afterwards with Lord Methuen's Column, and subsequently with General Plumer's Force.

The Contingent, small as it was, was split up; but saw a great deal of fighting throughout July, August, and September, 1900, in the district between Mafeking in the west, and Warmbad, north of Pretoria, in the east. At Koster's River (19th, 21st, 22nd July) there was a prolonged engagement in which parties from the different Australian Colonies took a large share. The 3rd Western Australians, with a strength of about 70, had Captain (Medical Staff) F. J. Ingoldby, and several others wounded. They were associated with the 3rd Victorians; and, as before stated, formed the 3rd (sometimes called the 2nd) Regiment of Australian Bushmen.

A few Western Australians, acting under Captain Ham, 3rd Victorians, were in the Australian garrison which made a stiff defence at Eland's River in the Rustenburg district, 4th to 16th August. (*Vide* New South Wales Citizen's Bushmen, p. 73, and 3rd Queensland Contingent.) Another small detachment were with General Carrington, when he attempted to effect Hore's relief from the west; while the first troops to march into the place as the advanced scouts of Lord Kitchener's force, which relieved the garrison from the south-east, were men of the 1st Western Australians.

During the last few months of 1900, and up to April, 1901, the 3rd, as part of the 3rd Australian Bushmen with General Plumer's Force, saw much fighting in many parts of the seat of war; and, under the fine leadership of Major Vialls, always did well.

Received from Lord Roberts, 3rd December, 1900 :—

"Lord Kitchener informs me that General Paget has brought to his notice the great gallantry of Major Vialls, 3rd Western Australians, and of the magnificent behaviour of that regiment in a recent engagement. I offer to their relations and to the Colony generally, my most hearty congratulations."

Captain Hurst remained in South Africa after the return of his Contingent to Australia. While attached to "G" Battery Royal Horse Artillery, then converted into Mounted Rifles, he was severely wounded in action at Boochbult, Western Transvaal, 31st March, 1902.

The 3rd left Cape Town on 9th May, 1901, in the transport *Morayshire*, and arrived in Fremantle on the 28th.

Disbanded, 18th August, 1901.

War Services and Honours.

Vialls, Lieut.-Colonel H. G.—Operations in Rhodesia, Transvaal, Orange River Colony, and Cape Colony, between April, 1900, and April, 1901. Despatches, *London Gazette*, 19th April, 1901. C.B. Queen's Medal with four clasps.

Hurst, Captain H. E.—Operations as stated. Served until the end of war. Action at Rhenoster Kop. Special mention in Commanding Officer's despatches, 19th November, 1900. Queen's Medal with four clasps. King's Medal with two clasps.

Vernon, Lieutenant R. R. C.—Operations as stated. Despatches, *London Gazette*, 19th April, 1901. D.S.O. Queen's Medal with four clasps.

Chipper, Lieut.-Quartermaster S. J.—Was present during operations in Rhodesia, and received Queen's Medal with two clasps.

Ingoldby, Major (Medical Staff) F. J.—Operations in Rhodesia and Transvaal. Despatches, *London Gazette*, 17th June, 1902. Queen's Medal with two clasps.

Lieutenants C. H. *Ord*, A. F. *Thunder*, and M. R. P. W. *Gledhill* were present during all, or portions of, operations stated, and received Queen's Medal with clasps. Lieutenant Ord was mentioned in despatches, *London Gazette*, 10th September, 1901.

Nominal Roll.

No. and Name.	Rank.	Remarks.
Vialls, Harry George	Captain	*Vide* " Promotions."
Hurst, Howard Edwin	,,	
Ord, Craven Harry	Lieutenant	
Thunder, A. F.	,,	
Vernon, Rupert R. Charles	,,	*Vide* " Promotions "
Gledhill, Major Reginald Percy Wm.	,,	*Vide* " Promotions "
Chipper, Stephen James	Lieutenant and Quartermaster	*Vide* " Promotions "
Ingoldby, Frederick John	Captain (M.S.)	Severely wounded at Koster River, 19.7.00
N.C.O.'s AND MEN.		
3. Malcolm, Norman Maxwell	Sergeant	Coy. Sergeant-Major
35. Nairn, Edward	,,	Coy. Sergeant-Major. Special mention in C.O. despatches, 12.4.01
24. Pilmer, Richard Henry	,,	Coy. Sergeant-Major
9. Deighton, Arthur Robert	Corporal	Reg. Quartermaster-Sergeant
64. Richardson, Arthur	,,	Sergeant. Broke arm at Bamboo Creek, —.6.00 ; left at Marandellas
89. Rollings, John Hamilton	,,	Sergeant. Invalided to Australia, and awarded pension
38. Day, George	Farrier-Sergeant	Farrier Quartermaster-Sergeant
63. Manning, Frederick Gibson	Farrier	Farrier-Sergeant
68. Gouly, Lionel	Corporal	Sergeant
66. George, William Augustus	,,	Sergeant. D.C.M. Despatches, *London Gazette*, 23.4.01
4. Shea, Michael James	,,	Sergeant. Special mention in C.O.'s despatches, 12.4.01
26. Monger, William Wigmore	,,	
44. Forbes, Bertram James	,,	
17. Alnutt, Frank Gustavus	,,	
53. Black, Alexander	,,	Special mention in C.O.'s despatches, 12.4.01
21. Bunning, Arthur Benjamin	Lance-Corporal	
23. Drummond, Alexander	,,	
10. McLeod, John Alexander Nicholl	,,	Special mention in C.O.'s despatches, 12.4.01
100. Andrews, Benjamin Henry	Private	*Vide* " Promotions "
45. Anderson, William	,,	
105. Angel, Thomas Hotspur	,,	Wounded at De Burg's Pass, 7.4.01 ; died, 23.4.01. Despatches, *London Gazette*, 23.4.01. D.C.M.

Nominal Roll—*continued.*

No. and Name.	Rank.	Remarks.

N.C.O.'s AND MEN—*continued.*

No. and Name.	Rank.	Remarks.
24. Bishop, Alfred Warner	Private	
40. Bushby, William	,,	
109. Byrne, Thomas James	,,	
58. Burrows, Charles	,,	
66. Burrows, Thomas George	,,	
92. Bucknell, William E.	,,	Sergeant. Invalided to Australia, and awarded pension
93. Bolitho, Richard	,,	Severely wounded at Wolventein, 14.2.01
71. Carroll, Charles James	,,	
5. Cowley, William David	,,	
7. Cowan, Robert	,,	
15. Cox, Edmund	,,	Slightly wounded at Koster River, 21.7.00
33. Cragg, Philip	,,	
43. Clair, William Alfred	,,	
47. Cotter, John Patrick	,,	
57. Coffin, James Edward	,,	
74. Cross, William Henry	,,	
108. Coatman, George Henry	,,	
18. Deveney, Gilbert	,,	
37. Davidson, Alfred	,,	
102. Dymock, Ernest Frederick	Bugler	
39. Fullarton, Allen	Private	
19. Griffith, Richard A.	,,	
72. Greeson, Arthur Ellis Wrixon	,,	
76. Glen, George Augustus	,,	Slightly wounded at Koster River, 21.7.00. Special mention in C.O.'s despatches, 19.11.00
97. Gilliland, Edward William	,,	Special mention in C.O.'s despatches, 12.4.01
31. Hardy, Edward James	,,	Special mention in C.O.'s despatches, 19.11.00
62. Hall, Ernest William	,,	
61. Hogarth, Joseph Hatchell	,,	
75. Hambly, Edgar Anthony	,,	Died of fever at Buluwayo, 26.6.00
88. Hooley, Hubert Edward	,,	
82. Hume, James	,,	Died at Fremantle, 1.6.01
95. Hall, Henry	,,	
104. Hazell, Charles Richard	,,	
6. Jones, William Oliver	,,	Slightly wounded at Koster River, 21.7.00
107. Jones, Arthur Thomas	,,	
73. Jones, George	,,	
96. Jackson, Frederick	,,	
99. Keenan, Edward	,,	Special mention in C.O.'s despatches, 19.11.00
52. Leeson, Joseph	,,	Slightly wounded at Koster River, 22.7.00
12. Lee, Sydney	,,	
59. Lefroy, de Courcy Gerald	,,	
83. Leitch, Dugald	,,	
85. Lyon, Charles Allen	,,	Reported missing at Koster River, 23.8.00
90. Leslie, Robert Clarke	,,	
106. Lindsay, John	,,	

Nominal Roll—*continued.*

No. and Name.	Rank.	Remarks.
N.C.O.'s and Men—continued.		
11. Laidlow, William	Private	
13. Muirhead, James	,,	
22. McMahon, Michael	,,	
30. McMurtrie, Robert H.	,,	
41. McManus, Robert John	,,	
49. Martin, Albert Edward	,,	
60. McDonald, John Fowley	,,	
67. McPhee, William John	,,	Died under an anæsthetic, Buluwayo, 2.7.00
28. McPhee, Hector	,,	Special mention in C.O.'s despatches, 12.4.01
70. Manners, John	,,	
77. Mahood, William	,,	
91. McKay, Arthur	,,	
103. Morton, Wilfred	Bugler	
84. Nicholls, Hedley Tresawna	Private	
93. Nugent, Robert	,,	
8. O'Donnell, Frank James	,,	
51. O'Hern, George William	,,	
80. O'Sullivan, Michael Joseph	,,	
27. Preene, Richard Lionel	,,	
42. Partridge, Frederick George	,,	
16. Ralph, John	,,	
81. Roscoe, John	,,	Died of wounds, Johannesburg, 3.11.00
79. Strickland, Frederick Philip	,,	Severely wounded at Wolventein, 14.2.01. *Vide* "Promotions." Invalided to Australia, and awarded pension
14. Saunders, George Albert	,,	Slightly wounded at De Burg's Pass, 7.4.01
20. Scott, Jeremiah	,,	Wounded at Koster River, 21.7.00
29. Stephens, Ernest Hubert	,,	
32. Smith, Alexander Robert	,,	Dismissed by C.M.
46. Smith, Walter Jackson	,,	
55. Stirling, Tom	,,	Special mention in C.O.'s despatches, 12.4.01
69. Sinclair, Sydney Howard	,,	
2. Thomas, Alfred A.	,,	
48. Tully, Harry Edward Moore	,,	
78. Thompson, William	,,	
94. Thomas, William Morris	,,	Sergeant. Severely wounded at De Burg's Pass, 7.4.01. Invalided to Australia, and awarded pension
86. Travers, Mark	,,	
34. White, Henry	,,	Died at Melbourne from exposure on service, 4.6.01
25. Wild, Richard Corke	,,	
36. Wilson, James Henry	,,	
50. Watkin, Edmund Hebblewhite	,,	
87. Ware, Herbert	,,	
101. Wallis, William	Bugler	
110. White, Alexander Patrick	Private	

FOURTH (MOUNTED INFANTRY) CONTINGENT.

BY the Western Australian *Government Gazette* of 16th March, 1900, it was notified that the formation of a fourth Company of Mounted Infantry had been authorized, with an establishment of 7 officers and 125 of other ranks. This was the first Western Australian Contingent of Imperial Bushmen. For pay, clothing, equipment, conditions of enrolment, and service, etc., *vide* Imperial Bushmen, New South Wales or Victoria.

By Army Order 150 (Imperial), July, 1900, it was intimated that N.C.O.'s and men of Australian and other Colonial Contingents in receipt of ordinary Army rates of pay, would obtain a gratuity of £5 when discharged medically unfit, or on account of their services being no longer required, or on the termination of their engagements. In the event of death during service, the gratuity would be credited to the estate. This gratuity was, also, to be in addition to the gratuity (if any) given to the troops at the end of the war.

Departure and Return.

The Contingent left on the 8th May, 1900, comprising—7 officers, 120 others, with 132 horses. Three were killed; 1 officer promoted from the ranks; 3 officers, 35 others were struck off in South Africa; 5 officers, 81 others returned to Australia.

Promotions, Etc.

Captain J. Rose was promoted Major, 15th March, 1900.

Lieutenant C. A. C. Newland, promoted Captain, 15th March, 1900.

Lieutenant E. Vernon, promoted Captain (Sup.), 1st April, 1902, attached to 6th Contingent.

Lieutenant E. R. Williams, promoted Captain, 8th March, 1901, and appointed to 6th Contingent.

Quartermaster-Sergeant H. N. Venn, promoted Lieutenant, 2nd March, 1901.

Corporal L. L. Reid became a Lieutenant in 8th Australian Commonwealth Horse.

For promotions of N.C.O.'s and men, *vide* nominal roll.

Service.

The squadron left Fremantle by the transport *Manhattan* on the 8th May, 1900, and arrived at Beira on the 28th. After having touched at Durban, the Contingent was landed at Port Elizabeth on 19th June, and was at once taken to the Kroonstadt district. They served with General Clements' Column; and they were present at Bethlehem, Rhenoster Kop, and Wittebergen.

On 23rd June they joined a force under Colonel Brookfield, which was to see some very severe fighting during the ensuing three weeks. They also formed part of the 4th Regiment of Imperial Bushmen, consisting of the 4th South Australians, the 4th Western Australians, and the 4th (or more properly 3rd) Tasmanians, under Lieut.-Colonel J. Rowell.

On the 3rd July, General Paget had a stiff engagement with the enemy at Leeuw Kop. In the course of the fighting the guns had been taken to the road; and, during a pause in the action, the escort had been removed to the rear. The Boers, with great skill and secrecy, delivered a sudden and furious counter-attack, in which they gained temporary possession of the guns. Captain Budworth succeeded in rallying the Australians, who had retired, and promptly brought them back. For some time there was cause for anxiety; but the period of imminent danger did not last long; it was over from the moment when, under the firing of the Australians, the Boers left the disabled guns and retreated. Colonel Rowell, having broken a rib through his horse falling, was unable to be present, and Major Rose commanded the Bushmen.

At the taking of Bethlehem, 7th July, 300 Bushmen, mostly South and Western Australians, joined in the attack, and behaved excellently. They were in the pursuit of De Wet from Bethlehem through Oliphant's Nek. On 4th November, the regiment, which had been split up, was together again, under Colonel Rowell. It was long in General Plumer's Force, and did very good work in the operations north of Pretoria and in the Eastern Transvaal.

Upon De Wet's intention to attempt an invasion of Cape Colony being manifested about the end of January, 1901, General Plumer's troops were entrained from Brugspruit in the Eastern Transvaal to Cape Colony; and it was in a great measure due to them that the Boer General was driven out. There were many casualties in the numerous rear-guard engagements with the commandoes. After pursuing the remnant northward, Plumer's men were again entrained at Brandfort for the district north of Pretoria, and took part in the expedition to Pietersburg.

On the Pietersburg trek, and after the occupation of that place, the 4th Imperial Bushmen contributed largely to the success of operations generally in advance of Plumer's Force; they took many prisoners and wagons, and one gun. Some of the 4th Imperial Bushmen were in the escort for a convoy which was sharply attacked by some 400 of the enemy, on the Bethel-Standerton-road, 25th May, 1901. "The escort under Colonel Gallway fought with great gallantry, and completely confuted the enemy's repeated efforts to press into close quarters."—(Lord Kitchener's despatch, 8th July).

On the 5th July, 1901, the Contingent departed from Cape Town in the transport *Britannic*, and arrived at Albany on the 20th. Disbanded on the 14th August.

WAR SERVICES AND HONOURS.

Rose, Major J.—Operations in the Transvaal and Orange River Colony between June, 1900, and July, 1901, including actions at Bethlehem, Rhenoster Kop, and Wittebergen. Queen's Medal with three clasps.

Newland, Captain C. A. C.—Operations and actions as stated. Queen's Medal with three clasps.

Barnes, Lieutenant C. A.—Operations as stated. Actions at Eland's River, Bethlehem, and Wittebergen. Queen's Medal with three clasps.

Vernon, Lieutenant E.—Operations as stated. Actions at Bethlehem, Rhenoster Kop, and Wittebergen. Police duty, under Military Governor, Pretoria. Queen's Medal with three clasps; King's medal with two clasps.

Lieutenants F. G. *Hume*, E. R. *Williams*, and H. N. *Venn*, and Captain (Medical Staff) W. *Gibson*, participated in the operations and actions generally, and obtained the Queen's Medal with clasps. Lieutenant Williams was promoted Captain, 8th March, 1901, and served with 6th Contingent, *vide* operations of that Contingent.

Nominal Roll.

No. and Name.	Rank.	Remarks.
Rose, James	Major, O.C.	Slightly wounded at Bethlehem, 8.7.00
Newland, Charles Albert C.	Lieutenant	
Barnes, Charles Albert	,,	
Vernon, Eustace	,,	
Hume, Frederick Gustavus	,,	
Williams, Edward Ralph	,,	
Gibson, Walter	Captain (M.S.)	
Venn, Harry Norman	Lieutenant	*Vide* " Promotions "
3. Wood, John	Sergeant - Major (W.O.)	In hospital with typhoid, 15.7.00

N.C.O.'s AND MEN.

No. and Name.	Rank.	Remarks.
73. McAlpine, James Henry	Sergeant	C. Sergeant-Major, 1.11.00
110. Moore, Hugh Augustus	Quartermaster-Sergeant	Slightly wounded at Krugersdorp, 4.10.00
41. Stewart, Sinclair Moody		
44. Lee, John	Quartermaster-Sergt. (Farrier)	In hospital with typhoid, 14.7.00
20. McRae, Arthur Worthington	Farrier	Farrier-Sergeant, 26.7.00
37. Chambers, Charles Herbert	Orderly - room Sergeant	
60. Connole, John	Sergeant	
6. Colls, Edward Joseph	,,	
14. Williams, Frederick James	,,	
28. Watson, John	,,	
109. Houston, John James	Private	Corporal, 21.6.00 ; Sergeant, 1.1.01
7. Johns, Henry Alexander	Sergeant	
51. Benson, Richard Moore	,,	
46. Duggan, Dennis	Corporal	Sergeant, 21.6.00
17. Grimes, John	,,	
52. Reid, Lester Livingstone	,,	*Vide* " Promotions "
24. Stone, Edward	,,	
23. Richardson, James	Lance-Corporal	Corporal, 1.1.01
111. Porter, Thos. Hedley	Corporal	
89. McKenzie, Andrew	Lance-Corporal	
63. Robinson, Arthur	,,	
58. Arundell, Edward William	Bugler	
104. Harper, Warabea Forrest	,,	
2. Anderson, Arthur William Hall	Private	
86. Anderson, Norman McLeod	,,	
15. Atkinson, William	,,	
62. Baptie, James	,,	
30. Bell, Thomas	,,	
71. Bellchambers, Walter	,,	
117. Bown, Archibald Joseph	,,	
4. Browne, John	,,	
97. Browne, Edgar Mercer	,,	
79. Bryant, Ernest William	,,	
101. Byrne, Michael Cyril	,,	
107. Campbell, Dalmahoy	,,	
59. Cane, Patrick James	,,	
32. Carmody, Ernest	,,	
49. Cavender, Charles	,,	
12. Chandler, Frederick Henry	,,	Slightly wounded at Stinkontboom, 24.7.00
91. Christenson, Alexander	,,	
120. Clow, John	,,	
83. Cook, Thomas Henry	,,	

Nominal Roll—continud.

No. and Name.	Rank.	Remarks.
N.C.O.'s AND MEN—*continued.*		
98. Coulls, Albert Edward	Private	Slightly wounded at Stinkontboom, 24.7.00
5. Cree, Henry	Farrier	
82. Curtis, William Stewart	Private	
78. Datson, Frederick William	,,	
34. Dawson, Richard	,,	Corporal, 1.6.01
54. Dwyer, Francis Edward	,,	
10. Eccles, Percy Joseph	,,	
96. Evans, Edward	,,	Severely wounded at Bethlehem 5.7.00
99. Ewins, Charles Henry	,,	Dangerously wounded at Bethlehem, 3.7.00
80. Farrell, William	,,	
77. Franklin, William	,,	
70. Fraser, William	,,	Lance-Corporal. Killed in action near Pietersberg, 8.4.01
102. Grave, William Arthur	,,	
106. Gray, Henry Dickenson	,,	
21. Growden, Frederick Henry	,,	
112. Gutteridge, Harry	,,	
65. Hackett, Ernest John	,,	
105. Hales, Maurice Day	,,	
29. Hicks, Charles James	,,	Wounded slightly at Bethel, 22.5.01; reported missing at Durban, 16.6.00
95. Hodgkinson, Arthur Frederick	,,	
47. Holding, Oliver Arthur	,,	
56. Horner, Frederick	,,	
36. Horsfall, Edward James	,,	
66. Hunt, James Alfred	,,	
43. Iles, Ernest George	,,	Killed in action at Jagersfontein, 24.8.00
94. Inkpen, Lawrence Henry	,,	
67. Johnson, William Joseph	,,	
16. Kain, Archibald	,,	
119. Kay, James	,,	Killed in action at Palmietfontein, 19.7.00
26. Knight, George Frederick	,,	
90. Larkin, James Charles	,,	
85. Le Couteur, Henry	,,	
64. Lee Steere, Wilfred	,,	
87. McGrath, John	Corporal	
68. McIntyre, Andrew	Private	In hospital with rheumatism 8.7.00
31. Maguire, James Arthur	,,	
114. Mahood, James Wallace	,,	
108. Malcolm, Laurence Stuart	,,	
27. Maskell, Luke	,,	Wounded slightly at Grasfontein, 13.2.01. Invalided to Australia, and awarded pension
76. Mills, Ernest	,,	
93. Monger, Herbert George	,,	
61. Morgan, Francis James	,,	
92. Morrell, Arthur Hubert	,,	
8. O'Connor, J.	,,	Broke leg accidentally
22. O'Brien, Michael	,,	In hospital with pneumonia, Bethlehem, 28.7.00

Nominal Roll—*continued*.

No. and Name.	Rank.	Remarks.
N.C.O.'s AND MEN—*continued*.		
69. Ottey, William	Private	
35. Page, Algernon Montford Treherne	,,	
40. Page, Albert James	,,	
84. Patterson, Frederick	,,	
116. Pechey, Edward Alfred	,,	
48. Perry, Thomas	,,	
75. Plunkett, George Andrew	,,	
118. Porter, Hubert Walter Grave	,,	
88. Rank, Joseph George Alexander Whartin	,,	
100. Robinson, Joshua John	,,	
33. Rollestone, George Reginald Aubrey	,,	
53. Russell, David Lowrie	,,	
39. Ryan, Ernest	,,	
38. Saunders, Alfred Solomon	,,	
11. Scheurer, Herbert John	,,	Wounded at Machadodorp, 14.10.00
18. Scott-Murray, Colin Campbell	,,	Discharged medically unfit, 4.7.00
9. Searle, Robert Charles	,,	
1. Shaw, Alfred	,,	
55. Shepherd, Albert Ezekiel	,,	
74. Shepley, Walter Thomas	,,	
42. Sims, Frederick	,,	
81. Slattery, Austin	,,	
45. Solomon, Bertram Marcus	,,	
13. Stanley, Arthur	,,	Wounded at Stinkhontboom, 24.7.00
50. Thompson, Ernest William	,,	
113. Thompson, William Alexander	,,	
25. Walker, George William	,,	
103. Ward, William	,,	
72. Wheildon, William Henry	,,	
57. Williams, George Horonda	,,	
115. Woodward, William Henry	,,	

FIFTH AND SIXTH (MOUNTED INFANTRY) CONTINGENTS.

ALTHOUGH these two Contingents were separately raised and left Western Australia at different times, they agreed to amalgamate after arriving at the front, and thus to form one battalion of four or five companies, instead of remaining distinct units of two companies each (*vide* "Service.") Authority for enrolment was published in December, 1900, and January, 1901. Conditions of enlistment, pay, clothing, and equipment, etc., were as for previous Contingents.

Many of the N.C.O.'s and men had served in other Contingents at the war; and a large proportion of the remainder were, or had been, members of Australian Militia or Volunteer Corps. The *personnel* of these Contingents was, therefore, of a superior character.

DEPARTURE AND RETURN.

The 5th Contingent left on 6th March, 1901, comprising—14 officers, 207 others, with 239 horses. Six officers and 5 others were attached in South Africa; 1 promotion from ranks; 1 officer, 9 others were killed or died; 12 officers, 63 others were struck off in South Africa; 8 officers, 139 others, returned to Australia.

The 6th departed on 10th April, 1901. Establishment—14 officers, 214 others, with 237 horses. Two officers, and 6 others were attached in South Africa; 2 promotions from ranks; 2 officers, 13 others were killed or died; 7 officers, 48 others were struck off in South Africa; 9 officers, 157 others returned to Australia.

PROMOTIONS, ETC.

Fifth Contingent.

Lieutenant A. J. B. Brown, promoted Captain, 25th June, 1901.
Lieutenant H. M. Downes, promoted Captain, 18th January, 1902.
Sergeant F. H. Mackinnon, promoted Lieutenant, 8th February, 1902.
Sergeant-Major J. S. Teare became a Lieutenant in Johannesburg Mounted Rifles, 4th February, 1902.
Sergeant-Major S. G. McWhirter, Lieutenant, Johannesburg Mounted Rifles, 4th February, 1902.
Private C. M. Porter, promoted Lieutenant in Imperial Yeomanry, 3rd January, 1902.

Sixth Contingent.

Sergeant P. J. Daley, promoted Lieutenant, 18th January, 1902.
Sergeant-Major F. W. Bretag, promoted Lieutenant, 8th February, 1902.
Sergeant W. C. Mills, promoted Lieutenant, "D" Squadron, 8th Australian Commonwealth Horse.

For promotions of N.C.O.'s and men, *vide* nominal rolls.

SERVICE.

The 5th Contingent left Fremantle in the transport *Devon* on 6th March, 1901, and arrived at Durban on the 28th. The 6th embarked on the *Ulstermore*, which put to sea on the 10th April, reaching Durban on the 29th. As before stated, after the 6th arrived at the seat of war, both Contingents united, forming one strong battalion, the command of which was entrusted to Major (afterwards Lieut.-Colonel) J. R. Royston, D.S.O., who had seen the commencement of the war as a subaltern in the Border Mounted Rifles, a Natal Volunteer Corps, and had gained distinction at the defence of Ladysmith. Lieutenant A. J. B. Brown, an officer who obtained experience in the 1st Western Australian Contingent, was appointed adjutant of the combined battalion.

They served with Major-General F. W. Kitchener's Column in the Eastern Transvaal, Natal, and Orange Free State; and with Colonel Campbell's, Colonel Benson's, and Colonel Wing's Columns in Eastern Transvaal.

For a great part of the year 1901, the 5th and 6th were in the Column of Major-General Kitchener, who long operated in the Lydenberg district, and generally over the Eastern Transvaal. In April, the Column, working from Lydenberg, took part in the operations of Sir Bindon Blood to the north of the Delagoa railway, and in the Middelburg district. During April, the Western Australians were several times engaged, and made some captures of prisoners and stock.

On 13th May, Kitchener's Column crossed to the south of the railway and made for the Ermelo district to take part in another sweeping movement towards Ermelo, under the direction of General Bindon Blood, and back towards the Ermelo-Bethel district. Captain Campbell was complimented by General Kitchener during operations at Farne House. On the 15th, there was a severe fight at Grobelaar Recht, near Carolina, in which the 5th had Lieutenant Forrest and Sergeant Edwards and Corporal Bollinger killed, and four men wounded; and the 6th had four men killed, Lieutenant S. S. Reid and four men wounded, one of whom subsequently died.

On the 16th, there was more fighting in which Lieutenant F. W. Bell distinguished himself, and was recommended for the Victoria Cross, which he subsequently received. The following is the official report of his conduct (*London Gazette*, 4th October, 1901):—"At Brakpan, 16th May, when retiring through a heavy fire, after holding the right flank, Lieutenant Bell noticed a man dismounted, and returned and took him behind him. The horse not being equal to the weight, fell with them. Lieutenant Bell then remained behind, and covered the man's retirement till he was out of danger."

On the 23rd June, at Renshoogte, there was again fighting. Lieutenant Reid and two men were killed, and two wounded severely. During these operations a number of prisoners, and some carts containing ammunition were taken.

In July, Kitchener's Column was back at Middelburg, and after refitting, moved north of the railway, and had some encounters in which prisoners were taken. On the 16th August, there was fighting, with further casualties. Portion of the battalion was from August to October in Colonel Benson's Column, and got in some good work in the Eastern Transvaal.

Towards the close of 1901, and in the early months of 1902, both Contingents were acting under General Bruce Hamilton in the Eastern Transvaal, and took part in many of his most successful enterprises. They had a few casualties in various actions, notably at Waterval River, Rolspruit (where Lieutenant G. A. Moris was killed) and Roodepoort.

While with Colonel Wing's Column in February and March, 1902, the Western Australians undertook many arduous marches in the hope of getting in contact with the enemy, but they had been worsted so often that their desire was to keep out of sight.

In the Commander-in-Chief's despatches of 8th March, 1902, Lieutenant R. Clifton was mentioned for conspicuous good service in General Bruce Hamilton's operations in Ermelo district; and Lieutenant P. J. Daley for gallantry. It was stated that "in pursuit of superior force of the enemy, near Kromdraai, on 28th February, 1902, he was severely wounded, but with Lieutenant M. A. Shee, D.S.O., 19th Hussars, captured seven of the enemy." Also "as Corporal, for gallant service on three occasions with scouts, when parties of Boers were taken. Promoted Sergeant by Commander-in-Chief."

Both Contingents embarked in the transport *Columbian*, which left Durban on 7th April, 1902, and arrived at Fremantle on the 29th. Disbanded on 17th May ensuing.

War Services and Honours.

Fifth Contingent.

Darling, Captain H. F.—*Vide* 1st Contingent.

Brown, Captain A. J. B—*Vide* 1st Contingent.

Downes, Captain H. M.—Operations in Transvaal, Orange River Colony, and Natal between April, 1901, and March, 1902. Queen's Medal with three clasps.

Flynn, Captain J. I. (Medical Staff).—Operations as stated. Queen's Medal with clasps.

Scott, J. S., and *Davies*, A. (Lieutenants).—Operations as stated. Queen's medal with three clasps.

Ochiltree, Lieutenant J. L.—Operations as stated. Mentioned in Commander-in-Chief's despatches, 23rd June, 1902. Queen's Medal with three clasps.

Griffith, C., *Messer*, J. F., *Sherard*, N., and *Forbes*, H. D. (Lieutenants).—Operations as stated. Queen's Medal with clasps.

Forrest, Lieutenant A. A.—Operations in Eastern Transvaal. Mentioned in Commander-in-Chief's despatches, 8th July, 1901. Killed in action at Grobelaar Recht, 15th May, 1901.

Williams, Lieutenant C. W.—Operations as stated. Queen's Medal with clasps.

Clifford, Lieutenant G. S.—Operations as stated. Mentioned in Commander-in-Chief's despatches, 8th March, 1902. D.S.O. Queen's Medal with three clasps.

Morris, J. T., and *Mackinnon*, F. H. (Lieutenants).—Operations as stated. Queen's Medal with clasps.

Collick, Rev. E. M.—Was present during operations and received Queen's Medal with clasps.

Sixth Contingent.

Campbell, Captain J.—*Vide* 1st Contingent.

Williams, Captain E. R.—*Vide* 4th Contingent.

Reid, Captain F. B. (Medical Staff).—Operations in Transvaal, Orange River Colony, and Natal, between April, 1901, and March, 1902. Mentioned in Commander-in-Chief's despatch, 8th July, 1901. Queen's Medal with three clasps.

Young, W. H., *Hawkins*, J. F., and *Bardwell*, B. E. (Lieutenants).—Operations as stated. Queen's Medal with clasps.

Maley, Lieutenant A. E.—Operations as stated. Mentioned in Commander-in-Chief's despatches, 23rd June, 1902. Previous service with 1st Contingent. Queen's Medal with clasps.

Bell, Lieutenant F. W.—Operations as stated. Despatches, *London Gazette*, 4th October, 1901. V.C. Queen's Medal with clasps.

Reid, Lieutenant S. S.—Served with 2nd Contingent. Operations as stated. Mentioned in Commander-in-Chief's despatches, 8th July, 1901. Killed in action, 23rd June, 1901.

Clifton, Lieutenant R.—Operations as stated. Mentioned in Commander-in-Chief's despatches, 8th March, 1902. Queen's Medal with clasps.

McCormack, Lieutenant H. B.—Operations as stated. Despatches, *London Gazette*, 29th July, 1902. D.S.O. Queen's Medal with three clasps.

Moris, Lieutenant G. A.—Served with 1st Contingent. Operations as stated. Killed in action, 3rd February, 1902.

Wright, R. E., *Woodrow*, C. E., and *Bretag*, F. W. (Lieutenants).—Operations as stated. Queen's Medal with clasps.

Daley, Lieutenant P. J.—Operations as stated. Despatches, *London Gazette*, 31st September, 1902. D.S.O. Queen's Medal with two clasps.

Nominal Roll—Fifth Contingent.

No. and Name.	Rank.	Remarks.
Darling, Herbert Frederick	Captain	Previous service with 1st Contingent
Flynn, Joseph Ignatius	,,	Medical Staff
Brown, Arthur J. Bessel	Lieutenant	Previous service with 1st Contingent. Battalion Adjutant.
Downes, Harold M.	,,	
Scott, John Stuart	,,	
Davies, A.	,,	
Ochiltree, John L.	,,	
Griffith, Cottinghame	,,	
Messer, James Farquharson	,,	Previous service with 1st Contingent
Sherard, Norman	,,	Previous service with 1st Contingent
Forbes, Harold Dundee	,,	
Forrest, Anthony Alexander	,,	Killed in action near Carolina, 15.5.01
Williams, Claude William	,,	Previous service with 1st Contingent
Clifford, G. S.	,,	Supernumerary, 9.6.01
Morris, J. T.	,,	Supernumerary, 7.11.01
Collick, Edward Mallan	Chaplain, with rank of Captain	

N.C.O.'S AND MEN.

No. and Name.	Rank.	Remarks.
14. Abbert, Percy Henry George	Bugler	
49. Allen, Philip S.	Corporal	Sergeant, 17.5.01; Sergeant-Major, 9.1.02; Regimental Sergeant-Major, 4.2.02.
168. Alday, Robert	Private	Killed in action at Waterval River, 1.2.02
146. Angove, Harold	,,	
142. Ashmead, Arthur Henry	,,	
314. Bacchus, Archibald Samuel	,,	
122. Bailey, Harvey Inkpen	,,	
290. Bannon, Luke	,,	Lance-Corporal, 11.12.01
277. Bardsley, James Lee	,,	
274. Backman, Albert George	,,	
279. Battye, Crispin	,,	
139. Bambrick, Edward Vincent	Lance-Corporal	
233. Benbow, Henry	Private	
166. Bissett, Charles	,,	Severely wounded near Carolina, 15.5.01
109. Bickley, Samuel Absolom	,,	
115. Bollinger, William Frederick	Corporal	Died from wounds, near Carolina, 18.5.01
177. Brickley, Samuel Francis	Private	
227. Broomhead, Septimus	,,	
288. Brewer, Charles Headlam	,,	
309. Breeding, Joseph	,,	

Nominal Roll—*continued*.

No. and Name.	Rank.	Remarks.
N.C.O.'s AND MEN—*continued*.		
179. Bowers, Walter	Private	
167. Burrows, Henry	,,	
193. Buchan, Archibald	,,	
275. Bullock, Henry	,,	Corporal, 3.1.02
203. Cahill, Michael	,,	
252. Carroll, William	Lance-Corporal	Sergeant, 11.12.01
258. Campbell, Ivan Clifford	Private	Orderly-Room Sergeant, 15.1.02
319. Cole, Hector William	,,	
128. Chapman, William Henry	,,	
135. Collins, George Henry	,,	
147. Collins, Jeremiah	,,	Lance-Corporal, 19.5.01; Sergeant, 11.12.01
185. Connolly, William Walter	,,	
219. Counsell, Frederick	,,	
304. Coleman, James Francis	,,	
191. Clarke, George	,,	
225. Croneen, Seymour	,,	
259. Cramp, Frederick	,,	
212. Curedale, Edward	,,	
224. Day, Leonard Mitchell	Lance-Corporal	Sergeant, 10.12.01
236. Davis, Walter H.	,,	
211. Dance, Frederick	Private	
239. Dalliston, James George	,,	Lance-Corporal. Killed in action at Waterval River, 1.2.02
313. Dale, John Graham	,,	Sergeant. Despatches, *London Gazette*, 29.7.02. D.C.M.
136. Delaney, John	,,	
311. De Bude, Harry Norman	,,	
302. Dixon, Frederick	,,	
170. Dickens, John	,,	
157. Doak, Christopher	,,	
138. Donovan, James	,,	Lance-Corporal, 8.11.01
281. Dunstan, William John	,,	Died of enteric at Pretoria, 19.2.02
271. Dwyer, Thomas Edward	,,	
197. Dyke, Samuel	,,	
111. Edwards, Frederick Francis	Sergeant	Killed in action near Carolina, 15.5.01
292. Egan, William	Private	
181. Ellis, James Winton	,,	
175. Erwood, Charles	,,	
117. France, Levi	Sergeant	
278. Freeman, James Augustus	Corporal	Sergeant, 11.12.01
251. Frost, Montague	Private	Corporal, 1.9.01; Sergeant, 1.3.02
159. Finney, Dudley	,,	
256. Fisher, Cecil	,,	
287. Finlayson, Alexander	,,	Corporal, 11.9.01
196. Forrest, Cunningham Campbell	,,	Despatches, *London Gazette*, 29.7.02
134. Fletcher, William	,,	
285. Fyfe, George David	,,	Farrier-Corporal, 10.12.01
201. Furlong, Richard Joseph	Corporal	Missing at Brakpan, near Carolina, 15.5.01
200. Gandy, William	Private	
218. Gilmore, John	,,	
310. Goddard, William	,,	
235. Goodwin, Robert James	,,	Lance-Corporal, 21.2.02
321. Gorrie, John Brown	,,	

Nominal Roll—*continued*.

No. and Name.	Rank.	Remarks.

N.C.O.'s AND MEN—*continued*.

No. and Name.	Rank.	Remarks.
112. Grave, Gerald	Corporal and Orderly-Room Clerk	
127. Gray, Edward James	Private	
130. Graham, William James	Farrier	
298. Green, Arthur	Sergeant	
150. Hales, Louis Napoleon	Private	
149. Hammond, Arthur	,,	Died of wounds, Waterval River, 1.2.02
243. Hancock, Robert James	,,	Lance-Corporal, 19.5.01; Sergeant, 11.12.01; severely wounded near Carolina, 15.5.01
301. Hamilton, Samuel	,,	
264. Hanson, Kenneth Edward	,,	
116. Harris, John Noble Douglas	,,	
265. Harrington, Patrick	,,	
250. Harken, Ockey Michael	,,	Corporal, 11.12.01
153. Haynes, Harry	,,	
217. Hayden, John	,,	
232. Hayes, James Byron	,,	
297. Horsburg, Charles Walsh	,,	Quartermaster-Sergeant, 4.5.01
312. Horgan, Henry Grattan	,,	
155. Hill, Ronald	,,	
273. Hutchinson, George	,,	Lance-Corporal, 21.9.01
228. Hughes, Herbert	,,	
145. Iles, Francis William	,,	
318. Irving, John Gordon	,,	Saddler-Sergeant, 16.1.02
284. Jamieson, George	,,	
238. Jones, Edward	,,	
308. Jones, Walter Thomas	,,	Sergeant, 1.3.02
245. Johnson, James Patrick	,,	Lance-Corporal, 11.12.01
272. Julius, Francis	,,	
282. Kay, Martin Bulmer	Sergeant	
261. Kelly, Walter	Private	Lance-Corporal, 1.3.02
253. Kemble, Henry Robert	,,	
151. Kennedy, Finlaw St. John	,,	Severely wounded near Carolina, 15.5.01
162. Kennedy, James Cornelius	,,	
214. Kidd, John Edgar	Sergeant	
263. Kidd, Thomas Arthur	Sergeant	
240. Kiely, Francis Angus	Private	
316. Kirton, Rowland	,,	
268. Knapton, George	,,	
247. Lawrie, Robert	,,	Regimental Quartermaster-Sergeant, 1.2.02
207. Leake, Robert Maitland	,,	Lance-Corporal, 10.12.01
317. Leisk, John	,,	
299. Lee, Herbert William	Lance-Corporal	Sergeant, 1.9.01; Coy. Sergeant-Major, 4.2.02
237. Love, Alexander	,,	
264. McKinnon, Farquhar Hugh	Corporal	Severely wounded at Vaal Bank, 4.10.01; Sergeant, 8.11.01 *Vide* "Promotions"
267. Manton, John Stuart	Private	
158. Mansford, Augustus	,,	
174. Maltey, Frederick William	,,	

Nominal Roll—continued.

No. and Name.	Rank.	Remarks.

N.C.O.'s AND MEN—continued.

No. and Name.	Rank.	Remarks.
186. Marshall, James	Private	Corporal, 10.12.01. Dangerously wounded at Standerton, 10.11.01
187. Marshall, William	,,	
283. Marston, Lionel James	,,	
118. Messer, Arthur Stewart Brunton	Lance-Corporal	
280. Mewha, James	Private	
289. Miles, George	,,	
244. Middleditch, Frederick Hugh	,,	
199. Moulton, Harold Robert	,,	
270. Moulton, Charles	,,	
221. Morrell, Clem	,,	
169. Morgan, George Ferguson	,,	
163. Mofflin, Percy	,,	
276. Murray, Wallis James	,,	
291. Murray, Arthur Charles	,,	
294. Murphy, J. L.	,,	
123. McWhirter, Samuel George	Coy. Sergeant-Major	Vide "Promotions"
124. McDonald, Angus	Private	
156. Morrow, Charles Davis	,,	
126. McLaren, William John	,,	
144. McAffee, Alexander John	,,	
160. McGie, Richard Lawrence	,,	
173. McMahon, Peter Hamilton	,,	
183. McCaffery, William Ernest	,,	Lance-Corporal, 10.12.01. Severely wounded at Strankodspruit, 21.7.01
202. McNay, Henry	,,	
184. McGregor, Robert Henry	Farrier	Farrier-Sergeant. Died of pneumonia, Middelburg, 20.5.01
154. McFarlane, Thomas	Lance-Corporal	
188. Neale, Francis	Private	
299. Newton, Wilfred William	,,	
161. Nicholson, Harold	,,	
113. Norrish, William Wray	,,	
205. Noris, Henry Lewis	,,	
148. O'Connell, John	Sergeant	
120. O'Connor, James Henry	Private	
121. Parker, Harold Myborn	Lance-Corporal	
140. Parker, Walter	Private	Died of enteric at Standerton, 22.1.02
255. Passerini, David	,,	
206. Petch, Thomas	,,	
131. Phillips, George Henry	Lance-Corporal	
260. Porter, Charles Mansell	Private	Vide "Promotions"
210. Pruntey, Cairn Patrick	,,	
119. Reynolds, John	Quartermaster-Sergeant	
306. Ryan, Timothy Joseph	Saddler-Sergeant	
137. Ryan, Dennis	Private	
293. Rice, William Henry	,,	
320. Rice, Arthur Henry	,,	Severely wounded at Blinkwater, 1.9.01
165. Rowe, Samuel	,,	
305. Robinson, John Herbert	,,	
180. Rudd, Thomas Noble	,,	

Nominal Roll—*continued*.

No. and Name.	Rank.	Remarks.
N.C.O.'s and Men—continued.		
170. Ross, David	Private	
132. Shannon, Thomas	Coy. Sergeant-Major	
231. Shaw, Hugh Thomas	Lance-Corporal	Sergeant, 9.1.02
242. Stanvard, Frederick Charles	Corporal	
141. Stuart, Nathaniel	Private	
263. Stevens, Walter J.	,,	Severely wounded near Carolina, 15.5.01
296. Stewart, David Hall	,,	Lance-Corporal, 17.5.01
300. Stacey, William	,,	
315. Stewart, Edward	,,	
307. Stanford, Thomas Abraham	,,	
303. Slingo, Thomas	,,	Slightly wounded near Grentlingstead, 23.11.01. Invalided to Australia, and awarded pension
208. Smith, John	,,	
222. Smith, Thomas James	,,	Reported dangerously ill at Germiston, 20.7.01
241. Smith, George Henry	,,	
257. Smith, George Whitfield	,,	Invalided to Australia, and awarded pension
178. Shea, William	,,	
204. Sizer, John Thomas	,,	
248. Shaw, Donald	,,	Invalided to Australia, and awarded pension
266. Solomon, Herbert	,,	Treacherously shot near Jankanisteke Farm, 15.4.01
176. Summerhayes, Walter	Bugler	
226. Stone, Leolin Clive	Private	
269. Talbot, Isaiah	,,	
125. Teare, John Samuel	Sergeant	Sergeant-Major, 1.9.01. *Vide* "Promotions"
192. Teede, John Stirling	Private	
286. Thorpe, Albert Davis	,,	
152. Tipping, Victor	,,	
230. Tonulty, Arthur Tonulty	,,	
254. Totolas, Hector	,,	
172. Vance, John	,,	
216. Wansborough, Walter Ernest	,,	
295. Watson, St. Clair	,,	
213. Watson, William Abbott	Bugler	
220. Walker, Ernest Robert	,,	
133. White, Donald	Private	Farrier-Sergeant, 20.5.01
143. Wigg, Richard Horace	,,	
189. Wilcher, Reuben	,,	
164. Williams, John George	,,	
194. Williams, Pryce John	,,	
209. Wishart, John Henderson	,,	
198. Woods, Arthur Ellis	,,	
182. Woodall, John	,,	
223. Wright, William Hammond	Lance-Corporal	
80. Farrell, William	Private	Joined in South Africa. Lance-Corporal, 6.7.01
53. Russell, David Lowry	,,	Joined in South Africa. Corporal, 6.7.01; Sergeant, 11.12.01

Nominal Roll—Sixth Contingent.

No. and Name.	Rank.	Remarks.
Campbell, John	Captain	Previous service 1st Contingent
Williams, Edward Ralph	,,	Previous service 4th Contingent
Reid, Francis Bentley..	,,	Medical Staff
Young, William Henry	Lieutenant	Slightly wounded at Bladplaat, 16.8.01
Hawkins, John Frederick	,,	
Bardwell, Bernard Eversett	,,	
Maley, Albert Edward	,,	Previous service 1st Contingent
Bell, Frederick William	,,	
Reid, Stanley Spencer	,,	Previous service 2nd Contingent. Died of wounds at Middelburg, 23.6.01
Clifton, Reginald	,,	
McCormack, Harold Barry	,,	
Moris, G. A. ..	,,	Previous service 1st Contingent, Killed in action at Rolspruit, 3.2.02
Wright, Richard Evelyn	,,	
Woodrow, Claude Edward	,,	

N.C.O.'s AND MEN.

No. and Name.	Rank.	Remarks.
373. Abbott, Alfred Percy ..	Private	Dangerously wounded at Merrivaal, 1.2.02. Despatches, *London Gazette*, 29.7.02. D.C.M.
385. Adam, Francis Thomas	,,	Killed in action near Carolina, 15.5.01
326. Algie, Thomas Wilkins	,,	
364. Allen, William Hudson	,,	
504. Arnold, James	,,	
483. Backman, John Henry	,,	
456. Bailie, George Alexander	,,	
495. Barrett, Thomas Henry	,,	
361. Barron, Charles John ..	,,	
508. Benson, Horace	,,	
430. Birch, Walter Richard	,,	Lance-Corporal, 1.6.02
322. Bird, Bruce ..	,,	
372. Blair, Herbert Alexander	,,	
339. Blanck, Arthur	,,	Died of wounds at Middelburg, 18.5.01
510. Blight, Edward Norman	Bugler	
509. Blight, George Sydney	,,	
327. Blumenthal, Herbert Edgar	Private	
457. Boneham, Thomas	,,	Lance-Corporal, 11.12.01
480. Burke, Michael Daniel	,,	
522. Brennan, James	,,	Lance-Corporal, 13.10.01
323. Bretag, Frederick William	Sergeant	Sergeant-Major. *Vide* "Promotions"
342. Bright, George	Private	
505. Brooker, Thomas Henry	,,	
367. Brown, Oliver	,,	
419. Brown, Frederick Simon Cecil	Corporal	
451. Buswell, Henry	Private	
448. Bushby, William	,,	Sergeant, 19.2.02
534. Burston, William	,,	
532. Butt, George Rawson	,,	
453. Butler, Walter	,,	Lance-Corporal, 11.12.01
417. Campbell, Edward Robson	Sergeant	
381. Campbell, Samuel	Private	
526. Callaghan, Denis	,,	Corporal, 11.12.01

Nominal Roll—*continued.*

No. and Name.	Rank.	Remarks.

N.C.O.'S AND MEN—*continued.*

No. and Name.	Rank.	Remarks.
496. Callendar, Fenley James	Private	Lance-Corporal, 11.12.01
441. Carr, James	,,	
426. Carrington, Cyril Wellington	,,	
450. Cassidy, Edward	,,	
478. Chichester, Charles Oakeley	,,	
371. Christie, Mitchell Alexander	,,	
481. Cleary, Thomas Kevin	,,	
383. Close, John Hoskin	,,	
370. Clowes, Dennis Robert	,,	
348. Clifford, Clarence Chudleigh	,,	Killed in action at Renshoogte, 23.6.01
435. Cobb, Charles	Quartermaster-Sergeant	
479. Cobb, Cuthbert Harrison	Private	
362. Coles, Joseph Arthur	,,	
355. Cook, George John	,,	
527. Cook, Frederick	,,	Dangerously wounded (accident), 24.8.01
515. Connors, Thomas Arthur	,,	
498. Coward, Charles Lanham	,,	
422. Cunningham, James Michael	Corporal	
459. Dann, Thomas Vernon Hugh	Private	
535. Daley, Patrick Joseph	,,	Corporal. Promoted Sergeant by C.-in-C. for gallantry. *Vide* "Promotions"
333. Davis, Alfred	,,	
387. Delahunty, James	,,	Killed in action at Bladplaat, 16.8.01
408. Devon, John R.	,,	
389. Devon, Robert	,,	Lance-Corporal, 21.12.01
440. Dickman, Charles	Sergeant	
354. Dixon, Alexander McCully	Private	
331. Doughney, John William	,,	Corporal, 9.9.01
500. Doust, Clarence Raymond	,,	Lance-Corporal, 11.12.01
497. Dunn, Percy Henry	,,	Corporal, 13.1.02
475. Easther, Edwin	,,	
390. Eldridge, Edgar	,,	Specially mentioned in O.C.'s despatch, 22.12.01
382. Emke, Charles	,,	
384. Evans, John	,,	
472. Evans, John	,,	
499. Facey, Joseph Thomas	,,	Severely wounded near Carolina, 15.5.01
447. Fairweather, Alfred	,,	Quartermaster-Sergeant, 1.8.01
325. Finmore, George	,,	
335. Fisher, Benjamin	,,	Killed in action near Carolina, 15.5.01
461. Flynn, William Thomas	Saddler-Sergeant	Sergeant-Major, 11.12.01
416. Forsberg, Carl Alfred	Lance-Corporal	
393. Foley, Michael Buckley	Private	
514. Ford, Matthew Herbert	,,	
429. Fry, Oliver Edwin	,,	Died of enteric at Standerton, 22.12.01
466. Freeman, Edward	,,	
424. Gardner, William	,,	Lance-Corporal, 11.12.01
520. Gardner, James D. L.	,,	
521. Gardner, John	,,	

Nominal Roll—*continued.*

No. and Name.	Rank.	Remarks.

N.C.O.'s AND MEN—*continued.*

No. and Name.	Rank.	Remarks.
455. Garrett, Charles	Private	
337. Garland, Walter	,,	
347. Gast, Joseph Chandler	Lance-Corporal	Sergeant, 31.12.01. Special mention in O.C.'s despatch, 22.12.01
444. Gawith, Joseph Kitchen	Private	Sergeant, 11.12.01
378. Gelling, Geoffrey Hamilton	,,	
324. Geale, Alfred	Farrier-Sergeant	
533. Gibson, David Young	Lance-Corporal	Sergeant, 1.12.01
427. Giles, Philip	Private	Corporal, 1.12.01
473. Gregor, James	,,	
525. Greer, Joseph	,,	
329. Guthrie, Wemyss Manley	,,	
434. Hackett, Hugh	,,	Severely wounded at Renshoogte, 23.6.01
513. Harken, Martin Theodore	,,	
516. Harding, William	,,	
366. Harte, Henry	,,	Slightly wounded at Merrivaal 22.12.01
406. Hart, Nathaniel	Coy. Sergeant-Major	
377. Harrington, Albert	Private	
501. Hatter, James Robert	Lance-Corporal	
431. Henderson, James	Private	
464. Hehir, Alfred	,,	
519. Hepburn, Neil	,,	
388. Hogan, John Patrick	,,	
452. Hough, David	,,	
474. Honey, Albert	,,	
458. Hunter, Robert Thomas	,,	Accidentally shot himself
471. Hyne, Charles Frederick	,,	
386. Jacobsen, George Peter	,,	
414. Jeffery, Stanley George	,,	
507. Jenkins, Richard Thomas	,,	
343. Jones, Arthur	,,	
477. Jones, James Cavanagh	,,	
409. Joynes, George	,,	
530. Joyce, Thomas Redmond	Sergeant, Orderly Room Clerk	
415. Keenan, Edward	Private	
404. Kelly, Albert Edwin	Corporal and Officer's Orderly	Sergeant, 11.12.01
395. Kelly, Joseph Dennis	Private	
330. Keogh, William	,,	Sergeant, 13.10.01
410. Kindon, Frederick James	,,	
531. Kyle, John Austin Joseph	Corporal	
356. Lane, James	Private	
352. Lawrence, George Henry	,,	
488. Leary, Frank Cecil	,,	
332. Lee, John E.	,,	
359. Leeder, Henry D.	,,	
433. Loughton, Herbert	Sergeant	
375. Mackay, George William Lincoln	Private	Sergeant, 11.12.01
487. Marsden, Cecil Sydney John	,,	
468. Matthew, Charles James	,,	
392. Mayman, Edgar Ernest	,,	

Nominal Roll—continued.

No. and Name.	Rank.	Remarks.
N.C.O.'S AND MEN—*continued.*		
363. Mayes, Frederick	Private	
443. Mills, William Checkley	Sergeant	Severely wounded at Renshoogte, 23.6.01. *Vide* "Promotions." Invalided to Australia, and awarded pension
421. Minchin, Joseph Henry	Corporal	
360. Morrison, James	,,	Coy. Sergeant-Major. 11.12.01. Special mention in O.C.'s despatch, 22.12.01
511. Morgan, James	Private	
506. Morton, Robert	,,	
484. Monaghan, William	,,	
336. Murray, James Francis	,,	
454. Maccabe, John	,,	
470. Macdonald, George Charles	,,	Slightly wounded at Bladplaat, 16.8.01
368. Mackenzie, William	,,	
407. McManamy, Edward	Corporal	
394. Nankivell, Reginald Ashton	Private	
412. Neale, Alfred Howard	,,	
512. Nelson, Francis	,,	
350. Nickoll, John	,,	
391. Nicholas, Sydney	,,	Severely wounded near Carolina 15.5.01
437. Nichols, William	,,	
423. Norris, Wilfred James	Lance-Corporal	Coy. Sergeant-Major, 11.12.01
489. O'Connell, Daniel	Private	
369. O'Neil, William Barry	,,	
442. O'Neil, John	,,	
517. O'Shea, Daniel	,,	
346. Oughton, George	,,	
529. Paul, George Henry	Sergeant	
341. Page, Frank	Private	Killed in action near Carolina, 15.5.01
502. Panton, Frank	,,	
528. Pannan, James Albert	,,	
349. Pearce, George Henry	,,	
518. Penny, Ralph Brunker	,,	Corporal, 11.12.01
351. Pentzin, Ernest	,,	Lance-Corporal, 1.6.02
374. Pine, David	,,	
425. Powell, James John	,,	
432. Pollard, James	,,	
462. Pritchard, John Henry	,,	
469. Pryor, Havelock	,,	
379. Prew, Reginald John	,,	
490. Read, Edward	,,	
486. Richardson, James Eglanting	,,	
492. Richardson, John	,,	
493. Richardson, Charles Robert	,,	
328. Riddle, Charles	,,	
397. Robertson, George	,,	
365. Robinson, Charles	,,	Mentioned in C.-in-C.'s despatches, 23.6.02
396. Rowe, William	,,	
449. Russell, Walter Edward	,,	
438. Rutherford, Ernest Arthur	,,	

Nominal Roll—continued.

No. and Name.	Rank.	Remarks.
N.C.O.'s AND MEN—continued.		
353. Ryan, Patrick Henry	Private	
465. Ryan, John Thomas	,,	
485. Rule, Hedley	,,	Slightly wounded near Carolina, 15.5.01
344. Saddlier, Henry W.	,,	
411. Sanderson, John	,,	
402. Scholtz, Charles	,,	
428. Schultz, Arthur Henry	,,	
399. Seccombe, Frank William	,,	
403. Semple, John	,,	Killed in action near Carolina, 15.5.01
398. Shearer, Samuel Augustus	,,	
445. Shaw, David John	,,	
405. Shaw, Septimus Lachlan	Corporal	
357. Simpson, Thomas Edward	Private	
523. Siles, Thomas	,,	
340. Skinner, Percy	Lance-Corporal	Corporal, 11.12.01
436. Spencer, Richard Walter	Private	Died of enteric, 14.5.01
338. Stanley, Percy	,,	
467. Stephens, Albert Edward	,,	
446. Stokes, Ernest Henry	Lance-Corporal Saddler	Corporal, 5.12.01
491. Synan, James	Private	
345. Teehow, Otto	,,	
420. Thurston, John Bates Milne	Sergeant	Died of pneumonia at Standerton 30.12.01
439. Timms, Edward Arthur	Bugler	
380. Trebilcock, Henry	Sergeant	
460. Truscott, William Edward	Private	
334. Wallace, Robert Norman	,,	
418. Wark, Alexander	Corporal	
400. Watson, James Ellison	Private	
476. Watson, Henry Francis	,,	
413. Westcott, George	,,	Killed in action at Renshoogte, 23.6.01
463. Whiteside, Arthur Ferdinand	,,	Corporal, 11.12.01
524. White, William Richard	Coy. Sergeant-Major	
358. Wilkie, James	Private	
376. Wilson, Thomas Henry	,,	Died of enteric at Standerton, 12.12.01
482. Williamson, Francis Henry	,,	
401. Wight, Andrew	,,	Dangerously wounded at Middelburg, 14.6.01. Invalided to Australia, and awarded pension
494. Wright, Harry George	Lance-Corporal	
503. Wyatt, James	Private	
537. Hanna, Charles Edmund	Private	Joined in South Africa
1426. Foy, William	,,	Transferred from Kaffrarian Rifles, South Africa
823. Leach, David	,,	Joined in South Africa. Sergeant, 11.12.01

SECOND BATTALION AUSTRALIAN COMMONWEALTH HORSE.

WESTERN AUSTRALIAN UNIT.

THIS was "E" Company (or half Company) of the 2nd Battalion Australian Commonwealth Horse, composed of Western Australians. For pay, clothing, equipment, organization, service, &c., *vide* 2nd Battalion Australian Commonwealth Horse, Victoria.

Those who desired to join the Company were required to have had experience of country life in Australia, management of horses, and bush travelling; and to be of good character.

A captain, a corporal, and six privates of the Australian Army Medical Corps, Western Australian section, furnished that quota of the Commonwealth Army Medical Corps Contingent. Nominal roll subjoined. For service *vide* Army Medical Corps, New South Wales, p. 16.

There were no promotions of officers, nor casualties. Promotions of N.C.O.'s and men will be found in nominal roll. A proportion of them had served in previous Australian Contingents, or in South African Horse.

Departure and Return.

The Company left on the 26th February, 1902, consisting of 2 officers, 58 others, having in reality only the strength of about a half-Company. Sixty horses were taken. Fifteen N.C.O.'s and men were struck off in South Africa; 2 officers, 43 others returned to Australia.

Service.

The Company embarked on the transport *Manchester Merchant* at Fremantle, 26th February, 1902; the South Australian Company being also on board. Arrived at Durban on 14th March, and entrained for Newcastle, where they joined the Victorians on the 18th; Lieut.-Colonel M'Leish, C.M.G., in command. On 8th April, marched to Volksrust and entrained to Klerksdorp, where the battalion became portion of Colonel De Lisle's Australian Brigade, included in Lieutenant General Sir Ian Hamilton's Mobile Force. They took part in ensuing operations, including the "drive" (7th to 11th May), between Noitverwacht and the Kimberley-Mafeking railway line (Leeuwspruit, about 4 miles from Devondale Siding), the success of which contributed so much to the conclusion of the war. (*Vide* 2nd Australian Commonwealth Horse, Victoria).

The Company officers, of course, participated in the operations, and received Queen's Medal with clasps. Lieutenant and Quartermaster B. H. Andrews had seen previous service with 3rd Contingent. Lieutenant H. N. Venn, Paymaster, 1st and 2nd Battalions, who had formerly served in 4th Western Australian Contingent, returned to Australia by the *Drayton Grange*, 11th July; he was subsequently promoted Captain, and returned again to South Africa for final settlement of Australian accounts.

The Company embarked at Durban on 5th July, 1902, in the transport *Norfolk*, with the South Australians; arrived at Albany on the 25th., and were disbanded shortly afterwards.

Nominal Roll.

No. and Name.	Rank.	Remarks.
Davies, Charles	Lieutenant	Commanding
Pretty, Edward Percival	,,	
Andrews, Benjamin Henry	Lieutenant and Quartermaster	Battalion Staff. Previous service 3rd Contingent
Nyulasy, A. T.	Captain (A.M.C.)	Battalion Staff

N.C.O.'s AND MEN.

No. and Name.	Rank.	Remarks.
1101. Dunn, Mathew William	Private	
1102. Copeland, Thomas John	Quartermaster-Sergeant	
1103. Moore, George	Lance-Corporal	
1104. Ashmore, Thomas	Private	
1105. Main, George	,,	
1106. Woods, —.	,,	Promoted Lance-Corporal
1107. Battye, William Thos.	,,	
1108. Grimes, John	,,	Promoted Sergeant
1109. Jago, Sydney Broderick	,,	Promoted Quartermaster-Sergeant
1110. Cavanagh, William	,,	
1111. Cahill, George Percival	,,	
1112. Zaccheus, Gustavus Henry	Corporal	
1113. Shea, Michael James	Sergeant	
1114. Coatman, Geo. Henry	Private	Promoted Lance-Corporal
1115. Charteris, Jas.	,,	
1116. Martin, Wilfred	Bugler	
1117. Hicks, Geo. Bertrand	Corporal	Promoted Sergeant
1118. Bridgeman, John Samuel	,,	Promoted Sergeant-Major
1119. Knowler, John	Private	
1120. Messenger, Ernest John	,,	
1121. King, Frank Alderley	,,	
1122. Bradbury, Henry Ernest	,,	
1123. Clarke, Geo. Lawrence	,,	
1124. Kilmurray, Henry	,,	
1125. Johnson, Oscar Chas.	,,	
1126. Collins, James, junior	,,	
1127. Wiley, Robt. Thos. Pearson	,,	
1128. Rowley, Walter Vatian	,,	
1129. Collins, John Edwards	,,	
1130. Wilson, William	,,	
1131. Trathan, Henry Harold	Lance-Corporal	Corporal
1132. Smith, Walter James	Private	Corporal
1133. Matthews, James Harold	,,	Farrier-Sergeant
1134. Williamson, John Forsaith	,,	
1135. Monger, George	,,	
1136. Armstrong, Alfred	,,	
1137. McCarthy, John	,,	
1138. Smith, James	,,	
1139. Butler, Albert James	,,	
1140. Cahill, Walter	,,	
1141. Nicholls, John	Farrier-Sergeant	Farrier-Major
1142. McColl, Archibald	Private	
1143. Day, Henry Stuart	,,	
1144. Sommer, Adolph George	,,	
1145. Bell, Wm. Jas.	,,	
1146. Kells, Robt.	,,	
1147. Grass, Fredk.	,,	
1148. Wyatt, Joseph William	,,	
1149. Jones, David Henry	,,	
1150. Hughes, Patck. Percy	,,	
1152. Clarke, Geo. Fredck.	Lance-Corporal	Corporal

Nominal Roll—*continued*.

No. and Name.	Rank.	Remarks.

N.C.O.'s AND MEN—*continued*.

1153. Lee, Ed.	Private	
1154. O'Connell, Thomas	,,	
1155. Hearman, Walter Edgar	,,	
1156. Bitton, John	,,	
1157. Crouch, Robt.	,,	
1158. Bell, Edgar Watson	,,	
1159. Ridd, Alf. Geo.	,,	

AUSTRALIAN ARMY MEDICAL CORPS.

W.A. Section.

Nyulasy, Arthur John	Captain	Battalion Staff
1357. Jeffers, John Patrick	Corporal	
1358. Cunningham, Alex. Vincent	Private	
1362. Matthews, Samuel	,,	
1361. Reynolds, Sylvanus	,,	
1360. Waterman, Fredk. Thos. Samuel	,,	
1267. Yann, Fredck.	,,	
1269. Shrimpton, Jesse	,,	

FOURTH BATTALION AUSTRALIAN COMMONWEALTH HORSE.

WESTERN AUSTRALIAN UNIT.

CONSTITUTED "D" Company of the 4th Battalion Australian Commonwealth Horse; "A" and "B" Companies being Victorians, and "C" Company, South Australians.

For details of pay, establishment, clothing, equipment, &c., *vide* 2nd Battalion, Australian Commonwealth Horse, Victoria.

For service, *vide* 4th Battalion, Australian Commonwealth Horse, Victoria. Two of the Company officers had served previously (*vide* nominal roll); the others obtained the Queen's Medal with two clasps.

There were no casualties. For promotions, *vide* nominal roll. A proportion of N.C.O.'s and men had had previous service.

DEPARTURE AND RETURN.

The Company was divided and embarked in two transports, the *Templemore* (which carried the Victorian and South Australian units and staff), and the *Englishman*. Strength—5 officers and 115 others, with 122 horses. Embarked on 7th April at Fremantle. One officer, 47 others were struck off in South Africa; 4 officers, 68 others returned to Australia. Embarked on 11th July, in the transport, *Drayton Grange*, and arrived at Albany on 30th July.

Nominal Roll.

No. and Name.	Rank.	Remarks.
Robertson, John Ernest	Captain	
Esdaile, Ronald Douglas Walley	Lieutenant	Previous service in 2nd W.A. Mounted Infantry Contingent
Strickland, Fredk. Philip	,,	Previous service in 3rd W.A. Mounted Infantry Contingent
Messer, Kenneth Durward	,,	
Finnerty, Arthur John	,,	
N.C.O.'S AND MEN.		
2820. Hunt, James Arthur	Sergeant	
2821. Cragg, Phillip	Corporal	
2822. Brady, Edgar Vernon	Private	
2823. Dymock, Ernest Fred	Bugler	
2824. McAlpine, James Henry	Sergeant-Major	
2825. Balding, Gerald	Private	
2826. McMurtrie Robt.	Sergeant	
2827. Hannah, Robt. Jas.	Private	
2828. Salmon, Ralph	Bugler	
2829. Hamilton, William	Private	
2830. O'Mara, John Joseph	Farrier-Sergeant	
2831. Troedel, Charles	Private	
2832. Richards, Walter Jas.	,,	
2834. Eccleston, John Joseph	,,	
2835. Murray, Wm.	,,	
2836. O'Leary, Fred Joseph	Shoeing Smith	

Nominal Roll—*continued*.

No. and Name.	Rank.	Remarks.
N.C.O.'s AND MEN—*continued*.		
2837. Williams, Fred	Private	
2838. Hunt, Hugh	,,	
2839. Sullivan, Frank Arthur	,,	Promoted Lance-Corporal
2840. Ellis, Herbert John	,,	
2841. Crisp, Herbert	,,	
2842. Norris, George L.	,,	Promoted Lance-Corporal
2843. Wright, Alf. Jas.	,,	
2844. Hay, Jas. Arthur	,,	
2845. Stevenson, Chas. F. G.	,,	
2846. Luttrel, Sydney P.	,,	
2847. Dewar, Frank	,,	
2848. Samuels, Herbert	,,	
2849. Baldwin, John	,,	
2850. Messer, Arthur Stuart Brunton	Quartermaster-Sergeant	
2851. Burkett, Geo. Arthur	Private	
2852. Taylor, Edward Louis	,,	
2853. Cox, Edward M.	,,	
2854. Barry, John	Sergeant	
2855. Wilson, John	Private	
2856. Atkinson, William	Lance-Corporal	
2857. Davies, Arthur Geo.	Private	
2858. Blake, Jas.	,,	
2859. Owen, Robt. Ed.	,,	
2860. Cooper, James Geo.	,,	
2861. Charlton, Edwin	,,	
2862. Logan, William	,,	
2863. Brown, Albert S. J.	,,	
2864. Guest, Ernest Wm.	,,	
2865. Haigh, Arthur	,,	
2866. McLeod, John	,,	
2867. Morrish, D. K.	,,	
2868. Pearce, George R.	,,	
2869. Stratton, Wm.	,,	
2870. Atkinson, John	Shoeing Smith	
2871. Chapple, Alfred	,,	
2872. Pride, William A.	,,	
2873. Salmon, Algernon	Corporal	
2874. Lee, Sydney	,,	
2875. Bartlett, Henry	Private	
2876. Whrildon, William	Lance-Corporal	
2877. Outred, George Ed.	Private	
2878. Randford, Walter	,,	
2879. Earl, William	,,	
2880. Mutton, William	,,	Promoted Lance-Corporal
2881. Carlyon, John S.	,,	
2882. McGuinness, John	,,	
2883. Martin, Archibald	,,	
2884. Scheurer, Hubert J.	,,	
2885. Henderson, John Chas.	,,	
2886. James, Hamish S.	,,	
2887. Matheson, Donald	,,	Promoted Lance-Corporal
2888. Bird, John Fredk.	,,	
2889. Crain, Edwin C.	,,	
2890. Smith, Louis	,,	
2891. Bryant, Joseph S.	,,	

Nominal Roll—*continued.*

No. and Name.	Rank.	Remarks.

N.C.O.'s AND MEN—*continued.*

No. and Name.	Rank.	Remarks.
2892. Eccles, Percy Joseph	Private	
2893. Martin, Fred. J.	,,	
2894. Campbell, Chas. K.	,,	
2895. O'Donnell, Frank J.	Lance-Corporal	
2896. Howard, John	Private	
2897. Watts, Percy	Corporal	
2898. Hughes, Walter George	Private	
2899. Kemp, David	,,	
2900. Kemp, William	,,	
2901. Allwood, Frank C.	,,	
2902. Crothers, James	,,	
2903. Job, Herbert W.	Shoeing Smith	
2904. McRae, Francis	Private	
2905. Harrington, Patck W.	,,	
2906. Parry, Ernest	,,	
2907. Brown, Frank S.	,,	
2908. Davenport, Peter	,,	
2909. Wheeler, Edwin	,,	
2910. Brown, Edgar M.	Corporal	
2911. Stirling, Thos. F.	Sergeant	
2912. Judge, Joseph J.	Private	
2913. Murray, C. C. Scott	,,	
2914. Wilson, James	,,	
2915. O'Reilly, Phillip	,,	
2916. Husking, Albert	,,	
2917. Johnston, John D.	,,	
2918. Sackild, Clement	,,	
2919. Cotter, John P.	Corporal	
2920. Driscoll, Daniel	Private	
2921. Gardiner, Fredk. W.	,,	
2922. Warrington, Frank	,,	
2923. Tomlyn, Edwin	,,	
2924. Ferguson, John Maxwell	Lance-Corporal	
2925. McMahon, William	Private	
2926. Gallagher, Douglas	,,	
2927. Stewart, James	,,	
2928. Kiernan, William	,,	
2929. Jacobs, Edward	,,	
2930. Duff, Edward P.	,,	
2931. Jenkins, John	,,	
2932. Brissenden, Lawrence	,,	
2933. Wells, William Henry	,,	
2934. Culhane, James	,,	
2935. Husking, Richard	,,	

EIGHTH BATTALION AUSTRALIAN COMMONWEALTH HORSE.
WESTERN AUSTRALIAN UNIT.

THIS was "D" Squadron of the 8th Battalion, Australian Commonwealth Horse, which comprised two South Australian squadrons, one Western Australian, and one Tasmanian.

For particulars of pay, clothing, equipment, conditions of enrolment, organization, &c., *vide* 5th Battalion, Australian Commonwealth Horse, New South Wales, page 184.

No. 1 Troop comprised 29 N.C.O.'s and men, who were enrolled at Military Head-Quarters, Perth; No. 2 Troop of similar strength, enrolled at Geraldton (6), Bunbury (14), Northam (6), and Albany (3); Nos. 3 and 4 Troops, each of strength stated, at the Eastern Goldfields; enrolling centre, Kalgoorlie. Preference was given to men belonging to existing military units, to those who had served in South Africa, and to civilians that possessed most military qualities.

Horses fit for service were selected by local committees, at prices not exceeding £20; preference being given to horses brought by the men enrolled. Height, 15 to 15.3 hands; age, 5 to 12 years.

For service, *vide* 8th Battalion, Australian Commonwealth Horse, South Australia. There were not any casualties. Promotions as per nominal roll.

Departure and Return.

The Squadron embarked on the transport *St. Andrew* (which had on board the battalion staff and the other Squadrons), at Fremantle, 2nd June, 1902, and arrived at Durban on the 19th. Strength—4 officers, 116 others, with 120 horses. Forty seven N.C.O.'s and men were struck off in South Africa; 4 officers, 69 others returned to Australia.

Nominal Roll.

No. and Name.	Rank.	Remarks.
Roberts, Stephen Richard Harrick	Captain	Commanding Squadron
Healey, Walter James	Lieutenant (A.M.C.)	Battalion Staff

No. 1 Troop.—Central District.

Farmer, Herbert	Lieutenant	

N.C.O.'s and Men.

No. and Name.	Rank.	Remarks.
463. Birch, Walter Richard	Sergeant-Major	
376. Browne, Walter	Sergeant	
380. Rank, Joseph George Wharton	Corporal	
377. Williamson, Arthur	Trooper	
378. Broadbent, Alex. John	,,	
379. Williams, Arthur	Lance-Corporal	Promoted Corporal
383. Ford, Arthur	Corporal	
381. Morrah, James	Trooper	
461. Price, Charles William	,,	
401. Arnold, Robert	,,	
403. Edwards, Leonard Douglas	Lance-Corporal	Promoted Corporal
385. Airy, William	Trooper	
386. Hill, Ronald Loughton	,,	
387. Abbott, Ernest William	,,	
388. Eaden, James	,,	
389. Bince, Harry Linden	,,	
390. Gare, James Edwin	,,	
391. McRae, Alexander	,,	
393. Syers, John Drinkwater	,,	Promoted Corporal

Nominal Roll—*continued.*

No. and Name.	Rank.	Remarks.

No. 1 Troop—Central District—*continued.*
N.C.O.'s and Men—*continued.*

394. Many, Jack	Private	
395. Chapman, James	,,	
405. Moir, Charles Main	,,	
398. Grant, John Edward	,,	Promoted Sergeant
446. Prisk, Oliver Henry	,,	
399. Hampshire, Alfred James	,,	
402. Paleske, Ralph Von	,,	
384. Howard, George	,,	
404. Johnston, George	Quartermaster-Sergeant	
382. Floyd, Ernest	Trumpeter	

No. 2 Troop.—Gold-fields District.

Beresford, G. St. George Ross	Lieutenant	Previous service in 2nd Contingent

N.C.O.'s and Men.

392. Doig, Frederick John	Sergeant	
397. Brickhill, Walter James David	Corporal	
406. Dyson, Sydney	Trooper	
407. Merrett, Henry Charles	,,	
408. Rowe, John	,,	
409. Sayer, George Butters	,,	Promoted Lance-Corporal
410. Murdoch, Norman David McLeod	,,	
411. Gallaher, Henry Fletcher	,,	
412. Hawkins, James	,,	
413. Smalpage, Eugene Best	,,	
414. Lowther, Ernest William	,,	
415. McNabb, Donald	,,	
416. Pratt, William John	,,	
417. Thompson, John	,,	
419. Ninnis, George	,,	
420. Law, William	,,	
421. Flower, Marshall	,,	
422. Brown, Timothy	,,	
423. Thomson, William Laing	,,	
424. Foster, Edward Amor	,,	
425. Eadie, Thomas	,,	
426. Robinson, John Moore	,,	Promoted Corporal
427. Perks, Joseph	,,	
428. O'Neil, William	,,	
429. Scholes, Alfred	,,	
432. Hoskyns, Chandos	,,	
431. Langlands, Charles John	,,	
430. Challinger, William Frederick	,,	Promoted Corporal
433. McNeil, Angus	,,	

No. 3 Troop.—Gold-fields District.

Mills, William Checkley,	Lieutenant	Previous service in 1st and 6th Contingents

N.C.O.'s and Men.

400. Roberts, Matthew Henry	Sergeant	
454. Ramsay, Edward Dudhope	Corporal	
434. Lyon, Joseph Ithiel	Trooper	
435. Ruthven, Chas. William	,,	
437. Pearce, Frederick John	,,	
438. Castle, Henry	,,	

Nominal Roll—*continued*.

No. and Name.	Rank.	Remarks.
No. 3 Troop—Gold-fields District—*continued*.		
N.C.O.'s and Men—continued.		
439. Moxham, Thomas	Private	
440. Williamson, Frank	,,	
441. John, William	,,	
442. O'Sullivan, Michael Joseph	,,	
443. Lethlean, John	,,	
444. Phillips, Thomas Matthews	,,	
445. Carroll, Geo. Johnston	,,	
418. Treagus, Chas. Moon	Lance-Corporal	
447. Prisk, David	Trooper	
448. Carthew, Frank	,,	
449. McKinnon, Donald James Sommerville	,,	
450. Barrett, Edward John	,,	
451. Bennett, Chas. Edgar	,,	
452. Cavin, John	,,	
453. Flatt, Arthur John	,,	
436. Butler, John	Corporal	
455. Shakes, Valentine	Trooper	
456. O'Neill, John Peter	,,	
451. Sullivan, John Lawrence	,,	
462. Finch, Kenneth John Stuart	Lance-Corporal	Promoted Sergeant
459. Lamont, Niel	Trooper	
460. McIlraith, Samuel James	,,	
458. Beaumont, Edgar Bruce	,,	
No. 4 Troop.—Country Districts.		
N.C.O.'s and Men.		
396. Stotter, George Dexter	Sergeant	
487. Larkin, James Charles	Corporal	Promoted Sergeant
464. Vine, Charles William	Trooper	
465. Dawkins, Francis Richard	,,	
466. Buckle, Hugh Francis Arnund	,,	
467. Lloyd, Lionel Taylor	,,	
468. Mohr, Henry	,,	
469. Westh, Henry Morton	,,	
470. Carlilini, Joseph Lot	,,	
474. Branoberger, Peter	Lance-Corporal	
472. Bynon, David George	Trooper	
473. Barry, James	,,	
471. Coulter, Jason	,,	
475. Burgess, Gordon Angelo	,,	
476. Locke, Charles	,,	
477. Bristowe, William Henry	,,	
478. Robinson, Charles	,,	Promoted Lance-Corporal
479. Rowland, Albert Edward	,,	
480. Fleming, James Patrick	,,	Promoted Lance-Corporal
481. Beattie, Charles John	,,	
482. Flanagan, Richd. Augustus	,,	
483. Moore, Horace George	,,	
484. Thom, Albert Charles	,,	
485. Thom, William	,,	
486. Britton, John Clifford	,,	
488. Stephens, Thomas Richard	,,	
489. Page, Henry	,,	
490. Nelson, Robert John	,,	
491. Webber, John	Trumpeter	

List of Officers and Others of Western Australian Contingents who Died or were Killed.

Regimental Number, Rank, and Name.

1st Mounted Infantry Contingent.
- Major Moor, H. G.
- Lieutenant Hensman, G. G. W.
- 96. Private Conway, M.
- 18. Corporal Bishop, G. N.
- 30. Private Collett, M. W.
- 13. " Force, H.

2nd Mounted Infantry Contingent.
Nil.

3rd Bushmen's Contingent.
- 75. Private Hambly, E. A.
- 67. " McPhee, W. J.
- 81. " Roscoe, J.
- 105. " Angel, T. H.
- 83. " Hume, J.
- 34. " White, H.

4th Mounted Infantry Contingent.
- 43. Private Iles, E. G.
- 119. " Kay, J.
- 70. Lance-Corporal Fraser, W.

5th Mounted Infantry Contingent.
- Lieutenant Forrest, A. A.
- 184. Farrier-Sergeant McGregor, R. H.
- 115. Corporal Bollinger, W. F.
- 111. Sergeant Edwards, F. F.
- 266. Private Solomon, H.
- 147. " Parker, W.
- 168. " Alday, R.
- 239. Lance-Corporal Dalliston, J. G.
- 149. Private Hammond, A.
- 289. " Dunstan, W. J.

6th Mounted Infantry Contingent.
- Lieutenant Moris, G. A.
- Lieutenant Reid, S. S.
- 335. Private Fisher, B.
- 341. " Page, F.
- 385. " Adam, F. T.
- 403. " Semple, J.
- 339. Private Blanck, A.
- 436. " Spencer, R. W.
- 413. " Westcott, G.
- 348. " Clifford, C. C.
- 458. " Hunter, R. T.
- 387. " Delahunty, J.
- 376. " Wilson, T. H.
- 420. Sergeant Thurston, J. B. M.
- 429. Private Fry, O. E.

Summary of Contingents Despatched.

Transport.	Date.	Contingent.	Officers.	Others.	Horses.	Guns, Wagons, &c.
Medic	7th Nov., 1899	1st W.A.M.I.	5	125	17	2 maxims, 1 spring cart, 2 wagons
Surrey	3rd Feb., 1900	2nd W.A.M.I.	6	97	125	1 spring cart, 1 wagon
Maplemore	13th Mar., 1900	3rd Bushmen	7	109	127	..
Manhattan	8th May, 1900	4th W.A.M.I.	7	120	132	..
Devon	6th Mar., 1901	5th W.A.M.I.	14	207	239	..
Ulstermore	10th April, 1901	6th W.A.M.I.	14	214	237	..
Manchester Merchant	26th Feb., 1902	"E" Coy., 2nd A.C.H.	2	58	60	..
		A.A.M.C.	1	7	..	..
Templemore and *Englishman*	7th April, 1902	"D" Coy., 4th A.C.H.	5	115	122	..
St. Andrew	2nd June, 1902	"D" Sq., 8th A.C.H.	4	116	120	..
		Batt. Staff A.C.H.	4	..	..	..
			69	1,168	1,179	7

Disposition.*

	Officers.	Other Ranks.
Died or were killed	5	35
Discharged in South Africa, or embarked for England and struck off in South Africa	34	293
Commissioned in Imperial Service	2	
Returned to Australia	42	835
	83	1,163

* These figures are in some respects approximate only; it having been found impossible to obtain **exact** statements, owing to attachments, enlistments, and discharges, &c., in South Africa, of which adequate returns have not been made.

QUEENSLAND.

QUEENSLAND.

PREFATORY.

THE following appeared in the *Queensland Government Gazette* of 19th October, 1899 :—

"A PROCLAMATION.

[L.S.]
S. W. GRIFFITH,
Administrator.

" By His Excellency the Honourable Sir SAMUEL WALKER GRIFFITH, Knight Grand Cross of the Most Distinguished Order of St. Michael and St. George, Chief Justice of the Colony of Queensland, and Administrator of the Government of the said Colony and its Dependencies.

" WHEREAS the Government of the Colony of Queensland lately offered, in the event of hostilities breaking out between Great Britain and the South African Republic, the services of a Contingent of Troops, consisting of 250 Officers, Non-commissioned Officers, and Men of the Queensland Mounted Infantry, together with a Machine Gun Section of the Queensland Regiment of Royal Australian Artillery, for field duty with the Imperial Troops employed in South Africa : And whereas on the nineteenth day of October, instant, the Legislative Assembly of the said Colony resolved as follows :—

"' That this House renews the assurance of its loyalty and devotion to the Throne and Person of Her Most Gracious Majesty The Queen, and as evidence of its sympathy with Her Majesty's subjects in the South African Republic, who have for so long a period suffered burdensome disabilities and grievous injustice, desires to support the determination of Her Majesty's Advisers to secure the immediate recognition of British rights in that Republic. This House therefore views with approbation the proposal of the Government to equip, despatch, and maintain a Military Force volunteering for service with Her Majesty's Army in South Africa, consisting of 250 Officers, Non-commissioned Officers, and Men of the Queensland Mounted Infantry, together with a Machine Gun Section of the Queensland Regiment of Royal Australian Artillery.'

" And whereas Her Majesty has authorized a Force of Volunteers to be raised in the said Colony for the purposes aforesaid, and has directed that such Force shall, as from the embarkation thereof, be deemed to be serving with Her Majesty's Regular Forces : Now, therefore, I, Sir SAMUEL WALKER GRIFFITH, the Administrator of the Government aforesaid, do hereby proclaim and declare that a Military Force of Volunteers shall be and is hereby authorized to be raised and enrolled for Service with Her Majesty's Army in South Africa, consisting of 250 Officers, Non-commissioned Officers, and Men of the Queensland Mounted Infantry, including a Machine Gun Section, the detailed establishment whereof is more particularly described in the Schedule hereunder set out.

" Given under my hand and Seal, at Government House, Brisbane, this nineteenth day of October, in the year of our Lord One thousand eight hundred and ninety-nine, and in the sixty-third year of Her Majesty's reign.

" By Command
" JAMES R. DICKSON.
" GOD SAVE THE QUEEN ! "

This was the inception of the Queensland Contingents to the seat of war ; the First, Second, and Third of which were paid by the Colonial Government upon the following scale :—Officers, as in other Australian Contingents ; N.C.O.'s and men —Staff sergeants, 10s. per diem ; company sergeant-major, 9s. ; sergeant, 8s. ; corporal, 7s. ; artificer, 6s. ; bugler, gunner, private, or driver, 4s. 6d.

Equipment comprised uniform (khaki cloth F.S. jacket, cord pants, puttees,, field service hat, and cap), greatcoats, boots, and a full kit of underclothing, fatigue suits, necessaries, &c. Fully horsed, and supplied with saddlery, M.E. rifles and bayonets, bandolier and cartridge belt with supporting braces. It was provided, further, that all horses and saddlery would remain Government property. As matters turned out, however, they were handed over to the Imperial remount depots. Regimental transport was provided.

Pensions and compassionate allowances to widows and orphans were guaranteed upon the same scale as those granted in the case of persons of similar rank in the Imperial service, according to the provisions of the Royal Warrant for Pay.

Preference in the earlier Contingents was given to men who had been trained as Mounted Infantry, drivers in field artillery, or who had been accustomed to the care of horses.

Camps of Instruction, where the Contingents were enrolled, organized, drilled, and equipped, prior to embarkation, were established, under experienced officer and sergeant instructors, at Meeandah, the Exhibition, and Lytton.

FIRST (QUEENSLAND MOUNTED INFANTRY) CONTINGENT.

LIKE the early Contingents in other States, the first despatched by Queensland was ordered to be raised from officers and others serving in the local defence forces, namely, 250 of the Queensland Mounted Infantry, and a Machine Gun Section from the Royal Australian Artillery (Queensland). They were to be equipped strictly in accordance with the Field Service Manual for the equipment of a Mounted Infantry unit. With regard to this, however, Lieut.-Colonel Ricardo, who commanded the Contingent, stated in his report :—" Out of 262 of all ranks enrolled, 123 were then serving in the Queensland Mounted Infantry ; but 46 men, who had served, also joined ; this left 93 to be recruited from outside. Of this number, 25 N.C.O.'s and men of A Battery (Royal Australian Artillery), volunteered ; they were some of the best men we had, and their example had a very good effect on the Contingent. The remainder were made up of men who said they were, or had been, members of the Queensland Defence Force."

The Contingent was practically enrolled, organized, and equipped with arms, clothing, horses, saddlery, transport wagons with fittings and stores, between the 13th and 28th October—a record of the indefatigable way in which the Staff, the Comptroller of Stores, the medical and veterinary authorities, and the embarkation officers must have worked. The horses were selected and purchased by Veterinary Major Irving, P.V.O.

ESTABLISHMENT.

Staff :—One major, 1 sergeant-major, 1 quartermaster-sergeant, 4 privates ; total, 7 ; with 4 riding and 4 draught horses ; total 8.

Machine Gun Section (Royal Australian Artillery) :—One lieutenant, 1 sergeant, 1 corporal, 2 bombardiers, 5 drivers, 7 gunners ; total, 1 officer, 1 sergeant, 15 rank and file, with 6 riding and 14 draught horses ; total 20.

No. 1 Company :—One captain, 3 lieutenants, 1 company sergeant-major, 4 sergeants, 1 sergeant-artificer, 3 artificers, 2 buglers, 6 corporals, 92 privates ; total, 4 officers, 109 others, with 100 riding and 20 draught horses ; in all, 113 of all ranks, with 120 horses.

No. 2 Company :—The like.

Supernumeraries :—Two officers, 8 privates, with 14 riding and 18 draught horses ; in all, 10 of all ranks, 32 horses.

Grand total :—One major, 2 captains, 9 lieutenants, 1 regimental sergeant-major, 1 quartermaster-sergeant, 2 company sergeant-majors, 9 sergeants, 2 sergeant-artificers, 6 artificers, 4 buglers, 13 corporals, 2 bombardiers, 208 gunners, drivers, and privates ; in all, 12 officers, 248 others, with 224 riding and 76 draught horses ; altogether, 260 of all ranks, with 300 horses.

DEPARTURE AND RETURN.

The Contingent left on 1st November, 1899, comprising 14 officers, 248 others, with 284 horses, besides machine guns and wagons. Ten died or were killed, 1 officer was transferred, 1 commissioned in the Imperial Army, 7 were struck off in South Africa ; 12 officers, 231 others returned to Australia.

PROMOTIONS, ETC.

Major P. R. Ricardo, promoted to Lieut.-Colonel, 13th December, 1899.

Captain H. G. Chauvel was appointed Adjutant on 13th February, 1900, and held the local rank of Major in South Africa, from 30th November, 1900, to 21st January, 1901.

Captain R. S. Browne (Special Service Officer) held the local rank of Major in South Africa.

Captain P. W. G. Pinnock to Brevet-Major.

Lieutenant D. E. Reid, promoted to Captain, 13th February, 1900. Brevet of Major.

Lieutenant R. Dowse served as Captain and Adjutant at the Maitland Camp, 6th November, 1900, to 12th December, 1900.

Lieutenant H. Bailey, similar service, 18th April, 1900, to 12th December, 1900.

Lieutenant R. Gordon, promoted Captain and transferred to command of Mounted Infantry Company, 1st Battalion, Gordon Highlanders, February, 1900, to January, 1901.

Lieutenant (Supernumerary) C. H. Anderson-Pelham, was appointed 2nd Lieutenant, 12th Lancers, 18th April, 1900.

For promotions of N.C. officers and men, *vide* nominal roll.

SERVICE.

The Contingent embarked in the transport *Cornwall*, on 31st October and 1st November, 1899, and went to sea on the latter day. Arrived at Table Bay on 12th December; landed at Cape Town on the following day, and proceeded to Orange River in two trains. Their transport and ammunition wagons had been taken over by the Ordnance authorities at Cape Town, but fresh were issued at De Aar, comprising five buck wagons (nominal load 3,500 lbs.) and five Scotch carts for the ammunition. Subsequently, however, the Army Service Corps took over all transport. The wagons brought by the Contingent were used chiefly by the Royal Engineers, who spoke highly of them as being very handy, well and faithfully built, and very light in the draught; but, as every wagon required two drivers, it was more economical to have a vehicle that would carry a heavier load.

Owing to the weight of the machine gun carriage and the condition the horses were in, it was found that even with four horses per gun they could not keep up with the Column, and were, therefore, worse than useless. The machine guns were therefore handed over complete with harness and all spare parts to Colonel Chambier, Royal Artillery, at Kimberley, and, being required for further service, were retained when the Contingent returned to Queensland.

From Orange River the Contingent proceeded to Belmont, whence it took a prominent part in the engagement at Sunnyside (1st January, 1900) and the Relief of Douglas (2nd January, 1900), as part of an expeditionary force under Lt.-Colonel T. D. Pilcher.

In February, 1900, the Contingent took part in the Relief of Kimberley (Alderson's Brigade, General French's Division), and from thence proceeded to Koodoosrand, and was employed in the operations at Paardeberg (17th to 26th February).

After the surrender of General Cronje, the Contingent formed part of a mounted brigade under Lt.-Colonel Martyr (General French's Division), and took part in the engagements at Poplar Grove (7th March) and Driefontein (10th March), and the occupation of Bloemfontein on the 8th March, 1900.

At Bloemfontein, the 2nd Queensland Contingent joined by order of the Field Marshal Commanding-in-Chief. The regiment went into rest camp at Springfontein until the 31st March, when the two companies of the 1st Contingent under Lt.-Colonel Ricardo formed part of the earlier relieving force at the engagement at Sanna's Post (31st March).

During April, 1900, the regiment, then consisting of three companies, with the 3rd Mounted Infantry Regiment (Imperial) and the 1st and 2nd Contingents of New Zealand Mounted Rifles, formed the 3rd Mounted Infantry Corps under Lt.-Colonel T. D. Pilcher, joined the 1st Mounted Infantry Brigade under Major-General Hutton (French's Division), and left Bloemfontein on the 1st May, when the general advance on Pretoria commenced. The regiment took part in the engagements at Brandfort (3rd May), Constantia (4th May, 1900), Vet River (5th and 6th May), Zand River (10th May, 1900), Klipriversberg (28th May), Johannesburg (29th May, 1900), Pretoria (4th June, 1900), and Diamond Hill (11th and 12th June).

After the occupation of Pretoria, strong inducements were offered to Australians and New Zealanders to join the South African Constabulary, which was then being formed, and a considerable number of the members of the 1st and 2nd Contingents were transferred; and, though many afterwards rejoined their regiment, the strength of the two Contingents was much reduced.

Lt.-Colonel Ricardo, considering that he was left without a command corresponding to his rank, applied for other employment, which was granted in Pretoria, and handed over the command to Major Chauvel.

Reformed into two squadrons, the regiment was engaged in the operations at Reit Vlei (13th to 16th July, 1900), and was then transferred to Mahon's Brigade (Ian Hamilton's Division), with which it took part in the first eastern advance as far as Balmoral (25th July), the action at Zilikat's Nek (2nd August), the operations about Rustenburg (August, 1900), and the pursuit of De Wet's force northwards to Warmbad, including engagement at Oliphant's Nek (17th August). The regiment then returned to the Eastern Transvaal, and, with the exception of half a squadron which accompanied Mahon's Brigade to Barberton under Lieut. Glasgow, formed part of a mounted force consisting of the 3rd Mounted Infantry Regiment (Imperial), Queensland Mounted Infantry, and 3rd Brabant's Horse, under Major Chauvel, which was employed in minor operations in the Middleburg District (Brigadier-General Barker), including the action near Pan (11th October, 1900), subsequently joining General Smith-Dorien's command at Belfast.

Early in November, orders having been received for the return of the 1st Contingent, the horses and saddlery were handed over, and train taken to Cape Town. The men were, however, detrained at De Aar, under Captain Pinnock, and proceeded to Worcester, remaining there until the meeting of the Afrikander Bond had been held, when the journey to Cape Town was resumed.

On 13th December (anniversary of the day of disembarkation), embarked on transport *Orient*, and arrived at Brisbane on 17th January, 1901, after having called at Albany, Melbourne, and Sydney *en route*. Disbanded on the 23rd.

WAR SERVICES AND HONOURS.

Ricardo, Major P. R.—Operations in Cape Colony, Orange Free State, and Transvaal, 1899–1900, including Sunnyside, Relief of Kimberley, Driefontein Sanna's Post, Vet River, Zand River, Johannesburg, Pretoria, and Diamond Hill Despatches *London Gazette*, 16th April, 1901. C.B. Queen's Medal with four clasps

Chauvel, Major H. G.—Operations as stated, including Sunnyside, Relief of Kimberley, Driefontein, Vet River, Zand River, Johannesburg, Pretoria, Diamond Hill, Reit Vlei, and Zilikat's Nek. Despatches, *London Gazette*, 16th April, 1901. C.M.G. Queen's Medal with four clasps. Lieut.-Col. Chauvel subsequently commanded 7th Australian Commonwealth Horse.

Browne, Major R. S.—*Vide* Special Service Officers.

Pinnock, Captain P. W. G.—Operations as stated. Sunnyside, Relief of Kimberley, Driefontein, and Diamond Hill. Staff Officer, advanced base, Mounted Infantry Brigade, July to November, 1900. Queen's Medal with three clasps.

Reid, Captain D. E.—Operations as stated, including Sunnyside, Relief of Kimberley, Paardeberg, Poplar Grove, Driefontein, Vet River, Zand River, Johannesberg, Pretoria, Diamond Hill, Zilikat's Nek, and Reit Vlei. Despatches, *London Gazette*, 3rd February, 1901, and 16th July, 1901. D.S.O. **Queen's Medal with five clasps.**

Gordon, Captain R.—Tirah Expedition, 1897-98. Medal with two clasps. Operations as stated, including Sunnyside, Paardeberg, Poplar Grove, Vet River, Zand River, Johannesberg, Pretoria, Diamond Hill, and Wittebergen. Despatches, *London Gazette*, 16th April, 1901. D.S.O. Brev. of Major. Queen's Medal with six clasps.

Dods, Captain J. E. (Army Medical Corps).—Operations as stated, including Sunnyside, Relief of Kimberley, Paardeberg, Poplar Grove, Driefontein, Sanna's Post, Vet River, Zand River, Johannesburg, Pretoria, Reit Vlei, and Zilikat's Nek. Queen's Medal with four clasps.

Dowse, Lieutenant R.—Operations as stated, including Sunnyside, Relief of Kimberley, Paardeberg, Poplar Grove, Driefontein, Sanna's Post, Vet River, Johannesburg, and Pretoria. Queen's Medal with four clasps.

Bailey, Lieutenant H.—Operations in Cape Colony, including action at Sunnyside. *Vide* also 6th Queensland Imperial Bushmen.

Adie, Lieutenant A. G.—Operations as stated, including Sunnyside, Driefontein, Vet River, Zand River, Johannesburg, Pretoria, Reit Vlei, and Zilikat's Nek. Dangerously wounded at Sunnyside, 1st January, 1900. *Vide* also 6th Queensland Imperial Bushmen.

Black, Lieutenant C. H.—Queen's Medal with one clasp.

Anderson-Pelham, Lieutenant C. H.—Operations in Cape Colony, including Sunnyside.

Glasgow, Lieutenant T. W.—Operations as stated, inclusive of all actions (except Sunnyside). Despatches, *London Gazette*, 16th April, 1901. D.S.O. Queen's Medal with five clasps.

Cumming, Lieutenant C. A. (Supernumerary).—Operations as stated, including Johannesburg, Pretoria, and Diamond Hill. Queen's Medal with four clasps.

Nominal Roll.

No. and Name.	Rank.	Remarks.
Battalion Staff.		
Ricardo, Percy Ralph	Major	
Anderson-Pelham, Cecil Henry	Lieutenant	Supernumerary
Dods, Joseph Espie	Captain (A.M.C.)	
1. Price, James George	Regimental Sergeant-Major	Invalided to Australia, arr. 18.8.00
2. Wales, Albert Harvy	Regimental Quartermaster-Sergeant	
64. McLennan, Kenneth	Company Sergeant-Major	O.R. Clerk
Supernumerary Officer.		
Brown, Reginald Spence	Captain (Major in South Africa)	For special service
"A" Company.		
Officers.		
Chauvel, Henry George	Captain	Adjutant, 13.2.00
Reid, David Elder	Lieutenant	
Glasgow, Thomas William	,,	
Cumming, Charles Alexander	,,	Supernumerary
Adie, Alfred George	,,	Wounded at Sunnyside, 1.1.00 Invalided to England, 16.11.00

Nominal Roll—*continued.*

No. and Name.	Rank.	Remarks.
"A" COMPANY—*continued.*		
N.C.O.'s and Men.		
3. Walker, James John	Coy. Sergeant-Major	Regimental Sergeant-Major Awarded D.C.M. Despatches. *London Gazette,* 18.9.01
66. Ryan, James Bernard	Sergeant	Company Sergeant-Major. Despatches, *London Gazette,* 18.9.01
172. Walker, Harry Frederick	,,	Invalided to Australia, arr. 18.8.00
74. Macarthur, John	,,	Invalided to Australia, arr. 16.9.00
164. Saville, William Walter	Sergeant-Saddler	
27. Maddicks, Frederick	Corporal	Sergeant, 9.12.99
155. Brosnan, John Cornelius	,,	Despatches, *London Gazette,* 18.9.01
203. Lyons, William Michael	,,	Sergeant, 1.7.00
108. Kidd, Alexander	,,	Invalided to Australia, arr. 18.8.00
38. Covell, Henry Horton	,,	
46. Barker, James Frederick	Private	Corporal, 9.12.99
87. King, William Gillespie	,,	Corporal, 9.12.99
109. Bowdler, William	Lance-Corporal Bugler	Invalided to Australia, arr. 1.9.00
208. Morris, John Crisop	Bugler	
246. Dimmock, Thomas	,,	
162. Knudsen, Peter	Private	
161. Missing, Herbert Henry	,,	
144. Thomas, Ray Tabor	,,	Invalided to Australia, arr. 18.8.00
171. McDonald, Joseph	,,	Invalided to Australia, arr. 18.8.00
152. Harris, William	,,	
148. Martin, Thomas Bram	,,	
173. Suthers, Herbert	,,	
174. Chadwick, Edward Andrew	,,	
45. Drew, Conway Lovett	,,	
160. Brown, William Joseph	,,	
169. Durham, James	,,	
150. Punch, Thomas	,,	
163. Glasgow, Alexander	,,	
167. Lee, Thomas Broadford	,,	
153. Russell, George Edward	Shoeing Smith	
149. Mason, William	Private	
157. Gray, James Roderick	,,	Invalided to Australia, arr. 8.12.00
168. Counter, James Frederick	,,	
151. Bull, John Edward Newell	,,	Invalided to Australia, arr. 18.8.00
39. De Verdon, Nivel	,,	Invalided to Australia, arr. 18.8.00
212. Orton, Robert	,,	Invalided to Australia, arr. 19.11.00
206. Pirie, Robert Hill	,,	
227. Smith, George Thomas	,,	Invalided to Australia, arr. 1.6.00
209. Volkman, Arthur Gus	,,	
207. Mussett, Arthur	,,	
228. Miles, William	,,	
44. Brown, John William	,,	
82. Barron, William	,,	
196. Walker, George William	,,	
107. Sharp, Charles Octavius	,,	
31. McKenzie, Richard	,,	Invalided to Australia, arr 18.8.00
129. Farmer, Edward, Henry	,,	
158. Hill, Sydney Edward	,,	Invalided to England, 23.5.00; returned to Australia, arr. —.2.01

Nominal Roll—continued.

No. and Name.	Rank.	Remarks.

"A" COMPANY—continued.

N.C.O.'s and Men—continued.

No. and Name.	Rank.	Remarks.
146. O'Brien, Richard Nicholas	Private	
166. Alley, Albert Edward	,,	Invalided to Australia, arr. 19.9.00
226. McConkey, Peter	,,	Invalided to England, arr. 11.6.00
193. Rossiter, William	,,	Invalided to Australia, arr. 18.8.00
131. Millan, Alexander	,,	
189. Anderson, Edward	,,	
190. Hitchcock, John Henry	,,	Invalided to Australia, arr. 18.8.00
218. Cammack, William	,,	Invalided to Australia, arr. 18 8.00
195. Cox, William	,,	Invalided to Australia, arr. 1.9.00
194. Mundey, Joseph William	,,	Invalided to Australia, arr. 1.6.00
192. Butler, Bedford	,,	
216. Anderson, Ralph Andrew	,,	
214. Fellows, Isaac	,,	
238. Iszlaub, George James	,,	Invalided to Australia, arr. 18.8.00
104. Runge, Christian	,,	
13. Mackenzie, Albert William	,,	Invalided to Australia, arr. 1.9.00
20. Le Marchand, George James	,,	
10. Walsh, Walter	,,	
15. Fox, William	,,	
21. Kelly, James	,,	Invalided to England, arr. 11.6.00
175. Christie, William James	,,	
182. Banff, John Henry	,,	
180. Cumner, Thomas	,,	Died of enteric at Kimberley, 20.3.00
176. Holcombe, James David	,,	
179. Pitt, Robert Samuel	,,	Invalided to Australia, arr. 18.8.00
178. Fielding, Ernest Victor	,,	Invalided to Australia, arr. 18.8.00
117. Kraut, Julius	,,	
186. Hart, James	,,	Invalided to Australia, arr. 1.9.00
181. Smith, Robert	,,	Invalided to Australia, arr. 18.8.00
48. Washbourne, Sydney	,,	Invalided to Australia, arr. 18.8.00
156. Banks, Joseph	,,	Invalided to Australia, arr. 18.8.00
47. Stewart, Charles Rupert	,,	
122. White, Albert Joseph	,,	
83. Bourne, Charles Henry	,,	
79. Kennedy, Thomas	,,	Slightly wounded near Johannesburg, 28.5.00. Invalided to Australia, arr. 8.12.00
80. Burge, Joseph	,,	
78. Stewart, Wallace Highton	,,	Invalided to Australia, arr. 18.8.00
36. Thompson, Robert Samuel	,,	
50. Cameron, Arthur Archibald	,,	
120. Browne, Thomas	,,	
119. Turnbull, James Campbell	,,	
106. Grayson, James	,,	Invalided to Australia, arr. 18.8.00
202. Coogan, James	,,	
197. Willmett, Walter	,,	
201. Muir, Forrest	,,	
198. Hughes, John Stanley	,,	
199. Davidson, John Macintosh	,,	Corporal
215. Ross, John Smith	,,	Invalided to Australia, arr. 18.8.00
185. Morris, William Arthur	,,	Invalided to Australia, arr. 1.9.00
210. Fraser, Charles	,,	
225. Christensen, James Walter	,,	
121. Lambert, Edgar	,,	
49. Johnson, Augustus	,,	

Nominal Roll—continued.

No. and Name.	Rank.	Remarks.
"A" Company—continued.		
N.C.O.'s and Men—continued.		
211. Baulch, Henry	Private	
54. Sundmacher, George	,,	
25. Walker, Sydney	,,	Died of enteric at Bloemfontein, 25.6.00
30. Philipofski, Adolph	,,	Invalided to Australia, arr. 19.9.00
217. Chalmers, Allan	,,	
143. Munro, Alexander	,,	
154. Gale, William Henry	,,	
170. Lloyd, James	,,	Invalided to Australia, arr. 1.9.00
230. Payne, Stephen	,,	
188. Edwards, William	,,	Slightly wounded near Johannesburg, 29.5.00
205. McCarthy, James Joseph	,,	
220. Shaw, William	,,	
204. Solway, Thomas Henry	,,	
115. Barnes, George	Shoeing-Smith	
254. Luke, Arthur	Private	
255. Neale, Ernest William	,,	Invalided to Australia, arr. 15.9.00
"B" Company.		
Officers.		
Pinnock, Philip William Grant	Captain	
Dowse, Richard	Lieutenant	
Bailey, Henry	,,	
Gordon, Robert	,,	Tirah Campaign, 1897–8. Severely wounded at Brandewan River, 30.1.01
N.C.O.'s and Men.		
4. Breydon, Richard	Coy. Sergeant-Major	Prisoner of war at Sanna's Post, 31.3.00. Relieved at Pretoria, 4.6.00
65. Loynes, James	Sergeant	Company Sergeant-Major. Mentioned in C.-in-C.'s despatches, 31.3.00
81. Paten, Harry	Sergeant	
28. Hockey, Frederick James	,,	
43. McLeod, William	Corporal	Sergeant, 9.12.99
192. Wright, George	Farrier-Sergeant	
213. Lacey, John	Corporal	
56. Conley, George Bertram	,,	Killed in action, Sanna's Post, 31.3.00
116. Wriford, George	,,	Corporal. Joined Provincial Mounted Police, Bloemfontein, 1.5.00. Reported missing, 11.3.01; body afterwards found
35. Tancred, George Henry Lumsden	,,	Sergeant. Despatches, *London Gazette*, 18.9.01
41. Stevens, William Johnstone	Private	Corporal, 12.12.99. Despatches, *London Gazette*, 18.9.01
184. Scott, Charles John	Bugler	
177. Devitt, William	,,	**Corporal. Died of enteric at** Bloemfortein, 12.5.00

Nominal Roll—*continued.*

No. and Name.	Rank.	Remarks.
"B" COMPANY—*continued.*		
N.C.O.'s and Men—*continued.*		
29. Butler, William Melville	Private	
32. Thomson, Robert Jenson	,,	
33. Cathcart, John	,,	Invalided to Australia, arr. 18.8.00
34. Todd, Joseph	,,	
37. Wynne, William Cardinal	,,	
40. Morris, John James	Lance-Corporal	Corporal, 9.12.99
42. Walker, Gilbert Ramsay	,,	
51. Cooper, Frank	,,	
52. McIntyre, Robert	Private	
53. Starkey, Edward Robinson	,,	Invalided to England, 9.6.00
55. Strong, Charles Joseph	,,	Dangerously wounded at Sanna's Post, 31.3.00. Invalided to Australia, arr. 1.6.00
57. Scott, George Archibald	,,	
58. Neville, George	,,	
59. McDougall, John	,,	
60. Morrison, Donald Rogers	,,	
61. Spurway, Benjamin	,,	Prisoner of war, Sanna's Post, 31.3.00. Relieved, 4.6.00
62. Johnston, Harold	,,	Invalided to Australia, arr.15.9.00
63. Smith, Ralph Gordon	,,	
67. Maxwell, Thomas Robert	,,	Invalided, to Australia, arr. 18.8.00
68. O'Mahoney, Frank	,,	
69. French, William	,,	
70. Marley, Miles	,,	
71. Reed, Harold	,,	
72. Moore, James	,,	
73. Lacey, Ernest	,,	Invalided to Australia, arr. 1.9.00
75. Brady, Matthew Devine	,,	Invalided to Australia, arr. 1.9.00
77. Seymour, George	,,	Slightly wounded at Constantia, 5.5.00
84. Hutton, George Lionel	,,	
86. Locke, Jack	,,	Invalided to Australia, arr. 18.8.00
88. Goodchild, William	,,	
89. Egan, Michael	,,	Invalided to Australia, arr. 18.8.00
90. Armstrong, Thomas Henry	,,	
91. McLeod, David Cumming	,,	Killed in action, Sunnyside, 1.1.00
92. Breeze, Albert	,,	
93. Casey, James John	,,	Invalided to Australia, arr.10.12.00
94. McNeven, Hugh	,,	Invalided to Australia, arr. 18.8.00
95. Bryce, William Henry	,,	Corporal. Died of wounds, Spitzkopulei, 24.8.01. He was then serving as Sergt.-Major with Prince of Wales, L.H.
96. Neilson, John	,,	Invalided to England, arr. 5.8.00
97. Ridley, George	...	
98. Michael, George	...	Invalided to Australia, arr. 18.8.00
99. Pope, Daniel	,,	Corporal
100. Whelan, Thomas James	,,	
101. Betts, George	,,	
102. Cooper, Samuel Welsby	,,	
103. Palfrey, William	,,	
105. Fry, Albert Charles	,,	
110. Hinton, Herbert Gerald	,,	Invalided to England, arr. 16.8.00
111. Braithwaite, Thomas Farrer	,,	Slightly wounded at Constantia, 5.5.00

Nominal Roll—*continued.*

No. and Name.	Rank.	Remarks.
"B" COMPANY—*continued.*		
N.C.O.'s and Men—*continued.*		
112. Millard, William Holdsworth	Private	
113. Ingarfield, George Percy	,,	
114. Primrose, Victor	,,	Invalided to England, arr. 5.8.00
118. Daniels, John	,,	
124. Chamberlain, William Allen	,,	
125. Strong, William George	,,	Invalided to Australia, arr. 1.9.00
126. Crump, Charles	,,	Invalided to Australia, arr. 24.11.00
127. Penhaligon, William	,,	
130. Smith, William	,,	
132. Staines, Raymond Henry	,,	Prisoner of war, Sanna's Post, 31.3.00. Relieved, 4.6.00
133. Colquhoun, Joseph	,,	
134. Brodrick, Edmund St. John Vincent	,,	Died of enteric at Bloemfontein, 25.6.00
136. Hermann, Frederick Charles	,,	Invalided to Australia, arr. 8.12.00
137. Weise, Heinrich Carl Gustav	,,	Invalided to England, arr. 11.6.00
138. Baudinet, George	,,	
139. Jones, George Richard	,,	
140. Thomas, William	,,	
141. Swenson, Nicholas Theodore	,,	Invalided to Australia, arr. 1.9.00
142. Clark, James Ernest	,,	
145. Hodgkinson, William George	,,	
147. Knyvett, Frank Berners	,,	
159. Tomlinson, George William	,,	
165. Reece, Herbert Llewellyn	,,	Killed in action, Sanna's Post, 31.3.00
193. Moss, George William	,,	Zulu War, 1879. Invalided to Australia, arr. 8.12.00
187. Logan, Thomas James	,,	Slightly wounded at Sanna's Post, 31.3.00
219. Jones, Victor Stanley	,,	Killed in action, Sunnyside, 1.1.00
221. Jackson, Edward	,,	Invalided to Australia, arr. 17.7.00
222. McIntosh, Donald	,,	Invalided to Australia, arr. 18.8.00
223. Kavanagh, Patrick Joseph	,,	Invalided to Australia, arr. 18.8.00
224. Solway, Robert	,,	
229. Campbell, Colin Clyde	,,	
231. Hill, Charles	,,	
233. Greenwell, Richard	,,	Invalided to Australia, arr. 18.8.00
234. O'Brien, John	,,	
235. Smith, Ernest	,,	
236. O'Hagan, Thomas	,,	
237. Cain, John	,,	
239. Montague, Eugene Graham	,,	Invalided to Australia, arr. 19.9.00
240. Rose, Albert	,,	Wounded at Sunnyside, 1.1.00. Invalided to Australia, arr. 1.6.00
241. Evans, Walter James	,,	Invalided to Australia, arr. 18.8.00
242. Damrow, William Alexander	,,	Died of enteric at De Aar, 19.12.00
243. Arnold, John Henry	,,	Invalided to Australia, arr. 1.9.00
245. Teasdale, Charles	,,	Invalided to Australia, arr. 8.12.00
247. Wagner, August	,,	Invalided to Australia, arr. 18.8.00
248. Henry, Arthur Douglas	,,	
249. Graham, Archibald	,,	
200. Willmett, Percy	,,	
250. Munro, James	,,	Corporal. Invalided to England, **arr. 16.8.00**

Nominal Roll—*continued.*

No. and Name.	Rank.	Remarks.

"B" COMPANY—*continued.*
N.C.O.'s and Men—*continued.*

No. and Name.	Rank.	Remarks.
251. Summers, Louis	Private	
253. Conroy, John James	,,	Invalided to Australia, arr. 8.8.00
256. Whitehorn, H. S.	,,	
257. Jackson, W. H. G.	,,	

MACHINE GUN SECTION.

Black, Cecil Herbert	Lieutenant	Invalided to England, 16.11.00

N.C.O.'s and Men.

No. and Name.	Rank.	Remarks.
5. Price, Frederick	Sergeant	Invalided to Australia, arr. 1.9.00
6. Harris, Herbert	Corporal	Mentioned in C. in C. despatches. 31.3.00. D.C.M. Invalided to Australia, arr. 18.8.00
7. Lambert, George Egbert	Bombardier	
8. Wieck, George Frederick Gardles	,,	Prisoner of war, Sanna's Post, 31.3.00. Relieved, 4.6.00.
11. Beard, Edward	Gunner	
23. Buckback, Henry	Driver	
16. Harris, Herbert George	,,	
9. Irwin, Thomas	Gunner	
24. Mungall, Henry	,,	
26. Menah, Frederick James	,,	
19. Riddell, Peter	,,	Invalided to Australia, arr. 18.8.00
12. Rasmussen, John	,,	
18. Ryan, Thomas	Driver	Invalided to England arr. 5.8.00
22. Schultz, Charles Frederick	,,	Invalided to Australia, arr. 8.12.00
14. Smith, James	Gunner	Invalided to Australia, arr. 1.9.00
17. Williams, Albert	Driver	Invalided to Australia, arr. 1.6.00

SECOND (QUEENSLAND MOUNTED INFANTRY) CONTINGENT.

THIS constituted the 3rd Company, Queensland Mounted Infantry, and it was raised under proclamation, dated 29th December, 1900, authorizing a further "Military Force of Volunteers," for service with Her Majesty's army in South Africa, of the establishment detailed hereafter.

Commanding officers were directed to furnish lists of members of their corps, prepared to volunteer for service in South Africa. They were required to be trained men, expert shots, and good riders; and any man in possession of a suitable horse might have same purchased by the Government, if services accepted.

ESTABLISHMENT.

Staff :—One major, 2 staff sergeants, 4 rank and file ; total, 1 officer, 6 others ; with 4 draught, 4 riding horses ; total, 8.

No. 3 Company :—One captain, 4 lieutenants, 1 company sergeant-major, 4 sergeants, 1 sergeant-artificer, 5 artificers, 2 buglers, 6 corporals, 119 privates and drivers ; total, 5 officers, 138 others ; 12 draught, 130 riding horses ; total, 142. Grand total, 150 of all ranks, with the like number of horses.

Beyond the staff stated, however, there were a medical officer and a veterinary officer ; besides 1 captain, 1 lieutenant, appointed supernumerary.

DEPARTURE AND RETURN.

The Contingent left on 13th January, 1900, comprising 10 officers, 144 others, with 178 horses. Four died ; 27 were struck off in South Africa ; 11 officers (1 appointed in South Africa), 113 others returned.

PROMOTIONS.

Lieutenant H. J. I. Harris, promoted Captain, 22nd November, 1900.
Private F. G. Newton, promoted Lieutenant, 1st May, 1900.
Private N. T. Seccombe, promoted Lieutenant, " D " Company, 3rd Australian Commonwealth Horse.
Private C. B. Holme, promoted Lieutenant, 7th Australian Commonwealth Horse.
For promotions of N.C.O.'s and men, *vide* nominal roll.

SERVICE.

The Contingent left Queensland by the transport *Maori King* on 13th January, 1900, anchored in Table Bay 22nd February, disembarked at Cape Town on 24th ; went to Maitland Camp, and entrained for Modder River on 28th (10 officers, 142 other ranks, and 175 horses), arriving on 3rd March. It proceeded at once to join Lord Roberts' Field Force, and came under the command of Colonel Martyr.

The 2nd were present at the actions at Osfontein, Poplar Grove, Driefontein, and the various engagements leading to the occupation of Bloemfontein. They were then on outpost duties round Bloemfontein until 9th April, 1900, when this Contingent came under the command of Lieutenant-Colonel Ricardo, 1st Contingent, (*vide* that Contingent, under " Service.")

On the 8th April, the Australian Regiment (*vide* 1st Victorian Contingent), with several other corps, including the Queenslanders, was absorbed in the 1st Mounted Infantry Brigade, under the command of Major-General Hutton, C.B., A.D.C. ; this Contingent serving in 3rd Mounted Infantry Corps. The advance on Pretoria followed ; and subsequent operations, including Vet and Zand Rivers, near Johannesburg, Diamond Hill, Riet Vlei, and Zilikat's Nek (April to September).

Served to 9th November, under Major Chauvel ("Chauvel's Mounted Infantry"), in minor operations round Middelburg (Brigadier-General Barker's district), as far east as Belfast.

To 7th March, 1901, under Captain H. J. I. Harris (Australian Mounted Infantry), in minor operations, Machadodorp District (Brigadier-General Reeves), as far east as Krokodil Poort. Attached to Major-General W. Kitchener's Column, 12th to 18th February.

The Contingent was in orders for Colonel De Lisle's Corps, December, 1900, but was not afforded an opportunity to join.

EXTRACT FROM COLUMN ORDERS BY MAJOR-GENERAL E. T. HUTTON, C.B., A.D.C., COMMANDING.

"Pretoria, 8th October, 1900.

Major-General Hutton, in relinquishing command of the Force placed under his orders, desires to convey to the officers, N.C.O.'s and men of the various units who have served under his command during the campaign, his sincere and hearty congratulations upon the success that, under Providence, has attended their efforts throughout the operations in which they have been engaged. The units of Imperial troops selected for service with the Mounted Infantry and those of Colonial mounted troops, representative of Canada, of the six Colonies of Australia, and of New Zealand, have alike distinguished themselves, by their steadiness under fire, by their gallantry in the field, and by their uniform good conduct in camp. In the latter connexion it is a subject of the greatest satisfaction to note that since the formation of the 1st Mounted Infantry Brigade, on 7th April, there has been almost an entire absence of military crime.

The mutual sympathy, admiration, and good will which have been so conspicuous between the Imperial and Colonial troops composing the command, must in the Major-General's opinion necessarily be conducive to that unity and solidarity of feeling which is an important and essential factor in the success of the Army of the British Empire.

The Major-General desires especially to record his appreciation and thanks for the excellent service rendered by all members of the staff connected with his Force, both Imperial and Colonial, but especially to Lieut.-Colonel Martyr, D.S.O., Chief Staff Officer, and to those of his headquarters staff.

Lieut.-Colonel Hutchison, Q.M.I., performed the duties of assistant staff officer to the officer in charge of the 1st Mounted Infantry Brigade Transport, during the advance from Bloemfontein, Johannesburg, and Pretoria (inclusive).

(True Copy).

J. B. M., Major, C.S.O.,
General Hutton's Column.

Pretoria, 8th October, 1900."

The Contingent embarked at Cape Town in the transport *Tongariro* on 31st March, 1901, called at Fremantle, 20th April, and Sydney, 29th April; left by rail, 1st May, arrived at Brisbane 3rd May, and were disbanded on the 10th.

WAR SERVICES AND HONOURS.

Hutchison, Lieut.-Colonel K.—Operations in Orange Free State and Transvaal, 1900–01. Queen's Medal with three clasps.

Thompson, Captain W. G.—Operations in Orange Free State, Transvaal, and Cape Colony, 1900–01. Actions at Poplar Grove, Driefontein, Vet River, Zand River, Johannesburg, and Pretoria. Queen's Medal with three clasps. In command, April to November, 1900.

Richardson, Captain Sir Edward A. S., Bart. (Supernumerary).—Operations and actions as stated. Queen's Medal with three clasps. Sir Edward was an officer of 3rd Battalion, Black Watch (Royal Highlanders).

Harris, Captain H. J. I.—Operations as stated. Actions at Poplar Grove, Driefontein, Vet River, Zand River, Johannesburg, Pretoria, Riet Vlei, and Zilikat's Nek. Commanded Contingent, November to December, 1900; Australian Mounted Infantry, January, 1901, to March, 1901. Queen's Medal with four clasps.

Stodart, Lieutenant R. M.—Operations as stated. Actions at Polpar Grove, Driefontein, Johannesburg, Pretoria, Riet Vlei, and Zilikat's Nek. Queen's Medal with three clasps.

Crichton, Lieutenant A. F.—Operations and actions as stated, including Vet River, Zand River, and Diamond Hill. Queen's Medal with four clasps. Served in "D" Company, 3rd Australian Commonwealth Horse.

Walker, Lieutenant J.—Operations and actions as stated, exclusive of Diamond Hill. Queen's Medal with three clasps.

Fox, Lieutenant J. H. (Supernumerary).—Operations and actions as stated. Queen's Medal with clasps.

Newton, Lieutenant F. G.—Operations and actions as stated. Severely wounded with Pilcher's Force, 12th August, 1900. Queen's Medal with four clasps.

Nolan, Captain H. R. (Army Medical Corps).—Operations in Orange Free State, February to May, 1900, including actions at Poplar Grove, Driefontein, and Vet River. Queen's Medal with three clasps.

Barnes, Captain A. W., Veterinary Officer.—Operations and actions as stated. Queen's Medal with clasps.

Nominal Roll.

No. and Name.	Rank.	Remarks.
OFFICERS.		
Hutchison, Kenneth	Lieutenant-Colonel	
Thompson, William George	Captain	
Harris, Hubert Jennings Imrie	Lieutenant	
Stodart, Robert Mackay	,,	
Crichton, Archibald Frederick	,,	
Walker, James	,,	
Richardson, Sir E. Stewart	Captain (Supy.)	
Fox, John Henry	Lieutenant(Supy.)	
Nolan, H. R.	Captain (A.M.C.)	
Barnes, A. W.	Vet. Captain	
N.C.O.'S AND MEN.		
1. Cooney, Teddes	Quartermaster-Sergeant	Awarded D.C.M. Despatches, *London Gazette*, 27.9.01
2. Bruce, William Cunningham	Colour-Sergeant	
15. Winterford, Alfred Edwin	Sergeant	
19. Wollstein, Harry More	,,	
22. Midgeley, Stephen	,,	Invalided to England, 13.8.00
27. Berry, William Henry	,,	
3. Johnson, Edmund Teasdale	Private	
4. Heiberg, Helge	,,	
5. Midgley, Francis James	,,	
6. Sabine, William Randolph Eppes	Sergeant	Sergeant-Major

Nominal Roll—*continued.*

No. and Name.	Rank.	Remarks.
N.C.O.'s AND MEN—*continued.*		
7. Holme, Charles Bretheton	Private	Prisoner of war at Swartz Kopjes, 13.2.01; released, rejoined, 16.2.01. *Vide* "Promotions"
8. Moss, Frank Buckton	,,	
9. Munro, Thomas Gascoyne	,,	Corporal, 13.1.00
10. Winterford, William Henry	,,	
11. Gatland, Edwin Francis	,,	
12. Cavaye, James McLelland	,,	
14. Harris, Andrew Alfred	,,	Corporal. Awarded D.C.M. Despatches, *London Gazette*, 27.9.01
16. Newton, Frank Graham	,,	*Vide* Promotions. Invalided to England, 16.11.00
17. Hugonin, Claude	,,	Invalided to Australia, 25.8.00
18. Richards, Frederick Adolphus	,,	
20. Wikner, Gustaf Adolph	,,	
21. Lee, Arthur James	,,	
24. Locke, Robert Henry	,,	
25. Hanson, Edward Joseph	,,	
26. Evans, Richard Edward	,,	
28. Walker, George Edward	,,	
29. Waterton, George William Thomas	,,	Invalided to Australia, arr. 18.8.00
30. Tamblyn, Francis	,,	
31. Gabriel, William James	,,	
32. Stenhouse, George	,,	
33. Smith, Edward	,,	
34. Daly, John Florence	,,	
36. Trickett, James John	,,	Corporal. Awarded D.C.M. Despatches, *London Gazette*, 27.9.01
37. Robertson, John	,,	Invalided to Australia, arr. 18.9.00
38. Fisher, Walter Ingram	Shoeing-Smith	
39. Wilson, Lachlan Chisholme	Private	Acting-Corporal. Prisoner of War at Swartz Kopjes, 13.2.01; released, rejoined 16.2.01
40. Buchanan, William Samuel	,,	Corporal, 13.1.00; Sergeant, 8.5.01. Severely wounded at Swartz Kopjes, 13.2.01
41. Hives, George Hay	,,	Wounded at Klipdam Farm, 6.3.00
42. Rice, Cecil Edward	,,	
43. Blunt, Robert Henry Theodore	,,	
44. Halse, Kendon Jeffreys	,,	Invalided to Australia, arr. 8.12.00
45. Higginson, John Bingham	,,	
46. Evans, William	,,	
47. Gallwey, John William	,,	Invalided to Australia, arr. 8.12.00
48. Lloyd, William Moyston	,,	Severely wounded, Constantia, 5.5.00. In Netley Hospital England, Dec. 1900
49. Pasco, Montagu Gordon Charles	,,	
50. Campbell, Malcolm Livingstone	,,	
51. Venables, Harold	,,	
53. Gill, Joseph Samuel	,,	
54. Reimers, Charles Matthew	,,	Died of enteric at Bloemfontein, 24.4.00
55. Stibbards, Thomas	,,	Invalided to England, 13.8.00
56. Mantel, Harry	,,	Egyptian campaign, 1882-4; Corporal, 13.1.00; Sergeant, 9.4.01

Nominal Roll—*continued*.

No. and Name.	Rank.	Remarks.
N.C.O.'s AND MEN—*continued*.		
57. Price, Solomon	Private	
58. Thorburn, George Edwin	,,	
59. McMahon, John	,,	
60. Tidey, Albert George	,,	
61. Cran, Eric George	,,	Corporal, 13.1.00
62. Robinson, St. John	,,	Returned to Australia, arr. 19.2.01 discharged 26.2.01
63. Carpendale, Herbert Victor	,,	
64. Jones, Ernest Llewellyn	,,	Invalided to Australia, arr. 19.11.00
65. Black, Ralph Wemyss	,,	
66. Baker, Arthur	,,	
67. McCabe, Thomas	,,	Corporal
68. Vaughan, Charles Robert Geoghegan	,,	
69. Ford, Frederick	,,	
70. McDonald, John	,,	
71. Ramsden, Samuel Henry	,,	
72. Horley, Jesse	,,	Returned to Australia, arr. 25.3.01
73. Walsh, Richard	,,	
74. Schubert, Frederick Charles	,,	Invalided to Australia, arr. 19.9.00
75. Thomas, Francis James	,,	Invalided to Australia, arr. 1.9.00
76. Donkin, John Edward	,,	
78. McDonald, William Alexander	,,	
79. Reid, Charles	,,	
80. Prangley, Frank	,,	Invalided to England, 16.8.00
81. Gay, Henry	,,	Corporal
82. Hitchings, Frederick James	,,	Invalided to Australia, arr. 1.9.00
83. Gordon, George Fernando	,,	
84. White, Edward Tarplee	,,	
85. McSporran, Ewen	,,	
86. Enever, Joseph	,,	Farrier-Sergeant
87. Hopkins, Charles James	,,	
88. Dobson, John James	,,	Invalided to Australia, arr. 18.8.00
89. Bates, John Robert	,,	
90. Parnell, James	,,	Died of pneumonia, Pretoria, 21.7.00
91. Clutterbuck, Thomas	Bugler	
92. Connolly, John	Private	Corporal, 13.1.00; invalided to Australia, arr. 18.8.00
93. Nielson, Peter	Shoeing-Smith	
94. Douglas, Joseph	Private	
95. Bennett, William	,,	
96. McLeish, William Alexander	,,	Invalided to Australia, arr. 18.8.00
97. Seccombe, Norman Thorne	,,	*Vide* " Promotions "
98. Seccombe, William Thomas Thorne	,,	Slightly wounded, Swartz Kopjes, 13.2.01
99. Mills, Egerton Charles	,,	Acting-Corporal
100. Haylock, Alfred Atherton	,,	
101. Sargint, Harry	,,	
102. Bothamley, Alfred	,,	Invalided to Australia, arr. 8.8.00
103. Fordham, Henry George	,,	Invalided to Australia, arr. 18.8.00
104. Macfarlane, James Burns	,,	Acting-Corporal
105. Sanderson, John Emerson	,,	
106. Kerr, Archibald	,,	Corporal
107. Hamer, Arthur	,,	
108. Cronan, Edward	,,	Died of enteric, Bloemfontein, 2.4.00

Nominal Roll—continued.

No. and Name.	Rank.	Remarks.

N.C.O.'s AND MEN—continued.

No. and Name.	Rank.	Remarks.
109. McGregor, Charles	Private	
110. McAllister, James Cloheny	,,	
111. Halligan, Thomas	,,	Corporal. Invalided to Australia, arr. 1.9.00
112. Ross, Colin Hassel	,,	
113. Simpson, Young Peitland	,,	Farrier-Sergeant, 13.1.00
114. Innes, David	,,	Invalided to Australia, arr. 8.12.00
115. Birkbeck, Frederick George	,,	
116. Rawson, Lionel Reginald	,,	Prisoners of war at Swartz Kopjes, 13.2.01; released, rejoined 16.2.01
117. Warner, Timothy	,,	Invalided to Australia, arr. 8.12.00
118. Dutton, Richard Guy	,,	Invalided to England; returned to Australia, arr. 6.3.01
119. Myatt, Charles	,,	
120. Perry-Keene, Harold	,,	
121. Flewell-Smith, Malcolm	,,	
122. Kibble, Sydney George	,,	
123. Stevenson, Colin Graham	,,	
124. Dodd, Arthur William	,,	Invalided to Australia, arr. 18.8.00
125. Brady, William (junior)	,,	
126. Miller, James Herd	,,	
127. King, Archibald Edward	,,	Invalided to Australia, arr. 15.9.00
128. Landsborough, Sidney Lutrell	,,	Died of pneumonia, Johannesburg, 15.6.00
129. Evans, Harry John	,,	
130. Farnsworth, Herbert Jermyn	,,	
131. Drury, Noel Harnage	,,	
132. Shaw, William	,,	Returned to Australia, discharged 13.3.01
133. Corcoran, Thomas	,,	
134. Ward, George Abel	,,	Invalided to Australia, arr. 1.9.00
135. Schy, Frank	,,	
136. Fernleigh, Thomas Ernest	,,	
137. King, Wyndham Guy Fitzgerald	,,	Invalided to England, 16.8.00
138. Hosick, Frederick Harold	,,	
139. Wildman, George	,,	
140. Eves, Reginald Horace	,,	
141. Granville, Edward Leslie	,,	
142. Truman, Clifford Allan	,,	
144. Powell, Alfred Thomas	,,	
145. Smith, Rowland Siddons	,,	
146. Johnson, John Peter	,,	Invalided to Australia, arr. 4.7.00
147. Smith, Robert Campbell	,,	
148. Laffan, Thomas	,,	Invalided to England, 13.8.00
149. Cook, Charles	,,	
150. Heberdeen, Herbert William	,,	

Major C. D. W. Rankin and Captain F. W. Toll, Special Service Officers, accompanied the Contingent to South Africa.

THIRD (QUEENSLAND MOUNTED INFANTRY) CONTINGENT.

BY proclamation, dated 9th February, 1900, a third " Military Force of Volunteers " was authorized, constituting the 4th and 5th Companies, Queensland Mounted Infantry; the strength was slightly increased by subsequent proclamation of 2nd March. Conditions of enlistment were similar to those of the previous Contingent.

ESTABLISHMENT.

Staff.—1 major, 2 staff sergeants, 4 rank and file; total, 1 officer, 6 others, with 4 horses.

Nos. 4 and 5 Companies, each.—1 captain, 4 lieutenants, 1 company sergeant-major, 4 sergeants, 1 sergeant-artificer, 5 artificers, 2 buglers, 6 corporals, 126 privates and drivers; total, 5 officers, 145 others, with (for the two companies) 100 draught horses, (for each company) 119 riding horses—in all, for each company 150 of all ranks, with horses as stated.

At Base.—Storeman, 1 sergeant, 2 rank and file; total, 3. Spare horses, 58.

Total.—1 major, 2 captains, 8 lieutenants, 2 staff sergeants, 2 company sergeant-majors, 9 sergeants, 2 sergeant-artificers, 10 artificers, 4 buglers, 12 corporals, 258 privates and drivers; in all, 11 officers, 299 others, with 100 draught, 300 riding horses. Grand total, 310 of all ranks, with 400 horses.

PROMOTIONS, ETC.

Lieutenant J. R. Fowles held the local rank of Captain in Rhodesian Field Force.

Lieutenant E. M. Hockings also held such rank.

Private C. S. Abercrombie, promoted to Hon. Lieutenant and Quartermaster, 1st July, 1900, *vice* Fielden, invalided.

Sergeant C. H. Brand, promoted to Lieutenant, 25th June, 1900. Served as Captain with 7th Australian Commonwealth Horse.

Private H. E. Forrest, promoted to Lieutenant, 17th October, 1900, *vice* Leask, deceased.

Private R. Sleight, promoted to Lieutenant, 17th October, 1900, *vice* Annat, deceased.

Corporal G. A. C. Dods, promoted Lieutenant, 7th Australian Commonwealth Horse.

For promotions of N.C.O.'s and men, *vide* nominal roll.

DEPARTURE AND RETURN.

The Contingent left Brisbane on 1st March, 1900, comprising—14 officers, with 302 others, and 406 horses. Two officers, 5 others died or were killed; 3 were transferred; 2 officers, 52 others were struck off in South Africa; 14 officers, 242 others, returned to Australia.

SERVICE.

The 3rd Contingent left on the 1st March, 1900, by the transport *Duke of Portland*, calling at Albany on the 12th, and arrived at Cape Town on 2nd April; thence proceeded to Beira, and disembarked there. They were embodied in the Rhodesian Field Force, of which they became the 2nd Regiment, and participated in operations in Rhodesia, between the 11th October, 1899, and 25th May, 1900. As portion of the " Bushmen's Brigade " in Colonel Plumer's Column, they assisted in the relief of Mafeking. The Brigade served subsequently in General Carrington's Column.

Between July and November they were engaged in operations in Transvaal, east of Pretoria, including the action at Rhenoster Kop, 29th November. They were then in Craddock's Corps, General Paget's Column. As portion of the Bushmen's Brigade, General Baden-Powell's Column (but detached), they figured in operations west of Pretoria, including the defence at Eland's River, 4th to 16th August; Colonel Hore, officer commanding lines of communication, being in command.

At the engagement at Koster River on the 22nd July, the Queenslanders were under heavy fire for $6\frac{1}{2}$ hours; during which time bullets, the majority of them explosive ones, were whistling, singing, exploding, and hissing all round them, the enemy being posted on a line of kopjes, which afterwards proved to be within 800 yards of their position under cover, in the long grass near the main road. Here the Queensland Contingent bore the whole brunt of the fire, being in the lead, and the first to come in view of the enemy. Lieutenant Leask was wounded early in the day, but would not quit his post; he died of the wound afterwards. They were ultimately rescued by the garrison at Nogato's Nek, where Colonel Lushington telephoned into Rustenburg for reinforcements, with the result that portion of the Protectorate Regiment, under Captain Fitzclarence, with another force under the officer first named, came upon the scene; and the former poured volleys into the kopjes with such effect that the Boers were dislodged.

The Eland's River Camp (Ottoshoop, between Rustenburg and Zeerust) was attacked by Commandant De La Rey on 4th August, at daybreak.

For an account of this spirited defence, *vide* New South Wales Citizen's Bushmen. In this affair, Lieutenant Annat was killed, and twelve rank and file wounded. One of the Queenslanders, Trooper J. T. Masterton, was the first man hit. The casualties (amongst which were five deaths) were very heavy on the first day; and nearly all being from fragments of shells, were very bad wounds. Several men were hit a second time in hospital. It was fortunate that the Queenslanders marched in, as otherwise there would have been no medical officer, ambulances, or appliances, no water carts, and very few entrenching tools.

On the 29th November, General Paget made an attack on the enemy's very strong position at Rhenoster Kop (Rietfontein), and the whole force was engaged from 7.15 a.m. until nearly midnight. The 3rd Queenslanders were on the left flank with the Victorians and Western Australians, and were under shell, pom-pom, and rifle fire the whole time; but having a certain amount of cover, losses were not very heavy. Staff Sergeant Austen was hit on the leg with a pom-pom shell, and Trooper W. H. Earl on arm and thigh with mauser bullets.

As soon as they got back to camp they were ordered out again—being given 20 minutes only—to occupy and entrench the position extending along the crest of the hill about $1\frac{1}{2}$ miles. The men worked exceedingly well, although they had been practically carrying on two days and a night with very little food.

The enemy evacuated the position on the 30th.

The following is an extract from Force Orders by General Paget, on the 1st December :—

"The Major-General wishes to place on record his high appreciation of the gallant bearing of the troops under his command in the recent engagement.

"The enemy was in a strong, naturally defensive position, which he was forced to evacuate by the intrepid advance of our men, under an exceptionally heavy fire.

"The Major-General wishes to point out to the troops under his command that the moral effect of this engagement on the Boers must be very great, a force numerically no stronger than their own, having forced them to retire from a position of great natural strength, which it was most important they should not evacuate.

"The Major-General thanks all ranks for the gallant way in which they behaved, and wishes to express his admiration of their bravery and devotion to duty. In publishing the above to the mounted troops of the Force, Brigadier-General Plumer wishes to say how proud he is to have under his command troops who behaved so well in action as the two brigades did on 29th November."

From 29th November to 1st February, 1901, operations in the Transvaal, Craddock's Corps, General Paget's Column. February and March, under General Lyttleton's command, operations north of Cape Colony, and in the Orange River Colony. April, operations in the Transvaal, north of Pretoria, in Jeffrey's Corps, General Plumer's Column.

EXTRACT FROM REPORT OF CAPTAIN R. B. ECHLIN TO THE COLONIAL SECRETARY, BRISBANE, 17TH AUGUST, 1901.

"I have the honour to make the following short report on the conduct of members of the 3rd Queensland Mounted Infantry under my command in an engagement at Koster River, Transvaal, on 22nd July, 1900. On 24th July, I wrote an official report to my commanding officer, Major W. Howard Tunbridge, giving a detailed account of the engagement. Although I carried this document nearly three months, and eventually entrusted to an officer for posting, Major Tunbridge assured me he never received it.

"I particularly mentioned that it was very difficult to individualize bravery. For instance, Bugler Keogh was shot in the cheek when we were dismounting. The bullet came out at the nape of his neck; still he fought for $5\frac{1}{2}$ hours. Then Lieutenant R. Walsh was hit in the head, and wanted to continue on duty. Lieutenant Leask was wounded early in the day, and never left his post until the fight was over. He succumbed to his wound afterwards.

"The most notable act of bravery, not actually observed by me, but of which I have had ample evidence, was that of Bugler Forbes. This lad, then about 16 years old, took my horse and his own to what was supposed to be cover, behind a deserted farm house, and held these horses until they were both shot. During that trying time he had a bullet sent through his haversack. Forbes, with the other horse-holders, were compelled to take shelter in this farm house; and when, with the continuous fire kept up by its occupants, ammunition commenced to run short, Forbes under fire went out amongst the shot horses and ransacked the saddle wallets. A Mr. Toy, a war correspondent of a Western Australian newspaper, was one of those who took shelter in the farm house, and in writing to his journal, particularly referred to Forbes' action.

Two hundred and seventy (270) men were participants in this engagement, and when the roll was called at 4 p.m. on that day, the following was the result:—Six killed, 2 died (two days afterwards), 1 died (three weeks afterwards) (Lieutenant Leask), 9 severely wounded, 14 slightly wounded, 27 missing, of which 20 turned up. Total casualties, 59.

"The Queenslanders numbered seventy (70), and the rest of the troops were were composed of New South Wales, Victorian, and Western Australian Bushmen.

R. B. ECHLIN, Captain,
(late Officer Commanding "B" Squadron, 3rd
Queensland Mounted Infantry Contingent).

Bugler Forbes was mentioned in despatches and awarded the D.C.M., *vide* p. 473.

On 9th May, 1901, the Contingent departed for home in the transport *Morayshire* at Cape Town: called at Fremantle, Adelaide, Melbourne, and Sydney (7th June), thence by rail to Brisbane. Disbanded on 21st June.

WAR SERVICES AND HONOURS.

Tunbridge, Major W. H.—Operations in Rhodesia, Transvaal, Orange River Colony, and Cape Colony, 26th April, 1900, to 23rd April, 1901; including actions at Koster River, Rhenoster Kop, and Eland's River. Despatches, *London Gazette*, 16th April, 1901. C.B. Queen's Medal with five clasps. A.D.C. to His Excellency the Governor-General (*Gazette*, 8th August, 1902).

Kellie, Captain C. W.—Afghan war, 1880. Medal. Soudan, 1884-5. Actions El Teb (slightly wounded) and Tamai. Medal with two clasps, and Khedive's Star. 4th class Medjidie. Operations as stated. Relief of Mafeking. Action at Eland's River. Queen's Medal with three clasps.

Echlin, Captain R. B.—Operations and actions as stated. Queen's Medal with clasps. Commanded " D " Company, 3rd Australian Commonwealth Horse,

Duka, Captain A. T. (Army Medical Corps).—Operations in Rhodesia, and Transvaal, including actions at Eland's River. Despatches, *London Gazette*, 16th April, 1901. D.S.O. Queen's Medal with two clasps.

Annat, Lieutenant J. W.—Operations in Rhodesia and Transvaal. Killed at Eland's River, 6th August, 1900.

Dalgleish, Lieutenant G. W.—Operations in Rhodesia. Queen's Medal with four clasps.

Fowles, J. K., *Hockings*, E. M., *Harris*, H. J., *Walsh*, R. H., *Forrest*, H. E., and *Brand*, C. H. (Lieutenants).—Operations in Rhodesia, Transvaal, Orange River Colony, and Cape Colony, with actions as stated. Queen's Medal with five clasps.

Hanly, Lieutenant J. M.—Operations and actions stated. Queen's Medal with clasps.

Leask, Lieutenant J.—Operations in Rhodesia and Transvaal. Died at Pretoria from wounds received in action, 20th August, 1900.

Fielden, P. H. G. (Supernumerary), and *McColl*, M. G. (Lieutenants).—Operations in Rhodesia and Transvaal. Queen's Medal with two clasps.

Abercrombie, C. S., Lieut.-Quartermaster.—Operations in Rhodesia and Transvaal. Queen's Medal with four clasps.

Sleight, Lieutenant R.—Operations in Rhodesia, Transvaal, Cape Colony, and Orange River Colony. *Vide* also 6th Queensland Imperial Bushmen.

Nominal Roll.

No. and Name.	Rank.	Remarks.
OFFICERS.		
Tunbridge, Walter Howard	Major	
Kellie, Charles Wauchope	Captain	Afghan Campaign, 1880. Soudan, 1884-5
Fowles, John Kentwell	Lieutenant	
Harris, Henry John	,,	
Annat, James Whamond	,,	Killed in action at Eland's River. 6.8.00
Echlin, Richard Boyd	Captain	
Hockings, Edwin Morton	Lieutenant	
Walsh, Richard Henry	,,	Slightly wounded, Koster River, 22.7.00
Leask, John	,,	Severely wounded, Koster River, 22.7.00; died of wounds and pneumonia, Pretoria, 20.8.00
Hanly, John Matthew	,,	

Nominal Roll—*continued*.

No. and Name.	Rank.	Remarks.
OFFICERS—*continued*.		
Dalgleish, George Walter	Lieutenant	Supernumerary. Invalided to Australia, arr. 1.9.00
Fielden, Percy Henry Guy	,,	
McColl, M. G.	,,	Supernumerary
Duka, Albert Theophilus	Captain, A.M.C.	
N.C.O.'S AND MEN.		
1. Glass, Alexander John	Private	Sergeant-Major
2. Gordon, Archibald George.	,,	Sergeant-Major
3. Timms, David Walter..	,,	
4. Wright, William Leckey Ferguson	,,	Quartermaster-Sergeant. D.C.M. Despatches, *London Gazette*, 27.9.01
5. McIntyre, Donald	,,	Corporal, 20.8.00 ; Veterinary-Sergeant, 1.12.00
6. Dods, George Archibald Cowen	,,	Corporal, 17.2.00. Slightly wounded at Rietfontein, 30.11.00. *Vide* Promotions
7. Donkin, Leslie	,,	Sergeant
8. Mabbutt, Thomas	,,	Company Sergeant-Major
9. Gorst, Alfred John	,,	Sergeant, 17.2.00
10. Bennett, Henry William	,,	Sergeant
11. Chapman, Archibald Duncan Campbell	,,	Lance-Corporal, 1.11.00 ; Corporal
12. Leach, John ..	,,	Acting-Corporal
13. Gordon, William Francis	,,	
14. Jones, Harold	,,	Lance-Corporal
15. Brown, John Robertson	,,	Slightly wounded at Ottoshoop, East Rhodesia, 4–16th August, 1900
16. Unwin Charles King	,,	Corporal. Gunshot wound (accidental), Mafeking
17. McNulty, Edward Eugene	,,	Sergeant, 17.2.00
18. Williams, John Thomas	,,	Corporal .
19. Livesey, Charles Edward	,,	Returned to Australia, arr. 25.3.01
20. Parkinson, William	,,	Corporal, 17.2.00. Sergeant
21. Bartley, Herbert Wilfred	,,	Corporal, 14.7.00
22. Morrison, John	,,	
23. Denman, Emanuel	,,	
24. Mathie, Edwin	,,	
25. Anderson, Ernest William	,,	
26. Livesey, Hampden Gibbon	,,	Farrier-Sergeant-Major. Slightly wounded, Ottoshoop, East Rhodesia, 4–18th August, 1900
27. Elston, William Ernest	,,	Sergeant, 17.2.00
28. Macdonald, Douglas Kinneir	,,	Died of tubercle, Pretoria, 12.2.01
29. Campbell, Archibald St. Clair	,,	
30. Daly, Edward Arthur	,,	
31. Maude, Alwyne Edward Francis Cornwallis	,,	Died of pneumonia and measles Mafeking, 20.8.00
33. Christie, Arthur	,,	Invalided to Australia, arr. 19.9.00
34. Crick, Charles Henry	,,	Dangerously wounded at Pienaar's River, 21.8.00. Invalided to Australia, arr. 8.12.00
35. Bacon, James Rudkin	,,	Corporal, 19.7.00
36. Winthrop, Walter Thursby	,,	
37. Davidson, Leslie	,,	

Nominal Roll—*continued*.

No. and Name.	Rank.	Remarks.
N.C.O.'s AND MEN—*continued*.		
38. Deshon, Arthur Popham	Private	Corporal, 15.7.00
39. Forrest, Harold Edmonds	,,	*Vide* "Promotions" and "War Services"
40. Masterton, John Thomas	,,	Severely wounded at Eland's River, 6.8.00; died of wounds Krugersdorp, 11.9.00
41. Earl, Frederick Halson	,,	
43. McNish, Frank St. Clair	,,	Lance-Corporal, 16.11.00
44. Plummer, Sydney John	,,	
45. Herd, Robert Arthur	,,	Slightly wounded at Eland's River, 2.9.00. Invalided to England, 19.10.00
46. Faloon, David	,,	
47. Cossart, Sydney Joseph	,,	Acting-Corporal
48. Pott, George	,,	
49. Ross, William Carmichael	,,	
50. Cobb, John	,,	
51. Grant, Collingwood McKenzie	,,	
52. Barnes, Hiram	,,	
53. Nichols, Walter Lewis	,,	
54. Winniett, Chard Massey	,,	
55. Hoffmann, Andrew Joseph	,,	
56. Nott, Frank Ernest	,,	Corporal, 17.2.00
57. Hermann, Harry	,,	
58. Millett, Michael	,,	
59. Nowland, Walter Richard	,,	
60. Gorman, Thomas	,,	Lance-Corporal
61. Hallett, Robert James	,,	
62. Burns, William	,,	
63. Bocock, Edward	,,	
64. Barton, William	,,	Returned to Australia, arr. 25.3.01
65. Fallis, Richard	,,	Slightly wounded at Ottoshoop, East Rhodesia, 4–16th August, 1900
66. Evans, Edward James	,,	Sergeant, 17.2.00. Invalided to Australia, arr. 19.11.00
67. Caldwell, Erskine James	,,	
68. Goodwin, James	,,	Slightly wounded at Ottoshoop, East Rhodesia, 4–16th August, 1900
69. Kingsley, Louis	,,	
70. Fishbourne, Patrick John	,,	Sergeant, 17.2.00
71. Scovell, Robert	,,	
72. Harvey, Arthur Edgar	,,	Returned to Australia, arr. 25.3.01
73. Greenslade, Daniel	,,	
74. Nicholson, George	,,	
75. Greer, John	,,	
76. Rudhall, Benjamin	,,	
77. Spence, Archibald	,,	
78. Williams, Charles Gordon	,,	
79. Soden, William	,,	Acting-Corporal
80. Gorst, Albert Edward	,,	
81. French, George	,,	
82. Boyle, Henry Stewart	,,	
83. Davis, Arthur Wilson	,,	
84. Condor, Herbert Samuel	,,	
85. Evans, Alfred	,,	

Nominal Roll—*continued*.

No. and Name.	Rank.	Remarks.
N.C.O.'s AND MEN—*continued*.		
86. Boyes, Frederick	Private	
87. King, John	,,	
88. Bryce, David	,,	
89. Simpson, John	,,	
90. Atkinson, Charles Edwin	,,	
91. Brand, Charles Henry	,,	Sergeant, 17.2.00. *Vide* "Promotions" and "War Services"
92. McShea, John Joseph	,,	
93. Cairns, James Alfred	,,	Corporal
94. Garner, James	,,	
95. Davidson, Norman Alexander	,,	Corporal, 12.4.00. Severely wounded at Eland's River, 6.8.00. D.C.M. Despatches, *London Gazette*, 27.9.01. Invalided to Australia, arr. 10.12.00
96. Hartley, Harold Leslie	,,	Corporal, 17.2.00
97. Armstrong, John	,,	
98. Gore, William	,,	
99. Bradshaw, William	,,	
100. O'Callaghan, Charles	,,	
101. Pierce, John Joseph	,,	
102. Powter, Henry Carter	,,	
103. Hawes, Thomas William	,,	
104. Travers, Horace	,,	Quartermaster-Sergeant
105. Waltisbuhl, Anthony	,,	
106. Birkbeck, Arthur Francis	,,	
107. Ambrose, William	,,	
108. Harth, Frederick	,,	Severely wounded at Eland's River, 6.8.00. Invalided to Australia, arr. 8.12.00
109. Briggs, Charles	,,	
110. Crockett, Edward Francis	,,	
111. Clark, William Henry	,,	
112. Grubb, Henry	,,	Lance-Corporal
113. Davis, Frederick Joseph	,,	
114. Walker, David	,,	
115. Gittens, Thomas Chasely	,,	Slightly wounded, Buffel's Hoek, 16.8.00
117. Earl, William Henry	,,	Severely wounded at Rietfontein, 29.11.00
118. Barton, Newton Hastings	,,	
119. Corfe, Arthur Cecil	,,	
120. Burton, Thomas	,,	Slightly wounded at Bulkskop 24.8.00. Invalided to Australia, arr. 8.12.00
121. Henderson, Alfred John	,,	Invalided to Australia, arr. 8.12.00
122. Drew, Samuel Henry	,,	
123. Willoughby, Frederick Herbert	,,	
124. Copeland, William	,,	
125. Lax, John	,,	
126. Powell, James	,,	Returned to Australia, arr. 19.2.01
127. Welch, Edward Hutton	,,	
128. Wills, Alfred Henry	,,	
129. Molle, Eric Frederic	,,	
130. Cumming, Andrew Rudolph Leighton	,,	

Nominal Roll—*continued*.

No. and Name.	Rank.	Remarks.
N.C.O.'s AND MEN—*continued*.		
131. Tannock, Edward John	Private	Sergeant-Major, 16.11.00
132. Clarke, Edward Charles	,,	
133. Stupart, Ernest Robert	,,	
134. Ryan, Arthur Albert	,,	Corporal, 16.11.00
135. Rudd, Enoch	,,	
136. Culverhouse, Frederick	,,	
137. Bates, John William	,,	
138. Ferris, Charles	,,	
139. Craig, Frederick William	,,	Invalided to Australia, arr. 8.12.00
140. Dean, William James	,,	Corporal, 17.2.00
141. Koch, Felix Bernard Theodor	,,	Corporal, 17.2.00. Sergeant, 21.7.00. Slightly wounded at Koster River, 22.7.01
142. Twine, Leonard Sield	,,	Acting-Corporal. Severely wounded, Pienaar's River, 21.8.00
143. McKellar, Charles Richardson	,,	
144. Barker, John Charles	,,	Lance-Corporal
145. Rootes, Walter	,,	
146. Price, William	,,	
147. Crawford, John Adam	,,	Quartermaster-Sergeant
148. Benson, Jens	,,	
149. Langford, William Henry	,,	
150. Goodwin, Frederick	,,	
151. Hamilton, James	,,	Wounded, 12.2.01
153. Craven, Edmund Cecil	,,	
154. Flamank, John James	,,	
155. Stewart, Arthur Bradford	,,	
156. Farrell, William Robert	,,	
157. Bailey, Arthur Thomas	,,	Died of enteric, Pretoria, 29.1.01
158. Stone, Edward John	,,	
159. Farrington, Joseph	,,	Severely wounded at Rhenoster Kop, 17.12.00
160. Curtis, George Henry	,,	
161. Gordon, Henry Clement	,,	
162. McIntosh, David Gibb	,,	
163. Shaw, Charles James	,,	
164. Courtney, James	,,	
165. Pegg, Henry	,,	Corporal, 16.5.00
166. Watson, Albert Thomas	,,	
167. Kielly, Michael Patrick	,,	
168. Orchison, Alexander	,,	
169. Jury, Francis George Victor	,,	
170. Townley, Norman Vincent	,,	
171. Kirkpatrick, Robert	,,	
172. Sawdy, Alfred James	,,	
173. Pettigrew, John	,,	
174. Hutchinson, George	,,	
175. Black, Henry Wemyss	,,	Quartermaster-Sergeant. Returned to Australia, arr. 22.2.01
176. Coe, James Lloyd	,,	Severely wounded at Rhenoster Kop, 17.12.00
177. Abercrombie, Charles Stewart	,,	*Vide* "Promotions" and "War Services"
178. Wilson, John	,,	
179. Owen, George	,,	
180. Estaughffe, Charles Douglas	,,	
181. Wright, James	,,	

Nominal Roll—*continued*.

No. and Name.	Rank.	Remarks.
N.C.O.'s AND MEN—*continued*.		
182. Walters, Thomas	Private	Slightly wounded at Koster River, 22.7.00
183. Bell, Horace Walsh	,,	
184. Horton, George Cooper	,,	
185. Pickering, Charles Morrison	,,	
186. Walker, Harry Arthur	,,	
187. Skelton, Bruce Aloysius	,,	Corporal. Slightly wounded at Rietfontein, 30.11.00
188. Cowell, George	,,	Squadron Quartermaster-Sergeant
189. Hill, William Henry	,,	
190. Robinson, John Henry	,,	Farrier-Sergeant
191. Jorgensen, George Matthew	,,	Severely wounded at Koster River, 22.7.00. Invalided to Australia, arr. 8.12.00
192. Bray, Thomas William	,,	
193. Keogh, Herbert William	Bugler	Slightly wounded at Koster River, 22.7.00 D.C.M. Despatches *London Gazette*, 27.9.01
194. Virgen, Charles William	Private	Invalided to Australia, arr. 8.12.00
195. Dodds, Harold Nicholas	,,	Squadron Quartermaster-Sergeant
196. Cooper, Robert Edward	,,	
197. Massie, Hugh Aier	,,	
198. Jackson, Walter Thomas	,,	
199. Bryce, James	,,	Slightly wounded at Ottoshoop, Eland's River, 4–16.8.00
200. Trower, George Matthew	,,	
201. Gordon, Thomas Henry	,,	
202. Lenthal, Walter Frederick	,,	Returned to Australia, arr. 25.3.01
203. Groom, Charles William	,,	Invalided to Australia, arr. 25.8.00
204. McCarthy, Joseph	,,	
205. Cecil, Aubrey Bruce Cooper	,,	
206. Mortimer, Richard Charles	,,	Lance-Corporal, 16.11.00. Corporal
207. Gardner, Samuel John	,,	
208. Rush, Charles	,,	
209. Phillips, Charles Francis	,,	
210. Rankin, Thomas Alexander	,,	
212. Smith, William Henry	,,	
213. Byrne, Thomas	,,	
214. Arthur, Reginald	,,	
215. Howard, Thomas Patrick	,,	
216. Fitzgerald, John	,,	
217. James, Arthur	,,	
218. Mildown, George Alexander Robert	,,	Lance-Corporal, 14.12.00
219. Farrely, Bernard Joseph	,,	
220. Easdon, Sydney Ernest	,,	
221. Furness, Arthur	,,	Corporal 18.2.00; Sergeant, 16.11.00
222. Carver, John	,,	
223. Wallace, Frank James	,,	
224. Gray, Ernest Winser	,,	Acting Farrier-Sergeant
225. Woodard, Arthur William	,,	
226. Earby, Henry John	,,	**Corporal-Trumpeter**
227. Huxtable, Edwin	,,	**Sergeant**
228. Marsden, Harry	,,	

Nominal Roll—*continued.*

No. and Name.	Rank.	Remarks.
N.C.O.'s AND MEN—*continued.*		
229. Cope, Joseph Edward	Private	Sergeant, 18.2.00
230. Austen, Sydney	,,	Sergeant, 18.2.00. Severely wounded at Rietfontein, 29.11.00
231. Excell, Arthur Reginald	,,	Staff Sergeant, 8.3.01
232. Easlea, Thomas	,,	
233. Pott, Gideon William	,,	
234. Portus, George Davidson	,,	
235. Robinson, John James	,,	Slightly wounded at Ottoshoop, Eland's River, 4–16.8.00
236. South, Edwin Egerton	,,	Slightly wounded at Ottoshoop, Eland's River, 4–16.8.00
237. Shaw, Frederick Clement	,,	
238. Smith, David	,,	Corporal, 22.2.00
239. Hamer, George	,,	
240. Sykes, Henry Alexander	,,	
241. Vigors, Henry Manning	,,	
242. Wiltshire, James	,,	Invalided to Australia, arr. 15.9.00
243. Thorpe, John	,,	Slightly wounded at Rhenoster, Kop, 17.12.00
244. Doughan, John James	,,	
245. Wilson, Wylie Andrew	,,	
246. Hore, Benjamin	,,	
247. Gordon, Archibald Andrew	,,	
248. Davies, David John	,,	
249. Francis, John	,,	
250. Carlisle, Norman	,,	
251. Birmingham, Patrick	,,	
252. Callaghan, Charles Warwick	,,	
254. Butler, George	,,	
255. Bannister, Thomas John	,,	Lance-Corporal, 16.11.00
256. Deacon, Charles Edwin	,,	Corporal, 22.2.00; Sergeant, 10.12.00
257. Runcorn, Albert Edward	,,	
258. Lush, Alan Barling	,,	
259. Yapp, Albert	,,	
260. Richard, James	,,	
261. Watson, Robert	,,	
262. Brant, Thomas	,,	
263. Walford, William	,,	Corporal, 10.12.00
264. Isaacs, Norman Scott	,,	Lance-Corporal
265. Thomas, Charles Eric	,,	Invalided to Australia, 2.8.00
266. Innes, Joshua Clare	,,	
267. Carter, Wharton	,,	
268. Preston, Charles Alfred	,,	
269. Hurford, Robert Warrington	,,	
270. Wells, James William	,,	
271. Leighton, Charles Hill	,,	
272. Martin, James	,,	Farrier-Sergeant
273. Cumming, William John	,,	
274. Mayne, George Albert	,,	Lance-Corporal. Severely wounded at Hamilfontein, 12.2.01
275. Anderson, Robert	,,	Corporal, 22.2.00; Sergeant, 8.3.01
276. Ross, Thomas Brunton	,,	Corporal, 22.2.00
277. Wilmot, Matthew	,,	
278. Fowler, Morton	,,	
279. Flint, Thomas	,,	
280. Barker, Arthur	,,	

Nominal Roll—*continued.*

No. and Name.	Rank.	Remarks.
N.C.O.'s AND MEN—*continued.*		
281. Hanlon, William Lawrence	Private	Invalided to Australia, arr. 19.11.00
282. Hannam, Charles Henry Gonda	,,	
283. Christiansen, Martin	,,	
284. Forrest, George Richard	,,	Slightly wounded at Koster River, 22.7.00
285. Smith, John	,,	Corporal
286. Cumming, Donald	,,	Slightly wounded at Ottoshoop, Eland's River, 4–16.8.00
287. Blair, James	,,	Corporal. Severely wounded at Koster River, 22.7.00
288. Whitmee, Arthur	,,	
289. Robins, Albert Christopher	,,	
290. Fisher, Hugh Addison	,,	
291. Durman, Leonard	,,	
292. Harte, William Myers	,,	
293. O'Connor, John	,,	
294. Hull, George	,,	Died of enteric, Pretoria, 6.1.01
295. Sunner, John Phillip	,,	
296. Sleight, Rowland	,,	*Vide* "Promotions" and "War Services"
297. Forbes, Arthur Edward	Bugler	D.C.M. Despatches, *London Gazette*, 27.9.01
298. Brown, Archibald	Private	
299. Hammond, Frederick Grant	,,	
300. Carter, Edward Gregson	,,	
301. King, Mortimer James	,,	Slightly wounded at Jericho, 24.10.00
302. Buchanan, James	,,	
303. McLaren, W. A.	,,	Slightly wounded at Ottoshoop, 4–16.8.00
304. Midson, Charles Arthur	,,	
305. Lyons, Robert	,,	
306. Bowtell, William	,,	
307. Allan, Alexander William	,,	Returned to Australia, arr. —.3.01
308. Mellifont, James David	,,	

FOURTH (QUEENSLAND IMPERIAL BUSHMEN) CONTINGENT.

IT was the first Regiment of Imperial Bushmen raised in Queensland, and under conditions similar to those which obtained in New South Wales and Victoria (see under those States). Candidates were required to be good shots, good riders, and practical bushmen of experience, to have good eyesight and hearing and sound health. Age, 21 to 38 years; chest measurement, 34 inches; height, 5 ft. 6 in. to 5 ft. 11 in.; weight, not over 11 st. 10 lb.; to undergo physical examination and to be unmarried, for preference.

Rates of pay, until the Contingent came under the rates paid by the Imperial Government for service in South Africa outside Cape Colony and Natal, were as follows:—Lieutenant-colonel, £2 per diem; major, £1 10s.; captain, £1 5s.; lieutenant, £1 1s.; medical and veterinary officers, according to rank; staff sergeants, 10s.; company sergeant-major, 9s.; sergeant, 8s.; corporal, 7s.; artificer, 6s.; bugler, gunner, driver, or private, 4s. 6d.

For rates of pay when serving in South Africa beyond Cape Colony and Natal, *vide* 4th Victorian (Imperial) Contingent.

The companies were still numbered consecutively with those which had preceded them.

CLOTHING AND EQUIPMENT.

Uniform consisted of khaki cloth F.S. jacket, pants, puttees, hat, F.S. cap. Greatcoats and boots were also issued; and a full kit of underclothing, necessaries, &c.

Rifles and bayonets were supplied in South Africa. Cartridge belts (bandoliers) and braces issued in Queensland. Fully horsed and supplied with saddlery. Regimental transport provided. *Vide* Appendix II., p. 578.

ESTABLISHMENT.

This was as subjoined:—

Battalion Staff.—1 lieutenant-colonel, 1 major, 1 adjutant, 1 quartermaster, 1 medical officer, 1 veterinary officer, 2 staff sergeants, 1 sergeant, 1 corporal, 14 privates; total, 6 officers, 18 N.C.O.'s and men, 24 riding horses; in all, 24 of all ranks, 24 horses.

No. 6 Company.—1 major or captain, 4 lieutenants, 1 company sergeant-major, 5 sergeants, 5 artificers, 2 buglers, 6 corporals, 97 privates; total, 5 officers, 116 N.C.O.'s and men; 50 draught, 121 riding horses. In all, 121 of all ranks, 171 horses.

No. 7 and No. 8 Companies.—The same. Spare horses, 13.

Total.—1 lieutenant-colonel, 1 major, 3 company commanders, 1 adjutant, 12 lieutenants, 1 quartermaster, 1 medical officer, 1 veterinary officer, 2 staff sergeants, 3 company sergeant-majors, 16 sergeants, 15 artificers, 6 buglers, 19 corporals, 305 privates. In all, 21 officers, 366 N.C.O.'s and men; 150 draught, 400 riding horses. Grand total—387 of all ranks; 550 horses.

DEPARTURE AND RETURN.

Left on 18th May, 1900, comprising—26 officers, 368 of other ranks, with 512 horses. Fifteen were killed or died; 5 officers were transferred; 2 officers, 63 others, were struck off in South Africa; 2 were commissioned in Imperial Army; 20 officers, 288 others, returned to Australia.

Promotions, Etc.

Captain F. L. Jones was Adjutant, 17th November, 1900, to 7th August, 1901.
Lieutenant A. W. Butterworth, promoted Captain, 18th November, 1900.
Lieutenant W. I. Ferguson, Acting Adjutant, temporarily.
Sergeant A. Bailey, promoted Lieutenant and Quartermaster, 15th January, 1901, *vice* Crichton, returned to Australia.
Sergeant N. B. DeLancy Forth, received a commission in the Imperial Service, but returned invalided to Australia.
Private H. C. Morley received a commission in the Imperial Service; struck off Contingent, 17th January, 1901.
Private J. D. Henry became Lieutenant, "D" Company, 3rd Australian Commonwealth Horse.
Private V. B. Brodie became Lieutenant, 7th Australian Commonwealth Horse.
For promotions of N.C.O.'s and men, *vide* nominal roll.

Note:—The following promotions and transfers from 4th Queensland Imperial Bushmen, appeared in South African Army Orders, 7th July, 1901:—

Captain J. W. M. Carroll, to 6th Contingent (Major from the same date, Army Order, South Africa, 12th October, 1901).
Lieutenant M. A. T. Bell to 5th Contingent as Captain.
,, C. V. Sellheim   ,,   ,,   ,,
,, W. I. Ferguson   ,,   ,,   ,,
,, J. McLeod (Veterinary Officer)   ,,   ,,
Sergeant A. C. Robertson   ,,   ,,   Lieutenant.
,, H. St.C. Yaldwin   ,,   ,,   ,,
,, A. Smith   ,,   ,,   ,,
,, G. F. Livingstone   ,,   ,,   ,,
Sergeant-Major A. E. Pooley   ,,   ,,   ,,
All to be supernumerary to Establishment.

It does not appear, however, that all these officers joined the Contingents in question, *vide* nominal rolls of such Contingents; also, *vide* Note to "Promotions," 4th Victorian Contingent, p. 254.

Service.

The 4th Queensland Imperial Bushmen started for the war on the 18th May, 1900, in the transport *Manchester Port*, and arrived at Beira on the 14th June. Proceeded by order to Port Elizabeth; arrived there on the 20th; thence sent to Cape Town, and disembarked there on the 23rd, having anchored in Table Bay on the previous day, and sent ashore baggage and stores. After a short rest at Maitland Camp, entrained to Kroonstad towards Lindley, and from thence to Pretoria, and joined General Ian Hamilton's force.

On the 13th July at Honen's Nek, occurred their first casualty. A patrol having been sent out to escort guns to Wonderboom, Private Duggan was shot dead in a skirmish. 16th July.—Eastern advance, and engagement at De Waggen Drift. From 21st July to 20th August.—Advance to Rustfontein, and engagements at Honen's Nek and Zilikat's Nek. Returned to Commando Nek, marched to Rustenburg, up Maghatie's Valley, *via* Zeekoe Hoek, and Oliphant's Nek, in pursuit of De Wet. Advanced towards Warmbad, and skirmish *en route* at Krokodil Drift. Returned to Pretoria on the 28th, and remained until 10th September.

A detachment of 4 officers and 50 men then joined General French's eastern movement; the remainder, after refitting, joined General Ridley's Column, General Clements' command. 15th to 23rd September.—Operations at Maghatie's Valley; on 26th, skirmish at Zandfontein, where Lieutenant Higson was dangerously wounded. From that date to 15th October, Rustenberg, viâ Magata Pass; operations in Maghatie's Valley. Left General Clements' command, and joined General Paget's, as part of Colonel Hickman's corps; General Plumer's Column at Jericho. 24th October, a telegram was received from General Paget by Colonel Hickman, "Please inform Colonel Aytoun how gratified I am by the accounts of the results achieved by the Queensland Imperial Bushmen in so short a time, and I trust his wounded are doing well."

From that date, operations west of Rustenburg on Zelons, Koster, and Eland's Rivers, till 11th November; during which time there were several skirmishes with the enemy. Operations east of Pretoria and north of the railway; skirmishes at Oybrand's Kraal, Roodepoort, and Hartebeestfontein.

On 19th November, Lieut.-Colonel Aytoun was admitted into hospital at Pretoria, suffering from enteric; and was subsequently invalided to Australia. Major Deacon assumed command of the Battalion.

On the 29th, there was a heavy engagement at Rietfontein (Rhenoster Kop) with Ben Viljoen, from 5.30 a.m. until about 10 p.m. (*vide* 3rd Queensland Mounted Infantry "Service"), and the enemy evacuated the position on the night of the 30th.

Operations in the vicinity until 17th December; then between Rustenburg and Pretoria until 14th January, 1901. Colonel Hickman's brigade was broken up on the 18th, and the Battalion then became part of Lieut.-Colonel Craddock's brigade. Operations included a sweeping eastern movement as far as Balmoral; and operations in vicinity until 2nd February, 1901. On 24th January, by Divisional Orders, the Contingent was separated from Lieut.-Colonel Craddock's command, and formed part of Lieut.-Colonel H. B. Jeffrey's corps. Craddock's and Jeffrey's brigades were officially designated "Plumer's Force." On 31st, joined Colonel Jeffrey's corps above Balmoral, and camped there. On 1st February, 10 officers, 135 N.C.O.'s and men were available for the firing line; 53 dismounted men were shown in the weekly state. The Queenslanders had been in constant touch with the enemy, and there had been many casualties, both of men and horses; remounts being, of course, obtained from time to time.

On 3rd February, entrained at Balmoral to Naauwpoort, Cape Colony, arriving there on 7th; drew remounts, refitted, and started in pursuit of De Wet on 9th. Skirmishes, 12th, 13th, and engagement on 14th at Wolvekuilen. On the 13th the enemy were engaged twice during the afternoon, once very heavily. Lieutenant Kellaway was severely wounded. On 15th, De Wet's heavy transport ammunition wagons, over 30 (mostly full), and a maxim, were captured, having been bogged and abandoned. About twelve prisoners were also taken. Crossed the railway line at Houtkraal. Colonel Crabbe's and Colonel Henniker's Columns joined on the 16th; engagement at Geeluck's Poort on the following day. On the 23rd, the main body came in touch with the enemy about 12 noon, near Pompean Pan, Orange River, and pushed them very hard until 8 p.m.; they had to abandon a 15-pr. and a pom-pom. Thirty prisoners were taken; trekked about 40 miles this day.

Arrived at Hopetoun on 24th, obtained remounts, marched to Orange River station, and entrained there on 26th; and detrained at Springfontein on 1st March. From that date until 15th, the route was by Philippolis, Fauresmith, Pietersburg, to Winburg. Entrained at Smolldiel on 20th, and arrived at Pretoria on 22nd.

Commenced advance on Pietersburg on 26th; occupied Warmbad, **30th**; Nylstroom, 1st April; Pietpotgeiter's Rust, 5th; Marabastad, 7th; and Pietersburg, 8th; after slight opposition. Left Pietersburg, *via* Chune's Poort, 14th, to hold drifts in Oliphant's River, and operations in vicinity; returned to Pretoria, 6th May. Refitted and marched on 13th; sweeping movement towards Bethel, with almost daily skirmishes. On the 20th, orders were received to march at 6 a.m. to the vicinity of Bethel. Some resistance was made, and large parties of Boers could be seen on every skyline. Bethel was reached at 2 p.m., and a considerable number of the enemy surrendered when their stronghold was occupied. Orders were issued at 5 p.m. to burn the town; and after the women and children had been removed, the town was soon in a mass of flames.

Quitted Bethel on 22nd, and marched to Rietpan, *en route* to Standerton to replenish. The enemy was still seen in large numbers, and very daring; at one time charging up to within 250 yards of the pom-poms. Arrived at Standerton on 27th, after having been daily in touch with the Boers. Marched on the 30th; engaged in sweeping operations towards Piet Retief, which was occupied on 9th June. The 4th parted from General Plumer's force here, being under orders for Australia.

The following individual instances of gallantry in the field were specially rewarded by the General Officer Commander-in-Chief :—

Acting-Sergeant E. H. Shadforth, to be Sergeant. On patrol near Boschkop, Cape Colony, on 12th February, 1901, he brought Private Suter, whose horse had been shot, out of action under heavy fire.

Private J. Alford to be Corporal. At Driekuilen, Cape Colony, on 15th February, 1901, single-handed he took prisoners three armed and mounted Boers and a Kaffir.

Private E. Culliford to be Corporal. Same place and day, he took prisoners four armed Boers.

Private J. H. Rule to be Corporal. Same place and day, single-handed he took prisoners three armed Boers and two Kaffirs.

The 4th, escorted convoy and prisoners to Utrecht, and were involved in a half-day engagement *en route* at Elandsburg. Arrived at Utrecht on the 18th June, and on the 20th, orders were received to proceed with convoy to Newcastle, Natal, *en route* to Stormberg, for mobilization. General Plumer addressed the Regiment, and thanked them for their good service during the past 12 months. Arrived at Newcastle on 22nd; handed in all equipment on same day, and entrained for Stormberg on 23rd; arrived 28th, and on 4th July entrained for East London.

Embarked on transport *Britannic* on 5th July, together with members of Western Australian, Tasmanian, and New South Wales Contingents, with whom the 4th had served the whole time. Called at Albany (20th July), Adelaide, Melbourne, and Sydney, and arrived at Brisbane, 5th August. Disembarked on the following day, and disbanded on the 10th.

War Services and Honours.

Aytoun, Lieut.-Colonel A.—Operations in Transvaal, July to November, 1900. Despatches, *London Gazette*, 10th September, 1901. D.S.O. Queen's Medal with clasps.

Deacon, Major W. T.—Operations in Transvaal, Orange River Colony, **and** Cape Colony, July, 1900, **to** June, 1901, including actions at Rhenoster **Kop and**

Zilikat's Nek. In command from 19th November, 1900, to 7th August, 1901. Despatches, *London Gazette*, 16th April, 1901, and 7th May, 1901. C.B. Queen's Medal with four clasps.

Carroll, Captain J. W. M.—Operations as stated. Adjutant, 18th May, 1900, to 17th November, 1900. Subsequently attached to and commanded 20th Battery, R.F.A., 1st July, 1901, to —— December, 1901. Served until termination of war. Queen's Medal with three clasps. King's Medal with two clasps.

Berry, Captain J. K.—Operations as stated. Despatches, *London Gazette*, 29th July, 1902. Queen's Medal with four clasps. Commanded "D" Company, 1st Australian Commonwealth Horse.

Durham, Captain H. R. P.—Operations as stated. Queen's Medal with clasps.

Jones, Captain F. L.—Operations as stated. Despatches, *London Gazette*, 29th July, 1902. Queen's Medal with four clasps.

Joseph, Captain E. J.—Operations as stated. Queen's Medal with clasps.

Crichton, Captain A. E., Quartermaster.—Operations as stated. Queen's Medal with clasps.

Butterworth, Captain A. W.—Operations as stated. Queen's Medal with clasps.

Bell, Lieutenant M. A. T.—Operations as stated. Served subsequently with 5th Contingent. Queen's Medal with three clasps. King's Medal with two clasps.

Cowley, C., *Crichton*, A. D., and *Philp*, C. J. C. (Lieutenants).—Operations as stated. Subsequently proceeded to South Africa with details. Queen's Medal with four clasps.

Ferguson, Lieutenant W. I.—Operations as stated. Served subsequently with 5th Contingent. Queen's Medal with three clasps. King's Medal with two clasps.

Green, Lieutenant W. A. G. E.—Operations as stated. Subsequently served in "D" Company, 1st Australian Commonwealth Horse. Queen's Medal with three clasps. King's Medal with two clasps.

Kellaway, Lieutenant W. J.—Operations as stated. Severely wounded, 13th February, 1901. Queen's Medal with four clasps.

Sellheim, Lieutenant C. V.—Operations as stated. Served subsequently with 5th Contingent as Captain. Queen's Medal with three clasps. King's Medal with two clasps.

Graham, D. M. L., *Higson*, J., *Hyde*, C. E. W., *Kemp*, W. T., *Parker*, C. A., and *Pickburn*, W. H. (Lieutenants).—Operations as stated. Queen's Medal with four clasps. Lieutenant Parker served as Captain with 7th Australian Commonwealth Horse.

Nisbet, Major W. B. (Army Medical Corps).—Operations as stated. Queen's Medal with four clasps.

McLeod, Lieutenant J., Veterinary Officer.—Operations as stated. Subsequent service with 5th Contingent and 7th Australian Commonwealth Horse. Queen's Medal with three clasps. King's Medal with two clasps.

Bailey, Lieut.-Quartermaster A.—Operations as stated. Queen's Medal with four clasps.

Day, Rev. C. V. P. (Chaplain, Hon. Captain).—Operations as stated. Queen's Medal with clasps.

Nominal Roll.

No. and Name.	Rank.	Remarks.
Officers.		
Aytoun, Andrew	Lieut.-Colonel	Invalided to Australia, arr. —.12.00
Deacon, William Thomas	Major	
Carroll, John Walter Maxwell	Captain-Adjutant	
Jones, Francis Lionel	Captain	
Durham, Herbert Rowland Pasley	,,	Transport Officer
Joseph, Ernest Joseph	,,	
Berry, James Kinkaid	,,	
Butterworth, Archibald William	Lieutenant	Invalided to England, —.1.01
Sellheim, Casimir Vaux	,,	
Kemp, William Thomas	,,	
Kellaway, William John	,,	Severely wounded at Grasfontein, 13.2.01
Crichton, Aubrey De Pree	,,	
Bell, Marmaduke Alexander Thomas	,,	
Higson, John	,,	Severely wounded at Zandfontein, 25.9.00
Graham, Dugald Maxwell Lockwood	,,	
Hyde, Charles Edward Whithorn	,,	
Ferguson, William Isaac	,,	
Parker, Charles Albert	,,	
Green, William Alfred Goodall Esdaile	,,	
Philp, Colin John Campbell	,,	Supernumerary
Cowley, Campbell	,,	Supernumerary
Pickburn, William Henry	,,	Supernumerary
Crichton, Archibald Edward	Quartermaster-Captain	
Nisbet, Walter Blake	Major, A.M.C.	
McLeod, John	Veterinary-Lieut.	
Day, Rev. C. V. P.	Hon. Captain Chaplain	
N.C.O.'s and Men.		
1. Atwell, William	Sergeant-Major	
2. Wright, George Percival	Quartermaster-Sergeant	
3. Harris, Henry George	Company Sergeant-Major	
4. Upton, Charles Morris	,, ,,	
5. O'Brien, Charles David	Private	Invalided to Australia, arr. 8.12.00
6. Gill, John Frederick	Company Sergeant-Major	Mentioned in C.-in-C.'s despatches, 31.3.00
7. Bailey, Arthur	Private	Sergeant, 1.6.00. *Vide* " Promotions " and " War Services "
8. Decent, Thomas Fox	,,	Corporal, 1.6.00
9. Wienholt, Arnold	,,	Sergeant, 1.6.00
10. Livingstone, George Frank	,,	Sergeant, 1.6.00. *Vide* " Promotions "
11. Towner, Alfred George	,,	
12. Cuming, Percy Richard	,,	
13. Brown, David	,,	
14. Beatty, Wilson Dacres	,,	Corporal, 29.12.00
15. Morrice, George	,,	
16. Henry, John George	,,	

Nominal Roll—*continued*.

No. and Name.	Rank.	Remarks.
N.C.O.'s AND MEN—*continued*.		
17. Kercher, George James	Private	
18. Hobson, John Ernest	,,	
19. De Lancey-Forth, Nowell Barnard	,,	Sergeant, 1.6.00. *Vide* "Promotions"
20. Rowe, Frederick James	,,	
21. Moore, Thomas Peat	,,	
22. Remfrey, George Harold	,,	Invalided to Australia, arr. 15.9.00
23. Jordan, John	,,	Corporal, 29.12.00
24. Kingsmill, Herbert Cyrus	,,	
25. Anderson, William Albert	,,	Returned to Australia, discharged 5.7.01
26. Cottam, Robert Henry	,,	
27. Howard, Harry	,,	
28. Richardson, Robert	,,	Invalided to Australia, arr. 27.9.00
29. Barnett, James	,,	Returned to Australia, arr. 25.3.01
30. Smith, Albert	,,	Sergeant, 1.6.00 *Vide* "Promotions"
31. Gardiner, John David	,,	Wounded at Hamman Kraal. 17.7.00
32. Browne, William	,,	
33. Yaldwyn, Hamilton St. Clair	,,	Sergeant, 1.6.00 *Vide* "Promotions"
34 Robertson, Arthur Campbell	,,	Corporal, 1.6.00; Sergeant, 29.12.00. *Vide* "Promotions"
35. Mathison, William	,,	
36. Boyd, Robert	,,	Corporal, 1.6.00
37. Worrall, John Peter	,,	
38. Burn, William Castle	,,	
39. Bell, Malcolm	,,	
40. Whyte, Albert John	,,	
41. Thomson, James Reily	,,	Corporal, 1.6.00
42. Bernard, Richard	,,	
43. Smith, Clarence Sydney	Farrier	
44. Grimes, Thomas	Private	Invalided to Australia, arr. 10.12.00
45. Leach, Albert Forrest	,,	
46. Hackwood, Charles Wesley	,,	
47. Suter, George	,,	
48. O'Connor, Daniel Patrick	,,	
49. Thomas, James	,,	
50. Anderson, Hans Peter	,,	
51. Mann, John	,,	
52. McInnes, Colin	,,	
53. Henderson, Edward William	,,	Invalided to Australia, arr. 25.8.00
54. King, Ambrose Ernest	,,	
55. Smith, George	,,	
56. Harrop, George	,,	Corporal, 18.3.01
57. Ruttley, Charles James	,,	
58. Lamb, John Foster	,,	
59. O'Donnell, James	,,	
60. Dawson, George Henry Moss	,,	
61. Castles, Joseph	,,	
62. Achilles, Frederick	,,	
63. Dowzer, Nathan Esli	,,	
64. Keilar, Alexander	,,	
65. Culliford, Ernest	,,	Promoted Corporal, 15.2.01, by C.-in-C. for distinguished gallantry in the field. G.O. 386/01

Nominal Roll—continued.

No. and Name.	Rank.	Remarks.
N.C.O.'S AND MEN—continued.		
66. Naylor, Walter	Private	
67. Hastie, Peter Stewart	,,	Died of pneumonia, St. Vincent's Hospital, Sydney, 24.5.00
68. McIntosh, Charles John	,,	
69. Coleman, John	,,	
70. Rule, John Holland	,,	Promoted to Corporal, 15.2.01, by C.-in-C. for distinguished gallantry in the field. G.O. 386/01
71. White, Ernest Albert	Farrier	
72. O'Neill, John Joseph	Private	
73. McPherson, Alexander	,,	
74. Young, Lionel Hugh Wardell	,,	Killed in action, Doomlaagte, 28.9.00
75. Smith, Frederick Edward	,,	Invalided to Australia, arr. 19.11.00
76. West, John Henry Ernest	,,	Sergeant, 1.6.00
77. Duggan, James	,,	Killed in action, Honen's Nek, 13.7.00
78. Graham, Thomas Alexander	,,	
79. Power, James Charles	,,	Promoted to Sergeant, A.O., S.A. Gallantry and good service in action. G.O. 267/01
80. Raymond, Arthur Ernest	,,	
81. Bolton, Henry	,,	
82. Farrell, John Joseph	,,	
83. Greer, Joseph Norman	,,	
84. Graham, Thomas	,,	
85. Crawshaw, Robert Wilkinson	,,	
86. Turner, James Arthur	,,	
87. Gillespie, James McBride	,,	
88. Searle, Frederick Henry	,,	
89. Macdonald, John Kenneth	,,	
90. Bancroft, John	,,	
91. Bruce, William Robit	Farrier	
92. Gray, Arthur Alva	Private	Invalided to Australia, arr. 8.12.00
93. Stirling, Robert	,,	
94. Burton, George Alfred	,,	
95. Chapman, James Francis	,,	
96. Murphy, James	,,	
97. Miller, Andrew Reid	,,	
98. Horsburgh, George Turner	,,	
99. Townshend, Ernest	,,	
100. Buckley, George William	,,	
101. Rodd, Edward George	,,	
102. Taylor, Frederick Maurice Burden	,,	
103. Cave, Alfred Noble	,,	
104. Knox, William	,,	
105. Wilson, Frederick	,,	
106. Johnson, Louis Victor	,,	Corporal, 1.6.00
107. Johnston, William Henry	,,	Returned to Australia, arr. 19.2.01
108. Detmold, Percy George	,,	
109. Rumbelow, William	,,	
110. Miller, John	,,	
111. Reynallt, Matthew Henry	,,	Corporal
112. Perrett, Arthur	,,	Returned to Australia, arr. 25.3.01
113. Stibbards, David	,,	
114. Dwyer, Arthur Ernest Icly		

Nominal Roll—*continued.*

No. and Name.	Rank.	Remarks.
N.C.O.'s AND MEN—*continued.*		
115. Garden, James Alexander	Private	Slightly wounded at Jericho, 29.10.00
116. Dooley, Patrick Michael	,,	
117. Hollis, Joseph Dowling	,,	Invalided to Australia, arr. 1.9.00
118. Meek, Frederick Maurice	,,	
119. Thomas, Theobald Edmond	,,	
120. Nattrass, William Francis	,,	
121. Watkins, James Augustus	,,	
122. Kennedy, Patrick	,,	Orderly-Room Sergeant, 1.6.00
123. Tucker, Henry Frederick Wallace	,,	Invalided to Australia, arr. 8.12.00
124. Brodie, Vernon Bissett	,,	*Vide* " Promotions "
125. Hill, Vutor Austin	,,	
126. Hutchinson, Richard Charles	,,	Mentioned in C.-in-C.'s despatches, 31.3.00
127. Purcell, John Joseph	,,	
128. Elliott, Arthur Bowen	,,	
129. Costello, Martin	,,	
130. Sherman, Charles	,,	
131. Ellis, Aubrey Thomas	,,	
132. Jauncey, George Essex	,,	
133. Rutter, Arthur George	,,	
135. Riddell, Charles Henry	,,	
136. Shearer, John Hooks	,,	Invalided to Australia, arr. 8.12.00
137. Sturgess, Arthur	,,	
138. Murray, Alfred Douglas	,,	Corporal, 1.6.00
139. Crisp, Herbert Edward	,,	Corporal, 1.6.00 ; Sergeant
140. Perkins, John Joseph	,,	Sergeant, 1.6.00
141. Matters, William Adolphus	,,	
142. Greenaway, James Herbert	,,	
143. Plowman, Alfred	,,	
144. Robertson, Hugh Clive	,,	
145. Kelk, Eustace	,,	
146. Corner, Robert Henry	,,	
147. Lynd, James William	,,	Died of wounds, Jericho, 23.10.00
148. Cunningham, Joseph	,,	
149. Ross, Claudius Ralph Mackenzie	,,	
150. Hamilton, John Henry	,,	
151. Herkes, Robert	,,	
152. Herth, Harry Roy	,,	
153. Weatherley, George	,,	
154. King, Charles Ernest	,,	
155. Micklem, Lionel Offley	,,	
156. Volkman, Thomas Paul	,,	
157. Barton, Lionel Salter	,,	
158. Murch, Albert Charles	,,	
159. Barnes, Charles Grafton	,,	Mentioned in C.-in-C.'s despatches, 31.3.00. Returned to Australia, discharged, 5.7.01
160. Markwell, Edmondstone	,,	
161. Watson, Walter Henry	,,	
162. Wilson, Joseph Stephen	,,	
163. Gardiner, Alfred William Gabriel	,,	
164. Bennett, William Charles	,,	
165. Durack, James Edward	,,	
166. Giltrow, William	,,	
167. Sacre, Edgar Thomas	,,	
168. Huston, Robert Ernest	,,	Farrier-Sergeant
169. Schipkie, John Charles Frederick	,,	

Nominal Roll—*continued.*

No. and Name.	Rank.	Remarks.
N.C.O.'S AND MEN—*continued.*		
170. Maddock, George Hamilton Sydney	Private	Sergeant, 1.6.00
171. Cudmore, Henry Carrington	,,	
172. Brickwood, Robert Hugh	,,	Severely wounded at Heilbron. 19.10.00
173. Kelly, Michael Augustine	,,	
174. Anderson, Robert	,,	
175. Simpson, David	,,	
176. Howe, Samuel James	,,	
177. Jackson, John	,,	
178. Hannan, Michael John	,,	
179. Nolan, William Patrick	,,	
180. Downie, James Duncan	,,	Corporal, 1.6.00
181. Maitlend, Rhys	,,	
182. Myers, Alexander Stuart	,,	
183. Kelly, William	,,	
184. Broatch, William	,,	
185. Bennett, George Henry	,,	
186. Parker, Martin	,,	
187. Murray, Henry Baylis	,,	
188. Clarke, Arthur Hill	,,	Mentioned in C.-in-C.'s despatches 31.3.00
189. Yorston, Allan Bell Renton	Bugler	Corporal, 1.6.00
190. Wildie, Walter	Private	Corporal, 1.6.00
191. Marles, Leopold Baptist	Bugler	
192. Thompson, Victor Emanuel	,,	
193. Carter, William Robert	,,	
194. Purves, Godfrey Liddle	Private	
195. Strang, James	,,	Sergeant, 1.6.00. Died of wounds, Houtkraal, 16.2.01
196. Hanley, James John	,,	
197. Beatty, Sidney Stuart	,,	Corporal, 1.6.00
198. Wagner, Albert	,,	
199. Barclay, William	,,	
200. Perske, John Frederick	,,	Sergeant, 1.6.00
201. Christie, Albert William	,,	
202. Maxwell, Francis	,,	Sergeant, 1.6.00. Killed in action at Hamman's Kraal, 17.7.00, endeavouring to save a comrade
203. Smith, James	,,	
204. McLeod, Donald John Roderick	,,	Died of bronchitis, Pretoria, 19.8.00
205. Boydell, William Pearce	,,	Corporal, 29.12.00
206. Grieve, John Hay	,,	
207. Hore, Victor Thomas George	,,	
208. Galligan, John Joseph	,,	
209. Holdway, John	,,	
210. Cook, Edward Christian	,,	Wounded and taken prisoner at Doornlaagte, 29.9.00; escaped to Krugersdorp
211. Turner, Charles	,,	Corporal, 1.6.00
213. Hill, Onslow Frederick Stanley	,,	
214. Caller, Albert	,,	
215. Clark, Raymond Joseph	,,	
216. Rappel, John Robert	,,	Sergeant, 1.6.00
217. Skelton, John Telfer	,,	
218. Douglas, Theophilus Thomas	,,	

Nominal Roll—*continued.*

No. and Name.	Rank.	Remarks.
N.C.O.'s AND MEN—*continued.*		
219. Bolam, John Robert	Private	
220. Hockings, Frank	,,	Invalided to Australia, arr. 19.11.00
221. Vardy, Joseph Francis	,,	Corporal, 1.6.00; Sergeant, 29.12.00
222. Lindore, James William	,,	
223. Pooley, Alfred Ernest	,,	Sergeant, 1.6.00; Sergeant-Major. *Vide* "Promotions"
224. Lamrose, George	,,	
225. Baglietto, Eugene	,,	
226. Smith, Arthur	,,	
227. MacRae, Donald	,,	
228. Symes, Arthur Rowley Thomas	,,	Corporal, 1.6.00
229. Henry, James Douglas	,,	*Vide* "Promotions"
230. Gilbert, Richard Edward	,,	Invalided to Australia, arr. 8.12.00
231. Whipham, Arthur Guy	,,	
232. Noakes, George Tanner	,,	
233. Scougall, Percy Burdett	,,	
234. Lindley, Horace William	,,	
235. Meredith, Charles	,,	Died of enteric, Pretoria, 19.8.00
236. Flood, Luke	,,	
237. Sutor, August William	,,	Taken prisoner, Kailfontein, 12.8.00
238. Suter, Robert Ackland	,,	
239. Hood, John Stuart	,,	
240. Doyle, Graham	,,	
241. Seldon, Robert	Bugler	
242. Healey, James Joseph	Private	Slightly wounded at Oliphant's River, 26.4.01
243. Lehman, William	,,	Severely wounded at Rietfontein, 29.11.00
244. Goodwin, David John	,,	
245. Cousens, Harry Richmond	,,	
246. Stuart, William James	,,	Invalided to Australia, arr. 10.12.00
247. Thone, James	,,	
248. Helder, John Oliver	,,	Killed in action, Doornlaagte, 28.9.00
249. Bowes, Charles Henry	,,	
250. Phillips, William Henry	,,	Invalided to Australia, arr. 18.8.00
251. Bassman, Arthur Clarence	Shoeing Smith	Invalided to Australia, arr. 16.1.01
252. Bourke, John	Farrier-Sergeant	Invalided to Netley, England, arr. 4.12.00
253. Eales, Francis Edgar	Private	
254. Luxton, Charles	Farrier-Sergeant	
255. Ingram, William James	Private	
256. O'Brien, Jack	,,	
257. Ross, Reginald Roy Mackenzie	,,	
258. Mulray, Richard	,,	Invalided to Australia, arr. **8.12.00**
259. Wills, Cedric Spencer, jun.	,,	
260. Blank, Richard Henry	,,	
261. White, Alfred	,,	
262. Lawson, Charles Henry	,,	
263. Wood, Peter	,,	
264. McGladdery, William	,,	Corporal, 29.12.00
265. Livingstone, William	,,	
266. Clarke, Thomas	,,	
267. Robins, James Alexander	,,	

Nominal Roll—*continued*.

No. and Name.	Rank.	Remarks.
N.C.O.'S AND MEN—*continued*.		
268. Malcomson, Thomas James	Private	
269. Devine, Donald	,,	
270. Soden, John Adams	,,	
271. Beatty, Frank Percy	,,	
272. Luck, Guy Harold	,,	
273. Adamson, Charles Young	,,	Corporal, 1.6.00 ; Quartermaster-Sergeant, 6.4.01
274. McPherson, John Fraser	,,	
275. Sloan, William Christopher	,,	
276. Lovegrove, Arthur Sidney	,,	
277. Mitchell, George McPherson	,,	
278. Loder, Edward	,,	
279. Clancy, Peter James	,,	Killed in action, Zandfontein, 25.9.00
280. Shadforth, Ernest Hollinworth	,,	Corporal, 1.6.00 ; Sergeant by C.-in-C. for distinguished gallantry in the field, 29.12.00. G.O. 386/01
282. Colville, William	,,	
283. Daws, George	,,	Died of enteric, Pretoria, 15.8.00
284. Poole, William Shortly	,,	Died of enteric, Pretoria, 30.8.00
285. Bettany, Harry	,,	
286. Williams, Meredith George	,,	Corporal, 1.6.00
287. Bendall, Thomas	,,	
288. Leishman, James	,,	
289. Alford, John	,,	Promoted to Corporal, 15.2.01, by C.-in-C. for distinguished gallantry in the field. G.O. 386/01.
290. Dodds, Edward Swain	,,	
291. Daniels, William John	,,	
292. Richards, Frank	,,	
293. Crossman, James Knight	,,	
294. Montgomery, William Cumming	,,	
295. Clarke, James	,,	
296. Wright, Alfred Edwin	,,	Killed in action, Rietfontein, 29.11.00
297. Mitchell, Maurice	,,	
298. Mulholland, William John	,,	Invalided to Australia, arr. 8.12.00
299. Yeatman, Frederick	,,	
300. Greig, William Fraser	,,	
301. Thompson, Hiram Preston	,,	Invalided to Australia, arr. 10.12.00
302. Petersen, Charles Frederick	Farrier	Sergeant
305. Akred, James Allen	Private	Corporal, 1.6.00
306. Goddard, Stanley Jansen Prince	,,	
307. Frazer, Norman	,,	
308. Melon, John	,,	
309. Timewell, William John	,,	
310. Welch, Herbert Henry	,,	
311. Mumford, George Stealey	,,	
312. McDougall, Alexander	,,	Invalided to Australia, arr. 8.12.00
313. Lucas, Frank William	,,	Mentioned in C.-in-C.'s despatches, 31.3.00
314. Reardon, Peter William	,,	
316. O'Sullivan, Francis	,,	
317. Cunningham, John Thomas	,,	
318. Taggart, Thomas Henry	,,	
319. Wales, William John	,,	

Nominal Roll—continued.

No. and Name.	Rank.	Remarks.
N.C.O.'s AND MEN—continued.		
320. Hastie, Thomas	Private	
321. Cobon, Thomas	,,	Invalided to Australia, arr. 18.8.00
322. Busher, William James	,,	
323. Thorn, George	,,	
324. Smith, Thomas Hope	,,	
325. Butler, William	,,	Died of heart disease, Bloemfontein, 26.1.01
326. Payne, George Herbert	,,	
327. Glover, John Edward	,,	Severely wounded at Balmoral, 23.1.01
328. Butler, Robert Thomas	,,	
329. Holpen, Archie	,,	
330. Grogan, Martin	,,	
331. Derrett, Walter	,,	Invalided to Australia, arr. 16.1.01
332. Griffin, Louis Gerald	,,	
333. Saunders, William Frederick	,,	
334. Bartlett, William Henry Augustus	,,	
335. Clark, Alexander	,,	
336. Bourke, Arthur Clinton	,,	Died of enteric, Pretoria, 12.9.00
337. Morris, Herbert	,,	
338. Black, Archibald Syme	,,	
339. Morrison, William Wilson	,,	Farrier-Sergeant
340. Shaw, Frederick	,,	
341. Birt, George Howard, jun.	,,	
342. O'Connell, James	,,	
343. Micklethwaite, Richard Spencer	,,	
344. Cunningham, Alexander	,,	
345. Carter, Joseph Richard	,,	
346. Easton, Frank	,,	
347. Hair, Victor Arthur	,,	
348. Boyle, James McKenzie	,,	Returned to Australia, arr. 25.3.01
349. Hetherington, Cecil Somerville	,,	
350. Richardson, William Egbert	,,	
351. Wilkins, William James	,,	Sergeant, 1.6.00
352. Holpen, Frederick Ernest	,,	
353. Jarmain, Thomas Edward	,,	
355. Queale, Oliver	,,	
356. Robinson, William James	Bugler	
357. Blakeway, Thomas	Private	
358. McFadzen, Fergus George	,,	
359. Thomasson, William John	,,	
360. Block, Joseph	,,	
361. Richards, Thomas	,,	
362. Hood, Robert	,,	
363. Lunn, Richard	,,	Corporal, 1.6.00
364. Allen, George	,,	
365. Bridges, Thomas George	,,	Corporal
366. Webb, William George	,,	
367. Stewart, Ralph	Saddler	
368. Gamgee, Stewart Edward	Private	
369. Lake, Harry	,,	
370. Arlidge, Alexander John	,,	
371. Morley, Harold Collison	,,	*Vide* "Promotions"
372. Templeton, Samuel Shaw	,,	
373. Mackenzie, William Hogarth	,,	
374. Adams, Charles Langslon	,,	
375. Allen, Thomas George	,,	

FIFTH (QUEENSLAND IMPERIAL BUSHMEN) CONTINGENT.

THIS was another Regiment of Imperial Bushmen, similar to the preceding. For conditions of enlistment, clothing, and equipment, *vide* 4th Queensland Imperial Bushmen.

RATES OF PAY.

The following were the rates of pay from date of embarkation :—

Commanding officer, 25s. per diem; major, 23s.; captain, adjutant, and quartermaster, 21s.; lieutenant, 15s.; transport officer, according to rank; medical officer, 20s.; regimental sergeant-major, 9s.; regimental quartermaster-sergeant, 8s. 6d.; company sergeant-major, 8s.; other sergeants, 7s.; corporal, bugler, saddler, farrier, 6s.; private, 5s.

Field, Colonial, and any other allowance in addition. Each officer received £50 for his outfit.

ESTABLISHMENT.

Battalion Staff.—1 lieut.-colonel or major, 1 adjutant, 1 quartermaster, 1 transport officer, 1 medical officer, 3 staff sergeants (R.S.M., R.Q.M.S., transport sergeant), 1 clerk (staff sergeant), 2 clerks (rank and file), 3 medical orderlies, 6 batmen; total, 5 officers, 4 staff sergeants, 11 rank and file. In all, 20, with 10 private, 10 public riding horses.

Detail of a company.—1 major or captain, 4 subalterns, 1 company sergeant-major, 4 sergeants, 1 farrier-sergeant, 2 shoeing-smiths, 1 saddler, 1 bugler, 8 corporals, 115 privates, 5 batmen; total, 5 officers, 5 sergeants, 4 artificers, 1 bugler, 128 rank and file. In all, 143, with 10 private, 133 public riding horses, in all, 143.

Cyclist Company.—2 subalterns, 1 colour-sergeant, 2 sergeants, 2 artificers, 2 corporals, 42 privates (including 2 batmen); total, 2 officers, 3 sergeants, 2 artificers, 44 rank and file. In all, 51.

Draft to follow Contingent.—1 subaltern, 1 sergeant, 2 corporals, 22 privates, including 1 batman; total, 1 officer, 1 sergeant, 24 rank and file; with 2 private, 25 public riding horses, and 73 spare horses—100 altogether.

Recapitulation.—Battalion staff—5 officers, 4 staff sergeants, 11 rank and file; total 20; with 10 private, 10 public riding horses.

Three companies.—15 officers, 15 sergeants, 12 artificers, 3 buglers, 384 rank and file; total, 429; with 30 private, 399 public riding horses; total, 429.

Cyclist Company.—2 officers, 3 sergeants, 2 artificers, 44 rank and file; total, 51. Spare horse, 1.

Draft.—1 officer, 1 sergeant, 24 rank and file; total, 26; with 2 private, 98 public riding horses.

Grand total.—23 officers, 23 staff sergeants and sergeants, 14 artificers, 3 buglers, 463 rank and file—526 of all ranks; with 42 private, 508 public riding horses, or 550 altogether. (Veterinary officer was appointed for the voyage only, but obtained permission on arrival in South Africa to remain with the Battalion during the period of service).

Draught horses were to be supplied by the Imperial authorities in South Africa. It will be observed that the establishment of a company had been greatly increased; preference being given apparently to a detail of three large companies, rather than four smaller ones. *Vide* 6th Contingent ("Service") as regards this.

Each of the officers (except those of the Cyclist company) took 2 private horses.

Batmen were fully trained Mounted Infantry men, and rode spare horses.

PROMOTIONS.

Captain F. W. Toll, promoted Major, 17th April, 1901.
Lieutenant H. R. Carter, promoted Captain, 17th April, 1901.
Sergeant-Major F. B. Knyvett became Lieutenant, 7th Australian Commonwealth Horse.
For promotions of N.C.O.'s and men, *vide* nominal roll.

DEPARTURE AND RETURN.

The Contingent left on 6th and 10th March, 1901, comprising—23 officers, 506 others; with 476 horses. Two officers, 33 others, were killed or died; 12 officers, 58 others, were struck off in South Africa; 16 officers, 413 others, returned to Australia.

SERVICE.

This Contingent departed in the transport *Templemore*, on 6th March, 1901, and arrived at Port Elizabeth on 1st April. Left by three trains for Kroonstad on the same day, and reached there on the 4th; thence to Elandsfontein, and thence *viâ* The Springs to Pretoria, arriving on the 9th. From this city, the 5th entrained for Pietersburg, that being the terminus of the northern line held by the enemy, and on which the 3rd and 4th Queensland Contingents were marching. Arrived on the 11th; and on the following day the Battalion was attached to Colonel Jeffreys' Corps, of Brigadier-General H. C. O. Plumer's "Force," (consisting of Craddock's and Jeffreys' Brigades), with which it served continuously.

On the 10th March, a draft, consisting of 1 subaltern, 1 sergeant, and 24 rank and file, with 100 horses, left Pinkenba (Brisbane) by the transport *Chicago*; disembarked at Port Elizabeth on 20th April, and joined the Contingent.

Having received remounts and transport, the 5th started on trek south-easterly on 14th April, and were engaged on outpost and patrol duty in the neighbourhood of Oliphant's River, until 25th. Then the force under Colonel Jeffreys was divided into three parts, and came in contact with the enemy in the vicinity of Tabak Plaats Camp, when a brisk skirmish ensued. Since leaving Pietersburg, no less than 170 horses had either died or been destroyed, suffering from "horse-sickness." On 28th, trekked south-west, and joined remainder of Plumer's force at Badfontein. Passed through Coomassie Poort and Usekraal, and arrived at Silverton, 5 miles from Pretoria, on 6th May. Left on 14th; reached Bethel (then being burned) on 21st; and participated in action at Mooifontein on 25th. At Standerton on 27th, and marched on 30th; Hartab on 2nd June, having constantly encountered parties of the enemy, and brought in prisoners, sheep, horses, goats, and vehicles.

At Piet Retief on 10th, where the Cyclist company, having proved unsuitable, were all mounted (except six) with horses of the 4th Contingent, which was returning home. Thence to Zinderhoek; and on 15th, skirmish at Slaughn's Berg. On 17th, at Kopje Eileen; and operations as far as Utrecht on 23rd. Started on 28th to trek through Privaan's Poort; various operations, and halted at Bothwell, 7th July. Thence to Carolina and Klippan by 12th, and to Wonderfontein; at which place entrained on 16th in four trains, destination unknown, but on 18th detrained at Bloemfontein. Marched on 24th to Kruger Drift; arrived at Poplar Grove on 26th, and Modder River on 31st. Lieut.-Colonel Flewell-Smith here received notice to proceed to Cape Town by train to take up appointment as a District Commandant in Cape Colony. The command of the Battalion thereupon devolved upon Major F. W. Toll during the remainder of their campaign.

It would be needless to recapitulate, step by step, the treks taken, of which the foregoing offers a fair example. Suffice it to state, that during August, the Contingent went west and south-west (Orange River Colony), and north-west (Cape Colony). In September and October, south-east (Orange River Colony); operations on Caledon River, at Wepener, and Mokari Drift. November to January, 1902, south-east (Transvaal); January to March, north-east (Orange River Colony). Like other Contingents, they had large casualties in the horses, owing to sickness, over-work, scanty feed, and losses by the enemy. On 8th May only 92 were on strength; and since 14th April, 84 had been sent to sick depots, and 260 had died. In such emergencies, prior to remounts joining, the dismounted men were carried in wagons, or walked and rode alternately.

The 5th saw plenty of fighting. They were constantly in touch with the enemy, and besides innumerable small skirmishes, mention may be made of operations of 24th and 25th May at Klipfontein and Mooifontein; and Mokari Drift, Caledon River, 27th September, where Lieutenants Pooley and Caskey and two men were killed, and four wounded.

On 6th December, with Colonel Pultney's Column at Beelzebub (South-Eastern Transvaal). The force marched at 6 p.m.; Jervis's corps on left, Pultney's on right, Colvin's Corps, with General Plumer, in centre, with Jervis's and Colvin's guns and transport. At 4.30 a.m., the 5th in advance, sighted the enemy's outposts at Familie Hoek, and drove them into camp at a gallop, when they appeared in great force. On the supports coming up, the 5th again advanced, compelling the enemy to retreat, when they brought up their full force and charged; but Major Toll held his position until Colvin's corps came up with the guns and compelled the foe to evacuate the position, about 2 p.m. There were estimated to be 800 Boers present, including men from the Ermelo, Wakkerstrom, and Carolina commandoes. The casualty list of the 5th comprised 1 killed, 1 died of wounds on 16th, 9 wounded; 3 captured, disarmed, and released. The Commanding Officer was warmly complimented by the General, who regretted that he had been unable to support him earlier.

The disastrous affair at Onverwacht, 4th January, 1902, is remarkable as showing the determined stand made by the Boers, even at this late stage of hostilities, when they obtained an opportunity. The 5th were then in " Vallentin's Corps "; Major Vallentin (Somerset Light Infantry) having succeeded Lieut.-Colonel Sir John Jervis in the command of what had been known as " Jervis's Corps, Plumer's Force." All the mounted troops and light transport moved at 5 a.m. from Rotterdam, with two days' rations and forage. Vallentin's Corps with one pom-pom, was detached on left flank; with 110 of the 5th, under Major Toll, in advance. The country was very difficult, being mountainous and rough, and the enemy offered some slight resistance. On arriving at Onverwacht in the vicinity of Bankop, their scouts could be seen retiring. The officer commanding corps decided to halt on the high ground for a couple of hours. The Queensland Imperial Bushmen, except an advanced screen of about 20, held a semi-circle of about 3 miles as observation posts.

A patrol having reported some 50 Boers with cattle in a kloof on left about 2 miles off, Major Vallentin decided to attack; but, upon moving off, a number of Boers were reported about $\frac{1}{2}$ mile in front of posts, hidden in a deep hollow. Major Vallentin ordered a change of front with the pom-pom, and gallop. A small company of Imperial Yeomanry were put out as a screen, and the Queensland Imperial Bushmen, having moved off, took a little time to swing round. The party acting as support were ordered to support the Imperial Yeomanry, but had no sooner left the gun than a withering fire was opened on the advance, hitting the officer commanding the Imperial Yeomanry, whereupon the screen at once retired. The enemy galloped for the gun from the front and left flank; the supports under Lieutenant Reese were ordered to dismount and check their advance.

Major Vallentin retired with the pom-pom at a gallop, and opened fire from from top of the ridge. About 200 Boers appeared on the left, and Major Vallentin again ordered the retirement of the gun; but after limbering up the wheel-horses were shot. The right flankers, under Captain Carter and Lieutenant Higginson, came between the gun and the advancing enemy. They dismounted and held with great gallantry the position taken up, though absolutely without cover. Sergeant Power and Private Goodall were killed here; Captain Carter, Lieutenant Higginson, and six men wounded. The gun would have been captured but for the stubborn resistance of the Queensland Imperial Bushmen, aided by a few of the Hampshire Mounted Infantry.

The rapid advance of the enemy was temporarily checked; but to no avail, for they outnumbered the defence by five or six to one. A steady retirement was carried out on foot; all horses being sent back under cover of the ridge some distance in rear, upon which it was desired to fall back. Lieutenant Cook with a small party on extreme left, were cut off and captured in a tremendous rush by the enemy; Sergeant Berry killed, and all but Lieutenant Cook and two men wounded.

The remainder of the Queenslanders retired to the ridge overlooking the river; and here the Imperial Yeomanry were ordered to hold the position, and the Mounted Infantry to support the Queenslanders; the gun to be protected until the arrival of support from the main Column, halted about 5 miles on the other side of the river. A gallant resistance was now made. The Boers eventually secured the ridge in rear, from which they were enabled to shoot down the defenders with ease, firing from a range of 50 yards; though those in front had been two or three times repulsed, after getting within 30 yards, and two were killed only 10 yards in front. On the knob held, only about 40 feet long, and with very little cover from the front, 10 men were killed, and 14 N.C.O.'s and men wounded.

The Boers secured the position from the rear. They stripped the officers and men of all but clothing, and, in a few cases, boots and coats were taken. Shortly after this, the gun from the main Column opened fire, but with no results. The Boers retired, after collecting rifles, etc., and horses (about 30 of which they obtained alive out of nearly 100), and taking their dead and wounded away on these animals.

About an hour afterwards relief came with the ambulance; and it was reported that Major Vallentin had been killed and three out of four of his staff wounded. All the disarmed men were ordered back to the pom-pom. Captain Dodds collected about 30 armed men; the others picked up rifles which had belonged to killed and wounded, and with these, and the 5th Victorians, who had now arrived, a defensive position was taken up, and the ridge securely "sangared" (or a stone wall built round it) to hold the pom-pom.

The officers captured with Major Toll were Lieutenants Loynes, Hunter, Clerk, and Reese, Warrant Officer Price, and two officers of Hants Mounted Infantry; one wounded. On the field were found 19 of the corps, killed; and 39 wounded officers and men.

Lieut.-Colonel Vialls was placed in temporary command of the corps. On advancing about 2 miles, the enemy were again met, and made a determined dash, but 300 men were already in position, and the pom-poms did havoc. The Boers soon retreated in disorder, and were not again in action. General Plumer on viewing the position, assured Major Toll that he was quite satisfied that that officer and his men had done all in their power against terrible odds.

On 12th March, 1902, their campaign having drawn to a close, the 5th (being then part of Colonel Vialls' corps), arrived at Volksrust, where they handed over horses, wagons, &c., and on the 19th, entrained for Cape Town, picking up 80 details at Standerton. Arrived at Cape Town on 23rd, and proceeded to Green Point Camp. On 27th, embarked on transport *St. Andrew*. General Settle, commanding Cape Colony Defence Forces, spoke a few words of farewell, and read a complimentary telegram from Lord Kitchener, wishing the Australians a safe passage home. Arrived at Albany on 18th April, Melbourne 23rd, and Brisbane 30th; and were disbanded on 5th May.

WAR SERVICES AND HONOURS.

Flewell-Smith, Lieut.-Colonel J. F.—Operations in Transvaal, Orange River Colony and Cape Colony, April, 1901, to May, 1902. Commanded 5th Queensland Imperial Bushmen to 31st July, 1901. Area Commandant, Cape Colony, 1st August, 1901, to 30th November, 1901. Administrator of Martial Law, No. 11 Area, Cape Colony, 1st December, 1901, to 27th March, 1902. Commanded Artillery and Cavalry Depot, Cape Town, 29th March, 1902, to 3rd June, 1902. Queen's Medal with five clasps.

Toll, Major F. W.—Operations as stated. Commanded Contingent from 1st August, 1901, to 5th May, 1902. Despatches, *London Gazette*, 25th April, 1902. Queen's Medal with five clasps. King's Medal with two clasps. See also " Special Service."

Dodds, Captain T. H., Adjutant.—Operations as stated. Despatches, *London Gazette*, 29th July, 1902. D.S.O. Queen's Medal with five clasps.

Gehrmann, Captain C. G.—Operations as stated. Queen's Medal with five clasps.

Austin, C., and *Carter*, H. R. (Captains).—As above.

Ferguson, W. I., *Bell*, M. A. T., and *Sellheim*, C. V. (Captains).—See 4th Contingent.

Loynes, Lieutenant J.—Served previously with 1st Contingent, which see. Operations as stated. Queen's Medal with four clasps. King's Medal with two clasps.

Cowell, W. R., and *Clerk*, E. (Lieutenants).—Operations as stated. Queen's Medal with five clasps.

Caskey, Lieutenant L. J.—Operations as stated. Despatches of Commander-in-Chief, 8th March, 1902. Killed in action, 27th September, 1901.

Cook, B. W., *Benjamin*, H. A., and *Burnside*, G. H. (Lieutenants).—Operations as stated. Queen's Medal with five clasps.

Halse, K. J., *Higginson*, J. B., and *Hugonin*, C. (Lieutenants).—Had previous service with 2nd Contingent, which see. The two former Queen's Medal with three clasps, and King's Medal with two clasps; the latter, Queen's Medal with four clasps.

Hunter, W. S., *Joss*, A. W., *Keary*, G. A., *Koch*, G. H., and *Ogg*, G. R. (Lieutenants).—Operations as stated. Queen's Medal with five clasps.

Reese, Lieutenant C. G. B.—Operations as stated. Despatches, *London Gazette*, 20th August, 1901, and 25th April, 1902. Queen's Medal with five clasps.

Pooley, Lieutenant A. E.—Previous service with 4th Contingent, which see. Operations as stated. Killed in action, 27th September, 1901.

Koch, Lieutenant F. B. T.—Previous service in 3rd Contingent, which see. Operations as stated. Served with 7th Australian Commonwealth Horse. Queen's Medal with four clasps. King's Medal with two clasps.

Townley, Lieutenant N. V.—Previous service in 3rd Contingent, which see. Operations as stated. Queen's Medal with five clasps. King's Medal with two clasps.

Dutton, R. G., and *Cavaye*, J. McL. (Lieutenants).—*Vide* 2nd Queensland Mounted Infantry. Operations as stated. Queen's Medal with four clasps. King's Medal with two clasps.

Hutchens, Captain H. J. (Army Medical Corps).—Operations as stated. Despatches, *London Gazette*, 29th July, 1902. D.S.O. Queen's Medal with five clasps.

McLeod, Captain J, Veterinary Officer.—*Vide* 4th Queensland Imperial Bushmen.

Tucker, Lieutenant G., Veterinary Officer.—Operations as stated. Queen's Medal with five clasps.

Nominal Roll.

No. and Name.	Rank.	Remarks.
OFFICERS.		
Flewell-Smith, John Francis	Lieut.-Colonel	
Dodds, Thomas Henry	Captain and Adjutant	
Toll, Frederick William	Captain	Previous service as S.S. Officer
Gerhmann, Charles George	,,	
Austin, Colin	,,	
Carter, Hubert Reginald	Lieutenant	Severely wounded at Onverwacht, 4.1.02
Loynes, James	,,	Previous service with 1st Contingent. Slightly wounded at Familie Hoek, 6.12.01
Hunter, William Scott	,,	
Benjamin, Herbert Asher	,,	
Caskey, Lachlan John	,,	Killed in action at Mokari Drift, Caledon River, 27.9.01
Clerk, Edward George	,,	
Reese, Charles Gustave Burgoyne	,,	
Burnside, George Hamilton	,,	
Halse, Kenedon Jeffreys	,,	Previous service with 2nd Queensland Mounted Infantry. Severely wounded at Rietfontein, 14.6.01
Cook, Bernard William	,,	
Higginson, John Bingham	,,	Previous service with 2nd Queensland Mounted Infantry. Severely wounded at Onverwacht, 4.1.02
Hugonin, Claude	,,	Previous service with 2nd Queens- Mounted Infantry
Keary, George Alfred	,,	Transport Officer
Ogg, George Rusden	Quartermaster-Lieutenant	
Hutchens, Harold John	Captain (A.M.C.)	
Joss, Alexander Wynward	Lieutenant	
Koch, George Hilfers	,,	

Nominal Roll—*continued*.

No. and Name.	Rank.	Remarks.

Transfers from Various Queensland Contingents.

OFFICERS.

No. and Name.	Rank.	Remarks.
Ferguson, William Isaac	Captain	From 4th Queensland Imperial Bushmen
Bell, Marmaduke Alexander Thomas	Captain (Supernumerary)	From 4th Queensland Imperial Bushmen
Sellheim, Cassimir Vaux	,, ,,	From 4th Queensland Imperial Bushmen
McLeod, John	Veterinary Captain (Supernumerary)	From 4th Queensland Imperial Bushmen
Koch, Felix Bernard Theodor	Lieutenant (Supernumerary)	From 3rd Queensland Mounted Infantry (Sergeant)
Townley, Norman Vincent	,, ,,	From 3rd Queensland Mounted Infantry
Dutton, Richard Guy	,, ,,	From 2nd Queensland Mounted Infantry (N.C.O.)
Cavaye, James McLelland	,, ,,	From 2nd Queensland Mounted Infantry (N.C.O.)
Pooley, Alfred Ernest	Lieutenant	From 4th Queensland Imperial Bushmen (Sergeant). Killed in action at Mokari Drift, Caledon River, 27.9.01

Vide also " Draft" and "Enrolled in S.A."

N.C.O.'S AND MEN.

No. and Name.	Rank.	Remarks.
1. Shannon, James Patrick	Private	Saddler-Sergeant. Died of wounds at Onverwacht, 4.1.02
2. Ayscough, Arthur Leslie	,,	Sergeant
3. Fordham, Henry George	,,	
4. Vanza, Vincent	,,	
5. Fraser, James	,,	
6. Stack, Thomas Patrick	,,	
7. Jones, Horace Barkham	,,	
8. Busby, William Norman	Bugler	Severely wounded at Onverwacht, 4.1.02. Despatches, *London Gazette*, 29.7.02
9. Bell, Rae	Private	
10. Ford, Joshua	,,	
11. Ponting, William	,,	
12. Rossiter, William Leopold	,,	
13. Ruffin, Walter Joseph	,,	
14. Campbell, William Lachlan	,,	Wounded between Bethel and Standerton, 25.5.01
15. Priest, David William	,,	
16. Smith, Edmund Brierley	,,	Corporal, 20.5.01. Severely wounded, Onverwacht, 4.1.02
17. Horne, Robert Alexander	,,	
18. McGhie, Malcolm John	,,	Corporal, 20.5.01
19. Edgar, Walter Arthur	,,	
20. Wightman, William Alexander	,,	Corporal
21. Stuart, Charles Henry	,,	
22. Longland, Walter	,,	
23. Arnold, David Dalziel	,,	Dangerously wounded at Onverwacht, 4.1.02
24. Brook, Thomas Edward	,,	

Nominal Roll—*continued.*

No. and Name.	Rank.	Remarks.
N.C.O.'s and Men—continued.		
26. Young, James Aquilla	Private	Corporal, 1.10.01
27. Mason, James Edward	,,	Wounded between Bethel and Standerton, 25.5.01. Killed in action at Familie Hoek, South East Transvaal, 6.12.01
28. Cordingley, Frank	,,	Corporal
29. Robertson, John Charles	,,	
30. Easlea, George	,,	
31. Hendy, William Muir	,,	Killed in action at Standerton, 25.5.01
32. Locke, John	,,	
33. Hall, John David	,,	
34. Hunt, Edward Henry	,,	Killed in action at Oliphant's River, 26.4.01
35. Henrickson, Frederick	,,	Despatches, *London Gazette*, 29.7.02
36. Devitt, William Francis	,,	
37. Priddle, Charles	,,	Severely wounded between Bethel and Standerton, 25.5.01
38. Healy, William Patrick	,,	
39. Thomas, John	,,	
40. Clements, Robert	,,	Corporal, 1.11.01
41. Lucas, William John	,,	
42. Wylie, James	,,	Corporal, 30.4.01. Severely injured by fall from horse in action, Kopjesfontein, 6.8.01
43. Wylie, Allan Malcolm	,,	
44. Ziebell, Walter	,,	
45. Craig, Arthur Wilmot Napier	,,	
46. Elliott, Reginald Aynsley	,,	
47. Evans, John Joseph	,,	
48. Keightley, Frederick Martin	,,	
49. Garella, Thomas	,,	
50. Henderson, Thomas King	,,	
51. Parsons, William	,,	
52. Horan, Hugh Joseph	,,	
53. Henderson, Edward William	,,	
54. Dodds, Sydney Richard	,,	Acting-Corporal, 20.4.01. Slightly wounded at Amersfoort, 2.6.01
55. Hoyland, Thomas Ashton	,,	
56. Anning, John Harry	,,	Killed in action, Kopjesfontein, 6.8.01
57. Ellison, Charles Edgar	,,	
58. Wilson, William Thomas	,,	
59. Lang, Fred	,,	
61. Whitaker, James Augustus	,,	
62. MacGregor, Samuel	,,	Acting-Corporal, 1.6.01
63. Hennessy, Timothy	,,	
64. Wall, Arnold Conrad	Shoeing-Smith	
65. Daniell, Hubert John	Private	
66. Boyle, Joseph Francis	,,	
68. Barber, William Ernest	,,	
69. Davies, Walter Henry	,,	
70. Smith, Henry Francis	,,	
71. Downie, William Wallace	,,	
72. Doyle, Robert	,,	
73. Thatcher, Albert Ernest	,,	

Nominal Roll—continued.

N.C.O.'s AND MEN—continued.

No. and Name.	Rank.	Remarks.
74. Goodall, Frederick Thomas	Private	Killed in action, Onverwacht, 4.1.02
75. Curran, Patrick	,,	
76. Hamilton, Herbert George	,,	
77. Iselin, Kenneth	,,	
78. Allmann, Charles	,,	
79. Brace, William	,,	Slightly wounded Katdoombult Farm, 5.8.01
80. Dobe, John	,,	
81. Wyatt, Francis George	,,	
82. Booth, John	,,	
83. Fogg, Herbert John Harry	,,	Wounded between Bethel and Standerton, 25.5.01. D.C.M.: A.O. 33,'02.
84. Wood, William	,,	
85. Fulton, William Wilson	,,	
86. Whittington, Charles Frank Lewis	,,	Corporal
87. Walsh, George	,,	
88. Fry, George Philip	,,	
89. Slater, Charles William	,,	
90. Dickson, James	Shoeing-Smith	
91. Anderson, Olaf Peter	,,	Slightly wounded at Familie Hoek, 6.12.01
92. Orr, Henry	Private	
93. Pierson, John Stewart	,,	
94. Murray, Charles Gerald Templeton	,,	
95. Adams, Thomas Henry	,,	
96. Fielding, Arthur William	,,	Corporal, 28.9.01
97. Priest, Edward Raven	,,	
98. Byrne, Charles	,,	Severely wounded at Onverwacht, 4.1.02
99. Seales, William	,,	Returned to Australia, discharged, 16.1.02
100. Green, Arthur William	,,	
101. Roberts, Egbert Mead	,,	
102. Lawson, George	,,	
103. Forsyth, George Given	,,	Died of measles, hospital, Brisbane, 3.3.02
104. Carless, Joseph	,,	Wounded between Bethel and Standerton, 25.5.01
105. Murphy, Denis	,,	Acting-Corporal, 1.6.01. Died of enteric at Pretoria, 17.12.01
106. Taylor, Alfred Frank	,,	
107. Ross, William Hardy	,,	
108. Morley, John	,,	
109. Campbell, Andrew	,,	
110. Stirling, Colin	,,	Killed in action at Kopjesfontein, 6.8.01
111. Lahey, James Allen	,,	
112. Smith, Dielmann Jacob	,,	
113. Wall, William	,,	
114. Allen, Martin	,,	
115. Logan, John Christopher	,,	
116. Baartz, Frederick John	,,	
117. Neilson, Ernest	,,	
118. McGregor, Alexander	,,	Returned to Australia, discharged, 23.12.01

Nominal Roll—*continued.*

No. and Name.	Rank.	Remarks.
N.C.O.'s AND MEN—*continued.*		
119. Goodliffe, Robert	Private	Returned to Australia, discharged, 16.1.02
120. Kokkinn, Charles Harold	,,	
121. Beed, William	,,	
122. Macartney, Warwick	,,	Killed in action at Onverwacht, 4.1.02
123. Boyes, Tom	,,	
124. Jones, Henry Matthew	,,	
125. Lilley, David Robert	,,	
126. Owens, William Charles	,,	
127. Lilley, William	,,	Killed in action at Onverwacht, 4.1.02
128. Smith, John Clarence	,,	
129. Window, William	,,	Severely injured by fall from horse in action, Mokari Drift, Caledon River, 27.9.01
130. MacMahon, Patrick	,,	
131. Nicolaus, William Frederick	,,	
132. McLean, Alexander McKenzie	,,	
133. Hope, Clement	,,	
134. Parry, Albert	,,	Corporal
135. Kirkup, Frank Edgar	,,	
136. Provan, George Harvey	,,	
137. Mealing, Christopher Thornton	,,	
138. Heap, Albert James	,,	
139. Crump, William Robert	Shoeing-Smith	
140. Bedsor, Arthur Daniel	Private	
141. Rapp, Charles Samuel	,,	
142. Godfrey, John	,,	
143. Locke, James	,,	Corporal, 1.6.01
144. Huntley, Arthur	,,	Returned to Australia, discharged, 16.1.02
145. Adams, Charles Langlow	,,	
146. Maher, James	,,	
147. Walden, Charles	,,	
148. Macartie, John	,,	Severely wounded at Onverwacht, 4.1.02
149. King, Colin Baumgardt	,,	
150. Conway, John	,,	
151. Dinnar, John	,,	
152. Barker, John	,,	
153. White, William Henry	,,	
154. Stockwell, William Henry George	,,	
155. Palmer, William	,,	Severely wounded, Onverwacht, 4.1.02
156. Hughes, Arthur	,,	
157. Anderson, John Henry	,,	Killed in action at Oliphant's River, 26.4.01
158. Smith, William James	,,	
159. McIntosh, William James	,,	
160. Smith, John Edward	,,	
161. Henzeel, John Smith	,,	
162. Woolard, Albert Edward	,,	
163. Collins, Percy William	,,	
164. Macfarlane, John	,,	Acting-Corporal. Killed in action at Onverwacht, 4.1.02
165. Eagleton, Alexander William	,,	Killed in action at Onverwacht, 4.1.02

Nominal Roll—*continued.*

No. and Name.	Rank.	Remarks.
N.C.O.'s AND MEN—*continued.*		
166. Turner, Edward Vernon	Private	
167. Donald, George Olive	,,	
168. Latcham, George Arthur Thomas	,,	
169. Steele, William	,,	
170. Brook, Albert Ernest	,,	
171. Horstmann, Vincent	,,	
172. Gooch, Herbert Sherlock	,,	
173. Dale, Thomas James	,,	
174. Forbes, Alexander	,,	
175. Norman, Ernest William	,,	Severely wounded, Onverwacht, 4.1.02
176. Hinds, Joseph	,,	
177. Bell, William	,,	
178. Smith, Hilliard	,,	Sergeant. A.O. Gallantry and good leading in action
179. Nimble, Henry	,,	
180. Hoelscher, Alexander	,,	
181. St. John, Oliver Beauchamp	,,	
182. Little, William James	,,	
183. Billington, Frederick Harrison	,,	
184. Holland, Mervyn Arthur	,,	
185. Conti, Arthur Armitage	,,	
186. Neville, George	,,	Slightly wounded, Onverwacht, 4.1.02
187. Woods, Charles Keith Elphinstone	,,	Sergeant, 1.7.01
188. Stewart, Philip Graham Annandale	,,	
189. Lacey, Henry	,,	Sergeant
190. Jefferson, Thomas William Joseph	Bugler	
191. Ferguson, John Norman Victor McLean	Private	Sergeant
192. Oxford, Arthur	,,	Sergeant, 1.7.01
193. Smythe, Albert Thomas	,,	Corporal, 1.12.01
194. Davidson, George	,,	
195. Howes, William Henry	,,	Returned to Australia, discharged, 16.1.02
196. Bennett, Sydney Grace	,,	
197. Warlow, William	,,	
198. Price, Ernest Lesleigh	,,	
199. Moller, Cuthbert	,,	Killed in action at Oliphant's River or Malipo River, 26.4.01
200. Halley, Thomas	,,	
201. Beckett, William Joseph	,,	
202. White, George Henry	,,	Mentioned in C.-in-C.'s despatches 8.3.01. Killed in action at Mokari Drift, Caledon River, 27.9.01
203. McIlveen, John	,,	Died of accidental wound at Wakkerstroom. 9.12.01
204. Munro, Gilbert Bryce	,,	
205. Bretherton, Arthur	,,	
206. Carruthers, John Stewart	,,	
207. Lanfer, Charles Henry	,,	
208. Williams, Albert	,,	
212. Booker, John Nelson Tarplee	,,	
213. Armstrong, Frank Ayerst	,,	Sergeant, 4.1.02
214. Armstrong, Herbert Victor	,,	
215. Sketcher, Henry	,,	

Nominal Roll—continued.

No. and Name.	Rank.	Remarks.

N.C.O.'s AND MEN—continued.

No. and Name.	Rank.	Remarks.
216. Tibbetts, Frederick Richard	Private	
217. Brown, George	,,	
218. Moloney, Daniel	,,	
219. Coote, John William	,,	
220. Savill, Frederick Herbert	,,	
221. Linski, Alfred	,,	
222. Sutherland, John	,,	
223. Savill, George Daniel	,,	
224. Harvey, John	,,	Severely wounded between Bethel and Standerton, —.5.01
225. West, Stephen	,,	Corporal, 7.7.01
226. Stewart, Henry	,,	
227. Shadforth, George Stanley	,,	
228. O'Brien, Nicholas	,,	Corporal
229. Belin, Anders Gustav	,,	Died of wounds at Onverwacht, 4.1.02
230. Campbell, Colin	,,	Severely wounded at Familie Hoek, 6.12.01
231. Smith, James Olivant	,,	
232. Chapman, John Russell	,,	
233. Egan, Mickel	,,	
234. Heaslip, William George	,,	
235. Wakefield, James	,,	Acting-Corporal, 27.6.01
236. Ellenton, Frederick	,,	
237. Desmond, Andrew	,,	
238. McMahon, Michael	,,	
239. Mears, Henry Archibald	,,	
240. Beavan, William	,,	
241. Farmer, Arthur William	,,	
242. Pitt, Charles Henry	,,	
243. Monk, John	,,	
244. Harvey, James	,,	
245. Paton, Thomas	,,	Slightly wounded, Mokari Drift, Caledon River, 27.9.01
246. Lee, Patrick	,,	Slightly wounded at Familie Hoek 6.12.01
247. Whitlock, Frederick	,,	
248. Curtis, Matthew	,,	
249. Mulhall, John	,,	
250. Purtell, Thomas	,,	
251. Hutchison, James	,,	
252. Gallaway, William	,,	
253. Henderson, Henry	,,	
254. Eames, Edward	,,	
255. Mair, William	,,	
256. Blunt, Frederick Gregg	,,	Accidentally shot at Oliphant's River, 17.4.01
257. Freeman, Laurence Cartwright	,,	
258. Bleakley, Thomas	,,	
259. Bernard, Sidney James	,,	
260. McElwaine, Thomas	,,	
261. White, Herbert John	,,	Accidentally killed, Tabakplaas, 21.4.01
262. McLean, John Hector	,,	
263. Dimmick, Leonard	,,	
264. Pent, George	,,	
265. Forster, Claude Arthur	,,	
266. Ridgeley, James	,,	

Nominal Roll—continued.

No. and Name.	Rank.	Remarks.
N.C.O.'s AND MEN—continued.		
267. Mitchell, Charles Edward	Private	Wounded between Bethel and Standerton, 25.5.01
268. Smith, Harry	,,	Sergeant, 28.9.01
269. Robinson, Alfred	,,	
270. Smith, Harold Herbert Kennedy	,,	
271. Armstrong, William Joseph	,,	
272. Hinton, John Edward	,,	Sergeant
273. Johnson, Harold	,,	Acting-Sergeant
274. Walsh, William James	,,	
275. Thompson, James	,,	Returned to Australia, discharged 16.1.02
276. Benson, Percy George	,,	Accidentally injured at Pietersburg, 14.4.01. Returned to Australia, discharged 12.3.02
277. Hallahan, John	,,	
278. Carmody, John Patrick	,,	
279. Berry, Thomas Harold	,,	
280. Miers, James Graham	,,	
281. Plowman, Alfred James	,,	
282. Hall, John Joseph	,,	Lance-Corporal. Severely wounded, Mokari Drift, Caledon River, 27.9.01
283. Ezzey, George Ephraim	,,	
284. Symington, Quinton Leitch Anderson	,,	Severely wounded at Familie Hoek, 6.12.01
285. Naylor, Walter	,,	Staff Sergeant
286. Leetch, Frederick William	Corporal	Acting-Sergeant, 5.1.02
287. Quigley, James	Private	
288. Fox, James	,,	
289. Connors, Francis Patrick	,,	
290. Krause, Edward	Saddler	
291. Vaughan, Alfred Milchor	Private	
292. Potts, William	,,	Corporal, 5.1.02
293. Jones, Oswald Ker	,,	
294. Martin, John Gray	,,	
295. Murphy, James	,,	
296. Knyvett, Frank Berners	Sergeant	Company Sergeant-Major, 28.9.01. A.O. 512/02. For coolness and gallantry in action at Onverwacht, 4.1.02. *London Gazette*, 29.7.02. D.C.M. *Vide* "Promotions"
297. Fordham, Edward Arthur	Private	
298. Foulston, William Richard	,,	
299. King, Leonard Wallace	,,	
300. Muller, Francis Charles	,,	
301. Grant, James	,,	
302. Lissnor, Isidor George	,,	
303. Lapworth, Alfred James	,,	
304. Brookes, Langley	,,	
305. Lees, Frank Grant	,,	
306. Lancaster, Albert John	,,	
307. Sanderson, William	,,	Died of enteric at Newcastle, 5.7.01
308. Brown, Richard	,,	
309. Marmant, John	,,	Mentioned in C.-in-C.'s despatches, 8.7.01. Captured and released at Wonderfontein, 15.7.01

Nominal Roll—*continued.*

No. and Name.	Rank.	Remarks.
N.C.O.'s AND MEN—*continued.*		
310. McLeod, Frederick	Private	Returned to Australia, discharged 13.3.02
311. Price, James George	Sergeant-Major	Regimental Sergeant-Major, W.O., 30.4.01. Despatches, *London Gazette,* 29.7.02
312. Williams, George Alfred	Company Sergeant-Major	
313. Goode, James	,, ,,	R.Q.M.S., 6.11.01
314. Baumann, Carl William August	,, ,,	
315. Poole, Frank	Private	
316. Marks, Fred	,,	
317. Anderson, James	,,	
318. McKenzie, John William	,,	
319. Smith, Malcolm	,,	
320. Lambert, Henry William	,,	
321. Dear, James	,,	
322. Murphy, John Frederick	,,	
323. Fleet, Frederick William	,,	
324. Kells, Edward James	,,	Promoted to Corporal by C.-in-C. for distinguished gallantry in the field, A.O. 38/01
325. Bird, William	,,	
326. McCarry, Hugh James	,,	
327. Hind, Albert Joseph	,,	
328. Shepherd, Bertram Ormond	,,	
329. Weppler, Richard	,,	Dangerously wounded at Familie Hoek, 6.12.01
330. Mullen, Hugh Patrick	,,	
331. Milner, Benjamin	,,	Killed in action at Mokari Drift, Caledon River, 27.9.01
332. Armstrong, George	,,	
333. Ramsay, James William	,,	Reported dangerously ill at Springfontein, 7.9.01
334. Campbell, William Dougald	,,	
335. Maslen, Charles Henry	,,	Returned to Australia, discharged 13.3.02
336. McCormick, Patrick	,,	Slightly wounded between Bethel and Standerton, —.5.01
337. McCabe, John Edward	,,	
338. Henderson, Claud Graham Morphett	,,	
339. Taylor, Herbert Thomas	,,	
340. Batchelor, Uglow	,,	Slightly wounded at Onverwacht, 4.1.02
341. Frere, Charles	,,	
344. Heenan, Denis	,,	
345. White, Colin	,,	
346. Rogers, George Richard	,,	
347. Towers, John Frederick	,,	
348. Jackson, Robert Balfred	,,	Corporal, 14.10.01
349. Paton, James	,,	
350. Drew, William	,,	
351. Hyde, William Frederick	,,	Returned to Australia, discharged 13.3.02
352. Davies, Archibald Henry Clark	,,	
353. Burge, Joseph Alexander	,,	
354. Walsh, Charles James	,,	Corporal
355. Thompson, Alfred	,,	

Nominal Roll—*continued*.

No. and Name.	Rank.	Remarks.
N.C.O.'s AND MEN—*continued*.		
356. Hodge, William	Private	
357. Mathias, Harold Rolleston	,,	Slightly wounded at Familie Hoek, 6.12.01
358. Burton, John	,,	Pay Sergeant, 1.6.01
359. Kruck, Christian	,,	
360. Ferguson, James	,,	
361. Gourgaud, John Claudius	,,	
362. Chamberlain, Thomas	,,	
363. Carr, Thomas Edward Page	,,	
364. O'Connor, James Joseph	,,	
365. Thwaites, Robert	,,	
366. Corbett, Arthur Brownlow	,,	Sergeant, 10.7.01
367. Corbett, Cuthbert Brownlow	,,	
368. Jones, Harrison Dan	,,	
369. Meredith, Charles Laurence	,,	
370. Taylor, Sidney	,,	
371. King, Charles Frederick Victor	,,	Corporal. Mentioned in C.-in-C.'s despatches, 8.7.01
372. Cousins, John	,,	Died of inflammation of intestines, Pretoria, 15.5.01
373. Lyon, Herbert Thomas	,,	
374. McDonald, William Alexander	,,	
375. Bates, Albert	,,	
376. Casey, James John	,,	
377. Casey, Edward Chaplin	,,	
378. Furner, William Robert	,,	
379. Griffiths, Michael	,,	Captured and released at Palmietfontein, 25.7.01
380. Richardson, William	,,	
381. Turnbull, Reginald Francis	,,	
382. Crook, Charles Henry	,,	
383. Brown, George William	,,	
384. Sinclair, Frederick	,,	Severely wounded at Onverwacht, 4.1.02
385. McLeod, Donald	,,	
386. Tytherleigh, Arthur	,,	Served with New South Wales Contingent to Soudan, 1885. Medal with clasp. Khedive's Star. Acting-Corporal, 20.4.01
387. Jones, John William	,,	
388. Lock, Joseph	,,	
389. Wagner, Albert Alfred	,,	
390. Todd, William	,,	
391. Pfundt, Adolphus Ernest Alfred	,,	
392. Barnard, George	,,	
393. Wood, John Arthur	,,	
394. Alder, Joseph	,,	
395. Reiley, Owen	,,	
396. Clark, George Howard	Artificer	Died of enteric at Charleston, 14.2.02
397. Sweeney, Edmund	Private	Wounded between Bethel and Standerton, 25.5.01. D.C.M. Distinguished conduct in the field. A.O. 33/02.
398. Yesburg, William Henry	,,	Corporal, 5.1.02
399. Gatfield, Joseph Thomas	,,	Severely wounded at Mokari Drift, Caledon River, 27.9.01

Nominal Roll—continued.

No. and Name.	Rank.	Remarks.
N.C.O.'s AND MEN—continued.		
400. Allard, Frederick Albert	Private	Slightly wounded at Familie Hoek, 6.12.01
401. McCabe, Edward	,,	
402. Hardwick, Richard Knox	,,	
403. Strong, Thomas Henry	Corporal	Slightly wounded at Groothoek, 17.6.01. Sergeant, 1.12.01
404. Bassmann, Arthur Clarence	Private	
405. Byers, John Jones	,,	
407. Austin, H. Norman	,,	Seriously wounded (accident) Standerton, 25.5.01
408. Reed, Benjamin	,,	
409. Stephenson, William	,,	
410. Urquhart, Donald	,,	
411. Jeffrey, William	,,	
412. Mills, Charles Benjamin	,,	
413. Hutchison, William	,,	
414. Meibusch, Francis	,,	
415. Lee, Harry	,,	
416. Tallan, James John	,,	
417. Hobart, Minchen James	,,	
418. Wheatly, William John	,,	Slightly wounded between Bethel and Standerton, —.5.01
419. Roberts, Alexander	,,	Died of wounds, Wakkerstroom, 16.12.01
420. Loseby, Ernest	,,	
421. Olson, Charles	,,	
422. Damsiell, Charles	,,	
423. Tacay, Hesparus May	,,	
424. Johnson, John	,,	Severely wounded, Palmietfontein, 25.7.01
425. Gibson, Vincent	,,	
426. Hooper, Edgar	,,	
427. Lebherz, John	,,	Returned to Australia; discharged, 13.3.02
428. Armitstead, William Harold	,,	
429. Miller, Thomas	,,	
430. Carpenter, Charles	,,	
431. Parish, Charles John	,,	
432. Castles, William John	,,	
433. Marsh, Edgar George	Corporal	Sergeant, 5.1.02; severely wounded at Familie Hoek, 6.12.01
434. Whitworth, James	Private	
435. McNalley, Henry	,,	
436. Hamilton, James Alfred	,,	
437. Todd, Robert	,,	
438. Prince, Anselm Charles	,,	
439. Creedy, Mickall	,,	
440. Cody, Stephen John	,,	
441. Kelly, Robert Shaw	,,	Killed in action at Onverwacht, 4.1.02
442. Enever, Philip	,,	
443. Kenney, Eric Alfred	,,	
444. Crowley, George Andrew	,,	
445. Hobourn, John Henry	,,	
446. Matthews, Henry Thomas	,,	

Nominal Roll—*continued*.

No. and Name.	Rank.	Remarks.

N.C.O.'s AND MEN—*continued*.

No. and Name.	Rank.	Remarks.
447. Bedford, Arthur	Private	
448. Dudley, John	,,	
449. Fitzsimmons, John	,,	
450. Thompson, Frederick	,,	
451. Whiteside, Andrew	,,	
452. Berry, Robert Edwin	,,	Sergeant. Killed in action at Onverwacht, 4.1.02
453. Taylor, Frank Seddon	,,	
454. Justins, Albert Leura	,,	
455. Walters, James Oliver	,,	
457. Peppler, Otto	,,	
458. Murray, Arthur Ernest	,,	Severely wounded at Onverwacht, 4.1.02
459. Grant, Patrick Roger Fullerton	Acting-Corporal	Corporal, 14.5.01
460. Chisholm, Robert	Private	
461. Campbell, George	,,	
462. Hughes, Edward Beverley	,,	Acting-Corporal, 1.7.01
463. McDonald, Andrew John	,,	
464. Chardon, Charles	,,	Killed in action at Onverwacht, 4.1.02
465. Fenwick, John Frederick	,,	Corporal. Severely wounded at Onverwacht, 4.1.02
466. Frus, Andrew Darling	,,	
467. Dent, Osmond	,,	
468. Bauman, Joseph Maxwell	,,	
469. Worthington, Albert Henry	,,	
470. Wainwright, Ernest Ralph Percy	,,	
471. Adams, Henry James	,,	
472. Collins, William Henry	,,	Sergeant
473. Marsen, Alfred	,,	
474. Neary, John Thomas	,,	
475. Cumming, Robert Ross	,,	Accidentally killed at Katdoombult Farm, 5.8.01
476. Elcoats, Bertram Weatherly	,,	
477. Hobson, Edgar Septimus	,,	
478. Molloy, John	,,	
479. Bryce, Charles Chambers	,,	
480. Heinrich, Adolph Frederick	,,	
481. Waterton, George William Thomas	,,	Severely wounded at Onverwacht, 4.1.02
482. Clarke, William George	,,	Killed in action at Onverwacht, 4.1.02
483. Rayer, Arthur Albert	,,	
484. Gellan, William	,,	Slightly wounded at Katdoombult Farm, 5.8.01
485. Shann, Joseph	,,	
486. McCabe, William	,,	Dangerously wounded at Groothoek, 17.6.01
487. Rockley, George William	,,	Farrier-Sergeant, 9.12.01
488. Bodman, Herbert William	,,	
489. Anderson, Walter Andrew	,,	
490. Eva, Arthur Henry	Bugler	
491. Byrne, Edward James	Private	Colour-Sergeant. Broken arm (accidental), Standerton, 27.5.01

Nominal Roll—*continued*.

No. and Name.	Rank.	Remarks.
Draft.		
OFFICERS.		
Cowell, William Ralph	Lieutenant	
N.C.O.'s AND MEN.		
492. Derrett, Walter	Sergeant	
493. Kimpton, Mark	Corporal	Slightly wounded at Onverwacht. 4.1.02
494. O'Callaghan, Joseph McDall	Private	Died of pneumonia, General Hospital, Hobart, 1.4.01
495. Goss, Lionel	Corporal	
496. Hunter, Alpha	Private	
497. Coleman, Michael	,,	
498. Rudd, Henry	,,	
499. Fraser, Charles	,,	
500. Tierney, Thomas Morgan	,,	
501. Fox, John	,,	
502. Clements, William James	,,	
503. Swain, George Edward	,,	
506. Keane, Percy Darcy	,,	
507. Loeffler, Albert Joseph	,,	
508. Deschamp, Wallace Victor	,,	
509. Kimmins, William Charles	,,	
510. Dobe, Henry	,,	Severely wounded at Onverwacht, 4.1.02
511. Salt, Edward Hugh	,,	Killed in action at Onverwacht, 4.1.02
512. Lawson, James	,,	
513. Chatfield, George	,,	
514. Daves, Ernest Ronald	,,	
515. McDonald, James	,,	
516. Fincham, William Nathaniel	,,	
517. Partridge, Edgar George	,,	
518. Walker, Alfred William	,,	
Enrolled in South Africa.		
OFFICERS.		
Tucker, George	Veterinary-Lieutenant	
N.C.O.'s AND MEN.		
519. Wilson, Arthur	Private	
520. Morris, Thomas Henry	,,	
521. Gray, J. G.	,,	
522. Burgess, John	,,	
523. Harrison, Robert	,,	
524. Peart, James Alfred	,,	
525. Power, James Charles	,,	Sergeant, Army Order, gallantry and good conduct in action. Killed in action at Onverwacht, 4.1.02
526. Robertson, D. J.	,,	
527. Bettany, H.	,,	
528. Wilson, J. H.	,,	

Nominal Roll—*continued.*

No. and Name.	Rank.	Remarks.

N.C.O.'s AND MEN—*continued.*

No. and Name.	Rank.	Remarks.
529. Barlow, George	Private	
530. Craig, Robert W.	,,	
531. Bayles, A. C.	,,	
532. Roxburgh, M.	,,	
533. Chalmers, J.	,,	
534. Allen, M.	,,	
535. Dumbrell, W.	,,	
536. Ansten, Thomas	,,	
537. Doyle, G.	,,	
538. Caller, A.	,,	
539. Destree, L. H.	,,	
540. Robinson, C. S.	,,	
541. Green, R. R.	,,	
542. Warmington, E.	,,	
543. Wallis, F. W.	,,	
544. Alves, S.	,,	
545. Kingsley, Louis	Sergeant	

SIXTH (QUEENSLAND IMPERIAL BUSHMEN) CONTINGENT.

A REGIMENT raised under circumstances similar to those which governed the enrolment of the two which preceded it. For conditions of enlistment, clothing, and equipment, *vide* 4th Contingent. For rates of pay (stated to be upon joining camp in lieu of embarkation as previously), *vide* 5th Contingent.

ESTABLISHMENT.

Battalion Staff.—1 lieut.-colonel or major, 1 adjutant, 1 quartermaster, 1 transport officer, 1 medical officer, 4 staff sergeants (R.S.M., R.Q.M.S., transport sergeant, O.R. clerk), 2 rank and file, 3 medical orderlies, 6 batmen; total, 5 officers, 4 staff sergeants, 11 rank and file. In all, 20, with 10 private, 10 public riding horses. Veterinary officer appointed for the voyage.

Details of a company.—1 major or captain, 4 lieutenants, 1 sergeant-major, 4 sergeants, 1 farrier-sergeant, 2 shoeing-smiths, 1 saddler, 1 bugler, 8 corporals, 100 privates, 5 batmen; total, 5 officers, 5 sergeants, 4 artificers, 1 bugler, 113 rank and file. In all, 128, with 10 private, 118 public riding horses; total, 128.

Recapitulation.—Battalion staff, as stated.

Three companies.—15 officers, 15 sergeants, 12 artificers, 3 buglers, 339 rank and file; total, 384, with 30 private, 354 public riding horses. In all, 384. Spare horses, 296.

Grand total.—20 officers, 19 staff sergeants and sergeants, 12 artificers, 3 buglers, 350 rank and file; with 40 private, 660 public riding horses; or 404 of all ranks, with 700 horses.

Draught horses were to be supplied by the Imperial authorities in South Africa.

No record could be obtained of promotions except other than to Commissions; for which *vide* Nominal Rolls.

DEPARTURE AND RETURN.

Left on 4th April, 1901, comprising—17 officers, 384 others, with 615 horses. Eleven were killed or died; 4 officers, 60 others, were struck off in South Africa; 19 officers, 313 others returned.

The first draft (20th August, 1901), comprised—1 officer, 77 others; the second (26th September, 1901)—3 officers, 18 others. Two were killed; the remainder returned at various times.

SERVICE.

Like the other oversea Contingents at this stage of the war, the 6th were employed for the most part in constantly trekking over given districts, driving in and harassing the enemy, bringing to the various bases prisoners, horses, cattle, sheep, vehicles, etc., and laying waste the country—a service of much excitement and vicissitude.

The Contingent embarked at Pinkenba, and went to sea on 4th April, 1901, in the transport *Victoria*, arriving at Cape Town on 2nd May. Two drafts of details subsequently followed. The first, under Captain Echlin, who was detailed for the voyage, left Brisbane by rail on 18th August, embarked in the *Britannic* at Sydney, 20th August, and arrived at Cape Town on 22nd September. The second, officered by Lieutenants Crichton, Cowley, and Philp, entrained at Brisbane, 24th September, 1901; embarked at Sydney in the *Harlech Castle* on 26th September, and reached Cape Town on 26th October.

From Cape Town, the 6th proceeded, by order, to Durban; arrived on 7th May, and disembarked the following day. Entrained same day for Pietermaritzburg, leaving horses and 30 men, including farriers and smiths, at Durban, under Lieutenants Rich and Vaughan. Arrived at Pietermaritzburg on 9th, entrained on 14th, arrived at Volksrust on the following day, and Standerton on 16th. The horses arrived in six trains on the same day, having been starved and not watered since two and a half days before; and, as nothing could be done that evening, nearly all the animals were three whole days without food or water. Transport was drawn on the 18th, consisting of 9 buck wagons, 4 Scotch carts, and 1 water cart.

On the 19th, the Contingent was posted to Lieut.-Colonel R. Grey's Column, consisting of (in addition) the 7th New Zealand Regiment (six squadrons), 2 15-prs., 1 pom-pom (Royal Field Artillery), half-battalion 1st East Lancashire, and detachments of Royal Engineers, Army Service Corps, &c. Lieut.-Colonel Hon. H. F. White (a Jameson raider) commanded the mounted troops. The 6th served side by side with the 7th New Zealanders during the greater part of 1901 and the first three months of 1902.

Colonel Grey pronounced the companies of the 6th to be too large, and directed the Regiment to be reorganized into four companies, each of three divisions. This was accordingly carried out; Captain Wollstein being appointed to command No. 4 company, with Lieutenants Brown and Vaughan; Lieutenant H. F. Evans to act as quartermaster as well as transport officer.

Started to trek on 20th in the Standerton district, marching very light, without tents, wallets off saddles, &c.; and convoy for General Bullock having come up, the Column proceeded towards Ermelo on 21st. The enemy sniped daily at flank, advance, and rearguards, and there were a few casualties. Arrived at Ermelo on 27th, having captured 15 Boers, and much stock; handed over the convoy, began return journey to Standerton, the cold winds being so piercing that in some cases men fainted, one falling from the saddle in a swoon. On the 31st, the New Zealanders had a bad day, losing 3 killed, 3 wounded, and 9 prisoners.

On 2nd June, camped near Standerton, and sustained their first loss in the person of Private A. W. Davis, a cheerful and hard-working young soldier, who died of enteric. Formed horse depot at Standerton, and sent in 338 horses with Lieutenant W. D. Evans and 34 N.C.O.'s and men; 302 remounts were received.

During June there was constant skirmishing and both corps suffered casualties on many occasions. On the 11th, there was a brisk engagement near Kaffir's Spruit in the Ermelo district. Lieut.-Colonel Garratt, towards the end of the month, took over the Column which moved from The Springs east to Johannesburg. On 13th July, surprised and captured a laager at Kopjesfontein on the right of the Vaal; and on 21st, captured two Boer convoys. On the 22nd, there was fighting near Lindique Drift; and Colonel Garratt's force co-operated in some minor operations under General Elliott. Casualties were frequent about this time. In August substantial captures were made at Bultfontein. In September, October, and November, operations in the Wakkerstroom district and east of Transvaal.

In December, Colonel Garratt marched to Newcastle by Botha's Pass, and through Drakensberg, to cover the construction of blockhouses in that corner of the Orange River Colony. This task having been completed, the Column was, with that of Colonel Dunlop, put under the command of Colonel Hon. J. H. G. Byng.

On 2nd February, 1902, Colonel Byng, being then at Liebenberg's Vlei, to the west of Reitz, heard of a Boer convoy in the neighbourhood, and at once pursued. The 6th Queensland Imperial Bushmen and the New Zealanders charged the enemy's rearguard with much gallantry, whilst the South African Light Horse bravely rushed the centre. Three guns, 3 wagons laden with ammunition, 26 prisoners (including 2 captains and a field cornet), 150 horses and mules, and 750 cattle were taken; 5 Boers were killed and 8 wounded. After this, all the Columns in the district engaged in a big drive towards the railway; which operation ended on 8th February, when it was found that 300 prisoners had been taken.

During March, Colonel Garratt's command took part in further drives in the Orange River Colony; and in April in a concerted movement of many Columns, from the Standerton line to the Delagoa railway and back.

The 6th embarked at Durban on 17th May, 1902, in the transport *Devon*; arrived at Albany, 5th June; Sydney, 13th; Brisbane, 17th. Disbanded, 23rd June, 1902.

WAR SERVICES AND HONOURS.

Tunbridge, Lieut.-Colonel O. A.—Operations in the Transvaal, Orange River Colony, and Zululand frontier of Natal, 8th May, 1901, to 17th May, 1902. Slightly wounded, 22nd July, 1901. Despatches, *London Gazette*, 29th July, 1902. C.M.G. Queen's Medal with two clasps.

Bailey, Captain H., Adjutant; was Staff Officer, Australian and New Zealand Contingents, at the Depot, Maitland, May to December, 1900. Operations in the Transvaal, Orange River Colony, and Zululand frontier of Natal, between May, 1901, and January, 1902. Brigade-Major Colonel Gordon's Column, 1st February, 1902, to 1st June, 1902. *Vide* also 1st Queensland Mounted Infantry. Queen's Medal with three clasps. King's Medal with two clasps.

Adie, Captain A. G.—Operations as stated. *Vide* also 1st Queensland Mounted Infantry. Queen's Medal with three clasps. King's Medal with two clasps.

Wollstein, Captain H. M.—Operations as stated. *Vide* also 2nd Queensland Mounted Infantry. Queen's Medal with three clasps.

Geyer, Captain F. W. C.—Operations as stated. Queen's Medal with four clasps.

Whitehorn, Captain H. S.—Operations as stated. *Vide* also 1st Queensland Mounted Infantry. Queen's Medal with five clasps. King's Medal with two clasps.

Row, Captain E. R. (Army Medical Corps).—Operations as stated. Queen's Medal with two clasps.

Boland, Lieutenant S. B.—Operations as stated. Slightly wounded, 1st December, 1901. Despatches, *London Gazette*, 29th July, 1902. D.S.O. Queen's Medal with two clasps.

Nielson, Lieutenant T. C.—Operations as stated. Queen's Medal with two clasps.

Evans, Lieutenant W. B.—Operations as stated to 15th November, 1901. Queen's Medal with two clasps.

Rich, Lieutenant D. St. G.—Operations as stated. Despatches, *London Gazette*, 29th July, 1902. Queen's Medal with two clasps.

Evans, H. F., and *Brown*, V. S. (Lieutenants).—Operations as stated. Queen's Medal with two clasps.

Cameron, Lieutenant D. C.—Operations as stated. Despatches, *London Gazette*, 20th August, 1901. Queen's Medal with two clasps.

Vaughan, Lieutenant C. R. G.—Operations as stated. *Vide* also 2nd Queensland Mounted Infantry. Despatches, *London Gazette*, 25th April, 1902. Queen's Medal with three clasps.

Walker, Lieutenant G. W.—Operations as stated. *Vide* also 1st Queensland Mounted Infantry. Queen's Medal with five clasps. King's Medal with two clasps.

Curtis, Lieutenant B. W.—Operations as stated. Queen's Medal with two clasps.

Excel, A. R., *Elston*, W. E., and *Anderson*, R. (Lieutenants).—Operations as stated. *Vide* also 3rd Queensland Mounted Infantry. Queen's Medal with five clasps. King's Medal with two clasps.

Wright, Lieutenant W. L. F.—Operations as stated. *Vide* also 3rd Queensland Mounted Infantry. D.C.M. Despatches, *London Gazette*, 29th July, 1902. Queen's Medal with five clasps. King's Medal with two clasps.

Sleight, Lieutenant R.—Operations as stated. *Vide* also 3rd Queensland Mounted Infantry. Queen's Medal with three clasps.

Nominal Roll.

No. and Name.	Rank.	Remarks.
OFFICERS.		
Tunbridge, Oliver Allan	Lieut.-Colonel	Slightly wounded at Vereeniging, 22.7.01
Bailey, Henry	Captain-Adjutant	Previous service in 1st Queensland Mounted Infantry Contingent
Adie, Alfred George	,,	,, ,, ,,
Wollstein, Harry More	Captain	Previous service in 2nd Queensland Mounted Infantry Contingent. Quartermaster to 20.5.01
Geyer, Frederick William Christian	,,	
Whitehorn, Henry Saxon	,,	Previous service in 1st Queensland Mounted Infantry Contingent
Row, Edward Reginald	Captain (Army Medical Corps)	
Boland, Simon B.	Lieutenant	Slightly wounded at Tinter's Kop, 1.12.01
Nielson, Trevor Cottier	,,	
Evans, William Brynan	,,	
Rich, Douglas St. George	,,	
Evans, Harry Foster	,,	Transport Officer
Brown, Villiers Seymour	,,	
Cameron, Donald Charles	,,	
Vaughan, Charles Robert Geoghegan	,,	Previous service with 2nd Queensland Mounted Infantry Contingent
Walker, George William	,,	Previous service with 1st Queensland Mounted Infantry Contingent
Curtis, Bertram William	,,	

Captain B. O. Meek, Veterinary Officer, was attached for the voyage.

Nominal Roll—*continued.*

No. and Name.	Rank.	Remarks.

Supplementary (*Joined in South Africa.*)

OFFICERS.

Excel, Arthur Reginald	Lieutenant (Supernumerary)	From 3rd Queensland Mounted Infantry Contingent (Staff-Sergeant)
Elston, William Ernest	,,	From 3rd Queensland Mounted Infantry Contingent (Sergeant)
Anderson, Robert	,,	,, ,, ,, ,,
Wright, Willam Leckey Ferguson	,,	From 3rd Queensland Mounted Infantry Contingent (Quarter-master-Sergeant, D.C.M.)
Sleight, Rowland	,,	From 3rd Queensland Mounted Infantry Contingent (Lieutenant)

N.C.O.'s AND MEN.

1. Elston, Thomas	Private	
2. Renwick, Robert Lancelot	,,	Company Quartermaster-Sergeant, 1.5.01
3. Richardson, George Henry	,,	
4. Shaw, Farquhar	,,	
5. Seymour, George	,,	Severely injured on transport *Victoria*, —.4.01
6. Glazebrook, Frank	,,	
7. Doran, Michael Park	,,	
9. Kenna, George Leonard	,,	
10. Franks, Albert Edward	,,	
11. Treadwell, George	,,	
13. Louche, Howard Joseph	,,	
14. Lake, George William James	,,	
15. Sheehan, James	,,	Sergeant, 1.5.01
16. Smith, Alexander Johnston	,,	
17. Walker, William Towley	,,	Sergeant, 20.1.02
18. Daniels, John	,,	Corporal
19. Ireton, Richard	,,	Accidentally injured at Pretoria, 16.7.01
20. Howlett, Thomas	,,	
21. Wills, Andrew Ernest	Bugler	
22. Gorman, Jerome Thiege	Private	O.R. Sergeant, 6.6.01. Died of meningitis at Greenport, 17.2.02
23. Sutton, Geoffrey William	,,	
24. Francis, Alfred	,,	
25. Sullivan, William James	,,	
26. Smith, Flewell T.	,,	Slightly wounded at Paardeplatz, 21.9.01
27. O'Brien, Jeremiah	,,	
28. McCall, William Joseph	Saddler	
29. May, George	Private	Slightly wounded at Joedchoop, 25.6.01
30. Savage, William Henry	,,	
31. McDougall, Augustus Thyne	,,	
32. Corr, Alexander	,,	Corporal, 28.4.01
33. Gamble, James William	,,	
34. Cunningham, James Alexander	,,	Returned to Australia; discharged, 16.1.02
35. Smith, Henry	,,	
36. Ryan, Cecil Augustine	,,	

Nominal Roll—*continued*.

No. and Name.	Rank.	Remarks.
N.C.O.'s AND MEN—*continued*.		
37. Murphy, Michael	Private	
38. Cousins, Thomas Henry	,,	
39. Healy, Victor Eugene	,,	
41. McClintock, James Alexander	,,	
42. Lillie, Arthur Reuben	,,	
43. Whitford, Frederick Charles	,,	
46. Wadsworth, Harris	,,	
48. Weatherley, Ernest	,,	
49. Elmhirst, H. Augustus	,,	
50. Gardner, Joseph	,,	
51. McDonnell, Peter	,,	
52. Nielson, George Albert Edward	,,	
53. Birkin, William	,,	
54. Cotter, James	,,	
55. Hovey, George William	,,	
56. Tribe, Reginald Walter	,,	Returned to Australia; discharged, 16.1.02
58. Woodroffe, William Bennet Palmer	,,	
59. Clark, George John	,,	Slightly wounded at Depreez's Lager, 7.8.01
60. Memmott, Joseph	,,	
61. Willis, William	,,	
62. Hopkins, William James	,,	
63. Bates, Thomas	,,	
64. White, Charles Robert	,,	
65. Quine, John	,,	
66. Kendrick, Percy James	,,	
67. Davidson, Samuel	,,	
68. Andrews, Charles	,,	
69. Furness, Arthur Henry	,,	Slightly wounded at Mooifontein, 16.6.01
70. Kaspar, Charles Frederick	,,	
72. Greer, James Ramsey	,,	
73. Roberts, Henry Thomas	,,	
74. Whittick, Walter John	,,	
75. Mulholland, William John	,,	Slightly wounded at Paardeplatz, 21.9.01
76. Gregory, Edward	,,	
77. Hawkins, Robert Smith	,,	
78. Fern, William Henry	,,	
79. Davis, Albert William	,,	Died of enteric at Standerton 3.6.01
81. McDonnell, Joseph Edward	,,	
82. McKinnon, Hector	,,	
83. Green, James Henry	,,	
84. Mossop, Henry	,,	
85. Grainger, Lewis	,,	
86. Freeman, Harry	,,	
87. Weaver, Frank William	,,	
88. Cameron, William Stanley	,,	
89. Thow, Clan Euquart	,,	
90. Pitman, Robert	,,	
92. Price, Arnold	,,	
93. Goodfellow, William Watson	,,	
94. Moxley, Arthur Selwyn	,,	
95. McVinish, Colin John	,,	
96. Gill, Frederick Henry	,,	

Nominal Roll—*continued*.

No. and Name.	Rank.	Remarks.
N.C.O.'s AND MEN—*continued*.		
97. Ferris, Albert Abraham	Private	
98. McPherson, Neil	,,	Died of pneumonia, Rietfontein 3.8.01
99. Cecil, Egerton Burleigh Cooper	,,	
100. Newland, George Francis	,,	
101. Bailey, Richard	,,	
102. Cox, Thomas Henry	,,	
103. Keightley, Walter	,,	
104. Lambley, Charles	,,	
105. Devine, Arthur Ernest	,,	
106. Webster, William Francis	,,	
107. Brown, William Ernest	,,	
108. Little, Samuel	,,	
109. Ruthenberg, August	,,	
110. Wilson, George	,,	
111. Lochner, Edward Christian	,,	
113. Lascelles, Charles Henry	,,	
114. Greene, Thomas Peter	,,	
115. Hill, Stephen	,,	
116. Sargood, Timms Augustus	,,	
117. Hanlon, Patrick John	,,	
118. Grayson, John	,,	
119. Marr, Richard Sydney	,,	Killed in action at Sandwana Hill, 5.10.01
120. Salway, Edward	,,	
121. McLeod, Robert	,,	
122. Ingram, Alexander	,,	
125. Trevethan, Hercules	,,	Sergeant
126. Nisbett, James Creolam	,,	Corporal, 1.5.01
127. Mann, Edmund	,,	
128. McLeod, Arthur James Alexander	,,	
129. Aldridge, Edward Henry	,,	
130. Byrne, Thomas	,,	
131. Starkey, William Henry	,,	
132. Tripp, Charles	,,	
133. Bishop, Albert Edward	,,	
135. McCartney, Edward James	,,	
136. Allan, Alexander	,,	Corporal
137. Williams, Charles Edward	,,	
138. Pearce, Herbert Frederick	,,	Corporal, 13.12.01
139. Reading, Albert Edward	,,	
140. Miles, Joseph Alfred	,,	Slightly wounded at Tinter's Kop, 1.12.01
141. Grant, Henry	,,	
143. Rapkins, Herbert Tangney	,,	
144. McDonald, Silvester John	,,	Slightly wounded at Bosch Hoek, 27.12.01
145. Byrne, James Joseph	,,	
146. Seymour, Henry Edward	,,	
147. McLaughlin, Frederick Joseph	,,	
148. Byrne, Peter Paul	,,	
149. Moore, John	,,	
151. Nugent, George Thomas	,,	
152. Watt, Hedley Verner	,,	Despatches, *London Gazette*, 29.7.02, for gallantry
153. Gould, Albert Edward	,,	Slightly wounded at Mooifontein, 16.6.01
154. Blackford, Walter	,,	

Nominal Roll—*continued*.

No. and Name.	Rank.	Remarks.
N.C.O.'S AND MEN—*continued*.		
155. Thomson, Christian Albert	Bugler	
156. Volkman, Thomas Paul	Private	Quartermaster Sergeant, 19.7·01
157. Burnett, William Harlock	,,	Sergeant, 1.5.01
158. Petersen, William John	,,	
159. Russell, Samuel Keira	,,	Killed in action at Rietfontein, 14.6.01
160. Farish, Thomas	,,	
161. Scanlan, Albert Joseph	Shoeing-Smith	
162. Brockett, Thomas	Private	
163. Ward, Frederick	,,	
164. Whippham, Reginald Augustus	,,	Company Quartermaster-Sergeant, 1.5.01
165. Smith, Arthur Frederick	,,	
166. Lee, Arthur	,,	
167. Anderson, Charles Stuart	,,	Returned to Australia; discharged 20.1.02
168. Johnson, Arthur	,,	Slightly wounded at Lindique, 25.7.01
169. Beddell, Robert	,,	
171. Woods, Richard	,,	
172. Vale, John Joseph	,,	
174. Beaumont, William Arthur	,,	
175. Bassett, Abraham William C.	,,	
176. Chardon, Arthur	,,	
177. Barradale. Robert	,,	Corporal, 13.12.01
179. Anthony, Charles	,,	
180. Dempster, Robert	,,	
181. Spreadborough, Arthur Joseph	,,	Sergeant-Major
182. Munck, Julius Valentine	,,	
183. Sharland, William John	,,	
184. Nicoll, Alaric McDonald	,,	
185. York, Frederick	,,	
186. McDougall, Duncan	,,	
187. Perry, Douglas Herbert	,,	
188. Schneider, Joseph Albert	,,	
189. Mills, George Henry	,,	Killed in action at Paardeplatz, 21.10.01
190. Hartnett, George Augustus	,,	
191. Malcolm, John	,,	Quartermaster-Sergeant, 6.6.01. Died of enteric at Kroonstad, 22.7.01
192. Goodchild, Joseph	,,	
193. Richardson, Henry James	,,	Returned to Australia; discharged, 31.3.02
194. Sharkey, Thomas Bernard	,,	
195. Gardner, David John	,,	
196. Cameron, Vernon	,,	
197. Walsh, Archibald James	,,	
198. Adams, Robert John	,,	
199. Chard, James Arthur	,,	
200. Wilson, Archibald Frederick	,,	
201. McDonald, Peter	,,	
203. Cossart, Percy Nelson	,,	
204. McGahan, Augustus John	,,	
205. Kelleher, William Vincent	,,	
206. Green, Henry	,,	
208. Macleod, William Robert	,,	
209. Grayson, Thomas John	,,	

Nominal Roll—continued.

N.C.O.'s AND MEN—continued.

No. and Name.	Rank.	Remarks.
210. Bell, Arthur Henry	Private	
211. Cooper, Charles	,,	
212. Elcoate, Aubrey Tom Johnstone	,,	
213. Hall, David	,,	
214. Power, Maurice Charles	,,	Severely wounded at Joedchoop, 25.6.01
216. Farry, Michael	,,	
217. Buchester, William	,,	
218. Juchan, Ernest Townsend	,,	Died of pneumonia at Pietersburg, 21.10.01
219. Trenkner, Conrad Arnold William	,,	
220. Waugh, Donald	,,	Company Sergeant-Major
221. Brown, Percival Lyddon	,,	
222. McCormick, Thomas	,,	
223. Kielly, Patrick	,,	
224. Brennan, Michael, John	,,	
225. Ducrot, James	,,	Returned to Australia; discharged, 13.2.02
226. Young, Percy Norman	,,	
228. Davis, Michael	,,	
229. Robinson, David	,,	
230. Condrin, John	,,	
231. Cloherty, Frederick Charles	,,	Returned to Australia; discharged 13.3.02
232. Pluck, Patrick Christian	,,	
233. Geaney, Matthew	,,	Died of wounds, Vereeniging, 25.7.01
234. Byrne, James	,,	
235. Argus, John William	,,	
236. Phillips, Sidney	,,	
237. Muller, Charles	,,	Returned to Australia; discharged 13.3.02
238. Duel, George Ernest	,,	
239. O'Loane, Albert Edward	,,	
240. Lovett, Beresford Sackville	,,	
241. Rogers, Henry Malcolm	,,	Sergeant. Severely wounded at Boschman's Kop, 4.7.01
242. Ohmsen, Alexander	,,	Sergeant
243. Jones, Alfred	,,	Sergeant
244. Flanagan, Patrick Joseph	,,	Sergeant. Returned to Australia; discharged 13.3.02
245. Abell, William	,,	
246. White, Albert Edward	,,	Returned to Australia; discharged 16.1.02
247. Colquhon, Joseph	,,	
249. Furey, John	,,	Severely wounded at Rietfontein, 14.6.01
250. Carr, Henry James	,,	
251. Daly, Harry Ellis	,,	
252. Veitch, Robert	,,	
254. Schmidt, Adalbert Franz Hermann	,,	
255. Edwards, David Renfrew	,,	
256. Douglas, Herbert	,,	
257. Hincks, Thomas	,,	
259. Smith, Robert William	,,	
260. Jones, William	,,	
261. McErlane, James	,,	

Nominal Roll—*continued.*

No. and Name.	Rank.	Remarks.
N.C.O.'s AND MEN—*continued.*		
262. Wanless, Daniel	Private	
263. Thompson, Ernest Leslie	,,	
264. Wilson, John	,,	
265. Lee, John Joseph Francis	,,	Slightly wounded at Joedchoop, 25.6.01; returned to Australia; discharged, 31.3.02
266. Kelly, Robert	,,	
267. Terry, Frederick John	,,	
268. Doyle, Timothy Herbert	,,	Company Quartermaster-Sergeant, 1.5.01. Despatches *London Gazette*, 29.7.02. "For Gallant Conduct."
269. McDonald, Edward	,,	
270. Wyatt, Frederick Charles	,,	
271. Boyd, James. /	,,	
272. Regan, James Felix	,,	
273. Thomson, James Wood	,,	Corporal, 17.4.01; Sergeant, 1.5.01
274. Walpole, John Thomas	,,	
275. Summers, Edward	,,	
276. Milne, Phillip	,,	
277. Moynihan, Cornelius Johnson	,,	
278. Arnel, Edward	,,	
279. Cullen, Charles Joseph	,,	Corporal, 28.4.01
280. Edmonds, Charles John	,,	
281. Buckby, George Ernest	,,	
282. Lowe, Harold	,,	Corporal, 25.4.01
283. Matheson, John Ken	,,	Killed in action at Rietfontein, 16.6.01
284. Phillips, Harry	,,	
285. May, George Amos	,,	
286. Adair, Francis	,,	
288. Horton, Alfred Robert	,,	
289. Johnston, William	,,	
290. Flanagan, Eugene Joseph	,,	
291. Edwards, William	,,	Sergeant, 13.12.01
292. Evans, Rees	,,	
293. Palmer, Harry Woods	,,	
294. Richards, William Henry	,,	
295. Flower, Jonathan Thomas W.	,,	
296. Armstrong, John McGill	,,	
297. Waring, William	,,	
298. McIntosh, John Alexander	,,	
299. May, James	,,	
302. Sheehan, David	,,	Corporal, 1.5.01; severely wounded at Beginsel, 4.1.02
303. Tommassie, Bertie Ernest	,,	
304. Atkinson, George Thomas Charles	,,	
305. McGregor, John	,,	
306. McNall, George Francis	,,	
307. Bryer, Arthur Darlington	Saddler	
308. Elliot, William	Private	
309. Clelland, William	,,	Slightly wounded at Mooifontein, 16.6.01
310. Harvey, George	,,	
312. Flattley, William Forrest	,,	
314. Regan, Edward Joseph	,,	
316. Finn, Michael	,,	

Nominal Roll—continued.

No. and Name.	Rank.	Remarks.
N.C.O.'s AND MEN—continued.		
318. Sutton, Alfred Lindsay	Private	
319. Lawson, Robert James	,,	Returned to Australia; discharged 13.3.02
320. Sloane, William Bernard	,,	
321. Osborne, Arthur Charles	,,	
322. Juchan, Percy James	,,	
323. Smith, John Francis	,,	
324. Carr, Sydney Joseph	,,	Accidentally wounded at Standerton, 11.6.01
325. Mullahy, James	,,	
327. Wooley, Alfred Richard	,,	
329. Donaldson, Robert Philp	,,	Corporal
330. Smith, Charles Christopher	,,	
331. Nilson, Frederick	,,	Died of accidental injuries at Heidelberg, 6.9.01
332. Grevell, Arthur Rangwall	,,	
333. Pope, Rupert	,,	
334. Mackenzie, Charles Fleming	,,	
335. Cusack, James	,,	
336. Blandford, Joseph	,,	
337. Bradley, James Leopold	,,	
338. Fenner, Henry Williamson	,,	
339. Stapleton, Michael Joseph	,,	Corporal, 19.7.01
341. Johnstone, Henry	,,	
342. Sorrell, Walter	,,	Slightly wounded at Leeuwpoort, 28.8.01
343. Osborne, Samuel Francis	,,	
344. Hoey, Joseph	,,	
345. Dowling, John	,,	
346. Jensen, Thomas James	,,	Farrier-Sergeant, 1.5.01
347. Sinclair, William Charles	,,	
348. Shaw, George Walter	,,	Farrier Quartermaster-Sergeant, 1.5.01. Slightly wounded at Albertina Siding, 1.3.02
349. Mooney, James	,,	
350. Home, George Francis	,,	
351. McPherson, Andrew Percy	,,	
352. Sherwood, Harold Courteen	,,	Corporal, 1.5.01
353. Denison, John Taylor	,,	
354. Lunn, Arthur	,,	
356. Quinn, Lloyd	,,	Slightly wounded at Losberg, 23.8.01
357. Sinclair, Thomas Miller	,,	
358. Edward, William Patrick	,,	
359. Hopf, Ernest	,,	
360. Swenson, Charles John	,,	
361. Lee, Thomas	,,	
362. Crone, Robert Lyden	,,	
363. Nelson, Christian	,,	
364. Glassey, William	,,	
365. Grimstone, C. H.	,,	Sergeant
366. Trask, Frederick Herbert	,,	Regimental Sergeant-Major, despatches *London Gazette*, 29.7.02. For gallantry, D.C.M.
367. Alford, Ernest Pacil	,,	
368. Asche, Frichof Hearfold	,,	Sergeant. Returned to Australia; discharged, 20.1.02

Nominal Roll—*continued.*

No. and Name.	Rank.	Remarks.
N.C.O.'s AND MEN—*continued.*		
369. Davis, Henry	Private	
370. Evans, Henry George	,,	
372. Deuble, Frederick	,,	
373. Christie, Patrick	,,	
374. Rayner, Edward William	,,	
375. Francis, Edward	,,	
376. Wilson, James Carrie	,,	Company Sergeant-Major, 18.10.01
377. Little, John Kyle	,,	Sergeant. Returned to Australia; discharged, 16.1.02
378. Redhead, Thomas	,,	
379. Redhead, Reuben	,,	Corporal, 13.11.01
381. Logan, George	,,	
382. Brown, George Ernest	,,	
383. Wilson, Thomas	,,	
384. Durham, James	,,	Corporal. Slightly wounded at Waterval Hoek, 26.6.01
385. Bell, John Wilcox	,,	
386. Murphy, John	,,	
387. Innes, David	,,	
388. Harris, Thomas	,,	
389. Tiffen, John William	Shoeing-Smith	
390. Marsh, William	Private	
391. Mallon, Henry	,,	
392. Logan, Whitmore	,,	Slightly wounded at Mooifontein, 16.6.01
393. Christie, Arthur	,,	
394. McNamara, Percy Edgar	,,	
395. McCarthy, John Joseph	,,	
396. Bradford, Percy	,,	
397. Bray, Shannon	,,	
398. Smith, George James Bardo	,,	
399. Higginson, Charles Bingham	,,	
400. Moroske, George	Shoeing-Smith	
401. Aherne, Phillip Patrick	Private	
402. Nicols, Charles Maclaurin	,,	
403. Lilley, William John	,,	
404. Hegarty, Richard	,,	
405. Stoneham, John	,,	
406. Hansen, Arthur William	,,	
407. Gardner, Robert	,,	
408. Williams, Thomas Hastings	,,	
409. Mackay, John	,,	
410. Neale, Ernest William	,,	
411. Shaw, Albert	,,	
412. Brooks, Frederick John	,,	
413. Sullivan, Constantine	,,	Corporal, 13.12.01
414. Gregory, Cyril John	,,	Corporal, 24.4.01
415. Norris, Ernest Frederick	,,	
416. Jenner, Ernest	,,	
417. Worrall, George Edward	,,	
418. Andrews, Richard	,,	
419. Sullivan, Simon Charles	,,	
420. Luscombe, Garnet Mancel	,,	
421. Boyce, Samuel	,,	Returned to Australia; discharged, 2.3.02
422. Lonergan, Matthew Jeremiah	,,	
423. Hudson, Albert Ernest	,,	Corporal, 24.1.02

Nominal Roll—*continued.*

No. and Name.	Rank.	Remarks.
Details per "Britannic."		
OFFICER.		
Echlin, Robert Boyd	Captain	*Vide* 3rd M.I. Contingent
N.C.O.'s AND MEN.		
600. Graham, Thomas	Private	
601. Douglas, Joseph	,,	
602. Smith, George	,,	
603. Campbell, Malcolm Livingstone	,,	
604. Rudhall, Benjamin	,,	Killed in action, Amersfoort. 3.2.02
605. Glover, John Edwin	,,	
606. Lambert, George Egbert	,,	
607. Mantle, Harry	,,	
608. Connolly, John	,,	
609. Rush, Charles	,,	
610. Leighton, Charles Hill	,,	
611. Bradshaw, William	,,	
612. Macfarlane, James Burns	,,	
613. Thornburn, George Edwin	,,	
614. Flamark, John James	,,	
615. Harris, Andrew Alfred	,,	
616. Huxtable, Edwin	,,	
617. Daley, Florence John	,,	
618. Powter, Henry Charles	,,	
619. Smith, Ernest	,,	
620. Innes, Joshua	,,	
621. Reardon, Peter William	,,	
622. Kingsmill, Herbert Cyrus	,,	
623. Richardson, William Egbert	,,	
624. Bates, John Robert	,,	
625. Woodard, Arthur	,,	
626. Fallis, Richard	,,	
627. Stuart, William James	,,	
628. Montague, Eugene Graham	,,	
629. Caldwell, Erskin James	,,	
630. Horley, Jesse	,,	
631. Easlea, Thomas	,,	
632. Waltisbuhl, Anthony	,,	
633. Robinson, John Henry	,,	
634. Dodd, Arthur William	,,	
635. Willmett, Walter Henry	,,	
636. Hill, Onslow Frederick Stanley	,,	
637. Cain, John	,,	
638. Payne, George Herbert	,,	
639. Mellifont, Patrick James	,,	
640. Davidson, Leslie	,,	
641. Buchanan, James	,,	
642. Barton, William Leslie	,,	
643. Gilbert, Richard Edward	,,	
644. Pegg, Henry	,,	
645. Macauley, James	,,	
646. Davidson, Norman Alick	,,	
647. Smith, John	,,	
648. Flint, Thomas	,,	Killed in action, Amersfoort, 3.2.02
649. Issell, Charles	,,	
650. Keogh, Herbert William	,,	
651. Sundmacher, George	,,	

Nominal Roll—*continued*.

No. and Name.	Rank.	Remarks.
N.C.O.'S AND MEN—*continued*.		
652. Cook, Edward Christian	Private	
653. Whipman, A. G.	,,	
654. Briggs, Charles	,,	
655. Bell, Horace Walsh	,,	
656. Brickwood, Robert Hugh	,,	
657. Pope, Daniel	,,	
658. Clarke, James	,,	
659. South, Elwin Egerton	,,	
660. Trower, George Matthew	,,	
661. Walker, David	,,	
662. Towner, Alfred George	,,	
663. Burns, William	,,	
664. Wynne, William Cardinal	,,	
665. Forrel, John Joseph	,,	
666. Horton, George Cooper	,,	
667. Travers, Horace	,,	
668. Barker, John Charles	,,	
669. Eves, Reginald Horace	,,	
670. Shaw, Charles James	,,	
671. Kelly, Michael Augustine	,,	
672. Lax, John	,,	
673. Cavaye, James McLelland	,,	
674. Armstrong, John	,,	
675. Dutton, Richard Guy	,,	
676. Davidson, Frank	,,	

NOTE.—All the foregoing, except three, had served in previous Contingents.

Details per "*Harlech Castle.*"

OFFICERS.

Crichton, Aubrey De Pree	Lieutenant	*Vide* 4th (Imp. Bushmen) Cont.
Cowley, Campbell	,,	,, ,, ,,
Philp, Colin John Campbell	,,	,, ,, ,,

N.C.O.'S AND MEN.

No. and Name.	Rank.	Remarks.
676. Welch, Edward Hutton	Private	
677. Searle, Frederick Henry	,,	
678. Holpen, Frederick Ernest	,,	
679. Holpen, Archibald	,,	
680. Holdaway, John	,,	
681. Townsend, Ernest	,,	
682. Doughan, John James	,,	
683. Winniett, Chard Massey	,,	
684. Mansergh, Charles	,,	Returned to Australia; discharged 16.1.02
685. Cousens, Harry Richmond	,,	
686. Thompson, Victor Emanuel	,,	
687. Hannan, Michael John	,,	
688. Thompson, Hiram Preston	,,	
689. Micklethwaite, Richard Spencer	,,	
690. Broatch, William	,,	
691. Akred, James Allen	,,	
692. Maddock, George Hamilton Sydney	,,	
693. Farrell, William Robert	,,	

Note:—Every officer and man of these details, except one, had served in 3rd or 4th Queensland Contingents.

SPECIAL SERVICE OFFICERS.
Captain (now Colonel) R. S. Browne.

THIS officer was attached for Special Service to the First Queensland Contingent, and embarked with them in the transport *Cornwall*, which left Brisbane on 1st November, 1899, and arrived at Table Bay on 12th December. He obtained the local rank of Major, and was present at the relief of Kimberley, and operations in Orange Free State, February to May, 1900; including operations at Paardeburg, 17th to 26th February. Actions at Poplar Grove, 7th March; Driefontein, 10th March; Vet River, 5th and 6th May; and Zand River, 10th May. Operations in the Transvaal in May and June, 1900, including actions near Johannesburg, 29th May; Pretoria, 4th June; and Diamond Hill, 11th and 13th June. Operations in the Transvaal, west of Pretoria, July to 29th November, 1900, including action at Zilikat's Nek, 2nd August. Operations in the Transvaal east of Pretoria, July to 29th November, 1900, including actions at Riet Vlei, 16th July. Operations in Cape Colony north of Orange River, 1899–1900. Invalided to Australia, and arrived at Brisbane, 24th November, 1900 Despatches, *London Gazette*, 8th February and 16th April, 1901. C.B. Queen's Medal with five clasps.

Major (now Lieut.-Colonel) J. J. Byron.

Complete records of this officer's service could not be obtained. He was present at operations in Cape Colony, Orange River Colony, and Transvaal, 1899–1900 Advance on Kimberley, including action at Magersfontein (wounded). Aide-de-camp to Field Marshal Commanding-in-Chief. Despatches, *London Gazette*, 8th February and 16th April, 1901. C.M.G. Queen's Medal with four clasps.

Major (now Lieut.-Colonel) V. C. M. Sellheim.

Selected by the War Office as a Special Service officer. Embarked at Southampton in transport *Harlech Castle*, on 20th October, 1899. Attached 2nd Battalion, Northamptonshire Regiment. 20th November, 1899, with Methuen's (1st) Division. Present at actions at Belmont, 23rd November, 1899; Graspan, 25th November, 1899; Modder River, 28th November, 1899; Magersfontein, and reconnaissance there in force, 11th December, 1899.

Attached to Victorian Mounted Rifles, with Australian Regiment, 17th December, 1899, at Enslin. Attached to 1st Contingent Queensland Mounted Infantry, 13th January, 1900, as Transport Officer, and Officer Commanding Machine Gun Section. Present at Colonel Rochford Boyd's expedition against the rebels during January.

March to, and relief of Kimberley, with General French's Mounted Division, including the engagements at the crossing of the Riet and Modder Rivers. March to, and capture of Bloemfontein, with Centre Column, including the battle of Driefontein, 10th March, 1900. Action at Waterval (Sanna's Post), 31st March, 1900, and subsequent operations with Colonel Henry's Brigade, for the relief of Broadwood's Force.

Appointed to staff of Colonel Pilcher's Mounted Infantry Brigade, 15th April, 1900. Present at the operations of Major-General Hutton's Mounted Infantry Force during the general advance on Pretoria on the 1st May; including the capture of Brandfort, 3rd May, 1900; engagement at Constantia, 4th May, 1900; Vet River, 5th May, 1900; Zand River, 7th May, 1900; capture of Kroonstad, 12th May, 1900; action at Klip River Berg, 28th and 29th May, 1900; and capture of Johannesburg; subsequent advance to, and capture of, Pretoria.

Operations under Lieut.-General French to the north and east of Pretoria, including battle of Diamond Hill, 11th and 12th June, 1900. Operations northeast of Pretoria, under Major-Generals Hutton and Mahon. First general advance eastward with **Major-General Mahon's Force**, as far as Balmoral, 25th July, 1900, and subsequent return to Pretoria. March to relief of Rustenburg, 5th August, 1900, with Lieut.-General Ian Hamilton's Division; and pursuit of De Wet's Force northwards to Warmbad, including engagement at Oliphant's Nek, 17th August, 1900.

Appointed Staff Officer to Chauvel's Mounted Infantry, 14th September, 1900. Present at operations of the corps, including the engagement near Pan on 11th October, 1900.

Embarked for Australia per s.s. *Sophocles*, and arrived at Brisbane, 15th December, 1900.

Despatches, *London Gazette*, 16th April, 1901. C.B. Queen's Medal with six clasps.

Captain (now Major) F. W. Toll.

This officer proceeded to South Africa in the transport *Maori King*, with the Second Queensland Contingent, which arrived on 22nd February, 1900. He was appointed Railway Transport Officer at Cape Town; and after three weeks of this duty, joined Lord Roberts' army near Bloemfontein, which had been occupied before Captain Toll's arrival. He obtained charge of a company of infantry in the (44th) Essex Regiment, 18th Brigade, XI. Division, commanded by Major-General Pole-Carew; but vacancies subsequently occurring in the Brigade staff, became field-aide and acting aide-de-camp, and the former duty was carried out until the end of his service. He was in the advance from Bloemfontein, and operations round Leeuwkop and Paardekraal (horse shot under him), and in vicinity of De Wetsdorp. Proceeded in the general advance on 1st May to Johannesburg and Pretoria; present at Vet River, Zand River, Boxburg, Kroonstad, and Elandsfontein. At Boxburg he captured an armed Boer, whose rifle he was permitted to retain. In engagements round Pretoria, Diamond Hill, and Edendale, where he captured three armed Boers within 500 yards of a farm in which there were 50 or 60 Boers, about 9 miles from the British outposts. In addition to his other duties he became officer in charge of Intelligence and Signallers. He was with the advance upon Belfast and Barberton, including all sorties and engagements. At Belfast he was in charge of 14 sharpshooters selected to hold a dangerous position. Of these, 6 were killed by pom-poms and 2 by bullets; others were wounded. Ammunition became expended, and a man volunteered to go back for some, but was shot dead as soon as he rose. Captain Toll then made the attempt and secured enough to carry on with until dark.

On occupation of Nellspruit, Waterval Onder, he was appointed Provost-Marshal, which duty he performed until his service ended. He returned in command of time-expired troops by the transport *Wooloomooloo*, arriving at Brisbane on the 8th December, 1900.

See also Fifth Queensland Contingent.

Major (now Lieut.-Colonel) C. D. W. Rankin.

Embarked in the s.s. *Maori King* at Pinkenba, Brisbane, 13th January, 1900. Arrived at Cape Town, 22nd February, 1900. Returned to Queensland, 6th March, 1901.

Second in Command, Australian Regiment of Mounted Infantry, and afterwards D.A.A.G. First Mounted Infantry Brigade, South African Field Force. Operations in Orange Free State, February to May, 1900. Operations in the Transvaal, June, 1900, including action at Diamond Hill, 11th and 12th June. Operations in the Transvaal, east of Pretoria, July and August, 1900, including action at Riet Vlei, 16th July. Operations in Cape Colony, south of the Orange River, February, 1900.

In General Order, No. 467 of 1900 (6th October, 1900), it appeared that "Major Rankin, injured by horse falling near Belfast, has sailed for England."

Queen's Medal with three clasps.

FIRST AUSTRALIAN COMMONWEALTH HORSE.
QUEENSLAND UNIT.

CONSTITUTED "D" Company of the 1st Battalion, Australian Commonwealth Horse, consisting of three companies New South Wales, one Queensland, and one Tasmanian.

For details of establishment, pay, clothing, and equipment, &c., *vide* 1st Australian Commonwealth Horse (New South Wales), p. 166.

The Queensland officers of regimental staff were Lieut.-Colonel J. S. Lyster, commanding battalion, and Captain J. Gillies, Army Medical Corps. The company was short of one officer, in consequence of the resignation of a subaltern before embarkation.

Many of the N.C.O.'s and men had served in previous Contingents.

DEPARTURE AND RETURN.

The company left Brisbane 26th January, 1902; Sydney (with New South Wales Contingent), 18th February, 1902; with 7 officers, and 116 others; 124 horses. Of these, 1 officer resigned, 2 privates died, 1 officer 37 others were struck off in South Africa; 5 officers, 77 others returned.

SERVICE.

By rail from Brisbane, 26th January, 1902; embarked on transport *Custodian* (Sydney), 18th February, 1902. With Colonel De Lisle's, also Colonel Williams' Column. Took part in driving operations in Western Transvaal, in the former officer's Column, which formed part of a force consisting of 13 columns under Lieut.-General Sir Ian Hamilton. (*Vide* 1st Australian Commonwealth Horse, New South Wales).

EXTRACT FROM FIELD ORDER.

"Devondale, Transvaal,
12th May, 1902.

"The following telegram has been received from General Sir Ian Hamilton, K.C.B., D.S.O. :—

"'The following is the general result of recent operations.—Killed, 1; prisoners, 354; rifles, 212; horses, 326; mules, 95; donkeys, 20; wagons, 175; Cape carts, 61; cattle, 3,500; sheep, 13,000; small arm ammunition, 6,340; trek oxen, 106. Amongst prisoners is Jan de la Rey, elder brother of General.'

"Since telegraphing this information to Pretoria, General Ian Hamilton has received the following telegram from Lord Kitchener :—

"'Capital result. Tell troops I highly appreciate their exertions and consider result very satisfactory. We have now since Methuen's mishap taken 860 out of De la Rey's forces.'

"As there is a considerable proportion of new troops in the command, the General Officer Commanding Mobile Columns, W.T., thinks that Column Commanders would do well to explain to them that the General Officer Commander-in-Chief is not in the habit of bestowing indiscriminate praise; and that, on the contrary, the compliment which has been paid this force is a very rare occurrence."

The Company embarked at Durban on 11th July, 1902, in transport *Drayton Grange*; touched at Albany, 30th July; Melbourne, 7th August; Sydney, 10th; Brisbane, 13th.

Disbanded on 19th August, 1902.

War Services and Honours.

Two of the officers (Captain Berry and Lieutenant Greene) had served with the 4th Contingent, which see.

The officers who had not seen previous service were awarded Queen's Medal with two clasps.

Nominal Roll.

No. and Name.	Rank.	Remarks.
Officers.		
Berry, James Kincaid	Captain	Served in 4th Contingent
Woodcock, Charles Francis	Lieutenant	Lieutenant, Royal Australian Artillery
White, Cyril Brudenell Bingham	,,	Lieutenant, Royal Australian Artillery
Green, William Alfred Goodall Esdaile	,,	Served in 4th Contingent
N.C.O.'s and Men.		
818. Perske, John Frederick	Company Sergeant-Major	Regimental Sergeant-Major, 28.5.02
817. Parsons, John Williams	Quartermaster-Sergeant	
921. Abraham, Cyril	Private	
855. Allan, John	,,	
916. Angle, Charles	,,	
804. Barry, Lawrence	,,	
885. Beattie, John	,,	
862. Beetham, John James	,,	
819. Bernard, Richard	,,	
948. Allen, Robert	,,	
868. Bowdler, William	,,	
816. Blakeway, Thomas	,,	
874. Bliss, George	,,	
908. Brown, John Horace	,,	
856. Brown, William Joseph	,,	
940. Brown, John William	,,	
836. Burton, George Alfred	,,	
822. Blundell, John S.	,,	
886. Busher, William James	,,	
935. Cannon, John	,,	
882. Campbell, Thomas Bridge	,,	
917. Campbell, John Ormes	,,	
880. Carberry, James	,,	
853. Carter, Richard	,,	
869. Casey, Thomas Charles William	,,	
905. Brischke, Otto	,,	
941. Chesney, Frank Rawdon	,,	
891. Clark, James Ernest	,,	Corporal, 7.7.02
919. Cowley, John Peace Mornington	,,	
923. Creighton, William Allan	,,	
938. Cunningham, Joseph	,,	
829. Curtis, James Henry	,,	
864. Daye, Joseph Henry	,,	
913. Dawson, Geoffrey Charles	,,	
900. Dunlop, Adam James	,,	Corporal, 7.7.02
901. Dunlop, William Andrew	,,	
881. Easton, Francis Paul	,,	
925. Eiseman, John	,,	

Nominal Roll—continued.

No. and Name.	Rank.	Remarks.

N.C.O.'s AND MEN—continued.

No. and Name.	Rank.	Remarks.
918. Evans, David	Private	
894. Ferguson, William	,,	Corporal, 7.7.02
839. Flanagan, John Joseph	,,	
845. Flanagan, Thomas Michael	,,	
867. Forbes, Arthur Edward	Bugler	
858. Fry, Albert Charles	Private	
832. Gaffel, Richard William	,,	
860. Gillespie, Francis George	,,	
840. Glasgow, Daniel Robert	Lance-Corporal	Corporal, 7.7.02
820. Goodwin, James	Private	
815. Graham, Thomas Alexander	,,	
863. Greer, William	Lance-Corporal	Corporal, 7.7.02
813. Greig, William Fraser	Private	Corporal, 7.7.02
866. Hall, Arthur Ernest	,,	
944. Hall, William	,,	
897. Hally, John	,,	
934. Harper, Benjamin John	,,	
810. Hemming, Alfred Villiers	,,	
909. Hough, Thomas George	,,	
902. Hounslow, Joseph	,,	
933. Howell, George Frederick	,,	
911. Humphries, Archibald	,,	Died of pneumonia at Hospital, Portsea, Victoria, 9.8.02
895. Hunter, John	,,	
876. Irwin, Thomas	,,	
841. Jeffrey, John David	,,	
833. Jolly, David	,,	
947. Katting, Alfred	,,	Died of enteric at Elandsfontein, 27.6.02
906. Kerr, John Arthur	,,	
932. Kielly, Michael Patrick	,,	
838. Knipe, John Rogers	,,	
831. Lacey, William James	,,	
893. Lacey, Albert Victor	,,	
903. Loughman, Thomas	,,	
942. Lucas, Frank William	,,	
939. Macdonald, John	,,	
896. McLean, Hector	,,	
920. McLean, John Alexander	,,	
931. McLellan, John Robert	,,	
833. McLeod, William Duncan	,,	
801. McMillan, George	,,	
865. McMorrine, Livingstone	,,	
802. Mahony, Edward William	,,	
951. Morris, James	,,	
805. Meade, John	,,	
850. Moffitt, John James	,,	
807. Moss, Frank Buckton	Corporal	Sergeant, 7.7.02
946. Moss, Herbert Saville	Private	
847. Murtagh, Lawrence	,,	
823. Nicoll, Reginald McQuaril	,,	
828. O'Keefe, Edward	,,	
875. Owen, George	,,	
830. Phillips, Charles Francis	,,	
884. Quinlan, John	,,	
899. Raymond, Arthur Ernest	,,	
929. Reuben, Maurice Tasman Leonard	,,	

Nominal Roll—*continued*.

No. and Name.	Rank.	Remarks.
N.C.O.'s AND MEN—*continued*.		
842. Rowe, Frederick James	Private	
811. Ryan, Michael William	,,	
809. Saunders, William Huntley	,,	
827. Schroder, Frederick	,,	
943. Scudder, John	,,	
914. Shaw, William Fitzroy	,,	
910. Simpson, John	,,	
945. Skelton, John Telfer	,,	
806. Sparks, Alexander	,,	
936. Staunton, Peter	,,	
814. Stewart, Ralph	,,	
879. Stibbards, Thomas	Bugler	
926. Sykes, Charles John	Private	
857. Taylor, Alfred John	,,	
927. Thorpe, John	,,	
887. Todhunter, Ernest Percy	,,	
915. Toll, Osmond Harding	,,	Corporal, 7.7.02
844. Tutty, Victor Charles	,,	
852. Wall, Albert John	,,	
843. Warren, John Charles	,,	
872. Watson, James	,,	
949. Weir, James	,,	
870. Wheatley, William John	,,	

COMMONWEALTH ARMY MEDICAL CORPS.

FORMED the Queensland Field Hospital and Bearer Unit of the Commonwealth Contingent, Army Medical Corps. For details of clothing and equipment, establishment, &c., *vide* Army Medical Corps, New South Wales, 4th Contingent, p. 16.

It comprised—1 warrant officer, 1 sergeant, 1 sergeant-artificer, 1 corporal, 2 lance-corporals, 10 privates; 16 in all, of whom 3 were struck off in South Africa.

Left Brisbane by rail on 30th January, 1902, and Sydney on 12th February, in the transport *Manchester Merchant*. Arrived at Durban on 17th March, and participated in operations in the Transvaal between 19th March and 31st May, 1902.

Embarked on 10th July in the transport *Drayton Grange* at Durban; called at Albany, 30th July, 1902, and arrived in Brisbane on 13th August, having taken Melbourne and Sydney *en route*.

Disbanded on 19th August, 1902.

Nominal Roll.

No. and Name.	Rank.	Remarks.
1339. Walker, Frederick	Warrant-Officer	
1340. Lowry, Robert Alexander	Sergeant	Promoted Staff Sergeant, 1.4.02
1341. Holliday, James Owen	Collarmaker - Sergeant	
1342. Quinn, John	Corporal	
1343. Hair, Victor Arthur	Private	
1344. Miller, Andrew Reid	,,	
1345. Benjamin, Adolph Bertram	,,	
1346. Tunley, Arthur	,,	
1347. Farrell, William Arthur	,,	
1348. Dunsmore, William Wallace	Lance-Corporal	
1349. Armstrong, William Herbert	,,	
1350. Arnsby, Thomas William	Private	
1351. Polson, Alfred Henderson	,,	
1352. Cavanagh, Thomas	,,	
1353. Pringle, Alfred	,,	
1354. Adams, Henry	,,	

THIRD AUSTRALIAN COMMONWEALTH HORSE.

QUEENSLAND UNIT.

THIS was "D" Company of the 3rd Battalion, Australian Commonwealth Horse, consisting of three Companies, New South Wales, one Queensland, and one Tasmanian.

For details of establishment, pay, clothing, and equipment, &c., *vide* 1st Australian Commonwealth Horse (New South Wales), p. 166. For service, *vide* 3rd Australian Commonwealth Horse (New South Wales), p. 176.

Departure and Return.

Left Brisbane, 25th March, 1902, in the transport *Englishman*, comprising— 5 officers, 117 others (1 enrolled at Hobart); 121 horses. Called at Hobart; arrived at Durban, 10th May. Two left at Hobart and returned to Queensland; 1 died; 3 officers, 33 others were struck off in South Africa; 2 officers, 81 others returned to Australia.

Embarked 11th July, 1902, at Durban, in the transport *Drayton Grange*; Albany, 30th July; Brisbane, 13th August; having called at Melbourne and Sydney.

Disbanded 19th August, 1902.

Nominal Roll.

No. and Name.	Rank.	Remarks.
Officers.		
Echlin, Richard Boyd	Captain	Previous service in 3rd Contingent
Crichton, Archibald Fredk.	Lieutenant	Previous service in 2nd Contingent
Seccombe, Norman Thorne	,,	Previous service in 2nd Contingent
Henry, James Douglas	,,	Previous service in 4th Contingent
Bowman, Arthur Macarthur	,,	
N.C.O.'s and Men.		
1850. Mayes, Charles Aitken	Sergeant	Staff Sergeant-Major, 17.5.02
1872. Harris, Alfred Edward	Quartermaster-Sergeant	
1937. Schipkie, John Charles Frederick	Farrier-Sergeant	Farrier Quartermaster-Sergeant, 22.5.02
1928. Christie, William James	Sergeant	
1911. Turner, Charles	,,	
1931. Ryan, Arthur Albert	,,	
1909. Walsh, Walter	,,	
1862. Davis, Arthur Wilson	Corporal	
1906. Tracey, William Walter	,,	
1907. Brooks, Albert	,,	
1917. Millan, Alexander	,,	
1929. Stenner, George Henry	,,	
1967. Reid, Charles	,,	

Nominal Roll—continued.

No. and Name.	Rank.	Remarks.

N.C.O.'s AND MEN—continued.

No. and Name.	Rank.	Remarks.
1933. Bennett, George Henry	Lance-Corporal	
1958. Flood, Luke Hubbock	,,	
1876. Goodwin, George Taylor	,,	
1959. Huston, William John	,,	
1930. Mooney, Timothy	Saddler	
1881. McIntosh, Alexander	Shoeing-smith	
1887. Cordingley, John William	,,	
1827. Bell, William T.	,,	Farrier-Sergeant, 22.5.02
1889. Tighe, Charles William Alfred	,,	
1874. Aldham, Harcourt Byron Ernest	Private	
1877. Allen, John	,,	
1957. Archibald, Robert	,,	Left at Hobart, and returned to Queensland
1939. Barry, Joseph Hugh	,,	Left at Hobart, and returned to Queensland
1870. Bell, George	,,	
1981. Benwell, Francis Ross Lewin	,,	
1974. Blackshaw, Henry Aaron	,,	
1966. Blomfield, Albert Henry Charles	,,	
1863. Bolwell, Frederick William	,,	
1912. Bower, Samuel Henry	,,	
1858. Bowman, Charles Ernest	,,	
1924. Brannelly, John Patrick	,,	
1892. Brimstone, Bernard Barton	,,	
1955. Brocklebank, William Hann	,,	
1977. Bromhall, Lewis Charles	,,	
1948. Bryce, Patrick	,,	
1898. Cameron, Hugh	,,	
1980. Clarke, Bell Sheridan	,,	
1856. Clarke, Edward	,,	
1963. Coleman, Albert Bartholomew	,,	
1914. Connolly, John William Fitzroy	,,	
1921. Considine, Patrick	,,	
1888. Coutts, Wilfred James	,,	
1985. Davies, Robert John	,,	
1873. Dodd, John	,,	
1942. Donaldson, Ernest Robert	,,	
1962. Donovan, Frederick	,,	
1964. Edwards, Morris George	,,	
1905. Evans, Maurice John	,,	
1869. Gall, James	,,	
1916. Gall, John Charles	,,	
1954. Goos, Henry	,,	
1908. Grenier, George Alexander	,,	
1970. Harris, Joseph	,,	
1868. Hawkins, Giles Harrison	,,	
1891. Hayes, John Thomas	,,	
1938. Hermann, John Henry	,,	
1896. Hessian, Peter Joseph	,,	
1860. Hinz, August Henry	,,	
1918. Hoelscher, Geoffrey	,,	
1902. Jefferson, Frederick	Bugler	
1903. Jessop, George Henry Frank	Private	
1973. Jones, Charles Lewis	,,	
1976. Jones, Jess Richmond	,,	
1855. Keenan, William	,,	
1854. Kimpton, Stephen William	,,	

Nominal Roll—continued.

No. and Name.	Rank.	Remarks.
N.C.O.'s AND MEN—continued.		
1941. Laws, William Catchside	Private	
1895. Lee, Patrick	,,	
1867. Leney, Frederick Charles Hunt	,,	
1978. Lester, Henry	,,	
1866. Lewis, Charles Edward	,,	
1983. Lubke, William John Albert	,,	
1878. Lucas, Thomas Richard	,,	
1984. Lyons, John Thomas Daniel	,,	
1923. Maloney, Thomas Francis	,,	
1969. Marsden, Eric William	,,	
1880. Matheson, Murdock	,,	
1926. Mealing, Christopher	,,	
1882. Millers, Nicholas Henry	,,	
1952. Munro, John Thomas	,,	
1982. Murphy, John	,,	
1915. McCarthy, Ernest Henry	,,	
1965. MacDonald, Ralph Munro	,,	
1897. McGrath, Edward Joseph	,,	
1991. McSwaine, John Robertson	,,	
1932. O'Dwyer, James	,,	
1979. Parker, Peter Albert	,,	
1956. Randall, Frank	,,	
1968. Rickaby, Daniel	,,	
1971. Roberts, Charles David	,,	
1992. Robinson, William James	Bugler	
1861. Ross, Reginald Roy Mackenzie	Private	
1884. Ross, Alfred John Mackenzie	,,	
1899. Ross, Kenneth Stuart	,,	
1885. Ruffett, James	,,	
1859. Sacre, Edgar Thomas	,,	
1883. Scragg, George	,,	
1890. Smith, Charles Andrew	,,	
1922. Stacy, Ernest James	,,	
1904. Star, Charles Henry	,,	
1852. Star, William	,,	
1988. Storey, Algernon Gould	,,	
1986. Thomas, George	,,	
1871. Thompson, Burke Westwood	,,	Died of pneumonia, Melbourne Hospital, 8.8.02
1919. Thompson, William	,,	
1975. Todd, David	,,	
1961. Todman, Edmond Thomas	,,	
1947. Vaughan, Michael	,,	
1944. Vollmerhause, Otto	,,	
1945. Vollmerhause, Frank Ferdinand Jacob	,,	
1943. Vorm, Frederick Peter	,,	
1987. Wallis, Harry George	,,	
1910. Walsh, Frank Vincent	,,	
1989. Weir, George Herbert	,,	
1925. Wilkinson, Edwin	,,	

SEVENTH AUSTRALIAN COMMONWEALTH HORSE.

A BATTALION which differed from the preceding in being raised entirely in Queensland. For details of establishment, pay, clothing, and equipment, organization, etc., *vide* 5th Australian Commonwealth Horse (New South Wales), p. 184, and 6th Australian Commonwealth Horse (Victoria), p. 324.

Squadrons were raised in the following districts; as far as possible from local forces :—

"A" Squadron.—Southern Coastal District. 1st Troop, Logan ; 2nd Troop, Bremer ; 3rd Troop, Burnett ; 4th Troop, Moreton.

"B" Squadron.—Darling, Western Downs, and Border Districts. 1st Troop, Darling Downs ; 2nd Troop, Border ; 3rd Troop, Warrego ; 4th Troop, Maranoa.

"C" Squadron.—Northern District. 1st Troop, Kennedy ; 2nd Troop, Flinders ; 3rd Troop, Winton ; 4th Troop, Dalyrmple.

"D" Squadron.—Central District. 1st Troop, Mitchell ; 2nd Troop, Peak Downs ; 3rd Troop, Port Curtis ; 4th Troop, Leichardt.

Many of the N.C.O.'s and men had served in previous Contingents ; some in local South African Corps.

Departure and Return.

Left on 19th May, 1902, with 23 officers, 467 others (1 enrolled on board ship) ; and 493 horses. Four died ; 4 officers, 123 others were struck off in South Africa ; 19 officers, 340 others returned.

Service.

The Contingent steamed from Pinkenba (Brisbane), on 19th May, 1902, in the transport *Custodian*. Arrived at Durban on 22nd June ; and peace having been declared, did not proceed further than Newcastle, Natal.

Embarked on 28th June at Durban in the transport *Manchester Merchant*. At Albany, 18th July ; called at Adelaide, Melbourne, and Sydney, and arrived at Brisbane, on 2nd August.

Disbanded on 9th August, 1902.

Nominal Roll.

No. and Name.	Rank.	Remarks.
Battalion Staff.		
Chauvel, Henry George, C.M.G.	Lieut.-Colonel	Previous service, 1st Queensland Mounted Infantry Contingent
Plomer, William Henry Percival	Major	Egyptian campaign, 1884
O'Brien, James Charles	Captain-Adjutant	
Keogh, Peter Malachy	Captain and Quartermaster	
McLeod, John	Captain, Veterinary Officer	Previous service with 4th Queensland Imperial Bushmen
Nicholson, Frank Villeneuve	Captain	Paymaster, 5th and 7th Battalions
Webster, George Alexander	Lieut. A.M.C.	
1. Ryan, James Bernard..	Regimental Sergeant-Major	Previous service, 1st Queensland Mounted Infantry Contingent
2. Sabine, William Randolph Eppes	Regimental Quartermaster-Sergeant	Previous service, 2nd Queensland Mounted Infantry Contingent
3. Macrossan, John	O.R.C. Staff Sergeant	

Nominal Roll—*continued.*

No. and Name.	Rank.	Remarks.
"A" SQUADRON—SOUTHERN COASTAL DISTRICT.		
Officers.		
Hodgkinson, William Oswald	Captain	
Holme, Charles Bretheton	Lieutenant	Previous service, 2nd Queensland Mounted Infantry
Codd, Frederick Charles Edward	,,	Previous service, S.A.C.
Koch, Felix Bernard Theodor	,,	Previous service, 3rd Queensland Mounted Infantry and 5th Queensland Imperial Bushmen
N.C.O.'s and Men.		
462. Kidd, Alexander	Sqn. Sergeant-Major	
4. Hemmy, Frederick William	Sqn. Quartermaster-Sergeant	
5. Hodgkinson, William George	Sergeant	
6. Rutledge, George	,,	
7. Rappel, John Robert	,,	
8. Pepplir, Gilbert Otto	Private	
9. Purcell, John Joseph	Farrier-Sergeant	
10. Wardell, Bernard James	Shoeing-Smith	
11. Ekblad, Nils Peter	,,	
12. Ryan, Patrick	,,	
13. Smith, Edward	Saddler	
14. Stanley, Arthur Henry	Trumpeter	
15. Anderson, John	,,	Died at sea (s.s. *Custodian*) of fish poisoning, 9.6.02
16. Mealing, William Richard	Corporal	
17. Knudsen, Peter	Sergeant	
18. Christie, Charles	Corporal	
19. Christie, Albert William	,,	
20. Lloyd, James	,,	
21. O'Connor, Daniel Patrick	,,	
22. Bowden, Henry Fitzroy	Private	
23. Buckmaster, Denis John	,,	
24. Brosnan, Michael	,,	
25. Bartlett, William Henry Augustus	,,	
26. Boyd, Bernard	,,	
27. Bytheway, Samuel	,,	
28. Browning, Richard	,,	
29. Bryce, James	,,	
30. Blackburne, Edward Lee	,,	
31. Biddle, Henry	,,	
32. Boxhall, Frederick Lamont	,,	
33. Brown, Irving Stuttford	,,	
34. Bishop, Alexander	,,	
35. Carroll, Patrick	,,	
36. Carr, Patrick	,,	
37. Clements, Alfred Ernest	,,	
38. Carmody, William	,,	
39. Chatterton, Robert	,,	
40. Chapple, James Alfred	,,	
41. Clements, Edward	,,	
42. Cummings, Andrew	,,	
43. Condon, Dennis	,,	
44. Carless, Joseph	,,	

Nominal Roll—*continued.*

No. and Name.	Rank.	Remarks.
"A" SQUADRON—SOUTHERN COASTAL DISTRICT—*continued.* N.C.O.'s and Men—*continued.*		
45. Cloherty, Frederick Charles	Private	
46. Donald, George Oliver	”	
47. Deneefe, James	”	
48. Davies, John	”	
49. Dodds, Edward Swayne	”	
50. Duffy, Thomas Edward	”	
51. Dugdale, Walter	”	Died at sea (s.s. *Custodian*) of gastritis, 15.6.02
52. Drew, Samuel Henry	”	
53. Earl, Francis George	”	
54. Forman, James Glennie	”	
55. Gallwey, John William	”	
56. Gleeson, Bartholomew	”	
57. Harrison, William Ernest	”	
58. Hourigan, John	”	
59. Handy, John	”	
60. Holland, James	”	
61. Horgan, Daniel	”	
62. Holcombe, Alexander Essex	”	
63. Harper, Knollys	”	
64. Johnson, William Henry	”	
65. Johnson, Mulhall Francis	”	
66. Jackson, Leslie Lewis	”	
67. Johnson, Thomas Henry Grew	”	
68. Kettle, George Henry	”	
69. Kent, Ernest Alfred	”	
70. Knayer, Charles William	”	
71. Long, Samuel	”	
72. Lindsay, Harry	”	
73. Manwaring, James Hardy	”	
74. Morse, Alfred	”	
75. Meldron, John Patrick	”	
76. McCarthy, Joseph	”	
77. Madden, Stephen	”	
78. Matthews, Frank	”	
79. Moss, Reginald Charles	”	
80. Murray, William Wilson	”	
81. Maddock, Arthur Frank Vivian	”	
82. McNemay, James Barry	”	
83. McClelland, James	”	
84. Nielson, Jacob Peter	”	
85. Neller, Joseph William	”	
86. O'Hanlon, James Kemp	”	
87. Olsson, Frederick George	”	
88. Page, John	”	
89. Price, Arthur Farren	”	
90. Phipps, Edward	”	
91. Quinn, John James	”	
92. Rooks, Albert James	”	
93. Rogers, George Victor	”	
94. Risson, Henry	”	
95. Sheehan, William	”	
96. Stewart, James Stephen	”	
97. Shillito, George	”	
98. Savage, Norman Douglas	”	
99. Smales, Hugo	”	
100. Silvester, Albert William	”	

Nominal Roll—*continued*.

No. and Name.	Rank.	Remarks.
"A" Squadron—Southern Coastal District—*continued*.		
N.C.O.'s and Men—continued.		
101. Sachse, Clarence Otto	Private	
102. Smith, Edwin Percival	,,	
103. Spiden, Robert Aleck	,,	Died in Hospital, Brisbane, of pneumonia, 17.8.02
104. Stilgoe, William	,,	
105. Steele, Bert Danby	,,	
106. Stuart, James	,,	
107. Scott, John Ernest	,,	
108. Scanlon, John Patrick	,,	
109. Simpson, John Charles	,,	
110. Saunders, Henry	,,	
111. Smith, Alec. Jonson	,,	
112. Tregoning, Joseph	,,	
113. Von Holt, John Joseph	,,	
114. Whelan, John	,,	
115. Woosley, Ernest Harry	,,	
116. Wensley, William	,,	
117. Yates, Ernest Edwin	,,	
118. Riles, Frederick Samuel	,,	
"B" Squadron—Darling, Western Downs, and Border Districts.		
Officers.		
Yaldwin, Hamilton St. Clair	Captain	Previous service, 4th Queensland Imperial Bushmen
Wilson, Francis Henry David	Lieutenant	
Dods, George Archibald Cowan	,,	Previous service, 3rd Queensland Mounted Infantry
Knyvett, Frank Berners	,,	Previous service, 1st Queensland Mounted Infantry. and 5th Queensland Imperial Bushmen
N.C.O.'s and Men.		
119. Treadwell, Rubin John	Sqn. Sergeant-Major	
120. Cain, Joseph	Sqn. Quartermaster-Sergeant	
121. Chambers, James	Sergeant	
122. McDonald, Cecil Allan	,,	
123. Boyd, Robert	,,	
124. Macnish, Frank St. Clair	,,	
125. Ross, John	Farrier-Sergeant	
126. Funnell, Robert Henry	Shoeing-Smith	
127. Marshall, Thomas Joseph	,,	
128. Robinson, Henry Edwards	,,	
129. Matthias, William Albert	Saddler	
130. Gagen, John Thomas	Trumpeter	
131. Cox, Walter Henry	,,	
132. Chudley, Charles	Corporal	
133. Grayson, John Irwin	,,	
134. Stevens, Harry	,,	
135. Meritt, Harold Waldron	,,	
136. Arrell, Harry John	,,	
137. Hally, Thomas	,,	

No. and Name.	Rank.	Remarks.

"B" SQUADRON—DARLING, WESTERN DOWNS, AND BORDER DISTRICTS—*continued.*

N.C.O.'s and Men—*continued.*

138. Allen, Arthur	Private	
139. Atkinson, Percy Arthur	,,	
140. Armstrong, James	,,	
141. Brodie, John Garfield	,,	
142. Boughton, William	,,	
143. Bichsel, Samuel	,,	
144. Bishop, George	,,	
145. Blagg, Joseph	,,	
146. Brizzle, William Robert	,,	
147. Butz-Bennet, Henry Bowes	,,	
148. Barton, Edward Percy	,,	Died in Hospital, Portsea, Victoria, of pneumonia, 14.8.02
149. Cranston, George William	,,	
150. Connors, Thomas Patrick	,,	
151. Cox, George Eric Mackenzie	,,	
152. Clarke, Charles	,,	
153. Craig, John	,,	
154. Collins, Albert Thomas	,,	
155. Donohue, John	,,	
156. Dora, Harry	,,	
157. Dalton, John Patrick	,,	
158. Donnelly, John Francis	,,	
159. Ericksen, Gustav Aage	,,	
160. Evans, Edwin	,,	
161. Edwards, William Herbert	,,	
162. Fleming, Victor Robert	,,	
163. Flint, Sydney Joseph	,,	
164. Francis, Wilfred Everett	,,	
165. Fortescue, Charles	,,	
166. Fowler, Frederick Sydney	,,	
167. Gilkison, Aubrey Frederick	,,	
168. Harkiss, James Ramage	,,	
169. Gray, Arthur Henry	,,	
170. Gilmore, Alex.	,,	
171. Giltrow, Richard	,,	
172. Grant, Alexander Stewart	,,	
173. Goss, John Ernest	,,	
174. Hanlon, John	,,	
175. Head, Thomas Alfred	,,	
176. Johnson, John	,,	
177. Johnson, Frederick	,,	
178. Kearnan, Michael	,,	
179. Keys, Alfred George	,,	
180. Knowles, Richard James	,,	
181. Littlewood, William David	,,	
182. Le Feuvre, Sydney Edward	,,	
183. Lee, John Joseph	,,	
184. Lucas, Percival George Ashmore	,,	
185. Lucas, Guy Edgar	,,	
186. Lavercombe, Alexander	,,	
187. Marks, Charles Richard	,,	
188. Marler, Ernest Walter	,,	
189. Murray, Harry	,,	
190. Masters, Arthur	,,	

Nominal Roll—continued.

No. and Name.	Rank.	Remarks.

"B" SQUADRON—DARLING, WESTERN DOWNS, AND BORDER DISTRICTS—continued.

N.C.O.'s and Men—continued.

191. Mathison, William	Private	
192. Mousley, Raywood	,,	
193. Moore, Charles Frederick	,,	
194. Mackie, John Norman	,,	
195. Mackay, Eric Leith	,,	
196. McDonald, Alexander John	,,	
197. McLaren, William Alfred	,,	
198. McLaren, John Brown	,,	
199. McCarthy, James Patrick	,,	
200. Nicholson, William George Joseph	,,	
201. Nicholaus, Ernest	,,	
202. Nicholaus, Henry	,,	
203. O'Neill, William	,,	
204. Oliver, William John	,,	
205. Osmond, Benjamin Edward	,,	
206. Palmer, Ellis Richard	,,	
207. Pullen, Charles Richard	,,	
208. Power, Edgar Norman	,,	
209. Poncho, John	,,	
210. Quinn, Thomas	,,	
211. Rice, John Patrick	,,	
212. Scanlon, Daniel Joseph	,,	
213. Sheehan, Patrick	,,	
214. Spears, James	,,	
215. Scott, James	,,	
216. Starkey, Edward George	,,	
217. Sanderson, Ainslie	,,	
218. Smith, Hughent Ashley	,,	
219. Stewart, John	,,	
220. Tryhorn, Charles	,,	
221. Tamblyn, Francis	,,	
222. Thompson, Alfred Joseph	,,	
223. Thomas, Samuel	,,	
224. Taylor, William Charles	,,	
225. Taylor, Henry Arthur	,,	
226. Watson, John Robertson	,,	
227. Wilson, Richard	,,	
228. Wren, William Henry	,,	
229. Woodforde, Eric Redout	,,	
230. Wrigley, Alfred	,,	
231. Whitford, Arthur	,,	
232. White, Edward Matthew	,,	
233. Webb, Clement Cecil	,,	
459. Marden, John Charles	,,	

"C" SQUADRON—NORTHERN DISTRICT.

Officers.

Brand, Charles Henry	Captain	Previous service, 3rd Queensland Mounted Infantry
Brodie, Vernon Bissett	Lieutenant	Previous service, 4th Queensland Imperial Bushmen
Tolson, James	,,	
Turnour, John Monteith	,,	

Nominal Roll—*continued.*

No. and Name.	Rank.	Remarks.
"C" SQUADRON—NORTHERN DISTRICT—*continued.*		
N.C.O.'s and Men.		
234. Hudson, Cecil Raymond	Sqn. Quarter-master-Sergeant	
235. Price, Solomon	Private	
236. Morris, John Crisop	Sqn. Sergeant-Major	
237. Sweeney, Edmund	Sergeant	
238. Fogg, Herbert John Harry	,,	
239. Connors, Jack	Farrier-Sergeant	
240. Erixson, Louis	Shoeing-smith	
241. Quinlan, Patrick John	,,	
242. Simpson, Andrew	,,	
243. Solway, Thomas Henry	Saddler	
244. Dickson, William Robert Edgar John	Trumpeter	
245. Borrill, John Thomas	,,	
246. Bacon, James	Corporal	
247. Stockdale, Frederick Risley	,,	
248. Cheffins, Frederick	,,	
249. Lehman, William	Private	
250. Price, William	,,	
251. Locke, James	,,	
252. Anderson, William Francis	,,	
253. Armstrong, Alton	,,	
254. Badenock, William Frederick	,,	
255. Bagley, Alfred Young	,,	
256. Barr, George Preston	,,	
257. Biddle, Robert	,,	
258. Bogie, Robert Dixon	,,	
259. Boulter, Dennis	,,	
260. Brittingham, Rowland James	,,	
261. Bull, Walter	,,	
262. Campbell, William Leslie	,,	
263. Callow, Robert	,,	
264. Carrol, Patrick	,,	
265. Clough, George Henry	,,	
266. Clough, Thomas	,,	
267. Christensen, James Walter	,,	
268. Christie, Donald	,,	
269. Conway, James	,,	
270. Couper, Charles Frederick Atkins	,,	
271. Connors, Michael	,,	
272. Debney, George Ross	,,	
273. Diack, Henry Adam	,,	
274. Dippel, Christopher Henry	,,	
275. Dodgson, Sydney	,,	
276. Doonan, Thomas	,,	
277. Dunne, Albert Alfred	,,	
278. Dunne, Joun Canice	,,	
279. Dunne, William John	,,	
280. Douglas, George	,,	
281. Easton, Thomas	,,	
282. Ellson, Walter Henry	,,	
283. Emmerson, Norman	,,	
284. Erskine, Peter	,,	
285. Goldsmith, George Hassett	,,	

Nominal Roll—*continued.*

No. and Name.	Rank.	Remarks.

"C" SQUADRON—NORTHERN DISTRICT—*continued.*

N.C.O.'s and Men—*continued.*

No. and Name.	Rank.
286. Gore, Edward	Private
287. Hamilton, James Alfred	,,
288. Hammond, Harold Aubrey	,,
289. Heathcote, James Albert George	,,
290. Hammond, Walter	,,
291. Herring, John	,,
292. Harding, Richard George	,,
293. Hawkins, Thomas Bartholomew	,,
294. Holmes, David	,,
295. Hogarth, Joseph	,,
296. Hodges, George Douglas	,,
297. Hutchinson, William McAllister	,,
298. Jenkins, John Henry	,,
299. Jensen, William Francis	,,
300. Jones, William	,,
301. Kershaw, James	,,
302. Kidd, Herbert	,,
303. Knudsen, Christian	,,
304. Langford, Benjamin James	,,
305. Lawrence, Eric James	,,
306. Le Feuvre, Peter	,,
307. Lingard, Henry Arthur	,,
308. Luck, Samuel	,,
309. Matheson, Robert	,,
310. Matheson, Lewis	,,
311. Madigan, George	,,
312. Mahony, Cornelius	,,
313. Meredith, George	,,
314. Maitland, Thomas	,,
315. Moore, George Morton Tennyson	,,
316. Moody, William John	,,
317. Morrice, George	,,
318. Morgan, Alexander	,,
319. Newton, Charles Robert	,,
320. Coates, Joseph	,,
321. Mortimer, Ernest Leslie	,,
322. O'Dwyer, John Taylor	,,
323. Pill, James Edward	,,
324. Parker, Charles Edward	,,
325. Playfoot, John	,,
326. Prince, John	,,
327. Raine, Robert William	,,
328. Robertson, Sydney	,,
329. Robinson, Edward Albert	,,
330. Singleton, Thomas	,,
331. Scott, Richard Aston	,,
332. Sewell, John Thomas	,,
333. Smith, Joseph	,,
334. Sontag, August	,,
335. Suthers, Thomas	,,
336. Stevens, Michael	,,
337. Smythe, Charles John	,,
338. Sullivan, Edward	,,
339. Thomson, Alfred	,,
340. Turner, John Edward	,,
341. Wallace, Samuel	,,

Nominal Roll—continued.

No. and Name.	Rank.	Remarks.
"C" Squadron—Northern District—continued.		
N.C.O.'s and Men—continued.		
342. Watkins, Herbert	Private	
343. Williams, Ernest	,,	
344. Williams, Charles Henry	,,	
345. White, James Blackwood	,,	
346. Wilkie, Andrew	,,	
847. White, Herbert William	,,	
348. Whitehouse, Leonard	,,	
"D" Squadron—Central District.		
Officers.		
Parker, Charles Albert	Captain	Previous service in the 4th Queensland Imperial Bushmen
Wienholt, Frederick Edward	Lieutenant	
Black, Duncan	,,	
Moran, Frank	,,	
N.C.O.'s and Men.		
461. Paten, Harry	Sqn. Sergeant-Major	
349. Faine, Thomas Francis Gordon	Sqn. Quartermaster-Sergeant	
350. Prigg, William	Sergeant	
351. Arnold, John Henry	Private	
352. Sheppard, Frederick William Dankeld		
353. Slade, William	Corporal	
354. Bruce, William Robert	Farrier-Sergeant	
355. Neale, Arthur Drayton	Shoeing-Smith	
250. Ryan, Thomas Joseph	,,	
357. Johnstone, William	,,	
358. McIntosh, Edward Edwin	Saddler	
359. O'Brien, John Cahill	Trumpeter	
360. Thomas, Percy Lindon	,,	
361. Hodson, Arnold Weinholt	Corporal	
362. Robins, James Alexander	,,	
363. McDonnell, Alexander Joseph	,,	
364. McDonnell, John Joseph	Private	
365. Symington, Quinton Leith Anderson	,,	
366. Allen, George Henry	,,	
367. Anderson, William Alfred	,,	
368. Aylward, Herbert Alfred	,,	
369. Barber, Charles Joseph	,,	
370. Ballad, Abe	,,	
371. Benson, Barker Robert	,,	
372. Blogg, William	,,	
373. Buxton, Francis Joseph	,,	
374. Chisholm, Frederick John	,,	
375. Cody, John	,,	
376. Conroy, Joseph Patrick	,,	
377. Coker, Herbert Lisley	,,	
378. Collins, Conrad Carden	,,	
379. Considine, Patrick	,,	
380. Curran, Edward Lawrence	,,	
381. Deeley, Joseph Alonza	,,	

Nominal Roll—*continued*.

No. and Name.	Rank.	Remarks.

"D" SQUADRON—CENTRAL DISTRICT—*continued*.

N.C.O.'s and Men—*continued*.

382. Eames, Edward	Private
383. Fairbairn, William Noble	,,
384. Fitzgerald, Thomas Lattin	,,
385. Fitzgerald, Peter Nugent	,,
386. Fitzgerald, Gerald	,,
387. Fletcher, Sydney John	,,
388. Forrest, Henry	,,
389. Finney, Robert Edwin	,,
390. Galvin, Timothy	,,
391. Gamfield, Henry Charles	,,
392. Halligan, Thomas	,,
393. Harrison, Richard Mild	,,
394. Harle, William Myers	,,
395. Hazelton, Archibald	,,
396. Heath, Charles	,,
397. Heckley, Walter	,,
398. Henderson, Edward William	,,
399. Henderson, Selby Stuart	,,
400. Heatherington, Haysly Fairfax	,,
401. Herd, Robert Alfred	,,
402. Hegarty, Robert Claude	,,
403. Higginson, Irlam	,,
404. Higgs, James	,,
405. Humphreys, William	,,
406. Hunt, Edward Thomas	,,
407. Hutchison, Alfred	,,
408. Keefer, William Henry	,,
409. Klöpsch, Ernest	,,
410. Lancelotte, Edward Benjamin	,,
411. Locke, Hudson James	,,
412. Luck, Edward Charles Cecil	,,
413. Macarthur, John	,,
414. McCarthy, Peter	,,
415. McCabe, Peter	,,
416. Macaulay, James Booth	,,
417. Marsh, Leslie	,,
418. Marshall, Harry Richard	,,
419. Marshall, Charles James	,,
420. Mason, William	,,
421. Maxwell, George	,,
422. Mears, Henry Archibald	,,
423. Miles, George Edward	,,
424. Morgan, Thomas	,,
425. Monoghan, Edward	,,
426. Miller, Lewis Alfred	,,
427. Nesbit, James Stewart	,,
428. Norton, Francis Henry	,,
429. Norton, Robert	,,
431. O'Brien, Robert	,,
432. Perkins, Samuel	,,
433. Porter, George Henry	,,
434. Reynolds, William Arthur	,,
435. Reynolds, Daniel	,,
436. Redgwell, John George	,,
437. Robertson, Norman	,,
438. Rossiter, Joseph	,,

Nominal Roll—*continued.*

No. and Name.	Rank.	Remarks.

"D" Squadron—Central District—*continued.*

N.C.O.'s and Men—*continued.*

No. and Name.	Rank.	Remarks.
439. Ryan, George	Private	
440. Sanders, Frank	,,	
441. Sloane, John Henry	,,	
442. Smith, James	,,	
443. Stewart, William	,,	
444. Summers, Lewis	,,	
445. Dickson, William	,,	
446. Thorn, Stanley	,,	
447. Vivian, Richard Edward	,,	
448. Wakefield, Frederick	,,	
449. Ware, George Henry	,,	
450. Wildig, Benjamin Parte	,,	
451. Williams, Arthur Lynne	,,	
452. Williams, James Gordon	,,	
453. Williams, Thomas	,,	
454. Wanka, William	,,	
455. Wolstenholme, Walter	,,	
456. Wright, James	,,	
457. Wuth, Charles Theodore	,,	
458. Toomey, Arthur	,,	
460. Fraser, William Alexander	,,	
464. Collum, Hugh	,,	
465. Ungerer, Henry	,,	
466. Redman, Charles	,,	
467. Moore, Edward John	,,	

LIST OF OFFICERS AND OTHERS OF QUEENSLAND CONTINGENTS WHO WERE KILLED, OR DIED.

Regimental Number, Rank, and Name.	Regimental Number, Rank, and Name.

1st Contingent.
91. Private McLeod, D. C.
219. ,, Jones, V. S.
56. Corporal Conley, G. B.
165. Private Reece, H. L.
95. Corporal Bryce, W. H.
180. ,, Cumner, T.
177. ,, Devitt, W.
25. Gunner Walker, S.
134. Private Broderick, E. St. J. V.
242. ,, Damrow, W. A.
116. Corporal Wriford, G.

2nd Contingent.
108. Private Cronan, E.
54. ,, Reimers, C. M.
128. ,, Landsborough, S. L.
90. ,, Parnell, J.

3rd Contingent.
Lieut. Annatt, J. W.
,, Leask, J.
40. Private Masterton, J. T.
31. ,, Maude, A. E. F. C.
157. ,, Bailey, A. T.
294. ,, Hull, G.
28. ,, McDonald, D. K.

4th Contingent.
77. Private Duggan, J.
202. Sergeant Maxwell, F.
279. Private Clancy, P. J.
147. ,, Lynd, J. W.
283. ,, Daws, G.
235. ,, Meredith, C.
284. ,, Poole, W. S.
336. ,, Bourke, A. C.
204. ,, McLeod, D. J. R.
67. ,, Hastie, P. S.
325. ,, Butler, W.
74. ,, Young, L. H. W.
248. ,, Helder, J. O.
296. ,, Wright, A. E.
195. Sergeant Strang, J.

5th Contingent.
261. Private White, H. J.
199. ,, Moller, C.
157. ,, Anderson, J. H.
34. ,, Hunt, E. H.
31. ,, Hendy, W. M.
256. ,, Blunt, F. G.
494. ,, O'Callaghan, J. McD.
372. ,, Cousins, J.
307. ,, Sanderson, W.

5th Contingent—continued.
56. Private Anning, J. H.
110. ,, Stirling, Colin
475. ,, Cumming, R. R.
Lieut. Pooley, A. E.
,, Caskey, L. J.
331. Private Milner, B.
202. ,, White, G. H.
27. ,, Mason, J. E.
203. ,, McIlveen, J.
419. ,, Roberts, A.
105. ,, Murphy, D.
525. Sergeant Power, J. C.
452. ,, Berry, R. E.
164. Act.-Cpl. Macfarlane, J.
511. Private Salt, E. H.
464. ,, Chardon, C.
127. ,, Lilley, W.
122. ,, MacCartney, W.
482. ,, Clarke, W. G.
74. ,, Goodall, F. T.
441. ,, Kelly, R. S.
165. ,, Eagleton, A. W.
229. ,, Belin, A. G.
1. Sgt.-Sad. Shannon, J. P.
396. Artificer Clark, G. H.
103. Private Forsythe, G. G.

6th Contingent.
159. Private Russell, S. K.
283. ,, Matherson, J. K.
98. ,, McPherson, N.
191. Q.M.S. Malcolm, J.
233. Private Geaney, M.
79. ,, Davis, A. W.
331. ,, Nilson, F.
119. ,, Marr, R. S.
189. ,, Mills, G. H.
218. ,, Juchan, E. T.
604. ,, Rudhall, B.
648. ,, Flint, T.
22. Q.M.S. Gorman, J. T.

1st Battalion ("D" Company), A.C.H.
947. Trooper Katting, A.
911. ,, Humphries, A.

3rd Battalion ("D" Company), A.C.H.
1871. Trooper Thompson, B. W.

7th Battalion, A.C.H.
15. Trumpeter Anderson, J.
51. Trooper Dugdale, A. R. W.
148. ,, Barton, E. P.
103. ,, Spiden, R. A.

Summary of Contingents Despatched.

Transport.	Date.	Contingent.	Officers.	Others.	Horses.	M. Guns and Wagons.
Cornwall	1 Nov., 1899	1st Queensland Mounted Infantry	14	248	284	2
Maori King	13 Jan., 1900	2nd Queensland Mounted Infantry	10	144	178	
Duke of Portland	1 Mar., 1900	3rd Queensland Mounted Infantry	14	302	406	
Manchester Port	18 May, 1900	4th Queensland Imperial Bushmen	26	368	512	
Templemore	6 Mar., 1901	5th Queensland Imperial Bushmen	22	481	376	
Chicago	10 Mar., 1901	Draft	1	25	100	
Victoria	4 Apr., 1901	6th Queensland Imperial Bushmen	17	384	615	No record.
Britannic	20 Aug., 1901	Details	1	77	..	
Harlech Castle	26 Sep., 1901	Details	3	18	..	
Custodian	18 Feb., 1902	D Company, 1st Australian Commonwealth Horse	7	116	124	
Manchester Merchant	11 Feb., 1902	Details Army Medical Corps	..	16	..	
Englishman	25 Mar., 1902	D Company, 3rd Australian Commonwealth Horse	5	117	121	
Custodian	19 May 1902	7th Australian Commonwealth Horse	23	467	493	
		Special Service Officers	5	..	..	
	Staff	Australian Commonwealth Horse	2	..	..	
	Total		150	2,763	3,209	

Disposition.*

	Officers.	Other Ranks.
Died or were killed	4	88
Transferred	7	3
Discharged in South Africa, or embarked for England, and struck off in South Africa	29	499
Commissioned in Imperial Army	1	2
Returned to Australia	124	2,193
	165	2,785

* These figures are in some respects approximate only; it having been found impossible to obtain exact statements, owing to promotions to commissions, attachments, enlistments, and discharges in South Africa, of which no adequate returns have been made.

TASMANIA.

TASMANIA

PREFATORY.

AUTHORITY for the Tasmanian Contingents was conferred by Statute, namely, the *Tasmanian Military Contingent Act* 1899, 63 Vict. No. 11, and by regulations thereunder.

Pay was issued to the first and second Contingents, according to rates as stated, by the Tasmanian Government and the Imperial Government; to the remainder by the Imperial Government, the Tasmanian Government acting as agents.

Clothing, equipment, and necessaries were furnished upon a liberal scale; and horses and saddlery provided; but (as in case of the other Contingents) not returned from South Africa.

Camps of Instruction were held in the first instance at the Military Barracks Hobart; and afterwards at the Show Grounds, Newtown.

The period of engagement was twelve months, or the duration of the war. About twelve months was the average service of any Australian Contingent, though many officers, N.C.O.'s and men remained behind, and served in other Contingents or were employed.

Tasmania sent four Contingents to the war. A draft for the first Contingent is also sometimes counted as another; but this is manifestly erroneous, as will be perceived from the record of that Contingent. The State also contributed a half-company to First Australian Commonwealth Horse; a company to the Third, and a squadron to the Eighth.

The First Contingent was a company of Infantry, which was mounted in South Africa, and became part of the Australian Regiment. They were in General Clements' Force, and engaged in operations round Colesberg; were in the advance upon Bloemfontein; joined Colonel Henry's Brigade, and participated in the march to Pretoria, actions and operations. Thence to Komati Poort.

The Second Contingent (Bushmen) served with General Carrington's Column in Rhodesia and Western Transvaal; and afterwards under Lord Errol and Lord Methuen in Transvaal, Griqualand West, and Orange River Colony.

The Third (Imperial) Contingent were in operations in Eastern Orange Free State under General Paget; and also under him in North East Transvaal and Western Transvaal. Operations in Cape Colony with General Plumer.

The Fourth (Imperial Bushmen) Contingent served in Cape Colony under General French, and subsequently joined Colonel Gorring's Flying Column, and did excellent service in many operations and actions.

Although the number of men and horses despatched to the front was naturally comparatively small, yet the Tasmanians did excellent work wherever they went; and the proportion of honours and rewards distributed was relatively large—a circumstance which speaks for itself with significance.

FIRST (TASMANIAN) CONTINGENT.

THIS Contingent, which consisted of one company of Infantry (converted in South Africa into Mounted Infantry), was raised in October, 1899, under statute of the local Legislature, 63 Vict. No. 11, with an establishment of 4 officers, 1 warrant officer, 5 sergeants, 4 corporals, 2 buglers, and 64 privates. It was subsequently strengthened by a draft comprising 1 officer (Medical Staff), 2 sergeants, and 43 rank and file. Men were enlisted as far as possible from the local forces; and it was notified that officers and N.C.O.'s of such forces serving in the ranks whose position and seniority had been altered, would resume their original position and seniority on their return to Tasmania.

PAY.

The following were the rates of pay from date on which officers and others reported themselves in camp, to time of disembarkation in South Africa:—Privates and buglers, 4s. 6d. per diem; corporals, 7s.; sergeants, 8s.; colour-sergeants, 9s.; warrant officers, 11s. 6d.; lieutenants, 19s.; captains, 23s. 6d.

After the date of disembarkation in South Africa, the following was the rate of pay:—Privates, 3s. 6d.; buglers, 3s. 5d.; corporals, 5s. 4d.; sergeants, 5s. 8d.; colour-sergeants, 6s.; warrant officers, 5s. 6d.; lieutenants, 10s.; captains, 8s. 11d.

The difference between the two rates was paid by the Imperial Government. Any member of the Contingent was authorized to make over his pay to an agent approved by the Defence Minister. A personal allowance of £5 was granted to commissioned officers towards the cost of kit; and the cost of the valise was also defrayed from funds specially provided.

EQUIPMENT, ETC.

Uniform consisted of khaki cloth jacket, trousers, puttees, and field-service hat. Great-coats with capes, khaki cloth frock, and boots were also provided as well as field-service cap, worsted cap, haversack, and a very complete kit, comprising underclothing and necessaries, water-bottles, clasp-knives, and mess-tins.

Rifle M.E. ·303, with bayonet, &c., waistbelts, ball-bags, and V.E. braces. Regimental transport was furnished.

It was estimated that the total weight of equipment was as follows:—For an officer—Articles carried on the person, 37 lbs. 0¼ ozs; articles carried in kit bag and kettles, 19 lbs. 10½ ozs.; total, 56 lbs. 10¾ ozs. For others—Articles carried on the person, 49 lbs. 5¾ ozs.; articles carried in kit bag, 17 lbs. 3½ ozs.; total, 66 lbs. 9¼ ozs.

DEPARTURE AND RETURN.

The Contingent left on the 27th October, 1899, comprising—4 officers, 76 others, with 2 wagons. Six died or were killed; 2 were struck off in South Africa; 4 officers, 68 others, returned to Australia.

The draft was despatched on 18th January, 1900, of 2 officers, 45 others, with 2 wagons. Four died; 1 officer, 41 others returned. One officer was in charge to South Africa only.

PROMOTIONS.

Captain C. St. C. Cameron, promoted to Major, — December, 1899.

Lieutenant Wallace Brown, promoted to Captain.

Sergeants W. P. Lowther and F. B. Adams were promoted to Lieutenants, Bushmen's Contingent.

Corporal C. R. A. Chalmers, promoted Lieutenant, "E" Squadron, 3rd Australian Commonwealth Horse.

Sergeant H. Hallam, Privates C. O. Blyth, F. R. Chalmers, M. H. Swan, J. M'Cormick, and G. F. Richardson became Lieutenants in 4th Contingent.

SERVICE.

The First Tasmanian Contingent was under the command of Captain C. St. C. Cameron who, as an officer of the 9th Lancers, had taken part in Lord Roberts' great march across Afghanistan, and was therefore well qualified to lead them when they figured in the mounted branch. The Company left Launceston, Tasmania, on 27th October, 1899, and embarked on board the transport *Medic* at Melbourne on the 28th ; arrived at Cape Town on 26th November. (*Vide* 1st Victorian Contingent).

The Contingent were at first on the De Aar-Modder line, where, with the remainder of the Australian Regiment, they garrisoned Enslin and other posts protecting the railways. At Naauwpoort, Cape Colony, on 1st Feburary, 1900, they received horses, and joined General Clements' Force then holding the long line opposite the Boer position. They were engaged in operations around Colesberg, which was occupied on 28th February; but all their good service with the Australian Regiment has been narrated, under heading already referred to.

A draft of two sergeants and 43 rank and file, under Captain A. R. Riggall who took charge to Beira, and having with them Lieutenant (Medical Staff) S. C. Jamieson, left Hobart on 18th January, 1900 ; embarked in the transport *Moravian* at Melbourne on the 23rd., and arrived in South Africa on 20th February. They proceeded to Victoria West Road, where they were engaged on the lines of communication until the 5th April, when they entrained for Bloemfontein, and joined the company there.

After their arrival at Bloemfontein, the Tasmanians, with the 1st and 2nd Victorians and the South Australians, were put under the command of Colonel Henry, whose Mounted Infantry were about the outpost line north of Glen Station. They took part in many reconnoitering patrols before the advance to Pretoria ; and were in the action at Hout Nek, 30th April. Major Cameron, who had been wounded and taken prisoner (24th February) had been recaptured at Bloemfontein, and resumed command. During the march to Pretoria, which commenced on 2nd May, Colonel Henry's men were generally the screen in front of the centre and left-centre. They had very hard riding, often from 40 to 50 miles in a day, and took a prominent part in a number of skirmishes and engagements: notably Vet River (6th May) ; Zand River (10th May), when Major Cameron was again wounded ; at the coal mines on the banks of the Vaal ; and in the fighting outside Pretoria.

After the occupation of Pretoria, the Mounted Infantry were mostly stationed on the eastern front. They were at the battle of Diamond Hill, and in the eastern advance from Pretoria. They were in the actions at Balmoral at the end of July, and near Belfast on 7th September. After some very hard marching over rough country, where scouting was difficult, Komati Poort was entered on 24th September. They attended a review there on the 28th.

The total service may be thus summarized :—Operations round Colesberg under General Clements. Joined 4th Mounted Infantry Corps at Bloemfontein. Advance from Bloemfontein to Pretoria, with Hutton's Mounted Infantry Brigade and XI. Division; including actions at Karee Kloof, Brandfort, Vet River, Zand River, Elandsfontein, Johannesburg, and Diamond Hill. From Pretoria to Komati Poort with 18th Brigade, 11th Division ; including actions at Belfast, and occupation of Kapsche Hoop.

In October, the Contingent was taken to Pretoria and there inspected by Lord Roberts.

Lieutenant J. C. Walch, S.T.A., who accompanied the Contingent as a Special Service officer, served with the Royal Horse Artillery, and was present with "Q" battery on 31st March, 1900, at Sanna's Post, when he was severely wounded on the right arm. It was at this action that, owing to the gallant conduct of the battery as a whole, four Victoria Crosses were awarded, for one officer, one N.C.O., and two gunners.   Lieutenant Walch subsequently joined the Contingent.

The Contingent embarked on the transport *Harlech Castle* at Cape Town on 3rd November, 1900, and arrived in Tasmania on 7th December, having called at Albany, Adelaide, and Melbourne.   Disbanded on 8th December.

WAR SERVICES AND HONOURS.

Cameron, Major C. St. C.—Afghan campaign, '78–'79–'80, with 9th Lancers. Medal with clasps. Bronze star—" Kabul to Candahar." Operations in Cape Colony, Orange Free State, and Transvaal, between November, 1899, and October, 1900; including advance on Kimberley, actions round Colesberg, and at Vet River, Zand River, Karee Kloof, Brandfort, and Belfast. Twice wounded Despatches, *London Gazette.* C.B. Queen's Medal with three clasps. Aide-de-camp to Governor-General, 8th August, 1902

Brown, Captain W.—Operations as stated, including actions round Colesberg and at Belfast. Specially mentioned in Commanding Officer's report, 7th December, 1900.   Queen's Medal with three clasps.

Heritage, Lieutenant F. B.—Operations as stated; including advance on Kimberley, and actions round Colesberg, Karee Kloof, Brandfort, Vet River, Zand River, Johannesburg, Pretoria, Diamond Hill, and Belfast. Specially mentioned in Commanding Officer's report, 7th December, 1900. Queen's Medal with five clasps.

Reid, Lieutenant G. E.—Operations and actions as stated. Specially mentioned in Commanding Officer's report, 7th December, 1900. Queen's Medal with clasps.

Jamieson, Lieutenant S. C. (Medical Staff).—Operations and actions as stated except Colesberg. Specially mentioned in Commanding Officer's report, 7th December, 1900.   Queen's Medal with five clasps.

Nominal Roll.

No. and Name.	Rank.	Remarks.
OFFICERS.		
Cameron, Cyril St. Clair	Captain	
Brown, Wallace	Lieutenant	
Heritage, Francis Bede	,,	
Reid, George Elliot	,,	
N.C.O.'s AND MEN.		
Costello, James	Sergeant-Major	Despatches, *London Gazette.* D.C.M.; special mention in C.O.'s Report, 7.12.00
8. Giblin, Alan Vincent	Colour-Sergeant	Specially mentioned in C.O.'s Report
13. Barnes, Arthur	Sergeant	
1. Hallam, Harry	,,	*Vide* " Promotions "
14. Keys, Maurice	,,	
36. Lowther, William Ponsonby	,,	*Vide* " Promotions "
2. Chalmers, Cyril Roderick Alleyne	Corporal	*Vide* " Promotions "
45. Lee, Edgar Hepburn	,,	
49. Parselle, Frederick	,,	
41. Whitelaw, John Henry	,,	Joined Pretoria Police Force; struck off Contingent, 1.7.00
5. Armstrong, William Henry	Bugler	
43. Davis, Herbert James	,,	
68. Abbott, Herbert Benjamin Thomas	Private	
16. Anderson, Thomas	,,	
71. Bailey, Elliot Henry	,,	Killed at Witkornsk, 11.9.00
60. Ballantyne, Andrew	,,	
56. Barker, Thomas William	,,	Died of disease at Deelfontein, 15.6.00

Nominal Roll—*continued.*

No. and Name.	Rank.	Remarks.
N.C.O.'s and Men—continued.		
62. Barnes, Robert Henry	Private	
12. Betts, Henry Allwright	,,	Lance-Corporal. Killed near Donnerpoch, 20.6.00
46. Black, Henry Mitchell	,,	Died of disease at Bloemfontein, 18.4.00
61. Blower, James	,,	
48. Blyth, Charles Oscar	,,	*Vide* " Promotions "
26. Branagan, William Daniel	,,	
58. Brothers, Charles	,,	
3. Briant, Frederick Charles	,,	
30. Button, Alfred	,,	Killed at Rensburg, 9.2.00
10. Chalmers, Frederick Royden	,,	*Vide* " Promotions "
44. Chilcott, Charles David	,,	
51. Coles, William Richard	,,	
28. Collins, Claude Eustace	,,	
29. Collins, Vivian Gowan	,,	
25. Coombe, Archibald	,,	
42. Cox, Henry James	,,	
70. Dennis, Arthur Walter	,,	
69. Ducie, Stephen William	,,	
11. Edwards, John	,,	
38. Elliott, John Theop	,,	
24. Fremlin, Clarence Albert	,,	
32. Gaby, Reginald Wigmore	,,	
50. Gilham, Atherly	,,	Killed at Rensburg, 9.2.00
27. Gillies, Angus	,,	
67. Greenbank, Edward Leonard	,,	
40. Hall, Gordon Frank	,,	
37. Harris, Frederick John	,,	
47. Headlam, Lionel Vicary	,,	
22. Holmwood, Alfred Desormeaux	,,	
64. Hope, John	,,	
55. Hough, Alfred William James	,,	
53. Hutton, John	,,	
54. Hynes, Cecil William	,,	
4. Jephson, Alexander Hill	,,	
57. Lade, Cyrus	,,	
63. Lathey, Arthur James	,,	
52. Lynch, Francis Bernard	,,	
35. Lowther, George Markham	,,	
39. Maddox, Hugh Cathcart	,,	
17. McGuiness, Edgar	,,	
21. McGuiness, Hugh Charles	,,	
59. McGuire, Frederick	,,	
20. Morrisby, Frank Edward	,,	
65. Morse, James	,,	
66. Page, Julian Lambert Russel	,,	
18. Parker, Alfred James	,,	
19. Pedder, Charles Frederick	,,	
15. Peers, Victor Stanley	,,	
23. Reynolds, Alban John	,,	
34. Roberts, John	,,	
72. Smith, Fenton Magnus	,,	
75. Smith, Robert Arthur	,,	
33. Stephenson, Charles Morrison	,,	
9. Swan, Morton Henry	,,	*Vide* " Promotions "
73. Walker, George Arthur	,,	
7. Weeding, Frederick	,,	
6. Williams, Stanley James Salter	,,	
74. Wilson, Robert Benjamin	,,	
3. Wright, James	,,	

Nominal Roll—*continued*.

No. and Name.	Rank.	Remarks.
Draft.		
OFFICERS.		
Riggall, Arthur Horton	Captain	In charge to Biera
Jamieson, Stanley Connebee	Lieutenant (Medical Staff)	
N.C.O.'S AND MEN.		
84. Adams, Frank Bertram	Sergeant	Mentioned in C.-in-C.'s despatches, 8.3.01. *Vide* "Promotions"
99. Berresford, Cyril Walter	,,	
76. Doolin, Robert Percy	Corporal	Joined Imperial Railway Department. Died of disease
95. Smith, Richard Percival	,,	
103. Best, Frank	Private	
110. Best, Morris	,,	
93. Blyth, George	,,	
120. Burton, Walter	,,	
104. Butler, Joseph	,,	Died of disease at Germiston, 1.6.00
78. Chepmell, Henry Douglas	,,	
105. Chilcott, Arthur	,,	
100. Cheveux, Arthur Farrell	,,	Joined Imperial Railway Department
82. Douglas, James Angus	,,	
85. Ellis, Leslie Morton	,,	
88. Evans, Ernest Chambers	,,	
80. Facy, Hedley Hastings	,,	
90. Fitzallen, Thomas Henry	,,	
96. Galvin, Thomas	,,	Died of disease at Pretoria, 19.8.00
88. Hays, Edward Charles	,,	
77. Hortin, Algernon Babington	,,	
111. Johnstone, Leslie William	,,	
107. Judge, George	,,	
98. Larner, Harry Elvin	,,	
86. Lawson, Alexander	,,	
94. Lupton, Alfred	,,	
89. Lyon, William	,,	
101. Macanally, Samuel Charles	,,	
79. McCormick, John	,,	*Vide* "Promotions"
115. McGuinness, George Frederick	,,	
116. Murdock, Alexander Paul	,,	
108. Packett, Edwin	,,	
92. Parish, Charles Arthur	,,	
114. Pegg, Albert Edward	,,	
119. Pitt, Roland, Philip	,,	Died of disease at Norval's Pont, 11.6.00
106. Potter, Arthur William	,,	
118. Rafferty, Rupert Anstice	,,	
113. Richardson, George Fairbrass	,,	*Vide* "Promotions"
109. Riley, Samuel	,,	
117. Smallhorn, Herbert	,,	
102. Stagg, Pitman John	,,	
91. Tilley, Arthur James	,,	
81. Vaughan, Oswald De Wit	,,	
91. Wellard, Gilbert	,,	
87. Williams, William Joseph	,,	
112. Wilson, Reginald Colin	,,	

NOTE.—No complete record could be obtained of N.C.O.'s and men promoted, of casualties other than deaths, or of those invalided; either for this Contingent or the Draft.

SECOND (TASMANIAN BUSHMEN) CONTINGENT.

AUTHORIZED by the Tasmanian Government about February, 1900. It consisted of a half-squadron of Mounted Infantry. Establishment (leaving Hobart)—1 sergeant-major, 2 sergeants, 1 farrier-sergeant, 4 corporals, 1 farrier, 43 privates. Lieutenant-Colonel E. T. Wallack, Special Service officer, went in charge; and officers were posted in South Africa.

Pay and equipment were as for former Contingent, except (in regard to the latter), such slight changes as were requisite in providing for mounted men.

PROMOTIONS, ETC.

Sergeant A. M. Boyes, promoted Lieutenant 18th November, 1900; Adjutant, 2nd January, 1901.

Lieutenants Lowther and Adams were promoted from 1st Contingent.

Sergeant G. W. Kemsley became Lieutenant " C " Squadron, Australian Commonwealth Horse.

For promotions of N.C.O.'s and men, *vide* nominal roll.

DEPARTURE AND RETURN.

The Contingent embarked at Hobart, 5th March, 1900, comprising—52 sergeants and rank and file, with 58 horses. One was killed; 2 struck off in South Africa; 1 officer commissioned in the Imperial Army; 1 officer, 49 others returned.

SERVICE.

The Bushmen's Contingent, consisting as before stated, of about a half-squadron of Mounted Infantry. was sent to the theatre of war, under charge of Lieut.-Colonel E. T. Wallack. They embarked at Hobart on the transport *Antillian* on 5th March, 1900; arrived at Cape Town on the 31st, and proceeded thence to Beira, where Captain A. H. Riggall took charge, he being the officer who had previously brought out the draft for the 1st Contingent.

Their principal operations, and Corps or Columns served with, were as follow: —Formed part of General Carrington's Column, sharing in the operations in Rhodesia and Western Transvaal under him. Then under Lord Erroll in Transvaal Mounted Infantry Brigade and afterwards, under Lord Methuen, in Western Transvaal, Griqualand West, Orange River Colony.

Having crossed Rhodesia towards Mafeking, they took part in many operations, under the leaders named. They had several casualties near Ottoshoop in August, when Carrington was endeavouring to assist Colonel Hore. The Contingent formed part of a complete Bushmen's Regiment, with " D " Squadron, 1st New South Wales, one Squadron of New Zealanders, and three of South Australians.

For a long time the Regiment did excellent work in the Western Transvaal, as part of Lord Methuen's Force. At Buffel's Hoek (21st August), there was a sharp fight. They were in action at Ottoshoop (12th September), and Lichtenburg (26th). About the month of September, Captain Riggall was invalided home, and Lieutenant Lowther took charge.

Throughout the latter part of 1900 and the first quarter of 1901, the composite Bushmen's Regiment was in many engagements, chiefly in the Western Transvaal, but also in Northern Orange River Colony. In several of these the enemy fought with considerable determination; and, consequently, losses were frequent. For many months the Western Transvaal was dangerously denuded of troops; thus there was considerable strain on those who were there.

The Contingent embarked on the transport *Aberdeen* at Cape Town on 19th May, 1901, and arrived in Tasmania on 14th June; having called at Albany, Adelaide, and Melbourne on the way.

Disbanded on 16th July, 1901.

WAR SERVICES AND HONOURS.

Riggall, Captain A. H.—Operations in Cape Colony, Orange River Colony, Transvaal, and Rhodesia, between April, 1900, and September, 1900. Despatches, *London Gazette*. D.S.O. Queen's Medal with four clasps.

Lowther, Lieutenant W. P.—Operations as stated. Queen's Medal with clasps.

Boyes, Lieutenant A. M., Adjutant.—Operations as stated. Mentioned in Despatches, *London Gazette*, 29th July, 1902. Queen's Medal with four clasps.

Adams, Lieutenant F. B.—Operations as stated. Mentioned in Despatches, *London Gazette*, 29th July, 1902. Queen's Medal with four clasps.

Nominal Roll.

No. and Name.	Rank.	Remarks.
OFFICERS.		
Wallack, Ernest Townshend	Lieut.-Colonel	In charge to Beira
Joined in South Africa.		
Riggall, Arthur Horton	Captain	Invalided to Tasmania, —.9.00
Lowther, William Ponsonby	Lieutenant	Previous service in 1st Contingent
Adams, Frank Bertram	,,	Previous service in 1st Contingent
N.C.O.'S AND MEN.		
Goucher, Thomas	Sergeant-Major	
122. Boyes, Alexander Mackenzie	Sergeant	*Vide* "Promotions." Despatches, *London Gazette*, 29.7.02
136. Gardiner, John James	,,	Mentioned in Commander-in-Chief's Despatches, 2.4.01
160. Smith, Thomas	Farrier-Sergeant	
132. Cox, Harry	Corporal	
134. Dowling, Herbert	,,	
161. Smith, Vernon	,,	Quartermaster-Sergeant, 18.6.00
168. Towers, George	,,	
127. Barwick, William Henry	Farrier	Staff Farrier-Sergeant, 15.5.00
121. Adams, Edward Beuse	Private	
124. Beveridge, Henry David	,,	
125. Burgess, Eric Ethelbert	,,	
123. Butler, Hedley Salisbury	,,	
126. Brain, Frank Edward	,,	
131. Chant, Robert	,,	Mentioned in Commander-in-Chief's Despatches, 2.4.01
130. Chant, Walter Herbert	,,	
129. Coleman, John	,,	Lance-Corporal, 18.6.00
128. Cowen, Stanley Michael	,,	Invalided and awarded pension
135. Douglas, Ronald	,,	Mentioned in Commander-in-Chief's Despatches, 2.4.01
133. Dyer, Arthur Valentine	,,	
144. Gerrand, Robert Soamers	,,	
140. Hamilton, Alexander	,,	
141. Harrison, Archibald Oscar	,,	Lance-Corporal, 18.6.00
138. Heathcote, Harry Ward	,,	
137. Hillier, Albert George	,,	Mentioned in Commander-in-Chief's despatches, 2.4.01
139. Hood, Major Harry	,,	

Nominal Roll—*continued.*

No. and Name.	Rank.	Remarks.
N.C.O.'s AND MEN—*continued.*		
143. Jacson, Edward Roger	Private	Lance-Corporal, 26.5.00; killed at Ottoshoop, 22.8.00. Mentioned in Commander-in-Chief's despatches, 2.4.01
142. Johnson, Alfred Frank	,,	Corporal. Sergeant, 18.6.00
146. Kemsley, George William	,,	Corporal, 26.5.00; Sergeant, 2.1.01; Commander-in-Chief's despatches, 8.4.01; despatches, *London Gazette*, 29.7.02; D.C.M. *Vide* "Promotions"
145. Kerr, Peter	,,	
149. Lawson, Robert	,,	
148. Lee, Richard	,,	
147. Lette, Alfred	,,	
170. Mace, Rowland Thomas C.	,,	
153. McInnis, Ronald	,,	
152. McIntyre, William Keverill	,,	
150. Midgley, Samuel Hawksworth	,,	
151. Mitchell, Elvin Charles	,,	
154. Packett, Charles	,,	
155. Petersen, Louis	,,	
156. Phelan, Edward Thomas	,,	
158. Riley, James St. Clair	,,	Lance-Corporal, 18.6.00
157. Rockett, Hildreth Payton	,,	Corporal, 18.6.00
159. Royle, John Douglas	,,	
163. Sims, Arthur Edward	,,	Lance-Corporal, 28.3.00
165. Stanworth, James Benjamin	,,	Corporal, 18.6.00
164. Sullivan, Joseph	,,	
162. Sweeney, William	,,	
167. Tolman, Alfred Gibbs	,,	
166. Tolmie, Frank Malcolm	,,	Farrier, 14.5.00; Farrier-Corporal, 19.7.00
171. Wilkinson, Reginald Longworth Cave	,,	
169. Wood, Robert Rumney	,,	

SPECIAL SERVICE OFFICERS.

LIEUT.-COLONEL E. T. Wallack, Tasmanian Permanent Staff, was sent out to South Africa as a Special Service officer. He was placed in command of the 1st Tasmanian Bushmen to take them to Cape Town, where he was to hand them over to Captain Riggall.

He embarked at Hobart on the transport *Antillian* on 5th March, 1900. On arrival at Cape Town he was ordered to proceed to Beira, South-East Africa, to join Lieut.-General Sir Frederick Carrington's Staff. The Bushmen went with him, and were there handed over to Captain Riggall.

Colonel Wallack was at once appointed Staff Officer to disembark and forward to Marendellas the Rhodesian Field Force.

He then joined Sir Frederick at the camp at Marendellas, and was appointed to the Head-Quarters Staff of the Rhodesian Field Force.

While at this camp he trained the 4th and 5th New Zealand Contingents in the use of the magazine rifle, and assisted to raise the Rhodesian Field Artillery.

Colonel Wallack served with Sir Frederick Carrington until that General returned to Rhodesia, and was present at the operations against the Boers in the Elands River, Marico, Zeerust, and Ottoshoop districts, 1st August to 1st September.

He then joined Brigadier-General the Earl of Erroll, and served with that officer in the active operations at Ottoshoop and its vicinity, 1st September, to October. On 17th October, Lord Erroll's Command joined the 1st Division, and Colonel Wallack was attached to the Staff, and was present in the campaign in the Western Transvaal until 7th January, 1901. From 9th to 18th January in hospital from injuries to the eyes received near Jacobsdal. 19th January, appointed Staff Officer for Mafeking Command; held this position for six weeks, and then proceeded to Cape Town on duty in connexion with arrival of fresh Colonial Contingents. On 29th March, rejoined the 1st Division at Kimberley; and 8th April, proceeded to Fourteen Streams, and from thence to Doornfontein, Orange River Colony, and carried out the musketry training of the Imperial Yeomanry.

On 5th May proceeded to Cowan's Farm and rejoined Head-Quarters of the 1st Division, and was placed in command of the troops stationed there—about 1,200 of all ranks—until granted leave on 18th June.

Was invalided for ten weeks in England; returned to South Africa on 1st November, but was too ill to proceed to the front.

Left for Australia, 14th November, 1901.

Despatches, *London Gazette*, 2nd April, 1901. C.B. Queen's Medal with five clasps.

Lieut. J. C. Walch. *Vide* p. 547.

THIRD (FIRST TASMANIAN IMPERIAL) CONTINGENT.

PAID by the Imperial Government; the Tasmanian Government acting as agents. This was a corps, consisting of one Squadron of Imperial Bushmen, of the same character as those already specified. For pay, equipment, qualification for enrolment, etc., see New South Wales Imperial Bushmen. The engagement was for twelve months or the duration of the war. This Contingent gained the unique distinction of having won two Victoria Crosses.

Establishment was—1 captain, 4 subalterns, 1 sergeant-major, 1 quartermaster-sergeant, 5 sergeants, 1 farrier-sergeant, 2 buglers, 107 rank and file.

DEPARTURE AND RETURN.

The Contingent left on 26th April, 1900, consisting of—5 officers, 117 others, with 133 horses. Two officers, 4 others, died or were killed; 2 officers, 20 others were struck off in South Africa; 1 officer, 1 N.C.O. were commissioned in the Imperial Army; 4 officers were promoted from the ranks; 4 officers, 88 others returned.

PROMOTIONS, ETC.

Lieutenant A. A. Sale, to Captain, February, 1901.
Lieutenant G. G. E. Wylly, V.C., received an Imperial Commission.
Lance-Corporal G. A. Douglas received an Imperial Commission.
Trooper J. P. Egan was commissioned in South African Field Force.
Corporal L. S. E. Page, promoted Lieutenant, 5th December, 1900.
Corporal R. L. Williams, promoted Lieutenant, 8th February, 1901.
Sergeant A. Stocker, promoted Lieutenant, 10th April, 1901.
Sergeant H. R. Reynolds, promoted Lieutenant, 12th April, 1901.
Sergeant G. Shaw, promoted Lieutenant in 2nd Tasmanian Imperial Bushmen's Contingent.
Trooper L. H. Laughton, promoted Lieutenant in 2nd Tasmanian Imperial Bushmen's Contingent.
Trooper W. K. Barwise, promoted Lieutenant, "E" Company, 1st Australian Commonwealth Horse.
Sergeant E. W. Stephens, promoted Lieutenant, "C" Squadron, 8th Australian Commonwealth Horse.

For promotions of N.C.O.'s and men, *vide* nominal roll.

SERVICE.

Embarked at Hobart on the troopship *Manhattan* on 26th April, 1900; arrived at Beira on 28th May, and proceeded to Durban, arriving on 3rd June. From thence the troops, which included the 4th South Australians and the 4th Western Australians, were sent to Port Elizabeth, where they disembarked on 19th June. These three Contingents formed together the corps known as the 4th Imperial Bushmen, under Lieut.-Colonel J. Rowell, of South Australia.

About the middle of June, operations were commenced encircling the Boers who were in the Wittebergen or Brandwater Basin; a mountain stronghold in the North-East Orange River Colony. Rundle, with the VIII. Division, and Brabant, with the South African Colonial Division, were holding the line from the Senekal eastwards to the Basutoland border. Clements and Paget, on the middle frontier west, were about Lindley, the south-west point of the Boer stronghold. These masses of men either could not live, or were not allowed to live, on the country; hence huge convoys of supplies were required to be sent from the railway.

On 23rd June a very large convoy left Kroonstadt for General Paget's Force at Lindley. The escort was commanded by Colonel Brookfield, 14th Imperial Yeomanry, and consisted of 200 of that corps, 114 other Yeomanry, 400 Imperial

Bushmen (namely, two Squadrons South Australians, one Squadron Western Australians, and one Squadron Tasmanians), 27 of Rimington's Guides, 93 Prince Alfred's Guards, 2 guns 17th Royal Field Artillery, 4 guns City Imperial Volunteer Battery, half-battalion of Yorkshire Light Infantry, and the 3rd East Kent (Buffs) Militia. The Australians were considered as one Regiment, under Colonel Rowell.

On the morning of the 26th June, Theron's scouts suddenly attacked the convoy near Eland's Spruit, but they were driven off. In the afternoon, near Swartz Farm, Piet De Wet attacked. The Australians were ordered to dismount, and advancing with great dash, the enemy was again driven off. On the 27th, the convoy marched 18 miles; the escort being engaged practically all day. Near Lindley, the traction engines stuck in the spruit. The 4th were the rearguard, and were hotly pressed by the enemy who endeavoured to cut off the Tasmanians forming the rear screen, but the City Imperial Volunteer Battery did good work; and Colonel Brookfield, having sent fresh Squadrons to Colonel Rowell's assistance, he was able to keep the Boers off the convoy.

Next day Lindley was reached. In a despatch to General Kelly-Kenny, commanding in the Orange River Colony, the Chief of the Staff said that Lord Roberts was of opinion that the convoy had been conducted with skill and foresight, that no precautions were neglected, and that the behaviour of the troops was creditable to all ranks. "His Lordship is glad to observe that, besides the regular troops employed, the Militia Battalion, the Corps of Imperial Bushmen, the Imperial Yeomanry and the City Imperial Volunteers, distinguished themselves on this occasion."

Colonel Brookfield and most of his troops now joined General Paget's command. After doing some work about the Bethlehem-Winburg district, they formed part of the escort which took the Boer prisoners from Wittebergen to the railway. On the 14th August, the Contingent entrained for Pretoria; and, on the 16th, they marched past Lord Roberts, who was very complimentary. On the same day they marched out to join General Paget, under whom they were during the next three months, to see hard marching and stiff fighting. "We were constantly under the fire of the enemy; pretty well every day brought its contribution of experience in the shape of small engagements." (*On the Veldt*, by Captain R. C. Lewis, Hobart, 1902).

On 20th August, the Contingent was put into the Mounted Brigade of Colonel Hickman, under whom they acted, until he left the Column in December. He almost invariably asked them to act as his advanced guard when he expected to fight the enemy. On the 1st September, 20 men of the Squadron, under Lieutenant G. G. E. Wylly, went out after cattle; they were surrounded and retired with difficulty. Trooper Brown was killed, and Lieutenant Wylly and four others were wounded.

It was on this day that Lieutenant Wylly and Trooper J. H. Bisdee both earned the Victoria Cross. Lieutenant Wylly's conduct was thus officially recorded:— "Although wounded, this officer, seeing that one of his men was badly wounded in the leg and that his horse was shot went back to the man's assistance, made him take his (Wylly's) horse, and opened fire from behind a rock to cover the retreat of the others, at the imminent risk of being cut off himself."—(*London Gazette*, 13th November, 1900). Colonel T. E. Hickman, D.S.O., considered that "the gallant conduct of Lieutenant Wylly saved Corporal Brown from being killed or captured; and that his subsequent firing to cover the retreat, was instrumental in saving the other men from death or capture." Lieutenant Wylly subsequently obtained a commission in the South Lancashire Regiment, and was wounded on the night of the 7th January, 1901, when the Boers fiercely attacked the posts on the railway about Belfast. He was appointed an aide-de-camp to Lord Kitchener.

Bisdee's achievement is recorded as follows:—"On the 1st September, Private Bisdee was one of an advanced scouting party, passing through a rocky defile near

Warmbad, Transvaal. The enemy, who were in ambuscade, opened a sudden fire at close range; and six out of the party of eight were hit, including two officers. The horse of one of the wounded officers broke away and bolted. Private Bisdee gave the officer his stirrup-leather to help him out of action; but finding that the officer was too badly wounded to go on, he dismounted, placed him on his horse, mounted behind him, and conveyed him out of range. This act was performed under a very hot fire and in a very exposed place."—(*London Gazette*, 13th November, 1900.)

On 4th November, the South Australians and Western Australians joined Colonel Hickman, and the Regiment was together again. At Rhenoster Kop, 29th, the Tasmanians were escort to the guns. In December, Captain Lewis was invalided with enteric, and the command devolved upon Lieutenant Sale, under whom the Squadron, much reduced in numbers, took a prominent part in the pursuit of De Wet, through and out of Cape Colony. Captain Lewis rejoined before the march to Pietersburg took place. After the town was occupied (8th April, 1901), the Tasmanians being the first to enter, Captain Sale, with a small troop galloped to a ridge beyond; he was shot by a Boer concealed in the long grass, a few paces to the left; and Lieutenant Walter, going to his assistance was mortally wounded.

On 25th April, Sergeant Stocker gained great distinction for his share in the capture of 35 prisoners. In May, the Squadron operated under General Plumer, through the Eastern Transvaal to Bethel and Piet Retief.

Operations, and Corps or Columns served with, may be summarized thus:—
Operations Eastern Orange Free State, including actions at Lindley, Bethlehem, Twin Hills, and Slabbert's Nek, under General Paget.

Present at capture of Prinsloo's laager.

Operations in North-East Transvaal, around Sybrant's Kraal, Warmbad, Nylstroom, Rhenoster Kop (29th November, 1900), under General Paget.

Operations in Western Transvaal, Rustenburg, Selon's River.

Operations in Cape Colony, commencing February, 1901, to check De Wet's raid, under General Plumer.

With General Plumer to Pietersburg, April, 1901.

The Squadron embarked in the transport *Britannic* at East London on 7th July, 1901, and arrived in Tasmania on 5th August; having visited *en route* Albany, Adelaide, and Melbourne. Disbanded 14th August.

WAR SERVICES AND HONOURS.

Lewis, Captain R. C.—Operations east of Orange River Colony North-East Transvaal, Western Transvaal, and Cape Colony, between June, 1900, and June, 1901, including actions at Lindley, Bethlehem, Twin Hills, Slabbert's Nek, Wittebergen, Sybrant's Kraal, Warmbad, Nylstroom, and Rhenoster Kop. Despatches, *London Gazette*, 16th April, 1901. D.S.O. Queen's Medal with three clasps.

Perkins, Lieutenant R.—Operations and actions as stated. Despatches, *London Gazette*, 16th April, 1901. D.S.O. Queen's Medal with three clasps.

Wylly, Lieutenant G. G. E.—Operations and actions as stated. Despatches, *London Gazette*, 13th November, 1900. D.C. Queen's Medal with three clasps.

Sale, Captain A. A.—Operations and actions as stated. Mentioned in Commander-in-Chief's Despatches, 8th March, 1901. Killed in action at Pietersburg, 9th April, 1901.

Walter, Lieutenant C. H.—Operations and actions as stated. Killed in action at Pietersburg, 9th April, 1901.

Page, L. S. E., *Williams*, R. L., *Stocker*, A., and *Reynolds*, H. R. (Lieutenants.)—Operations and actions generally as stated. Queen's Medal with three clasps. Lieuts. Page and Williams returned to South Africa in October, 1901, and were commissioned in the Cape Colony Field Force.

Nominal Roll.

No. and Name.	Rank.	Remarks.
OFFICERS.		
Lewis, Richard Charles	Captain, Officer Commanding	
Perkins, Raymond	Lieutenant	
Wylly, Guy Geo. Egerton	,,	Wounded, 1.9.00
Sale, Arthur Arnold	2nd Lieutenant	Died from wounds at Pietersburg, 9.4.01
Walter, Crosswell Herbert	,,	Killed in action at Pietersburg, 9.4.01
N.C.O.'s AND MEN.		
117. Shegog, William Lowry	Troop Sergeant-Major	
1. Townley, Percy James	Quartermaster-Sergeant	Regimental Staff
2. Cracknell, William	Sergeant	
3. Stephens, Ed. William	,,	*Vide* " Promotions "
4. Shaw, George	,,	Wounded at Warmbad. *Vide* " Promotions "
5. Nettlefold, Arthur Wm.	,,	Invalided to Tasmania
6. Summers, Mervyn Alfred	,,	Invalided to Tasmania
7. Shaw, James	Farrier-Sergeant	Invalided to Tasmania
8. Stepnell, Joseph	Corporal	Invalided to Tasmania
9. Page, Louis Sydney Eccles	,,	*Vide* " Promotions "
10. Reynolds, Hubert Ross	,,	Sergeant. *Vide* " Promotions "
11. Brown, Edward Stanley	,,	Wounded at Warmbad and invalided
12. Lester, Harold Joseph	,,	Invalided to Tasmania
13. Williams, Robert Llewellyn	,,	*Vide* " Promotions "
14. Ward, William Henry	Bugler	Invalided to Tasmania
15. Turner, Charles Arthur	,,	
16. Adams, Angus Robert	Trooper	Promoted to Sergeant
17. Blackaby, Henry	,,	
18. Bellette, Ernest Amos	,,	
19. Brown, Albert Melton	,,	
20. Brownell, Eric Lindsey Douglas	,,	Corporal for gallantry. Commander-in-Chief's despatches, 8.7.01; invalided to Tasmania, returned with 2nd Tasmanian Imperial Bushmen
21. Brumby, Lewis Berkley	,,	Lance-Corporal. Sergeant-Major at camp in Cape Town
22. Brewer, William John Colin	,,	Promoted Sergeant
23. Butcher, Louis George	,,	Invalided to Tasmania
24. Bisdee, John Hutton	,,	Invalided to Tasmania. Returned as an officer of 2nd Imperial Bushmen. Despatches, *London Gazette*, 13.11.00. V.C.
25. Berwick, William	,,	Invalided to Tasmania
26. Bull, Allan Thomas	,,	
27. Bridley, Walter McIntosh	,,	Made prisoner, but escaped
28. Barwise, William Kenyon	,,	*Vide* " Promotions "
29. Burbury, Leslie Douglas	,,	
30. Brown, Godfrey Hugh	,,	Made prisoner; died of wounds at Warmbad, 20.9.00
31. Bostock, Daniel William	,,	
33. Cliff, James	,,	

Nominal Roll—*continued*.

No. and Name.	Rank.	Remarks.
N.C.O.'s AND MEN—*continued*.		
34. Crawford, Reginald Calder	Trooper	
25. Campbell, William James	,,	Invalided to Tasmania
26. Clark, Peter	,,	Despatches, *London Gazette*, 16.4.01. D.C.M.
27. Costello, Albert Edward	,,	
28. Chester, Alfred Victor	,,	Invalided to Tasmania
29. Cooper, Joseph	,,	Wounded at Warmbad; invalided to Tasmania
40. Crosby, Edward Barclay	,,	
41. Davis, Herbert Frank	,,	Lance-Corporal. Promoted Sergeant
42. D'Alton, Frank	,,	
43. Davis, William Walter	,,	Invalided to Tasmania
44. Dawes, William James	,,	Invalided to Tasmania
45. Dudfield, James	,,	
46. Douglas, Gordon Adye	,,	Lance-Corporal. *Vide* "Promotions"
47. Eddy, William Lawrence	,,	
48. Egan, James Patrick	,,	Made prisoner, 9.3.01; afterwards rejoined. *Vide* "Promotions"
49. Fleming, Percy James	,,	Invalided to Tasmania
50. Fergusson, Benjamin Thomas	,,	
51. Firth, Albert Alex. Crossley	,,	Wounded at Warmbad
52. Groom, Francis Arthur	,,	Despatches, *London Gazette*, 16.4.01. D.C.M.
53. Geeres, Leslie Harry	,,	
54. Gerrand, James	,,	Promoted Sergeant
55. Gardiner, Arthur Joseph	,,	
56. Garrott, Edgar Albert	,,	
57. Guest, Robert William	,,	
58. Green, Richard	,,	
59. Griffin, James	,,	
60. Gleeson, Denis	,,	
61. Hays, Albert Ernest	,,	
62. Herbert, Lewis Arthur	,,	Invalided to Tasmania
63. Harradine, Edward Francis	,,	
64. Heyne, Charles	,,	
65. Haiz, Albert Xavier	,,	
66. Hamilton, Henry Wm. Vere	,,	
67. Humphreys, Robert	,,	
68. Hodgkinson, Walter Frank Cecil	,,	Made prisoner, 19.3.01; afterwards re-joined
69. Hutton, Leonard	,,	
70. Itchins, Henry Gabriel	,,	Invalided to Tasmania
71. Johnstone, Clarence Albert James	,,	
72. Johnson, Alfred	,,	
73. Jackson, Charles Albert	,,	
74. Keogh, Peter	,,	
75. Kenworthy, William	,,	
76. King, Charles George	,,	
77. Litchfield, Arthur Frederick	,,	
78. Lawrence, Owen Effingham	,,	Invalided to Tasmania, and returned to South Africa
79. Laughton, Louis Horace	,,	*Vide* "Promotions"
80. Lawford, William	,,	
81. Lette, Louis Frances John	,,	Died of enteric at Pretoria, 18.10.00

Nominal Roll—*continued.*

No. and Name.	Rank.	Remarks.
N.C.O.'s AND MEN—*continued.*		
82. Luttrell, Darcy	Trooper	Invalided to Tasmania
83. Littlejohn, Mervyn James	,,	
84. Muckle, Robert	,,	
85. McClelland, William	,,	
86. McLeod, Albert Arthur	,,	
87. McLaren, Percy	,,	Killed in action near Bronkhurst Spruit, 22.1.01
88. McGuillan, Andrew	,,	
89. Mace, Trevor Ellis	,,	
90. Maguire, William Alfred	,,	
91. O'May, Sydney Robert	,,	
92. Pilsbury, William George	,,	Invalided to Tasmania
93. Rye, Edward John	,,	
94. Shields, James Robert	,,	
95. Simpson, Charles	,,	Invalided to Tasmania
96. Simpson, Walter John	,,	
97. Simpson, Arthur Whitfield	,,	
98. Skinner, Harold	,,	
99. Smith, Norman Banks	,,	Invalided to Tasmania
102. Stocker, Archie	,,	Sergeant. Special mention in General Plumer's despatches, 8.5.01. D.C.M. *Vide* "Promotions"
101. Storey, Cameron Richard	,,	
103. Taylor, George Ernest	,,	Invalided to Tasmania; returned with 2nd Tasmanian Imperial Bushmen
104. Viney, Arthur Edward	,,	Invalided to Tasmania; awarded pension
105. Wright, Andrew	,,	Invalided to Tasmania
106. Williams, Herbert Mouat	,,	
107. Ward, Kenny	,,	Promoted Corporal
108. Weber, Gustav Henry	,,	Promoted Corporal
109. Whitmore, John William	,,	
110. Wyatt, Robert Oliver	,,	Invalided to Tasmania
111. White, George	,,	
112. Willoughby, Samuel	,,	Wounded at Warmbad
113. Whelan, William Patrick	,,	
114. Wadley, William Isaac	,,	Died of disease, 18.4.01
32. Walton, Thomas	,,	Invalided to Tasmania
115. Westbrook, Charles Walter	,,	
116. Walters, George Albert	,,	
100. Walker, —	,,	

FOURTH (SECOND IMPERIAL BUSHMEN) CONTINGENT.

CONSISTED of two Companies (or Squadrons), enrolled upon a system similar to that which obtained in constituting the previous Contingent. Rates of pay, equipment, &c., as before. The establishment comprised a small Battalion staff, consisting, in the first instance, of 1 lieutenant-colonel (commanding), 1 lieutenant (Medical Staff), 1 regimental sergeant-major, 1 regimental quartermaster-sergeant, and 1 transport sergeant. To these were added an adjutant, appointed from the Company officers, and an orderly room sergeant, also drawn from a Company. Each Company establishment included 1 captain, 4 subalterns, 1 colour-sergeant, 1 quartermaster-sergeant, 1 farrier-sergeant, 3 sergeants, 2 buglers, and 109 rank and file.

DEPARTURE AND RETURN.

The 2nd Tasmanian Imperial Bushmen left on 27th March, 1901, comprising —12 officers, 241 others, with 289 horses. Six were killed or died; 10 officers and 6 others were struck off in South Africa; 2 officers were appointed from the ranks; 1 N.C.O. obtained an Imperial commission. The remainder returned to Tasmania.

PROMOTIONS, ETC.

Lieutenant J. M'Cormick, to Adjutant, 27th March, 1901.
Lieutenant H. Hallam, to Transport Officer, 6th June, 1901.
Lieutenant M. H. Swan, to Paymaster, 1st August, 1901.
2nd Lieutenant F. R. Chalmers, to 1st Lieutenant, 1st August, 1901.
Colour-Sergeant A. J. P. Suche, to 2nd Lieutenant, 27th April, 1901.
Corporal G. L. McIntyre, to Provisional Lieutenant, 19th February, 1902.
Sergeant G. Shaw, promoted Lieutenant from 1st Tasmanian Imperial Bushmen.
Trooper L. H. Laughton, promoted Lieutenant from 1st Tasmanian Imperial Bushmen.
Lance-Corporal Brownell received an Imperial commission.
For promotions other than Commissions, *vide* Nominal Roll.

SERVICE.

The Contingent embarked at Hobart on the transport *Chicago*, on 27th March, 1901, and landed at Port Elizabeth on 24th April.

Their service was in Cape Colony, under General French; and may be summarized as follows:—8th, 9th, and 10th May—Ganna Hoek, driving Scheeper's Commando out of Craddock District; joined General Scobell's Column, operating still about Craddock; joined Colonel Gorring's "Flying Column." 1st June—Fight at Aliman's Fontein. 8th June—Fight at Rietfontein, Malan's Commando. 3rd July—Fight near Zuurberg. 29th July—Fighting near Schilder Kranz. 1st August—Chased enemy into Munro's Column. 13th August—Fight at Roodepoort, captured Commandant Erasmus, Cachet, and others of Kruitzinger's Commando. 14th August—Fight with Kruitzinger at Lamenkronst. 16th August—Chased Kruitzinger across Orange River. 16th September—Surprised Commando at Wildeschutt's Berg, capturing some prisoners; operations against Smut's Commando in Drakensberg district. 21st October—Fight with Van Reenan's Commando. 23rd November—Captured Commandant Besters and ten others. February, 1902—Operations with 17th Lancers in Bamboo Mountain. On the 18th—Captured and shot Commandant Judge Hugo at Grootfontein. 10th March—Captured Commandant Rhudolph at Klein Taffelberg.

Soon after landing, the Corps was engaged with Scheepers at Ganna Hoek Cape Colony, where Trooper Warburton was killed. Trooper Brownell distinguished himself in this affair and afterwards received a commission in the Imperial Army. On the 19th May, the Tasmanians joined Scobell's Column, which was one of the most successful. On the 1st June, they passed to Colonel Gorring, whose force was formed into a Flying Column, without wheeled transport.

On 13th February, 1902, Colonel Doran took over the Column, and the Contingent served under him until 4th May. On 18th February, they suffered several casualties, and the strain on men and horses was very great; but the Column did excellent work, and was frequently complimented by General French and Lord Kitchener. The various leaders commended the Contingent for fearlessness, good horsemastership, and cheerful endurance of the greatest hardships. On 13th August, 1901, Sergeant-Major Young, of the Cape Police, with Quartermaster-Sergeant Lynes, Sergeant Coombes, and eight other Tasmanians, charged a kopje where the enemy were strongly entrenched, and captured Commandant Erasmus and others. Young obtained the Victoria Cross.

The Contingent were several times successful in capturing influential Boer leaders. For twelve months they were incessantly employed; long marches often being undertaken by night, followed by actions with the Commandoes of Kruitzinger, Scheepers, Myberg, and others.

On the 22nd May, 1902, the Contingent embarked on the transport *Manila* at Durban, and arrived in Tasmania on 25th June, having called at Albany, Adelaide, and Melbourne *en route*. Disbanded on 30th June.

WAR SERVICES AND HONOURS.

Watchorn, Lieut.-Colonel E. T.—Operations in Orange River Colony, August to September, 1901. Operations in Cape Colony between April, 1901, and May, 1902 Despatches, *London Gazette*, 17th June, 1902. C.B. Queen's Medal with clasps.

Henderson, Captain C.—Operations as above. Queen's Medal with two clasps.

Spencer, Captain T. A.—Operations as above. Queen's Medal with clasps.

McCormick, Lieutenant J., Adjutant.—Served also with first Contingent. Operations with 2nd Tasmanian Imperial Bushmen, as stated. Despatches, *London Gazette*, 31st August, 1902. D.S.O. Queen's Medal with five clasps.

Mattei, Lieutenant C. (Medical Staff).—Operations as stated. Queen's Medal with clasp.

Richardson, Lieutenant G. F.—*Vide* 1st Contingent. Operations as stated. Despatches, *London Gazette*, 31st August, 1902. Queen's Medal with five clasps. King's Medal with two clasps.

Blyth, Lieutenant C. O.—Service as above. *Vide* 1st Contingent.

Bisdee, Lieutenant J. H., V.C.—*Vide* 1st Tasmanian Imperial Bushmen. Operations as stated. Queen's Medal with three clasps. King's Medal with two clasps.

Hallam, H., *Swan*, M. H., and *Chalmers*, F. R. (Lieutenants).—As for Lieutenant Blyth.

Brent, R. D., and *Suche*, A. J. P. (Lieutenants).—Operations as stated. Queen's Medal with two clasps.

Nominal Roll.

No. and Name.	Rank.	Remarks.

BATTALION STAFF.

No. and Name.	Rank.	Remarks.
Watchorn, Edwin Thomas	Lieut.-Colonel	
McCormick, John	Lieut.-Adjutant	Previous service in 1st Contingent
Mattei, Charles	Lieutenant	Medical Staff
266. Bruce, William	Sergeant-Major	
221. Robinson, Edward William	Quartermaster-Sergeant	
259. Coombe, Archibald	Transport Sergeant	Commander-in-Chief's despatches, 8.12.01 and 23.6.02

No. 1 COMPANY.

Officers.

No. and Name.	Rank.	Remarks.
Henderson, Carlisle	Captain	
Richardson, George Fairbrass	Lieutenant	Previous service in 1st Contingent
Blyth, Charles Oscar	,,	Previous service in 1st Contingent
Bisdee, John Hutton	,,	Previous service in 1st Tasmanian Imperial Bushmen

N.C.O.'s and Men.

No. and Name.	Rank.	Remarks.
250. Winfield, Charles William	Sergeant-Farrier	Farrier Sergeant-Major, 17.7.01
148. Drew, John	Sergeant	Acting Colour-Sergeant; acting Regimental Sergeant-Major, 17.2.02
122. Brewster, Frederick Vincent	,,	
150. Dixon, Robert	,,	Acting Squadron Sergeant-Major, 17.2.02
129. Branagan, William	,,	Colour-Sergeant, 28.4.01
235. Sandison, William	Corporal	Sergeant, 28.4.01
185. Johnston, Roy	,,	
131. Blacklow, Richard Albert	,,	Sergeant, 3.6.01
160. Facy, Wilfred James	,,	Sergeant, 27.3.01
204. McIntyre, Gilbert Langdon	,,	*Vide* " Promotions "
193. Lyne, Douglas M.	,,	Quartermaster-Sergeant, Commander-in-Chief's despatches, 8.12.01; died of disease, 4.5.02
178. Holmwood, Cecil Archibald	Lance-Corporal	Corporal, 1.3.02
255. Wilson, Robert Benjamin	,,	
213. Orr, John	,,	Corporal, 28.4.01; killed in action 18.11.01
194. Laughton, Sydney Thomas	,,	
166. Green, Hedley Laurence	Shoeing-smith	
139. Coleman, Herbert Norman	Shoeing-smith	
133. Billing, Phillip David	,,	
243. Thomas, Vernon Samuel	,,	
164. Glover, George	Saddler	
169. Goucher, Frederick Thomas Henry	Bugler	
240. Thompson, Frank William	,,	
118. Anderson, George Alexander	Private	
119. Abery, Robert George	,,	
120. Abery, Henry Percy	,,	
121. Adams, Gordon Cyril	,,	Lance-Corporal, 27.12.01
124. Brooks, George Robert	,,	
125. Burton, Charles William	,,	
127. Brown, Alfred	,,	

Nominal Roll—continued.

No. and Name.	Rank.	Remarks.
No. 1 COMPANY—continued.		
N.C.O.'s and Men—continued.		
128. Barker, Walter George	Private	
130. Blackburn, Harry Stanley	,,	
134. Byrne, William Joseph Samuel	,,	
135. Brewer, Geo. Martin Frederick	,,	
136. Baker, Arthur	,,	
258. Blyth, George Herbert	,,	
137. Cox, Leslie Thomas	,,	
138. Cassidy, William Robert	,,	
144. Coleman, Newell Hay	,,	
140. Coates, Ernest Thomas	,,	
142. Carlin, William Cameron	,,	
145. Cooley, Robert Golding	,,	
146. Cox, Herbert	,,	Lance-Corporal, 3.6.01
151. Dobson, William Michael Henry	,,	
152. Edwards, John William	,,	
154. Fitzallen, Charles Edward	,,	
155. Foreman, Frederick William	,,	
156. Fegan, William Patrick	,,	
157. Fergusson, Albert Ernest	,,	
158. Ford, Frederick Wilbraham	,,	
159. Ferguson, Tom Tierney	,,	
161. Frost, Norman Lewis	,,	
162. French, Claude	,,	
163. Greer, Harold William	,,	
165. Gee, Harold William	,,	
167. Groom, Charles Gresham D'Oyley	,,	Lance-Corporal, 28.4.01; Corporal, 27.12.01
168. Guthrie, Robert	,,	
170. Hewitt, Elmslie Fayrer	,,	
173. Hull, Robert Edward Morrisby	,,	Acting Quartermaster-Sergeant, 28.6.01
174. Harris, George Albert	,,	
175. Hewitt, Arthur Reginald	,,	
176. Howard, Thomas Chas. Herbert	,,	
177. Hill, George William	,,	
179. Harrison, Ronald Wilberforce	,,	Acting-Sergeant. Orderly-room Sergeant, 26.4.01
180. Harrison, George Francis	,,	
182. Jardine, Thomas Foster	,,	
183. Joyce, John Martial	,,	
184. Johnstone, J. H.	,,	
186. Jeffrey, Tasman	,,	
187. Kirk, Joseph Edward	,,	
188. Lutrell, Albert Walter Frederick	,,	
189. Little, Alfred Richard	,,	
190. Lyall, Thomas	,,	
191. Lyne, William Henry	,,	
195. Macdonald, Malcolm	,,	
198. Morrisby, Raymond Clark	,,	
197. Murrell, Edward R.	,,	
199. Mundy, Thomas	,,	
200. Monson, Albert Joseph	,,	
201. Maroney, Joseph Harland	,,	
202. McIntyre, Walter Archibald	,,	
203. Murray, David James	,,	
205. Marsden, Thomas Henry	,,	
206. Maddox, Cyril Lakeland	,,	

Nominal Roll—continued.

No. and Name.	Rank.	Remarks.

No. 1 COMPANY—continued.
N.C.O.'s and Men—continued.

208. Manser, John Albert	Private	
209. Nation, Herbert	,,	
210. Nicholson, Claude Anthony	,,	
211. Neal, Allan Henry	,,	
212. Oldham, Frank Hedley C.	,,	
214. Peacock, Frederick	,,	
216. Patterson, John Hugh	,,	
217. Parker, Arthur James	,,	
218. Paul, Richard Arthur	,,	
219. Pegg, Arthur Charles	,,	
220. Patrick, Thomas Henry	,,	
222. Riley, John Temple	,,	
224. Robertson, Thomas	,,	
225. Ramskell, Ernest Florestan	,,	
226. Ross, Harold	,,	
228. Simmonds, Frank Ernest	,,	
229. Shearing, George	,,	
230. Saunderson, George	,,	
231. Street, James Robert	,,	
232. Street, Robert Edward	,,	
233. Shegog, Albert Edward	,,	
234. Smith, Charles James	,,	
236. Thompson, Richard Horace	,,	
237. Tucker, Alfred Sorell	,,	
238. Tilley, Edward Tom	,,	Lance-Corporal; Corporal, 3.6.01
241. Templeton, Robert	,,	
242. Tucker, William George	,,	
244. Vincent, Alfred Henry	,,	
246. Williams, Percy Augustus	,,	
247. Whiting, Stephen Daly	,,	
248. Williams, Francis Hyld	,,	
249. Watson, Frederick	,,	
251. Wade, Percy	,,	
252. Warburton, John	,,	Died from wounds, 9.5.01
253. Whiley, Harry	,,	
254. Witherington, Laurence Hernsted	,,	
255. Wilson, Reginald Collins	,,	
257. Youl, Thomas Arndel	,,	
112. Willoughby, —.	,,	Lance-Corporal, 28.4.01; Acting Quartermaster-Sergeant, 22.5.01
103. Taylor, —.	,,	Lance-Corporal, 28.4.01
20. Brownell. —.	,,	Lance-Corporal, 28.4.01. *Vide* "Promotions"
359. Phegan, J.	,,	Died of disease, 3.12.01

No. 2 COMPANY.
Officers.

Spencer, Thomas Alfred	Captain	
Hallam, Harry	Lieutenant	Previous service in 1st Contingent
Swan, Morton Henry	,,	Previous service in 1st Contingent
Chalmers, Frederic Royden	2nd Lieutenant	Previous service in 1st Contingent
Brent, Rupert Delamere	,,	

N.C.O.'s and Men.

334. Suche, Alfred James Parnell	Colour-Sergeant	*Vide* "Promotions"
196. McLean, Murdie	Farrier-Sergeant	
290. Manning, William James	Sergeant	

Nominal Roll—continued.

No. and Name.	Rank.	Remarks.
No. 2 Company—continued.		
N.C.O.'s and Men—continued.		
328. Wise, Percy Frederick	Private	Acting Quartermaster-Sergeant, 22.5.01
357. Meredith, Charles Christopher	,,	
342. Beresford, Cyril Walter	,,	Quartermaster-Sergeant, 7.10.01
141. Chepmell, Henry Douglas	Corporal	Sergeant, 22.6.01
308. Page, Julian Lambert Russell	,,	
313. Sherrin, Oscar Herbert	,,	
298. Morgan, Evan	,,	
264. Birchall, Stephen	,,	
278. Hunt, Arthur Erskine	,,	Sergeant, 6.2.02
292. Murphy, James	Lance-Corporal	Corporal, 1.8.01; Sergeant, 16.10.01; Commander-in-Chief's despatches, 23.6.02
272. Edwards, William Alfred	,,	Corporal, 10.10.01
271. Evans, Alexander Arthur	,,	Corporal, 6.2.02
143. Chilcot, Chas. Ernest	,,	Corporal, 21.9.01
265. Bingley, Arthur	Shoeing-Smith	
263. Blackwell, Walter	,,	
267. Coombe, Edward	Saddler	
287. King, Jacob Archibald	Bugler	
262. Ballantyne, Robert	,,	
261. Bell, Rd. Patrick	Private	
123. Bevan, Archibald Joseph	,,	
132. Breward, George	,,	
343. Barnard, Walter	,,	
126. Barron, Edward	,,	Corporal, Field Hospital, 22.6.01
147. Curtain, Edward Allan Michael	,,	
266. Corrigan, Leslie James	,,	
268. Cawthorn, Charles	,,	Commander-in-Chief's despatches, 23.6.02
269. Cleary, Walter James	,,	
344. Cowell, Francis Gilbert	,,	Died of disease, 25.11.01
270. Dowd, Thomas	,,	
338. Donnelly, Daniel	,,	
153. Emery, Percy Alexander	,,	
273. Froot, Alfred Leslie	,,	
340. Grant, Archibald James	,,	
149. Hughes, James Leigh	,,	
171. Hunter, Albert Ernest	,,	
172. Huttley, Leonard Percy	,,	Died of disease, 14.2.01
274. Higgs, Edmund	,,	
275. Hunt, Algernon Ashbury	,,	
276. Hildyard, George Gerald	,,	
277. Hewitt, Walter	,,	
279. Hart, Richard John	,,	
280. Hill, John	,,	
356. Haines, Edward Ernest	,,	
281. Iles, Richard	,,	
282. Ibbotson, Frederick Nelson	,,	Shoeing-Smith, 1.7.01
355. Ibbot, Stephen Mears	,,	
181. Jones, Harold Percival	,,	
283. Johnson, James William	,,	
284. Johnson, Hedley Mitchell	,,	
285. Joyce, Joshua James	,,	
337. Jones, Archibald	,,	
358. Joyce, Joseph Clarence	,,	
286. Kearns, Thomas	,,	
192. Leslie, Thomas Henry	,,	
288. Loane, Norman Edward	,,	
289. Lyall, Alexander George	,,	

Nominal Roll—*continued*.

No. and Name.	Rank.	Remarks.
No. 2 COMPANY—*continued*. N.C.O.'s and Men—*continued*.		
351. Lawler, Harry	Private	
207. Mason, William	,,	
291. Maxfield, James	,,	
293. McKercher, George	,,	
294. Moyle, William Thomas	,,	
295. Morley, George	,,	
296. Matheus, Stewart	,,	
297. Murray, Aubrey	,,	
341. McGrath, Martin	,,	
345. Munro, James Lindsay	,,	
346. Massey, James	,,	
350. Moore, James Laurence Armitstead	,,	Acting Orderly-Room Sergeant, 22.5.01
353. Marshall, George	,,	
299. North, Joseph	,,	
300. North, William Henry	,,	Invalided and awarded pension
301. Nolan, Aron	,,	
302. Norman, Sydney Herbert Louis	,,	Lance-Corporal, 28.4.01 ; Corporal, 22.6.01
354. Nicholson, Alfred	,,	
303. O'Shea, James	,,	
304. Olding, John Thomas	,,	
215. Page, Francis Neville	,,	
305. Pedder, Joseph	,,	
306. Page, Dudley Harold	,,	
307. Page, Charles Hale	,,	
223. Reardon, James Tasman	,,	
309. Reid, Ernest Charles	,,	
310. Richardson, Montague Claude	,,	
311. Reading, Patrick	,,	
312. Reid, John	,,	
227. Scoll, Wm. Charles Stewart	,,	
314. Stewart, Kenneth Henry	,,	
315. Salter, William Hobart	,,	
316. Smith, William Arthur	,,	
317. Scritchley, William Edmund	,,	
318. Smith, John Robert	,,	
319. Scadon, Robert William	,,	
320. Sutton, Roland Thomas	,,	
321. Scott, Alfred Henry	,,	
335. Sommervill, William	,,	
339. Sargeant, Dudley Herbert	,,	
352. Suitor, Alban	,,	
239. Tayler, Walter Alfred Chas.	,,	
322. Thompson, Percy Robert	,,	
323. Thompson, William	,,	
324. Turner, Albert Edward	,,	
245. Waddle, Percy Chas. Emanuel	,,	
325. Webb, Frederick Henry	,,	
326. White, George	,,	
327. Watson, Robert	,,	
329. Wilson, John William	,,	
330. Wright, Francis William	,,	
331. White, Edward Henry	,,	
332. Weeding, John James	,,	
333. Waller, William Albert	,,	
336. Wilkinson, Harry George	,,	
347. Whittle, John Woods	,,	
348. Wilkins, John William	,,	
349. White, William	,,	

NOTE.—No complete record could be obtained for this Contingent of casualties other than deaths.

FIRST BATTALION AUSTRALIAN COMMONWEALTH HORSE.
TASMANIAN HALF-UNIT.

TASMANIA furnished one company (or more strictly one half-company) as her quota to the First Battalion, Australian Commonwealth Horse. For organization, equipment, pay, etc., *vide* that Battalion, New South Wales, page 166. Men selected were required to be good shots and good horsemen; those of previous service in South Africa had preference if medically fit. Married men were not enlisted; and unmarried officers had preference, other conditions being equal.

Establishment:—1 captain, 2 subalterns, 1 sergeant-major, 1 quartermaster-sergeant, 2 sergeants, 1 farrier-sergeant, 2 shoeing-smiths, 1 saddler, 1 bugler, 3 corporals, 47 privates, including 2 paid lance-corporals; total, 62. There were not any Tasmanians on Battalion staff.

The condition of enrolment was 12 months or the duration of the war; and payment was by Imperial Government, Commonwealth Treasurer's authority, No. 7, 1901-2. Many of the N.C.O.'s and men had served in previous Contingents.

DEPARTURE AND RETURN.

The half-company left on the 16th February, 1902, comprising—3 officers and 59 others, with 63 horses. Two died; 3 officers, 57 others returned.

There were not any promotions of officers. For promotions of N.C.O.'s and men *vide* nominal roll.

SERVICE.

"E" Company, 1st Battalion, Australian Commonwealth Horse, embarked at Hobart on transport *Manchester Merchant*, 16th February, 1902, and arrived at Durban on 14th March.

From 15th April to 28th June, served with the Australian Brigade, under the command, first of Colonel De Lisle, and latterly of Colonel Williams; the Brigade forming during the same time part of Colonel Thorneycroft's Force. Participated in operations in the Transvaal, and the great final "drive," *vide* 1st Australian Commonwealth Horse, New South Wales.

Embarked on transport *Drayton Grange* at Durban, 11th July, and arrived in Tasmania, 9th August, having visited *en route*, Albany and Melbourne.

Disbanded, 19th August, 1902.

WAR SERVICES AND HONOURS.

One officer had passed through previous service in the First Tasmanian Imperial Bushmen, which see; the others were awarded Queen's Medal with clasp.

Nominal Roll.

No. and Name.	Rank.	Remarks.
OFFICERS.		
Perceval, Arthur Wm. Bernard	Captain	
Riggall, Herbert	Lieutenant	
Barwise, William Kenyon	,,	Served in 1st Tasmanian Imperial Bushmen
N.C.O.'S AND MEN.		
1181. Briant, Frederick Charles	Company Sergeant-Major	
1184. Morrisby, Frank Edward	Company Quartermaster-Sergeant	Died of disease, 25.6.02

Nominal Roll—*continued.*

No. and Name.	Rank.	Remarks.
N.C.O.'s AND MEN—*continued.*		
1238. Lade, Cyrus	Sergeant	
1186. Tilley, Lionel John	,,	
1242. Lette, Alfred	Farrier-Sergeant	
1234. Smallhorn, Herbert Ernest	Corporal	
1185. Storey, Cameron Richard	,,	
1236. Larner, Harry Elvyn	,,	
1193. Lawson, Robert	Lance-Corporal	
1237. Joyce, Joshua James	,,	
1188. Maning, Athol Talbot	,,	
1194. Williams, Herbert Mouat	,,	
1229. Barnes, Robert Henry	Saddler	
1191. Costello, Albert Edward	Shoeing-Smith	
1190. Bransgrave, Henry Edward	,,	
1207. Kent, Harry	Bugler	
1211. Browne, Clifford Styant	Private	
1221. Brownley, Alfred James	,,	
1192. Berwick, William	,,	
1199. Blacklow, Norman Fergus	,,	
1233. Blyth, Arthur Allen	,,	
1213. Brooke, Walter Arnott	,,	
1241. Blackett, Mortimer Cephas	,,	
1182. Clerkson, John Henry	,,	
1218. Crooks, Thomas Ray	,,	
1222. Dunlop, Morton John	,,	
1220. Dineen, Arthur Ernest	,,	
1212. Fitzallen, Albert Edward	,,	Died of disease, 30.5.02
1235. Fitzgerald, Francis Arthur	,,	
1183. Gourlay, Garnet Rupert	,,	Quartermaster-Sergeant, 26.6.02
1195. Goyen, John Leslie	,,	
1228. Guerin, James	,,	
1223. Haigh, Edward Leslie Simpson	,,	
1208. Hepburn, Alexander McGregor	,,	
1206. Hanigan, Harold Leslie	,,	
1207. Hopkins, Thomas James	,,	
1202. Jepson, Charles	,,	
1203. Joyce, Aloysius	,,	
1239. Johnson, Joseph Thomas	,,	
1225. Lloyd, Mitchell	,,	
1227. Morgan, Henry Arthur	,,	
1201. Marshall, Henry James	,,	
1189. Morley, Reginald Alfred	,,	
1200. McCrea, John	,,	
1231. McInnes, Malcolm Charles	,,	
1240. McGuire, William Alfred	,,	
1230. Owen, Francis Stephen Bygrove	,,	
1210. Pitstock, William Herbert	,,	
1198. Pegg, Albert Edward	,,	
1204. Reardon, Lionel Lewis	,,	
1224. Richardson, Charles Mowbray	,,	
1197. Shadwick, Frank	,,	
1217. Swifte, Allan Henry	,,	
1196. Ward, Charles William	,,	
1205. Willmott, George	,,	
1187. Williams, John Langley	,,	
1216. Williams, Edward Oliver	,,	
1219. White, Eric	,,	
1214. Wright, Herbert Ernest	,,	

C.4720. 2 O

THIRD BATTALION AUSTRALIAN COMMONWEALTH HORSE.
TASMANIAN UNIT.

ONE Company of Tasmanians constituted their unit of the 3rd Battalion, Australian Commonwealth Horse, composed besides, of three Companies (or Squadrons) from New South Wales, and one from Queensland. Organization, equipment, pay, qualifications, condition of enrolment, etc., as for the half-company for 1st Australian Commonwealth Horse.

Establishment:—1 captain, 4 subalterns, 1 sergeant-major, 1 quartermaster-sergeant, 1 farrier-sergeant, 4 sergeants, 6 corporals, 8 lance-corporals (4 paid), 1 saddler, 3 shoeing-smiths, 2 buglers, 89 privates. There were not any Tasmanians on Battalion staff.

Many N.C.O.'s and men had served in other Contingents and Irregular Corps.

DEPARTURE AND RETURN.

Left on 8th April, 1902, comprising—5 officers, 116 others, with 121 horses. Two died; 4 were struck off in South Africa; 5 officers, 110 others returned. There were no promotions of officers in South Africa. For promotions of N.C.O.'s and men, *vide* nominal roll.

SERVICE.

" E " Squadron embarked at Hobart on transport *Englishman*, 8th April, 1902, and arrived at Durban, 10th May. Entrained to Newcastle, and joined the Battalion at Kitchener's Kop. Remained in camp there awaiting orders. Engaged in exercising the Squadrons, recuperating the horses, marching expeditions through the adjacent country, etc., until the termination of the war. *Vide* 3rd Australian Commonwealth Horse, New South Wales, p. 176.

Handed over horses, &c., and entrained to Durban; there embarked on transport *Drayton Grange*, 11th July, 1902, and arrived in Tasmania on 9th August, having visited *en route* Albany and Melbourne.

Disbanded, 19th August, 1902.

Nominal Roll.

No. and Name.	Rank.	Remarks.
OFFICERS.		
Morrisby, Arthur	Captain	
Swan, Ronald Arthur	Lieutenant	
Chalmers, Cyril Roderick Alleyne	,,	Previous service in 1st Tasmanian Contingent
Shaw, Henry Ashburner	,,	
Stourton, Reginald Norman Joseph	,,	Previous service in 1st Leith Horse
N.C.O.'S AND MEN.		
2020. Adams, John Edward	Company Sergeant-Major	
2038. Whitham, John Lawrence	Company Quartermaster-Sergeant	
2114. Smith, Thomas	Farrier-Sergeant	
2088. Ward, Kenny	Sergeant	
2128. Walker, George Arthur	,,	
2115. Clarke, James Mortyn	,,	

Nominal Roll—*continued.*

No. and Name.	Rank.	Remarks.
N.C.O.'s AND MEN—*continued.*		
2132. Ferguson, Benjamin Furney	Sergeant	
2034. Smith, Charles	Corporal	
2021. Duke, Richard Darby	,,	
2137. Wallack, Ernest Francis	,,	
2047. Jackson, Charles Arthur	,,	Sergeant, 11.7.02
2135. Matthews, Lionel John	,,	Lance-Sergeant, 11.7.02
2138. Gage, Henry Cleburne Ogle	,,	
2081. Guest, Robert William	Lance-Corporal,..	Paid rank
2050. Archer, Thomas Kentish McRae	,,	Paid rank
2071. Page, Eustace Amstey	,,	Paid rank
2133. Phillips, Percy George	,,	Paid rank
2029. DeLittle, William Vernon	Lance-Corporal ..	Unpaid
2100. Rapp, George Morres	,,	Unpaid. Squadron Quartermaster-Sergeant, 11.7.02
2134. Mitchell, Godfrey Ormerville	,,	Unpaid. Corporal, 11.7.02
2077. Cooper, Arthur Charles	,,	Unpaid. Sergeant, 11.7.02
2119. Scott, James	Saddler	
2084. Newton, Walter	Shoeing-Smith	
2048. Gibson, William	,,	Squadron Farrier-Sergeant, 11.7.02
2074. Thompson, Norman	,,	
2087. Sharp, Charles	Bugler	
2032. Pegus, Wroughton John	,,	
2107. Able, Leonard Guy	Private	
2141. Andrews, Herbert Edward	,,	
2059. Aitchison, John Joseph	,,	
2060. Aitchison, William	,,	
2042. Bransgrove, Percy Lauss	,,	
2043. Burton, Edward Charles	,,	
2055. Bailey, Charles	,,	Shoeing-Smith, 11.7.02
2061. Bryan, John Henry	,,	Lance-Corporal, 11.7.02
2063. Bell, Charles	,,	
2064. Brennan, Michael	,,	Lance-Corporal, 11.7.02
2097. Brannagan, Thomas Patrick	,,	Lance-Corporal, 11.7.02
2098. Breen, George	,,	
2124. Brambley, Albert Edward	,,	
2128. Barber, Walter Charles Henry	,,	
2144. Blacklow, Harry Tierney	,,	
2149. Brown, Albert Henry Josiah	,,	
2150. Bellette, Archibald	,,	Shoeing-Smith, 11.7.02
2155. Carter, John Charles	,,	
2156. Clarke, George Lewis Augustus	,,	
2065. Cundy, Charles	,,	Died of disease on transport *Drayton Grange*, 2.8.02
2146. Dunkley, Edgar Leslie	,,	
2152. Dineen, Frederick William	,,	
2066. Edwards, Henry William	,,	
2067. Evans, Francis John	,,	
2022. Ferguson, Charles Vernon	,,	
2069. Fox, Bertie Cecil	,,	Lance-Corporal, 11.7.02
2080. Farley, Alfred Joseph	,,	
2106. Fitzgerald, Frank Percy	,,	
2139. Field, Daniel Newbury	,,	
2143. Fuller, Charles Frederick James	,,	
2023. Goss, Herbert	,,	
2024. Gillow, Arthur	,,	
2090. Gill, Frederick Thomas	,,	
2103. Green, Henry Richard	,,	

Nominal Roll—*continued.*

No. and Name.	Rank.	Remarks.
N.C.O.'s AND MEN—*continued.*		
2111. Gibson, Tremlitt	Private	
2142. Hardy, Alfred Ernest	,,	
2025. Hudson, George Arthur	,,	
2026. Hodgman, Vincent Lade	,,	Died of disease on transport *Drayton Grange*, 5.8.02
2070. Horsley, William Francis	,,	
2096. Hannigan, George Henry	,,	
2109. Husband, Leslie	,,	
2116. Hamilton, Archibald Victor	,,	Lance-Corporal, 11.7.02
2117. Hawkes, Samuel	,,	
2118. Heron, James Alexander	,,	
2121. Herbert, Ernest George	,,	
2125. Hope, Garnet John	,,	
2127. Headlam, Rupert William	,,	
2147. Hanstein, Alfred Adolphus	,,	
2154. Haines, Wm. George	,,	
2131. Jordan, John	,,	
2028. Keogh, Martin	,,	
2030. Ludbey, Wilfred	,,	
2052. Lewis, Arthur	,,	
2053. Lewis, Benjamin	,,	
2054. Lyne, Percy Burton Phillipson	,,	
2099. Lamb, Gilbert Rumney	,,	
2082. Laird, William	,,	
2031. Manning, Henry William	,,	
2042. McLoughlin, William John	,,	
2083. Mortyn, Tertius	,,	
2112. Morse, Esrom	,,	
2153. Madsen, Charles Joseph	,,	
2157. Madsen, Weils Peter	,,	
2158. McGree, Denis Patrick	,,	
2145. Newman, Lavington Philpot	,,	
2056. Pennefather, Charles Francis	,,	
2072. Paul, Charles Herbert	,,	
2033. Reynolds, Thomas Walter	,,	
2086. Roberts, Benjamin Horace	,,	
2092. Rust, Walter Hall	,,	
2148. Rust, Henry	,,	
2113. Rogers, William Lynton	,,	
2123. Radford, Edward	,,	
2057. Smith, Albert	,,	
2073. Street, Harold Sydney	,,	
2102. Swan, Henry	,,	
2136. Stuart, Robert Charles Andrew	,,	
2151. Stagg, Frederick George	,,	
2037. Tribolet, Benjamin Castles	,,	
2046. Thompson, Jas. William	,,	
2093. Turner, Joseph	,,	
2095. Thomson, Cecil James	,,	
2130. Thollar, James Raywood	,,	
2079. Venton, Henry	,,	
2126. Vince, Louis	,,	Lance-Corporal, 11.7.02
2045. Williams, Alfred	,,	
2101. Webster, David Samuel	,,	
2110. Wilson, Gordon	,,	
2129. Wilson, Thomas Alexander Scott	,,	

EIGHTH BATTALION AUSTRALIAN COMMONWEALTH HORSE.
TASMANIAN UNIT.

ONE Squadron "C." The Battalion comprised besides, two Squadrons of South Australians, and one of Western Australians. For organization establishment, equipment, conditions of enrolment, pay, etc., vide 5th Australian Commonwealth Horse, New South Wales, page 184. The enrolment was carried out under the State Commandant by the commanding officers of the Battalions and Squadrons in the districts or localities selected to furnish a quota of men. Preference in selecting men was given to those serving in existing military units, to those who had had experience in South Africa, and to civilians possessing the most valuable military qualities. Qualifications were :—Height, not less than 5 feet 3 inches ; chest measurement, not less than 34 inches ; age, not under 20 ; passing a medical examination ; and capability to ride and shoot well. Single men were preferred, but married men and widowers with children were eligible on the understanding that there would be no separation allowance; and that they were willing to allot not less than two-fifths of their pay to their wives or children. Term of engagement, one year, or until termination of war.

The first troop, comprising 29 N.C.O.'s and men, was raised in Hobart ; the second, of a similar number, in Launceston ; the third, of a similar number, on the North Coast ; and the fourth, of a similar number, on the West Coast. Each troop was commanded by a subaltern officer ; but one vacancy was left to be filled in South Africa.

SERVICE.

"C" Squadron, comprising—4 officers, and 116 others, with 121 horses, embarked at Hobart on the transport *St. Andrew*, on 21st May, 1902 ; and, on 26th May, put into Port Adelaide for the Battalion staff and South Australian Squadrons, Called at Fremantle, 2nd June, for the Western Australian Squadron, and arrived at Durban on 19th June. Two officers and 10 others were struck off in South Africa. Embarked again (2 officers, 106 others) on the transport *Manchester Merchant* on 1st July ; and arrived at Hobart on 28th July, having called at Albany, Adelaide, and Melbourne *en route*. *Vide* also 8th Battalion, Australian Commonwealth Horse, South Australia.

There were not any promotions nor any casualties. Contingent disbanded, 9th August, 1902.

Nominal Roll.

No. and Name.	Rank.	Remarks.
Battalion Staff.		
Osborne, F. W.	Major	Second in Command
Brown, Henry George	Captain, Paymaster	Also for 6th Battalion
Squadron Officers.		
Ogilvy, Kenneth Arthur	Captain	
Cruickshank, Maynard Hayes	Lieutenant	No. 1 Troop
Kemsley, George William	,,	No. 2 Troop. Previous service in 2nd Tasmanian Contingent
Stephens, Edward William	,,	No. 3 Troop. Previous service in 1st Tasmanian Imperial Bushmen

Nominal Roll—continued.

No. and Name.	Rank.	Remarks.
No. 1 Troop—Hobart.		
N.C.O.'s and Men.		
251. Walker, Alfred	Sergeant-Major	
254. Crosby, Edward Barclay	Sergeant	
261. Breen, George	Corporal	
269. Dobbie, Robert	Lance-Corporal	Paid rank
270. Crooks, John	,,	Paid rank
304. Douglas, Rupert Oswald	,,	Unpaid
306. Farrar, Julian Gordon Knowles	,,	Unpaid
266. Bailey, Harry	Shoeing-Smith	
273. Blair, Arthur Vernon	Bugler	
283. Beck, Percy Isaac	Private	
285. Bezette, George Robert	,,	
287. Brock, Clarendon	,,	
294. Clarke, Kenneth	,,	
298. Cotton, Adam Jackson	,,	
307. Featherstone, Percy George	,,	
309. Gill, Archibald John	,,	
317. Headlam, Geo. Arthur Bayles	,,	
321. Holloway, Frank	,,	
324. Johns, John Charles	,,	
328. Martin, Alfred Christopher	,,	
333. McDonald, James Anderson	,,	
337. Pearman, John	,,	
340. Pickett, Frederick Albert	,,	
343. Porter, Clarence Hedley	,,	
346. Proctor, William	,,	
348. Saunderson, Thomas	,,	
356. Stewart, John Charles	,,	
358. Teague, Hugh	,,	
361. Umfreville, Gilbert Fraser	,,	
No. 2 Troop—Launceston.		
252. Lee, Walter Percy	Quartermaster-Sergeant	
255. Gaby, Reginald Wigmore	Sergeant	
263. Emery, Percy	Corporal	
262. Burnett, Robert Alexander	Lance-Corporal	Paid rank
272. Judge, Poyntz	,,	Unpaid
267. Drake, Thomas Percy	Shoeing-Smith	
274. McPherson, Herbert	Bugler	
279. Badcock, Edward	Private	
293. Clarke, Aubrey	,,	
292. Chillcott, Walter Theodore	,,	
295. Connell, Wm. Anderson	,,	
303. Dawkins, John Chas. Allen	,,	
300. Dalton, Alfred Ernest	,,	
305. Edmunds, Wm. Thomas	,,	
308. Fitzallen, Harold Herbert	,,	
367. Griffiths, Clarence Lorenzo	,,	
319. Hinds, William Robert	,,	
325. Knight, Alfred	,,	
365. Laird, James	,,	
330. Miller, Edgar Harold Christopher	,,	
334. McIntee, Francis	,,	
329. Mathews, Percy Montford	,,	
366. Phillips, Percy George	,,	
296. Parker, Robert	,,	
350. Simmonds, William John	,,	
351. Shepherd, John	,,	
352. Shepherd, Joseph	,,	
357. Taylor, George	,,	
364. White, Frank Sandberg	,,	

Nominal Roll—*continued.*

No. and Name.	Rank.	Remarks.
No. 3 Troop—North Coast.		
N.C.O.'s and Men—*continued.*		
256. Smythe, Alan Blackmore	Sergeant	
260. Facy, Cecil Clyde	Corporal	
258. Wilson, Benjamin Arthur	,,	
271. Stewart, John Alexander	Lance-Corporal	Paid rank
335. Oliphant, Harold William	,,	Unpaid
264. Johnstone, Leonard	Saddler	
275. Abel, Sidney	Private	
276. Adams, Geo. Edgar	,,	
282. Bear, Joseph	,,	
284. Berry, William	,,	
286. Boyd, William	,,	
288. Brown, Stanley John	,,	
291. Chaplin, Wm. Wenton	,,	
299. Cuthbert, Joseph Henry	,,	
302. Dawes, Reuben Thomas	,,	
313. Gardain, William	,,	
311. Good, David Hector	,,	
315. Hart, Richard John	,,	
326. Krebs, Wm. Patrick	,,	
327. Marsten, John Francis	,,	
332. McDonald, William	,,	
338. Peck, Arthur Frederick	,,	
339. Perger, Alfred Garnett	,,	
336. Padman, Clive	,,	
347. Richards, Reuben	,,	
349. Sibley, Walter	,,	
354. Smith, William Thomas	,,	
353. Smith, William Henry	,,	
362. Walters, William James	,,	
No. 4 Troop—West Coast.		
257. Crawford, John	Sergeant	
253. Pratt, John Courtney	Farrier-Sergeant	
259. Littlejohn, Mervyn James	Corporal	
360. Tynan, Michael	,,	
265. Lane, John Russell	Shoeing-Smith	
277. Anderson, Alexander	Lance-Corporal	Paid rank
301. Davis, Oscar Stephen	,,	Unpaid
278. Anderson, James Charles	Private	
280. Badkin, Ernest Albert	,,	
281. Bateman, Charles	,,	
289. Bull, Benjamin	,,	
290. Burdon, Ernest Theodore John	,,	
297. Cooper, Henry	,,	
310. Gill, Francis Morris	,,	
312. Goodchild, Louis Phillip	,,	
314. Grubb, Frederick	,,	
316. Hawkes, William Richard	,,	
318. Hearne, John Edward	,,	
320. Hinkley, Thomas	,,	
322. Howard, Thomas Arthur	,,	
323. Hughes, Noel Thomas	,,	
331. Mitchell, William Albert	,,	
341. Pilkington, William Charles	,,	
342. Pitt, Arthur Henry	,,	
344. Power, Patrick	,,	
345. Prior, Percy	,,	
355. Staples, George Lyndon	,,	
359. Tyler, George	,,	
363. Wills, John	,,	

Officers, N.C.O.'s, and Men of Tasmanian Contingents who died or were Killed.

Regimental Number, Rank, and Name.	Regimental Number, Rank, and Name.
1st (Mounted Infantry) Contingent.	*2nd Imperial Bushmen.*
71. Private Bailey, E. H.	193. Q.M.S. Lyne, D. M.
56. ,, Barker, T. W.	213. Lance-Cpl. Orr, J.
12 Lance-Cpl. Betts, H. A.	252. Private Warburton, J. E.
46. Private Black, H. M.	344. ,, Cowell, F. G.
30. ,, Button, A.	359. ,, Phegan, J.
50. ,, Gilham, A.	172. ,, Huttley, L. P.
104. ,, Butler, J.	
96. ,, Galvin, T.	
119. ,, R. P. Pitt	
76. Corporal Doolin, R. P.	"E" Company, 1st Battalion, Australian Commonwealth Horse.
2nd (Tasmanian Bushmen) Contingent.	
143. Lance-Cpl. Jacson, E. R.	1212. Private Fitzallen, A. E.
	1184. Q.M.S. Morrisby, F. E.
1st Imperial Bushmen.	
Captain Sale, A. A.	
Lieut. Walter, C. H.	"E" Company, 3rd Battalion, Australian Commonwealth Horse.
30. Private Brown, G. H.	
81. ,, Lette, L. F. J.	
87. ,, McLaren, P.	2065. Private Cundy, C.
114. ,, Wadley, W. I.	2026. ,, Hodgman, V. L.

Summary of Contingents Despatched.

Transport.	Date.	Contingent.	Officers.	Others.	Horses.	Wagons, &c.
Medic	28 Oct., 1899	First (Infantry)	4	76	4	2
Moravian	23 Jan., 1900	Draft	2	45	..	2
Antillian	5 Mar., 1900	Bushmen	..	52	58	..
Manhattan	26 Apr., 1900	1st Imperial Bushmen	5	117	133	..
Chicago	27 Mar., 1901	2nd Imperial Bushmen	12	241	289	..
Manchester Merchant	16 Feb., 1902	"E" Company, 1st Australian Commonwealth Horse	3	59	63	..
Englishman	8 Apr., 1902	"E" Company, 3rd Australian Commonwealth Horse	5	116	121	..
St. Andrew	21 May, 1902	"C" Squadron, 8th Australian Commonwealth Horse	4	116	121	..
		Special Service Officers	2	..	..	..
		Battalion Staff, Australian Commonwealth Horse	1	..	..	..
			38	822	789	4

Disposition.*

	Officers.	Other Ranks
Died or were killed	2	25
Discharged in South Africa or embarked for England and struck off in South Africa	14	44
Commissioned in Imperial Service	1	2
Returned to Tasmania	23	745
	40	816

* These figures are in some respects approximate only; it having been found impossible to obtain exact statements, owing to attachments, enlistments, and discharges, &c., in South Africa, of which adequate returns have not been made.

APPENDIX I.

GRAND TOTAL OF CONTINGENTS, ETC.*

State.	No. of Contingents.	Officers.	Other Ranks.	Horses.	Guns and Wagons, &c.	Remarks.
New South Wales	15	327	6,000	5,877	150	
Victoria	8	191	3,401	3,873	27	
Queensland	9	150	2,763	3,209	..	No record
South Australia	9	84	1,450	1,430	..	No record
Western Australia	9	69	1,168	1,179	7	
Tasmania	7	38	822	789	4	
	57	859	15,604	16,357	188	

* This is exclusive of drafts, but inclusive of the numbers contained therein.

APPENDIX II.

CLOTHING AND EQUIPMENT.

The subjoined list, which was published in General Orders in connexion with Commonwealth Horse, shows the outfit supplied to Imperial Bushmen and Commonwealth Horsemen, and paid for by Imperial Government; and also the scale of rations in Camp of Instruction:—

CLOTHING AND EQUIPMENT SUPPLIED TO N.C.O.'S AND MEN.

Uniform.

One field service hat (with chin strap); 1 field service jacket; 1 pair pantaloons (with loop for belt); 2 pairs boots and 1 pair laces (spare); 1 great coat; 1 field service cap (with chin strap); 2 pairs puttees.

Kit and Sea Kit.

One pair canvas shoes, with leather soles, and 1 pair laces (spare); dungaree suit, comprising 1 jacket, 2 pairs pants; 1 white hat (with strap); 1 blue jumper; 2 shirts (flannel); 2 under vests; 3 pairs socks; Crimean cap, woollen (to come down over face, with hole for mouth) belt, leather, in lieu of braces; 2 towels, 1 razor, 1 shaving brush, 1 comb, 1 knife, 1 fork, 1 spoon (the last 7 items in holdall); housewife (fitted); jack knife and lanyard; kit bag (number to be marked on in large letters); 1 "Jack Shea" pot (with strap); 1 section bag, to hold four kits; 1 pair spurs (with straps complete); 2 pairs drawers (woollen); 2 cholera belts (flannel); 4 small badges (for collars of tunics); 1 large badge (for hat); shoulder-strap badges; 1 book (note) and pencil; 1 bottle (water, aluminum, with strap); 1 calico bag (for ship use); 1 brush (clothes); 1 field dressing (with description cards); 1 haversack (tanned); 1 tin vaseline; 2 pieces soap.

Saddlery.

Saddle; bridle, complete, with ring bit; leathers (stirrup); irons (stirrup); girts, leather (folded); wallets, with 3 straps; straps, baggage, sets of three; 1 blanket, horse; 1 surcingle; 1 bag, water, canvas; 1 bag, nose; 1 brush, dandy; 1 brush, curry; 2 cloths, sponge; 1 rope, head; 1 net, forage; 1 sponge, water; 1 picket, hoof; 1 tin saddle paste; 1 chamois leather.

Equipment.

1 bandolier, leather (66 rounds); 1 waterproof sheet, 6ft. 6in. by 3ft. 6in., with seven eyelet holes, each side; 1 pair blankets (say from 4¼ to 5 lbs. each); 1 pair wire cutters to each group; field glasses to non-commissioned officers (4 per squadron).

Scale of Rations in Camp.

Bread, 1¼ lbs.; meat, 1½ lbs.; tea, ½ oz.; sugar, 3 ozs.; coffee, ¼ oz.; salt, ½ oz.; pepper, 1/36 oz.; potatoes, 1 lb.; vegetables, ½ lb.; with the addition of the following extras twice a week:—Jam, 1 tin to 4 men; pickles, 1 bottle to 8 men; rice, ½ oz. per man; curry, ½ oz. per 8 men.

The daily scale of forage comprised 6 lbs. of oats, 12 lbs. chaff, 4 lbs. of lucerne hay, and 3 lbs. of bran. Daily scale of fuel:—8 lbs. of wood, or 2 lbs. of coal per man.

Officers allowed £30 to provide all equipment, uniform, and saddlery for themselves, as might be approved by State Commandant. Swords not taken, but officers required to provide themselves with following articles of equipment:—Sam Browne belt; revolver, Imperial pattern, or to take Imperial Government ammunition; pair field glasses; watch; compass; haversack, water bottle, (which two latter might be issued from store on repayment).

INDEX.

"A" Battery, Royal Australian Artillery, 48; under Imperial discipline, *ib.*; equipment, reference to orders, clothing, establishment, pay, embarkation and return, *ib.*; service, 49; war services of officers and promotions, *ib.*; extracts from Report of Colonel S. C. Smith, 50; nominal roll, 53; draft, 56.

"A" Squadron, New South Wales Mounted Rifles, 28; draft from New South Wales Regiment *ib.*; establishment and draft, departure and return; reference to orders, clothing, &c.; promotions, *ib.*; war services and honours, 29; principal operations, *ib.*; contact squadron after De Wet, 30; Corps Order by Colonel De Lisle, 30; letter from General Ridley, 31; letter from General Alderson, *ib.*; clasps earned, extracts from diary of Captain Antill, *ib.*; nominal roll, 32; draft, 34.

Abercrombie, C. S., private. 3rd Queensland, 470; hon. lieut.-quartermaster, 463; war service, 466.

Abbott, J. H. M., corporal 1st Australian Horse (New South Wales), 46; commissioned in Imperial service, 42.

Adams, F. B., sergeant, 1st Tasmanian, 550; lieutenant, 2nd Tasmanian, 552; war service, *ib.*

Adie, A. G., lieutenant, 1st Queensland, 450; war services, *ib.* 508; captain, 6th Queensland, 509.

Adrian, R. E., lieutenant (supernumerary), 2nd New South Wales Mounted Rifles, 107.

Ahern, A. P., sergeant, 1st Victorian Infantry, 228; 2nd lieutenant, 223.

Akins, C. H., lieut.-quartermaster, 5th Victorian, 281; war service, 280.

Airey, C. F., lieutenant, 2nd New South Wales Mounted Rifles, 110; war service, 109.

Airey, H. G., sergeant, New South Wales Citizen Bushmen, 83; lieutenant, 71; war service, 73.

Airey, H. P., lieut.-colonel, commands New South Wales Citizen's Bushmen, 75; war service, 72.

Alderson, E. A. S., brigadier-general, letter from, 31.

Alford, J., corporal, 4th Queensland, gallantry of, 477.

Alfred, W., captain-quartermaster, 4th Victorian, 259; war service, 257.

Allan, G. H., lieutenant, New South Wales Lancers, 10; war service, 8.

Allan, W., lieutenant, 2nd South Australian, 349; war service, *ib.*

Allen, P. S., warrant-officer (regimental sergeant-major), 5th Western Australian, 421.

Allen, R. R., 2nd lieutenant, staff, 3rd New South Wales Mounted Rifles, 125.

Allen, W. B., lieutenant, New South Wales Citizens Bushmen, 75; war service, 72.

Anderson, C. G., lieutenant, 1st New South Wales Mounted Rifles, 64; captain. 58; war service, 59.

Anderson, E. O., lieutenant, 2nd Victorian, 234; commissioned Royal Field Artillery, 230.

Anderson, G., corporal, 1st New South Wales Mounted Rifles; Soudan, 1885, 65.

Anderson, H. A., lieut.-adjutant, 5th Victorian, 281; war service, 280.

Anderson, J. B., nursing sister, Victorian, 241.

Anderson, R., lieutenant (supernumerary), 6th Queensland, 510; war service, 509.

Anderson-Pelham, C. H., lieutenant (supernumerary), 1st Queensland, 450; commissioned in 12th Lancers, 448; war services, 450.

Andrews, B. H., private, 3rd Western Australian, 410; lieut.-quartermaster, 2nd Australian Commonwealth Horse, 432.

Annat, J. W., lieutenant, 3rd Queensland, 466; war service, *ib.*; killed in action, 464.

Antill, E. A., lieutenant, "A" Battery, 53; at Vryburg, 51; Schweizer-Renche, 52; captain, and major (local), 49; war service, *ib.*

Antill, J. M., captain, "A" Squadron, New South Wales Mounted Rifles, 32; major, 28; extracts from diary of, 31; with 2nd New South Wales Mounted Rifles, 110; war service, 29, 109.

Antill, S. R., lieutenant, 1st New South Wales Mounted Rifles, 65; from sergeant, 58; captain, 1st Australian Commonwealth Horse, 172; war service, 60.

Appendix I., total of Contingents, p. 578; Appendix II., Clothing and Equipment, *ib.*

Appleby, H. O., sergeant-major, 4th Victorian, 267; lieutenant, 5th Victorian, 281; war service, 279.

Apps, J., lieutenant, 1st Australian Commonwealth Horse, 172.

Army Medical Corps, Australian Commonwealth, 16; nominal roll, 25; New South Wales details, 175; Victorian details, 317; Queensland details, 526; South Australian details, 378; Western Australian details, 433.

INDEX—*continued.*

Army Medical Corps, New South Wales, 13; efficiency of, *ib.*; reference to orders, clothing, pay, *ib.*; establishment, summary of Contingents, nursing sisters, 14; promotions, 15; service, 1st Contingent, *ib.*; 2nd Contingent, 16; Imperial draft, *ib.*; Australian Contingent, *ib.*; war services and honours, 17, 18; extract from Colonel Williams' report, 19; attached to Field Army, *ib.*; complimented by Lord Roberts, 20; nominal rolls, 20, 22, 24, 25.

Army Order relative to continued service, 254.

Arnot, W. O., lieutenant, 3rd South Australian, 353; war service, *ib.*

Arundel camp, attack upon, 217.

Atkinson, S. H., lieutenant, 2nd New South Wales Mounted Rifles, 110.

Atwell, W., warrant-officer (regimental sergeant-major), 4th Queensland, 479.

Auld, Rev. J. H. G., chaplain, New South Wales Citizens Bushmen, 75; war service, 73.

Austin, A., nursing sister, New South Wales, 14.

Austin, C., captain, 5th Queensland, 492; war service, 491.

Australian Commonwealth Horse, 1st Battalion, *vide* First Battalion, Australian Commonwealth Horse.

Australian Commonwealth Horse, 2nd Battalion, *vide* Second Battalion Australian Commonwealth Horse.

Australian Commonwealth Horse, 3rd Battalion, *vide* Third Battalion, Australian Commonwealth Horse.

Australian Commonwealth Horse, 4th Battalion, *vide* Fourth Battalion, Australian Commonwealth Horse.

Australian Commonwealth Horse, 5th Battalion, *vide* Fifth Battalion, Australian Commonwealth Horse.

Australian Commonwealth Horse, 6th Battalion, *vide* Sixth Battalion, Australian Commonwealth Horse.

Australian Commonwealth Horse, 7th Battalion, *vide* Seventh Battalion Australian Commonwealth Horse.

Australian Commonwealth Horse, 8th Battalion, *vide* Eighth Battalion Australian Commonwealth Horse.

Australian Horse, First, *vide* First Australian Horse.

Australian Regiment, The, 214; how composed, inspected by Sir Alfred Milner, and camp visited by Major-Generals Brabazon and Babington, *ib.*; arrives at Belmont, 215; New Year message from Melbourne, *ib.*; first casualty, *ib.*; inspected by Major-General Kelly-Kenny, 216; forms part of Major-General Clements' "Force," *ib.*; fully mounted, operations at Slingersfontein, Bastard's Nek, and Pink Hill, *ib.*; order by General Clements, 217; praised by Lord Kitchener, *ib.*; fighting at Arundel, reconnaissance towards Norval's Pont, crosses into Orange Free State, advance to Donkerpoort, Longkop, Philippolis, and Fauresmith, *ib.*; detachment to Jagersfontein, 218; arrives at Bloemfontein, *ib.*; Major-General Hutton inspects and addresses, *ib.*; Colonel Hoad bids good-bye, *ib.*; absorbed in 1st Mounted Infantry Brigade, 219; general officers served under, *ib.*; casualty list, killed or died, 219, 220; casualties, summary, 221; mentioned in despatches, honours, *ib.*

Ayliffe, G. G., lieutenant, 5th South Australian, 368; war service, 366.

Aytoun, A., lieut.-colonel, commands 4th Queensland, 479; invalided to Australia, 476; war services, 477.

Baden-Powell, Major-General, thanks New South Wales Citizens Bushmen, 71.

Bagot, C. G. S., lieutenant, 6th South Australian, 374; war service, 367.

Bailey, A., sergeant, 4th Queensland, 479; lieut.-quartermaster, 475; war service, 478.

Bailey, H., lieutenant, 1st Queensland, 453; captain-adjutant at Maitland camp, 448; war service, 450, 508; captain-adjutant, 6th Queensland, 509.

Bailey, H. S., lieutenant, 4th Australian Commonwealth Horse, 319.

Baker, A. B., captain, New South Wales Citizens Bushmen, 82; major, 71; war service, 72.

Barbeta, E., veterinary-lieutenant, New South Wales Imperial Bushmen, 90; with 1st Australian Commonwealth Horse, 167; war service, 87.

Barclay, A. H., sergeant, 2nd Western Australian, promoted lieutenant, 403; war service, 405.

Bardwell, B. E., lieutenant, 6th Western Australian, 426; war service, 420.

Barker, T. H., civil surgeon, attached to Army Medical Corps, 24; hon. lieutenant, 18; war service, *ib.*

Barnard, J. F., lieutenant, Medical Staff with 2nd Australian Commonwealth Horse, 309.

Barnes, A. W., veterinary-captain, 2nd Queensland, 459; war service, *ib.*

Barnes, C. A., lieutenant, 4th Western Australian, 415; war service, 414.

Barnett, —., sergeant, 3rd New South Wales Mounted Rifles, lieutenant, 124.

Barracks, Military, Hobart, camp at, 545.

INDEX—*continued*.

Barwise, W. K., trooper, 3rd Tasmanian, 558; lieutenant, 1st Australian Commonwealth Horse, 568.
Basche, C. O., lieutenant, 1st New South Wales Mounted Rifles, 62; died, 60; war service, *ib.*
Bastard's Nek, engagement at, 216.
Bates, J., corporal, 1st New South Wales Mounted Rifles, Soudan, 1885, 67.
Bathgate, J. D., lieutenant, 5th Australian Commonwealth Horse, 188.
Battye, A. E. M., lieutenant, New South Wales Citizens Bushmen, 80; war service, 72.
Battye, R. R., lieutenant, 2nd New South Wales Mounted Rifles, 110; 3rd Imperial Bushmen, 147.
Bayly, M. W., major, special service officer, New South Wales, 195.
Bean, H. K., lieutenant, Army Medical Corps, 24; war service, 18.
Bearer Company, Army Medical Corps, engagements, 15.
Beattie, J. P., lieutenant, 6th Australian Commonwealth Horse, 329.
Beatty, K. J., lieutenant, 5th Victorian, 281; war service, 279.
Beck, Rev. E. C., chaplain, "A" Battery, 53; commended by commanding officer, 51; war service, 49.
Belfast, 1st Australian Horse (New South Wales), at, 43.
Bell, F. W., private, 1st Western Australian, 400; lieutenant, 6th Western Australian, 426; obtains Victoria Cross, 419; war service, 420.
Bell, G. J., lieutenant, 5th Victorian, 281; captain, 274; war service, 277.
Bell, G. L., lieutenant, Army Medical Corps, with 5th Australian Commonwealth Horse, 186.
Bell, H. H., sergeant, 5th Victorian, 283; lieutenant, 274; war service, 279; with 2nd Australian Commonwealth Horse, 309.
Bell, M. A. T., lieutenant, 4th Queensland, 479; captain (supernumerary), 5th Queensland; 493; war service, 478.
Bell, W. R., lieutenant, 6th Australian Commonwealth Horse, 330.
Benjamin, H. A., lieutenant, 5th Queensland, 492; war service, 491.
Bennett, A. J., captain, 1st New South Wales Mounted Rifles, 67; major, 58; supernumerary, 3rd Mounted Rifles, 123, 137; war service, 60, 124.
Bent, J. B. L., sergeant, 1st New South Wales Mounted Rifles, 65; lieutenant (supernumerary), 3rd Mounted Rifles, 58, 123.
Beresford, G. St. J. R., quartermaster-sergeant, 2nd Western Australian, 405; lieutenant, 8th Australian Commonwealth Horse, 438.
Berry, J. K., captain, 4th Queensland, 479; war services, 478; commands "D" Company 1st Australian Commonwealth Horse, 523.
Bethel, town of, burned, 477.
Bethel-Standerton road, fight at, 414.
Bethlehem, taking of, 357, 414.
Bickford, W. J., veterinary-lieutenant, 2nd South Australian, 349; 4th South Australian, 358; war service, *ib.*
Bidmead, M. S., nursing sister, South Australia, 378; obtains Royal Red Cross, *ib.*
Bidstrup, C. N., lieutenant, 2nd Australian Commonwealth Horse, 310.
Binstead, J. W., 2nd lieutenant, 3rd New South Wales Mounted Rifles, 137.
Bisdee, J. H., trooper, 3rd Tasmanian, 558; obtains Victoria Cross, 556; lieutenant, 4th Tasmanian, 563; war service, 562.
Black, C. H., lieutenant, commands Machine Gun Section, 1st Queensland, 456; war service, 450.
Black, D., lieutenant, 7th Australian Commonwealth Horse, 538.
Black, J., warrant-officer (regimental sergeant-major), 3rd Australian Commonwealth Horse, 177.
Blair, F. M., lieutenant, 1st South Australian, 344; Australian Regiment, 214; recommended, 343; war service, 344.
Blow, E. A., captain, 5th Australian Commonwealth Horse, 186.
Blue, S., trooper, 2nd South Australian, 350; lieutenant, 6th, 374; war service, 367.
Blyth, C. O., private, 1st Tasmanian, 549; lieutenant, 4th Tasmanian, 563; war service, 562.
Boardman, Rev. J., chaplain, New South Wales Citizens Bushmen, 75; war service, 73.
Boland, S. B., lieutenant, 6th Queensland, 509; war service, 508.
Bond, J., warrant-officer, Army Medical Corps, 20.
Borwick, W. H., private, 4th Victorian, 262; lieutenant, 254; war service, 258.
Bossby, F. V., lieutenant, 3rd New South Wales Imperial Bushmen, 147.
Bossley, F. V., lieutenant, 5th Australian Commonwealth Horse, 188.
Bothaville, "A" Squadron, New South Wales Mounted Rifles, at, 30.
Bowden, T. L., lieutenant, 3rd New South Wales Imperial Bushmen, 147; 1st Australian Commonwealth Horse, 168.
Bowker, H., veterinary-lieutenant, 1st New South Wales Australian Horse, 42.
Bowman, A. M., lieutenant, 3rd Australian Commonwealth Horse, 527.

INDEX—*continued*.

Boyd, C. J. K., lieutenant, 4th Victorian, 259 ; war service, 258.
Boyes, A. M., sergeant, 2nd Tasmanian, 552 ; lieut.-adjutant, 551 ; war service, 552.
Brabazon, J. H., sergeant, 2nd Victorian, 238 ; 2nd lieutenant, 230 ; with 5th Victorian, 281 ; war service, 233, 279 ; captain, 6th Australian Commonwealth Horse, 325.
Brace, C. F., lieutenant, special service officer, New South Wales, 199.
Brace, E., lieutenant, 5th Victorian, 281 ; war service, 279.
Brakenlaagte, heroic defence at, 304.
Brakfontein, Cameron's Scouts engaged at, 243.
Brand, C. H., sergeant, 3rd Queensland, 469 ; lieutenant, 463 ; war service, 466 ; captain, 7th Australian Commonwealth Horse, 535.
Braun, C. L., sergeant, 1st New South Wales Mounted Rifles, 65 ; lieutenant (supernumerary), 3rd Mounted Rifles, 58, 123.
Bree, R. S. R. S., lieutenant, 2nd Victorian, 234 ; war service, 233 ; died, 231.
Brees, W. A., sergeant-trumpeter, 3rd New South Wales Mounted Rifles, 135 ; lieutenant, 124.
Bremner, H. M., 2nd lieutenant, 2nd New South Wales Mounted Rifles, 110.
Brent, R. D, 2nd lieutenant, 4th Tasmanian, 565 ; war service, 562.
Bretag, F. W., sergeant-major, 6th Western Australian, 426 ; lieutenant, 418 ; war service, 421.
Bridges, W. T., major, Royal Australian Artillery, special service officer, New South Wales, 197.
Brigade under Colonel Hoad, 215.
Broadwood, General, telegram from, *re* Palmeitfontein, 398.
Brock, D. W., corporal, 2nd South Australian, 349 ; lieutenant, 5th South Australian, 368 ; war service, 367.
Brodie, V. B., private, 4th Queensland, 482 ; lieutenant, 7th Australian Commonwealth Horse, 535.
Broinowski, F. J., quartermaster-sergeant, New South Wales Citizens Bushmen, 75 ; lieutenant, 71 ; war service, 73.
Bronkhurst Spruit, typical trek, 275.
Brooke, H. E., 2nd lieutenant, 3rd New South Wales Mounted Rifles, 137.
Brown, A. J. B., sergeant, 1st Western Australian, promoted lieutenant, 396 ; war service, 399 ; captain, 418 ; with 5th Western Australian, 421 ; adjutant, 5th and 6th Western Australian, 418.
Brown, H. G., captain-paymaster, 6th and 8th Australian Commonwealth Horse, 573.
Brown, V. S., lieutenant, 6th Queensland, 509 ; war service, 508.
Brown, W., lieutenant, 1st Tasmanian, 548 ; Australian Regiment, 214 ; captain, 546 ; war service, 548.
Browne, H. H., captain, New South Wales Imperial Bushmen, 101 ; major, 3rd Imperial Bushmen, 107, 144, 147 ; war services, 89.
Browne, R. S., captain, special service officer, Queensland, 450, 520.
Brownell, —., lance-corporal, 4th Tasmanian, 565 ; obtains Imperial commission, 561.
Bruce, G. O., lieutenant, 2nd Victorian, 234 ; war service, 233.
Bruce, W., warrant-officer (regimental sergeant-major), 4th Tasmanian, 563.
Bruche, J. H., captain, special service officer, Victorian, 306 ; joins Australian Regiment, 214 ; with 2nd Australian Commonwealth Horse, 309.
Buchanan, D., lieutenant, 3rd New South Wales Imperial Bushmen, 147.
Buckeridge, T. W., lieutenant, 3rd New South Wales Imperial Bushmen, 147.
Bullock, C. C., 2nd lieutenant, 3rd New South Wales Mounted Rifles, 127.
Bullock, J. A., corporal, 2nd Western Australian, 406 ; lieutenant, Bushveldt Carbineers, 403.
Burnage, G. J., major, 3rd New South Wales Mounted Rifles, 127.
Burnie, R. M., lieutenant, 5th Victorian, 281 ; war service, 279.
Burns, J. L., veterinary-lieutenant, with 3rd South Australian, 353 ; war service, *ib.*
Burnside, G. H., lieutenant, 5th Queensland, 492 ; war service, 491.
Bushmen Brigade, 3rd Queensland, with, 463-4 ; at relief of Mafeking, 463.
Bushmen, composite regiment of, 352, 551.
Bushmen.—*New South Wales*: Citizen, 70 ; Imperial, 85, 144. *Queensland*: 4th Imperial, 474 ; 5th Imperial, 487 ; 6th Imperial, 506. *South Australia*: 3rd Bushmen, 352 ; 4th Imperial, 356 ; 5th and 6th Imperial, 364. *Tasmanian*: 2nd Bushmen, 551 ; 1st Imperial, 555 ; 2nd Imperial, 561. *Victoria*: Bushmen, 240 ; Imperial, 252. *Western Australia*: 3rd Bushmen, 408.
Butler, W., warrant-officer (regimental sergeant-major), New South Wales Imperial Bushmen, 91 ; lieut.-adjutant, 87 ; captain, *ib.*; war services, *ib.*
Butterworth, A. W., lieutenant, 4th Queensland, 479 ; captain, 475 ; war service, 478.
Byron, J. J., major, special service officer, Queensland, 520.
Cadden, R., lieutenant (supernumerary), 3rd New South Wales Mounted Rifles, 123.
Cade, D. D., lieutenant, Australian Army Medical Corps, 26 ; hon. captain, 19, 317 ; war service, 19.

INDEX—continued.

Cahill, T. S., lieutenant, 2nd Australian Commonwealth Horse, 310.
Caine, Rev. C., chaplain, New South Wales Imperial Bushmen, 91 ; war service, 87.
Caines, H., lieutenant, New South Wales Imperial Bushmen, 94 ; captain, 87 ; with 3rd Imperial Bushmen, 144, 147; war service, 88.
Cameron, C. St. C., captain, 1st Tasmanian, 213, 548 ; Australian Regiment, 214; major, 546 ; war services, 548.
Cameron, D., lieutenant, 3rd New South Wales Imperial Bushmen, 147.
Cameron D. C., lieutenant, 6th Queensland, 509 ; war service, 508.
Cameron, J. McL., lieutenant, commanding Scouts, 251 ; captain, 241 ; major, *ib.*; war service, 244.
Cameron's Scouts, 240 ; service, 243 ; nominal roll, 251.
Campbell, D. G., lieutenant, 2nd New South Wales Mounted Rifles, 110.
Campbell, J., lieutenant, 1st Western Australian, 399 ; Australian Regiment, 214 ; captain, 396 ; war services, 398 ; commands 6th, 426.
Campbell, N., lieutenant, 5th South Australian, 368 ; war service, 367.
Camps of Instruction : *New South Wales*, 3 ; *Queensland*, 446 ; *South Australia*, 342 ; *Tasmania*, 545 ; *Victoria*, 212 ; *Western Australia*, 395.
Cape, C. S., lieutenant, New South Wales Citizens Bushmen, 82 ; captain, 71 ; war service, 72.
Carington, Hon. R., major, 2nd New South Wales Mounted Rifles, 110 ; lieut.-colonel, 144 ; commands 3rd New South Wales Imperial Bushmen,147 ; war service, 146.
Carroll, J. W. M., captain-adjutant, 4th Queensland, 479 ; major, 475 ; war service, 478.
Carstairs, H. G., lieutenant, 3rd Victorian, 245; captain, 5th Victorian, 281 ; war service, 244, 278.
Carter, A. C., lieutenant, 5th South Australian 367 ; war service, 366.
Carter, H. R., lieutenant, 5th Queensland, 492 ; captain, 488; war service, 491.
Carter, W. B., lieutenant, 3rd New South Wales Imperial Bushmen, 147.
Carthew-Yorstoun, A. M., lieut.-colonel, report on Lieutenant Grieve, 197.
Caskey, L. J., lieutenant, 5th Queensland, 492 ; war service, 491 ; killed in action, 489.
Catchlove, G. E., sergeant, 4th South Australian, 359 ; lieutenant, 356 ; war service, 358.
Cavaye, J. McL., lieutenant, (supernumerary) 5th Queensland, 493 ; war service, 492.
Chalmers, C. R. A., corporal, 1st Tasmanian, 548 ; lieutenant, 3rd Australian Commonwealth Horse, 570.
Chalmers, F. R., private 1st Tasmanian, 549 ; 2nd lieutenant, 4th Tasmanian, 565 ; 1st lieutenant, 561 ; war service, 562.
Chalmers, H. B., captain, 4th Victorian, 259 ; major, 5th Victorian, 253 ; war service, 257.
Chapman, A. E., captain, 3rd New South Wales Mounted Rifles, 130.
Chauvel, H. G., captain, 1st Queensland, 450 ; major, 447 ; commands 1st and 2nd Queensland, 449 ; war services, *ib.* ; commands 7th Australian Commonwealth Horse, 530.
Cherry, C. C., veterinary-lieutenant, New South Wales Citizens Bushmen, 75 ; war service, 73.
Chipper, S. J., sergeant-major, 3rd Western Australian, promoted lieut.-quartermaster, 408 ; war service, 410.
Chocolate, Queen's, distributed, 215.
Chomley, G. G. F., lieutenant, 1st Victorian Mounted Rifles, 223 ; Australian Regiment, 214 ; captain, 5th Victorian, 280 ; war service, 277.
Chomley, W. B., lieutenant, 4th Victorian, 259 ; war service, 258.
Chrisp, H. McD., corporal, Cameron's Scouts, 251 ; lieutenant, 5th Victorian, 242.
Chrisp, J. G., lieutenant, 5th Victorian, 280 ; killed in action, 276 ; war service, 278.
Christian, S. E., lieutenant "A" Battery, Royal Australian Artillery, 53 ; at Petrusville, 52 ; war service, 49.
Christie, A. J., lieutenant, special service officer, Victorian, 306.
Christie, H. B., 2nd lieutenant, New South Wales Citizens Bushmen, 80 ; South African constabulary, 71 ; war services, 72.
Christmas beer intercepted by Boers, 52.
Citizens Bushmen, New South Wales, 70 ; establishment, pay, departure, and return, reference to orders, clothing, campaign, &c., *ib.* ; General Order by Major-General Baden-Powell, 71 ; promotions, *ib.* ; war services and honours, 72 ; extract from report of Major W. H. Tunbridge, 73 ; nominal roll, 75.
Clark, W. F., lieutenant, 5th Victorian, 281 ; war service, 278.
Clark, W. J., major, 3rd Australian Commonwealth Horse, 177.
Clarke, C. W. St. J., lieutenant, 4th Australian Commonwealth Horse, 319.
Clarke, L. F., major, 4th Victorian, 259 ; lieut.-colonel, 253 ; war service, 257.
Clarke, W., lieutenant, 3rd New South Wales Imperial Bushmen, 144, 147.
Clements, G. J. H., lieutenant, 5th Victorian, 280 ; captain, 274 ; war service, 278.
Clements, Major-General, orders *re* Slingersfontein, 216, 217.
Clerk, E. G., lieutenant, 5th Queensland, 492 ; war service, 491.
Cleveland, L. A., lieutenant, 4th Victorian, 259 ; captain, 5th Victorian, 253 ; **war service, 258.**

INDEX—*continued.*

Clifford, G. S., lieutenant (supernumerary), 5th Western Australian, 421 ; war service, 420.
Clifton, R., lieutenant, 6th Western Australian, 426 ; gallantry of, 419 ; war service, 420.
Clothing, &c., sent to Lancers by Viscountess Hampden, 9.
Clothing and equipment, South Australian Contingents, 342.
Cochrane, W. J., sergeant, 5th Victorian, 274 ; lieutenant, *ib.* ; war service, 279 ; with 6th Australian Commonwealth Horse, 328.
Codd, F. C. E., lieutenant, 7th Australian Commonwealth Horse, 531.
Code, F. G., lieutenant, 4th Victorian, 259 ; captain, 5th, 253 ; war service, 258.
Coffey, E. N., warrant-officer (regimental sergeant-major), 1st Victorian Infantry, 226.
Coggins, H. C., lieutenant (supernumerary), 2nd New South Wales Mounted Rifles, 107 ; 3rd New South Wales Imperial Bushmen, 147.
Coghill, A. J., lieut.-quartermaster, 6th Australian Commonwealth Horse, 325.
Coleman, W., sergeant-major, "A" Battery, 53 ; Soudan, 1885, *ib.*
Collick, Rev. E. M., chaplain, 5th Western Australian, 421, war service, 420.
Collins, A. E., lieutenant, 3rd South Australian, 353 ; in command, 352 ; captain, *ib.* ; war service, 353 ; commands " C " Squadron, 4th Australian Commonwealth Horse, 382.
Collins, P. C., corporal, 2nd Western Australian, 406 ; lieutenant, South African Constabulary, 403.
Colquhoun, W. J., commander, transport officer, 1st Victorian, 213 ; Australian Regiment, 214.
Coltman, C. S., lieutenant, 4th Victorian, 259 ; captain, 5th Victorian, 281 ; war services 258, 278.
Commandants, Conference of, 211.
Commonwealth Army Medical Corps, *vide* Army Medical Corps, Australian Commonwealth.
Companies, 6th Queensland, re-organized, 507.
Comrie, A. N., warrant officer (regimental sergeant-major), 2nd Western Australian, 405.
Connolly, J. B., lieutenant, 3rd Australian Commonwealth Horse, 177.
Conroy, J. M., captain, special service officer, New South Wales, 202.
Contingents, grand total of, *vide* Appendix I., 578.
Contingents, summary of, New South Wales, 206, 207 ; Victorian, 337 ; Queensland, 542 ; South Australian, 392 ; Western Australian, 441 ; Tasmanian, 577 ; three classes of, 341.
Cook, A. E., lieutenant, 4th South Australian, 358 ; war service, 357 ; captain, 8th Australian Commonwealth Horse, 386.
Cook, B. W., lieutenant, 5th Queensland, 492 ; war service, 491.
Cope, W., lieutenant, New South Wales, Citizens Bushmen, 75 ; war services, 72.
Copeland, H. P. R., captain-adjutant, 3rd New South Wales Mounted Rifles, 125 ; major, 124 ; special service officer, 201.
Cornish, A. F., captain, 6th South Australian, 374 ; war service, 367.
Cornwall, C., 2nd lieutenant, New South Wales Citizens Bushmen, 75 ; South African Constabulary, 71 ; war service, 72
Cortis, W. R., captain, Army Medical Corps, 22, 62 ; works under heavy fire, 61 ; war service, 18.
Cory, G. C., lieutenant, 3rd Australian Commonwealth Horse, 177.
Cosgrove, A. R., lieutenant, New South Wales Imperial Bushmen, 98 ; war service, 88.
Cossins, G. H., lieutenant, 6th South Australians, 374 ; war service, 367.
Costello, J., warrant-officer, 1st Tasmanian, 548.
Coulter, S. R., lieutenant, 5th Victorian, 280 ; war service, 278 ; killed in action, 276.
Cowell, W. R., lieutenant, 5th Queensland, 504 ; in charge of draft, *ib.* ; war service, 491.
Cowley, C., lieutenant (supernumerary), 4th Queensland, 479 ; war service, 478 ; with details, 519.
Cox, C. F., captain, Lancers, 4, 10 ; war services, 7, 124 ; major, commands 3rd New South Wales Mounted Rifles, 125 ; lieut.-colonel, 124.
Cox, C. M., lieutenant, 3rd New South Wales Imperial Bushmen, 147.
Cox, F. W. S., lieutenant (supernumerary) 2nd New South Wales Mounted Rifles, 107.
Coyle, J. E. F., 2nd lieutenant, 2nd New South Wales Mounted Rifles, 110 ; war service, 109.
Crane, F. W. C., captain-quartermaster, 5th Australian Commonwealth Horse, 186.
Creer, R. C., captain, 3rd Australian Commonwealth Horse, 177.
Crichton, A. De P., lieutenant, 4th Queensland, 479 ; war service, 478 ; commands details, 519.
Crichton, A. E., captain-quartermaster, 4th Queensland, 479 ; war service, 478.
Crichton, A. F., lieutenant, 2nd Queensland 459 ; war service, *ib.* ; with 3rd Australian Commonwealth Horse, 527.
Cronje, General, his laager and prisoners, 29.
Cross, E. H., lieutenant, 3rd Australian Commonwealth Horse, 177.
Cruickshank, M. H., lieutenant, 8th Australian Commonwealth Horse, 573.
Cudmore, R. H., lieutenant, 5th South Australian, 367 ; war service, 366.
Culliford, E., corporal, 4th Queensland, gallantry of, 477.

INDEX—continued.

Cumming, C. A., lieutenant (supernumerary), 1st Queensland, 450 ; war service, *ib.*
Curr, H., lieutenant, 1st Australian Commonwealth Horse, 168.
Curtis, B. W., lieutenant, 6th Queensland, 500 ; war service, *ib.*
Cyclist Company, 5th Queensland, 487 ; proves unsuitable, 488.
Daley, P. J., sergeant, 6th Western Australian, 427 ; lieutenant, 418 ; gallantry of, 419 ; war service, 421.
Dalgleish, G. W., lieutenant, 3rd Queensland, 467 ; war service, 466.
Dallimore, J., captain, 4th Victorian, 259 ; captures Boers, 255 ; war service, 257.
Dallimore, P. J., lieutenant, 5th Victorian, 281 ; war service, 278.
Dangar, F. H., sends cases to Lancers, 9.
Dangar, H. P., major, New South Wales Citizens Bushmen, 75 ; war service, 72.
Dangar, H. W., captain, Royal Australian Artillery, 48 ; special service officer, N.S.W. 199.
D'Apice, J. C. F., trooper, 1st New South Wales Mounted Rifles, commissioned in Imperial Army, 58.
D'Arcy, A. E., lieutenant, 3rd New South Wales Imperial Bushmen, 147.
D'Arcy, C. B., private, 4th Victorian, 261 ; lieutenant, 253 ; war service, 258.
Darling, H. F., lieutenant, 1st Western Australian, 399 ; Australian Regiment, 214 ; captain commands 5th W.A., 421 ; war service, 398.
Dart, G. A., 2nd lieutenant, 3rd New South Wales Mounted Rifles, 137.
Davies, A., lieutenant, 5th Western Australian, 421 ; war service, 420.
Davies, C., lieutenant, commands "E" Squadron, 2nd Australian Commonwealth Horse, 432.
Day, A. T., lieutenant, 2nd Australian Commonwealth Horse, 309.
Day, Rev. C. V. P., chaplain, 4th Queensland, 479 ; war service, 478.
Deacon, W. T. major, 4th Queensland, 479 ; in command, 476 ; war service, 477.
De Castilla, J., lieutenant, 2nd Western Australian, 405 ; war service, *ib.*
De Haviland, T. L., sergeant, 3rd Victorian, 246 ; lieutenant, 241 ; adjutant, *ib.* captain, 5th Victorian, 281 ; war service, 244, 278.
De Lancy-Forth, N. B., sergeant, 4th Queensland, 480 ; commissioned Imperial service, 475.
De Lisle, H. B., colonel, Corps order by, 30 ; congratulates 5th and 6th South Australians, 365.
Delohery, H. C. M., civil surgeon, 24 ; hon. lieutenant, 18 ; war service, *ib.*
De Mestre, H., lieutenant (supernumerary), 2nd New South Wales Mounted Rifles, 107 ; 3rd Imperial Bushmen, 147.
Dempsey, J. I., sergeant-major, 3rd South Australian, 353 ; lieutenant, 352 ; war service, 353.
De Passey, W., warrant officer (regimental sergeant-major), 2nd South Australian, 349 ; lieutenant, 347 ; war service, 349 ; captain, commands "D" Squadron, 2nd Australian Commonwealth Horse, 379.
De Reyher, G., trooper, 4th South Australian, 360 ; lieutenant, 4th Australian Commonwealth Horse, 382.
Desmond, J., veterinary-lieutenant, 5th South Australian, 368 ; war service, 367.
Diamond Hill, 30, 61, 448, 547.
Dibbs, T. B., captain, special service officer, New South Wales, 202.
Dick, J. A., lieutenant, Army Medical Corps, 22 ; war service, 18.
Dickson, B. B., lieutenant, 5th Australian Commonwealth Horse, 192.
Died or were killed, *vide* Killed or Died.
Dixon, J., lieutenant, 3rd New South Wales Imperial Bushmen, 144, 147 ; honours, 146.
Dobbin, W. W., captain, 3rd Victorian, 245 ; major, 241 ; war service, 244.
Dobson, D., lieutenant, 6th Australian Commonwealth Horse, 334.
Dodds T. H., captain-adjutant, 5th Queensland, 492 ; war service, 491.
Dods, G. A. C., corporal, 3rd Queensland, 467 ; lieutenant, 7th Australian Commonwealth Horse, 533.
Dods, J. E., captain, Army Medical Corps, 1st Queensland, 450 ; war service, *ib.*
Doudney, G. L. H., lieutenant, 3rd New South Wales Mounted Rifles, 132.
Doudney, R. V., lieutenant, 3rd Australian Commonwealth Horse, 177.
Douglas, F. J., lieutenant, Medical Staff, 3rd South Australian, 353 ; war service, *ib.*
Douglas, G. A., lance-corporal, 3rd Tasmanian, 559 ; receives Imperial commission, 555.
Dove, F. A., lieutenant, "E" Squadron, New South Wales Mounted Rifles, 38 ; Australian Regiment, 214 ; detailed to scout, 38 ; captain, 37 ; in command, 36 ; adjutant, 3rd Australian Commonwealth Horse, 177 ; war service, 37.
Dowling, W. V., lieutenant, 1st Australian Horse, 45 ; missing, 8, 45 ; captain, 42 ; war service, *ib.*
Downer, J. H., lance-corporal, 4th South Australian, 359 ; lieutenant, 4th Australian Commonwealth Horse, 382.
Downes, H. M., lieutenant, 5th Western Australian, 421 ; captain, 418 ; war service, 420.
Downes, H. M., captain, 4th Victorian, 259 ; major, 5th, 253 ; war service, 257.

INDEX—continued.

Dowse, R., lieutenant, 1st Queensland, 453; captain-adjutant, Maitland Camp, 448; war service, 450.
Doyle, R. D., lieutenant, New South Wales Imperial Bushmen, 91; captain, 3rd Imperial Bushmen, 144, 147; war service, 88.
Drage, P. W. C., lieutenant, 1st New South Wales Mounted Rifles, 67; killed in action, 61.
Dransfield, A., lieutenant, 3rd New South Wales Imperial Bushmen, 144, 147.
Driefontein, 1st Australian Horse (New South Wales), at, 45.
Drive, great, which ended war, 167, 308, 522.
Drummond, D., 2nd lieutenant, 3rd New South Wales Mounted Rifles, 135.
Duff, Lady, sends tobacco to Lancers, 9.
Duffy, J. S., sergeant, 2nd Western Australian, promoted lieutenant, 403; war service, 405; in charge, 404.
Duka, A. T., captain, Army Medical Corps, with 3rd Queensland, 467; war service, 466.
Duncan, G. C., warrant-officer (regimental sergeant-major), 1st Australian Horse, 45.
Duncan, R. L., sergeant, 4th Victorian, 264; lieutenant, 5th Victorian, 281; war service, 279.
Dunn, S. S., captain, Medical Staff, with 4th South Australian, 358; war service, ib.
Durham, H. R. P., captain, transport officer, 4th Queensland, 479; war service, 478.
Dutton, R. G., lieutenant (supernumerary), 5th Queenslanders, 493; war service, 492.
"E" Squadron, New South Wales Mounted Rifles: Raised as infantry, 35; how recruited, embarkation, &c., orders, clothing, establishment, service, converted into mounted rifles, ib.; casualties, 36; engagements, ib.; services and honours, 37; extract from, Captain Legge's report, ib.; from Captain Holmes' report, 38; nominal roll, ib.
Eames, W. L'E., major, Army Medical Corps, 22; war service, 17.
Ebeling, G., lieutenant, 5th Victorian, 281; war service, 279.
Eberling, R., warrant-officer, Australian Army Medical Corps, 26, 175; lieut.-quartermaster, ib.
Ebsworth, A., 2nd lieutenant, 1st Australian Horse, 45; killed in action, 42.
Echlin, R. B., captain, 3rd Queensland, 466; extract from report, 465; in charge of draft, 518; commands "D" Squadron, 3rd Australian Commonwealth Horse, 527; war service, 466.
Eckford, A. G., lieutenant, New South Wales Citizens Bushmen, 78; captain, major, 71; attached (supernumerary) 2nd Mounted Rifles, 107; war service 72.
Eddy, G. A, major, commands 1st Victorian Infantry, 213, 226; second in command, Australian Regiment, 214; honours 221; killed in action, 216.
Edie, J. G., 2nd lieutenant, 2nd New South Wales Mounted Rifles, 110; war service, 109.
Edney, J. R., warrant officer (regimental sergeant-major), 1st Australian Commonwealth Horse, 168.
Edmunds, W. H., lieutenant, 5th South Australian, 367; war service, 366.
Edwards, C. A., captain, Army Medical Corps, 20; with "E" Squadron, Mounted Rifles, 37; war service, 17.
Edwards, J. H. V., sergeant, 1st New South Wales Mounted Rifles, 63; commissioned in Bushveldt Carbineers, 58.
Edwards, V. H., major, special service officer, South Australian, 377.
Egan, J. P., trooper, 3rd Tasmanian, 559; commissioned in South African Field Force, 555.
Eighth Battalion, Australian Commonwealth Horse, 385: *South Australian details*, how raised establishment, troops of, where enlisted, service, nominal roll, ib.; *Tasmanian unit*. 573; details, enrolment, qualifications, troops, service, ib.; nominal roll, 573; *Western Aus'ralian unit*, 437; pay, troops, men preferred, horses, service, departure, &c., ib.; nominal roll, ib.
Eland's River, New South Wales Citizens Bushmen, at 71, 73; Victorian Bushmen at, 241 3rd Queensland at, 464; 3rd Western Australian at, 409.
Eland's Spruit, attack on convoy, 556.
Elston, W. E., lieutenant (supernumerary), 6th Queensland, 510; war service, 509.
Embling, H. A. A., lieutenant, 4th Victorian, 259; war service, 258.
Equipment, Queensland Contingents, 445.
Erasmus, Commandant, capture of, 562.
Erroll, Brigadier-General, Lord, Brigade Order by, 256.
Esdaile, R. D. W., private, 2nd Western Australian, 406; lieutenant, 4th Australian Commonwealth Horse, 434.
Esler, H. J., sergeant, 4th Victorian, 260; lieutenant, 5th Victorian, 281; war service, 279.
Evans, H. F., lieutenant, transport officer, 6th Queensland, 509; war service, 508.
Evans, T. G., lieutenant, 3rd New South Wales Imperial Bushmen, 147.
Evans, W. B., lieutenant, 6th Queensland, 509; war service, 508.
Everett, W. F., captain, 5th Australian Commonwealth Horse, 188.
Excel, A. R., lieutenant (supernumerary), 6th Queensland, 510; war service, 509.
Exhibition, camp at, South Australia, 342; Queensland, 446.
Fagan, Rev. P., chaplain, 1st New South Wales Mounted Rifles, 62; war service, 59.

INDEX—continued.

Familie Hoek, engagement at, 489.
Farlow, F. C. E., lieutenant, 5th Victorian, 280; war service, 278.
Farmer, H., lieutenant, 8th Australian Commonwealth Horse, 437.
Fawns, J. R., lieutenant, 4th Australian Commonwealth Horse, 319.
Ferguson, C. C., lieutenant, 5th South Australian, 367; war service, 366.
Ferguson, R. H., lieutenant, 4th South Australian, 358; war service, 357.
Ferguson, W. I., lieutenant, 4th Queensland, 479; acting adjutant, 475; war service, 478; captain, 5th Queensland, 493.
Ferry, R. J., warrant officer (regimental sergeant-major), 5th South Australians, 368.
Fetherstonhaugh, C., lance-corporal, 1st New South Wales Mounted Rifles, 65; lieutenant, 3rd Mounted Rifles, 58.
Fetherstonhaugh, R. S., major-general, letter from, 146.
Ffrench, E. A. W., lieutenant, 4th Victorian, 259; commissioned Royal Artillery, 253; war service, 258.
Fiaschi, C. F., lieutenant, 1st Australian Commonwealth Horse, 172.
Fiaschi, T. H., major, Army Medical Corps, 20; war service, 17.
Fielden, P. H. G., lieutenant (supernumerary), 3rd Queensland, 467; war service, 466.
Fifth Battalion, Australian Commonwealth Horse, 184; establishment, organization, *ib.*; qualification, pay, reference to orders, clothing, service, 185; nominal roll, 186.
Fifth Queensland (Imperial Bushmen) Contingent, 487; conditions, clothing, equipment, rates of pay, establishment, *ib.*; promotions, departures and return, service, 488; draft, *ib.*; war services and honours, 491; nominal roll, 492; draft, 504; enrolled in South Africa, *ib.*
Fifth and Sixth South Australian (Imperial) Contingents, 364; how recruited, establishment, departure and return, promotions, *ib.*; service, 365; war services and honours, 366; nominal roll, 367, 374.
Fifth Victorian (Mounted Rifles) Contingent, 274; conditions, enlistment, pay, clothing, establishment, departure and return, promotions, &c., *ib.*; service, 275; regiment divided into two wings, *ib.*; Lieutenant Maygar obtains Victoria Cross, 277; war services and honours, *ib.*; nominal roll, 280.
Fifth and Sixth Western Australian (Mounted Infantry) Contingents, 418; authority for, *personnel*, departure and return, promotions, service, *ib.*; both Contingents unite, *ib.*; Lieutenant Bell obtains Victoria Cross, 419; war services and honours, 420; nominal rolls, 421, 426.
Finlayson, G. J., lieutenant, 3rd New South Wales Imperial Bushmen, 145, 147.
Finnerty, A. J., lieutenant, 4th Australian Commonwealth Horse, 434.
First Australian Horse (New South Wales), 41; origin, uniform, *ib.*; despatch of two Contingents, orders, conditions, *ib.*; clothing, &c., 42; promotions, war services and honours, service, *ib.*; engagements, 44; extracts from Captain Thompson's report, *ib.*; nominal roll, 45.
First Battalion Australian Commonwealth Horse, 166: *New South Wales details*, establishment, men selected, horses, details, orders, clothing, &c., *ib.*; departure and return, operations, promotions, war services, nominal roll, 167. *Queensland unit*, 522; details, regimental staff, departure and return, service, extract from Field Order, *ib.*; war services and honours, 523; nominal roll, *ib. Tasmanian half-unit*, 568; details, establishment, &c., *ib.*; nominal roll, *ib.*
First Mounted Infantry Brigade, under Major General Hutton, 348; Colonel Gordon, D.A.G., *ib.*; how composed, *ib.*
First New South Wales Mounted Rifles, 57; establishment, orders, clothing, embarkation and return, *ib.*; promotions, &c., 58; commissions awarded, commands, principal operations, *ib.*; war services and honours, 59; extract from diary of Lieut.-Colonel Knight, 61; nominal roll, 62.
First Queensland (Mounted Infantry) Contingent, 447; how raised, rapid despatch of, establishment, departure and return, promotions, *ib.*; service, 448; joined by 2nd Queensland, *ib.*; at Diamond Hill, *ib.*; summary of operations, 449; war services and honours, *ib.*; nominal roll, 450.
First South Australian (Mounted Rifles) Contingent, 343; class of recruits, establishment, promotions, service, *ib.*; war services and honours, 344; nominal roll, *ib.*
First and Second South Australian Contingents formed into one Corps, 343.
First Tasmanian Contingent, 546; establishment, draft, how recruited, pay, equipment, departure and return, promotions, *ib.*; service, 547; mounted at Naauwpoort, *ib.*; draft joins at Bloemfontein; Henry's Mounted Infantry, *ib.*; war services and honours, 548; nominal roll, *ib.*; draft, 550.
First Victorian (Infantry and Mounted Infantry) Contingent, 213; merged into Australian Regiment, 214; afterwards joins 4th Mounted Infantry Corps, 222; supplementary lists, *ib.*; promotions, &c., *ib.*; nominal rolls, 223, 226.

INDEX—*continued*.

First Western Australian (Mounted Infantry) Contingent, 396; authorization of, pay, clothing, and equipment, departure and return, promotions, *ib.*; service, 397; war services and honours, 398; nominal roll, 399.

Fisher, C. E., warrant-officer, lancers, 10.

Fitzhardinge, A. F., corporal, New South Wales Citizens Bushmen, 80; receives Imperial Commission, 71.

Fletcher, S., veterinary-lieutenant, 3rd Victorian, 245; transferred to South Australian Imperial Bushmen, 241; war service, 244.

Flewell-Smith, J. F., lieut.-colonel, commanding 5th Queenslanders, 492; takes appointment in Cape Colony, 488; war services, 491.

Flying Column, 230.

Flynn, J. I., captain, Medical Staff, 5th Western Australian, 421; war service, 420.

Foley, W., transport-sergeant, New South Wales Imperial Bushmen, 91; lieut.-quartermaster, 87.

Forbes, A. E., bugler, 3rd Queensland, 473; bravery of, 465.

Forbes, H. D., lieutenant, 5th Western Australian, 421; war service, 420.

Foreman, Rev. H. C., chaplain, 3rd New South Wales Imperial Bushmen, 147.

Formby, H. H., lieutenant, Australian Army Medical Corps, 26; hon. captain, 19, 317; war service, 19.

Forrest, A. A., lieutenant, 5th Western Australian, 421; war service, 420; killed in action, 419.

Forrest, A. E., captain, 1st Australian Commonwealth Horse, 170.

Forrest, G., gunner, "A" Battery; Soudan 1885, 54.

Forrest, H. E., private, 3rd Queensland, 468; lieutenant, 463; war service, 466.

Forster, G. B., lieutenant, 2nd New South Wales Mounted Rifles, 110.

Forsythe, W. A., lieutenant, 3rd Australian Commonwealth Horse, 177.

Fortescue, F. A., lieutenant, 3rd New South Wales Imperial Bushmen, 144, 147; honours, 146.

Foster, E. G., lieutenant (supernumerary), 3rd New South Wales Mounted Rifles, 123.

Fotheringham, R. S., lieutenant, 5th South Australian, 367; war service, 366.

Fourth Battalion Australian Commonwealth Horse, 318: *Victorian details*, departure and return, service, war services, *ib.*; nominal roll, 319. *South Australian Unit*, 382; authority for, strength, service, return, nominal roll *ib.* *Western Australian unit*, 434; pay, &c., service, casualties, promotions, departure and return, *ib.*; nominal roll, *ib.*

Fourth Australian Imperial Bushmen, 356, 413, 555.

Fourth Mounted Infantry, Henry's, 231.

Fourth Queensland Imperial Bushmen, 474; qualifications, pay, clothing, equipment, establishment, departure and return, *ib.*; promotions, &c., service, 475; war services and honours, 477; nominal roll, 479.

Fourth South Australian (Imperial Bushmen) Contingent, 356; pay, &c., establishment, departure and return, promotions, service, *ib.*; war services and honours, 357; nominal roll, 358.

Fourth Tasmanian (2nd Imperial Bushmen) Contingent, 561; establishment, departure and return, promotions, service, *ib.*; joins Flying Column, 562; captures Boer leaders, *ib.*; war services and honours, *ib.*; nominal roll, 563.

Fourth Victorian (Imperial) Contingent, 252; qualifications, clothing, pay, establishment, *ib.*; departure and return, promotions, &c., 253; Army Order relative to continued service, 254; service, *ib.*; extract from orders by Lieut.-Colonel Henniker, Lieut.-General Lord Methuen, Brigadier-General Lord Erroll, 256; telegram from Lord Kitchener, 257; war services and honours, *ib.*; nominal roll, 259.

Fourth Western Australian (Mounted Infantry) Contingent, 413; when authorized, strength, pay, clothing, &c., gratuity, departure and return, promotions, &c., service, *ib.*; portion of 4th Australian Bushmen, *ib.*; war services and honours, 414; nominal roll, 415.

Fowles, J. K., lieutenant, 3rd Queensland, 466; captain Rhodesian Field Force, 463; war services, 466.

Fox, J. H., lieutenant (supernumerary), 2nd Queensland, 459; war service, *ib.*

Francis, H. E., quartermaster-sergeant, 2nd South Australian, 349; lieutenant, 347.

Fraser, C. S., lieutenant, New South Wales Citizens Bushmen, 78; war service, 72.

Fraser, J. A., warrant officer (regimental sergeant-major), 1st Western Australian, 399.

Frater, Penelope, nursing sister, New South Wales, 14.

French, G. A., Major-General, telescopic sights of, 197.

Freyer, J. K., lieutenant, Army Medical Corps, 24; war service, 18.

Fullerton, A. Y., captain, Army Medical Corps, 3rd Australian Commonwealth Horse, 177.

Garden, A. G., nursing sister, New South Wales, 14.

Gardiner, C. A. P., lieutenant, 5th Victorian, 280; captain, 274; war service, 277.

Garibaldies, worn by 3rd Victorian, 240.

Garland, R. R., lieutenant, 5th Victorian, 280; war service, 278; with 2nd Australian Commonwealth Horse, 309.

INDEX—*continued.*

Gartside, R., lieutenant, 3rd Victorian, 245 ; war service, 244.
Garvan, J. C., lieutenant, 1st New South Wales Mounted Rifles, 65 ; war service, 60.
Gates, T., private, 1st New South Wales Mounted Rifles ; Soudan, 1885, 68.
Gayer, A. V., private, 3rd Victorian, 248 ; commissioned Imperial Service, 242.
Geary, G. G., lieutenant, 5th Australian Commonwealth Horse, 190.
Gehrmann, C. G., captain, 5th Queensland, 492 ; war service, 491.
Gell, S. L., lieutenant, New South Wales Citizens Bushmen, 78 ; war service, 72 ; captain (supernumerary), 2nd Mounted Rifles, 107.
Germaine, T. H., lieutenant, 2nd Australian Commonwealth Horse, 309.
Geyer, F. W. C., captain, 6th Queensland, 509 ; war service, 508.
Gibson, C. H., 2nd lieutenant, New South Wales Imperial Bushmen, 94 ; captain, (supernumerary) 3rd Mounted Rifles, 123 ; war service, 88.
Gibson, W., captain, Medical Staff, 4th Western Australian, 415 ; war service, 414.
Gilchrist, H. W., lieutenant, 3rd Australian Commonwealth Horse, 177.
Gillies, J., captain, Army Medical Corps, with 1st Australian Commonwealth Horse, 167.
Gilpin, A. G., lieutenant, 4th Victorian, 259 ; war service, 258 ; killed in action, *ib.*
Gilpin, T. J., lieutenant, 4th Victorian, 259 ; war service, 258.
Gjedstead, C. E., lieutenant (supernumerary), 2nd New South Wales Mounted Rifles, 107 ; 3rd Imperial Bushmen, 147.
Glanham, T. D. Y., private, 1st New South Wales Mounted Rifles ; Soudan, 1885, 63.
Glasgow, T. W., lieutenant, 1st Queensland, 450 ; war service, *ib.*
Gledhill, M. R. P. W., lieutenant, 3rd Western Australian, 410 ; commissioned in Imperial service, 408 ; war service, 410.
Gleeman, T. W., lieut.-quartermaster, 5th South Australian, 367 ; war service, 366.
Glenie, —., nursing sister, South Australian, 378.
Gordon, A. G., sergeant, 3rd New South Wales Mounted Rifles, 128 ; lieutenant, 124.
Gordon, J. M., colonel, special service officer, South Australia, 377.
Gordon, L. W., trooper, 2nd South Australian, 350 ; granted Imperial commission, 347.
Gordon, R., lieutenant, 1st Queensland, 453 ; captain, 448 ; war services, 450.
Gosse, W. H., trooper, 2nd South Australian, 350 ; granted Imperial commission, 347.
Goucher, T., sergeant-major, 2nd Tasmanian. 552, warrant officer (regimental sergeant-major), 8th Australian Commonwealth Horse, 386.
Gould, A. C. M., sergeant, New South Wales Imperial Bushmen, 104 ; 2nd lieutenant, 87.
Gould, E. J., lady superintendent, nursing sisters, New South Wales, 14 ; in charge at Orange River district, 20.
Gould, G. E., lieutenant, 5th Australian Commonwealth Horse, 186.
Grace, H. G., lieut.-quartermaster, 1st Australian Commonwealth Horse, 167.
Graham, D. M. L., lieutenant, 4th Queensland, 479 ; war service, 478.
Grahame, E. P., lieutenant (supernumerary), 3rd New South Wales Mounted Rifles, 123.
Grand total of Contingents, *vide* Contingents, Grand total of.
Gratuity. Imperial, of £5 on discharge, 413.
Green, Rev. J., chaplain, New South Wales Citizens Bushmen, 75 ; 1st Australian Commonwealth Horse, 168 ; war service, 73.
Green, T. A., captain, Army Medical Corps, 20 ; major, 15 ; commands Australian Army Medical Corps, 16, 25, 175 ; war service, 17.
Green, W. A. G. E., lieutenant, 4th Queensland, 479 ; war service, 478 ; with " D " Squadron, 1st Australian Commonwealth Horse, 523.
Greenwell, G. M., 2nd lieutenant, 3rd New South Wales Mounted Rifles, 137.
Greig, F. E., lieutenant, transport officer, New South Wales Imperial Bushmen, 90 ; captain (supernumerary), 3rd Mounted Rifles, 123 ; war service, 87.
Gregg, A. N., sergeant, 4th Victorian, 263 ; lieutenant, 5th Victorian, 281 ; war service, 279 ; with 6th Australian Commonwealth Horse, 330.
Grey, R., lieutenant-colonel, 6th Queensland, posted to Column of, 507.
Gribben, A. P., veterinary-captain, 1st New South Wales Mounted Rifles, 62 ; war service, 59.
Grieve, G. J., lieutenant, special service officer, New South Wales, 196 ; extract from report, *ib. ;* killed in action, *ib.*
Griffen, G. A., squadron sergeant-major, 1st Australian Horse, 45 ; first Australian killed, 6, 8, 42.
Griffith, C., lieutenant, 5th Western Australian, 421 ; war service, 420.
Griffith, J. De B., captain, Medical Staff, 3rd Victorian, 245 ; war service, 244.
Griffiths, C. T., 2nd lieutenant, 2nd New South Wales Mounted Rifles. 110 ; war service, 109.
Griffiths, O. R., lieutenant, commands Machine Gun Section, 2nd New South Wales Mounted Rifles, 110 ; war service, 109.
Grobellar Recht, fight at, 419.
Grover, H. C., lieutenant, 5th Victorian, 281 ; war service, 279.
Gubbins, S., lieutenant, 5th Victorian, 281 ; war service, 279.

INDEX—continued.

Gunning, T., private, 1st New South Wales Mounted Rifles; Soudan, 1885, 68.
Hallam, H., sergeant, 1st Tasmanian, 548; lieutenant, 4th Tasmanian, 565; transport officer, 561; war service, 562.
Hallett, J. W., regimental sergeant-major (warrant-officer), New South Wales Citizens Bushmen, 75; lieutenant, 71; war service, 73.
Halse, K. J., lieutenant, 5th Queensland, 492; war service, 491.
Ham, D. J., captain, 3rd Victorian, 245; commands at Rhenoster Kop, 243; war service, 244.
Hamilton, Sir Ian, lieut.-general, telegram from, 145; telegram with results of last great drive, 522.
Hamilton, R. A., trooper, 2nd South Australian, 350; lieutenant, 347.
Hampden, Viscountess, sends clothing, &c., to Lancers, 9.
Hancock, P. J., farrier-sergeant, 1st New South Wales Mounted Rifles, 66; commissioned in Bushveldt Carbineers, 58.
Hanly, J. M., lieutenant, 3rd Queensland, 466; war service, ib.
Hanley, C., lieutenant, New South Wales Imperial Bushmen, 103; war service, 89.
Hanover Road Field Force, 230.
Harriott, W. R., lieutenant, 1st New South Wales Mounted Rifles, 64; killed in action, 60; war services, ib.
Harris, G. H. S., lieutenant, 1st Australian Commonwealth Horse, 168.
Harris, H. J. I., lieutenant, 2nd Queensland, 459; captain, 457; war service, 459.
Harris, H. J., lieutenant, 3rd Queensland, 466; war service, ib.
Harris, N. S., nursing sister, South Australian, 378.
Harris, S., lieutenant, 2nd Western Australian, 405; captain, 403; war service, 405.
Harteb, operations at, 255.
Harvey, A. K. Le R., lieutenant, 6th South Australian, 374; war service, 367.
Hawker, J. C., major-adjutant, 4th South Australian, 358; war service, 357.
Hawkins, J. F., lieutenant, 6th Western Australian, 426; war service, 420.
Hayter, F. J., major, 6th Australian Commonwealth Horse, 325.
Healy, J. W., sergeant-major W.O., 1st Victorian M.I., 223; lieutenant, 4th Australian Commonwealth Horse, 319,
Healey, W. J., lieutenant, Army Medical Corps, with 8th Australian Commonwealth Horse, 386, 437.
Heidelberg, occupation of, 61.
Helbert, G. H., regimental quartermaster-sergeant, New South Wales, Imperial Bushmen 91; lieut.-quartermaster, &c., 87.
Henderson, C., captain, 4th Tasmanian, 563; war service, 562.
Henessy, V. J. P., lieutenant, 5th Victorian, 281; war service, 278; captain, 6th Australian Commonwealth Horse, 328.
Henniker, A., lieutenant-colonel, Column Order by, 256.
Henry, Colonel, regiment of Mounted Infantry under, 547.
Henry, J. D., private, 4th Queensland, 484; lieutenant, 3rd Australian Commonwealth Horse, 527.
Hensman, G. G. W., sergeant, 1st Western Australian, 396; lieutenant, ib.; war service, 399; died of wounds, 397.
Henty, J. R., lieutenant, 6th Australian Commonwealth Horse, 332.
Henwood, H., lieutenant, 5th Victorian, 280; captain, 274; war service, 278.
Heritage, F. B., lieutenant, 1st Tasmanian, 548; Australian Regiment, 214; war service, 548.
Heron, R. M., 2nd lieutenant, Lancers, 10; war service, 8; captain, 3rd Mounted Rifles, 132; honours, 124.
Heywood, P. G., private, 4th Victorian, 267; lieutenant, 254; war service, 258.
Higginson, J. B., lieutenant, 5th Queensland, 492; war service, 491.
Higson, J., lieutenant, 4th Queensland, 479; war service, 478.
Hill, C., lieutenant, 3rd Victorian, 245; captain, 241; war service, 244.
Hill, N. G., lieutenant, Machine Gun Section, 3rd New South Wales Mounted Rifles, 142.
Hilliard, M. A., captain, 1st New South Wales Mounted Rifles, 64; war service, 59.
Hindmarsh, H. E., lieutenant, 3rd New South Wales Mounted Rifles, 137.
Hines, F. E., nursing sister, Victorian, 241; dies in South Africa, ib.
Hipwell, M. G. P., captain, 5th South Australian, 367; war service, 366; died, 365.
Hoad, J. C., colonel, secretary Conference of Commandants, 211; special service officer, Victoria, 213, 305; entertained by Sir Alfred Milner, 213; commands the Australian Regiment, 214; visits Lord Methuen, 215; commands Brigade, ib.; takes mounted party to Rensburg, 216; bids farewell to regiment, 218; lines of communication order, 219; honours, 221.
Hoadley, E., nursing sister, New South Wales, 14.
Hockings, E. M., lieutenant, 3rd Queensland, 466; captain, Rhodesian Field Force, 463; war service, 466.
Hodgkinson, W. O., captain, 7th Australian Commonwealth Horse, 531.
Holborow, G. A. H., lieutenant, 1st New South Wales Mounted Rifles, 67; war service, 60.

INDEX—continued.

Holdsworth, A. A., lieutenant, 2nd Victorian, 234; war service, 233.
Holdsworth, J. H. B., lieutenant, 3rd Victorian, 245; captain, 5th Victorian, 241; war service, 244.
Holland, F. H., 2nd lieutenant, 3rd New South Wales Mounted Rifles, 137.
Holland, T., sergeant, "A" Battery; service, Soudan, 1885, 53.
Holman, R. C., warrant officer "A" Squadron New South Wales Mounted Rifles, 32; lieutenant, 2nd New South Wales Mounted Rifles, 110; captain, 109; adjutant, honours, *ib.*
Holme, C. B., private, 2nd Queensland, 460; lieutenant, 7th Australian Commonwealth Horse, 531.
Holmes, A., captain-quartermaster, New South Wales Imperial Bushmen, 90; war service, 87.
Holmes, F. J., lieutenant, 2nd Australian Commonwealth Horse, 310.
Holmes, R. J., lieutenant, 1st Australian Commonwealth Horse, 172.
Holmes, W., lieutenant, "E" Squadron, 1st New South Wales Mounted Rifles, 38; Australian Regiment, 214; captain, 37; in command, 36; extract from report of, 38; war service, 37.
Honman, A., major, Medical Staff, with 2nd Victorian, 234; war service, 233.
Hood, G. H., corporal, 2nd Victorian, 239; 2nd lieutenant, 230; war service, 233.
Hopkins, W. F., captain, Medical Staff, with 1st Victorian Infantry, 226; Australian Regiment, 214; died, 218.
Hopkinson, E. F., farrier-sergeant, 3rd New South Wales Mounted Rifles, 130; lieutenant, 124.
Horne, H. R., sergeant, Cameron's Scouts, 251; lieutenant, 242; war service, 244.
Horsfall, A. H., lieutenant, Army Medical Corps, 22; war service, 18.
Houston, J. J., lieut.-quartermaster, 4th Australian Commonwealth Horse, 319.
Howe, R. W., sergeant, Cameron's Scouts, 251; lieutenant, 241; captain, *ib.*; war service, 244.
Howland, F. H., captain, 1st South Australian, 213, 344; Australian Regiment, 214; major, 343; war service, 344.
Howse, N. R., lieutenant, Army Medical Corps, 22; captain and major, 15; with Australian Army Medical Corps, 16, 25, 175; war service, 18; Victoria Cross, *ib.*
Hubbe, S. G., captain, commands 3rd South Australian, 353; war service, *ib.*; killed in action, 352.
Hugonin, C., lieutenant, 5th Queensland, 492; war service, 491.
Hume, F. G., lieutenant, 4th Western Australian, 415; war service, 414.
Humphris, J. F., lieutenant, 2nd South Australian, 349; captain, 347; war service, 348.
Hungerford, T., sergeant-major, New South Wales Imperial Bushmen, 101; 2nd lieutenant, 87; captain (supernumerary), 3rd Mounted Rifles, 123.
Hunter, W. S., lieutenant, 5th Queensland, 492; war service, 491.
Hurcombe, F. W., lieutenant, 4th South Australian, 358; captain, 356; war service, 357; with 5th and 6th Contingents, 365; major, *ib.*
Hurst, H. E., captain, 3rd Western Australian, 410; war service, 409; attached to R.H.A., and wounded, *ib.*
Hutchens, H. J., captain, Army Medical Corps, with 5th Queensland, 492; war service, *ib.*
Hutchings, F. H., lieutenant, 4th Victorian, 259; war service, 258.
Hutchison, K., lieut.-colonel, commands 2nd Queensland, 459; staff, 1st Mounted Infantry Brigade Transport, 458; war service, *ib.*
Hutton, A. W., 2nd lieutenant, New South Wales Citizens Bushmen, 82; war service, 73.
Hutton, C., captain, 5th Victorian, 280; commands right wing, 276; commands regiment, 277; major, 274; war service, 277.
Hutton, E. T. H., major-general, addresses Australian Regiment, 218; commands 1st Mounted Infantry Brigade, 219; Column Order, by 458.
Hyde, C. E. W., lieutenant, 4th Queensland, 479; war service, 478.
Hyndman, J. A., lieutenant, 3rd New South Wales Imperial Bushmen, 144, 147.
Imperial Bushmen, New South Wales, 85; pay, establishment, orders, clothing, &c., *ib.*; departure and return, service, principal operations, promotions, 86; war services and honours, 87; extract from Major Miller's Report, 89; nominal roll, 90.
Imperial Government, outfit supplied by, *vide* Outfit Supplied by Imperial Government.
Infantry, Mounted at Naauwpoort, *vide* 1st Contingents, except Queensland.
Infantry, New South Wales, *vide* "E" Squadron, Mounted Rifles.
Inglis, S., lieutenant, 2nd Western Australian, 405; war service, *ib.*
Ingoldby, F. J., captain, Medical Staff, 3rd Western Australian, 410; major, 408; war service, 410.
Innes, P. S. L., lieutenant, 5th Australian Commonwealth Horse, 186.
Irish Brigade, defend Vereeniging, 231.
Irving, G. G. H., lieut.-colonel, commands 6th Australian Commonwealth Horse, 325.
Irving, G. R., lieutenant, New South Wales Imperial Bushmen, 94; war service, 88.
Ives, C. M., lieutenant, 3rd South Australian, 353; war service, *ib.*
Ivey, I., nursing sister, Victorian, 241; mentioned in Despatches, *ib.*

INDEX—*continued.*

James, W. A., lieutenant, Australian Army Medical Corps, 26; hon. captain, 19, 317; **war** service, 19.
Jamieson, S. C., lieutenant, Medical Staff, 1st Tasmanian, 550; war service, 548.
Jasfontein, fighting at, 216.
Jeffrey's Corps, 5th Queensland attached to, 488.
Jenkins, D. H., captain, 2nd Victorian, 234; war service, 233.
Jenkins, R. L. H. B., captain (special service officer), New South Wales, 199; commands Machine Gun Section 2nd New South Wales Mounted Rifles, 110; war service, 109.
Jermyn, F. D., lieutenant, Medical Staff, 2nd South Australian, 349; captain, 347; with Australian Army Medical Corps, 25, 378; war service, 18, 349.
Johns, D. N., captain (supernumerary), 2nd New South Wales Mounted Rifles, 107; 3rd Imperial Bushmen, 147.
Johnson, C. F. M., lieutenant, 2nd Australian Commonwealth Horse, 379.
Johnson, S. B., lieutenant, 1st Australian Commonwealth Horse, 170.
Johnston, A. G., lieutenant, 5th Victorian, 280; war service, 278; killed in action, 275.
Johnston, A. W., regimental sergeant-major, Australian Regiment, 214.
Johnston, G. J., major, special service officer, Victoria, 305; lieut.-colonel, commands 4th Australian Commonwealth Horse, 319.
Johnstone, A. W., sergeant, 1st South Australian, 344; lieutenant, 343; war service, 344.
Johnstone, J. B., superintendent nursing sister, New South Wales, 14.
Jones, D. T., veterinary-lieutenant, 4th Australian Commonwealth Horse, 319.
Jones, F. L., captain, 4th Queensland, 479; adjutant, 475; war service, 478.
Jones, P. W., captain-quartermaster, 8th Australian Commonwealth Horse, 386.
Joseph, E. J., captain, 4th Queensland, 479; war service, 478.
Joss, A. W., lieutenant, 5th Queensland, 492; war service, 491.
Kambuladraai, action at, 276.
Kane, F. W., lieutenant, Army Medical Corps, with New South Wales Imperial Bushmen, 90; war service, 87.
Karrakatta, camp at, Western Australian, 395.
Kater, E. D., 2nd lieutenant, 2nd New South Wales Mounted Rifles, 110; war service, 109.
Keary, G. A., lieutenant, 5th Queensland, 492; war service, 491.
Keckwick, H. L., sergeant-major, 4th South Australian, 358; lieutenant, 356; war services, 358.
Keeble, —., sergeant-major, 5th Victorian, recommended for bravery, 275.
Kellaway, W. J., lieutenant, 4th Queensland, 479; war service, 478.
Kellie, C. W., captain, 3rd Queensland, 466; war service, *ib.*
Kelly, A., private, 2nd Victorian, 235; commissioned Scottish Horse, 230.
Kelly, G. E. E., lieutenant, 3rd New South Wales Imperial Bushmen, 144, 147.
Kelly, J., captain, 5th Victorian, 280; died of wounds, 275; war service, 277.
Kelly, J. P., private, 4th Victorian, 271; lieutenant, 254; war service, 258.
Kelly, N. W., lieut.-colonel, commands 4th Victorian, 259; war service, 257.
Kelly, R. H. V., lieutenant, 1st New South Wales Mounted Rifles, 62; commissioned in Royal Field Artillery, 58; war service, 60.
Kelly, R. V., major, Army Medical Corps, 22; lieut.-colonel, 15; commands 2nd Contingent, 16; commands Imperial Draft, 24; war service, 17.
Kemp, W. T., lieutenant, 4th Queensland, 479; war service, 478.
Kemsley, G. W., sergeant, 2nd Tasmanian, 553; lieutenant, 8th Australian Commonwealth Horse, 573.
Kendall, E. A., veterinary-captain, 1st Victorian, 223; Australian Regiment, 214; 5th Victorian, 280.
Kennedy, J. D., sergeant, "A" Battery; with Soudan Contingent, 1885: 53.
Kennedy, N., warrant officer (regimental sergeant-major), 3rd Victorian, 251.
Keogh, H. W., bugler, 3rd Queensland, 471; bravery of, 465.
Keogh, P. M., captain-quartermaster, 7th Australian Commonwealth Horse, 530.
Kessell, H., lieutenant, 5th Victorian, 281; war service, 279; with 6th Australian Commonwealth Horse, 333.
Kilk, W. B., warrant-officer (regimental sergeant-major), 3rd New South Wales Imperial Bushmen, 147.
Killed or died, New South Wales, 203; Queensland, 541; South Australian, 391; Tasmanian, 576; Victorian, 336; Western Australian, 440.
King, A. E. G., 2nd lieutenant, New South Wales Imperial Bushmen, 98; war service, 88; lieutenant, 5th Australian Commonwealth Horse, 190.
King, A. T., private, 4th Victorian, 265; commissioned in Royal Artillery, 253.
King, R. G. C., lieutenant, "A" Battery, 53; commands draft, 48; war service, 49.
Kirby, M. T., lieutenant, 2nd Victorian, 234; captain, 230; dashing exploit of, 231; **war** service, 233; with 2nd Australian Commonwealth Horse, 309.

INDEX—*continued*.

Kirkpatrick, H. J., trooper, 1st Australian Horse, 47 ; commissioned in Imperial Service, 42.
Kitchener, General Lord, visits Australian Regiment at Arundel, 217 ; telegram to 4th Victorian, 257 ; to 5th Victorian, 277 ; despatch, *re* 4th Western Australian, 414 ; *re* 5th and 6th South Australian, 365 ; compliments 1st Australian Horse, 43 ; telegram, *re* the great drive, 308, 522.
Knight, G. C., lieut.-colonel, commands 1st New South Wales Mounted Rifles, 62 ; extracts from diary, 61 ; war service, 59.
Knyvett, F. B., private, 1st Queensland, 455 ; sergeant-major, 5th Queensland, 499 ; lieutenant, 7th Australian Commonwealth Horse, 533
Koch, F. B. T., lieutenant (supernumerary), 5th Queensland, 493 ; war service, 492 ; with 7th Australian Commonwealth Horse, 531.
Koch, G. H., lieutenant, 5th Queensland, 492 ; war service, 491.
Komati Poort, review at, 232, 348.
Koster River, 3rd Queensland at, 464 ; 3rd Western Australian, at 409 ; New South Wales Citizens Bushmen at, 71 ; 3rd Victorians at, 242.
Krygger, A., private, 1st Western Australian, gallantry of, 397.
Kuilfontein Kopje, shelling of, 230.
Kyngdon, L. H., captain, Royal Australian Artillery, special service officer, New South Wales, 200.

Laing, J. B., Chief Paymaster. New South Wales, good management of, 3.
Lamb, C. W., captain, Royal Australian Artillery, special service officer, New South Wales, 199.
Lamb, E. A., 2nd lieutenant, 2nd New South Wales Mounted Rifles, 110.
Lancers, New South Wales, 4 ; pay, establishment, *ib.* ; orders, 5 ; clothing, arms, units, service, *ib.* ; actions, war services and honours, 7 ; extract from Major Lee's report, 8 ; nominal roll, 10.
Lang, P. H., lieutenant, Medical Staff, with 4th Victorian, 259 ; war service, 257.
Langlands, E. A. V., nursing sister, Victorian, 241.
Langley, E. J. F., sergeant, 2nd South Australian, 349 ; lieutenant, 5th, 367 ; war services, 366 captain, 8th Australian Commonwealth Horse, 388.
Langwarrin, Victorian training camp at, 212.
Lascelles, G. R., captain, Royal Fusiliers, with 1st South Australian, 343 ; adjutant, Australian Regiment, 214 ; at Arundel, 343 ; honours, 221.
Lassetter, F. O., 2nd lieutenant, 2nd New South Wales Mounted Rifles, 110 ; war service, 109.
Lassetter, H. B., lieut.-colonel, commands 2nd New South Wales Mounted Rifles, 110 ; war service, 109.
Laughton, L. H., trooper, 3rd Tasmanian, 559 ; lieutenant, 4th Tasmanian, 561.
Lawson, G. L. L., lieutenant, Army Medical Corps, with New South Wales Imperial Bushmen, 90 ; captain, 87 ; war service, 87.
Laycock, F., sergeant, 1st South Australian, 344 ; lieutenant, 8th Australian Commonwealth Horse, 387.
Leane, E. T., lieutenant, 4th South Australian, 358 ; war service, 357.
Learmouth, F. L., corporal, 1st New South Wales Mounted Rifles, 58 ; lieutenant, 62 ; war service, 60.
Learmouth, M. C. L., 2nd lieutenant, New South Wales Imperial Bushmen, 103 ; war service, 89.
Leask, J., lieutenant, 3rd Queensland, 466 ; war service, *ib.* ; died from wounds, 465.
Lee, C. A., corporal, "A" Squadron, New South Wales Mounted Rifles, 33 ; lieutenant, 28, 58 ; with "B" Squadron, 62 ; captain, 2nd Mounted Rifles, 110 ; 3rd Imperial Bushmen, 147 ; war service, 60.
Lee, G. L., major, commands Lancers, 6, 10 ; complimented by General French, 6 ; extract from report of, 8 ; war services, 7.
Lee, J. H. A., major (Royal Australian Engineers), 1st Australian Commonwealth Horse, 167 ; lieut.-colonel, *ib.*
Leeuwfontein, convoy captured at, 275.
Leeuw Kop, engagement at, 414.
Legge, G. H., lieutenant, 1st New South Wales Mounted Rifles, 67 ; war services, 60.
Legge, J. G., captain, commands "F" Squadron, 1st New South Wales Mounted Rifles, 38 ; Australian Regiment, 214 ; extracts from report, 37 ; major, *ib.* ; war service, *ib.*
Leitch, J. B., veterinary-lieutenant, 4th Victorian, 259 ; war service, 257 ; veterinary captain, with 3rd Australian Commonwealth Horse 177.
Le Mesurier, H., captain-adjutant, New South Wales Imperial Bushmen, 90 ; major and lieut.-colonel, 86 ; commands 8th Australian Commonwealth Horse, 385 ; war service, 87.
Lenehan, R. W., captain, 1st New South Wales Mounted Rifles, 62 ; major, Bushveldt Carbineers, 58 ; war service, 59.
Lewis, G., quartermaster-sergeant, 4th South Australian, 358 ; commissioned in Imperial service, 356.
Lewis, R. C., captain, commands 3rd Tasmanian, 558 ; **war service, 557.**
Liggins, F. P., sergeant-major warrant-officer, 1st New South Wales Mounted Rifles, 38.

INDEX—*continued*.

Lilley, J. L., lieut.-adjutant, 2nd Victorian, 234; war service, 233.
Lister, E. W., nursing sister, New South Wales, 14.
Livingstone, G. F., sergeant, 4th Queensland, 479; lieutenant, 475.
Lockett, H., lieutenant, 2nd Australian Commonwealth Horse, 309.
Loel, B. B., veterinary-lieutenant, 2nd Australian Commonwealth Horse, 309.
Logan, M. W., lieutenant, " E " squadron, 1st New South Wales Mounted Rifles, 38; Australian Regiment, 214; war service, 37.
London, Lord Mayor of, telegram from, 215.
Lovely, L. H., corporal, 2nd Australian Commonwealth Horse, 380; lieutenant, 4th Australian Commonwealth Horse, *ib*.
Lowther, W. P., sergeant, 1st Tasmanian, 548; lieutenant, 2nd, 552; in command, 551; war service, 552.
Loynes, J., sergeant-major, 1st Queensland, 453; lieutenant, 5th Queensland, 492; war service, 491.
Luscombe, A. P., captain, special service officer, New South Wales, 200.
Lyddite shell, small effect of, 198.
Lydiard, C. G. S., lieutenant, 1st New South Wales Mounted Rifles, 62; captain, 2nd Mounted Rifles, 58, 110; major, 109; war service, 60, 109.
Lynch, G. H., lieutenant, 2nd South Australian, 349; war services, 348.
Lynch, T. J., lieutenant, New South Wales Citizens Bushmen, 78; captain, 71; war service, 73.
Lyons, G., lieutenant (supernumerary), 3rd New South Wales Mounted Rifles, 123, 124.
Lyons, M., 2nd lieut.-quartermaster, 2nd New South Wales Mounted Rifles, 110; war service, 109.
Lyster, J. S., lieut.-colonel, commands 1st Australian Commonwealth Horse, 167.
Lytton, camp ground, Queensland, 446.
Macarthur, L. G., lieutenant, 3rd Australian Commonwealth Horse, 177.
MacBain, Rev. S., chaplain, 3rd Victorian, 245; war service, 244.
Macdonald, A. C., lieutenant, 4th Victorian, 259; war service, 258; captain, 4th Australian Commonwealth Horse, 319.
Macdonald, H., sergeant-major, 2nd Victorian, 234; lieutenant, 4th Australian Commonwealth Horse, 319.
Macdonald, H., lieutenant (supernumerary), 2nd New South Wales Mounted Rifles, 107; with 3rd Imperial Bushmen, 147.
Macdonald, Sir H., major-general, letter from, 196.
Macdonald, P., lieutenant, 3rd New South Wales Mounted Rifles, 132; captain, 124.
Macfarlane, G., lieutenant (supernumerary), 2nd New South Wales Mounted Rifles, 107; with 3rd Imperial Bushmen, 147.
Macfarlane, J., sergeant, 4th Victorian, 266; lieutenant, 5th Victorian, 281; war service, 279.
Macfarlane, S. C., lieutenant, 6th South Australian, 374; captain, 364; war service, 367.
Macgregor, N. A., lieutenant, 3rd New South Wales Imperial Bushmen, 144, 147.
Machattie, T. A., captain, New South Wales Citizens Bushmen, 80; war service, 72.
Machine-guns used by 1st Queensland, 447-8.
Mackay, J. A. K., colonel, commanding New South Wales Imperial Bushmen, 90; entertained by Mayor of Cape Town, 86; war service, 87.
Mackellar, K. K., lieutenant, 1st Australian Horse, 45; commissioned in 6th Dragoon Guards, 42; killed in action, *ib*.
Mackenzie, K. D., lieutenant, New South Wales Imperial Bushmen, 91; war service, 88.
Mackenzie, S. L., 2nd lieutenant, New South Wales Imperial Bushmen, 103; captain (supernumerary), 3rd Mounted Rifles, 123; war service, 89.
Mackinnon, F. H., sergeant, 5th Western Australian, 423; lieutenant, 418; war service, 420.
Maclean, A. L., 2nd lieutenant, New South Wales Imperial Bushmen, 101; war service, 89.
Macpherson, C. M., 2nd lieutenant, New South Wales Imperial Bushmen, 101; acting adjutant, 87; war service, 89.
Mafeking, New South Wales Citizens Bushmen at, 71.
Mailer, W., captain-adjutant, 4th Australian Commonwealth Horse, 319.
Maley, A. E., lance-corporal, 1st Western Australian, 400; lieutenant, 6th, 426; war service, 420.
Mann, F. W., lieutenant, 4th Victorian, 259; war service, 257.
Marshall, G. A., captain, Army Medical Corps, 22, 53; war service, 18, 49.
Marshall, J., captain, Army Medical Corps, 22; war service, 18.
Martin, J. H. B., veterinary-lieutenant, 5th Australian Commonwealth Horse, 186.
Martin, M. P., nursing sister, New South Wales, 14.
Martin, T. M., captain, Army Medical Corps, 20; promotion, 15; war service, 17.
Martin, W. P., lieutenant, 5th Australian Commonwealth Horse, 192.

INDEX—continued.

Mason, C. J. C., lieutenant, 4th Victorian, 259 ; captain, 5th, 253 ; aide-de-camp to Lord Methuen, ib. ; war service, 258.
Mason, E. P., warrant-officer, Army Medical Corps, 20 ; to Soudan, 1885, ib.
Mason, J. W., private, 4th Victorian, 271 ; lieutenant, 253 ; captain, 5th, ib. ; war service, 258.
Matchett, A. L., nursing sister, New South Wales, 14.
Mathews, J. R., regimental quartermaster-sergeant, 2nd Victorian, 234 ; lieutenant, 230 ; war service, 233.
Mattei, C., lieutenant, Medical Staff, 4th Tasmanian, 563 ; war service, 562.
Maygar, L. C., lieutenant, 5th Victorian, 280 ; obtains Victoria Cross, 277 ; war service, 278.
Mayor, Lord, of London, vide London.
McColl, J. P., 2nd lieutenant. 2nd New South Wales Mounted Rifles, 110 ; war service, 109.
McColl, J. T., warrant officer (regimental sergeant-major), 3rd New South Wales Mounted Rifles, 125.
McColl, M. G., lieutenant (supernumerary), 3rd Queensland, 467 ; war service, 466.
McCormack, H. B., lieutenant, 6th Western Australian, 426 ; war service, 420.
McCormick, A., major, special service officer, Army Medical Corps, 14, 22 ; war service, 18.
McCormick, J., priv te, 1st Tasmanian, 550 ; lieutenant, 4th Tasmanian, 563 ; adjutant, 561 ; war service, 562.
McCulloch, W., 2nd lieutenant, 3rd Victorian, 245 ; commissioned Imperial service, 241.
McDonnell, E. P., lieutenant, Army Medical Corps, 20 ; with " A " Squadron, Mounted Rifles, 29 ; war service, 17.
McDonnell, Rev. G. N., chaplain, 5th Victorian, 280.
McEwen, J. F., warrant-officer, Australian Army Medical Corps, 26.
McGillivray, J., warrant-officer (regimental sergeant-major), 5th South Australian, 368 ; killed in action, ib.
McGlinn, J. P., captain-adjutant, 1st New South Wales Mounted Rifles, 62 ; war service, 59.
McInerney, Rev. J., chaplain, 2nd Australian Commonwealth Horse, 309.
McInerney, T. M., lieutenant, 1st Victorian Infantry, 226 ; Australian Regiment, 214 ; capt..in, 222 ; major, ib.
McIntosh, H., sergeant, " A " Squadron, New South Wales Mounted Rifles, 32 ; lieutenant, 28 ; with 2nd Mounted Rifles, 110 ; captain, 109 ; war service, ib.
McIntyre, G. L., corporal, 4th Tasmanian, 563 ; provisional lieutenant, 561.
McIntyre, H., sergeant, 4th Victorian, 266 ; lieutenant, 5th Victorian, 281 ; war service, 279.
McKaige, E. J., sergeant, 4th Victorian, 265 ; lieutenant, 5th Victorian, 281 ; war service, 279.
McKnight, W., captain-adjutant, 3rd Victorian, 245 ; major, 5th Victorian, 281 ; war service, 244, 277.
McLean, A. A., lieutenant, " A " Squadron, New South Wales Mounted Rifles, 32 ; captain, 28 ; with 2nd Mounted Rifles, 110 ; major, 109 ; war service, 29.
McLeish, D., captain, commands 1st Victorian Mounted Rifles, 213, 223 ; Australian Regiment, 214 ; major, 222 ; honours, 221 ; lieutenant-colonel, commands 2nd Australian Commonwealth Horse, 309.
McLeod, J., veterinary-lieutenant, 4th Queensland, 479 ; veterinary-captain, 475 ; supernumerary with 5th Queensland, 493 ; war service, 478 ; with 7th Australian Commonwealth Horse, 530.
McMasters, R. T., lieutenant. 2nd Western Australian, 405 ; captain, 403 ; war service, 405.
McMillan, M. E., lieutenant, 3rd Australian Commonwealth Horse, 177.
McWhirter, S. G., sergeant-major, 5th Western Australian, 424 ; lieutenant, Johannesburg Mounted Rifles, 418.
McWilliams, G. F., major, Medical Staff, 1st Western Australian, 399 ; Australian Regiment, 214 ; lieut.-colonel, 396 ; war service, 399.
Meadows, A. J. H., captain, 5th Victorian, 280 ; war service, 277.
Meeandah, Queensland, training camp at, 446.
Meeham, M. R., lieutenant, 3rd New South Wales Mounted Rifles, 130.
Meek, B. O., veterinary-captain, 6th Queensland, 509.
Melbourne, New Year Message from, 215.
Melhuish, F. W., veterinary-lieutenant, Lancers, 10 ; veterinary-captain, 2nd New South Wales Mounted Rifles, 110 ; war service, 8, 109.
Meredith, J. B., lieutenant, Army Medical Corps, with New South Wales Citizens Bushmen, 75 ; war service, 73.
Messenger, R. W. J., warrant-officer, New South Wales Imperial Bushmen, 101.
Messer, J. F., lance-corporal, 1st Western Australian, 400 ; lieutenant, 5th, 421 ; war service, 420.
Messer, K. D., lieutenant, 4th Australian Commonwealth Horse, 434.
Methuen, Lord, lieut.-general, Imperial Bushmen bodyguard, 86 ; Divisional Order, 256 ; lette from, 352.
Michell, H. C., 2nd lieutenant, New South Wales Imperial Bushmen, 96 ; acting-adjutant, 87 ; war service, 88.

INDEX—*continued*.

Middleton, C. E. A., lieutenant, 2nd New South Wales Mounted Rifles, 110 ; captain, 3rd Imperial Bushmen, 147 ; honours, 146.
Miell, A., lieutenant, 5th South Australian, 367 ; war service, 366.
Military Contingent Act, Tasmanian, *vide* Tasmanian Military Contingent Act.
Millard, G. W., lieutenant, 3rd Australian Commonwealth Horse, 177.
Miller, D., major, New South Wales Imperial Bushmen, 90 ; extract from report of, 89 ; war service, 87.
Miller, D. F., lieutenant, New South Wales Imperial Bushmen, 101 ; war service, 89 ; captain (supernumerary), 3rd Mounted Rifles, 123 ; died, *ib*.
Mills, C. G., 2nd lieutenant, 2nd New South Wales Mounted Rifles, 110 ; lieutenant, 3rd Imperial Bushmen, 147.
Mills, W. C., sergeant, 6th Western Australian, 429 ; lieutenant, 8th Australian Commonwealth Horse, 438.
Milne, Rev. F., chaplain, 4th Australian Commonwealth Horse, 319.
Milner, Sir Alfred, entertains Australian officers, 213 ; inspects Australian Regiment, 214.
Mitchell, C. H., private, 1st New South Wales Mounted Rifles; with Soudan Contingent, 1885, 69.
Mitchell, J. B., lance-corporal, 1st New South Wales Mounted Rifles, 64 ; commissioned Imperial service, 58.
Moffitt, W., 2nd lieutenant, 3rd New South Wales Mounted Rifles, 127.
Mokari Drift, action at, 489.
Molloy, L., 2nd lieutenant, 2nd New South Wales Mounted Rifles, 110 ; war service, 109.
Moor, H. G., captain, 1st Western Australian, 213, 399 ; Australian Regiment, 214 ; major, 396 ; war service, 398 ; killed in action, *ib*.
Moore, G. A., lieutenant, 3rd Victorian, 245 ; war service, 244.
Moore, T. M., 2nd lieutenant, New South Wales Citizens Bushmen, 82 ; war service, 73.
Moran, F., lieutenant, 7th Australian Commonwealth Horse, 538.
Morgan, J. S., lieutenant, 3rd Australian Commonwealth Horse, 177.
Moris, G. A., private, 1st Western Australian, 402 ; lieutenant, 6th, 426 ; war service, 420 ; killed in action, 419.
Morley, H. C., private, 4th Queensland, 486 ; commissioned in Imperial service, 475.
Morris, A. G. H., captain, Royal Australian Artillery, special service officer, New South Wales, 202.
Morris, J. T., lieutenant (supernumerary), 5th Western Australian, 421 ; war service, 420.
Morrisby, A., captain, commands " E " Squadron, 3rd Australian Commonwealth Horse, 570.
Mortimer, H. S., quartermaster-sergeant, 1st New South Wales Mounted Rifles, 67 ; lieutenant, Bushveldt Carbineers, 58.
Moseley, F. W., lieutenant, 4th Victorian, 259 ; captain, 5th, 281 ; war service, 258, 278.
Mounted Rifles : *New South Wales*, 1st, 57 ; 2nd, 106 ; 3rd, 123. *South Australian*, 1st, 343 ; 2nd, 347. *Victorian*, 1st, 213 ; 2nd, 229 ; 5th, 274.
Mountjoy, E. L., lieutenant, 6th Australian Commonwealth Horse, 331.
Moy, P. J., squadron sergeant-major, 3rd New South Wales Imperial Bushmen, 158 ; lieutenant, 145.
Moyes, A. H., lieutenant (supernumerary), 2nd New South Wales Mounted Rifles, 107.
Muhs, A. C., lieutenant, New South Wales Imperial Bushmen, 96 ; war service, 88.
Muir, F. B., lieutenant, 5th, South Australian, 367 ; war service, 366.
Mullins, T. L., lieutenant, New South Wales Citizens Bushmen, 80 ; captain, 71 ; 1st Australian Commonwealth Horse, 170 ; war service, 72.
Murphy, A. E., lieutenant, 5th Victorian, 281 ; killed in action, 275 ; war service, 279.
Murphy, C. T., warrant-officer (regimental sergeant-major), 5th Australian Commonwealth Horse, 186.
Murray, A. C., captain, Scottish Horse, 304 ; wounded at Brakenlaagte, *ib*.
Murray, J. H. P., major, special service officer, New South Wales, 200.
Murray, P. F. L., lieutenant, 2nd New South Wales Mounted Rifles, 110 ; war service, 109.
Mylne, G. E., lieutenant, New South Wales Imperial Bushmen, 103 ; captain, 3rd Imperial Bushmen, 144, 147 ; war service, 89.
Naauwpoort : New South Wales, South Australian, Tasmanian, Victorian, and Western Australian Infantry mounted at, 35, &c.
Neald, W. J., lieutenant, 5th Australian Commonwealth Horse, 188.
Newland, C. A. C., lieutenant, 4th Western Australian, 415 ; captain, 413 ; war service, 414.
Newlands, R. G., lieutenant, 3rd New South Wales Imperial Bushmen, 144, 147.
Newman, J., quartermaster-sergeant, " A " Squadron, New South Wales Mounted Rifles, **32 ;** lieutenant, 28 ; captain, 2nd Mounted Rifles, 110 ; 3rd Imperial Bushmen, 147.
Newman, W. A., lieutenant, 1st New South Wales Mounted Rifles, 65 ; war service, 60.
Newmarch, B. J., captain, Army Medical Corps, 22 ; war service, 18.

INDEX—*continued*.

New South Wales: *Prefatory*, 3; Lancers, 4; Army Medical Corps, 13; "A" Squadron, Mounted Rifles, 28; Infantry, 35; 1st Australian Horse, 41; "A" Battery, Royal Australian Artillery, 48; 1st Mounted Rifles, 57; Citizens Bushmen, 70; Imperial Bushmen, 85; 2nd Mounted Rifles, 106; 3rd Mounted Rifles, 123; 3rd Imperial Bushmen, 144; 1st Australian Commonwealth Horse, 166; Australian Army Medical Corps, 175; 3rd Australian Commonwealth Horse, 176; 5th Australian Commonwealth Horse, 184; Special Service officers, 195; pensions, 202A; killed or died, 203; summary of Contingents, 206; classification, 207.
New South Wales Citizens Bushmen, *vide* Citizens Bushmen, New South Wales.
New South Wales Imperial Bushmen, *vide* Imperial Bushmen, New South Wales.
New South Wales 3rd Imperial Bushmen, *vide* Third Imperial Bushmen, New South Wales.
New South Wales Mounted Rifles, commended by General Hutton, 32.
New South Wales Mounted Rifles, 1st, *vide* First New South Wales Mounted Rifles.
New South Wales Mounted Rifles, 2nd, *vide* Second New South Wales Mounted Rifles.
New South Wales Mounted Rifles, 3rd, *vide* Third New South Wales Mounted Rifles
Newton, F. G., private, 2nd Queensland, 460; lieutenant, 457; war service, 459.
Newton, N., nursing sister, New South Wales, 14.
Newtown show grounds camp, Tasmanian, 545.
Nicholl, J. A., lieutenant, 4th Victorian, 259; war service, 258.
Nicholson, C. E., lieutenant, Lancers, 10, 6, 9; captain, 8; war service, *ib*.
Nicholson, F. V., captain-paymaster, 5th and 7th Australian Commonwealth Horse, 530.
Nicholson, S. H., captain, 3rd Australian Commonwealth Horse, 177.
Nield, J. H., lieutenant (supernumerary), 2nd New South Wales Mounted Rifles, 107; quartermaster, 110.
Nielson, T. C., lieutenant, 6th Queensland, 509; war service, 508.
Niesigh, J. W. N., captain, special service officer, New South Wales, 202.
Nisbet, W. B., major, Army Medical Corps, with 4th Queensland, 479; war service, 478.
Nixon, E., nursing sister, New South Wales, 14.
Noblett, G. E. H., corporal, 1st South Australian, 344; lieutenant, 5th, 343.
Nolan, H. R., captain, Army Medical Corps, with 2nd Queensland, 459; war service, *ib*.
Nordman, W. G. R. P., corporal, 2nd South Australian, 351; lieutenant, 8th Australian Commonwealth Horse, 390.
Norris, C. T., lieutenant, 1st Australian Commonwealth Horse, 170.
Norton, A. E. M., captain, 4th South Australian, 358; war service, 357.
Norton, E. S., lieutenant, 2nd Victorian, 234; captain, 230; war service, 233.
Nunneley, W. A., lieutenant, 6th South Australian, 374; war service, 367.
Nursing service, New South Wales, 16, 20.
Nursing sisters, New South Wales, 14, 20; South Australia, 378; Victoria, 240.
Nylstrom, captured, 243.
Nyulasy, A. J., captain, Australian Army Medical Corps, 25; with 2nd Australian Commonwealth Horse, 432, 433; war service, 19.
O'Brien, H., lieutenant, 1st Australian Commonwealth Horse, 172.
O'Brien, J., private, 4th Victorian, 260; lieutenant, 254; war service, 258.
O'Brien, J. C., captain-adjutant, 7th Australian Commonwealth Horse, 530.
O'Brien, W. E., captain, New South Wales Imperial Bushmen, 94; major, 86; 5th Australian Commonwealth Horse, 186; war service, 88.
O'Farrell, M., captain-adjutant, 4th Victorian, 259; major, 5th Victorian, 253; war service, 257.
O'Loghlen, B., lieutenant, 5th Victorian, 281; war service, 279.
O'Reilly, T. S. L., lieutenant, 5th Victorian, 280; captain, 274; war service, 278.
O'Shea, W. A., lieutenant, 3rd New South Wales Imperial Bushmen, 144, 147.
O'Sullivan, J. R. B., lieutenant, 5th South Australian, 367; captain, 364; war service, 366.
Oakes, Rev. S., chaplain, 1st Australian Commonwealth Horse, 167.
Ochiltree, J. L., lieutenant, 5th Western Australian, 421; war service, 420.
Officers for special service, *vide* Special Service Officers.
Ogg, G. R., lieut.-quartermaster, 5th Queensland, 492; war service, 491.
Ogilvy, H. L. S. B., sergeant, 2nd South Australian, 351; lieutenant, 2nd Australian Commonwealth Horse, 379.
Ogilvy, K. A., captain, commands "C" Squadron, 8th Australian Commonwealth Horse, 573.
Oliver, S. A., lieutenant, 2nd Western Australian, 405; captain, 403; gallantry of, 404; **war** service, 405.
Onslow, A. J. M., lieutenant, "A" Squadron, New South Wales Mounted Rifles, 32; **war** service, 29.
Onslow, J. W. M., lieut.-colonel, special service officer, New South Wales, 202; **commands** 5th Australian Commonwealth Horse, 186.
Onverwacht, disastrous engagement at, 489.

INDEX—*continued*.

Ord, C. H., lieutenant, 3rd Western Australian, 410; war service, *ib*.
Ordish, H., warrant-officer (regimental sergeant-major), 6th Australian Commonwealth Horse, 325.
Osborne, F. W., major, 8th Australian Commonwealth Horse, 385.
Osborne, H. H., lieutenant, 5th Victorian, 281; war service, 279.
Osborne, J. B. N., lieutenant, 1st Australian Horse, 45; war service, 42; Imperial commission, *ib*.
Osborne, S. F., 2nd lieutenant, Lancers, 10, 6; war service, 8.
Otter, A. E., colonel, at Langwarrin, 212; commands 5th Victorian, 280; invalided, 275; war service, 277.
Ottoshoop, action at, 252.
Outfit, supplied by Imperial Government, *vide* Appendix II., 578.
Owen, P. T., major, special service officer, New South Wales, 201.
Oxley, J. E., lieutenant, New South Wales Imperial Bushmen, 98; captain, 87; war service, 88.
Page, L. S. E., corporal, 3rd Tasmanian, 558; lieutenant, 555; war service, 557.
Paget, Major-General, Force Order by, 464; telegram from, 476.
Palmer, H. A., lieutenant, Medical Staff, 5th Victorian, 281; war service, 280; killed in action, 275.
Palmer, R. W., lieutenant, 3rd New South Wales Mounted Rifles, 135.
Parker, C. A., lieutenant, 4th Queensland, 479; war service, 478; captain, 7th Australian Commonwealth Horse, 538.
Parker, F. M. W., lieutenant, 1st Western Australian, 399; Australian Regiment, 214; captain, 396; war service, 398.
Parkin, T., lieutenant, 4th Victorian, 259; captain, 5th, 253; war service, 258.
Parrott, T. S., lieut.-colonel, special service officer, New South Wales, 200.
Patterson, J. H., lieutenant, Medical Staff, 5th Victorian, 281; captain, 274; war service, 280.
Patterson, W. G., major, 4th Australian Commonwealth Horse, 319.
Paul, J., regimental quartermaster-sergeant, Australian Regiment, 214.
Pay, issued by South Australia, 341-2; by Queensland, 445; New South Wales, Tasmania, Victoria, Western Australia, *vide* Contingents.
Pearce, J. W., lieutenant, 4th Australian Commonwealth Horse, 319.
Pearce, N. M., lieutenant, 3rd New South Wales Mounted Rifles, 125.
Pearce, R. St. J., captain, special service officer, New South Wales, 201.
Peek, J. H., lieutenant, 3rd New South Wales Mounted Rifles, 125; captain, 124.
Pendlebury, H. W., lieutenant, 1st Victorian Infantry, 226; acting quartermaster, Australian Regiment, 214; captain, 222; with 2nd Australian Commonwealth Horse, 309.
Pensions authorized by Queensland Government, 446; by New South Wales Government, 202A; also *vide* Nominal Rolls.
Percival, A. W. B., captain, commands "E" Squadron, 1st Australian Commonwealth Horse, 568.
Perkins, A. E., major, Army Medical Corps, 20; war services, 17.
Perkins, R., lieutenant, 3rd Tasmanian, 558; war service, 557.
Perske, J. F., warrant officer (regimental sergeant-major), 1st Australian Commonwealth Horse, 523.
Philipstown, surprise of, 255.
Philp, C. J. C., lieutenant (supernumerary), 4th Queensland, 479; war service, 478; with details, 519.
Pickburn, W. H., lieutenant (supernumerary), 4th Queensland, 479; war service, 478.
Pietersburg, capture of, 243; officers shot at, 557.
Piet Retief, cyclist company broken up at, 488.
Pilkington, H. L., captain, 2nd Western Australian, 403; major, *ib*.; lieut.-colonel, *ib*.; war service, 405.
Pink Hill, fight at, 216.
Pinnock, P. W. G., captain, 1st Queensland, 453; war service, 449.
Pipes presented by Queen Alexandra, 108.
Plomer, W. H. P., major, 7th Australian Commonwealth Horse, 530.
Plumer, General, thanks 4th Queensland, 477; compliments 5th Queensland, 489; his "Force," 476.
Pockley, H. R., 2nd lieutenant, New South Wales Citizens Bushmen, 80; war service, 72.
Pocock, M. A., nursing sister, New South Wales, 14.
Pongola Bosch, great capture at, 276.
Pontin, A., warrant officer (regimental sergeant-major), 5th Victorian, 285.
Pooley, A. E., sergeant-major, 4th Queensland, 484; lieutenant, 5th, 493; war service, 491; killed in action, 489.

INDEX—*continued*.

Porter, C. M., private, 5th Western Australian, 424; lieutenant, Imperial Yeomanry, 418.
Porter, J. W., warrant officer (regimental sergeant-major), 3rd New South Wales Imperial Bushmen, 147; lieutenant, 145.
Portuguese frontier, Komati Poort, 232.
Potgeiter, Commandant, capture of, 276.
Potter, L. D. P., sergeant, 2nd Western Australian; lieutenant, 403; war service, 405.
Pounds, H. H., lieutenant, 4th Victorian, 259; captain, 5th Victorian, 253; war service, 258.
Powell, J., lieutenant, 2nd Australian Commnowealth Horse, 310.
Powell, J. W., lieutenant, 1st South Australian, 344; Australian Regiment, 214; war service, 344; killed in action, 343.
Power, J. E., lieutenant, 6th Australian Commonwealth Horse, 326.
Power, T. H., lieutenant (wing adjutant), 5th Victorian, 280; war service, 278.
Prefatory: New South Wales, 3; South Australian, 341; Queensland, 445; Tasmanian, 545; Victorian, 211; Western Australian, 395.
Press, A. H., lieutenant, 2nd Australian Commonwealth Horse, 310.
Press, W. J., warrant officer (regimental sergeant-major), 2nd South Australian, 349; lieutenant, 347; war service, 349.
Pretoria, Victorians first to enter, 232.
Pretty, E. P., lieutenant, 2nd Australian Commonwealth Horse, 432.
Price, D. C. W. H., 2nd lieutenant, 3rd New South Wales Mounted Rifles, 135.
Price, J. G., warrant officer (regimental sergeant-major), 1st Queensland, 450; 5th, 500.
Price, T., colonel, raises Victorian Mounted Rifles, 229; commands 2nd Victorian, 234; commands Hanover Road Field Force, 230; marches on Bloemfontein, 230; carries man out of fire, 222; war service, 233.
Priestly, P. H., lieutenant, 5th South Australian, 367; war service, 366.
Proclamation, loyal by Queensland Government, 445.
Public and private riding horses, 5th Queensland, 487; 6th Queensland, 506.
Puddings, &c., sent to Lancers, 9.
Pulteney's Column, 489.
Purcell, F. G., lieutenant, 4th Victorian, 259; captain, 253; major, 5th, *ib.*; war service, 257.
Queen's chocolate, *vide* Chocolate, Queen's.
Queensland: *Prefatory*, 445; 1st (Mounted Infantry) Contingent, 447; 2nd (Mounted Infantry) Contingent, 457; 3rd Mounted Infantry Contingent, 463; 4th (Imperial Bushmen) 474; 5th (Imperial Bushmen), 487; 6th (Imperial Bushmen), 506; drafts, 518, 519; Special Service officers, 520; 1st Australian Commonwealth Horse unit, 522; Australian Commonwealth Army Medical Corps unit, 526; 3rd Australian Commonwealth Horse unit, 527; 7th Australian Commonwealth Horse, 530; officers and others killed or died, 541; summary of Contingents, 542.
Queensland Mounted Infantry, 1st Contingent, *vide* First Queensland Mounted Infantry.
Queensland Mounted Infantry, 2nd Contingent, *vide* Second Queensland Mounted Infantry.
Queensland Mounted Infantry, 3rd Contingent, *vide* Third Queensland Mounted Infantry.
Queensland 4th Imperial Bushmen, *vide* Fourth Queensland Imperial Bushmen.
Queensland 5th Imperial Bushmen, *vide* Fifth Queensland Imperial Bushmen.
Queensland 6th Imperial Bushmen, *vide* Sixth Queensland Imperial Bushmen.
Queensland unit, 1st Australian Commonwealth Horse, *vide* First Australian Commonwealth Horse.
Queensland unit, 3rd Australian Commonwealth Horse, *vide* Third Australian Commonwealth Horse.
Rainey, A. P., 2nd lieutenant, New South Wales Imperial Bushmen, 94; war service, 88.
Ranclaud, E. B., lieutenant, New South Wales Imperial Bushmen, 145, 147.
Randwick, training camp at, New South Wales, 3.
Rankin, C. D. W., major, special service officer, Queensland, 521; joins Australian Regiment, 214.
Rankin, J., lieutenant, 3rd Australian Commonwealth Horse, 177.
Rauchle, G., quartermaster-sergeant, " A " Battery; service in Soudan, 53.
Rawson, M., nursing sister, Victoria, in charge, 241; awarded Royal Red Cross, *ib.*
Reade, C. J., captain, commands 2nd South Australian, 349; major, 347; war service, 348.
Redford, P. W., lieutenant, 5th Victorian, 280; war service, 278.
Reese, C. G. B., lieutenant, 5th Queensland, 492; war service, 491.
Regimental Transport, abolished, 199.
Reid, D. E., lieutenant, 1st Queensland, 450; captain, 449; war service, 450.
Reid, F. B., captain, Medical Staff, with 6th Western Australian, 426; war service, 420.
Reid, G. E., lieutenant, 1st Tasmanian, 548; Australian Regiment, 214; war service, 548.

INDEX—*continued.*

Reid, H. A., sergeant, 4th South Australian, 358 ; lieutenant, 356 ; war service, 358 ; captain-adjutant, 8th Australian Commonwealth Horse, 386.
Reid, L. L., corporal, 4th Western Australian, 415 ; lieutenant, 8th Australian Commonwealth Horse, 388.
Reid, S. S., private, 2nd Western Australian, 407 ; lieutenant, 6th, 426 ; killed in action, 419 ; war service, 420.
Reitz, fighting at, 507.
Rensburg Siding, engagement at, 6.
Reynolds, H. R., sergeant, 3rd Tasmanian, 558 ; lieutenant, 555 ; war service, 557.
Reynolds, Rev. J. A., chaplain, New South Wales Imperial Bushmen, 91 ; war service, 87.
Rhenoster Kop, fighting at, 241, 275, 464.
Rhodesian Field Force, 463.
Ricardo, P. R., major, commands 1st Queensland, 450 ; remarks on enrolment, 447 ; hands over to Major Chauvel, 449 ; lieut.-colonel. 447 ; war service, 449.
Rich, D. St. G., lieutenant, 6th Queensland, 509 ; war service, 508.
Rich, W. S., private, 1st New South Wales Mounted Rifles, commissioned in Imperial Army, 58.
Richards, T. R., lieutenant, 3rd New South Wales Mounted Rifles, 137 ; captain, 124.
Richardson, Sir E., supernumerary captain, 2nd Queensland, 453 ; war service, *ib.*
Richardson, G. F., private, 1st Tasmanian, 550 ; lieutenant, 4th Tasmanian, 563 ; war service, 562.
Richardson, J., warrant-officer (regimental sergeant-major), 2nd Australian Commonwealth Horse, 309.
Richman, E., lieut.-adjutant, 5th South Australian, 367 ; war service, 366.
Ridley, C., General, letter from, 31.
Riggall, A. H., captain, commands draft for 1st Tasmanian, 550 ; commands 2nd Tasmanian, 552 ; war service, *ib.*
Riggall, H., lieutenant, 1st Australian Commonwealth Horse, 568.
Rignetti, E. E., sergeant, 1st Victorian Mounted Rifles, 224 ; lieutenant, 223 ; captain, 5th, 280 ; war service, 277 ; with 6th Australian Commonwealth Horse, 333.
Ritchie, A. McL., lieut.-quartermaster, 3rd New South Wales Imperial Bushmen, 145, 147.
Roberts, Lord, field marshal, *re* Army Medical Corps, 20 ; message from, 409 ; *re* convoy, 576.
Roberts, C. W. F. P., 2nd lieutenant, Lancers, 10 ; war service, 8 ; to Imperial Cavalry *ib.*
Roberts, E. A., lieutenant, 4th South Australian, 358 ; war service, 357 ; captain-adjutant, 2nd Australian Commonwealth Horse, 309.
Roberts, J. C., lieutenant, 1st Victorian Mounted Rifles, 223 ; Australian Regiment, 214 ; died of wounds, 216.
Roberts, S. R. H., captain, commands "D" Squadron, 8th Australian Commonwealth Horse, 437.
Roberts, W. F. E., lieutenant, 1st Australian Commonwealth Horse, 168.
Robertson, A. C., sergeant, 4th Queensland, 480 ; lieutenant, 5th Queensland, 475.
Robertson, C. W., captain, New South Wales Citizens Bushmen, 78 ; killed in action, *ib. ;* war service, 72.
Robertson, D., private, 1st New South Wales Mounted Rifles ; Soudan service, 66.
Robertson, J. E., captain, 4th Australian Commonwealth Horse, 434.
Robertson, S. A., lieutenant, 5th Victorian, 280 ; war service, 278.
Robertson, W. St. L., lieutenant, 4th Australian Commonwealth Horse, 319.
Robinson, G. M., lieutenant (supernumerary), 2nd New South Wales Mounted Rifles, 107 ; 3rd Imperial Bushmen, 147.
Robinson, H. F., 2nd lieutenant, New South Wales Imperial Bushmen, 91 ; war service, 88.
Robson, H., lieutenant, staff, 3rd New South Wales Mounted Rifles, 125.
Rodd, F. C., lieutenant 4th Australian Commonwealth Horse, 319.
Rogers, J., lieutenant, 6th Australian Commonwealth Horse, 334.
Rogers, R. S., civ. surgeon, 6th South Australian, 374.
Rose, J., captain, commands 4th Western Australian, 415 ; major, 413 ; war service, 414.
Rose, Rev. J. H., special service officer, New South Wales, 200.
Roth, R. E., major, Army Medical Corps, 20 ; war service, 17.
Rouse, T. H., lieut.-quartermaster, New South Wales Citizens Bushmen, 75 ; war service, 73.
Row, E. R., captain, Army Medical Corps, with 6th Queensland, 509 ; war service, 508.
Rowan, A. H., lieutenant, 6th Australian Commonwealth Horse, 327.
Rowan, A. P., lieutenant, 5th Victorian, 281 ; war service, 279.
Rowell, F. M., lieutenant, 2nd South Australian, 349 ; captain, 347 ; war service, 348.
Rowell, J., lieut.-colonel, commands 4th South Australian, 358 ; commands composite regiment, 356 ; war service, 357.
Royal Australian Artillery, "A" Battery, *vide* "A" Battery, Royal Australian Artillery.
Royal Red Cross, awards of, 14, 241, 378.
Royal salute fired by "A" Battery, 52.
Royston, J. R., lieut.-colonel, commands 5th and 6th Western Australian, 418.

INDEX—*continued*.

Rudduck, H. S., veterinary-captain, 2nd Victorian, 234; war service, 233.
Rudkin, C. M. C., lieutenant, New South Wales Imperial Bushmen, 96; war service, 88.
Rule, J. H., corporal, 4th Queensland, gallantry of, 477.
Russell, C. S., lieutenant, 3rd New South Wales Imperial Bushmen, 144, 147.
Russell, H. J., sergeant, 4th South Australian, 359; lieutenant, 356; captain, *ib.*; war service, 358.
Rustenburg, operations at, 71, 241.
Ryan, J. B., warrant-officer (regimental sergeant-major), 7th Australian Commonwealth Horse, 530.
Ryder, A. O., lieutenant, 5th Australian Commonwealth Horse, 190.
Ryrie, G. de L., captain, New South Wales Imperial Bushmen, 91; major, 86; war service, 88.
Ryrie, O. B., sergeant-major, New South Wales Citizens Bushmen, 80; lieutenant, 71; war service, 73; captain, 5th Australian Commonwealth Horse, 192.
Ryrie, S. S., lieut.-adjutant, New South Wales Citizens Bushmen, 75; captain, 71; war service, 72.
Ryrie, V. W., 2nd lieutenant, New South Wales Imperial Bushmen, 91; war service, 88; captain, 5th Australian Commonwealth Horse, 190.
Sale, A. A., 2nd lieutenant 3rd Tasmanian, 558; captain, 555; war service, 557; killed in action, *ib.*
Salmon, R. W., lieut.-adjutant, 1st Victorian Mounted Rifles, 223; captain, *ib.*; Australian Regiment, 214; died, 217.
Samuelson, G. S., lieutenant, Army Medical Corps, 22; captain, 15; war service, 18.
Sanders, F. G., trooper, 2nd South Australian, 351; commissioned in Imperial service, 347.
Sandford, D., sergeant, 4th Victorian, 261; bravery of, 256; lieutenant, 2nd Australian Commonwealth Horse, 310.
Savage, A. H. P., major, Royal Australian Artillery, special service officer, New South Wales, 202.
Schwabe, J. H., lieutenant, commands Machine Gun Section, 3rd New South Wales Mounted Rifles, 142.
Scobie, R., lieutenant, 3rd New South Wales Mounted Rifles, 127; captain, 124.
Scott, E. I. C., lieutenant, 3rd New South Wales Imperial Bushmen, 145, 147.
Scott, J. S., lieutenant, Western Australian, 421; war service, 420.
Scottish Horse, recruits for, 304.
Scott-Skirving, R., major, special service officer, Army Medical Corps, 14, 22; war service, 18.
Scriven, W., major, special service officer, South Australian, 377.
Sea Cow River, affair at, 255.
Seacombe, N. T., private, 2nd Queensland, 461; lieutenant, 3rd Australian Commonwealth Horse, 527.
Second Battalion Australian Commonwealth Horse: *Victorian units*, 307; how composed, qualifications, clothing, pay, establishment, departure and return, *ib.*; service, 308; war service, 309; nominal roll, *ib. South Australian unit*, 379; details, recruits, service, war services, nominal roll, *ib. Western Australian unit*, 431; pay, clothing, conditions, Australian Army Medical Corps; promotions, departure and return, service, *ib.*; nominal roll, 432; do., Australian Army Medical Corps, 433.
Second New South Wales Mounted Rifles, 106; establishment, orders, clothing, departure and return, *ib.*; draft, 107; officers attached, operations, *ib.*; pipes sent by Queen Alexandra, 108; N.C.O.'s and men to attend Coronation, *ib.*; extract from Column Orders, *ib.*; honours, 109; promotions, war services, *ib.*; nominal roll, 110.
Second Queensland Mounted Infantry Contingent, 457; proclamation, establishment, departure and return, promotions, service, *ib.*; Column Order by Major-General Hutton, 458; war services and honours, *ib.*; nominal roll, 459.
Second South Australian (Mounted Rifles) Contingent, 347; establishment, departure and return promotions, service, *ib.*; war services and honours, 348; nominal roll, 349.
Second Tasmanian (Bushmen) Contingent, 551; establishment, pay, equipment, promotions, departure and return, service, *ib.*; forms part of a Bushmen Regiment, *ib.*; war services and honours, 552; nominal roll, *ib.*
Second Victorian (Mounted Rifles) Contingent, 229; qualification for, clothing establishment, rates of pay, departure and return, *ib.*; promotions, &c., service, 230; becomes part of Colonel Henry's 4th Mounted Infantry, 231; war services, 233; nominal roll, 234.
Second Western Australian (Mounted Infantry) Contingent, 403; engagement, establishment, clothing, pay, pensions, departure and return, promotions, *ib.*; service, 404; war services and honours, 405; nominal roll, *ib.*
Sellheim, C. V., lieutenant, 4th Queensland, 479; captain (supernumerary), 5th Queensland, 493; war service, 478.

INDEX—continued.

Sellheim, V. C. M., major, special service officer, Queensland, 520 ; joins Australian Regiment, 214.
Selman, S., lieutenant, 5th Victorian, 281 ; war service, 279.
Sergeant, J. E., lieutenant, 5th Victorian, 281 ; war service, 278.
Sergeant, T. H., lieutenant, 2nd Victorian, 234 ; captain, 230 ; war service, 233.
Seventh Battalion Australian Commonwealth Horse, 530 ; details, squadrons, how raised, departure and return, service, *ib.* ; nominal roll, *ib.*
Shadforth, E. H., sergeant, 4th Queensland, gallantry of, 477.
Shadler, R., captain, 3rd Australian Commonwealth Horse, 177.
Shaw, G., sergeant, 3rd Tasmanian, 558 ; lieutenant, 4th Tasmanian, 561.
Shaw, H. A., lieutenant, 3rd Australian Commonwealth Horse, 570.
Shaw. L. J., 2nd lieutenant, 3rd New South Wales Mounted Rifles, 137.
Shea, major. Indian Staff Corps, commands 5th and 6th South Australian, 365.
Shearer, J. H., trooper, 1st South Australian, 346 ; lieutenant, 5th, 367 ; war service, 366.
Sheppard, N. H., lieutenant, 3rd New South Wales Imperial Bushmen, 145, 147.
Sherard, N., private, 1st Western Australian, 402 ; lieutenant, 5th, 421 ; war service, 420.
Sherlock, H. H., regimental quartermaster-sergeant, 3rd Victorian, 249 ; lieut.-quartermaster, 242 ; war service, 244.
Sherlock, S., veterinary-lieutenant, 4th Victorian, 259 ; veterinary-captain, 5th Victorian, 281 ; war service, 280.
Shields, D. A., captain, Medical Staff, 6th Australian Commonwealth Horse, 325.
Showground, Newtown, Tasmania, camp at, 545.
Siekman, F. C., quartermaster-sergeant, 4th South Australian, 358 ; lieutenant, 2nd Australian Commonwealth Horse, 379.
Simes, C. N., lieutenant (supernumerary), 2nd New South Wales Mounted Rifles, 107.
Simmons, T. E., lieutenant, 3rd New South Wales Mounted Rifles, 137.
Sindel, A., sergeant, 1st Victorian Infantry, 226 ; lieutenant, 1st Scottish Horse, 223.
Sixth Battalion Australian Commonwealth Horse, 324 ; organization, establishment, troops, how raised, departure and return, *ib.* ; service, nominal roll, 325.
Sixth Queensland (Imperial Bushmen) Contingent, 506 ; enlistment, clothing, equipment, pay, establishment, departure and return, service, *ib.* ; drafts, *ib.* ; war services and honours, 508 ; nominal roll, 509 ; details, 518, 519.
Sixth South Australian Contingent, *vide* Fifth and Sixth.
Sixth Western Australian Contingent, *vide* Fifth and Sixth.
Sleight, R., private, 3rd Queensland, 473 ; lieutenant, 463 ; war service, 466, 509 ; supernumerary with 6th, 510.
Slingersfontein, fighting at, 6, 42, 216.
Smith, A., sergeant, 4th Queensland, 480 ; lieutenant, 5th, 475.
Smith, D. F., nursing sister, Victorian, 241.
Smith, E. M. B., nursing sister, Victorian, 241.
Smith, N., private, 1st Victorian Infantry, 227 ; 2nd lieutenant, 223 ; lieutenant, 5th, 280 ; war service, 278.
Smith, R., sergeant, 2nd N.S.W. Mounted Rifles, 120 ; lieutenant, Imperial Bushmen, 145, 147.
Smith, S. C. U., colonel (major, Royal Field Artillery), commands " A " Battery, 53 ; extracts from report of, 50.
Smith, W. R., captain, Medical Staff, 5th South Australian, 368 ; war service, 367.
Soane, E. W. R., captain, New South Wales Imperial Bushmen, 103 ; captain-adjutant, 5th Australian Commonwealth Horse, 186 ; war service, 89.
Solly-Flood, F. F., corporal, 2nd South Australian, 349 ; lieutenant, South African Light Horse, 347.
Soudan, New South Wales Contingent, 1885, men who served in, *vide* chiefly Nominal Rolls, " A " Battery, and 1st New South Wales Mounted Rifles.
South Australia, 340 : *Prefatory*, 341 ; 1st (Mounted Rifle) Contingent, 343 ; 2nd (Mounted Rifle) Contingent, 347 ; 3rd (Bushmen) Contingent, 352 ; 4th (Imperial Bushmen) Contingent, 356 ; 5th and 6th (Imperial) Contingents, 364 ; Special Service officers, 377 ; Australian Army Medical Corps, 378 ; 2nd Australian Commonwealth Horse, 379 ; 4th Australian Commonwealth Horse, 382 ; 8th Australian Commonwealth Horse, 385 ; died or were killed, 391 ; summary of Contingents, 392.
South Australian Mounted Rifles, composed of 1st and 2nd Contingents, 348.
South Australian Unit, 2nd Australian Commonwealth Horse, *vide* Second Australian Commonwealth Horse.
South Australian Unit, 4th Australian Commonwealth Horse, *vide* Fourth Australian Commonwealth Horse.
Southby, H., warrant-officer (regimental sergeant-major), with 4th Australian Commonwealth Horse, 319.

INDEX—*continued*.

Southey, C. M., lieutenant, 3rd New South Wales Imperial Bushmen, 147.
Special Service Officers: New South Wales, 195; Queensland, 520; South Australia, 377; Tasmania, 554; Victoria, 305; remarks upon, 195.
Spencer, T. A., captain, 4th Tasmanian, 565; war service, 562.
Spencer, W. F., sergeant, 4th South Australian, 358; lieutenant, 8th Australian Commonwealth Horse, 386.
Stacpoole, A. R., captain, Medical Staff, 4th Australian Commonwealth Horse, 319.
Stapleton, J. H., lieutenant, 1st South Australian, 344; Australian Regiment, 214; captain, 343; war service, 344.
Staughton, S. T., lieutenant, 1st Victorian Mounted Rifles, 223; captain, *ib*.; Australian Regiment, 214.
Stebbins, J. F., lieutenant, 5th Victorian, 281; war service, 278; 6th Australian Commonwealth Horse, 325.
Steel, M., nursing sister, New South Wales, 14.
Stephens, E. W., sergeant, 3rd Tasmanian, 558; lieutenant, 8th Australian Commonwealth Horse, 573.
Stevens, A. G. V., lieutenant (supernumerary), 2nd New South Wales Mounted Rifles, 107.
Stewart, D. J., quartermaster-sergeant, 1st New South Wales Mounted Rifles, 67; lieutenant, 2nd Mounted Rifles, 58, 110.
Stewart, J., lieutenant, 3rd New South Wales Mounted Rifles, 132.
Stewart, J. M. Y., captain, Medical Staff, 2nd Western Australian, 405; war service, *ib*.
Stirling, N. W., veterinary-lieutenant, 6th South Australian, 374; war service, 367.
Stirton, P. E., lieutenant, 1st New South Wales Mounted Rifles, 58, 62; war service, 60.
Stock, D., lieutenant, 5th Victorian, 281; war service, 279.
Stocker, A., sergeant, 3rd Tasmanian, 560; distinguished, 557; lieutenant, 555; war service, 557.
Stodart, R. M., lieutenant, 2nd Queensland, 459; war service, *ib*.
Stokes, S. F., captain, 3rd New South Wales Mounted Rifles, 135.
Stourton, R. N. J., lieutenant, 3rd Australian Commonwealth Horse, 570.
Strickland, F. P., private, 3rd Western Australian, 412; lieutenant, 4th Australian Commonwealth Horse, 434.
Strong, C. D., veterinary-lieutenant, 5th Victorian, 281; war service, 280.
Strong, W. J. W., lieutenant, 3rd Victorian, 245; war service, 244; captain, adjutant, 6th Australian Commonwealth Horse, 325.
Stuart, F. W., lieutenant, 3rd New South Wales Mounted Rifles, 125.
Sturdee, A. H., captain, Medical Staff, 4th Victorian, 259; war service, 257.
Suche, A. J. P., colour-sergeant, 4th Tasmanian, 565; lieutenant, 561; war service, 562.
Sullivan, E. J., transport-sergeant, 1st New South Wales Mounted Rifles, 62; Soudan, 1885, *ib*.; died at Kroonstadt, *ib*.
Summary of Contingents, *vide* Contingents, Summary of.
Sutton, H. B., 2nd lieutenant, 2nd New South Wales Mounted Rifles, 110; 3rd Imperial Bushmen, 147.
Swan, M. H., private, 1st Tasmanian, 549; lieutenant, 4th Tasmanian, 565; paymaster, 561; war service, 562.
Swan, R. A., lieutenant, 3rd Australian Commonwealth Horse, 570.
Swartz Farm, attacks on convoy, 556.
Sweetland, H. St. J., lieutenant, " A " Battery, 53; at Prieska, 52; war service, 49.
Symonds, S. L., veterinary-lieutenant, 3rd New South Wales Mounted Rifles, 125.
Tasmania: *Prefatory*, 545; 1st Contingent, 546; 2nd (Bushmen) Contingent, 551; Special Service officers, 554; 3rd (Imperial) Contingent, 555; 4th (2nd Imperial) Bushmen, 561; 1st Australian Commonwealth Horse (½-unit), 568; 3rd Australian Commonwealth Horse (unit), 570; 8th Australian Commonwealth Horse (unit), 573; died or killed, 576, summary of Contingents, 577.
Tasmanian Military Contingent Act, 545; authority for Contingents, *ib*.
Tasmanian Unit, 1st Australian Commonwealth Horse, *vide* First Australian Commonwealth Horse.
Tasmanian Unit, 3rd Australian Commonwealth Horse, *vide* Third Australian Commonwealth Horse.
Tasmanian Unit, 8th Australian Commonwealth Horse, *vide* Eighth Australian Commonwealth Horse.
Tasmanians, good work done by, 545.
Tatchell, E. C., lance-corporal, 1st Victorian Infantry, 228; 2nd lieutenant, 223; captain, 5th, 280; war service, 277; with 6th Australian Commonwealth Horse, 330.
Taylor, H. J. C., lieutenant, " A " Battery, 53; captain-adjutant, 1st Australian Commonwealth Horse, 167; war service, 49.
Taylor, J. S., lieutenant, 3rd New South Wales Imperial Bushmen, 147.

INDEX—*continued.*

Taylor, T. G., lieutenant, 3rd New South Wales Imperial Bushmen, 145, 147.
Taylor, O. A., sergeant, 3rd New South Wales Mounted Rifles, 125; lieutenant, 124.
Teare, J. S., sergeant-major, 5th Western Australian, 425; lieutenant, Johannesburg Mounted Rifles, 418.
Tedder, J. G., lieutenant, 2nd New South Wales Mounted Rifles, 110; war service, 109.
Thaba Mountain, affair at, 38.
Third Battalion Australian Commonwealth Horse, 176; conditions, commissions, orders, orders, clothing, summary, service, *ib.*; nominal roll, 177. *Queensland Unit*, 527; details, service, departure and return, nominal roll, *ib. Tasmanian Unit*, 570; details, establishment, departure and return, service, *ib.*; nominal roll, *ib.*
Third New South Wales Imperial Bushmen, 144; record, promotions, *ib.*; service, 145; Force Orders, *ib.*; letter from Major-General Fetherstonhaugh, 146; war services and honours, *ib.*; nominal roll, 147.
Third New South Wales Mounted Rifles, 123; orders, clothing, departure and return, supernumerary officers, *ib.*; service, promotions, honours, war services, 124; nominal roll, 125; do., draft, 137; do., machine-gun section, 142.
Third Queensland (Mounted Infantry) Contingent, 463; proclamation, establishment, promotions, &c., departure and return, service, *ib.*; extract from Captain Echlin's report, 465; war services and honours, 466; nominal roll, *ib.*
Third South Australian (Bushmen) Contingent, 352; qualifications for, establishment, departure and return, promotions, service, *ib.*; war services and honours, 353; nominal roll, *ib.*
Third Tasmanian (1st Imperial) Contingent, 555; details, establishment, departure and return, promotions, service, *ib.*; part of 4th Imperial Bushmen, *ib.*; complimented by Lord Roberts, 556; two Victoria Crosses, *ib.*; war services and honours, 557; nominal roll, 558.
Third Victorian (Bushmen) Contingent, 240; how recruited, *ib.*; qualifications, rates of pay, Cameron's Scouts, establishment, clothing, *ib.*; nursing sisters, 241; departure and return, promotions, *ib.*; service, 242; part of 3rd Rhodesian Field Force, *ib.*; Cameron's Scouts, 243; return, 244; war services and honours, *ib.*; nominal roll, 245; do., Cameron's Scouts, 251.
Third Western Australian (Bushmen) Contingent, 408; gazetted, strength, pay, clothing, horses, conditions, departure and return, promotions, &c., service, *ib.*; portion of 3rd Australian Bushmen, *ib.*; war services and honours, 409; nominal roll, 410.
Thomas, E. H., lieutenant, New South Wales Imperial Bushmen, 101; war service, 89.
Thomas, G. A., sergeant, 1st Australian Horse (New South Wales), 45; commissioned in Imperial service, 42.
Thomas, H., 2nd lieutenant, 3rd New South Wales Mounted Rifles, 135.
Thomas, H. W., lieutenant, 3rd New South Wales Imperial Bushmen, 144, 147.
Thomas, J. F., captain, New South Wales Citizens Bushmen, 75; major, 71; war service, 72.
Thompson, A. C., sergeant, New South Wales Imperial Bushmen, 103; 2nd lieutenant, 87; captain, 3rd Imperial Bushmen, 144, 147.
Thompson, J. A. M. W., lieutenant, 3rd New South Wales Mounted Rifles, 130.
Thompson, R. R., captain, commands 1st Australian Horse, 45; extract from report of, 44; war service, 42.
Thompson, W. G., captain, 2nd Queensland, 459; war service, 458.
Thomson, A. E. H., nursing sister, Victorian, 241.
Thomson, W. H., lieutenant, 2nd Australian Commonwealth Horse, 310.
Thorn, G. F., lieutenant, 1st Victorian Mounted Rifles, 223; Australian Regiment, 214; captain, 223; with 4th Australian Commonwealth Horse, 319.
Thorne, F. O., lance-corporal, 4th South Australian, 362; lieutenant, 356; war service, 358; with 2nd Australian Commonwealth Horse, 379.
Thunder, A. F., lieutenant, 3rd Western Australian, 410; captain, 6th, 408; war service, 410.
Tiddy, D., nursing sister, Victorian, 241.
Tilney, L. E., lieutenant, 5th Australian Commonwealth Horse, 186.
Timoney, Rev. F., chaplain, New South Wales Citizens Bushmen, 75; war service, 73.
Tivey, E., captain, 4th Victorian, 259; surprises Philipstown, 255; major, 5th Victorian, 253; war service, 257; with 2nd Australian Commonwealth Horse, 309.
Tobacco sent to Lancers by Lady Duff, 9.
Toll, F. W., captain, special service officer, Queensland, 521; with 5th Queensland, 492; major, 488; commands at Onverwacht, 489; war services, 491.
Toll, J. T., captain, Medical Staff, 1st South Australian, 344; Australian Regiment, 214; war service, 344; died at sea, *ib.*
Tolmer, H. A., trooper, 2nd South Australian, 351; lieutenant, 5th, 368; war service, 366.
Tolmer, J. D., trooper, 2nd South Australian, 351; lieutenant, 5th, 347.
Tolson, J., lieutenant, 7th Australian Commonwealth Horse, 535.

INDEX—*continued.*

Tooth, D. K. L., lieutenant, " A " Squadron, New South Wales Mounted Rifles, 32 ; war services, 29 ; commissioned in 9th Lancers, *ib.*
Townley, N. V., lieutenant (supernumerary), 5th Queensland, 493 ; war service, 492.
Trask, F. H., warrant-officer (regimental sergeant-major), 6th Queensland, 516.
Treatt, G. V. D , lieutenant, 3rd New South Wales Mounted Rifles, 130.
Tremearne, A. J. N., lieutenant, 1st Victorian Infantry, 226 ; Australian Regiment, 214 ; joins Ashanti Field Force, 222.
Trew, H. F., lieutenant, 3rd Victorian, 245 ; captain. 5th, 241 ; war service, 244.
Tucker, G., veterinary-lieutenant,, 5th Queensland, 504 ; war service, 492.
Tunbridge, O. A., lieut.-colonel, commands 6th Queensland, 509 ; war service, 508.
Tunbridge, W. H., major, commands 3rd Queensland, 466 ; war service, *ib.*
Turnour, J. M., lieutenant, 7th Australian Commonwealth Horse, 535.
Ulbrich, F. W., lieutenant, 4th Victorian, 259 ; war service, 258.
Umphelby, C. E., lieut.-colonel, Royal Australian Artillery, special service officer, Victorian, 305 ; died of wounds, *ib.*
Umphelby, T. A., lieutenant, 2nd Victorian, 234 ; war service, 233 ; with 5th Victorian, 281, 279.
Umphelby, T. F.. lieutenant, 2nd Victorian, 234 ; captain, 230 ; major, 5th, 281 ; war service, 233, 277.
Ussher, N. J., trooper, 1st Australian Horse, 47A; 2nd lieutenant. 5th Australian Commonwealth Horse, 192.
Valkheuval Poort, severe action at, 6.
Vaughan, C. R. G., lieutenant, 6th Queensland, 509 ; war service, *ib.*
Vaughan, P. W., 2nd lieutenant, 1st Australian Horse, 45 ; war service, 42.
Veldt ponies, caught and broken by 5th and 6th South Australians, 366.
Venn, H. N., quartermaster-sergeant, 4th Western Australian, promoted lieutenant, 413 ; war service, 414 ; captain, paymaster, 431.
Vereeniging, defended by Irish Brigade, 231.
Vernon, E., lieutenant, 4th Western Australian, 415 ; captain, 413 ; war service, 414.
Vernon, R. R. C., lieutenant, 3rd Western Australian, 410 ; commissioned in Imperial service, 408 ; war service, 409.
Vet River, action at, 231.
Vialls, H. G., captain, commands 3rd Western Australian, 410 ; major, 408 ; lieut.-colonel, *ib. ;* fine leadership of, 409 ; war service, *ib.*
Victoria, *prefatory,* 211 ; camp of instruction, 212 ; First (Infantry and Mounted Rifles) Contingent, 213, 222 ; the Australian Regiment, 214 ; Second (Mounted Rifles) Contingent, 229 ; Third (Bushmen) Contingent, 240 ; Fourth (Imperial) Contingent, 252 ; Fifth (Mounted Rifles) Contingent. 274; *recruits for Scottish Horse,* 304 ; Special Service officers, 305 ; 2nd Australian Commonwealth Horse, 307 ; Australian Commonwealth Army Medical Corps, Victorian details, 317 ; 4th Australian Commonwealth Horse, 318 ; 6th Australian Commonwealth Horse, 324 ; killed or died, 336 ; summary of Contingents, 337.
Victoria Cross obtained by Lieutenant F. W. Bell, 419 ; Private J. H. Bisdee, 556 ; Captain N. R. Howse, 18 ; Lieutenant L. C. Maygar, 277 ; Lieutenant G. G. E. Wylly, 556.
Victoria, Queen, message from, 215.
Virginia Siding, action at, 231.
Wagons, 1st Queensland, 448 ; taken over by Royal Engineers, *ib.*
Waite, W. C. N., corporal, 1st South Australian, 345 ; lieutenant, 6th, 374 ; war service 367.
Walch, J. C. lieutenant, special service officer, Tasmanian, 554, 547.
Waldron, T. W. K., captain, New South Wales Imperial Bushmen, 98 ; war service, 88.
Walker, F., warrant-officer, Australian Commonwealth Army Medical Corps, 26, 526.
Walker, G. W., lieutenant, 6th Queensland, 509 ; war service, *ib.*
Walker, J., lieutenant, 2nd Queensland, 459 ; war service, *ib.*
Walker, R. C. H., lance-corporal, 2nd South Australian, 351 ; lieutenant, 8th Australian Commonwealth Horse, 387.
Wallace, R., lieut.-colonel, commands 3rd Australian Commonwealth Horse, 177.
Wallack, E. T., lieut.-colonel, special service officer, Tasmanian, 554 ; takes out 2nd Contingent, 552.
Walsh, R. H., lieutenant, 3rd Queensland, 466 ; war service, *ib.*
Walter, C. H., 2nd lieutenant, 3rd Tasmanian, 558 ; war service, 557 ; killed in action, *ib.*
Walter, E., nursing sister, Victorian, 241.
Walter, G. J. R., lieutenant, 2nd South Australian, 349 ; captain, 347 ; war service, 348.
Walton, E. R. N., lieutenant, 5th Victorian, 280 ; war service, 278.
Wanliss, E., private, 4th Victorian, 267 ; lieutenant, 253 ; war service, 258.
Ward, B. T., lance-corporal, 4th South Australian, 363 ; lieutenant, 8th Australian Commonwealth Horse, 389.
Warmbad, captured by 3rd Bushmen, 343.

INDEX—*continued*.

Wasson, J., warrant-officer (regimental sergeant-major), 2nd New South Wales Mounted Rifles, 121; honours, *ib.*, 108.
Watchorn, E. T., lieut.-colonel, commands 4th Tasmanian, 563; war service, 562.
Waters, H., lieutenant (supernumerary), 3rd New South Wales Mounted Rifles, 123.
Watson, W. W., lieutenant, 4th Australian Commonwealth Horse, 382.
Watson, W. W. R., lieutenant, 1st New South Wales Mounted Rifles, 58; captain, 67; war service, 60.
Watt, J. A., captain, 5th South Australian, 367; war service, 366.
Watts, B. A. G., regimental sergeant-major, 4th Victorian, 262; lieutenant, 5th, 281; war service, 279.
Way, J., trooper, 2nd South Australian, 351; commissioned in Imperial service, 347.
Wearne, A. E., lieutenant, 2nd New South Wales Mounted Rifles, 110; 3rd Imperial Bushmen, 147.
Wearne, W. S., lieutenant (supernumerary), 2nd New South Wales Mounted Rifles, 107; 3rd Imperial Bushmen, 147.
Webster, G. A., lieutenant, Army Medical Corps, with 7th Australian Commonwealth Horse, 530.
Wedd, W. S., lieutenant, 5th Victorian, 280; war service, 278.
Weinholt, F. E., lieutenant, 7th Australian Commonwealth Horse, 538.
Weir, F. V., lieutenant, 1st Australian Commonwealth Horse, 170.
Wentworth, F., 2nd lieutenant, New South Wales Imperial Bushmen, 98; war service, 88.
Western Australia: *Prefatory*, 395; First (Mounted Infantry) Contingent, 396; Second (Mounted Infantry) Contingent, 403; Third (Bushmen's) Contingent, 408; Fourth (Mounted Infantry) Contingent, 413; Fifth and Sixth (Mounted Infantry) Contingents, 418; 2nd Australian Commonwealth Horse (unit), 431; 4th Australian Commonwealth Horse (unit), 434; 8th Australian Commonwealth Horse (unit), 437; died or killed, 440; summary of Contingents, 441.
Western Australian Unit, 2nd Australian Commonwealth Horse, *vide* Second Australian Commonwealth Horse.
Western Australian Unit, 4th Australian Commonwealth Horse, *vide* Fourth Australian Commonwealth Horse.
Western Australian Unit, 8th Australian Commonwealth Horse, *vide* Eighth Australian Commonwealth Horse.
Westgarth, J. E., lieutenant, New South Wales Citizens Bushmen, 82; commissioned in Royal Field Artillery, 71; war service, 73.
Whidborne, H. E., lieutenant, 4th Victorian, 259; captain, 5th 253; war service, 258.
White, C. B. B., lieutenant, Royal Australian Artillery, with "D" Company, 1st Australian Commonwealth Horse, 523.
White, R. J. L., 2nd lieutenant, New South Wales Imperial Bushmen, 96; killed in action, 89; war service, 88.
White, S. A., lieutenant, 4th South Australian, 358; war service, *ib.*
Whitehorn, H. S., captain, 6th Queensland, 509; war service, 508.
Wilkinson, J. F. M., lieutenant, 1st Australian Horse, 45; in command, 43; captain, 42; war service, *ib.*
Williams, C. W., private, 2nd Western Australian, 407; lieutenant, 403; with 5th Contingent, 421; war service, 420.
Williams, E. F. C., colonel, Column Order by, 108, 145.
Williams, E. R., lieutenant, 4th Western Australian, 415; captain, 6th, 426; war service, 414.
Williams, R. L., corporal, 3rd Tasmanian, 558; lieutenant, 555; war service, 557.
Williams, W. D. C., colonel, places Army Medical Corps in efficient condition, 13; commands 1st Contingent, 15, 20; surgeon-general, Principal Medical Officer, 15; extracts from report of, 19; war service, 17.
Wilmansrust camp rushed by Boers, 275.
Wilson, A. C., veterinary-lieutenant, 6th Australian Commonwealth Horse, 325.
Wilson, F. H. D., lieutenant, 7th Australian Commonwealth Horse, 533.
Wilson, H. L. D., captain, 4th South Australian, 358; major, 356; war service, 357.
Wind, cold, causes men to faint, 507.
Wintle, W. E., lieutenant, 3rd New South Wales Imperial Bushmen, 145, 147.
Wollaston, H. N. S., captain, 4th Victorian, 259; war service, 257.
Wollstein, H. M., captain, 6th Queensland, 509; war service, 508.
Wolmaranstad, occupation of, 255.
Wood, J., warrant-officer (regimental sergeant-major), 4th Western Australian, 415.
Wood, M., corporal, 2nd Victorian, 237; 2nd lieutenant, 230; war service, 233.
Woodcock, C. F., lieutenant, Royal Australian Artillery, with "D" Company, 1st Australian Commonwealth Horse, 523.
Woodrow, C. E., lieutenant, 6th Western Australian, 426; war service, 421.

INDEX—*continued*.

Woods, C. T., private, 1st New South Wales Mounted Rifles, 67; commissioned in Imperial service, 58.
Woods, H. B., lieutenant, 3rd Australian Commonwealth Horse, 177.
Woodward, T. E., nursing sister, New South Wales, 14.
Wray, Rev. F. W., chaplain, 2nd Victorian, 234; war service, 233.
Wray, K. M., captain, New South Wales Imperial Bushmen, 96; war service, 88.
Wright, R. E., lieutenant, 6th Western Australian, 426; war service, 421.
Wright, W. L. F., lieutenant (supernumerary), 6th Queensland, 510; war service, 509.
Wylly, G. G. E., lieutenant, 3rd Tasmanian, 558; obtains Victoria Cross, 556; receives Imperial commission, 555; wounded, and appointed to Lord Kitchener's staff, 556; war service, 557.
Wynne, G., captain-quartermaster, 3rd Australian Commonwealth Horse, 177.
Yaldwin, H. St. C., sergeant, 4th Queensland, 480; lieutenant, 5th, 475; captain, 7th Australian Commonwealth Horse 533.
Young, W. H., lieutenant, 6th Western Australian, 426; war service, 420.
Zand River, action at, 29, 231, &c.
Zeerust, Cameron's Scouts engaged at, 243.
Zouch, R. E., 2nd lieutenant, New South Wales Citizens Bushmen, 75; captain, 1st Australian Commonwealth Horse, 168; war service, 73.

By Authority: ALBERT J. MULLETT, Government Printer, Melbourne.

www.ingramcontent.com/pod-product-compliance
Lightning Source LLC
Chambersburg PA
CBHW051123230426
43670CB00007B/647